BLACK RACE, WHO ARE YOU?

The Great Black Race Chronoholocaust Cataclysm

R. M. Dipanda

ISBN 978-1-954345-82-9 (paperback)
ISBN 978-1-954345-83-6 (digital)

Copyright © 2021 by R. M. Dipanda

All rights reserved. No part of this publication may be reproduced, distributed, or transmitted in any form or by any means, including photocopying, recording, or other electronic or mechanical methods without the prior written permission of the publisher. For permission requests, solicit the publisher via the address below.

Rushmore Press LLC
1 800 460 9188
www.rushmorepress.com

Printed in the United States of America

CONTENTS

Foreword... v
Introduction vii

Chapter 1:   The Cosmic Matrix 1
Chapter 2:   Egypt..21
Chapter 3:   The Origin of the Bible 125
Chapter 4:   Slavery..349

About the Author 726
Acknowledgments and Gratitude 727

*E*very being on earth is a thought, and that mode of thought is God, the voice of numbers, echoing song and harmony in spheres, and in the infinity of space and time. To know his thought in the immense universe, know yourself and you will know the thought of God, the beyond, where innumerable souls of the world spring up.

For He who constantly creates worlds is threefold: the Father; the mother; and the essence—the substance of life is their son.

In ourselves, we carry a sublime friend, the thought of God, the Divine Liberator—the Divine Light, who knows the source and the end of life, but whom we do not know.

Each of us encloses two of these three worlds, and all three are one in the ineffable, because God dwells in the interior of every man.

He who finds him in himself, the supreme precious spirit of awakening will be born in him, and he will live his happiness, his joy, and in him, the light of God will no longer degenerate; and where it has already appeared, love will grow more and more.

Men named this harmony love because it has wings and the virtue to give.

The soul that found God, its light is one with God; and it will drink the water of immortality and be delivered from pain, old age, rebirth, and death.

To ascend to heaven is learning and seeing; to descend on earth is to remember; for every being on earth is a thought, and that mode of thought is God.

R. M. Dipanda

FOREWORD

I was born in a great rich country, which was first colonized by Portugal from 1472 to 1578, and then from 1578 to 1840 colonized by the Netherlands, from 1840 to 1883 colonized by England, and finally from 1883 to 1918 colonized by Germany. The Germans lost the Great War in 1918 and also lost their colony at the same time. And my country was divided into two by the League of Nations.

The eastern part was given to France and the western area to the United Kingdom. After the Second World War, my country, which had its independence in 1960, continued its long sappy road under the tutelage of France and England. Cameroon is part of several countries that constitute our famous, happy, and rich continent.

In addition, our African countries, buffeted in a Western culture with sometimes concepts that date from the nineteenth century, have chosen to adopt foreign languages for their administration, economics, education, justice, and politics but known as languages that more than 70 to 80 percent of the populations of all African countries do not understand, and which disintegrate Africa with the complicity of their leaders.

Everywhere, this Western model, forcing black Africa to educate itself to their concept, is a model clad on African realities, resulting to the impure soul of our rightful people and that some Westerners already described fundamentally unfair as a huge gulf, an abyss, between the reality that African populations are living but surely full of anger.

The cradle of humanity, known as the history of humanity, teaching us about man, hominid, the evolution of man by the DNA extracted from the bones of our human ancestors, is found in Africa; and if Adam and Eve are the first human beings, as some religions said, they could only be Africans, therefore black; so are the first inventions, the work of the black humanity, and all the scientific researchers of the whole world believed this opinion.

For centuries, blacks themselves, not far from believing that they're submen, resulting from a particular ideology that forms the basis of debasement, of moral indoctrination and humiliation, established by Arabs and whites in favor of slavery and colonization, was practiced to make blacks believe that they have brought nothing to human civilization.

It must be said that in all countries of black Africa, Africans in the twenty-first century, still in the hands of those ruthless white predators who are plundering our wealth, are still struggling to make their way toward the construction of strong and united nations, where it would be good to live; yet they deserve to be a society built on their own values but are forced to direct themselves toward all their political plans, to identify themselves with their economic system, to eat like them, to think culturally, socially like them, and to live like them.

Thousands of years ago, Ancient Egypt was considered as the civilizing nation of the world, whose whites, like Aristotle or Herodotus, claimed to be the land of "blacks with frizzy hair, and whose philosophy and science was taught to the Greek scholars as the essence of their knowledge; that Ancient Egypt, which has also left us gods of all kinds, has nothing to do with the Egypt of the present Egyptians.

But these gods were betrayed by Africa, which sold its soul on the religious level; and consequently, only believes in the belief or set of beliefs taught in their foreign languages and in their churches as a group of Christian theological doctrines of predestination; a concept according to which God would have chosen from all eternity, in the secret of faith, those who will be pardoned and will have the right to eternal life. So how can one be sure of being heard by God if we Africans are praying with tongues that we do not understand the meaning of our prayers? Thus, our stolen teachings, which should lead us to have more confidence in ourselves, are reducing us and make us feel ashamed of our race.

Consequently, it is the consciousness of what one has been that determines the construction of a future nation, because the eminent role of blacks in human civilization could fill pages of the history of humanity; even if black men are lagging behind mankind, our "debasement to the rank of "beast" or subjecting us to "the omnipresent spittle" is not important; the importance is what we do with what they're doing with us and not what they do to us.

It is essential that Africans "overcome complexes," revalorize themselves, and know that they cannot build a future with the ideas or the vision of others, but as great wonderful people, they can only build a future with their own vision of the world. They should know that accommodating nonsense in human history and the grossest mounted prejudices still widely shared in the West up to their political class, to make the black man the personified negation, will not advance Africa as long as Africans will believe in what the Westerners make of them.

INTRODUCTION

CHAPTER ONE

THE COSMIC MATRIX

I am sitting silently in the region of the concrete thought of the world of thought before an altar of earth in the open sky, where a blazing fire of the mystifying dry grass is burning, with only harmonious birdsong filling the atmosphere, immersed in the immense blue ocean of my thought; thought forms that mold and shape all forms of the physical world, being first a thought. My mother, the womb of the great earth, is where my father, the sky—the divine star, the principle of the unity of the universe; an invisible hyperphysical order—the intellectual eternal, embracing all the immeasurable spaces and time, the essential cosmic—fertilized the highest part of its surface, the uterus, and generated me with a deep soothsaying of truth and the breath of an imposing consciousness, containing secrets of my dual origin. Anterior and superior to earth is my divine type of man. Heavenly is my origin of soul. And my body is a product of terrestrial elements, an organizing principle; otherwise, the material could have been an inert mass and diffuse.

Oh, Africa! The creative light is dim in your old country, and it illuminated all manuscripts that thou hast given me there are some million years ago. And that I convey to the world through my mummified hand of the Great All. The secret of his subtle impenetrable smile of erudite professes to me a sacred prophecy, from island to island and from one coast to the other, He, the Most High, whispers the revelation of the old black race.

Oh, Africa! You're a sublime cosmic matrix fertilized by the cosmos to generate the black race, and humanity is born.

The black race called Halasiou by the pharaoh of the New Kingdom Seti I, of the nineteenth dynasty of Egypt, consecrated priest of the god Sutekh or Seth, indicating that his name Seti means "Set," but his known birth name, meaning "man of Set, beloved of Ptah," is "sty mry-n-pth" or Seti-Merenptah; and his vocalized name Menmaatre is his praenomen "mn-m3 t-r," taking upon his ascension to the throne. This son of Ramesses I and Sitre, and the father of Ramesses II, is the one who named the other three races that currently occupy the rest of the continents of the earth, represented by four different colors on the tomb of the oldest priest of Egypt at Thebes.

The red race called Rot, a color used in Egypt to represent the mulatto, was used to represent the male Egyptian. Could it be probable that the red mulatto race came from Egypt, in Africa?

The yellow Asiatic race was Amou, and the white Lybico-European race was Tamahou. This human variety, the result of your crisscross combination and degeneration or selection, was divided into four original and successive races and representing the natural distinct species of the human race.

The wise human at work is devoted and tossed between civilizations, and tired—yes, tired of being a prisoner of this world, in his Africa of palms, where the sun is beaming down its kisses, dancing solemnly in the shadow of the curved drums, under a curse without end, where man lives in a painful ever imagined manner with suffering crammed on him.

Oh, Africa, where will you go? But where will you go, Africa? Backward, but to what? Or forward to the inhuman workshop to painfully find the only hour of the day that speaks of obscure time, with the primary message of the sky echoing about its great history forever? Oh, Africa, every night, you are talking about the glory of your verifiable truths with all power.

You're the powerful silent voice never heard aloud but that works as an invisible flash, if only evoked secretly before the thunder. Your recognition is powerful and your truth a bliss. Africa!

Oh, Africa! You're a great, beautiful story—a beautiful authentic story that opens the hearts and minds to the harmonious and humanitarian cause for democracy, freedom, peace, and justice. Your letters of nobility give some disturbing revelations to crimes of thy lese-majesty.

After deploying all your attention to understand all your intelligible cares within reason, to express from one end to the other the very idea of love, which reaches the expansion of consciousness, corresponding to the nature of your kingdoms, you set out the truth of the fact without asking it as necessity.

Your verb, which gives the clearest definition ever found, is supremely used everywhere. More simply, as accurately and precisely as possible, it eliminates all ambiguity.

Is it in the same sense of your verb "love," of thy clearer definition ever found, that you're used but absolutely contradictory and controversial because of serious misunderstandings—misunderstandings that embrace all things in the visible and invisible worlds? Oh, yes, learn Africa, to leave the dense body by your will for the growth of your soul. Practice intelligible cares of love within reason for the expansion of your consciousness corresponding to the nature of your kingdoms—a correct understanding throughout that allows you to see in yourself.

You have been a student and guardian of the teachings of all occult schools of philosophies and sciences. Board not in the skepticism that obscures the truth or that attitude of calm confidence that prevents inner education and intuition; it's the only way to cultivate a sense of perception and to discover the truth in a given proposal of the absolute truth.

Cultivate a state of mind that admits that everything is possible. Do not let yourself be carried away by the consideration of the established fact. Search another perspective and keep adaptability in your mind. Always desire light, always more light.

Verify by yourself and find the most basic knowledge. If you have observed the facts as such, be satisfied. You will advance in the broader perspectives of the truth—perspectives that will illuminate you. And many mystery doors are going to be opened, one side dark and the other side illuminated, like in a mirror in which we see ourselves more in firm conviction than all other philosophies because, in this mirror, you absolutely reflect your true conviction—the mystery of the world. A truth revealed once and for all, to all other existences—the extreme limitlessness of occult knowledge, like being the alpha and omega of the man before his birth in the inner worlds, in his life, and after his death, for he is here to die. Possess a state of mind with great benefits that perfectly reconciles opinions that are seemingly absolutely contradictory.

Possess impartiality as the basis for your final judgment until the moment that your inner self allows you to judge knowingly because it is a free and wide-open spirit that discovers the bond of harmony that exists between all things. Aim your appealing only to reason, in the desire and hope to clarify some obsessive difficulties encountered.

Know that, under the sun, down here on earth and even high beyond the sky, there is no infallible revelation as complex as what embraces all things that do not prevent serious misunderstandings. Study very deep philosophies of the past, oh, Africa, and impregnate yourself with this idea to only give the last word on the mystery of the world as a philosophy containing nothing less than the teachings that have for many years devoted their knowledge exclusively to the widest and most logical conception.

The nonjustifiable alternate policies, to which you have been a target for its despots, will sooner or later be justified. Our thoughts will always be with you until the day of your victory against this underworld system yet inked in your spiritual triangle. You're passionate for freedom but perpetually living a polemic postcolonial political history unworthy of esteem. Your life is constantly persecuted by a reprehensible feeling of a deep and distinctive footprint of your story.

It is a story of a system of invasion and occupation of your ancient land of the pharaonic Egypt and the entire African continent, followed by the theft of your intellectuality, your genuine procedural knowledge, your epistemological, gnoseological and ontological knowledge, your irreproachable ancient literature supported and carefully styled to the level of a literary language, your instructive religious work, etc. In addition, as if all this was not enough, they continued with slavery, colonization, and a policy worthy of contempt, which are still inscribed on the velvet of our skin and echoing in our environment. Where the atmospheric darkness of your night comes to ravish the sun from the day affection and imprison it. However, you are very attached to your noble children by sincere love. You're an adept of controversy but a free thinker ready to give everything for the triumph of truth, love, freedom, and peace.

You're the light where the day is born; you're the understanding mother of wisdom and science. You're the tenacity born from the conviction. You're the order and desire where love is born. You're the satisfaction where resignation rises. You're patience, mother of great courage, the entire firmament, and the stars are your children. And it's from you that came all that exists. Oh, yes, go beyond the tops of the highest mountains of the universe, beyond the edge of the desert, far from where the beam that administers the space so immeasurable governs the earth; you're Africa, the matrix of humanity.

Africa, you feel, see, and hear sounds of the hyperphysical worlds—the one of causes, forces, and the physical world and the one-off affects that affect all other realms where nature reigns. Light and color are to you understandable but as incomprehensible as the existence of reality born of thee.

Your hyperphysical worlds awaken the superior senses of other realms where nature reigns, hidden from their eyes, more convinced by the reality of the invisible existence of those worlds than the entire truth immediately accessible to the belief. You alone know everything concerning these superior worlds to the application of the tangible world, which nobody thinks of acquiring an infinitesimal knowledge. You're what is above, like what is below—a physical hyperbirth without pain, which must be the same in your modest world, established at the infinitesimal with which we come into contact in our life on earth.

At first, you're a real occult value. The existence of the hyperphysical plans and the reasoning to your everyday life provide accurate descriptions and better sources. There will not be one exactly like you. You're unique by nature; you're abundance and development. Your differences are according to personal views, confusion, and disorder in the spirit, contrary to a better understanding and a better description of the spirit, each of them complementing the other in your higher planes, each being so faithful but different from each other.

Your noble children are called to reside in distant countries already for many years, living in new and strange conditions without any doubt possible with impatience, eagerly accepting the conditions of mediocre existence that are reserved for them in life. But having the knowledge acquired with one certainty of passing into the afterlife, after death is certainly a huge advantage for your beloved children; your mysterious agent causes phenomena that remain invisible to everyone. But a force in itself, allowing us to perceive its manifestations, is filled with crystals of the beginning, forming the visible and invisible worlds that act on us at all times. Your more durable and indestructible hyperphysical planes, still pretending to be something less tangible, are much more real than the tangible material world. And certain understandings of all your material things, causes, and forces are just effects that we cannot really understand without knowing the other.

The Great Architect (God) first conceived you in His mind, where you gradually took shape and finally existed as a well-defined idea. Your thought form started with materials placed on top of each other, with a divine plan and an invisible order for all. Thus, you're exactly an edifice edified as the thought form of your Grand Architect that becomes an objective reality. Now you're much more real and sustainable by the material object than in the mind of the Great Architect in thought form—a thought form that will never be destroyed; its duration is as long as life itself, and its existence can be read in the memory of nature, without violence to the reason, convinced of its utility, of its permanence, and of its reality.

Suddenly, the absolute was torn in two equal parts: darkness and light—what isn't and what is. Then, without a body or a specific face, appeared the highest and the most powerful creative of spirits, which imagination could not imagine. By pronouncing his name, "The one who Is," let His grave voice thunder universally. Then, in the molt, He announced the period of the puberty of times—the renewal of His skin in the human species—and more importantly, He turned at the side of the light so that what must be seen, be seen. Then at the side of the darkness, He erased from sight what must not be seen. So, He pronounced the visibility and the invisibility. Then He spread his first creation, water, between light and darkness, where sprang a content invested with three species: (1) "spirit," you seat corporeally in the human brain; (2) the "soul," sitting in the heart; and (3) the "heart" shield in a body, invested with physical sensations. These are three entities known to be the headquarters of perception.

He created heaven and earth through the eternal essence (the energy of the space); the light thrown in the beginning and on the evolution of our dual form of earth and heaven. The firmament, a star launched necessary to obtain a complete and definite conception, considered by whatever truth to be examined from several points of view. That man —"that first dual form of energy, the double sky," a source of light—possessed the key: the vowels and words suitably divided and put in place to hide and obscure the significance of the great and sublime mysteries. He demonstrated the transcendent wisdom of initiated intelligences, which inspired some wonderful interpretations unveiling time that only He could understand—the open conception of God, a true method to follow, the right to possess an occult truth out of reach.

Your brain is a keyboard, an instrument on which the human spirit plays a harmonious symphony for the pleasure of love, pain, hatred, joy, and the sadness of life. And the sensation is for the immortal spirit conscious of itself, a self-knowledge. But all depends on what we mean by sensation, isn't it? Because the position taken by each of the opposing camps is partly correct, if it means the ability to respond to shocks, like a bouncing rubber ball. Like your brain, all tissues of the human body, living or dead, are gifted with sensitivity and perceive the pain of the toe or the injured finger.

I had never had so much need of thoughts—thoughts as tangible as any material object in the physical world. Yes, just need of thoughts without time and without existent distance. Yes, I only thought of thought, thought conceived of thoughts, thoughts of countless hierarchies of spiritual beings.

Yes, my conceived thought! I had never had so much need of thoughts that materialized desires, passions, wishes, and feelings when I had my shoulders emerged, despite my efforts to be released, plunged into the huge painful path and arduous blue ocean of my thought. Without hesitation, my only supreme desire was just my thought, composed of material thought power. I had never had so much need of thoughts, where colors and light were changing constantly. Well, you must so desire an active spiritual thought with so much burning thirst and also be determined to know and to find expression in the substance of the different regions divided into seven regions existing under seven states and acquire it throughout all other kingdoms of nature because it is my sole and unique aspiration.

As intensely as I desired my thought power, acting on my physical body a while ago, when I had my shoulders plunged into the huge painful path and arduous Blue Ocean of my thought, revitalized, I struggled day and night for it by excluding any other ambition in the life of the four denser subdivisions to concretize my thoughts.

Certainly, because I was looking for the concrete thought with such fervor, through every fiber of my vitalized body, by appropriate methods that I had developed, I became wise—a result obtained by an effort to act on the knowledge provided by the intellectual substance.

A fundamental idea of your occultism, not easy to wander through and acquire a personal knowledge of the beyond; there is neither existing luck nor special gifts in that path that leads to knowledge but just the development of the latent senses in your being. Because all that you're is a primordial necessity for any other ambition in life, whose supreme motive must be to do good to mankind in complete disregard of oneself; otherwise, the painful and arduous path of your occultism is dangerous to tread. And the truth that makes us free and eternal cannot be discovered or revealed once and for all but should be sought forever. To learn some basic occult powers that remain immutable, human conditions before his birth and after his death are necessary. Do not despair of acquiring knowledge for the lack of occult powers. Subtle and superior senses of this world allow the African man to perceive the invisible worlds of creation. Your creation is composed of various plans of consciousness called inner worlds.

The hyperphysical plans and other dimensions of the multidimensional universe are hidden because of your state of slumber. They're nonexistent and incomprehensible to the white man, like a man born blind unable to perceive light and colors surrounding him in the sensible world. He feels things by the sense of touch, the sense of sight being default to him. These subtle bodies correspond to the plan of your conscience that I determine as follows: for the astral body, the astral plane that allows the soul to project itself to the celestial spheres, dissociating itself from the physical body and moving from one plane to another to freely explore the surrounding space and live an autonomous existence; for the mental body, qualified to be below the causal body, but above the astral body, the etheric body, and the physical body, man; the dense physical body, which is in itself the cause of nothing, nor a principle, is the consequence of everything. From the point of view of the soul, it goes from the top to the bottom; and as a vehicle for the soul-the spiritual man, it allows its involution, a retreat movement inward, preventing it from experimenting, to live experiences, and to evolve; but offers it the opportunity to express and radiate on the physical plane, etc. The African man distinguished all these aspects, including the physical and spiritual world. This is what religions appoint as the afterlife or heaven.

Your inner worlds can be defined as the states of energy/matter that interpenetrate your entire material world but not listed in the physical bodies, and their vibration on the extremely high-frequency bands are enabling them to coexist with your physical universe. The esoteric literature gives precise descriptions to this true nature of your underworld-the unknown (the hereafter), not more or less the fanciful representations of mythologies and religions. You're the soul, where the deepest mysteries of the immortal divine spark and which are at the base of the hyperphysical world that puts God in a relationship with the man.

The soul assimilated by the spirit, which develops its divine powers, is all that there is as the best and the most perfect in humans. Its ethereal and subtle substance liberated from the four thicker elements, drawn from the body that encloses it, is part of the realized experiences that the spirit harvests from its pilgrimage in the material.

Your pain is sufficient to everyday life oh Africa. But the versions of your sentences differ superficially from each other, showing how many times this reasoning is false in connection with the identical descriptions of your reasoning. Easily, it is much easier to conclude and recognize your sentence according to testimonies without penalty. Avoiding serious mistakes to have real value does not mean to be trustworthy. It is more than modest to speak in detail about what is found, against necessary investigations to know what is connected to your existence.

But the existence of reality, extremely opposed to your respect, only presents the truth immediately accessible and to the contrary understanding, to reveal reality that nobody sees. Consequently, the existence itself that possessed all life, far beyond knowing it completely, knows everything concerning the truth of its existence; it is able to provide descriptions as rich and accurate than those one would expect from the supposed better source, uniquely for the nature of their desires of abundance for developments. In your world of desire, the sixth world, the forms easily avoid gravity. Time and distance are nonexistent, and there is neither hot nor cold there. It is also tangible than any material objects are in the physical world.

In your world of desire, animal and human energies mingle with those of countless hierarchies of spiritual beings. And forces emanating from that huge legion of various beings mold the substance of your world of desire, constantly changing in countless varied shapes. In a world where color and light are constantly modified and where spiritual beings are as active as they may not appear, its substance serves to concretize desires, emotions, passions, wishes, and feelings, and find their expression in the substance of the different regions divided into seven regions and existing under seven states, corresponding to the seven subdivisions like any other kingdoms of the nature.

Two great faculties of the soul, the forces of attraction and repulsion, which manifest themselves differently in the three superior regions, are acting within the three denser regions; the region of feeling is the central region, the neutral zone. In a sense or in the other, the forces of your world of desire act on the dense body, vivify it, and push it to action through every fiber of the vitalized body.

The region of passion is the lowest in the world of sensual desires, and the region of impressionability is the second subdivision where the forces of attraction and repulsion are combined. Without your active cosmic forces in your world of desire, there wouldn't be any experience or moral development possible, and evolution would have been impossible for the form, for the individual, and for life. Because the forms evolve toward the superior states just to respond to the requirements of the development of the spiritual life; and this is why this kingdom of your nature is of great importance, according to what preceded. In your physical world, the seventh world, time and distance govern the existence, and material is submissive to gravity—to the phenomenon of contraction and expansion. Among the seven, the physical world is the densest. It is also divided into seven regions or subdivisions of your material.

Your gases, your liquids, and your solids are the three densest subdivisions that constitute the basis of all tangible forms, which we call the chemical region. Your four other different densities are occupied by the ether—a nonhomogeneous physical material but existing under four different states, the most subtle of the physical world called the etheric region, where the spirit vitalizes forms of the chemical region.

Your three superior subdivisions in the world of thought – your region of abstract thought -- provide the basis of the abstract thought. Your region of the concrete thought – your four denser subdivisions that gives body to your thoughts and concretize them, provides the intellect substance.

The occultist devotes much attention to the characteristics of your physical world, considering everything from a point of view very different from the one of the materialistic. Your chemical bodies are derived from the truly chemical constituents of your earth, like the air we breathe, the water that quenches our thirst, the cloud enveloping the top of your mountains, where you collect the sap of the creative energy, the blood of animals and humans, and manifest your energy to plants and on all forms of minerals. These forms of minerals, whether animals, human, or vegetables, constituted of your chemical substance, must also logically be inert, deprived of sensation as the chemical material in its primitive state.

It is the shaping of your fundamental substance—your unique universal spirit, that creates the diversity of forms that man observes their manifestation around him at various stages of development in the visible world, under the four major aspects of life torrents, constituting a spiritual impulse of the four kingdoms—animal, human, mineral, and vegetable—in various forms of the earth; and which are disintegrated by your chemical forces, when their shape is no longer usable and returns to their primary state, to build new forms of material. So being unable to understand the attitude of your hyperphysical worlds or to consider your physical world with contempt by a superficial knowledge is as incorrect as materialism. The substance of each of your worlds or the seven states of your material differs, not arbitrarily but is necessarily submissive to the laws practically inoperative in your other worlds, where the substance of which they're composed does not have a uniform density.

In your kingdom of nature, you're "ether." Let's penetrate into this Kingdom of the invisible and intangible world, where your senses are lacking to human. In that part of your physical world, unexplored by the materialistic, you exist. And your existence is of a substance more subtle than those known. You cannot be measured or collected. You're uncatchable at the will of scholars, and no one can isolate you, like the invisible air that can be measured at the speed of the wind, weighed or made visible under the form of liquid air, and be analyzed. It is not the same for you, oh, ether. But you exist despite all knowledgeable ingeniury.

We are placed in this material environment by the sublime wisdom that executes your will. Each of our vehicles has a special seed-atom - an atom that the spirit retains from a body between two incarnations. Our vehicles are rebuilt from these seed-atoms during a new birth. The densest etheric body of angels and archangels is formed with a "substance of desire." The "wave of life" of archangels precedes the one of angels. And the one of angels precedes ours.

The spirit groups of animals found among some archangels and in some spirits of different race of people or "gods," assisted Jehovah, their leader, in His tasks of governor of humanity. The kingdom of Thy will is established. And it is said that we must receive will—the will of your kingdom—like a little child. To learn, on the contrary, subject to other conditions, we could not learn the existence of your worlds, not inflicting violence on reason. We must use the knowledge of your superior worlds and strive to put it into practice in daily life to better take advantage of our education in your material world. Let us make mistakes in the school of your physical world by great valuable experiences because we learn more from committed mistakes, the path that leads to development. Such is a state of mind that presents great advantages.

The individual spirit, the triple spirit and divine body, directs our bodies and spirits through the means of intellect. The material of the materialization of the divine spirit is the physical body. The material of the materialization of the vital spirit is the vital body. The material of the materialization of the human spirit, an individualized parcel of the universal spirit that directs the personality from the interior, is the body of desire.

The manifestation of evolution is the stage in which the human being develops his consciousness into the divine omniscience known to humanity. But the manifestation of involution, a phase devoted to the building of the vehicles of the spirit and for the awakening of one's conscience, is a phase that humanity completely ignores. Man has used the highest less crystallized forms and the missing link, and has developed the current physical body, capable to receive the intellect. And the activity of the vital spirit in the intellect develops the intuition.

Five schools of major mysteries and seven of minor mysteries make a total of twelve mystery schools on earth, and their school is the Western school of minor mysteries. The minor mysteries have nine degrees, and the major mysteries have four degrees. The minor mysteries (the fourth period) refer to the evolution of humanity during the earth period. The major mysteries (the seven periods) of which all the Elder Brothers of the Rose Cross are initiates, lead to a development that will be reached by humanity at the end of the manifestation.

Scientists tell us about Pangaea, a unique mass that existed around 180 million years ago, when the first terrestrial human beings appeared in Australia, when all the terrestrial continents were still one big globe. It eventually split into two: Laurasia in the north with the northern continents, and Gondwana in the south, including Australia, Antarctica, India, Africa, and South America. India and Africa drifted from there sixty-five million years ago, leaving Antarctica in the south and Australia and South America in the middle.

Five eras are known to us. The polar epoch was the first terrestrial era, where the physical body was rebuilt and in which the material forming the earth today was still part of the sun and vibrated naturally in a very high temperature. It is in this polar region of the sun that our evolution immediately began to develop the most evolved beings who became the first humans. Since fire could not burn the spirit in that gaseous atmosphere, man recapitulated his mineral phase of existence again in the substances that were all in fusion and that formed the current earth.

Humanity began its evolution on over three planets before coming to earth. By relying on the occult teaching, we can imagine that all souls of our present humanity were once divine sparks that animated the mineral reign of the first planet, and then the vegetable reign of the second planet, and finally the animal reign of the third planet, the moon, to be finally ready to pass into the human reign on earth. *The Secret Doctrine* tells us that the current corpus, which is the moon, is the remnant of a great planet that was our last home. With the help of the lords of form, man built his first mineral body by the subtle chemical substance of the sun, like the maternity of a mother, unconscious of the construction of the child' body within her bosom.

The "conceptors — gods," wanted the expansion of the "firmament" in waters and separated water with water for the conditions of the period of the moon. A mass of water was formed around the burning core by the cold of the outer space and by the cloud of incandescent fire. From the process of water expanding, steam was produced by the contact of water and fire. A steam that was rushing outward was replaced by relatively cool water, which constantly gravitated toward the burning hot center, leading to a constant flow of water held in suspension.

This expansion was complemented by an atmosphere of the fog of fire formed by the steam escaping from the burning center toward the exterior, condensed by the contact with the space. To accomplish another cycle, this steam returned to the center to be heated again. The dense water was near the burning center, and water in expansion was outside. The invisible heat and the incandescent nebula followed later by moisture outside and the heat inside, eventually formed the solid part—the solid body of our current globe.

They wanted the separation of water from the dry ground, for the dry land to exist. This first formation of the earth's crust was called "the Earth by the Elohim—the ethers, the etheric region of the physical world.

There are four ethers in total. The first, the chemical ether, maintains the form. Here, all the forces that ensure the growth and the maintenance of bodies are acting. The second, the vital ether, maintains species where all forces that ensure the reproduction are acting. In the third, the light ether, all forces that produce movement and the perception are acting. The late comer, which is added to the other three ethers, is the reflective ether, where—through—the ego directs its vehicles and also registers all events that occur in the world. These four ethers form the vital human body. Here, the construction of the body and the descent of the spirit into matter have ended. Now that we have become humans, the spiritualization of the body in the soul begins the activity of the vital spirit in intellect and intuition.

The hyperborean era is the second, where the lords of creation—the Elohim, the "gods," the directors—created the reign of the stars, of the moon, of the sun, and of the vegetation. It succeeded minerals—Mineral that existed before the first solid formation of the whole crust called mineral or vegetable, which was made in the central sun, even as the material and dense substance did not exist at the time when the earth was thrown out of the central mass; the vital body was added to the physical body. Note that the crust melted in the form of a ring, which disintegrated when it was thrown out of the central mass to be assembled later again. With a relatively short required time, our earth, such a small body, recrystallized itself.

When the moon was separated from the earth, the melting process was repeated. But the melting process did not destroy the ethereal plants found on the solid part of the cloud fire of the central heat that came to give them the vital force necessary to attract the denser material to them. These ethereal vegetal forms, buried in the geological layers of our globe attracted solid materials to form the substance of the plants existing presently, when the heat came from outside after the separation of the earth with the moon and the sun. Let the waters produce things and all things that have the breath of life, according to their species, forms of big amphibians, "and all birds that have wings," said the Elohim. This reminds us of Gen. 1:20–21 of the Bible because the things that were formed were not alive but things that breathe and yearn for life.

The word *nephesh* (meaning "the living soul") and which refers to the creation of mammals in verse 24; is explained by saying that mammals breathed life. It fails to mention the asexual and hermaphrodite phase of humanity—the Lemurian era, during which the differentiation of sexes occurred—and goes directly to the creation of man in verse 27, where it is said that God—the Elohim— formed man in their image. It describes the Atlantean Epoch — the phase of evolution that humanity had reached, where beings without sex or hermaphrodite no longer existed, and goes directly to the separation of sexes that says, "He created them male and female, Gen. 5:2." And they finally said, "Be fruitful and increase in number to repopulate the earth, Gen. 1:28."

Generally, the identity and mission of Jehovah — the Eternal, just as it is found in the first chapter of Genesis, which attributes the creation of man at the end of all creations, mainly deals with the creation of the form; and in the second chapter placed at the first place where every living being took life in consideration. Both chapters probably find an agreement between the two seemingly contradictory descriptions. While the fifth chapter deals with consciousness. In any case, they're establishing a well-defined distinction between the physical form and the life that built this form, and its own expression is the key to the enigma. Thus, if we consider the human in the point of view of life, he was created first. But considered from the point of view of form, he was created last.

The Bible, the occult teachings, and the modern science agree and harmonize on the bisexual subject that was formerly the man; like a fetus which is at first bisexual before passing through the stage of development of intrauterine life corresponding to our era; on the other hand, accepting the story of the "rib of Adam" from which Jehovah created the female Eve, who will give birth to the living human being in a latent state, and from which one of the two sexes will predominate and the other will remain in a latent state, is not conceivable.

In a rudimentary form, each person still has the organs of the opposite sex. As was the primitive man, every person is actually bisexual. At the time of the separation event, Jehovah executed the change. When this creation took place, He breathed the breath of life into man, from the beginning to the middle of the Lemurian era, where the forms were more ethereal.

After the separation of the moon from the earth, to the generation of bodies, Jehovah did not intervene before the separation of humanity into two sexes. The skeleton became firm and solid because there was no individual spirit, and the man to become still had gills. His skeleton was as soft as cartilage. He had no red and hot blood. His entire shape was still soft and flexible, and he did not breathe through the lungs. It was in the first half of the Lemurian era, with the assistance of the lunar forces that crystallize and harden, that his dense and concrete body was built.

The third Lemurian era, prehistorically very distant, referring to the development phase of humanity, was to develop the will and power of conception. It is respectively designated on earth but in our sense of the word, this time has no dwellings. Lemurians had no eyes or desire, and their language consisted of sounds like those of nature. The body of desire was added to the physical and to the vital body. And during the latter part of the Lemurian era, the terrestrial crust in some places began to become hard and solid.

Biblical narrative described the same water conditions; fog of fire producing thick cloud in the air, obscuring visibility in the atmosphere at the earth's surface, and the first attempts of movement and breathing endowed with life, similar to those that existed during the period of the moon, referring to the origins of the "human race" corresponding to the Lemurian period of the lost continent; subsequently incorporated into the philosophy of the proto-New Age of theosophy and subsequently into the general marginal belief. Even if there is no known geological formation under the Indian or Pacific Oceans, or any valid scientific hypothesis that corresponds to the hypothetical Lemuria is no longer considered, the occult science believes that this continent existed in ancient times but sank beneath the ocean after a cataclysm. Man lived in the moaning of the wind, the thunder of the cataracts in the hypertropical climate, with the howling of the storm and the whispering of the stream batten by the storms, and surrounded by vast forests of giant ferns and animals of gigantic size, growing in an extremely luxuriant way. For him, the rumblings of the volcano were like the voices of the gods of which he knew he was a descendant. The birth of his body was unknown to him. He perceived the presence of his fellows but could not see them. However, he had an inner perception, such as the way we perceive things and people in a dream, but his perception of dream was clear and logical, with a very important difference. To a large extent, the same man had the power to shape his own body. He had a sense of hearing and touch at his birth, but his ability to perceive light came later. As the light shone weakly through the fiery atmosphere of the ancient Lemuria, he had two sensitive points that were affected by sunlight. And it was only toward the end of the Atlantean era that he obtained the ability to see as we do today. Man did not need the external light before that time, when the construction of the eye was in progress, because the earth was still part of the luminous mass, and sun was internal. Then man, who was himself bright, had no need of external light. It became necessary for man to perceive light when he became aware of the rays of light. And to meet the demand of an existing function, nature built the eye to make the perception of light possible. The perception of light thus caused the formation of the eye because there could not be an eye where there was no light.

The Atlantean era is the fourth era—the era of volcanic cataclysms that destroyed a large part of the Lemurian continent to replace it with the Atlantean continent, the current Atlantic Ocean. Ego could begin directing its vehicles, thanks to this era. It represented the end of involution, the phase of the construction of the body and the descent of the spirit into the material, and the beginning phase of the evolution of the spiritualization of the body into the soul. We then became men, followed by the present era called the Aryan epoch — where the activity of the human spirit in the intellect produces reason. Of these five eras are added two others mentioned in the Bible. The one of New Jerusalem is the Galilean era, where the world will live in the etheric region of the physical world and develop intuition through the activity of the vital spirit in the intellect.

And the last one is for the activity of the divine spirit in the intellect to give the spiritual consciousness to men.

Finally, when a flash of inspiration showed its face, the Creator said to the angels while thinking, "Everything is not yet in order or fully functioning. The universe is in the process of being created. However, there is a final task to be completed in the making of the universe. The real meaning of the human life—his purpose, his objective, and his death—are his treasure and the valuable object of his life, is beyond the description for all that I have created." For the human beings to know its immeasurable value, the Creator hid this treasure. Nevertheless, He did not hide it on the highest mountain peak, nor in the great desert wilderness, nor in the vast expanses of the universe. Instead, He hid this treasure of life within the human being, knowing that—this secret treasure being hidden in the human being—man will never search for it in the ultimate reality within himself, to know how precious it is. That is the beginning of time; a secret thought that reveals the meaning of life and the mystery of death; a perpetual cycle of births that created life functioning temporally until death, just with an invitation to do it over again and again, in the endless pattern of death and the rebirth, seeking in oneself who is eternal. The individual—the pure self, the likeness of God, the hidden treasure within the soul—not recognizable by the mind or senses—existed at the beginning of creation, subtly exists now and will continue unfathomably to exist in the future, dwelling in the innermost chamber of the heart and in the depths of the soul, waiting to tame the inner superior power and achieve self-mastering to conquer the world with a beautiful poetic explanation of the mystery of life and the eternal death. "He who overcomes, I will make him a pillar in the temple of my God, and he shall go out no more," "Revelation 3:12." The smallest spirit cannot contain the great superior spirit in evolution for a full liberation from the concrete existence. He is established by his actions, to accomplish many times a small period of time on earth and continue to live his irreparable destiny after the physical death. The soul follows its line that continues straight ahead, having achieved progress in this world; the soul can then discover the reality of things and the mysteries of existence. It continues to progress toward perfection after death, in its eternal journey to become a divine tree. Having a small amount of experiences without progress after death, it cannot return to correct its mistakes, but just an eternal repetition of the same experiences of the natural progress, not following a circular path or a straight line but using two spatial dimensions. Thus, the transmigration of souls is not an authority sustained by any doctrine.

Note that, in the Hebraic version of the Bible, the name Adam in the first chapters of Genesis—written in the form *ha'adam* (הָאָדָם)—means "human being" and not necessarily a masculine being. In the translated version of Gen. 2:21–23, it is often used without the article and designates the first created human simply called "man" as his proper name. He was still alone; thus, still androgynous, he was male and female. Adam is the symbol of the state of humanity as a whole.

The androgynous being is a human being who does not permit to know which sex or gender he belongs. Regardless his physical appearance, his identity is neither male nor female. Therefore, the representation of androgyny was in certain cultures and at specific periods, a story considered as a sign of the anger of the gods. The ancient people were making a clear difference between the androgynous rituals, which do not merely lie within the temple, or a compartmentalized model envisioning the divine. It is the coincidence of the opposite, living in a holistic manner, bringing together the magical and religious powers related to each of the two sexes than the concrete hermaphrodite. In the heart of the gospel, the two-becoming-one is regarded principally as a part of an early baptismal rite. This mystery rite was ensuring the initiate of the unity with God. It was a question of removing the darkness from the body of "the initiate to put the light in it, and bring back the primitive human—the primal Adamic androgynous human being"—to the sexual unity, and to his heavenly companion.

Therefore, hermaphrodism is a biological phenomenon wherein the individual is morphologically male and female. That generic human (the first man) in the Hebraic text, harmoniously overtone by most people as referring to a male human, was not specifically referred to as a male human (*ish*) until the creation of (*ishshah*)—the woman, taken from the rib of Adam—the man. After the creation of the female, God presented her to the human male. Then he saw the female human and said, "This one is the bone from my bone, and the flesh from my flesh! She will be called 'woman' [*ishshah*], because she was taken from 'man'[*ish*], Gen. 2:23." The first woman and the first man were therefore part of the same human, or one side of the first human being (*ha'adam*). This indicates that they shared the same flesh and bone.

Many traditions around the world reported that this primordial man was androgynous or, again, hermaphrodite. So, if all human beings were androgynous and were not yet divided into male and female, that separation was realized in the gradual transition, when the spiritual evolution of humanity required the division into two sexes of mankind. Thus the myth of Genesis, according to which Eve was born from a "rib" of Adam, means that the primordial being manifested itself as androgynous or the birth of the astral body before the physical body. The primordial Adam, who in the androgynous state was Adam and Eve, meant that the first human was undifferentiated at the origin of the "man - ish." In fact, the ancestor of humanity was an androgynous being. He was transformed by the rabbis who compiled the book of Genesis as *ish* (man). Translated correctly, the text indicates that a woman was born from an androgynous being and not from man. From that moment, the individuals, with the division into sexes became independent; and through marriage they were united, had children, education them, and this education of children and many other demands of life, represented a source of shared responsibilities. Capable of sharing these responsibilities, they could then learn life lessons necessary for their spiritual evolution.

Prior to his separation into two male and female human beings, androgynous was a sign of creation, of fertility, of fullness, and of totality; the union of the exterior and the interior, the outside and the inside; the union of the sky and earth, of the celestial and the mortal; and the union of male and female. So it is said, "When you turn these two beings into one, the inside as outside, up as down, and if you turn male and female into one, so that the male is no longer male and the female no longer female, then you will enter into the kingdom of God." Thomas says, "The inside I have made outside and the outside inside; and thy whole fullness has been fulfilled in Me." He recited this long prayer before his martyrdom with efforts to carry out his mission. Peter says, "Concerning this—the Lord says in a mystery, Unless you make on the right hand as what is on the left and what is on the left hand as what is on the right and what is above as what is below and what is behind as what is before, you will not have knowledge of the kingdom." This was to explain why he is being crucified upside down in the apocryphal Acts of Peter.

A letter from Pope Clement I in Rome to the church at Corinth called 1 Clement quoted these words as coming from "the master Jesus himself," saying, "When the two shall be one, and the outside as the inside, and the male with female, so that there is neither male nor female, they will automatically become on"; and in 2 Clement, he says, Both are one when we speak truth to each other; the inside is the soul and outside the body, and we should let the soul be evident in good works just as the body is visibly evident. As for "neither male nor female," by striping it mystical meaning and giving it a bland interpretation, the two entities become an anti-Gnostic preaching acceptable to Christians. But although there is no connection in date, origin, or subject of importance between the two texts, possibly from the Egypt of the second-century, that simply means that a Christian brother should not think of a sister-Christian as female, nor the sister think of him as a male. He said, "When you do these things, my father's kingdom will come." This passage of *2 Clement* saying authentically endorsed the words of Jesus, acknowledged the writer.

The Hermetic androgyny is as much the sun as the moon; at the beginning of the beginnings, the Androgyny appears to Alpha - to the Cosmic Emission, and to the Reintegration - to Omega. In other words, to form the hermetic androgynous, the male becomes female and the female becomes male; therefore, the human hermaphrodite (XXY), is neither male nor female but both at the same time. And he does not produce gametes capable of fusing with another gamete of the complementary type to generate a new living being and therefore is sterile. A reproduction of a sexual haploid cell is an effective reproductive system that all species possess. It is indeed necessary for the perpetuation of species in time, allowing the sexual reproduction of eukaryotes that include all unicellular or multicellular organisms. Therefore, it literally means a living organism characterized by the majority of the genetic cellular material contained in a nucleus.

This mechanism of sexual reproduction is related to eukaryotes and consists of a nuclear membrane (a "true nucleus")—"a true core" characterized by the alternation of two phases: (1)-diploid— when a biological cell contains two complete sets of chromosomes (2n chromosomes) in the core; and (2)-haploid— when a biological cell contains chromosomes, each having one exemplary of (chromosomes "n") in the core. These two phases are separated by meiosis and fertilization, thus forming a sexual life cycle to divide the living world into two major groups involving a genetic exchange that involves mechanisms of the reduction of (meiosis) and increases (fertilization) of chromosome repetition (ploidy), the number of copies consisting in a fusion of male and female gametes into a single cell named egg or zygote.

Two types of cell divisions exist in eukaryotes. Meiosis, the first, results in the production of a sexual cell or gametes for reproduction. And the second gene that retains information concerning the somatic cells and ensures the birth of cells, is identical to the mother cell during the asexual multiplication. Necessarily, the life cycle of a eukaryotic organism comprises an alternation of stages with different levels of chromosome repetition when we speak of alternating phase of life cycle.

The philosopher's stone is a double being called "Rebis" by alchemy. A transcendent principle being represented by embracing its own figurative power in feminine divinity, reveals the traces of androgynous in Adonis, Cybele, or Dionysus as a final product of a double matter, united once again in what is sometimes described as the divine hermaphrodite; when one has gone through the stages of putrefaction and purification, separating opposite qualities, a reconciliation of the spirit and matter indicating a being both male and female in a single body.

In China, the yin and the yang are the interconnected contraries or interdependent opposing forces in the natural world, interacting on each other and giving birth to each other. The physical manifestations of the yin-and-yang concept are thoughts considered as life and death, as above and beneath, fire and water, light and dark, hot and cold, and so on. In the Indian Sanskrit, Shiva is a composite form of the androgynous Hindu deity known as Ardhanarishvara. And in Japan, two powers go hand in hand; Izanagi the (husband and brother) is the one who changes the destiny, and Izanami the (wife and sister) is the decider. Izanami is both the kami of creation and death and the multitude of kamis of heaven and earth; she created the islands and deities of Japan, according to *Kojiki* and *Nihon Shoki*.

This double being first evolved in Africa; in that imperishable, sacred land, the first mystical enterprise on firm ground, on which the first black race spawned by our divine progenitors and where the simultaneous evolution of seven human groups on seven different parts of our globe occurred; it symbolizes the wealth and happiness beyond the contradictions of humanity; its pseudo-values and deterioration are the original unity. The cradle in which the first man discovered happiness led him to find the survival issue through thousands of years of labyrinth when he did not yet know where to enter, neither to exit.

The history of humanity begins like in all texts of Genesis by the final return to that original unity referring to the principle, and not only with the primordial androgynous but also the beginning, where man was separated into two distinct human beings: the unity of "man" and "woman," the relationship between two people of the opposite sex. In ancient Greek, the words invented from the names γαμέτης (gametē) and γαμέτις (gametēs), respectively denote husband and wife. Something that may involve the manifestation of aspects within an individual is in the dissolution of the masculine and feminine, where a whole unitary is found. And it is in the mutual achievement of men and women that that whole unitary is found. Of the two presented ways of androgynous, we find that androgyny is a divine primordial state to be found. And it is through frenzied love in that divine androgynous state, that the human existence is found—the unity of the cosmos—namely, the unity with God.

Chromosomes that come from parents are twenty-three from the mother and twenty-three from the father. Genetically, the nucleus of every cell in the human body contains twenty-three pairs of chromosomes constituted of genes that determine our physical characteristics (gender, skin color, hair color, eyes, etc.). Very special is the pair that determines sex. Men have an X chromosome from the mother and one Y chromosome from the father (XY). Women inherit two X chromosomes, one from each parent (XX).

Clearly, we see that the scribe who wrote the previous creation sentence of revolutions had the knowledge and the occult information of the wave of life that had evolved on the globe during the earth period.

The story of creation contains two chapters that give two different names to God. The first name is Elohim, and in the fourth verse of the second chapter of creation is Jehovah, in the Hebrew text. But not being monotheistic, to conceive God as merely a superior man was for him an acquired knowledge.

Jehovah is the leader in charge of the special part of the work of creation. As the dispenser of children, He builds bodies or concrete forms using the hardening lunar and crystallizing forces. He is one of the Elohim. The leader, having the responsibility, governed angels who are his messengers in this work of humanity of the period of the moon—the regent of the current moon—and is in charge of the degenerated and evil beings that are therein. Having the heaven as the throne and the earth as a musical instrument, the spirits of race as archangels who were the humanity of the sun period, were and still are with him.

When humanity began his independent career, the Elohim rested from their work as creators and guides. As a feminine name meaning a single female being, the adding of the masculine plural termination "im" to the feminine name "Eloh" indicated a legion of female and male beings, a negative expression and positive dual creative energy. In the formation of the universe, seven other entities that belong to our evolution, collaborating with God, are added to the creative hierarchy list called "Elohim." They worked voluntarily on our evolution, according to the first chapter of Genesis. This set of scholarly discussion simply wants to explain how forms were designed; and it is depending on the needs of the development of a race that archangels are fighting for or against a nation as spirits and heads of race.

Several masters of the earth have each their own role and are natives of various places. The creative leaders are the main group, originating from the constellation of Sagittarius. The Arcturians and Ashtars, whose mission is to take care of the youngest, left the earth in 2013, eleven years after the departure of Kryeon in 2002. These groups, belonging to the Pleiades of the seven sisters who are watching over us, are located in the same dimension as we are; they speak to us, and help the rulers to lead the world. The group of angels who is watching over us is the solar group. All the great masters, like several pharaohs and other well-known guides, assigned as guides at the beginning of our life, lived as humans on earth to solve our problems and to avoid us the worse behavior of certain influential leaders who claim to be our masters. It is through theunique intermediary of those who know them that they can orientate the leaders without them realizing it.

The presence of the Pleiades group of Sirius, Vega, the constellation of Lyra, and many others present in this world, is to try to help us make the least mistakes possible at this so important moment of their great passage on earth to teach us that we all come from one part of the universe; and to let us know with much more certainty at the appropriate time that our divine being will give us all information still awaiting in us. Our initiators will allow us to tap into the faculty of the motionless dichotomy of their consciousness—the positive and powerful knowledge than all the elements of forces of our determinisms united. It was from the son of mental that man received the divine spark eight million years ago. This spark allowed him to think and to differentiate himself from the animal. But since then, he hasn't managed to master this mental body, physical or astral.

However, the wisdom that comes from the heavenly sky is above all very pure and then affectionate. Nevertheless, it is sincere, peaceful, soft, open to reason, attentive, flexible, full of good fruits of pity, considerate, and finally impartial. So, if the physical heredity was a fact and if having the genius as a natural ability of great creative faculty was not a quality of the soul, a genius even greater than the one of an ancestor in all scholarly works would have been born, but this is not the case; consequently, it is a process of the progress toward the evolution of humanity. If he should be a genius even greater than his predecessor, to resolve all problems that the laws rationally combine, he must seek a way to progress toward the next phase of his evolution and achieve a high quality of the soul, the one of a superman whom the law rational twinned, to become an even greater genius than his ancestor.

Nature has created two camps of life to be lived, enjoyed and manifests an ardent need to know our inner being, and well after to know the other. Since the separation into two distinct humans in the beginning, we are possessed by that mysterious desire for closeness to the other, which expresses in us the enjoyment of nature. Is it a metaphor or a tangible reality? A fullness of love that all human beings seek, and happy when they find their half? Man has the capacity to reach the ultimate stage of evolution; but he is not yet at that final stage. The angelic divine state is the next step in the evolution of man. All kingdoms allow everyone to experience the material in a gradual manner. And from a different angle, in the human kingdom where man lives as an angel, in the so-called inferior reign, everything is as developed as the other.

Our world is a world of four dimensions (width, height, thickness, and time). There is also a fifth dimension, the consciousness of time (the ability to identify our temporal future or the energy toward which we are heading). The sixth dimension is the consciousness of speed. And the seventh dimension is the consciousness of the vibratory rate. The highest mode, by which God expresses himself through man, is the highest degree, left in the kingdom of God.

According to the chiliastic doctrine, the history of our planet—marked by periods of cataclysm—is an eternal beginning. It believes that there will be an end of the world and that Christ will return to the earth in a visible form to establish a kingdom that will last one thousand years. This disruption of the cosmic origin always occurs at the end of the evolution of time, of a civilization that will last seven thousand years. And a complete cycle will include four periods of the same duration, making a total of twenty-eight thousand years of the cosmic origin because of the intense solar activity. Many gigantic catastrophes have been orchestrated by the intervention of beings from outer space, by the fault of men, and by the disruption of natural laws.

Your mystery has not yet been solved, oh, Africa. Your first human movement is like the movements of celestial stars. Your matrilineal ancestor, the mother of all human beings, has been identified through the mitochondria organelles" found in most eukaryotic cells and passed on from mother to mother by your child living in Africa around 150,000 years ago to all human beings living today. It appeared to be a fact that your religion is the oldest known mythology in the world, long before humans moved from Africa to other continents. Your faithful children—faithful to their religion—took their mitochondrial fragments all over the world with them and worked their way into associations like Rosicrucian, sects such as Freemasonry, and religions of different denominations today.

Oh, Africa! You're a membrane-bound organelle, a specialized structure with a specific function in most eukaryotic cells of the world. You're known as the nucleus, and your mitochondria make organelles representing the human on earth; by tissue and type of cell, the numbers per cell vary considerably by species; but you're still barely visible to the Western world today. Oh, yes, your mystery has not yet been solved, oh, Africa.

CHAPTER TWO

EGYPT

Oh, yes! I am Africa, the cradle of humanity. I am the land of the ancestor of your ancestors. I am Africa. As "Mother of Humanity," the oldest "Garden of Eden and the only one of indigenous origin," I am known as Africa, and I was called Alkebulan by my ancestors. Alkebulan, my ancient African name was used by Khart-Haddans who in fact were called Carthaginians, the Ethiopians, the Nubians, and the Numidians; they also gave me names like Corphye, Ethiopia, Libya, Groppelli, and Africa; but Africa, my current inappropriate name, was adopted by the ancient Greeks and the Romans.

I am Africa. Even if I am qualified to use multiple names proving my dignity, I am the freedom full of dignity and peace. Latin calls me *Africus*— yes, a province of my region since my origin. But just call me Africa. I am a northern part of the continent for some. And for others, I am just a historical curiosity today. From the Latin *aprica* to the fictive Greek name *aphrike*, solely call me Africa.

I am Africa for the Ifren Bantu tribe, and Ifri is my ancestor. Ifren, you're the ancient inhabitants of Ifriquia or Ifuraces; Afar and Afridi are all my children. Long ago, my land was also called Taferka or, again, Ifriqiya, the present-day Tunisia. In my land, Ifren, a supreme deity, lives in an area of flatland crowned with mountains. I encompass many climates—temperate at the north and south, hot and dry along the tropics, and wet and hot on the equator. Yes! I am the natural exception, a reason to be, a rainy windy system, sunny and of cold blood. Oh, yes! I am Africa; I am a type of nature by excellence.

According to historians and Egyptologists, the start of the Egyptian chronology was in 49214 BC. And the First Dynasty began in 4246 BC, according to the natural order of the world by the Canopus decree—a decree issued by the meeting of Egyptian priests gathered at Canopus in 238 BCE. In 1815, the church accepted the pharaonic dynasties raised by Champollion in the year 5285 BC. They also indeed existed before the birth of Adam.

Obtaining the exact date of Egyptian chronology of July 27, 9792, BC and the cross-checking of texts from the breaking point of the balance of our globe established mathematically, accords almost perfectly with the historical narratives of Herodotus. But Manetho traced the history of Egypt to 23200, or 3700 BCE; these predynastic years of the royal line and the anterior line of Horus kings, preceded by a dynasty of demigods, date back to 15,150 additional years. And because these datings are contradicting the version of Adam and Eve's creation as the first human beings, the Western archaeologists rejected them.

Very regrettable for them since a Hermetic manuscript dating back to 1400 BCE came to support Manetho's claim as the most reliable existing lists of the Egyptian kings. Prerequisite to the familiar dynastic era of Egypt, Manetho dated three distinctive historical periods. The first dynastic period, known as the predynastic period, is reasonably close to the figure 13777 of Manetho, and lasted 13,420 years; the second period is the Horus period of ninety-nine kings, opposed to the figure 15,150 of Manteo, and which lasted 23,200 years, was longer than what Manetho imagined.

The era of the demigods was also recognized by the Turin Papyrus; unfortunately, the canons reconstructing the evidence interpreting the list of its kings, constituted by Manetho, is henceforth assigned as missing; but a third-century church historian by the name of Bishop Eusebius reproduced Manetho's timescale as follows: 30544 BCE for the dynasty of gods; 16644 BCE for the dynasty of demigods; 15380 BCE for the first line of kings; 13572 BCE for the reign of thirty kings; 11782 BCE for the reign of ten kings of Thinis; 11432 BCE1 for the human kings; 5619 BCE2 for the dynasty of Mena; 5319 BCE3 for dynasty of Boethos; 5065 BCE4 for the dynasty of Necherofo (Necherofes); 4851 BCE4 for the first royal dynasty of Soris (Snofru); 4829 BCE4 for the three-king Khufu/Cheops Calso dynasty, known as Fura; 4766 BCE4 for the three-king dynasty of Chepren/khafre/khafura; and 4700 BCE for the dynasty of four kings Merikara/myerkinos, all attested by Manetho, the ancient classical historian, including other erudite searchers. Finally, a disaster destroyed the first Egyptian civilization.

Manetho started his chronology with the Hyksos, who infiltrated the delta region of Lower Egypt, threatening its extinction during the middle kingdom from 2055 to 1650 BC, mentioning that these Semitic shepherd kings including the Jewish patriarch Abraham, who adopted many Egyptian ways and traditions of a civilization that already existed for 1,500 years—namely, by renaming their god Seth, the brother of Osiris as Sutech or Satanuka, and for their rulers, the Egyptian dynastic titles, invaded Egypt.

He mentioned that gradually, around 1750 BC, these settlers became more established and wealthier, after sacking Egypt and driven out the Egyptians; that they coexisted quite amicably with the Seventeenth Theban Dynasty, emerging in the eastern strongholds that was ruling from Elephantine, the first cataract, opposite Aswān city to Abydos, one of the oldest cities in Egypt by preserving the ancient culture and traditions during an era. It is known that the ancient Ethiopian Empire was established by the south of Elephantine, the most southern city in Egypt known as "the South Gate."

The Thebans (Egyptians of Ethiopian), who became more confident in their power after having simply waited for their time, seeming content to allow the existence of strangers in their country without much fuss, gradually began to arm themselves to begin a campaign, rose against the Hyksos; and finally expelled them, and as thoroughly as possible wiped them from the delta and from the history of Egypt. It is also known that during their infiltration, the son of Jacob (Israel) known by the name of Joseph became the prime minister of Egypt. The group known as the children of Israel, liberated by Moses, was captured and enslaved after expelling the Hyksos; Moses, the founder of the Jewish nation, liberated them after a civil war. The New Kingdom from 1550 to 1069 BCE was established by the Eighteenth Dynasty, after the Seventeenth Egyptian Thebans Dynasty liberated the Delta region of Egypt. He continued in his chronology of Egyptian kings with one of the last local kingdoms of the Theban region of Egypt by the name of Seqenenre Tao I, who reigned over the Seventeenth Dynasty. After the brutal killing of Seqenenre Tao I, Kamose, the last king of the Theban Seventeenth Dynasty, became king, and avenged the death of their father, and reunited Egypt. But Kamose, the immediate successor and elder brother of Ahmose, only reigned for three years; although today, some scholars are approximately giving him a longer reign of five years, his attested highest regnal years are those mentioned by Manetho.

Kamose died just when he was about to expel the Hyksos out of the northern Egypt. After the death of Kamose, Ahmose being still a boy of only ten years old, it was his mother Ahhotep, who reigned as regent; she continued the campaigns and educated him for his future duties for ten years until when he was ready to rule. Not enduring the humiliation of foreign occupiers on their land, he then made the final conquest, defeated the Hyksos by marching on Arvaris to finally liberate Egypt from foreign occupation, and united Egypt. Now a pharaoh of a united Egypt, he married his sister Nefertiri and expanded the county's borders in the south, from the borders of Nubia to the north of the Mediterranean.

From his great victory, he became a hero and worshipped as a god when he returned to Thebes. He extended the borders of Egypt in the northeast, beyond the Sinai desert and in the south deep into Nubia by laying the foundations for a new empire and a golden age of a united Egypt before his death. The Thebans (Egyptians of Ethiopian) regained the Ethiopian territory up to the second cataract, where they turned their attention southward. They established a new administration with a viceroy at its head, named Djehuty–Pharaoh Ahmose. Ahmose, the first ruler of the Eighteenth Dynasty, the liberator of Egypt, who reigned from c1550 to 1525 BC during the northern occupation, started the new Egyptian empire after liberating his country before his death in 1525 BC.

His successor was one of his children by the name of Dr Djeserkara I, Amenhotep I, from 1525 to 1504 BC, who was replaced by Akheperkara, Thothmose I; he is the one who extended the Egyptian sovereignty beyond the fourth cataract by pushing the borders of Egypt further into Ethiopia and Palestine. And in a campaign against Mitanni, he crossed the Euphrates while in Sinai. To honor Amun, he remodeled the great temple of Karnak; Thothmose I reigned from 1504 to 1492 BC. He was married to the daughter of Ahmose I to legitimize his claim to the throne. Mutneferu, Thothmose II, his son, succeeded him.

He reigned from 1492 to 1479 BC and was married to his fully royal half-sister, Hatshepsut, royal daughter of his father. Consequently, at his death, his son at an early age inherited the throne, and his aunt, Queen Hatshepsut, who later made her own bid for the throne, became regent and accumulated enough support from her officials to declare herself queen from 1473 to 1458 BC.

As a strong woman, she built herself a temple, a unique and magnificent temple dedicated to the Ethiopian god Amun in Deir el-Bahari. Featuring a "birth relief, this temple was showing Amun visiting his mother involving his own immaculate birth." At Thebes, she continued adding expeditions to temples, to Amun, and restoring other temples fallen into ruins or that suffered during the Hyksos' war. The legitimate pharaoh Thothmose III, who was reduced to a junior co-regent, inherited the throne after the death of Queen Hatshepsut, and the largest Egyptian empire that extended the Egyptian boundaries to the Middle East, Ethiopia, and Palestine. His establishment, known as the great solar (Kara) society, created as a spiritual man, inherited the legacy of Shemsu Hor as the ancestor of Mena from 5619 BC and as the founder of Egypt.

From 1427 to 1400 BCE, Amenhotep II succeeded his father, Thothmose III, known as Aakheperura, was the best Pharaoh that Ancient Egypt has ever seen. He was often considered as a great and brilliant sovereign, responsible for the establishment of great peace and prosperity for his people; in general, it was the golden age of Ancient Egypt before his death; he was succeeded by Thothmose IV, who fulfilled the dream promising him kingship if he cleared away the sand surrounding Ra Harakhte (or Xpakhte). He then legitimized his reign by the dream stolen between the paws of the Giza sphinx and from 1390 to 1352 BC Amenhotep III, his son succeeded him. As a hybrid pharaoh, he was the son of one of the chief wives of Thothmose IV, the daughter of the Mitanniah king known under the name Mutemwiya. Thus, Amenhotep III was a pharaoh with Asian and Egyptian blood, who was married to an Ethiopian woman named Tiye, the daughter of Yuya and Tjuyu.

This great royal wife was the mother of Amenhotep IV, who later on baptized himself as Akhenaton, and she was also known to be the grandmother Tutankhamun. When Pharaoh Akhetaton came to power, the affairs of the empire were managed by the great solar (Kara) society, headed by the priesthood of Amun, and were the maker of kings. Amenhotep IV became the prophet of the god Amun-Ra-Harakhty, under the well-established priesthood of the Ethiopian Amun. Then, as the sole god of the empire, he adopted the Piscean god Aton (or Aten), symbolized by the sun disc, and built a new capital city at Armana.

The Ethiopian god Amun-Ra-Harakhty or Xpakhty, who was not a human god, pronounced Xpictoc in Greek, became the Roman Empire god and later on, in 325 CE, gave the name Christos to Yeshua (the Greek Jesus), and from then, Yeshua is known as Jesus Christ. Two branches were established by the great solar (Kara) society during the reign of Pharaoh Akhetaton—namely, the Nazarene society, called Essenes and the Therapeutae. Moses, the founder of the Jewish nation, headed both branches, having been a learned student in all arts, sciences, and philosophy of the Egyptians; he adopted the god Eichton or Aton of the African Piscean and renamed him Adon or Adonai.

Within the Egyptian empire, a great unrest was caused by those religious changes of Pharaoh Akhetaton, who's the Piscean (Atenist) religion was abolished by his successor and reinstated the god Ptah, Amun-Ra-Harakhty. From 1332 to 1322 BCE, during the reign of Tutankhamun, the living image of Amun and son of Akhenaten lifted the ban on the cult of Amun, and traditional privileges were restored to its priesthood and in the entire African Pantheon. It was during the excavation of his tomb that archaeologists made the discovery of the golden statue of god Ptah. Egyptologists are speculating that after the death of Tutankhamun, his successor named Ay, who from 1323 to 1319 BC or 1327 to 1323 BC held the throne of Egypt for a brief period of four years depending on the chronology followed; he could have been a descendant of Tiye, the mother of Amenhotep IV.

From 1323 to 1295 BC, Horemheb, who inaugurated the beginning of the nineteenth dynasty of Ramesside, succeeded Tutankhamun. In accordance with the Egyptian Pantheon, restored by Pharaoh Tutankhamun, Pharaoh Rameses II dedicated the temple of Abu Simbel to himself, to Ra-Harakhty, to Amun, and to Ptah. With four pharaonic characters representing the four children of Horus, he placed the picture of god Ra-Harakhty or Xpakhty, the Greek Xpictoc, above the door of the temple.

The Ramesside unstabbed dynasties made a Libyan military commander by the name of Shesong I, to join the Ramesside dynasty by marrying the daughter of Pharaoh Psusennes II, named Maatkara, and legitimized himself as the Libyan pharaoh Shesong I. A path opened by that instability allowed the Libyan settlers and other foreigners to settle in the Delta region, adopting the native Egyptian culture and traditions. And the mystical or Gnostic Christianity can be found as early evidence at Abu Simbel.

Once Shesong I felt more united to Egypt, he placed his three sons in the key position of authority in power: as the governor of Upper Egypt and high priest of Amun, the one called Iuput; as the third priest of Amun to support his brother, Djeptahaufankh; and as the military commander of Heracleopolis, the one named Nimlot. King Solomon of Judea was even married to the daughter of that Libyan pharaoh Shesong I during its reign. After the death of Solomon, King Shesong I saw his chance and invaded Judea and Israel during the dispute of Judah and Israel and managed to defeat both of them in a magnificent campaign. Then at Thebes, on the walls of the great temple of Amun, he celebrated his victory.

It is also good to know that King Solomon studied in Egypt during the reign of Shesong I and that the kingdoms of Lower and Upper Egypt were fragmented into city states at the time when Ethiopia in the south was growing in power. Finally, a war broke out between the ruling Libyan dynasties of the Twenty-Third and Twenty-Fourth Dynasties with the ancient Ethiopia that defeated the Libyan army and established the Twenty-Fifth Ethiopian Dynasty to unite the Lower and Upper Egypt.

At Gebel Barkal, the high priest of Amun, Pharaoh Piankhi, a Kushite founder of the Twenty-Fifth Dynasty of Ancient Egypt, was married to the daughter of the seventh king of Napata, known as Pharaoh Alara. Pharaoh

Piankhi, who ruled his country from the Nubia city of Napata, nowadays modern Sudan, from 747 to 716 BC, led the war against the Libyans. After the death of his father-in-law, he succeeded him. They continued their roles as city-state kings after defeating the Libyan prince of Sais in the battle for the control of Lower Egypt. Tefnakht, who was defeated by Piankhi, reigned from 727 to 720 BC as the Libyan leader.

Bakenrenef succeeded his father Tefnakht, the second ruler and the head of Sais. Bakenrenef was allowed under the lordship of King Piankhi to also rule in Sais as the only Twenty-Fourth Dynasty pharaoh recognized universally. Pharaoh Piankhi changed his position against the kings' coalition of the North around the twentieth year of his reign at Heracleopolis and defeated them. Note here that these datings are solely from the period of the Manethonian history of Egypt; the modern scholars can include other datings.

Then at Thebes, he allowed his sister be consecrated the divine wife of Amun and established her influence; he started the restoration work at the great temple, and incited the building project from Napata his preferred city, where he was ruling. The one known as Neferkara, Pharaoh Shabaka, from 716 to 702 BC, succeeded his brother Pharaoh Piankhi, buried in a pyramid at Gebel Barkal at his death. And in the main centers of Amun at Thebes and in various religious centers, extensive construction projects and the restoration of temples were undertaken by Shabaka at Abydos, Dendera, Edfu, Esna, and Memphis. He managed to contain the growing threat of the Assyrian empire, especially under Sargon II, during his reign by consolidating the Nubian kingdoms. He made Thebes the capital city of his kingdom and undertook enormous construction work throughout Egypt; especially in Thebes and in Karnak, where he erected a pink granite statue of himself bearing the twin crowns of Egypt. He was buried at Gebel Barkal near the religious center of Napata, like his brother.

The son of Piankhi, Pharaoh named Shebitku, succeeded Shabaka. Like his nephew, he reigned from 702 to 690 BC. And against the Assyrian king, he managed to make an alliance with the Palestinians and the Phoenicians during his reign, a period known as the more complicated part of the Assyrian empire threat. But from 690 to 664 BC, Sennacherib of the Assyrian domination soon defeated them. With the death of Sennacherib in 681 BC, the Assyrian threat faded slightly, when from 673 BC the reign of the seigniory of Taharqa, went through several Assyrian campaigns starting at the border, to finally invade and captured Memphis, the Egyptian capital in 671 BC.

Consequentially, Pharaoh Taharqa led a brief resurgence against the Assyrians in Memphis that they sacked eventually, where he was again beaten, forcing him afterward to retreat all the way to Napata. And with Esarhaddon, the youngest son of Sennacherib who succeeded him took Memphis again; and effectively, ending his short reign in the Kushite Empire, he fled back to Nubia, his homeland. Intrigued in the affairs of Lower Egypt, Taharqa fanned numerous revolts to free Egypt until the death of Esarhaddon. But once again, Ashurbanipal, the heir of Esarhaddon invades Egypt, forcing Taharqa to flee in

Thebes after his defeated, where he built its spiritual priest-kings center known as Thebes, by restoring temples throughout Egypt and Ethiopia. Around 690-656 BC, Mentuemhet, the fourth Prophet of Amun and Prince of the City was Taharqa's mayor, who carried out extensive extraordinary works for the King at Thebes. Taharqa was succeeded by the last Nubian king Tanutamun from 664 to 653 BC; during his reign, the named Ba-ka-Re, his royal nomen meaning "Glorious is the soul of Re," tried to take Egypt back when he controlled only the area between the third and fourth cataracts. He then decided to descend the Nile, killing the representative of the Assyrians named Necho I in his campaign and reoccupied all Egypt, including Memphis, and for about eight years he reigned throughout Egypt and Nubia. As a result of that victory, Assyrians returned to Egypt in full force, attacked Thebes by plundering all the holy places, and defeated the army of Tantamani. Thus, Assyrians also forced him to f lee to Napata, stopping his hopes of liberating the entire country, until 653 BC. He was succeeded by the son of Taharqa named Atlanersa, after his death in 653 BC. In all of Upper Egypt until his eighth year of reign in 656 BC, when Psamtik I peacefully took control of Thebes and effectively unified all Egypt, Tantamani's authority was still recognized, although the Ethiopian influence in Egypt ended. And it is indeed their reconquest that put an end to the Nubian control of Egypt. As a result, the Kushite kings never entered Egypt again, according to Manetho.

Note that this little walkthrough in the chronology of our history is necessary to understand what the reign of the Kushite race went through up to the end of its control over Egypt.

The first pharaoh of the world who established the First Dynasty in about 5500 BC was Menes (Narmer) of Ancient Egypt, originally from Hierakonpolis, the southern kingdom; he was also the one who formed an alliance between the two kingdoms of Egypt (north and south) after conquering the Lower part (north) at the end of the fourth millennium BC and crowned with a double diadem: red crown of the north, worn by the kings of Lower Egypt, and the (white crown) of the upper South worn by the kings of Upper Egypt, which resulted in a large country that he divided into provinces. And since it is said that "Behind every great man, there is always a great woman," a lady of great cosmetic talent and of extraordinary rank, known as Neithhotep, was his wife.

To take advantage of the northern breeze that was blowing across the Egyptian desert from the Mediterranean, Menes built the city of Men-nofre (Memphis in English) exactly where he wanted it, on a site earlier known as the "White Walls," where the Nile's flooded the plain, located in the center of the white kingdom or the upper kingdom, only a few miles from the present day Cairo on the west side of the Nile. Hikuptah, the "home of the soul of Ptah," the Black God is the original name from which the English name of Egypt derived.

Menes constructed a gigantic dam to avoid the water overflow and diverted the annual floods that made the Nile delta so fertile to accumulate surpluses of food. Then he built the temple of Ptah, the potter and craftsman of the gods, who dreamed creation through his heart and spoke it out, and the word became existence. In his new city, he founded the cult and taught the most refined tastes such as the elegance, (covering the tables and sofas with beautiful and sumptuous fabrics), as well as the manners and the graces of decoration. He brought radical changes in the way of life conferred on humanity and was noted as the first person to initiate the idea of living elegantly and considered sumptuous life as a gift from the gods.

The falcon-headed god Horus himself—one of the oldest gods, the most powerful and significant god worshipped in the ancient predynastic Egypt—gave him the kingship with the throne and crown of Egypt, making him the first human pharaoh and the ruler of the two kingdoms: the kingdom of Upper Egypt and the kingdom of Lower Egypt. His establishment was a huge influence on the advancement of technology and government. Good nutrition, luxury, security, and stability contributed to that advancement.

Hor-Aha was the second pharaoh of the First Dynasty of Ancient Egypt in the present-day Egyptology, often combined with the Second Dynasty under the group title the Thinite dynastic period of Egypt, "or the archaic period of the first dynasty of Egypt," when the capital was Thinis, near Abydos in the Upper Egypt; and assigned as the place of origin and designated as covering the first two dynasties by Manetho. His name was frequently in the yielding of the name of Pharaoh Horus, associated with the god Horus—an element of the royal title— entirely given as Horus-Aha, meaning "Horus the Fighter." The tomb of Hor-Aha was revered as the tomb of Osiris.

Very important was the burial complex of First Dynasty, including the tomb of Djer, in the Ancient Egyptian culture and the religious tradition of the Eighteenth Dynasty to the following. According to Manetho, during the First Athothes Dynasty that reigned in Memphis—the creator of the hieroglyphic writing system, sometimes identified as Djer—wrote a treatise on anatomy.

Hor-Aha, the most ancient king of Egypt, who led many religious activities, ascended to the throne and became a pharaoh of a single kingdom at about the age of thirty, probably in the late thirty-second century BC or the early thirty-first century BC, and ruled until he was about sixty years old. Djer, the third pharaoh of the First Dynasty of Ancient Egypt, who reigned for fifty-seven years, was a son of the pharaoh Hor-Aha (or Horus Aha), son of Narmer and his wife, Khenthap—a name meaning "musician of the god Hapi," the god who made the flood of the Nile — and a queen consort of Ancient Egypt, pointing her toward a religious and sectarian role since she was connected to a god, linking her to the king's title "bull of his mother."

His grandfather was Narmer. His grandmother was Neithhotep, meaning "the goddess Neith is satisfied," who was the first queen of Ancient Egypt. She was the early woman in history whose name was known as the cofounder of the First Dynasty, and she was originally a princess of Lower Egypt before her marriage to Narmer, a king of the Thinite period of Upper Egypt, a period covered by the first two dynasties, the thirty-first century BC.

Sextus Julius Africanus, from a family originally from the province of Africa, gave Djer a reign of sixty years, unlike the version of Eusebius of Caesarea, who reduced his reign to thirty years. The mother, spouse or the grandmother of Djer named Neithhotep, bore the title of consort of the two ladies before any woman; these two titles were usually given to the queens during the first dynasty), (and particularly, she was the foremost pious spouse of a reigning monarch).

Women carrying titles such as "the Great One of the Hetes-sceptre" were later on associated with queens of the complete royal families known from Ancient Egyptian hieroglyphics and thought to be the wives of Djer. Narmer lived around the mid-thirty-first century BC, according to current Egyptology. In almost every respect, Ancient Egyptians who lived on the banks of a river like the Nile and in Egypt itself, nicknamed (the "gift of the Nile") adopted different customs and manners from those of other men. From the Mediterranean, the Nile River began its journey of some four thousand miles deep into the African interior.

Its first five hundred miles—stretching from the first cataract at Aswan, known as Upper Egypt, f lowing from the south—are nothing more than a channel that runs through the Sahara Desert, about some twelve miles wide at its most large dimension. Its last six hundred and sixty-five miles constitute the land of Egypt. The Nile broadens suddenly in the Memphis region into the delta—the northern region called Lower Egypt—and then at the Mediterranean seaboard it becomes sixty miles wide.

Oh, Egypt, since the creation of your way of life and the style of your civilization, a remarkably accurate summary civilization, twenty districts in the Lower Egypt and twenty-two located in Upper Egypt marked your union into forty-two administrative districts called nomes. Your clan leaders controlling these nomes venerated a protective deity. Thanks to your earliest political and economic situation, your high level of technology and artistic achievement, your religious and cultural awareness that in less than five hundred years defined the well-thought-out concept that governs and which later will be taught throughout the whole world, are still governing the world.

In that formation of your way of life, gods and goddesses were usually depicted as human beings. Amon-Re, the sun god, was the leader of the gods among gods. Geb—the father of Osiris, who allowed crops to grow and whose laughter was earthquakes—was the earth god. Nut, his sister, was the goddess of heaven. Nut, whose union with her brother Earth engendered Isis, the mother of Horus.

In various cosmogonies, the creator is the deity responsible for the creation of the physical universe. The one that we qualify as the organizing God, creator of the world from the preexisting material, is the demiurge. On the same belief of a creative principle, the demiurge is at the origin of that creation in which each nome sees its patron god. Thus, Thoth is the founder of the world for the Hermopolitans and Re for the Heliopolitans, etc. In this divinity system, each local demiurge is a manifestation of the same divine power in a multitude of forms to explain coherently that system; hence the creation of the world looks simpler since Ptah, the unique God, is the actor in the creation of the world by his thought.

In the Nile delta, the name given by the Greeks to the ancient city of Onou (or Onou-Iounou-Onou-Iunu) is Heliopolis, which was the capital of the Thirteenth Nome of Lower Egypt, known as "the city of the sun," (the "eye of the sun"), today called Ain-ech-Chams in Arabic.

The nine deities called the nine gods are a group of the oldest creations first created by the demiurge, and they gather all forces of the universe. After Ptah created himself and sat on the primordial mound emerging from the water, he gave birth to a couple: Shu (the air god, an anthropomorphic male adorned with an ostrich feather) and Tefnut (the goddess of moisture, a zoomorphic female with a lion's head). Then Ptah said: I am the master of light, the Eternal Ra, who came out of the primordial ocean called Nouou.

According to my desire, I created myself and brought my body into existence by the word and thought and by my magical power. This is how I wished to be constituted in an autogenous manner from Nun—the personification of the primordial ocean, the ocean that made life and that will make death—by becoming aware of myself. But before my birth, the ennead of the primordial gods still in me did not exist, and the first corporation of gods was not yet brought in the world.

I was inert and lonely in the Nouou because there was still no place to stand up; (my place of residence, the city of Heliopolis, was yet not founded) or a place to sit since my throne was not yet formed, and I had not yet created Nut—the mother of all the stars, the goddess of the sky, symbolizing the firmament above me, said the demiurge Atum to the kingdom of Egypt.

Both Shu and Tefnut, as part of the great ennead, were born of the seed of Atum-god Re, the creator. Having a single parent, he protects them and maintains their demonic powers of chaos, represented as snakes with his two children: Geb (god of the earth) and Nut, daughter of Shu, the god of the air (goddess of heaven). Together, they represent the four primordial elements. When men no longer respected and obeyed Re, Nun, the primeval force from which creation sprang, destroyed humanity through its journey and killed all mortals. It is not surprising to notice that all the myths of creation have one thing in common as a concept rather than a God concerning this Nun, who begot the creator-God of Shu, who was spit, and Tefnut sneezed by the demiurge Atum.

The primordial god Atum engendered the first divine couple constituted of the god of air, Shu—the vital breath, creative principle of life—and his wife and twin sister, Tefnut, occupying the atmospheric space, arms raised, separating the sky from the earth. He was usually represented in the main sanctuary at Heliopolis by a man capped with a feather. Shu and the goddess of moisture, Tefnut, were born by the spit of his mouth or by masturbating. Tefnut was the mother of Geb (earth) and Nut (the sky).

Like her husband, who embodies his life as dry air, Tefnut embodies the changing elements (moist air) under the form of a lion-headed woman or a lioness, taking the appearance and attributes of dangerous goddesses, so she embodies the eye of Ra, the burning and devastating sun. Shu and Tefnut are worshipped as a pair of lions. The faraway daughter of the sun, Tefnut, who gives free rein to her ferocity, once fled into the Nubian Desert.

The demiurge Thoth deposited a strange egg recently sprung from the Nun on the primordial mound, where only mounds emerged, which were brooded by the eight elementary entities. Shu—the god of the air and the breath of life, husband and twin brother of the lioness goddess of moisture, Tefnut, symbolizing water or rain—was charged by Ra to bring her back after intoxicating her with wine. Therefore, the faraway daughter of the sun appeased found the flood, its beneficial aspect of the river; the Nile in rise, said the myth.

He who was born on the primordial hill decided the multiplicity of creation in his heart by the word and thought and created the first distinction between male and female at the origin of all things. The tears that Re-Atum shed after finding his children, brought by the goddess of air and the breath of life, formed the first humans.

The Heliopolitan cosmology began before the creation of the world. The first mythical story tracing the creation of the world was created in Heliopolis three thousand years before Christ. This mythical story told us that, in the beginning, there was a vast expanse of water where a hill called the benben emerged, the sacred stone, sheltering an egg created by eight creative forces composed of four frogs and four snakes and their female counterparts with snake heads.

The Hermopolitan cosmogony was composed of Nun and Naunet (liquid element), Heh and Hauhet (infinity), Kek and Kauket (darkness), and Amun and Amunet (mysterious element or hidden), called Ogdoad of Hermopolis. This egg hatched Atum, the sun, who rose immediately to heaven. Atum (the "wholeness" and "nothingness"), who from the top of that original mound created the world, was the only god created by this chaos. He was the protector of the monarchy and the royal pyramid under the ancient empire; "Sovereign of the two lands" who could again create the world. Holding a scepter in one hand and the ankh form of the original mound or (sign of life) in the other, as a man wearing the double crown, known under the name of pschent, Atum revealed to Osiris that he would destroy and transform all he had created to eel or to primordial serpent at the end of the world.

Associated with the setting sun, but also with several feminine deities as Temet or Nebethetepet, he was assimilated to the sun as the star of the evening Ra-Atum, under the guise of an old man and became the snake of the journey in the afterlife. His main sanctuary at Heliopolis, where he lived and worshipped, has today disappeared. In that principal place of sun worship of Ancient Egypt, there are only few vestiges left.

The earth god Geb and the sky goddess Nut (represented by the body of a woman or by the body of a cow); and the space in which the diurnal and nocturnal celestial body evolved—the stars, the moon, and the celestial vault, were in turn engendered by the two deities; both bodies of Nut illustrated the journey of the sun god (Ra) during the day and night. In addition, like the great one who gave birth to the gods, she was represented as an archedwoman who, every evening, swallows the star to engender it in the morning.

Standing with arms stretched upward, she gives back life that she brought out from the depths of the underground to the sun. She is found represented on the sarcophagi in her main sanctuary at Heliopolis as a major funerary deity. Noun was described as being an absolute darkness, which was neither darkness nor night— "what doesn't exist," the zero, the nothingness. While God is in everything, so is he in this nothingness.

Both deities Geb and Nut were separated from Shu, the mother of Nut, jealous of their union, for a period of 360 days. But Nut, the daughter of Shu and the granddaughter of the sun god Atum, gained five additional epagomenal days at the dice game against the god of time (Thoth) to correct the mismatch between the discrepancy between the indications of the calendar and the astronomical cycle; the time interval of the equinoctial year or the tropical year on the earth that the sun needs to return to the same position in the cycle of seasons could be explained by those five days. So cursed by the sun god, who feared that Nut do not seize his power by his eternal presence in heaven, Thoth, the god of time, agreed to extend the year for five days, making a total of 365 days a year.

It was during those extra five days that Nut (the sky goddess) unites with Geb (the god of the earth). Despite that separation, they will have five children from their union: Osiris and Isis, Seth, Nephthys, and Horus. They constituted the nine primitive gods, descendants of the demiurge Atum that constitute the ennead of Heliopolis, which also included Geb, Nut, Tefnut, and Shu. The mass of continental land that appeared from the bosom of the primordial ocean, where the eight who came into existence brought forth a lotus, from which Re is assimilated to Shu; Re saw and desired a lotus bud from which emerged a dwarf, as a necessary female auxiliary, and from their union, Thoth was born, and the world was created by the verb. A text of Edfu described their appearance and its initial impact on the organization of the world.

The blue lotus means beauty above all – "purity," the symbol of fertility, the sunlight, the transcendence, and the wisdom of knowledge. The Fourth Egyptian Dynasty greatly valued the "sacred lotus." It is from the lotus petals that the sun-god was formed, and from the chaos of Nun, he emerged as Ra. It is the victory of the spirit over the senses and one of the most ancient and deepest symbols of the planet.

The Egyptian calendar of twelve months of thirty days each, equaling (360 days), increased from 360 days plus the last five days making (365 days), which is what a year counts nowadays. In the Kemitic ancient mythology, the god of wisdom, and the god of the moon, which was Djehuty, the inventor of writing and numbers, divided the Kemitic calendar with the standard division of 365 days, composed of twelve seasonal divisions; and to keep the lunar calendar coherent according to the seasons, he used the forms of intercalation by taking into account the lunar cycle; and from the Sothic cycle, the Kemite usage is 1,468 years, dating back to 4241 BC, and known as one of the oldest civilization in the world, according to Herodotus.

These five epagomenal days were considered "evil" by the Egyptians. Also, harmful, these last five days of the Aztec calendar, composed of eighteen months of twenty days each making (360 days), were days of misfortune for the Aztecs. And in the Ethiopian calendar, additional five days were added to a thirteenth month on a calendar counting twelve months of thirty days each, making a total of thirteen months.

Thus, Nut who symbolized the ribbon of the Milky Way spread her body over the earth to protect it; and touching the ground her limbs represented the four cardinal points. Her tears were the rain, and her laugh was the thunder. The word is not just a simple element of language. Besides being an expressed thought, the word, pronounced by an oath or commitment, is creative. I assert that the word in the African philosophy of the pharaonic period was a constant strongly internalized ethical that gave to every human being, the full feeling that he can accomplish his activities in life as a form of supreme morality. This also leads me to suggest that the word in the African tradition of the ethical essence manifested itself in ritualized practices. According to this vision, the word to say must be true, in accordance with that of the ancestors, and in communion with the cosmos and with Maat.

Nun does not tend to manifestation, actualization, materialization, realization, specialization, or temporality. Nun is eternal (*djedet*)—a state of no state existing before the appearance of the current transformations of the nature (*kheper*); it contains everything and is in everything (*ta*), heaven, earth, and the Duat, the world afterlife.

This concept of the Creator-God, which extends around the world without a creator, is from Noun, the primordial ocean, which first created the first god Amen, Ptah (Apis), etc., from its bosom, and then followed the god Atum, Atum-Re, and Amun, also known as Amen, which means "hidden," associated with Re, and later named Amun-Re, expressing his fusion with the god of the sun; and all known God since the ancient Ethiopian empire of several pharaohs up to the Egyptian temples. He is this creator of life and death who embodied the God Elohim. From God Elohim, who became the God of the covenant with Abraham, was mutated in harmony with the god of Akhenaton. His reign is compressed by Moses, and called Yahweh, considered as the Semitic God or the Christian God, today called the Father.

Nun contains a floating genetic potential in itself, which spontaneously is transformed from the state of latency to the birth of activity. In opposition to the dark and confused waters, it will first give light and then life. The absolute absence of all activity or differentiation is a thought of quality. Nun and the nothingness should not be confused; Nun is both preexisting and nonexistent before the creation, a sort of non-real but just a virtual neutral state, a kind of very different nothingness from our emptiness, our zero. It's the nothingness that defines nothing and therefore does not relate to anything.

For an initiate, the virtual nonexistence still holds the possibility, the potential of a new ordered series of elements, a cause without resistance. In the sense of the absence of all manifested thing, it is not a vacuum or a zero but contains the virtual nothingness of the autogenous genetic potential, univalent and singular in itself, completing the creation in the water environment without limits by action on itself. The Demiurge is the creation represented by Nun; it operates within and on the preexisting substance, eternal, dark and inert virtual state—the "form" that crystallizes itself in the Nun before the space and time—the creation of the sky, of the horizon, of the Duat, of everything and their dynamics; it is closer to our notion of a cellar unity, which is divided according to the karyokynesis process, but far from our current concept of zero. The Nile flows from south to north regularly, with an annual flood pouring life into a dying and dry land. As if appointed by the gods, an annual miracle took place in June. Every June in spring, rains and melting snow filled the Nile, covering the soil on either side of the river and across the delta with black fertilizers that gave richness to the life of the Nile.

A green wave bearing incalculable tons of decaying vegetation shaped your landscape, with a paradisiacal divine architectural design that drew the sons of the midnight sun. A second wave a month later, bearing the rich humus silt, a partial decomposition by microorganic of the soil, full of minerals and potash, nourished the dry and cracking soil. In addition, the desert also threatening to swallow the population was rushing around the descending water of the Nile, unknown to the Ancient Egyptians; they nevertheless pushed away the threat of being swallowed by the desert for another year. Then from every city of Egypt resounded this great cry of praise: "Peace, healing, and wisdom are exalted."

Your civilization reached its maturity around 2600 BC. Although little was recorded from 3100 to 2600 BC, your hereditary dynastic system was accurately developed and which governed the world by the first dynasty of King Narmer, ended in the thirty-second century; foreign dynasties will govern Egypt under the Macedonian and the Roman domination until AD 395. And at the death of Cleopatra, your magnificent and mysterious spark that Egypt had was eternally extinguished; finally, your light of Amon-Re and the wisdom of Thoth ended in 311, in the ancient land that was your Egypt, after Jesus Christ. Nevertheless, several developments took place. Naturally, the craftsmen of Memphis, who were worshiping a ram-headed God, the potter Khnum, fashioned beings with the mud of the river in his city of Memphis, where Menes had established his capital, in a town well known for its pottery; the hieroglyphic script was conceived, and the monumental architecture, of which Egyptians were so well-known and proud of, was constructed.

In the history of humankind, the Medu Neter (or Medu Netcher, Medou Neter, Medou Netcher) gave birth to the history of the oldest and longest language. It is the oldest writing in the world of which we kept traces than any other languages. This Negro-African writing was a pharaonic writing of the Nile Valley of that period. We're unaware that the Medu Neter imitates existing objects in the African nature with great accuracy. Additional evidence for the origin of Kemet indigenous inhabitants of your Africa is the fauna and flora that we find in the African Medu Neter.

Practically, all the great prophets of creation of which the Christian Bible tells us about, from Abraham to Jesus up to Muhammad—those who made Moses so majestic and superhuman went to Egypt, the land of the pharaohs, to learn techniques and the wisdom of the Kemetic philosophy, an esoteric and cosmic knowledge enabling them to understand and master the positive visible energies and the obscure invisible side as mystical forces dedicated to our humanity; to live in harmony with its manifestation in the daylight as in the darkness of the night; and to understand the Medu Neter, the divine word, the codes of reading sacred texts that our African ancestors left us.

That creative science is still present in the true Kamite tradition, still alive everywhere on the African continent and in the worldwide. Its codes are still present, enjoying a subtle powerful and beautiful spirituality, which reveals Maat to a people of the sun. Maat is at the heart of a marvelous and dedicated millennium of civilization. Moreover, its mystical force with various terrestrial and astral energies of the universe of Maat flows in each of us.

However, we can see that the sacred texts that our African ancestors left us include deliberately maintained gray areas, and many unspoken truths crying out in the same logic as the founding myths. It is in those codes where the divine words are found as our ancestors themselves named them that we must seek a central point transmitted by our ancestors to understand the Medu Neter, not the apparent naivety, often the source of confusing, and the improbability of their words. Maat—the goddess who governs the equity, the balance, and the harmony of creation—is the symbol that decreed the commands of respect that open the gates of truth to obtain the ultimate reward.

Around 9000 BCE, the humanity of the Egyptian Nubian history of black Africa covers a period up to the appearance of the first urban centers in the region of Nabta (west of Abu Simbel). The history of Africa allows the understanding of the new dating of their history, their cultures, their philosophies and African descendants. Remarkable thinkers, black men and women and architects with burned skin by the sun of your continent, possessed a mysterious and intelligent science. That spiritual science was more than physical, more than magical, and more than hypnotic. They wrote the most beautiful historical lines of our next life with "hieroglyphics;" indeed, with a particular accuracy of the "hieroglyphics" as a primitive writing of the Kamites were established; its signs were true drawings, sometimes complex, to only be applied to sacred, painted, sculpted, or engraved characters. They represented natural objects, characters drawn with the greatest care, as cursive, hieratic, demotic, linear and abbreviated scriptures, with very few exceptions.

All Kamite monuments bore hieroglyphics, usually used for monumental inscriptions, either in public buildings or in beautiful private mansions. From right to left or left to right, they can be written in rows or columns. Signs looking toward the beginning of the text are the orientation of signs indicating the direction of reading, and the signs turned to the right show a reading from right to left, and vice versa. The "hieroglyphic graphic" following from left to right is the Kamite language script known as the Medu Neter. The "Neter" sign at the left (sort of pennant or f lag), used as an emblem or as an identifier, is the writing of the word *God*; the middle sign (a walking stick) means "word," and the three lines on the right, indicate the mark of plural, with the stick, "Medu." This script (Medu Neter) expresses the uniqueness of God—the "words of God" and not "words of the gods." Here, the thesis of passing Akhenaton or Moses as the fathers of "monotheism and the divine words, implies a hidden meaning of "a unique God expressed by the Medu Neter."

In the oldest sacred texts of Kemet, God must be understood in masculine and feminine. The primordial ocean that emerged, being alone in the Nun, close to the singularity of the big bang, is incorrectly called the primordial ocean. He, God, then created his hypotheses of a rational nature, including his various divine manifestations. It is from his various divine manifestations that "the Father, the Son, and the Holy Spirit speak," of which the Christian monotheism.

Nevertheless, by calling their language Medu Neter—meaning, "language of the gods, sacred world inspired by the great architect of the world, the creator—made the Medu Neter eternal through hieroglyphics.

Over centuries, the Medu Neter has survived and retained its meaning and deep roots, unlike all other human languages; disturbed by the horrors and vicissitudes of human history at a distant period, the Medu Neter, which kept its deep roots, allowed the disoriented descendants to draw inspiration from its greatness. Here, also, we found the deep root of *Medu*, which means "words" in the Bamileke language; "Medu Mba" (Medumba) in Cameroon.

This language is the mother language of all Bamileke languages spoken in west Cameroon. To demonstrate the greatness and the genius of the African people, the origin of the history of mankind, the Medu Neter has survived to restore their cultural integrity in the history of their descendants and cock a snook at the falsified history.

Western Egyptologists deny the motherhood of Ancient Egypt to Africa through various and varied ideological falsifications; but through the palpable linguistic argument, the black African origin of the Medu Neter is incontestable proof. Thus, the Medu Neter brings linguistic proofs of its belongingness to the Bamileke language of Africa. Exceptionally, the Bamileke (Medu MBa) has retained all the roots of Medu Neter. Here, the divine truth of the word *Truth*, with a capital *T letter*, having the form of a beautiful well sharpened knife is exposed. In the phonetics and interpretation terms in the Bamileke language in Cameroon, all the key words explaining the way of thought are identical to the mythology of Ancient Egypt. I must also say that there are many striking similarities between the Bamileke language and the ancient Hebrew language.

As we know, the Ancient Egyptian language having (hieroglyphics) as the ancient script was deciphered far from the African linguistic and cultural context but transcribed and transliterated according to the English and French linguistic conventions of the Western European languages, using the Roman alphabet of twenty-six letters.

It is Jean-Francois Champollion—an illustrious French scientist, born on December 23, 1790, in Figeac, considered as the father of Egyptology—who deciphered the hieroglyphics. Jean-Francois Champollion was saying of himself that "he was all for Egypt and that Egypt was everything to him" before he died on March 4, 1832, in Paris. In accordance with an understanding based on their cultural model and psychology, hieroglyphs were finally transliterated and interpreted by the Western Egyptologists.

After visiting numerous tombs in the Valley of the Kings, Champollion said the following about whites: "Real savages tattooed on various parts of the body. . . Finally, (and I am ashamed to say it, since our race is the last and the most savage of the series,) the Europeans, who at those remote times, we must be fair, were not a good figure of this world. We must herby include all the people of blonde race, white and yellow-skinned people, living not only in Europe but also in Arabia and Asia, have their point of departure. . . I certainly did not expect, arriving at Biban-el-Molouk, to find sculptures that could serve as vignettes to the history of the primitive inhabitants of Europe, if we have not had the courage to undertake that journey. Their sight, however, has something flattering and consoling, since it makes us appreciate the path we have traveled since."

Jean-Francois Champollion, known as Champollion-le-Jeune, revealed to us the past history of grandeur and perfection of the Egyptians, down to the smallest detail, and its surprising riches. From then on, the hieroglyphic wall was collapsed, and in front of that past of grandeur and perfection that scientists and adventurers discovered, they were petrified with admiration, recognizing it little by little, like the one that engendered all the other civilizations. He referred to Herodotus, who said that, "for me, I consider the Colachs to be a colony of the Egyptians, because, like them, they have black skin and frizzy hair;" that is to say, the Ancient Egyptians were real Negroes of the species of all naturals of Africa.

Hieroglyphs lost their original meaning of guttural sounds characterizing the sacrificed African languages, and which disappeared in the course of writing by modifying and neglecting the words. The vowel 'e', nonexistent in the Medu Neter language, was added between two consonants by convention to facilitate the reading to the Western Egyptologists. That interpretation has seriously lost the original sense of the meaning of the words; in linguistics, the same word could have several senses or meanings according to the context in which it was used. It had several meanings, including the figurative sense (the rational and objective sense). They have simplified the word to easily identify it and translated it from one language to another so that it could be easily understood by everyone, especially by those who are not part of the language community in which that word belongs.

The literal meaning, the sense by the sound of the word, the sound of the letter-for-letter meaning, which often confirms the figurative meaning allowing to see through it, the way of thought, the psychology and the wisdom of the people who spoke that language, more richer in teachings and most important than the figurative meaning, was evacuating anything that was "the mode of thought of the language." The community meaning was the sense that the members of a linguistic community gave to a word. To understand the meaning, one has to be culturally part of that community. And the double meaning was the fundamental characteristic of the Medu Neter. A word still has several meanings as in the Bamileke language. The double understanding therefore has a figurative and literal meaning, symbolic and semantic.

Since the Ancient Egyptians spoke in parables, the double understanding and the literal meaning of the sacred African language are the most important approaches in the interpretation of the hieroglyphics. In addition, in the Bamileke and other African languages, Ancient Egyptians used images and symbols to express themselves. Many African languages have also been transliterated by changing their scriptures or by suppressing their phonetic sounds, the guttural sounds existing in the African languages and absent in the Western languages through the prism of the European languages.

In the Bamileke Medu MBa, where the predominance of sounds and consonants are found, retained the same consonantal structure as the Medu Neter. These letters, *K, M, N, T, P, H*, as the letters of the Ancient Egyptian language, are also letters used in the Bamileke language. Sound by sound, this is the literal meaning of the word *Bamileke*: ('BA' – is equal to –"the ones," those of, to designate the geographical origin of someone); ('Mieh –"brothers;") (*'Lah'* – "country, region;") and (*'Ke'* – "high, what is at the top of a place, a region, a land.") High is about Upper Egypt, speaking of a country or region in Africa. Remember that for modern Egyptologists the appropriate name of "Egypt," KEMET is, just like Ancient Egyptians called their country KEMET, or "High Country" and "Low Countries" and not "Egypt," as it is called today.

Therefore, 'Khe Mieh,' justified by the Bamileke thought, is equal to KEMET, which means "the brothers of the upper region, or the brothers of the High Country, if one refers to Upper Egypt." Among the Ancient Egyptians, the high was the low, and the low designated the high in the present understanding; implying that the high designated the south as the original cardinal point of all their culture and source in the understanding of the Ancient Egyptians. Thus, the double understanding of "the land of the blacks, the land of those who are black or burned," in the Ancient Egyptian meaning is Kemet.

To summarize and conclude, I must say that Upper Egypt at the ancient time was the place of all KEMET powers. Therefore, the literal sound by sound meaning of Bamileke means "the brothers from the south of Egypt," – of Upper Egypt – the brothers who come from the High Country or from the Highland, by sound by sound put together. Consequently, since we know that an Ancient Egyptian word like an African word possessed and still several meanings, the word '*Khe*' in the Bamileke language, depending on the context, has therefore several meanings and interpretations; in this case, it means "burnt, black, blacken, darken," etc.; as always, to facilitate the reading of African words in Western languages, the word "*Bamileke*" has been transliterated into a modern name. This south and its words of sound by sound, founded by African thought as the original cardinal point of all our culture and source, have been changed by Westerners.

The white supremacy has to collapse like a castle of cards. The Meroitic, which was a spoken language since the end of the third century BC to the fifth century at the north of present-day Sudan in the kingdom of Kush, must replace the Latin and Greek in the educational programs to edify the new African humanities to the Egyptian Nubian civilization. The Ancient Egyptian law must take the place of the Roman law over the subbasements of the ancient pharaonic culture, if we want to build a body of human sciences in all fields with power because Egypt is for the rest of the black Africa, and Greece and Rome for the West. The ancient Greeks never deny the Kemet anteriority and the Negro origins of the Ancient Egyptian writing, which appeared almost three thousand years before the Greek European writing. If the West wishes to whitewash Ancient Egypt, it is because in reality, there was no European civilization at that time. The Egyptian Nubian civilization marks the earliest stage of our culture.

The two systems of Heliopolitan and Hermopolitan cosmogonies of the Egyptian philosophy should be taught in conjunction with the Greek philosophy, especially that one of Democritus, born around 460 BC in Abdera and died in 370 BC; of Epicurus, founder of the philosophical school antiquity in 306 BC, born in the late 342 or early 341 and died in 270 BC; of Plato, contemporary of the Athenian democracy, born in 428/427 BC in Athens and died in 348/347 BC; of Aristotle, logician, philosopher, and scientist in the Greek kingdom of Macedonia in Stagira, born in 384 BC and died in 322 BC in Chalcis in Euboea; etc.

To better highlight the contribution of black Africa to the Western thought systematically, African education must integrate the civil and military architecture, music, sculpture, painting, the study of art in etc., throughout Africa.

No erudite has ever reconstructed the historical method of a primitive linguistic predialectal of an ancestor, common to the comparative and inductive Egyptian language; on one hand, to the Semitic languages and the Berber languages; and on the other hand, to the Indo-European languages, there is no linguistic genetic kinship between the Egyptian, the Berber and the Semitic, as there is none existing between the Egyptian and the Indo-European; neither an Indo-European language like the Hittite or the Greek, nor a Semitic language like the Assyro-Babylonian Akkadian, the Arabic or the Hebrew, nor a Berber language like the Berber of Siwa or the Riffian; an Afro-Asian language of the

Amazigh language family, spoken in Western Europe and the Rif, in the region of northern Morocco, in the Riffian diaspora and in the rest of Morocco.

Genetically, by sticking to the rigorous scientific plan, the Egyptian language is only related to the other languages of the old and modern Negro-African of the African continent. During the first Egyptian religious texts, Buddhism and Brahmanism did not yet exist. For this fact, these two religions cannot explain the Egyptian religion. The texts that were found inside the pyramids in Africa are the oldest religious texts in the world. Any resemblance with the Indian religious texts would be copies made by the Indians, on the ancient religious texts of the Negroes of Africa, centuries later. In the course of that period, the priesthood became entrenched; the power accrued in the priesthood of Ra. Khnum grew from his potter's wheel and became the creator of the universe when Menes assumed the throne. At a time, Khnum replaced Ra, the sun god, the head of the Egyptian pantheon. In your ancient priesthood, the social culture inbreeding, known as endogamy, greatly reduced the chances of the external claims upon the throne or upon the royal property.

In addition, the pharaohs frequently married their own daughters to preserve the divine lineage; for a nobler motive, the Ancient Egyptian priesthood was determined to continue this practice to the extreme, so that the royal house with the divine lineage of Horus remains pure. Corruption was not to be tolerated; the possibility of claiming the direct descent of blood was revealed by the marriage of Osiris to his sister Isis, to protect the divine blood that ran in the veins of the royal family. That union begot Horus, the presumed ancestor of the pharaoh. Hathor, his wife, who personified the principles of joy, was the goddess of dance, beauty, love, music, fertility and motherhood, and she helped women in childbirth. Pharaohs who compromised the divine lineage died from mysterious causes. Admittedly, these practices are still prevailing among royalty today, but certain, members of royal families are strongly declining them.

In Jos. 11:13–21, Hathor was worshipped in Canaan in the eleventh century BC; then ruled by Egypt at Hazor or Tel Hazor his holy city, supposed to be destroyed by Joshua in the Old Testament.

Oh, Ancient Egypt, your highly organized and civilized society lasted for more than three thousand years, until the arrival of Alexander the Great in Egypt before finally being absorbed after 30 BC by the Roman Empire. Your end was the beginning of Christianity. Your heart, placed in a balance to be weighed after death, swung against an ostrich feather, (the symbol of truth and justice). Because of your goodness, your heart will not cease to exist but will be granted eternal happiness. The gods themselves preserve your dead body in the temple of Ptah, the god of craftsmen, where the god's spirit lives. The spirit of God inhabits your dead body so that you can use it in the next life.

The cycle of the Nile is a conscience carefully carved in the African history like the legendary Pharaoh Osiris, who represents the river; Set, his brother, is the chaos, the desert, and the darkness. Isis, Osiris's wife and sister, represents the priesthood; and Horus, her son, the pharaoh. By efforts, the creation of a vast personified network brought back life. The formation of thought here is equal to the sun; the feeling of permanence, if less than the Nile (water), is the sense of predictability and the benevolence of the general phenomena of the world, because orderly and benevolent is the universe. The marvelous work of the pharaohs was ensuring the constant brilliance of the sun's rays on the solar disk and the stability of everything upon which it radiated.

Ra, the god of the sun was the first king of Egypt. After the creation of the world, gods themselves ruled the land of Egypt. The other members of their family then followed them until the kingship eventually passed to Osiris, who was in charge of the underworld. The falcon-headed god Horus, Osiris's son, who avenged him, bequeathed the throne of Egypt at the end of his life and then gave the assumed divinity to Menes, the first pharaoh.

A remarkably optimistic consciousness that avoided the feeling of anxiety; factors created within the reach of experiences with rivers of beliefs, for the relatively unchanged civilization, to be the best of all possible worlds. Simply love life with no fear of death; seek no paradise even after life. Accumulate desire energies to not overwhelm the inevitable foe. It is an extension of this thought that knew love. Use the term *Maat*—the concept of balance, justice, truth, or harmony—to express this concept and to maintain favors of the gods. The gods take care of your people because man himself was a god. Since he was a god himself, his authority, as well as his divinity, was unquestioned; the law was his word, and humanity's land of unprecedented prosperity was his domain. Isn't it amazing, the pharaoh, being just a man and at the same time a God-King? And being the center of the Egyptian religious thought was the incarnation of Maat. An expression of the cosmos harmony was everything that he spoke.

Your undisputed divine work of civilization lasted for more than five hundred years, combining the double crown into one great crown, symbolizing the divine authority. The foundations of your arts, philosophy, religion and politic institutions were laid during that time of your "golden age." The symbolic manifestation of the dual nature of the pharaoh's power was to hold a shepherd's staff in one hand and a flail in the other. Conquering by love, he was the master of graciousness, rich in sweetness and triumphant; none can come close to him, he the crusher of foreheads.

I will also like to add this very important information: all women around the world should rejoice and be proud of themselves because this great African man known as the first unifying pharaoh was also a great liberal, who had the first prime minister in the history of mankind, a Kamite/African woman under his reign in about 3200 BC; it is of very great importance to the woman in the history of the African antiquity and a truth by which we should hold on. The first queen, Neithhotep, was the wife of Narmer/Menes and a cofounder of the First Dynasty.

The unique and first great empire of the planet earth that the world had never seen, with its powerful, beautiful, elegant, well-cared, wise and disciplined pharaohs; these great masters, sometimes considered as aliens or gods, founded the first and worthy civilization, which up to today, still guides us by revealing us secrets of their lives to the lives we lead nowadays, thanks to excavations without borders and the discovery of their mummies unearthed after three to four thousand years. The Ancient Egyptian priests created multiple forms of thoughts to protect the mummified bodies of the great pharaohs and queens against those who might consider one day, desecrating their graves.

The technical sector of mummification at the time of Ancient Egypt dates back from about 3000 BC. Moreover, in the sixteenth century BC, it reached the highest degree that man could achieve. Upon death, several professionals were required for the funeral ritual, and the duration of various operations of mummification was seven decades or seventy days.

This time of the embalming process was very important to the Egyptians because they considered all constellations' movements, but especially of the star named Sirius, and knew that, between the appearance of Sirius up to its disappearance and its return to the starry sky, the duration was seventy days, the time required for the dead to be reborn in another life. It is known that the mummification process was very expensive, so it was necessary that the propositions of several series of mummifications in an order of social hierarchy be presented to the family of the deceased by the priests-embalmers. This classification of functions according to a relationship of subordination was to determine the prices of the mummification according to the rights of the deceased ranking and the value of his respect in society.

After a mutual agreement on a series of mummification chosen by the family, the embalming priests were taking the body in their mummification workshop solely for that purpose. To begin the process of mummification, they first had to remove the intestines and various organs by slicing the abdomen with a well-sharpened Ethiopian stone. After removing the abdominal organs, they thoroughly washed the inside of the abdomen with palm wine and made sure that all ointments were of good quality. Then they sprinkled the body with crushed perfume and filled it with crushed cinnamon and pure myrrh. They added other aromatic and embalming containing natron as substance of baking soda with hygroscopic properties, to absorb moisture of the air. Then they put back the seat of thought and feeling known as the heart back in the abdomen before mummification.

The liver, the stomach, the intestines, the spleen, the kidneys, the viscera of the chest, the abdominal cavity, the cranial box, etc., were thoroughly cleaned. These organs were then packed in packages; if they were not put back in the body, they put them in four sacred vessels, which were of course placed in the burial chamber of the tomb, near the sarcophagus, before closing the grave. The closure of the incision was followed by the coating of the body with several layers of powerful animal and vegetable oils to effectively preserve the body.

The Egyptian funerary custom required that the eviscerated body be dried in the sun, so after all the mummification operations, the body was taken to a high place, west of the city, for this purpose. Finally, amulets were placed on the deceased, and then they proceeded on the laying of strips, covering the face with a mask that married the features of his appearance and placed him in an engraved and painted sarcophagus. Indeed, this work of art involved several professional specializations—namely, embalming, biology, chemistry, surgery and general physician in medicine. Good knowledge was needed in the areas of weaving for the bandage, painting to decorate linen strips and the sarcophagus, carpentry of high quality for the sarcophagus, metal fabrication for amulets reflecting the beliefs, metallurgy for the manufacture of iron tools, and gold sarcophagi. Thus, mummification was a great influence of advanced artistic techniques of their time.

Therefore, it was the advent of Christianity that stopped the art of mummification in Egypt in the second century after Christ by saying that the bodies of the dead must return to the state of dust to release the pure soul to eternal life. However, considering mummification as a reprehensible manifestation of human vanity, its traditional elements of anterior Egyptian beliefs enriched the new religion. Gradually, the Egyptian mummification technique influenced more precisely, Europe. They who were able to extract various balms from the Egyptian mummies that supposedly could cure all sorts of evils ailments; a technique of such a great civilization, both artisanal and scientific, treated the body of the deceased previously by skillful masters of prosaism, and would have dissipated hypochondria.

Cabinets of curiosities, erected by scholars and princes of Europe to expose all kinds of objects and the works of art coming from the counties of that mysterious distant Egyptian civilization, fed the curiosity of the enthusiasm and the keen interest of Napoleon to begin his campaign in Egypt. A mummy was for scholars, an object of remembrance and a perfect witness of their time. Today, we continued to learn a lot of information from mummies, such as their affections, their life expectancy, their daily lives, etc., thanks to advanced radioscopy analyses of new cutting-edge techniques. The belief that was reinforced for over three millennia was extinguished by a new belief that used the same techniques of the pharaonic era to influence the Asians, the Incas, and the Western fascination today for the preservation of the body after death.

In Canada, the United States of America, France, Great Britain, etc., the body conservation process or the art of embalming in science and modern technology, succeeded the Egyptian art of the conservation of the body – the Egyptian embalming, which allows the preservation of natural decomposition of dead human body. Since every Egyptian had to reach life after death, even the less fortunate was entitled to a cheaper mummification at death. The funeral ritual of setting the deceased continued with the removal of the body from the place of mummification.

A religious procession of priests and faithful followed assiduously by the family in pain and painfully by mourners in grief, were taking the body of the deceased by the performance of a solemn ritual. A religious ceremony was passing from one place to the place, singing and praying in devotional acts before closing his coffin: and finally, toward his last resting place, the place of burial. After all, the priest proceeded with the burial through a well-defined ritual, with a sacred gesture to revive his senses, the priest touched the seven openings of the mummy's head for his ultimate incantation; and the journey of life after death was about to begin. But first, the family and relatives of the deceased provided offerings, and then the tomb was sealed.

This mummification technique created naturally by the desert was observed on the preserved mummy of the nicknamed Ginger because of his red hair, and naturally mummified. He was surrounded by his personal items when he was found in Upper Egypt, in Gebelein, at the end of the nineteenth century around 1896, and display in a showcase of the British Museum; the Gebelein Man died in 3100 BC and was perfectly preserved by the hot desert sand for more than five thousand years after his death. He was discovered accidentally by Africans who used their knowledge and created a technical mummification practice that quickly evaporated water from the body, draining the corpse by covering it with the warm sand. Before the artificial mummification was developed in the world, this natural method was widely used in the Egyptian pre-dynastic period, at the time of the pharaohs'original belief for a better passage in the next world-the after-death. The African who found the mummy approached the English Egyptologist, Orientalist, and philologist named Sir E. A. T. Wallis Budge in 1896, who was working for the British Museum, to help build its collection by buying antiquities like manuscripts, papyri, and cuneiform tablets. He immediately recognized the Gebelein Man as the first complete mummified body and identified as being from the Ancient Egypt presynaptic period, brought to England since over a hundred years ago.

This mummification technique was performed as a machine between the dissociation of the impalpable container containing the "soul" and the container—the carnal envelope—the "physical body," to cross the passage between life and death without hindrance; but smoothly, the body after death must also be preserved to ensure the eternity of life. The technique of mummification, which is a science and a proper art, is a real expertise of technicians resulting from a long process of manufacturing activity involving other objects and tools to accomplish the mission of ensuring the existence of souls beyond.

The mummification technique went through all forms of invasion; but resisted, among other things, Arabs, Assyrians, Kushites, Lagids, Libyans, Macedonian of Alexander the Great, Persian, Roman, British and many others; including the Egyptian religious reforms and the preponderance of the church in the second century after Christ, and did not stop to improve for more than three millennia. Their tombs were built with the intention of repelling tomb robbers; for that purpose, harmful waves, created artificially were implemented in tombs or inserted in mummies, especially in the one of Tutankhamen. These harmful waves found in mummies, inserted as a powerful violent poison, acted with all intensity of venom when absorbed by the body of the living and struck the consciousness of the profaners, causing such a terror resulting to they're fleeing, to protect the mummified corpse of pharaohs.

Their very effective technical methods are continually making their well-preserved mummies to live after five thousand five hundred year. Until today, Egypt, as we know it, is the only civilization in the world that produced us so many technical methods and secrets of mysteries that allowed archaeologists to make numerous discoveries for the development of all scientific elements that we know in the actual world.

The particular position of the mummy's statuettes and the mummies themselves – (legs together and arms crossed high on the chest) made that his emitted waves were very strong on the side. The embalming of the deceased had a sacred character for the people of the Nile. This technique of the Egyptian priests, which completely lost its scientific values, was already a deteriorated rite in time, of which they had lost the essential of the most sacred keys that they had as objective to revive the deceased on the physical plane instead of the invisible world. Thus, the conservation of the physical body made that the vibrations of the dead, were still radiating intact in his grave related to our dimension all over the country, and therefore, all over the Earth, to continue his mission beyond the physical death.

So even though he will no longer be incarnated on earth, his "mission" and influence could continue beyond the physical death. Mummification was not only to keep the physical body. Knowing that, "the limits we imposed on ourselves are the only limited limits;" those of the physical body stop right where the limits of the boundless soul start. Therefore, the process of mummification that kept the connection between the physical body and the soul was accomplished by high initiates. It is also an unimaginable process today.

This great work made in Egypt is better known to us today than any other civilization that preceded Greece because it opened its written history on stone pages to us. Therefore, we owe Egypt an absolute respect. The explanation of the "name or the title *Pharaoh*" *is* established to express the desire of heaven and earth, which would mean in one word: "powerful leader born from heaven." As you have already noticed, this history, I will say the history of Africa, but which is generally known as the history of the entire world is not at all told in a fair manner. Even the nonsense they show us on TV and what the media tell us is a very poorly conceived history and poorly known throughout the Western world, particularly to all black people in the world. Yes! I mean all the Negroes in this world because even if you find yourself today in North America or in South America, the Caribbean, or the French and British Indies, or wherever you're in the four corners of the world, where you were cruelly transferred against your will by force and brutality to destroy the power, the intelligence, the wisdom, the sovereignty, the pride, and the wealth that Africa possessed to better govern us, you're and will always remain the cherished and loved children of Africa.

In addition, everything about your past, you're supposed to know it. I bet the majority among us do not know that blacks once ruled the world and that everything that is legislation today was inherited from our ancestors and the black pharaohs of a very distant period. Well, you know it now, and that is what makes us proud. In the primitive times, writing was a privilege for the priesthood and at the same time considered as a sacred thing in the religious practice and was primarily functioning as a source of inspiration. In the Southern Hemisphere, specifically in Sudan, where black priests began to write, they traced their mysterious signs on the skin of animals or on the stones from right to left.

The white priests, or the Nordics, who had learned the black priests' writing, also started to write. But the consciousness of their origin was developed in them. And with their racial pride and national consciousness, they too invented their own signs; and instead of turning to the south, toward the black countries as the blacks, they turned to the north, toward the lands of their ancestors by writing from left to right. I also assert that it is the first stammering of words that gave birth to society and at the same time, awakened a vague hint of the divine order in humanity. The principle of social policy, therefore, appeared the day when a number of half-savage people, and a small primitive tribe, assembled their instincts and their wisdom and selected the most powerful sage and the most intelligent among them to defend and govern them. That day, a civilized society and a well-organized religious ideology were born. This took place for the first time in the African continent and specifically well-organized in Egypt.

The principle of the domestic government of the first men in Africa is the legacy of the principle of a father in Africa, who was first of all a husband for a woman and a father for his children, and his children, in turn, fathers for their families. When the family expanded and developed branches, he becomes the head of the family; and when the branches multiplied and then move away from the trunk to finally generate a large family tree, he became a king of a large family society. Thus, a nation was born. But even as the paternal power has never engendered government societies ruled by the will of fathers' law, fathers in the early ages have given birth to small common circles presided by an elected authority over everyone, who governed separately on the model of the original legislation for the progress.

This kind of government of the people received natural humanitarian dispositions and sociocultural arrangements, knowing more or less the price or the value of their existence and respect for the human being. Highlight everything that led to the happiness of the people. Becoming responsible for experimental efforts until the moment when things could be developed to the satisfaction of all concerned entities and be more or less attentive and sensitive to the interests of the people. The representation of the succession from father to son is a very old tradition, representing 341 wooden statues. Herodotus (*Histories*, II, 143) says that 341 wooden statues were shown to him by the priests of Thebes, representing the high priests who succeeded each other from father to son for over eleven thousand years. The declaration of Solon, asserting that Egyptian priests told him about a chronology dating back to nine thousand years before his time, was confirmed by Plato in the *Timaeus*, presupposing the existence of historical archives covering vast periods in Ancient Egypt.

It emerges in almost perfect agreement with the one told by Herodotus. The Egyptian origin is an origin dating back for more than twelve thousand years, according to Herodotus. Thoth ruled the earlier empire of Egypt with Osiris, known in the Egyptian pantheon as a dictator and usurper of the rights of the people, who disciplined royalty and never accepted to be ruled by despots.

He tried to maintain the doctrine of Osiris, which was already at its highest stage as a culture and achievement, practiced by the Israelites attached to the Hebrew race. It was after the succession of Thoth that the following dynasties departed from the doctrine of Osiris, who became a pharaoh himself until the kingdom fell. And Thoth, who proclaimed the Egyptian empire, was in the eighteenth century abandoned by the hordes of blacks of the South who brought him to power, seeing the material and obscure conceptions appearing to increase their influence, despite his good governance. But for centuries, a splendid civilization of brotherhood and unity was maintained by the directives of Osiris and his successors. Here is the revelation of a progressive and continuous history, multiform as nature, identical to its source as truth, and immutable as God. So let's say these pharaonic priests, those Africans who traced signs on skins and stones and who knew how to found religions since the dawn of time were not animists but astronomers who founded their worship at the precession of the equinox cycle.

They had the oldest known solar calendar of ancient Africa, comprising 365 days per year, based on the star Sirius, a star that has an extremely dense dark companion. Furthermore, that the duration of this cycle was not determined by awakened humanity before the seventeenth century of our era (an assumption mentioned in all books of astronomy). By following a step-by-step foundation of their religious and the sovereignty of the first absolute civilization of Egypt in Africa, we discover not only that the truth has been hidden from us but also that our knowledge was stolen from us to finally use it against us.

On March 21, 1950, according to the exercise book of Moses, the vernal equinox point passed from Pisces to Aquarius. Well, to better understand this process, let's make a leap into the previous lives of those pharaohs—a journey of a millennium in the past—to find ourselves between 4530 and 2370. During that period of equinox, the sun rose on the Bull; while the sun was on the Bull-Taurus, the pharaonic priests professed the cult of Apis the Bull. The god of fertility and fecundity and a royal god in the shape of a Bull was considered as a manifestation of the God Ptah. Thus, Ptah (Apis the Bull) is usually presented as a black statue, also associated with the sun and Osiris, renascent through the Nile flood.

Ptah is the creator of the world, the creator of creators, and the one who awaits the prayers of men. God Ptah (Apis aka Apis or Hapi-ankh) is a very old God not only for the modern world but also for the first Egyptians. He became Osorapis and then Serapis and borrowed the solar disk image to Re or Ra, that he bore between his horns. And when the equinox moved by the force of precession and was found in Aries, the god Khnum (Aries)—the same ancient local God-creator represented with a human body and a ram's head with horizontal horns—shaped a couple of small dolls with clay on a potter's wheel before breathing life into them.

The worship associated with the frog goddess Heqet, who engendered and protected newborns from the primitive aquatic environment, which the Heliopolis clergy of the Fifth Dynasty associated with the sun god under the name of Knouhm-Re, was supplanted from the beginning of the New Kingdom and succeeded Apis at around 2370.

Then another cult appeared in Egypt, the one of Amon, which also meant "God Aries" and who declared a ferocious competition to Khnum. But when the competition between the two gods became very demagogic, Apis began to play the third thief. And it was in that period that Moses appeared, he who was to consecrate his supposedly chosen people in the worship where the symbolism of Aries-RAM, plays a crucial role.

And then when the vernal point was found again in Pisces, the symbol of his supposedly chosen people, the conclusion of the New Covenant was settled, resulting in the foundation of the Christian religion in which the symbolism of fish is essential. But first of all, take in consideration that a first cult existed, called "the cult of the Mother Goddess" possibly six thousand years before the cult of Apis and before the discovery of agriculture.

Ptah (also called Apis and Hapi) was recognized as one of the greatest Egyptian gods, and he was declared not only the creator of the universe but also the creator of everything from which all things sprang. The priests recognized Apis from other bulls by the mystical marks he was given. Namely: His forehead marked with a white triangle, his back with a figure of a vulture with outstretched wings, his right side with a crescent of the moon, his tongue with the image of a scarab, and finally his long fluffy tail with doubled hairs on itself with additional details around the tip. His head raised upward toward the sun and his chest pushed forward in most of his statues was considered a very noble and strong position.

During the beginning of the dynastic periods, which unified the Upper and Lower Egypt, God Hapi, God of the Nile, was or is still portrayed as having the breasts of a woman and the penis of a man, and his prominent full belly indicated fertility, his ability to feed the earth through the Nile's annual floods; a symbol of (hermaphrodite), related to the lotus flower. Called "Hap-Meht," the Nile god of Upper and Lower Egypt, since Egypt was divided into two parts, (the north and the south), he was represented wearing the papyrus plants on his head—a symbol of Lower Egypt—as a northern god— the god of the plants of the Nile, and the lotus plants, a symbol of the Upper Egypt, as a southern god.

Apis or Hapi was always represented holding both lotus and papyrus plants in his hands and two vases as a god of the entire Nile. Eventually, he was identified with Osiris, who also was originally a water or river god. God Hapi, associated with Nun (or Nu) as the Nile source, was believed to be somewhere in the watery chaos of the domain of Nun and Naunet. Nun was related to the creator God Ptah; the two were considered as the father of the sun god Atem.

However, the Egyptians had no idea on how or why the Nile flooded each year. They only believed that the Nile was coming out of the earth between two mountains (Qer-Hapi and Mu-Hapi), between the islands of Elephantine and Philae, and the floods—then commonly known as the arrival of Ptah (Hapi)—created a mysterious belief about him. Hapi was a God of both Upper and Lower Egypt, and Egyptians believed that the source of the Nile was guarded by the gods Khnemu, Anqet, and Satet. Khnemu (also Khnem or Khnoum) was one of the oldest gods, originally a water god; he was an important god who remained important in some semi-Christian sects, two to three centuries after the birth of Christ.

In Africa generally, Ptah is the oldest God creator of the universe of gods. It is by Ptah that Thoth, one of the divinities of the Egyptian pantheon, depending on the phonological interpretation of the emphatic consonants of the Egyptians that Thoth is known as the God of the alphabet, the God of knowledge, hieroglyphics, intelligence, logic, magic, meditation, mind, moon, measure, reading, reason, deeds, thought, secrets, scribes, wisdom, and writing.

Thoth was the seat of intelligence or spirit, the language of the sun god Ra, and the means by which the will of Ra was translated into speech. The scribe wrote the story of our reality and then placed it in the networks for our experience and our learning, thanks to the alchemy of time and consciousness. Later in the history, at the level of Ancient Egypt divinity, Thoth became strongly associated with the arbitration of different stakes of arts and of magic, the writing system, the development of science, and—in the legend of Osiris—the judgment of the dead in the hall of Maat as a god of the moon. Linked to the will of God Ptah, Thoth and Maat played many essential leading roles in the maintenance of the universe, notably including one of the two deities known as Seshat, who was the wife and sister of Maat, and sometimes his daughter begotten by the goddess Nehemetaouay; she was also his assistant; they're the two deities who stood on each side of the boat of Ra (the sun god/goddess).

A sky deity representing the sun, the power, and strength of the sunlight in the solar deities, like a story recorded under various clichés. The Ancient Egyptians believed that Seshat, Thoth's daughter or wife, invented writing, while Thoth taught it to mankind. Known as the "mistress of the house of books," she took care of Thoth's library of spells and scrolls. Seshat was the essence of the cosmic intuition, the creation of the geometry of the sky, alongside Thoth. In the Egyptian mythology, Seshat was originally the deification of the concept of wisdom and became a goddess of writing, astronomy, astrology, architecture, and mathematics.

The cult center of Eshmunen or Hermopolis in the earlier period, known as the city of Khmun, was where Thoth wrote the worship of the sun and the important religious texts, such as the *Book of the Dead*, truly called the *Book of the Coming Forth by Day and by Night* in the Ancient Egypt era. This day of all luminous principle opposes darkness, forgetfulness, annihilation, and death, like the "missing sun" found in many cultures in Africa and around the world. For example, the Tiv or Tivi people, an ethnolinguistic group or nation in West Africa numbering over two million individuals in Nigeria and Cameroon, consider the sun as the son of the Supreme Being Awondo and the moon, is the daughter of Aondo or Awondo.

Others believe in the sky deities representing the sun god or goddess are known in the Barotse tribe. The Lozi people—an ethnic group inhabiting the region of Barotseland in western Zambia and also found in Namibia (Caprivi Strip), Angola, and Botswana—believe that the sun is inhabited by the sky god Nyambi, and the moon is his wife. Also believed to reside inside the sun is the Ancient Egyptian god of creation, Amun. An Akan ethnic group today in the southern regions of the Republic of Ghana and Ivory Coast, with the largest ethnic population of roughly twenty million people, believes in the sky deity Nyame, the creator in both countries of West Africa, and in Nommo, the mythological deity of creation of the Dogon of Mali.

The South American cultures, the Incan considered the ancient sun god Inti, since the Incas divided their identities according to the stages of the sun, commonly known as the son of Kon-Tiki (also Con-Tici Viracocha), the god of civilization; the great creator God in the pre-Inca and Inca mythology, as the supreme god and the most important deity, similar to the sun worship in the tradition of their civilization. In the ancient Slavonic church, Svarog, the Slavic god of the sun and spirit of fire, is the subject of the sun worship.

The solar boat concept associated with Re, the Supreme Solar God, symbolizing the Egyptian mythology, was linked to the daily cycle of the sun, traversing the sky during the Neolithic period with Ra and Horus in the ancient myths of Egypt; and each night on another solar boat, he was passing through the realms of the underworld, the (Duat), to reappear every morning in the east.

The boat in which he traveled from the sunrise to noon was called Atet or Matet, and the one he traveled from noon to sunset was Sektet. Apep, the mighty snake god who typified evil and darkness, attacked the solar god in hell according to the Ancient Egyptian mythology, and he fought with the help of his fellow gods to defend him against the evil snake Apep and defeat him, representing the victory of good over evil.

In a crescent-shaped boat, the depicted falcon-headed man, Anti – occasionally depicted on the solar boat and known as a lesser god, was the "guardian of the sunrise." Atum (Ra), Geb, Isis, Nephthys, Nut, Osiris, Set, Shu, and Tefnut were the nine different gods in the sun boat as the companions of the solar god Ra; they were called the Ennead of Heliopolis. The extended "divine family," the sons of Osiris, are known as the gods Horus and Anubis.

The sun within the lioness Sekhmet, warrior goddess of healing, known as the most ferocious hunter who formed the desert by her breath, is also a solar deity who bears the solar disk. Sekhmet is closely associated with the cow-headed goddess, the goddess of dance, joy, music, sexual love, pregnancy, and birth;

Sekhmet is one of the twelve daughters of the sun god Ra. It is said that when the sun is within the lioness, it can be seen reflected in Sekhmet's eyes at night or that it is within the cow, to which she is associated, Hathor, the cow-headed goddess, during the night, and reborn each morning as her (bull) son, and eventually used as an address to royalty during the Bronze Age. Wadjet, Sekhmet, Hathor, Nut, Bast, Bat, and Menhit are the earliest deities associated with the sun. The first, Hathor and then Isis gave birth to breastfeed Horus and Ra.

The sun has been traversing the sky in a chariot; note here that with this sentence, the Proto-Indo-European religion has a solar chariot. In the Vedic Surya, the son of Āditi and Kashyapa, is the sun god; in Greek, Helios (sometimes son of the Titan and sometimes assimilated to Apollo, also means "sun"); and in the Germanic, Nordic, or Roman mythology, Helios corresponds to Sol; these gods also lead the chariot of the sun; at dawn, Ra travels across the sky in his solar boat by driving away the demon of darkness Apep, the opposite of the order and the exterior of maat, representing the "solarization" of several local gods like Hnum-Re, Min-Re, Amon-Re, etc., who have reached their peak; Ra passes through the Duat (the underworld) – (Hades), where his deceased stayed after his death and where he resurrected at the same time as the sun for his solar barge to emerge in the east.

Osiris, an Egyptian god usually identified as the lord of the dead and the god of the afterlife and the underworld with his green skin symbolizing rebirth, is considered the oldest son of Geb, the earth god, and of Nut, the sky goddess; Osiris is sometimes considered as the brother and the husband of Isis, with his posthumously begotten son Horus, the falcon-headed god of war and protection. Thanks to the hope of a new life after death, at the beginning of the New Year, his links with Orion and Sirius are associated with him to the cycles of vegetation and the annual flood of the Nile as the lord of the dead, widely worshipped until the suppression of the Egyptian religion of paganism during the Christian era.

The worship of Isis, a goddess in the Ancient Egyptian religious belief and a name meaning "throne," spread throughout the Greco-Roman world as the ideal mother and wife, the patroness of nature and magic, and the friend of artisans, the patroness of the oppressed, slaves, and sinners, who also listened to prayers of aristocrats, maidens, rulers, and the wealthy. She was also known as the goddess of children and the protector of the dead. The cult of Isis was introduced to traditional centers of worship in Greece in cities like Athens, the capital and the world's largest and oldest city, with a recorded history spanning around 3,400 years, where the Delphic oracle ordered the purgation of all dead bodies and that no one should be allowed to either give birth or die on the island. Because of its sacred importance and to be fit for the proper worship of the gods, purification was performed to attempt to purify the island in the sixth century BC.

On the island of Delos, like the ancient Oracle site of Delphi, marked by the marble monument said to be thrown from the sky by Zeus and known as the omphalos navel of the earth, the ancient city believed to be determined by Zeus, who sought it to find the center of his "grandmother, creator and giver of birth to the earth," Earth (Ge, Gaea, or Gaia the personification, and the great mother of the entire universe), Delos is an ancient archaeological site; an island that had a position as a holy sanctuary for a millennium. The temple of Delos was built before the temple of Delphi by Apollo.

Eleusis is a city in Greece that housed a sanctuary of great renowned for its mysteries, and as a city named after the hero Eleusis, son of Hermes, and in a municipality in West Attica Greece, at about twenty kilometers northwest of Athens; it is a city of a great historical and mythological mysteries of great importance according to tradition, and it is founded by Triptolemus, the son of Celeus. The cult of the mysteries of Eleusis was an agrarian cult for the worship of Demeter; when she came to Eleusis during the time Persephone, her daughter, was kidnapped by Hades, this agrarian worship was held to her honor after meeting the king of the place named Celeus; it extended throughout Greece and the Roman Empire. Its origins have exceptional eminent merits. In 395 after Jesus Christ, the barbarity of the Visigoths of Alaric I destroyed Eleusis.

King Alaric I was a nobleman from 395 to 410, particularly known for his invasion and plundering of Rome in 410; he was born around 370 in the Peuce Island at the mouth of the Danube Delta, the present-day Romania, and died in Italy in 410. His people, a Germanic people from the Goths (wise Goths), were Indo-European ethnic groups people of the forest, originally established in Northern Europe on the shores of the Black Sea, covering an area of 413,000 km2 between Europe, the Caucasus, and Anatolia. The Goths, who first originated from the corded ware culture of Southern Scandinavia, are people who spread on the southern shores of the Baltic Sea, 432,800 km2, an intracontinental sea located in Northern Europe and connected to the Atlantic Ocean via the Nordic Sea.

In the Bronze Age, Southern Scandinavia formed the first settlement generally described as "Germanic," and the Finnish who populated Northern Finland, Norway, and a large part of Sweden. But the term *Germans* did not include the first Scandinavians to the point of attaching them in the same population. From the beginning, a woman was chosen to act prophetically on the white race by the invisible. They had their salvation from a prophecy of a woman in a state of ecstasy, the "Voluspa"—the prophecy of clairvoyance in the Norse mythology; a famous work among the mythological poems contained in the *Poetic Edda*, probably composed in the tenth or eleventh century.

It is known as a poem with cosmogonic value, defined as a system of the formation of the universe and eschatology—a discourse on the end of time, referring to the theology and philosophy in relation with the last period, which takes the form of a long monologue where a clairvoyance exposes the history and the destiny of the world, of gods and men to the god Odin, since the origin of the world in a series of visions rich in details up to "Ragnarok"—a series of future events including various natural disasters like a great battle resulting in the death of a number of great figures, and the submersion of the world in water as a prophetic end of the world in the Norse mythology; and which will bring about a renewal of the universe, after the returned of gods.

Indeed, two great white leaders with red hair and blue eyes from the north were about to fight each other fiercely. Suddenly, a wild visionary woman rushed between them. To separate them, this woman prophetess in the mystical state, directly unifying her soul to God, spoke with an authoritative and accentuated voice with eyes full of passion, projecting an unfathomable glow. She articulated breathless words, warning the two warriors saying that she had seen their ancestor, the victorious warrior of the young white race in the forest, evoking their union against the common enemy and their sworn enemy—the warriors of the old black race, who only waited the end of their war to destroy them.

Convinced about what she said, the exalted woman believed in herself; speaking in tone with emotion, she convinced the two brother warriors, surprised and moved by an invincible force to unite and exterminate the black race. Of the two leading warriors, one was the brother of the woman and the other her spouse; overwhelmed by the supernatural revelation of the inspired women, they regarded her as a kind of deity, and then suddenly stopped to fiercely fight between themselves. This is how the ancestor worship was established among the white races. The early civilizations of the people of white race were based primarily in Asia, specifically Iran and India. Since it was the woman who was chosen to act prophetically on the white race at the beginning, the fact of religious inspiration led men to be regarded as prophets, rishis, and sages, and quickly took over on women. And for that same fact, people of various colors were mixed, including the Aryan race.

The one whom men submitted at home and repressed is no longer a priestess and no longer directs the world, but among the people of the same origin in Europe, Europeans remained barbarians for thousands of years in Scandinavia, believed in the Pythonesses with powers of divination through the enlightened forest of the Northern Hemisphere and granted a prominent role to the women of the "Voluspa" of *Edda*. Women with golden hair and blue eyes, accompanied by reckless leaders deciding the day of battle of the German armies, were Celtic druidesses. The soothsayers, who were beneficent at first to the Thracian Bacchae in the legend of Orpheus, continued their prehistoric clairvoyance in the Pythia of Delphi; then these great visionary prophetesses, prophesying the cruelty of the evil magic, to the sinister songs of priests, were pouring human blood on the dolmens with the acclamations of the wild Scythians, without interruption, since the earliest times.

On the monitoring of the elderly-educated druids, these primitive druidesses of the white race were organized into colleges of prophetesses and gave impetus to the race of brutal force and violence of the sign of Thor, whose war of prejudices several centuries secular with the black race had just began their imaginary intuition and their imaginary divination. The druidesses wanted to dominate the people at all costs by terror and by huge abuses of power and corruption to be mistresses of destiny. The essential element of their worship was human sacrifice, inspiration lacking in them; the heroic instincts of their race despising death favored the courageous to throw themselves on the knifes of the bloodthirsty priestesses on the first appeal and hurry themselves to the dead, thinking to obtain favor of their ancestors by living sacrificed as messengers.

Druidesses became a perpetual threat in the minds of the first leaders of the white race as a formidable instrument of domination. This perversion of the human nature of nobler instincts was a lack of mastering, of scholarly authority, of a higher consciousness directed toward the good, and was an inspiration that degenerated into superstition ambition, and personal passion, using ferocious sacrifice as a cruel instrument of tyranny and treacherous exploitation to engulf their people as well as others.

The genius blood of the black race, with superabundant force and passionate energies, has unfortunately generated, refined, effeminated its characteristics, has faded the special color of India, and deprived it of a part of the blood energy of the black race. This ethnic base of course from India, has maintained the dominant barbaric ideas of the white race at the top of their civilization through so many revolutions with its metaphysical aspirations to the sublime prejudices up to its moral sense of domination.

The ancient religious history of this crossbreeding of India is that double genius resulting in two ancient traditions: one as lunar dynasty, a descendant of the son of the moon; and the other as solar dynasty, a descendant of the son of the sun, covering two symbolic religious conceptions.

Two categories of cults different from the sovereign creator, known as the male God of the universe, around whom the woman is respected and considered as a sacred fire, practicing the worship tradition of their ancestors, qualified as the elective esoteric kingship science of their supreme God.

The religions of the Aryan cycle, attributing divinity to the female were under the lunar sign. The lunar cult, the adoration of nature, was a blind worship in its violent terrible and terrifying manifestations, where the cult leaned toward idolatry and black magic, tyranny, and popular unconsciousness on passions, from where polygamy originated. Bringing the sickness of the sky to the world, the white race of the wild scene was to be liberated to befall to a distinctive self-awareness of individual freedom, thoughtful sensibility, the power of sympathy, and a domination of the intellect.

The repartition of Angles, the Germanic people in the first century after Jesus Christ in Europe, is an original expansion of the Germans, attesting the Danish Bronze Age. The region of origin of the Angles, where the name of England derives, is limited by the waters of the Baltic Sea (Kieler Forde) to the east, the Eckernforde Bay in the southeast, and the Flensburg Fjord and the border with Denmark in the north. That region is where a small human group was found in a primitive society of the current historical region, originating from the peninsular known in German language by the name of Angeln, and in Danish as Angel; it was developed at the expense of the Jutland peninsula, located on the northeastern coast of the city of Kiel, capital of Schleswig-Holstein; and known as one of the components of the federated states of Germany, with the capital the city of Schleswig. As a vassal of Denmark, this region existed during the late Middle Ages until the War of the Duchies in 1864.

Two countries opposing the German Confederation—the Austrian Empire and the Kingdom of Prussia—declared war on Denmark. Already in the memory of the people, it was known that they had obviously caused the First Schleswig War in 1848, opposing the German Confederation to Denmark. The second conflict was caused by the succession of the greedy Duchies in power. These people, who expanded to Danube and the Nordic areas of Western Germany, replaced the corded ware culture of their ancestors in around 2400 BC. Denmark and Southern Sweden were invaded by another related branch.

Many searchers associated with the corded ware culture with some families of the Indo-European languages, encompassed a vast area, from the west, the Rhine River, to the east, the Volga River, to the present day of modern Germany; it was associated with countries like Belarus, Czech Republic, Denmark, Estonia, Finland, Latvia, Lithuania, the Norwegian coast, the western Romania, the European part of Russia, Slovakia, the southern part of Sweden, and in the north of Ukraine. It is also believed that these Indo-European families of languages are related to the Catacomb culture. It is from its characteristic pottery ornamentation that the corded ware culture received its name. At the beginning of the late Neolithic era (New Stone Age), this culture flourishes through the Copper Age and reaches the highest point of development in the early Bronze Age.

It is also characterized as the battle-ax culture or single grave culture, a tomb burial under barrow, a characteristic custom of offering a tombstone to the dead, generally including a custom indicating that the amber beads, a battle-ax, and pottery vessels will accompany the deceased in his last resting place. The battle-ax culture is derived from a prehistoric stone tool hand ax, the longest-used tool in human history, in use since the Paleolithic period for hundreds of thousands of years. During the Mesolithic period around 6000 BC, the first hafted stone axes were produced. In the Neolithic period, technological development continued with the battle-ax people of Scandinavia; their axes were cultural objects of high rank, characterizing the time that humans adopted the use of cut stone, wood, and bone tools.

The early members of the genus *Homo*, such as *Homo habilis*, gradually evolved from the simple use of stone tools up to a modern human, *Homo sapiens*, having a fully anatomical behavior during the Paleolithic era. Specifically, humans began to produce the works of art during the end of the Paleolithic period and engaged in religious and spiritual behavior, such as the burial ritual, spreading in the great European plain southward toward Germany; the one that on the geographically terms designates the plain of North German, and without interruption extended toward the west of the Netherlands, up to a part of Belgium, to the north of Denmark and the east of Poland. Finally, going up to the beginning of the second Iron Age around 500 BC, they formed their own kingdoms in the fifth century during the period of the great invasions of the late antiquity.

The two branches of the Goths that are known are the Ostrogoths and the Visigoths. It is known that these two branches were repeatedly engaged in wars against Rome. The Visigoths settled in Dacia in the Roman Empire (now Romania) from 270 to 275 in a province colonized and abandoned by the Romans from 106 to 256, and from 376, they migrated back toward the west in the Western Roman Empire in Hispania and in ancient Aquitaine, a territory limited to the Pyrenees Atlantic triangle. Their brothers, the Ostrogoths, who during the third and fourth centuries established a kingdom at the north of the Black Sea, chose the actual land of Ukraine, more precisely Sarmatia.

Till then, almost empty of men, the demographic expansion equally contributed to generate a new settlement, since Germans were only mentioned at the time that the formation of people took place, from the third century BC, a period ending when the Germans entered in history. Because the Greeks or the Romans did not leave any written testimony, could their ancient name be that of the Germans Celts, would it have been confused with the names of the Celts by the ancient historians?

Herodotus tells us that in the middle of the fifth century BC, the Celts inhabited the regions of the Pillars of Hercules up to Danube, starting from the Iberian Peninsula up to Romania; and across the southern Germany, Austria, a region attested by the presence of populations with Celtic character, traditionally recognized as the original Celts of Hallstatt, which takes its name from an archaeological site located in Hallstatt, a village in the Salzkammergut, a region of the Eastern northern Pre-Alps.

From 1100 to approximately 400 of the civilization of Hallstatt, the said Celtic civilization was a period that succeeded the late Bronze Age, which was used to designate the first Iron Age in Europe. Their territory continued toward Bohemia, the Netherlands, Belgium, France, Northern Italy, Moravia, Slovakia, Slovenia, and Hungary. The Bohemia and Moravia bordering the Third Reich had a border at the time when Czechoslovakia existed, designating the Sudetenland, currently a historical region of Central Europe.

They had a religion with a well-developed polytheistic religious system, several years of sustained economic growth, and the authority of an omnipotent priestly class, generally referred to by the term *druid* that was gradually dissolved from the first century before Jesus Christ, in the culture of the Roman Empire. That diversified polytheism religious system continued to exist until the fifth century in Ireland and was the Celtic culture as early as 900 BC, and it was the introduction of Christian evangelization that ended the Celtic religion out of Europe. Nevertheless, only having a system of priestly class that favored oral thought and verbal expression in societies where most of the population was unfamiliar with writing, their beliefs, their gods, and their rites are not known to us. Apart from the Welsh and Irish medieval literature, the archaeological remains, and finally their neighbors (the Greeks and Romans), their writings as direct evidence did not reach us.

Since the late third century, when the Visigoths occupied the ancient Roman province of Dacia, they had from the year 341, adopted Arianism, a form of theological thought of early Christianity affirming that Jesus Christ was in no way God, the "divine Father." Nevertheless, that Jesus Christ, God's unique Son, was first of all human, a distinct human being begotten, not created directly by the divine Father, therefore having a part of his divinity. In the early fourth century, this form of Christianity was attributable to Arius, an Alexandrian theologian born in Cyrenaica; nowadays a traditional region of Libya, located around the ancient Greek city of Cyrene, whose name came from ancient Cyrenaica, a Roman province.

The simple priest Arius supported his prophecy. In addition, he maintained the Father's superiority over the Son, against other bishops of Alexandria, who were saying that Jesus Christ was an incarnation of the God of Israel, according to the Christologist Alexander.

Alexander of Alexandria sustained the doctrine of the eternal immutable Son of the same nature as the Father. Other theories at that time were established when the first regional council convened by Alexander in 318 excommunicated Arius. It was at a time when no dogma had yet occurred in Christianity, so the theological debate was still normal. From 284 to 305, Emperor Diocletian, who was reigning over the Roman Empire, was the last great persecutor of Christians. Those persecutions that destroyed books and Christian properties also made many martyrs from the period 303 to 305.

In 306, specifically after July 25, 306, when Constantine was proclaimed emperor by the soldiers of his father, Maxentius—his rival—contested his proclamation; he did the same and took power, relying on the discontent of Rome and the Senate.

The bursting of the empire occasioned a battle known as the Battle of the Milvian Bridge in the northern Rome, which cost Maxentius's life on October 28, 312, at the gates to the city, where he had before radiated with power for many years. Constantine I, the thirty-fourth Roman emperor, was the first emperor to end the persecution of Christians in Rome. Moreover, he put his role as emperor below the Christian God by adopting Christianity as the state religion. He established freedom of religion, favoring the extinction of Mithraism through the promotion of Christianity. Thus, the Orthodox Christian Church was able to grow by considering him as a saint. His Edict of Milan, issued in 313, restored the confiscated property from Christians and officially put an end to their persecution.

When the Visigoths settled in the Roman province, they remained faithful to their faith and their belief in Arianism before the First Council of Nicaea, convened by Constantine I in 325, came and qualified Arianism as heresy.

The Trinitarian Christians from the First Council of Nicaea of the early Christianity was held from May 20 to July 25, 325, under the dignity of bishops such as Alexander of Alexandria, Alexander of Constantinople, Eustathius of Antioch, Macarius of Jerusalem, and Sylvester of Rome, all gathered at Nicaea in Bithynia, an ancient kingdom in the northwest of Asia Minor, today Iznik, located in Turkey.

It was in that council that the dogmatic problems highlighted by the controversy between Arius and his bishop Alexander, the disciplinary problems, and the problems which then divided the Eastern Churches, were solved.

These Germanic people, with their kings qualified as tyrants and as bloodthirsty invaders, were not sparing those who opposed them either. Vortigern, king of the Britons in the fifth century after Jesus Christ, asked the Angles to fight alongside him against the war of the Picts. The subjugated lord of the kingdom was the king, and shortly after his ascension to the throne, his withdrawal became sure by the Picts, allied to the Scots and Saxons Picts of Scotland, and the quotas Angles, of Jutes who were forming a coalition in Albania, the ancient name of Scotland, to answer the call of the Breton king Vortigern in 449. His dream of seizing the royal treasures, as well as fortified cities, under the pretext of foreign threats, was crowned with success.

And the territories over which the Breton king Vortigern reigned were threatened by the Scot invaders from Ireland, presented as a descendant of a certain general Woden in Old English; and in the Germanic mythology, Woden is the main god of the Norse mythology of death, victory, and knowledge; serving as an instrument of the divine retribution against the heretical Britons, the Angles, the opposite of the future England by the "angle" Symbolically, the world was considered as a square with a representation that came from an "angle" (in Latin, *angulus*), representing the four cardinal points—namely the Roman church in the center. Thus, the Angles attached to the Christian tradition were portrayed as a new chosen people, even knowing that their origins were pagans.

The proposal of the Saxons to bring other Germany warriors, considering the dangers that were threatening the kingdom, was accepted by the king, and his promise to reward his warriors with land, the right to construct was in accordance with the law on which the fortress of Castrum Corrigiae was built. On the island of Brittany, a wedding was held not to the taste of girls and boys of today, placing love at the center of marriage. Here, the king fell instantly in love with the beautiful young daughter of Hengist, visiting the new home of her father. The king, after meeting the girl for just some few hours, married the beautiful Ronwen in exchange with the territory of Kent, whose county town was Maidstone, located at the southeast of London in England. Katigern, Pascent, and Vortimer—his first three sons—were not also happy with the marriage of their father, which was neither to the liking of other lords.

Scotland was facing a new fear of Saxon invasion and the cunning of the Hengist of Germany, worried the Breton Vortigern. It was at that moment that a request of the Bretons to Vortigern occurred, exhorting him to get rid of the Saxon allies already settled in Scotland. So he was dethroned from his sovereignty, and Vortimer—his son—was proclaimed king consequently for his reluctance to get rid of that mighty army of Saxon allies, which allowed the king to defeat his enemies but terrifying the population. Hengist, who was preparing to leave with three hundred thousand soldiers for Scotland, finally decided to make peace without bloody violence and convened a conference at Ambrius. However, Vortigern was attacked by Hengist in a meeting where peace should have been the agenda of the day; he grabbed his throat and slaughtered him with four hundred and sixty other Breton lords. Vortigern was buried in Kaercaradoc, the current Salisbury.

At that time, a developed doctrine professed that freedom should regulate the relationship between God and man, from the second half of the fourth century by the ascetic Breton Pelagius, Celestius, and Julian of Eclanum. Pelagianism, a doctrine characterized by the insistence of the free will of man that the Auxerre of Saint Loup and Troyes were coming to fight on the island of Brittany, was rather a set of philosophical positions without homogeneity; it was a concept of teaching that the Fathers of the Church rejected as not being a religious ideology in itself, which marked the opposition of the African episcopate.

At the beginning of the sixth century, the term *paganism* (in Latin *paganus*) (pagan), the religion of those who were not Christians or Jews, was used by Christians; thus, the world was not limited, and was not going to simply be limited to the perception of the early Christians or the Jews. There were some people who had no priestly caste but bore great importance to particular beliefs and deities that produced effects.

The Germans were in fact one of those people without priestly caste. The Celts and the Gauls had a priestly caste; they organized their society around a belief in both the sacred and the temporal. The druids believed that it was necessary to submit the individual to the regulation of litigations before getting the favor of the deities. The Greeks of the middle ages in the fourth century designated their polytheist ancestors by the term *Hellene*, equivalent of *paganus*. The word *gentiles*, which referred to all non-Christian beliefs, had a rapprochement with the word *pagani* of the bishop St. Augustine of Hippo, used from 395 until his death in 430. Hippo was an ancient name of the city of Annaba, in northeastern Algeria, which became one of the principal cities of Roman Africa. It was definitely replaced by the word *pagan* in 409, and the old term *gentile* was not used anymore in the current state of knowledge.

Already opposing the philosophical positions without homogeneity and its concept of grace rejected by the African episcopate Augustine of Hippo, who condemned the Pelagianism doctrine of Pelagius, and many works of Celestius in 411; he was followed by the Western Roman Emperor Honorius, whose reign was precarious and chaotic; then, in 418 by the Sixteenth Council of Carthage with the approval of Pope Zosimus. This second Christian heresy fought by Augustine, who was practicing a naturalist religion and rationalist doctrine, was an idea of the grace that took off in the fourth and fifth centuries in the diocese of Roman Africa.

Donatism—a Christian doctrine considered schismatic and heretical by the Catholic historiography of the Trinity Church, concerned the issue of whether a Christian who has abandoned the Christian faith could be reconciled with the church. This question became a matter of great controversy in the Catholic Church, caused by many Donatists, who refused the validity of the sacraments issued by the bishops who had risked their lives in the Diocletian persecution from 303 to 305—they were condemned by the Council of Rome in 313, confirming the excommunication of Donatus. The last repression of Christianity under the tetrarchy, "a system of four governments of the Roman Empire" set up in the late third century by Diocletian and especially in the early fourth century under his reign, was to deal with the barbarian invasions.

Donatism was appointed by a schismatic bishop of *Cellae Nigrae,* the Black House of North Africa in Numidia, by the name of Donatus the Great, who died around 355. Around 305, Donat le Grand–Donatus Magnus, provoked a schism in the community of many traitors of church members, who turned over sacred scriptures to be burned or betrayed their fellow Christians to the pagan threat of the Roman authorities during the Diocletianic Persecution. These traditors, eventually pardoned under Constantine, returned to positions of authority like bishop Mensurius of Carthage during the early Christian Church in the early fourth century. However, the less pardoned Donatists proclaimed that all sacraments celebrated by these traditors priests and bishops were invalid, by refusing to admit having delivered the holy books and sacred vessels to the gentiles.

The bishop of Hippo, the African theologian Augustine, had a few years later developed the arguments to counter Donatism, criticizing the narrow and puritan religious attitude of Donatists from 395 in a climate of repression of Roman Christians in Africa and from the 295 to 299, where the persecution took a systematic form in the early fourth century of the great persecution of Diocletian.

In 307, the appointment of the deacon saint Miltiades, a native of North Africa, changed the Christian situation in Carthage; he was ethnically of the Berber origin. So, it was Maxentius who put an end to the vacancy of the episcopal seat, when he was the Roman emperor; he lifted punitive measures against the Christians and allowed the election of Miltiades as bishop of Carthage in 311. Miltiades became pope on July 2, 311, and condemned Donatus after acquitted Caecilian of Carthage in the Lateran Synod of Rome that he presided in 313.

As the thirty-second African pope of the Catholic Church, who condemned Donatus, the follower of Majorinus, the leader and founder of the Donatist sect particularly developed and grown in North Africa, for the origin of the schism within the Church, Pope Miltiades dealt with these splitting problems of the Church caused by Donatist followers during his papacy, until his death on January 10, 314; and was the first pope to enjoy the favors of a Roman emperor. Some members of the community of the Cecilian bishop of Carthage changed to be traditors like Felix of Aptunga, who consecrated him, were against his ordination as a bishop. This conflict, which divided African Christians during the fourth century, brought by his supporters to the greatest excess, was referred to an appeal at the Council of Arles (314), on their condemnation at a Council of Rome in 313. After the unfavorably appeal for the Donatists, they presented the feeling of war against nonschismatic Christians under the reign of Constantine and became enemies of the Roman authorities of the seventh and eight centuries, up to the Arab invasions. The feeling of civil war against Christians, presented in this African region because of the schism developed by the Donatists desolated Africa.

In 429, the Vandals, a Germanic tribe of Scandinavian origin, arrived in Africa during the great invasions period in the fifth century. In 439, ten years after their arrival in Africa, Carthage fall and was detached from the Roman Empire. Around 425 BC, the exploration of West Africa was for the first time from Carthage by the navigator Hannon. The only source of the voyage of the Carthaginian explorer off the west coast of Africa comes from the Greeks. Depending on the case, he may have reached Cameroon, Gabon, or Sierra Leone. Vandals had successively conquered southern Spain; according to the testimony of Julius Caesar, they occupied the south central of ancient Baetica and Galaecia, located in the northwest of the Iberian Peninsula, ulterior Hispania; the region of Hispania comprised one of the three main provinces of Gaul; the Gaul, located at the northwest tip of Spain, was a name given to an occupied territory by Aquitaine people, known as Gallic Celts, Belgian, and Romans, the islands of the Western Mediterranean and North Africa in the fifth century, during the Great Invasions. They first established a "vandal kingdom in Africa" from 439 to 534.

In 270 BC, the Ptolemaic Egyptian king Ptolemy II Philadelphus hired four thousand Galatians Celts mercenaries "to seize Egypt." According to Pausanias, "they perished one after another or by the heat of the desert or by famine" on a deserted island of the Nile River where they were abandoned by Ptolemy. The Visigoths' brothers, Visigoths who at the same time settled in southern France, were expelled from France in 531. But having already extended their jurisdiction to the northeastern Spain, they migrated southward in the Iberian Peninsula to also found the first Hispanic monarchies at their entry into that territory that lasted up to 711 during the Muslim invasion. That part of Africa, a part of the provinces of African so much requested by the Western, was once more conquered by the Byzantines in 533 to 535. And in 535, the law of Justinian came to put an end to the practice of any religions, "Arians, Donatists, Jews, pagans and any other heretics." Emerging from their wild forests and their lacustrine dwellings, inhabited by an imbalance, the fight against the black race oscillated for very long centuries, from the Pyrenees to the Caucasus and the Caucasus to Himalayas. At the beginning of that war, the half-savage whites only had their bows and arrows with stone points and their spears. The inequality in the level of knowledge in science was evident since the industrialized civilization of the black race and their cyclopean cities were developed.

The black race had brazen armor of brass, iron weapons, and at the first shocked captivated white slaves in mass and was forcing them to work as porters of ore in their ovens and to work on stone. During their captivity, two capital things were taught to them by blacks: the sacred art of writing mysterious hieroglyphic signs on skins, on the bark of ash trees, and on stone; and metal smelting, which the escaped captives brought back to their homeland. But they had only fragments of our sciences and arts and their uses. Nevertheless, the sacred scripture of the black race, the masters' educators of the white race and conquerors, became the origin of the religious tradition and secret science of the Celts.

And the art of forging the molten metal of the black race became the resource for making their instrument of war. Ready to conquer, they bounced once more at the right time, better armed from their forest, where they hid like wild beasts. They overthrew the black cities from the coastal region of Europe, hunted blacks, and invaded North Africa and Central Asia occupied by dark-skinned tribes and then, in turn, invaded the whole Africa from century to century. It was by war and conquest on blacks that the Aryan civilizations were formed. These so-called Aryan and Semitic people originated from the submission of their bellicose settlers to the peaceful black people, who were dominating and were accepting religious initiation from black initiator priests.

These Aryan people remained in a state of barbarism, which included Scythians, Dacians, Sarmatians, Celts, and Germans, who were mixed with black humanity first by a bloody conquest and then by a pacific colonization with an erroneous cartographic code to change humanity and the prehistoric past of the black race. In a more specific manner of denomination, Egyptian priests initiated Arabs, Chaldeans, Etruscans, Hindus, Iranians, Greeks, Jews, Phoenicians, and many nomads of antiquity to "the primitive hidden absolute secrecy of God." The principle of intellectuality—the unity of "God," formless and its secret initiation—were presented as one of the essential moral principles of the black priests, considered universally. It is for that reason that we can note a tendency toward monotheism and popular idolatry among the Semites, where the black race has dominated royally.

The tendency to polytheism among the white winners considered the nature by mythology, the passion for the worship of ancestors, and the personification of the deity; by that fear before the nature, the white man realized that there was something superior, and the charitable spirit was linking him to an unknown past mystery, and he adored the highest. One part of the Celts fleeing the authority of druidesses sowing terror by human sacrifices, forced them to expatriate around 10,000 BC and wandered like Bodhones in the wilderness; then later on, with one of the Sumerian tribes, almost a family that suffered from consanguinity, they became the Semites to form the Hebrew people after a thousand vicissitudes, nearly four thousand years ago.

It was a revelation to a druid by the name of Ram, received in the forest that allowed Ram to pluck up the sacred mistletoe of the oak, of the "Mother's Night," during the sixth night of the winter solstice, the first of the Celtic year.

Dressed in white and with a golden sickle, he prepared the mistletoe of oak, all received spiritually in a linen cloth of an immaculate whiteness. This plant with medicinal properties should not touch the ground; otherwise, it lost its powers and virtues, because according to the prophecy its purified souls.

Mistletoe is a legend and a reality; it is said that mistletoe is a healer of epilepsy, hypertension, and leprosy and acts on the immune system. Let us note that by this healing of leprosy, the druidesses' authority saw mistletoe come and free the druids' college from its cruel prophetesses. Mistletoe fell from heaven, and in which we attributed magical powers ensured the fertility of herds and neutralized poisons. Other legends also attributed other virtues to mistletoe, associated with the symbols of love, eternity, and prosperity; the famous plant means "cure-all" in the Celtic language.

Among other things, the custom of kissing under mistletoe was known as the sacred plant of the goddess of love named Frigga. She became the Queen of Heaven and belonged to the highest hierarchy of Ases by marriage to Odin. Therefore, as wife of God Odin, she could predict the future, and she was the goddess of love, marriage, and motherhood. After making the gods to promise her as the mother of Balder, imploring them that no harm should happen to her son, when she dreamed of his death. She didn't know that her son had Loki, the daemon as enemy, who out of jealousy was planning to kill the sun god Balder with an arrow poisoned with mistletoe he made. By the cunning of the evil god Loki, Hoder, the blind god of winter and the Brother of Balder, shot the arrow and became the unintentional killer of Balder. Suddenly, all life on earth stopped, the sky paled, and heaven and earth wept for the sun god for three days. His mother resurrected him after multiple attempts of each element to bring Balder back to life three days later. She had to kiss anyone who passed under the mistletoe. And it was the resurrection of Balder as legend in Scandinavia that the symbol of love and forgiveness came to mind. This is how the tradition of kissing under mistletoe came to existence. Mistletoe is found in several places such as North Africa, the British Isles, the Iberian Peninsula, Russia, Ukraine, Scandinavia, Lebanon, Syria, Korea, Japan, the Indian subcontinent, and Indochina.

Around 6700 BC, the expatriation of Ram with several thousand of Celts gave birth to the Ram Empire. Later on, its influence on all traditions of the white race, known in Latin as (Aries), Ram founded the Lamique cult in Tibet by changing its name to lamb (Lam). But since the outspread of Buddhism, also called the Lamaism cult as the main religion in Tibet from India in (618-649 CE), it is believed that Buddha in his prior rebirth was Rama or Ram declares the Buddhist text.

For nearly 250 years, the Visigoths continued to play an important role in Western Europe, after the fall of the Roman Empire in 476. The traces that they left for a long time in people's minds qualified them as being the most prestigious barbarian people in Europe through their mythical origins and their long history. Consequently, the divine and human nature of Jesus Christ still caused controversies, even after centuries of early Christianity. However, even after time, it would always be questioned. Moreover, Eleusis, in mysteries, would remain a sanctuary of great fame as Delos.

Delos had a particular place for a millennium as a holy sanctuary, mainly dedicated to Artemis, Apollo's twin sister associated with the moon. This place is considered the cradle of the twin gods.

In Greek mythology, Apollo is the god of light and the sun; he can bring the plague by his bow, being a god of healing, purification, and medicine. As god of arts, he is the god of song, music, and poetry, with the lyre that Hermes created for him as an instrument that became an attribute for him; Hermes made this lyre with the carapace of a turtle he killed on his way in search of the f lock of Apollo to celebrate the modest wisdom of his mother and his own birth remembrance, just a few moments after his birth. It is also known that he is the inventor of the pan f lute or syrinx. Apollo is also the god of masculine beauty and conductor of the nine muses. His two sites of oracle worship were already fully established around 650 BC, when the written sources began. At Delos and Delphi, Apollo practiced the cult Delos Apollo and Apollo Pythian, meaning the divine-God, before Olympian Greek mythology.

The origin of the inhabitants—identified by Thucydides as Carians pirates expelled by King Minos of Crete, son of Zeus and Europa, who became a judge of the dead in the underworld after his death—indicated that the island was inhabited since the third millennium BC.

The Titaness Leto, the mother who conceived after her hidden beauty accidentally attracts the eyes of Zeus, the father of the above-mentioned twins'deities, by the name of Apollo and Artemis, Leto was the goddess of motherhood and the protectress of young people. This womanly demure and goddess of modesty was relentlessly pursued by the goddess Hera, the Olympian queen of the gods, wearing a crown and holding a royal lotus-tipped scepter, was leading her from land to land. This goddess of marriage, of the sky and the stars of heaven, was preventing her from a place to rest and give birth when she was pregnant with the twins. But finally, the floating Island of Delos provided her with that facility. That sacred Delos was a major cult center between 900 BC and the year 100.

Eventually, Dionysus, who was worshipped in mystery religions, considering that his death and rebirth were events of mystical veneration, was also the proof of the island's religious significance. Temples were built in Rome in his honor and obelisks were erected. His inscriptions were found on the Arabian Sea and the Black Sea, indicating followers in Arabia, Asia Minor, Germany, Gaul, Pannonia, Portugal, Spain, and numerous sanctuaries in Great Britain.

The Egyptians' great Ra, the primary name of the sun god of Ancient Egypt, was almost the universally worshipped king of gods and the father of all creation. He was considered as the king of gods and as one of the central gods of the Egyptian pantheon and the patron of the pharaoh. Zeus, the god of the sky and thunder, closely identified with the Roman Jupiter in Greek mythology, was the "father of gods and men" in Mount Olympus, who ruled as a father ruled the family according to the ancient religion.

Hermes, the god of transitions and frontiers, the sons of Zeus and Maia of the Pleiade from the antiquity of the nocturnal skies, clear and unpolluted atmosphere, who moves freely between the worlds of mortal and divine, with interest and much wonderment as the messenger of the gods; he is the emissary intercessor between the mortals and the divine who leads souls into the hereafter in the Greek religion and mythology. He guides heroes and thieves and gives the chance to men. It is Hermes who invented weights and measures. As the god of travelers, he keeps traders, orators, prostitutes, crossroads, and roads.

Dionysus, the god of wine, winemaking, theatre, and religious ecstasy, the only one to have a mortal mother to become an example of a dying god, is the god of the grape harvest; a Greco-Roman name deriving from the name of the Greek god Dionysus. He is for some cults from the south, precisely from Ethiopia and to others, a foreigner who arrived from the east as an Asian, and some ancient sources described him as Thracian.

Usually, an ecstatic experience is interpreted in the particular religious context and particular cultural traditions, because religious people believe that it cannot be induced by natural human activities, but that true religious ecstasy, as a gift of the supernatural being they're following, can only occur in their religious context. Without any known reason, or by contact with something or someone perceived as extremely beautiful or holy, an ecstatic experience may occur on occasion, with the particular religious and cultural traditions of an individual. The particular individual uses ecstatic techniques or practices, generally associated with psychotropic drugs, a substance that alters the functioning of the brain and causes changes in perception, mood, consciousness, cognition or behavior; including prayer, religious rituals, meditation, breathing exercises, physical exercise, sex, music, dancing, sweating, fasting and thirst. These deliberately induced techniques or ecstatic practices in trance states are often interpreted as religious ecstasy; and this includes statements about contacting supernatural or spiritual beings, to receive new information as revelation.

To guide or interact with spirits, clairvoyance and healing; to travel to heaven or the underground world is a shamanic activity of the realization of ecstatic trances. Some shamans take plants such as Ayahuasca, cannabis (drugs), peyote and some mushrooms, while others rely on ascetic practices, dance, music, rituals or visual conceptions to help the mental discipline as a means to reach ecstasy. There are different stages of ecstasy, the highest being Nirvikalpa Samadhi. A state of ecstasy called samādhi is a yoga technique, provided to reach ecstasy. There are eight trance states also called absorption, known as a preliminary transition that leads to final saturation; especially in the Pali Canon, in Buddhism; the first four materially oriented states are Rupa, and the non-materials of the other four states are Arupa. Usually, communion and the unity with God are associated with the monotheistic tradition; without any meaning, the person who lives such experiences can also live them as a personal mystical experience. However, in that process, "believers who fall touched by the spirit and remain unconscious, semiconscious or fully conscious for a time," are interpreted by charismatic Christians who practice ecstasy as the work of "the Holy - Spirit." In Greece, during the annual Anastenaria, the dancers on fire do so in a state of ecstasy, believing to be under the influence of Saint Constantine.

There is a distinction between the summits of theology, the mystical theology, the supreme degree of the knowledge of God, corresponding to a secret revelation. The ascent to God, is a rise in silence and darkness, it is expressed with words, but having a higher knowledge. Beyond all understanding, we enter the total absence of speech and understanding by the poverty of words, plunged into the darkness that allows to make the invisible visible, and to say the unspeakable. The speculative theology, a theological theory not resting on the Bible, but on the imaginary paradigm of its creator; and symbolic theology, the lower degree of theology, is an image that goes beyond itself, and examines the experience of sensible things, derived from the expressions of the Bible; so God revealed himself as the God of jealousy, anger, drunkenness, sleep, etc. In order to suppress inhibitions and social constraints, initiates used intoxicants and other trance-inducing techniques (such as dance and music) to free the individual to return to a natural state in the Dionysian Mysteries.

Demeter, named Ceres by the Romans, was the goddess of agriculture, the daughter of Cronus and Rhea, the sister of Zeus, and the mother of Persephone. She presided over the sacred law, grains and the fertility of the earth, and the cycle of life and death. Persephone, the daughter of Demeter and Zeus, was abducted by the god Hades while she was picking wild f lowers, with the permission of Zeus, to be his wife in the underworld where the dead live. Hades had a claim on her and decreed her to spend four months each year in the underworld because she ate the food of the dead while in the underworld.

By trying to find out what happened to her daughter, she wandered over the face of the earth without success. Then the anger of the loss of her daughter made Demeter laid a curse on the world. Thus, she created winter from the grief of her daughter's absence during the winter seasons, and her returns brought the spring to mark the withdrawal of her gifts from the world. She sought the help of the goddess Hecate, the goddess of witchcraft, who told her to ask Helios, the sun, because she heard the calling of Persephone one day, and if in his daily journey of the sun across the sky, Helios had maybe seen what happened to her; to that question, the reply of Helios was Hades, who was Zeus's brother, was at the same time, the brother of Demeter and Zeus, Persephone's father.

Consequently, the reply of Helios complicated the complaint of Demeter to Zeus, concerning her abducted daughter by Hades, which remained without intervention. And it was at that moment that the one who presided over the sacred law, over grains and the fertility of the earth, decided to withdraw from her role as goddess to prevent seeds from germinating, resulting to the threat of the human race extinction by famine because no crops could grow anymore.

Seeing all this, Zeus, the brother of Hades, had to intervene by asking him to free his daughter. Eventually, the reunification of Demeter to her daughter allowed crops to grow again after she admitted having eaten a pomegranate seed of the dead.

Here lies the explanation of the religious founding mysteries and some details of Demeter's cult of important events; it also explains the harvest, winter, and the annual growth cycle, for many centuries, because those who attended the worship of Demeter swore the secret of the winter's death, like the yield grain every spring, so that the soul be reborn again after the harvests of the body of death in winter.

Demeter of the Greeks, the goddess of the earth and harvest, was credited for the reward of cultivation of the soil, beloved for her service to mankind to have giving him the gift of harvest. She was a mature motherly figure with a veil over her head, showing her very beautiful face; she gave life after death to those who learned her mysteries—the mystery rites believed to derive from those of the Egyptian goddess Isis.

Cybele—the Phrygian goddess native of the mythology of ancient Anatolia, whose worship spread to the cities of ancient Greece and the Roman Empire—was worshipped as a goddess of fertility and represented Mother Earth and nature, caverns, mountains, as well as walls and fortresses.

Sometimes, they're considered to be the same goddesses or at least strongly similar to the goddesses in the Greco-Roman times; and Manitou, the primitive force that produces effect containing the living inherent spiritual power in the spirit world, is the great supernatural spirit or God; generally a religious characteristic system of many Amerindian indigenous people, in their animism theories is a belief in innumerable spiritual beings concerned with human affairs and capable of helping or harming human interests; also believed to be present in natural phenomena (animals, plants, geographic features, and meteorological). This world of deities in general, known as a religious characteristic system of many nation in the world, has followed its course up to America, especially in North America, among the numerous Algonquian languages where we find the Arapaho, the Blackfoot, the Cree, the Cheyenne, the Fox-Sauk-Kickapoo, the Mi'kmaq (Micmac), and the Ojibwa, whose member languages were or are still spoken in Canada, New England, the Atlantic coastal region southward to North Carolina, the Great Lakes region, and surrounding areas westward to the Rocky Mountains. All believe in the same gods, and these gods are the same spirit with the same value but with different levels of divinity.

This belief in the unique God of different names, having the same value but different levels of divinity originated in Africa, where He, the great supernatural spirit, built the first egg from which the sun sprang. With Ptah, he built up the material universe under the guidance and direction of Thoth, the creator of the will of the dying, known as the oldest son of Ra in the ancient books of the pyramids and the child of Geb – god of the earth and Net or Neith; attested as early as the First Dynasty like the prime creator of the universe, and Osiris, the inventor of agriculture and religion, regularly holding the scepter Heka and the nekhekh flabellum in his hands crossed on his chest.

He was a divine keeper of all history and archives; he had an absolute knowledge of all arts and sciences, including arithmetic, surveying, geography, astronomy, soothsaying, magic, medicine, surgery, music, drawing, and writing. Put in charge for the protection of "Aah-tehHuti" – the moon, he created the five intercalary days, the ruse of the moon by giving it seventy seconds. He escorted Horus on his journey after every twelve hours of daylight until the nighttimes could come. "Ra spoke, Thoth has written, and the humanity read."

Khoum had seven forms as an architect. The father god Khnemu, as the name indicates, has the root *khnem*, which means "to build." He is the "beginning," the father of fathers, the maker of heaven and earth, the father of the fathers of the gods and goddesses, and the source of life of all things that exist. He is known as a symbol of fire, air, earth, and water with an attribute of the four great gods— Ra, Shu, Geb, and Osiris—and has four rams' heads upon a human body, united within himself. The four rams are also the symbols of the life of Ra, the life of Shu (god of air), the life of Geb, and the life of Osiris.

Anqet, the local Nubian goddess, is the daughter and the sister of the goddess Satet, the eye of Ra and the wife of Khnemu. She is the goddess of the island of Sahal, near the first cataract of the Nile. The origin of the cult of Anqet, daughter of Khnemu, can be traced back to the Old Kingdom. Her name means "to embrace;" during the annual floods of the Nile, her ceremonial festival was held to give thanks to the Nile water for its gift to life, and the fertilization of fields, by people throwing precious gifts like coins, gold, and jewelry, into the river. This act was as a symbol of returning the wealth provided by the goddess fertility derived from the benefits of the Nile water as thanksgiving. Together, the three deities Khnemu, Anqet, and Satet formed the triad of Elephantine, the principal deities of that city.

And Satet is the mother of the goddess Anqet, goddess of the yearly flood of the Nile and fertility, worshipped on the island of Sahal, two miles south of Elephantine, connected with the star "Sept," which marked the beginning of the flood season by its return to the night sky. She is described in the Pyramid Texts as cleansing the king with four jars of water and protecting the pharaoh with her arrows. In Egypt, her temple in Elephantine is known as one of the holiest places.

Knouhm-Re was the god who formed the breeding males; he gave birth to females and united the body in the maternal uterus. To make those young beings that were still in the maternal womb, he softened breathing in the throat of pregnant women. He made the heart to organize the circulation of blood throughout the body to lead the human being; the head, hair, and face for identification; the eyes to see; the nose to breathe; the ears to hear; the mouth to eat and to speak; teeth to chew; the two jaws that moved apart from each other; hands with fingers to work; feet, shins, and thighs to walk; the anus for extracting wastes from the body; and testicles and the phallus to complete the manly sexual act and the matrix to receive the seed for the purpose of multiplication of generations. Finally, he impregnated the breath of life in all things from the beginning, given life to all that exists, and placed the souls of the gods in him. He was the god of gods, the god who dominated the gods, the father of fathers and mother of mothers, greater than the previous gods, the greatest of all, and the noblest of nobles.

Before the European religious campaigns era on the African continent, Africans did not know Western science. They practiced the worship of traditional religion. We must also remember that we are a people that was nutritionally self-sufficient, and culturally, religiously, economically, politically, socially, and spiritually independent. We also know that Africa reveals another truth. It is in Africa—the continent that knows the oldest God of gods of all time—specifically in the Olduvai Gorge area of Kenya, Uganda, Tanzania, and Ethiopia that the oldest fossils of the first people of humanity, known by thename of Twa, were found. These Twa have worshipped the god of the most ancient original form of Horus I, the God of gods Ptah. It is these same Twa that are known as the first migrants along the 4,100 miles of the Nile River, thus, establishing later on the Egyptian civilization, where the black God of gods Ptah symbolized the mystery system of mysteries of the whole universe.

All names of God that all religions in the world are advocating, from Apis to the monotheism god of Moses or Judaism to Islam, which made the black man a slave to white, etc., are just a transformation of a well-developed belief, implemented and practiced before the Jew who claims ownership of the Bible, puts his foot in Africa, or evermore, imagines that one day he will settle in Israel.

Ptah, master of the eternal, Ptah, master of justice, Ptah, master of truth, is the excellent creator God by excellence who existed before all things and known as the God of gods behind the creation of the universe by the thought and by the verb.

We know that by the effort and fury of the great Nubian pharaoh Shabaka, the founder of the Twenty-Fifth Dynasty before Jesus Christ, a native of Napata (Kusch kingdom), from 716 to 702, who during a visit to the temple of Ptah discovered the destruction of the most sacred papyrus comprising the myth of God the creator. So it was Shabaka who gave the order to engrave the accession of Horus I to the throne of Egypt and the myth of God the creator on a block of black granite, putting an end to the Twenty-Fourth Dynasty of Sais, after crushing the reign of King Bakenranef by capturing him and burning him alive at the stake. He was also the one who promoted the cult of Amun, and by arranging his own burial on his death, he revived the custom of pyramid burial.

The period known as the history of the Twenty-Fifth Dynasty of Ancient Egypt was the third intermediate period, during which was composed of a succession of Nubian rulers in time. As the first Nubian king of the Twenty-Fifth Dynasty, Shabaka chose Memphis, as his first place of residence, and then Thebes, where he himself honored gods, before initiating the construction in Karnak, his pyramid and new temples. By establishing settlements up to the Syria-Palestine region, in a period known as the most stable period of his new

Kingdom in the history of Ancient Egypt, he extended his empire up to the borders of the Assyrian Empire by restoring the function of the high priest of Amun and fell into oblivion at Karnak.

Africa knows another very ancient God named Amen. In the remote period of the Fifth Dynasty, Amen was numbered among the primitive gods. In hymns, we often read or utter "Amen" at the end of a prayer to express our affirmation—meaning, that we do not disapprove of anything and that we agree with all that has been said; we confirm that So be it. "Amen." Amen is then a description of God. That description can be summarized by a passage of the scriptures: "The Father of lights, with whom there is no variation or shadow of change" (James 1:17). He is hidden to his children, hidden to gods and men.

The black God Amen is symbolized in the mystery texts of the Ancient Egyptian Empire, soon after the pairs of gods Nau and Nen, equivalents of the aqueous abyss, from which all things sprung. From the God Amen, the God Ptah was born in Egypt, even before the Egyptian civilization. He was described as the God who created his own body by the verb. So, we have the creation by the verb. He is the God, who was created by his own thoughts, God who first created the light (Ra), who manifested himself like the sun, and who finally exercised the rest of creation by the expressions of thought. Amen means what is not seen and what cannot be seen. This is what Amen said: "The faithful and true witness, the principle of the works of God" (Rev. 3: 14.) "Whoever wishes to be blessed on earth, will be blessed by the God of truth" (God Amen) and "whoever swears on earth will swear by the God of truth - (the God Amen) "(Is. 65:16); "For as there are promises of God, it is in him the affirmation - yes and in Amen, the glory of God through us" (2 Cor. 1: 20).

History tells us that, some eight thousand years before Jesus Christ, there was desertification of the Sahara, a very important fact in the history of migration in Africa. After the sudden drying of that depression that divided the Maghreb from Black Africa, people migrated toward the Nile valley, which later on generated one of the most glorious civilizations of the world—Egypt of the pharaohs.

The large group of Bantu people, whose migrations were the most important and from whom the Twa people belonged, was believed to have left the Nile valley to different regions of Africa to the south of Sahara—East Africa, Southern Africa, Central Africa, and West Africa. The move of the Bantu people was marked by the iron civilizations. The exact start of the spread of the Bantu people from their base is not known. But as an assumption, it was placed around five thousand years ago. The Bantu speaking communities reached the great Central African rain forest to the west in 3,500 years—1500 BC.

Before the expansion of agriculture and livestock, South Africa of the equator was populated by Neolithic people, having some ancestors of modern forest people called Pygmies of Central Africa in search of food, speaking Bantu languages nowadays. That is why the current scientific knowledge is placing the distribution of this people from Eastern Cameroon across Central Africa and East Africa up to Southern Africa and tracing the edge of their ancestral land near the southwestern modern Nigeria and Cameroon, four thousand years ago (2000 BC) and recognizing the Bantu languages as a branch of the Niger-Congo family languages. Note that the Bushman was there for at least twenty-five thousand years in the caves of the prehistoric and paleoanthropological sites of Sterkfontein, Swartkrans, Kromdraai, and Makapansgat, located in the province known under the name of Pretoria Witwatersrand-Vereeniging and which was officially renamed Gauteng in May 1994 to June 1995, in the northwest of Johannesburg.

Fossils found in that Highveld indicate that australopithecines lived there since about 2.5 million years. One hundred thousand years ago, *Homo erectus* was replaced by modern humans, *Homo sapiens*. In the Eastern Cape, the province where the site of Klasies River Mouth is located, they found fossils that indicated that, ninety thousand years ago, modern humans were already living in South Africa. In the southern savannas, which are today known as the Democratic Republic of Congo, Angola, and Zambia, the pioneer groups emerged over 2,500 years ago (500 BC). Toward the east, near the Great Lakes region, another current of migration was for a creation of a large new population center where a rich environment supported a dense population three thousand years ago (1000 BC). At the southeast of the Great Lakes region, movements in small groups were faster, scattered near the coast and near rivers by early settlements, because of harsh farming conditions in the remote areas of the water, and which created a mixed genetic ethnicity for Bantu people, that came from this region. In South Africa, in the year 300, the pioneer groups reached the long modern KwaZulu-Natal coast; and in the year 500, the modern Northern Province was encompassed in the former Transvaal Province.

Since millennia of the prehistoric times, Khoisans are the indigenous people of the South Africa region coming from the Great Lakes region before its history was marked by the European immigration, who also consider themselves as citizens of South Africa, including Indians, Asians, and Jews; their Metis, created the ethnic conflict opposing the colonists since 500 years BC, fearing the loss of their lands, since they held no legal title and were considered like squatters in their proper country. The black South Africans had solidified and expanded community structures. Their developed chiefdoms and their pastors became known as the Khoikhoi.

A historical division of the Khoisan, an ethnic group of indigenous people in southwestern Africa—closely related to the Bushmen, called San by the Khoikhoi—practiced extensive pastoral agriculture with the large herds of Nguni cattle, the preferred breed by the indigenous Bantu people of South Africa, Swaziland, Namibia, Zimbabwe, Botswana, and Angola and known for their fertility and disease resistance in the Cape Province before the colonizing settlers in the region in 1652. While small groups of Sans continued living within the regions, the Khoikhoi were established along the coast over time by the ancestors of certain groups of the current Nguni people, like the Ndebele, Swazi, Xhosa, and Zulu. The Tswana-Sotho, a group of Basotho communities of Pedi and

Tswana communities, settled in the Highveld of Botswana, Lesotho, Zimbabwe, and Zambia; the Lemba, the Vanda, and the Tsonga Shangaan people are groups living today in areas northeast of South Africa.

The Bantu people to whom I am referring to are a group of three hundred to six hundred ethnic groups in Africa and represent about one-third, 335 million of more than a billion of the African population. The word *Bantu* means "people," if we trust its many names in the Bantu languages: in Swahili, *wa-tu*; in Lingala, *ba-to*; in Douala, *ba-to*; and in Zulu, *aba-ntu*. For the most part, they live together in peace, though researchers know little about this period, not connecting them to any method of writing, apart from archaeological artifacts. Their expansion was a long series of small waves of physical migration. A creation of new social groups involving intermarriage between communities allowed a diffusion of the language and knowledge in small mobile groups to communities and small neighboring population groups passing to the new domain. Their diffusion of new methods of agriculture and metallurgy in both iron and copper, the development of new techniques, allowed them to colonize new regions of more ecologically very different densities and of higher-yielding crops.

The powerful Bantu-speaking states started to emerge between the fourteenth and fifteenth centuries in the Great Lakes region, where kings of Monomotapa built the famous grand complex of Zimbabwe on the Zambezi River, south of the tropical savannas of Central Africa. Because of the dense population, the process of states formation, including military power, increased in the sixteenth century, leading to several specialized divisions in labor with new techniques, to the technological developments in the political and economic activity, in the spiritual ritual of royalty as the source of national strength of health, and making emigration more difficult to increase exchanges between African communities with European, Arabic, Indonesian, and Chinese traders on the coasts.

On March 6–8, 1986, in London, the Greater London Council, its agglomeration gave a conference for the ethnic minority unity. This conference was mainly addressed to Africans from Africa and blacks from the Caribbean and consisted to educate all black communities in England and participants from different parts of the world; it was a question of identifying on the 4,100 miles of the civilization of the Nile Valley, the beginning of the birth of what is today called civilization in Africa. Satisfactory proofs were given since the discovery of African works in Egypt. The London Museum is housing artifacts of Egypt. The document called the Papyrus of Hunefer is the document that Sir E. A. Wallis Budge used in his translation as a part of the Egyptian Book of the Dead. A copy of this document is found in the library of Syracuse University in New York. In this sacred document, we can read this: "We the Egyptians came from the beginning of the Nile." But where is the beginning of the Nile? The beginning of the Nile is where the ancient God Hapi dwells at the foothills of the Mountains of the Moon.

The farthest point of the beginning at the south of the delta of the White Nile is in Uganda, which spreads out in west Ethiopia, where the Blue Nile and White Nile meet at the other side of Khartoum, the capital and largest city opposite Omdurman, the second-largest city in the Republic of Sudan, lying on the western banks of the River Nile, where it f lows from the south down north and meets with the Atbara River, the last tributary of the Nile before it flows completely through Sudan in the part of the ancient kingdom in Nubia, and continues to f low toward Egypt and the Mediterranean Sea.

It f lows completely through Ta-Nehisi, Ta-Zeti, or Ta-Seti, known as Sudan, which was once neighboring the nation called Meroe or Merowe, and continues into the southern part called Nubia by the Romans, parallel to the part of the Nile called Egypticus by Greeks, Egypt by the English, Mizrain by the Jews, and Mizr/Mizrair by Arabs. It ends and empties its delta in the great sea of Sais, known as the Mediterranean Sea, nowadays. The part that was called Nubia, belonging to Sudan nowadays, included three Kushite kingdoms during antiquity; the first had its capital at Kerma (2400 to 1500 BC); Napata was the capital of the second (1000 to 300 BC), and the capital of Meroe was the third kingdom of Kush (around the fourth century BC to the third century after Jesus Christ). If I use Egypt as a starting point, I will conclude that Egypt has more ancient documents and other artifacts than any other ancient civilization in the world that one can speak of.

Theoretically, places like Babylon, Sumer, and all other places you hear historians talk about can't show you any artifacts as the best proof before firsthand information. In terms of artifacts, you can find them in archaeological discoveries along the Nile and all over Africa; you can find artifacts of human fossils that existed thousands of years ago. Historical research and science concluded that the migration of the human beings out of Africa really occurred very long ago in different prehistoric periods. The first period was the one of *Homo erectus*, etc., and the second period was the one of *Homo sapiens*, who traveled to different parts of the world, including Europe, to populate the world.

In the time of the Grimaldi people, countries connecting Africa to Europe were known to be much closer than they are today, especially in the earlier stages of evolution of modern races and the evolution of typical white race, which derived from the black race. Certainly, certain bodily characters of Negroid traits are assigned to the Combe-Capelle man of that period to represent a common ancestor of Europeans. But the skeleton of a *Homo sapiens* named Chancelade man, dating from twelve thousand to seventeen thousand years before Christ, discovered buried in a strongly flexed position, as do the Bushmen of South Africa and some Australian tribes, is a proof to the modern researchers today. This skeleton is discovered in a cave of Raymonden at Chancelade in a French commune located in the department of Dordogne, Aquitaine region in 1888. According to the index of its skull, its high cranial capacity was 1,670 cm3; therefore, literally meaning that it is a dolichocephalic skull. The ratio between the maximum width and the maximum length of the vertebrate skull measured in the horizontal plane was 72 in epic index and very high (hypocephalus) with ellipsoidal-subrectangular shape, different from that of Combe-Capelle than the one of the Cro-Magnon man.

He had a high, broad and very large face, a broad and raised forehead, with little pronounced arcade eyebrows, a well-developed chin and strong bones, and high orbits that are closely spaced and rectangular. He was generally a fairly small-sized individual of 155 centimeters.

So the ancestor of the black race was the man of Grimaldi and the Negroid, who presents some of the characteristics of the black race, is nothing but a nigger, representing the fossils the Cro-Magnon man, who became the ancestor of the white race, and the Chancelade man, an ancestor of the yellow race; all these fossils are evidences of African migration in these regions, and they're confirming the black ancestor as the ancestor of the entire humanity.

The prehistory of African hominids presents the sedentarization leading to the birth of the human being about seven million years ago, in an occupied and continuous habitat, at the opposite of the nomadic or seminomadic migration, corresponding to the beginning of the Neolithic period (about nine thousand years before Christ). Nomadism was imposed by the lack of resources; for example, Japan sedentarized at the beginning of the Jomon period between approximately 15,000 until 300 BC and before the Neolithic period. The human being has gone through many transformations from the Uruk period, the protohistoric stage of development of Mesopotamia, which covered approximately the fourth millennium before Christ.

In Mesopotamia, during the Ubaid period ranging from about 6500 to 3750 BC, sedentarization spread in three directions: along the shores of the Gulf to Qatar in neighboring Khuzestan, toward the north in the Hamrin, and to Tepe Gawra, where we see in the ancient levels the particularities of El Obeid mix with those of Tell Halaf and Samarra. More broadly, at the same time, this period also concerned the neighboring regions of the Middle East that experienced some Mesopotamian influence, like Syria, western Iran, and southeastern Anatolia, during certain phases of development of the Uruk culture. In those peripheries, this period also tended to be better known in Mesopotamia. The Neolithic began around 9000 BC in the Middle East and ended around 3300 BC, with the spread of metallurgy and the invention of writing.

In the conquest of the American West, "frontier" referring to the contrasting region at the edge of the line of the European sedentarization in America, was focused primarily on the conquest and the settlement of Indian; this sedentarization occurred generally in the ancient civilization of Mesoamerica in a set of geographic areas, occupied by the ethnic groups of the Aztecs and Incas, the Mayas and the Tarascs. These ancient civilizations of Mesoamerica are mainly known for their progress in the fields of art, astronomy, architecture, agriculture, writing, and mathematics. The sedentarization process involved many theories and multiple causes: firstly the demographic reasons related to the climate, and then the need for irrigated agriculture in food growth, the search for Fertile Crescent before they settled down in various parts of Mesoamerica, and finally the sedentarization of the oasis.

One sticking example known to scientists and researchers is the analysis of the bone remains of the man of Grimaldi, the oldest Negroid type so far discovered, which reveals the presence of a black man who engendered the man called Cro-Magnon, the first white man, after a period of twenty thousand years of climate adaptation to populate Europe. The Grimaldi people were found with a civilization of fauna assigned to the end of the Mousterian or the beginning of the Aurignacian period of forty thousand to twenty-eight thousand years ago.

The extermination of the Grimaldi man by Europeans to seize their lands in Europe is unfortunately, the history phase never told for Africans to know who the European really is. The Grimaldi man was known to Europeans as the Khoisan inhabitant of Europe. The same British, Dutch, and Germans: the Celts, who migrated into Europe from place to place for their evolution by exterminating the Khoisan in Europe, are the same invaders who after (ca. 500 B.C.), repeated what already happened as event to eventually commit other Genocides of Herero and Namaqua. Proofs of their migrations across Asia, Europe, Mongolia, and Siberia Russia, are provided artifacts placing them in these territories sometime around 45,000 B.C. Just like the Andamanese Negritos of the Andaman Islands and the Pygmies of Central Africa, the matrilineal transmitted Mitochondrial DNA of the Khoisan people is shown in the largest genetic diversity of all human populations of the world. Some of the Khoisan artistries in a cave near the southern Cape shoreline in South Africa are around 75,000 years ago.

In Dar es Salaam, Tanzania, at the National Museum, for example, the bones and other remains of *Zinjanthropus boisei* from about 1.75 million years ago are exposed to the public; those of Lucy are at the National Museum of Ethiopia, associated with Addis Ababa University. We also know that scientists discovered the oldest fossil skeleton of a human ancestor more than a million years before Lucy that walked on the earth 3.2 million years ago. The fossils of Ardi were discovered in the harsh Afar Desert of Ethiopia just forty-six miles (seventy-four kilometers) from where Lucy's species were discovered in the Middle Awash region at a site called Aramis. This discovery was far more important than Lucy and revealed that Ardi lived 4.4 million years ago. In Chad, older hominid fossils were uncovered, including a skull of at least seven million years old.

To my knowledge, you cannot find any skeleton of Adam or any skeleton of Eve in any part of the world. Artifacts along the Nile revealed that two groups of Africans, the Hutu and the Twa, existed before writing came into being, taking us back to at least 400,000 before the common Christian era. The Twa and the Hutu were the people who used the most ancient and one of the most important symbols called the ankh in Egypt, adopted by Christians and called the crux ansata or ansata cross. Twa and Hutu were named pygmies by British anthropologists, but this name never existed before in Africa.

It is good to mention that Captain Bartolomeu Dias came to Monomotapa, the southern tip of Africa, in 1486 at the Christian era with the Portuguese before the first Europeans. Ten years later, in 1496, Captain Vasco da Gama also came with his group. They met a group of people there whom they called

Kaffirs, the racist name given to African Bushmen and Hottentots by the British and Dutch when the Boers came to Africa in 1652. These Africans were known by the name of Khoikhoi, the little people, and the Khalaharis, which takes us back at least thirty-five thousand to forty thousand years to another group called the Grimaldi, who traveled up the entire western coast—leaving their writings, their pictures, and their drawings in caves along the way to the northwestern coast of Africa—and crossed into Spain all the way up to Austria. You can see the Grimaldi paintings that are at least thirty-five thousand years old at the Natural History Museum in New York City.

It is very important that you realize that this was about thirty-one thousand years before Abraham, the first Jew, and before Adam and Eve, who started the world according to the Jewish—the Jewish world. The southern tip of Africa takes us back to a period called the Sibellian period—a period of the hieratic writings that no one in the modern time has been able to decipher, twenty-five thousand years before the birth of Jesus Christ (Sibellian II) existed. Ten thousand to six thousand years before the Christian era (Sibellian III) lead us to the stellar calendar and the predynastic period, when the high priest Manetho attempted to present the chronological history of the Nile valley imposed upon him by the Greeks in about 227 or 226 BC.

We forget the rest of the Nile valley and only deal with Egypt, not knowing that Egypt is not at the beginning of the Nile's high cultures but the end because European historians changed Manetho's chronological history of the Nile valley. They said the first cataract of the Nile River is at a place called the city of Aswan, instead of the last; in fact, the Sixth Cataract is Aswan Upper (or Southern) Egypt. The pyramids of Egypt are the world's largest monuments that will blow your mind, but they're not the first of Africa; they're the last. However, if you go on the Nile, you will always hear about them because the high culture came down the Nile.

The size of these pyramids in Africa increased in sophistication when Africans became much more competent in engineering, etc. That is why you could see different forms and the colossal pyramids at the end of the Nile. The largest of the pyramids, the Great Pyramid of Giza, built in 2589 to 2566 BC in the Fourth Dynasty (2613 to 2498), called Cheops by Herodotus, was built by the great pharaoh Khufu and originally stood 481 feet (146.6 m). The step pyramid in Sakkara is the first built by Imhotep for Pharaoh Djoser, the third pharaoh of the Third Dynasty. Imhotep was the multigenus architect who simultaneously introduced the first structure ever built with stone to mankind without mortar or any other compulsory materials.

African engineering is not only known for the building of pyramids by the multigenus Imhotep but also equally known for the time of Senwosret II, the fourth king of the Twelfth Dynasty, ruler, king, and pharaoh of Ancient Egypt from 1842 to 1836 BC. He conducted many agricultural projects in Faiyum that transformed thousands of marshlands into fields with the division of the Nile to stop the rush of water. His goal was to establish a strong economic base for Ancient Egypt.

Far back to 2200 BC, his many military campaigns in Nubia extended his kingdom's border further south and protected minerals in Nubia and Sinai to extract natural resources from them. He also built a pyramid near Faiyum that was destroyed by Ramses II, and most of its fragments were taken off the site to build a structure for him. In total, there are seventy-two in Egypt and thirty-two pyramids in Sudan. The pyramids in Sudan are built by two methods; silt pyramids and mud-brick pyramids are older than the pyramids in Egypt. The silt pyramids appeared following the flooding of the Nile River, at the period when the Nile River was overflowing its banks, bringing down the silt from the highlands of Ethiopia and Uganda and from the Mountains of the Moon, called Kilimanjaro by the people of Kenya. It must be clear that these pyramids are not those types of bricks made of mud and straw mentioned in the Hebrew Torah, specifically in the book of Exodus. You can see artifacts of all this period I am talking about in museums all over Europe and the United States of America.

In this perspective, let us go back to the Egyptian temples dedicated to the worship of Sobek, the crocodile god, and Haroeris, the falcon god, in the second century before Christ, and I will reveal some facts about medicine to you. The temple of Haroeris and Sobek is located in Kom Ombo, the ancient Nubba, in a town called Nubt, which means "city of gold" in Egyptian. Haroeris is the Greek name of a god in the Egyptian mythology, Horour (hr-wr) is Haroeris, probably the oldest form of the god Hor (Horus in Greek), meaning "Great Horus" or "'Horus the Elder," represented by the cobra; and Sobek, the son of the aquatic goddess Neith and the twin gods Senwy, represented by the Nile crocodile.

At the rear of that temple, drawings of medical instruments dating back to the time of Imhotep can be found, taking us back to about 285 BC during the Greek rule. They're medical instruments in the exact dimension, styles, and shapes and still in use in medical practices today. All kinds of symbols related to the use of incense, the beginning aspect of the calendars (the dating process for the farmers), and the one still used by the Coptic farmers, are there to be admired. The thirteen-month calendar, twelve months of thirty days each and one month of five days, is still in use by the Ethiopian government and officially still a means of telling time to date.

History tells us that Hippocrates, born 458 years before Christ in Kos, Greece, was never the father of medicine. At the age of nineteen, he went to study in the temples of Isis and Osiris, which contained the sacred book of all medical precepts in Egypt. In the original text, the researchers discovered that the great initiates of the remote pharaonic times revealed that they had benefited from a long chain of knowledge from a certain ancestral past of genetics, medicinal science, and the finest surgery cosmic mathematics.

They admit that between monuments, pyramids, etc., the Papyrus Calberg no. VIII contains medical describe; the Berlin papyrus contains several papyri, like mathematical knowledge, ancient pregnancy test procedure, and other medical information of the Middle Kingdom; the Ebers Papyrus, dating to c. 1550 BC and known as the most important among the oldest medical papyri of Ancient Egypt, is a herbal medical knowledge; the Kahun Papyri, dating from around 2000 years BC, are a collection of mathematical and medical topics, like contraception, fertility, gynecological diseases, pregnancy, etc., and constitute the oldest known medical treaty. The papyrus of Luxor, the Smith's Papyrus, and other sources of knowledge concerning other subjects have not been revealed to the uninitiated world; but these papyrus, specifying to us that each disease be only treated by a specific medical specialist for the illness, such as a doctor for unknown disease conditions, a doctor for strangury, or a doctor for trachoma and gonorrhea, are of an ingenious precision. The fathers of medicine in the temple had the Sacred Book containing all medical precepts. The great black Egyptian pharaohs, initiated at the genetic temples of the most remote times, had medical knowledge. The original texts in papyrus like the Berlin Papyrus, the Papyrus Calberg no. VIII, and the Ebers Papyrus, those revealed to initiates as the Kahun Papyri, the papyrus of Luxor, of monuments of pyramids and the papyrus of Smith, revealed much of the Egyptian medical science knowledge to the world.

Furthermore, a papyrus that thoroughly described the specific gestures to be performed during operations to save lives of people having a severely smashed, less serious or cracked skull, is the papyrus of Smith. The injury to the head itself is dating back before the recorded history. Trepanation and cesarean section are a work of more than three hundred sheets, dating from Hor-Aha, the son of Menes, and the second king of Egypt, who reigned four thousand years before our era, is an exquisite work. Proofs of used trepanation treatment of the skull fractures in the line of battleground are found in graves with holes drilled on the fracture lines during these ancient times. This papyrus, written around 1650 to 1550 BC, is divided into two and is kept in two museums: the British Museum and the Berlin Museum, each possessing one-half of the papyrus.

This singular operation with the trepan is still practiced by a few people with savage wild manners and bizarre medical practice who have no access to the ideas of modern medicine. The successes of their practice still astonish the modern medical world. Their iron tools for trepanation of ten thousand years old are the pride of modern medicine. The famous Ancient Egyptian medicine known of his doctors was scientific but had a magical character that led foreign kings to appeal to them for various health problems. They had medicine specialization in surgery, very good doctors with a good knowledge of the human body; they treated stomach-ache cares, skin irritations, wounds, broken bones, etc., and other purely psychological problems. Egyptian doctors had drugs with undeniable healing effects. Thanks to the knowledge of surgery and the human anatomy, Egyptian doctors became a better source of expertise already in the fifth century BC and a source of accurate knowledge for mummification, which no people of that time could have.

The process of drying and the preservation of skin were their precise knowledge of embalming bodies with creams and products with aromatic essences extracted from soft consistency substances, like fat or paste for specific use of which they scented and perfumed the bodies; they were transmitted to the world by Ancient Egyptian people. From the purgatory, that ugly infernal fire of healing the sick became an infirmary covered with animation and the ointment of a dozen masses, made of a third and two-thirds, throwing a kind of black page of the sanguinary desquamation of epidermis.

The beginning of what is known nowadays as the zodiac was located at a place called Dendera, in the temple of the goddess Het-Heru (Hathor). The original zodiac of a rectangular shape was stolen by the French, who dropped it in the river Nile during a hot pursuit by the Arabs of Egypt on their way to France. The circular one is the false zodiac; the one said to be remembered in detail by a Frenchman, was reproduced within two weeks and placed in the temple of goddess Het-Heru for tourists to contemplate nowadays. Once again, even in those early days, Africans along the Nile were already dealing with astronomy, and Europeans had not yet gone one inch further than them. However, remember that the Papyrus of Hunefer deals with the Africans who descended on the Nile and who were already using that type of science but not having enough artifacts to put together evidence for the transition to be seen today. We have the best records going back even before Pharaoh Necho II, who saw the navigation of the entire continent with a map of Africa in almost the same common shape it has today. Navigational instruments, which were used to navigate, were used by referring to the sun and stars as navigational tools, dating back to about 600 before Christian era, before Herodotus came to Egypt in 457 BC, and Erastosthenes, between 274 and 194, before Christian era with the rectangular world map in shape.

To our knowledge, they had no concept of Africa from southern Ethiopia to Monomotapa because they reflected the end of Africa where the Sahara is—the southern end of the Sahara, the actual Republic of South Africa. This distortion is mostly attributed to the important major role played by England.

Agriculture is another subject proper to Africa before the arrival of writing, when man observed the germination of seeds and supported religious conflicts to one of the most secret symbols of the religiosity of Egypt and other parts of Africa. Regarding the observation of Africans along the Nile, we get to the twenty-eight-day hibernation of the dung beetle otherwise called the scarab, which goes into the manure of a donkey, horse, and cow, the only animals with grass manure. The death of the beetle in the mind finally became a better symbol of resurrection when it came out of hibernation. So, the beetle became the symbol of resurrection in the Egyptian religion, which spread to other parts of Africa and subsequently into Judaism, Christianity, Islam, and so on.

I believe that religion itself started in some mind or by some reason when men experience the birth of a child. Witnessing the birth of a child, sets them thinking, allowed them to transcend thought, standing there and seeing this baby come out from the woman's organ. When the pelvic region of a woman expands for about four or five inches in diameter for the head to pass through, made them immediately to start to transcend their thought, and start attributing this action to something beyond any imagination, and then they started to believe.

Because your experience came from a woman, she became your first deity, the goddess of the sky Nut, and a man became the god of the earth, Geb. Suddenly, the sun appeared in the entire universe, and you realized that the sun and the moon made the river rise. When the sun rose, there is light; and when it goes down, there is no more light. When the moon rose, you see no light because there is no light shining on it. Without this great attribute of God, crops and vegetation don't germinate, and then finally, man realized that there is a God.

Regarding these factors, Africans created the science of astronomy, the table of scientific data, the planetary table, and so forth, up to each of the astrological nature influences, a physical relation of astronomy having nothing to do with your love life, but the water rising at high tide, and the separation of the two disciplines that the ancients spoke to us about becomes clear. In those days, the Greeks like Plato, Aristotle, and others came and learned these sciences in Africa for their education.

In Egypt, only one book was read because there were no publishing houses like today, and most of its subjects were taught orally, mouth to ear, shoulder to shoulder, with certain instructions given toe to toe, under strict conditions to obey. The English took twenty-two tablets from Egypt to England and set up what they called Freemasonry today. Sir Albert Churchward, in addition to being a doctor, was a great man in England and one of those who made the English Freemasonry what it is today. His book titled *Signs and Symbols of Primordial Man* is a cornerstone of Freemasonry.

As founders of the Western Freemasonry, they did not only falsify the human history, but they also equated the great and supreme power of Neteru, the god of the first time (Zep Tepi), the hidden mysteries of Creation with human gods. He created heavens and earth, sea, and sky, men and women, animals and birds, and all that is and all that shall be, including the creeping things in it. Also, Neteru - is a force of cosmic energy, a cyclical transformation of energies in different forms, a brilliant representation of the universe-not thought of as gods and goddesses.

Ptah, Ra, Shu, Geb, Osiris, Seth, and Horus are the gods (Neteru), considered to have emerged from an infinite, when the sun rose for the first time, known as (Zep Tepi) of the African timescale, who reigned on earth including the founding of Egypt; followed by Thoth, Maat, and Horus as the gods of the first time, according to the Turin Papyrus, revealing us African gods. But we are treating the Ancient Egyptians today as if they had a barrier that prevented them from going to other parts of Africa and as if they were a special race in Africa, forgetting that they were moving along the entire continent in the first place, and then throughout the world to engender multiple civilizations of present-day Africa.

So it isn't because when you go to Egypt and in most of the world's museums and notice that the Ancient Egyptians are not represented by the artist as the ancient Nubians, Ethiopians, or anybody else that they're not black, because they purposely erected the statues of the Greeks, the Romans, the Persians, the Assyrians, and the Hyksos, but none of the Africans. Consequently, by their guilty conscience, once in a while, they make the nose of Pharaoh Mentuhotep III flat, to look like a typical African.

When this couldn't be done, they said Negroes came into Egypt in the Eighteenth Dynasty. What imbeciles. They even forgot that Negroes had a place they called Negroland BC, which was in fact the Songhai Empire, which existed between the fifteenth and sixteenth centuries in West Africa, founded at Koukia in the seventh century before the Portuguese arrived in Africa in the late fifteenth century. Knowing that Negroland could be seen in the map, I am still asking myself how the Portuguese placed Negroes in Egypt in the Eighteenth Dynasty, with Akhenaton as a figure or the father of Amenhotep IV, called Amenhotep III (Amenophis III) by the Greeks.

Perhaps because the Portuguese didn't create Negroes until the seventeenth century after Jesus Christ; indeed, they forgot that Africa was not only the cradle of humanity but also the cradle of civilization that spread from the banks of the Nile into all writings, documents, and belief systems around the entire world. History revealed to us that Etruscans, who later on became the Romans, and the people of Pyrrhus, who later on became the Greeks, did not exist until these people came from the island of the Mediterranean or the Great Mediterranean Sea.

It is known that when they left, Egyptians were colonizers of other parts of Africa by setting up the first educational system for the people of Pyrrhus, a little enclave that later became Africa, where the borders of Libus, the present day Libya meet Egypt. The educational system for the Greeks occurred there. This educational system was moved from there by Africans to the city of Elea. The Greeks came there after leaving the African Greek peninsula to the Italian peninsula to meet other people who came illegally, sneaking over to (Libus) - Libya. Note that from this period until Homer, there was no record to deal with because there was no writing in Greece yet.

But whatever the case is, they learned because the students eager to learn were coming from everywhere, from Babylon, Europe, etc., to Egypt. The Greek and the Babylonian writings, which originated from Egypt during the First Dynasty period of documentation, dating to some extent from at least 4100 BC, are not when writings started along the Nile.

This period was known as the period of war between the north, headed by King Scorpion, and the south, headed by King Narmer, when King Narmer started to unite and reorganize Egypt under two viziers. The introduction of religion, mathematics, sciences, engineering, law, medicine, and so forth, was in the predynastic period.

The period of the belief in a unique God started when King Narmer defeated Scorpion, the leader of the north, in 4100 BC, and then he decided to unite the deity of the north known as God Amen, which we still say at the end of every prayer today, with his own deity of the south, the God Ra, to become a unique god (Amen-Ra). So always remember that you are still nowadays praying to the African God Amen and that the belief in a unique God did not really start with Akhenaton. In that respect, God Amen-Ra became Ptah, and the goddess of justice presented as a balance became Maat—which is the same symbol until today used in the United States for justice but falsely used because one scale is up and the other down. After stealing the African knowledge, the Greeks implemented it in Europe by changing the Egyptian divine names. Thus, Maat, the representation and the symbol of justice became Themis, venerated as a goddess in Athens. She became the personification of the divine and natural law, of order and justice, as the Egyptian Goddess Maat.

This representation of justice is not justice at all; that is why there is no justice in the United States or elsewhere in the world. Justice is when both scales are on the same level. But the symbol of the system of justice being foolish around the world, said no, you African-Americans will never have justice, including all immigrants in the United States of America, and anyone around the world, who are asking for justice. The forming foundation of justice had forty-two admonitions called the "forty-two laws of the Goddess Maat, found in chapter 125 of the Book of the Dead of the Ancient Egyptians before the remonstrances to the goddess Maat, goddess of justice, of law on morality, and the advent of human behavior.

Incantations for the coming forth toward the light, equally known as the *Book of the Coming Forth by Day and by Night*, are centered on the ritual of the coming forth by day of the law of a unique God, in a book generally called the *Book of the Dead* by Egyptologists, because it was found in the sarcophagi indicated that the Ancient Egyptian religion was monotheistic, to the belief in a unique God named Ra or Amun-Aten-Re according to times, and to the worship of his multiple manifestations; hence the worship of many gods.

An Osirian religious reform, initiated by the high priest Imhotep at the end of the ancient period around 2750 BC, was held in Egypt. Osiris, who represented the Nile, was to disappear by the misdeeds and jealousy of his brother Seth, the incarnation of evil and disorder, who killed Osiris, the incarnation of good, and enclosed him in a box of an extreme beauty fabricated to contain his corpse to throw him into the Nile. The goddess of family and marriage, Isis, immediately began to search for her husband and brother after she learned of his death. She managed to recover the body of Osiris in the box designed on his measurements and aground in the territory of Byblos in Phoenicia to bury him in Egypt.

Already in Egypt, Seth, who became aware of the return of his brother's corpse, was not happy at all. So once again, Seth undertook another evil idea to really eliminate his brother Osiris from the planet earth; he took the corpse of his brother to cut it into thirty-six pieces and scattered them across the world. The mythical queen and the funerary goddess Isis of Ancient Egypt began once again to look and find the remains of her late husband to do her mourning. She then managed to gather all the parts of the body except the phallus. In this case, she found thirty-five pieces, instead of thirty-six pieces. In addition, gathering his parts allowed Osiris to ascend on the ladder of Nut, his mother, for safety and eventually became king of the dead in the land of Egypt, the gift of the Nile, in the world.

The conductor of souls and god of the dead, the jackal-headed Anubis, anointed him with Holy Ghost unction of life to separate the man in him for God's work; then he took the form of a falcon and fecundated Isis of the child who became the sun god, commonly known to the world under the name of Horus. He who resurrected Osiris from the dead, Anubis—the master of embalmers—wrapped his mummy with bandages, for him to radiate into the eternal kingdom of the beginning of life as the god of the dead. Here, this ritual of embalming is showing us that the origins of this ancient funerary practice of the first Egyptians were officially adopted in the religious practices that gave birth to an entire empire. Our physical body can contain a new breath of life if it is prepared after the death of a human being to reach the divine world, the afterlife, by religious practices.

The permanent conflict between light and darkness, a struggle of worship created by Amenhotep IV (also known as Amenophis or Akhenaton) on the one hand, and by the established clergy in Egypt on the other hand, was that great illumination of a unique eternal God against a multiplicity of deceptive gods. For the first time in the history of civilization, this new revelation, the true principles of the existence of a unique, eternal God, aroused a violent reaction across the country. Amenhotep IV devoted his influence, his fortune, and his time to the development of the monotheistic religion, building temples and altars to the eternal God by destroying all that was devoted to ancient beliefs, such as statues, temples, inscriptions, and walls.

That movement, considered a dangerous rival, was overthrown by cunning clergy. This success occasioned the overthrow of the young pharaoh, who had spread his religion by accomplishing so many things throughout the nation.

By an extreme suffering more or less satisfactory, he rapidly left this world, leaving a development of a new revelation that hundreds and even thousands of years of religious cataclysms on the earth could not obscure the brilliance of its inscriptions, beliefs, doctrines, and prayers to the God of all creatures nor could destroy the statues and temples, preserved for posterity.

The Black Race Religious Centers that invaded the south of Europe, which were implanted in Central Asia, Africa, Caucasus, and Upper Egypt, dominated the world. The teachings of Amen-em-eope existed since one thousand years earlier before Solomon plagiarized them word for word, paraphrased them, and stole them, to later on be called the Proverbs of Solomon.

The beginning of the Western civilization of the Judeo-Christian-Islamic and the Greco-Roman theosophy is indeed from the Seventeenth Dynasty, around c. 1360 to 1353 BC, known as the teachings of Pharaoh Amenhotep IV, a fundamental concept attributed to Pharaoh Akhenaton, popularly known as Akhenaton, from an Amarna papyrus, points and certifies this fact:

> When you set in the Western horizon of heaven the world is
> in darkness like the dead.
> Every lion comes forward from his den.
> The serpents all sting, and darkness reigns.
> Light falls over the earth when you rise in the horizon
> The two lands are in daily festival
> Then all over the world they do toil.
> How fruitful are your works!
> They're hidden from our presence.
> Oh my only God, whose powers no other has.
> You alone created the earth as you desired, and alone:
> All that are upon the earth.

This fundamental concept, attributed to Pharaoh Akhenaton but represented in Psalm 104, and called hymn to the order of cosmogony in the Old Testament, including the Psalm of David, the one of Solomon, Ecclesiastes or the holy Hebrew Torah, were without existence seven hundred years before the Christian era. It is obvious that Solomon, the author of Psalm 104 in the Bible, knew about the worship of the unique God of prehistoric times before the invasion of the white race and before slavery, thereby prior to fifteenth century BC, when the holy book was published for the first time. This shows us how the teaching of Africa was resumed in the Hebrew mind, deformed and plagiarized, if we compared this ancient use of English in most of our familiar versions.

> Thou makest darkness and it is night, wherein all the beasts
> of the forest do creep forth; the young lions roar after their
> prey; they seek their meat from God.
> The sun ariseth; they get them away and lay them down in
> their dens.
> Man goeth forth unto his work and to his labor until the
> evening . . .
> Oh Lord, how manifold are thy works! In wisdom has thou
> made them all;
> The earth is full of creatures.

The plagiarism of the African work by Hebrew writers came from a literary work of a flourished tradition known beyond a solitary piece of specific geography, covering an extensive period. For an exciting evaluation between these two quotes, I could only refer you to Barbara Mertz's *Temples, Tombs, and Hieroglyphs: A Popular History of Ancient Egypt*, page 237, referring to the African antiquity scholars, not the Western contemporary African scholars. The revelation made here is on one of a series of papyrus called "The Great Hymn to Aten," written by Amenhotep IV, using the same terms of previous texts for the praise of Osiris and Amun.

The deity attached to this teaching of basic law is known as the jurisprudence that the harboring suspicion port of our knowledge cannot conceal from the penalty of the thief in Africa. King Uri, the first king of the earliest time of the kingdom of Ethiopia, considered justice as morality of the state of event, not based on force. The fundamental laws that could be called democracy derived from Amen-em-eope laws, spread from North Africa into Numidia, today called Tunisia; not the absurdity stated by Plato, saying that Greece supposed to have democracy. No, sir, never the people of Greece had democracy in the past and don't have anything called democracy today.

Augustine's family continued to practice the Manichean religion in Numidia; when Augustine born in Thagaste in 354, left his education in Carthage or Khart-Haddas, in the Roman province of North Africa, today known as Souk Ahras, the present territory of northern Tunisia, the North East of Algeria, eighty kilometers from the Mediterranean Sea; from the modern coast of current western Libya, along the Little Sirte that the Arabs later named Ifriqiya. He then later on took the Manichaean religion in Rome during the Christian era. While in Rome, the twenty-nine-year-old boy spoke to Ambrose, the greatest Christian scholar in all Europe, who became one of the most influential ecclesiastical figures of the fourth century and was considered one of the first four doctors of the church from his education in Carthage. Ambrose, born between 337 and 340, became stunned by his education in Carthage and treated him with great respect.

After his conversion to Christianity, Augustine developed a variety of methods and different perspectives by framing the concepts of the original sin, sometimes called the ancestral sin, resulting from the fall of man, known as a transition of the first humans from a state of innocent obedience to God, to a state of disobedience to God; then they fabricated arms and just engaged in war, known as a doctrine of military ethics of Catholic origin in Rome; but philosophically believing that the grace of Christ was indispensable to the freedom of mankind.

His thought of the Augustinian religious order, known as the Rule of St. Augustine, profoundly influenced the vision of the medieval world. The Manichaean teaching was the same as the one that the monk Guido taught at the University of Salamanca in the time of the Moors. From the Manichaean idea, Augustine wrote against the Stoics, about the Holy City of God, and the fundamental principle that was to govern modern Christianity in its moral, called *On Christian Doctrine*. He was one of the most important figures in the development of Western Christianity, heavily influenced by Manichaeism.

The theological Christian Teaching of his book describing how to interpret and teach the Scriptures consists of four books. In 397 he published the first three and in 426, he published the fourth. His writings about the Scriptures were to defend the scriptural truth when it was attacked, to discover the truth in the contents of the Scriptures, and to teach the truth from the Scriptures as the three tasks set for Christian teachers and preachers, are oeuvres of Saint Augustine of Hippo.

The Cameroonian theologian Engelbert Mveng even supported a PhD graduate in theology devoted to the African Augustine in 1964 before graduation. By these erudition words, one could notice an indigenous humble African, who was saying: Islam supposed to bring something new when it's started, but did it bring something new at all? No. According to Islamic literature, Islam started in Africa with an African woman from Egypt called Hagar and Abraham, who was from Asia, the city of Ur in Chaldea. The Elamites, a group of African people, were ruling at the time of Abraham's birth. The Ganges, a sacred river that still bears this name, was named after an African general Ganges from Ethiopia.

Indians kept the symbolic worship of the cow, representing the worship of goddess Het-Heru or Hathor—the golden calf of the Jews. The obelisk copied by Hindus is still there. In 1836, Sir Godfrey Higgins published a two-volume work. He spoke about all deities of the past as being black, particularly in one volume. The religion of Ngai, the Supreme God who came from the religion of the Nile valley, at the basis of the same river, is practiced by the Kamba and Kikuyu of Kenya.

While praying by worshipping Ngai, the monolithic Supreme God, the omnipotent creator of the universe and all it contains; they performed goat sacrificial rituals under the sacred Mugumo tree facing the Mount Kenya called Mount Kirinyaga, meaning the mountain of brightness; during the human life stages such as birth, death, the times of drought, epidemics, harvesting, marriages and planting. In prayers and sacrifices within Ngai spirituality, the late president Jomo Kenyatta and anthropologist, qualified the "Gikuyu as Mwene-Nyaga (Possessor of Brightness) or (The Owner of the Dazzling Light)."

So, they believed in a unique God, feminine and masculine, therefore, androgynous, who is the creator in the entire Africa. In Ancient Egypt that they left a thousand years ago, Osiris or Usirey, the Ngai Narok, who represents God's goodness, is a black man; while Seth or Sutey, the Ngai Nanyoke, who disobeyed God by incarnating evil, is a white man with red hair. The invention of philosophy by African occurred during these fundamental questionings in the nature where they were placed, were such as: when was I created? If yes how and why? He then observed his environment for a long time to answer these philosophical questions. Note also that throughout Africa, there is only one genuine religion called animism and base on scientific research.

The Amazulu of the Zimbabwe River adopted it as time changes. The Yorubas of West Africa had the same structure of the deity system as the Nile valley since the earliest teachings in their folklores. It is known that the Deity/God was addressed as a shepherd in Africa and elsewhere in the ancient Nile valley or in Egypt; but the Negroes who believed that their Egyptian civilization descends from Egypt, are forgetting that their ancestors, who were adapted to the material conditions of the Nile Valley, are the oldest guides in the path of civilization.

Commonly, the creation of man attributed to Western academicians, describing the system of mysteries taught in the Nile valley is referred to the sun

God Re. You can find this story of creation in Judaism doctrines in the first book of Moses; God Re is traced in Gen. 1:26–27, 5:1, and 9:6. The three texts are where the real statement is quoted, saying that man was created in the image of God; and where Paul explains that man, here understood in the narrower sense of male, is "the image and glory" in 1 Cor. 11:7.

Therefore, as Western historians always seek ways to appropriate all stories that mostly concerned Africa, they assumed once again that Egyptians could be the descendants of Atlantis without any concrete evidence. Simply because four thousand years before our era, they discovered an extraordinarily flourishing civilization in Africa, whose origins they did not know. Therefore, they tried to make us believe that the children of Africa, Egyptians, were descendants of the son of Thoth; then asserting further that many elements were referring to the extreme Western origins. And because their civilization was very quickly developed, it was not the result of evolution but a legacy that came from their ancestors, descendants of Thoth's son, who came to Egypt after a great cataclysm, feeling the near end of their continent. These historians or teachers forgot that everything that was created was first established in Africa. This fruit, the result of an evolution and an extraordinary civilization, was inherited from our ancestors. And it was only from Africa that everything was set up for the rest of the world.

Historically, how do you define a civilization or a period between a primitive society and an advanced society? I believe that if this transition period remained an incomprehensible period for you, it is because of your complex; I will not say superiority, but of different feelings of inferiority and representations, fully conscious of unconsciousness provided by the emotional power that organizes your personality.

But one fact will always remain ineffaceable concerning the pharaonic civilization. The pharaonic civilization was the first civilization in the world established by the black pharaohs. Today, everyone knows that this civilization was a knowledge that existed before the descendants of Thoth's son in Africa; where specially sorted adult African ancestors were initiated until they reached wisdom, according to an imperative age limit to reign or exercise knowledge in their society, to transmit that means of illumination to their elder sons, then pass it from son to sons, and one day carry that intact same torches of knowledge to the ultimate next generations.

Ancient Egypt was the heir of that knowledge in the already existing kingdom of African ancestors, not that mambo jumbo of Europeans who described Ancient Egypt as the heir of the Atlanteans. Once again, a personification of African history, but this time, I am sorry and would like to my knowledge clarify a shade concerning the African know-how—a know-how that the white man do not want to attribute to a black man, simply because he considered this know-how very important to assign it to a black man and claimed that my grandfather was a descendant of the son of Thoth. No Sir, my grandfather was not a descendant of the son of Thoth; but a wise initiated man who was practicing his rituals at the planetary hours, like if he had a table of the planetary hours and the nature of planetary influences engraved in his head or in the sky; he could give me the exact time of the day without any watch, just by looking at the sky. He knew the dates and months of the year without a calendar and had the notion of all yearly seasons of our African countries without Western education. The Egyptian calendar itself was based on the star Sirius and used for more than ten thousand years ago. Already, they knew that Sirius had an extremely dense and dark companion. And even after the destruction of Egyptian first African civilization, enough evidence survived to enable its development. The Greek philosophers drew all their astronomical knowledge from Egypt.

After all this been said, it is not strange to me that Egyptians, who were naturally too advanced in this know-how, had multiple developed sciences, especially in astronomy, medicine, and architecture; and they already knew metals around ten thousand years ago.

Egyptians used astronomical techniques to calculate the length of a degree of latitude and longitude at a few centimeters, millennia before Christ. And before nearly four thousand years, this exploit was not equaled by any civilization. Remember that the Dogon from Mali also possessed a great knowledge of astronomy, the existence of certain stars, and a cosmogony so fantastic for generations, even before they were discovered by European telescopes.

The Egypt of Kush, the image of heaven, received the entire order of the heavenly things from Sirius, the celestial equivalent of Isis and Orion, the celestial equivalent of Osiris, for the projection down here on earth. And the divinity spoke to his disciple before the eyes of the sphinx, the great guard, fixing the immutable point where the sun rises at the equinox of spring, to prevent the loss of ancient wisdom during cataclysm. It is that tradition that conceived pyramids like the one of Cheops, as the center of the inhabited world with equal distance from the Bermuda Triangle and the Devil's Sea.

For example, Herodotus said in the fifth century BC, "Clearly, the Colchians are an Egyptian race . . . firstly because they have black skin and frizzy hair," 'in Book II, of his history, chapter 104.' And then secondly, he added by saying that, for this reason, among all these Colchian men, only Egyptians and Ethiopians practiced circumcision since the beginning of the world. The civilization of Ancient Egypt was exclusively black, a convincing African genius in the history of mankind. Diodorus, Strabo, Aeschylus, Apollodorus and Seneca affirmed it unanimously.

The African culture is forever linked to an ancient strain of humanity, endowed with a civilizing mission; but today suspended above the dark abyss of the past by a troubling historical night of the most horrible nightmare of domination ever lived; which transformed its kingdom destiny into almost all necessary discomforts that exists to annihilate it, and has afflicted its population with a deep cultural illness difficult to identify.

In the beginning, time was of irrelevance, so immortality was a normal thing at the beginning of human existence, when Nommo came to earth. Life and death were like a snake shedding its skin for them. Nommo reemerged after death and remembered everything from their previous lives. This characteristic of remembering everything from their previous lives made them immortal beings. These elder Africans of the Dogon tribe described Nommo as androgynous hermaphrodites identified as feminine beings and said that no intelligent life existed on our planet during their arrival. For them to live on earth, they decided to create new life with intelligence by combining their DNA with the animal DNA.

Did they get the result expected from their experiment? No one could tell. But what was certain was that humans were born from that experiment and were linked forever to them spiritually. However, that characteristic, the rebirth after death and remembering all from the previous lives is latent in man and is still is today. So, it is remembering our previous life that makes human being becomes immortal. Nevertheless, we are not immortal as they were, and we do not also look like our celestial ancestors because they spent more time in water than on land, with serpent like bodies ending with fish tails. On their heads, they had horns with noses like cows, holes for ears, and slanted eyes; and they communicated using sonar as dolphins. In southern Iraq, some ancient statues were found dating back to 4500 BC and matched the description of Nommo.

The Dogon people's precise origin, like many other ancient cultures with the history of early oral traditions, was lost in the mists of time. In the ancient literature, they're most often called *Habe*, meaning "stranger" in Fulbe language; and in French language, they're called Peul. But generally, they're called Dogon. They're mainly located in West Africa in Mali, in the districts of Bandiagara and Douentza. From southwest to northeast, there are three distinct topographical regions composed of cliffs, plains, and plateaus roughly parallel to the Niger River.

The Dogon population within these regions is about three hundred thousand, concentrated in villages built on sandstone cliffs attaining the heights of up to six hundred meters (two thousand feet), most with less than five hundred inhabitants, and providing a spectacular physical setting of approximately seven hundred villages. They're an expression of the cosmological ideas. Their rituals and symbolisms are complex. The Dogon religious ideas including the ancestors worship, which is a complex belief and knowledge, primarily defined by the ancestors' spirits who lived in the legendary era before the appearance of death in humans and who slowly migrated from their obscure ancestral homelands to the Dogon sacred places used for the worship of a mythological ancestor of great importance for the practice of their worship; the cult of Nommo, the first living being created by Amma, known as the supreme creator God, was also called Amen in the Dogon religion. Their religion explains the genetic engineering of human beings, and their mythology is older than the Egyptian, Christian, and Greek mythologies. Principally, three cults are known to be religious beliefs of the Dogon.

The cult of Awa that leads souls of the deceased to their final resting place in the family altars and consecrates their passage to the ranks of the ancestors is a cult of the dead. During the funeral and death anniversary ceremonies, worshippers of this cult dance with sculpted, painted, and highly ornated masks to reorganize the spiritual forces disturbed by the death of Nommo, with their seventy-eight different types of ritual masks used as symbols to represent the same subject around the same theme; by their discipline to perceive the senses and the beauty of nature through the rituals of art and send their messages beyond the realm of religion and philosophy.

The cult of Lebe concerns the agricultural cycle. Its shrines with a little earth incorporated in their altars encourage the continued fertility of the land. To guard the purity of the soil, the Dogon believe that, every night, Lebe—the god of agricultural cycle—visits the hogons, the chief priests guarding their shrines. The agricultural god is then transformed into a snake and then breathes the life force in him by licking his skin to purify him; then after purification, he officiates him responsible at many agricultural ceremonies with purity.

The third cult is called Binu, a practice of worshipping ancestors associated with the Dogons' sacred places, where they communicate with the spirits and carry out agricultural sacrifices. Binu is a totemic complex practice related to the myth of the creation of the world, like all their major sacred beliefs in the first living being – the deity named Nommo, created by Amma – (the God of heaven and creator of the universe). His creature quickly multiplied to become four sets of twins. And then the disobedience of the order established by Amma came from one of the rebellious twins.

Then the God of heaven and creator of the universe sacrificed another Nommo; cut off his body and scattered his parts throughout the universe to purify the cosmos and restore the order in the destabilized universe as a source of proliferation of the mythic ancestors in the Binu shrines; where blood sacrifices and the harvest millet are made. Spirits often make themselves known to their descendants in the form of an animal and transmit the ancestor force to them through these rituals in each Binu sanctuaries to become the clan's totem throughout the Dogon country. All secret myths told by the Dogon priests about the star Sirius happened to be true because modern science asserted the existence of the star Sirius and all stars around it.

The Dogons tell us that our ancestors came to earth millennia ago, aboard *Nomo* (a lunar smoke spacecraft similar to *Apollo*), and are from a planet in orbit around a third star called Sirius C; in addition, they knew two other star companions of Sirius, the brightest star in the sky, located only 8.55 light-years away from the sun, including Sirius A (the star of Sigi) named Sigi Tolo, a white star visible to the naked eye, aged about 250 million years; furthermore, Sirius B (the fonio Star or Po) named Po Tolo, signifying the star of the beginning, the most important of all stars before Sirius A.

The Dogons consider it as the egg of the world, the reservoir, the source of all things, and the center of the stellar world. This white dwarf star, three times hotter than its companion, is found below on the left and revolves around Sirius A. Sirius C (the star of the female Sorghum), also named Emme Ya Tolo, is still not yet discovered nowadays by astronomers. The Dogons, the Bozos of Niger, and the Bambaras of West Africa attach great importance to this dual system.

This knowledge remained incomprehensible to the white man for many years until the discovery of Sirius A. New observation techniques testified that Sirius A had a twin that revolved around it. According to them, the entire universe, spiraling conically was created by Amma's voice, their supreme God and the central core from the constellation of Sirius – A Supreme God, as the Bible said: "In the beginning was the Word of Yahweh." According to them, Amma–the Creator God threw dumplings in space, which were transformed into stars. Then He modeled two white potteries.

The sun, encircled by a spiral of red copper, was the first white pottery. And the moon, encircled by white copper, was the second. From the clay column of the earth, eight little Nommo geniuses with green bodies, supple limbs, and red eyes gave birth to eight families and the eight tribes of the Dogon people. The body of a woman lying north to south represents the earth, and the altar of the village, where the collective oil stone is found, symbolized the female and male. The universe is infinite for them, and it moves away from us in a very high speed, making a spiral motion by a combination of translation and rotations motions.

They said that infinitely small elementary structures (cells, molecules, and atoms that make up the body of men on the earth) have the same configuration as those infinitely big as planets, solar systems, galaxies and milky ways; however measurable and gradually increasingly similar to Einstein's theories. And concerning the expansion and the structure of our universe, they anticipated on the latest most modern discoveries of the universe without any application of high-tech mathematical equations or superior telescopes or microscopes at their disposal; but having a great religious tradition and an extraordinary cosmic knowledge on the celestial maps of the sky; preserved by their high priests, great masters initiated of the most sacred mysteries, inherited from the celestial travelers from the space, and transmitted from generation to generation, since the beginning of the history of their existence.

In the Dogon villages of mud, at the foot cliff steeps, they were able to elaborate a mythology as well as complex than alive; peacefully, imbued with myths from the depths of time, rhythmed by festivals and rituals that sing a quiet philosophy of existence during seasons. Their sanctuaries home a particularly fascinating cosmogony. At the same time, their magical drawings, invoked in their secret rites, constitute a kind of writing of several hundred sacred characters. And some of their drawings look curiously like the traditional form of the zodiac signs nowadays. For over seven hundred years, the Dogons of Mali claimed that Sirius, a star located in the Orion belt, has a small moon, making a revolution in fifty years – knowledge that the NASA discovered gracefully through the development of satellites in 1970.

In black Africa, polytheism—the belief in space travelers, to the physical plural gods of flesh and blood—is a belief that black beings have always known and is a source of the truth of our "authentic religions."

A troubling accuracy inherited from this people who came from heaven, who created all life on earth with science and art, is henceforth registered; but that the Western Christian religious principles took from us, assimilated it like a newborn, to finally transform us as slaves, and colonize us by abusing it unscrupulously with every force. These people who came from heaven to earth very long ago, brought the vegetable fibers from the plants of the "field of heaven with them," to establish plants, animals, and the first human couple, who will subsequently engender eight major ancestors of humanity. After creating life on the earth, Amma and the other gods returned to heaven on board of their vessel (*Nomo*).

The Catholic Church hides this truth that reveals the most sacred mysteries and maintains us in the darkness, with a power based on a blind belief, the ignorance of the masses by the belief of a mysterious God, immaterial and omnipotent; but who does not exist in their huge cathedrals of obscurantist mysticism with an attitude opposing the spiritual education of man to the reason and to the progress in this infinite universe and to the infinity inhabited world by human beings; but nowadays resembling humans called humanoids in science-fiction language—a human creation in human form, who represents the human characters graceful to science, are today found everywhere in the life of the infinite universe, as a banal phenomenon to infinity, and lacking all senses of reasoning.

For an African tribe living in a self-folded life, it still possessed much other astronomical knowledge that seems astonishing. Historically, it knows the four largest satellites of Saturn, though invisible to the naked eye. It knows the different phases of Venus and said that Venus has a "companion" by the name of Toro, which can be the asteroid recently discovered between Earth and Venus and divides the sky into 22 equal parts and 266 constellations.

The Dogons said that our solar system is somehow attached to the Sirius system, which has two "sister" satellites: Sigi Tolo (Sirius A) and Po Tolo (Sirius B). They asserted that Nommo was the ancestor of men and that he came from Sirius at about eight light-years from Earth. Also, that Sirius C (or Emma Ya) possessed several other planets in orbit around it; that Po Tolo, which was photographed in 1970, is made of one of the densest materials in the universe, and that the destiny of Earth is intimately linked to the one of Sirius. The third star, Sirius C—the star of woman (Sorghum) or Emma Ya—has a period of revolution of thirty-two years around Sirius A on an elliptical perpendicular orbit to the one of Sirius B. It represents the celebration of women, when the festival of Sigui is held every fifty years. The Sigui festival, celebrated every fifty years by the Dogons, is underlined to regenerate the world and wish for good harvest, hence its importance.

Po Tolo (Sirius B), the oldest of the stars, confirmed by the science of our time as the companion of Sirius, is the name of a very small and very heavy African cereal seed. Regularly used, it completes its elliptical orbit around Sirius A in fifty years. Its name means "deep beginnings" and the Twin of the

Black Hole by the name of Po. Through the use of a powerful telescope, Alvan Clark discovered the second star called Sirius B in 1862. The first to suspect its existence in 1844 was the German astronomer, geodesist, mathematician, and physicist named Friedrich Bessel. While theoretically the theoretical orbit of Sirius B, known invisible to the naked eye, was clarified in 1851 by Peter, and in 1960, Bas Van Den explained his period of revolution of 50,090 years, just like the Dogon specified it for the first time.

But how did they know it? That remains and will always remain a cosmological myth to the Western world. The African people living in Mali on the Bandiagara Plateau and in Hombori Mountains know gravitation, the perfect and the concrete position of the orbits, of the invisible stars rotating around the solar system of Sirius since time immemorial. Americans discovered a dwarf star; whose density is 55 kg/cm2 that rotates around Sirius for 50.1 years thanks to a probe.

The Aztecs told the same story similar to the one of the Dogon, a vessel of dolphins that descended into the Lake Titicaca, several thousand years ago. According to the Dogons, seven hundred years ago, a spacecraft landed in their territory. Giants got out and dug a big hole filled with water to allow the crew, who looked like dolphins and whales, to come out of the vessel and facilitate communication with them by diving into the pool, telling them that they came from Sirius B to transmit them a wealth of information. This story also reveals to us that there are two types of people on Sirius: individuals of four meters in height and a race of dolphins. And together, we describe a double spiral of a figure traced in the cosmos and which makes us strangely think of the structure of our DNA today.

The confirmation of the two French astronomers Daniel Benest and J. L. Duvent saying they observed and conducted a thorough analysis to conclude in 1995 that they found Sirius C—a red dwarf gravitating at a very short distance from Sirius A, drowned in his light—does not confirm its discovery, and no astronomer has yet proved its existence. Thanks to the new hyperpowerful telescopes, these two French astronomers are confirming most of the sayings of the Dogons, except the existence of what they're not yet able to verify and see as planets or stars until today because of the lack of technical means. Other astronomers confirmed a few years before that our solar system is bound by a fixed invisible link with the Sirius system and that we all are tracing a spiral identical to that of the DNA molecule in space.

The Dogons tell of how their arrival five hundred million years ago in Mali so marked them, to the extent that on July 27, this tribe of Mali celebrates the New Year. Egyptians celebrated the New Year on July 19 and the Maya on July 24, on the first reappearance of the heliacal rise of the invisible Sirius during one part of the year. And because of the revolution of Earth, it appears during the day. Its cycle brings it back into the night sky, and his rising is programmed at the same time as that of the sun. The human being came from the grand central sun, somewhere around five million years ago. Tens of thousands of years ago, humans accepted to be hiding behind the universal physical system that only has one sun, behind the duality of the human being energy that prevents him from seeing who he is. The physical universe is not the place where the great central household of the sun is located.

The star Sirius has all astronomical descriptions that very precisely defined a long year of 1,461 solar revolutions, the most important of all referred to as the year of God, not having a steady rise on the horizon that rhythm the walk of time; it appears each year with a little more than six hours late in Dendera, and returns every four years with a day late, suitable to deduct an extra day in some way with a much better accuracy of the bissextile year than with the sun; since after 1,461 solar revolutions, Sirius appeared 1,460 times, very accurate in conjunction with our daytime star, but the countdown time, however, remains inaccurate with our leap year; therefore, all ends of two centuries, we must add a few hours. So exposed, I do not think that the Dogons possessed such knowledge because they're also descended from the son of Thoth.

The entities in the physical world of this household provide us with one part of our biology allowing the balance of their spiritual evolution. And it is this preprogrammed information for their spiritual evolution in human DNA that causes aging, disease, and death. Humans lost their way already for more than ten million years, and more than eighteen million years after the arrival of the big brothers of stars on Earth. They also specified that Earth was populated by animals before being inhabited by man and that the colors of the skin of the five races (white, brown, black, yellow, and red) are explained by the influence of their natural environment and correspond to the five senses of our body. But the spirituality entrusted to Egypt by the extraterrestrial masters was guarded by the Rosicrucians and Freemasons. Its sustainability and universality are memories of some people in the Middle East.

Regarding the Illuminati, their purpose is to defend all human beings, and all generations, in every corner of the earth. The Illuminati operate for the advancement, prosperity, protection, and to secure the ongoing survival of the human species as a whole. Their advice is against the restriction imposed on the human species to live a true freedom in our planet. Free from rules and laws, every human being wants to be freed from hardship, hunger, oppression, and poverty.

As a map to follow, our symbols are placed on the Cathedrals and on multiple official buildings of our cities in many countries of the world, for the humanity to follow the light, and a better quality life, which is the greatest concern of our organization, not placed in the world for our own glorification. The human species must find himself the path that leads to the light because at the center of the light resides the Eye, representing the Eye of God - the omniscient Eye - The Eye of Providence - exercising its oversight over Humanity - focus and fixed on the truth, revealing the truth and orientation when faced with decisions. Know that every human is guided by an inner compass that points toward the light; it completes those who follow it.

Our organization will never pull you down the path like a slave for our whims, even if it is not praised in any history books. The Illuminati have guided the human species through every threat of extinction and will continue to stand into eternity for the human species, but still knowing that human will perish and fade into the annals of time.

Its best-known symbol on the back of the U.S. dollar bill is a floating eye over an unfinished pyramid. It is also depicted in a triangle representing a pyramid, surrounded by rays of light. Also, the eye of providence is visible in the Declaration of the Rights of Man and the Citizen of 1789 and present on the Great Seal of the United States of America.

The Oudjat eye, a most ancient symbol of protection in the Egyptian mythology, with the attribute of divinity, is a representation of an omniscient eye, taken up by several religions and philosophical societies of the world, participating in the ceremonies of secret societies where the cult of the Egyptian and Babylonian gods is perpetuated: Isis, Osiris, Baal, Moloch, or Semiramis. This absolute knowledge of the eye that sees everything is attributed to the gods of India, Indra or Varuna, to those of Iran, like Ahura Mazda, and more than five thousand years ago, the "Brotherhood or the Fraternity of the Snake," in the Mesopotamian civilizations, whose origin goes back to the roots of the Western civilization, in Sumer and Babylon. Today, the goal of the Illuminati, known in Latin as the "ANNUIT COEPTIS," meaning "our project will be crowned with success," the project of "NOVUS ORDO SECLORUM," meaning the "new order for centuries;" in other words, all this means: the new world order is close to its final realization. Throughout the ages, multiple names of organizations that are attached to the organization of the Illuminati, include the Egyptian "mystery schools," the ancient and mystical Order of Rosa Crucis, the Freemason, the esoteric or "occult" organizations of the Greeks, the Christian Church of Rome established in Europe, Islam, the Priory of Sion, the Order of Malta, the Military and Hospital Order of St. John of Jerusalem, and the successive political powers, in a long filiation, to designate the resulting system, the core of the "masters of the world," used their symbols as "vehicles" by "fraternity." The Illuminati organization exerts its influence within these multiple organizations in its current form, since the founding of the Illuminati Order in Bavaria by Adam Weishaupt in 1776.

Thus, beyond the borders of the Egyptians' old cultural activity of various examples, known as the transcendent qualities of pharaohs, the importance of verbalization and the moral depth of great wisdom and discernment in the Hermopolitan and Memphite schools, the Greek, eager to acquire knowledge, pushed their very young fertile minds to enable the development of their own intellectual and technological skills. They adapted the Egyptian ingenuity and incorporated it into Greek philosophy.

Seriously, why is no one really questioning where the Greek civilization and philosophy derived from, or the chief way in which they were transmitted? However, the answers to these questions assert that it was through the colonization of Egyptian by Greece that later led Greek to study in Egypt. In the Ancient Egyptian lore, Thoth was later adopted by the Greeks as Hermes; the syncretic representation and the combination of the Egyptian god Thoth and the Greek god Hermes, as the god of wisdom, writings upon papyrus, attributed series of early Egyptian books to Hermes and consequently regarded him with great respect. Because he was considered the greatest of all kings, the greatest of all priests, and the greatest of all philosophers, the title "Thrice Greatest" was given to him.

Almost all Masonic symbols are of Hermetic in character, borrowed from the mysteries established by him; because he was the author of the Masonic initiatory rituals, as he is of first importance to Masonic scholars. Hermes Trismegistus of the Druze, the Greek messenger of the gods, was then identified with the Egyptian god Thoth, the god of knowledge, known as the Hermetic discipline, that strives toward a full spiritual awakening. To the Egyptian pharaoh high priest and god Thoth Imkopech, who was the teacher of the Sacred Mysteries in Ancient Egypt, was the father who built the great initiatory center of antiquity, best known of all pharaohs as the first architect of the Step Pyramid of Djoser at Saqqara, who clearly illuminated pyramid; the founder of astronomy studies and as a doctor.

Imhotep was considered a man, but (other than the pharaohs), he was one of the few Egyptian gods; and in Khemnu, called Hermopolis by the Greeks, in the Temple of Thoth, Thoth was a deity, the heart and tongue of Ra, by which his will, was translated into speech. Consequently, as the same personage, the two gods were worshipped as one. Imhotep was first honored as a god and as a wise man. We also know that the pyramids were built by paid workers from all continents of the world, not by slaves. The initiation of Pythagoras was accomplished there.

As students, pharaohs were crowned insiders and instruments of initiators. They never acted against people who had acquired intellectual superiority and wisdom, which enabled them to live in accordance with their desires and in harmony with the unseen nature that they never equaled since its degraded kinds. The tyrant pharaohs were overthrown by people who formed a single entity.

Preparing to become a pharaoh left little room for leisure, and we must also say that the education of a prince in the houses of life—where the scribes taught him the basic science, the secrets of all things of nature, and hieroglyphs containing the mysteries of heaven and earth—was not a cakewalk. Thus, it is known that all the kings of Ancient Egypt were scholars where all Greek philosophers and other Western nations drew all their knowledge of surgery, astronomy, mathematics, etc.

Cagliostro said, "All light comes from the East, all initiation from Egypt." This meant that even some celestial beings, beings above all rites and initiated beings became leaders, officers and were worshipped as gods after their departure. Osiris became a striking example on that subject.

Since pyramids were a place of initiation and symbolized the transformation of men into gods, it opened its doors of the firmament for mortals to enter, make their way to the heavens, and come out as illuminated or simply as gods. Entering the great pyramid—khuti, its Ancient Egyptian name signifying light of glory—was to be capped with the nodes of telluric forces to accentuate the origin of the royal deity, enjoy its baths, its waves of radiant faith, and the divine status dedicated to religious.

At the end of initiation, the adept had to undergo the ritual of initiatory death in an empty sarcophagus to know life and death and be transformed from a simple man into a god. The transformation of man into a god was a symbolic knowledge of death; man should experience and understand that this death had nothing to do with the physical death. For the initiates, death must be understood as a divine order, a journey toward the knowledge of wisdom, a total purity achievement toward light, not a long physical sleep.

Khuti—the great pyramid as a center of many magnetic anomalies, representing all known mathematical data—astronomical or prophetical, sought by several Egyptian pharaohs and strangers from all over the world, was transforming many adepts at a point in time; this transformation of man into a god is the survived secret of the civilization of a black race that disappeared ten thousand years ago, leaving behind a fabulous energy of an unsuspected science for the purpose of human rescue and the state of things in our time; that most recognizable symbol of ancient civilization known as Egypt has become a narrow region located between two isolated deserts of Africa.

There, a great history is told by its numerous mysterious monuments, built with great accuracy and precision, which are still envied today. The Great Pyramid is an example of one of the grandiose passionate handiwork not only for religious and commemorative purposes but also to reinforce the wide-ranging power and the divine right of pharaohs with a perfect passionate astronomical engineering that led them to construct a reduced model of the Northern Hemisphere of the Earth and used its reduction scale (1/43 200th) as one of the fundamental phenomena of the celestial mechanics.

The fourth century BC reports that the Egyptian already observed the stars since ten thousand years ago. Their connection mechanics of concrete energy sensors with stars and their initiatory teachings have generated an architecture based on sacred numbers: designating what opposed the utility of a profane and the common. Its program is placed outside the ordinary and mundane things but allows humans to learn the complex knowledge and technology brought from the stars.

The year 10500 corresponds to the first time of Orion before Christ; the exact time to build the Great Mystery was propitious and especially pretentious. The process to create the Great Pyramid that began in 2584 BC, in year 10500, took one hundred years to be completed in 2500 BC. But according to Herodotus, an Egyptian priest informed him that the pyramid was built by a team of ten thousand workers and that the monumental and colossal work only lasted twenty years.

Diodorus, on the other hand, stated that the works on the beautifully pyramid of Khufu, who lived around 4,600 years ago, only lasted for twenty years and was built by a total of three hundred thousand workers, he estimated. This estimation of the construction of the Great Pyramid given by Diodore, believing that the works have only lasted twenty years, requiring the laying of a stone block every two minutes, is absolutely absurd because of the precision involved. As the one who commissioned one of the Seven Wonders of the Ancient World, known as the Great Pyramid of Giza, he is generally accepted as Khufu, the second pharaoh of the Fourth Dynasty, during the twenty-sixth century BC, the period in the first half of the Old Kingdom. The other two pyramids do not match the craftsmanship of the Great Pyramid but are still standing tall and very impressive.

At the time of its creation, the astronomical and the pure mathematical calculations made by scientific laws and the standard guide for navigational observatory were unknown. The sacred origins of the Great Pyramid, the pure applied mathematics, and the crucial measurements of their aging are "three keys" of mystery that still baffle several investigators and scientists who have explored and studied the Great Pyramid in great length during the past two thousand years.

The complex mathematical and scientific laws used to build the Great Pyramid of Giza for mystical and religious purposes, which have been the object of intense speculation for the past 4,500 years, were discovered in 1700 BC, brought to Greece after their education in Egypt; these mathematical and scientific laws were later rediscovered by the Europeans. The Great Pyramid of Giza itself was built in the middle of the third millennium before Christ.

The Great Pyramid is specifically built at a parallel equidistant from both the equator and the North Pole; the longest parallel land on the globe is the east-west axis (thirty degrees north), and the longest meridian land is the north-south axis (thirty-one degrees east of Greenwich); its crossing of diagonals divides the Nile delta; at the same time, it also divides while crossing the maximum continent into two equal fractions, the emerged parts of our earth. The observatory of Greenwich in the Meridian Building is nine apart but so much less accurate than the Great Pyramid of Giza, which is three apart away with its north-south alignment. Their reproduced natural angle is 51°51' of the crystal quartz. It has been also demonstrated that the Great Pyramid is exactly located in the center of the world and at the center of the continent's gravity.

The sun in itself presided over the gigantic construction of the pyramids, noted the royal scribe of the Pharaoh at the Just Way, dedication of Khufu on the Temple of Ptah at Giza. This inscription claiming that the sun which resided the origin of Ptah, and which was lost in the mists of time, is his statement on an earlier document preserved in the museum of Boulac in Egypt. The Great

Pyramid as the stars gate at the north gallery, pointing toward the polar sky, canalized energy from space and was the first giant telescope.

For this fact, they were all built by architects demonstrating a sustained reasoning of science on the left bank of the Nile to cap telluric nodes forces that are signified and those who signified. Scientifically supported, they're located near the epicenter with mathematical precision of lines of force on the surface of the earth; with an ingenious and laborious spirit, which all together specified data that are imposed and requirements. These architects were educated in astrology, philosophy, jurisprudence, arithmetic, geometry, history, music, and medicine and had fully learned to attract cosmic energy from the cosmos. Using electromagnetic waves on the earth to serve as a gateway to the underground kingdom; its proportion as the mode of modulated communication, and its perfect pyramidal shape as vector; as energetic architecture, it could bring back to life a dead physical body. The pyramid lost its metal top (copper, brass, gold, etc.,) over time.

The Pyramid of Cheops, as a radiesthesic headlight, was the sending station that allowed the pharaohs to communicate with the celestial to finally dictate their royal and humble orders to the people at that time. Their wireless transmission mechanism, a remote communication mode hitherto never discovered, was generally using modulated electromagnetic waves as a vector.

Unusual objects such as a small double-pointed metal hook, a gigantic crystal radio transmitter, a piece of cedar of twelve centimeters long and adorned with engravings, photoelectric cells, metal walls, a rough stone sphere, and a round flying object were found in some rooms. That powerful sound force that Egyptians used is stronger than our modern electricity and reacted to ultrasonic vibrations. Today, the use of sonar equipment to make a radio still prevents researchers to explain the true radiation of the pyramid. It is an indestructible bibliographic document; a stone bible revealing all facts of the past, it testifies an advanced technology.

It is a memory intended to conserve the recordings of all events of the earth since the beginning of ages and some knowledge for the public education following the tradition, and especially to not allow the loss of ancient wisdom until the new world order comes; it is like an empty tomb never filled but known as a tomb of archives never found and where one cannot enter without having the understanding its mysteries.

A chamber of the king, called Queen's Chamber, was used for the mummification process but did not shelter the mummy of the queen nor the mummy of Cheops, neither another pharaoh's mummy in the king's chamber. You had to cross the queen's chamber as a preliminary stage of sexual initiation to reach the king's chamber. And countless rooms existed above the same king's chamber. Those of Giza never served as a tomb to any pharaoh.

The three pyramids, considered as tombs, didn't deliver royal remains. The discovery of galleries and statues in the Great Pyramid of Giza and the sphinx was held secret. During the flood, the pyramids were supposed to preserve secrets like the science of art, the science of religion, the mysteries of esoteric science, astronomy, geometry, physics, and a good deal of other knowledge of ancient wisdom for future education. Initiation opened the doors of the firmament by its hieroglyphics inscribed on the walls of the pyramids, for anyone who knew the secret writing to make its way to heaven and symbolically be transformed from man to god.

Symbolically, the disposition of the sediments of masonry by the color of stones, and especially by the direction in which the space of the corridor leading to the tomb turns, described the memory of the earth on the walls. In addition, the process by which these sediments are disposed in tracts, according to the national legislation, decreed that before reaching his liberation, each entity as an insider must go through what is indicated therein.

Another fingerprint replica of gods in the soil of Egypt is the magnificent representation of the sky in connection with the three stars of the "belt of Orion" by the three pyramids of Giza, under the form of fifteen million tons of rock; however, corresponding exactly to the configuration of the sky around 10450 BC; and disposed in the same manner regardless of the height and altitude of the land and conceived as a permanent architectural fingerprints signature of the eleventh millennium BC.

This marked the episode of "Jacob's Ladder" connecting heaven and earth. The Tiwanaku civilization in the Andes, according to *Nature* and *New Scientist*, seems to have been destroyed around 12,400 years ago, at the last geomagnetic inversion; also at the period of the eleventh millennium before the Christian era, many thoughts that its ruins were probably thirty thousand years old. The spirit took shape and began to descend on this earth. During their stay on that continent, the development of people followed the first destruction cost by the people themselves, and then changes followed. Changes caused by earthquakes and hurricanes raised the water of seas, and suddenly, in the whole world, large mammals disappeared for their existence to just become history; but finally, water gave life back to the world, and then in Egypt, the agriculture in expansion emitted strong echoes of success, leading to the end of the first stammering.

The upheavals related to the structure of the terrestrial crust occurred in a large scale within it bosom around four thousand years before Christ. These tectonic movements caused a global superelevation and a deformation of the constituent materials of considerable magnitude of the Alps and the Himalayas, the Andes of South America, and the Rocky Mountains of North America. Thus, a longer year of 360 days was established after 4000 BC, when the zodiac was revised.

This history of the earth with its nations, its religion, its initiation, its tradition, its culture, its economy, its politics, its justice, and its ordinances, as well as the dates, places, names of individuals, and the construction of the Great Pyramid are archived since the beginning of time but are not found in the Great Pyramid. These ordinances stipulate that before these archives are opened again, the temple must rise again. The change of times will be seen by the sunrise above the water; and when the shadow of light radiates between the paws of the sphinx, they will testify. And when the experience of man had seen great changes occurring on the earth, times will be fulfilled, and the sphinx—guardian of the threshold, portrait of Asrarion, prior to the Great Pyramid—will allow entrance by its right foot in a hallway to the archives room.

The Great Pyramid of Giza, the second largest in the world, at equal distance from the famous Bermuda Triangle and the Devil's Sea, included a king's chamber named Hall of Initiates. As an initiate to the great mysteries, it was obvious that, for the king, the transformation of man into a god became evident. And as it was used to send messages, there was an empty initiation sarcophagus in radiant blue as a symbol of initiatory death in the king's chamber; since the place of initiation into the great mysteries was in the building, the pyramid was housing adepts from different African countries and from different part of the world.

The Egyptians of antiquity entered the pyramid as mere mortals; illuminated in the heavenly mystery and being already equal to the light of the glory of the gods, they left it knowing the secret teachings of all ages, realizing that in Egypt, where deities spoke to their disciples, is the projection of the celestial order and the image of heaven here below; in one word, Orion is the celestial equivalent of Osiris, and Sirius is the equivalent of the heavenly Isis; the initiate of great mysteries, lying down in a sarcophagus, accepted the ritual of voluntary death understood as a divine order in the secular life.

In the sarcophagus, he experienced a symbolic death—a temporary separation of body and soul—to show him that he was a dual being in a state of particular consciousness, and by the mystical processes, he had to resuscitate in a new life full of knowledge and ensured communication with a place called second life, between life and death. Many followers tried to change certain rituals without success, but only Jesus knew how to break the law of the ritual discipline that required insiders to be sealed during their initiation in the tomb.

The blue color of the king's chamber increased the intensity of thoughts; it was radiesthesic, and it rendered the process of detection based on that ability to receive radiations that certain bodies emitted; so it facilitated communication telepathically with the mystic.

The initiation of mages to the "sacred sleep" was used to treat patients spiritually. The patient was put so deep into sleep that he was able to perceive the etheric forms in the spiritual world. I mean real visions and not chaotic dreams. The art of acting of mages, who knew these visions, directed powerful spiritual forces to enter the sick body through the attenuation of the inner consciousness and ordered the vital forces in disharmony and disorder in the body to harmonize. The help of external remedies was not often requested, and it rarely existed.

Pyramids like the Pyramid of the Moon, the Pyramid of the Sun, and the Pyramid of the Feathered Serpent are also known as the greatest pyramids of the spiritual world. The first largest pyramid in the world is the Great Pyramid of Cholula; a temple dedicated to the god Quetzalcoatl, the Aztec god of wind and learning, from the classic to postclassic period in Mexico. Its construction started from the third century BC and was built in four stages, through the ninth century AD. The Pyramid of the Sun is the first largest pyramid at Teotihuacan, founded in 200 CE, and was abandoned in 750 CE; it is known as the third largest ancient pyramid in the world. This structure in Teotihuacan is the second largest in Mesoamerica.

The Pyramid of the Moon in Teotihuacan is the second-largest pyramid in Mexico. Its construction was between AD 200 and 250, and the structure is also older than the Pyramid of the Sun.

The Temple of the Feathered Serpent is the third-largest pyramid at Teotihuacan, dated between 150 and 200 of CE. As the earliest-known representations of the feathered serpent, the deity is often identified with the much-later Aztec god Quetzalcoatl, also known as the Temple of Quetzalcoatl, and the Feathered Serpent Pyramid; and the Temple of the Feathered Serpent, the Pyramid in Xochicalco, is founded in about AD 650 by the Olmeca-Xicallanca, Mayan group at the late classic period.

The Teotihuacan culture, which reached its peak in 450 after Jesus Christ, was the first culture to use the feathered serpent as an important political and religious symbol when it extended its powerful cultural influence through much of the Mesoamerican region. These pre-Columbian societies had flourished, extending from central Mexico to Belize, the northern Costa Rica, El Salvador, Guatemala, Honduras, and Nicaragua before the Spanish colonization of America in the fifteenth and sixteenth centuries with multiethnics like the Maya, the Mixtec, the Nahua people, the Otomi, the Totonacs, and the Zapotec; defined by a mosaic of cultural features, Mesoamerica developed its indigenous cultures and shared it among them. The Mesoamerican pyramids were built in the pre-Columbian period, and that construction continued until about the year 250. Sometime between the seventh and eighth centuries after Jesus Christ, the city of Teotihuacan lasted until around 550 after Jesus Christ when its major monuments were sacked and systematically burned to ashes. We cannot determine the size, height, and altitude of the one located forty miles southwest of Zion in Shensi, China, being in a prohibited area, despite claims qualifying it larger than Cheops. But except the one that fit a mountain in Cholula, Mexico, they were all constructed and arranged in the same manner as the pyramids in Egypt.

Pyramids are a great example of analogous destinations used by architects today for construction as in every other science. But cathedrals, the great religious centers that radiate faith and dolmens, offering exposure to vibrational energies, all enjoy their bath, the wave form of telluric forces as the work of our ancient Theurgy, meaning "God and Work," to raise the level of consciousness by increasing the psychic faculties, improving the health of their adepts and invoking the supernatural powers for the laudable purposes of reaching God and communicate with "good spirits"; this practice, the characteristics of the sordid Ars Goetia, is the opposite of Theurgy, say some.

These buildings are built by ancient builders, constructors of cathedrals, megaliths and pyramids, who had the sacred knowledge of the cosmo-telluric subtleties. They used this knowledge to reach higher states of consciousness to build those sacred edifices. The crypts of some of these buildings such as cathedrals were also formerly used as places of burial. Therefore, until today, under various slabs of some cathedral crypts in the world, we can still find at least one tomb of respected individuals.

Thoth, the great Egyptian priest and the inspirer of Ra, is the Hermes of the Greeks and has the same value as Manitou of the Native Americans; the Egyptian Osiris is the Dionysus and the Neptune of the Greeks. The Egyptian Isis is the Demeter, Cybele, or Ceres of the Greeks. The Egyptian Ptah is their Zeus. Enoch or Thoth is the Egyptian god of wisdom. Before the flood, he taught the art of building to men. And to preserve the essential Great secret key in the bowels of the earth, he engraved it on a slab of oriental porphyry.

Blacks lived for hundreds of years because they knew the spiritual practice and medicinal techniques of rejuvenation separated from psychology and religion. Their life expectancies were more than one hundred years. Dams, surgery, electricity, medicine, and psychology, to only quote a few, were their religion. The origins of the arrow of Twa, believing in the god Ptah, are traced back on the edges of the Nile valleys centuries before the white man dreamed one day to come to Africa.

Almost intact, they have maintained their old tradition of black race initiation near the Ethiopian Plateau, resulting from a great tradition above all rites. Remember that all initiation came from Egypt and all enlightenment from the East, according to Cagliostro in the eighteenth century. The old tradition practiced by the black race for ages was transmitted to the red race and then picked up in insufficient pieces by the Atlantean. We know that the Celt Bodhones, which are up to today in Palestine called Hebrews, passed through Ethiopia, a country inhabited by blacks. A great part of these Bodhones spread in the desert, and they were known as the nomadic people.

The most sacred of all initiation temples is at Dendera, a small town in Egypt on the West Bank of the Nile about five kilometers south of the current Kenah (or Qena) and sixty-five kilometers north of Luxor, where Osiris, Isis, and their son, Horus, were worshipped. All the symbolism of the resurrection of the Christ, the Holy Trinity, and a zodiac reproducing the map of the sky without context of a specific day of a pastime, and the one of the lion as a pilot of the twelve constellations were there engraved in hieroglyphics, and dated from 9792 BC. A golden circle with a radius of 7,545.60 m, a two-story round block, was also found there. The original temple was directly connected by corridors to the golden circle, comprising all mechanisms of the global articulation of the celestial vault; its variable geometry and its extremely accurate calculations, most sumptuous than the sixth monument rebuilt, are contemplated by its today's visitor. The sphinx, that huge monument of a face with open eyes fixed at an immutable point where the sun rises at the spring equinox, was named by the Greeks when they saw it for the first time. The word *monument* means "to warn or warning."

According to Albert Slosmann and Ch. Dupuis (astronomers), the Ancient Egyptians sphinx, a mythical creature known as the "father of terror," was the name given to it by the Arabs, who until today called it Abul Hol.

Dominique Vivant Denon told us this about the Sphinx: "I just had the time to observe the Sphinx, which deserves to be drawn with the most scrupulous care, and which has never been in this way. Although its proportions are colossal, the contours which are preserved are as supple as pure: the expression of its head is sweet, graceful, and tranquil: the character is African-but the mouth, whose lips are thick, has a softness in movement and a delicacy of execution really admirable; it is of the flesh and of life."

"As for the character of their human figure, borrowing nothing from other nations, they copied their own nature, which was more graceful than beautiful; in all, the African character, of which the Nigger is the charge and perhaps the principle." Dominique Vivant Denon wrote this truth which disturbs the white, by showing an African princess with her white servant, and commenting on Egyptian art, on the occasion of his drawing of the famous Sphinx of Giza.

It was a precious testimony for the African history. His words are part of his many sketches, drawings and artistic prints, during the expedition of Napoleon in Egypt from 1798 to 1799. Since photography did not exist at that time, the fauna and flora objects like the stelae, statutes, monuments, boats etc., and all the heritage of Egypt had to be collected through its artistic expertise, to make the Egyptian civilization better known in the hexagon.

Refusing to be a part of the great falsification of the history of humanity, Count Volney, one of the great Western scholars, inhabited by justice, wisdom and good faith, bequeathed a very emotional testimony to the posterity, in the middle of the slavery period. Constantin-Francois Chasseboeuf de La Giraudais, called Volney, manifested in all conscience, an awareness, to not plunge into the nauseating Caux of prejudices, concerning the African origin of the Ancient Egyptians.

He said: "Before the great Sphinx of Giza, the Nigritic features attenuated today were notoriously distinctive in my day; therefore, the French scholar preferred to adhere to the reality of the facts of a Negro Egypt, and clamored it loud and clear to the scientific community of his time, rather than indulging in the lie of conscious falsification of history." Volney made the findings about the indigenous people of the country, the Copts of Egypt at that time, who were under the Arab occupation for nearly a millennium and a half, and who are the mixed descendants of the Egyptians: according to him, falsification should absolutely not show the Afro cut; he said: "All have puffy faces, swollen eyes, crushed noses, and fat lips; in a word, a true face of a mulatto; and that he was tempted to attribute it to the climate, when, having visited the Sphinx, its appearance gave him the word of the enigma.

By seeing this Nigger characterized head in all its features, the Europeans said: hide us its African features. Thus, the father of Ankh Aton (Akhenaton IV, Ekawase nema-re, the name of enthronement of Amenhotep III, and Ankh Aton

(Akhenaton IV, himself, of Negroid traits and aquiline nose, the Egyptologists made them appear as whites. His mother Tiyi, with Negroid traits and an aquiline nose inherited by Akhenaton IV, has never been shown by Egyptologists. They erased black hair to disguise black-kamites-skinned in whites.

It became more and more inadmissible to continue to accept the hitherto obvious thesis of a Negro Egypt. So, to destroy the memory of a Negro Egypt at all costs and more completely in all minds, the birth of Egyptology was necessary. Thus, in subjective interpretations, facts and historical documents, they really strove to find a white origin for Egyptian civilization.

Everything was therefore passed over in silence, being unable to find any contradiction in the formal testimonies of the ancients; and consequently, not been unable to refute them by an objective confrontation with all Egyptian reality. How could they go astray at this point, to create so many difficulties and delicate problems to modern specialists, by the fabrications unworthy of normal men as were these ancient Europeans? Or we reject them dogmatically with indignantly while regretting, or we keep the entire universe in ignorance, for the pleasure of feeling superior, bogged down in these contradictory remarks.

However, by repeating the initial dogma, believing therefore to have demonstrated the white origin of Egyptian civilization to the eyes of all honest beings in the world, they then slipped on the difficulties of the problem, after so many intellectual acrobatics more gratuitous than extensive knowledge; but knowing that the facts do not deceive. Henceforth, the profound affinity of the intimate kinship, known as the common denominator of Egyptologists and their theses, will be reduced to a desperate attempt to refute the thesis of a Negro Egypt.

The original documents of the Tomb of Seti I show us blacks with frizzy hair, but those falsified by the whites show us the whitened Kamites, having frizzy hair; does this lie reassure you? Desperately, the war with Nubia became a conflict between whites and blacks for falsifiers; all Kamites, as well as Ramses himself in the tale of Moses are white. The historian Henri Stierlin highlights a collection of proofs at a just title, following a meticulous investigation, in his titled book: "The false bust of Nefertiti a sham of Egyptology."

He discovered by denouncing its manufacture by an artist named Gerardt Marks, on the initiative of the German Ludwig Borchardt, the archaeologist who was responsible for the excavation in 1912. Gerardt Marks thus manufactured this fake bust of Nefertiti right on the site of excavation. To reassure them and cover up the inconvenient truth, all the noses of almost all Negro-Egyptian statues were broken by the falsifiers, to soften the African character of the Ancient Egyptians.

The falsity of Egypt's Negro thesis is a business of almost all Egyptologists, despite the education and the abundance of facts. To cut the valley of the Egyptian-Nubian Nile from the rest of Africa culturally, the Hamito-Semitic - more descriptively called Afro-Asiatic was invented from scratch, since in the materiality of the linguistic facts, this family does not exist, and has never been reconstructed.

According to the cenacles of the Western scientists, the Egyptian and Ethiopian civilizations, those of Ife (Ile-Ifẹ in Yoruba), Benin, and the basin of Chad, that of Ghana and all those called Negro-Sudanese - Mali, Gao, etc., that of the Zambezi - Monomotapa, and that of Congo in full Ecuador etc., were created by the mythical whites, despite the formal testimony of the ancients. These whites then faded away like a dream, to let the Niggers perpetuate the forms, as technical organizations etc.

Discovering at the beginning of the nineteenth century that black Egypt was the country that brought all the elements of civilization into Europe and the world, they could not contain this truth. Its imperialism, seeing itself in charge of the civilizing mission in Africa, discovered that, it was precisely that Black Africa that they submitted in slavery, that black Africa which they have regressed that was the source of all they could imagine as a civilization by digging into the past; so, this truth, all Western scholars could not accept it; consequently, committing the worst intellectual crime against humanity. In page 67 of his book, Volney says: but by returning to Egypt, the fact that it gives back to history, offers many ref lections to philosophy. What subject of meditation, to see the present barbarity and the ignorance of Copts, resulting from the alliance of the deep genius of Ancient Egyptians, and the brilliant spirit of the Greeks; to think that this race of black men, today our slave and the object of our contempt, is the very one to whom we owe our arts, our sciences and even the use of the word.

In 2500 to 2532 BC, Pharaoh Khafra created the Great Sphinx. The sphinx—built in the image of Anunnaki's head placed on a body of lion, representing the age of lion in 10,500 BC—was the first monument built. It was the symbolic representation of leonine, a race of the second-degree density, that was active in the original edification of the Anunnaki culture; it was the sentinel protecting the main entrance to the inner earth and the passage leading directly to the Ark of the Covenant, between the river and the sphinx, one of the undiscovered pyramids that served as archives, containing information on Christ.

In 1380, the nose of the sphinx was in very good condition before Napoleon's campaign in Egypt came to destroy it. History tells us that a drunken French artillery officer of Napoleon's army, who wanted to see if he could aim well, had as target the nose of the sphinx with a beaming face and smashed it. Or even, according to others, it could be as ordered by the Koran, which declared a religious war to destroy the Christian idols of the pre-Christian era that destroyed the nose of sphinx; because at that period, the Muslim fanatics began destroying its nose, before destroying its brand-new bright-red-varnished face.

It is also written that this very beautiful figure, smiling in a gracious manner, with a mouth bearing the seal of grace and beauty, had its face disfigured by a man named Saim-ed-Dahr and has remained in that state until today. This was brought to us by a fourteenth-century Egyptian historian commonly named Al-Makrizi. Al-Makrizi who was a mamluk, designating slaves, Muslim rulers of slave origin, or Muslim slave soldiers in Arab, who thought that by disfiguring the sphinx's face, he was fixing a religious error.

Finally, even as Egypt being the cradle of the Western civilization, France still wanted to bring the ideas of the enlightenment to the Egyptian people; and Muslim fanatics still think that they're the center of all religions in the world. Today, the sphinx, which has gone through countless hurricanes and earthquakes, suffers from erosion, which is flushing its rock under the form of blades.

You're an ancient megalithic monument and a mysterious ancestral Stonehenge, oh, sphinx! You're several large stones in dimensions throughout the world; but you particularly was erected between 2500 and 1100 BC, corresponding to the Mesolithic of the average age of the stone in the Neolithic Era that began around 10,000 BC and ended between 4500 and 2000 BC in various parts of the world to the New Stone Age; emphasizing the age of polished stone already known in the Upper Paleolithic Era; a prehistory period from about 2.6 million years to about 10,000 years, the Old Stone Age in the Chalcolithic and Bronze Age. You're a Stonehenge in the United Kingdom, a circular structure, a set composed of concentric suspended stones that start from the four corners of your building.

Countless generations of illustrious scientists have studied your existing cavities, where you reside in the west, four miles from Amesbury, famous for all its monuments and prehistoric sites. The small town in the county of Wiltshire is across the river Avon and is also immediately close to the site of Woodhenge, located one kilometer north of Amesbury, and to the north, eight miles from Salisbury, a city dating back to the Iron Age retaining some Arthurian legends. The United Kingdom housed another site called Men-an-Tol, erected in the Penwith region at the western tip of Cornwall. This site is known for its round stone pierced with a large round hole in the center and comprising a small alignment of three stones in the southwest of the United Kingdom.

By your condition of conservation, we cannot ignore your presence in one of the world-recognized sites in England by the name of Stonehenge. A scientific work notably fixed; still unable for scientists and historians to come to a solid theory of when, why, or by whom your structure was built, and not easily allowing any terrestrial to fully reach your understanding. Depending on the region, you describe various earlier periods of the planet, dating back to the tenth millennium BC.

In the southern Ethiopia and throughout the African continent, you're a great seniority, and some of your dolmenic cists are dating from the second millennium up to the tenth millennium BC. In the Shoa and the Ethiopian Sidamo, you decorate the unfathomable region with most recent elegance of the first millennium of our era. In the south of Addis Ababa, specifically in the districts of (*wereda*) Soddo and Tiya, you're a brand of funerary use. In North Africa, your age is of the third millennium (2200) BC; at the fifth millennium BC (4500) or the seventh millennium BC (6500), in the Upper Egypt (Abu Simbel), a town 290 kilometers southwest of Aswan on Lake Nasser in Nabta Playa, oh,

Africa! You're sheltering with honor, dolmens, and menhirs. You're recognizable near the small town of Thibar by dolmens in the necropolis of Djebel Gorra on the road to Teboursouk in Tunisia; including many prepunic megalithic tombs of ancient Carthage people, originally traced from the Berbers and Phoenicians.

Nobly set up in the site of Tundidaro in Mauritania, a mysterious structure of a wonderful dome measuring forty kilometers in diameter is to be seen in the Sahara Desert. This geological giant eye of the Sahara Desert in Mauritania is of unknown origin. On the Adrar Plateau, several other monuments of standing stones arranged in circle are also found, and their megaliths retained the original characteristics, settled in the Neolithic era. To mention only a few countries in the Maghreb, Algeria, Morocco, and Tunisia are added to the list as countries that also home megaliths. The site of Tundidaro comprises 150 erected stones in the region of Niafunke in Mali.

Oh, ancestral stone protecting tombs in Niger, Togo, Chad, and on the right bank of the Gambia River in Senegal, of a period extending from the third century BC, identified in a limited space between the rivers Gambia in the south and Saloum in the north. From the sixth century BC in Bouar, Central African Republic, you're sublime and majestic. And in other countries where dolmens are also edified, such as dolmens of British America, from the sixth century BC up to the fifteenth century, at Alto de los Idolos, a few miles from San Augustine are sublime. In Brazil, the Calcoene site of the ancient time in Amapa, near French Guiana; in Peru, a fortress made of carved stones of more than one hundred tons in Cuzco, Koricancha, and Sacsayhuaman are also majestic.

Near Tihuahuanaco, its unexplained stones precisely cut and fit together in Bolivia are incredible; as a vast cultural complex, the temple of Puma Punku, located in Tiwanaku, was surely there from 1320 to 1533 before the arrival of the Incas, as one of the most significant complexes in the history of the pre-Columbian Americas. At Tiahuanaco, one of the largest stelae measures 7.3 meters high and weighing 20 tons, and some blocks are estimated to weigh from 100 to 150 tons. In addition, the Puma Punku skill is filled with mysteries that baffle one's mind, and as one of the most incredible ancient ruins, there, we find incredible evidence of precision-cut stone, precise engineering, perhaps the biggest mystery involving Puma Punku. This wonderful place makes people to lose the notion of space and time with its high-level evidence of astronomy, geometry, and mathematics.

The biggest mystery involving Puma Punku is these huge blocks of stones cut in precision and placed in such a perfect manner that attract engineers and constructors around the world today. How did they manage to achieve this type of precision work that architects and engineers around the world today cannot construct or replicate? And how did this ancient mankind manage to transport these huge blocks of quarry stones within ten to one hundred kilometers as an achievement accomplished thousands of years ago that human knowledge cannot answer? These mysteries remain unanswered. Still in Bolivia, at Puerta Del Sol, Gate of the Sun in the Cordillera of the Andes, you're sheltering a Venusian calendar, the oldest of the earth with 225 terrestrial days, testifying no era seen in the city of Tiahuanaco by man.

Your door pierced in your existence has a pediment and a frieze with three rows; with stratospheric suits, equipped with jet and propulsion engines that pierce the peace of the second layer of the terrestrial atmosphere, lying above the troposphere and under the mesosphere, covered with engravings of winged effigies of human heads and the Inca god Viracocha. These fortresses made of large stones demonstrate by excellence the best Neolithic architecture representing the sun god because of the linear marks that surround your face. This human knowledge without any known descendant and difficult to grasp, but much too precious as artifacts of the prehistoric cultural traditions, is scattered between generations and carefully preserved to be passed from one generation to another are rediscovered as cultural traditions, marking their heritage for human to learn from other humans thought encrusted in words.

As the potter, the divine Khnum received the order of Amun to shape the child and his *ka*, the one of the parts composing the human being in his lifetime, known as the spiritual dual, the vital energy nascent at the same time as a human being, which thanks to funerary worship and food offerings, survives after death in the grave; and the other part, the *ba*, known as the soul, a spiritual principle, separates from the body after death. So is the Bolivian god of the Sun on the Gate of the Sun, known as Viracocha in the Andes region of South America, representing the great creator deity in the pre-Inca and Inca mythology and who, despite the facts remains a mystery.

A group of nine deities—Geb, the first divine king of the earth, represents one of the cosmic elements; at the origin, Geb organized the element and the divine royalty, and then the four cosmic elements of creation (Atum = fire, Shu = air, and Tefnut = water) and Geb = earth, were finalized by him on Earth. Gen. 1:9 is considering that God created the earth from water as the secondary material creative element, like a mother gives life to a baby. Shu, the sky and wife of Tefnut, humidity, is associated with water, the morning dew, and order. Shu supports Geb, the earth, by its arms. She represents Tefnut, the masculine atmosphere of the upper world, spat out by Atum; Tefnut is the sister of the air god Shu, the feminine lower world and the mother of Geb and Nut. In 1 Gen. 1:6, associated with water, the primary material creative element, God said "Let there be a firmament in the midst of waters, and let the waters separate waters from waters." And in John 3:5, associated with air Jesus said, "One must be born of water and air to enter the kingdom of God."

Air, the primary nonmaterial creative element, considered as the spirit of the gods is an animating element, and the soul of humans; not being visible but can be felt, seems very mysterious. Gen. 2.7 said, "God formed man from the dust of the earth and breathed the breath of life into his nostrils; and man became a living soul." Air, "spirit" as Jesus called it, means *ruach*, in Hebrew, translated as "wind, breath, or from nephesh," meaning "breathing creature." Spirit (with a capital *S*) is referring to God, and spirit (with a small *s*) as the soul is referring to humans. Nut, the sky, symbolizing the firmament and considered as the mother of all the stars, is far above life. And separated from Geb, her brother and husband by Shu, the father, she is close to those who leave the earth. As a daughter of Shu and Tefnut, Nut, and Shu created the space, differentiation, order, and life. The space is a cosmic element called ether by ancient astrologists.

Nut is the substance that filled all space, the vital breath as the first sigh of creation, where the idea of a self-created God came from; thus the first natural differential of the first time, the single element from which the other four elements came from, the Lord of the (four) Winds and the principle of life itself. Isis, mourning her brother Osiris, sought his members to reanimate him; Osiris, reanimated by his wife and sister Isis, became the king of the Duat and the dead. And through the magic of Isis, his wife and sister, she became pregnant of their child Horus, who by offering his left eye made his father a whole. Magic itself is rejected by religions because of it works "beside" God; and because a priori magic cannot work, the modern science refutes it because it cannot be understood or controlled even if it does happen to work.

Nephthys, as an incessant help of Isis and often coupled with her, is the sister and the wife of Seth. Nevertheless sterile, she was able to give birth to Anubis; he became one of the many sons of Osiris after Osiris took over his position as the original god of dead and chased him away for him not to hurt Horus, his nephew. This son of Nephthys is the one testing the faith and the knowledge of the gods after watching over the process of mummification to be ensured that it's properly done. During the judging of the heart, Anubis, having the same animal totem like Set, places the heart of the death on the scales of justice to feed the souls of the wicked people to Ammit and conduct souls through the underworld.

Ammit, a demon goddess in Ancient Egyptian religion, and in some beliefs, was living near the scales of justice in Duat. She was a funerary deity, the "Devourer of the Dead," "Eater of Hearts," and "Great of Death." Against the feather of Maat, she was weighing the heart of a person in the Hall of Two Truths. The person undergoing judgment had his heart devoured, judged not to have a pure heart. Once devoured, which meant "a second death;" after Ammit swallowed the heart, the soul dies for a second time and becomes restless forever and will no longer be allowed to continue its journey toward immortality and in the light of Osiris.

Seth is evil, known as sexual perversities (like sodomy) associated with violence. As the sworn enemy of Horus, the lord of the desert storms who nevertheless serves Re and who also serves the divine king who sits on the throne of Geb was worshipped as the god of wind. To Isis, his sister, and Osiris, his brother, Set was believed to be their ally who also defended Ra, their father, and to Nephthys, his sister and wife, a counterpart. Although being always a dark and moody god, he granted the strength of the storms to his followers. And the demiurge Atum, the eternal cosmic is differentiated, isolated, luminous, and singular; the first moment of creation started with Atum self-creation before things emerged as a perfect differentiation of perfect energies.

Tefnut, his daughter, representing the identity of life, and Shu, her brother, representing the identity of Maat, existed in the "first moment" of space and time. The "psychic mechanism" representing the core of the original creative intention of Atum as the first moment is the "zep tepi" period, a period that emerged from the primordial chaos of timelessness, when earth was ruled by gods. According to the Pyramid Texts, when the "old" sun dies, it rejuvenates creation to be reborn as the "new" sun; and he regenerated the source of life and order, both in this life and in the afterlife. This group of nine deities representing the sun god Atum and worshipped at Heliopolis was arranged in three rows of three, radiating all forces present in the universe, when the supreme power, Atum, opened the maternal womb of the royal wife to give birth to the child who was in the egg (uterus) of his mother, would reign in the future.

These deities, as the great ennead of Egyptian Heliopolis mythology, surrounded the child that Amun promised royalty at its birth. The androgynous demiurge Atum, the father of Shu, the first exclusively male god, and Tefnut, his sister, like the first couple of sexual gods, gave birth to Geb and Nut, and their children, Osiris, Isis, Set, and Nephthys; so the indestructible bibliography of the great ennead stands as a stone, an ancient megalithic monument and the mysterious ancestral Stonehenge. In your representation, oh, Stone, many scholarly works devoted an intellectual part of their time to you. Having evoked all sorts of hypotheses from the nineteenth century, poetic signs well before the ancient civilizations were assigned to you, because near the dolmen dominating humanity, the soul meditates and consents with the spirit, on what says the shadow of his mouth, concerning the presence of the large ancestral stone. A poetic erudite work in which the ancestral monuments intersect, which involved earth, air, fire, and water, known as the four elements that the earth has to offer us in terms of simpler earthly substances to explain the nature and the complexity of all matter. Today, thanks to technological advances, men have used your works of art, the work of God, his mysterious natural energy of the past, and proudly erected windmills, bunkers, bridges, and huge building projects, as witness of the one who has tamed a teaching of time.

As inspirer of popular legends, you have been assigned more diverse origins, as the virgin or a saint divine supernatural miracle, or even more, the devil work of Gargantua, the giant advocacy of humanist culture, to the exploits of the Epicurean philosophy—a relative doctrine, first of all seeking the pleasure of senses and which consists of profiting from the good things of the universe. Morally, it said: "Be collegially and studiously unlimited to acquire the key of wisdom, understand that we can be happy beings if we desire it, and live in good society; and not be reduced to the restricted dimension of silence needs and the horror of darkness, of a degenerated man, burning with the pleasure of senses, and the intellectual enjoyment of our body."

You're an ancient background that shines through countless popular traditions, a very ancient hidden deity, but benevolent, dating back to a much earlier period. Like a pixie of all pixies, you detain control of forms, and you transform yourself into enormous telluric energies, attributed to that sublime gigantic dimension, also ordering the primordial chaos. The primordial chaos is "in the likeness" of the infinite light and infinite space in certain cosmogonic conceptions; it is often viewed as the disordered state of unformed matter, which preceded the world that existed before the ordered universe, and hidden in the process of creation. This chaos is translated by the opposition of the bad king Picrochole, filled with hatred in an absurd and ridiculous conflict in the Picrocholine war with futile motives, representing much crudity and violence in relation with the thirst for conquest against the good king Grandgousier.

In that conquest, Picrochole attacked the kingdom of Grandgousier, the father of Gargantua, against an insult and the evil attitude of the giant Gargantua toward the neighboring Lord Picrochole. Gargamelle, the daughter of the king of butterflies, a serviceable female with a fine good-looking face, and Grandgousier, who married her, are your parents. You advocate peace, a description that reflects the appetite of life by all excellence. Born of their union, you came out of the left ear of your mother, who bore you in an unusual way in the world. As a child aware of the desired pleasure, you immediately asked for a drink as delicacies. Genealogically, by giants of the past, the pregnancy that lasted longer depended on the perfection of the newborn.

According to custom, your parents were big spenders and eaters. So much milk was needed—yes, much milk, hundreds of thousands of cattle, about seventeen thousand nine hundred and thirteen cows, to feed you, you the child called "Grandgousier as your father cried out at your birth." To breastfeed you and calm you was your Shrove Tuesday, called "Mardi Gras" in French translation, and meaning the day of "fat eating" or "gorging" day. You're a masterpiece, the newborn of perfection conceived for eleven months.

Two colors of the blazon of thy father, white and blue, dressed you, oh, Gargantua! The blue symbolizes heavenly things. The white represents the delights, joy, pleasure, victory and the gaiety of life. Since the ancient times, your colors symbolize contradicting emotions of another color—the one of mourning, symbolizing sadness is the pain experienced at death. Before the intelligence, you learned under the orders of the teachings of the pedagogue Ponocrates, oh, Gargantua! He who made you drink a potion to clean your brain for you to learn subjects like crafts, art, fencing, herbalism, metallurgy, rhetoric and develop your taste of critical spirit for justice.

As a humanist preceptor of the body hygiene, moral and physical exercise, your disciples speak with such ease and such force. Gargantua gives rise to fecundity, to cults of a deity and of the phallic fecundity; the penis being a conscious energy associated with deities such as Osiris, sometimes with a ram's head. Your worship, the fecundity of your stones, was demonized by baptizing your ancient places of worship as diabolic. In a more literary form concerning the day of your legend, attributed by Merlin de Robert de Boron in the late twelfth century to the early thirteenth century, your legend is defined by the erection of your famous enchanter to commemorate the victory of the recovered kingdom of the King Pendragon Uther, the dragon head; he who was branded by his Christianization as an evolution of the myth of King Arthur made the grail a Christian relic by the name of Holy Chalice.

According to him, after the crucifixion, it is known as the vessel of the Last Supper, which collected the blood of Jesus. The Last Supper is therefore, by Christians, the last supper of Christ with his apostles before his death on the evening of the Holy Thursday, three days before his resurrection and before the Jewish Passover. Your whole, forming an alignment of megaliths located in the southwest of England is special. As calculator of observed eclipses at a period distant, you reproduce the configuration of the celestial vault on earth. Formerly, Choir Gaur was your name, meaning "the dance of giants." Your lodge as a discernment was a term of firm convention, used as a place of initiation; and as the stones so large of a past civilization so distant, the human being of great civilizations came to a determinable conclusion of your unknown origin of this world as being from a distant land of Africa, where you were transported to Ireland by the giants for your majestic chastity: the medical point of view generating various important properties related to religious rites, formerly kept secret by your followers.

Your adept, believers and worshippers were feeding you with the element (water) to collect your healing powers. This same element (water) served as baths, prepared at your feet, to heal the sick who were suffering from any disease. And to heal their wounds, this water was mixed with medicinal plants (roots, seeds, bark, and wood) for the extraction of active principles.

You teach wisdom to reason the small canal unable to receive an education, by the transmission system of the first and seventh chakra of the crown and the root located at the top of the skull; vertically oriented upward, connecting your spirit to the cosmic. Your chakras are considered as vortexes energy of the body – the centers of mental energy and the emotional health–the vitality that penetrate the body and the aura of the body to fuel the physical with matured energy and all other elements mentioned here above, to solve our problems at the root level and lead us to spiritual awakening.

The Egyptian priests' knowledge was extremely wide, and the proof is that the most illustrious scholars and philosophers of the world went to learn in their temples. Among those few were Aristotle, Diodorus, Herodotus, Plato, Solon, Thales, and Pythagoras, who drew the best from their teaching. The Egyptian priests of the early dynasties were few and just as Moses said in the Bible; they had direct access to the divine.

The scriptures give us the echoes of the high priests or great initiates of ancient times in the history of the Bible, like Moses himself, who was born in Egypt, in North Africa, who fought Ramses II, the pharaoh who was reigning in Egypt from 1298 to 1232, and who had occult means. Were you not surprised to know that the literary form between the mythology and the Bible—long accounts of creation, the flood, the existence of early man, and his dealings with the gods—is really curious? I think that under these various names, certain biblical and mythological characters are the same. Moses, who was initiated to all mysteries of the Egyptian priesthood, used it for the constitution or otherwise, I will say, reconstitution of the Bible. I assert that the Hebrew Pentateuch and hieroglyphic characters that enabled him to write the first three chapters of Genesis were the sacred writing of the pyramids and the sphinx.

The obelisk of Luxor, which is today found at the Place de la Concorde in Paris, is crowned with mysterious characters belonging to the sacred writings of the Egyptian priests. "Let us make man in our image," as Moses said, is a representation of two eternals, appearing on the two obelisks of Luxor.

Where the first eternal is titled "Ancient of Days, Eternal Soul, and Elohim"— a principal eternal and master of all things, represented as the Lord; the second eternal is titled "the Eternal Pacificator, Second of Glory, and Adonai." As a result, the second person is contained in the first and wrapped with eternal love, and the whole of which constituted the Essential Trinity, "Father, Son, and Holy Spirit." For good reason, I summarized them as such:

> The Eternal Soul is equal to the Father.
> The Eternal Pacificator is equal to the Son.
> And the Eternal Love is equal to the Holy Spirit.

From which Moses, son of one of the pharaohs, founded his monotheism, based and what constitutes the Christian dogma. Here is another striking example of these three symbolic nicknames:

> The King of Fire, the elder (represented by the sun), is the Father.
> The King of Fire, the peacemaker (represented by the moon) is the Son.
> And the King of Fire, very gracious and very charitable (represented by the planet Venus), is the Holy Spirit.

The truth here is that the initiation of Moses pushed his precautions so far that it masked the esoteric doctrine alive in him, and that is why the monotheistic prophet made that the external religion reigns over esotericism. It is under this principle that, for the common man, the shape conceals the substance. In a way, if an Egyptian priest of ancient times enters in a Catholic shrine today, he will have the surprise of his life to see the Passover Lamb as a diminished replica of the memphistic ox and the dove of the Holy Spirit of Thoth, with the ibis head, which will remind him the divine intelligence.

What would the initiate of Serapeum think, he who combined the aspects of Osiris and Apis in a humanized form accepted by the Greeks of Ptolemy of Alexandria, considering the fish as a symbol of the early Christians on the walls of the catacombs; and the uninitiated Romans of the ancient times, who interpreted the Eucharistic communion in the literal sense, and accusing the followers of Peter of eating a little child? Unless you are ignorant or warned, one should not confuse symbolism and idolatry.

One is first struck by the fact that the points of resemblance are not those of an Egyptian but of a Nubian. The prototype of the Great Sphinx is neither a child of Japheth nor a child of Shem but a son of Ham. Nimrod, the son of Kush, was the first father of dictatorship, who later became the first king of mankind, founder of the first empire that came into existence after the flood, around two thousand years before Christ. Like it is said generally and more specifically, he was the inaugurator of wars and the one who grouped men into tribes. Furthermore, I would say that the plan of the pyramid was much anterior to the construction and that the entire knowledge that it contains was the great well of great biblical inspirers like Melchizedek or Enoch. In the Egyptian tradition, the one who brought this plan in Egypt was Sisithros, the grandson son of Enoch. But the architect of the pyramid, said others, was of Nimrod, the most extraordinary builder of the Bible.

Nimrod was the son of Kush, and Kush himself was the son of Ham, the youngest of the sons of Noah. This was what Moses tells us in Genesis: "Kush begot Nimrod: who began to be very mighty on earth. He was a mighty hunter before the Lord." It is from there that this striking formula that said of him, "As Nimrod the mighty hunter before the Lord," came from, and it is a good slogan.

The beginning of his kingdom was Babel, Erech, Akkad, and Kalne, the land of Shinar. He left the country of Assyria and built Babylon, Nineveh, and the streets of the city of Calah and Resen, a city between Nineveh and Calah. This is how Nimrod got the reputation of a great builder across the East. And that was why he was assimilated to Ninus in the construction of Nineveh.

But his greatest and considerable enterprise was that of Babel. According to the texts, the one who was represented as a giant in body and spirit, Ninus (Hercules, Nimrod, or Adonis) was abandoned by his people and was forced, after his architectural failure, to take refuge in other countries.

The great hunter therefore surveyed the primitive earth up to Egypt, where his passage resulted to the first messianic tradition under the guise of Osiris. I'm then permitted to believe that Nimrod (Osiris) was also probably the first reformer of all the pharaohs of Egypt. I must also say that the Egyptian priests had three ways of expressing their thoughts. The first was clear and simple; the second, symbolic and figurative; and the third, sacred or hieroglyphic. This way of expressing thoughts had the key to the high universal primitive language and at the same time, an initiative before Babel. The language of heroes and gods that Moses applied in the first chapter of Genesis, and the key revealed three meanings in the same text.

Fabre Olivet, the author of the restored Hebrew language, says this: "The bad or good interpretations given to the word Beroeshith, offer three distinct meanings. Moses followed the method of the Egyptian priests. The word Beroeshith in Hebrew means: "In the principles of all what follows the principles of abstract principles." Because the same word took at their discretion, the proper sense, the figurative sense or the hieroglyphic sense.

"According to the Essene tradition, every word in this Sepher of Moses contains three meanings—the positive or simple, the comparative or figurative, the superlative or hieratic. When one penetrate to this last sense, all things are revealed through a radiant illumination and the soul of the one enlightened reaches heights than those who are bound to the narrow limits of the positive sense and satisfied with the letter that killeth, will never know that solemn majesty of the sacred things."

Maurice Bardier also said, "After the Babylonian captivity, around the year 536 before Christ, the Jewish nation had completely lost the essential meaning of the texts of the Hebrew language." Fabre Olivet also wrote about it: "He asserts plainly and fearlessly that the Genesis of Moses was symbolically expressed and ought not to be taken in a purely literal sense." Saint Augustine recognized this, and Origen states that "if one takes the history of the creation in the literal sense, it is absurd and contradictory."

"Fabre d'Olivet claims that the Hebrew contained in Genesis is the pure idiom of the Ancient Egyptians, and considering that nearly six centuries before Jesus Christ, the Hebrews having become Jews no longer spoke, nor understood their original tongue, he denies the value of the Hebrew as it is understood today, and undertook the means to restore that language lost for twenty-five centuries. The truth of this opinion does not appear doubtful, since the Hebrews according to Genesis itself they were in Egypt for four hundred years."

"This idiom, therefore, having become separated from a language which attained its highest perfection and was composed entirely of universal, intellectual, abstract expressions, would naturally fall from degeneration to degeneration, from restriction to restriction, to its most material elements; all that was spirit would become substance; all that was intellectual would become sensible; especially everything that was universal." They were just a large body without a soul, and at the very time of Ezra, men had to explain everything as well as they could to the Jewish people in Aramaic, which was their living spoken language. The ancient Hebrew had henceforth passed to the state of a dead language. Claims made by the Anglo-Saxon for the benefit of the recent times were for the exclusive benefits of their race.

Changing the Jesus hair of Kush to blond hair with blue eyes was just a false image or a religious conception of nationalism and spiritual personification. All was already there, well-founded, before any people came to appropriate it. So, there are no elected people.

The chosen people of the Holy Hieroglyphic Scripture or the Holy Scripture itself is general and is certainly not this one or the other because every nation is an ethnic amalgam and at the same time, a spiritual mixture. Here is one of many proofs of the central idea of the Messiah's system, very identical to the Egyptian traditions. I would quote Jesus asking his disciples.

"Have you never read in the scriptures that the stone that the builders rejected has become the cornerstone"? It came from the Lord's doing, and it was a prodigy in our eyes. Of which other stone was it about then? If not, the stone that crowned the Great Pyramid and that could not be both the angular stone and the capital stone equal to the summit? A stone from the top that Jesus specifically indicated, when speaking about his kingdom saying, "You're Peter (which means 'rock'), and upon this rock I will build my church" Yes, Peter became that cornerstone as one of Jesus' disciples in the world.

The church of Jesus, the Christian religion, is built by all qualifications and personification on the basis of an Egyptian stone, highly regarded by insiders, including the sacred writings of all time and the principle of the high initiation. The original teaching of Jesus was unconsciously deformed and folded for material necessities. The more churches became mental and formal, the more they lose sight of the spiritual concept. Each church saw its spiritual primacy decrease to the detriment of the material authority. Jesus agonized at Golgotha only to escape from the miseries of life by ascension. The great eternal myth of the Messianic deliverer was the one of the open grave that no power could longer close.

Luke the Evangelist said, "When the Sabbath was over, Mary Magdalene, Mary mother of James, and Salome bought spices to go and anoint Jesus. And very early on the first day of the week, at the sun rising, they went to the tomb. And they say to one another, 'Who will roll away the stone for us from the entrance of the tomb? And looking up, they saw that the stone was rolled away from the entrance—even though it was very large. And entering the tomb, they saw a young man sitting on the right side, dressed in a white robe, and they were alarmed.

"And he said to them, 'Do not be alarmed. You seek Jesus of Nazareth, who was crucified. He has risen; he is not here." It was the morning of the third day, like the Egyptian recipient after the third night waiting in the sarcophagus, and who have accomplished the three-day ritual of the Secret Mysteries of Isis, representing the resurrection in Christianity.

The three-day ritual, the Secret Mysteries of Isis, experienced in the sarcophagus was practiced for the initiate to free his spirit from his mortal coil and for his soul to fly through the spiritual spheres, wandering from space at the gateways of eternity, to reach illumination. At the end of third day, he returned to himself again after realizing that his body was a house that his soul could slip out without the physical death, and discovering that all the universe was life, progress, and the external growth; and having experienced the great mystery, he achieved the real immortality, indeed an initiate twice born in the light of God.

It is said that "the illuminated Freemason of antiquity, having reached the thirty-third degree" went through these three days mystical passage in the chambers of the Great Pyramid, like many Ancient Egyptian pharaohs, prophets, and scribes of the priesthood entered the portal of the Great Pyramid as men and were coming out as the "Twice Born Ones"—as gods, related to their secret rite of immortality in the sarcophagus. In the Christian religion, it is said that Jesus fulfilled this rite bringing him to the resurrection—to the light of God. It is relative to this resemblance that we must measure the error of theology that made the living Christianity a religion of the crucifix. In the memory of the Crucifixion and under the sign of the crucifix, new crucifixions were fulfilled. The Christian world was completely filled with the idea of the fall and death. Yet, being nailed on the cross and dying on Golgotha, only took place to prepare the liberation of the body, the soul and the spirit from life.

Let us mention that before the resurrection of Jesus, there were at least three resurrections that the Bible presents to us in the Gospels: (John 11) presents us the resurrection of Lazarus; (Luke 7:11-17) that of a young man at Naim; and lastly (Mtt. 5:21-42), the resurrection of the daughter of a certain Jairus; therefore, Jesus was not the firstborn from the dead to resurrect himself. The only difference between these resurrections tells us that the one of the three resurrected is a return to earthly life, unlike that of Jesus, indicating the entry into eternal life, not a return to earthly life.

Christ was not the crucified. In initiation, he was the Risen One, winner over death and tomb in his holy resurrection. Incorruptible, he announced the final fate of all men; through him, death would be no more. On the other hand, Jesus Christ, despite his Eastern origin and despite having played his role in Asia, he mainly exerted an influence in the West. The true Christic territory is Europe, whether in a reformed Catholic form or orthodox. Striking therefore, is the other name of the great Osirian divinity of death that was called Amentiou—which means, "Chief of the Westerners." In the history of humanity, more than ten thousand years before Jesus, the first resurrected among the dead was "Amentiou" (Osiris) Wosire, the one who is, the master of Eternity, the lord of the Maat (truth-justice), and the "Great" and "Mighty" Ancestor. This divine being, perpetually good, was sent to earth by Amun to fight against evil, and he triumphed over evil.

In fact, to decimate kamites, the Semites used Jesus of only two thousand years ago, to claim the paternity of this divine being that the Kamites already knew more than ten thousand years ago in Africa. Jesus is not therefore the only one sent by God or the only resurrected from the dead, if we must believe in this story diverted from Osiris by the Semites. "Amentiou" (Osiris) Wosire, which means hidden region, is one of the names of Hell in Egyptian, where souls go after death. In Egyptian, that underworld stay by the lord and god of the Amentiou was also called the country of truth, and the word.

So, the whole world knew that the knowledge of God was only found in Egypt. They had of course heard of the prodigious knowledge of Egyptian priests and their great mysteries. So, the world had well understood that it wanted that knowledge of God to penetrate into the depths of nature and that it would only find it in the temples of Egypt, in Africa.

From then, the resolution was taken, and the humanity of the four corners of the earth was going to Egypt to be initiated there. Initiation sometimes lasted twenty-two years under the supervision of the pontificate of the high priest Sonchis, who exposed tests, temptations, terrors, and ecstasies to the insiders of Isis, up to the apparent and cataleptic death of followers, and to their resurrection in the light of Osiris. Insiders crossed all these spheres that allowed them to realize the doctrine of the verb *light* or of the universal word and the one of human evolution through seven planetary cycles, not as a vain theory but as a lived thing; cruel but instructive lesson of the history of life after the lessons of the science of God.

Finally, many of these insiders reached the top of the Egyptian priesthood and were only thinking of evil for Egypt. They said to each other, "Let's go erase them from this world for them to cease to be a sovereign nation, a very powerful empire, and so that no one could have remembrance of the name Egypt anymore. Let's take possession of their knowledge, their creations, and their dwellings." From that moment, a serious problem more poignant than a dagger and sharper than the sound of lyre was in front of Egypt, particularly in front of Africans.

The entire earth started shouting, "Fatality! Fatality! Oh! What Fatality!" And heaven was saying, "Providence! Providence!" And the humanity who was floating between the two, was answering, Madness! Madness! Madness!

Oh! What pain! But deep inside itself, Egypt heard another invincible voice of the whole Africa, responding from the deep channels of the earth and the blaze of the heavenly starry sky with this cry: Freedom! Freedom! Freedom! What facts? What reasons? But who therefore had the reason to want to destroy the providential Egypt, which was the sovereignty of the African continent, the educator of the whole wide world in the true sense of the word, and which is still the pride of Africa in the South of all time, squatting in its dense and sandy forest, still questioning the future of its mutilated advent? The invaders, the fighters or the humanity; the craziest, the uneducated or the educated people; were they unhappy men or righteous men endowed with reason but rendering themselves silent to become insensitive objects by the whims of a single being, a mankind, with a power of mind? One thing was certain because all these voices were all telling the truth. Each one triumphing in its sphere, but none delivered it its true purpose.

What an image of the animal nature, unleashed in man who has renounced the dignity of the spiritual state that he received from the creator, and rejecting the greater expensive and beautiful gift of nature to lead to that monster of despotism, which treads everything at its feet, and imposes the reign of the most implacable destiny to humanity, by its ugly apotheosis? It is difficult to understand that for a long time, especially in the primitive centuries, despots of Asia—men jealous of the excess of natural freedom—meditated the loss of that precious freedom rights, which was the grand prize of the existence of Egypt; when the war was declared by one of the previous insiders of that Egypt high as its sphinx, felled in Egypt, and came to melt upon the Nile basin with all its evils and dragged the country of Narmer and Osiris into a new whirlwind. Their brutal and cruel assaults, repeated for centuries, had failed before the invincible wisdom of the Egyptian initiations, before the power of the glorious priesthood and the providential energy of the pharaohs. But the immemorial kingdom, asylum of the knowledge of God, was not to last forever.

Finally, the son of the conqueror of Babylon, Cambyses II from 529 to March 522, king of Persia (the former name of Iran), the successor of Cyrus II from 530 to 522 BC, came to fall upon Egypt with his countless armies, and hungry as swarms of locusts, to put an end to the pharaonic institution in 525, whose origin was not lost in the mists of time. It was a disaster in the eyes of the wise and to the world. It was the beginning of ferocious injustice and an establishment of absolute inhumanity toward the black race; until then, Egypt had covered Europe against Asia. Its protective influence even extended throughout the basin of the Mediterranean by temples of Phoenicia, Greece, and Etruria, with which the high Egyptian priesthood was in constant contact. This boulevard once overthrown, its Egyptian bull was about to melt head down to the shores of the Hellenic convivial establishment on a good night. The great king of Persia Cyrus II of the Achaemenid Empire, from 559 to 550 BC, the father of Cambyses II, was the founder of the Persian Empire after the Median Empire.

To conquer Egypt, Cambyses II appealed to Polycrates after consolidating his possessions in Phoenicia, an ancient region in the north of ancient Canaan. Nowadays, this territory is in Lebanon and certain portions of Syria and Syro-Palestine, of which one side became Israel. Geographically, Cambyses II occupied the classical Phoenicia, the Palestinian region of Western Asia bordered on a course to the west by the Mediterranean Sea, oriented by Mount Taurus to the north, forming the southeast edge of the Anatolian plateau, the sources of the Euphrates to the east, with Arabia in the southeast and south, essentially favorable to the development of ports installation, known for its great sailors at that time to control territory in the eighth century.

Deliberately oriented toward the sea, Cambyses II also occupied Cyprus to continue his threatening hostilities of the Persian army toward Egypt. Thus, Cambyses II secretly concluded an alliance with Polycrates of Samos to properly lead his war project, carefully planned for the conquest of Egypt. His tactic was surely to have the reinforcement of Syloson, the brother of Polycrates of Samos, who commanded the fleet of the island for Egypt, with its two maritime forces of Phoenicia and Cyprus. And by a powerful fleet, Cambyses II marched on Egypt and overthrew the last pharaoh of the Twenty-Sixth Dynasty, Psamtik III, who reigned from 526 to 525 BC.

The circumstances of this war were caused by the same errors of the pharaoh Psamtik I, also spelled Psammetichus (664 to 610 BC), who embraced the same Carian mercenaries. The head of the Carian troops by the names of Phanes of Halicarnassus and Polycrates of Samos, whom the last pharaoh Psamtik III considered as his allies and who particularly had an extensive knowledge of the access roads of Egypt, betrayed him at the end to join Cambyses II.

They first conquered Gaza; Gaza Strip, as a bridgehead between the doors of the delta, became their access routes for all their campaign against Egypt.

Cambyses II crossed the Sinai with his army, helped by Arab tribes who were supposed to be friends of Egypt, but replenished the water supply to its enemies. And in spring 525, with reinforcements and the aid, Cambyses II's victory was only a matter of time to achieve.

The Persian army then invaded the delta after crushing the Egyptian army at Pelusium and continued its progress toward Memphis without great resistance. Polycrates, the all-powerful master of the Cyclades and its first Carian inhabitants, Phanes of Halicarnassus, an important mercenary, head of Carian troops of the pharaoh and Arab tribes rose to overthrow Egypt and past its reign under the control of Persians. The end of Saite Egypt by conquest against the Kushites was proclaimed by Cambyses II, and Egypt became an administrative division of the Persian Empire by founding the Twenty-Seventh Dynasty with Cambyses II, established as pharaoh by the clergy of Sais. After only six months of reign, Psamtik III, who had already taken refuge, was defeated; and by this new defeat, he lost the reign as pharaoh forever.

Its students, after all, have decided to demolish its monuments and share its obelisks and its valuable art objects among themselves to finally decorate the monuments of Western countries. On top of that, they have already decoded their hieroglyphics but still remains for them to penetrate in the deep vault of their thoughts. It is these hieroglyphics in these demolished temples, its crypts, and its pyramids that the famous doctrine of God was developed and elaborated as a universal word that Moses reformed in his Golden Ark and from which Christ became a living torch.

The fall of our Egypt was caused by the same mistakes we still commit until today: selling the land of our ancestors and revealing their most intimate secrets. These mistakes took effect since the year 663 BC, when the Assyrian king Ashurbanipal, from 669 to 627 BC, invaded for the total conquest of Egypt, the submission of Babylon, and the destruction of the Elamite Empire, forcing the Kamite king of Kush Tanutamun, king of Napata and pharaoh from 664 to 656, to live in exile.

His successor, the Kamite Psamtik I, a black pharaoh from 663 to 609 BC, considered by the Egyptian people as a traitor, committed mistakes that we regret until today. It was during the Ionians' and the Carians' escapade in search of booty that they approached Egypt. Pharaoh Psamtik I, who wanted to get rid of his Kamite brothers and the Assyrian invaders, began to give them parts of our ancestral land for the service of these mercenaries. Apart from these few infiltrations, the pharaonic Egypt belonged entirely to the entire black African world until 525 BC.

These mercenaries that Pharaoh Psamtik I had kissed consisted of two groups. The first group, the Greeks, was only interested in our scientific knowledge (mathematics, geometry, astronomy, philosophy, etc.). The second group, the Carians, which according to some historians were Semitic (Jews), was only interested in acquiring the basics of our religion to establish their religious philosophy. Thus, Psamtik I opened the gates of the mystery of mysteries of our ancestral land to these two groups, which could no longer be deported because they were already landowners.

They also had our knowledge, which made that, from a few teaching bridges of the history of our Fera Akounaatona, Greeks were able to invent *Oedipus* by Sophocles, from 495 to 405, and the Jews Moses—by (Ezra) in 398 before Christ. So we can understand that the primary responsibility for the propagation of our knowledge was Psamtik I; and we can agree that when a people gives out its scientific knowledge, its land, and its religion to another, there is nothing secret remaining for this people and its nation is no longer safe from assault.

This explains the great miracle of the Greek knowledge by Thales of Miletus, who was the first student of the Egyptian Kamite priests from 640 to 547 BC; Pythagoras of Samos, who was the favorite of the Kamite priests of Egypt and who well knew how to keep the sacred side of our knowledge from 580 to 490 BC; and Archimedes from (287 to 212).

That is why I conclude that black people are politically the most naïve nation in the world, and this is historically true because we practically take in everything that comes to us and everybody presented to us without question. We can see this naivety in Psamtik I, who gave his land to strangers and opened his secret mystery castles. After being taught, they then insulted us with bad offending language by saying that the African continent has made no contribution to civilization and that it started in Greece. For centuries, Africans accepted the praise and honor given to the Greeks, while the true authors of civilization rightfully belonged to the people of Africa.

Many of the false information are found in the historical thought of erudite scholars, resulting on the historical falsifications and racial prejudices. The theft of this great African legacy is an unforgivable act, a legacy wrongly credited to the arrogant Europe, and it is what made them feel superior to other races.

You cannot come to someone's home and steal his civilization, his arts and sciences, his philosophy, his cultural patrimony and use it as an insult to enslave him. Conversely, these great ancient achievements have led them without embarrassment to cling at the altar of the supposed superiority, to not admit the works of the ancient African continent in the civilization of the world. The intellectual theft of African heritage is the greatest crime that Europe committed against the world, and we, as Africans, have no choice but to vigorously argue and contest it. The European arrogance would have been diminished if their scholars had not falsely claimed what is certainly not theirs or had correctly indicated with truth, the contribution of Africa to the human civilization. The truth would have set Africans free and not be held in such self-contempt. But our strengths and weaknesses are the reasons of our betrayal.

Quite frightening is that those who still solicit our help today, by telling us a lot of good things, will turn against us tomorrow after obtaining it. At that early period, they came back and conquered us to better destroy our so wellfounded civilization. In the same vein, without learning from our mistakes, we repeatedly invite the wrong strangers to dinner, gave them our wealth and our women, and forbade them to tell about what they experienced as sentimental lyric. We continue being hospitable to the wrong strangers around the world, just like we have been with the latecomer, the white race, to whom we taught all inspirations. Before they were allowed into our temples, we first invited them to dinner and educated them by initiation as neophyte members of our secret order. They obtained grades through teaching administered orally with a pledge on oath to secrecy for what was given to them; but without manifesting any loyalty to our relationships, they instead went to unveil the strengths and weaknesses of Africans to the one called Alexander the Great to come and conquer Africa. The invasion of Alexander the Destroyer let the Greek gain access to all our ancient books by plundering libraries and temples. He allowed Aristotle, who was his tutor until the age of sixteen, to build his own school with African knowledge and gained the reputation of the wisest man who ever lived. For over two hundred years, the Greeks stayed in Africa and were initiated into great indigenous African mysteries from 2,500 to 3,000 years ago.

In the same sense, indigenous African mysteries created religion that the Jews finally used as base for slave trade against us. Arabs turned against us after we created Islam for them; they used it against us to justify the Arab slave trade after years of fruitful partnership. We created socialism, which an African king was preaching around 1,300 years before the birth of Christ; they also found our strengths and weaknesses and then again finally turned against us when they newly discovered the concept.

This is the truth about our past that we didn't sooner discover to not be cringing to their altar or the characteristic practice of the people of the West, who are using almost every stolen ideas from us, particularly the complex religious system called the mystery of mysteries that we taught to the world, to finally urge them, to a supposed son of an imaginary god; a sacrilege, I may say.

The Chaldeans and the Babylonians refused to publish all secret teachings they had studied under the Egyptian masters, not like Aristotle and Plato, the usurpers, who published all the Egyptian secret teachings into book forms and claimed their authorship. Aristotle was credited with a number of books that the age of our word-processing software could not write and that a single man could not imagine writing. Which made him be regarded as the greatest erudite of antiquity. But on the other hand, just being the original source of a false idolized model of intellectual greatness and his death marked the death of philosophy among the Greeks.

You see, the black man's hospitality to strangers is the best humanitarian relationship in the world. But by revealing the simple fundamental truth about the theft of his legacy by the Greeks and other nations in the world, his hospitality to strangers sucks; it is objectionable, offensive, and arousing disapproval.

When Ionia was a colony of Egypt, Egypt held sway over a large part of the known world at the apex of its glory. After the fall of Egypt, Ionians became the Persian subjects before becoming Greek citizens, from the eighth century BC., where the first forms of science and philosophy were developed in the West.

The manifestations of the black man's hospitality to strangers gave an opportunity to a partly African group of people living in Asia, considered shepherd kings, after being raised from their former slave status about 1,600 years ago. These shepherd kings invaded Egypt for many years. Egyptians broke their backs during their stay in Egypt and then finally drove them out to take the destiny of their lives in possession and at last establish peace throughout Egypt.

CHAPTER THREE

THE ORIGIN OF THE BIBLE

The African is the innovator in the traditional field of spirituality, the sacred and religion. So, let's go back to the time when our ancestors determined the enterprise of spirituality, the sacred, divinity, religion, and civilization from a technical and practical point and study their technique to understand their workings. Because the terms "African," "Nigger," and "Black" came from abroad, which transformed our history into folklore because of the absence of truth; compared to the daily experiences inflicted on blacks by the Jewish, Christian, and Islamic religions, basically, African religions diverted by the invaders, borrowed to slavers and to colonizers, who blasphemed them. So why are the "mysteries" of the earliest indigenous written texts of African origin, as well as the first documentation of the monotheistic religion developed in Africa, not recognized as the indigenous works of African, indeed illuminating the world?

However, it is ultimately known that the indigenous traditional African spirituality of sub-Saharan Africa—from Egypt, the high cultures along the Nile, and other parts of Africa—forms the Western religions today and that the Greek philosophy, stolen from Africans, is full of racism. That philosophy, our "love and wisdom," existing since the Antiquity of knowledge and human existence, was known as our mode of life of rational activity in the world.

How much longer are we to remain its outsiders? Do we really want an approval from the whites to acknowledge our influence and creativity of what is really called religion today? I have many questions but have no answer. Literally, we all know that it is the history of African philosophy that led to critical ref lection and questioning about the world and allowed to apprehend its evolution. From ancient times, our ancestors conceived philosophy as an activity of creation and meditation; a concept considered as a search for truth for the definition of good, evil, beauty, happiness, peace, and justice in the meaning of life. At the time when our ancestors conceived its definitions, wisdom was the science of the first principles and the first causes, and today its remains known as at the time of our ancestors. Historically, it is linked to a set of disciplines such as the human and social sciences, the formal sciences and the natural sciences.

It engendered the theory of ethics and logic, the theory of knowledge, metaphysics, and political philosophy as fundamental studies. Ramifications like philosophical anthropology, or language philosophy, aesthetics and spirit philosophy, philosophy of law, (epistemology) and the philosophy of science. All these branches were conceived by our ancestors for the search of truth at the course of time. Very early, they were understood not only as a theoretical ref lection but also as a way of life.

Our ancestors were not content merely to confront abstract questions; they acted and lived in a certain way because they tended toward wisdom, according to the etymology of the term *philosophy*, as philosophers. They were especially looking for happiness, therefore sought to live properly, by emphasizing on the application, understood as a way of life in their own lives, to guide others and help them lead on their lives in good manner. Around a philosopher in antiquity, a real community of life was constituted and had a collective project or even political.

Around the epic of Plato or Aristotle for example, philosophical schools were generated, which partly explains these "collective" ambitions of philosophy. From the pre-Socratics, who lived before Socrates from the middle of the seventh century BC until the fourth century BC, and especially from Socrates (470–399 BC), the Stoics, Plato, Aristotle, Epicurus, Descartes, Spinoza, Sartre, or Russell, this conception of philosophy as a fashion of life was forbidden.

They cannot deny the indigenous African origin of their religions because numerous ancient manuscripts were preserved in African libraries, as in Ethiopia and Timbuktu; but today they're disillusioned and conceived as a mind-numbing drug by whites to anesthetize people's minds just to fill up their unscrupulous pockets.

It is known that great amount of books with useful information about African religion and spiritual beliefs were written before the dark ages of European colonialism that came and destroyed the aspects of our traditional culture and eventually stole and modified our written texts to rewrite them for scholarly purposes; but with false statements of our traditional cultures, misrepresentations, and numerous racist characterizations; if we refer to Christianity, Islam, and Judaism, we could notice that Africa is the home of a rich religious heritage, primarily written in Ancient Egypt by African.

For over three thousand years, the Ancient Egyptian civilization lasted longer than the entire accepted recorded history in the world, which developed esoteric practices, as well as a multitude of gods and goddesses and then, under the pharaoh Akhenaton, the first true monotheistic religion propaganda of the world.

The early Ancient Egyptian pyramids at Sakkara, where we could find funerary inscriptions written on the walls, dating back from the Fifth and Sixth Dynasties, are believed to be the oldest sacred texts known in the world, approximately from 3000 BC.

Through thousands of years of Egyptian history, the evolution of religious belief covers religions from the earliest Osirian beliefs up to the ground-breaking monotheism of Akhenaton. Therefore, I essentially refuse the ideas of those who say that African religious beliefs are similar to those of the European people because to me, European religions are the belief systems taken from Africa to the rest of the world.

Oh, Africa! There is no continent that can rival the most romantic and the most tragic mystery that you have lived. Africa! You're the refuge of God Almighty and the gods, and your name reveals mysteries of the celestial kingdom. In your land, the land of blacks, which represent one of the most ancient human being in human history, your typical race is rare among Negroes. You're the potential source of richness with wealth like ebony, diamond, gold, ivory, rubber, and so forth.

Oh, Africa! You're the land of Kush, which nevertheless wrote the universal history. The old kingdom of Punt, the trading partner of your Ancient Egypt, betrayed you. But the sphinx is still sitting at the entrance of your land to protect you from the lotus-eater's race. The Arabian, Beja, Bedouin, Tuareg, etc., are you children.

A widespread assumption of inferiority marks the loss of humanitarian humanity throughout the domination of your land by whites, with unreasonable prejudice against your color, assumed to be the harmful truth to the white men. Your pacific cultures particularly detailed as taboos in divination, magic, prophecy, sorcery, sexual practices, and sacrifice are just as much as cultural and spirituality progressive view of my time that can be developed if allowed.

The roots of religions like Judaism, Christianity, and Islam are exclusively indigenous traditional African religions, preached by Africans of Central Africa and along the Nile River water course. The rite of passage involving a change of status in society, known as *okuyi*, is practiced in Equatorial Guinea and by several Bantu ethnic groups. Across the west coast of Central Africa, different countries like Cameroon and Gabon practiced this same rite of passage. Among the Lundas, the popular gods are frequently invoked; but the Nzambi god, a higher entity considered as the highest deity of the pantheon, is rarely invoked.

In West Africa, Shango is one of the most popular religions in the history of Africa. Its god (Olodumare) is the supreme god with three manifestations: he is the creator (Olorun), the ruler of the heavens (Olofi), and the channel between heaven (Orun) and earth (Aye).

In their spiritual or indigenous, traditional religious system, Orishas is a deity or spirit manifestation of god known as the god of fire, lightning, and thunder; originating from different regions of Africa as a mixture of traditions from the Bantu people; with an area geographically stretching eastward and southward from Central Africa across the African Great Lakes region down to Southern Africa.

The core of the Bantu family itself was located in the region that is today known as Cameroon and eastern Nigeria. About three thousand years ago, they began their expansion, one of the largest in human history, from the original core of the African continent; first introducing Bantu people to the center, which included Burundi, the Central African Republic, Chad, the Democratic Republic of Congo, and Rwanda; they continued across the African Great Lakes, a series of lakes constituting the part of the Rift Valley lakes, and around the East African Rift, including Lake Victoria, the second largest freshwater lake in the world bordering three countries; and Lake Tanganyika, the second largest in volume and the longest freshwater lake, as well as the second deepest in the world and the deepest in Africa. Bantu people were introduced in all these regions.

The African Great Lakes region includes countries like Burundi, the Democratic Republic of Congo, Kenya, Rwanda, Tanzania, and Uganda. And they were all along introduced in the region down to Southern Africa, the southernmost region of the African continent, including the Republic of South Africa; the regions where no Bantu people were originated previously at all.

The Bantu groups nowadays include millions of people known as the Luba of the Democratic Republic of Congo, indigenous to the Katanga, Kasai, and Maniema with over 13.5 million people; the Zulu of South Africa, the largest ethnic group in South Africa, with an estimated ten to eleven million people living mainly in the province of KwaZulu-Natal; and the Kikuyu of Kenya, with over six million people. A small number also live in Zimbabwe, Zambia, Tanzania, Mozambique, etc., counting over three hundred to six hundred ethnic groups and 535 languages spoken by most populations of sub-Saharan Africa, nowadays Bantu regions.

The indigenous Africans who once occupied the lands around the major great lakes of Central Africa, known as the Nile River, were the ones who developed the "mysteries of Egypt." God Ra (Egypt) was the brother of the god Olodumare and many other known divinities.

God Ra (Egypt) gave birth to the Christian, the Judaic, and the Islam gods; and the god Olodumare gave birth to several religions of the New World, like Santeria in Cuba and Puerto Rico, voodoo in Haiti, and candomble in Brazil and most of the Caribbean countries. According to the Yoruba legend, Olodumare, the supreme god, was the creator of the world. St. Augustine is the one who developed the early Christian Church. Moses, who is represented as Hebrew of the Jewish religion, was an indigenous African; I will not have enough to repeat that. The river Nile, where they said they found Moses floating down in a bulrush basket, begins in Uganda. He is the one who created that catastrophic consternation among theological racists.

What is today known as the Koran of the Islamic faith was the work of two indigenous Africans from East Africa, precisely men from Ethiopia. These two former slaves and educated men put down the basic documents of Islam and many of their original prayers and doctrines worshipped by Muslims. The so-called Western religions are offering us the incorrect history of our African religions' origin by presenting us Jesus Christ with blue eyes and blond hair as our deity—a representation of a white man, our suppressor—and it is accepted universally. After the destruction of African civilization, white folks defined our reality by dehumanizing us for our souls to be saved. African religions find their way throughout the world and are today expressed in practices of a number of related religions developed among enslaved Africans in countries such as Argentina, Brazil, Cuba, Colombia, Dominican Republic, Guyana, Haiti, Jamaica, Puerto Rico, Panama, Suriname, Trinidad and Tobago, United States, and Uruguay, including some European countries like Germany, Italy, France, Portugal, Spain, and Asia.

These religions were derived from the traditional African religions, especially of West and Central Africa, generally involved in the veneration of ancestors and/or a pantheon of divine spirits such as the Loas of the Haitian voodoo and in Louisiana, known as the New Orleans voodoo; developed by the Central and West Africans populations of the United States, as traditions of the African diaspora. Voodoo is a collective folklore term for "African traditional religions" practiced by the Ewe people of eastern and southern Ghana, the Kabye people, Mina people, and Fon people of southern and central Togo; the southern and central Benin, under a different name from the Yoruba of southwestern Nigeria.

The Candomble Jeje is practiced primarily in Brazil; the word *Jéjé* means "stranger" in Yoruba language, thus representing the Yoruba slaves in that region. As one of the major branches of Candomble, Candomble was developed by Ewe and Fon people. Orishas is also a Yoruba religious tradition, originating from Africa. Anago, Oyotunji, and Umbanda are all spirits or deities of a Brazilian religion that mixed African religions with Catholicism spiritism and considerable indigenous traditions, like Winti in Suriname, based on three principles: first, the belief in Anana Kedyaman Kedyanpon as the supreme creator; second, the veneration of the ancestors; and, third, the belief in Winti pantheon spirits.

Apuku is also a belief among the Afro-Surinamese traditional religion known as the anthropomorphic forest spirits. Both men and women can be possessed by Apuku. They're also known to be water spirits, such as Watra Ampuku, because it can also pass itself off as another spirit. This religious belief originated from the Akan slaves of the Dutch Empire in South America. Akan populations are mainly settled in Ghana and Ivory Coast in West Africa.

The spiritual religion called Obeah is designating occult magic; Obeah is a religious practice derived from West African, specifically from the Igbo origin, and it is a term used in the West Indies territory to refer to folk magic and sorcery; note that Obeah is a word of African origin; Obeah is practiced in Suriname, Jamaica, Trinidad and Tobago, Dominica, Guyana, Barbados, Grenada, Belize, the Bahamas, and other Caribbean countries.

Because slaves were not authorized to practice their own religions, African people in the New World syncretized their deities with the Roman Catholic saints, so voodoo altars frequently have Catholic figures displayed, such as Ayizan, meaning "Holy Land" or "Sacred Land," syncretized with the Catholic Franciscan St. Clare, St. Peter or St. Lazarus, Saint Philomena, St. Michael the Archangel, St. Jude, and John the Baptist became Loa-spirit in their own most notably right. Santeria, a syncretic religion of West Africa, also known as La Religion, Regale de Ocha, La Regla Lucumi, or Lukumi, was syncretized with Roman Catholicism. Lucumi is a liturgical language known as Yoruba with prayers, chants, and songs spoken by practitioners of the Santeria religion, originally from the language still spoken in Nigeria today.

Various traditional African religions from Congo to Angola are syncretized with Christianity. The indigenous African religions' lineage grows worldwide with over one hundred million adherents to its spiritual systems. It is suggested by some scholars that Yoruba dynasties are descendants of the aristocracy of ancient Assyria because of their shared Afro-Asiatic and Indo-European roots.

Between the Yoruba religion, the ancient Mesopotamian religion, Egyptian religion, Berber religion, Arabian religion, Semitic religion, Indo-Iranian religion, Greek religion, and Roman religion, there are numerous similarities, like St. Peter or St. Lazarus, Ayizan or St. Clare, St. Philomena, Archangel Michael, St. Jude, and John the Baptist. The myth of African belief is a notion of traditional African religions practiced in the sub-Saharan Africa and represents all religions not attached to the Old Testament. African societies have religious practices since their creation. Its believers were working on the consistency of virtue of revelation to revelation and from knowledge to knowledge, up to the most sublime discovery of oneself.

They were rising to the gods and descended among the dead, as living and humans by the force of their will. They preserved the truth that was not vainly giving to all as worthy initiates, who have reached the highest degree of science and sacred doctrine, after a silence oath on the law of mysteries. Their traditional African religions, the (sacred doctrine) did not practice any syncretism, resulting in a change of elements and its fundamental principles or a mixture within its religious system was not assimilated to any another religion among practices of the said African religions.

Traditional ancient African religions are full of mysteries; their belief in reincarnation, characterized by the ancestor worship that remains an initiatory aspect, is a single model and a common basis; in the majority of lineage cases, several elements in the traditional conception are considered, such as the matrilineal kinship and the totemism system—the practice of regarding a totem as mystically related to a family, a clan, a group, or a system of tribal division according to tribal organization based on the principle of totem.

Totem is feared because it is sacred, and we do not use it, and it is not to be consumed. View religion, its pattern of behavior, an organizational requirement, represents the foundation of the institutions of esoteric science, its integral science and religious principles, and its indestructible foundations. If you know the law of life, you will evaluate it. If you know the law of the universe, you will know the number; and if you know the law of God, you will have unity. Moreover, where the science of the soul and art of divination comes, it shall open the three doors of the hereafter for you. In addition, you will recognize yourself there as a knowledge of sleep, dream, and ecstasy.

Europeans became the owners of our African Christian religion developed by St. Augustine. It was known that in the mother church, a black woman was teaching Christian catechism to white people at the first school of catechism of all North Africa in the first monastic order of monks. This black woman was killed by Zealot who could barely read or write with violence without advocacy in her academy.

And for her not to be made a martyr, her bones were thrown into the sea by that fanatic person. One of the Zealots group known as a Jewish sect was the "fourth Jewish Zealots sect," founded by Judas of Galilee. They have an inviolable attachment to liberty and fanatically uncompromising in pursuit of their religious, political, or other ideals. It was marked as a group having some thought during the period of the first Jewish-Roman war of 66 to 73 CE, by Josephus. In the Acts of the Apostles (Acts 1:13) and in the Gospel of Luke (6:15), the one selected by Jesus as his apostle by the name of Simon was a Zealot. The other three Jewish sects founded by Judas are: Pharisees, Sadducees, and Essenes.

When the father of the history of Christendom named St Augustine died in 430 CE, the mother church started its decline and lost control. Africans are the only nation in the world who allows this sort of hospitality to strangers year after year, now over three thousand years.

"I am the Eternal. . . I am the Word [verb] which *IS* before the scripts" is the gospel of St. John, found in chapter 85 of the first verse of the Book of the Dead. According to these great royal funeral rituals of the Old Kingdom, the deceased after death had to travel; the spirit had to be prolonged by a formula better adapted to express its journey in the afterlife and reach its true home in heaven. Its goal was to reach the light, the beneficent sun generator of life, and to ensure a better access to the eternal life and safeguard its soul and its body in the heart of light and melt with it and into it under its protection. The expression "coming forth by day" symbolized life and represented the supreme desire of the dead to unite with the many blessed celestial entities around the sun during the hours of sunlight.

The references that I'm going to mention here are based on countless written and published versions of the Bible since the true original version was written by Africans about 3,400 years before the Old Testament and more than 4,200 years before the New Testament. These references follow sequence, both originals and versions of the Old and New Testaments. From the Ninth to the Twelfth Dynasty, the period of 2160 to about 1700, it was first named "the Book of Two Paths" or "the Sarcophagus Texts" under the period of the Middle Kingdom by Pharaoh Unas, the last ruler of the Fifth Dynasty of Egypt, from 2353 to 2323 BC. He succeeded Djedkare Isesi, around 2381 to 2353. The pyramid of Unas, the first pyramid with texts, was discovered by Gaston Camille Charles Maspero in 1881, when he was the director of the Egyptian Archaeology Museum in Bulaq and the Egyptian Antiquities Service in Cairo.

The funerary temple, the shrine of Unas, in the north of Saqqara, defying time on the edge of the desert, is covered with hieroglyphs, forming the first copies of the Pyramid Texts. These first copies of the texts are shown on the walls of the burial chamber and widely developed in the Sixth Dynasty of Teti, the first king and founder of the Sixth Dynasty, around 2323/2321 to 2291.

The pyramid of Merenre I, among others, also revealed the funerary texts to us—namely the religious and ritual texts of the edges between two dimensions in which one of the limits is the world of the death, concerning several religious pharaohs such as Unas, Pepi I, and Pepi, the high priest of Ptah under the reign of Psousennes I, to only name those few, who are the ones who formed the set of functions as the most appropriate spiritual ritual formulas to accomplish the funeral passage after the living dimension. Some of these Pyramid Texts represent numerous testimonies about the lives of many pharaohs; on everyday life and on ancient religious life, throughout the history of Ancient Egypt, in the royal and burial tombs, and in Temple's radiating spiritual knowledge dating back from the first dynasty, the reign of the second king Hor-Aha, (numbered 3357) as the oldest tomb, representing all these elements and images.

These images of everyday life and representations of food, used things, and cultural elements in the form of little statuettes given as servants to the dead, were to defend them in the ancient tombs and perform their civic duties in the life beyond. These practices, evolving from the Second Dynasty, were born for the first time and after many changes, led to a new type of burial. They had to be left in their graves, representing all the things that the deceased had used, for the deceased to find them on his way in the afterlife. Admittedly, the first African, the Egyptian, and the first pharaohs really believed in immortality of the human beings in their time to honor the deceased in such manner.

Toward 2600, the first stone pyramid of Egypt was built by Imhotep, meaning "the one who comes in peace is with peace"; he was the great priest of Heliopolis who worshipped the sun god Re; he entered the history of architecture as the architect of Djoser, first king of the Third Dynasty in the history of Ancient Egypt BC after the archaic period—the Thinite period of Ancient Egypt, around 3000, and ending around 2700; then the appearance of state was established, including the time of the Third, Fourth, Fifth, and Sixth Dynasties of the kings in Egypt.

At that time of the Third Dynasty, after dethroning Nefertoum, the powerful son of Ptah, Imhotep—who in all regions took care to cure all diseases by a call—historically reformed the Egyptian religion, introducing the Osirian myth. Considered the founder of Egyptian medicine, he was the oldest known pharaoh in history who left us writings about treating several diseases and surgery. The oldest document, the Edwin Smith Papyrus, was probably written by him.

This first known written document dealing with surgery was the oldest known document that used the word *brain*. It was probably copied in the Sixteenth and Seventeenth Dynasties of the New Kingdom of Ancient Egypt, around 1500 BC. A vendor sold this papyrus in 1862 to Edwin Smith at Thebes. It established the link between the brain and body functions. And it was the Egyptologist James Henry Breasted who translated this papyrus and published it in 1930, recognizing in particular the functions and the provision in functional anatomy of forty-eight medical conditions. Apart from various references of surgical procedures, including anatomical and clinical procedures like the skull bones, the external surface of the cerebral cortex, the cerebrospinal fluid and intracranial pulsation, suture of chest wounds, meninges, and trauma, it describes preventive or curative treatments to be applied on numerous cases in great detail; and its prognosis, associated with its treatment of the head, closure of surgery, cognitive functions, immobilization of head injuries and spinal cord, etc., concerning the body of living beings that we know today, reached us by this oldest medical text.

This Edwin Smith Papyrus, known hitherto, that contains a practical guide of medical care, was also one of the first to theorize medicine based on magic by a copy of a text, the first writing for specific surgery, and is dating as more ancient as seven hundred years. His translation demonstrated the medical knowledge of the Ancient Egyptians to the Western world, compared to what it thought complacently, up to the various incantations and various receipts.

According to the composition of the human being, every human has some ten tangible and intangible components in him. These components, integrating him into the earthly sphere of the sensible and the ethereal realm of the ancestors and gods, are beyond the simple duality between the soul and the body. So, the human being, who is hoping for a posthumous survival in the grave gracefully with its ethereal components after death, besides the supernatural powers regulating in the cosmic phenomena, survives an immortal existence.

This attainment of the breath of life (Ankh) is only possible through the effective control of Heka magic and respect of the truth of the principles of Maat (truth and justice) during human life—namely, by an inner power allowing him to assimilate himself to the gods judged to be free from sins. So, from the underworld to heaven, Imhotep wants to symbolize the ascension of his deceased body, rising by a gigantic staircase, in the form of a pyramid erected toward the sky.

It is from the one at the point of Philae, known as Imhotep, the father of the Egyptian spirituality, that we also owe the three words *Akh*, *Ba*, and *Ka*, which form the three elements of the triangle of African spirituality in Egypt; *Akh* represents the point, *Ka* the base, and *Ba* the mounted energy on the body of a bird in the form of a human head, ready to fly freely, circulating between the other two.

For the rehabilitation of the soul, it can reincorporate it in a new mortal body until the soul's consciousness become conformed with the sublime light of the perfection of the divine *Akh* and make it rise to the Creator after death. Imhotep perpetuated this religious instruction, which already started four hundred years before him. And the multitude of Ancient Egyptian gods would grow by his descendants, who worshipped the cult of the great, unique, invisible God (Ptah), long before the Bible was written. Thus, the mystery of the message of the eternal, the existence of one unique and invisible God, inspiring them the story of the resurrection, was known in Africa, especially in Egypt, before the birth of the patriarchs.

I would also like to mention that Abraham and Ishmael bequeathed a famous black stone that also bore these two sacred syllables of *Ka* and *Ba* of the Muslim posterity. It was even said that it was Abraham and his son Ishmael who rebuilt the Kaaba, the sacred mosque of Mecca, which means "cube" in Arabic. This concept of reincarnation appeared in the Pyramid Texts found in the royal tombs, and it was not new.

Despite the changes of many civilizations, many similarities exist in this imbroglio of mysteries. Let's simply say that everything is not solely random! That's why the sea that is located between the eastern parts of Sinai is today called the Gulf of Aqaba, and it is the same name given to the city of Aqaba, between Sinai and Saudi Arabia. The two spellings of *Ka* and *Kha*, under the same consonance, have two similar nuances. It is under the form of two hieroglyphs or different phonetic drawings that these words are written. *Kha*, which represents the mortal body, is symbolized by a migratory bird (stork), while *Ka* consists of two human arms raised toward the sky in a prayerful attitude.

The *Ba*, an immaterial component of gods, is the soul of men, and the body of man, like the *Ka*, is translated by the expression "*Soul-Ba*." The *Ren*, a part of the individuality of the deceased Vital for his journey to the afterlife, was often alongside of *Ba*, including the body and the shadow, recognized existing in heaven, the soul could then live a blissful esprit in the afterlife like *Akh*, as long as the given name at birth was spoken; and if he fulfills these aspects inscribed on multiple places of the tomb, protected by formulas and preserved with satisfaction, he becomes a glorified spirit, the breath of life.

A postmortem status of more than one element like the psychic elements *Ba*, which represents a bird with a human head, the aspect of the free soul of the deceased, is the coming forth by day out of the tomb with more important relationships, presently united with the mummy. And *Ka*, the body, the principle of life, evolving in the tomb, nourished on food, water, incense, and formulas as funerary offerings, to maintain itself for the coming forth by day and continue to satisfy *Ka* unlikely to the soul-ba free of movement. *Ren,* the name and *Shut*, the shade, among other elements of personality, are closer to our conception of the soul, in the Book of the Dead.

After being glorified in the regeneration and solarization in his glorious apparition assimilated to RA, to the annihilation of death, his consciousness in itself and the fullness of his vital energies are evoked by words, repulsing the powers of destruction and mastering the elements (water, fire, etc.) of the cosmic, regenerating the emergence in the divine light, an accomplishment of the total transfiguration of the deceased is realized. Now is the time of the test of the divine judgment, and the guarantors of the divine law of Maat, the forty-two gods, known as supreme judges before Osiris, will judge him.

If he passes the test, the sacred bark will lead him to the mysteries in the Duat, where he will move under all forms desired as he pleases; to enter in the house of the god Osiris and render him homage in the Duat. Solarized at his embarkation, the deceased becomes multiple cults rendered on the occasion of certain festivals in the universe as the manifestation of Noun; an auto-generated primary substance of abyssal water from which emanated Atum-Ra, the demiurge himself by a long-term complex gestation, entirely alone in Noun, when he emerged from the womb, before he gave birth to other gods of the Ennead; and when he began to govern what he created and other deities such as "the masculine principle, the god of air Shu," "the feminine principle, the goddess of moisture

Tefnut," "the masculine principle, god of earth Geb," "the feminine principle," goddess of the sky Nut," and two couples named "Osiris and Isis," and "Nephtys and Seth, symbolizing the four consort couples in the Heliopolitan cosmogony, in which he became Re in his glorious apparition.

In the state of forgetfulness, annihilation, and death, the soul of the deceased during regeneration crosses through the kingdom of the diurnal and nocturnal sun toward the sun god Ra. Thus, the human being is from the Noun, more or less directly from Ra. In the Pyramid Texts, Ra, who rose day across the sky, having won his victory over the forces of darkness at night, through the underworld of Hades, was considered as the master of the year; but Apophis the serpent, the personification of chaos, of evil forces and the darkness of the night, who sought each night to destabilize, to destroy the divine creation in the world, to swallow it and to plunge it into darkness, was fought by the warrior god Seth, the god of confusion, disorder, and disruption.

The master of thunder and lightning, particularly fear, and in the eternal rivalry with Horus, perpetuating heterosexual aggressive sexual behavior with beautiful goddesses, and as homosexual with Horus, is linked to blind destructive forces, very disturbing, but participated in a positive role in the running of the world and was like the protector God to pharaohs. On the boat of Ra, Pharaoh Khufu, the second pharaoh of the Fourth Dynasty, took his place in the kingdom of the dead.

After his death, the death of his son, Crown Prince Kaouab, son of Re, death before his brother made that king Khafre his successor, was the first to include the name of Sa-Re, in his titulature; thus preceding the birth name and connecting it as the son of Re, the cosmic power of the universe. By developing the affirmation of the importance of Atum toward Re, Khafre therefore retained the title of son of the (sun god Re).

Amenhotep IV, who succeeded his father, after his reign filled with artistic splendor and unprecedented period of prosperity, continued the religion of Aten, a solar god of Ancient Egypt, introduced by his father Amenhotep III. Ouaenre, the "Unique of Re," better known as Akhenaton, ascended the throne of Egypt, crowned at the age of less than sixteen, by the name of Neferkheperoure (the manifestations of Re are perfect), toward 1355/1353.

As testified and attested by the Pyramid Texts of the Old Kingdom, the origin of the worship of the god Aten is much older as a principle than the visible radiance of the god Atum-Re, who occupies the place of the demiurge in the Heliopolitan cosmogony. Particularly in the very ancient cosmogony of Atum, the origin of the sun God Re, quickly assimilated to Re, is known as the one that engendered the male god Shu and his twin sister, the goddess Tefnut, the first divine couple, by his seed. Hence, the great Ennead, the principal gods of Ancient Egypt; according to the Pyramid Texts, Atum didn't exercise creation from scratch, therefore did't create the world, but exercised his creation from a material or a preexisting substratum; well, Re eventually replaced Atum in the Egyptian pantheon.

After a religious syncretism between the gods of Egypt and those in Asia during the reign of his father Amenhotep III, his son Amenhotep IV, both the incarnation and prophet of the exclusive worship of Re-Horakhty (who is in Aten), worshipped alongside Re as the manifestation of the sun between its morning rebirth during its terrestrial glory and the setting sun, he imposed the worship of the sun disk Aten as the first propaganda of the monotheistic religion belief in a unique God.

A form of belief of the gods, in which the greatest attested divinity is unique in the context of its worship, played a predominant role according to the logic of the henotheism and received preferential worship compared to others. He continues in his reign by imposing this solar tutelary God, both physical and spiritual according to him; and the principal gods of the exclusive worship of the sun disk Aten, irradiating heat within and radiating his light outside and on all living beings on earth; like the solar star at the center of our galaxy is physical, so rayon the esprit.

Thus, the first polymorphic monotheism that presented a unique God, under different aspects attested and considered as such, was born by the cult of Aten that lasted about eighteen years of history; at first, a tendency of this cult was born during the reign of his father but attested by others and disputed by some in the history of religions. His proclamation of the supremacy of the sun god Aten, in favor of the state, led him to close all temples of the Theban god Amun by confiscating church properties and forbidding the worship of the traditional gods.

The logical outcome of the god of the solar disk Ra, as the creator of the universe, is based on an attested reconstruction by explaining the recoating of different forms of the solar star during its course in the sky in three unique deities: the triad of Heliopolis, the religious capital of the sun signifying the rising sun Khepri, the sun at its zenith, and the setting sun Atum-Re. And it is by the gradual assimilation of the form of Re of the Egyptian theologians and the association with several other gods that Re-Atum, the god of creation of the nine major gods, is attested as Amun, who became Amun-Re, a specific and unique god from a mixture of several deities, as syncretism. Religiously, this conception, according to which several gods or divine beings exist, is a form of primordial (asexual) polytheistic of Egyptians, existing and able to manifest itself only through a multitude of infinite divinities because the eternal is infinite. Like the rule of polytheism, Ancient Egyptians rejected any tendency dedicated to the monotheistic sun god of Akhenaton, denoting a kind of rotation of worship of several gods.

The absolute of beliefs is the one where the universal soul is at the center of all, eternal and immutable, transcending the infinite temporal cycles in time and space. But by accelerating the theological evolution, began by his predecessor father, the complete establishment of Atum in the Egyptian clergy upsets the balance and natural order, the justice and the existence of deities in the history of Ancient Egypt, and in the world during the time of a reign. Thus, Amenhotep IV then decided to abandon the worship of the dynastic hidden god Amun to favor the cult of the sun disk Aten.

To establish his future capital, he chose a desert location on the eastern bank of the Nile, the Middle Egypt. The virgin Theban god was present during his first visit at that place in year four of his reign to build his temple, aiming at the point where the sun rose at some three hundred kilometers north of Thebes, known as the city of Akhetaten, at the present Amarna. Finally, Amenhotep IV took the name Akhenaton, in Ancient Egyptian meaning "The Horizon of Aton," thus changing his name in the year six of his reign. The new residence, still under construction, dedicated to the unique god Aten, allowed the beneficent rays to penetrate in the temple like what happened on November 22, when the sun's rays hit the altar, to have that mixture of golden and silver rays from the sunlight in the future building at the open sky between Thebes and Memphis; like when the sun passed the doors of the carved rock of the temple of Ramses II, occurring also in February, showing the commonalities of traditional African architectural culture across Africa. This new residence was occupied, when he left the city of Amun with his entire administration and the royal court, to the new city that he founded still devoid of any cult, in the year nine of his reign.

After the founding of the city of Akhetaten, quickly erected with mudbrick and talatats (around 1360), as the capital of the Egyptian empire in the fourth year of his reign, his power lasted for four centuries. The establishment of the worship of the unique god Aton in the single city of Ancient Egypt put forward a belief system in which the verb is the creator. Its occult influences, such as the faculty of incarnation, invalidated the expression of ancient principles, destroying images of the ancient deity's worship in the main critical areas of the kingdom, to make way to the unique god of the solar disk—the universal god Re, known as the demiurge without equal.

The celestial kingdom of Aton, inscribed in the cartridges, presented a true religious revolution in the ancient "Re-Horakhty," the new god incarnated in a new function in that new residence, where he conducted his magical operations properly. As one of the biggest "mysteries," he left us a detailed knowledge of the history from the year three of his reign in the only city of Ancient Egypt.

Oh, Egypt! From your first formulas of the cult of Aten, established in the fourteenth century BC by Pharaoh Akhenaton in complete copies of the Saite recession, a registered distinction of elements separation, constituting personalities in the funerary ritual of the coming forth by day occurred. Unlike the darkness, but with all luminous principle; *Ba*, the soul of the mummy, must be separated from the deceased, where the body remains hidden in the Duat, representing that underground world before rising to heaven.

Your dichotomy sums this ritual: "Your mother's heart has been restored to you, and the viscera of the heart of your body have been given back to you; we have put your body in the earth and your *Soul-Ba* in heaven"; this dichotomy is a formula of prime importance. These ritual formulas, used to put the mummy in the ground, are found in chapter 1B, mentioning the importance of the heart, in the summary of chapter 169; and to live after death for the coming forth by day in both chapters and chapter 3 of the funerary ritual formulas.

During the reign of Amenhotep III, Aton had a prominent role, but his son Amenhotep IV will make the solar disk belief of a unique God a personification, transforming Karnak as the great temple of the god Amun-Re. He added an entire religious complex dedicated to the solar disc at the east of Karnak. One could perceive the decisive importance given by these consecrations to the solar worship, literally to the one useful to Aten, in the year five of his reign.

For the first time, the deceased was remembered at each feast of the coming forth by day toward the Twelfth Dynasty and did not cease to mark so many spirits. The coming forth by day of the deceased was then associated with the faculty to be transformed into the living *Ba*, in the Nineteenth Dynasty. It was after his death that the cult of Aten (Amenhotep IV, known as Akhenaton) was extinguished, after distancing himself from God Amun and his clergy, already attested by the reign of Amenhotep III, his father. Until now, Christianity is the only religion so close to the faith of Akhenaton worldwide. The *Book of the Dead* of Ancient Egypt, a book of initiation and its doctrines outlined in the Pyramid Texts, explicitly represents the Anu doctrines of Nubia (Kush). It is well known that in Egypt, the famous pharaoh Narmer, at the origin of civilization, was originally from the Anu of Sudan. These Anu Negroes, the only perpetrators of these sacred texts, professed these doctrines so old in Egypt at the time when these texts were collected and written into one body as the Book of the Dead and the Pyramid Texts. In volume 2, chapter 1 of the *General History of Africa*, Cheikh Anta Diop demonstrated the origin of these veterans (Anu) of Egypt to us as authentic Negroes from Sudan.

The Shabaka Stone, named after the Nubian pharaoh Shabaka, was originally erected as a monument at the Temple of Ptah in Memphis in the late eighth century BC by the Twenty-Fifth Dynasty, as a relic incised with an Ancient Egyptian religious text. Shabaka considered that God Ptah, created by thought and by the verb, and at the origin of the creation of the universe, believed that in the Twenty-Fifth Dynasty. The information reached us from that old theological document named Memphite Theology discovered in the archives of the library of the temple of the same god in Memphis. This Ancient Egyptian deity was absorbed by the syncretism of the ancient deities of the Memphis region, under the form of Ptah-Patek, one of the multiple aspects of the God Ptah, presented as a naked and deformed dwarf.

During the late period, the popularity of Ptah-Patek figurines, associated with the god Bes, the god of the home, originating from Sudan, grew in the Egyptian New Kingdom; this god—represented as a dwarf with long arms, short legs, a tail, and a lion face—was established in Egypt in the Twelfth Dynasty, and his cult spread throughout the eastern Mediterranean and exceeded borders of the country up to Carthage.

Around 5500 BC of the Neolithic era, the thought of the Egyptian religion existed already in Africa as the longest religious experience in the history of humanity; when the Edict of Theodosius ordered the closure of all temples of Egypt in 384 of our era, at that time, religious practice or other solemn beliefs of the same gods that men worshipped, including funerary beliefs, were older than three and a half millennia.

From 3100 BC, monuments appeared in the Nile valley, with the complexity of its religious writings and multiple deities. Three thousand years later, the Roman emperors and the Ptolemeans had them rebuilt and continued the African religion in Egyptian temples. It is thus the Ancient Egypt that fathered the one who goes down in history as the high priest Khaemwaset, great Pontifex of Ptah, the God of god's artisans; the god of goldsmiths and architects, who was following the worship of his ancestors, in Memphis. The prince Khaemwaset followed the religious career of his father Ramses II, whose glory passed through centuries, and his grandfather Ramses in the land of Kush at the end of their reigns.

Ptah, master of the jubilee celebrations, the Sed festival ceremonies, which began under the reign of Pepi I, also known as "Heb Sed," was traditionally celebrated when the reign of pharaoh reached the first thirty years in the pharaonic tradition; Ptah is known as the imperial god with Ra under the Old Kingdom; he was part of the five great Egyptian gods with Amun, Ra, Isis, and Osiris of the Middle Kingdom. Khaemwaset was buried in the Serapeum of Saqqara after his death. Death before his father, Khaemwaset left us steles containing reliefs of perfect quality, describing inscriptions qualifying him as a great magician and describing the restoration of the tombs of the cult of Apis of the Old Kingdom.

Therefore, inaugurating the great catacomb to accommodate the mummified remains of sacred bulls and those dedicated to Anubis, a family of carnivorous mammals such as dogs, jackals, wolves, or foxes with many molars, and nonretractile claws, Khaemwaset was thus indicating the future of Ptah; and to Bastet, with the features of felines, the Egyptian goddess of the warmth of the sun, the joy of home, and maternity; whose religious center was in the city of Bubastis in Egypt; he wanted to retain its importance to the end of the Egyptian history for the sacred animals cults, beside the catacombs, from the first dynasties of kings and members of the aristocracy, well after the influx of Greek settlers into the delta.

Since then, the royal necropolis site of the Old Kingdom, built under the First Dynasty, developed around the royal pyramids of the Fifth and Sixth Dynasties, did not stop expanding with many mastabas, Egyptian funerary buildings from the burial of the first two pharaonic dynasties to the senior dignitaries of the archaic period and the Middle Kingdom of Egypt. This most beautiful temple of the country, the most faithful in its time, later became the royal residence in 943 before the Christian era; where the first ruler and founder of the Twenty-Second Dynasty by the name of Shoshenq I, the son of Nimlot A, the great chief of Ma, became pharaoh.

"Ma" means Meshwesh, dating back to the eighteenth Egyptian dynasty of the reign of Amenhotep III. Like an ancient Libyan tribe of Berber origin located beyond Cyrenaica, they were in almost constant conflict with the Egyptian state, during the nineteenth and twentieth dynasty (around 1295 - 1075 BC). In the Western Delta region of Egypt, a growing number of Libyan Meswesh settled and controlled the country at the end of the twenty-first dynasty. Under pharaohs as powerful as Shoshenq I, Osorkon I, Osorkon II, and Osorkon III, they ruled Egypt during the twenty-second and twenty-third dynasties, after a 38-year interregnum during which the Egyptian kings Siamun and Psusennes II took the throne of the country.

In the region of Aswan, on the left bank of the Nile in Lower Nubia, the ancient city of Abu Simbel housed the two most famous temples of Ramses II of the Nineteenth Dynasty, facing the Nile with rooms dedicated to the gods Ra, Amun, and Osiris and a small temple for Hathor. One of the rooms of the temple was dedicated to God Ptah. These two temples are carved in sandstone in the western mountains.

The high priests of the cult of Apis, who worked with the vizier as the first magistrate after the pharaoh, was a title defined as the ears and eyes of the king, created at the time of pharaoh Snefru for his son Nefermaat I; together, they fulfilled the role of architect in chief and master of craftsmen, responsible for the decoration of the royal funerary complexes at the Sixth Dynasty in Ancient Egypt; often known as a prime minister, his duty was to supervise the functioning of the country. This title was first held by Kagemn I, a vizier of both Pharaoh Huni and Pharaoh Snefru, the half-brother of Khufu from the end of the Third Dynasty to the beginning of the Fourth Dynasty. The site of Snefru, the first king of the Fourth Dynasty who ruled for twenty-four years according to the Turin Papyrus, demonstrated its longevity by the oldest mastaba used until the Sixth Dynasty. The Westcar Papyrus, as its name indicates, was brought from Egypt in 1824 by Henry Westcar, the British traveling in the region.

Henry Westcar entrusted this manuscript to Ms. Westcar, his niece, who in 1838 offered it to Karl Richard Lepsius, who by his expedition began the study of pyramids by long months in Giza. More than 130 private tombs were discovered and a list of pyramids recorded. He continued toward Saqqara and discovered the step pyramid of the great pharaoh Djoser Netjerikhet.

Going up toward Thebes, where mainly three gods were worshipped, grouped in the Theban triad, known as the "hidden god Amun the father; the mother goddess Mut, associated with the waters from which everything was born, and the traveler, the moon god Khonsu, son of the god Amun," who is related to the nightly travel of the moon across the sky, where alongside the pharaoh, Khonsu was fighting against the forces of darkness as a fierce protector in Thebes by honoring the god Amun. But Khonsu, as both divine child and devourer of hearts, meant the evolvement of Egyptian deities that had many aspects over a very long time. As deities, they were worshipped in the massive temple complex at Karnak and were primary favored by both the Eighteenth and the Twenty-Fifth Dynasties. Often the builder of Karnak, known as pharaoh Amenhotep I, was depicted among these gods.

It was therefore in the middle of a hedge of honor that Karl came out of an impressive temple with a big smile and full of emotions. And then Karl Richard Lepsius crossed the monuments of Tell el-Amarna, one of the greatest cities of Ancient Egypt, which only lasted for a short moment in history, precisely for a quarter of a century; where talatats, typical stone blocks of the Amarna period, were used for the construction of two temples of Aten at Karnak; and for the construction of the monuments of the city of Tell el-Amarna, built by Akhenaten.

The temple of Karnak is more than a temple; it is an immense complex of old buildings, courtyards, and several temples that have perpetually evolved for more than 4,500 years. It is a unique place, probably the largest temple in the world and one of the most beautiful in the whole valley of the Nile. It was considered like the Vatican of that time, which covers almost all the important stages of Ancient Egypt.

For Karl Lepsius, to find certain sites of more than five thousand years old or to look at a temple with ancient writings and, moreover, a statue of that era so distant, still allowing him to touch that old stone so elegantly carved, stuck him the vertigo so disturbing to still be able to feel emotions. By their majesty beauty and a visual striking spectacle that marks the spirit, it was difficult for him to form a simple idea and think that this civilization so far back in time erected these majestic sites. However, he discovered the labyrinth at Hawara; not far from the pyramid of the last king of the Twelfth Dynasty, who reigned from c. 1855 to 1808 BC, named Amenemhat III; where in 1843, Karl Lepsius made his first excavations, going through Deir el- Bahri, the "Monastery of the Sea," known as a complex of mortuary temples, and tombs; it was first built by Mentuhotep II of the Eleventh Dynasty, who reigned from c. 2061 to 2010 BC. Deir el-Bahri is located opposite the city of Luxor, at the West Bank of the Nile.

That same site of Hawara was excavated in 1888 by William Flinders Petrie. Desirous of seeing the wonders revealed to him, he found the Greek papyri of the first and second centuries of our era; comprising legal records and many other types of document, revealing a great deal about life in Egypt, as the result of his labors.

Karl Lepsius then fatally fell in love, amazed by the charming attractions of the best beautiful memories of Philae, the spells of the ultimate island, and the witchcraft of the sacred temple of the cult of the goddess Isis, imposing and magnificently preserved, still retaining the power of expression to impress its visitors.

His too short stay in that beautiful country, but an opportunity almost truth, made him discover the impressive beauty of most of the high places of that Ancient Egypt, in a word as in a hundred unforgettable words. And there, on the island of Philae, by a spectacle even more beautiful, with a heat particularly appreciable of the sun always at the rendezvous, that very pretty country particularly required his attention by the glaring sunlight shows of the setting sun, which rendered the show even more beautiful. And for those old stones of those temples, that "crowd bath" of its visitors, was for them a more interesting attraction. By the beauty of the landscapes, the most enchanting of all the temples made him stop for a few moments to admire some lines that a little too much, summed up all its beautiful presentations. But particularly dissipated by the beauty of the landscape, he failed to captivate that real heart blow of that Egyptian connoisseur and lover, where every test was detailed to revive the history of the ancestors of that country.

Through his interest in finding the ancestor of Egyptian pharaohs and the civilization of African origin, Richard Lepsius went through Abu Simbel, the temple of Ramses II in the region of Aswan, up to Ethiopia. The temple of Abu Simbel highlights both the breathtaking of the Egyptian escapades and the wonderful engineering ambition of the colossal stone statues, portraying the propaganda of pharaoh's immortality. Until today, the work of these kings is still crowning their effort beyond their majestic temples so that the visitors burst into laughter with pure delight. The temple inner guard is represented by the deified finely carved features of Ramses II colossus in stylized harmony.

Walking along the rocky promontory of Nubia, which dominates the site of the relief of the temple of the Mount Napata, located at the foot of Mount Gebel Barkal, with magnificently carved granite and embellished with gold ornamentation in which resided the god Amun himself, Richard Lepsius was amazed by the overwhelming beauty. This place was considered sacred by the local population and as one of the larger temples in the region. On the edge between the living, the dead of the desert and the lands of Gebel Barkal, the site of the capital of the Kingdom of Kush, where a temple of Amun, dating from the early Eighteenth Dynasty to the Twenty-Fifth Dynasty, identified as the birthplace of god Amun, this temple built on the banks of the river, at the shadow of the "Pure Mountain," was dedicated to the god Amun.

He penetrated the north of Khartoum toward the royal cities of Meroe, along the White Nile up to the center of Sudan, where the cult of Amun of Napata with a ram's head, identified as the main deity was worshipped. The same main god is confused with the Egyptian Amun, but their shared history began with the Egyptian colonization of the Nubian province. During that period, the cult of Amun depicted as ram's head grew subsequently and gained importance. Thus, after the Egyptians conquered Nubians, they were also attracted by the main deity of the Kushites, identified as Amun. Amun became a thought of fertility deity, and since rams were considered a symbol of virility, its deity became associated with virility. As the Egyptians expanded their control of Nubia, they built numerous temples to god Amun. One of those temples stood at the foot of a holy mountain called Gebel Barkal, as the largest of all in the region.

This identification of the Nubian Amun led to another fusion of identities with Amun, becoming Amun-Ra. And subsequently, that Kushite deity is described in the Hymn to Amun-Ra as "All gods are three-Amun, Re and Ptah," that no one equals. He who hides his name as Amun, and who appears with the face as Re, his body is Ptah. The Amun of Napata sat on his throne with a uraeus cobra dressed on the forehead of his headdress, of which he is one of the attributes in the very heart of the sacred mountain. This ancient local deity capped with two high feathers of the Theban god, whose sacred animal was the ram, has been absorbed by the syncretism developed from the Eighteenth Dynasty.

From the Nile valley, his expedition, which lasted from 1842 to 1845 in Egypt, was directed toward the starting point. From the heart of Africa and the coast of the Red Sea, he saw an orthodox monastery by the name of St. Catherine's Monastery of Sinai, built at the foot of Mount Sinai, one of the oldest monasteries in the world still in operation and whose monastic activity seems to have started very early. The solitude life chosen by the Egyptian monks, from the end of the third century, flourished in that secluded place at the south of the Sinai Peninsula in Egypt.

Karl Richard Lepsius was the first translator of the *Book of the Dead*. But before this translation, he first published his facsimile from the first copy of the Book of the Dead, known of the Papyrus Cadet, in 1805. This papyrus was brought from Egypt at the return of the military campaign from Egypt led by Napoleon between 1798 and 1801. It was executed for Egypt during the Ptolemaic period before our era. This same copy was a reproduction of an old manuscript, gotten from the army by Mr. Cadet of the Freemasons, to whom we owe the current mounting of the original papyrus. This military campaign of France was headed for the continuation of the destruction of Egypt, then regarded as the cradle of civilizations. Egypt was then discovered, accompanied by a scientific expedition with hostile culture.

Thereafter, the fruit of his entire African trip resulted in a first translation, which he named *Book of the Dead*, based on the *Papyrus of "Iouef-Ankh or Iufankh,"* different from the other copies of the *Book of the Dead*. His translation into German language was published in 1842. At that time of Ancient Egypt, the *papyrus of Iouya* counted forty formulas, and the *Papyrus of Kha*, dated from the reign of Amenhotep III, of the Eighteenth Dynasty, which counted thirty-three chapters, out of the 150 formulas, then used as one of the oldest copies known under the title of the *Book of the Dead*, was actually titled - r(3) w nw pr. t m hrw, known as the "*Book of* the Coming Forth by Day," as its transliterated name of the Ancient Egyptian. Gathering literally all "Formulas for the Coming Forth into the Daylight," it is also the oldest illustrated book throughout the world history of religions. These different magic formulas—of one of the most complete papyri, that exist—dating from the Ptolemaic period, were divided for the first time in 165 chapters by Karl Richard Lepsius, each chapter to a numbered magic formula, all preserved in the Museum of Turin till today. There is another papyrus dating from the reign of Amenhotep III. The papyrus of the queen of Mentuhotep of the Thirteenth Dynasty, preserved in Berlin, was the oldest version known to date.

In Ancient Egypt, the *Book of the Coming Forth by Day* was the real title given to this book. It was from its original hieroglyphic text that an English translation was produced by Sir Ernest A. Wallis Budge, published in London, England, after the Christian era. Under the title of the book known as the Book of the Dead, Sir E. A. Wallis Budge published an edition of all its chapters and named it the *Book of the Coming Forth by Day*, in 1898 from the *Papyrus of Ani*; one of the oldest known copies, dating from the reign of Amenhotep III, of the Eighteenth Dynasty, discovered in a tomb in Thebes in 1887 and preserved in the British Museum; increasing its volume with the *Papyrus of Nu*, it contained chapters 187–190.

The *Papyrus of Ani*, written by one or more royal scribes containing divine offerings to the lords of Thebes, the divine offerings with declarations and spells to all the gods; manufactured in specialized workshops to obtain a funeral ceremony to help the deceased in his life after death, this stolen papyrus in Egypt also undergoes a division into thirty-seven leaves, thus separating the vignettes of its text. An anarchic division made some vignettes to be cut into two parts, from a papyrus that measured twenty-three meters long and about thirty-nine centimeters wide. Under the pen of a pleiad of authors, we henceforth find numerous versions after his transliterated *Book of the Dead*. This English Egyptologist also translated an epic story of the early fourteenth century precisely known by the name of *Kebra Nagast*, written in Ge'ez, meaning the "Glory of Kings."

The Westcar Papyrus, also famous, is registered under number 3033 at the Egyptian Museum of Berlin in 1886 at the death of the Egyptologist. The period of its dating is placed between the end of the Seventeenth and the beginning of the Eighteenth Dynasty, in accordance with the hand of the scribe. According to the grammar of Middle Egyptian, the text was copied from an original text, describing a magical spectacle probably written in the period of the reign of the Twelfth Dynasty, and it is inscribed as the oldest script ever discovered. In this papyrus, many legends are registered as erudite stories concerning pharaohs; for instance, concerning the first three kings of the Fifth Dynasty; named Userkaf, from 2494 to 2487; Sahura, from 2487 to 2475; and Neferirkara from 2475 to 2455; and in total, the Fifth Dynasty, which started its reign from 2494 BC, lasted up to the reign of Unas from 2375 to 2345 BC.

The fulfillment of the prediction of their birth and their advent as first kings is described in a passage called: "The theogamy principle of allowing God to come into the world of man, raised to the ranks of the gods and physically take the place of the pharaoh, to unite with his spouse the Queen in order to fecundate the future heir of the pharaonic throne," was a frequent principle in the Egyptian belief. This principle was an ancient practice to justify the royal and celestial origin of his heir, legitimizing an accession to the throne, and to express the dual nature of God living on earth.

An important strong theology of ancient royalty was the divine birth of the future queen, the first great woman called Hatshepsut of the Eighteenth Dynasty, whose history kept the name, represented on high reliefs of the temple of Deir el-Bahari, corresponding with a theology of Amenhotep III of the Eighteenth Dynasty and Ramses II of the Nineteenth Dynasty. She headed the high clergy of Amun, proclaiming his great name and propagating the myth of the divine birth engendered by god Amun, who took her father's traits to be given greater legitimacy. This beneficent royal function was promised to her by Amun in the entire country. The Egyptian mythology continued with the visit of god Ra and his union with the priestess Reddjedet of the city of Sakodou, who fathered the first three kings of the Fifth Dynasty. Ra sent his divine goddesses Heqet, Isis, Khnum, Meskhenet, and Nephthys to help Reddjedet give birth, thereby legitimizing their ascension to the throne. Tales of this papyrus were qualified as tales of magicians of very great importance.

That older tradition of magic and the principle of theogamy, the (meeting of God and man) became a religious political formula adopted by some rulers of the Eighteenth and Nineteenth Dynasties, legitimizing the intervention of the divine affiliation, strengthened in its resolution to the power of the throne. Amenhotep III of the Eighteenth Dynasty and Ramses II of the Nineteenth Dynasty followed this form of important royalty theology to generate future terrestrial heirs. And indeed, in the beauty of its palaces, the intervention of the divine coupling was accomplished, and the divine incarnation was manifested.

The Hyksos invasion with a horde of strong foreign barbarians subjugated the regions of black people without effort to their will by military superiority and caused the fall of the regions in the east of the Nile delta and Middle Egypt. They gradually took power by breaking the unity of the country, and toward 1650, they definitively seized Memphis, concretizing their takeover without difficulty or a fight. But in the year fifteen of his reign, Ahmose I, the founder of the Eighteenth Dynasty and the first king of Thebes from (1550/1549 to 1540), took Memphis after the conquest of Lower Egypt from Khamudi, the last defeated king of the Hyksos Fifteenth Dynasty, and became the king of all Egypt until 1525/1524.

At his coronation, Ahmose took the title of Neb-Pehty-Re after the death of his brother Kamose at the throne of Thebes, who died from unknown causes after only three years of reign; a death that followed the death of their father, killed by foreign rulers ruling over Lower Egypt during the conflict, when he was only seven years old. In turn, he ascended the throne and reaffirmed the Egyptian power beyond its borders successfully.

One of the most successful pharaohs' reigns was the one of an indigenous woman, the fifth pharaoh of the Eighteenth Dynasty of Ancient Egypt, who reigned longer in the Egyptian dynasty than any other indigenous woman; she was known as the daughter of Thutmose I, who drove the Hyksos out of Egypt when she ascended to power. For Queen Hatshepsut to succeed in eliminating the invaders from her country, Egyptians fought and finally defeated the Hyksos people, invaders of their land who made themselves lords of the Lower Egypt, continuing what her ancestor Ahmose I had already started.

The period of the New Kingdom, the most prosperous of all Egyptian history, was a period that will end the occupation of the Hyksos' reign and the taking of South Canaan under the achievements of Thutmose I. The first king of that period was the initiator Ahmose I, Amosis I, Amenes, or Aahmes; his divine name was Ah or Iah, meaning "moon," and Aahmes means "born of Iah;" thus the combination of "Iah" and "mosis" means "born of the moon." This empire was composed of three dynasties and covered periods from about 1500 to 1000 BC; from 1552 to 1292 BC of the Eighteenth Dynasty, known as the heyday of Ancient Egyptian civilization; from 1292 to 1186 BC of the Nineteenth Dynasty; and from 1186 to 1069 BC of the Twentieth Dynasty, when the golden age of art and the new Egyptian literature of love came to an end.

We must remember the names of Amenhotep, Thutmose, Hatshepsut, Akhenaton, Tutankhamen, Horemheb, Ramses, Seti, Taousert, and Sethnakht, among the famous people of that time. This period also testifies the most beautiful architectural temples built, for example, the one of Luxor used to worship kings or the tombs like those of Seti I, Ramesseum, Abu Simbel, to the dead kings in worshipping their *Ka*, etc. This African invasion caused a disruption within Africa itself and its religions. The Kingdom of Kush located on the confluences of the Blue Nile, and the Atbara River, led by King Kashta from 760 to 747, and today the Republic of Sudan, invaded Egypt in the eighth century BC. The Twenty-Fifth Dynasty of Egypt was ruled by Kushite kings for a century until Psamtik I expelled them in 656 BC. This African kingdom was established after the Bronze Age collapsed. The Middle East people, who were buying iron from the Kushites of Meroe, learned how to melt iron and manufactured weapons.

With the blind trust of Africans, they manufactured iron-tipped weapons and managed to drive the Africans with their magnificent army of softer bronze-tipped weapons out of the Middle East and began the decline of Egypt. The disintegration of the New Kingdom of Egypt was centered at Napata, an ancient Nubian city-state founded by Thutmose III in the fifteenth century BC. Napata was on the West Bank of the Nile River at the site of modern Karima, a town in the Northern State in Sudan, some four hundred kilometers from Khartoum on a loop of the Nile.

Meroe was the imperial Kushite capital for several centuries during the classical era known as Ethiopia in the early Greek geography. Meroe was located about six kilometers northeast of the Kabushiya station, approximately two hundred kilometers northeast of Khartoum, near Shendi, Sudan, on the east bank of the Nile. The Meroitic kingdom disintegrated because of the internal rebellion until the fourth century after Christ, when it weakened.

It was customary to give a new name to the new pharaoh at the coronation, consisting of a sacred royal title of five different names, beside the name usually given by the mother of the child at birth from the Old Kingdom. In the sphere of the sacred, the cosmic harmony of Maat, equity, peace, order, solidarity, truth, and justice were translated as governors; therefore, this cosmic harmony of Maat and his governors were part of the equilibrium of the world, thus connecting the pharaoh to the cosmic power of the universe, conferred him power, the skill of depth knowledge, the fecundity and vitality, as concepts, throughout the African civilization.

The legal texts and religious inscriptions designated the pharaohs of Ancient Egypt by all its names of the royal titulature, constituting simultaneously an ideology of power, which succeeded on the throne for more than three millennia. On the other hand, the term *pharaoh*, in the present emblematic languages of Ancient Egypt, has never been part of the titulature in the civilization qualified as the pharaonic Egypt. The word *pharaoh* in Greek (in Egyptian *per-aa*, meaning "palace or large house of the king" in hieroglyphics) became known by the tenth king Akhenaton (Amenhotep IV) of the Eighteenth Dynasty, who used the title *per-aa*, assigned to him. So, the named Akhenaton was the first king to bear the title of *pharaoh*.

The book of Genesis in the Bible is one of the first sources that introduced us the character of pharaoh as kings of Egypt by designating it as an institution rather than a specific monarch. Furthermore, it was during the first meeting of the pharaoh opposing the prophet Moses and Aaron, pleading to release the Israelites from their servitude in Egypt in the book of Ex. 5:1–5, that Moses continued to introduce the word *pharaoh* in the Bible. But the word *pharaoh* itself first appeared in Gen. 41:1–36). Moses started his introduction by saying in Ex. 1:2–8 that a new king came in Egypt who did not know Joseph; and on his death in Ex. 2:23–25, where the Israelites were still complaining to be forced to be slaves. The Bible also cites the word *pharaoh* in Jr. 46:2 and 2 Kings 23:29–35.

In 650 of our era, a real return to spirituality happened under the Twenty-Sixth Dynasty and gave a final shape to the *Book of the Dead*. More complete titles were also present on other papyri, known as the "Formulas for the *Coming Forth by Day*" or "Instructions, Hymns, Formulas of Transfiguration, Glorification and Spells to Cross Obstacles in the Empire of the Dead." Thus, since the creation of the *Book of the Dead* in the papyri of spirituality, its first translation up to the very authentic secular history, the particular methods of the divine providence in its stories, proved the evidence of successive spiritual secrets and its substances drawn from the great royal funerary ritual, some centuries before the Christian era, concerning the chronology taken from the Bible.

The recognition, the respect to the honor of the divine and to the creator of the entire humanity must be solemnly awarded to Africans and Egyptians of the Nile valley and the Great Lakes, the regions of the center, of the East and North Africa, where the first "Bible" was written. This absolute truth that I invoke with right is known by all the great translators of the scripture and shared by senior officials in matters concerning the Bible. All ecumenical black leaders in the ecumenical council of churches—in which participated, among others, Rev. H. George Polk of *the Memorial Baptist Church*, Rev. William F. Hawkins of *the Metropolitan African Methodist Episcopal Church*, Rev. Hawkins J. Plummer of *the Salvation Baptist Church*, and Rev. James Gunther of *the Lutheran Church of the Transfiguration*—certified the authenticity of this information to us.

Obviously, we seem to forget that all the Bibles that we use for the Word of God contained the works of various writers, men and women, but mostly men, and that all works or compositions are compiled in what is today our different versions of the Holy Bible or Holy Writ. We also failed to realize that that same Bible is the result of a period of hundreds of revisions and translations; in brackets, the relevant data points that it was translated in the time of Solomon in Phoenician, and then, after the captivity of Babylon, Ezra wrote it in Chaldean Aramaic language; each of them marking the use of words or figures as to separate them from their real context. Let's be categorical and unambiguous to say that when the Greeks also translated the Bible, the Jewish priesthood poorly controlled its keys, and St. Jerome, who in turn translated it from Hebrew to Latin, could not penetrate the true original meaning of the Bible, which covered approximately three thousand years, 700 before to 2015 after Christ. Despite innumerable English versions before, the Authorized Version of the Old and New Testaments, King James Version was the only true Bible that Christian Protestants used and still use today. We called it the Authorized Version because King James, being the king of Great Britain, forced all its colonies in the world by military power to adopt his version, much later published in 1611.

While all in that period was preceded by much more essential principles previously created and developed by Africans, its core principles later became the basis of the teachings of Judaism and Christianity. Since blacks, especially in Africa and some parts of the world, did not know that the Old and New Testaments are an integral part of their own heritage and legacy, geographically, historically, and racially, a real Bible study will give a better understanding of the power exercised by Africans for the foundation of Judaism, Christianism, and Islamism.

Indeed, even Moses—the father of the Old Testament, an African who used the ancient teachings of his African teachers of the Nile and the system of the mysteries of the Great Lakes region of central, eastern, and northern Africa—knew it. He finally passed this legacy to other African Jews, who converted its essential principles into what later became the Pentateuch or the Old Testament (the first five books of Moses or the Torah). So I conclude that the first Bible or scroll ever recorded on a document and produced by man, regarding the recognition of a work of such magnitude to honor and respect the divine, a creator of the entire mankind, was that of the African of the Nile valley and Great Lakes regions of central, eastern, and northern Africa. I would also like to mention that these Africans were not different from the Africans we see today in the streets of Amsterdam, Bronx, Brooklyn, Brussels, Harlem, London, Montreal, Paris, Timbuktu, South America, South Africa, or in the rest of the world, whom we wrongly call "Niggers," "black men," or "black people."

The striking suggestion of Rev. George H. Polk saying that it would be of utmost importance that an average parishioner have some form of understanding of the chronological development and in what order the authorized version of the Old and New Testaments of King James came to life—was an idea that immediately was supported by the Reverend Hawkins and Reverend Plummer to formulate a chronology concerning the origin and evolution of the Old and New Testaments. I will therefore say that my book is a glorious privilege to discover a heavenly truth that was hidden from us simply to oppress us. So, let us make a jump of few years back, at the beginning of the history of the Bible, where the "Sacred Scripture was written by the inspired scribes by God."

Well, but what is the Bible? It is a written collection of sacred texts particularly considered by a religion; for example: as the only faith, the Old Testament for Hebrew; the New Testament for Christians, and for Muslims, the Koran, as religious guides in divinity. Relatively to the history, the origin of the Bible, the only religious guide in the divinity to Christians, Jews, parishioners, and to Muslims, the Koran, are by most nation's unknown books.

So, my little journey begins with the new order of the world according to the Bible, by Noah and his descendants for the repopulation of the earth. That is why I chose to begin this draft after the flood of Noah. But it should be mentioned that, from the creation, a more spiritual notion of the Divine Generator (the Father) already existed and still exists in the black beings, from generation to generation on earth before the flood of Noah; because he made Noah see his deep bosom in the depths of the earth, and the heaven's tangible things as the celestial vault, the stars shining in the firmament, and gave him a ravishing Beatitude thought.

The continuation of the human being existence on earth by Noah, as a natural principle of God's forgiveness; God, who contains all kind of eternals, invisible and hidden from the eyes of the flesh, but Black Mother as the universal soul, grandmother of worlds, and God of gods, who takes multiple forms in the ether; vibrating under the fire of the eternal male under the starry sky, as the sower of sun with the subtle light. Let's enter in her nuptial field, and let's drink death with life, in the divine bed of the heavenly liberator.

He took a decision to eradicate the corrupt humanity, who each day bore all thoughts that solely tended toward evil in its heart and its growing wickedness on earth only forming bad drawings all day long. So men, cattles, beasts, all tiny creatures and birds of the sky, were to be wiped off from the face of the earth; Gen. 6:1–8, where God, who created, ordered a flood to the devastating waters, ordering Noah, a patriarch related to the biblical story, qualified as a preacher of righteousness, to do as he said. Noah (in Hebrew, נ ח [nōa'h]), built the famous ark that bore his name (*Tebhath Noah* [ת.ב.ת נ ח] or "ark of Noah") for the continuation of the existence of the human being on earth. Gen. 7:1–4 said, "Enter the ark, you and all your households, for you alone I have seen to be righteous before Me in this time. You shall take with you every clean animal by sevens, a male and female; and a couple of the animals that are not clean, a male and female; also of birds of the sky, by sevens, male and female, to perpetuate the offspring alive all over the earth. Because for another seven days, I will send rain on the earth for forty days and forty nights; and I will blot out from the face of the earth every living thing that I have created." These events are less known to be the motivation of God to destroy his own creation. Noah escaped the devastating waters and saved his family and pairs of animals of each species, thanks to the ark.

Admittedly, several elements rather unusual of his story in Genesis correspond to the legend of the epic story of the Sumerian Gilgamesh. We place the beginning of the writing of the Akkadian recital in the second millennium BC for the elaboration of the oldest massive recital of the myth called the *Epic of Gilgamesh* in the ancient Mesopotamia. The one consisting twelve tablets found in Nineveh, which emerged around 2300 BC, is the most complete version as a better source to determine the course of the text sometimes called standard version.

Several recitals of the *Epic of Gilgamesh*, recounting the history of a flood decided by the gods, were a great success of high antiquity. According to the tradition that reported the epic, Ziusudra in Sumer, Outa-Napishti or Atrahasis in Babylon, indicated that the man Noah who built the ark bore different names, compared to other flood legends of the Middle East like Noah of the biblical story.

The Sumerian Noah was Ziusudra, known as the first writer of the flood myth much later taken by the Babylonians. Many passages of his writing were borrowed by the Bible. Among others, we may quote the Sumerian Dilmun engraved in cuneiform writing in the *Epic of Gilgamesh*, like the fable of the Garden of Eden during the third millennium BC, and the Eden, the Hebrew terrestrial paradise; both quotations represent the same subject; the Mesopotamian mythological texts attribute the creation of this island to their main god EA-Enki, and the myth of the flood to the hero Ziusudra; the subject of the origin of man, describing the original sin, and Eden, the Hebrew terrestrial paradise garden, describing the same idea of the original sin of the first woman named Lilith, first wife of Adam, of the Jewish tradition, but originally a Mesopotamian demon before Eve, associated with the wind and storm. Lilith revolted openly, rejecting the most classic practices of sexual intercourse, all of which gave man the superiority during the sexual act, and which would impose on the woman a lower position. Thus, she clearly claimed her status as "equal" from her companion Adam, who wanted to practice sexual relations of classical postures.

In the book of Genesis, evoking creation, there are two passages indicating the creation of woman. Gen. 1:27 says, "God created man in his image, in the image of God he created him," man and woman, male and female, "he created them." Note here that this passage, rarely interpreted correctly, indicates an "original androgyny," for "he created them male and female." Note that neither names of Adam nor Eve are mentioned in this first chapter. And Gen. 2:7 says that after God created Adam, the first man in his image from the dust of the earth, he animated him with his breath on the sixth day of Creation.

Then God created the animals considering that Adam had to have a companion, but he found no companion among them, after giving a name to each one of them. So, to create a woman for him, God put him to sleep and created the woman from Adam's rib, whom Adam later called Eve. Thus, referring to the original androgyny, Eve therefore came out from the side of Adam asleep, and not from Adam's rib. In St. Jerome's translation of the "rib," the creation of Eve from the "rib," indicates a subordination of woman to man; but in the Bible, the Hebrew word *ṣela* takes more the meaning of "side."

Thus, Eve, meaning "the one who gives life" in the Hebrew literal sense, has an absence of the letter yod in her name. On this subject concerning the translation of the expression "one of his ribs" in Hebrew, an exegetical debate still exists. The original sin was the consumption of the fruit from the tree of knowledge, of good and evil, forbidden by God to Adam under death penalty, which Eve ate under the disobedience of God, for the promise of the serpent (Nahash), and which she gave to Adam, who ate it eventually.

This disobedient serpent to God the Creator, concerning the forbidden fruit promised them the opening of their eyes and a new knowledge related to the gods, but due to their fault, they hid themselves because of their nakedness; thus introducing the original sin into a world where everything was unity and harmony, resulting in division, suffering, and all that follows. Lilith, who does not appear by name in scripture, was succeeded by Eve, according to some Jewish mystical legends.

It is the twelfth tablet of the Gilgamesh Epic, dating back to 2000 BC., which relates Lilith to us in the Sumerian poem of Gilgamesh in the land of the dead, under the form of lillake at the third millennium. Her Hebrew root is layla, "night," shaped with the impure earth at the same time as Adam, according to Kabbalistic literature. According to other narratives, Lilith and Samael, in fact, are a single androgynous being, in the image of God, who emerged spontaneously at the same time, says the masterpiece of Kabbalah, called Sepher ha-Zohar. According to Gen. Rabbah 18:4 of Yehuda Bar Rebbi, the Holy blessed be He—first created a first woman, but the man parted from her, seeing her rebellious, full of blood and secretions. Gen. Rabbah 22:7–30 relates that she incited Cain to kill Abel, for the possession of his first mother Eve, being the little Lilith, for him to be the sole owner.

As Adam and Eve engendered the beneficial portion, Cain and Abel engendered the diabolical portion of humanity. The fact that Lilith was created at the same time from clay as Adam, and rebellious to Adam's authority, inspired feminist movements as the torchbearers of their struggle; taking the figure of Lilith and her simultaneous creation to the one of man, at the contemporary time of the 1970s; therefore, placing the woman in a status of parity-equality with men, and not the subordination. Unlike Eve, conceived from a rib of Adam according to the Bible, she was created to depend on him therefore submissive. Eve, further seen as an ideal docile woman to the man than a genitor, is the opposite of Lilith, who functioned, alternately, morally and psychically as a sexual demon and as a fatale femme and sterile.

To pervert Eve, Lilith pushed Satan, disguised as a snake, by possessing her carnally to engender Cain, the first human being umbilicated, endowed with a navel, unlike his various parents. Then Lilith could enjoy evil for evil, because through man, she betrays Adam; through the scorned mother, she deceived Eve; through Cain, the child she perverted, and he became an assassin; and by the child, Cain killed Abel. So far beyond revenge, Lilith quadruply took revenge according to Jewish tradition, because she was punished by infertility.

Gen. 1:27 presents the explanation of a double account of creation; the first narrative would correspond to the creation of Lilith as the first woman of Adam; and would concern Eve to the second story in Gen. 2:22. Lilith became the disobedient serpent to the creator God, concerning the fruit of the forbidden tree; and the same suffering in the same place mentioned in the Bible caused the fall of Eve.

The story of the founder of the kingdom of Akkad by the name of Sargon I, the first great Mesopotamian king abandoned on the Euphrates at birth in a floating basket and found by Akkis, the gardener, was also taken to form the story of Moses. All these legends are copied into the Old Testament, inscribed in the writing of the Sumerian legends. So, Noah's ark in Gen. 6:13–15 is inspired by the Sumerian text, identically copied, describing the plagiarism of the Sumerian texts in the Bible.

They said that the god Utu came in a dream to warn a king and priest by the name of Ziusudra, after the decision of the assembly of the gods to destroy the seed of mankind with a terrible flood. Ziusudra, the priest and king, was to build a huge boat before the flood invaded the whole country. There were five cities existing before the flood.

The first was Alulim, the city of the king Eridu, ancient city of the first king of Sumer in southern Mesopotamia, today located in Iraq on the bank of the Euphrates, fifteen kilometers southwest of Ur. Nudimmud, its god, was the leader. Eridu came down from heaven, and his city was the first to receive royalty.

Second was Bad-tibira, an ancient city between Ash Shattrath and Tell as-Senkereh, identified as modern Tell al-Madain at the south of Iraq. The name Bad-tibira appears on a piece of the lost tablet. Bad-tibira was the second city to receive royalty.

Larak was the third-important city of ancient Sumerian to have exercised royalty but not yet accurately localized from its antediluvian era. The fourth city, Sippar, was one of the oldest to have sheltered one of the main sanctuaries of the sun god Shamash. The city of Sippar in Mesopotamia was one of the ancient sites that provided us tens of thousands of cuneiform tablets and the penultimate city that exercised kingship before the flood. The last city was the city of Suruppak, where the last of the prediluvian kings Ziusudra reigned in Sumer. Ziusudra was transported by the Hebrews to illustrate the story of the flood of their patriarch Noah later for the prolongation of life after the destruction of the world.

However, from the ninth century BC, Aramaic adopted the principles of the Phoenician writing like the Hebrew of another linguistic family. Assyrians considered Aramaic as a second language in the eighth century. Aramaic became, from the sixth to the fourth century, the official language of the Persian Empire from Egypt to India.

To qualify the Hebrew, simply note that it is from the Aramaic script that the basis of the "square" writing derived; the square writing, which survives barely transformed in the manuscripts of the Samaritans, is generally supplanted by the square Hebrew, derived from the Aramaic; it so called because it contains only consonants; and each of its letters seems to be drawn on the periphery of a square, not containing small signs above or below letters, forming the basis of the square writing script, still used today by Hebrew and believed to have flourished around the sixth century BC. Many Aramaic documents of a Jewish community of the fifth century were found in Elephantine, near Aswan in Egypt. The Hebrew, who is not content of what he learned in Hebrew school such as: ethnicity, morality or spirituality - God, but analyzed Jewish history as a parable of a corporate politics, and the land of Israel as a piety, entered in a country where yesterday the entrance was blocked by a yellow ribbon with Hebrew lettering. Aramaic was a Semitic language quite similar to Hebrew. The Babylonian influence was just as their language, the Aramaic; it possessed a grammar having more affinities with Hebrew. Hebrew used the same alphabet for writing, and Aramaic became the language spoken throughout the old East at a time.

Many books of the Bible, written or reworked during the exile in Babylon from (587 to 538), express an event that profoundly affected Judaism; referring to the Hebrew Bible, concerning most of the books written after their return from exile, apart some few chapters of Daniel are written in Aramaic and Hebrew, like chapters 1–6 written in Aramaic, chapters 8–12 written in Hebrew, and chapter 2:4 written in Hebrew, where Daniel (also called Belteshazzar) accepted to reveal mysteries to "King Nebuchadnezzar and let him know the interpretation of his dream and his visions concerning what will happen at the end of days;" Then Daniel, who implored God about the mysteries of Nebuchadnezzar had a nocturnal vision, and the mysteries were revealed to him by God in heaven, so that the king might know the interpretation that Daniel gave him for him to understand what was going through his mind; from chapter "2:41" where the second kingdom is mentioned up to verse "45," representing the fourth spiritual age of Nebuchadnezzar's dream about a giant statue of four metals and a mixture of clay and earth, Daniel successively explained the division of the world into four parts of ages, of which each age of the empires is morally inferior to the preceding one; from chapter 7:28 written in Aramaic, the text continues up to chapter 12, partially translated into Hebrew.

At the beginning of the book of Daniel 2:3, originally written in Hebrew and concludes in Aramaic, his language of origin in which over a period of about seventy years, he was the beneficiary of a series of five visions, moving from general to specific, known as the prophecy of Daniel. Then there's Ezra 1:1–7 and 6:19–22 written in Hebrew and 4:7–8, 12, and 26 in Aramaic. One verse in Gen. 31:47 and Jer. 10:11 were also written in Aramaic. We can only find a few texts written in Aramaic in the Bible, but the influence of this language in many texts written in Hebrew is sensitive and palpable as in Dan. 1:4, which uses the term *Chaldean* to designate Aramaic.

Although few texts were written in Aramaic, the Hebrew texts adopted words or phrases of the Aramaic language; moreover, as many Jews were speaking Hebrew with difficulty (or not at all), upon their return from exile, it was necessary to translate the Hebrew text of the Bible into Aramaic. The translator, the metourgman, immediately gave the Aramaic translation of the passage in a loud voice and in a strictly oral manner. It was this translation in a strictly oral manner that was written; those translations were known as Targum.

Originally, the text did not include any vowels, but the Bible being a sacred book, it appeared necessary to permanently fix the pronunciation, and consequently, its meaning. The pronunciation, fixed by the erudite Masorete rabbis, the word *massore* in Hebrew, meaning "translation," was retained. This work was completed around the eighth century after Jesus Christ—meaning, well over a thousand years after the texts were written in consonant script.

Several codification systems of vowels came into competition. Finally, the Masoretes of Ben Asher's school of thought opted for additional signs above and below the line of consonants as a form of fairly Modern Hebrew. Indeed, a member of the congregation was reading passages of the law of the prophets during the Sabbath service; he was reading aloud a free version of a biblical passage in use in synagogues in Hebrew that a Turgeman translator had to adapt for the public. In some passages of the books of Ezra and Daniel, the impact of Aramaic appeared, as well as in the *targumim* (plural of Targum, meaning "interpretation") of the Hebrew Bible in Aramaic. In 330 BC, after the conquests of Alexander the Great, Aramaic was supplanted by Greek as the official language but would still survive for a long time, especially in Judea and Syria, in the culture of the Middle East; for the Jewish communities, of which the use of their language was lost in most, the Targum was essential.

While the clergy and notable Jews spoke Aramaic but preferred Hebrew in the first century, Aramaic became the language of the people. The *targumim* offered a ref lection of the rabbinic interpretation of the Bible, compiled or written since the days of the Second Temple up to the High Middle Ages in the land of Israel or in Babylonia. No matter how faithful the translator was to the Masoretic text, the official version of the Hebrew Bible was nothing but just simple translations, because originally, the entire book was written in Aramaic. The traditional Syriac Christians Bible was the nearest source of the original version of the New Testament.

Many manuscripts of Qumran testified few words transmitted by the gospels (literary genre proclaiming the Word of God) written in Greek, such as *Ephphatha*, meaning "open up" or "be opened," in Mark 7:34; *Golgotha* ("place of skull") in Mark 15:22; "Eloi, Eloi, lama sabaqthani" (My God, my God, why have you forsaken me?) in Mark 15:34; etc. This indicates that Aramaic became the language of the people. These indications suggest that Jesus and the apostles spoke Aramaic.

From the third century of our era, the Jerusalem Talmud and the Babylonian Talmud, a collection of discussions and commentaries on the Torah, known as the monuments of Jewish erudition, were all written in an Aramaic dialect. Syriac was another Aramaic dialect that became the liturgical language of the

Eastern Christians. They also had Aramaic as a distant ancestor in the sect of the Samaritans, near Mount Gerizim (Israel) with the Samaritan spoken today.

Translation continued in all Aramaic writings, to judge which was most adapted for the public. The hidden Christian Apocrypha writings—writings whose authenticities aren't established literally; writings considered not authentic because they were judged by religious authorities as not inspired by God; or books represented as inspired by God but not part of the Jewish biblical canon, and distinguished from the protocanonic books contained in the Hebrew canon; whereas the Catholic tradition considers them as deuterocanonical books "belonging to the second canon."

The word *canon* refers to books derived from the biblical canon in Greek meaning "rule, model, or decree law of the Church;" and in Hebrew, "qaneh," means in all religions, all as texts considered sacred and governing cults as opposed to noncanonical Apocrypha. Its main acts of worship are sacrifice, the offering of an animal or a human as bloody sacrifice, offering a liquid, an object, food as nonbloody sacrifice, or the offerings of libation and education to one or more deities.

Originally, the term *sacrifice* means "making sacred." Education in brief for the Catholic school, was the evangelization and catechesis, "instruction by word of mouth," became generally institutionalized;" the "molding of networks" in the act of looking at the mystery of life and engage what its resources to its congregations was an important establishment in the religious education historically; but today, they're not schools for Catholics only. Invocation in a religious or spiritual context consists of making an appeal or asks help from God, a divinity, a spirit, a genius, or a saint, for a rescue by a prayer; prayers of praise, prayer of intense religious immersion services of the moments of joy and other faith-related events like mourning and weddings, etc. The reading of sacred texts answers the universal question of every spiritual seeker, "How to live a spiritual life every day for a sacred meaning" and experience spiritual perspectives on animals, bodies, creativity, community, leisure, nature, places, relationships, and things; to see the world with inner eyes, to discover the meaning of spiritual key practices in everyday life from the spell to zeal, described in spiritual texts.

Finally, there is preaching: "to preach," "The action of spreading the divine word," which has an important role, especially in the Abrahamic religions and Buddhism, but "preaching can also be done through missionary activity, which is not linked to a worship properly said." Songs are added to the list as tone of solemnity, chanted as prelude to fit the disparate elements together; music follows to demonstrate the emotional intensity and the spiritual significance of that comfort, encouraged in various ways and upliftment, as a fundamental belief of human nature. Pilgrimage is a voyage performed by a believer to a place of devotion, a place held sacred according to his religion. And the religious procession is a solemn parade of faithful for an accomplishment of a ritual as a religious act, while praying, singing, or performing other acts of devotion in Catholicism. Its religious ceremony can be held inside or outside places of worship; these are both processions of priests Trinity and faithful Christians. In orthodoxy, religious procession also exists.

We all know St. Jerome, a monk, doctor of the church; the Bible translator, founder of religious orders, and one of the four Fathers of the Western Church with Ambrose of Milan, doctor of the church, writer and poet, the quasifounder of hymnody, meaning "singing or composed hymns"; both saints were in the fourth century, the most influential ecclesiastical figures of Western Christianity, who are known among the Latin fathers who wrote about the "defense," the "explanation," and the "doctrinal of Christianity." Several major areas of theology were developed by them during that Patristic period, like the establishment of the New Testament canon to achieve the consistency of faith; they sought the doctrine of the church and the doctrine of divine grace; they fixed the ecumenical creeds and the two natures of Christ, to establish the doctrine of Trinity. In the liturgy of the Roman Catholic Church, we distinguished hymns from psalms. It is to the honor of God, of the Virgin Mary or of the Saints that the hymns, poems or songs, were composed; a distinction was made between the Latin Christian and the reader of Cicero on the rebirth of the religious tolerance in the seventeenth century from the one of the Greek fathers, whose methods of allegorical interpretation were taken by the Roman Catholic Church. Other than Greek or Latin, several other fathers of the church wrote in different languages like Aramaic, Coptic, Ge'ez, and Syriac. In AD 382, St. Jerome's best known translation of most of the Bible into Latin, (known as the Vulgate) at the late fourth-century became officially promulgated as the Latin version of the Bible by the Catholic Church during the sixteenth century. After Augustine of Hippo as the first ancient Latin Christianity writer, Jerome was the second most voluminous known ancient Christianity Latin writer among others. He was also one of the protagonists of debates against Arianism, a man who was in possession of potentially limitless intellectual capacities. The Mastering of various disciplines through the quest of knowledge was necessary for the proper use of one's faculties. Under him, Augustine of Hippo was converted to Christianity. Augustine of Hippo (St. Augustine) was from the municipality of Thagaste (known today as Souk Ahras, Algeria) and was a Christian theologian, philosopher and bishop of Hippo in late antiquity.

A Berber Latino Romano-African writer, born from a Roman African father named Patricius, (an African Romanized), therefore a Roman citizen, and from a non-Romanized Berber mother, by the name of St. Monica, who was a devout Christian, and not like her Pagan spouse, who on his deathbed was converted to Christianity. St. Augustine was one of the thirty-three doctors of the church. Gregory I, doctor and father of the Western church, became the sixty-fourth pope in 590; his influence during the middle ages was considerable. It was from him that we owed the name of Gregorian chants. Since the Vatican II, the Roman Catholic Church celebrated him on the September 3; but before, it was on the day of his death on March 12, 604. St. Gregory the Great was a pope from

September 3, 590, to his death and was declared to be the last good pope of the Catholic Church.

Augustine, after reading the *Hortensius* of Cicero, compared to the reading of the Bible, concluded that the stories that the Bible abounds are seen as gross and immoral and lacking subtlety. He continued by saying that the language of Cicero was very far from the slang words filled in the Bible of the African church and that it was rather an apprenticeship of wisdom, which in any case stated to be a thought only at the seventh century BC in the West. Or like those Westerners who received that wisdom, the quality of having experienced knowledge and good judgment; we quote: "Bias of Priene, a politician and legislator of the sixth century BC; Cleobulus of Lindos in c. 600 BC on the Greek island of Rhodes; he governed Lindos as tyrant; Chilo of Sparta, a Spartan politician from the sixth century BC; Periander of Corinth, a tyrant of Corinth during his rule in the seventh and sixth centuries BC; Pittacus of Mytilene, who governed Mytilene (Lesbos) along with Myrsilus; Solon of Athens, a famous legislator and reformer, who framed laws that shaped democracy in Athens in the early sixth century BC.; he was born around 638 BC and wrote poetry up to his death in 558; and Thales of Miletus, the first well-known philosopher and mathematician; they're well known as the Seven Greek wise men recognized for their wisdom in the early-sixth-century BC."

At that time, Christ was seen as a teacher of wisdom, not as the Savior for African Christians, and no study of the fundamental nature of knowledge or the reality and the existence, considered as a technical academy in the discipline of philosophy did not exist at that time. Whoever was to combine the biblical conception of God to the neoplatonic conception of the Greek tradition, believed in the will of God: is that will, the righteousness, the temporal goal, as the God of Abraham, Isaac, and Jacob, and Jesus Christ have the compassion for the Eternal? Because the truth that directs the spirit from within is not a voice that resonates outside.

While the immutable virtue of God and his eternal wisdom consulted by Christ, whose teaching is included in the gospel according to Thomas 83, about the hidden words of Jesus in the page of the early Christian writings, Jesus said, "The images are revealed to man, but the light which is in them is hidden in the image of the Light of the Father, a reasonable soul. He will reveal Himself, but His image is hidden by His light." And the light of God and power are none other than God Himself, manifesting Himself according to good or bad of man's own will, as the source of our consciousness and our experience is our inner being, and subjectively, those who are intuitive or spiritually perceptive recognize it.

Being the creator and ruler of the universe, he manages animals, the birth, growth, aging of men, plants, and movements of the stars, like His creations, partly natural, partly voluntary, and the condemnation of sinners by the trial of the righteous and the perfection of the blessed. He, the Creator and Governor of the universe, who inspired the rule through Saint Augustine, also promoted him as one of the architects of the Western thought of the "inner self" by "establishing the new ancient Christianity Faith and by developing the Western philosophy." The Anglican Communion, the Catholic Church, and the Eastern Christian Church recognized him as a patron saint of the Augustinians. Generally, his writings, qualified as a contribution in the Western Christianity and known as masterpieces that covering various fields including theology, philosophy, and sociology, are still governing many orders and religious congregations today. He said to the Jews of Genesis Rabbah (Midrash Rabbah) that they cannot deceive God, the Sovereign Judge, and that if Pilate pronounced the sentence and gave the order to crucify Christ, the Jews also put him to death by shouting, "At the cross! At the cross! Crucify him! Crucify him!" He strongly objected the translation of the entire Bible by St. Jerome in Latin, under the name of the Vulgate, because for the interpretation of certain terms of the Tanakh, he used to rely on the advice of the rabbis to remain as faithful as possible to the Hebrew truth.

Genesis Rabbah: Midrash Rabbah and the Sefer haYashar, found in the King James Bible of 1611, mentioned in Jos. 10:13 and 2 Sm. 1:18, is an unknown book mentioned in the Hebrew Bible; it bears the title of "Book of the Correct Register;" and in the English tradition, it is known as the *Book of Jasher.*" The book is describing the biblical history of the creation of Adam and Eve and the descendants of Cain as a basic mythology concerning the origin of the various forms of civilization, references which correspond those cited in the biblical texts like Naamah, daughter of Lamech and Tsillah (for the first), and the daughter of Enoch, the great-grandfather of Noah; including the common tale of accidentally killing of Cain by Lamech and his son Jabal, requiting his wickedness for the slaying of Abel. As mentioned in the Bible, Lamech is the first polygamist personage to take Adah and Zillah (Tselah) as his wives. For the second, the three sons, Shem, Ham, and Japheth, Gen. 6:9, outlines the history of the righteous man who found grace in the eyes of Yahweh.

The second epistle of Peter 2:5–6, refers to nonlegalistic exegetical texts concerning Noah's name, meaning "rest" according to (Midrash Agadah); Noah, who spared the ancient world and that we rank among the biblical patriarchs, is qualified as a preacher of righteousness who found favor in the eyes of Yahweh. From where could have Peter know that Noah was a preacher of righteousness in the action of spreading the word of God—to say in front of—to preach? Noah was much talking of the righteousness of God by "primarily proposing to the faithful what to believe and do for the glory of God, and the salvation of men," says chapter 7:20–39 of the Jewish book of Jubilees; apart from the second epistle of Peter 2:4–5, and about Peter himself, no reference is mentioned in the Old Testament, neither in the New Testament, so where did he get that information? Just to conclude that, Peter knew this information by reading the book of Enoch.

Gen. 4:17 and 5:18–24 tell us that Enoch (in Hebrew חנוך [hānokh]), father of Irad, was the son of Cain and the great-grandfather of Noah, the seventh of the patriarchs of the lineage of which Adam was the first and Noah the tenth. Enoch lived in all 365 years. Enoch walked with God and was no more because God took him. A whole cycle was placed under the patronage of Enoch, including in particular his books and jubilees. In the Apocryphal writings, he rose from his human body to that of an angel. And in the epistle of Jude, he prophesied the last days.

Enoch, the first man copyist of the seventh generation of Adam, who prophesied about them, said, "The Lord is coming with thousands upon thousands of his holy ones," which is a quote from Jude 1:14. According to the words of Moses in Dt. 33:2, "The Lord came from Sinai and dawned over them from Seir; like the sun on the horizon, and he shone forth from the Mount of Paran. He came with the myriads of holy ones from the south, from his mountain slopes." He was born among men on earth, and to whom writing, knowledge and wisdom were taught, is an extracted quote from the *Book of Jubilees concerning Enoch*; Enoch described the signs of heaven according to the order of their months. In his book, seasons of the years were according to the order of separation of their months so that they could be known to men. He described the history of the creation of the world up to the flood; his history subtracted from the Bible is described as a retrospective work with a detailed vision. The book of Enoch was presented and deposited in its integrity written in the Ethiopian language called Ge'ez.

Among the generations of the earth, he wrote a testimony; he was the first to testify to the son of men; of a conflict that occurred between the son of God—the dethroned angels banished from heaven to earth by a judgment. We can still read these words today in the book of Enoch: "Since the beginning, the Son of Man existed in the mystery." The Most High preserved him beside his power and revealed him to his elected. He was appointed in the presence of the Lord's all mighty power, before the creation of the sun, the stars, and the signs in heaven. Kings, princes, and rulers of the earth were afraid and will bow before him. And they shall worship him, and terror will be with them, when they shall behold and perceive the Son of a Woman seated upon the throne of his glory. He shall be a staff of support for the righteous, the hope of those who are troubled at heart and the light of the Gentiles. He saw an inexhaustible fountain of righteousness in the ether, a very great sea where he was placed with many fountains of wisdom, larger than the terrestrial sea where all thirsty souls who drank of it were filled with wisdom and their dwellings were with the holy and elected. Then he, the elected will call all the powers of the earth, all the saints of heaven, and the all mighty power of God.

If you're able to understand the Elected One, open your eyes and lift your horns. Then the Cherubim, the Seraphim, the Ophiuchus, all the angels forces, all the angels of the Lord, the power of the Elected and the other powers serving on earth and in heaven will raise their voices; and the power of the Elected shall remain over the sinners and the ungodly; and with the son of man shall they dwell, eat, lie down, and rise up for ever and ever. This quoting is from the book of Enoch, chapter 48 and 61. Enoch has another work attributed to him called "The Book of the Secrets of Enoch." The undeniable confirmation of its authenticity is due to some fragments in Aramaic, found at Qumran. Its distant past registered it among the apocryphal books and gave it a dominant place among the old books.

1 Enoch, or Ethiopian Enoch, a pseudepigraphic writing of the Old Testament attributed to Enoch, was part of the canon of the Old Testament of the Ethiopian Orthodox Church, rejected by the Jews, and not included in the Bible, called the Septuagint.

Toward 364, a conference concerning the council involved in regulating the conduct of church members in the regional council of Laodicea, whose participated number of bishops is unknown, its leadership, even its organization unregistered, took place at the city of Laodicea, the metropolis of Phrygia in the province of Minor Asia. It expressed its decrees in the form of written rules or canons. That date of 364, noted by Justel in the Code of the Universal Church he published in 1645, is a date that the rights and obligations of all Christian faithful qualified uncertain; that Council of Laodicea officially excluded some "apocryphal" gospels and certain writings that did not form part of the canons of the Christian churches, which are writings that were not retained.

Among the sixty canons, the sixtieth canon listed retained four canonical gospel books by omitting certain parts of the book of Revelation from the Bible and listing the twenty-six books of the New Testament; including the Hebrew Bible, containing twenty-two books of the Old Testament that must be read; and adding the book of Baruch plus the epistle of Jeremy to it as accepted books by the Christian churches. And the uncanonical books, books composed of private authority, and books to the infantry were forbidden to be read in church by the fifty-ninth canon. The book of Enoch is believed to have been demonized, leading to its degeneration. And another list matching the one of the Council of Laodicea was produced by Cyril of Jerusalem, around AD 350.

We find its influence in the Hiberno-Latin texts, as in *Altus prosator*, on the passages devoted to the calendar. The sixty canons retained a list of scriptures accepted by the church, like the four canonical gospels constituting the New Testament, by rejecting the other texts in the category of Apocrypha. Canonical books were excluded from the Apocalypse of St. John. The Church of Laodicea rejected an apocalypse treasure intended for it and also rejected the book of John buried in Ephesus. Certain parts of the book were written in Hebrew, some in Aramaic, before the discovery of the fragments in Aramaic among the Dead Sea Scrolls.

Its composition was estimated in the third century BC. Chapters 1 to 5 were composed in Hebrew by using the version of the recognized text as authoritative within in Judaism called the Masoretic Text of Deuteronomy, which was traditionally regarded as an exact replica of the original Bible but having differences with other older versions in meaning. Like the Samaritan Bible, the version of the Pentateuch or the Torah in use among the Samaritans, is relatively close to the Christian and Jewish versions of the Pentateuch but incorporating a significant difference with the Greek Septuagint version of the

Tanakh, the Hebrew Bible or Old Testament, including the Apocrypha in the Greek language, conceived for Jews in Egypt speaking Greek, and adopted by the early Christian churches, which has some changes of nearly two thousand textual variations, in agreement with the one written in the Samaritan alphabet. And with the Latin Vulgate, some changes are shared between versions.

The Letter of Aristeas (second century BC) reported that the translation of the Torah was made at the request of Ptolemy II, toward 270 BC, by seventy-two translators. Also, the Septuagint is the ancient Greek version of the entire biblical Scriptures of (the Christians Old Testament) and the Qumran Scrolls or the Manuscripts of the Dead Sea. A series of scrolls and fragments of a Jewish papyrus were written in Hebrew, some in Aramaic, and a few in Greek around the first century BC. These nine hundred manuscripts were officially discovered between 1947 and 1956 in eleven caves, frequently attributed to the Essene groups without definitive proof; and between them, they have similarities in some places, where they diverged from the Masoretic Text. The first scroll of Isaiah, the major discovery of Qumran, written in fifty-four columns of seventeen sheets of leather, containing the entire book made in the second century BC, with a total length of approximately 7.30 meters, is the oldest complete manuscript written in Hebrew, known from the Bible as the book of Isaiah, which became famous worldwide.

A quarter of these manuscripts were copies of portions of the Hebrew Bible. The rest were nonbiblical Jewish writings, including Apocrypha. These many writings reflected customs and opinions indicating that the texts were copied or composed between the third century before our era and the first century of our era. Qumran presumably housed a school of copyists. Their authors were in disagreement with the religious authorities of Jerusalem before the destruction in year 70 of our era. A wide range of thoughts that did not necessarily reflect their religious beliefs and convictions was adopted. These writings revealed the existence of extremely strict rules on the Sabbath and an almost obsessive concern for ceremonial purity (Matt. 15:1–20, Luke 6:1–11); as Luke wrote in Luke 3:15, they also believed in the imminent coming of the Messiah. The Essenes, who lived away from the society, believed in the destiny and the immortality of the soul. They rejected marriage and attached great importance to the mystical ideas, relating the participation to the cult rendered by the angels. Their teaching was incompatible with that of the early Christians and the one of Jesus.

Mtt. 5:14–16 said, "A lamp should be lighted to be put on the lampstand so that it shines on the whole house and for all those who are in the house, and not to be put under a bushel." For as the light of the world, people's light must shine like the flavor of salt, because if it loses its flavor, it is no longer good for nothing. Thus, their light must shine in the eyes of men so that their works may be seen by rendering glory to the father in heaven. These words of beatitudes are the words of the evangelical discourse. Col 2:18 says to not "let no one come to frustrate you by indulging you in humble practices and in the worship of angels: such a person also gives great detail about things they have seen; they're puffed up with vain pride by their unspiritual thought." Summarizing that, we should not practice the worship of angels, against the false asceticism, and according to the elements of the world; and 1 Tim 4:1–3 says, "Some spirits in the last days, will explicitly renounce faith in order to attach themselves to deceitful spirits and diabolical doctrines, seduced by hypocritical liars, marked with a red-hot iron in their consciences. These people forbid marriage and the use of food that God created to be taken with thanksgiving by believers and those who have knowledge of the truth."

All these are to qualify all those who rejected marriage and attached great importance to mystical ideas, concerning the participation in the worship given by angels. To conclude that, idolatry is prohibited by the Christian assemblies; to not leave the church of God and follow the false teachers who invoke the angels in the worship rendered by the angels.

In 1773, three copies of this book were taken from Ethiopia to Britain by a Scottish explorer and geographer, James Bruce, the famous traveler and adventurer who traveled all over North Africa, exploring unfamiliar area, to discover the source of the Nile. Let us note that European scholars have long sought this book. For Mormons, it is Enoch who founded the city of Zion.

In the Bible, Zion means, at the same time, the geographical locations, such as the fortress of the Jebusites, and all that personifies the presence and the blessing of God. "The Lord's hand was heavy against the people of Ashdod, and its vicinity; He terrified them and afflicted them with tumors. And when the people of Ashdod saw what was happening, they said, 'The ark of the God of Israel must not stay with us, because His hand is heavy against us and against Dagon our god" (1 Sm. 5:6–7).

By dint of the Jebusites' ban on David to enter Jerusalem, he decided on taking Zion (2 Sm. 5:6–7), so Solomon summoned the elders of Israel to Jerusalem to build the city of David, which was Zion (1 Kings 8:1, 2 Chr. 5:2), the holy mountain of God (Ps. 74:2). And finally, the survivors of Mount Zion left the city of Jerusalem (2 Kings 19:31). Because of the righteousness of Zion, he was abducted and taken to heaven by the righteous who lived there, according to the book of Moses (Heb. 12:22). And Psalm 132:13 tells us that, figuratively, Zion was the headquarters chosen by God and represented the emblem of His presence and His blessing and simultaneously, may designate everywhere enjoying the divine presence (Ps. 9: 12, Ps. 48:2–3).

The founder of the Church of Jesus Christ of Latter-day Saints, who founded Mormonism in 1830, said he witnessed a series of spiritual manifestations when he was fourteen years old. He said that, in the spring of 1820, God the Father and Jesus Christ his Son appeared to him in his first vision for the restoration of the church of Jesus Christ. He reported that, several times, Moroni—the son of Mormon and the last Nephite prophet who lived in the early fifth century after Jesus Christ—appeared to him and revealed the place where the book written on gold plates were buried in 1823, accompanied by the Urim and Thummim. This religious personality of a political life also made known to the religious world that three of the original apostles of Christ by the names of James, John, and Peter, accompanied by John the Baptist, who was not an apostle, appeared to him in 1829 to transmit the keys of priesthood to him. It was through their recommendation that he organized the church of Jesus Christ on earth. And it was by the help of the Urim and Thummim that he was able to translate the gold plates that were handed over to him in 1827, which later became the Book of Mormon. So, it was Joseph Smith, from the United States, who reestablished the original church of Jesus Christ in the world. According to the Mormons, God prepared the translation of the plates through the Urim and Thummim; and after the translation, the angel Moroni recovered them.

In Ezra 2: 1–63, Ezra cites the list of Zionists on their return from exile after being deported from Babylon to Jerusalem by King Nebuchadnezzar. Back to Jerusalem, since they were not appearing in the genealogical register, they were excluded from the priesthood and treated as unclean and were also prohibited to eat sacred foods, until a priest got up for the Urim and Thummim.

Dt. 33:8 says: give your Thummim and your Urim to Levi thy holy one, the man whom you gave thanks and whom thou didst prove. In Ex 28:30, Aaron was to put the Thummim and the Urim at the breastpiece to appear before Yahweh. Lv 8:1–8 tells us that Moses washed Aaron and his sons to clothe him and placed the breastpiece on him, where he put the Urim and Thummim. In Num. 27:21-23, Moses took Joshua and presented him before Eleazar the priest, after laying his hands on him, so that Eleazar could consult him according to the rite of the Urim at the recommendation of the Lord for him to have a share of his dignity to be obeyed by the whole community of Israel after giving him his orders. So as these Bible chapters are mentioning, the disguise of the true origin of the laws could not completely erase the ancient features of the Egyptian truth by its fables.

The Mosaic Code of truth, hidden by the laws of the Hebrews, bore a title in the Egyptian language—called a hierarchical writing system used on papyrus, stones, and wood, in religious literature. Since the art of carving stone is older than the New Testament itself, the Egyptians used it to record most sacred and important events that touched every aspect of life in their time.

This religious literature of classical Egyptian antiquity, practicing the expression of divination considered its pharaohs as wise, judicious and insightful counselors to whom gods spoke directly. Properly said, the word *oracle* refers to— "to speak" or from the Latin verb *ōrāre*. The signification of "oracle," meaning uttering the "Most Holy" words, practiced in the innermost room of the temple, originated in Egypt. It was evoking the higher powers to influence the lives of men and women in Egyptian language; its ordinances were carved on natural objects as pieces of hardwood, on metal, into leather, stones, or in all created things on earth to embody sacred powers.

This divination language, combined with logographic, syllabic, and alphabetic elements as first Glyphs, was used since the sun appeared at the horizon; and it was incorporated into the interpretation of the cult of the Blank Stone as the Great Amun-Ra. So the art of divination, the oracular tradition combined with the ancient art of stone casting and stones carving, originated from Africa; it was conceived to emphasize the light in spiritual things stemming back for millions of years before the Greek temples of prophetic predictions or precognition of the future inspired by the gods, got a hold of our ancient art of stones carving, and then propagated it in the European culture and throughout the world. The oracular site of the snake-headed woman—eye of the moon, known as the renowned temple in Per-Wadjet, of the goddess Wadjet in Egypt, was the source for the oracular tradition. Wadjet was depicted as a woman with two snake heads considered as one of the aspects of the Great Mother, a form of deity of the snake goddess, a chthonic deity of the underworld, especially in the Greek religion. But the Europeans finally took the ancient art of stone casting and stones carving and eventually changed its proper name to Runes, distorted it, and made it their own. Since the art of stone is still a mystery like in the ancient times, the word *Runes,* also meaning "mystery or secret," is quite suitable indeed to the Egypt religious literature.

And concerning the word *oracle,* when it is translated into the Aramaic Hebrew language, it also has the same meaning as the Egyptian. But to our knowledge, nothing was written concerning the name Runes as a contemporary mystery of El-Eloh. However, the first existence of casting stones appeared in the Old Testament as the Urim, meaning "stones of lights," and the Thummim, meaning "perfection" in Aramaic, which is found in Ex 28:30. In pre–Christian era, Runes took on a ritual aspect serving divination, and the symbols were carved into pieces of hardwood, incised on metal, cut into leather, or carved on stones with an alphabet script called "Runes" for divination purpose as the Urim and Thummim. Thus, the word *truth,* which was known as an oracle among Egyptian, became a word similar to that of the Urim and Thummim in the religion code of the one who was saved from the waters in Egypt, known as Moses.

So, the Urim and Thummim were among the many garments worn by the high priests of ancient Israel. The two carnelian stones called Urim and Thummim, with the names of the twelve tribes of Israel engraved on both stones, were each placed in a pocket square near the shoulders in the breastplate of the high priest.

The historian Josephus told us that when God was present, the two stones began to shine brightly in a supernatural way. According to the description of this same historian in book 3, chapter 7 entitled: *Jews Antiquities,* the Thummim consisted of twelve stones of an extraordinary size and beauty inserted in the breastplate of the high priest, with the name of a tribe engraved on each stone, which began to shine with splendor when God indicated to them that they would be victorious in battle, book III, chapter 7 and 8). As ordained by God, the Hebrew high priests consulted these instruments of oracles of perfection and light prepared by God, to interpret and translate in the Septuagint version, therefore a sortition was invoked and realized by these manipulated objects to designate the principal characteristic of the truth and reveal the supernatural entities, to obtain a revelation and a truth via divination, by transmitting a request to God in public or national emergencies, and by placing his hand on the Urim and the Thummim, to determine the will of God in certain situations. This Septuagint version was made in the third and second centuries BC, for Greek-speaking Jews in Egypt. As the Greek version of the Old Testament or the Hebrew Bible adopted by the first Christian churches, it included the Apocrypha.

The book of John in the Bible, known under the name of Apocalypse, evokes an angel in chapter 14:6, saying that "the apostle John saw another angel flying at the zenith, having a good and eternal gospel to proclaim unto all people who dwell on the earth, and unto every nation and languages of all tribes;" this flying angel was considered as Moroni by the Mormon theology. Peshitta is the Hebrew Old Testament text translated into Syriac, and its New Testament was translated from Greek. The translated version in Syriac dialect or group of dialects of Eastern Aramaic is the standard version of the Bible for churches in the Syriac tradition. The Syriac version, in all likelihood, is the earliest translation made from AD 160 to AD 180 at Antioch, the capital of Syria during the Seleucid reign. The first Christian Disciples of Christ made the first translation at the literary capital called Edessa. Its text of the New Testament in Aramaic exists in two forms: (1) the Syriac New Testament as part of the Peshitta Bible in the classical Aramaic, or (2) the "Peshitta," as the "Assyrian Modern" New Testament; the Peshitta is the name reserved for the Aramaic oral text, as composed of multiple small speeches and by witnesses transmitted in evangelical collars in Jerusalem to the Jews. It contains a complex system that gives description between its lines still untapped till today.

Its methods of memorizing its oral application, still specific to African civilizations, are preserved in Africa, particularly in the Middle East. This assumption is originally because the Aramaic vernacular language was the primary language spoken by Jesus and his twelve apostles. These memorizing methods of oral application rendered the apostles' words and their accents revealing the revelation of what was unknown or secret in theatrical actions; and its mimetic rhythm was engraved with such easiness in the hearts of the first Christian communities. This evangelical orality, discovered very recently, was the work of a few intrepid pioneers who were not afraid to face misunderstandings and maintained an emotion of love contained in their original expression, which no important particular theology can reproduce among all languages that have translated the Bible—namely, Hebrew, Greek, Arabic, French, English, and other languages, which remained helpless beyond its simple evangelical orality meaning.

Rightly without any dispute related to the phonetic form of Peshitta, not having the same phonetic form as the Westerners, they nevertheless considered it as a Phonetic material which is a language used to form the oral made of simple concepts. Since an evangelical text has never gotten so much expressiveness as the Aramaic gospel text, it only has expressiveness when it is recited in Aramaic. This demonstrates enough that it was originally composed in that language. And the first translator of the oral recitation, known under the name of Marc, has himself left several sentences in the original language. The form that preaching can take may change according to the New Testament writings, as well as the type of apostolate (the ministry of an apostle and the place where it is preached) and by extension, the propagation of the faith. To preach is comparably and totally independent of the day of the week or even the time of day. In other words, any Christian lay religious or "professional" religious (man or woman) can a priori engage in preaching when Protestantism took it over because the New Testament does not require that a preacher be consecrated; these few biblical foundations of preaching mark a sure separation between Roman Catholicism and Protestantism.

Several New Testament texts revealed some interventions of the first great preachers, who were the apostles, as well as the early Christians of primitive congregations. Evangelization was done at the same time as the witness by preaching. The intellectuals of the Greco-Latin civilization of that time advocated the extension of all knowledge, even religious. The purpose of that evangelization was to spread the divine word, and to make it accessible to everyone, of all origins, and in all languages. One of the volumes of the Midrash Rabbah or Genesis Rabbah explains interpretations, words, and phrases rather distant from thoughts reproduced in various exposed text after translation.

This rabbinic literature, often referring specifically to the literature of the Talmudic era, is in various compilations of Midrash Haggadah; but primarily, the first collection of the rabbis of the Talmud, of which Midrash Rabbah is one of the best-known, as the first collection or part of the Midrashim of rabbis on the books of Tanakh, designating the aggadic midrashim as a whole, represents the last word given as an "explanation" of the Holy Scriptures. Generally, "Rabbah" as part of their name means "great." And on the five scrolls, like other writings of the Hebrew Bible, after the (Torah-Pentateuch) and the writings of the (prophets-Nevi'im), comes what forms the third and final part of the (Tanakh-Hebrew Bible) called the Ketuvim as a subdivision of the writings. In this subdivision, there are books like various compilations of Midrash Haggadah. One of the best known in these various compilations is the Midrash Rabbah, as well as the Hebrew texts in various practical functions and in different fields of the corpus of rabbinic literature, most used during divine service, including the Song of Songs, Deuteronomy Rabbah, Exodus Rabbah, (Genesis Rabbah-Bereshit Rabbah), Leviticus Rabbah, Numbers Rabbah, the book of Ruth, the book of Lamentations, Ecclesiastes, and the book of Esther, designating a set of ten collections of midrashim haggadic. In an identical context in the Bible, the word Midrash appeared only twice, in the second book of Chr. 13:22, where it is mentioned that the rest of the history of Abijah was written in the midrash of the prophet Iddo, and in the second book of Chr. 24:27, concerning the restoration of the temple of God, duly recorded in the midrash of the Kings. The Midrash of the book of the Kings is mentioned among the noncanonical books in the Bible.

As a whole, it designated the teachings of the Jewish tradition and the nonlegislative teachings. Since the giving of the Torah at Mount Sinai, the Midrashim were taught as an oral tradition; toward the ninth and tenth centuries, after the closure of the Talmud, they were put into writing. Also, as in the Talmud, the comments attributed to this or that rabbi of the Talmud were written in Aramaic. In the translation of the Bible into the vernacular language by Erasmus in 1516, it is said, "You will be at the origin of all the people of the Earth." But according to the Bible, on the divine plans, all humans are descendants of Noah, the terrestrial animal with a chemical body as Adam II, in the second creation by Yahweh, the God of Israel. Noah's father, Lamech, said his son will bring solace in work and painful toil of the hands of humanity, from the ground that God cursed, by naming him Noah, Gen. 5:29.

Let's note that according to the Jewish sacred books, the creation of Adam II, second creation of the chemical terrestrial man, descendant of Yahweh (in chapter 4 of Genesis) up to Methushael, was not to have longevity because this creation was illegal. Compare this to chapter 5:1 of the first creation of Adam I, the galactic man and the descendant of Elohim up to Methuselah, gave us the proof of his double creation.

This union between the first creation, meaning the notion of spirituality, descending into the depth of the consciousness up to Lamech, the terrestrial man, is his formation with a form of psyche life, and referring to the human soul called ishshah is known as a proto-plasma type, driven from the Garden of Eden, and not existing anywhere in the universe; and it is perhaps a cosmic necessity that completely overturned the whole cosmic cycle. Gen. 3:23–24 said, "And Yahweh expelled the man out of the Garden of Eden, out casted him, and posted the cherubim and the f lame of lightning sword to protect the way of the tree of life, of which fruit He forbade the man to eat for an eternal life; finally, he let him live on earth simply to cultivate the soil, where he was taken."

The Old Testament exhibits the chronology in chapter 5 of Genesis, citing ten generations between Adam and Noah, son of Lamech, born in the year 1056, after the creation of Adam, tenth of the lineage from Adam through Seth. And it reveals that Noah lived 950 years, but the chronology of creation and all created things can only be a normal moral to the satisfaction of all entities, if the consciousness included in the text of the Torah, solely read and understood by oral tradition, can be read and understood by all entities with satisfaction.

A very traditionalist reading of the Bible is necessary to discover that the recital of Genesis, translated from the hidden Torah, also called "Torat Ha-Sod," the secret Torah is "the teaching of the secret," known as the Kabbalah; mistranslated as a "secret teaching," Kabbalah is "the teaching of the secret." The inner practice, the breath in the body, known as the soul: an inner wisdom of a person; providing the knowledge of wonder, the knowledge of the wisdom of mystery, a sense of the beyond, of that which cannot be known, or understood.

From its integral Judaism religious origin, its New Age of Christian part, to the concepts of a set of esoteric teachings, Kabbalah explains the mortal and finished creation of the universe of God, the relationship between the unchanging eternal, and the endless mysteries. It seeks the nature and the purpose of existence, to define the nature of the universe. Kabbalah also teaches methods for the adept to understand the concepts leading to attain spiritual realization and various other ontological questions. It is not a religious denomination in itself but forms the foundations of mystical religious interpretation of the Akkadian or Sumerian ancient traditions; it is copy to only be read as a narrative recital but having a true substance in the used language or in the figurative language that gives importance independently to each of its letters. The Bible tells us that its emblematic character known as Noah lived as a righteous man in a degenerated and degraded world but walked with the true God.

Noah (Nun Het, the one with the ark) was seeing himself as in a mirror, looking himself into the eyes of Yahweh; he found grace (Hen Het Nun) in the eyes of Yahweh, so said the Word of God in Gen. 7:1–2.

In Hebrew, the God who spoke to Noah is *Anochi*, the feminine god of the masculine *Ani*, meaning "I am the Lord your God." These two names are used in many verses of the Torah. The female God *Anochi* is referring to his own opposition by saying that there is no other God than him, with a desire to get closer to his interlocutor. On the other hand, the masculine God Ani is a personification of his person. His conception of both polarities is accessible to human understanding. In Gen. 15:1, the same God spoke to Abram in a vision and heard by Moses at the top of Mount Horeb in the Sinai Desert.

The theonym of the divinity of Israel, transcribed in French as YHWH הוהי)), in the form of the sacred tetragrammaton composed of the masculines *Yod* and *Waw*, and twice the feminine letter *Hey*, making a total of four Hebraic letters: *yōḏ* (י), *hē* (ה), *wāw* (ו), *hē* (ה), are letters constituting the name of the God of Israel and Judah. The Hebrew Bible, the Tanakh, presents them as the invariable proper name of God: its root is composed of three *letters* היה *(HYH)* of the verb "to be," "to exist," "to happen," "to take place," "to occur," "to cause to become," or "to engender." This most marvelous and fundamental word is used for "the identification of person, a thing or to denote the simple existence."

Augustin Crampon—the canon of the cathedral of Amiens, regarded as the Catholic exegete, and translator of the Catholic Bible—directly translated the first edition of the biblical study compiled in French throughout a lifetime, since the medieval times of the Christian religion and all canonical books up to the early twentieth century, published by him in 1899. The Jehovah transcript of the tetragrammaton YHWH was preserved by Father Crampon; and it is by combining the Hebrew consonants with the vowels of the Hebrew word *Adonai*, "Lord" that the theonym of the divinity of Israel was obtained. From the Hebrew, Aramaic, and Greek texts, the Catholic priest Crampon, born on February 4, 1826, in Franvillers in la Somme (France), made his translation of the "Crampon Bible" from the canonical books. He died on August 14, 1894, in Paris.

You will not pronounce the name YHWH in vain, which the mortals thought to be so holy, but that the translators of the Old Testament translated by Lord God, under the virtue of the Third Commandment, which well accords with the importance attached to the name YHWH in the Hebrew scriptures. In

Ex. 20:2–17, some verses cover this expression, containing the idea underlining a list of forbidden things to do like: "not to pronounce the name of God in vain, not to make any image, in the likeness of anything in heaven above, or in the earth beneath, not to have no other gods, not to covet or bear false witness against thy neighbor, not to do unworthy things, not take this name YHWH 'in vain' and so on, and so on, according to Moses, and if you do these things, He would elevate you to the rank of liar." The third commandment is the law of YHWH, meaning "I am the One who IS and who will be the Eternal;" it is transliterated into English as "Yahweh," and in German as "JHVH." These Ten Words in Ex. 20:2–17 about not pronouncing the name YHWH in vain were also mentioned by Father Crampon. Gen 4:26 reveals that the name YHWH that should not be used in a disrespectful, profane, or blasphemous manner was the name given to Enosh, the son of Seth, who started to invoke it for the first time as practiced more than two millennia earlier. Thus, to avoid having to pronounce it, the Jews substituted the name by superstition much later.

And its punctuation "יְהוִֹה" of the tetragrammaton pronunciation from which the English name "Jehovah" derived is more accurately represented than the Hebrew Bible. So wherever the name YHWH appeared in the text, the reader would pronounce the word Lord: Adonai in Hebrew; and to a point in time, the wonderful pious idea of the personal name of God vanished from the human consciousness. This tetragrammaton had to do with the name of the oldest Semitic deity, Yah (the eternal), having its explanation in Ex. 3:13–14 in the Bible, where Moses saw a blazing fire sprang from the burning bush but was not consuming.

Moses, who was grazing the sheep of Jethro, his father-in-law, priest of Midian, saw God, who appeared to him and said, "Tell your people that I am the God of your father, the God of Abraham, the God of Isaac, and Jacob, that I have seen the misery of my people." Moses answered to Elohim by saying, "Behold, suppose I go among the Israelites and tell them that the God of your fathers has sent me to you, but what shall I say if they ask me, 'What is his name?'" God said to Moses, "I am Elohim. I am He who Is. I am what I Am" (Ehyeh Acher Ehyeh [הָיָה אֲשֶׁר הָיָה] in Hebrew). And He said, "This is what you are to say to the Israelites: I Am has sent me to you to tell them that 'I Am the one that future generations will remember." The TOB, the ecumenical translation of the Bible, presented Him as "I am THAT I am."

In Ex. 6: 3, Ps. 83:18 and Is. 12:2 and 26:4, the Catholic Church of the early twenty-first century replaced YHWH with IEHOVAH and Lord God; Elohim (ALYHM) in Hebrew is composed of *A* for Aleph and *Y* for Yod and viewed naturally as consonants originally, and considered as a sacred name of God in Hebrew. First Cor. 8:5–6 tells us that there are many gods and lords in heaven and on earth. Here are two examples taken from the Bible: Gen. 3:22–23 reports that the Lord said, "The man has now become like one of us, knowing good and evil." The word "*us*" proves the existence of many gods.

"So he must not be allowed to reach out his hand and also take from the tree of life and eat, and live forever." And Gen. 11:7–8 says, "Come, let us go down and confuse their language, so they will not understand each other." As already mentioned above, the first epistle of Corinthians continues its chapter 8:5–6, by telling us that "Although there are so-called gods in heaven or on earth—yet for us there is one God." You must know that, in Hebrew text, it is written *lords* instead of *God*. And from the modern translation of Adonai, Elohim is the plural of Eloah, the Supreme Being; Jehovah is the plural of the name Yahweh; El Shaddai and so on are plural. We can notice this plural by these biblical passages.

The big book, clearly giving a lot of information known as the Bible, is originally a book of few words, brief but comprehensive, and of a concise root of impenetrable mysteries. An Egyptian genius that Moses wrote with the initial fire, between the trembling verses by the breath (Ruah) of Elohim; manifestly, he was revealing the *true* Egyptian God-Creator of heaven and earth to the Israelites by turning the heavy pages of the history of the universe, after his Egyptian initiation.

Moses, to whom Egypt had opened the doors of its underground occult temple, to be initiated as a true illuminator by the light of its immobile lamps; revealing him the succession of worlds in time, and time in time; at the end by his acquired intellectuality, he lost its true root; known as the comprehensive mystery of its gigantic and brilliant construction between two blocks of larva—the mystery of the secret of time and the secret language of the temple that generated the Bible. And when the Bible was first translated into Phoenician, it lost its esoteric keys and the oral explanation that Moses received from his initiators.

The Jews in turn, poorly controlled its esoteric keys, already lost in majority, when Ezra wrote a new version in Chaldean Aramaic. And when the translation of the Bible was published in Greek, its translators had just a vague idea of the true esoteric text of the Bible. The three translations of the Old Testament in Greek, realized toward 170, by the one whom St. Jerome qualified as Ebonite, Symmachus, and Theodotion, a Jewish scholar of the Hellenistic culture of the first century or second century, were intended for Jews of the Diaspora unable to read Hebrew.

Thus, the Latin version of St. Jerome, translated from the Hebrew text already very poor in the primitive sense that was the true sense, had completely escaped him. The Bible, our holy book, has lost its prodigious language, an eloquent language expressing things as clearly as possible with a limited number of words, which evoked the principles and causes in the consciousness of the adept, who then as the result saw the rays of the divinity radiating in him in the invisible and visible nature, awakening his senses no longer reason; its phonetic structure, its universal meaning of each vowel and consonant, its acoustic value of the letter, reasoning like a plucked string musical instrument called lyre reasoning in the ear of the learner, leading him to think, understand, and form a judgment by a logical process no longer exist. That phoneticism of the sacred language of the ancient temple no longer has the magic formula of its sparkling syllables of the text, which was transforming the fire letters into the thought of light.

We quail them like brass in a great darkness, wrapped in a secret priesthood of the ancient religion cycles, up to the Christian initiates of the first decade, determined by the esotericism since the dust of time, but having the mother idea as the living thought that admits the immutability of the universal law—a gradual evolution, the development of the inner-self, an extension and the notion of reasoning with copper foundations of the world. I will simply say that without initiation, we would not have a religious constitution as it is known today. As the Bible usually tells us stories, this leads us to Ex. 18:13–25 for the religious constitution and the establishment of fundamental principles, according to which a state or another organization is recognized to be governed. It cites Moses in this sense: "The next day, when Moses sat to judge the people, the crowd stood every day around him from morning till evening, awaiting his judgment."

When Moses's father-in-law saw that he was doing overwhelming work for the people, he asked him these questions: "How do you go about dealing with people's affairs? Why do you sit alone, and all the people standing around you from morning till evening?" Moses said to his father-in-law, "People come to me to consult God; they come when they have a dispute. I then determine an alternative resolution of the disputes between them and I teach them the laws of God and his decisions to implement the reign of the law." Moses's father in-law said to him, "What you're doing is not good. You and the people will certainly wear yourselves out, because the task exceeds your strength. You will run out and exhaust those people around you, because you're not able to do it alone for your people. Now obey my voice; I will give you some advice; then he gave him the following advice: let God be with you! But for God to assist you, you shall represent the people before God and bring their disputes to God, and you will teach them statutes and laws, and let them know how they must walk and what they should do.

"Moreover, look for able men from all the people, men who fear God, who are trustworthy and hate bribes, and place such men over the people. Instruct them on how to resolve problems, disputes or contentious issues; the law regulations and decisions of peaceful resolution of all disputes; let them know the path to follow and the conduct to consider carefully.

Make them chiefs of thousands, chefs of hundreds, chefs of fifties, and chefs of tens; an institution of judges, which will be available and at the service of the people, to deliver justice at all times. And let them judges the people at all times. Every great matter they shall bring to you, but any small matter they shall decide themselves. So, your task will be lightened, and they will bear the burden with you. If you do this, God will direct you, you will be able to endure, and all these people will also go to their homes in peace." So, Moses listened to the voice of his father-in-law.

This advice of his father-in-law (the initiator) was an initiation to Moses, as the notion of reasoning having the mother idea, known as the living thought of the universal law, leading to the founding of the religious constitution, and the civil legislation that existed in Egypt, since the dust of times, were at that period born in the Jewish community by the facts of Moses, who did everything his father-in-law gave him as advice. He chose capable men among the Israelites and made them leaders of the people—rulers of thousands, of hundreds, of fifties, and of tens—as he was advised by his father-in-law. His father-in-law was a high priest of one of the cave temples of Midian. But what the Bible did not tell us is that this high priest was also a former treasurer of the pharaohs and one of the former ancient magicians of Ancient Egypt.

This Ethiopian, initiated into the secret great mystery with typical rituals by the name of Jethro, was a great sage who has accumulated knowledge and treasure of sciences in his memory. He knew his old tradition, ascending from the oldest race in the world, a race that had ruled for four or five thousand years before Ramses. He immediately recognized a predestined man in the person of Moses as a man with a particular belief and faith, predestined by God to go to heaven or to hell to get what he needed, and who wanted to undergo atonement imposed on initiated murderers. According to the Bible, he previously killed an Egyptian soldier who was violently beating a Jew. Known as a wise priest and doubly initiated, in two separate educations in the Mansion of Life, or House of Life, he was housing an integrated administrative and architectural institution, and a temple of importance for initiation; a separate place of school education where the progeny of elites, civil servants, and clergy received education tailored to their social status in Ancient Egypt. Moses was educated in Egyptian temples to the monotheistic belief, the belief in one universal God, a belief born in Africa and then from Osiris as the same God that everyone knew before he could cross borders.

Because he knew all their sciences, he was raised among Egyptian priests, where he stole the Ten Commandments of the law of a unique God, which already existed, written on papyrus scrolls kept in sanctuaries well before he updated them in the Sinai. He was well-educated in their schools in theurgy in the temple of mysteries of the ancient city of "On" known today as Heliopolis (the city of the sun), linked to its veneration of the sun deities, where he who was known as Moses was called Hosarsiph. Beth-Smees is the city of the sun that celebrated the worship of the god Ra, the solar god; the temple of the sun is the form under which Jer. 43:13 designates this city). Asnath, Joseph's wife, whom Pharaoh gave him in Gen. 41:45, was the daughter of a priest of "On" named Potiphera; and in Gen. 46:20, Manasseh and Ephraim were born to Joseph by Asenath the daughter of Potiphera, priest of "On."

On the way in search of a land to take refuge, fleeing from the pharaoh who wanted to kill him, he met the seven daughters of Jethro, which are revealed to us by the Bible, probably having a symbolic meaning. This was what Num. 12:1 said: "Miriam and Aaron spoke against Moses because of the Kushite woman whom he had married, for he had married a Kushite woman." Ex. 2:16–20 continues by saying, "Now the priest of Midian had seven daughters, and they came and drew water from the well, and fill the troughs to water their father's f lock. At that instant, the shepherds came and drove them away, but Moses stood up and saved them, and watered their f lock.

When they came back home to their father Reuel [Jethro], he said, 'How is it that you have come home so soon today?' They said, 'An Egyptian rescued us from the shepherds and even drew water for us and watered the f lock.' He said to his daughters, 'Then, where is he? Why have you left the kind-hearted man? Call him to come and eat bread.' So, the girls went looking for him and invited Moses in their family house, where he eventually settled and finally fell in love with one of Jethro's daughters.

Now concerning the magic wand; the story that I'm going to tell you reveals to us that when Moses asked to marry Zipporah, she replied by saying, "My father has a tree in his garden. His orders are that anyone who would like to marry one of us must uproot that tree. But know that it devours anyone who will try to uproot it. Will you try to uproot it to marry me?" Indeed, this Ethiopian had a very old magic wand (a magic rod) that the Supreme God created and that he initially kept very preciously in the ancient pharaonic treasury for a long time when he was their treasurer. And that he decided to take and keep it personally when he was leaving Egypt for it to be a support of his old age of labor on earth as he saw it supporting Joseph, worn-out by time in Egypt.

This wand was inherited by the oldest human on earth up to Adam; Adam passed it on to Seth, his third son. Then from Adam's family, it was passed as inheritance to Enosh, the son of Seth, and Enosh passed it to Enoch, son of Cain. This wand was passed through generation to generation up to Noah, son of Lamech who was the son of Methuselah, and from Noah to Shem. It continued its route from Abraham to Isaac, from Isaac to Jacob, and finally from Jacob to Joseph, who died in Egypt.

After being an unspeakable support to so many generations to an indefinite pursuit of progress in existence, where man lives as if he was never going to die, with painful secrets of the past events and an absurd present without aim on earth, where he died as if he had never lived, deceived by time, an unknown future, where in the memory of the living, he is just something passed and erased like an air current that erased nature meanders on the sand; he is then only inscribed in the memory of the living as a shadow and remember as a history.

So one day, Jethro was walking in his garden, leaning on that magic wand as support. But without paying attention, he struck the ground with the wand; and suddenly, the magic stick mysteriously rooted deeply in the soil in his backyard. By Jethro's error, it suddenly became a tree with lots of fruits. At the moment, he knew that only an initiated could uproot it. Jethro himself did no longer bother to uproot it anymore because his days on earth were already numbered. And having fathered only girls without heir, he thenceforth took the decision to hand it over as heritage to the one who would marry one of his daughters, and Zipporah knew it. To the question of Zipporah, "Will you try to uproot it to marry me?" Moses answered yes and asked, "Where is that tree?" And Zipporah went and showed him the tree in question in the garden of her father.

Thereby, once again, Moses found himself facing another dreadful test; he had to uproot this magic rod, which was killing the suitors of the daughters of Jethro, at the request of one of them; this time, it was at the request of Zipporah; and it was his turn to prove that he was capable of uprooting this magical rod before marrying Zipporah. So as he was a person of conviction, he wisely succeeded to uproot the tree; then all of a sudden, the tree once again became a magic wand, and he passed the test, which now gave him the right to inherit it and marry Zipporah.

Moses held this wand very high as to give thanks and praise to the Creator, now that it has once again became a magic rod, having the color of sapphire with an unimaginable glow of glory, partly reflecting the surface earth and partly the celestial vault, and bearing at its top the most sacred name of the Most High that no human here on earth had ever pronounced. That famous rod—the magic wand that he inherited in Ethiopia during his refuge by Jethro, one of the Ethiopian elders of the purest race who had not lost the oldest tradition ascending the earth—helped Moses later on in his enterprises. Thus, it was the same way that Moses also took the Golden Ark of the Covenant from the Egyptian temple, which was essentially an Egyptian ritual object that he remodeled at will to become a central vehicle for communication with Yahweh. This Ark was used to protect the arcane book of theurgy in the Egyptian temple. It is to this day used by the Hebrews.

The throne of Elohim that contained the book of cosmology called Sefer Bereshit in Hebrew was also an initiation instrument of the Egyptian arcane secrets, reserved for initiates, transformed by Moses as an instrument producing a phenomenal magic, especially of a nature that manifested a luminous legend. During the Exodus, according to the Bible, it was that famous magic wand and the ark that allowed water to spout from the rock in Horeb when Moses led the Israelites out of Egypt.

Jethro was therefore the one who continued to initiate Moses up to the end. He also led him in the ritual of expiation of sins imposed by the cosmic law to a murderer, at the end of his initiation, engaging him to go and ask the authority of Osiris to raise him to a supreme power by the treasure of knowledge of science that Jethro had accumulated and the one of the rituals in the library of his temple. He led him into the cave of his temple, an underground place containing a sarcophagus with inscriptions of all names of the gods of the universe on the temple walls, revealing the history of the past cycles and the prophecy of future cycles.

Moses submitted himself to death to discover his inner light; a cruel proof that put him in a lethargic sleep for days or even weeks with the help of certain prepared especially for that ritual after a long abstinence. Moses, the priest of Osiris, emerged victorious from that test after a resurrection in the light of Osiris. On his mystical journey, he found the soul of his victim into the abyss but still wandering in the atmosphere of the earth and help his spirit to pass beyond his unknown death to the afterlife; after Moses's test of resurrection in the light of Osiris, he expiated his astral body from his injustice after helping his victim to pass beyond. But sometime, after the physical dead, consisting to clear out impure elements from the astral body, most initiates undergo a slow decomposition to form the spiritual body on earth, resulting to a complete regenerated man who possess his own heaven. Nevertheless, now that his past has been completely washed from his conscience, he returned in the light of the earth as a completely changed man.

Now in his inner eye, he knows (the verb of the word *IEVE*), with its root "I," the creative spirit by excellence, and the unique one from which all others are derived; he then took the ultimate figures of the word *IEVE*, and those fire letters will define his most bold action, which will allow him to write his book of principles; known as Sepher Bereshit—the key of mysteries—a torchlight of initiates, as a concentrated synthesis of the past science, and the framework of future science, to connect the point of all nations, hence the Bible. Jethro, the black man, also bequeathed him an absolute knowledge of the said science—a divine faculty containing all the mystical powers, simultaneously ordered in its revelation, and its soul as a veil of light, shining like an immortal lamp, it awakens an intimate music in the hearts of initiates, when from the bosom of God, the holy oil of love is thrown on its heart.

Consequently, to the tetragram already explained here above, here is another view concerning that sacred name of God in the Hebrew Bible: in the Judeo-Christian intellectuality, the symbol that corresponds to Isis is Eve, Heva, also known as the eternal woman. On the crowd monuments of Ancient Egyptian temples, where a crowned woman was seen, she was holding a jug cross and on the other hand a scepter with a lotus f lower, as the symbol of initiation; a symbol of an eternal life, the sacred language of temples enlightening its brilliant centuries like gold. Superlatively, she symbolized the celestial invisible nature, the proper element of souls and spirits, and she properly typified a woman, a universal feminine kind. Comparatively, to Eve, she is the goddess Isis, the spiritual light and the understandable sacred language that conferred initiation by itself.

So, these examples will enlighten what the sacred language of Ancient Egyptian temples was all about and how the three primary theology senses of Egyptian symbols correspond with those of Genesis. The eternal name of JEVE is composed by the code letter *Jod* and the name of Eve. Its ineffable representing the divine essence occurred in the name IEVE, having at the right hand, the first letter "I ׳," known as the potential manifestation and the eternity. Eve, Heva, is not only known as the woman of Adam but also as God's wife. So, the divine essence in the greatest abstraction of the name JEVE is explained as follows: it first offers us the double life indication and at the same time forms an essential living root known as EE—ππ; it is the only name enjoying the prerogative of never been used as name. From its unique verb are other verbs derived, since the formation of its root. To conclude, the verb *Eve*—π ר π—means existing being. In this explanation, the intelligible sign, Vau—I—as a verb by excellence, found in the middle of the root of life, was taking by Moses, to form the proper name of the Being of beings; and to it, he added the potential sign of manifestation and eternity—I - ר —; to obtain—JEVE — π ר πι — in which the optional exist is found placed between a past without origin and a future without expression. Exactly, this admirable name then means He who IS, who WAS, and who will BE.

By articulating it word by word, it is pronounced as follows: "Yod, He, Vau, He." - "Yod-He-Waw-He" - (הוהי) - is the most sacred name of God the Heavenly Father who spoke to Moses and said, "I am the Lord." As a divine name, the first letter expressed the divine thought, the theogonical science and the natura naturans of Spinoza. The three other letters expressed three nature orders, natura naturata, the three worlds in which this thought is realized, and by the continuation of the cosmogonical psychical and physical science that correspond with it, making four letters in total as the theonym of Israel divinity.

It contains the ineffectual eternal masculine and the eternal feminine name in its deep bosom, constituting their indissoluble union of power and mystery. The one who is known as the sworn enemy of all divinity images by the name of Moses didn't transmit this knowledge to his people but consigned it figuratively in the structure of the divine name by explaining it to his adepts. So, Moses's idea came out brilliantly in Genesis by wanting to hand to the posterity the secret testament of the Sepher Bereshit, determined by the esoteric point of view.

Is the veiled nature in the Judaic cult hidden in the name of God? "Jod-he-vau-he," the four sacred letters representing God in his eternal fusion with the nature, embracing every creature in the living universe, was in reality pronounced "he-vau-he" by all initiates of Egypt, Judea Phoenicians, Middle Age Asia, and Greece, as a sacred cry. Jod is equal to Osiris—meaning, the highest divinity, the intellect creator, which is in everything, everywhere, and above all, known as an eternal masculine. And He-vau-he represented an eternal feminine Eva known as (Isis); she represented the nature under all visible and invisible forms fecund by her.

Now here is a map of the good book of books of the Christian scriptures, consisting of the sixty-six books of the Old and New Testaments on earth, initiated in Africa up to Asia and followed much later by Europe, and a chronological order of the two originals of what we call the Bible and the major released versions highlighting the historical events that have influenced them.

From 10,000 to 6000, Africans of the ancient Nile valley and other Africans in the region of the Great Lakes were already using the stellar calendar, providing particular seasonal information indicating the days, weeks, and months of a particular year before the Christian era.

The revised version of the book that was called the Book of the *Coming Forth by Day and by Night* by Africans was introduced in 4000, when the stellar calendar yielded its place to the solar calendar, also put in place by Africans of ancient Nile valley. The same book, also known by the name of the *Book of the Dead*, was translated in 1895 from hieroglyph into English by an English Egyptologist by the name of Sir Ernest Alfred Thompson Wallis Budge, born on July 27, 1857, in Cornwall, England, and died on November 23, 1934, in London.

The history of the bringing the universe into existence, especially considered as an act of original creation by God, according to the Hebrews, begins in 3700 and much later on the adoption of the Pentateuch, the first five books of the Hebrew Bible are traditionally ascribed to Moses and compiled from texts of the ninth to fifth centuries BC even as biblical exegesis of this century does not recognize Genesis as his work.

The beginning of the dynastic period is placed at thirty-one centuries before our era, under the reign of the Nubian pharaoh by the name of Aha Narmer, king of Ancient Egypt who reigned during the Thinite period and whom the Greek Herodotus called Menes, toward the end of the ancient Predynastic kingdoms of 3100, and ends around 2700. Abraham, the first Hebrew of the Semitic people of the ancient Orient, descended from the nomadic tribes of the eastern edge of the Syrian Desert and was born, according to Annunaki, in 2123; according to the civil year, in 1813; according to the Jewish year, in 1948 BC; and according to the Holy Scriptures, in 1770 in the city of Ur, Chaldea, during the period of African colonial rule. Faithful to the worship of the sun and known today as Jewish, from which all Jews traced their descent, immigrated to Africa around 1850, according to the Holy Scriptures; in 2023, according to the Jewish year; and in 1738, according to Annunaki.

The first foreign invaders in Africa, the mixed people of Semitic and Asian, known as the Hyksos kings of the desert and the Eastern shepherds of the regions of Mesopotamia and the Levant, invaded the ancient Near East of Egypt in circa 1675 BC, corresponding today to the modern Middle East. They entered in the black region by this first foreign invasion, invading Egypt (Africa) and coming from the banks of the Oxus River around the Fertile Crescent.

They were the first known Semitic people who peacefully first settled in Egypt, Africa, from 1730, until being driven out in circa 1532 BC. Thus, taking advantage of the weakness of the Egyptian government, they drove them from power and seized the northeast of Egypt around the second millennium BC and formed the Fifteenth and Sixteenth Dynasties of Egypt. Before crossing to Greece, they ruled a large part of the Egyptian country. This member of the Judah tribe, belonging to the Jewish people of antiquity, existed in Palestine by a conversion of descendants since the sixth century BC until the first century after Christ, since a Jew is considered Jewish just by a Jewish mother. Lev. 24:10 gives credibility to this belief. Originally, the *Jewish* name comes from the name Judah of the Hebrew patriarch, the fourth son of Jacob and Leah and one of the twelve sons of Jacob of the twelve tribes of Israel. Since commonly, the first Jew, Abraham, was described as a Hebrew in Gen. 14:13.

Toward 2030 of our era, during the splendor of Ur, Abraham lived his childhood in Ur, Chaldea, with his family. The family of Terah, well-known in Ur, was a shepherd. Terah fathered three sons: Nahor, Abraham, and Haran, who died in Ur. Ur was presented by the Bible as the hometown of the patriarch Abraham. Before the destruction of the royal city of Ur, by incursions of the nomadic Amorites and a coalition led by the Elamite king Kindattu of Simashki, they invaded the land of Sumer and managed to take it in 2004 BC. It is said in the Bible that Terah left with Abraham and his wife, Sarai; Nahor and his wife, Milcah (the daughter of the deceased Haran, who was also the niece of Nahor); his grandchildren Lot and Jisca, the brother and sister of Milcah. He took them out of Ur of the Chaldeans to migrate in the land of Canaan; at their arrival in Haran, a city mentioned in (Gen. 11:27–32), the whole family stayed there during its great journey from Ur to the Promised Land, probably fleeing from famine, war, and other reprisals (Gen. 12:10–11). Ur, located on one branch of the Euphrates River and near the Persian Gulf, was one of the oldest and most important cities of the ancient Mesopotamia, the present Iraq. After leaving Ur, Terah and his whole family, his small tribe, settled in a small town known today as a district in south-eastern Turkey; the ruins of this city are located on the Balik region (a tributary of the northern Euphrates), named Harran and forming the heart of a rich culture, linking Syria to the valley of Tigris, in the course of history.

The name Harran, besides being the name of Lot's father, was also the name of a flourishing city; and according to the same principle, cities like Terah, Nahor, Serug, and Peleg were named after Abraham's ancestors, since his family consisted of a very powerful dynasty and not extraordinary; and on the whole, represented the great commissioners of the region.

Terah died in this small town that the Bible called Harran. Laban—the great-grandson of Terah, stepfather of Jacob, and the brother of Rebekah—continued to live in this city of Harran, which since 2400 BC knew how to retain its Semitic name. After the death of Terah, the legacy of the deceased and the family herd were to be shared. The first part was given to Nahor and the second part to Abram and his godson Lot, who shared it equally thereafter.

A third family—that of Eliezer, whom Abram, in the absence of a personal posterity, presented to the Lord as his designated heir—added to these two families (Gen. 15:1–4), mentioned this probable cousin of Abram remained in Damascus.

Filled with great satisfying ideals, his conception of what is perfect, Abram had an appropriate right heart, most sensitive, desirable or perfect for his ideals, but not likely to become a reality because they only existed in his imagination. In love with justice and peace, he dreamed of a family blessed by God like those living with Him in heaven, a large expanse of space and a great mass of flock, which he dreamed of bequeathing to his posterity. Therefore, God spoke to him, asking him to go to Canaan, a neighboring country inhabited by the Canaanites and where pastures were abundant, with his cousin Lot. God, whom Abram trusted, called him Abraham, according to the Bible, to entrust him posterity as numerous as the stars of heaven; and like a surprising prediction, He also promised him material prosperity and protection.

Abram set out for the land of Canaan after taking all he had amassed; he then took his staff and all what he had acquired in Harran. He took Sarai, his wife, and his nephew Lot and came to Canaan (Gen. 12:5). At their arrival in the land of Canaan, Sarai took an Egyptian servant by the name of Hagar. Lot settled in the cities of the plain; he set up his tent up to Sodom. And Abram settled in the land of Canaan (Gen. 13:12). It was from the name of the character of Canaan, son of Ham and grandson of the patriarch Noah, according to the Hebrew Bible that this territory was named, cited in Gen. 10:6 and 1 Chr 1:8. His three brothers—Kush, Mizraim, and Put—were respectively eponyms of Ethiopia, Egypt, and Somalia.

The term of the old name *Canaan* first appeared in human history in the third millennium BC. El—the primordial God, the father of mankind and every creature of the belief and the worship of a superhuman controlling power, especially a personal god or gods—was the god of the Canaanite religion before any foreign migration. His name Abram, popular since the second millennium BC in the ancient Middle East, received an - h - ה, like an addition to the verbal roots of his name. This phenomenon was known in Aramaic and other languages. The biblical writers kept the name Abraham to distinguish the Hebrew patriarch from multiple Abrams of the ancient Middle East. "You will no longer be called Abram but Abraham," in Hebrew, said El Shaddai in Gen. 17: 5.

After asking his wife to tell the pharaoh that she was his sister, and presented her as his sister, Abraham received many gifts from two protagonists, who claimed Sarah as their wife; this story is revealed in Gen. 12:13–17; to remedy this situation, the Lord will intervene, first by striking the first protagonist who didn't know that Sarah was Abraham's wife. Gen. 12:17–20 reveals that for the sake of integrating her into the Pharaoh's harem as his wife, he and his entire household were struck by plagues. And the second intervention of the abduction of Sarah by King Abimelech of the city of Gerar took place in a dream in Gen. 20:1–7.

So the kidnappers saw themselves being threatened by God for the release of Abraham's wife; He then represented himself by the human form that God can take to visit human to prove that He exists in all forms to His listener as Master of Creation and that He is hidden under an anonymous human aspect that exceeds our level of understanding too materialistic. The listener then received the visit of the Lord to prove to him that he was not dreaming. God and two angels took human forms to visit Abraham, after reproaching him for his lie. Two identical episodes are mentioned in the Bible concerning Sarah, the half-sister and wife of Abraham.

The proclamation of posterity to Abraham, the first patriarch of the Bible by God, is revealed to us by the Bible in a banal and boring story of inheritance on this earth, lacking evidently originality. God's posterity, promise to Abraham as the future generation of nations, to an old man married to a woman also too old, and at the same time barren with good heart, but who knew jealousy, was a promise very difficult to believe. For Abraham, this promise was impossible to be fulfilled; however, he was put to the test of faithfulness by God, according to the Bible. Let us not forget that, at that time, patriarchs could have several wives and several concubines. And the daughters of the tribal chiefs had one or more maidservants, who could also be the concubines of the master. So even with a jealous heart, Sarah gave Hagar, her Egyptian servant, in accordance with the custom of that time, as concubine to her husband Abram, after ten years that Abraham lived in the land of Canaan so that he could get a son as heir (Gen. 16:3). Finally, the servant of Sarah gave a child to Abraham by the name of Ishmael, the eldest of his family.

Abraham was faced with another problem—the sacrifice of his firstborn to the god Moloch, which was a common occurrence in Canaan and in Phoenicia. A thousand years later, children sacrifices were still mentioned in the Bible and in Israel. This tradition was later turned into the sacrifice of animals to satisfy the symbolic tradition of a cruel bloody sacrifice that God did not like.

The very young and too pretty servant of Sarah, Hagar, Ishmael, and Abraham lived a peaceful life until the birth of the child named of Isaac, who had just been born from Sarah announced their separation. This birth was also a fulfillment proclaimed to Sarah in a dream by God in response to her prayers to have a child. Abraham had happiness, now having two children that he so much loved, but his two children will not last long together; this time, he was going to lose his first son at the request of Sarah, requesting to expel Hagar her servant, and the firstborn Ishmael; after the departure of his eldest son Ishmael, and his mother by jealousy and the fear of Sarah, not wanting Ishmael to claim his birthright inheritance from Abraham, Sarah was satisfied.

So now that Ishmael was gone, Abraham was convinced that the god Moloch would take his youngest son to satisfy the tradition of sacrifice, forgetting that God the Eternal, who proclaimed posterity of two children to him, did not like blood sacrifices, even less the cruel sacrifices of children; but noticing that God did not allow that cruel sacrifice relieved Abraham. Sarah died in Hebron at Kiryat Arba in the arms of Abraham, where all religions were to come together to pray together. He buried her in Hebron, in the cave of Machpelah near Mamre, which became the tomb of the patriarchs for posterity (Gen. 23:19).

Abraham had knowledge of the stories of the Garden of Eden, located between the Tigris and Euphrates (*Eden* means "plain"), and transmitted from mouth to ear since thousands of years, before Abraham left the city of Ur in Chaldea for his immigration in Palestine. This Sumerian nation received the spiritual and scientific cultures of countless black tribes from Africa, transmitted to the people of Mesopotamia and throughout the Middle East from centuries to centuries, for millennia. In the biblical account of the Creation, the disobedience of Adam and Eve by eating the fruit of the tree of knowledge of good and evil led God to expel them from that place where they were living.

Having lived in Egypt, Abraham learned about the resurrection of the soul and many other occurrences like circumcision, suffered by Ishmael when he was thirteen years old (Gen. 17:25–26) and by Abraham when he was ninety-nine years old (Gen. 17:24–25), like a sign of the covenant made between Abraham, his descendants, and God. So, all the males of the house of Abraham, the Bible tells us, were circumcised by removing the skin that covers the glands of their penis (Gen. 17: 23–24). Circumcision was originally only practiced in Africa among black people, particularly by Egyptians and Ethiopians.

(Gen. 17:7 to 8) said: I will establish my covenant between me and you and your seed after you in their generations for an everlasting covenant, to be your God, and to your seed after you. And Gen. 17:9–12 revealed that circumcision was imposed to Abram by God Yahweh. Yahweh appeared to him and said, "This is my covenant which you shall keep, between Me and you and your descendants after you: all your male children must be circumcised; and you shall be circumcised in the flesh of your foreskins, this shall be a sign of the covenant between Me and you." Becoming circumcised at ninety-nine years old became his covenant with God Yahweh, and then he became Abraham.

Thus, (Gen. 17:12–15) affirms to us that: it was an African custom from Egypt that became the sign of the covenant between Yahweh and the Hebrews by circumcision, requiring Abraham to circumcise all newborn males at the age of eight days, specifying even those bought with money, therefore those purchased like properties belonging to the buyer; in conclusion, once again promoting slavery in the Bible.

This symbolic practice, represented in texts found among the Pyramid Texts, was practiced already in Egypt around 2400 BC. And certainly, the worship of the unique and invisible God and a notion of spiritual rebirth and life after death were already honored since the past eight hundred years by the Egyptians. In both countries of Ancient Egypt and Mesopotamia, there were individual conscience and humanitarian principles. Thus, extending the traditional doctrine, Abraham continued his belief on the ways of the divine providence of Imhotep.

He who arrived in Egypt at the end of the period of the pyramids, coinciding with the first interim period, Abraham arrived in Egypt after the end of the Old Kingdom; but despite various inconsistencies between the biblical revelations pointed out by the data of archaeological studies and regular problems that the Christian religion was facing and still face, some priests and preachers still present us the gospels as if we call God for our problems or repentance, he will respond to us instantly, and our problems will be solved. The problem is that this is not the case, considering that this faith sees the world living without care and without being happy at all times, and has done nothing so far, financially or spiritually, to solve our problems.

And this is how the Bible presents the story of Abraham to us—a descendant of Shem, son of Noah, as a character who received everything from God with a click of the fingers. Let's note that the divine providence of the multiple and impenetrable stars is the smallest details that God has not left at random, from our infinitesimal smallness to the stars around their core, tirelessly turning around our great universe of galaxies, colliding with each other from time to time. It also tells us that upon Abraham's death, one of the five great prophets of Islam— including, Noah, Moses, Jesus, and Muhammad—had two sons known as Ishmael and Isaac, who gathered at his bedside, buried their father in the tomb where Sarah already was resting in peace in Hebron, said (Gen. 25:7–9).

Driven by famine, disease, and war, Abraham, the Bible character, arrived in Africa with his family. But the biblical accounts did not give us adequate indications of a patriarchal period; later on, these Hebrew, renamed Mizraim families are today Muslim of Mizrair and Christian; then the alleged Father Moses of the Old Testament was born in Africa as the prince of Egypt. Moses's birth is not exactly known since the rabbinic Judaism placed his birth in 1391 to 1271, some scholars in 1320, St. Jerome in 1592, the Annunaki in 1393, James Ussher in 1571, the Jewish year in 2368, and the biblical chronology around 1527 BC.

The one, who was said to have led a military campaign against the land of Kush (Ethiopia), after invading Egypt, led it on behalf of his stepfather, Khaneferre; Moses was heir to the throne of Egypt, under the name of Thutmose II. But after killing an Egyptian, he lost that title. And according to the Bible, against the pharaoh Ramses II, Moses led a civil war leading to the Exodus of the Hebrews. He crossed the Red Sea by a spit of land, with his oppressed people living on both banks of the Nile, well composed of Jews and Egyptians like him, voluntarily between 1250 and 1230 before Christ, up to Mount Sinai in Egypt, where he received the Ten Commandments, a single significant element distinct from speech or writing in the biblical tradition. Gen. 23:12–13, Dt. 5:6–21, and Ex. 20:1–17 formed a brief synopsis of the Ten Commandments, of the Laws regulating all aspects of Jewish life, on the 613 commandments found in Leviticus and other books.

The first prophet of Judaism, Moses, the founder of the Jewish religion according to tradition, to whom God reveals his name by this formula: (Ehyeh Asher Ehyeh) הִיָה אֲשֶׁר הִיָה, (I am the One who Is-who-Was-and-who will Be), in continuity with the ancient African tradition, is explained in Gen. 3:14 by the tetragrammaton YHWH), meaning Yahweh. He was the mediator who prepared the meeting between Yahweh and Israel, an unexpected meeting, during which God spoke directly to Hebrews in a crash of lightning and thunder to seal a new Covenant. This character, the most important of the Hebrew Bible, is for Christianity a foreshadowing of Jesus Christ and for Islam a precedent of the prophet Muhammad.

The one who led Israel out of Egypt died at 120 years old on the threshold of Canaan in 1190. But before dying completely, ending the function of his organism and falling asleep in the sleep of earth, he cursed the whole race of Judah by these terrifying words of terror: "Let the people of Israel be dispersed around the four corners of the world for betraying my God." So Moses called on the vengeance of Elohim, irritated against his people; he sanctioned them by consecrating them to the misfortune of hell by this solemn utterance of a curse, invoking a supernatural power, intended to inflict harm and punishment on his people. This curse is still following this people, dispersed around the four corners of the world, up to this day.

These words came out from the mouth of the prophet, raising his weighing arm weakened by death for the last time, like if he wanted to say a final word; he was honorably attended by Joshua and the Levites, terrified by hearing these last words from Moses the initiator, after noticing the transformations of the Pentateuch, the depths of Genesis in legendary story that the Jewish priesthood gives us today.

After the prophesied curse of Moses on his Jewish people, known as not having a common language, a homeland, or a shared history, says Dt. 4:26–28, and promising their annihilation, Dt. 28:63–64, is indicating that as the Lord had taken pleasure to procure them a land, so he would snatch it from them and scatter them among all people of the world from one end to another. Thus, knowing this fact, they're fighting so hard by drinking the blood of the innocent people of Palestine in their homeland to exterminate their nation just for them to have a small portion of land. The house of Israel, whose inhabitants were taken captive in Assyria after the reign of Solomon, has therefore distorted the original gospel of Creation, the Word of God, written in year 66 after Jesus Christ, almost a century later, after the bloody hours of the Roman legions that destroyed thousands of Jews by looting and destroying the temple and completely razing Jerusalem.

The *Book of the Coming Forth by Day and by Night*, also known as the *Book of the Dead* and the book of initiation from Ancient Egypt, was distorted by the Hebrews living in Egypt in 700 to 500. The Torah, the five books of Moses, were put into circulation in a version of Pentateuch and supposed to be the Word of God. According to Jewish tradition, the Torah contained 613 commandments, serving as the charter and doctrine to the Orthodox Jews.

The book of Genesis, of the legislator of the prophet known as the work of Moses, which contains the essence of the Mosaic tradition and the law intended for Israel, took centuries before it penetrated the whole nation. The Christian law is intended for the whole world; it knew times of religious fervor without violation of the law, and there were periods of religious fury where the law was violated like today; including a greater part of the world still un-Christian, violating the Ten Commandments at the expense of their legal promulgation in the history of the Christian Church; nevertheless, either Mosaic or Christian today are not astonished by those laws, but never imply their nonexistence.

The existence - "essence," implying nature, is its total sum absolutely necessary; being as a whole that never ends, all that exists must be considered as nature in its totality. "The essence of God" and other static parts like every "cosmic organism" and the "unique creation of beings" or the "sap" that nourishes trees are called "natural naturata"; its cosmic force is always at work in things of the universe; the term *natura naturans* means embracing dynamic components present in its static, penetrating its ingredients in the inner workings of all cosmic things, each linked to its "genes," displayed in each human as unique in every aspect, and continuing its unity among diversities.

The conception of the cosmic existence in Africa defined this aspect as God manifesting his spiritual existence, possessing the same spiritual "genetics" extracted from his substance and f lowing in the substance of "being," spirit and matter, in an unconditional natural state of reality and true love specifically disposed as all laws created by God. The mosaic tradition contained pieces of spiritual "Essence Elements" of the African conception, and the supernatural Europeans claimed that everything outside of nature does not exist, depending on nothing for its existence.

Its characteristics and its "Mark" begin by the knowledge of nature, by ordering the cosmic force to express its meaning in the essence of the thing and by displaying its rational mathematic power. Its rules as principles of a life after earthly death came from the brilliant idea of the cosmos subdivisions into the visible subdivision, where a transition separates the plane of existence to the invisible plane, where nothing dies but rather a transition into another dimension.

A luminous coronation of a stunning science of the Supreme God was snatched from the initiation of Isis and Osiris, at the Solar Temple in Memphis, to constitute a monotheistic religion: the tradition of the divine origin; its current drafting that the Jewish priesthood (Elohist and Jehovist) present to us is composed of various Egyptian fragments made after the exit of the Israelites from Egypt; therefore, posterior to four or five centuries.

The depths of the light of his torches are revealed in Genesis; so even the Pentateuch of the prodigious Moses initiatory career underwent some transformations by the people of Israel, who betrayed the Mosaic tradition, the religion of the prophet Moses and the judges, containing the esoteric essence. From that distortion of the Hebrews, appeared the first Greek Septuagint Version of the Pentateuch, written by seventy-two writers in Alexandria, who took office in the year 250 to 100.

Parents Joseph and Mary announced the birth of Jesus Christ in Bethlehem as a Jewish child in the year 8 BC, according to the details of his birth, because Dionysius Exiguus, the religious Christian scholar, the Eastern and Western Christian, is the one who invented the Christian era, or the Common era, five hundred years after the birth of Christ, and used the date of the birth of Jesus Christ for dating used to the present day. This sixth-century monk invention is used to number the years of both the (Christianized) Julian calendar and the Gregorian calendar. This dating of the church time started from the recognition of Jesus as the Lord by the Christian Church of Rome, placed in the sixteenth century by Dionysius Exiguus, and which became two centuries later, a general use.

This time, placed exactly or not, since the creation of Adam, and knowing that six thousand years of earth history, having no year zero in the scheme, ended in 1872, and the AD (anno Domini) era—meaning "in the year of the Lord" in Medieval Latin—started. The conception of counting years from the start of this epoch, based on the birth of Jesus of Nazareth, immediately after "the year AD 1," followed by "the year 1 BC," denoted the years before the start of the era. This counting started 536 years after the first year of the Persian king Cyrus, started before the AD year, 1872 years have passed after Jesus, since the Domini year.

Entering the seventh millennium, the day of distress will see the beginning of the setting to pieces of the kingdoms of this world and the establishment of the Day of the Lord, the Kingdom of God, in heavens and earth, believed by Christianity or cultism that the thousand-year reign of Christ, the resurrection of the righteous, will take place before the seventh millennium; my seventh millennium; the day of the sun of the seventh day; a day of boredom full of anger, my distress and indifference.

It is true that some questioned the year one of our era as the birth of Jesus and have placed four years behind our era to indicate the real date of the birth of Jesus Christ; relatively to the reign of Herod the Great, exposed by the Jewish historian Josephus, setting his date of birth on October of the year 2 before Jesus Christ; one year and three months before our era. But till then, all those manipulations of dates by scholars are just presumptions, without any sure evidence, since Mary, the mother of Jesus, will never return from the dead to give us the exact time of the birth of Jesus.

The English Bible translated by Louis Segond, in its review version of 1910, published after his death in 1909, and the version of John Nelson Darby had both determined the theory of dating the birth of Jesus to four years before the year 1 of the Christian era, which was generally accepted. Jesus grew up as a rebellious, intelligent young man, who knew the ins and outs of the temple, to find himself in the temple of Jerusalem, where he challenged the corruption of his rabbi teachers, concerning the central principle of Judaism in the twelfth century. The evidence of their practices reached us by the copper roll discovered in 1952, containing enumerations of sixty-four hiding places, attributing them to cult objects in gold and silver with priestly clothes in the temple of Jerusalem, destroyed in year 70 after Jesus Christ.

In accordance with the teachings of Christianity, only a marginal current called Messianic Judaism considers the historical existence of Jesus; his beliefs as the son of God, the redeemer of mankind, and other topics announced in the Old and New Testament as the messiah, are irrelevant in Judaism. According to the beliefs of Judaism and Islam, with a strict monotheism, the idea of God as a duality or trinity of God the Father, God the Son, and God the Holy Spirit, assimilated to polytheism, is excluded in the Torah because he said to Israel that he is the only Lord our God, Dt. 6:4. The repentance of sins and salvation are not also the beliefs of Judaism.

Theoretically, everyone should be condemned for his own sin and not the children for their father's sins, or vice versa. Since repentance and salvation can't be obtained by the sacrifice of another person, we need to focus on personal repentance. In the first century after Jesus Christ, Christianity began its history as a Jewish movement in Palestine, since the Council of Jerusalem, held around AD 50, on discussions sanctioning the Christian Jewish community to have opened Christianity to the pagans converted to Jesus's followers. Those discussions led by James the Just, his decision is described in chapter 15:23 to 29, of the book of Acts of Apostles, under the name of the apostolic letter maintaining a separation between Jews and pagans.

A debate was called in that meeting suggesting that male Gentiles converted to the disciples of Jesus were not required to be circumcised; since circumcision, the Abrahamic "eternal sign," was considered repugnant during the period of Hellenization of the Eastern Mediterranean. However, Jewish people circumcision, associated with Abraham, is cited as "the custom of Moses," traditionally considered as the lawgiver in a whole; and Jesus's words are reporting in John 7:22 that Moses made it clear by giving more official binding for the Jewish people circumcision in its law covenant.

But to make it easier for the Gentiles to join the movement, the circumcision of males was mandated to not be obligatory for all Gentiles converted; being Jewish Christians by birth or converted, they were all considering the early Christians as a part of Judaism. We can also find a description in Galatians 2 describing the same event. In 325 after Jesus Christ, the Council of Nicaea finally came and unified the church, affirming that Jesus is divine by the belief in Trinity - God the Father, the Son, and the Holy Spirit. Jesus died, killed by the Jews and the Romans in the year 33 after Jesus Christ, after a brief religious life evidently, according to the gospels.

The appearance of the first edition of the New Testament in the Christian Bible, written in a form of ancient Greek, a common dialect that became a literary language, and known as the Koine version of a Septuagint translation of the third century before Jesus Christ, and before the Greek translation of the Bible, is propagated in the year 52 to 100 of our era.

In that New Testament, a collection of works written in common Greek of the first century, translated from the Aramaic language spoken by Jesus Christ, recounted events in the first century of Christianity and the teachings of Jesus. And as a version of the Pentateuch, it was elaborated by the Synod of Jamnia. The canon of the Hebrew Bible was defined under the supervision of Rabbi Yohanan ben Zakkai, who was in charge of a school that became a source of academic hypothetical proto-rabbinic Judaism, in the city of Yavneh/Jamnia, hence the name of Synod of Yavne. From there, the Judaism standard was structured and acknowledged from the second to the sixth century of the Christian era, after the destruction of the second temple in year 70 after Jesus Christ.

The New Testament accounts twenty-seven books, written by nine different authors, and authorized by the church. In an alphabetical order of works of each author, officially recognized as canonized saint acknowledged as holy, generally regarded as a virtuous and considered being in heaven after death, I first quote Saint-Jacques, who wrote one epistle of the New Testament. But no specification is referred to define which one, since in the New Testament, several James are mentioned. But some sources describe him as the brother of Jesus, the first bishop of Jerusalem, and the presumptive author of the epistle of James.

St. John, who was among the twelve apostles, was a professional fisherman. Jesus called upon him when he was repairing his fishing nets. He wrote one gospel around the year 95 after Jesus Christ, three epistles, and the Apocalypse. Being on the cross, Jesus entrusted him his mother. The esoteric text of John, a mystery from the ancient knowledge of the Egyptian pharaohs, summarizing the mysteries of the universe and life in a few words by the gospel, reveals mysteries; in his revelations, we could penetrate in the deep depth of the doctrine, its secret teachings, and its sense of promise in an esoteric reserve.

His gospel, the gospel of the spirit, has a deep view of the transcendent truth revealed by the master and known as the science of mysteries, the secret of religions, which the wise Essenes taught him, and it was a powerful way of summarizing it. He also had an eagle as a symbol, which, with its wings deployed, gave it the look of a king who was traveling through spaces with a blazing eye that possessed the sky of the planet Earth and the solemn hour of the world, dark and full of spooky signs.

Its mysteries cannot be understood or apprehended by the understanding only. St. John speaks of the existence of the Divine, as a great secret of the origin of the verb—the divine intelligence—an emanation of the great mystery of God, as the origin of the beginning of time and creation of all things: he speaks of the mystery of life as a reality to experience; he speaks of the spiritual process as crucial, difficult to define and as problem to be solved.

St. Jude wrote one epistle. He was considered to be one of Jesus's four brothers by the Eastern Church tradition, known as his half-brother and son of his father Joseph, and we could find their names in the New Testament. Not knowing the exact identity of Jude created disagreement in different traditions; some considered him the brother of James and some as his son. James was also mentioned in the gospel of Mtt. 13:55, which called him "Judas the Zealot," qualifying him as the brother of Jesus. He was one of the twelve apostles.

St. Luke was not part of the twelve apostles. He was just fascinated by the aspect of Christ's work since his gospel quoted the miraculous healings performed by Jesus in large numbers but did not know or see Jesus during his earthly life. Mark and Paul were his traveling companions. He was a doctor by profession, according to the epistle of Paul to the Col. 4:14, in the twelfth book of the New Testament. He wrote one gospel, dating back from the year 50 after Jesus Christ, and the book of the Acts of the Apostles.

As the disciple of the apostle Paul, he followed Paul loyally to his martyrdom. He was also the first icon painter of the eighth century, according to the Christian tradition of that period. He who was considered as the soft Luke, elaborated the senses of mysteries in his gospel; but under the veil of the legend of poetry, he wrote the longest most grammatically correct gospel in polished Koine Greek, among all writers of the New Testament; it was regarded as the gospel of the soul, of woman and love, full of the broadest sense of peace, reconciliation with God, and apart from faith, the salvation from sin; he explained its use in the opening of his narrative.

St. Mark, who was not part of the twelve apostles, wrote one gospel, literally precious with fact, containing acts and public words by an editorial testimony of Peter, whom he helped with Paul in their missionary works, dating from year 65 after Jesus Christ. This author, to whom the Gospel of Mark is attributed, close to the apostles Peter and Paul and called John at birth and then nicknamed Mark to become John Mark, is said to have founded one of the main episcopal churches of Early Christian Church of Alexandria, about nineteen years after the ascension of Jesus, precisely in the year 49 after Jesus Christ. That original community is today claimed by both the Coptic Orthodox Church and the Greek Orthodox Church of Alexandria. However, it is good to mention that his gospel did not claim direct witness of reported events or to be written by Mark. Honorably, as the founder of Christianity, Mark became the first bishop of Alexandria in Africa by composing the aspects of the Coptic liturgy.

St. Matthew was serving in his office of the Roman government when called him. The one who accompanied Jesus during his earthly ministry, listed among the twelve apostles, wrote one gospel, also literally precious with fact containing acts and public words, dating from the year 50 after Jesus Christ. Without underlying his work as a tax collector from the Jewish people for Herod Antipas, Luke 5:27 only described the calling of the Levi by Jesus after a scene of miracle performed on the paralytic, first by telling him that the son of man has power on the entire earth, Luke 5:24–25. Matthew, known as one of the four evangelists who witnessed the resurrection and the ascension of Jesus to heaven, was also one of the two disciples to preach God's message up to Ethiopia with Andrew.

St. Paul, up to his dramatic conversion to Christianity around the year 32, persecuted Christians and Christianity after abandoning Judaism, his traditional religion, which taught him to persecute the early followers of Jesus of Nazareth.

For the edification of Christianism, his meeting with Jesus, which made him blind deeply, overwhelmed him, and this manifestation persuaded him permanently. And by the name of that same Christ whom he persecuted; he was baptized three days later after that spectacular meeting during his trip to visit Damascus. According to tradition, the baptism took place in the house of Saint Ananias, who performed the baptism himself, followed by worship in the same crypt formed by two bedrooms and attested from the first century, which gave him his sight back. And probably thinking he had received a revelation, he decided to break up with the observance imposed on the faithful of the Torah for the salvation of God, whom he persecuted. Thus, 1 Cor. 15: 8 tells us that being designated directly by Christ, his apostolic function was confirmed as the last to whom Jesus appeared.

Paul crossed borders with the knowledge of Jesus Christ up to the West. Act. 28:23 relates the arrival of Paul in Rome to us, when he was trying to persuade the Jews of Rome about Jesus, rendering them the witness of the kingdom of God by starting from the Law of Moses.

And the Acts of the Ap. 28:30–31 recounts the two years he spent in Rome to us. So, becoming one of the greatest missionaries, Paul wrote thirteen epistles, maybe two years after his exodus, dealing with various subjects, from the epistle to the Romans to the epistle to Philemon.

St. Peter, who after the arrest of Jesus denied him, was like John, a professional fisherman. He too, was in Rome with Paul. The works of this great missionary are two epistles on the Christian life and hope, maybe written two years after the exodus. And this was after fully repented. Peter was the best known of the twelve apostles of Jesus. This leader of the early Christian Church ordained and appointed as the fundamental "rock of the church of Jesus" by Jesus himself, was the founder of the Church of Antioch as one of the five major churches that composed the Christian Church. In Mtt. 16:18-19 Jesus said thou art Peter, upon this rock I will build my church. But Eph. 2:20 tells us that this construction of his Church, based on the apostles and prophets, has Christ Jesus himself as the main cornerstone. He was known as one of the first disciples of Jesus, and his church was referred to as the first church for the Christians. He migrated in the city of Antioch because of the persecution of the first so-called Christians in Jerusalem before the breakdown of the communion between the Eastern Orthodox and the Roman Catholic churches; this East-West schism began in the eleventh century.

This major Christian center was during the Hellenistic Greece period, and well after the period of the Roman Empire, marking the city as the third most important city, founded near the end of the fourth century BC at the east coast of the Orontes River. At the late Roman period, Antioch became part of the province of Syria at a time; it is nowadays a city in Turkey, called Antakya, and totally in ruin. As a result of its role played in the longevity of the emergence of early Christianity and Hellenistic Judaism, the city kept the name of "the cradle of Christianity." Thus, the first so-called Christianity influence started in Turkey near the Syrian border. Later on, St. Peter also founded the church in Rome and considered the first bishop of the state church of the Roman Empire. St. Peter the Apostle, the first pope, ordained by Jesus himself, was considered as such by the Roman Catholic Church but crucified under Emperor Nero Claudius Caesar in Rome. Let us note that his church was totally differed with the present-day Christianity.

And the last of these authors of the New Testament is an author of one epistle to Hebrews, a Christian stranger very close to Paul. Among these writings, the three synoptic historical values of the gospels that I have taken like reference are from Matthew, Mark, and Luke as the basis, and John as the mysteries of the esoteric doctrine of Christ, by admitting the posterior writing and the symbolic objective of this gospel. And these four gospels—equally authentic but known with different titles as the gospel of John, the gospel of Luke, the gospel of Mark, and the gospel of Matthew—are gospels that we must control and rectify, by each another.

In the conception of Christ, they esoterically interpreted the history texts by enlightening the everyday questions that were found in the life of Jesus, who did the work of the Holy Spirit toward craziness, with his life floating between an ambitious dream of an illuminated who became a Messiah without wanting and almost without knowing it. It is for the delight of the apostles and for the popular desire that this name was inadequately imposed on him because a prophet must have a strong faith to found a new religion that could change the soul of the world, not with such weak faith of Jesus, enlightened by a pale sun of the planetary system without any magnetism, which provided no vitality and without any enthusiasm or ardor of the creative fire.

These gospels are today recognized by the church as direct witnesses of Jesus's life. Its word of exhortation is reporting the "radiance of the glory of God and the exact imprint of his nature, and he upholds the universe by the word of his power;" opening the exaltation of Jesus as an exalted "priest," a "high priest," and the "Son of God"; and describing the doctrine of Christ to exhort Christians to persevere in faith his role as a mediator between God and humanity, in the text of the New Testament.

According to that house, these Jewish Christian authors who wrote the books of the New Testament and other books of the Bible, living in Jerusalem, referred to themselves as the first race to inhabit the earth and as the pure white race; Israel, meaning the crystal race and called the Aryan race. Is it true? Not at all. Let's notice that these are the kinds of lies that the holy book of the Western circulates since decades to allow them that evil ego and a maleficent spirit exercised all over the world.

From 335 to 323 BC, the conquests of Alexander the Great up to the Byzantine evolution (c. 600) besieged Egypt. The history of Egypt is a fascinating story, if one follows its long, horrible road that Westerners subjected it, after the victory of Alexander the Great from his attack in Gaza. It must be said that from his priests of the god Amun, to the implantation of Hellenism in the valley of the Nile, the foundation of the city of Alexandria to the west of the delta by Alexander, up to the handover of the administration of the entire country to several Macedonian civil and military leaders, the eyes of the natives saw the title of "son of Amun," once bore by the Pharaohs, be attributed to the foreigners. Thus, Alexander the Great received the title of "son of Amun" from the priests of the god Amun, after consulting the oracle.

The emperor Constantine brought together a group of bishops of the Roman Catholic Church to decide on the birth of Jesus Christ and his mother Mary, as virgin; to decide about the books of the Bible under the Council of Nicaea in the year 322; and to determine the nature of the relationship of Christ to the Father. Jesus Christ was declared to be God in the year 323 by the group of Nicene bishops of the Roman Catholic Church.

The first twenty-seven books of the New Testament, the canonical version according to the order of the Western canon, saw the day in the year 350 to 400, from an original version of forty-five Books in total. This agreement was reached by the authority of all the churches in the fourth century. Finally, they declared the twenty-seven books of the New Testament as canonized in 367 and decreed by the churches as the only divine Holy Scripture, which must be read in Christian churches.

Many works of Christian authors of the second century (and even of the late first century) that we know and that were read in some churches by many Christians of the second century were not retained by the canon of the New Testament. The Last Supper, the pastoral instructions of baptism, and the teaching of the Twelve Apostles, transmitted to nations and known as the Didache, meaning the "doctrine of the Lord," dated from the early second century. This teaching was a collection of Christian moral precepts and the one that revealed the Father's love. For example, around the year 96, the epistle of Clement of Rome, known as the disciple of Peter, was read in the Church of Corinth as a letter addressed to the Christians of the city.

The Vulgate, the Latin version of the Bible translated by St. Jerome, which is based on the Septuagint version, was published in the year 400. The publication of the racist version of the Pentateuch, in the sixth century of our era, by European rabbis and other scholars of the religion, is located in the year 550. And it is on the same date that the Babylonian Talmud was translated into a European version.

The prophet Muhammad ibn Abdallah was born in the year 570 before the year of Hegira. And it was outside Medina that the religion of Islam was established, from the first day of the year of the Hegira, at the oasis of Yathrib, the Medina of today. After criticizing the polytheistic religion of Mecca and then exercising a power of supreme authority over the pre-Islamic Arabia, which mostly tortured nomadic Christians and followers of Islam to force them deviate from their belief, the prophet Muhammad was forced to f lee to exile from Mecca in the year 622 after Jesus Christ. The fundamental teachings of the Old and New Testament are modified by Islam, like the story of the twelve sons of Ishmael. It is modified and repeated to the satisfaction of the prophet, compiled in a bible of Islam called the Koran and put into circulation in the year 670. It even appeared that one of the two sons of Ishmael by the name of Kedar, who settled in Mecca, was the ancestor of Quraysh, the tribe of Muhammad, descendants of Adnan up to Ishmael. The Muslim prophet therefore had black blood because the mother of Ishmael was from Ancient Egypt.

The first section of the Koran was written by Bilal, one of the first companions of the prophet, who traveled through time, since the early days of Islam up to today. It was to Bilal, an Ethiopian prince, improperly qualified as a former black freed slave from East Africa, was the one that the prophet entrusted the heavy task of calling the hours of daily prayer, precisely on the Kaaba of Mecca, five times a day, every day of the year. So, he was then known as the first muezzin after he and the prophet built the first mosque of Medina. At the heart of the sacred mosque in Mecca, the place that became the great center of pilgrimage for all Muslims since the seventh century, housed a large black stone. This stone was found by Abraham and his son Ishmael and transported to Mecca after the death of Sarah. At least once in their lives, every Muslim dreams of going there to become an accomplished Muslim.

Here are some examples of the blacks at the origin of the Abrahamic religions. In the first place, Melchizedek, a Canaanite black, the monotheist king of Jerusalem, was the one who initiated Abraham. The prophet Idris, a black inventor of writing and sewing like Mahomet, had the gift of prophecy at the age of forty. His father's name was Yered, the son of Mahalalea, according to the Shafi'i jurist historian Ibn Kathir, in his book titled *Histories of the Prophets*, which preceded the advent of the apostolate of the prophet Muhammad of Islam.

Idris was raised to a high rank by Allah because he was a prophet and veracious, according to the Koran Chapter 19: Mary Maryam–verses 56–57. To identify Idris with Enoch, the exegetes relied on one of these main points, mentioning that Enoch was also elevated to a high rank by God. Luqman, whom God gratified with wisdom, was a pre-Islamic black man whom the Koran just described characteristics than speaking of him as a prophet. The mother of Ishmael, the second wife of Abraham, who was black, she was called Adiara. Since Ishmael was from the Quraysh tribe, Ishmael was the ancestor of the descendants of the prophet Muhammad.

At the time of the prophet Mohamed, Ethiopia, which dominated Arabia, was an African kingdom. Moreover, all the southern Arabia and the region of Mecca were under the control of the Black Sabeans, the first inhabitants of Arabia at the time. Bilal, one of the princes of the Ethiopian nobility, was not a slave. At the time of the prophet Muhammad, the black hegemony excluded the slavery of Bilal, since Mohamed was only protected by blacks because of the Islam he brought; so the Qurayshs, his tribe, did not want him anymore. Thus, the black leader, Ayoba Lansar, who controlled Medina, welcomed the prophet Mohamed at that time. The falsification of the Persians, of Aryan White origin from Iran, was the race that wove that invention concerning the slavery of Bilal, after the Ethiopian domination of Arabia, conquered by these Persians.

Along with the Radhanite Jews, they were the first to enslave blacks and practiced racism. It is also necessary to know that the present royal family of Arabia is of Aryan Persian origin and not the descendants of the prophet Mohamed. The first tribe of God, as an example of the black race, at the origin of the Islamic religion, is the Shabazz Tribe, which means "glorious powerful people" in Arabic; it is a tribe from which all blacks descend. Shabazz means "the throne of the beginning of the soul" in Ancient Egyptian.

This tribe appeared on earth after it was separated from the moon; therefore, it is of divine origin; moreover, the sura 15: 26–28 in the Holy Koran, clearly states that the black man is the first creation of Allah. Originally, many words are from Ethiopia, Kushite, and globally; the birth of the Arabic language itself, was a contribution of the Canaanite and Sabean blacks. The Muslim bonnet, the taqiyah, the fasting, the hours of prayer in relation to the position of the sun, and the prayer itself were inherited from the blacks of Egypt, Ethiopia—ancient—Nubia, and the black Sabean community of Arabia.

The version of the Masoretic Text of the Jewish school, written by Jewish scribes in Hebrew in years 600 to 900, is the version translated into Bible by many Christian generations in different languages. Like the one of the professors of theology who rejected the spirituality of the institutional Roman Catholic Church and many of its distinctive teachings, known as the precursor of the Protestant Reformation, the Englishman John Wycliffe boldly undertook the translation of the Vulgate into English and brought out that English version in 1382. His Bible is known today as the Wycliffe Bible.

The first version of the Bible printed by the composition of an arrangement of physical type of text in an edition of the Vulgate, Latin version composed of two volumes in folio, is put in circulation by Johannes Gutenberg in 1456. It is a text reproduction of the Latin Bible translated by St. Jerome. The official translation of the Torah, the first five books of Moses, is placed in the year 1460, according to the agreement of all and according to Moses ben Maimonides, the Spanish Jew and the Andalusian rabbi of the twelfth century, who was trained by his father to the Talmud at the base of his Halacha law of the rabbinical Judaism. This physician, philosopher, and theologian, who excelled in all these fields and became a lawyer on Jewish law, is the one who compiled the Torah in a complete clear code and a style expressing itself in few words. The scholar Maimonides, known by the nickname "Eagle of the Synagogue," left among his many works, a commentary on the Mishna, compiled in 1168, as one of the works of exegesis and theology, and a second Torah of philosophy compiled in 1187, and he headed the Jewish community of Egypt.

In the third century BC in Egypt, the Old Testament could not escape being translated in the Greek language because it was listed as the first language; it was known as the Septuagint. So, St. Erasmus came well after to translate its own proper version of the New Testament from Greek into Latin in 1516 after printing the Greek New Testament and corrected some parts of the Bible that were found in the Vulgate. This Latin writer, philosopher, doctor of theology, regular ecclesiastical dignitary of St. Augustine, and native of Gouda but born in Rotterdam, a well-known city of the Netherlands, was one of the greatest humanists of the Renaissance, who wrote the New Testament in Latin. Hoping that the sacred text would be available in all languages, he was considered the second Moses of Judaism.

A translation of the Bible into German language was also carried out by Martin Luther, an ordained priest in 1507. The father of Protestantism and reformer of the church faced the Church of Rome protesting against the edict Diet of Worms, a general meeting of the states of the Holy Roman Empire in the small town of Worms, Germany, leading to his excommunication.

The Augustinian theologian brother, holding just the Bible as the only legitimate source of Christian authority, challenged the papal authority over the repentance of sins and the salvation of the soul. He said that man, fatally imperfect before God, must accept his sinfulness state and that to want to solve the problem of sin by indulgences was a practice incompatible with the piety of God. Without the intercession of the church, man received the salvation of the soul as a gift of God, and he could only receive the repentance of sin by a sincere, genuine faith. Finally, he said that this fatal imperfect state of man before God does not prevent penance.

This practice has its roots in the writings of St. Paul, possessing a history and a specific meaning in Christianity. It is revealed to us in the Epistle to the

Rom. 8:13 that: if man lived according to the flesh - sin, he would die; but if he lives according to the power of Spirit - the spiritual - the law of righteousness is fulfilled, and the works of the body die, sin would be forgiven, and man would live in the righteousness of reason, having God in him.

In the tradition of the Roman Catholic Church, the partial or total forgiveness of human sin before God, dating back to the third century, was fulfilled by a worship—by fasting, explicitly recommended in the gospel; by prayer and obedience to superiors; by an act of donation, piety, or imposing oneself to suffering; by accepting the sufferings sent by God; or by the deliberate deprivation of a desire, etc. This pain inflicted to oneself in the context of the Catholic religion is qualified by the term *corporal mortification*, done to advance in the spiritual realm. In everyday language, this expression is mentioned in the Catholic bibles and best known in the Protestant Bible of Segond as "sackcloth and ashes," to cover the heads with ashes or to be clothed with a poor and rough cloth as a penitential act, and this is what King David did after his adultery with Uriah's wife and the murder of her husband, the Hittite, and taking his wife for her to become his. "Now that the sword of justice turned against him in misery, the child that the woman gave to David fell seriously ill, struck by God and David besought God. Strictly, he was clothed with sackcloth, sleeping on the bare ground by fasting; to repent," revealed 2 Sm. 12:16–20. This outward expression of King David was a confession to his sins to receive absolution.

In Mtt. 3:4, John the Baptist ate the locusts that cause extensive damage to crops and wore camel skin in the wilderness as a model of an ascetic life oriented toward the coming of the kingdom of God in the New Testament.

Mtt. 4:1–2 tells us that, before starting his preaching, Jesus Christ retired to the desert to fast and pray for forty days. This garment of mourning or a sacred garment to be worn after being washed with water was also mentioned in the Old Testament. The rough clothes, mourning dress in Lv. 16:3–25, originated from the cilice. For the purpose of mortification and penance, the Latin form of the hair shirt was used to recognize the kingdom of God for all his creation in a practical manner, to express the consciousness of sin and to repent, to amend oneself, and to show firmness in one's decision, described in the book of Leviticus as a fundamental of sacrifice. There are many examples concerning this practice in the Old and New Testaments.

This system of ascetic religious practices and beliefs concerning the relationship between humanity and God, a superior nature that we called divine, which became a legal definition for the papal decree in the twelfth century, was transformed into a lucrative business over time by indulgences as the idea of Pope Leo X to resell it to individuals and raise the necessary funds for the construction of the new St. Peter's Basilica in Rome from 1513 to 1521, diverting sinners away from their real duty of charity and penance.

Martin Luther, the Protestant, fiercely opposed this idea of diverting sinners from their true duty of charity and penance, denouncing it as being transformed into a lucrative business for the purgatory of souls. This repair of souls inhabited by sins has nothing to do with the price Jesus paid for his sins; however, justice requires that compulsory reparations must be performed, necessarily for our own salvation, since God is merciful. But in this world or in the other, nobody knows purgatory, yet the church informs us that purgatory exists; therefore, each of us must repair the harm he did to his brothers for the salvation of souls temporarily separated from God, because of our sins by multiple temptations on earth, has made us understand that our mere and only honor is to do good—translated into God. Therefore, lost in the midst of all these questions of knowing if God exists, does he really care about us?

And does he know us? If he is so merciful, does he forgive us? And will he really understand our temptations? All these questions concerning God and purgatory depress us; but it seems to me that there is only one truth—death—and before this truth, the time to ask God's forgiveness is not giving to us. And if the possibility of making a definitive choice to clean up the dirt deposited on our "spiritual garments" and to repair the faults of our lives through purgatory, real death would not exist. So what the church is asking us, to present ourselves first to their holy priests—God, to make a great toilet while praying for our poor souls, by the indulgences granted by the pope in favor of the living, for the remission of the temporal punishment in purgatory, or again awarded after the absolution granted by a priest as a result of the confession, represents a disappointment to souls.

For the profit of the church, the unlimited sale of indulgences was a widespread abuse by the godfathers of the Roman Catholic doctrine, taking advantage of the money thrown into their coffers by the fear of man to go to hell and by the sinners who expiated their sins, believing that as soon as the necessary funds were monetized, the soul will fly from the purgatory and enter heaven. I must say that, in the Bible, this idea is nowhere mentioned. These practices of pretensions and beliefs of Catholic priests to monetize access to paradise, granted to anyone, are opposed to the secret divine will of God—the theological concept of the predestination of God, who secretly chooses those to be pardoned and those who have the right to be qualified for eternal life. The sale of indulgences by the priests of the Roman Catholic Church was already denounced by John Wycliffe a century and a half earlier.

This conflict with the papacy, which erupted in 1517, only accelerated Martin Luther's process of reform and generated the great revolution in the Roman Catholic Church and the formation of the foundation of Protestantism in 1529. He provided the new Christian Church with teaching tools intended for pastors such as *The Great Catechism,* and for the people, *The Small Catechism*, abolishing the priestly celibacy, most of the sacraments, cultural rites, recoating a sacred dimension, and the monastic vows to priests; thus distancing the new Christian Church more and more from the Roman traditions in a sense but retaining the baptism and the Eucharist, the liturgical celebration, as the main Christian worship; the predicator of justice—the action to spread the divine word, and to say before—the action of preaching. In Protestantism, its other name is homily, an occasional comment uttered by the priest or deacon at a Catholic Mass intended primarily for spiritual edification rather than doctrinal instruction.

The Centurion edition of 1968, pp. 173 to 174 on the Constitution of the Sacred Liturgy of the Second Vatican Ecumenical Council, Paris, specified that the homily is to explain from the sacred text the mysteries of faith and the standards: or rules of the Christian life by following the development of the liturgical year. Often, the Protestants' insistence on the knowledge of biblical writings encouraged evangelizers and pastors to promote literacy. So, the course of the history of the Western civilization was changed to the influence of the great ideas of Rev. Martin Luther on the Protestant Reformation. The first English language version used for other English translations, etc., was written by the famous English Protestant William Tyndale, the first translator of the New Testament from the Greek text in 1535. Since in the Middle Ages, possessing the scriptures in English without authorization was punishable by a death sentence; thus, the publication of the Bible by John Wycliffe was condemned, even as several partial or fictionalized versions of the biblical stories already existed in English from the seventh century onward.

The first version of Tyndale's translation was translated from the original texts of the Hebrew version of the Old Testament to English and for the New Testament from the Greek text. Since he spoke Spanish, French, Greek, Hebrew, and Latin, the translation of this brilliant scholar was the first Protestant Bible and the first printed English edition, influenced by the reforming ideas of Martin Luther. It should be noted that, by his position concerning the divorce of King Henry VIII, William Tyndale wrote a pamphlet titled *"The Practice of Prelates"* in 1530, denouncing the divorce as being contrary to the Holy Scripture. Already, his first translation of the Holy Scriptures challenged the English religious legislation and the authority of the Catholic Church. He also wrote *The Obedience of a Christian Man*, read by King Henry VIII in 1534.

He was arrested after seceding with the Catholic Church of Rome and thrown in prison in the castle of Vilvoorde in 1535. William Tyndale was executed by strangulation, and his body was burned at the wooden stake after being judged in 1536 as guilty of heresy. Those who were engaged as staunch opponents of Lutheranism, opposing all changes in the doctrines of the church, the clerical marriage, and remaining hostile to the English Bible of Tyndale, were the London Bishop John Stokesley, Sir Thomas More, King Henry VIII himself, and Thomas Cromwell, the chief minister to the King, a lawyer and statesman, to only name few who hunted Tyndale and judged him guilty of heresy concerning the divorce of King Henry VIII.

But after engineering the divorce of Queen Catherine to the king that Pope Clement VII disapproved in 1534, and allowing him the annulment of his own marriage, Cromwell lawfully arranged the marriage of Anne Boleyn, the pregnant mistress from her future husband as the fourth wife to the king. Six months later, the German princess Anna von Kleve was found unattractive by the king. Therefore, he was also executed for treason and heresy by an arraigned under a bill of attainder on the Tower Hill on 28 July 1540, because the marriage turned into a disaster, ending in an annulment.

After his death, his wishes to the king of England, telling him to open his eyes, concerning his first translated version of the Old and the New Testament used for other English translations, etc., before his strangulation, his last words were to be approved by the king. His vow was granted when the first authorized version of the Bible, the Great Bible of King Henry VIII, largely repeating the text of Tyndale, prepared by Myles Coverdale, working under the commission of Thomas, Lord Cromwell, appeared less than two years later in 1538, intended for the Church of England.

He made a contribution throughout the British Empire and in the English-speaking world through his Bible, which contributed to the development of the Reformation of the Church of England. This version of the first completed edition of the English Bible, the Old and New Testaments, was written by Miles Coverdale, ordered by King Henry VIII, published in Antwerp, Belgium, in 1535, and the version strengthening this earlier version was published in 1538, relying in particular on the translation of Tyndale. And the King James Version, compiled by fifty-four scholars, ordered by the king, was also inspired by the translation of Tyndale, taking up to 76 percent of the Old Testament from the Bible of Tyndale and 83 percent of the New Testament in 1611.

In 1537, the first Bible ever printed in Great Britain was printed in England, the English version of St. Matthew translated according to the Tyndale and Coverdale versions. Henry VIII, the monarch of Great Britain, authorized another version of the Bible. The first Bible translation officially approved in English was published in a fusion of the two bibles of Tyndale and Coverdale in 1539, and it's known under the name the Great Bible of Coverdale.

The first version of the Holy Bible in English with chapters divided into verses was printed in Geneva in 1560 by Rowland Temple. It was written in Geneva by three great Bible translators, supporters of the Reformed theology. So, we would quote their respective sponsors as—Miles Coverdale; John Knox, the founder of the Presbyterian denomination in Scotland; and William Whittingham, a Reformed Protestant and Anglican reformer—for this version. Members of the English College of Douai, a college founded by Cardinal William Allen in 1561 as a Catholic seminary, created to form the English Catholic clergy, undertook a translation of a Bible into English, known under the name of Douai Bible. Their work resulted in a translation of the New Testament in one volume, published in 1582 in Reims. And almost thirty years later, the version of the Old Testament was translated in two volumes. In 1609, Genesis to Job was published as the first volume; and in 1610, the second volume — Psalms to 2 Maccabees, with the Clementine Vulgate Apocrypha — was also published by the University of Douai in France; both translations were translated from the Latin Vulgate into English.

To maintain his kingship polygamous behavior and satisfy the conditions set by himself for the royalty of his kingdom, he mandated his subjects for the writing of the Old and New Testaments, the Authorized King James Version of Great Britain, in 1611, even after the pope in Rome rejected its aspects. Most black believed that this version of the Bible was the only true scripture, written by scribes inspired by God. To continue to manipulate their African colleagues, this myth was perpetrated by members of the clergy and some black theologians.

For the first time in the history of the United States, Europeans inviting researchers from America were once again authorized to cooperate and to participate in the distortion of the original teachings of the Nile valley and the Tigris-Euphrates valleys; in correspondence, they produced another version, This version, known as the revision of King James, was the first and remains as the only officially authorized revision that contains the original Word of God.

The revised version of the New Testament was published in 1881; and in 1885, the Old Testament. Later on, in 1894, the Apocrypha followed. The revised version, now known under the name of the American Standard Version, published by Thomas Nelson & Sons in 1901, was based on a formal translation equivalence method of the Bible into English. Another production of this version was made in English and produced in 1995 by the American Committee brought about by the jealousy between Europeans of Europe and Europeans of America.

The one of James Moffatt, revised and written in modern English, dates from 1924; it is known under the name the Holy Bible: The Revised Version of Moffatt.

The version of Goodspeed and Smith was translated by different characters in 1931; among them were Edgar J. Goodspeed of the University of Chicago, who translated the New Testament, and J. M. Powis Smith as editor, and also from the University of Chicago, who translated the Old Testament. The New Testament in Greek translated into English was published by the Brotherhood of the Episcopal religious of the Roman Catholic Church of the Christian doctrine congregation, and the Old Testament remained according to the Latin Vulgate version. This version of the Holy Bible of 1941 was the Douay-Rheims Challoner Revision.

Bishop Ronald A. Knox also wrote an Authorized Version of the Bible in English by the Roman Catholic commandment of Wales and England according to the version of the Latin Vulgate to counter the King James Version. This version, from 1945 to 1949 is known by name Knox Bible. Under the sponsorship of the National Council of the Churches of Christ, another standard version was written by a group of Europeans of the United States of America, calling themselves inspired scribes of God. Called Standard Version of the Holy Bible, it was dated from 1952.

Under another sponsorship of the Protestant churches of Great Britain by the Protestants of Oxford University Press of Cambridge University Press, a version of the Holy Bible was written in New English by a group of English writers in 1961. In the United States of America, a version approved by a group of rabbis, priests, ministers, and theologians, finding all its content satisfactory to the teaching of Judaism and Christianity, was published in a common American language version in 1973, etc. Many other well-known older versions exist in the biblical chronology, which I did not mention.

The oldest known version of the Bible that we have dates from 1669. It was then edited in Amsterdam by the Elsevier brothers and validated by the pastors of Geneva. It was then translated into Italian and then in English before David Martin published a new version in 1707.

Thus, the preferential worship of one God received a most remarkable, distinctive quality of the religion of Ancient Egypt in the polytheistic systems, whose influence or competence between gods functioned according to the logic of henotheism, of which the first case dates back to Akhenaton, about the cult of Amun – a specific and unique God conceived from a mixture of several deities in a monotheistic tendency.

So Yahweh, the God of Hebrews, is not universal because, for a long time, they remained polytheists; therefore, they're not also the first monotheists since the work of the Kamite – black people, born in the Nile valley and creator – of the word *God* by hieroglyphics – known as the Medu Neter, from which monotheism was born. It is from the word *God* in Gen. 14:18–20, mentioning the name of Melchizedek, as king of Salem, who blessed Abram and who supposedly was a Canaanite who knew God the Most High of black origin that Melchizedek, the priest of God the Most High pronounced his benediction to bless Abram.

The high priest of God the Most High brought bread and wine to bless Abram, the head of the priesthood, and his descendants, who received blessing from the priest of God the Most High by these words: "Blessed be Abram by God the Most High, who created heaven and earth, and blessed be God the Most High, who delivered your enemies into your hand." And Abram gave him the tithe of all as a practice adopted by many black families, contributing 10 percent of their incomes to the church.

In the Phoenician pantheon, the name of the Most High God, of which each element is attested as two distinct deities (El and Elyon, the Highest God that the priest-king Melchizedek adored). In the Canaanite religion, El was known as an ancient Supreme God and compounded of these two words, *El* and *Elyôn*, which also mean "God the Most High." In the Hebrew Bible, these two words also usually mean "God the Most High" in English, similar to the Septuagint version. Second Sm. 22:14 identified Elyōn as Yahweh; in a very mystical context, Is. 14:13–14 used the word *Elyōn*, known as the word that originated during the time of the Maccabees, to provide the basis of the speculation on the fall of Satan.

According to the number of interesting gods found in the verses of the Holy Scripture, the boundaries were to be set in the New Revised Standard Version, which was itself an updated translation of the American Standard Version, using the tetragrammaton of YHWH to identify God that Jacob inherited. Jacob, son of Isaac (son of Abraham), told his family and all those who were with him Gen. 35:2, "Put away the foreign gods that are among you." And Gen. 31:19–34 shows us the constant polytheism at the time of the Old Testament.

In the Bible, *Elohim* (plural) means "gods." In Gen. 1:26, it is said, "Let us make man in our image, after our likeness." The words *let us make* implies other gods in the divinity, if one well understands the chapter of the Bible, integrating gods like Elohim, Jehovah, Yahweh, in the creation, and so on.

Here are proofs of other gods in the Bible: Ex 18:11, "Yahweh is greater than all gods." Ex 20:5 "You shall not bow down to them, nor serve them, for I, Yahweh your God, am a jealous God." Ex 34:14, "The Lord, whose name is Jealous, is a jealous God." Dt. 27:15, "Cursed be anyone who carves and casts an idol and secretly sets it up." Dt. 5:9, "I, the Lord your God, am a jealous God." These eras expressed in majesty the polytheism practiced by the Hebrews in the Bible. All these references recognized polytheism; therefore, the existence of other gods venerated between them. The fears of polytheism among the Hebrews led Joshua to set up recommendations within the populations. According to the Bible, he forbade them to not pronounce the name of other gods; nor should they invoke them in their oaths, to serve them and not worship them, and that if they serve other gods, Yahweh, their God, would be inflamed with anger against them. So Yahweh's anger, with whom they bound the covenant, would strike them, and they will disappear for good from countries where they're now roaming if they transgress this covenant Jos. 23:6 to 9 and chapter 23:16. But the people who made this covenant with Yahweh, the God of Israel, despite all Joshua's warnings, served other gods. They denied Yahweh and served foreign gods, like the god Milcom – the deity of the Ammonites – the gods of Aram – the gods of Moab – Chemosh – the deity of the Moabites, the Philistine gods like Baal worshipped by the King Ahab of Israel from 874 to 853, who built an altar for Baal 1 Kings 16:29–33, and Asherah, the goddess of the Sidonians. And Yahweh was inflamed with anger against them Judg 3:7–8.

Joshua continued to recommend to them to only bow their hearts to Yahweh and exclude foreign gods and that if they were to abandon Yahweh and serve other gods, which were among them, Yahweh would mistreat them again, and will destroy them, after he has done good to them. Polytheism is constant in the Bible; it shows us that other gods at all time existed despite the requirement of good behavior by the Law in the eyes of Yahweh. But the great God, whose name is not known by all, appears on the Pyramids Texts (three thousand years before Jesus). He is like a reality of a unique divine power, clearly and inaccessible to the human spirit.

The PT 456 formula of the Kemet Pyramid Texts described the unique monotheist God in some documents as such: "Salute to you, the Unique God," God the unique said the sarcophagus texts. "Like Atum, his name is Unique; O Thou, the Unique God, there is none other than you," acknowledged the Great Hymn to Aten; "You, the Unique," asserted chapter 15 of *the Book of the Dead*; "You, the Lord"; and so on, in different papyrus, like the one of the hymn to Osiris; the one of the hymns and prayers to Ra; the *Bulak papyrus*, and the *Leiden papyrus*, to name just a few, describing the unique God well before the unique God of Judaism.

At the Creation, the conception of a previous initial principle existed already for more than two thousand years before the Bible in the theology of Memphis in Egypt. And the creation of the world is revealed in the papyrus titled "Teaching of the King of the Upper and Lower Egypt," used by individual students or groups to focus on language, writing, and to produce chosen sentences or teaching ideas of everyday life, just like they retained his teaching to his son Merikare, up to the initiation of Moses. It was written by a scribe called Khamwese during the Middle Kingdom.

These instructions of the father Wahkare Khety with greater freedom, describing the limits of royal authority, were referred to kings of a unified Egypt; the first of its kind was effectively a treatise on royalty in the form of a royal testament for the teaching of King Merykara. And as the foundation of the biblical religion of the present monotheism contains the Little and Great Hymn of Akhenaton, numerous passages in the Bible were modified to the will of emperors and kings who dominated the Hebrews, to hide the historical reality. Thus, the Old Testament contains outdated data and imperfections, recognized by the Vatican Council II.

Contrary to secure data of hieroglyphic texts, the Elohist used the name Elohim for God; and the Yahwistic used the name Yahweh of the sacerdotal irretrievably pattern, which offers us a multiplicity of sources that emit a lot of contradictions. In vain, archaeologists have excavated and searched Palestine, of all the lands of the globe, but has not found the slightest concrete evidence susceptible to the existence of the Hebrews as they're described in Genesis and in Exodus; no other evidence exists that can confirm a specific event of the biblical narrative. On the other hand, in the hieroglyphic writings, a multiplicity of evidence exists describing the existence of the Ancient Egyptians of the Nile valley, like the Kametes, who invented monotheism; and eventually, numerous writings containing more wonderful sources than any other countries describing multiple events, if we compare them to the sources of Egypt, concerning henotheism as the worship of a single God, but at the same time, accepting the existence or possible existence of other deities.

Henotheism, the starting point of all religions, is a religious system in which a unique God more important than others dominates. Monotheism is the worship of a unique God, which became the belief of many Europeans, since the nineteenth century after Jesus Christ, but it was not excluding the worship of other gods, contrary to monolatry, consisting in the worship of a single deity but recognizing the existence of many gods. Referring to other gods, the Old Testament reveals numerous passages to us leading us to consider that the transformation of the old religion of the Hebrews to monotheism was performed from monolatrism. These belief concepts are registered in the same book titled the Book of the Dead by Egyptians and known as the easiest book to read.

The worship of Elohim, the patron God, also characterized as the heavenly leader, as the protector of the human race, and as the father, is a cult to which all attributes of divinity are attributed as an expression of a religious feeling, evoking the monolatry in Elohism with the name of Elohim; grammatically the plural of "God" or "deity" in the biblical Hebrew Literature; Elohim is known as their tribal cult or national religion of Jews. The existence of this patron God is at the origin of the theology of Ancient Egypt; He is also known more accurately as the patron God of the city.

In Gen. 17:1–8, "El-Shaddai-a powerful God," who revealed himself to Abraham as his patron God—Elohim, is another God who promised him that "He will bless him, will establish His covenant with him and that if he's honest, He would multiply his prosperity, and will extremely increase his assets." We could notice here that this God did not reveal himself to Abraham as a unique God. In Ex. 20:1–5, another powerful God, delimiting the Mount Sinai to priests only, and barriers to the people, declaring it sacred, spoke these words to the people of Moses: "I am the Lord your God, who brought you out of the land of Egypt, out of the house of slavery. You shall have no other gods before me. You shall not make for yourself a carved image . . . You shall not bow down to them," plunging us into the roots of henotheism in the biblical revelation. Dt. 6:4 also tells us that it is in the monotheistic circles that the existence of a unique god was manifested.

A manifestation of King Mesha of the ninth century BC registered many other gods worshipped as the principal deity. On its stele, at the time of King Omri, king of Israel, dating from about 850 BC, the Mesha Stele was described as having the longest engraved inscription, so far ever discovered, in the time of ancient Palestine. This stele, written in Moabite by a type of Phoenician alphabet, is the oldest of the Semitic alphabet. And the Moabite language used in the inscription of this stele is identical to the form of primitive Hebrew, presenting us the god Chemosh honored by human sacrifice as the main Moab deity. It inscribed among others, in the middle of the ninth century BC, two references of the ancient dynasty of David.

It was therefore necessary to slaughter defeated populations to consecrate them to Chemosh. In the Bible, the character of Jephthah, one of the judges of Israel of the book of Judges, offered him his daughter as a sacrifice following a careless vow; (Judg. 11: 29–31), is giving us reason concerning that vow to his victory, promising Yahweh to offer him a burnt offering. "Then the spirit of the Lord came upon Jephthah, and Jephthah made a vow to the Lord." "If you deliver the Ammonites into my hands, the first to come out of the door of my house to meet me, if I return victorious from the battle against the Ammonites, shall surely belong to the Lord," and I will offer him as a burnt offering. And when the allies of the army of king Joram of Israel, and king Jehoshaphat of Judah besieged the city of Kir-hareset of the Moabite king Mesha, he also offered his son as a sacrifice to the god Chemosh, according to the Bible.

It was before Kamosh's face that Yahweh's vessels were dragged into a war fought by two hundred men. After taking Yahas, built by the King of Israel, to annex it to Dijon, Eglon, the king of Moab, annexed over hundreds of cities on his territories; inscribing thereby the context of the conquered conflict, opposing the Moab to the kingdom of Israel. The Bible is describing the same event in chapter 3:4–27, of the second book of Kings in very different terms, concerning the request of Joram to the king of Judah, to know if he will come to war on his side.

Thus, among the Moabites, the conception of divinity and royalty is a parallelism of conceptions found in the Old Testament. By the Ammonites, the same god is named under the name of Milcom. Readers of that period were personal witnesses of events revealed on the Mesha Stele like the first document warmly written in the lifetime of Mesha, contrary to the Old Testament, which is telling us obsolete historical writings and written imperfections in a different context from that of the epoch concerned, revealing us old traditions of several centuries.

This is the big difference between the Mesha Stele and the Old Testament. Several military campaigns took place reported the Stele of Mesha to us, which duly stretched for multiple years, while, besides the activity of the king, to ignore the Old Testament, the Bible only reported the campaign of the war that occasioned the coalition of Israel, Judah, and Edom, waged against Moab.

A unique campaign of the war in which the major city of Moab (Kir Hareseth), was destroyed by the anger of god Chemosh, according to the Bible; but also by the failure to besiege the royal city of Mesha, relate Is. 16:7–11, Jer. 48:31 and 36, and the second book of Kings 3:21–25 to us. Judg. 10:3 tells us that, after the death of Jair, a worship of Baal and Astarte, which displeased God, was still the belief of the children of Israel. This provoked the anger of God, therefore throwing them in the hands of the Philistines and the Ammonites, declaring war to the Hebrews. To save them, Jephthah, who succeeded Jair, made an unwise vow to the god Chemosh.

Genesis, the first book of the Bible, is the book that presents us the character of Moab, the Moabite origin as the son of Lot, begotten with his oldest daughter, who, before mating with her father, made him drunk without his knowledge. She became pregnant after having sex with her father and gave birth to a son that she named Moab, known as the descendants of the Moabites, an incestuous son of Lot, engendered by his eldest daughter. And her younger sister, whom she encouraged the next day, also had sex with her father, who wasn't conscious of his bedtime or the rising day, after making him drink wine. She got pregnant and gave birth to Ben-Ammi, a son known as the descendants of the Ammonites, an incestuous son engendered by the youngest daughter of Lot. Gen. 19:31–38 refers to this incest behavior of the daughters of Lot. The kingdom of Moab is an attested historic land existing alongside most of the eastern shore of the Dead Sea. And the "children of Ammon" or "Ammonites," occupying the east of the Jordan River in present day, were a Semitic language speaking nation of Iron Age, between the torrent valleys of Arnon and Jabbok. The gods of Ammon are named in the Hebrew Bible as Milcom or Molech.

The book of Ruth tells us the story of a famous Moabite, Ruth, converted to the values of Judaism. Chemosh was honored by the Moabites up to the Persian period. Finally, Gad, Manasseh, and Reuben, the three of the twelve tribes of Israel, shared the kingdom of Moab between them. Gradually, the period of henotheism of the god Chemosh of Hebrews, qualified as a filthy abomination, treated and regarded as something of lesser importance, was subordinated to YHWH by the authors of the Hebrew Bible. Its cult was put to end by the pious king Josiah before the Babylonian exile by the last great religious reform, and in that occasion, the temple of Chemosh was declared unfit to all religious use.

Among the Hebrew, the utensils of Elohism that Jehovah defeated, does not differ from the one inscribed on the stele of King Mesha; while this god of henotheism, to describe the disconcerting picture of Jewish spiritual traditions, was born above all need among other nations. He was antidemonic and anthropomorphic with human characteristics and labeled with other entities, drowning the organized empires of polytheism, and subordinating the foreign gods of the three Abrahamic religions. He is the founding father of the covenant between the Jewish people and the God in Judaism; he is the prototype of all believers, Gentile or Jewish in Christianity; and he is considered as a link in the chain of prophets in Islam, beginning with Adam and culminating in Muhammad. All these groups are known as the adherence to the henotheism of the mighty Elohim, one particular God out of many as the God of Abraham, the God of Hebrews. Note that the God Most High Elohim was worshipped in the temple consecrated to Osiris, most popular about his legend as a resurrected god who reigned in the afterlife. The acting God of Moses, the monotheism God: a God without equal, who does not have his similar, Is. 46:9 and who will not yield his place to another God, Is. 48:11, is a God who reveals the future of what is not yet accomplished; and according to the reference, as the only God of Israel in Dt. 6:4; where Yahweh reveals to us that he is the God of monotheism, said by his mouth to his people by saying that "I am the only God," is a God who will give his glory only if we walk in his name and love him with all our heart, with all our soul, and with all our power. He said he was the First and the Last, and there was no one else besides Him. This God of monotheism became the eternal God from the eighth century, according to the prophets of Israel. In his faithful elements, Mic. 4:5 reveals Elohim to us as the monotheism God of Israel by these words: "All nations may walk in the name of their gods, but we will walk in the name of the Lord our God." There was, therefore, a starting religious point throughout the evolution and the experience of humanity. The doctrine of henotheism led to polytheism at one stage; and when the men of God of the Bible finally wanted divine initiative, henotheism became monotheism and gave way to a necessarily revealed divinity known and understood as a unique God.

One unique God, who deserved to be called divine, required true monotheism, with a strong individual involvement on the part of the faithful, who must know that his God is the only one with certitude. The founder of this monotheism was the Hebrew Bible in the Jewish tradition, wanting that the faith in a unique God be for all functions, necessary for their life and for all human beings of the universe. This veneration of a unique God of monotheism, followed by Christianity and Islam, differed from henotheism.

Akhenaton was the first propagandist in the fourteenth century BC for this veneration of a unique monotheism God and universally known as God of the solar disk. Historically, this exclusive cult of Aten was only a temporary phenomenon, which was not emblematically imposed because, without real implementation, it arose from nowhere in the Egyptian religiosity, bounded by the space of time, forgetting that monotheism offered an example of a generalized polytheism in a slow process from henotheism toward the monotheism of our days in the Old Testament.

The chapter 9 of Daniel in the second century BC provides a testimony to the gods of nations from the appearance of literary sources of the oldest prebiblical religious texts, discovered since three quarters of a century, at Ras Shamra/Ugarit. Since, the necropolis of Ugarit has revealed a prehistoric city dating back to c. 6000 BC. Ugarit is mentioned in the el-Amarna tablets. Most of the clay tablets unearthed from the site identified that they were written in a special alphabetic scripture, revealed as the "Ugarit writing," very similar to Hebrew. They also contained fragments of mythological epic poetry and religious literature.

Joshua, who confessed that he and his house served Yahweh, confirmed to us that their ancestor Terah—father of Abraham, Nahor, and other members of their family—served other gods, in Jos. 24:2, and chapter 15), urging them to choose either the gods of their fathers or the gods of the Amorites. It was certified by these chapters that the biblical tradition was well aware of the adoration of other gods by Israel's ancestors. But the Deuteronomic Reform in chapters 12–26, consisting of removing idols from the temple and pagan altars, destroying fertility cults and rural sanctuaries by centralizing worship at the Temple of Jerusalem, will lead the national religion in community cohesion, to consider idolatry as a form of betrayal, from the seventh century.

Around 640–609 BC, it was the reign of King Josiah of Judah that instituted this great religious reform, because (c. 622 BC) the book of the law found in the Temple of Jerusalem is considered as the basis of the reform by scholars, as the same code of law in the book of Deuteronomic Reform.

God the Father of the patriarchal narratives of Genesis, who addressed his anointed in Ps. 2:7 addressed him by these words: "Today I have begotten you as my son." It was a proto-history testimony of the believer as the only personal God Yahweh, to the exclusion of any other god. But between monotheism and this personal God, his existence should not obscure the universal character of God, considered Unique, as mentioned in Ep. 4:4 to 6, I quote: "There is one body and one Spirit, just as you were called to one hope when you were called . . . a unique God and Father of all, who is over all and through all and in all."

This was how the polytheist Egyptian people, not wanting monotheism, which just plunged the country of the Nile in calamity, were taken out of Africa by a foreign people—the Hebrews, who lived for a good period in Egypt, became descendants of Ancient Egyptians. And being worshippers of the God Aten —

Elohim, they preserved him so that, one day, He would reign as monotheism all over the world in a new faith. This intolerant monotheism, invented by Akhenaton, was briefly continued by his successor, the obscure pharaoh Ai-Aton, after the death of Akhenaton; Ai, the predecessor of Tutankhamun, who married his widow by the name of Queen Ankhesenamon. It was in the holy city of the god Aten, city of gold and light, located at the north of the current Asyut on the Nile, that he adored the unique God, creator of heaven and earth. He reigned there as an absolute supreme master, breaking with the deities of the Egyptian pantheon. This city, Akhet-Aten, the capital of the empire of Egypt from 3,350 years ago, is today known as Tell el Amarna.

When Akhenaton died, his successor—although just a high priest by the name of Ai—took the reins of power by ensuring the regency and waiting for Tutankhamen who was only eight years, to grow. He became pharaoh by name of God the Father — Divine Father Ai. So, this god Aton, who was proclaiming that men were equal and that only wickedness differentiated them, was erased by Ai and Tutankhamen, restoring the orthodoxy, the ancestral cult of Amun, of multiple gods. Inscriptions resembling a form of pronunciation and symbolic value to the Hebrew alphabet, written in unusual hieroglyphics, were discovered in the tomb of Tutankhamen, opened in 1923. The engraved signature of the obscure pharaoh Ai was found on a wall of the tomb in hieroglyphics, resembling that of the god pronounced as Adonis (Aton-Ai) in the Aramaic Bible.

Ra-Moses I became pharaoh in turn under the name of Ramses, fifty years later as the emissary of Pharaoh Aton-Ai and was close to the "people." The Bible called him Moses, the worshipper of the unique God (Adon). To worship this unique God Adon, this people lived an exodus, which drove the monotheistic priests of Adon out of Egypt under the Seventeenth Dynasty, according to Moses in the Bible.

Is it true? It remains to be verified, since the name of Moses does not appear on the list of Egyptian pharaohs. Moses, the Egyptian who inherited the Egyptian religion, therefore transmitted his own Egyptian religion of the god Aton to the Hebrews as a final phase of each successive periods of the history of Ancient Egypt. All other universally accepted phases expressing undeniable facts in the biblical world concerned the universe of Ancient Egypt with Egyptian histories. They would thereby write the Bible during their exile in Babylon, where that troublesome Egyptian origin no longer appeared, by inventing the names of its characters and their births and remodeling it many times, again and again.

From the first three thousand years, the Bible provides us with the story of God, elaborated by our ancestors as facts that existed already with the perception of objects left as evidence to humans, especially accepted by the senses of the spirit, and identified as the most interesting artefacts of over four thousand years old; or objects having undergone a minimal transformation by man, thus being distinguished from any object whose modification would be due to the events occurring or to a natural phenomenon; inscribing Adam as the first human race progenitor, and created by God-Elohim at the beginning of creation.

According to the book of Genesis, he lived with Eve, the first woman in the Garden of Eden, mentioning the time of his death at the age of 930 in the biblical Abrahamic religions; and the Koranic traditions are reporting that God created Adam out of clay and ordered that angels should bow to this human. And about the "original sin," Islam has no notion of it, and its point of view about Adam and Eve's "original sin," the Islamic religion concludes that they were repented and forgiven.

The word *Adam* was derived from the Sanskrit word *Adima*, meaning "progenitor." Its masculine form of the word *adamah* means "ground" or "earth." Its masculine noun, *'a-d-m*, meaning "red," "fair," "handsome," means "man," "mankind." Next to Noah and Methuselah, Adam is the third longest-living person who died about 127 years before the birth of Noah. The deuterocanonical books, the book of Genesis, the Book of Iqan, the Book of Mormon, the Koran, and the New Testament also mentioned the name of Adam.

During a period of nearly four thousand years, the age of each of the offspring of Adam and the name and age of each of the periods are given to us. The year 536 BC is well established and generally accepted date known to be the first year of Cyrus, as an indication of the chronological end of the Bible. Naturally, man already lived on earth hundreds of thousands of years ago, different from what the Bible tells us. A chronological indication extending up to the present day is testifying a clear present of life on earth to us, and as profane, he became worthy to the trust of God. Beyond the year 776 BC, the invention of epochs or eras slowly followed an exact method essential for the establishment of dates, like the farthest time dating defining the era of Nabonassar, decreed in Babylon in 747 BC.

In 776 BC, the first victory won in the Olympic Games, which took place every four years, dated from about three hundred years before Christ by the Greeks. And the dating of the history of Rome started from 753 BC, a few centuries after its founding. Rome was founded only twenty-seven centuries ago, wrapped by uncertain tradition, dating as far back as its first centuries; so were the traces of the Bible chronology followed beyond the year 776 BC, as history. Up to three thousand years ago, there were only obscure or uncertain traditions unworthy of fabulous myth, difficult to understand in various parts of the world; but they were of trust, of belief that one could depend on and perceive their intended meaning, emerged in Africa; then the history of chronology of the oldest pagan nations, not being able to clearly and distinctly trace back their past of around three thousand years, emerged.

The history of the Babylonians, of Syrians, and Egyptians was beyond three thousand years ago, followed by a period in which history, wrapped in a great darkness, was fragmentary. Not beyond the last 2,600 years, Greeks gave us the exact dates of the past 3,000 years inherited in Egypt. The claims of the origin of man on earth, the sole fact of the divine guidance and preservations found in the Bible, are the fabulous prehistoric mythical age giving to Greece, known as our first six million years of human civilization; and man on earth like our ancestors existed around six million years, which tend to progress from an original long-gone age in which humans enjoyed an almost divine existence than the current age of the modern form of humans, who only evolved around two hundred thousand years ago, and in which humans are beset by innumerable pains and evils. Genesis takes us from the lost paradise to the restored paradise of Apocalypse, and when the new era of eternal bliss rises, humanity will continue on the path that leads to eternity, according to prophecies.

A panoramic view of Creation, the fall of man up to his reconciliation and his resettlement in the Bible, is offered on the whole of its history and prophecy. The Bible history is thus similar to unknown rivers of Africa, which flow from unknown sources of the continent toward unknown seas. But up to their glorious effusion in the ocean of eternity, their sources can be traced under the direction of the Bible itself. The reestablishment of the Jewish world is best seen as the great sabbatical day, illustrating the six thousand years of the history of the earth since the creation of Adam, during which the creation of well-established childbirth was to be followed by a day of rest, a holy day, the seventh day of the week as the Sabbath day, according to Ex. 20:8–11, mandated by the Torah on the land of Israel. He said, "Remember the Sabbath day for sacrifice. Because for six days you will work; but the seventh day is the Sabbath day for Yahweh your God. For in six days Yahweh created the heavens, the earth, the sea, and all that they contain." That's why the Sabbath day is dedicated and blessed by the Lord your God.

It was with the hope of being therefore liberated by the law prescribed to them, in Rm. 8:21– to free themselves from corruption and fatigue, under the servitude of sin and death, and to enter into the freedom of the glory of God that this spring celebration was introduced. But the *Passa'h*–Passover was a religious institution in the pharaonic Egypt. And it was this African Passa'h that gave birth to the famous paschal festival that the Jews celebrate as the beginning of the annual agricultural cycle of the barley harvest season, said Moses in Ex. 13:3–4, forbidding the Hebrews to eat leavened bread on the day of the Exodus out of Egypt.

And for Christians, the Easter celebrated today meant the feast of unleavened bread and the paschal offering as it was called by the Pharisees, according to the gospels of the apostles. It was never of Jewish origin but an Ancient Egyptian ritual of priestly tradition, copied by the Bible writer. It was considered as a spiritual preparation for the Jewish custom since the Talmudic times for a beginning without sin.

Indeed, the sufferings of this present time are not worth to be compared with the glory of God that must be revealed in us. Because up to God's law given to Adam and Eve, there was no sin in the world; but sin entered the world through one man by the name of Adam, who sinned and transgressed the law according to the desires of the flesh, which was death. Rm 8:7 said, "The law according to the desires of the flesh, which is death, and which does not submit itself to God's law." This flesh, in the offing of sin, was condemned for the justice of the law to be fulfilled and incarnates itself in the spirit of sin or the spirit of human soul by opposition to material or physical things to live a spiritual life and peace with his conscience.

It is impossible to do what God's standards require because of the weakness of our human nature—the flesh. Consequently, this was also something impossible for the Law itself to do. But God sent his own Son in the likeness of sinful flesh to be a sin offering. That way, God condemned sin in our corrupt nature—the flesh—so that the righteous requirement of the Law might be fulfilled in us, who do not live according to the flesh but according to the Spirit, Rm 8:3–4.

Good. Now that there is no more condemnation, the law of the Spirit gives to those freed by the law of sin and death. The profane history having lasted from 536 up to the date known as the year 1 after Jesus Christ is not indicated in the history of the Bible. Thus, establishing this chronological line from the Creation to the Christian era, we find a total of a period of 4,128 years. A period of 6,000 years is obtained by adding 1,872 years of the Christian era, going from the Creation to the year 1873 after Jesus Christ.

So it is a fragment of the Yahwist tradition, inherited from the Egyptian high priest, collapsed after six thousand years of prosperity that the Bible presents us; it is known that the Egyptian priesthood was in constant contact with Europe and Asia; therefore, it inspired us this principle in the priestly context of very distant outskirts by the name of Noah, Shem, Ham, and Japheth.

The Yahwist tradition is unrolling the great mysteries of the earthly and heavenly Isis before our eyes; referring to a popular legend about the giant, born from the union between the mortal daughters of men and the heavenly beings, sons of God by veiling its mythological aspects. Gen. 6:1–4 presents us Nephilim and Gibborim as sons of God who came to earth as supernatural characters in the Holy Bible, and in Num. 13:33, it is revealed that: "We saw the Nephilim (the descendants of Anak come from the Nephilim), and we seemed like grasshoppers in our own eyes, and we seemed the same to them."

In the Holy Scripture, these brief passages, telling us the story of their origin, are the only two representations the Pentateuch refers to as fallen angels, creatures that corrupted the souls of men on earth. YHWH saw that his son continued to have strong reputable sons of bygone days with the daughters of men, so he decided that the man of flesh would only live 120 years of his life on earth because his spirit would no longer judge him for his faults. The Bible is only remembering the insolent race of supermen, "the Nephilim," as the Hebrew name for supernatural characters in the Bible; those "angels who are dethroned and who corrupted the souls of men" were of a perversity that motivated the flood. As the sons of God, the lineage of Seth, and the daughters of men; as descendants of Cain, to a discerned commitment, whose punishment and salvation are for the destiny of man, and whose wickedness has corrupted the whole creation. It was the return of chaos because the pure dikes that God put for them here on earth were broken from those in heaven.

It was a judgment of God that prefigures the end of times. And it was in the technical language of rituals that the laws of the world are restored, but the heart of man always remains wicked. Despite all, His creation was saved from the flood; and He will lead it where He wants. The salvation granted to Noah means the calming of His anger and the withdrawal of His threat. The feeling of contrition or regret for the past mistakes is for the repentant, the action of expressing the human renewal for sins, committed under the Holiness Mother of gods, who cannot stand sin but directly connected to men, who love to sin. The Noahide covenant, with a symbol of the rainbow, is extended to all creation. It is transformed by the covenant of Abraham with the symbol of circumcision, the black ritual, and will be limited to only Israel through Moses with in return, the obedience to the law, for those who disobey it.

The lamb means purity–the word of God–knowledge–the Seven Seals–the descent of the cosmic consciousness–the cardinal virtues–the elevation of the human consciousness and the rapid f light of time; these principles are the fugitive periods of human life leading toward the perfection of the spirit and the material world; to the simultaneous unison of the perfect cosmic wisdom, up to the perfect universe–the human death. Any symbol of universal natural principles is the beginning and the representation of the great law. Man is again the blessed and consecrated king of creation, as in the beginning, but not in a peaceful reign. In this new order, he will fight for his liberation.

Men will fight among themselves, and souls will report to God on the Judgment Day. But will that heavenly peace blossom in man? The last days of man will tell and will revenge the state of man by justice. God said to Noah, "I am putting my covenant in the cloud, and it will become a sign of the covenant between me and the earth. Such is the sign of the covenant that I am putting between all flesh on the earth and me." Discover here a compiled checklist of genealogical resources assigned to people for various reasons.

The announcement of the entry of the Gentiles (Japheth) and his descendants after the flood was: Gomer, the eldest child of Japheth, was the ancestor of the people of Indo-European origin from the south of Russia, identified to the Cimmerians. Magog was one of the patriarchs, one of the seven sons of Japheth. Madai was a designated son of Japheth, who was married to a daughter of Shem, according to the book of Jubilees; generally, the Madais were identified with the Iranian Medes by the biblical scholars. Javan was the fourth patriarch of the seven children of Japheth and considered the ancestor of the Greeks. Tubal, a son of Japheth, according to the Bible, was the ancestor of the Iberian people and the ancestor of the first tribes that populated the Italian peninsula. Meshach, which means "prince" or "precious," was another son of Japheth. And Tiras was the last of the seven children of Japheth, who according to Flavius Josephus was the ancestor of the Thracians, and according to the Midrash Bereshit Rabbah, the ancestor of Persians.

The sons of Gomer were as follows: Ashkenaz, the eldest son of Gomer, was the ancestor to the people established in the south of Russia, the Black Sea at one side and the Caspian Sea on the other, not too far from Armenia and near the upper Euphrates River in Asia, according to the Hebrew Bible. Riphath, the biblical patriarch and son of Gomer, was qualified by the Jewish historian Flavius Josephus of the first century, as the ancestor of Paphlagonians in a historical region of Asia Minor. And Togarmah, the third son of Gomer, was the father of a legendary hero by the name of Haik, and according to the legend of the Armenian mythology, he was an ancestor of the Armenians and Kartlos, ancestor of Georgians.

The sons of Javan were the following: Elishah, Tarshish, Dodanim, and Kittim. Among the four sons of Javan, Kittim sometimes designated the Romans, Macedonian, or Assyrian in Hebrew literature; one of the manuscripts of the Dead Sea, describing the "War of the Sons of Light against the Sons of Darkness," designated the Kittim as originated from Ashur; and in some manuscripts of the Dead Sea, Kittim seems to designate the Romans; the Dodanims, in the Christian community are Hebrews of origin and designate (Shem), known as the ancestor of Abraham and the Israelites; they're associated with the people of the island of Rhodes as their ancestor.

The Old Town of Rhodes, which abounds with beaches, wooded valleys and ancient stories of the worship of the sun, engaged on a cultural journey through the past civilizations, is by far the largest and still the most powerful old city of that country. The Dodanims were considered either as the original Greeks or simply as family members of the Greeks. It seemed that the tribe of Dan was originally from the Danaans of the Hebrew tradition, the sea people, who left the surroundings of the Atlantis Ocean to settle on the island of Rhodes. They could metamorphose, had the power to heal, and could modify the weather conditions as they wished, according to Diodorus, known as a Greek historian for writing the monumental universal history.

Even as the origin of the Dodanims seemed still to be unknown, they appeared to be from the north of the Orontes, a river of the Middle East, which ran through western Syria after taking its source in central Lebanon to settle in the Mediterranean, near the port of Samandag. Today, Syria claims this region of Hatay at the southeast of Turkey.

In the Bible, priestly traditions, responsible of the two stories of creation, the genealogy of Adam, part of the Flood story, the Table of Nations, and the genealogy of Shem, inscribed in chapter 10–27, to 32 of Genesis, for example, Abraham's ancestry, resumed the priestly traditions of the congregation without representation, and these passages aren't performing an action from start to end; these resumed priestly traditions in the Bible are abandoned since 1032.

According to the irretrievable model of the priestly genealogy of chapter 5 of Genesis, the origin was restricted to the direct ancestors of Abraham; while the priestly genealogical table in the Bible less summarized people groups according to their ethnic affinities than their historical and geographical relations. Thus, the sons of Japheth populated Minor Asia and the islands of the Mediterranean; the sons of Ham, Kush, the firstborn of Ham, at the origin of the human race existence on earth, are Micrayim, the younger brother of Kush and elder brother of Pout followed by Canaan; together, their families constituted the Hamite; a member of a group of North African people, including the Berbers and the Ancient Egyptians, supposedly descended from the son of Noah. This son of Ham, second son of Noah, was the ancestor of the Hittites, the Girgashites, the Amorites, the Canaanites, the Perizzites, the Hivites, and the Jebusites.

The sons of Kush included Seba, cited as the people of East Africa, is by extension attached to Egypt and Ethiopia, according to Is. 43:3; we also know Havilah; apart from being the name of a country, defined as a territory inhabited by the Ishmaelites, it is extending at least "from Havilah to Shur—to the ancient Persia or the modern Iran up to the Arabian Gulf, opposite Egypt, and going toward the direction of Assyria;" Genesis mentioned Shur by saying, "The angel of Yahweh met Hagar, the maid of Sarai, near a certain spring in the wilderness; the spring that is on the way to Shur, fleeing from her mistress Sarai. He ordered Hagar to return to her mistress, promising her multiple offspring (Gen. 16:7–11); Marah is located in the "wilderness of Shur," according to Ex. 15:22–23; then 1 Sm.15:7 is letting us know that "from Havilah all the way to Shur, near the Egyptian eastern border, Saul slaughtered the Amalekites;" followed by the father of one of the seventy postdiluvian families by the name of Sabteka, as the fifth son of Kush, and Sabtah, the third of his sons, referring to the name of the country occupied by his posterity in his genealogy. Raamah was quoted in a unique verse of the book of Gen. in 10:7, as a patriarch. And finally, Nimrod, the first hero on earth, was among the six sons of Kush. Sheba and Dedan were the sons of Raamah, who, according to Gen. 9:18–19, 10:1–32, and 1 Chr. 1:9, founded the three great groups of the seventy postdiluvian families' generation in the biblical revelation. Mizraim, which means "Egypt," the younger brother of Kush and son of Ham, fathered the Ludim people, mentioned in Gen.10:13. But the indication that 1 Chr. 1:11 is giving us concerning this people did not give them any African origin. It was said that they founded and occupied the land of Libya at the west of Egypt. They were first designated as Ludim and well after as Lehabim.

According to Josephus, they were near the put tribes of the most mysterious sons of Ham in the country of the Moors, originally of the Arab Berber populations, populating the Maghreb toward the extreme west of Africa and the Atlantic Ocean, followed by the Anamim people, of which the same chapters mentioned here above concerning the Ludim people were telling us that they were of the Egyptian race, attached to the people of North Africa.

Ezek. 29:14 is qualifying Pathros as the country of Egyptians origin; Ezek. 30:14 announces that Jehovah decided that he will perform the acts of judgment and make Pathros desolate, associating it also to Egypt. And Is.11:11 seems to confirm that Pathros of Kush had a border with another Kush country known as Ethiopia.

The Bible continues with the Lehabim people of minor notability, of which little or nothing is known out of all family connections but considered as minor biblical figures in the Bible. The Naphtuhim people are perhaps established initially in Egypt or immediately at the west of Egypt as mentioned in Gen. 10:13. According to these chapters and verses here below, but already mentioned here above, the Bible is presenting us Pathros as a country that Yahweh decided to destroy, but it is nowhere found as locality; however, according to these prophets, the Bible is also presenting us its people as the inhabitants of Pathros, in the country of Upper Egypt, said Jer. 44:15.

And in the literature, Casluhim, a name and people that are also not found anywhere exactly, were Egyptian ancient people mentioned in the Bible, where the Philistines and Caphtorim came from. Apart from Mount Casius and the province of Kassiotis in Egypt, they have no other link anywhere in Africa. The Casluhim race and the Pathrusim race of different social structures, determined by the class of heredities and recognized autonomous branches of religions, who became connected by practicing endogamy, resulted in the birth of the Philistines, the Azathim, the Gerarim, the Githim, and the Akronim, according to the 10:23, of the book of Jasher, which Jos. 10:13 and 2 Sm. 1:18.

The historical truth presented in the Hebraic Bible about the Egyptian tradition, initially about the colony of the father of Egypt (the *Mitzrayim* in Hebrew), has a weak echo compared to the historical truth expressed by the Greek historians concerning the descendants, whose names refer to Egypt, according to the Mosaic genealogy of Gen. 10:13–14.

Canaan fathered Sidon, his firstborn and the founder of the ancient city of Lebanon also named Sidon, one of the oldest cities and the capital of the Canaanite kingdom at the Phoenician coast, around the fifteenth century BC. Then Heth, his second son, was the ancestor of one of the seven tribes in the land of Canaan, the Jebusites, which the second book of Samuel 5:6 mentions as the descendants of Canaan, and known as the first inhabitants of the city of Jerusalem, named originally "Jebus," which he founded before its capture by King David toward 1004.

The Amorites were known toward the mid-third millennium BC. This Semitic people of ancient Syria first occupied large parts of southern Mesopotamia from the twenty-first to the end of the seventeenth century BC; then these uncivilized nomadic people associated themselves with the lands west of the Euphrates, including Canaan toward 2400.

The Girgashites were said to be descendants of Canaan, inhabiting the land of Canaan but not listed among the other Canaanite tribes. According to some sources, they were a branch of the great family of the Hivites, who left the land of Palestine before the return of the Israelites from Egyptian servitude. From these revelations of some chapters of the Bible, enumerating the list of nationalities or tribes inhabiting the country of Canaan, nothing was certainly established or accordingly known about their geographical position.

However, Gen. 10:1 6; 1 Chr. 1:14; Gen. 15:21; Dt. 7:1, Jos.3:10, 24:11; and Neh. 9:8 are giving us the light of the historical records, identifying the

Girgashite people or tribes as inhabitants of the ancient land of Canaan in the Old Testament.

The Bible mentioned the Hivites as the inhabitants of the mountainous regions of Canaan at Mount Hermon, a mountain of the anti-Lebanon extending from Lebanon to the north of Jerusalem. These inhabitants of tents dominated the region of Shechem and existed at least until the time of David and Solomon as an ethnic group. It was during the collapse of the "Syro-African Depression," that this mountain chain of Mount Hermon was born.

Since the Israeli conquest of the Six Day War in 1967, Israel occupied this mountain as a strategic place to ensure the control of a vital source of drinking water in the region at the southern end of the border between Syria and Lebanon. This sacred place, according to Luke 9:29–36, was considered by some as the place where Jesus metamorphosed accompanied by his disciples James, John, and Peter, when Elijah and Moses appeared at his side and when his clothes became dazzling white, and his face changed to a total transfiguration, while he spoke to them. Gen. 34:13–17 tells us that they did not practice male circumcision. The Hittites were recognized as one of the few people of the Canaanites region that were erased from the surface of the earth.

The Arkites are ranked among the patriarchs of the Bible as the inhabitants of the land of Canaan and as the descendants of Canaan. Their city, known by the name of Arqa, is located in the northernmost governorates of Lebanon near the village of Minyara in Akkar district, currently known as a city in Lebanon, twenty-two kilometers northeast of Tripoli as capital, near the coast. Their city is called Arqat in the Bible. Concerning the Sinite people as the descendants of Canaan, there are various localities with similar names, possibly as people of the northern part of Lebanon. However, most authoritie consider their identity uncertain, compared to the biblical literature.

Arvadites were a part of nowadays Syria, and Arvad was as an island city that they inhabited. In the early second millennium BC, the settlers on that island were the Phoenicians until it became an independent kingdom, and then it was named Arvad, mentioned by the Bible in Ezek. 27:8–11 as the Canaanite progenitor of the Arvadite people at the north of Tyre. The town of Arwad covered the entire island located in the Mediterranean Sea and was the only inhabited island on the coast of Syria.

The Canaanite people named Zemarites occupied a location named Saumur, called Sumra today on the Mediterranean coast, between Arvad and the seacoast of Tripoli and Ruwad. This Canaanite tribe may be identified with some certainty in that modern town as a place where the Zemarites lived. This Zemarite tribe or branch of the Canaanites, partially from an unused name of a place in Palestine, was designated not only as one of the Phoenician tribes but also as one of the most important Phoenician cities, disappeared from history, and their families spread abroad, according to Gen. 10:18.

The Hamathites, descending from Canaan, were located in what is today western Syria and at northern Lebanon as the kingdom of Hamath, where they inhabited. The city was located on the banks of the Orontes River at the north of Damascus and at the north of Homs, with Hama as its provincial governorate capital.

These seven greater and mightier nations known as the Hittite, the Girgashite, the Amorite, the Canaanite, the Perizzite, the Hivite, and the Jebusite were founded without any institution or special organization nor an originated covenant, therefore destroyed by God without showing any mercy, according to Dt. 7:1–2.

The southern countries of Egypt, Ethiopia, Arabia, and Canaan attached them in memory of the Egyptian domination on that region. Between these two groups are the sons of Shem. The son of Shem Elam, a country and descendant of the sons of Shem, has a very long history; this part of southwestern Iranian Plateau occupied two main regions, corresponding to the region of Susa, known in the Bible as an ancient Elamite civilization. Its city became the capital of the Achaemenid Persian Empire in the fifth century BC and the region of Anshan/Anzan, the former capital of the Elamite kingdom. After the fruitful and unfruitful periods of Anshan, it became the first capital of the Persian Achaemenes kingdom. In the proto-Elamite period, it became the main conurbations country of Elamites in the late fourth millennium BC in the province of Khuzestan, known today by the name of Tall-i Malyan, corresponding to Anshan, an ancient city in Iran. This ancient Elamite country around the current provinces of Khuzestan and Fars was a territory that was occupied by the sons of Elam at the east of the Tigris basin on the Persian Plateau in the Mesopotamian plain originally identified with Abraham as coming from Ur of the Chaldeans and known as the Hebrew's location.

Ashshur, the second son of Shem, is a biblical character mentioned in Genesis and refers both to the land of Assyria and to its people, identified with the Akkadian groups; according to the biblical text of Gen. 10:11, Ashshur, who came out of Shinar, originally a region located between the Tigris and Euphrates, built Nineveh, Rehoboth, and Calah. Later on, this region was called Babylonia, where the temple tower of Babel was built by Nimrod, who established his kingdom on Babel, Erech, Accad, and Calneh. The original capital of Assyria was Ashur on the West Bank of Tigris up to the early ninth century BC in an ancient region of northern Mesopotamia.

Arpachshad is a character from the Biblical chronology known as the third son of Shem. This name is also known as a region where he was established and was an Ancestor of Abraham. These believers, Christians through Isaac, Muslims through Agar, or Jews of the Abrahamic religions considered themselves descendants of Abraham. Eventually by some of the sons of another wife of Abraham named Keturah, married after the death of Sarah, is mentioned in Gen. 25:1–5 and by the sons of the sons and daughters of the daughters of Abraham and Keturah's children in Gen. 25:4–6.

Regarding Lud, as I have already said above concerning this name, even the identification and location of his sons remain the sources of much uncertainty, since the names of various people are established well before the Greeks came and gave them alternative names. But certain sources are considering the Lydians who lived at a time in Asia Minor, as people who were descendants of Lud. Nowadays, most of the people in that Asian part speak Turkish. That peninsula also called Anatolia—surrounded by the Black Sea, the Aegean Sea, and the Mediterranean Sea—is known as the modern Turkey and as the Armenian mountainous region.

Finally, Aram is the father of the Arameans, an ancient people of the Middle East, who are identifying themselves nowadays as the Syriacs, Assyrians, Assyrian-Chaldeans, and Chaldo-Assyrians, or as Aramaic- Assyrian-Chaldeo-Syriac. The language of the people of this child of Shem is the very first language that Christ used to preach. The river Aram-naharaim, mentioned in the three tablets of Amarna, is generally identified with the Nahima region, the land or the city of Haran between the Tigris and Euphrates Rivers in ancient Syria, and the birthplace of Abraham, according to the Jewish rabbinical tradition.

The sons of Aram included Uz, Hul, Gether, and Mash; "and in the country of Uz, lived a man named Job," said Job 1:1; Hul's house was Bochart in Armenia at the Hylatae of Syria; the house of Gether was uncertain, and the house of Mash was also Bochart in the Mous Masius of Armenia. In Genesis, Aram is the name given to Syria.

Arpachshad fathered Shelah, and Shelah begot Eber. To Eber were two sons born; the first was called Peleg, the ancestor of Hebrews because it was in his time that earth was divided, and his brother was called Joktan. The Elamites, Assyrians, and Aramaeans are all associated with various Arabic people who occupied the whole eastern part of the Arabian Peninsula, according to Gen. 10:21–32. So if we are to believe the story lines, the genealogical tables of the Bible, the origin of nations is a mixture of the sons of Noah, Ham, Japheth, and Shem, mixed between their sons and daughters to populate the earth. One thing is certain today, and everyone knows it: it is from one generation of parents with black skin that all other colors were generated to fulfill the promise of God.

Despite numerous proven rejections relating to a historical account of a false chronology, hypocrites of many Orthodox Jews and some Christians up to the half of the nineteenth century, still consider the entire population of the world as the descendants of the three sons of Noah. The family tree of people of the descendants of the patriarch Noah in the Old Testament is a guide of local ethnic groups of the ancient Near East, aiming to explain the historicity of the relations between those different groups toward the seventh century BC, at the time of the final Bible text writing.

So unless God comes and reveals the divine sparkling light of our farthest origin to us to a specific understood point of truth, this creation knowledge of the Holy Scriptures will remain an uncertain knowledge to us human beings; and as creatures of limitless impiety, disfigured by sin, we will continue to live without the knowledge of God, and no Holy Scriptures revelation can come and change that. The Yahwists, the Elohists, the Deuteronomic source, and the priestly source are simply bringing changes, personifying the original knowledge, on the already inhabited world that existed in Israel around the time of Solomon, affirming the human unity, divided into groups, from a common black parent tree.

The Tower of Babel built well after the patriarchs' period, therefore during the reign of Hammurabi toward 1780 of our era, does not at all favor this diversity but the complementary aspects of world history. The story behind which a Mesopotamian mythical hero is hidden, is a slogan that says, "As Nimrod the mighty hunter before the Lord," was at a period of pastoral life; he had Accad, Babel, Calneh, and Erech, cities that are all in the land of Shinar as the first fruits of his empire (Gen. 10:9–12); these cities were located near Babylon—a name used to designate the southern part of Lower Mesopotamia by opposition to the country of Sumer of Sargon II, the Neo-Assyrian king from 721 to 705. Kush, the founder of ancient Babylon, is the father of the famous Nimrod, under the name of Bel, meaning "Lord" in an ancient Semitic dialect.

The ancient Akkadian king Sargon, founder of the dynasty of Akkad in the twenty-fourth century BC, extended his domination over the entire Middle East by uniting the southern Mesopotamia for the first time. It is from Sumer, the first urban civilization of one of the most important and most brilliant periods of the Mesopotamian history, relating to the art and civilization that it evokes, that we owe the sexagesimal system of that bygone world; identifying itself by the division of the hour into sixty minutes and sixty seconds. Their numeral system with sixty as its base, passed down to the ancient Babylonians, originated in the third millennium BC. The superior number sixty, highly composite, involving the sexagesimal numbers simplified in one hour, can be divided evenly into sections of thirty minutes, twenty minutes, fifteen minutes, twelve minutes, ten minutes, six minutes, five minutes, four minutes, three minutes, two minutes, and one minute.

After thousands of years, this division of the hour is anyway still directly a tributary on the daily existence of human destiny on earth, used—in a modified form—for measuring time, angles, and geographic coordinates; Sumer, the southern part of Babylonia, comprised a people whose exact origin is unknown at the southern Iraq; according to the reference of the chronological tables of the late fifth millennium to the beginning of the fourth millennium, their language, not akin to any classical or modern language, remains a mystery, like the cities that are in the land of Shinar.

The story of the Creation of man, described on the seven tablets, revealed to us that Father Sky and Mother Earth made the history of the Sumerian creation. It was in their name that Marduk, the great god of war, was incorporated. In numerous Negro-African languages, this proliferated root retained the same sense of etymological origin. Kush and his biblical descendants were commonly recognized as black, the ancestors of the current Abyssinians.

Marduk (god of Babylon, a gifted son with an astonishing nature and remarkable forces) was the eldest son of Ea, known by Akkadians or by Sumerians as Enki, an agrarian deity, the strong source of violent human life and the personification of the fertilizing action of water in the Sumerian mythology. He was a god associated with fresh water, the creation, destiny, wisdom, intelligence, prosperity, and technical inventions, known as the third Mesopotamian god of the triad—guardian of the sacred "Me" (laws) of civilization—code of sacred powers associated with wisdom, and was the patron of exorcist possessing magic abilities.

Well after the disappearance of what constituted the Mesopotamian religious building in the biblical story of the Tower of Babel, inspired by the ziggurat Etemenanki "the house of the foundation of heaven and earth", the ziggurat of Babylon, the most spectacular monument of the Mesopotamian civilization, rose to the sky in a series of stair steps, consisted of several terraces supporting a temple built at its top. Its graphic symbol representing the word U6.NIR in the Sumerian ideograms, which derived from the verb *zaqāru*, meaning "to raise or "build at the height," has always had a house believed to be the polytheism belief and worship for thousands of years as the only religion.

Esagila was the main temple of the god Marduk with its sacred tutelary deity that protected Babylon. Its Sumerian name E.SAG.IL meant "the temple on the elevated pinnacle." It was erected in the center of the world on his honor, but also to all gods, where he created the world; it was located in the holy district of Babylon, at the same spot of the battle to gain power over the city of which he was the patron deity. It was around that temple that the holy city of Babylon was developed.

There afterward, it was where Enki (Ea), a representation of Marduk's father, who was considered as the master of freshwater, created man, the substitute, from the blood of Kingu; Enki executed the creation by taking the responsibility of the heavy behoving burden of deities, his masters, and allowing them to not work anymore. But since man is born from the blood of Kingu, a sinful god, even if it is not an idea of the type of punishable sin, he was a willingly sacrificed god, and man, the substitute, bears Kingu's guilt. He was the son of Anu, the sky god and the father of gods, and Nammu, the goddess of water and creation, and the virgin goddess of the Sumerian mythology, who corresponded to Tiamat in the Babylonian mythology, who gave birth to Ki, the god of the earth and An heavens, associated with the kingdom of Apsu, and to the goddess Damkina, the cosmological god and the protector of Babylon, who was dwelling in Babylon in the sanctuary in Esagila—*É.SAG.IL*; at the first lights of hope during our era, the main temple of god Marduk, which sunk into oblivion with Babylon was attached to ziggurat Etemenanki, passed to posterity as the Tower of Babel.

It was under the reign of the first king Ishbi-Erra of a city of ancient Mesopotamia called Isin, located at the southern Iraq that he reigned as founder of the first dynasty of Isin, from -2017 to around 1985, and was considered as the greatest ruler of the Babylonian dynasty of Pashe. Ancient Mesopotamia had other gods like the one named Sin or Nanna/Sin, representing the Moon, and who never played a major role in the Mesopotamian mythology; however considered one of the most important deities throughout the history of Mesopotamia, its main sanctuary retained a prominent place in the great city of Ur. They were also gods like the great god Enlil, his father, and his children, the goddess Inanna/Ishtar, and Utu/Shamash, the sun god. But at the time of Nebuchadnezzar I, of the Second Dynasty of Isin, from 1125 approximately to 1104, before Jesus Christ, Marduk associated with the planet Jupiter, worship at the Neo-Babylonian era, absorbed all their attributes; this god Marduk, the chief god of Babylon, after conquering Tiamat, the monster of primeval chaos, who became lord of the gods of heaven and earth, that he acquired all its importance; also, he was represented as Baal, the Phoenician a god of Canaanite origin. Since the third millennium BC up to the Roman times, his cult Jah, as a deity— "YHWH" "Yah" and "Jehovah" known as Baal was celebrated. "Jah" or "Yah" is known as the first syllable of the word Yahweh, the consonantal spelling of the proper name of God (YHWH), representing the four letters that form the tetragrammaton in the Hebrew Bible. For Jews, articulating the word "Jah"/ "Yah" was allowed because it was forbidden for them to pronounce the proper name of God "YHWH."

In the divine yard, "YHWH"/ "Yahweh"/"Yah"/Jehovah," is the "son" of God; the "assigned" Lord God of Israel is "Yahweh," not Elohim the Most High God. These names are known as pagan names. Among the sons of Elohim in the heavenly yard, Yahweh "YHWH" is the lesser "son" of the Most High God Elohim. But since the Hebrew Bible considers Baal as a fake foreign god, the name of Baal became blasphemy and Punic for numerous original Semitic gods, putting the uniqueness of God into questioning from the standpoint of the Hebrew religion. From the ninth century, the veneration of the divinities of Baal was opposed to the Israeli deity "YHWH" (the Lord) or Elohim. To deceive mankind, the original "sons of God" was changed to "sons of Israel" in some bibles, and distorted in some cases; completely altering the meaning of the "sons of God;" believing that the Most High is "Yahweh," "YHWH," Yah, and that the name of the Son of God is Yeshu(a) or Yehoshua, destroying the belief. Jesus as a name is an Anglicized variation of Yeshu, considered as a curse to erase the name of the Messiah. Immanuel is the Son of the Most High EL.

Under the dynasties of Ramses, extending on the Nineteenth and Twentieth Dynasties, these deities are assimilated in Egyptian mythology to Seth and to Montu. Between the reigns of Nebuchadnezzar I, from 1125 to 1104, on Babylon and the one of the best known sovereign of Babylon Nabuchonosor II, from 604 to 562 before Jesus Christ, they were passed into posterity in the Western tradition; and the second book of Kings, chapter 25, is revealing the names of ten other kings of Babylon intercalating in the Hebrew Bible to us. Like the lord of Apsu, the primordial aquatic abyss of the origin of time and the underground ocean of freshwater encircling the earth, which existed before the creation of man, he guided the course of great rivers and freshwater of irrigation canals by spreading happiness and abundance across the earth. Apsu constituted a source of knowledge and wisdom.

The turbulent birth of the great gods, followed by the one of the world's monstrous creatures engendered by Tiamat—the natural feminine element with her union to the husband Kingu, who preexisted the creation of gods, of the world and man; Kingu's life was put to death decided by Ea, residing in the abyss on which the earth is resting, as a punishment for him trying to annihilate his own offspring.

Becoming Anu or AN, the heavens, the attested sky, the father deity in Sumerian religion, was considered as being the "spirits, the demons," and the "supreme ruler of the kingdom of heaven." In his highest heavenly regions, Anu himself wandered in his kingdom of heaven. The biblical Shamayim—the Hebrew word for "heaven"—is known as the dwelling place of God and other heavenly beings; Ki, the earth, the home of the living, the biblical Eretz, is created as the so-called land of Israel (ץרא לארשי in Hebrew); concerning the story of Adam and Eve creation in the Bible, they're known as being the firstborn of gods; and sheol, considered as the kingdom of the dead, are all presumably stories from the Sumerian creation history.

Marduk was created by EA and his wife Daminka, the goddess of ancient Mesopotamia (in Assyria and Babylon), or Damgalnuna (in Sumer); but when EA discovered the stratagem of Apsu, the fresh water of abyss, lying beneath the earth and his wife Tiamat, the oceans of salted water, where chaos reigns, as wanting to destroy their offspring known as Lahmu and Lahamu, the first two gods, parents of Ansar and Kisar, grandparents of Anu, considered the father of all gods, and Ki (the earth), who ultimately were irritating their parents and other residents, the god of fresh water Ea, decided to put asleep Apsu and executed him.

Crying for the loss of her beloved husband and seeing her tears becoming the source of Euphrates and Tigris, Tiamat decided to avenge her dead husband. To avenge him, Tiamat and his son Kingu, who became her new husband, created an army of snakes and monstrous creatures that Kingu commanded. So the great Mesopotamian god Marduk, the vindictive warrior god, whom the divine king of Babylon represented, felt himself up to the task as a superior entity capable of defeating that monstrous primordial Sumerian entity by the name of Tiamat the tumultuous Sea, terrible female dragon of the great ocean of saltwater. Marduk had a stature so great and full of moral confidence that one could not imagine; view his gigantic limbs, his head with four eyes and four ears; his wide mouth maw with lips that when he stirred, a flaming fire came out of his terrifying mouth.

Because of her reign of chaos, Marduk was to face the terrible female Tiamat, who represented the gigantic snake; and for that, the requirement of more power was necessary. So, from the high council of the divine assembly and other gods, whom he exhorted these full powers, they gathered all their powers that they could have and awarded him fifty titles corresponding to all the divine attributes. So, with all his army of snakes and monsters, Marduk went to meet Tiamat, the terrible female dragon, to destroy her. Upon arrival at the destination, Tiamat immediately got rid of Marduk by swallowing him. What to do now in the belly of the terrible dragon? Without thinking long, he found that only a storm could destabilize Tiamat.

So, without hesitation, Marduk began to cause such a terrible storm that forced her to always maintain her wide mouth open for Marduk to come out. Thus, with a deadly arrow shot in the stomach, Marduk killed the monstrous primordial entity by getting rid of her other monsters as well. And to present his respect to his father, he decided to petrify them into star stone statues and transported them in the gardens of the temple of his father as ornamental pieces. He placed them around in harmony, blossoming in the sunshine of a merciless wind for them to become the soul of the garden. Marduk appropriated himself the tablets of destiny that Kingu kept as a wedding gift, given to him by his late wife Tiamat. He smashed the skull, and by separating her body, he began to create the world.

He created the sky from her head, and from her chest, he created the earth; from her lower limb parts and others limbs, he created the constellations of the celestial vault, the natural elements of the earth, and mountains; the ligament from the eyes of the dragon that he busted filled the two rivers of Euphrates and Tigris. The hair of Tiamat became vegetation; he transformed her bones into stones and her blood into ocean. With the corpse of Tiamat, he created the first humans and humanity with the blood of the god Kingu for them to take care of the universe that he just created. The god Kingu represented a reasoning that was very well characterized by the spirit of aggressiveness, destruction, and enslavement, leading to terrible wars.

It is not surprising to notice the spirit of aggressiveness, the reign of chaos, and the destructive instinct of the human nature, knowing that humans were created from these two evil entities. These barbarian conceptions fit perfectly with the cruel mentality of our religious leaders and leaders of our countries, the invaders of our peaceful spirits; they make us live cruel times through millennia by imposing us all kinds of beliefs and laws whereby, to have the right to survive, we must conquer or be submissive.

Apsu, the primordial ocean of fresh water of the beginning of time, mixing together with the salty ocean water of Tiamat, formed the waves, Mummy, and generated the first primordial couple, Lahmu, the snake, firstborn, and Lahamu, firstborn daughter of Tiamat and Apsu. *Ab* is "water" and *zu* is "far" in Sumerian. The couple Lahmu and Lahamu, which emerged from the original vase as feminine and masculine principles, existed at the beginning.

They generate the great gods Anu and Ea and other gods populating the sky, the earth, and the underworld in Eridu, one of the oldest cities in the world and the oldest in Mesopotamia, originally the home of Enki. He lived in Absu in E-Abzu (Deep Ocean), home of the cosmic water or, again, in the holy water tanks in the yards of his temple located at twelve kilometers southwest of Ur, present town of Tell Abu Shahrain, Dhi Qar Governorate, Iraq. These first two gods are parents of Elohim, the pivotal axis of heavens in Gen. 1:1, answering to the name of Anshar, god of heaven. He and Kishar, his sister and his wife at the same time, are gods of the second generation. Anshar and Kishar are parents of Anu.

These holy water tanks, typical for the purification of the Assyrians and Babylonians, are also called Abzu, similar to baptism in Christianity and the washing of the foot and other parts of the body for the preparation of prayers in Islam. For the first time, this religious term, referring to a divine promise, is used in 1 Sm. 13:19.

According to the writings of Sumer, AN, the creator of earth and the Cosmos, was seen as a well-ordered whole; AN reigned over his kingdom, assimilated to a high mountain, where heaven and earth were generated from the primordial ocean of infinite Origin—the beginning—the primordial sea that engendered the Annunaki, assembly of gods; but still united, they separated our earth, incarnated with evil in the universe, under the combined action of his son Enlil and the brother of Enlil, lord of the wind in Sumerian. This sky-father deity had the power to judge crimes committed by men, and the stars that he created as soldiers destroyed the wicked. He divided the universe between two of his sons—Nudimmud, the god of the sky; and Enlil, his favorite son and the lord who decided to produce what was useful, whose decisions were immutable, and who received the highest authority after the one of his father, An.

When heaven was distant from the earth (Ki), when the earth was separated from heaven, when the name of man was fixed, when (An) took heaven, and when Enlil, the beneficent god, took earth, he germinated the land through the seed of the country. The mother goddess of fresh water, Ammou, whom (An) created among the other obliged gods, asked his son Enki, the god of fresh water, to create humanity. He shaped the first men with clay, so that by their work, they could provide food and offer it to the gods in the form of offerings and sacrifices. The benevolent fertility goddess Ninhursag, wife of Enki, wanted to destroy her work with her power after creation, but her husband stopped her because she could not take away the power from him to create monsters, giants, or deformed and sterile human beings. We therefore find similarities between the stories of different cultures, presenting us different stories of creation.

Several versions of "manufactured humanity" by Elohim-the totally asexual planning deities are found denatured in Gen. 1:26. This chapter of Genesis is about a model of the mixture of the primordial human Namlu'u, the original being, and the Neanderthal, manufactured by Elohim by Nammu, the mother of Enki. This version of the first "manufacturer" the "life designers," obedient to laws, was rendered asexual by the clan of Yahweh, like Usumgal-Anunna, the Sumerian gods.

Enki separated sexes for humanity to be autonomous so that man could be multiplied compared to the authoritarian regime of Anunna. In the Mesopotamian plain of Eden, a gigantic agrarian industry was sitting where we would find the oldest traces of wheat in the world. By very specific terms via sexuality, to the initiation of the secret of the dark stars, and with the secret attached to sexuality, you will be able to reproduce yourself. This gift of sexual reproduction made for men by Enki was a taboo that the Bible presents us through the temptress Eve, like the notion of sin. Enki wanted men to be autonomous and initiated. But when sexual humanity found itself facing gods in Edin, it was very difficult to fully control it.

It had to secretly manage its autonomy to continue its work and to meet its obligation. A deliberate distortion was found in the Bible, recounting that the woman was created as a kind of by-product from the left side of the man and created second. This contradicted the importance of the thought of the eternal feminine. The Bible also denatured Enki (the serpent), presented as a symbol of authority and as an instructor in Mesopotamian belief and not reversed as a tempter.

Enki, in a form of a serpent, said to the serpent, initiate humanity, because a woman knows the secret trees and the sign of the moon of god (Digir) for procreation. Thus, between gods and men, there existed peaceful relations, almost familial and friendly, a spirit of society based on respect and justice, at an unknown archaic period, which degenerated considerably under the pressure of different reigns of foreign invaders.

Enlil, made of the terms *En* (Lord) and *lil* (the universal breath), without attributes or specific place of attachment, is one of the main gods and the supreme deity of the pantheon of the ancient Mesopotamian religion and considered the king of gods during the second half of the third millennium and most part of the second millennium BC, assigning supremacy to human kings by his decisions. He often plays an important role as a leader of the gods, the spirit allowing beings to live. As the god of justice who possesses both energy and power, he mediates between his father (An) and the humans on earth. He is the executor of celestial decisions and the master of worlds, who possesses the tablets of destinies on which the fate of humanity is engraved. Among the Akkadians, he is found under the name Ellil.

The will of Enlil, and his followers to extend their dominance over humanity, constituted the establishment of a new global religion. With his brother Abgal, he decided to recompose the language of the genus *Homo* (*Ukubi*). He said, "From the matrix language [Emesa], we will create hundreds of abundant particles of this matrix language, and each ethnic group in each nation will speak its own dialect so that the whole genus *Homo* [*Ukubi*] will be unable to communicate clearly with Kharsag and his great Satan." We will replace certain terms placed in the language with new ones and move them from time to time when humanity will have decoded them. Thus, since the dawn of time, our work will bear fruit in all their languages so that the great Satan and his followers gradually lose ground.

An, Enlil, and Enki—the triad of the three basic divinities, as the symbol of a protective Trinity of human life—seems to be well united. So Enli, who married the same goddess Enki, comes from the same cell as two twin brothers and are not to be mistaken, because from a point of view, they're two half-brothers and did not get along at all; it is rather basically one and the same deity with the same prefix (En), the Lord, king and high priest, to whom we attributed different and variable exploits since the beginning of the times of legend according to the location and consideration, as a personal honor to each of their gods and their mythology. Like most of the Egyptian cities choose their protective god at the predynastic times for the creation of the earth arose from the cosmos, the creation of man shaped by clay, compared to the power of the Sumer god of water, there are many similarities with the Bible.

Endowed with considerable force, the immortal gods possessing supernatural powers shaped man and woman in the image of gods; or understandably in the shadow of gods, a word used in Hebrew. From their entity emerged a brilliant kind of dazzling, luminous splendor that plunged mortals in a feeling of great respect and fear. The whole earth belonged to this God; his faithfuls brought food to the temple for this God, which the high priest received in his name. This rite, celebrated in the temple of Ur remind us the union of Dumuzi, the shepherd king, and Inanna, the goddess of love and the high priestess who each year married a local king; it resembled the one of Thebes. The vengeful warrior god Marduk and the progenitor of the violent humanity, represented by the divine king of Babylon, became the supreme god of the Mesopotamian pantheon.

Gilgamesh, the fifth king of Uruk (at the beginning of the Second Dynasty), was also the name of the ancient city of Sumer and well after Babylon, nowadays Iraq. He was a character of the First Dynasty of Ur, who reigned for 126 years. He was the central character in an epic poem among the oldest works in the Mesopotamian literature. He was also known under the name of Bilgames in the oldest Sumerian texts. He was the main character in many epic stories, of which the most famous was the "Epic of Gilgamesh," which was awarded a huge success during the antiquity.

Gilgamesh was a demigod, a being with partial or lesser divine status, such as a minor deity, commonly used to describe mythological figures who were the offspring of a god and a human being and not a mortal raised to divine rank. The Sumerian king Gilgamesh, god-human hybrid, was supposedly described as two-thirds god and one-third human. The list of Sumerian kings placed his reign around 2600 BC.

His father was Lugalbanda, from Sumerian words meaning "young king" (*lugal*), and "young, junior, or small" meaning (*banda*). He was the second king of Uruk who reigned for 1200 years, and his mother was Ninsun (wild cow lady), whom some call Rimat Ninsun, who was the goddess of Gudea of Lagash in Sumerian mythology. He and his son Urlugal, the sixth king of the First Dynasty of Uruk (c. twenty-sixth century BC), rebuilt the shrine of the goddess Ninlil (lady of the full field of the storm or the lady of the air) at Tummal, a sacred area in the city of Nippur. After building the legendary walls of Uruk, to defend his people against external threats, the beloved companion of superhuman and the personification of all human virtues, Enkidu died of a slow, painful and inglorious death. He was punished by the gods for having killed the demon Humbaba and the bull of heaven. Bored with pain and looking for answers to the mysteries of life and death for his own extinction, he traveled up to the ends of the earth to meet the wise Utnapishtim, who, through the waters of death, divided the garden of the sun and paradise, where Utnapishtim, who survived the great flood, lived. Just to find the plant of eternal life, the hero descended to the bottom of the waters of Apsu for him to be immortal. Becoming Anu ("heavens," the biblical Shamayim) and Ki (the earth), all these mythological figures were created as being the firstborn of the gods.

The great Sumerian race, which history says was placed on earth to acquire knowledge, its kingdom in Sumer suddenly disappeared from the country of the two rivers, where it appeared on earth thousands of years ago, and left us a vast culture, science, and spirituality. Its powerful kingdom, around 4000 BC, scattered its culture throughout Mesopotamia, leaving no records. Like the hieroglyphs of Ancient Egypt with a whole pictographic origin, representing a concrete thing, mainly used as a phonetic or symbolic character drawing, reminding us of the gigantic enigmatic building of the pyramids of Egypt, distinguished by their cosmic and mythical appearance and their function, so were the appearance of the cosmic and mythical buildings of Mesopotamia and Babylon distinguished.

Babylon actually meant "Gate of God," and Babel was explained by the root *bll*, which meant "confused." The Bible says, "The Lord scattered them over the face of the whole earth from the place called Babel, after He confused the language of the whole world (Gen. 11:9)." According to their lineages and from the nations, such were the clans of the descendants of Noah, where everyone spoke the same language. And when they found a plain in the land of Shinar, they settled there for them not to be scattered over all the earth and they decided to build a city with a tower of brick and bitumen, of which the top penetrated the heavens. But as man proposes and God disposes, He then disposed, marked by the experiences of jealousy and envy with regard to man success, the city and the tower that men built in harmony, God said, "Come! Let's descend and confuse their language so that they no longer speak it and no longer understand each other, now that no design is unrealizable for them."

In the Bible, Gen. 11:1–9 reveals the same decision taken by Yahweh like the one taken by the brothers Abgal, Enlil and his followers, who, after revealing the arts, sciences, and techniques to men before the flood, decided to extend their domination over humanity by recomposing the language of the genus *Homo* (*Ukubi*) in the Mesopotamian mythology.

This space project in the history of the Tower of Babel that the crossed man inaugurated, hoping to ascend to heaven, displeased the gods as told in Genesis. According to the Bible, many dialects appeared after the construction of the Tower of Babel, and that time made that the only race, united as one nation, speaking a single language in the world before the construction of the Tower of Babel, ceased to understand each other, losing sight of the spiritual aspect and the concept of God, manifested in personal and material aspect.

Believing themselves to be authors of the works of earth, governmentally, hierarchically, and a leadership demonstrating ability and an influence to unite and to mobilize energies around a collective action, provoked an extreme diversity of thoughts leading to the great schisms; through their personal conceptions, they forgot that everything comes from a single source of God, who was speaking through them. This myth became a historical fact in 1898, when Robert Koldewey discovered this ancient ziggurat after conducting excavations at a site in Mesopotamia. For us, such was the meaning of the Tower of Babel. It was from them that people were scattered on earth. God blessed Noah and his children, and He said to them, "Be fruitful and multiply and fill the earth," according to the Pentateuch (Gen. 1:28). You may notice that the holy writings of the three religions were revealing the name of our continent and its inhabitants in the entire African territory before the arrival of whites in Gen. 2:11–14.

Our continent, which was known by the oldest name of all languages, is named in Wolof, a language mainly spoken in Senegal, as *khem*, meaning "charcoal used in cooking," therefore as black by extension; and in Fula, Fulani or Fulfulde, as *Kembu*, meaning "coal."

In Cameroon, Congo-Brazzaville, and Gabon, it was known as *Kami*, meaning "burned," and as *Fima*, meaning "black," in Bambara, a national language of Mali or dialect and language in Burkina Faso, Ivory Coast, Gambia, and Guinea. It is named Mossi in Niger Republic, and Burkina Faso as KiM, meaning "burned." In Aramaic, it was called *KaMa*; meaning "burned, heat, or blackened."

From Kama, the people of Kama are called Kamites or Hamitic, a member of the Chadic group of languages of a subfamily of the Hamito-Semitic family of languages. And it was formerly composed of the Berber, the Ancient Egyptian, and the Kushitic languages today recognized as independent branches of the Afro-Asiatic family.

In Hebrew, it is named *Kam*, meaning "burned," and in Coptic *KaMa*, meaning "black." Kemet, the black countries of the earth, and the rest of the ancestor continent with all intellectuality are and always remains a perfect image of the universe. But the name Africa, which our continent currently bears, did not exist on the geographic maps of 1600 to 1700 after Jesus Christ. It was referred according to the Bible as the land of Kush, the black descendant of Noah; of Cham, who was black; or again, Ethiopia, derived from Ityopp'is, an unknown son of Kush in the Bible.

The land of Sheba, the kingdom of the Arab king of Yemen, located in the southwestern tip of the Arabian Peninsula, who seized the northern Maghreb lands, etc., was called Ifriqos bin Qais bin Saifi. Since then, after the invasion of these lands, this northern part of our ancestor continent bore the name of this king. It is therefore how Ifriqya, corresponding to the provinces of the Roman Africa, was named Africa by the Romans at the period of the Western Middle Ages. Ifriqiya today corresponds to Tunisia (off-desert areas) at the east of Algeria and Tripolitania, the current Libya.

Oh, Kali, you're black. You're Africa. You're also white, yellow, red, and black at a time; the sister of Lulua and the wife of Cain; from the people of Central Africa, in the Democratic Republic of Congo; in the center south province of Kasai-Occidental; at the west and the Kasai Oriental border at the east, in between the Kasai River at the west, and also across the border at the northeastern Angola, you're black! You are all Africa!

Oh, Goddess Kali, you're the direct source of the celestial fire of priestesses, the root that divides time according to seasons, periods, and cycles. Your red color is synonymous with gold metal, the secret and the origin of secret knowledge, the seat of the soul, the organ that regulates the currents of thought, and a point where the body and the spirit meet.

Your ritual truth that defines the sacred ceremony is black and white at the same time. Your red and black color materialized itself into a physical substance of the purest and noblest precious stone named diamond, formed of a colorless crystalline, the brightest and the hardest stone of all; under the form of gold, you're showing the "supreme truth," as the living essences of the physical natural species and not metaphysical nature. Oh, black princess and beautiful girl, your voice, which is born during puberty, is the mysterious word spoken by the voice of the uterus.

Africa! Sacred black woman, beloved woman, secret thing where the occultism that obscures the hymn of gods is hidden; mystical secret links related to science that secretes growth hormones, your two links—secrets and mystics—considered as ominous, bore witness of a great veneration, never interchangeable. In your terrestrial environment, your lunar essence is menstrual blood—the f low of eternal wisdom, supreme source of the manifestation of light, equal to the mystical waters of creation, is the original celestial fire of the active longevity of the tree of life. Oh, sacred virgin priestess, in your mystical circles, your f lower loses blood and fades.

Your menstrual celestial fire, a pure lunar essence, is the gold of gods, collected by the heavenly, sacred ceremony venerated by gods. Being an essential basis, it is only given to kings and queens of the lineage as a beverage of knowledge and the longevity of life.

You have gone through hell and the purgatory in search of paradise, where awaited beatitude, the adept of the faithfuls of love. Graceful to love, you're pursuing your way by decreasing the volume of bodies, leading to the summit of yourself and allowing you an access to the highest degree of initiation—the guide that leads to salvation and wisdom.

Wisdom, or the creative genius is born from the union of souls; the soul of the one who fertilizes thy womb, with the spirit of a liberating joy, the soul of the hero; finally, allowing you to live the sexual act, up to its vocation, conversing with the mental habits that it requires to live that love that nourishes the human soul, still bound to a mortal body and assisting him to affranchise the order of time; at a depth where the soul opens to what surpasses it, and which isn't of the order of time.

Spiritually, in an unlighted person, light remains somnolent. And by a constant individual observation of the consciousness itself, of a plan without a pure existence, the somnolent light awakens the consciousness actually liberated of thought and spiritual energy of an unwavering will. At that moment, your true sacred black and white ritual is accomplished by the celestial fire of the goddess Kali, and then you became Africa—the organ regulating all thoughts, secrets, and mystics; the root of all knowledge; and a point where the body, the spirit, and soul meet. Oh, Kali, you're black. You're Africa.

Egyptian texts of ancient civilization usually translated the word *Africa* as "black land," and when nominating its inhabitants, the name of Kamite or Kemi (*km.t*) was applied by the good vital artery of the civilization of the Nile in Ancient Egypt, known as an excellent priestly power.

This name is also found in the esoteric foundation of the kemitist beliefs of Ancient Egypt, a completed sum of an education that perfectly reflects that of Egypt (Kemet). That word of two roots means "root" (*km*) and "black" (*t*) or "feminine" (*km.t*). The black land is a place inhabited by black people. The country of Kush, the fertile black earth, and by extension, Egypt, *Km.tjw* means "those of Egypt." In the Egyptian symbolism, Seth, the sterile, associated with the color of an area of land, especially covered with sand, characterizing an isolated place without water and vegetation, is commonly called the desert, and means "violence and chaos;" while Osiris symbolizes rebirth and fertility, associated with the black and green of the valley.

In a hymn to the glory of Sesostris III (from 1878 to 1842), pharaoh of the Middle Kingdom, a period of the history of Ancient Egypt, which followed the first intermediate period and preceded the second intermediate period, Kemet was represented as a man and a woman sitting, an exceptional variant designating a place inhabited and qualifying the skin color of its inhabitants. The *kmt.yw*—those of the black land, the inhabitants of Ancient Egypt, a black civilization of all people of Africa—are directly related to the history of Ancient Egypt and are particularly designated by the name KaMtou, meaning "black." Genesis quoted the continent of Africa and tells us in chapter 5:32, that Ham, brother of Shem and Japheth, born when Noah was five hundred years old before the flood, is the ancestor of the black kingdom of Kush. And that Kush, Mizraim, Put, and Canaan were his four sons. He was the ancestor of the Hamites, black people of Africa, and the Canaanites, according to Genesis. His biblical roots (Kam), or the ancient Jews (Ham), also spelled (Cham), known as the ancestor of the South Hamitic people, tell us that its meaning is related to the Semitic root meaning "hot" and classified the name of Mizraim, as a black person, as one of the son of Ham, and grandson of Noah, in Egypt.

The story in Genesis said that Noah, as a good farmer, began to cultivate the land, planted vines, and conjured Bacchus, the Greek god of wine and celebration. And after producing wine, he began to drink. And it was due to his state of being intoxicated and excited that he stripped off in his tent and fell asleep in the middle of it.

Ham, father of Canaan, saw the nakedness of his father and reported it to his two brothers outside. So in general, the descendant of Arabs, of the Jews, and the Semites Shem, and the one of the white Europeans, etc., by the name of Japheth took a coat, put it on their shoulders, walked backward, and covered the nudity of their father. They did not see the nakedness of their father since their faces were turned away. Cham, therefore, might have done more than just looking his drunk, naked, and sleepy father — but could have raped him. Too bad for the human being, since the violence and the evil spirit that God wanted to completely eliminate on earth by the flood persisted after it.

Now he came out from among the ten thousand saints, and from his right hand, he sent them the fire of law, for—in delirium—they continue to defile the flesh contemptuously by blaspheming the glories of God. Let the seigniory of the Lord Almighty condemn them for ignoring the laws of nature on the earth like beasts without reason. And it is in this distraction of Balaam that they went in the path of Cain.

Cain, the eldest son of the first couple of humanity, according to the Jews, is the son of Adam and Eve. This character of the Bible and the Koran is the founder of the Judeo-Christian and Muslim beliefs. His name is a significant ancient word in the process of self-awareness for the followers of a philosophical and religious school of thought of the eighteenth century, focusing on the mystical quest.

The Illuminists are based on an idea of illumination, proposing a reading of the occult sciences of a direct inner divinity inspiration and putting Christian texts in the light; those of Rosicrucian followers, like the epiphysis, are considered secret and the supreme source of light, since all spiritual light emerged from the same source. The philosophical doctrine of illuminism gives importance to the oldest prime principle responsible for the cosmic order of the universe, the assimilated concept of God and causal reasoning. Through mystical experiences, generally in metaphysics (the study of the principles of nature), completely separated from the material, the pure activity of the intellect in action and the intellect in power lies beyond the physical realities and focuses on the problems of knowledge, reality, truth, and freedom of the human being, graceful to its great spiritual depth and its great philosophical rigor.

For centuries, its polytheistic conception, in its most orthodox version combined with those of Parmenides and Plato, characterized the essential of the Greco-Roman philosophy of the late antiquity of the Plotinus Neoplatonism, which deeply influenced the Jewish philosophy, the Christian philosophy, and the Islamic philosophy. Especially the first principle, (the A), in perfect coincidence with good became the reason and faith whereby generally, the reason is considered a proper faculty of the human spirit, allowing him to discern good from evil, to set the criteria of error and truth, and to direct his will toward a particular given end purpose of the ethical, technical, and scientific point of view. And faith is the belief that human decides to adopt, but not fully manifesting a rational reason, it simply allows us to go beyond the given "natural."

Cain represents that original cause and material nature of everything, the confusion between different ways of understanding the first principle. First understood as evil, its initial spelling (*ayin*) means "the one of the inner eye." If it is represented with a *K*, it means "king"; and with a *Q*, it means "queen" but not considered as we know it today. With this eye, a truly spiritual person automatically perceives the subtle third eye of intuition without being deceived by his earthly physical eyes, developed without any importance of time and space, known by the name of the "Plan of Sharon," thousands of years ago as the plan of the circle of light, but not being a recent discovery of modern science. Thus, the first pendragons of the messianic lineage were Cainite kings of Mesopotamia, fed by the supplements of celestial fire, as mystical bread made from white powder of alchemical gold, to improve their awareness, intuition, and perception on the way to become gods themselves. Therefore, their immune system, at the endurance levels, rendered the antiaging properties possible.

They had extraordinary life expectancies, considerably strengthened in the royal member lineages, living for hundreds of years as confirmed by all the documents of that time to us. This heavenly fire ritual also told us that the lineage of the kings was also fed with the milk of the goddess, containing an active enzyme leading to longevity. This telomerase enzyme possessed unique antiaging properties, according to current genetic researchers. This longevity allowed them a transcendent life and multiple descendants. It is this multiple principle that controls the transcendence, the principle of immensity, ensuring multiple descendants, constituting a union between the surrogate for father Adam and mother Eve, who plays the role of a sex goddess for engendering a murderous son by the name of Cain as the first descendant, and it was between him and his sister Awan that he had his son Enoch, according to the Book of Jubilees.

She was considered as Yahweh, from the verb *qanah* in Hebrew and meaning "to create," according to Gen. 4:1, which said, "I have gotten a man with the help of the Lord." Consequently, she said that she nobly made love with Adam but not with Yahweh. Nobly, Cain or Qayin was also presented as the creator of civilization, having a bad heart full of jealousy, an excess of anger and practicing quarrel. So, this multiple principle "A" continued between people, by whom the transcending of the descendants occurred, assimilated to the notion of truth and to the "natural light" and as an innate idea of God put in man. But this first murderer of mankind has a very strong symbolic range and explains the origin of wars and the sources of violence and reveals the hatred that inhabits the heart of humanity. Cain represents the evil that evokes the fall and the original sin. It must be said that the orientation of prohibition murdering toward the morals by the religious interpretation, did not really prevent human to use his cognitive capacity of hatred, even as stupid as this prohibition is at the beginning of the Bible, it is considered as the first drama on the religious rite.

The Eye of God or the anger of God represents a guilty expression of two tendencies known as individual and collective, which are still opposed inside the human being. According to the Bible, notably rabbinical, Cain's lineage ends with the flood in Noah's time; it was considered as a mark of repentance to stigmatize the Jewish deicides that the Pope Innocent III, associated with the nomadic Jewish people, destined to remain stateless and "murderer of God." This term "*deicide*," meaning literally "murderer of God," also refers to the crucifixion of Jesus Christ.

In the epistle of St. Jude, verse 14 to 15 says that Enoch, the seventh from Adam, prophesied, saying, "Behold, the Lord is coming with thousands upon thousands of his holy ones, to execute judgment on all and to convict all the ungodly for all their deeds of ungodliness that they have committed in such an ungodly way, and of all the harsh words that ungodly sinners have spoken against him." But without any repentance on their part, they continued to utter insulting words against the continent of Ham, the father of mankind, by a singularity of the biblical myth compared to the archaic mythologies of the divine curse. So, the fault of Cham, if it were real, was not intended just to see the nakedness of his father because seeing the nudity did not deserve such a curse. Therefore, the biblical text concealed the true sense of the expression that would be appropriate to express "what he did to him and not what his youngest son, Ham, did."

If we refer to chapter 18 of Leviticus, which lists all sexual taboos, we immediately understand the exact meaning of the expression "to discover the nudity of someone." And immediately, the act of the son against his father becomes more than an action of seeing his nakedness. To summarize, "what his youngest son did to him" is undoubtedly the action of having sex. By taking advantage of the drunkenness of his father, Ham committed a homosexual incest and had not only seen the nakedness of his father. The Qumran manuscripts merely refer to the issue of grace—to give thanks to God after the flood to the consecutive celebration of the first harvest. And concerning this subject, they make neither the state of drunkenness nor of nudity.

Lev. 18:6–7 says, "None of you shall approach any one of his close relatives to uncover nakedness. . . You shall not uncover the nakedness of your father or the nakedness of your mother, she is your mother, and you shall not uncover her nakedness." These laws in Leviticus are the laws of God prohibiting certain practices on incestuous sexual relations among his people. There obviously would have been incest therefore, between Ham and Noah since, from an etymological point of view, the biblical expression "seeing nudity" in Hebrew was translated as "give his marital bed," therefore to make love; thus covering the nakedness of their father represents both the paternal anger; and having understood the secret of his birth explained a demonstration of the divine. In Gen. 9:22, this term "to see" in English is not translated into the Greek by γύμνωσαν (gumnosin) but by the word ασκεμοσυνη (aschemosune), designating homosexual relationships identified in several Midrashim compiled in Israel, admitted them as evidence and are known by the bishop Theophilus of Antioch. No indication of this interpretation was specified in the biblical text. Lev. 18:3 said, "You shall not do as they do in the land of Egypt, where you lived, and you shall not do as they do in the land of Canaan, to which I am bringing you and you shall neither walk in their ordinances." The Jewish historian Josephus said that God did not curse Ham, son of Noah, with whom He concluded an alliance. But in reality, the descendants of his son Canaan would suffer the curse of God—a biblical story in which Noah, the grandfather, cursed Canaan for a sin committed by Ham to his father.

This violation of the law, the natural law of good and evil, justly seems to be part of the human being since his creation. The process of several Midrashim, which instead of simply clarifying the immediate meaning of a verse and its spirit, but rather defines the laws of the biblical text, affirms that Cham rather castrated his father than the incestuous rape described in the Bible. In the Greek Bible translations of Aquila of Sinope, Theodotion of Ephesus, and Symmachus the Ebionite, this interpretation of the homosexual act appears more explicitly. Noah awoke from his drunkenness and learned what his youngest son did; he said, "Cursed be Canaan and his descendants! He will be a servant of servants for his brothers!" And then he said, "Blessed be Yahweh, the God of Shem; and let Elohim exalt Japheth" Gen. 9:18–27. The text said, "Here is the only righteous, Noah, after better presented him to us throughout the history of the flood as the builder, competent navigator and the ancestor of all farmers, and who in few verses mentioned here above spoke with God."

In Gen. 9:1–10, according to history, this patriarch who made a covenant with God was also represented dead drunk and completely naked in the Bible, and it was his sons—Shem, Japheth, and Ham, the father of Canaan—according to the illuminated manuscript of 1320, who populated the earth after the flood. It is good to know that in the latter days of Noah, men were eating, drinking, marrying, and giving their children in marriage. Man prefigures the advent of the Son of man, which preceded the flood but became at the end, the wicked man himself. And it is what will happen in the future times of the Son of man up to the destruction of the human race.

Noah pronounced a curse on his son, affirming that the descendants of his son Canaan, the four sons of Ham, would be servants because he dishonored him, which was interpreted to define Ham as the ancestor of all Africans. Canaan generated the Canaanites, while Mizraim generated the Egyptians; from Kush came the Kushites and Put the Libyan people, according to the Bible. This curse created one of the visible racial characteristics of the black-skinned offspring. The Babylonian Talmud of the sixth century, according to Edith Sanders, states that the descendants of Ham are cursed for being all black and depicts Ham as a sinful man and his progeny as degenerated.

The Arab slave traders took advantage of this barbaric attribution, and later on, the Europeans and the Americans also used this cruel act known to history to justify their evil spirit toward the African ancestor—one of the sons of Ham and grandson of Noah, in Egypt. The so-called religious people, the Islamic dignitaries, Jewish rabbis, priests, cardinals, and popes, with the degree of perversion ideas, carpet in the comfortable shade of their churches, threw an entire black nation in pasture, and easily armed the brains of wicked slave traders and racists all over the world.

This insignificant passage served as a trigger element to priests, ordained to perform certain rites and administer certain sacraments; to the Jewish rabbis, specially educated to teach the Jewish law; and to the expert theologians, claiming that theology gives a justification of religion and gave them a free rein for their fertile racist imagination to blacken Ham, following this legend; forgetting that from the top of their postulate, they're affirming that Cham sodomized his father, or more seriously again, probably castrated him. This legend that goes against the miracle of human evolution, already proven by science, asserted that Africa was the cradle of humanity; but the religious people of this legend have pretended not to discern the master idea of creation, and ignored the evidence and the truth of science with a sword in hand by applying justice without any force that could enforce it. But with the traditional attributes of violence characterizing their definitely conflicting state of mind, consisting to judge, adjudicate, and punish without any intellectual thought to legitimize a final prejudicial pain, and determine the suffering of others by prejudices. The modern black man was attached to a particular curse, inherited because of the darkness of his skin. This attaché of God was kidnapped, sold, put in servitude, and reduced to a slave by those very people who claimed to be men of God in all nations of the world.

Nevertheless, the Old Testament cannot prove the authenticity of the legend of Ham, for it is written in a time much later to the supposed facts in Roman times; that is to say, around four hundred years before Jesus Christ. I especially interrogate myself in these unequivocal terms by asking myself where the intellectual and spiritual scam came from.

The trade in human beings—the slavery, especially of the ancestors of Negroes, having suffered the barbarity of slavers, their extreme cruelty beyond the bestiality empire of inhumanity, the atrocity prepared by the wickedness of the same savage people, with the absence of culture and civilization for centuries, up to their global amnesia in the world, and turned to a state of ignorance that caused and still causing a lot of damages to African countries. All this after destroying the black civilization, recognized the slave trades, justified their brilliant cruel spirit, and then later on recognized the profound genius of Negroes centuries of education and their evolution during the ancient past of Egypt; where knowingly, a high civilization of intellectual institution was producing pharaohs of ancient times without difficulty; and which they chose to exploit, evidently by their famous legend.

Generally, the Old Testament was more than enough for this mission. The Negroes, made of weak spirits, were indoctrinated by the priests, the great admirals, giving an idea of respectable personality, and of a majestic nature of a pontificate worthy of nobility but consequently pedophiles and homosexuals, who said they were leading a civilization mission, but instead destroyed the root of humanity; denying the love of God, defined as a moral expression of personality to the sons of God—the black man; and denying him dignity, freedom, and honor, as what he has as best in life. Yet those who truly carried out that mission, to bring places and people to a stage of social, cultural, and moral development called civilizers in life, were those men known as the black race people; considered to be more advanced, but who became your contempt, your meditation object of barbarism, and at your eyes, your slaves; they're the very ones to whom we owe speech, thought, sciences, and arts, and who completely contrasted with the thought of their time.

These men of God, the slave supporters, dusted in just few verses, the passage of Noah drunk from his cup of alcohol, and in all his nakedness, to think of organizing projects for the depreciation of black people, and executed their religious justification in slavery and in the barbarity of colonization, for fundamentally inhuman motives. Through a tendentious interpretation of this legend, humanity has known various exegeses, which have had historical impact, quite simply to stifle the glorious past of Negro Egypt that civilized the world.

The authors wanted to reduce them as slaves for a religious bond. Gradually, as the slave trade was growing, first by the Arabs, followed by the Westerners, it persisted and became a controversial phenomenon of society and a serious social disagreement of personal characteristics and of beliefs against cultural norms. We must mention that, according to the Bible, the Egyptian people, a nation of Negroes and descendants of Ham, were the ones who inflicted so much suffering to the Jewish people while in Egypt. So, knowing these causes, we can no more ignore the causes of the legend of Noah, drawn from the Jewish literature, to punish the black man. But even after so much manipulation by the people hiding their evil intentions and poorly concealing their own destiny, they finally proved who they were by the propagation of the curse of Ham, which did that tens of millions of blacks were murdered, slaughtered without pity, shot down, chained, and savagely tortured for centuries despite their cries of distress.

In his fight against his opponents, Ham, the grandfather of the Babylonians, aimed to give strength and audacity to Israel by their supposed ancestor Shem, blessed by their God, and to the Hebrews, reduced in servitude in the sixth century BC in Babylon. This motif was their courage and hope of happiness in their misfortune of hideous chrono, and a destiny wrongly realized by this people and viewed as an omen of their future misery—an omen of a divine message from their gods. It may only seem a simple criterion to know that this Jewish people decided that a living being—the black man, known to be endowed with reason, be classified and maintain slave in their mind by acting in their way of doing without empathy, without feeling emotions in relations to other humans; and without difference, the looting without shame; the mass destruction, accompanied by rape, and by extension, implementing all type of civil relations determined by acts of cruelty.

Here are some defenses of the main masters of scholastic philosophy, and in the Catholic theology environment of popes, doctors of faith, who established a certain doctrine concerning slavery and racial prejudice, to try to correct the inhumanity that theology had woven. It was the case of this first pope historically assassinated in 882; Pope John VIII, elected pope on December 14, 872, who wrote to the princes of Sardinia, commanding and summoning them to free all slaves with a paternal love, for the salvation of their souls, in 873.

In surprise anger and pain, this one among them suddenly exclaimed by these words, "Let him be classified, but not according to his color;" this was said and affirmed by St. Thomas Aquinas, in the thirteenth century, concerning the color of the black man. He was a religious of the Dominican order, one of the leading masters of scholastic philosophy and Catholic theology. In 1567, he was proclaimed doctor of the church by the 223rd pope, Pius V, and in 1880 patron of the Catholic universities, schools and academies by Leo XIII, the 257th pope of the Catholic Church, who succeeded Pope Pius IX on February 20, 1878. St. Thomas Aquinas also held the title of angelic doctor and was of peaceful reasoning; and Pope Eugene IV, the Italian Benedictine monk who became the 207th pope of the Catholic Church on March 3, from 1431 to 1447, having a heart full with the love for the other, he defended the black slavery by emitting papal bulls to categorically forbid enslavement. It was by a form of excommunication that Pope Eugene IV was punishing anyone who was practicing slavery in 1435.

Meanwhile, the human being, composed of a soul and a body, was to be integrated into all moral inclinations, sensitive to the passion of love for the universal order, and accurate to the reality of nature; reassuring him the divine help—that is, to know and love God with all his creation and develop a conduct of natural reason at the highest point of human possible capacities; and to be open to the supernatural life offered by God to know happiness in the natural and realistic order in all his integrity; and receive bliss in the supernatural order for each created being and for a supreme end. As an example, that human being has to be an angelic doctor in this religious pontificate.

But despite the denial of respect of certain religious personalities of that pontificate, the curse in the Bible concerning blacks and the slavery of mankind persists up to the present day, granted by the legend of the so-called blessed in the eyes of Yahweh. Let us be unanimous here regarding Noah and say that the notables, the majority of idolaters and polytheists, treated him as a liar, something common in the prophecies. The Koran, consisting of 114 units of varying lengths known as suras, contained several different notable additional details concerning Noah, such as he preached for 950 years among his people with legendary patience, and that only a handful of poor people followed him; finally at the end, probably because of his sin, Allah told him that nobody else would follow him.

In various Hadith, known as not being a single same collection of "account," "narrative," or "report" unlike the same literary work recognized as the Koran by all Muslims, Hadiths are important tools to understand the Koran; they're known as describing the words, the Islamic prophetic language, the actions, the habits, the prophetic account of the Prophet Mohammed and his companions, narrated that God asked the whole humanity to be grateful for having saved them from the flood, condemning all others to perish; various Hadith narrates that "the story of Noah's drunkenness is not found in the Koran, because according to them, prophets are placed in harm shed against the capital sins like drunkenness, adultery and lying, by God." What unusual? Don't you think? Well, let it be so.

In the sura of the same name, "Wudd," "Soua'a Souwa'a," "Yaghouth," "Ya'a'ouq," and "Nasr," known as the chapter of the Koran, quotes the idolatrous deities worshipped by the people of Noah. The universality of the flood is a fact upon which all Muslim scholars have agreed without divergence. Islam qualify Noah (*Nuh* [نوح] in Arabic) as a prophet (*nabi* or *rassoul*), he who received the mission to convey the divine message on earth under the form of revelation (*Risala*). The Koran quotes him several times.

In sura 11, in an abbreviated manner, the flood story is repeated. The number 71 Sura, which evokes Noah's sermon to his contemporaries, was a call for the submission to God alone but bore the name disobedient. And in a shorter way of numerous other suras, compared to the story of Noah, written in the Bible, Muslim scholars said that it was just good people who believed in God but not belonging to any of his close family who were saved by Noah in the ark. One of his sons, who had not boarded in the ark, believing to be safe on the heights, was carried away by a wave that came between him and Noah, wanting to assist him. And that his wife was left behind like the wife of the prophet Lot, during the destruction of Sodom and Gomorrah. But when he invoked Allah for his child, it was revealed to him that he was not of his family.

Therefore, to give an additional argument to the story, Israel, Muslims, and European Christians maintained a confusion by subsequent comments as a way to criticize the dissolved morals of Canaanite descendants, forced to defend a land then called Palestine. They distorted the text to justify the reason of slavery in the Bible and in the Koran. At that time, the justification of the Canaanite territorial conquest by the Jews, who became the people of Palestine at the time, became remarkably possible by this justification of the curse of Ham to purchase a country much sought in the territory of another. Let us first underline that Moses and the authors of the sacred texts were not the inventors of the Bible, and the passage of the Hebrews in Egypt preceded the Jewish literature speaking of the time. It was entirely after the order of time, between the time of Moses and the date of the writing of the first texts of the Old Testament, around 400 BC, and the gap was about one thousand years. Hebrews let their anger appear in filigrees on the transparent plates linked to the worship against the black people, who, according to them, reduced them to slavery.

The slavers and other slave traders gave some consideration to this legend; hungry of power and the wealth of our countries, they used it to justify all atrocities still inflicted on black people until today. This nonsense that we read in the Bible prove that Christianity and any other religion that considered the words of a drunken prophet of the Jewish god were not the true religion, in this case also not the one of blacks since, for them, blacks were comparable to animals, even knowing that, from the beginning of creation and its evolution, it was proven that black civilizations were the brightest at certain times in the history of humanity in all areas. For this, they remain condemned until the end of time, and as an irony in the history of civilization of mankind.

We let ourselves be dominated by other civilizations of primates with animal tendencies, who overthrew us by excuses in the sacred texts with racist traditions, by the color of our skin, and to the detriment of the extraordinarily rich African cultural identity. The human being, in the operation of domination, grants credits to those dominating us for the simple aim of letting other human's work justify their domination and harvest the rewards. In this world of domination and the enslavement of man by man, man still needs hope, because—from father to son—man fades and disappears forever from this earth. The fathers of these seventy nations composed the semantic humanity that has always existed in the sermons of the fathers. Various exegeses of its author's self-conscious efforts, with historical repercussions, wanted the reduction of black Africa as slaves. Its descendants occupied the "land of Canaan," a land that was subsequently offered by God to Abraham, a Jewish descendant of Shem. This confusion of the confinement writing is found in the fragments of literary archeology of the Yahwist document; one of the four sources of the Torah as a fusion in a single text, consisting of various stories and traditions; and the priestly document, also one of the four sources of the Torah, written around the period of exile and after the Babylonian exile. Catholicism, a colonial religion, is the organizer of the transatlantic slave trade, and it is also known that Christianity is not recent in Africa. In the ancient Christian history of Africa, it is known that the first African country to host the gospel was Egypt before spreading to Ethiopia and Nubia, the current Sudan. According to the holy writings, Jesus Christ, fleeing the persecution of Herod, took refuge for some time in Egypt. And St. Mark, the apostle born John, nicknamed Marcus, one of the first converted to Christianity in charge of the evangelization of the Roman Empire by the apostle Peter, and evangelist disciple of the apostles Peter and Paul, was the preacher of Egypt. The church founded by him had headquarters in Alexandria.

The relics of Cairo were restored by the order of Paul VI, after the Second Vatican Council, in the new Cathedral of the Coptic Church. Thus, in the venerable monasteries of Wadi Natrun, the spirituality of one of the fathers called the Desert Fathers, consecrated St. Anthony the Great of Egyptian origin was the founder of the Christian eremitism, often approaching mysticism. In its spiritual component, eremitism seeks the higher truths of essential principles in voluntary isolation through prayer, meditation, or asceticism, a form of renunciation or self-abnegation, tending toward the discipline of the body and spirit seeking perfection; it was as a new way for the souls of elites to reach the holiness of the "Great eagle"— Saint like St. Pachomius the Great, raised in paganism but converted by Christians in Thebes; and then formed by the hermit named Palamon after he received baptism around 313; he was completely isolated in a deserted place and led an ascetic life in an integral face-to-face with God.

Many Christians for several decades were then retiring to the desert, like St. Anthony the Great. Through Palamon, Pachomius experienced the spiritual conduct of an elder and benefited from his advice and teaching. He himself became a guide for several anchorite disciples who felt the desire to place themselves under spiritual guidance. Seven years later, after he studied the scriptures in depth, Pachomius founded the first monastery and realized his dream around the year 320; gathering those who came to him into an organized community at Tabennese in Upper Egypt; then most faithfully, he began to seriously consider how to fulfill the obligations he had contracted by introducing the monastic rule of cenobitic life in his monastery. As the founder of cenobitism, the "common life" was born as a form of the "monastic life in community," unique to the cenobites of the early days of Christianity, Acts 2:44–46; the "common life—*koinos bios*" of the Greek cenobitism, derived from the primitive Church of Pachomius. And Theodoret of Cyr, connected to the School of Antioch, remains alive in the south of the delta of the Nile and in the monasteries of the Red Sea. On the other hand, Ethiopian Christianity survived all vicissitudes, thanks to its implementation in the inaccessible countrysides.

During the Arab invasion and the arrival of Islam in the seventh century, North Africa was a region actively Christian, with more or less six hundred bishoprics in the fifth century and great theologians among the fathers of the most fruitful churches, like St. Augustine, who died in 430. The perverse Judeo-Christian belief of the curse of Ham and Canaan mentioned in Gen. 9:18–27, is alienating for all blacks and all humanity. It is the foundation of the Arab-Muslim slave trade, the slave trade in the Indian Ocean, and the odious transatlantic slave trade. The propagation of such anti-Kamite religious teachings should be taken seriously by the Kamite community to support victims of those cruel sects and to honor religions created by the Kamites. After so much research on this subject, I came to the conclusion to no more believe in Jesus Christ, as the Catholic Church is presenting him, a legend based on a religious tale taken from the Egyptian Kamito myth of Horus, his father Osiris and the goddess mother, the virgin Isis; and by rejecting the Jewish and Christian Bible, which crushed and stole the precious indigenous tradition by stifling the Kamite people civilizations. The reasons behind this rejection are based on the organization of the world based principally by Western colonialists, guilty of crimes against humanity and against the divinity, perpetrated in the name of Jesus Christ and the Bible, and imposing its rules throughout the planet. The Bible and the Koran are false books, prejudicial to all Kamites, since the Western oppressors have Christian and Muslim faith.

By fear of upheaval and convictions that such research will lead the world to, a superfluous rigorous reflection of intellectual connotation and renouncement is maintained in the darkest and the most sensitive depths of our history, forcing some honest intellectual Kamites to close their eyes and letting not only the Kamite people without compassion—the optimal wellbeing, the awareness of what is essential to restore love and a natural corporal balance—but also all other people of the world to remain in ignorance, knowing the techniques used more or less secretive, concerning practices in the slavery book of the western religions. Therefore, these intellectual Kamites do not become conscious by closing their eyes; they do not find their dignities by being the marionettes of these same slavery supporters, and do not honor the memory of our dear indigenous animist ancestors, for the rebirth and the reawakening of Kamite people. The historical truth and the authenticity of the Kamite civilization, the global black community, are not in compliance with these criminal European nations of slavery, which systematically imposed the names Africa and African on us.

The Kamite revolution, henceforth adopted, must be found on the revelations based on historical truth of indigenous kingdoms and authentic people who were victims of the slave trade, the black Africans who were the legal property of another and forced to obey for their deportation, their genocide, their colonization, for the dismantling of their indigenous kingdoms, and for the disorganization of their civilizations; they promulgated the establishment of a religious ideology, advocating the inferiority of the black race in Judaism, Christianity, Islam, etc., revealed by the adoption of the rabbinic myth in the Bible and in the Koran by the curse of (Ham), and his son Canaan, in their so-called holy books.

This revolution makes that the number of conscious and determined Kamites increased day by day to restore the cultural, political, economic, educational, and religious ideological foundations without any concession, because there is a true animist indigenous ancestors religion of the Kamite kingdoms, and as a right and legitimate sovereign power in our territory, as we transmitted it to the Sumerian civilization. Thus, the book of Genesis—narrating the story of the creation of the world, the ark of Noah and the flood, the Tower of Babel, and the patriarchs Abraham, Isaac, Jacob, and Joseph—is also the home of countless stories of tribes transmitted to the Mesopotamian people and its alluvial plains.

The Sumerian civilization was absorbed by civilizations after offering its leaven to earthlings. It implanted its cultures in the immense mass of people of the earth.

Ancient legends tell us that there is only one tribe among all the tribes of the world, which is at the origin of man; this tribe can't be other than the black tribe since black is at the origin of humanity and not the twelve tribes of Israel. It is known that from the twelve tribes of Israel—among which ten were deported in captivity in Assyria in circa 720 BC, known as Asher, Dan, Gad, Issachar, Levi, Manasseh, Naphtali, Reuben, Simeon, and Zebulun, considered as the lost tribes—only two tribes were remaining, known as the tribes of Judah and Benjamin; and from the two tribes, only one tribe, the tribe Judah, was at the origin of man as a black tribe. So among the tribes generated by this first tribe, there was a tribe that suffered from inbreeding and tended to disappear; it was therefore why the "gardeners of the earth" placed the Sumerian race in that part of the world to strengthen the weakened tribe with the eleven successive cultures that were brought and placed on the earth. That race of the early Hebrews which was of black origin engendered their Semitic tribes, according to the file radiating with pure, impassive, and unalterable light of the esoteric Akashic concept.

Esoterically, the Ancient Egyptian representation of the ring with no beginning or end, dating for more than six thousand years ago before Christ, is known as its oldest representation of the ring. It was a woven papyrus, hemp, or reeds to be worn around the finger to symbolize eternity or an exchange to signify an endless love between wedded couples. According to the Ancient Egyptians, the ring is worn specifically on the fourth finger of the left hand because they believed that this finger housed a special "vein of love" directly connected to the heart. Traditionally, to symbolize the ring, Ancient Egypt used the feared belief of the endless circle of the sun and the moon, worshipped as gods, symbolizing the spirits of the eternal nature linked to the heart – Earth, and the open center meaning the doorway of the unknown things. The recurring symbol of the lords of the ring was also the ring. At the beginning of the Sumerian and the Scythian eras, over five thousand years ago, the ring was also a representation of unity and eternity. For Ancient Egyptian, the circle was a representation of power and control, a symbol the omnipotence of witchcraft, promising immortality to men. It is often known under the name of ouroboros, a snake biting its own tail, mentioned at a very early period in the texts of the pyramids in Egypt. Its cycle of time is surrounding the entire existing world and originally considered as marking the boundary between Nun and the ordered world.

If a cross is placed under the ring, it becomes the symbol of Venus, a familiar emblem of woman. Lay the cross above it, and it becomes the regalia of the masculine order, and when placed at the center of the ring, it symbolizes the cup of dew or the water cup known as the Holy Grail and known as the Rosicrucian symbol discovered in Mesopotamia and dating from 3500 BC.

This symbol has been for very long distinguished as a mark of the Sangreal, certifying the purity of the royal blood or the Holy Grail. It is also known that Rosicrucians are the adepts of the ancient association called the Ancient Mystical Order Rosae Crucis (AMORC), devoted to the study of the elusive mysteries of life and the universe. Traditionally, it originated in Ancient Egypt and is the largest and the oldest existing fraternity in the world currently. Several legendary stories of the island of Britain are presenting us texts of the Gaelic world—the history of the greatest kings of the island of Britain known under the name of Pendragon, meaning "dragon chief" or "dragon head" as a Celtic that several kings bore as magister equitum, an equivalent of the Roman title of a magistrate appointed as lieutenant to a dictator; one of them by the name of Merlin is commonly called Merlin the Magician, born of a human mother and a devil father. Even as Merlin tamed the dragons, he represented the form of the dragon after using a sign of the shape of a living dragon, to help Arthur.

Merlin became one of the most important figures of the imagination after his introduction in the Arthurian legend in the literature of the Middle Ages. To conceive Arthur, he played a secondary advisory role for Uther Pendragon, thanks to his wisdom; furthermore, in the literature of Middle Ages, his references are related to Welsh Celtic mythology and Irish literature as well as England and France. To allow the birth of King Arthur and his accession to power, he used magical incantations. Merlin also predicted the course of battles, helping and supporting King Arthur by advising the king and his knights, affecting the development and leading to an arduous long search of the Holy Grail. It is said that it was his father who was the builder of the Stonehenge. And the Uther Pendragon was another key character of the greatest kings, also meaning "dragon head" and the father of King Arthur. These kings were also named lord or king of the ring, according to the ring of their responsibility, which symbolized justice inspired by the divine.

Talking about divine inspiration, Ancient Egyptians believed that each morning, to represent the rebirth of the star of the day, it was the ring that was shown encircling the rising sun on the horizon of the sky. Therefore, from the setting up of Nun, it represented a symbol of rejuvenation and resurrection. And because it ate its tail, it was sometimes seen as a symbol of annihilation and of self-destruction and sometimes assigned a protective role. In its evolutionary cycle, there is truth in false and false in truth, signifying "the union of both opposing principles of day and night, good and evil, heaven and earth and it is half black, half white born of the earth in certain representations." For more than ten thousand years ago, the earliest use of jewelry was established by Egyptians, who already knew metals for the fabrication of chains and bracelets. In 332 BC, after Alexander the Great conquered Egypt, the tradition of the ring was assimilated to the Greeks.

They continued to use hemp, leather, bone, or ivory, not having the metal technology to produce metal rings, up to the time of betrothal rings. After Egyptians taught them the developed science of melting metal, the use of metal rings began to take over; and gradually, iron replaced materials used back then. And on rare occasions, gold and silver rings were given to women as valuable property of betrothal by men to prove their devotion and love. This circular image applied to infernal gods, one represented by the serpent, and the other representing the celestial world, represented by the circle, also represent a logo used in numerous French Masonic obediences, such as the Grand Orient, the oldest and most important obedience of the continental Europe born in 1773.

This justice inspired from divine was a symbol known to Canaan. Canaan, who had ten sons listed in Gen. 10:15 to 18, will give his name to the land of Canaan. Phoenicia was a classical term used by the Greeks to designate the major Canaanite region of port cities. This term described the part of the Middle East situated between the Mediterranean and the Jordan in the biblical narrative before its conquest by Joshua and the tribes of Israel out of Egypt. The seven ethnic groups that inhabited this land of Canaan were the Amorites, the Canaanites, the Girgashites, the Hittites, the Hivites, the Jebusites, and the Perizzites. They were all known under the generic name of Canaanites, whom the Jews subsequently exterminated.

It is a region that corresponds more or less to the territories of Israel today—the West Jordan, Lebanon, Palestine, and southern Syria; while his three brothers, Kush, Mizraim, and Put, sons of Ham, are identified in the scripture to the kingdom of ancient Ethiopia; Misraim, son of Ham, occupied among others the country that the ancient Jews considered as Egypt. And Put, the son of Ham and the father of Mazigh, the patriarch of the Amazigh people, was a set of indigenous ethnic groups from North Africa, which occupied a wide area from the west of the Nile valley up to the Atlantic and the whole of the Sahara at a certain time.

First Chr. 1:8 and Gen. 10:6 are describing his descendants as warriors. In ancient times, their powerful kingdoms formed of confederated tribes are usually known by the names of Libyans (or Libiques), a set of people living in the north of Africa before the arrival of the Phoenicians (between the Atlantic and Tripolitania); Moors or formerly Mores, designating the base of the Berber populations inhabiting the western part of North Africa in ancient times; and Gaetulians, ancient people of North Africa, who appeared in the third millennium BC, formed the Zeneta Berber people and the Branis Berber people. Their oldest references are probably those of the Carthaginians, indicating that their prince offered to marry Elissa (or Dido for the Romans), the founding queen of Carthage (modern Tunisia), toward the year 815 BC; of the Garamantes, a former Libyan Berber people who lived as nomads since the third millennium before our era, between Libya and the Atlas, especially around the oases of Djerba; or again of the Numidians of which the best known of Berber kingdoms was Numidia in the northern Algeria of our days and overflowing to the east end of the current Tunisia and west of the current Morocco up to Moulouya, with its kings such as Gaia, the Amazigh king and the last king of the eastern Numidia of Massylii, before his reunification with the western Numidia by his son Masinissa.

Gaia referred to the history of Carthage, the chronology of the Numidian kingdoms; it also means earth—primordial goddess—identical with the goddess mother, maternal ancestor of the divine races; also numerous characters like Syphax, king of the Western masaesyli, opposing Gaia, king of the eastern Numidia, and to his son Masinissa, allied with the Carthaginians, who annexed the territory of Gaia at the death of Syphax; and Masinissa, son of King Gaia, the first king of the unified Numidia after contributing to the victory over Syphax in 204 before Jesus Christ, succeeded his father; these names are respectively eponymous of Ethiopia, of Egypt and Somalia, as brothers; this account was given to us in Gen. 10:6. They then experienced the Roman conquest, the Christianization, the Vandal invasion, the Arab conquest, and conversion to Islam.

The land of Canaan, an expression of the Hebrew Bible that means "the Canaan area," is today called Palestine, divided into two, including the state of Israel. The inhabitants of Canaan from the Bronze Age were called Canaanites. Joshua, son of Nun, whom we have already mentioned above concerning the conquest of Canaan, was a member of the tribe of Ephraim who initially was called Hoshea and to whom Moses gave the name of Joshua; he was born in Egypt at the time of servitude of the Hebrews, which they qualified as the period of slavery in Num. 13:16.

In Dt. 3:21, Joshua (in Hebrew, Yehoshua [יהושע] meaning "God saves") witnessed the Israelites out of Egypt, led by Moses. He was his assistant in the ascension of one part of Mount Sinai. Ex. 32:17 cited that period when Moses ascended Mount Sinai, ready to receive the Ten Commandments. Numerous ancient Christian writers made a parallel between "Joshua" and "Jesus," particularly in Heb. 4:8-14; Luke 3:29; and Acts 7:45; in Islam, Joshua was regarded as a prophet by the name of Yūsha' ibn Nun (عشوي ن ب نون, sura 18:60) in Arabic.

"You must not take a wife from the Canaanite women," Isaac said, who firstly blessed and gave this command to Jacob (Gen. 28:1). The discrimination among men of God began to appear by this commandment. "Esau then realized how displeasing the Canaanite women were to his father Isaac" (Gen. 28:8); "Esau took his wives from the women of Canaan" (Gen. 36:2). But Jacob—son of Isaac and Rebekah, twin brother of Esau, and grandson of Abraham, the biblical patriarch and the said prophet of Koran—went and took wives elsewhere to come and live in Canaan. The story of Jacob, a twin born second, began when Rebekah learned from God that she would engender two people and that the elder shall serve the younger, contrary to the birthright.

It all began when the senior brother, Esau, executed and sold his birthright to the demand of the younger brother, Jacob, tricking him out of his father's blessing. Rebekah, who loved Jacob, took advantage of the total visual disability of Isaac, her husband, who preferred Esau for his birthright; and she made him give his blessing to Jacob before his death. Upon the death of Isaac, their father, who wanted to restore Esau in his rights without success, Esau decided to kill his brother, who deceived him, to take his due from him. His intentions were very soon discovered by their mother Rebekah, who implored Jacob to immediately f lee to his uncle Laban in Harran. Fleeing from his brother Esau, Jacob spent the night in Bethel during his trip to Harran. Being in Bethel, the patriarch Jacob had a dream known as the "dream of Jacob."

Gen. 28: 10–19 describes that Jacob took a stone and put it under his head and fell asleep. He had a vision of a ladder resting on the earth and reaching the heaven, where God told him, standing at the top of that scale, "I am the God of your father Abraham and Isaac. I will give the land on which you lie to you and your descendants, which will be numerous as the dust of the earth. And you will spread to the west and to the east, to the north and to the south, and by you and your descendants shall all nations on earth be blessed. I will protect you wherever you go, for I am with you. I will not leave you until I have done all that I have just promised you."

Jacob, frightened, woke from his sleep and said, "Surely, God is present in this place, and none other than his house it is the gate of heaven. I do not know it. But from now on, I will name this place Bethel," meaning "house of God, but it was first called Luz." After having fought with the angel Gabriel, identified as an angel of God, he arrived by his uncle Laban, the brother of his mother Rebekah, at Harran and worked for his uncle for seven years and married Leah.

Actually, Laban refused to marry his younger daughter Rachel, to whom Jacob was interested, as long as the eldest was not yet married. Finally, deceived by Laban, Jacob eventually married Rachel in exchange for seven new years in his service. After twenty years of exile, Jacob had twelve sons and a daughter and decided to return to Canaan with his family. Leah, his first wife, got Reuben the eldest; Simeon the second; Levi the third; Judah the fourth; Issachar the ninth; Zebulun the tenth; and Dinah, the only daughter mentioned; Rachel his second wife, got Joseph the eleventh, and Benjamin the twelfth and last. Bilha the maid of Rachel and Jacob, as his concubine got Dan the fifth, and Naphtali the sixth. Zilpah the maid of Leah and Jacob's concubine, got Gad the seventh, and Asher the eighth.

In Gen. 32:28, Jacob would fight once again against an unknown entity during his return trip. That night, the unknown entity refused to give him his name, but on the contrary, named him Israel, and Jacob will henceforth be called Israel, meaning "the one who fought with God." In Gen. 32:2–3, the angels responsible to lead him up to the borders of Canaan—the future land of Israel, the Holy Land—left him and went to heaven, and Jacob met those responsible for other lands, descended on the earth. He was received by the angels assigned to the Holy Land at his return to Canaan.

The two tribes of Judah and Benjamin formed the kingdom of Judah in the south; the other ten tribes formed the Northern Kingdom, the kingdom of Israel, during the division of the kingdom in two. The twelve sons of Jacob were the descendants of the twelve tribes of Israel, except the Levites, scattered in other tribes, known as the descendants of the tribe of Levi, who did not receive a land after their establishment in Canaan but still considered as one of the twelve tribes of Israel because Levi was the third son of Jacob and Leah. The best known of the children of Levi was Jochebed, mother of Aaron, who became the first grand priest of Israel, and of Miriam, who followed the cradle in which her younger brother Moses was deposited on the Nile up to his collection by the pharaoh's daughter and who proposed Jochebed the mother of Moses to her as a nurse, whose identity was ignored by the daughter of the pharaoh (Ex. 2:1–10).

Amram, the nephew of Jochebed and father of Moses, belonging to the tribe of Levi, is the one who promulgated the laws of the Jewish wedding and divorce when Israelites were still enslaved in Egypt, according to the Talmud. Moses, who implicitly condemned the marriage of his parents, evoking the Leviticus marriage prohibition between nephew and aunt, is the one who led the children of Israel out of Egypt unto the land of Canaan, the countries of the eponymous ancestor of blacks.

Gen. 33:19 and 34:2, 4, 6, 8, 13, 18, 20 states that Dinah, the only daughter of Jacob, was raped by one of the son of Hamor, a Hivite prince of the country who sold him the land at Shechem at the time of the return of Jacob in Palestine. To enable the union of the two children, he later agreed to circumcise all men of the city. But Levi and Simeon, the brothers of Dinah who were not satisfied, plundered and then killed all the men of the city by surprise. The Hivites are descendants of Canaan, the sixth generation of the son of Ham, who lived at the north near Mount Hermon in the land of Canaan. Luke 9:29–36 described

Mount Hermon as the sacred place where Jesus metamorphosed. He went on this mountain with his disciples John, James, and Peter; and then when Jesus was conversing with Elijah and Moses, who appeared at his side, he was transfigurated. His face changed, and his clothes became dazzling white. Jesus Christ was the descendant of Judah, and all Israel's kings were from David's lineage of the Judah tribe. Judah was the son of Jacob. The lineage of Jesus's family was mentioned in Mtt. 1:1.

Gen. 37:12–36 tells us the story of Joseph and his older half-brothers, the eldest of Rachel; he was the eleventh and most loved son of Jacob who was sold to street vendors by his jealous half-brothers, pretending that he was dead. During a period of drought and famine over the land of Canaan, his half-brothers went to Egypt. Joseph, who had reached high positions in Egypt, recognized his brothers; he had doubled his tribes by his sons: Manasseh, the first, meaning "forget," referred to his integrity put to test in captive in a foreign country, sought to eradicate all memory of his home by oblivion and the alienation of its roots. Ephraim, the second son, was born in that obstacle that allowed his soul to exceed the maximum of admirable actions of great reliability and great expertise of all forces.

Ephraim meant "the one whom God permitted to fructify in the land of my affliction." He named him so after stimulating his latent forces and exploited the hidden powers in the depths of his being; he transformed them into a divine force to manifest his potential concentrated energies. Thus, the battle and the challenge were won in that land of affliction called Egypt. According to Gen. 37–50, the history of the Hebrew people constitutes a primordial role played by Joseph, who became a viceroy in Egypt. In this regard, the book of Exodus is the prelude to the history of Hebrews in Egypt. Upon the arrival of his half-brothers in Egypt, Joseph hides his identity and speaks harshly with them (Gen. 42:7).

Gen. 42:5, 13, 29, 32; 44:8; 45:17, 25; 46:6, 12, 31; and 47:1, 4, 14–15 described the several back and forth of Joseph's brothers to us between the land of Canaan and Egypt. On that occasion in Egypt, Joseph asked them this question: "Where do you come from?" And they answered from the land of Canaan to buy grain and foodstuffs. They told him that, from their father Jacob, they were twelve sons and that the youngest stayed with their father in Canaan, and one of them was no more. They gave all this information to Joseph without them knowing that they were speaking to their brother, but Joseph recognized his brothers and pretended not to recognize them. They continued to inform him of everything that had happened to them, saying, "We, your servants, found money near the opening of our bags of wheat, and we have brought it back from the land of Canaan because we cannot steal silver or gold from the house of your master."

Joseph got the permission of the pharaoh to let his brothers get stocks of wheat and foodstuffs and spur their animals before returning to Canaan. Joseph sold them the grain, draining all money that was in the land of Canaan and Egypt to fill the treasure chests of the pharaoh, leaving all Egyptians without money or food to eat (Gen. 47:14).

They arrived by Jacob their father, in the land of Canaan and told him about the wonders of Egypt. From that moment, Jacob took all his descendants and their livestock and possessions they acquired in Canaan and went to Egypt. Joseph went once more to notify the pharaoh of the arrival of his brothers and his father's house, who came to him with their little and big herds and all that belonged to them in the land of Canaan. "Now, please let your servants dwell in the land of Goshen," for in the land of Canaan, there was no more food throughout the country, and famine weighed heavily there. Faced with this famine of the land of Canaan, Egypt no longer knew what to do. Er and Onan, sons of Judah, died in the land of Canaan before coming to Egypt. Num. 26:19–20 revealed to us that Judah had five sons, who are Er, Onan, Shela, Perez, and Zerah; and his son Perez had two children: Hezron and Hamul. Gen. 48:7, 49:29–33, and 50:1–14 focused on the death of his wife Rachel, on the return of his ashes in Canaan after his death, and on his death in Egypt. Jacob told Joseph how the death of his mother, Rachel, hit him on the road to Canaan at some distance from the entrance of Ephrata, where Rachel's tomb is located at the entrance of the city of Bethlehem, the siege of a holy place of Judaism, the place of birth and coronation of King David of Israel, and the place of birth of Jesus of Nazareth, according to Christians. In Gen. 48: 3–6, Jacob said to his son Joseph that the Almighty God has blessed him when he appeared to him at Luz in the land of Canaan and made his son take an oath to bury him in Canaan in a tomb that he had dug in the cave of Machpelah, facing Mamre, a field acquired as a funeral property by Abraham, bought from Ephron, the Hittite. Other occurrences were included in the rest of the Bible: three in Exodus, three in Leviticus, eleven in the book of Numbers, and two in Deuteronomy and in the book of Joshua. Canaan reappeared when the children of Israel ate manna for forty years up to their arrival in the country they settled and currently live, where, for the first time, they ate products of Canaan (Jos. 5:12).

Upon their arrival at the borders of Canaan, where they were received by Eleazar, the priest who performed the ritual of the red heifer also known as red cow for sacrifice according to the Torah; and Joshua son of Nun, the successor of Moses, and the heads of the tribal clans of Israel, who settled in the land of Canaan and received the country as patrimony, and shared it between them, (Jos. 14:1). The Book of Jos. 10:28–43 described their conquest on the country of Canaan to us. The neighborhood problems started here and there on both side of Jordan by Joshua and all Israel for the establishment of two tribes and a half, which were the sons of Reuben, the sons of Gad, and the half tribe of Manasseh, who left the sons of Israel at Shiloh in Canaan to return home to the land of Gilead, the mountain range that ran along the Jordan, where they owned land, acquired by themselves.

In Num. 32:29–32, Moses determined the conditions and decreed the participation of the sons of Gad and the sons of Reuben to Eleazar, to Joshua, and to the leaders of the patriarchal tribes of Israel, concerning the conquest of Canaan and the right of the two tribes and the half tribe of Manasseh concerning the possession of land. All course of events told by the Bible from the exile out of Egypt up to the conquest of Canaan are evidences of the occurrences of the protohistory of Israel workers from Mesopotamia on the construction sites of the Nile delta, and who finally got completely out of Egypt; these Bene Israels finally settled in the land of Canaan in the land of the blacks. After the collapse of the great Egyptian empires dominating the Middle East, began the history of Israelites in the current territories of Israel and Palestine at the last centuries of the second millennium before Jesus Christ. Being from the same family, its descendants divided into twelve tribes were first independent and then became federated into a unified kingdom before splitting.

In the north of Palestine at the Iron Age, a kingdom was born from the late tenth to the eighth century BC (about 930 to 720 BC); the kingdom of Israel of the ancient Middle East, led by several successive dynasties for about two hundred years, was established by the Israelites. It was, of course, different from the kingdom of Judah, which appeared at the south in 931 after the death of King Solomon, son of King David, and formed around Jerusalem by the tribe of Judah and the tribe of Benjamin. Up to its fall, it had two capitals; Shechem was the first and later Samaria, founded by Omri.

The land of Israel (in Hebrew, ירא לארשי) is the land that included the ancient kingdoms of Israel and Judah. Its main chronological historical periods up to the name of Jerusalem, referring to the worship of a unique god of the Canaanites, are presented below. After the death of Saul, who reunited the twelve tribes, the second king David reigned as one of the two founders of the ancient Jewish state with his son Solomon. The second book of Samuel described his reign from 1010 to 970 BC at the cost of numerous wars. His long reign allowed him to conquer, to expand, and to pacify the kingdom, more accurately called "the city of David"; Jerusalem was the city that he made his capital. David wished to dedicate a temple to God, but he was not allowed to build the temple in Jerusalem. After a period of struggle between the numerous descendants of David himself from the tribe of Judah, Solomon reigned from 970 to 931 BC.

According to the Bible, the kingdom of Judah, in the land called Palestine, is a kingdom of the ancient Middle East that existed from 931 to 587, at the same time as the kingdom of Israel, and in competition with the other kingdom; and it was during a campaign of Nebuchadnezzar II against Jerusalem in 587 that this kingdom disappeared. The occupation of Bethar, an ancient fortress city of Judea in 135, is known as the last resistance of these Jewish populations who said they were the twelve tribes of Israel, after a fierce war that left Judea devastated to the Roman Empire.

From a preaching perspective, Islamic tradition preserves some significant elements concerning David. It quotes him as a judge imbued with wisdom and a great prophet-king. David (or Daoud [داود] in Arabic) is the fulfillment of the will of Allah by the biblical narrative.

His succession was mentioned in the first book of Kings concerning the division of the unified kingdom into two distinct kingdoms, the one of Israel and the one of Judah. Among his sons, his father David, who chose Solomon, prepared the investiture ceremony for his son as king. It was he who built the temple of Solomon, the first Jewish temple in Jerusalem. The cedar and the workers were supplied by his friend Hiram I, king of Tyre (the present-day Lebanon), for its construction in the rectangular shape of fifty meters by thirty meters approximately, and which lasted seven years. He who enriched the country by regional trade was criticized by the people for collecting too heavy taxes toward the end of his reign.

First Kings 11:3–5, 9–13 first quotes the seven hundred wives and three hundred concubines that Solomon had, evolving in his entourage as a fact, developed pagan religions in the country. His infidelity did not allow him to keep the covenant with God the unique eternal, but turned his heart to other gods worshipped by his wives, who influenced him; this led to the divine anger, who promised to snatch the kingdom from him but not in his life because of his father David, according to the Bible. Traditionally, a multitude of representations and artistic evocations of all kinds over the centuries were practiced. Thus, he was assigned the title of musician and poet, and numerous of his psalms are compiled in the book of Psalms. What the Bible does not tell us is that he was a Freemason; and its temple of 965 before Christ had many links with Freemasonry. And Freemasonry has several numbers frequently consecrated to the construction of the temple of Solomon. One can, for example quote the number 9 as the best known. Masonry itself has an origin of the art of building attributed to black architects. The professor of anatomy, an American doctor known for his founding principles on Freemasonry appointed "Secretary General of the Supreme Council" of the Southern Jurisdiction—"mother of the world"— of the ancient and accepted Scottish rite, to administer the highest degrees founded in 1801 in Charleston (South Carolina) in the United States, was Albert Gallatin Mackey; he was also the Secretary of the Grand Masonic Lodge of the same city; he declared that Nimrod was one of the major founders of Freemasonry. This son of Kush, the first hero on earth and the first king after the flood, was also known as a great builder who had the idea to build Babel (Babylon).

His initiatic brother in this esoteric sect, that illustrious character of American Freemasonry, who passed from the external "darkness" to the interior "enlightenment" and who was answering by the name of Albert Gallatin Mackey, left us numerous Masonic works, especially on its main founders. The historic and legendary origin of Freemasonry, which appeared in the seventeenth century in Scotland, is symbolic and older. Symbolically, it is positioned in an age where the study of the fossil remains of living things did not exist. This study of the scientific discipline of the past and its evolutionary implications by the name of paleontology establishes the prehistoric species and allows their reconstruction. That is why this mythical origin of Masonry was placed at the time of the first man of the Hebrew Bible named Adam, and passed to the one who built the ark, who was considered as the ancestor of all mankind and the first religion, and whom the tradition called Noah; finally, to the one whom many people attribute the construction of Solomon's temple more frequently, depending on the conception of the time by the masonry itself, but that some people moved the symbolic origin at the time of the pyramids building, and what the Westerners called the rediscovery of Ancient Egypt.

After the death of Solomon, this religious and political animosity used by Jeroboam I caused a schism between the kingdoms of Israel and Judah. Jeroboam I, the founder of the kingdom of northern Israel and the first king of Israel who reigned as monarch for twenty-two years, from 931 to 910, and originally an officer at the court of King Solomon, was the one who would end the unified monarchy of Israel. The kingdom of Israel succeeded the united kingdom of Israel and Judah. The unified monarchy as described in the Bible was proclaimed by the Israelites at the time of the judges of Israel around 1050 BC by the wish of the people to have a king like other nations. As idolatrous symbols of God, he put the golden calves at both ends of his kingdom to worship his religion.

In 1 Sm. 8, God accepted the principle of kingship desired by the people to choose a king, and chose a king in the land of Israel; and through the prophet Samuel, Saul, from the tribe of Benjamin, was designated as the first king of the Israelites from 1020 to 1010 BC. His population, accused to have let down the teaching of Moses by falling into idolatry, was condemned by a rather negative view in the Bible. And around 720 BC, the kingdom of Israel was conquered by the Assyrian Empire. The city of Ashur, guardian of the deity of god Assur, was where Assyria took its name, known as an ancient region of the northern Mesopotamia.

A powerful kingdom was formed in that region at the second millennium BC. From the eighth and seventh centuries BC, this powerful Assyrian kingdom later became an empire and was controlling territories of several current countries such as Iraq, Syria, Lebanon, Turkey, and Iran, extending over one part or the total territories of these countries. Let's take a wink on the evolution and decline in the history of that ancient region of Mesopotamia to briefly dissect their civilization. More widely known as ancient Mesopotamia, the history of ancient Assyria distinguished three phases, which are from the twentieth to the early fourteenth century BC, the Paleo-Assyrian period; up to 911 BC, the Middle Assyrian period; and from 612 up to 609 BC, dated the end of the Assyrian kingdom, the Neo-Assyrian period. You should know that the dates are approximate before 700 BC.

The period of the beginning of the second millennium BC up to 539 before BC marked the beginning of the rivalry of the kingdom of Babylon in the southern Mesopotamia with Assyria, the neighbor kingdom located in the north. During the eighteenth-century BC and under the leadership of Hammurabi, the sixth greatest king of the First Dynasty of the Amorite origin, the city of Babylon was its capital. This great sovereign was the first king to establish domination of the Babylonian kingdom in Mesopotamia and completed the conquest of Sumer and Akkad. He was considered one of the great artisans, most prestigious by the scale of his political and legislative work, and the power of his reign was one of the longest of the antiquity of the Near East of his time.

The state was assured from the city of Babylon between 1100 and 800 BC. After several centuries of instability, Babylonia passed for more than a century, from 728 to 626, under the control of Assyria. Gradually, the initiation of its reaction destroyed Assyria; and from 626 to 539 BC, its dominance resulted to a very brief formation of the Neo-Babylonian Empire by Nabopolassar I and Nebuchadnezzar II, soon conquered by the Persian king Cyrus II, according to the latest phase in the history of the kingdom of Babylon.

During the reign of Nebuchadnezzar II, the historical city of Babylonia, one of the largest cities of the Neo-Babylonian Empire, reached its peak in the sixth century BC and was dominating a large part of the Middle East at that time. It was under the reign of King Cyrus II that the Judeans, exiled in Babylonia, received the permission to return to Jerusalem. Cyrus also ordered to rebuild the temple of Jerusalem that Nebuchadnezzar destroyed during the capture of the city of Jerusalem, according to the Old Testament. The capital of this kingdom of Babylon was taken by King Cyrus II of Persia in 539 BC and extended its domination to the entire lower Mesopotamia and even beyond. Babylon was therefore no longer dominated by a dynasty of autochthon. The fall of the last king of Medes was imminent from 539 to 331 BC, submitted by the Achaemenid dynasty, the first of the Persian Empires, successor of the Median kingdom.

Successively dominated, Media was the popular of the empires; and from 311 to 141 BC, it passed to the Seleucid Greeks. From 141 BC to AD 224, the Parthian Empire took Media and Mesopotamia from the Seleucids. Finally, from AD 224 up to the Muslim invasion of the Arabs in 651, the Sassanids reigned in Iran. For more than four hundred years, the Sassanid kingdom was one of the two great powers in the western Asia. Up to the beginning of our era, the millennium culture of Babylonia, who nevertheless retained its prosperity, was slowly extinguished. The first of the Persian Empires to reign over a great part of the Middle East was the Achaemenid Empire, dating from around 556 BC with the founding clan liberated from the domination of the Medes.

The Hellenistic period was a period during which the region called Coele-Syria, one of the channels allowing access to Egypt, was dominated. In the Hellenized version of Aramaic, the term *Coele-Syria* meant with the exception of Phoenicia, the interior of Syria, and more exactly the entire Syria. The six conflicts that followed that period were corresponding to the Syrian wars and were opposing the Ptolemaic kingdoms and the Seleucid kingdoms. After the death of Alexander the Great, conflicts occurred between his successors in 323 BC for the sharing of the empire.

In Lydia in 281 BC, the Battle of Corupedium, the last battle of Diadochi, was between the army of King Lysimachus of Thrace and the one of King Seleucus of Syria. Ptolemy I of Egypt had established its dominance over Coele-Syria after the Battle of Ipsus, which took place in Phrygia (nowadays Turkey) in 301; and the sharing between the Ptolemic and the Seleucid dynasties during the Syria wars followed.

The Battle of Ipsus was considered in Western history as the greatest battle of elephants and as one of the greatest battles of the Hellenistic period. These two empires were exhausted humanly and in resources, and their conquest by Rome and by Parthia led to their final destruction. This historical region located in northeastern Iran—under the name of Parthia, the Old Persia, also known as Syrian Antioch—was a region that Ptolemy III seized, the capital called Antioch, after the death of Antiochus II, the Greek king of the Hellenistic Seleucid Empire. It eventually rivaled Alexandria as the chief Christian city of the Near East, which historians referred to Jewish Christianity of the first part of the period, during the lifetimes of the twelve apostles from a small movement in Galilee and Judea, where the origin of the Christian Church originated in Palestine.

During the Maccabean revolt, a dynasty came to power in Judea, joined by the Hasidim—the Hasmonean dynasty, initiated from 168 to 167 BC by a priest of the Jewish priestly line and a politico-religious leader of Yehoyarib named Mattathias, founder of the Hasmonean dynasty in the second century BC. According to the Christian tradition of the first book of Maccabees, this dynasty, also called Maccabaeus, informed us that Mattathias was succeeded by his son Judas Maccabaeus after his death, a year after the outbreak of the revolt. Even as Judas Maccabaeus was not the eldest of his family, he managed to seize Jerusalem after several battles in December 164 BC and restored the Jewish cult in the temple. In October 152 to 142 BC, he was succeeded by Jonathan, son of Mattathias and the brother of Judas Maccabee.

Judas Maccabaeus is considered as the first to reign with the title of high priest, and the Hasmonean dynasty is also considered to have figures of the rebellion against Antiochus IV Epiphanes of the Seleucid Empire, who tried to seize the treasure of the temple in Jerusalem from 176 to 175; he plundered, seized the treasure of the temple of Jerusalem in 168, after submitting Egypt and Cyprus on the same year to his domination. After stopping the persecution on the same year of his death in 164, the worship of YHWH was invested in the sanctuary and the altar after the purification of the temple by Judas Maccabaeus, who seized Jerusalem. The Seleucid Empire already had a vast territory known as Syria-Cilicia, Palestine, Mesopotamia, and part of Iran. Between 27 BC and AD 476, the ancient Roman domination of the Empire dominated to the point of encompassing a territory ranging from Mesopotamia up to the African province of Mauretania Tingitana (Morocco) and the Roman province of Britannia, covering England, Wales countries and the south of Scotland, from the first century to the early fifth century up to Egypt, during the period of five centuries. While preserving the tradition, the ancient Greek civilization received as a heritage, the ancient Roman domination, which deeply influenced the Mediterranean world culturally, linguistically, and religiously as one of the largest political entities of the Roman history, founded by Augustus, the first

Roman emperor from January 16 of the year 27 BC, who died in Nola on August 19, of the year AD 14.

This nascent empire ended the Roman Republic at the last civil war. It was in the third century BC that the Roman tradition fixed the history of the founding of the Roman monarchy, founded in 753 BC, according to the legend, by Romulus and Remus, followed by a series of seven kings, including other sovereign of ephemeral reign; and it was abolished in 509 BC at the year of the advent of the republic, corresponding to the fall of Tarquin the Superb. As military dictator, Augustus governed by sharing the territory of the Roman Republic and developed a model of government in which the republican state was ruled by him alone. In some representations, the name Augustus was attached to the founder of Rome, Romulus.

He had a territorial administration based on a powerful military and a bureaucracy ever more developed up to the deposition of Romulus Augustus, who reigned for only ten months, marking the end of the Western Roman Empire at his fall. The Western Roman Empire never recovered from its division by Diocletian in 285, and a new era of the Middle-Ages was marked at his fall in the history of Europe. Up to 402, Milan was its capital. Officially, the Western Roman Empire disappeared on September 4, 476, at the time of the abdication of Romulus Augustus, the last Roman emperor of the West. Its history, from the republican era to the imperial period, was initially characterized by a certain complex in and outdoor of political stability from the foundation of its empire by Augustus. Over long periods, population movements of very large scale called the barbarian invasions, confronted Rome from the end of the second century.

An increasingly important instability caused the crisis of the third century from 235 to 275 and succeeded the Principate period, particularly designating the power and position of the monarch always having a Senate holding more power than it had ever had before; however, not politically independent, since it was dominated by the emperor and finally by the assembly which was losing a large prestigious part of its power like "consuls," magistrates elected for one year by the people, or "praetors," an inferior colleague of the consuls - magistrates elected for a period of one year by the people's assembly of the Roman Republic - "comitia centuriate," to the Senatorial row, occupying the curule seat, wearing the toga, they had the power to punish; followed by "aediles," two magistrates elected each year by the "comitia centuriate," among the people; they were the assistants of "the plebeian tribunes," magistrates elected to defend the rights and interests of the weak and poor classes, and their primitive function were linked to the city administration. That college was elected by the people under the guise of restoring the republic to maintain existing institutions, which disappeared toward the reign of Alexander Severus. The form of the principate government was established by Augustus around 27 to 285. The second of the two phases of the government of the ancient Roman Empire was the Dominate, the "despotic" later phase of imperial government; it lasted approximately from 285 up to 476, the official date of the fall of the Western Empire. This period was a period in which the empire's inhabitants were only considered as slaves. Coups followed, and civil wars were multiplied, confronting more and more enemies at its borders.

The imperial expansion of the Roman Empire began with its founder Augustus, and during his reign from the year 27 before Christ up to his death in the year AD 14, he initiated the territorial annexation. Before his death, his empire was considerably enlarged by the annexation of some countries such as Africa; among his conquests, we already quoted Egypt; Dalmatia—the Eastern Adriatic coast in the classical antiquity, much larger than the current Dalmatia, encompassing much of the present Albania, Croatia, Bosnia and Herzegovina, Montenegro, Serbia, Kosovo, etc., were also annexed by the Roman Empire. . . In the first century BC, Germania, a geographical area inhabited mainly by Germanic people—the Noricum—became his possession at the first century of our era. In the ancient times, this area was a tribal federation in a Celtic kingdom and included present-day Austria and part of Slovenia; the Pannonia, an area encompassing the current western Hungary; eastern Austria; northern Croatia; northwest of Serbia; northeastern Slovenia; western Slovakia; northern Bosnia; and Herzegovina.

Raetia was located on the territories of the present eastern and central Switzerland, Bavaria, Upper Swabia, Vorarlberg, the most part of Tyrol, and part of Lombardy. He completed his conquest with the Iberian Peninsula, more commonly known under the name of Hispania. Among these territories, Judea was also counted as the possessions of the Roman Empire. The annexation of this region dated from the year 63 before our era, when Pompey the Great occupied it after his successful Third Mithridatic War. It was the period when the Roman Republic conquered the independent kingdom of Israel before its fall. The kingdom of Judah in the south was separated from the kingdom of Israel in the north.

These two kingdoms were created after the outbreak of a problem caused by members of the northern tribes of the united kingdom of Israel, refusing to accept the son of Solomon by the name of Rehoboam as their king, but the tribe of Benjamin joined Judah shortly after he remained loyal to the house of David with all his tribe, according to the Bible. From that siege of Jerusalem in the year 63 BC, which ended the Jewish independence and incorporated Judea into the Roman Republic, there were several rebellions against the Roman domination.

The very first, was the one that led to the destruction of Herod's temple and ended with the siege of Jerusalem. Josephus related that, despite the opposition of a part of the priestly class, following the increasing religious tensions between Greeks, Jews, and Romans, the First Jewish-Roman War, sometimes called the Great Revolt, took place sixty years later, between 66 and 73.

The Roman legions of Titus besieged the province of Judea in the year 70. They destroyed Jerusalem and the temple of Herod in that year 67; Gamla, the strongholds of the Jews, and in the year 73, Masada on the southwestern shore of the Dead Sea in the first century BC. The name Judea drew its origin from the Canaanite Hebrew of the tribe of Judah and today corresponded to one part of the West Bank and southern Israel. The one of Kitos took place from 115 to 117, during the Jewish-Roman war from 66 to 135; it was the second insurrection of the Jews from the province of Judea. And the last of these three great Jewish-Roman wars against the Roman Empire was referred to as the Bar Kokhba revolt; it took place from 132 to 135 of our era. These cities besieged, destroyed, and looted from the first revolt, ended as soon as these legions long considered in terms of military tactics as a model of efficiency and potential, entered in these cities of the province of Judea. The instigator of this fall was a revolt initiated from 132 by the Jewish patriot Shimon bar Kokhba, who led the Jewish-Roman war up to his death. In December 135, the one who was hailed as the Messiah was killed in his refuge at Bethar. For the third time, Jerusalem was largely destroyed, and the Jewish people, after slaughtering them, were forbidden to stay in the area around the city; and Hadrian was hailed as impecator after the victory in Judea for the third time.

At the end of that Bar Kokhba revolt in Judea, the name of the province was changed to Syria-Palestine, named by Emperor Hadrian, of Punic origin, a Tunisian city known under the name of Carthage and located northeast of the capital Tunis. And then the last residents of the Jewish people were once again scattered throughout the Roman Empire. Thus, Judea was renamed Syria-Palestine on August 9, 135, at the traditional date of the capture of Bechar and Jerusalem, newly put into the bag of Roman domination. Let us say immediately before continuing that it was in the second century BC that Roman domination became the master of ancient Greece. During antiquity, Greek culture was mixed with the earlier cultures of Egypt, Mesopotamia, and the Roman culture, which was developed earlier and known as the one that gave birth to the civilization of the Hellenistic kingdoms. This Greek culture also gave birth to another protagonist known in the history of the world—the Macedonian "half barbarian," who was easily carried away by anger and terrible violence. He was named Alexander the Great, who conquered beyond Greek borders throughout ancient times before the Roman domination. In the medieval civilizations, he remained undefeated on the battlefield.

Historians tell us that he was a king in Babylon by the will of Marduk, the principal god of the city; he proclaimed himself as pharaoh in Egypt as the living god Horus. During that period, where the superior feudal lords of the Achaemenid Empire joined the Medes of Iran and the ancient neighbor of the Persians, it resulted in a great empire founded by the Achaemenids, uniting into a single political entity in a sustainable way all the oldest civilizations of the Middle East and extending to the north and the west of Asia Minor, in Thrace and on the most coastal areas of the Black Sea, in Afghanistan to the east and in one part of nowadays Pakistan, on the present Iraq, in Syria, in Egypt to the south and at the southwest to Saudi Arabia, Jordan, Israel, and Palestine, Lebanon to the north, up to the northern Libya.

By undoing the ancient country of Asia Minor called Lydia, it seized Anatolia, conquered the Babylonian Empire, and captured Egypt. It was at that moment that Alexander the Great got the idea of seizing all the Achaemenid territories and began his conquest, which ended by the victory on the first of the Persian Empires, to reign over a large part of the Middle East. In 330 BC, the Achaemenid Empire ended, defeated by Alexander the Great, after threatening to take the ancient Greece for two successive times. Before the chaos created by Alexander's invasion of Persia, Artaxerxes IV Arses succeeded Artaxerxes III; then Darius III, a nephew of Artaxerxes IV, was placed on the throne by Bagoas before the total fall of the empire. Traditionally, Bagoas was a castrated man of Egyptian origin but born in Persia. In the old days, the practice of castration was not limited to the removal of the testicles but sometimes also to the removal of the penis to become a eunuch without the reproductive organs, to be a complete "bed keeper," and to be considered a harem keeper among Muslims.

Since Alexander the Great madly loved and devoted his love to boys, Bagoas was his favorite and equally loved Artaxerxes III, according to Plutarch. Bagoas generally played the role of the wicked with the mercenary named Mentor of Rhodes, a Greek who at the same time fought alongside Artaxerxes III to subdue Egypt again in 342 BC to the Persian Empire; and against him, he first fought in Sidon, during the revolt of the city of Tenes. Thus, after the defeat of Egypt, Bagoas was the real master of the country after being awarded full power. In Egyptian temples, he confiscated the sacred manuscripts; and to return them, he demanded bribes, which greatly enriched him. After murdering Artaxerxes III, his father, to keep his position as the powerful minister of Persia, he replaced him with his son, throwing pieces of the body butchered of his late father to cats, which ate him with voracity, for killing of the sacred bull Apis in 338.

His son Artaxerxes IV on the throne, unhappy with the killing of most of his family and his brothers with his exception, generally saw the threat to his reign. So, with the nobles of his royal court, despising the influence of Bagoas, he planned his murder, but this famous minister took the decision to poison him immediately after hearing of his attempt; he put Artaxerxes IV to death after only three years of reign in 336. And Darius III, his cousin, was brought to the throne of the Achaemenid dynasty. Finally, the first act of Darius III was to get rid of this dangerous minister.

In turn, Bagoas carefully elaborated another poison for Darius, realizing his intractability and his inflexibility. But as forewarned was forearmed, he quickly remembered the fate of his predecessors. Informed by the previous assassinations of his cousins, Darius was faced with the poison that Bagoas intended for him, but he forced him to drink it in 336 BC. Nevertheless, when Alexander approached Persia, his cousin Bessus, known by the royal name of Artaxerxes V, killed Artashat, the original name of Darius III, the last king of the Achaemenid Empire from (336 to 330 BC). Then as his successor, he declared himself the superior feudal lord of the throne of the Achaemenid Empire. Darius III was killed fleeing in the confines of Media before Alexander could reach him.

Historically, he was officially conquered by Alexander the Great. In 329 BC, Alexander the Great executed Artaxerxes V and faced the same tragedy, just like what he did to his cousin Darius III. The Persian Empire of Alexander was finally divided into small states to his generals. One of his generals was Seleucus I Nicator, who was appointed commander of the companions and the regent of Alexander's empire. He established the Seleucid Empire, which Alexander conquered, on much of the territory in the Near East, after Alexander's death in June 323 BC. And at the course of the second century BC, the reign of Iranian origin will be restored by the Parthians in the northeast of Iran after subsequently defeating their first enemies known as the Seleucid Empire and their complete loss of power and control of Persia. The Arsacid dynasty gradually extended their control, settling itself in Parthian from 253 until the middle of the second century BC.

However, a high priest of the Zoroastrian temple of Anahita, in the ancient city of Istakhr in Persia (Iran), by the name of Sassan proclaimed himself to be the Persian sovereign as the descendant of Darius III; and from that moment, multiple revolts settled in the country. The son of the lord Sassan, named Papak, started to kill kings of small towns and King Gozirh of Istakhr and declared himself king in his place. And the youngest son of Papak by the name of Ardashir was also the master of several cities in the province of Fars, and the great king of Parthia Arsacid at the time was the king Artabanus V. After so many revolts led by Papak against the lord of the Kingdom, and wars waged by his son against neighboring territories, both coast to coast, conquered territories and his father Papak took control of the kingdom, but theoretically, the vassal of the kingdom of Persia was still under the control of the king of kings, Artabanus V.

After the death of Papak, Ardashir succeeded his father as the head of the powerful kingdom in Persia; what the king of kings, Artaban V, did not accept, and made it known by asking Artaxerxes Ardashir I to return to the rank of the hierarchy applied in several domains, physically and morally in the kingdom of Persia by a formal notice; but intending to unify Iran, Artaxerxes (Ardashir I, the successor of Satan) replied by asserting its power and denouncing his allegiance and launched a challenge to the king of kings, Artabanus V. Sassan was more or less the one who started the foundation of the Sassanian dynasty at the end of the third century. The victory over Artabanus V, the last king of the Parthian dynasty, dethroned and killed on April 22 or 28 of the year 224 by Ardashir I, really began the Iranian Sassanian period after the decisive battle, whose origin was found in the heart of the Persian country, like the founder of the Sassanid dynasty, from the third to the seventh century, and dominated the Middle East to the east of the Euphrates until the Arab Muslim conquest.

From 224 up to the Muslim invasion of the Arabs in 651, the Sassanids reigned on Iran during the period constituting the golden age. This power of western Asia ended with the defeat of the last king of kings, Yazdegerd III (emperor), from the beginning of his reign on June 16, 632, to his assassination in the autumn of 651 in Persia. Before his death, he faced the invasion of the Muslim Arabs, which already, during the period of the dynastic conflicts in 628 to 632, raided Iraq. He failed to push the first of the Islamic empires of the Arab caliphate after fourteen years of struggle. In the history of Iran, the Sassanid era was considered one of the most important periods.

His empire encompassed the whole territory of Iran, Iraq, the present-day Armenia, the South Caucasus, also called Transcaucasia, including Georgia, Azerbaijan and, the region of Kars—Turkey, Dagestan, the southernmost part of Russia, located today in the North Caucasus Mountains; extending to the Central Asia southwestern territory, the western Afghanistan, fragments of (Anatolia), present-day Turkey and Syria, a part of the coast of the Arabian Peninsula, the Persian Gulf region and fragments of West Pakistan. This empire represented the fulfillment to the highest degree of Persian civilization, called Eranshahr Empire in their time. The Iranian Empire or the empire of the Aryans was the last great empire before its conquest by Muslims. Its cultural influence extended far beyond the borders of the empire before the adoption of the Muslim religion and reached Africa, China, Western Europe, and India. Iraq was ruled by the Sassanid Persians, and Syria and Egypt were part of the Byzantine Empire. The Western historians named one of the two states that emerged from the partition of the Roman Empire in the third century since modern times. This state, which lasted up to the fifteenth century, was called the Byzantine Empire, and its capital was formerly called Byzantium. Historically, May 11, 330, was the date of the founding of its capital Constantinople and marked the beginning of the Byzantine history. And up to 1930, Constantinople, the present-day Istanbul in Turkey, was the former name of the Ottoman Turkish authorities.

This division into two parts, resulting in the Eastern Roman Empire and the Western Roman Empire, was established by Diocletian after the death of Theodosius I in 395 and marked its final division into two empires. Its citizens never designated themselves as Romans but by the term *Roum*, historically a generic word used to describe the ethnocultural minorities by the Muslims; the Persians, Arabs, and Turks took this term as the name for its inhabitants. Marking the history of Europe and the Middle East, the Byzantine Empire gave birth to a brilliant civilization, during a period of over thousand years of existence, and had its origins in the foundation of the Roman Empire. Even if it is difficult to precisely date the beginning of the Byzantine history, current historians are dividing its history into three major periods, which are from the fourth century to the seventeenth century, the Paleo-Byzantine period, maintaining the classic characteristics of the Roman Empire (or the Eastern Roman Empire); from the seventh century to the twelfth century, the Meso-Byzantine period; and from the thirteenth century to the fifteenth century, the late Byzantine period, where the empire was reduced to the rank of a minor regional power, bequeathing various elements of its civilization to the Orthodox country and to the Ottoman Empire before disappearing as a state.

The East Roman Empire played a great role in the mixing of populations and the transmission of cultural values; in the economy and in the knowledge of the ancient ideas of its time, as a "shield" of Europe; its military plan first faced the Persians, the people of various steppes ethnic origins, who populated the vast eco region of Eurasian—from the classical antiquity of Scythia—usually nomadic people, going from the north of the Black Sea and Anatolia to Mongolia; originally the first hypothetical doctrine of the steppe corresponds to the mythology of the Indo-Europeans; the Turko-Mongol nomads who appeared during the early fourteenth century, among the ruling elites of Mongol Empire, later introduced "Tangrism;" from the Tarim Basin to China, Manichaeism and Nestorianism spread but never became the predominantly established religions. Buddhism, which found a new house in China, stretched from India in the north to the Tarim Basin; and the Tibetan Buddhism was adopted by Dzungaria and Mongolia. Islam was adopted by all steppes of the west of Dzungaria, around 1400, and in the basin of Tarim, Islam was established around 1600; afterward, the Persians finally faced the spread of Islam.

In 1204, this protective function of prosperity, rendered obsolete, ended by the devastating looting of Constantinople by the crusaders, marking the first occupation and leading to the capture and looting of the capital of the Byzantine Empire. In the Saint Sophia Cathedral, Baldwin I of Constantinople saw himself crowned as emperor of the Latin Empire of Flanders, founded after the fall of the Byzantine Empire, after the Fourth Crusade and lasted up to the reconquest of the city in 1261 by Michael Palaeologus, co-emperor of Nicaea from 1259 to 1261, usurped from the legitimate sovereign John IV Laskaris at the throne. He became the Byzantine emperor from 1261, the year of the restoration of the Byzantine Empire, up to 1282.

The eastern part of the Roman Empire generally called the Byzantine Empire, which was known as the "Lower Empire," was one of the two parts of the Roman Empire. This designation dated from the second half of the nineteenth century. After the death of the emperor in the western part, Rome then remained with a single emperor in the eastern part of Constantinople up to 1453, the date of the occupation of its former territory by the Ottomans. In 1299, Oghuz, one of the original branches of the Turks people under Osman I founded the Ottoman Empire in the northwestern Anatolia. After the conquest of Constantinople by Mehmed the Conqueror and now master of Islam on three continents of the world, the Ottoman Empire decided to continue the Achaemenid royal titulature, the title of the monarchical nobility of the Persian language, by naming their sultans by the name of Padishah in the fifteenth century and in the sixteenth century, as the successor of Muhammad, by the name of caliph.

In Islam, it is known that the title "Shah" (Shah of Iran, for example) is a title held by the emperors of Persia, and "sultan" is a title existing since the year 1000, held by Muslims and Ottoman monarchs. These are titles adopted by the three great Islamic empires known to Muslims, which are the Sunnite Turkish Ottoman Empire, founded in 1512 by Sultan Selim I and encompassing Arabia, the Balkans, Egypt, Iraq, Syria, and North Africa; the Shiite Safavid Persian Empire, founded by Safi ad-Din—the Sunnite mystic. The name of this Sufi order was Safaviyeh, and in the fourteenth and fifteenth centuries, in the society and politics of northwestern Iran, this order held a prominent place in the society.

The original precepts of all Sufi orders are traced from the prophet Muhammad through his cousin and son-in-law Ali ibn Abi Talib of the Islamic tradition, including the last of the three great Islamic empires known as the Grand Mughal Empire of India, which was founded in 1526 by Zahir-ud-Din Muhammad, nicknamed Babur, after the Battle of Panipat, in which he defeated the last sultan Ibrahim Lodi of Delhi. This empire is known as the second largest to have existed in the Indian subcontinent. In 1169, Saladin, who reigned from Egypt to Syria, founded the dynasty of Ayyubid "sultans." It was from the caliph of Baghdad that he received orders and commanded several emirs in the Muslim communities. The Ottoman caliphate was indeed the most perfect known usage of this title, like the one of the Turkish sovereign, at the same time spiritual leaders as caliphs and temporal rulers as sultans. These qualifications provided them a character of power equivalent to the one of emperor in the universality.

In the Sunni Islam, the term *caliph* was used to refer to the first four caliphs who carefully followed the way of Muhammad and were considered leaders. Muhammad said, "Hold fast to my Sunna [path or practice(s)] and the Sunna of the rightly guided caliphs." The term *Sunna* meant "unchangeable law" of God under the "rules of God," prescribed to all the prophets and to Muhammad, the prophet of Islam. From their ancestor of the Umayyad dynasties, the Umayyads were named after Umayyah ibn'Abd Shams, the caliph who ruled the Islamic world from 661 to 750. He was the great-uncle of Muhammad, originally from the Arab tribe of Quraysh, and a first cousin of Abd al-Muttalib, the paternal grandfather of Muhammad. Abd ibn Manaf Qusai was the common ancestor of Muhammad and the Umayyads.

Hasim, the son of Abd ibn Manaf Qusai, was at the origin of the clan of Banu Hashim, where Muhammad, the prophet, came from. And Abd Shams was at the origin of the Umayyad dynasty through his son Umayyah. It was Abu Talib (the son of the uncle of Muhammad, the prophet of Islam) and his grandfather Abd al-Muttalib (his uncle) who raised Muhammad at the death of his mother Amina in 577, when he was only six years old, and his father's death before his birth in 570. The son of Hashim ibn Abd al-Manaf, the great-great- grandfather of Muhammad, gave birth to Abdullah ibn Abd al-Muttalib (Muhammad's father); Abdullah ibn Abd al-Muttalib was the son of Abd al-Muttalib and the brother of Abu Talib.

The caliph Ali ibn Talib'Abi, the uncle of the prophet of Islam, Muhammad, who protected him as his own son, was succeeded by Abu al-Hasan Ali ibn Abi Talib, Muhammad's uncle, who henceforth headed the Hashim clan; he invaded Damascus, nowadays capital of Syria, and founded the Umayyad caliphate. Damascus is mentioned several times in the stories of the prophets in the books of Kings and in the book of Genesis as one of the continuously inhabited oldest cities and in its history, became the largest Muslim state, stretching from the Indus, the source of a river in Pakistan that gave its name to India in the ancient times, up to the Iberian Peninsula, the southwestern tip of Europe.

Muhammad—an Arab soldier of the Quraysh tribe, religious leader, founder of Islam, and considered as the major prophet born in Mecca around 570—married Khadija, the first wife of the prophet and considered as the mother of all Muslims in Islam. And according to the Islamic tradition, Muhammad died in 632 in Medina. The revelations of the words of Allah made to Muhammad, the prophet and messenger of Islam, sealed and determined the Islamic belief, thus assigning him the title of the last of the prophets of monotheism. Its origin is just like the monotheism revealed to prophets who came before him by God to Adam, to Noah, Abraham, Moses and to Jesus; that monotheistic revelation, according to the Abrahamic tradition that Mohammed presented as the word of God called (Allah in Arabic), was transmitted to him by the archangel Gabriel.

And it was in a world that did no longer know Jesus and in the internal quarrels of Christianity that Islam was born. For the Arabs, the cult of "baetyl" stones and the astral polytheism were not more attractive at that time of Muhammad. And like other tribes, the influence of the Judaic monotheism profoundly marked the Arabs, some of whom embraced a form of Christianity or Judaism, worshipping one God called the Merciful. Thus, at the crossroads of various beliefs in Mecca, the conservatory of pagan deities, the formula "Allahu Akbar" was more heard than all other spiritual power phrases of Islam meaning "Allah Is Greater!" Also, we would find the same controversies about the real nature of Christ and the same instrumentalization of religions, the same Jewish and Christian monotheistic influences, in countries where Islam established itself in master.

Only seven years after the death of the prophet Muhammad, specifically in 639, Africa saw itself taken by the Arabs to introduce the law and the faith of the Islamic belief there. They founded their first city in Al-Fustat, nowadays known as the city of Cairo in Egypt, after conquering it in 641, and implanted their first mosque there. Their conquest continued in a city of present Tunisia, center of Kairouan, meaning "Camp," and they built the Great Mosque of Kairouan in the same year 670, by the Arab general Oqba Ibn Nafi Al Fihri.

The Arab general Uqba ibn Nafi, born in 622, was sent by Muawiya I, the Umayyad caliph of Damascus, at the head of the Muslim armies to continue their raids to expand its territories and propagate Islam. Uqba ibn Nafi died in 683 after establishing the entry point for the Arab conquest of North Africa and Africa in general. Kairouan was designated as the first holy city of North Africa and the fourth holiest city of Islam until the eleventh century. In the early seventh century, after a brief occupation by the Vandals, who ravaged Gaul, Spain, and the North Africa from 439 to 534 and sacked the Roman Empire in 455, followed by the Byzantine influence, corresponding to the ancient provinces of Africa and Numidia up to the islands of Corsica and the four regions of the medieval Sardinia, the Muslim religion appeared, causing the occupier disappearance by the Arab conquest during the reign of the Umayyad dynasty of the Christian era. For several decades, the Vandal pirate kingdom outlived the imperial Rome at Carthage.

The name of Abbasids comes from a Sunni caliphate dynasty, founded by Abu al-As-Saffah'Abbas, a great-grandson of al-Abbas, the uncle of Muhammad from whom they descended.

From 750 to 754 in Kufa, Abu al-As-Saffah'Abbas ruled the Muslim world after overthrowing the last Umayyad, Marwan II, of the first Muslim dynasty of the more distant family ties to the prophet of Islam. By moving into their new capital, Baghdad, in 762, the triumph of the Abbasids over the Umayyads moved the power from Syria toward Iraq. The Iranians converted to Islam from that moment, had an equal share as the one of the Arabs for a deeply Muslim state. Their leader Abu Muslim gathered little people, ran away slaves around him, and triumphed in the Battle of the Zab in 750, after more than three years of war during the bloody revolution against the Umayyads.

Thus, during five centuries, the Abbasid dynasty became the head of a vast empire from the Atlantic shores of Iberia to the banks of the Indus and gave birth to illustrious caliphs like Al-Mansur, Al-Ma'mun, who became the second in 754 by succeeding his brother Abu al-Abbas as-Saffah, or the legendary Harun al-Rashid, the fifth Abbasid caliph who extended Muslim religion, the Arabic language, and a universal conscience of Islam that characterized the Muslim medieval world and took the Arabo-Muslim civilization at its apogee. The slow decline of this Arab Muslim civilization began when, within the empire, the Turkish tribes, freshly converted to Islam, became increasingly important and when the Mongols destroyed the great capital Baghdad by hitting the coup de grace to the Abbasid dynasty, all this in the indifference of the Muslim world toward the Abbasid dynasty, which survived up to the thirteenth century despite its difficulties.

It was through Fatima, the daughter of the prophet Muhammad, and Ali Ibn Abi Talib that the Fatimids traced their origins. Since the manifesto of Baghdad, those who formed an Ismaili Shiite caliphate dynasty were also called Obeydides. They reigned between 909 and 969 from Ifriqiya and between 969 and 1171 from Egypt. A great part of North Africa, Sicily, and part of the Middle East were included within this empire. The Fatimid came from the Shiite religious branch of Ismailis among the descendants of Ali, where the caliph should be chosen, considering the Sunni Abbasids as usurpers of this title in 909, by Abdullah al-Mahdi Billah, the dynasty of the Ismaili Shiism (Ismaelism), which claimed to be from the Alawite Ismaili lineage, founded and converted the tribes of Kabylia Kotamas to Shiite Islam.

On the Tunisian Sahel, Abou Abdallah chose a capital by founding the city of Mahdiyya by proclaiming himself a caliph in 909 and managed to enthrone the Ismaili imam Ubayd Allah, whom he delivered. An Umayyad caliphate, Cordoba Emir, did the same by establishing themselves in Spain in 929. The Fatimids conquered Egypt in 969 and extended their conquests up to Syria and managed to establish themselves in Malta and Sicily, with one foot in the southern Italy. The Fatimid Empire collapsed under the blows of the Frankish kingdom of Jerusalem. The decline of the Fatimid territory was reduced up to the only territory of Egypt, from 1060 up to its annexation by Saladin, the first Ayyubid caliphate, after the death of the last Fatimid caliph al-Hadid, who died on September 13, 1171, to the one of Baghdad.

He gave back the city of Ashqelon, which was controlled by the crusaders and recovered by Saladin in 1187, to the Sunnis. Saladin was known as the first leader of the Ayyubid dynasty, who ruled Egypt from 1169 to 1250 and Syria from 1174 to 1260. The Abbasids quickly took control of the Umayyad power by initiating an open insurrection against the Umayyad power, defeated in early 750. Because the Abbasid dynasty was less interested in the coast of Egypt, Israel, Lebanon, and Syria, the capture of much of Israel, including Jerusalem and other parts of its coast like Lebanon, was very easy for the First Crusade. Because of their gradual decline, the Mongol siege, led by Hulagu Khan in Baghdad, led to the capture of Al-Musta'sim, the last caliph known as the descendant of an immediate uncle of Muhammad by the name of Al-Abbas ibn Abd al-Muttalib. After his capture, they wrapped him in a carpet to put him to death by trampling him with their horses to put an end to the power of the Abbasid dynasty in Baghdad in 1258 after the Christian era.

The southernmost Latin state of the Orient created during the First Crusade in the East, was called the kingdom of Jerusalem. This Christian kingdom, created in 1099, extended from the reign of Baudouin I, going up to the Jordan Valley inland into Palestine, dominated the Gaza coastline from Daron up to Beirut. The Oriental Christians, especially from France and Italy (Syrians, Greeks, and Armenians), were called by Kings Baldwin I and Baldwin II to populate Jerusalem. In the kingdom of Jerusalem, the forms of rural settlement were areas of immigration. One could observe these areas to those fairly close at the same time in Mediterranean Europe. In August 1291, after the departure of the last crusaders of Tortosa, less than two centuries later, the kingdom of Jerusalem disappeared.

In its history, from 1099 to 1187, one could distinguish the period where the title of king was associated with the stranglehold of crusaders on the city of Jerusalem and the period during which the city itself was not under the crusader soldiers from 1229 to 1244 but where the title of sovereignty of crusaders in the Holy Land represented the highest level. Among the Western kings who will claim Jerusalem posterior to the disappearance of the Christian states of the Holy Land, Godfrey of Bouillon became the first prime sovereign of the kingdom of Jerusalem, born around 1058, with a place of birth not known with certainty but perhaps located between Boulogne-Sur-Mer in France and Baisy in Lower Lorraine (nowadays Belgium). His reign began on July 15, 1099, and he died in Jerusalem on July 18, 1100.

The reign of Baudouin I, born around 1065, began on July 18, 1100; he died on April 2, 1118, in the northeastern Sinai in el-Arish, on the way repatriated to Jerusalem after falling ill in the city of Farama, a city of ancient Lower Egypt located at the northern extremity of the Nile delta. His cousin Baldwin II of Bourcq, known as Baldwin of Edessa, succeeded him on April 14, 1118; he died on August 21, 1131. On September 14, 1131, Melisende succeeded her father and reigned until November 10, 1143, and was a regent as queen of Jerusalem from 1143 to 1152 because Baldwin III was still very young. Melisende was born in 1101 and died on September 11, 1161. The son of Fulk V of Anjou and Melisende of Jerusalem by the name of Baldwin III was proclaimed king at the age of thirteen on November 10, 1143, but under the regency of his mother; he was crowned king of Jerusalem on March 30, 1152. Born in 1131, he died on February 10, 1162, in Beirut. His brother Amalric I, born in 1136, succeeded him as king of Jerusalem, crowned on February 18, 1162, because he had no children. He died on July 11, 1174, of typhus. The son of Amalric I and Agnes of Courtenay by the name of Baldwin IV, "the Leper," started his reign from July 11, 1174, to March 16, 1185. The son of William of Montferrat and Sybil, daughter of Amalric I, who reigned under the regency of Raymond III of Tripoli, under the name of Baldwin V, surnamed Baudouinet, aged eight years old, who succeeded him, reigned from November 20, 1183, and died in September 1186. Sibyl, daughter of Amaury I of Jerusalem and Agnes of Courtenay, reigned as queen of Jerusalem from 1186 to 1187. The sister of Baldwin IV, "the Leper," died in October 1190, during the Siege of Acre, which was the first operation of the reconquest of the kingdom of Jerusalem, the third military Crusade from 1189 to 1191.

In August 1186 began the reign of Guy of Lusignan as king of Jerusalem up to 1192 and from 1192 to 1194 as king in Cyprus, leaving Cyprus to his brother Amalric II; Guy of Lusignan died in April 1194. Isabella I, the daughter of Amalric I and Agnes of Courtenay, was born in 1172; the love life of Isabella I had some storms. During the Third Crusade, after the death of Guy of Lusignan, who was king by marriage to Sibyl, the barons had no other choice but to accept the advent of Guy to avoid the loss of the kingdom.

Since the monarchy of Jerusalem was semielective and semihereditary, it was the assembly of barons who used to choose kings; he had to be the closest relative of the deceased king, and the assembly of barons had to approve the choice of this king. At the death of Guy of Lusignan, the situation was to change; and legally, the crown was to come back to Isabella, who was already married to Humphrey of Toron in 1190. At that time, a problem arose because the assembly of barons did not like the husband of Isabella; thus, an annulment was immediately undertaken by the papal legate—a member of the clergy, especially a cardinal, representing the pope. In this case, the pope sent an archbishop of Pisa and officially known as the legate of the ancient Rome under a pretext that Isabella was only eleven years old at her wedding; therefore by this fact, it was to be canceled.

This reason for not having yet reached the legal age for marriage was required to protect a king not being chosen outside the royal family; because if that was to be the case, it could create conflict between the royal families or cause a civil war. After this cancellation, Isabella was forced to marry Conrad of Montferrat eventually, who was older than her, and left the man she loved and preferred and with whom she formed a well-knit relationship. Conrad, who claimed to marry Isabella only for the throne, married her on November 24, 1190, and obtained the throne with the support of the barons and the lordship of Ibelins of the kingdom of Jerusalem. Isabella of Jerusalem, sister of Baldwin IV and Sybil, died shortly after her last husband in 1205. Conrad of Montferrat, who ensured his rights to the throne by marrying Isabella of Jerusalem, was born in around 1145 or 1147. He was the king of Jerusalem at the time that the Siege of Acre was lifted, on July 12, 1191, after a siege of twenty-two months. The main port of the Holy Land then became the capital of the kingdom of Jerusalem in the thirteenth century. He was assassinated by two Nizarites or Nizarians or Ismaili on April 28, 1192. These mystical Ismaili Shia communities were active since the eleventh century until 1257.

They professed the secrets side of the Koran—an esoteric Koran reading leading to the identification of their currents as initiated members of Batinians or Batin sects; the main thought designates at first, the Batin conception of the occult literal reading, containing a detailed description of the different Islamic sects, and several other hidden meanings in the esoteric Koran, accessible only to initiates. Clandestinely, under the cover of Sufism, this Ismaili community continued its development at the end of the middle ages and nowadays having over twenty-five million faithfuls as the eastern Ismailis progress. The esoteric heart of the Islamic tradition is known under the name of *Tasawwuf*, Sufism in Arabic; in a general manner, correctly translated, it means "the initiation;" and to both Shiite and Sunni orthodoxy, it is from the origins of the prophetical revelation of Islam. It is intimately linked to the esoteric initiatory organization, considering that *el-haqîqah* is the "truth" that vivifies life and allows deep inner understanding of the great road *es-shariyah*—the internalization of the love of God and the contemplation of wisdom. Batin باطن means "occult," inner," "secret of the depth," the esoteric interpretation of what is intimate and hidden; and zahir ظاهر, "the form" - the obvious side of the outside - opposing - the invisible - (the depth - the essence, the one whose - existence - is - hidden; one of the ninety-nine names of Allah—He is the Omniscient, the First and the Last, the Visible and the Hidden, verse 3, sura 57 of Iron (Al-Hadid) in the Koran. The inner, the Self of the individual is a Batin in the world of souls; it elevates a person spiritually, when a person is connected to Allah and cleansed with his light spiritually; because Allah, who cannot be seen but exists in every realm, has the attribute of the Hidden One.

Within the religious circles of Islam, the reason, which is a matter of spiritual intuition, is inaccessible to the faithful who oppose the Sufism, but the concepts of Sufism are of expert natures with on their head the Persian Aga Khan of the Ismaili Nizaris imam, a characteristic of an esoteric doctrine leading the faithful to less focus on form than substance. The Sufi Muslims are people who are searching for the inner "truth" that vivifies the love of God. And often placed in opposition with traditional Islam, Sufism gladly cultivates the idea of the mystery, at the same time believing that the Koran and Muhammad received the esoteric revelations. These ancient practices of a very orthodox teaching of Sufi "paths," Muhammad only shared them with some of his companions; he taught them how to approach the Koranic book, its representation of practical progress of meditation and wisdom; he taught them how to break down the symbolized barrier by "Qaf," the cosmic mountain that separates man from God, and reach the tree of knowledge, the alleged invisible presence of God, through the ascetic experience and the ecstatic union of physical love, and reach the love and knowledge of the Creator, present in the heart of the Sufis believer; and he could put his knowledge in practice without transgressing any kind of law. The Sufi scholar is a fulfillment of truth, knowing that the heart is full of righteous thoughts; he becomes so pure from all imperfection; to devote himself to the service of God and the love of God, he must be detached from the great world in the face of the earth, where all kinds of impurities are thrown. On an equal footing, he must consider the gold coin and the clod of earth without discrimination in comparison to the cloud, which pours its waves everywhere, similar to a motionless and impassive man when the villain tramples. But although subjected to the harshest treatments, it only gives compliant ideals to reach that stage of knowledge.

The British colonial regime of the Indian subcontinent had a British Raj, under the direct administration of the princely states under the suzerainty, headed by a viceroy. Graceful to a certain number of benefits and powers that the Aga Khan had from the hereditary title bore by Nizari Ismaili imams and princes, they benefited from the recognition of the British Raj.

The faithful of the first Aga Khan attributed miracles to Hasan Ali Shah, covering this Iranian born in 1804 with donations and venerated him as a god up to India, where he died in Bombay in 1881. After going through this initiatory method established by the great masters, describing different degrees of spiritual realization, where the soul governed by its passions is called to the degree of the soul that blamed itself to the elevation of the essence, or the embodiment of a specified quality toward the knowledge of God and the appeased spiritual or the immaterial part of a human being, all harmoniously in a calm and sweet feeling, it is difficult to believe that Conrad I was assassinated by those Ismailis or Nizarite Sufis, who instead speak of the extinction and the annihilation (*al-fana*) of the ego to reach the awareness, the action of the presence of God.

In the vocabulary of Islam, these projects corresponding to the recommendations of the detachments that a human must escape to reach all ideas of mystical fusion between man and God consist to the elevation of the spirit in the contemplation of the divine things. On the death of Conrad of Montferrat, assassinated on April 28, 1192, Isabella of Jerusalem, yet pregnant of Maria of Montferrat, was married to the barons of the kingdom Henry of Champagne. He became the king of Jerusalem from 1192 to 1197, chosen for marring the widow of Conrad on May 5, 1192. Henry of Champagne, born on July 29, 1166, died instantly in Acre when he accidentally fell from a window of his palace on September 10, 1197, while the city of Jaffa was besieged by the Sultan Malik al-Adil of Egypt.

Aimery II of Lusignan also married Isabella I of Jerusalem; he also was a widower of Eschiva of Ibelin, the queen consort of Cyprus since 1196. After his marriage, he became king of Jerusalem from 1198 to 1205 since it was necessary to find a reluctant king urgently according to the barons and since the city of Jaffa was in the hands of the Sultan Malik al-Adil. Aimery II of Lusignan was born around 1145 in the Poitou and died on April 1, 1205, at Acre. After his death in the prime of life, Maria of Montferrat, daughter of Conrad of Montferrat and Isabella I of Jerusalem, succeeded him in Jerusalem and became the queen of Jerusalem in 1205 while she was thirteen years old. But it was John of Ibelin, lord of Beirut, who exercised the regency on behalf of the daughter of Henry of Champagne. At the age of seventeen, her uncle, regent John of Ibelin, thought of finding her a husband in 1208; the council of barons decided that it must be John of Brienne.

On September 14, 1210, Maria of Montferrat married John of Brienne; and on October 3, 1210, he was crowned king of the kingdom of Jerusalem with his wife, after giving birth to a daughter by the name of Isabella II of Jerusalem, sometimes called Yolande of Brienne, in 1212; Maria of Montferrat died sometime later. John I of Brienne was king of Jerusalem from 1210 to 1225; after the death of his wife, Maria of Montferrat, in 1212, John of Brienne was accepted by the barons as regent of the kingdom from 1212 to 1225. Born around 1170 to 1175, John of Brienne died on March 27, 1237, in Constantinople, after he definitively left the kingdom of Jerusalem.

Isabella II of Jerusalem, the daughter of John of Brienne and Maria of Montferrat, was the queen of Jerusalem from 1212 to 1228. Born in 1212 as Yolande of Brienne, her birth name, she was also an empress consort of the Holy Roman Empire and a queen consort of Sicily from 1225 to 1228. At age fourteen, multiple enterprises were undertaken without her knowledge to organize her wedding. It turns out that her father wanted to encourage the knights of the Holy Roman Empire to interbreed in large numbers with his family, and the pope was in favor of that same idea, whereas Frederick II, the Germanic emperor, who was to marry the young Yolande of Brienne, just simply wanted to settle in the East to give his empire a Mediterranean dimension and the opportunity to expand his states by that marriage. Without hesitation, the fourth grand master of the Teutonic Knights, the Order of Brothers of the German House of Saint Mary in Jerusalem founded in the year 1190 to help Christians in their pilgrimages to the Holy Land and to establish hospitals; its fourth Grand Master was called Hermann von Salza and served from 1209 to 1239; he was known as the advisor and faithful friend of Frederick II of the Holy Empire and had twenty years of experience for serving repeatedly as a mediator between the emperor and the papacy; that experience led him this time also in mediation representing the pope to organize the wedding of Isabella with Emperor Frederick II, while Jean de Brienne, Isabelle's father, was still king of kings of Jerusalem. The bishop

James of Patti, brought to Acre by sea, equipped with fourteen imperial ships, immediately celebrated the marriage by proxy of Isabella and Frederick in August 1225. On the other hand, the crowning of the new empress followed their marriage, and the imperial ships set sail toward the direction of Brindisi in Italy, taking Isabella, her father, and several family members. Upon their arrival in Italy, a wedding worthy of nobility between the daughter of John of Brienne and Emperor Frederick II of Hohenstaufen was again celebrated on November 9, 1225, to seal their alliance. Without waiting for anything, Emperor Frederick II, who saw the opportunity to expand his states, dryly requested with a stone-face expression indicating his greedy desire to take control of everything, and urgently required by a theory of vanity and a doctrine of perverse opinion that the kingdom of Jerusalem be immediately ceded to him, the day after their marriage in luxury manners, knowing that John of Brienne was still the regent of the kingdom of Jerusalem. By the choice of his ideas in the deep hollow of his head, in the more or less distant areas of the recesses, were evolving other empty perverse theories that one would qualify today as pedophilia; ignoring what this great man, who paid no attention to anything was capable of doing; thus despite the young age of Isabella, he decided immediately to consume his newly married wife at the age of fourteen by having sex with her, causing damage to the higher and critical level of the forebay. After these perversions, he added another imperfection in his record covered with burrs by raping one of his cousins who came to attend the wedding.

This characteristic smudge committed by a distinctive character produced three illegitimate children in his clandestine relations with Bianca Lancia while married to Yolande of Brienne. The excommunicated since September 28, 1227, who took the kingship of Jerusalem from John of Brienne despite promises that he would remain king until his death, got the pope's decision to lift his excommunication in 1230.

In the history of the kingdom of Jerusalem, the life of Isabella II of Jerusalem, her reign, and her marriage marked a turning point, rising above the mediocrity in the so-called Holy Land. On April 25, 1228, she died, leaving a son by the name of Conrad IV to her husband.

Frederick II or Frederick of Hohenstaufen, whom Pope Gregory IX called the Antichrist, was born near Ancona, specifically in Jesi, on December 26, 1194. He reigned as king of Sicily from 1198 to 1250 and emperor of the Romans from 1220 to 1250. He was king of Germany from 1212 to 1250 and king of Jerusalem from 1225 to 1250. He became the prodigious pacificator, the transformer of things, the amazement of the world, the one who could not disappear.

During or after his death, the emperor, asleep of a magical sleep characterizing Etna, the highest volcano in Europe and one of the most active in the world, located near the city of Catania in Sicily, an autonomous region of Italy, was not dead asleep in the depths of a cave in the collective consciousness. Frederick II died near San Severo on December 13, 1250, in Fiorentino. And despite the expectation of his return after his death, he still remained dead. Let's note here that the list of the kings of France are not included in the list of the Western kings who posteriorly claimed to be kings of Jerusalem from the disappearance of Christian states of the so-called Holy Land.

The Arab family of Kurdish origin was occupying a vast region called Kurdistan, nowadays divided between the central and eastern Turkey, western Iran, northern Iraq, and northern Syria. And in that region, the descendant of Ayyub—a Kurdish officer who was serving the Zengid dynasty of emirs of the Turkish dynasty—reigned on the Muslims of the East from 1127 to 1222. Ayyub was also known as the father of Saladin, the chief executive of the Ayyubid dynasty, who ruled Egypt from 1169 to 1250 and Syria from 1174 to 1260, including the ancestor of the Ayyubid dynasty. As a craftsman of the reconquest of Jerusalem, Saladin was known as the main opponent of the Franks by Muslims installed during the last third of the twelfth century in Jerusalem. The recapture of the Christian kingdom of Jerusalem took place on July 4, 1187, during the Battle of Hattin, near Lake Tiberias in Galilee, between the forces of Saladin and the armed forces of the Christian kingdom of Jerusalem, directed by Guy of Lusignan.

The Battle of Hattin ended by the overwhelming victory of the forces of Saladin, opening wide the doors of Palestine. The one of Jerusalem to the crusaders started by Saladin's army on September 20 and ended on October 2, 1187, by the siege of Jerusalem. That Third Crusade brought the almost total collapse of the kingdom of Jerusalem. It allowed the imprisonment of King Guy of Lusignan and the fine f lowers of the nobility of the kingdom. In the history of the nobility of the kingdoms, Genghis Khan is recognized as the one who founded the Mongol Empire or the Turco-Mongol Empire in the early thirteenth century. This largest contiguous empire that ever existed stretched from the Mediterranean to the Pacific and from Siberia to India and Indochina. Genghis Khan was proclaimed King Khan between 1187 and 1196. To enable him the control of eastern Mongolia, he attacked the Tatars (Turkic people of Eastern Europe and northern Asia) and Tayichiud (members of a Mongol tribe present in central and southern Mongolia) before the formation of the Mongol Empire; the present Buryatia, Siberia, after defeating the territory of Merkit, members of a Turkish Mongol tribe present in central Mongolia, from which his mother originated; and the Naimans, also members of a Turkish Mongol tribe present in central Mongolia at the west of the current Mongolia in 1204.

The members of a Kereit tribe known as the Turkish Mongol, present in central Mongolia, were already regrouped in 1203 after killing Toghril, who was the chief of the tribe of Kereit in Mongolia at the end of year 1100 before the formation of the Mongol Empire. They were overwhelmingly Nestorian Christians—a doctrine claiming Christianity and saying that two entities, one divine and the other human, coexisted in Jesus Christ. They served as the spiritual guides to princes and emperors and had the titles as "Supreme Teacher" given by a Tangut Xixia King. The conquest of the Tangut kingdom, a people of Asia, whose history dates back from the Tang Dynasty, and who formed an empire known under the name of Western Xia, also known as Xixia of the Xia Western Dynasty, reigned from 1032 to 1227, and its conquest began in 1205.

It was the Chinese who were governing the kingdom of the Western Xia while the Tanguts governed the Tangut Empire and the Minyak by Tibetans. The Tanguts lived on the Tibetan Plateau in the seventh century and migrated in the Gansu Corridor in the thirteenth century in the northwestern province of the People's Republic of China, stuck between the Mongolian Plateau in the north and the foothills of the Tibetan Plateau in the south. This people of Tibeto-Burman language were located in the northwest of China, corresponding approximately to the Chinese provinces of the current Gansu, Shaanxi, and Ningxia, which founded the state of the territory of Tanguts and was the first country conquered by the Mongols led by Genghis Khan. The kingdom of Tangut Xixia resisted until 1209 and submitted itself to the Mongols in 1227, who founded the Yuan dynasty. In these territories, under the Yuan dynasty, slavery affected a large part of the Chinese population, according to certain authors. The Mongol Empire did not include the territories of the former Russian Empire, Indochina, or China, which was only one part subjected to the superior authority force of the Mongol Empire; and China is not also assimilated to the Mongol Empire.

The freed slaves, who were forming a militia in the service of various Muslim sovereigns, receiving a salary at the end of their training, were Mamluks. In Baghdad, the guard of the Abbasid caliphs was formed by the first Mamluk members at the ninth century. The Mamluks are non-Muslim captives recruited into the source of the current Turkestan, the Caucasus (Circassians, Georgians, etc.), the eastern Slavs of the Eastern Europe, or the Kipchaks of southern Russia.

The highest functions of the Mamluk system were reserved for men born slaves, and it was a system of a ruling class highly original and unique to Islam. Some Mamluks occupied important positions of command, although their positions were not hereditary among the captives of Muslim slaves. The caliphs took power from the Umayyads in 750 of our era; they reigned from the present Iraq, in their capital called Baghdad, for most of their ruling period that the caliph Al-Mansur founded in 762, after the capital Kufa. The name of the Abbasid dynasty was taken from Abbas ibn Abd al-Muttalib, the youngest uncle of Muhammad, and is a descendant of the third of the Islamic caliphates, who succeeded Muhammad, the prophet of Islam.

After the decline of their dynasty, they refocused in 1261 in Cairo, the capital of Mamluks up to 1517, during the conquest of Egypt by the Ottoman Empire. Muslims were recruiting children among those captured in non-Muslim countries so that they could latter wage war against Muslim countries since the rules prohibited Muslims from waging war between them. So to circumvent these rules, they selected children on the criteria of the absence of bonds, the lake of capacity resistance, and raised them as future Mamluks by inculcating them a religious and military education, far from their countries of origin.

They were freed in adulthood, and equipment and wages were provided by the sultanate or the emir—military leader, linked to his house, the house of

Mamluks, formed at the same time by him and his boss; Mamluks preserved the strong spirit of body that characterized them throughout their lives, and this system lasted from the ninth to the nineteenth centuries. Then at the service of the Ayyubid dynasty of the sultan, they were enrolled in the servile guard in Egypt; and on the Seventh Crusade, they overthrew the Ayyubid sultan in 1250 under the leadership of King Louis IX of France, the forty-fourth king of France also known under the name of St. Louis.

It was of course in accordance with the will of Louis VIII—his father, the one called "Louis the Lion"—that Queen Blanche of Castile exercised the regency of the kingdom until the adulthood of the new monarch at the death of his father, whereas only twelve years old. The Seventh Crusade from 1244 in Egypt was decided by the king; he and his mother left the kingdom of France in 1248 and in 1244, landed in Egypt. And it was until 1250 that the army regained its freedom, and France, which had no power to defend itself, spent four years to organize a defense against the Mamluks for the release of the kingdom of Jerusalem. In 1254, after the death of Queen Blanche of Castile, his mother, the crusade ended with the return of the king to France. King Louis IX of France died of dysentery during the Eighth Crusade on August 25, 1270, in Tunisia.

This nonhereditary Mamluk dynasty had a history of two lineages. From 1250 to 1382, Bahrites were known in Egyptian history as the first Mamluk dynasty to rule Egypt. They were young Turk Kipchaks sold as slaves to Egyptian merchants. And from 1382 to 1517, the Burjites formed the second dynasty of Mamluks reigned in Egypt. Because of their origins, they were also called the Circassian Mamluks, slaves taken in Circassia, a region of Caucasus. The Ayyubids dynasty, of the sultan as-Salih Ayyub, bought a thousand of these Bahrite Mamluks from Egyptian merchants and taught them the profession of arms for his protection. But in 1250, they were responsible for the fall of the Ayyubid dynasty of sultans at the death of Sultan as-Salih Ayyub by killing his heirs. And for Shajar al-Durr, the slave favorite wife of the sultan as-Salih Ayyub, to be maintained in power, she was forced to marry Izz al-Din Aybak, the first Mamluk sultan of Egypt, and she reigned with the title of sultan from 1250 until her death in 1257, killed by the order of her husband in Egypt. The reign of Aybak, founder of the Bahri Mamluk dynasty from the Turkish origin, lasted from 1250 to 1257, assassinated by the Mamluks. That same year of 1257, his son Al-Mansur Nur ad-Din Ali, at eleven years old, was proclaimed sultan of Egypt. Their dynasty was established by him, helped by the Mongol forces and allied troops in 1258, destroying the Abbasid caliphate and making Cairo the capital of the empire, until November 12, 1259, when he was overthrown by Qutuz, his tutor. The power of the Mamluk dynasty in itself was multiplied many times by forty-nine sultans. The most powerful power of its time stretched from 1250 over Egypt, Syria and the Arabian Peninsula up to the seizure of power in 1517 by the reign of Sultan Selim I of the Ottomans. They reigned over the Islamic state and retained an important role in the province until 1811, during the massacre of their leaders by Mehemet Ali.

From 1299 to 1923, the abolished Mamluk dynasty on November 1, 1922, which gave way to the Republic of Turkey, as well as part of its former national multilingual and multiterritories, passed under many other states of domination, and granted various types of autonomy during the course of centuries; and its type of autonomy before its independence in the second half of the twentieth century, was the Ottoman Empire and lasted for almost 624 years. Then gradually reduced until the end of the First World War, it extended over three continents and occupied all the ancient territory designating all Anatolia; nowadays 97 percent of the territory of all the Asian is part of Turkey and the 3 percent located in Eastern Thrace; a plain in Armenia, the Armenian high plateau in the western part of Azerbaijan, from the Nakhichevan enclave to the south of Georgia, at the northwestern Iran, to the eastern part of Turkey; one of the three "peninsulas" of the Southern Europe in the Balkan, a region bordered on three sides by seas: to the west, by the Adriatic and Ionian; to the south, the Aegean and the Sea of Marmara; and to the east, the Black Sea; the region of communication at the perimeter of the Black Sea represents Syria, the Arab country of the Middle East, located on the eastern coast of the Mediterranean Sea in the Levantine Basin. The current Syria, current Lebanon, the current Jordan, and Palestine were in a region of countries that were at a time grouped during the Ottoman Empire.

They were distinctly known under the name of Phoenicia, Palestine, Assyria, and part of the western Mesopotamia. Palestine, located between the Mediterranean Sea and the desert at the east of Jordan and the northern Sinai, designated the Middle East region, attested since Herodotus. Galilee, Judea, and Samaria were known as its regions, limited by Phoenicia and Mount Lebanon at the north and to the south by Edom and Philistia.

The history of this region would not cease to intrigue us by its occupation dating back for centuries already. We know that, from 390 up to the seventh century, Judea, Perea, and Samaria were part of the Byzantine province, with the capital as Caesarea. In 614, the Sasanian Empire became the master of the place; but before its loss by the Syrian conquest of 634 to 636, it was reannexed in 628. At that period, it was called "The first Palestine."

From 390, the Beit She'an Valley, the ten cities of the Decapolis at the east of Jordan, Galilee, and the Jezreel Valley were part of the Byzantine province, including the southern Golan Heights and the Jordan Valley; this time, Scythopolis was its capital, also known as Beit She'an, one of the oldest cities in Palestine as part of Capernaum and Nazareth, like the big cities of the province, as the second Palestine. And the third covered the area of Negev, covering the largest part of the district of Palestine and Edom and Jordan at the south, with the capital as Petra. The Roman emperor diocese of the East, the Roman Empire of the late time was the master, up to its final loss by the Muslim conquest of the seventh century. To the present day, Palestine is not known as a clearly defined area; Mesopotamia, located in the Fertile Crescent between the Tigris and Euphrates, is a historical region of the Middle East, and its biggest part corresponds to the current Iraq.

The edge of the Arabian Peninsula is at the junction between the southwest continent of Asia and Africa. Because of its large reserves of natural gas and oil, this vast peninsula plays a fundamental political role in this region, which is part of the Middle East. Egypt located on the southern coast of the eastern Mediterranean—the Levantine basin—is essentially a country northeast of the African continent. Its current space was once geographically the one of Ancient Egypt, and the part consisting of the Sinai Peninsula, which is located in Asia, is the northeastern Egyptian territory and a part of the coast of the North Africa at the north of the Sahara Desert and the Sahel—a biome of natural community of flora and fauna, corresponding to grasslands of savannas with few trees, and of temperate shrub lands from mild to the warm summer, and cool like the winter in the West.

This Sahara region, located at the northernmost part of Africa, covers huge tracts of territory from Algeria to Egypt, Libya, Mali, Mauritania, Morocco, Niger, Sudan, Chad, Tunisia, and the disputed territory of Western Sahara, claimed by Morocco, which controls 80 percent. These ten states cover an extensive eco desert region open to the galaxies of planets and stars, naturally with its large community of flora and fauna.

The prefecture "Imperial Gate" of the department of Istanbul today, was known as a synecdochic metonym for the central government of the Ottoman Empire; it became known as the "High Gate," referring first to a palace in Bursa. According to its origins, it was at the gate of his palace that the ruler announced his official decisions and judgments in the old Oriental practice. The name given to this gate to qualify the monumental honor "Gate" leading to the great vizier courtyards, seat of the Sultan's government in Constantinople, was the "Sublime Ottoman Porte" or simply the "Sublime Door" during the period of the Ottoman Empire. The Western state diplomats used it in the context of diplomacy, as a metaphor for the Ottoman Empire, and as part of its international relations.

Let me first clarify these terms, "international relation" used in the context of diplomacy by the Westerners to avoid certain ambiguities before continuing. During the second constitutional era, revolution and reformed replaced Imperial governments with this list composed of territories that were at various times Dominions; they were known as territories of Australia, South Africa, Canada, Ceylon, rebaptized Sri Lanka in 1972, India, Ireland, New Zealand, Pakistan, and Newfoundland. Colony countries are state powers, called metropolis, established in a region more or less distant, occupied by settlers of a stronger country, initially a foreign control of another country, maintaining a political, economic, cultural, and social process in the country called colonized country.

Their implantations in a foreign country consisted of the exploitation of resources in that area; at the same time, its development value was permanently integrated in a colonial empire. This exercise of the grabbing of regions was a stranglehold on an ideology whose precept was conquest. Protectorates are one of the forms of colonial subjugation of a political regime. These political regimes are considered as being under the close influence of the powerful, protective states, assuming the management of diplomacy, foreign trade, and eventually the army of the protected state. It is clearly and simply different from colonization. Mandate is an official order or the authority to carry out a policy under the League of Nations.

German colonies or possessions of the Ottoman Empire before World War II were entrusted to victorious colonial powers, which were Australia, South Africa, Belgium, France, Japan, New Zealand, and the United Kingdom, by article 22 of the Covenant of June 28, 1919, of the League of Nations. The British Empire or British Colonial Empire, under the sovereignty of the British Crown, met all the criteria mentioned above as the first world power that progressively established colonies overseas from the late sixteenth century. In 1922, at its peak, it had about four hundred million inhabitants—that is, a quarter of the world population. In the fields of politics, law, linguistics, and culture, its colony settlement and population extended over 29.8 million km2 about 22 percent of the emerged land, and its heritage migration was staggering.

In the Arava Valley at the north of Aqaba, Israel shares a border with Jordan as an Arab country of western Asia. Surrounded at the west by the West Bank and Israel, its territory is a constitutional monarchy along the Jordan River and the Dead Sea. Its region at the west of the Jordan River includes Jericho, Hebron, Nablus, Bethlehem, and other colonies. In 1948, this region became part of Jordan; and since the Six-Day War of 1967, it became occupied by Israel, which was granted an autonomy limit to Palestine in 1993 by a signed agreement. And since then, this area continued to be a conflict region caused by Israel.

Even as some data placed the origin of the Jewish state in that region in the eleventh century BC, don't forget that Jews are never native of that territory, which in its early history was also dominated by other known powerful nations, like the Babylonians, Persians, Greeks of Alexander the Great, Syrians, Romans, etc., as Western civilizations, which reigned there, except a brief period of domination by the Crusaders and under the British mandate. Saudi Arabia is to the south, Iraq at the east, and Syria at the north, with access to the Red Sea through the Gulf of Aqaba. This region was culturally Arab and Muslim from the seventh century. The Ammonites, Edomites, and Moabites, as historical people, established their capitals there. The Akkadians, the Assyrians, the Pharaonic Egypt, and the Jewish Hasmonean dynasty, which came to power in Judea during the Maccabean revolt, also dominated this region.

Israel is living in the contestation of the world opinion since 1948. The Jewish state fought a war by the name of the Six-Day War against Egypt, Jordan, and Syria, from June 5 to 10, 1967. The jostling of their opponents on all fronts ended in the loss of the Gaza Strip and the Sinai Peninsula, known before that war as the territory of Egypt. The Golan Heights was amputated from Syria and Jordan, from the West Bank and East Jerusalem. We must a thousand times say that no Arab country had recognized the existence of the Israel state, yet some annexed territories such as part of the West Bank are still occupied by Israel and still influenced the geopolitics of the region up to today. Despite the adoption of the resolution "242 1967" of the United Nations Security Council, demanding the immediate end of the military occupation, it is still not applied and frequently invoked in peace negotiations in the Middle East.

These territories, which were under the Jordanian and Egyptian control before 1967, originally known as the "Palestinian Territories," are territories that the United Nations Security Council is asking the evacuation of Israel up to today in vain; knowing that the majority of the powerful Western decision makers have Jewish blood and nationalities of those countries; and by scrutinizing the American parliament in majority Jewish, this issue of occupation is far from being settled.

Comprehensively, the green line formerly separating the city of West Jerusalem, the official capital of Israel since 1949 and East Jerusalem, the part that was to be the Palestinian state—marking the line of demarcation of the Armistice Arab-Israeli Agreements of 1949 signed between February 24 and July 20, 1949, between Israel, Egypt, Lebanon, Transjordan, and Syria, known as the neighboring countries of Israel, establishing the temporary armistice lines—are not respected under the Israeli Civil Administration but occupied these territories since 1967. As the UN Security Council is saying loudly, the acquisition of territory by force is inadmissible, and the legislative administrative measures taken by Israel have no legal validity in law, thus constituting a flagrant violation of the Geneva Convention. Israel must end the occupation of Jerusalem as reaffirmed by resolution 476 and resolution 478. Moses, the greatest legislator of the desert tribes, reveals that the name Lebanon, the state of the Middle East western Asia, shares its borders with the state of Syria at the north and at the east on 376 kilometers and at the south on 79 kilometers with Israel, bordered at the west by the Levantine basin, the eastern part of the Mediterranean Sea with 220 kilometers of coastline. These markings, found everywhere in the Bible, are found at the very heart of the so-called Promised Land. The Levantine Sea is bordered by the Asian coasts of the Middle East and Africa and the islands of the Hellenic arc. Almost all major Hebrew prophets, who announced the coming of the Messiah, in the shadow of this ancient Syrian massif, known as "Mount Lebanon," was also revealed by Moses, but so little is mentioning Lebanon in the history of civilization, if not the only citation with a kind of ideal fervor in Deuteronomy, in the book of Kings and Chronicles, up to the Psalms. We forget that this country that we all know at the end of the First World War only became a country in 1920. Since the division of the Ottoman territory on the basis of the autonomous entity of Mount Lebanon, called the "Greater Syria," the Western camp plays the same partition in the Palestinian region: Lebanese, Persians, and Berbers.

This division accredits the idea of the Saudi Arabian Sunni, willing to endorse an expedition against the eternal Persian and Shiite enemy, headlight of the world of Islam, which is expanding its competition. Rightly, Iran has the strongest supporters in the region, with the Shiite majority represented by the Hezbollah in Lebanon, described as the land of milk and honey in the region of

Greater Lebanon of the biblical times, and the Hamas in Palestine. This strong cleavage that already resisted for more than fifteen centuries in North Africa and that always existed between the first Berber occupants and the Arab conquerors tends to be recovered with mixed success to the benefit of the imperialists of the nineteenth century.

The West still thinks that it will be possible to isolate good number of components of powers from the traditional resistance lines to then slaughter them more easily at the open sky, with a great fineness of spirit and ingenuity of no-guilt; it is difficult to understand, to grasp because of its given character. These traditional lines of resistance of the Middle East—which are Iran, Libya, Palestine, Afghanistan, Pakistan, and Lebanon, which were the homeland of the Phoenicians, a branch of the Canaanite people—made the Western policy fail in the usual logic.

Since the dawn of time, world governance so functioned to prevent Africa and these countries to have a well-oiled relationship, but the West finds itself obliged to remove the mask of a simple supporter to the negotiation of a minimum agreement; on the other hand, the posture of the military operations process of yore to arm the rebellion was not new and was accomplished once more in Iraq and with the same tactics to later on justify the war delivered in the open sky against Iraq, against Libya, and today against Syria.

On September 17, 1978, two framework agreements were signed. One was for establishing peace between Israel and Egypt, and the other the Palestinian question aimed at solving the crisis in the Middle East. The path of Anwar el-Sadat negotiations with Israel had two factors: the situation resulting from the 1973 War ended by a defeat of a deep economic crisis and the breakdown of very serious famine riots in January 1977 in Cairo and in other Egyptian cities. Henry Kissinger offered an honorable way out to Anwar el-Sadat in a peace conference in Geneva. This proposal was a massive help to let Egypt come out from the economic slump. Several agreements were therefore passed from 1973 to 1975. Thus, allowing Egypt to recover the Suez Canal and oil wells; in particular, the Suez Canal was opened to Israeli ships by Egypt. On November 19, 1977, Anwar el-Sadat delivered a speech before the Knesset during his famous trip to Jerusalem. He decided to consider a completely new method, to bypass all the formalities after the failure of another American-Soviet initiative in October 1977, described in his autobiography. And then Jimmy Carter, the U.S. president of that time, invited Menachem Begin, the Israeli prime minister, and Anwar el-Sadat in September 1978 at Camp David. These negotiations ended by an accomplished signature of peace agreements. The basis of a separate peace treaty between Egypt and Israel was the first, signed in March 1979. The other guaranteed autonomy to the Palestinians, living in the West Bank and Gaza, and the final status of the territories was to be negotiated separately after the administration of local elected officials during an interim period of five years. This last one was rejected by the Arab countries because it guaranteed neither the possibility of an independent Palestinian state nor the withdrawal of Israeli troops from the occupied territories since 1967. Clearly, Menachem Begin made it clear that he would continue his politics of land confiscation for the implementation of Jewish settlements and categorically opposed any restitution of territories. The negative consequences of this failed separate peace were the exclusion of Egypt from the Arab League and the transfer of the headquarters in Tunis, which was only reinstated in 1987. His betrayal to the Camp David negotiations prevented the existence of the Palestinian state, referred to in the UN agreements of November 1947, and cost him his life. He was assassinated on October 6, 1981, by a commando of an Islamist group during a parade celebrating the victory of 1973.

Israel became a traditional ally of the United States and NATO, cooperating for a military goal and other political purposes. Since then, having a strong nuclear power with tens of billions of U.S. dollars, which are delivered to them every year by the military-industrial complex of the United States, Israel believed to be above all in the land of someone else, occupying their territory so-called their Promised Land.

You would have not come to me if I did not love you and if I had not given you that unconditional love and if I would have not been content to see you in my land when I met you for the first time; because the heart that loved is not a knee that can be bent, so let that heart that love, love the one that the eye of the heart loves. Therefore, contrary to you, I have loved you; because the eye goes where the eye of the loving heart does not ask it to go but goes where it wants to go.

And if you refused to the heart that loved to love what it loved, it will hate you and be content to love what it loved. Because the foot does not go where it does not want; unless it is forced, just like you were forcing your way in my land; but no matter the heart that loved, skinny or fat, because it is said that only the son of thy mother, who truly and unconditionally loves you, could tell you that your mouth has a bad breath, not as a fatality, but to correct the situation. And only a true friend would be content to warn you of your faults, not as an insult, but for you to be aware, without compromising your qualities. Only your spirit and discernment, which apprehend an awareness and wakefulness, may result in a tangible reality and conceive a logical projection. The Kamite community of the world has already conceived that logical projection since it received you with opened arms for a better future. It is a fact of realities appearing concrete to us today, which was not there at the time of the civilizing foundation by our ancestors, as real as the state of Israel today, which takes its very gracious host for granted, since its projection effort to form a Jewish state of Israel by Theodor Herzl, known in Hebrew as Ze'ev Binyamin (וְיָמִינְב בָּאז); an Austrian Jew journalist and writer, born on May 2, 1860, in Budapest (Austria-Hungary), and considered as the father of the state of Israel, who promoted the Jewish migration to Palestine. He was the founder of the Zionist movement from August 29 to 31, 1897, at the Basel Congress in Switzerland as a higher institution of the World Zionist Organization; he was the founder of the Jewish National Fund for the purchase of lands in Palestine and the author of *Der Judenstaat* (*The Jewish State*) in 1896 up to its realization by the UN in 1948. He died on July 3, 1904, in Erlach, Austria.

Thou hast received them, thou hast given them hospitality, and thou hast given them lands. But know that as a Kamite descendant from the cradle of humanity, the right to dream for a world corresponding to your reality cannot be denied because you're the first race placed in this world, but you never proclaimed to be elected. And neither your black children nor mixed race children like Arabs will never proclaimed to be elected. The history of the chosen race started in Gen. 12:7, when God promised its land of hosts to all the seeds of Abram and Sarai, whose names are changed to Abraham and Sarah, and not to his family members, known as the grandfather of Rebekah, Nehor, and Lot, the ancestor of the Moabites. The books of Kings in the Bible mentioned that kingdom, following the military encirclement of the Moabites.

Ramses II spoke of Moab (*mu' bu*), ruled by kings from an uncertain time, by two inscriptions of his time. They descended from Amor, son of Canaan; migrated toward the land of Canaan; and were submitted by Moses, Gen. 19:36–38. Therefore, if this land was promised to all Abram's posterities, then it must really be to all the seeds of Abraham and Sarai and the child of the servant by the name of Hagar, the mother of Ishmael, from which Muslims and Arabs have descended, according to the Bible. We must once again specify that we are talking about the Canaanite land, therefore the land of a black tribe, which became the land of Israel. Isn't that funny?

Today we still see the opposite of the actual facts, the legend of the emergence of the Israeli people in a country that is not theirs and of which no other recorded reference is mentioning the entry in the delta or other foreign people living in that region with a known Israeli ancestor, but just the data from the Bible. In any case, one thing is certain, and it is shouting out in a loud voice that the people of Israel, who are claiming Jerusalem today, have no ancestor descended from Judea.

The three kingdoms, Edom, Judah, and Israel, which Num, 21:31 quotes as Reuben, Gad, and Manasseh, from the twelve tribes of Israel, shared the kingdom of Moab between them. And 1 Kings 9:20–21 said that they were the servants of Solomon. And the Amorites, a group of Semitic nomads scattered in tribes in Mesopotamia and Syria, were—according to Gen. 13:18—those who settled at Mamre, where Abram bought the land for them. These Amorites were living in southern Canaan, in the city known as Hebron. They controlled the upper Mesopotamia, and their main centers were known by the names of Assur and Mari in the Middle Euphrates, in Mesopotamia. Let's note here that the word *Semitic*, used since the 1770s, referring most commonly to the Semitic languages, is forged from the proper name "Shem" (שֵׁם in Hebrew, سام in Arabic) as one of the sons of Noah, is a name, a renown and a prosperity. Elam, Asshur, Arphaxad, Lud, and Aram were his children in addition to daughters. Such are the descendants of Shem, according to their families and their languages, according to their territories and their tribes (Gen. 10:31); Bereshit, meaning "in the beginning," a great mystery of the divine determination; suggesting the division of time, of light and darkness, and good and evil (Gen. 1:1–6:8); the Semitic language family is a name of African Proto-Semitic origin, currently present in North and East Africa, West Asia, and Malta. In the first millennium BC, after the expansion of a range of other languages, grouping languages as Aramaic, Semitic dialects, found in several languages in Ethiopia, of which Amharic and Tigrinya are attested from the third or fourth century of our era, and not the Western Aramaic, the dialect of the Jews of the European origin, was in no way part of the original descendants of the Judean people, who were an ethnic group of the black race. The texts written in Ge'ez are the first appeared writings of the Ethiopian Semitic languages. And they explained the entire outflow of the first migration from Ur in Mesopotamia in search of a promised land because, according to them, God called Abraham and his barren wife and promised him prosperity. The existence and the future of the so-called chosen people depend on this act; it is not simply a matter of a carnal descendant, but to all those who the same faith has made sons of Abraham as indicated in Rom. 4:11–12; an age when moral, the consciousness, the inner-self, did not always intentionally reprobate false statements, but the humanity of God, my God, gave him the law, and he took the moral law as a progressive knowledge. The forgers used the pen mightier than the sword for the forgery of the black history, and everyone believed that their forgery was the truth. They forgot that the value of history resides in the perception of those who evaluate it as a scientific model—a truth that a white scientist was not willing to accept as being of nature.

Really, what I am is not important in the eyes of the white race, who qualifies me as a monster, searching himself in me. As a first illustration, they decided to replace my genius by a Caucasian in this world and named me Nigger, controversial and pejorative, and promoted to mask my specific universality of the human cultural aspirations. So generally, for you, white racist, I willingly accept that I am a Nigger, and what can you do about it? Nothing. But the black history is more powerful, and its contributions throughout nature will still well live long after death. And after your death, I will remain your shadow, your black shadow forever. The history of Ameru, the one I am referring to, possessed a principal ancient oral tradition that may seem a fable but contains more detailed elements of truth in the Jewish mythology. Surprisingly, the tribes of Kenya intrigue the Westerners. The biblical similarities concerning the ancient history of Ameru have a close true narrow link to the one of the Israeli tribes, adopted by the Judaic religion, if we follow the example of the time of the Jewish Falasha from Ethiopia; in Amharic, *falasha*, meaning "exiled" or "immigrants," the Beta Israel, the "house of Israel" (Falasha in Hebrew מישאלפ, in Ge'ez ፈላሻ, or Beta Israel in Hebrew אתיב לארשי, and in Ge'ez ቤት እስራኤል, is an origin poorly defined, but in the sense of the "family of Israel," the term *esra'elawi* (Israelites) represents my return to Israel.

Even as my strong original religious particularisms are reduced by a thorough redefinition of my identity, to consider myself henceforth as the Orthodox

Judaism, a big part of the Old and New Testament tells us the story of Moses, a leading figure, similar to the one of the Ameru at the Ancient Egypt (Misiri). The Misirian origin of People's Oral Tradition of Ancient Egyptian, known as a concept of ancient black African genealogy, presents the story of a baby in a reed basket that became a leader and a prophet; the killing of newborns by a tyrannical king, and Aaron, represented as a magic spear, an exodus, the splitting and the crossing of water by an entire nation. Shameful but true, it tells how the Amerus were made slaves by the red men, "redcoats," the Nguuntune at Mbwaa or Mbwa.

The anthropological research concerning this Meru story led to determine that these Nguuntunes were probably of Arab origin and possibly on the island of Mbwaa or in the current Yemen at the Lamu Archipelago or the island of Kenya at the coast of the Indian Ocean, composed of Lamu islands, where the island cities of Kiwayu, Manda, Manda Toto, Ndau, Pate, and Uvondo are located. Their exodus was done through a large portion of water. Graceful to the use of magic on a dry corridor, they crossed to the Tana Basin, the longest river in Kenya. At seven hundred kilometers long, it takes its source at the west of the Nyeri from the Aberdare Mountains up to the hills of Marsabit, before its final settling in the Mount Kenya region. A red volcano was born there about three million years ago at the opening of the East African Rift. Their stories seem to agree with the two versions of the northern and eastern branches. This story is trivialized by the Westerners, who in any case have falsified the great mysteries of Africa and wrapped them in a white sheet. But the great Meru Empire, which draws its origin from the ancient Nilotic and which is known as a kingdom that developed a civilization toward 300 BC up to AD 100, their story has not been proven beyond doubt by European scholars. On the other hand, without any doubt, they confirmed the history of black slavery in the Bible, generally accepted since the dawn of time. I will also quote the story of a factual truth concerning Euclid, the greatest mathematician of all time, who was born, grew up, was educated, and worked in Africa, and whom the European scholars qualified as Greek knowing that he could in no way be Greek or white since he had never traveled outside the African continent. But Thomas Jefferson, the third President of the United States, said that the work of Euclid would be difficult to the understanding of a black man, forgetting that he was educated by blacks in Africa.

Let's not forget that many scientists qualified as ancient Greek scientists were born, raised, and educated in Africa. Their fake portraits were drawn after their death and probably were all black Africans, the authentic Negroes. In the case of Euclid, his portrait was made 2,000 years after his death, 2,300 years ago in Africa. It is time for us to teach the truth to our children, to review and clear the erroneous statement that fills our history books. They must know that science is a gift of ancient Africa to the modern world, that it is an African who is the father of architecture, that it is an African who is the first scientist in recorded history, that it is an African by the name of Imhotep who is the father of medicine, that Africans were the bearers of light and still are light, and that it is foreigners in darkness who were coming and still come to look for light among African, that is why he is belittling. And it is known that the one who belittled the other is nothing because you have to belittle to feel superior. So, Greece is not the place where the Western civilization was born, knowing that all the early Greek scientists lived in Africa. The Ahmes Papyrus, renamed Rhind after a name of the mathematician who bought it, measuring about thirty-two centimeters wide and five meters long, was our primary source of the older information on the mathematics of the ancient civilizations of the Nile valley. This papyrus was found by the Scottish Egyptologist Alexander Henry Rhind in the ruins of a small monument near the Ramesseum at Thebes in 1858.

It is from the Fifteenth Dynasty, at the end of the second intermediate period, around 1680 to 1620 BC, and written around four thousand years ago by an African named Ahmes and dated by himself in year 33 before our era. This papyrus was carefully assembled in a roll of fourteen leaves. The prejudices of the European scientists made all texts of African books, be Europeanized, according to persons or European cities, to control the thought of man and for him to remain at the door of servitude and for him not to care about his actions. My goal is to make the black history known as the history of the world, responding deeply to the universal questions, for Africa is the birthplace of the native of all human beings, black or white. Our history is the compass that tells us who we are, where we come from, and where we are going.

The Bible and other holy books do not tell the truth and contribute to maintain and put people in confusion. They lie by telling us that ancient Africa practiced slavery, while there is no document showing a slave in Egypt since the word *slave* does not exist in hieroglyph. In reality, the word *bak*, which means "servant," is a free man and paid for his work, not a slave in Ancient Egypt as implied by historians. The falsifiers of our history want us to believe that the word *hm* is designated as "master" and "slave" at the same time. *Hm* is applied to pharaohs, priests, artisans, etc., in a religious sense, denoting the "servant." From the scribe, *hm* = *f* is translated as "king" - His Majesty and the wife as *hm.t* (Hemet).

It is normal that dissatisfaction be expressed for a vigorous change and more equitability in our history to the common interest of all and not just of a tiny handful of the wealthy people that have changed the reality of history, seized by fear and selfishness. I do not know how to express myself better concerning the authors of the Bible with the first racist text, better known by the title of the curse and prejudice against the ancient black African, established with the heart of power and by the ways of domination. Religion, representing God, which urged its members to bring all their support of the invisible to the visible world for the needs of spirituality, has demonstrated its strong desire to reduce one of His creatures as slave. But your secular moral authority will be evaluated in the light of your standpoints, between the living and the dead, by that spirituality. The cosmic gave a specific and honest history to blacks as a worthy ancestor of humanity. But the peregrinations of the Jewish people in the Christian religion and Arabs in Islam without any spiritual religious basis wanted the father of human history to have a particularly deceptive destiny for him to influence his culture for the benefit of a political history, which certainly breathes geography economic, taken hostage by their fraternities. I predict that this global start of the third millennium will let most blacks realize the characteristics of this society, jealous of their freedom and deeply breathe a breath of revolt, to lift them out of its barbarism and savagery, experienced in the old days but still lived today, and reveal a truth as a strong symbol of love, of the faith of the soul, of unity and of total freedom; the only and true happiness, the joy and the great honor of life, the only necessary things needed by all humanity, and by black man, proud to be in the cradle of his ancestors in Africa, and those in the peregrinations against their will, at the north to the south and at the east to the west, in the four corners of the world, taken there by force, by the barbarian white peregrines in Africa.

In the application of my truth, love is the strength of the soul. My truth does not have to admit acts of violence generally inflicted on humans. And it is only patience and compassion that separate the slave from the foot of his opponent, to whom the state of serf seems to be a truth. Thus, the patience of the other is requesting the truth by the self-suffering nonviolent means of humanity, inflicting voluntary psychic sufferings on the limp opponent, lacking strength and internal structure. My goal is to conquer, to convert that idea of the slavery supporter's violence of daily racism, of colonization, of colonialism, and to hamper his actions and his objectives.

For a just end, the perpetrator should not be constrained but simply converted to a defined success of cooperation, without obstructing the truth, for him to cease that traditional violence. This end is wrapped in my black linen skin by the inseparable means from the truth, forbidding me the use of any unjust means of violence to obtain an end attached to that aim, to obtain justice, and for peace. I believe that the humanity to which you have inflicted this terror, qualified as an error in his suffering, has neither deprived you of your monster nor wanted to buy it from you, and did not even fight with you for that monster, known as the evil spirit, which is his gift included all humanity and his property, however qualified as unhealthy, but used specifically to oppress him.

You oppressors, you genocidals, you who threw me into the dungeon of ships to export me as a commodity and submitted me to discriminatory treatment, you used unjust violent means since time immemorial; to integrate that injustice in my humanity was unjust and is still unnecessary. The calculated violence and the characteristic massacre of my spirit in general, have been transformed into a day of thanksgiving and joy, forged by the deliverance of the Lord.

I have confidence in me by telling myself that, at the end, death has no terror, but it is prescribed to all human beings, and that instinctive prescription that was imposed on me cannot be worse than now. So, I voluntarily accept my suffering, and know that it brings me joy and inner strength. But know also that there is always a choice between cowardice, violence, and the truth. To you who have chosen cowardice and violence toward the powerless who will never defend his honor, infinitely superior to your cowardice and violence, the punishment to your own dishonor is even more virile than forgiveness. Here, I want to eliminate the antagonisms without harming the antagonists, by the truth of love, which is the strength of the soul and which causes damages to the antagonist.

However, my truth purifies the antagonist; it will never destroy at the lower or higher level and will never put an end to their relationship. It will be transformed the strength of the soul, into a silent strength of the soul. My truth is a weapon, a universal force more powerful than the physical, with a moral power that armed individuals.

Holding to my truth, humanity is held by the power of the Almighty to cultivate a true spirit of love because no barbarism is without insolence, and impatience is a form of pressure. Truth is a virtue of the law on suffering. The moral elevation to this truth is an end of suffering. And love is in accordance with the truth, justice, freedom, and peace. It is not intolerant or unfair, but a lack of faith in its cause, betrays the intolerance of its cause. The active fidelity to obedience without discipline is disobedience to natural laws, and discipline leads to the voluntary obedience of its laws. We have to tolerate them and endure the sufferings that they can extraordinarily inflict on us against our will, even if we do not practice them; we are faithful to natural laws. A compulsory respect of the law is not a willing obedience that the truth requires as a universal solvent of injustice and prejudices. To strongly believe in that love, the strength of the soul is to lead a life of truth. To have faith in the inherent goodness of human nature is to have a living faith in the freedom of untouchability and self-esteem.

Honesty is devotion, a subordination of desires to what is true and what it means living fully in accordance with the truth. Let us suffer the abusive anger of the immoral opponent without anger, without ever exercising the penalty of retaliation, of a given order in anger by aggression. Don't let us insult him or curse him; we must not swear words to defend him from the chastisement for the deliberate aggression of the confiscation of our lives. He is himself a prisoner of his behavior, and the penitentiary regulation of self-respect is contrary to courtesy, to self-love. Only a manifestation to respect the rights of our lives is the respected action to obey the orders of those in danger, to protect them and help them change the process that hurts immoral feelings as a whole.

In the application of my truth, love is the strength of the soul. My truth is a remedy against evil and the great renunciation of violence in a determination of the power generated by the pure heart, which sterilizes all combination of weapons. The victories won by the slave supporters for the very cheap cost of slaves and the loss of several millions of lives did not worth that glorious price. We admitted psychically and physically that we were submitted passively without defenders to your technical violence, without measures of retaliation, even as the cost to pay was enormous; but fortunately, after all that sacrifice, we found a new sense of strength, dignity, and courage in ourselves because the application of my truth is love, and love is the strength of the soul.

Our true tradition, the work of esoteric Christianism at the forefront of humanity, is neither the popular Christianism, nor Judaism, or Buddhism, the light of Asia, but a true Christianism of the sun, which surpasses in brightness the brightest star in the heavenly sky. Coming out from a tradition of our ancestors, it dispels all traces of darkness. Instead, the Christianism of our days is full of darkness; and the heart of man, in the present state of our civilization, relegated more and more in the second plan, is further digging a wide and deep gulf between his intellect and him, forgetting that, by their union, they will be recognized as the "light of the world" and strong at the same time. The esoteric teachings are based on deep truths of a tradition that formed the basis of Christianism, exposed to the light. Its truths are incompatible and hidden to most Catholic and Christian theologians. All occult philosophy asserts that man has the opportunity to experience different degrees of reality, allowing him to access the superior principle through an illumination process as a philosophical thought. This sense of deep philosophical thought, which has animated the initiatic movements, since emblematic centuries, is aiming a state of spiritual and moral perfection—an unprecedented illumination, evoking the relation of the soul, the body, and the spirit to God. Thus, the esoteric dimension and Christianism are both facets of the same rich tradition from their marriage, and which no one can oppose the esoteric dimension.

Esotericism virtually became a pejorative word and also exposed to three major cyclone eyes nowadays; these three cyclone eyes are Power, Vampiristic, and Antagonistic; located outside the prevailing public opinion, and in the radical right, the extreme right, marked by the defense of tradition against the modern era; these two acceptations under the same word of very heterogeneous sensibilities, are aiming at a certain verticality as a form of elitism in the aristocracy, monarchy and in mysticism; reactionary ideas of the doctrine based on the ultras royalist of a spontaneous order. A concept used in many disciplines of science, particularly in biology, economic and sociology.

Numerous Catholic traditionalists are those who, up to today, referred themselves to those ideas, where we find the vision of the organic nations' unity of all races in believers' communities, obscured by an economic policy. It is the beginning of the refusal of the permanent revolution of our time, which does not stop just to the simple belief of the intangible laws, natural or supernatural, and replace all other religions by affirming that it is for the eternal good of humanity.

Terms became more and more nourished and almost became mundane; terms that are subject to the same ostracism; a form of social exclusion of certain groups in sociology, it is established as a prevailing rule in our social life. Esotericism covers very old notions, and its complex contours are often misunderstood, therefore discredited. Thus, without knowledge and according to the tradition of each, we never managed to define the concepts of the first absolute principle, or God, with precision, forgetting that man, who possessed a soul and a body, also possessed a spirit as an entity of a superior dimension and the divine breath in which he can participate, and must conquer everything that is at the origin of his being, but which isn't acceptable by moral reason, however which helps him to discover his origin-the loving soul. For the restoration of the original man, the soul and the body must maintain the relationship of unity through initiatic revelation, which puts into perspective the exegesis of the mysteries of various initiatic degrees to the state of glory, the revelations of the visible cosmos, which veils an infinite ocean of clarity, of the true civilization belonging to man; the history of the prophets, intended to deliver primordial revelations on humanity, is supposed to be the sign of the last hour, which must come back at the end of time, like the symbol of the mystical ascension to be raised from the dead.

The mystical ascension of a mystical text of apocalyptic and angelologic is one of the porticoes of the esotericism of ancient Judaism on the heavenly ascension of Rabbi Ishmael and his meeting with Metatron. In the "Book of Palace," the "Sefer Hekhalot," named the "Book of Enoch," is the oldest text of humanity that reveals the creation of the world to us.

Enoch is considered as the first man to have reached purity up to the path of union with God, according to Essene tradition. Third Enoch relates the gems of the medieval kabbalah of Jewish mysticism, considered as the first work of the rabbinic literature (the Mishnah), the first and most important of rabbinic sources, or the Talmud, the foundation of the Jewish law, gathering together all prescriptions and the entire collection of traditions and customs. It enlightened how other men were caught after their union with the divine world by the forces of the power of avidity and destruction; throughout the ages, these sacred texts with disconcerting simplicity have built mankind up to the knowledge of our days. The object of his mystical visions is to unveil the ecstatic of the seven celestial palaces during the mythical ascension. Its main sources of inspiration, consisting of short treatises and numerous variations between various communities and Jewish factions, reveal the facts of their dispersion in the world and narrate the problems in time and in space of their present generation, as the life ritual guide of the Halacha laws, based on the achievements of previous generations, encompassing civil, criminal, and religious law, the "way" a Jew should behave in every aspect of life, and those who followed its numerous laws, make of its aspects their daily lives.

The civil and religious rules of Halacha govern many Jewish communities up to this modern era of Jewish emancipation. The translation of the *Haskalah* literally means the "wisdom," "erudition," often termed Jewish enlightenment thought, which favors ideas of an inner "illumination," practicing "separation of church and state;" their intellectual members within this Jews movement find themselves citizens of other countries. To propose more flexible alternatives and to be less faithful to the sources, new trends moved away from the traditional model and proceeded to the advancement of the renewal of the ethical knowledge and on the aesthetics of their time. But in its quality of a "Jewish modern state," the Orthodox Halacha was the partial foundation of its state on the laws of personal status and family concerning divorce. On religious law, the Halacha is applied for the Israeli Jews.

The work of the world progress, which relentlessly fought against the arbitrariness, the evil will of man, who does not particularly care about equity or justice, the obscurantism, opposing the diffusion of knowledge and superstition, the worship of false gods, which was irrational in past centuries, still continues until today. From the book of Genesis, the Israeli law of various sources of the elements of Halakha, specifically includes the mosaic laws; the obligation of circumcision in the life of their progenitor, and the custom of not eating the sciatic nerve, technically called nervus ischiaticus as the second special ordinance imposed on Abram by God; these are various laws given to the first couple, and they bore a remarkable testimony as data.

In addition to the fundamental data of the Israeli laws, their modern codification of private law, is divided into two separate legal systems, one applies to Israeli settlers and the other to the Palestinians. It is through Ex. 12: 2 that the specific Mosaic laws are prescribed. The sanctification of the new month, however, is recapitulated in the book of Deuteronomy, in the book of Numbers, in Leviticus in the Torah, and many other unusually incongruous rites without further detail. Numerous exegetical comments on the subject of nature and the law, narrate disputes between Jesus and the doctors of the law in the New Testament. In the biblical references of the Gospel, Mtt. 5:17 relates this to us for that purpose: "Do not think that I came to abolish the Law or the Prophets; I did not come to abolish but to fulfill." However, there is a controversy, between the Christian positions and Judaism, going toward a form of simplification and systematization of the law; in Judaism, there is a certain tendency toward legalism in the interpretation of the law, indicating that the rabbis are focused on legalism to restrict and rigid moral codes. The angel Metatron, according to Jewish tradition and mystical literature, is a power of the divine world linked to the patriarch Enoch of the Bible, who appears in the Talmud and Midrash. The angel Metatron is in the immediate vicinity of God as a servant of the divine throne, hence the title of "Prince of the Face." Its text tells the mystical ascension of Rabbi Ishmael toward the divine palace. At the beginning of the quotation from Gen. 5:23–24, it is said that the whole lifetime of Enoch was 365 years.

Enoch walked with God, and then he disappeared, because God took him, meaning that Enoch entered alive in the Garden of Eden, relates the Talmudic treaty to us concerning the mystical ascension of Rabbi Ishmael. Upon his arrival in the seventh palace, the angel who was introduced to him was the archangel Metatron. At that instant, Metatron revealed to him that he was the son of Yared, a listed character among the patriarchs of the Old Testament, Gen. 5:18–19 and in the Hebrew Bible. He revealed that he was the transfiguration of the patriarch Enoch. The patriarch Enoch, who became divine, was literally explaining to him the steps that his soul had to cross, like his encounters with the hostile angels and the tests he underwent from one palace to another that he was able to subjugate with the divine names before reaching the seventh palace gate. And he revealed the divine secrets to him, which were revealed to him by God in the angelology, the cosmology, and the eschatology, and that when the men of Adam's generation became idolaters, the Eternal left the earth after Adam was driven from the Garden of Eden, and that to remove him in the middle of that perverse generation, the Creator made him ascend in the celestial heights. And above all in Jewish mystical literature, Metatron appears in the Talmud, the Midrash, where he is related to the biblical patriarch Enoch. Enoch finally explained to Metatron, known as the power of the divine world according to Jewish tradition concerning the governor of the seventy angels of Nations, and the unanswered questions of Jacob, asking God the angels' names, Gen. 32:30.

In Gen. 32:25, the "man" who appeared to Jacob, generally interpreted as an angel or God himself, wrestling with him throughout the night till daybreak, gave him no name; in Gen. 32:25–32, Jacob asks the "man" his name and receives no answer but progressively revealed himself as the Living God. In Gen. 32:9–12, he prayed to God at a difficult and challenging time and asked him to show grace and mercy to him in his time of need, revealing his growing in grace and spiritual knowledge in his life, and God answered his prayer. "He who struggles with God," known literally as "Israel," described Jacob, as wrestling with God. God gave grace to Jacob, and he revealed a trust in God in his struggle, mixed with apprehension, often too arrogant; depending upon God with boldness before him, mixed with his own independence, yet mixed with sin but full of righteousness from God.

Manoah, the father of Samson, also wanted to know the name of the angel of the Lord that spoke to his barren wife, "promising her that if she did not eat anything unclean, take strong liqueur or wine, she shall bring forth a son, consecrated to God from the womb of his mother, who shall deliver Israel out of the hand of the Philistines, until the day of his death;" and what was said to his wife was confirmed to him by the angel, Judg. 13:3–5, and 12–18; their names are still mysterious.

So, Metatron revealed the most glorious names of all the seventy names of God known to the Bible, frequently used in the Old Testament, in response to the question of Rabbi Ishmael. Metatron evoked the tetragrammaton, consisting of four letters yōd (י), hē (ה), wāw (ו), hē (ה), as the divine name of the most glorious of all gods, the one of the Almighty God, YHWH (יהוה This testimony is an account of Rabbi Ishmael's conversation with Metatron. The purpose of this example is to demonstrate his kindness, his humility, and the additional wisdom that Enoch managed to acquire through initiation for his union with the soul and the enlargement granted directly by the saint to the rank of God. The angel Metatron primarily appeared within the Kabbalistic mystical texts as a central figure, the highest angel of angels, traditionally the celestial scribe servant in the rabbinic literature. The human soul opposed to material or physical things wants to soar on the wings of the ethereal intuition. But chained down here silently, it remains powerless and does not manage to reach the eternal sources of light and the spiritual love to exist forever, without end or beginning. The human soul knows that there is something higher, the Creator. Blessed be he who feels instinctively the heart that aspires to the highest truths than those that can be embraced by the intellect alone, but the intellect imperatively demands to be given rigorous explanations from the material point of view on man and the creatures that surround it, to show it what form the phenomenal world is, for it to be satisfied.

This intellect, which imperatively requires the demonstration of the eternal phenomenal world and the source of the spiritual light to be satisfied, is science. The relationship of the intellect among others, greater than a single substantial form in the body, allows the understanding of senses—the whole mental faculties, the intelligence of the mind, which seeks to discover things and facts to achieve the conceptual and rational knowledge. In the soul of the entire humanity, intellect is a divine reason but is not a part of our soul and presumably escapes the conscious thought of man.

Modern scientists have cut off its wings; as in the field of science, the intellect f lies from discovery to discovery, and its unfulfilled aspirations, disturb it, causing anxieties and persistent distress. There must be a ground where the heart and the head can meet, each of them receiving equal satisfaction, one assisting the other in the search for the universal truth to unite. Just like the eye was created to help the human beings perceive the light that existed before creation, its primordial desire for growth formed the digestive organs and the assimilation to achieve it. Thought existed before the brain built it, and still builds it, to be able to express itself.

The intellect is today making its way and snatching secrets from the nature by the power of its audacity. So, the heart will find a way to break its shackles and realize its desires. The day it will concentrate enough powers to break the bars of its prison, chained by the dominating brain, it will become more powerful than the intellect, for, there can be no contradiction in nature; neither one nor the other can work in isolation. The intellect, helped by the intuition of the heart, probes deeper into the mysteries of the being. And the heart united to the intellect preserves error.

Each of them, having full freedom of action without doing violence to the other, finds equal appeasement. Man could only reach the highest and more accurately understanding of his own nature, of which he is a part in this world, only when this union, which will give him a broad mind and a great heart, is accomplished and made perfect.

At birth, the being appears in a small living form among us. This new life is beginning to grow for days, months, and years and then becomes an element of our existence. Then without exemption, the death skeleton begins to project its frightening shadow on him and sounds its pitiful clamor through the ages. Whether young, sick, healthy, old, poor, or rich, the pitiful clamor of the enigma of death demands solution to the enigma of life. Without exception, the form dies, and it disintegrates at the end of life.

Life, which came from I don't know where, passed into the invisible beyond; painfully, we do not know from whence comes this life. Why it was here, and where it went. Is there life after death? Unfortunately, these questions are without answers to the uninitiated humanity up to this day. This does not exclude that humanity, endowed with the supreme senses, and possessing dormant faculties more distant from the truth, cannot directly obtain information of the spirit on these enigmas. But to awaken them, a persistent effort on those existing faculties is necessary to accomplish the tasks of the Most High. Thus, awake and conscious, a great virtue could be obtained. And the gift of entering the afterlife to discover God; the relationship of the soul to God—of God to man and man to death—must be accomplished; if this discovery and the relationship of God to man takes place, then the deepest mysteries of immortality and the divine spark are realized; in our tradition, these same words are words that African sages uttered at the end of initiation; they were pronounced as a supreme confidence, and solemnly affirming the end of the ignorance of the adept, and leading him toward the path that leads to the personal knowledge of the afterlife, to perceive the human spirit, before birth and after death, and everything existing in our being. It is imperative for the being to acquire this knowledge to perfectly capture what proceeds. The basic idea of the occultism is to acquire this wisdom with persistent effort to better understand its contents.

John 1:1 says, "In the beginning was the Word, and the Word was with God, and the Word was God." On the other hand, 1 Cor. 8:6 says, "One God by whom all things were created, and one Lord, Jesus Christ, through whom all things exist and through whom we live." "And finally, for this very purpose God has prepared us, and has given us the Spirit as a pledge of what is to come, for we walk by faith, not by sight, therefore always being of good courage, and knowing that, while we are at home in the body, we are in exile far from the Lord," says 2 Cor. 5:5–7. But neither more nor less, Jesus isn't God but just as every man is God, according to *The Da Vinci Code*. Such is the primordial tradition, the original thought, the idea of a transcendent God, creative and personal under different exegeses of life. These exegeses shaped the teachings of Christianity, while defining what religious and spiritual beliefs are. Between Satan, Lucifer, the demons, the devil, and the Prince of this world, there is a definition or an extremely accurate theological position on God's relationship with man and of man with God.

In the caves of temples, a mystical laughter resounded for millennia; announcing the birth of the prodigious man, the gods of temples made man in their image, raising the children of earth to the rank of immortals in the likeness of God.

The great mythical characters were evoking this liberating laughter of initiates as a sign of self-accomplishment, a sign of joy to beings that have entered the dynamic universe, a presence of God who also embodies the sacred authority, manifesting in turn by turn the loneliness of the human being and its vocation to act. This initiatic laughter became a portcullis of dogmas from the institutionalized churches, attempting to fertilize the horizontal secularist, which shaped our academies and our religious teachings. To ensure a better understanding of the sacred texts, we carefully translated and canonized certain chapters of the Bible, as well as other sacred books of the world, in Latin, Greek, Hebrew, English, and even Arabic to teach a false story. But we have not yet understood that history and myth have become very dense for two thousand years of Christian interpretation, specific to the sacred time, from which we can no longer distinguish the truth from false and what is a legend to history.

The circumstances of the birth of Jesus were eloquently revealed by Matthew, who did not seem to agree with Luke in any point at all. Matthew described in his gospel that an angel appeared to Joseph in a dream after discovering that his fiancée, Mary, was pregnant. So, to prevent him from repudiating her, the angel informed him that she was pregnant by the Holy Ghost. But according to Luke 1:34, the archangel Gabriel announced the pregnancy and the birth of Jesus personally to the Virgin Mary. Therefore, the gospel took and personified the myth of virginity well-known in ancient temples, expressing the belief of a suffering mother Isis of Ancient Egyptians, who gave birth to Horus, considered as the protector of the monarchy, born by the breath after the death of her husband and brother of Osiris. This posthumous myth, dating back for over five thousand years, was the one used as the central tenet of Christianity to confirm the miracle of the birth of Jesus. It is surprisingly remarkable to see the resemblance of this myth in the ancient Christian belief, but with the Egyptian representation, specified on the obelisks at Sais by these words: "I am that I am; I am all that has been and is and shall be. Nobody has ever lifted my veil and I gave birth to the Sun, as the ancient mystery initiations dedicated to Isis." In this declaration of pantheism, nature and divinity are identical, designed to reveal the deeper, pantheistic truth to elite initiates, different from the public Egyptian polytheistic religion. In the book of Exodus, the Jewish God, "I am that I am," is the same as the Saite inscription, thus enough evidence to indicate that Judaism was a descendant of the Ancient Egyptian belief system.

These ancient mystery initiations were practiced in the Greco-Roman world, under the influence of earlier Greco-Roman mystery rites, an interpretation influenced by the ancient mystery initiations dedicated to Isis, developed in the Hellenistic times by the Greco-Roman mystery rites. In the early eighteenth century, many Freemasons and members of a European fraternal organization that reached its modern form and came to believe that their rituals could be traced back to the mysteries of Isis adopted the Egyptian motifs of the ancient mystery initiations dedicated to Isis, to reconcile Freemasonry's traditional origin story. The veiled Isis, an impenetrable symbol enigma, represents nature and truth considered as a deity. On the corridors of the temple, we see Isis, the devoted mother, breastfeeding her son Horus, surrounded by the solar disk. This ancient African belief and everything written on Egyptian obelisks remain indisputable.

Also, the church chose this theme for all Christian paintings to depict Jesus breastfeeding in the arms of Mary, also surrounded by a halo, representing the sun. But did Mary also become a queen of heaven, surrounded by the zodiac and other symbols specific to Isis, the goddess mother of earth? All miraculous birth data by mortal women pregnant by the breath or the spirit of Zeus, pronounced

"Zdeus," the supreme god in Greek who brings order and justice on earth, are also myths adopted by the Greeks after their education in Egypt, especially like those of Hera, Artemis, Demeter, and Persephone. We recognize the sign of ancient initiations in them, familiar to Egypt and preserved by the Essenes before the Christian era.

Christianity has managed to eradicate the cult of the Virgin with Egyptian roots, inculcated to the Greco-Roman and the Middle Eastern to make it its own. Furthermore, the indispensable psychological service of an essential complement to the Catholic faith is not qualified. But this theme has been used by the church to confirm the divinity of Jesus and to promote celibacy, yet Jesus was married. It had the audacity to add that after the birth of Jesus, Mary was sixteen years old and that she remained a virgin until the age of twenty-six years old, ten years after the birth of Jesus, according to some sources. But the church decided that Mary remained a virgin after the birth of Jesus until her own death. She was venerated as the purest of women who knew the suffering of human beings and the perfect mother who saw her son being crucified and humiliated in public. Even Father Jerome of Stridon, a monk doctor of the church and one of the forefathers of the Latin Church and translator of the Bible, denied the perpetual virginity of Mary, evoking the brothers of Jesus.

After preaching the gospel of the kingdom of heaven and lived an ascending order of marvelous power of humility, the intimate goodness of the heart, the thirst of justice followed by the sadness of the inner wickedness of the heart of the world, as the four well-known painful virtues; then the militant kindness, radiating the purity of the heart, raised by the divine grace to the fruits and seeds of good moral acts; and in the practice of good, man purified and helped by God, communicates with the divine love, and according to his deep vocation, he receives the divine mercy of God to become a renewed human being, capable to be merciful in his dignity; and then at his proclamation of the gospel, totally devoted to the poor, came the martyrdom for justice as the active and triumphant virtues; bringing the great mysteries in broad daylight in Galilee; translating the doctrine of initiation, the doctrine of the Verb and Trinity, which existed long before Jesus himself, and which came out from the depths of the esoteric prophetism, as the organization of the order and community; and all that pertains to the morality of man, cosmogony or physics, and the universal science of principles or theogony.

This doctrine of love toward one's neighbor, put forward as the first duty, is found in the Gospel of John with a new meaning. It hates hatred and lies; it promotes humility and consecration to attest the truth. But linking the original text of the Bible to Hebrew and Greek version concerning virginity, nothing is miraculous since the word *Halmaa* in Hebrew means "young girl," without any connotation of virginity. The same word is used by Mathieu and Isaiah to reinterpret the original meaning of the biblical text, which also means "young girl" and "a virgin" at the same time. Without these explanations, the change of meaning and the confusion of terms are installed.

At that time, the virginity of Mary was not hidden because she had other children as brothers and sisters of Jesus, the firstborn of Mary. And concerning the birth of Jesus, the Essene brotherhood certified that, at the birth of Jesus, he had a divine influence beyond the intervention of Joseph and Mary. The gospels consistently exonerated Joseph from this divine influence at the time of the procreation of Jesus from his paternity.

This aspect of the human body, which had to meet a certain criterion for a consecration, is simply erased by Christianity, for various reasons, but that Mary had to answer between her virginity at the level of the soul and the virginity on the physical plane, which is considered compulsory on the physical plane; the level of "karma zero" of Mary refers to a being reincarnated up to the end of all turns of incarnations but returned to earth (in a body) without karma, invested by a divine type of consciousness sufficiently pure, without remembering an anterior charge, without sin and without task, with a consciousness of extreme purity to welcome and carry a being within her, already energetically strong, and as exceptional as Jesus.

It was during the time when Herod was king that Jesus was born, if one believes in Mtt. 2:1; it is the year that Emperor Caesar Augustus ordered a census of all inhabitants of the Roman Empire, said Luke 2:1. Meanwhile, Quirinus was the governor of the province of Syria, Luke 22. So please note that it was the gospels that allowed us to date the birth of Jesus. Now for the general understanding, Quirinus was not a governor of the province of Syria during the reign of Herod because he was already dead, four years before the Christian era. And the census ordered by Emperor Augustus was also already held six years before the Christian era.

This information led us to conclude that Jesus was already a big boy long before the official date of his birth. Mathew 2:1 indicated Bethlehem of Judea as his birthplace and where he spent his childhood, which also posed problems, if we rely on this comparison of Mark 1:9 and John 1:45–46, revealing to us that Nazareth was the place of his birth. However, if the year and place of birth of Jesus were not known, December 25 could not also be the day of his birth.

December 25, designating the day of the birth of Jesus, is known as one of the two moments in the year that correspond to the time of the longest and the shortest day of the period of the solstice, marking the beginning of the winter solstice (December 22) in the Northern Hemisphere as the shortest day of the year. And as the longest day of the year, the summer solstice begins on June 21 in the Southern Hemisphere.

In the Southern Hemisphere, the winter solstice is the summer solstice, and the summer solstice is inversed in the Northern Hemisphere, just as the dates and seasons of solstices are inversed. In this case, December 25—when Persia (nowadays Iran) celebrated the anniversary of Mithras, the central figure of the cult of Mithraism, the sun god of truth and honor in antiquity—was of Persian origin.

Taken by the Romans under the name of Saturn, he embodied the pagan god Sol Invictus or the invincible sun god of the Gentiles. In Egypt, in Alexandra, this day represented the birthday of Osiris, the god of resurrection. The same month of December was for the Romans the month they were distracted all night long. It is the Roman emperor Aurelian who set the date of December 25, also corresponding to the day of birth of the solar deity Mithras as a great feast of the undefeated sun (Sol Invictus, BC). He chooses this date the next day at the end of the Saturnalia, wishing to religiously unify the empire religiously in the continuity of the traditional Roman festivities and by satisfying the followers of Sol Invictus and the worship of Mithra.

Furthermore, it was the successor of Pope Julius I, by the name of Liberius, the first to designate Rome as the apostolic headquarters, who also decided in the year 354 to make the transition between the pagan festival of December 25, which existed long before the Christianization of the West, designating this day as the official date of the birth of Jesus. Christians definitely adopted this day of December 25 sacred, as the date of his birth, three centuries after his death. January 1, traditionally considered as the year that followed the Nativity of Jesus, is the date of his circumcision and also marks the first anno Domini of the Christian era in the Gregorian calendar. This feast of Mithra symbolized the grace of light winning over darkness, taken by the church after the birth of Jesus, incarnating the sacred day of the sun on the night. The New Testament is the main source of information of an intense feeling of deep affection of love on the earth, which encompassed the gospels of the apostles on the great spiritual master.

The histories of his childhood are presented by significant events in the world history, but no precision of these events is mentioned in the gospel texts, giving us the time of the year when the birth of Jesus took place. According to Matthew and Luke, some chapters of the gospels were presented in a succinct manner. They put into account a number of familiar events like his conception and his birth, the Annunciation, the arrival of the Magi, the arrival of the shepherds, the vision of the temple in Jerusalem, the escape into Egypt where his family inhabited until Herod's death, and the return to Nazareth, emphasizing the genealogy of Jesus. But between twelve and twenty-nine years, Jesus stayed in the temple without the knowledge of his parents. Note that absolutely no detail was given on the life of Jesus when he was between twelve and twenty-nine years old in the Bible.

Seventeen years in this biography of Jesus are missing, in which we know anything about him, after all that presentation of those extraordinary events on his life. He had already learned what he wanted to know from the Essenes before meeting John the Baptist. And around the age of thirty, Jesus was baptized in the Jordan River by John after these seventeen years. After receiving the esoteric tradition of the prophets, Jesus chose its own historical and religious orientation. He received the higher initiation of the fourth degree of the order of the Essenes, granted only in the special case of a prophetic mission. He learned the secret of religion and the science of mysteries.

As you all know, the life of Jesus, of him being God or man, and his mission at a time, has raised numerous popular issues in books and movies. However, it is important to study the whole history and the universal spiritual in a broader context, from which its teachings emanated to understand the teaching of Jesus, as it is related to each filiations or the potential of Christ. At the time of Jesus, there were two main Jewish sects: Essenes and Pharisees. The principle of the Essenes was the immortality of the soul as separated from the body to pursue the mystical union of man with God. The principle of the Pharisees sect, known as believing in reincarnation, was the one that also dominated the temple of Jerusalem during the ministry of Jesus. Reincarnation was a popular belief among the Jews. Many ancient manuscripts revealed that Jesus received direct training in Egypt and in the East.

The ministry of Jesus was influenced by Judaism, as well as by Buddhism, Hinduism, Taoism, the Egyptian mysteries, cabala, and the Essene mysticism. Shrines of St. Issa found in India and Tibet revealed that Jesus spent seventeen years in India and Tibet from thirteen to twenty-nine years old, where he was both a professor and a student of Buddhism, Hinduism, hence his name St. Issa. In the masses of people living in Judea, in the quasi-deserted conditions, a cosmopolitan trade center of people more than illiterate led simple activities like fishing and carpentry in a political, cultural, philosophical, and very religious melting pot. Judea was strongly influenced by Orphism, which taught a spiritual belief system of reincarnation and which awakened a divine spark within man during the Greco-Roman influence.

Nicolas Notovitch, the Russian writer who first discovered the Tibetan manuscripts in the nineteenth century, went to Rome with his documented story titled *The Unknown Life of Jesus Christ*, the secret information revealing that Jesus spent six years of his life between the ages of fourteen and twenty-one traveling to Tibet and to the Indian holy cities like Juggernaut, Rajagriha, and Benares.

While in Rome, a high-ranking cardinal told him that sixty-three complete or incomplete documents brought back by Christian missionaries concerning Jesus's activities in the East were already possessed by the Vatican. The Apocryphal texts, discovered in 1945 near Nag Hammadi, Egypt—the secret book of John, the secret gospel of Mark, the gospel of Thomas, the gospel of Mary Magdalene, and the gospel of Phillip—recorded Jesus's mystical teachings.

The discovery of the Dead Sea Scrolls in Israel near Qumran in 1947, which contain over two hundred documents, provides us predated biblical evidence of gospels, saying that Jesus spoke of reincarnation; that he performed secret initiation rites, like those of the ancient mystery schools; and that he taught the precepts found in the Buddhism and Taoism and the Tibetan spiritual traditions, including the biblical commentaries, the prophecy, and the community rules.

The key concepts of the state or the fact of being Christ is a karma leading to the opportunity to improve the lifespan of the soul for our present-day personality to only live once, and the reincarnation of the soul after death, to return, clothed with a new body and personality, to experience the next higher level in the classroom of humanity on earth; successively, the ascending and descending human immortal soul by essence, through alternately spiritual and corporeal existences returns to God, to the pure spirit; having reached its perfection, the soul rises above the law, the law of reincarnation.

At its evolution, when it becomes aware of its divinity and when it becomes aware of its humanity, it rises in the fullness of its consciousness. The balance of karma is to fulfill a divine purpose. We can only be ready for the permanent reunion with God when the alchemical marriage takes place between the soul and Christ, freed from the cycle of rebirth. The state or the fact of being Christ was taught to Gnostics, followers of the ministry of Jesus for several hundred years until the ministry of the church hierarchy shut it down for political gain and human power. Thus, to reach the invisible sanctuary that leads to divine humanity, the soul of the white race is split into two and freed from the roaring animality.

The Roman emperor by the name of Trajan Decius arrested, tortured, and imprisoned Origen during the persecution against Christians, under his rule in 250, after torturing and beheaded the twentieth pope, Fabian, on the Via Appia Antica on January 20 of the same year.

Origen taught the preexistence of the soul, which passed through the successive stages of incarnation before finally reaching God, in the second century of our era, explaining his defense of the personal spiritual freedom, saying that the earth was a place of free experience to man. His mystical doctrine—which represented the literal moral and spiritual sense—was closer to a system of thought known as the one of Gnostics, claiming generally that God Yahweh, called the Demiurge, was a bad and an imperfect God who created the divine souls of human beings and imprisoned them in this material world. He could be considered a good, imperfect creator, or to the sense of evil, the incarnation of evil as an archangel. The Father of church Jerome of Stridon translated the homilies of Luke as a work of Origen, by which many of the church fathers were inspired. To manipulate the common knowledge, the church fathers voted centuries later to set apart Jesus from other men as the only begotten Son of God. The doctrine of the original sin was turned to shame by the church father St. Augustine, depriving the consciousness of man from the innate potential of Christ by substituting it with a vengeful god of impersonal divine laws of karma and reincarnation.

The works of Origen, the secret gospels, and the Apocryphal texts were declared anathema, thus destroyed and buried. The selfish dogma of man became the foundation of the spiritual thought throughout centuries. All the legacies of the previous mystic who sought mysteries, like the Cathars, proposing a different interpretation of the Gospels, rejecting in particular all the sacraments of the Catholic Church baptism of water, Eucharist, marriage, etc., were persecuted as heretics and destroyed. That Cathar religion was giving man the opportunity to reach the perfect purity of the soul, during the period of his earthly life, because his name taken from the Greek term catharos means pure. By an appropriate conduct, man must strive to break away from matter, gross desires, representing the Evil to which Good - the purified soul, ignoring the desires of the body is opposed in the physical world, considered as a test. For the Cathars, death signifying deliverance was not feared, because those who failed to purify their souls had to reincarnate indefinitely, and those who succeeded in purifying it rested forever in Good after death. In 1208, after the assassination of the pope's legate, the break between Cathars and Catholics was total. Yet an orthodox interpretation of many Catholic and Protestant churches, still considering Jesus as the only son of God, an arbitrary despotic in the image of man, unfortunately to this day, still prevails. The adepts of the state or the fact of being Christ must understand that the only begotten Son of God is the consciousness of Christ and not Jesus as flesh and blood. The Jewish texts like the book of Levi and both the Old and New Testaments are narrating the reign of King David, the one of Melchizedek, and many other biblical characters; they're related to other sons of God, and the revelation of how to become a son of God can be found in the Bible. The consciousness of Christ is the way; Jesus tells us by these felicities in the New Testament: "Whoever does the will of my Father in heaven is my brother and sister." The will of God is the truth, the life that saves us from our human ignorance and the separation from God.

If you fulfill this consciousness and reunite with the presence of "I am what I am," souls become immortal. By the rediscovery of these ancient teachings and the freedom of religion, we have an opportunity to follow the footsteps of our elder masters and teachers to become the divine Christ potential that lies within each one of us, like our own right allowing us to ascend back to God. The death of Christ, which edified souls and proliferated the faith, is reproduced in the soul of every Christian faithful, because his mystical and spiritual death was proven, so that the Church can finally spread on the earth. He was already here on earth among us, where he tasted the bitter time of life, measured in hours, minutes, months, and years as an indefinite point, the point of continuous progress of existence, filled with events of the past, of the present, and the future as a whole through distance, time, and space. He drank it, ate it, walked on it, slept on it, and sinned in earth; he tasted the joy and the pain of love on earth, like every other human. We disconcerted him with God, but from his sins, he died crucified on the cross, the symbol of shame, later on transformed to the symbol of salvation. He was born in sin by a woman who has a womb as the highest part of her surface, who tasted the flaming dry herb fire during nine months, and from a man who crossed the multiple waves of painful life to eat by the sweat of his brow by fecundating the terrestrial germs.

Jesus was an initiate, a high initiate, and a master adept of the ancient Judaic mysteries, who—after discovering the therapeutic effect of his knowledge—freed spirits from the unjust action of ritualists. He sought to establish justice by affirming the equality of masculine and feminine authority principles in both spiritual practice and social tradition; re-establishing tradition, particularly in the sacrament and social contract of marriage; a rite well known to the early church as the sacrament of the bridal chamber in which the union of man and woman in one energy was conducted and consumed almost exclusively by the spouse, implying the union of sexual intercourse the same evening; through an engagement ceremony and the teaching of secrecy through an initiation rite of sexual union; known as the conception of spiritually advanced offspring, fertility, and means of giving birth, in the ancient time.

Before continuing, here are some important explanations of the word *mystery*. It does not designate anything scary; it is rather linked to a gnosis, a mystical knowledge that may be revealed only by means of initiation. In Latin, *mystery* means "initia," and *mysties* means "mystae." The word *Initiare* means to "inspire," and *initium* means "the beginning, the teaching, or the education." The highest secret of the three grades of initiation, possibly in the early Christian faith, was laid down by Jesus. We know that the Jewish dissident fraternities born in Egypt, which sought to bring back the ancient Judaic mysteries forbidden by the temple in Jerusalem before his birth, initiated him. It was Jesus's teachings in the light of the sacred consortship that revealed what happened to the Gnostic, a movement that practiced yoga, a spiritual and physical discipline that aimed to free the spirit by perfect body control, known as the Apocrypha Gnosis of the heart, the heart knowledge, or the prophecy of Christianity that he incarnated.

This version of spiritual practice based on mystical wisdom of selfinitiation, which raised his consciousness to a new spiritual level, differs from the one that the church offers us. Christians were in the old days, very famous in higher spiritual knowledge based on miraculous deeds of healing and empowerment. This knowledge quickly became unpopular in the official circles of the church because it bypassed the authority of the powerless bishops in the higher spiritual knowledge.

Therefore, the original three-grade system of initiation was abandoned, and the sacrament of the bride chamber was also abolished, subsequently forbidden by the church, and in general anathematized the Gnostic worship. It is very important to note that the nonexistence of the bride chamber mysteries snatched the true heart of the Christian religion and left it with a little system of tribal superstition, cut off from the living participation that the great spiritual traditions of antiquity were exercising. The Christ mystery that Jesus established, which the Christianity inherited, is not the official faith that the West today celebrates but its pallid simulacrum—a representation or imitation of a thing or of a person.

Among the northern people, with whom Jesus was permanently in contact, where he spent seventeen years of initiation that transformed his body and life to accommodate Kristos, the sun, we found divinities as Aesus, Hukadern, and Karito Winda—the principle of the Celtic Trinity, which he assimilated for about a year and a half during his trip with his uncle Joseph of Arimathea in the country of Wales. This principle is still well known in esoteric tradition. The father, the cosmic ancestor of Jesus on the maternal side, was represented by

Aesus (Teutates). The Word (Verb), the Son of God, the spiritual and physical sun, was represented by Hukadern. The black virgin, the true Egyptian mystical Isis, symbolizing the material and the respect of nature, was represented by Karito Winda (or Korid Wen).

The black virgin cult, the Templar heretical cult of Isis and Horus, was born in Egypt. Isis, the black Egyptian goddess associated with wisdom and gnosis, was traditionally represented as the mother of the god Horus. For the occultists, the black mother became the god of the invisible and subtle work, which was developed underground. She was also linked to the respect and veneration consecrated to Mary Magdalene, the wife of Jesus, under her proper role. This cult of the black virgin, which dated back for more than ten thousand years, first formed the greatest Egyptian men and then the Hebrews, the Greeks, and the Romans in Egypt by initiating them into the little mysteries, followed by the great mysteries.

According to Jacques Huynen, the black virgin is a flash appeal about her miraculous work that was greatly venerated by the Middle Age people for having a comprehension that indicated everything about us across centuries. Her noble statue measured seventy centimeters high, thirty centimeters wide, and thirty centimeters deep; and her black color symbolized the occult caution that must surround the insiders. He said that the Christians, the druids, and the Easterners have fed us, and that if we know where to look, she would tell us that we were insiders of the great tradition and occultists who know the magic of certain numbers. She taught us alchemy, and we practiced it, and she proclaimed and described it for operators of the great work.

It was often in the crypt of the temple that we found the black virgin, placed beside a well, on a height, in a very mysterious and withdrawn place. Solomon wrote a poem for us in the Song of Songs; his first poem tells us about a black girl who was the joy and gladness more delicious than wine, full of pleasing perfumes, aromas, and having a name of a purified oil that flows—a spouse, introduced by the king to his apartments, kissing her with kisses of his mouth. He presents her to us in the Song of Songs 1:5–6 with these words: "I am black but lovely, O daughters of Jerusalem, like the tents of Kedar, like the curtains of Solomon." My beauty is a sealed source, and my name is oil that pours from an open heart with sincerity, tenderness, and confidence. She is proudly telling the world to not stare at her because she is swarthy, because it is the sun that burned her skin. Her assertion is universal to all black nations, and her charm intoxicates the heart. Symbolically, the black color was never the connotation of evil that the white attributed it; it is generally compound of these three senses in the history of mankind, attributed to the black people.

Ultimate, it is about the initial sense, literally evoking blacks as the original creature, hence the body, which was to grow and multiply to engender other nations of different colors in the world. In the second place, it is the moral sense, hence the spirit, the principle of life, which has no body and cannot be perceived by the senses of material existence and the immaterial element embodied in the human being. It designates the affectivity, the intuition, the judgment, the perception, the conceptual thought, etc., that some religions call soul. In the first human being, the body constituted of matter and spirit, formed a unique united nature but not two united natures. And in the third place, the soul is the spiritual principle in the material body, the intangible mystical sense of the human body; it is through the spiritual soul that the body, constituted of material lives, and their union is a deep mystical sense. In the ancient times, the Egyptians, at the time of the first pyramids, believed in the material and immaterial components of the human being and were using a set of specialized terms to describe them.

Psychically, in the earthly sphere of the sensitive and in the intangible realm of our ancestors and of gods according to their beliefs, the Egyptian initiates were imbibed with these nine essential elements of being as components of the soul: The first element (*djet*), the physical body, submissive to the physical decline that comes from old age, is considered as the material image of the great celestial body. The second element, the vital energy, the creative spiritual dynamism, is *ka*, which survives in the grave after death and represents a double that was born at the same time with the human. The third element, the possibility of incarnating the divine on the earth, is *ba*, improperly called soul, and is an intangible component of gods and men, representing an inherent transformation of energy in each person. The fourth element (*shut*) is a component representing the shadow as a reflection of the truth. The fifth element, the efficient light of the spirit, is known as *akh*, a state of being that reached the status of higher spiritual power after death. The sixth element, the siege of consciousness, called *ab* or the heart, is an organ symbolically evaluated on the balance of the court of Osiris at the ell of Maat. The seventh element, the power of realization, represents *sekhem*, a manifestation of selfenergy that is used to develop our faculties in the radiance of its light. The eighth element is the ultimate truth of all creation, the *ren* or the name, a primary part that designated the name of being. And finally, the ninth element is the body spiritualized, the *sakh*, which serves to preserve the karmic fruits of an existence for the next incarnation in its various bodies.

Death, a definitive rupture in the coherence of the vital processes, marking the end of life as opposed to birth, was influenced by the belief in immortality among the Egyptians of antiquity. These ethereal components helped the dead survive in the tomb and hope for an immortal existence. For them, death was a temporary interruption and represented an important part of their lives. Their beliefs about death were of religious order, and they believed that after death, the deceased soul was reborn.

For that, the preservation of *ankh*, the breath of life, was conditioned by the respect of the principles of truth and justice of Maat and the efficient mastery of Heka, known as magic; graceful to this last component, black humans assimilated themselves to the gods by an inner power and knowledge gained from a long observation of tradition, different from book learning. For Christianism, the soul, body, and spirit of the whole being must blamelessly be kept for the advent of the Lord; and every spiritual soul, marked by the original sin, was immediately created by God. As you could see, these very important aspects represented the very first religion in Africa, particularly among Egyptians of antiquity.

Black is a secret science—a science of absolute principles, a science of numbers—the sacred mathematics applied to the universe; he is the involution of the spirit into matter, the realization of eternal principles in space and time; the evolution of the soul through the chain of existences, and the science of the reigns of earthly nature, and its properties; the constitution of the black man is theosophical and not to a certain extent, the emblem of evil, as it is always presented, but as the one who brings joy and gladness. Its black virgin is Mother Earth—the matrix, the nourishing drink that all alchemy drinks, a symbol of the earth locked in a secret crypt but applying the power vibration of the earth that allows the access to the path of knowledge and demonstrates the regenerative principle, where life is propelled from the cosmic womb, from which sprang the light of the world.

A conscientious chronology of adepts, initiated into the mysteries of Ancient Egypt, told us that a complete civilization existed in Egypt for more than ten thousand years before Menes. Plato had the evidence before his eyes. When it came to Osiris (god of the ancient synthesis and the former world alliance), Herodotus confirmed and asserted the same fact. The priests of Egypt assured us that Egyptians had evidence of a complete social status well before Menes, which lasted up to Horus.

For 6.883 years just from the threshold of Menes, several huge civilization cycles succeeded in Egypt long before the Indian viceroy sovereignty as reported by a thorough chronology of the Egyptian priest Manetho. It is here concerning Egypt; of its knowledge of the mysteries, its existence in antiquity; of so a powerful science in its effects, which became the sectarianism libraries in India, in China, in Tibet, and around the world, for the obscurantism of the spirit by the mask of Theology, but that our ancestors considered the study with high instruction and civilization in temples, which was locked in the basements of the temples. The origin of this initiation placed at the start of any instruction—with physical tests, moral tests, and intellectual tests—was lost in the midst of primitive cycles.

It was some of these evidences of initiates and other characters who have good knowledge related to Jesus, the Christ known by different names, who revealed to us that in Egypt, the one who climbed the multiple curves leading to different levels in which there was a small chamber inside the pyramid, up to the highest initiation chamber, practically located in the center of the pyramid, was known by the name of Joseph. It was there that the royal crown—the high diadem, known as the symbol of knowledge—was placed on his forehead during the closing ceremony, which enthroned him as the greatest master of masters of the brotherhood.

According to tradition, after the birth of the child, the family was the main sovereign pontiff initiator of the child education up to elementary initiations of our religions; religiously constituted of rites of the ancient ancestors cult, it was after that period of elementary initiations that the vocational training began, allowing him to have a title in the society; initiation in the temples of the Little Mysteries in the ancient sense appointed the adept to titles like "Son of Woman," "Son of Man," or "Hero," after acquired the natural and human knowledge of Little Mysteries, sometimes after many long years of initiation. So in all these therapeutic branches, Jesus already had some healing powers; thus, his initiation was pursued in the Great Mysteries, after his elementary initiations, and in the secondary education of adulthood; in the Great Mysteries, the insider completed another hierarchy of sciences and arts. At the end of the most comprehensive studies, the pontiff of the temple was to crown him with some priestly and royal powers. He was then called the "Son of the gods" or the "Son of God" because he had sought the existence and knowledge of this science and many others contained in the temple. Jesus held the title of "Son of God" or "Son of the gods" because he was a consecrated child to a prophetic mission by the desire of his mother Mary, who was affiliated to the Essenes, before his birth.

Before our eyes, your word and the sight of the great being that you evoked terrifies and crushes us. Oh, blind soul, you're a Master who discovered his heavenly soul; arm yourself with the torch of mysteries in the terrestrial night, and follow thy divine guide, your luminous double; because the key to our past existences and future reasoning belongs to that Genius. He had now reached the superior degree and would bear the name of Jesus and be recognized as the Christ. The members of the supreme council harmoniously surrounded Joseph, honoring him, paying him homage by proclaiming that he was the incarnation of a supreme and living rationality. This part of Jesus' life was wrapped in a veil of legend by the gospels and left in the shade.

Once reached the messianic consciousness, the great Nazarene started to show the initiatic traditions and the esoteric truths, the meaning and the transcendent significance of its dual education. Jesus came to share the gospel of the kingdom of heaven, the thought of the prophets that he had conquered with men, to change the face of the world after so many meditations. He had just torn the veil of the traditional old religion from the beyond, that our ancestors implanted on earth, by evoking a more perfect life in the world of souls beyond this earth, and to achieve it, humanity must first begin to realize it by love and active charity here on earth. The young prophet from Galilee was preaching at the edge of the Lake of Gennesaret. He preached near fountains, in the boats of the fishermen, and in the green oasis between Capernaum, Bethsaida, and Korazim.

Already, crowds were following him; already, he was practicing by charismatically performing powerful miracles in a glowing and joyful sense. By the imposition of hands, he healed the sick by a command, or his mere presence, and often by a simple glance. He recruited fishermen and peasants among common ardent, believing and straight men, chosen by the help of his proper second sight gift to capture men of action. As a religious initiator, a glance was enough for him to make his choice. Irresistible, many disciples clung to him at all times. After probing a soul, he said, "Follow me." He was calling the hesitant and the timid to him with a decisive gesture.

He wanted thus by this gathering, to establish the kingdom of heaven on earth, with the teaching that he had already lived by a sermon in the Essenes Mountain. The popular teaching of Jesus showed the master sitting at the top of the hill, summarizing the teaching formed of esoteric germ, intended for only few people and likely to be understood by people with a specialized knowledge, with the future interested initiates gathered at his feet. The poor women and emaciated men in gray robes of penance, dirty and sick obviously welcome his words by seeing humble virtues in them. "Blessed are the poor in spirit, for the kingdom of heaven belongs to them. Blessed are those who mourn, for they shall be comforted. Blessed are the pure in heart, for they shall see God," Jesus said.

Mtt. 6:27–30 transmits this to people of little faith: "But if God so clothes the grass of the fields, which today is alive and tomorrow is thrown into the oven, will he not much more clothe you, O you of little faith?" Let us put full trust to our Heavenly Father for our earthly needs because the lily teaches us dependence upon God. Why do you worry about clothing? Consider yourself like growing in the lily fields, since even Solomon, in all his glory, was not dressed like you.

"Which of you by the thought of worry can add a single hour to his lifespan?" Jesus said furthermore. In Rom. 13:14, to elaborate on all our needs, Jesus said, "Clothe yourselves with the Lord Jesus Christ, and do not think about how to gratify the desires of the flesh." Your spiritual beauty is far superior to the splendor of the earth. Let us not be impressed by the judgment and appreciation of this world.

Your clothing is Christ himself, and God is the one who clothes our soul, not as a reward for our works but in response to our faith. One little f lower of the fields is more beautiful than all the glory of the great king Solomon, who, despite all his glory, was not clothed like the fields of lilies, Jesus said to the audience, with the starry sky on his head. The brilliance splendor of his words, resounding as the sound of a golden bell in the atmosphere with the fragrance of lilies, appears very clearly in the Bible in Song of Songs 2:1: "I am a rose of Sharon, a lily of the valleys," and the poem on the glory of Solomon, transforming poor women in virgins, in the beatitudes of light, altered with the perfume of lilies, pleasant and refreshing from the celestial kingdom. They felt elected like the words of Solomon to the Shulamith, expressing the modest opinion that they had of themselves, a humble expression of humility of the lilies of valleys.

Me, a wild girl of the fields, could I be better than the others? Because I feel nothing in myself, I was not born in the cities; I was born in a room constituted of the floor between joists in our house of cedars; my greenery is my bed and cypress my paneling. I am a country girl, a lily of the valleys, a flat area of the land worked by farmers, known as desperate impure, incredulous, unfaithful and ugly living being, but where lilies in the valleys of this world live; and it's the least of Solomon's luxurious palace that attracted me. And I simply explained my preference by giving my identity. Entering in the thought of the young girl,

Solomon corrected her and changed the Shulamite's words to praise. Concerning wealth, Jesus answered when the twelve disciples asked him the meaning of his parables; he said to the twelve and the crowd around him that the mystery of the kingdom of God has been given to them but that to those outside that mystery, the word comes to them in parables.

Marc says that it was always in parables that Jesus spoke; for example, when he wanted to explain the word *sower*, he was asking his interlocutors by saying, "How could you understand all these parables, if you do not understand the parable of the sower? Mark 4:13–14; in 4:18–19, he continued to explain that "those who are receiving the seed in the thorns, are those who hear the word, but the worries of this World, the deceitfulness of wealth, and desires for lusts come in and muffled the word, preventing it from fructifying." Jesus was the lily in the whimsical child's valley, and then on the Mount of Transfiguration, impregnated with the magnificent glory, he was set free; so is the vocation of the church.

But Solomon opposed the action of the Word of God and the lily of thorns as the emblem of all that is tedious. In this verse of the Song of Songs, the word "*thorns*" evokes the golden thistle that invaded the earth. By its form, its color, and its fragrance, which make lily to be the figure of miracle fact in its bushes, in the middle of thistles bushes, where the house of Caesar was found at the time of the Apostle Paul, there were saints on earth like lilies of God, says Phil. 4:22, adding that principally, those of the house of Caesar were a miracle of the Holy Spirit, and that they greet you.

And Phil. 2:14–15 confirms that we are surrounded by vanity, impurity, and wickedness. With this acclamation, we can read this on his chapters: In the middle of corrupted and perverse generation, "Do everything without grumbling or arguing, because the work of salvation must be undertaken without contestation, so that you may become blameless and pure, as the children of God without fault. Then you will shine among them like stars in the sky, Paul exhorted us."

James 2:5 declares to us in the scripture that God has chosen the poor in the eyes of the world for them to be rich in faith and be heirs of the kingdom, which he promised those who love him. And 2:6–9 said that it is the rich who oppress us and dragged us in front of the courts, blaspheming the beautiful name. It continued by saying, "If you really fulfill the royal law found in the Scripture, which says 'Love your neighbor as yourself,' you're doing right." "But the royal law will condemn the transgressors, and it was this law that Narcissus transgressed."

This handsome young man Narcissus, who rejected the nymph Echo, who was inflamed with love for him and followed his trace to find out that he preferred to die than to surrender himself to the desires of the nymph Echo. Shortly after sinking into the woods, Narcissus fell in love with his own reflection at the edge of the water table, synonymous to the river that brought him into the world; mad of passion for his own image, he transformed himself little by little into a flower, unable to detach himself from his reflection in the water.

Since he could not reach it, he became the lily that bears his name in the summer, the beautiful season where the sun hatches its f lowers petals at a spectacular aspect in all colors and makes them exhale sweet scents like the sun that blooms love in the soul, seized by a strong feeling of emotional relation and love; he forgot to drink, but being in the middle of water, where he struck himself in front of his own ref lection and dies of thirst devouring his heart; he forgot to eat, charmed by his beauty in the limpid water of the place, and rooted at the edge of the shallow pond colonized by vegetation; and by crying, shedding tears that disturbs the limpidity of the crystalline waters, made him see the image of his face erase.

And in his soul, his love slowly faded away, dried by the secret fire of desire. Gradually, Narcissus lost his strength and saw himself fading, wasted away by time in summer, losing that youthful air he once had. And the nymph Echo who could only repeat the last words that she heard by the punishment of Juno because of jealousy, was both the sister and wife of Jupiter, her twin brother. Because she helped the nymphs in Jupiter arm to escape, the anger of Juno made her lose almost all the power of words to the point that she could no longer express her love for Narcissus. Repulsed, she lived in the lonely lairs, her love for Narcissus still living in the depths of her heart since that time. Is.35:1–2 thunder by declaring that, "Like Narcissus, she shall blossom as the rose and will flourish abundantly when she blooms. The loneliness would brighten when that spring f lower will announce the summer. And with the songs of gladness and the cries of triumph, she would be filled with joy, and the wilderness and the arid land shall rejoice; they would see the glory of the eternal, the splendor of our God, and the glory of Lebanon shall be given to it as the magnificent of Carmel and Sharon."

John 3:2–3 is assuring that what shall be has not yet been revealed, but now we are the beloved children of God. Jesus has announced the spiritual summer to us for when he will be revealed, we shall be like him, for we shall see him as he is. And all those who have this hope fixed on him will be purified as he is pure.

In Phil. 1:6, Paul says he is confident that the one who began that good work in us will carry it on to completion at the day of Jesus Christ. The sublime, wonderful work of Christ is a unique work and considered as the rose, the queen of flowers, the rose of Sharon as the rarest and most beautiful of flowers. The work of the grace of its creature will lead us to purity and divine perfection. No moral, philosophy or religion can be compared to it. Notice that this too many quotations that I am obliged to apply in this book is to have a solid foundation for what I'm saying; I appeal for your understanding. Ezek. 2:3–4–6 clarifies with these words: "I am sending you to the Israelites, to a rebellious nation that has rebelled against me; they and their ancestors have been in revolt against me to this very day. The people to whom I'm sending you, are obstinate and stubborn. Say to them, 'This is what the Sovereign Lord says. 'Though they're a rebellious people, do not be afraid of them or their words. Do not be afraid, though briers and thorns are all around you and you live among scorpions," "Said God to Jesus, by adding that although they're a rebellious people, whether they listen or fail to listen—they will know that a prophet has been among them.

The act of the apostle Peter, who visited all the saints, led him to those dwelt at Lydda. Acts 9:32–35 said that the apostle Peter found a paralyzed man named Aeneas bedridden for eight years already, and he ordered him to stand up; "Get up and make up thy bed. Jesus Christ will heal you," and immediately, Aeneas got up. Faced with disability, suffering, ignorance, and sin, all the inhabitants of Lydda and Sharon who saw him healed were converted to the Lord. That act of the apostle Peter was qualified as a rose of Sharon. Its good smell of the narcissus rose of Christ in the Sharon region embalmed the whole of that country. The sweet scent of Jesus also spread through Peter and Paul and many others.

God always makes us triumph in Christ, according to 2 Cor. 2:14–15. He is spreading the smell of his knowledge everywhere through us. Indeed, we among those who perished and among those who were saved are the good aroma of Christ for God. Let us keep the perfume of Christ in us; even if we are persecuted, our persecutors strip us of their hatred in the vessel of trial; even if the narcissus petals are one by one removed, the Lord allows our despoliation in the vessel of trial; then we are dressed with the redemptive red color, radiating a striking image, the beauty of the lily f lower, symbolically, the spiritual beauty purified by the blood of Jesus; we owe it our spiritual beauty. By preaching his struggles, his infinite pains, and his joys without limit and spreading the soft wind of palms in their hearts, Jesus was gradually realizing his small group of the kingdom of heaven on earth, first with the twelve apostles. But in these gospel accounts, concerning the public life of Jesus, there is a legend—the exaggeration of certain mysteries, contradictions, divergences, and the joined-together pieces comprising such a unity, as an original character so powerful in action and thought, that makes us feel invincible faced to the reality of life. Love your neighbor as yourself, and be perfect, as your Heavenly Father is perfect.

By exhibiting the means necessary to reach that marvelous kingdom, he started with the depth of morals and science. First, Jesus wanted to reproduce the divine perfection, the invisible above the visible in the perfection of the soul, the inner life of the soul above all external practices by his public teaching—the supreme commandment of initiation—his proper experience of spiritual truths of the esoteric tradition of the Essenes that he held. The circles: the finite and the infinite, particular to the universal, and where the secret of science resides, Jesus went through it. Jesus was also saying that man should be reborn by water and by spirit, for the soul and spirit to be purified, to be baptized with water and fire, representing the truth intellectually perceived in the kingdom of God. This summary marks under this form the doctrine of the ancient mysteries of Egypt, known as the regeneration, after being baptized. Water represents purification; the spiritual germ of the soul is developed by water. And this internal development and the spiritual development of man are two different stages of development and two degrees of initiation of the mysteries of Egypt. Some poor in spirit, who understood nothing of all that great knowledge of the temples that Jesus was evoking, were astonished at such a marvel, exchanging gazes between them. The esoteric thought of Christ animated those who had a thorough knowledge in the mystery doctrines of Egypt, like those of India, and Greece had an understanding of its double and triple primary or literal sense, which pierced deeply into the gospel.

Above all the goods of the earth, Jesus placed the kingdom of heaven at a very high level, known as a principle of the mysteries, considering the spiritual rather than the material substance of the world. From the second century, the church violently suppressed this esoteric tradition of the Essenes—the true significance of the words of Christ and his knowledge of the extraordinary things. Most theologians no longer know this true esoteric thought, and they simply blurred the right words.

Here is Jesus Christ, considered as a great bodhisattva, who completed the ten steps of the spiritual path, and who accomplished the ten grounds for the realization of the awakening to reach the illumination according to the tradition; it is an authorized fact empowered by a testimony of a Tibetan master, scholar, and teacher known by the name of Kalu Rinpoche, who taught meditation at the order of Situ Rinpoche of the Palpung Monastery.

He was called Issa, an evidence of a superior lama attesting that he left home at the age of thirteen to fourteen years old, after he left Mount Carmel, to go to India where he lived for six years and in Nepal and Himalayas for six years also. When this Russian journalist, who was an initiated Buddhist searching for inner peace went to the Moulbek lamasery in Ladakh, a Tibetan province of India, in the nineteenth century, precisely in 1887, he had the surprise of his life when a learned man, the prior of the monastery, showed him a book he claimed to be the story of Jesus's youth.

He cautiously translated this very curious old book in French with the help of an interpreter of the Himis monastery and discovered that Jesus was called Issa in the text. Jesus was also the subject of a book written by the journalist Nicolas Notovitch, the author of a book about his journey in the East. He indicated then by saying that Jesus left Nepal and the Himalayan Mountains, descended in the valley of Rajputana, and continued toward the west by preaching the supreme perfection of mankind to various people.

The manuscripts, written and signed by the hand of Jesus and certified by a very great lama, testified that Jesus stayed in the monastery of Ladakh of the same ecclesiastical community of our days. At that period of his life, all great knowledge of the temples taught to him, he taught it by leaving traces of his passage.

He was entrusted and assigned to the school of Carmel of the Essene brotherhood at the age of six, where he stayed for over a year before his departure for India, Tibet, Persia, Euphrates, Babylon, Greece, and Alexandria. Dr. H. Spencer Lewis, founder of the Rosicrucian Order (AMORC) in the USA, also declared that the Pyramid of Cheops was the temple where his sublime, ultimate initiation took place and that he survived the Crucifixion. Dr. H. Spencer

Lewis was the first responsible Imperator in the world for the Old and Mystical Rosicrucian Order (AMORC), from 1915 to 1939.

The registry of the school of Carmel indicated that Jesus, son of Mary and Joseph, was registered there under the name of Joseph. The Mount Carmel was originally an Essene sect founded at Mount Carmel; this school was called the "School of Prophets" by Edgar Cayce the Rosicrucian, who indicated the same registration of Jesus at Mount Carmel. The indication of Jesus birth was also confirmed by the writings of one of the church first historians, known as "the founder of the Western theology" named Quintus Septimius Florens Tertullianus; the Tertullian of Berber origin, 200 after Jesus Christ, who was also a prolific and the early Christian author from Carthage in the Roman province of Africa; including Saint Jerome, 375 after Jesus Christ, and other eminent fathers of the early Christian Church, reported that Jesus was born in an Essene cave, on the main road near Bethlehem.

Numerous affirmations of initiates' revendications of secret cults, known as the Templars, confirmed his initiation by an attested veneration; and by the certified worship of the mythical queen and a funerary goddess, under her Christianized form of the black virgin made Jesus an initiate of the Egyptian cult of Osiris and the faithful of the goddess Isis; a secret revealed by the erudite scholars, the learned who acquired knowledge through the Freemasonry studies, known as, A. E. Waite of the early twentieth century, and Eliphas Levi in the nineteenth century.

Many wise nobles also testified that he went to the East, where he was known under the name of Youssef and where he died in Kashmir, according to A. Faber-Kaiser; at the south of Calcutta, on the Bengal coast in the city of Puri, at that period, he taught and organized the Brahmin castes of Indian society in the freedom of conscience.

By the members of the Essene brotherhood of Mount Carmel, he was sent to the East before his departure for India at the age of sixteen years for three years. Then via Persia, he returned to Egypt for his final initiation after his first trip to the south of Great Britain. This was revealed to us by Edgar Cayce (1877–1945). He was also the one who placed the appearance of man on earth in five different places at the same time around ten million and a half years ago. A manuscript describing secrets on the life of Jesus was discovered at Nag Hammadi in 1945. This manuscript was considered as a heresy by the Vatican, which refused to recognize it. The gospel of St. Thomas was judged as one of the most accurate documents on the word of Christ, asserted by scientists and by scholars all over the world.

Here is an extract from his multiple messages: "The kingdom of God is within you and around you; not in stone and wooden buildings. Fend the piece of wood and I'm there. Raise the stone and you will find me." But because St. Thomas also doubted the resurrection of Jesus Christ as one of his twelve apostles, the Christian tradition considered him as the symbol of religious disbelief. The one who carried the "good news" to the south of India also founded his church in

India, where he arrived in 52. It was on the hill called Mount St. Thomas today that he died as a martyr around the year 70, and he was buried in the crypt of the basilica of his church, near the town of Mylapore.

The Acts and the gospel of Thomas are both Apocryphal works attributed to St. Thomas. His disbelief toward Jesus Christ earned him the nickname of "Doubting Thomas." Concerning his disbelief, the Bible says: "Put your finger here and see my hands; and take your hand and place it in my side. Do not disbelieve but believe. Blessed are those who have not seen and yet have believed" (John 20:27, 29).

Two graves exist in Shingo, partly called Herai, derived from the word *Heburai*, in the Aomori Prefecture in Japan, presumed to be those of Christ (Kourisuto) and his brother Isukiri. "Hebrew" is pronounced "Heburai" in Japanese pronunciation.

In 1903, in the prefecture of Ibaraki, a parchment was discovered explaining that Jesus would have returned to Japan after being saved from the Crucifixion, graceful to the death of his brother in his place. After he settled there, he lived for 22 years, and he left this earth at the age of 118 after making only one trip abroad.

There are many versions that claimed that Jesus survived the Crucifixion. Thomas says he crossed the Indian border in the company of a character who strangely resembled Jesus after his Crucifixion on the symbol of the great mystery, at the same time of his life with all joys, love, and all his wonders; having developed a sign of earthly and heavenly fire, a sign of death with all pain within him; the resurrection, the fact of coming back to life; and finally, a sign dominated by the Unity of Trinity. Another shared version is that Simon of Cyrene took his place as explained by the irrefutable evidence of the Priory of Sion which was in possession of many provided proof that can be verified. Simon of Cyrene is mentioned in the first three gospels named synoptics since the works of Griesbach in 1776, according to the order they appear in the New Testament which are: "1 - the gospel according to Mtt. 27:32, where Simon of Cyrene carries the cross of Jesus while he was led to Calvary to be crucified there; 2 - the gospel according to Mark 15:21, where Simon of Cyrene, the father of Alexander and Rufus, takes the cross of Jesus on his return from the fields; 3 - the gospel according to Luke 23:26, where they put their hand on Simon of Cyrene returning from the fields, loaded him with the cross, and carried it behind Jesus." However, the New Testament contains four gospels quoting on the crucifixion of Jesus; apart from the first three synoptic Gospels quoted here above, the Gospel according to John 19:16-37 also speaks of the crucifixion of Jesus, but does not mention Simon of Cyrene. And apart from these four gospels, Simon of Cyrene, is not mentioned anywhere else in the Holy Scriptures.

Manuscripts containing more than two hundred illustrations of the alphabet, found by the family of Takeuchi, derive other forms of Greek, Egyptian, and Chinese writing. He was called Jesus of Nazareth, but at the time of his birth, there was no city or town in Galilee named Nazareth. Because researchers wanted, at any price, to see one place by that name in Galilee, the town known as Nasira was renamed Nazareth from the third century after Jesus Christ. So, the name Nazareth was therefore given by Jews to anyone not belonging to their religion. Jesus was not from Nazareth, but it was Pilate who wrote an inscription in Hebrew, Greek and Latin, and fastened it to the cross, and it read: Jesus of Nazareth, king of the Jews John 19: 19-20. He was an Essene like John the Baptist and Elis, known insiders of a branch of the illuminated fraternity, an occult influence on the countries surrounding the Himalayas and the Nile, with a high character of the Brotherhood of the White Lodge, which originated in Egypt some years before the reign of Pharaoh Amenhotep IV, the great founder of the first propagation of the monotheistic religion, which possessed most of the apostles of Himalayas and initiates of Egypt.

Nazarenes and Essenes had numerous common similarities; they had the same tendency to mysticism and were similarly treated as heretics by Jewish scholars, knowing that the mystics of Palestine awaited the coming of a great master, who was the reincarnation of one of their anterior leaders. At that period, the secret teachings of the East were saying that the Essene brotherhood represented a group of more advanced, more developed beings spiritually on earth and were at the origin of Christianity.

Very young, Jesus followed most of the teachings of the four sects widespread in the first century: the Sadducees sect of Judean society, which was active in Judea; the Pharisees sect, whose numerous teachings were incorporated in the rabbinic tradition, was from the descendants of the sages of the Great Assembly, opposing Sadducees by their submission to the oral law, which reveals the rabbinic tradition; the Essenes sect, a group originated from a group of priests; and the Zealot sect (whose leader was the master of justice), founded by the philosopher named Judas of Gamala and by the Pharisee called Zadok. He was also the first to serve as a high priest in the first temple built by Solomon in Jerusalem; known as one of the rabbis of the high-priesthood generation of wise, and as the second generation of five in the group of the Tannaim, teachers who assembled the Oral Torah, known as the Mishna, which eventually formed the Talmud; this period came after the period of the Zugot "pairs" and was immediately followed by the period of the Amoraim "interpreters."

This Mishnah compiled by Rabbi (Judah I or Judah the Prince), editor in chief and publisher in the second century of our era, is nowadays used for the rabbinic teachings. This movement of the Zealot sect, the fourth philosophy, founded in the year 6 after Christ, is distinguished from the three other Jewish sects; and the "third Essenes sect," which daily practiced intense concentration, frequently in a psychological state of immersion into virtual reality, as a perception of being physically present in a nonphysical world; accompanied by abstinence of worldly pleasures in a psychological state of piety and holiness; and in a physical voluntarily poor society state and a disturbed sense of reality and time.

The manuscripts called the Dead Sea Scrolls, discovered in 1947, evoked that they were more ascetics and more esoteric than the other three movements. Their conceptions and beliefs, long remained a secret, were hiding their knowledge; well coded, only initiates had codes to recognize the true from false. The Essene order was of Pythagorean origin, practicing a severe morality, and was invested in a particular Jewish form and national belief. This order existed right from the time of the Maccabaeus and was not at all of Jewish origin. Between the second century BC and the first century, these four main sects of Judaism were the members of the priestly class in ancient Judea. To render tribute to the human organization and considering the knowledge belonging to the secret domain of the higher ranks of their order, they leaned on the studies of nature, the practice of medicine, to know the properties of the infinite effects of plants, minerals, virtue, and wisdom. They were meeting in sections of grades to finally make their practice a duty to the physical and intellectual development of their fellow creatures. In many sacred writings, including the Christian Bible, Essenes were often regarded as Gentiles, and they were not Jews by birth, or by blood or by religion. The one who was called Jesus of Nazareth was born by Gentile parents, who lived in Galilee, and imbued with the teachings of the Essene brotherhood, with the privilege to learn the secrets of the Great White Brotherhood, a precise and simple truth from all Rosicrucian archives.

The similarity between the Essenes and the early Christianity is the most important revelation of the contemporary Jewish sect of early Christianity. There are innumerable confirmations about the gospels and Acts of the Apostles qualifying them to be Essene texts. The teacher of righteousness true identity and the organizer of the Essene community could not be revealed. He wrote the rule, the Manual of Discipline, and hymns. Constantly harassed, after being sent among Jews to let them hear the language of the prophets, he was betrayed by one of his own spiritual brothers. Persecuted by the impious priest for his achievement, he died a violent death. Jesus, the master, was the prototype of the Essene messiah. The discovery of these manuscripts was the most sensational thing that ever happened. The origins of Christianity were described in it in page 123 of the 1957 Dead Sea Scrolls.

In Mtt. 12:11, Jesus asked this to the Jews: "Which one of you who has a sheep and it falls into a pit on the Sabbath, will not take hold of it and lift it out?" He continued in Mark. 4:11 and said to them, "The mystery of the kingdom of God has been given to you, but to those on the outside, everything is done in parables." And as a final example, in Luke 8:4–10, Jesus quoted a parable of the sower to the crowd that was gathered from all cities. He said that some of the seeds fell from the sower's bag on the edge of the road; these seeds were trodden down and finally eaten by the birds of the air. The one that landed on the rock as soon as it sprung up dried immediately, because it lacked moisture. The other fell among thorns, and sprang up with it, stifled after grown. And the one that fell on good ground sprang up and bore fruit a hundredfold. So, at the end of this quote, he said, "Whoever has ears to hear, let him hear," for it is given to you to know the mysteries of the kingdom of God. Such was his answer to the question of his disciples, who did not understand anything about this parable, and like the others, they saw without seeing and heard without understanding as those who had only parables outside the kingdom of God. These parables were related to the secret teachings that Jesus explored during his years of initiation. To better understand, Jesus gave the explanation of the parable of the sower in Luke 8:11–18.

The uncertainty of Jesus's date of birth also raises issues, which are making a lot of ink f low. According to the Hebraic calendar, the only one valid during the time of Jesus Christ, the year began at the season that follows winter, more precisely on the holy day of spring, the season before the summer. It is very pleasant to contemplate the buds that announce the growth of the leaves and the development of the first f lowers in this season. Luke 2:1-14 says he is born in the spring, at the time of the grazing of cattle. And in the rabbinic literature, April was the first month of the ecclesiastic year, and it was the first day of that month that the celebration of "Easter" (named Pesach in Hebrew) occurred. For St. Clement of Alexandria (the master of Origen Adamantius of Alexandria), the nativity took place on April 18.

Others think that it is on March 25. Traditionally, in the Jewish year, since the Exodus of the Hebrews from Egypt, the twenty-fifth day of the ninth month of the Hebrew calendar is consequently equivalent to December 25. However, some sources believe that he is born on January 6, the day of Epiphany, held by St. Epiphany. It was known that this great and unique Christian fete representing the manifestation of Christ in this world was first celebrated by the Magi, who came to pay homage to the Messiah incarnated in this world, was celebrated up to the late fourth century. But the origin of the feast of Epiphany was anterior to Christianity; it came from pagan festivals of light, celebrated on December 22, marking the longest night of the year, the winter solstice, before the day of the celebration of Christmas.

Then a prolongation of days announced the extension of the celebrations, considered as the manifestation or the rebirth of light at the origin of all things, going from December 22 up to twelve days and twelve nights highly symbolic. So, January 6, the date that ended this cycle of the prolongation of days, was the day that the Father of the Epiphanius Church of Salamis in Cyprus chose as Jesus's birth date. And since December 25 was introduced as Jesus's Nativity and Christmas feast, this date only remained symbolic but considered for other celebrations. In the gospel and the Jewish tradition, epiphany is also celebrated under the form of a child begotten within the Jewish people in the lineage of David, in a given historical time. And the first Christian churches of the East, heirs of the ancient Church of the East founded by the apostle Thomas, also think that it was the sixth day of the tenth month that Jesus was born.

Jesus was born in Palestine about two thousand years ago. His name, Jesus, originated from Aramaic and Greek, the two main languages spoken by Jesus. *Yehoshuah* or *Joshua* in Greek means "Yahweh saves." The word *Christ* came from the Greek word *Christos* that the first apostles used and was later on used by the church with the name Jesus included to be that name we know today as

Jesus-Christ. The *mashiach,* or Messiah in Hebrew, means "the one who was anointed." The gospels, the epistles of St. Paul, and the Acts of the Apostles gathered evidences attributed to the apostles Thomas and James that certified the existence of Jesus under the name of the Apocryphal gospels. A lot of research of various people and historians were made on his life without evidence of historical significance of historians. But it is known that the Talmud contained elements of the life of Jesus. It is also known that most of his speeches were pronounced in Greek and in Aramaic, the language of the hidden initiation. And when he was to speak to those who did not understand these languages, he used Hebrew.

Historians concluded that Jesus was born around the year 6 BC, and his death was placed on April 7 toward the year 30 of our era. Between the actual birth of Jesus Christ and the year 0, there is a difference of about seven years. It seemed that the Mayan calendar, based on the conjunctions of Jupiter and Saturn, coincided with a large number of religious or political events, such as the birth of Christ in the year 7 BC. Jesus himself was not speaking of his birth, but all we know is what said of him. On the other hand, the story of the Magi was invented to give more authenticity to his story.

From the Essene memory, Lamaas was an astrologist who very early came to see the family and without a doubt gave birth to the famous symbolic image of the visit of the Magi, whom the Christianity of the first centuries never spoke of but, at the origin, placed there as an esoteric key of the alchemical teachings. The town of Nazareth was also added to the story of the Magi, just like it was told to us. Furthermore, Lamaas followed Jesus for a good part of his life, even when Jesus began to manifest the traits of hereditary human temperament in various characteristic types and to talk. He who closely followed him could notice pretty quickly that Jesus was not like other children because he was developing quite exceptional faculties of teaching. At that time, the Essene brotherhood was saying that the son of Mary and Joseph had something special.

Jesus deeply learned the principles of Buddha discipline: the word (verb) of Krishna, the healing techniques, the transmutation of elements, and the breath control, equal for total concentration were part of his initiation. His sublime initiation was completed in the heart of the Great Pyramid. He was the last really known initiate initiated in the Great Pyramid, a place where all energies at the time of our ancestors were focused at one point connecting the atom and the germ of every human being, with the supreme spirit of creation. It is also well known that he reached the highest degree of initiation after the completion of all tests indicated in the corridor leading to the tomb, representing what each entity as an initiate must go through before reaching his total liberation. Only Jesus was able to successfully complete the test of the empty tomb that was never completed before by other initiates sealed in the coffin of a tomb during his final initiation.

Jesus was quite normal at the age of six to sixteen years old, when he learned the commandments of the Essene brotherhood, before deciding to travel to India, Persia, and Egypt in search of different perspectives. At the age of thirteen to sixteen years old, having already had the esoteric knowledge, he pledged purification before continuing his initiation. Therefore, to purify and detoxify the physical and mental body, he went to India. To learn medicine and coordinate energy, he went to Persia for a year and appropriately spent most of his proper time in Egypt, where true knowledge and high initiation was and where he was finally initiated.

The prophetess named Judy during Jesus's lifetime, which headed and led the Essene Brotherhood, was healing those affected with physical or mental illness by the thought. This secret order had two objectives within Judaism: (1) the preparation of certain individuals and (2) the training of missionaries. Graceful to each of the twelve apostles of Jesus, consciousness started to become conscious of his body on earth, symbolizing a major center of regions or kingdoms that each of us finds in our innermost depths, linked to the reactions of people and stones, and the twelve things that disappoint and disgust us. This awareness is the price of the flesh in the matter and the transitional material that passes and leaves a permanent place to beauty, love, hope, and faith. Jesus, the Christ and the one whose personality we usurped, was very well initiated in the Great Pyramid with so much knowledge.

For his intelligence, justly superior to the one of certain beings on earth, he had the privilege of being initiated in certain very privileged places of the world and be prepared to live certain energies for the Christic dubbing doctrine, and continue his mission of teaching the natural laws governing life and transmit the universal concepts, neglected and forgotten by terrestrial humanity in the cosmos. As a human being like everyone else but with a sublime understanding and knowledge of initiation, he was severely tried by the lower class of sinners on earth; sparing no one with such erudition by the lack of understanding, they crucified him. Having accomplished his realization and his union with the divine in a way that all men could live, he became the perfect receptacle of light. However, the Gospel of John was not an expression of the transcendent person but ultimately a transcendent quality finally accessible to all men in the universe.

Jesus learned very quickly that, to change the world, he had to change himself. In this regard, to achieve his goals, he took all paths that led him to knowledge to reveal the whole truth that had to be revealed for life to be beautiful for those who know how to contemplate it. He wanted not to impose anything; he just wanted to teach and give the opportunity for everyone to take what seemed true and reject what seemed wrong. What escaped Jesus was the disadvantage of being hated when he was telling the truth useful to him. By telling the truth, Jesus felt a sense of mystery, the true source of all true science, known as the occult science, which has already revealed so many proven authentic facts in the world.

They have so much repeated to human that he lived in a democracy, that he finally believed in things very incomprehensible from the comprehensible ideas of the world—that most humans have lost the habit to think for themselves. But instead of learning, rather than teaching how to think, all rely on memorizing facts that are not necessary to the thought. God drew one from zero, as he drew the earth from nothingness. "There is nothing concealed that shall not be revealed, neither hidden that shall not be made known" (Luke 12:2).

If mankind wants to survive and reach a higher plane, he should indispensably search for a new way of thinking to master the mental body, the astral body, and the physical body. He must think of the past evolution of man, his present constitution, his intellect balance, and his sensitive heart and healthy body for his future development. All scholars have agreed, recognizing the current wrong way of human thought. It is must necessary that a latecomer who possesses a gift of wonder comes, to defend up to death and solve the impossible of those who are wrong but believed to be right. Blessed is the ignorant who do not believe in the universe that moves similarly through time because if he searches, he will find the time. Let those who no longer think that time exists, believing that they know everything about time, no longer seek it and be complacent in their ignorance. Is it not true that a wise man is considered mad in the kingdom of ignorance? Achieving perfection is everything, and time is nothing for nature hastening slowly.

By the knowledge he accumulated from his initiation, the great master and the soul of the teacher has shown us that human being was God but at the same time a very bad kind of animal and that God exists full of kindness, wisdom, and truth in all. Better known to us as God who was not only on the outside but also inside us, he never parted from us or any of his creations; and one of his sides knows everything and contains all truth. The lost gospel according to St. Peter affirmed that Jesus, the Grand Master, came here to reveal the truth, not to redeem.

His creation is what is called by Hindu Kryia "action" and Shakti "intelligent energy" considered as the "voice and spirit," derived from the creative verb. Jesus used "I" as the pure impersonality in John 14:6, saying, "I am the way, the truth, and the life." He could do things that he already created in his thought because everything could be done by the thought. And each of his speeches was an initiation. That is why when he was saying, "This is my body," or, "This is my blood," to his disciples and the 120 men who were around him during the Last Supper, he wanted to demonstrate that the spirit was in everything and that it should not be confused with the body, although interconnected but detached from the body.

Before the inclusion of "King of the Jews" being inscribed on the cross by Pilatehe, he was commonly called the son of a carpenter or Yeshua. Matthew is telling us about his birth, saying that only three Magi were asking where the child, the king of the Jews was, but the version of Edgar Cayce said that there were several visits of the Magi from Persia, India, Egypt, Chaldea, Gobi, Indochina, and Thailand. The title of mage was only conferred to mystical masters—highly advanced distinguished dignitary scholars in all areas of major academies and schools of mysticism of the East—who have mastered the arts and sciences and reached the highest degree of initiation into the mystery schools. The Magi mentioned in the Bible were consulted not only on matters of astrology, astronomy, medicine, history or spirituality, but also by kings and powerful intellectual elites of all countries, particularly in the field of natural laws and hundreds of other topics that required deep reflection and thorough knowledge.

The Messiah, coming from the prophecies in the Old Testament, is described as a divine person. The child that would be born of a virgin would be called "Emmanuel," which means "God is with us," according to Is. 7:14, and not the assertions of the New Testament about the nature of Jesus. Jesus in the New Testament is considered as a "mortal prophet" by his disciples and as just a man, a great and powerful man. But he was also considered as God, as every man is God.

The nature of the divinity of Jesus—the doctrine of the present Christianity—was invented and imposed by emperor Constantine in the Council of Nicaea in the year 325. Acts 10:25–26, 14:12–18, and Rev. 19:10 forbid us to bow down in a gesture of adoration before a created human being and simultaneously presented us Jesus considered as a mortal prophet, a man consecrated to a worship that belonged to God alone, as the Gospel of John 20:28 presents us this adoration to the crucified: "My Lord and my God!" said Thomas after the resurrection of Jesus. In Rev. 5, elder men bowed down to worship him; in John 3: 16, John proclaimed him as the only begotten Son of God. In 1 Cor. 8:6, he is presented in the image of the invisible God, a Lord by whom all things were created and through whom we exist. In Matt. 8:2, he is called the Lord, and before him, a multitude of sick people came and bow down to ask if he could heal them.

Truly, in all this admiration, Jesus was never God in the highest sense of the term God but created, engendered, and received a religious consecration so far inferior to God because he could not put the biblical monotheism and God's transcendence in failure. On the other hand, the fathers of the Council of Nicaea (325), the 220 to 250 participating bishops at the council, specified that Jesus was the Son of God, not created but begotten. Almost unanimous, the rejection of the Aryan doctrine qualified of a truth contrary to the integrity of the faith (a heresy) but supported by almost 99 percent of the participating bishops at the council, which only had two votes against the "credo." Is he of the same nature as the Father? The answer is no. But the divine boost given by Constantine made Jesus be considered as God in the Council of Nicaea. Chaired by the pope, that assembly of bishops was like the first council of the church from the twenty-one councils that the Catholic Church has known, including the latest one known as the Vatican II.

Jesus' divinity and his oneness with the Father, officially proclaimed by the Council of Nicaea, was the result of a vote of some 220 to 250 bishops of the Council of Nicaea. But the prologue of the gospel testimonies of John and the epistles of St. Paul in the New Testament are forceful. By introducing the personal idea of a creative and transcendent God, the thought of the original and the primordial tradition from which all religious founders got their inspiration was deformed. That thought of the original tradition—belittled in common by Judaism, Christianity, and Islam—was reinstated under the form of a great planetary religion by esotericism. Their God, an impersonal energy, designates the character of what contains a principle in itself to the nature that manifests itself in everything that exists around us. In the beginning was the Word, and the Word was with God, and the Word was God.

In the United States of America, in connection with the oppression of blacks, a religious culture was developed. In 1863, the abolition of slavery gave rise to separate black churches in the south. The freed slaves, the spiritual Negroes in majority Protestants, perpetuated their own religious traditions. Especially since the whites closed all the doors of educational institutions to them, they sought the gospel, the incantation of God's spell—the gospel and the blues in the African essence. It was in that instruction that their revolt was born, and the dream of social justice expressed in a religious language.

The black churches were founded in the late eighteenth century; traditionally the home of the black militancy as their only place of reunion and a space of comfort to the community legitimacy; a place of calls to the word of God and to the resistance. Finally, a prophetic theology of liberation was developed in those American black churches, having as roots the collective suffering of the community as experience. Combined with a prophetic theology of the faith of man, it incarnated the causes that it espoused, adopted the belief, and supported the way of life by practicing the pedagogy of action of moral and religious convictions.

The black community in the United States was drawing its sociopolitical substance in view of its liberation in that religious tradition of the community, legitimizing and inspiring universal transcendent principles. During centuries of oppression, forgiveness and tolerance were at the origin of its principles, incarnated by figures defending dignity and the human personality. The suffering of the black man highlights the deep spirituality of this one. It has not been destroyed by the inhuman sufferings he has undergone. He is able to draw the power of resistance from self-control in his deep spiritual resources specific to his culture.

The word of Christ conveyed is the universal experience of love, the image of God, the identification of every man in the image of God; that idea recommends decent treatment to humans, a phenomenon of divine humanization and a sacralization of the human, a deification of the human by the increased valorization of love, with the instruction to improve the personal morality intellectually. These transcendent forms are the great traditional, sacrificial entities of the country and nation, mobilizing values above the human. As human projects: a revolution, a progress to the point of achieving sanctification.

In that tradition, there is joy in the individual who recognizes the values above himself, exceeding his own subjectivity. Because the sacred is by definition more important than his life individually, ready to be sacrificed; but how to imagine that the human spirit could function without the necessary conviction to a belief in the sacred, without the experience or the idea of a religion as an irreducibly real thing in this world, while the discovery of the sacred is intimately linked to the consciousness of a real world? Thus, this consciousness gives meaning to the impulses and to the experiences of the black man.

Crucified by the slave trade and colonization, sufferings have settled for five centuries in the African continent. Contributing to the germination of a new civilization of panhuman, to a state of intense anxiety badly defined and specific in objective in which insecurity existed before any cause; but to the most insignificant reason observed, fixing fear in fear and a foreboding feeling of apprehension forever; Africa finds an attenuating balm against its painful past, oppressed by an indescribable apprehension that freezes its feelings, and throws it in a continual numbness faculties of its spirit. But the right arm of the tyrant is still extended to the heart of that Africa already crucified, claiming the black man's tepid reawakening of his consciousness, having reasons to hope for a better future; but on its side is the face of the shadow of America and Europe upright before it as a German soldier. And it is its acquired crystallized faith that will rejuvenate difficult tests of the man of the black continent.

This institution of slavery became aware of its condition of oppressing the freedom by reading the Bible in secret to give slavery the consolation of God. The myth of the exodus to the promise of love was confounded with a journey to the divine, the liberated, and the sacred disciples around the master having faith in him. When I hear mount the supplications of the wishes of our love toward the sky, of the return so tender of spring, I think of you; at the farewell of your love of September; and as my religious principle of enumeration, I count the actions that are repeated as a means of giving thanks to that love; invoking the action that engages its freedom to better confront and praise it with dignity.

Inspired, my conscience embodies a generation marked by the practice of evocation in general and by the natal sound of love for man, for the black man, giving him the hope to escape his ineluctable and fatal fate because the black man knew and was able to demonstrate the proof of exceeding the hatred causing his suffering imposed by the tyrant, without the temptation of revenge. The African and African American dimension of suffering inspired traditional and spiritual transcendent African values to not succumb to desperation. According to natural justice, religious faith must find a founding act internalizing the values and principles of life, hatred, and evil to accept suffering and resist their perversion. But the existentialism of tolerance among the black men engendered reconciliation between the meanings of suffering assumed by the African and the colonial oppressor.

Our experience has followed the spiritual path toward faith, to answer with good the evil inflicted on us. Our evangelical message has the solidarity that unites the oppressed human suffering to love. Our disposition of the soul and spirit opposes the absolute immorality of the oppression of black people, of the spring of the will inspired by evil for another. But the love in us is the highest virtue; the mercy generosity virtue of forgiveness of the principal criminal pleasure is to satisfy its desire to obey that principle of love; the basis of evil and the selfishness of man are the basis of human misfortunes.

The slavery of man for the purpose of forced labor, the central organism of gulag, managing the forced labor in the camps of the Soviet Union, and the destruction or slaughter of a mass scale of people, especially caused by fire or nuclear war known as Holocaust, are eruptions of the singular cruelty of evil of the Western global society that the culture of the principles of freedom and the human rights does not question but continues their unprecedented barbarism in a so-called civilized society. In other words, the reason for slavery, raising the same racist subjugation of colored people, made man believe that modernity has no sign of civilization.

The negation of the Western moral responsibility is obvious—a moral that still requires barbarism to its neighbor and to all humanity. Know that good is not done by selfishness but by the moral conscience. The cruelty of suffering imposed on black people testifies the nuances that underlie the moral efficacy of Western civilizations, placing this selfish morality above racial ideology. The racist identity, on the other hand, is placed above morals and is contrary to the social and moral progress to distinguish good from evil. The construction of violence of these great civilizations is not solely of moral judgment but is also due to the definitions of good and evil developed in the principles of all their civilizations to nourish inhuman feelings of contempt and hatred against blacks.

The voices of my tears are deposited in the marrow of their bones and mourning the souls of my ancestors, sacrificed black heroes, men of heaven. I admit to you that I feel sadness when I look at myself. I see that all my senses, like the morning and spring sun, and like the midday sun and the summer solstice, are awakened and dictate tolerance and the meaning of forgiveness to me; now that Shamash (the sun god) of justice, morality, and truth, has exposed the evil and the injustice in full light.

Sin, the god of the moon and father of the gods, is the creator of all things, the divinity of divinities, to whom I ally myself with deep faith. And I feel death settling in my blood in front of the priests of your clergy. The inspirer of the laws under the auspices of a king is represented by a worshipper and places his code several centuries before me, and I am crying to death, the death as a notion, as a biological link, innate of a common and inseparable genetic history. Thus, my memory is giving me a sense to the event of death, and my remembrance values its life and existence.

And since the voices of my tears are deposited in the marrow of your bones, they're mourning the souls of my ancestors, sacrificed black heroes, men of heaven. But instead of asking the cosmos to give us the wealth of the power of spirit, the wealth of health, the richness of the joy of living to discover the wealth of happiness that exists, the richness of the peace of life itself that the universe gives to all its creatures, allowing to know what we are, which defines that we are what we are, we prefer doing bad and turn to evil. Today, the man who has a good idea that can be put into execution, the creative mind that can dominate and visualize this idea, is a man who has wealth, a limitless wealth, a powerful wealth.

But, no, not to the cosmos but only supplications of praise to powerful kings and princes, like those who believe they own the earth. Know that the angel of peace in me is revealing me mysteries, mysteries of angels that differ, misleading, and destroying the Son of man; mysteries of angels measuring the faith and indicating me the day of final judgment, a day when all spirits will praise the Lord of spirits, sitting on his throne of glory with a unanimous voice. The Judgment Day of sinners and the impious is the day that the voice of an angel who shows salvation to those who taught iniquity to saints and to the elected will be heard.

I see a disaster establishing the truth of a fact; are you not seeing that an imminent catastrophe of impious and sinners has tilted the earth? And that it is time to seek advice from the grandfather of our ancestors, the heaven? From the pure angels of this disaster, ordered by God, who reveals their secrets to me about the preparation of the chastisement of the unrighteous angels of the human beings on earth convicted for the secrets that they have given to man? For me, the leader of the spirits was unable to execute the power of his will on the son of men, for their wickedness is always and always great. His justice was not endured, and no one has walked in righteousness. The human being is only subject to an evil spirit, which with his curse, the herbs of the earth cannot cure. But speaking here only of my own kidnapping, what else can I do than to ask the salvation of the holy angels and the glory of the Lord of spirits, God? It is a transfiguration by faith removed so that I should not see the point of death, for I am a being who was taken alive from the earth, and I do not invoke the death in the eyes of God's justice.

Since the creation of the human being, African beliefs have always given great importance to plants, to its barks, to its leaves, and to its roots, because— endowed with extraordinary therapeutic properties—they're used to heal the sick body, to purify the body and soul, to protect them against devilries, to favor love in accordance with the healing, to attract luck, and to institute protection. They use certain minerals such as consecrated crystals, charged with divine power. And then these entities, geniuses of the forces of nature, are taking different forms in the animal diversity in rivers, under and above the ground, mountains that pierce the starry sky, hills, and trees, which are mysteriously watching the shadows of the pitiful humanity, spending a short time on the surface of the earth. The birds in heaven, their bones and the human bones are great for bewitchment and for healing.

Thus, for Africans, object on earth is endowed with magical powers because it shelters geniuses of the earth, water, fire, and air, known as entities of the nature. Generally, as in all beliefs in the world, the African knowledge and practices conceived animal sacrifices, destined to satisfy geniuses and entities of the nature and to collaborate with the traditional healer. The ancestor worship is therefore dedicated to the entities of natural forces since the human being, from his dual constitution, is endowed with spiritual and intellectual faculties. So, through the cooperation with the geniuses, the souls of the deceased can be invoked to cure diseases, etc. Unfortunately, this good African religious practice has a side that can harm. It invokes, above all forces, a sublime power—the power of God, which purifies and unbewitches the bewitched to liberate him and protect him. It therefore allows casting a spell to destroy, cause misfortune, and cause death knowingly.

Consequently, death is a magical thought, connecting us to life and to the afterlife—the final goal of all life. As long as this afterlife persists in the memory of the living, our dead are among us. Our ancestors, who practiced these multiple rites of meditation, prayer, and other rites to extend the memory of our dead, are living cleaner and closer to the nature. To provide an intercessor between man and the gods, an intercessor in contact with human beings was necessary. Thereby an action of a magical thought is manifested in the modeling of clay statuettes, in the painting of parietal art or tableau, etc. A knowledge in statuary art on wood or stone was putting its engineering in work and was producing representations intended to define the positive vision and the faults of the human being; since the name of the supreme God is at the same time indefinable and just an approach of the unknown, therefore, unnamable, it could not be represented, nor the supreme God be defined.

We must above all carefully think about the vision of a field on other, find it interesting and choose it, if we accept its action by the magical thought. For example, prayers or meditations are chosen for the rituals of mummification, particularly known through the Egyptians. The skull, an indefinable magical thought being the symbol of death, which has long been in relation with certain practices of liaisons between the different planes of existence, is also related to postmortem rituals—rituals occurring for meeting death. The next period after death, indicating a thought in the spirit is to pass the dead from the world of spirits, to the one of the living; what an indefinable magical thought of the black man.

It was by the cosmos evidence (magic) that man was born, very certainly with magic. The evening at the vigil, he was very certain that the one who spoke of one other was he himself; so, he created numerous gods for himself. Having been unable to free himself from one or the other, led him to find refuge in an imaginary and illusory world. Suddenly, he experienced death throughout his history. So, he lived the reality of separation from his family. A lethal cause, owner of a toxic gene that called itself death, allowed the body to escape disease and epidemics, taking away the soul on a journey without return toward a country with a wonderful belief, covered with closed parallel lines of celestial horizon.

Already, wide beams of a boundless aurora were breaking the veil; already, the hearts of glorious spirits who had reached an eternal rest, were singing for those who are in the boat toward the spirit of Ra—the spirit of the sun in exaltation, uttering exclamations in the boat of millions of years. Already, raised up in the ethereal space, souls were floating in an intersidereal region of the great divine cycle, full of joy in the mysterious chapel, by these vain glorious words—I, "soul," have reached the land of truth and justification, and I shone in the hearts of gods who are in heaven, because, I woke up from dead like a living god, by giving thanks and glory to the great sacred boat; because I am from their race. Under the dazzling light, the night seemed no more than a dream to me, but what an unforgettable dream in an impalpable and invisible night, in this first journey that revealed my tomb on earth? Ah, I was far from the term *dream*, because the long journey on the boat of millions of years was far from a vision of the other world of the word dream; it is set for the final aim. But still feeling that juvenile imagination in me thickened by earth's smoke, nevertheless, the mystical ceremony of resurrection was just beginning. I, "soul," doubted the other consciousness that just hatched in me, that double mystery of the celestial inner "me," which appeared to me in a beautiful astral light like a living form had spoken to me in my sleep. Was it my sister's soul, was it my genius, or was it just a reflection of my deep spirit, a forewarning of my future being? Wonderful and mysterious, and if it is science, it is a true one. And what would I not do to live for millions of years? To not forget that divine hour, where I have seen my other pure and radiating inner "me"? Now considered like having consciousness, my spiritual soul and my divine spirit then at a germ unconscious stage, is now developed after my life on earth? I solemnly promised to follow and know about the journey in the light of Osiris, covered with celestial lines.

Let's try to penetrate it with the key of initiation by taking a look at its strange mysterious symbols that generated atoms by universal soul's vibrations, occurring in particular concentrical circles from the invisible to the visible, and from pure spirit to an organized substance from God to man. This descending order of proportional forces, an ontology or science of the intelligible principles, is the foundation of cosmogony, under different forms of power, descending from the first cause of an ineffable Father. Its descended order of incarnations is simultaneous to the ascending order of life; it is its involution that produces the evolution of the ascending order of life and death; and only it makes it clear opposed to souls and explains it. Krishna, Hermes, Moses, and Orpheus, as great initiators of India, Egypt, Judea, and Greece, knew this order of principle under different forms of power.

It is translated as a trip to the light of Osiris, in the form of a dream vision to Hermes, to know the origin of things; the great revelation of the secret of death; to know the continuation of the soul's life and its destiny after death or resurrection are revealed to us by Osiris.

This journey, a chapter in the Corpus Hermeticum, known under the name of *poimandres*, and found at the head of Hermes books, Osiris, the sovereign understanding, revealed things beyond understanding and let us contemplates the source of beings with satisfaction; his reassuring words poured a certain reassuring feeling in us and filled us with delicious light. In that reassuring feeling full of delicious light, Osiris explained the sound of light. He took us in spaces with a subtle fire that arises from the damp depth and reaching the ethereal spaces with the confusion unrolled in the depth; the chorus of heavenly body spread in the sky, and the voice of light filling the infinite, suspended between heaven and earth in a dream.

We beings of beings, made of "Haur," signifying light, and "Ruah," signifying breath, the divine breath that creates the intelligible light, just learned about the sound of light. In this summary, the word *Haur* is the reversed word *Ruah*, the eternal breath that palpitates under a veil, like a translucent form of the astral worlds, in the waves of the divine ether, spreading deep love in the infinite. Let us remember that these names, found in the second and third verses of Genesis, are hieroglyphic summaries.

Yes, we just learned about the sound of light; but at first, like a recent adept in a secret crypt of the temple, marked by the great revelation only known by the pontiff; summarizing sparkling words that he pronounced and which shined in the dark, Osiris taught us by explaining all eternity above and beneath us; to develop the superior part of our being: the spiritual soul, and the divine spirit that exist in us at a germ unconscious stage, and that will become Osiris after this life.

Osiris explained that the light is the divine understanding that contains everything by power and the pattern of every being; the darkness where we are plunged in is the material world where earthmen live. God is the Father, the word is the Son, and their union is life; and that the fire from the depths is the Divine Word. After this marvelous opening in us, how can we not close the eyes of our body and only see with those of our spirit, because the word is in us, we children of dust?

The word itself, the sacred fire, and the creative power in your being, is what in you that listens, sees, and behaves. Osiris let us see life of worlds and the way of souls, where man comes from, and where he is returning, done according to our desire. Through Hermes vision, Osiris showed us a marvelous spectacle of the infinite space of starry sky, enveloping the seven luminous spheres.

Osiris occupies the sidereal center of the seven heavens ranged on our heads like seven transparent concentric globes, the last one having as girdle the Milky Way. In each planet turning on its axis in a sphere, accompanied by a genius form, sign, and different light, we can contemplate their dispersed prosperity and their majestic movement in the heavenly starry sky with dazzling surprise.

Look, listen, and understand, while the seven spheres of all life are taught by Osiris; it is through them that the fall and ascension of souls are accomplished; the seven geniuses are the beams of the Word-Light. He taught us about of the moon genius, the nearest to us, crowned with a silver sickle, and having a restlessness smile. In the phases of the soul's life, each of them commands a sphere of the Spirit. The moon presides over births and deaths, because souls are extracted by it from the bodies and attract them into its beams. Above us, the pale Mercury with its caduceus that contains science is showing the way to the ascending and descending souls. The brightest Venus, holding the mirror of love, where turn by turn souls are alternately forgetting each other and recognizing themselves, is higher up.

The genius of the sun raises the triumphal torch of eternal beauty above it; and Mars, brandishing the sword of justice, is furthermore the highest. Jupiter holds the scepter of the supreme power, which is divine intelligence, enthroning on the azure sphere. Saturn carries the globe of universal wisdom, under the signs of the zodiac, at the limits of the world. These gods had other names in Egyptian languages, but the seven cosmogonical gods correspond to all mythologies, by their meanings and their attributions. Western tradition having adopted Latin names, we conserved them for more clarity. Osiris showed us these seven regions that encompass the visible and invisible world, the seven rays of the verb light, and the unique God who crosses them and governs them through them. Then the master showed us how the journey of men is accomplished through all these worlds. Osiris continued his teaching by showing us a luminous seed that he qualified as germs of souls from the regions of the Milky Way falling into the seventh sphere.

In the region of Saturn, these souls live like light vapors, carefree, happy, but not knowing their happiness. And they put on envelopes ever heavier by falling from sphere to sphere. Conformable to the environment they inhabit, they acquire a new corporeal sense in each incarnation, and their vital energy increases; but they lose the memory of their heavenly origin as they enter into thicker bodies.

The fall of soul's accomplishment, which comes from the divine ether, is accomplished in that process intoxicated by life; they rushed like a fire rain with shiver of sensual delight, more and more captivated by material, through the regions of pain and love, in their terrestrial prison up to death; where they groan in men, held back by the igneous center of earth, and where the divine life seems a vain dream to us. As earthly beings eager to know, Osiris taught us that in their fatal descending, as daughters of heaven, many souls perished in that fatal-proof journey.

Our soul is a veiled light; it shined like an immortal lamp when the holy oil of love is thrown on it; it could hear its voice, the voice of light that reveals intimate music in its being, at some choosing hours. Floating on the white vision above the muddy river troubling its life, it darkens and goes off when it is neglected.

It loses the memory of its origin by its unrestrained love for material. It returns to the ethereal region of the lifeless atom, having lost the divine spark that was in it, the memory of its origin that could become brighter than a star, and disintegrates in the whirlwind of coarse elements.

Suddenly, in the middle of groans and nameless blasphemies, in a roaring storm with a black cloud enveloping the seven spheres, everything disappeared under the thick haze. Then Osiris showed us the human specters, carried away by monsters, phantoms, and animals. Torn apart, they were uttering strange cries.

The destiny of irremediably low and wicked souls, who are tortured, said Osiris, ends in a process of destruction, resulting in the total loss of consciousness. Then at his command, the seven spheres reappeared under the firmament to show us the swarm of souls that was trying to ascend toward the lunar region. Some are knocked back down in fold toward earth like a whirlwind of birds under the storm strokes. By great f laps of wings, others are reaching the superior sphere, which led them to rotate. They recover the sight of divine things, once reached there. They will not reflect a dream of powerless good fortune of divine things. At this point, they become saturated with the clearness of their consciousness.

Through pain, they're impregnated with the lucidity of enlightened consciousness. Now they shine in their deeds. They possess the divine within themselves, for with the energy of the will acquired in their struggle, they become luminous. Let's strengthen our souls then and clear up our darkened spirit by contemplating this faraway fight of souls, which have reached the seven spheres and scattered like a shower of sparks, because it is the soul's destiny.

This knowledge is enough for us if we want to rise up to see how they're trying to leave the mother hive by describing divine chorus to be ranged up under their favorite genius. Among this group of souls wishing to leave their mother hive, some among them, the powerful of powerful, go back to the Father; Saturn hosts the most powerful, and the solar region houses the most beautiful; because everything begins eternally where everything ends, being power itself.

Therefore, the seven spheres that the ancient Hermes saw, and that our ancestors transmitted to us, together indicate "Love! Beauty! Immortality! Justice! Wisdom! Splendor and Science! "They all contain music, and their words are like the seven notes of the lyre with all numbers containing universal law.

An unfathomable depth that looks like a starry sky spangled with constellations in a space without ends, where the worlds rotate with their rhythm and their marvelous motions, just as a vault of golden nails for the child. They contain magic keys with eternal numbers and evocative signs for the wise. We will see its limits extend as we learn to contemplate and to understand it, because the same organic law governed all worlds. According to Osiris's explanation concerning the doctrine of the "word light," he demonstrated its triple nature, which is the spirit, the soul, and the body, encompassing understanding, power and material; light, word, and life, at the same time the intelligence.

By excellence, their union, the law of ternary unity, constitutes the divine and intellectual principle that dominates creation from top to bottom. Osiris thus led us to the generative principle of being flourishing in time and space, shaking the multiple f lowers of the ideal center of the universe. In this generative principle of being, seven round solid figures or surfaces, who's each point of its surface equidistant from its center represent seven planets, symbolizing seven different worlds, seven different spiritual stages, and seven principles. Across this solar system, each man is forced to go through it in his evolution. Their guiding power of all spheres without evidence of evolution and descending from themselves are seven geniuses or seven cosmogonic gods known as superior spirits. From their sphere, each great god, a spirit head of legions and leader of all spheres, who could exercise an action on man and on terrestrial things, reproduces his type under thousand variants.

Thus, Hermes penetrated to the threshold of the great arcana, where under the phantoms of reality, the divine life appeared to him. In his initiatory vision with Osiris, the hidden God, who animates bodies in labor in the wandering globes and breathes by millions of souls in the universe, made us discover the great septenary that embraces the universe and vibrates in the seven colors of the rainbow, in the seven notes of lassie; the seven gods of the Devas of India, the seven Amshapands of Persia, seven great angels of Chaldea, the seven Sephiroth of Kabbalah, and the seven archangels of the Christian Apocalypse.

In the constitution of man, which is triple in essence and sevenfold by its evolution, this great septenary also manifests itself. And now, in its invisible heaven, the light of Osiris, and henceforth belonging to the resurrected living, he makes us know, "The exterior which is like the interior of things; The small which is like the large; and that, in the divine economy nothing is small, and nothing is large; he who works is One; and there is only one law, as the first principal key of science." The second tells us that "gods are immortal men and men the mortal god." He invites us to choose our way to ascend to the pure Spirit, for the law of mystery covers the great truth. If we learn and work on these main keys of science, "this science will be our strength, our faith our sword and our infrangible armor, our silence." Of all the assumptions of life, death remains the only absolute truth of all truths, more than love on earth. It still represents and will always represent a journey toward the divine order, toward purity, and toward the knowledge of the divine intimacy, hence the initiation.

For the initiators of Moses, the insider, writer of the book of Genesis, borrowed a summary of the stories transmitted by word of mouth in Africa to reach the huge mass of civilized nations of the earth from centuries to centuries up to the Mesopotamian people for millennia. Unfortunately, the living in front of the unknown, which is death and who is always and forever losing the one for whom he felt so much affection, seems to have still not accepted this separation. And neither the deceased, leaving those for whom he also felt so much affection, remains in constant contact with us the living, without knowing it and exercising a certain application of a return of affection.

Thus, his children, a malignant spirit, the consciousness, the soul, and the creator, who came to enlighten the world of the living, created a god in this cosmic (magic) and imaginary world. So was the cult of the skulls born, an excellent way to effectively use the skull—the superior part of being, the vibrant human bone in resonance with the spirit of a deceased—to spiritually be in contact with the soul, the "spark of life" of a deceased person who is beyond in the afterlife; the skull is then used as a magical thought, a prayer for its accuracy, strongly linked to our problems for a resolution with a magical thought; the resonance with the spirit of a deceased is performed to overcome all obstacles and the fiascos of humanity; then an art by which we recognize the reincarnation of such or such of our ancestors, to be in contact with the deceased soul, is practiced for his return in a different physical body, preferably in the same family lineage, after a variable time of life in the world of the ancestors.

They were practicing the cult of the spirit of the ancestors, and very important are their masks and statuettes in the practice of their religious services. After their conversion to Christianity of their king Ibrahim Njoya in the early tenth century and then to Islam, he created his own religion by the name of *newt kuete*, meaning "who seeks and finds." He allowed the development of writing system, invented by him in the early tenth century with a school he built so that his writing system can be taught.

Cameroon is known as one of the few African nations to have invented writing. It is the French who terminated its writing system and its monarchy by uncontrolled slaughter of its people upon their arrival in Cameroon. In the cave of the ancients among the Bamileke of Cameroon for example, considered as neo-Sudanese by some historians, the deceased ancestor was dug up after a few months or years. The skull was placed in a sacred place, and it was the legitimate successor of the family lineage who secured its guardianship. A spiritual contact was to manifest itself to those who experienced a need.

They were coming humbly to submit their supplications in severe circumstances or on certain occasions to these skulls so that all the wise prayers performed in a loud voice should be answered. Through these prayers, they invoked the energy and the consciousness of their ancestors, followed by some symbolic gifts, such as sacrifices, for the fulfillment of all demands. After this spiritual communion in the world of the ancestors, the followers would return to continue their life on earth in a new physical body; with an external validation of the constructed body; with a psychic coherent satisfying manner; and desirably from the same family lineage; they believed in this practice, and an estimation of fidelity was respected by the alpha coefficient, which led our ancestors to believe, and for his people to still believe in reincarnation. Death did not exist for them. Human beings simply leave an earthly plane to continue another level of life beyond our earthly sphere.

This belief and practice have existed in Africa for millennia before the Tibetan Buddhism appropriates it for themselves as a practice and their guide as a choice. In some cemeteries in Cameroon, precisely among the Bamileke, we can still read the inscription "The dead do not die." Another Bamileke saying, whose construction presents a complete sense, and which determines all religions of the world, says, "Blessed are the dead, who have living beings." The excited intellectual curiosity led me to this spiritual thought: the memory responsible for remembrance reminds itself of the previous thought, left to its own curiosity. Thus, many authors still consider the manifestation of the alpha value as desirable and satisfying, designed as a generalization to the case of continuous variables of the formula, although the scientific literature does not make a state of consensus on the subject.

This scientific activity of disciplines and knowledge of occult precision with the use of technical tools to interrogate the past to know the truth is African. Such is the truth that must guide us and help us regain pride but also help us ensure absolute peace and indisputable solidarity between our African people. The cosmic body is the power of creation. God first created water as the first child of nature; it encompasses everything. Water holds all living things alive, including man, and holds the human life, and nothing is visible to its nature.

In Africa, an old water civilization in the Dogon environment, expresses the cultural conceptions of water through a traditional representation of the world.

The story of the genius of this Dogon people is less and less known by the young generations today. And the opening of their country to malicious tourism, as in so many other African countries, came and reinforced the loss of their tradition through their conversion to monotheism. First Islam, and second Christianity—two great religions of total oppression to the intellectuality to the detriment of ancestor worship and the tradition associated with the humanistic conception of the natural universe, very widely shared culturally by the Mandingo. In this culture, local cults and the authority system were closely associated with the control of water. And for its preservation, the collective existence respected prohibitions for collective identities, such as a ban on access to sacred wells, the annual purification by rain rituals to certain categories of persons, and the control of water sources by the hierarchy power and local political parties.

Here is an understanding of this tradition of the West African society. The Dogon said that the invisible beings called Nommo and Nyerum, to whom Africans offer sacrifices, live and animate wells and our existence. So Nommo is a philosophical system and a purely African concept—a wealth, a magical power of the active speech of the intelligence and poetry, a universal life force in evidence. The true meaning of the word *wealth*, the unlimited wealth that man possesses, is only man's powerful wealth when he creates a dominant thought and executes it by a creative spirit that visualizes that cosmic thought to live with happiness and wealth, the spirit of peace, health, and life itself, granted to all creatures in the universe as a thought, a cosmic thought.

Monotheism is that same heritage of our stolen African spirituality and wealth. That African spirituality thought and still believes that thinking words with words in the house of words contributes to the construction of the passive thought by thought.

In the mythology of the Dogon, Nommo holds water that holds man. This tradition is identical to the one practiced by the Sawa people of Cameroon. The spirit of their secret society—the Jengu, demi-human water spirits living in the waters—is the mediation between its worshippers and God, believing in the influence of witchcraft in everyday life. Their other evil spirits live in the forests and also in the sea. The pre-Christian ancestor worship, holding that their ancestors live in the sea, is a belief still persisting and also plays an important role in their faith.

Water would have not existed without these water geniuses in this world of the most extraordinary and most powerful creatures. And that is why we respect the crocodile, a large reptile of great waters, and the python, one of the largest nonpoisonous snakes, special and sacred, currently living on earth and which can transform itself into Nommo at an advanced age and recognized as a kind of snake of the family of *Pythonidae*, in addition to the sixteen species of catfish of the family of *Siluridae* known today, constituting a suborder.

Of all creatures that live, they made an ancient pact with their geniuses to satisfy them, and there are only insiders who can see this water genius that the common uninitiated cannot see. Failure to make the planned offerings is a transgression of the natural law prohibitions, and disrespecting it, offenses it. Considered as an avatar of immortal ancestors, its anger will not let us live in peace.

The water genius is a very important worship among the Dogon. One of their myths about death states that, before the birth of death, our ancestors simply underwent a transformation and became water geniuses and then in pythons. They then continue their life in a water puddle cave until the birth of death. At the origin of death, they presented themselves to one of their descendants in an animal form and contracted a covenant with one of them by giving him a stone bead. Consequently, in this clan, each individual took the lining of that animal species in which the immortal ancestor metamorphosed, since then became a sacred animal, like the one who became the first responsible for the cult of ancestors.

The elected officials of the village, who are practicing the cult of water genius, still meet till today before the Togu Na, the house of the verb, the seed of knowledge, also known as the home of the mother, although entry is not permitted to women. This meeting place in the center of the life force and cosmology, built at the same time when a regulation was founded, is used for learning the art of rhetorical persuasion through, the use of logical reasoning. They deal with all kinds of social problems there; education is also held there, as well as numerous spiritual initiations. For a comparative analysis of cosmology, this model is an African model of cosmology in the world scene. From that moment on, they were sharing a spiritual principle with him.

That sacredness of the totem animal of the Dogon clan is also practiced by the Masa and the Koumi clans of Chad and Cameroon. They believe that the genius of water by the name of Mununda and the genius of the bush are protective deities of extraordinary events of the cosmic, manifesting themselves as supernatural powers to humans, to animals, and to plants. Their tradition and others in Africa teach us that to have an understanding of the spirit of water; its sacrificial share must be given to it.

The nastiest of the water geniuses is the female, highly regarded and respected by some African religions; this female wants the woman to die and then be reincarnated to experiment and know death. Each water genius protects its citizens against attacks from other geniuses of water. On the other hand, if sacrifices are not offered to it, it takes revenge in evidence by eating and drinking the blood of those who come to drink its water.

The first to begin these rituals is from the clan of Sokolo, a small very ancient village founded since the time of Ouagadou, a community in the center of Nara in the Koulikoro region in the southwest of Mali. This phenomenon, widespread among other people in Africa, terribly resembles the one in Genesis. Its manifestation in the solar plexus, elaborated posteriorly by the brain, is transmitted to the cerebellum in the form of images, colors, and vibrations, and without words in the inner voice. The human soul is delicately enveloped in an essential and subtle material.

The entities of nature, elemental beings from the lower planes of the kingdom of essentiality, are known as geniuses in Africa. These geniuses of ancestor worship, dedicated to the spirits and to a multitude of deities, live in the waters of the earth, the mountains, the hills, plants, etc. The Bible, which forms polytheism, says, "I am the Lord your God; you shall not have other gods than me."

Polytheism is the worship and the belief in the existence of a multitude of deities—God, gods, goddesses of earth, water, fire, air, etc.—and also gives rise to the cult dedicated to these deities. But contrary to the will of God, the entities of their planes in the kingdom of essentiality are by their egos eventually superior to the African kingdom of essentiality. The most interesting descriptions of this belief are multiple rituals dedicated to their geniuses. To seek the support of the cosmos and our ancestors, the accredited sacrifices should occur, authorized by the master of the village at the banks of the river, accompanied by circle dances in the village and cloaked by the rhythm of drums and hands clapping. Only one rite allows the collective presence of the public, and it is the rite of the rain. In case of the rain problem, the soothsayers practicing divination will then find the lost soul without a body, still alive in our earthly sphere preventing rain because it does not want to get wet without a body. They catch it, attach it in the branches of a sacred tree, and put it into a sacred place of the village. The old man who lost this soul in a living body dies at the end of this rite, thus solving the problem of water and the fertility of soil.

The rainbow—composed of seven colors, which are red, orange, yellow, green, blue, indigo and violet is also a belief still existing in several clans in Africa. Its clan totem is a special and sacred snake as water geniuses. The Bible tells us that, after the flood, God made the everlasting covenant between him and every kind of living creatures on the earth, indicating that the rainbow represents the decision taken by Him to no more destroy life by flood, He told Noah in (Gen. 9:13–17).

In the Sawa tradition, mainly the coastal people inhabiting the littoral region of Cameroon for example, Bommo, the spirit of the snake in the cult of water, which lives in wells, metamorphoses itself into a beautiful young woman with a clear complexion and very smooth, shiny, and silky hair—known as something very common in the Kribi region. It can also be transformed into a ram, black dog, rooster, hen, python, or bull and travel from place to place; it reveals itself to uninitiated as inanimate objects, such as beautiful pottery; pretty jewelry, such as rings, chains, and bright bracelets in red gold, its favorite color; kitchenware, such as cups, spoons, pots, and dishes; and everything that the spirit can designate as well sculpted.

This tradition therefore practices a mysterious cult of the water spirit. Given its nature with water, it transforms itself and settles into the rainbow. This snake is called Gnoungou among the Sawa. The female geniuses of water quit their initial cradles and go and marry in any distant place, provided there is a pool of water in that place to accommodate the spirit.

The rainbow is sometimes represented in the sky in four noble and divine colors. We divinely see it designed in the sky by the spirit of water when the atmosphere forms the red clouds. Its male spirit appears most often in the sky and descends from the sky by cosmic vibrations, growls, and the sudden fall of torrential rains, guided by the rainbow itself, up to its female down on earth, initially conceived with water only, recognized and considered as the master of rain, harvest, and wind.

Thus, it draws energy in a fountain in a very distant horizon by manifesting itself to humans and nature, exposing its divine colors majestically in the infinitely large sky, in an atmosphere reddened by its cosmic power to discharge that same energy—the magical power of the creation of the universe in another place in the nature that requires that energy.

The pact between water geniuses and men was undone—if they got angry and if men did not offer them more sacrifices and offerings. That is why they travel and manifest themselves as the rainbow when it rains to go and reside in a river, a water jump, a well, or a pool of water. In that tradition, if one of the adherents receives the other with a sheep, the visitor must also offer a sheep in return. You should know that, in all eventualities, some people in high witchcraft (black magic of this tradition) go so far as to sacrifice a human being for their host. This act often concludes a covenant between hosts.

This means that you who received this human sacrifice should reciprocally repay it in due time to the one who offered it to you. But sometimes this reciprocity is broken because some members possessing this spirit of water were not condoning human sacrifice, which in turn has constraints, aiming to only offer a clan member and not a stranger. Therefore, offering a stranger does not honor the promises of this rule for the simple fact of protecting their clan, or the son of the country, that they baste as notabilities. The one who devours a son of the country as a sacrifice, defiled for having eaten a forbidden food or for the transgression of a religious prohibition will be offended and immediately returned from his visit with a hungry stomach; thus, instead of accepting to devour a foreign human being than anything else, he will undo the sociability of his covenant with the other. From that moment on, at the rise of the waterfront of a river or a water jump near the indebted village, the water path is traced by his installation in that place. He then takes action and will often catch all human beings depending on the other person because the way is open to this water genius but only if his genius is more powerful than the other. It turns out that an unpaid debt from one village to another, leads to severe restrictions between the two water sources of these two villages. They forbid themselves entering the water source of the other, even to wash their hands or feet. Failure to respect these restrictions may cause many deaths by drowning.

It is known that this liberal spirit draws its adherents to the deep of its damp abyss to initiate them to things of the mysterious world and to the most sacred secrets of the infinitely small and the infinitely large. It provides advice, transmits knowledge, and remedies against diseases to a few elected officials. It guesses the thought in the heart of its followers and their ability to keep a secret. But to the one whom it doubts, it makes him an idiot; those who are mistakenly taken in its house are released and can no longer speak.

Unfortunately, this tradition has inevitably disappeared nowadays because of the evil profaned by its heirs, who were killing for the pleasure of material. For this reason, we do no longer find noble guardians of this tradition like before. Today, it transforms itself into a very beautiful thing to attract people by manipulating water and kills them. It swallows children mercilessly. Their females, very beautiful women with fair skin and very smooth, shiny, fine, and soft hair come out of their environment and get married in villages by hiding their odd shape with a well-pronounced tail, which are appropriate in the water. Its interior cosmic eye can be destroyed by the potash, which transforms them into humans, if the host discovers its nose, which is not like the nose of a human.

In the Sudano-Sahelian regions, especially among the Dogon, this tradition is of utmost importance and a very rich conceptualization for access to water and its control. Its essence is expressed in the notion of the water genius and as a major cultural symbol of their identity, related to the religious field of their worship. Its history of the water spirits occupies a place in the economic and political hierarchy. And the role of the contemporary history for scientific purposes remains a problem that conditions and modifies their ability to perpetuate their traditional cults nowadays like yesterday. Thus, the males and the females of the water geniuses accompany each other to accomplish the mystical natural law in the universe of human beings and in a world infinitely small.

From his creative power, God created the world in all its majesty. He created the planets, the sun, the moon, the earth, and others again and again. The separation of water and earth represented the separation of light and darkness. The creation of Adam in the terrestrial paradise of the Hebrews in the Bible relates the famous creation of Eve, taken from the rib of Adam asleep, and the story of Noah. They're three more dynamic first scenes of the biblical narrative, in the chronological order, revealing his love, floating in his creative power, with open arms, at that very moment that the beauty of God formed the contours of beauty and placed them throughout the universe; and the hand of the Creator, rather than the drawing brush of a mortal, was supreme in itself.

In the history of blacks, people exterminations took place in Africa certainly, by those who hoisted at the summits of the world and who previously exterminated themselves through different beliefs. So, the trade of blacks was not an obstacle for the development of the Kamite. The promotion of classical African humanity must be open up for an African belief as the designer of Africa as in Ancient Egypt; which was an assembly of people of Africa, the oldest known home of knowledge, which so inspired the Greeks regarding the scientific plan, politics, architecture, medicine, arts, and culture. Their civilization was born in Africa through Egypt. But this knowledge was not a biological imprint; it has been interpreted and transformed. They first insidiously appropriated it and badly taught it.

But our historical legacy remains a credible characteristic in the history of mankind. Nowadays, they do it in an ineluctable way with the Dogon, obviously for the scientific purposes and all that follows, for the African descendants to no longer have access to it, for it to lose its identity, and for it to be left without a mark, thus shaping its permanent decline as was the case of Egypt. And the demonstration of intellectual dishonesty of many Western leaders and authors who are trying to rewrite history will not be taken seriously. It is therefore not a hidden fact of history since the Western archaeologists glorified and recognized the great civilizing sculpture of black Africa, like the one that greatly influenced the Greek entities.

All Western scholars also know that what was accomplished by Africa remains without pretext its work, not as theirs, for we know in fact very pertinently who we are, where we come from, and where we are going. However, multiple gurus of Western historians have expressly deceived Africans and generally the rest of the whole world for years, for the sole purpose of brainwashing and to cause misery and the lethargy of Africa by hatred that animates their souls. At that, I issue a gloomy sneer before these mysterious sinister characters of the West who are still clinging to these lies that have just lasted too long. And through which since some time already, a change is occurring against them, my respect for the Negro scholars for this great undertaking of awareness for the awakening of the black community. Unfortunately, there are still many questions about the history of Africa, its current situation, and its future in short- and long-term progress is facing the rest of the world without answers.

My synthesis comprises a masterly elaboration rich in teachings, a source of knowledge for the black pride, and an impressive erudition on the history of the world. I am not a historian, but I'm just quite simply trying to pick up the missing pieces of the African history, reveal clues from the bottom of the ink of my heart, to contribute thereby to the knowledge, and open spirits to the realities, with so much humility, for an instructive return to the purely African spirituality. Be very careful because I am not referring to Christianity, a white man religion, which is estimated above its real value, badly taught to better penetrate us, misunderstood to lull us to sleep, used to annihilate our potential and finally to exploit us for an indefinitely period, but thereby, still hermetically well sealed for the common mortals.

Know that a syncretism of African cults, which exist as a gift of God involving the mastery and the practice of principles, is still held by Africans, and this practice is a religion that cares about the very existence of humanity on earth. Here, I want to draw your attention to some of these African cults.

I'm speaking for example of the cult of ancestors, the cult of skull, and the cults of water geniuses, to only name a few. The African religious beliefs include some foundations and are revealing a certain traditional view on the existence of ghosts, demons, spirits, genies, gods, and goddesses transmitted from generation to generation for millennia. They reveal mysteries to certain traditionally initiated people—the elected officials who indeed see their forms and speak to these entities. Through their fears, they vow them cults so that they can often communicate with them.

According to the grail, these deities actually exist in the realm of essentiality, on the inferior planes of creation, and in the four inferior planes of that kingdom. In the three superior planes of this kingdom, these entities are primarily known under the name of God and as guides of elemental beings in Africa. Well after, by the German, Greek, and Islamic traditions, they were widespread. They're gnomes among the Jews; they're qualified as small misshapen spirits who live inside the earth and keep riches in the cabalistic tradition; they're elves, merfolks and mermaids, water spirits, in the Germanic, Scandinavian mythology, etc., committed to the administration and the maintenance of nature, the heavens, watercourses of earth, animals, and plants; all these geniuses are geniuses of multiple African traditions.

This sententious example expresses the moral truths by proverbs and poems, a form truth of my time and a time when the esoteric knowledge and the African doctrine were expressing an idea to express a truth. I assert that the human intuition, noble or despicable, manifests love, compassion, hatred, and all forms of benevolent and demoniac thoughts. They're the souls of our dead who in the material world of the three superior planes of subtle matter and in the four inferior planes of dense matter, where the disembodied spirits and the incarnated spirits linked to the earth, govern our thought forms of spiritual maturity in the primordial spiritual realm and in the divine sphere, where the archangels and angels live.

The effect of having taken this knowledge away from us has unfortunately reduced our inner spiritual life and our African religious beliefs to a very limited level. But as the first creation, Africans have always recognized the existence of God and the existence of the superior planes of creation. Everyone knows that the African religious belief, according to which everything lives—thanks to the cosmic powers or divine neutral power, spirit, soul, and entities of nature—is a highly respected belief in Africa. The belief in the powers of the cosmic bodies that animate the elements—human beings, animals, plants, and so on—is built by animism, a religion and a belief that attributes a soul to animals, phenomena, and natural objects. Polytheism is a religion that acknowledges the existence of many gods. Fetishism is credited with extraordinary powers or magical powers of certain objects. And witchcraft allows certain people—men, women, or children—to endow themselves with extraordinary powers, innate or acquired.

The divine neutral force penetrates human beings, interpenetrates and impregnates with the existence of this divine power, which f lows and penetrates everything. The cosmic bodies—the power of creation, God, water, earth, air, and fire—are considered as the natural philosophy or a theory of the four elements—a traditional way to describe and analyze the world. These four supporting stones, whether in the water, in the heavens, or on earth, contain a spirit—the spirit of God, until the death of human beings on earth. Then comes the cult of skulls, a symbol of death; a spiritual foundation by excellence to spiritually get in touch with the soul of the deceased to whom this bone belongs, and who is in the afterlife; long practiced before in Cameroon by the Bamileke people, well before the eleventh century by the Egyptians, the Mayan, the Nazca, etc., to extend the memory of the deceased who preceded the living, still closer to nature; a distinctive sign belonging to a state of mind; a magical thought connecting us to the life and death of the disappeared person, vanished without leaving traces; it consisted of modeling clay statuettes, the statuary art of wood and stone, and painting tableaux and parietal art.

A mummification ritual that was well known throughout the medieval Egypt and considered as a vehicle of preparing the body of the deceased for the return of his soul to purity, revived the past thoughts of our ancestors, and served the living to pass from our conscious world to the one of spirits—the one of God—with the sole purpose of providing contact between the human being and the unknown gods, indefinable to the knowledge of man. This practice, an intercessional action also known under the name of craniology, was adopted by the science studying all techniques and measures practiced in psychology, but why the representations of the skull, since the ram's skull is found on the ceiling of the famous Sistine Chapel, built between 1508 and 1512 in the Vatican, under Pope Sixtus IV, painted by Michelangelo, and known as a masterpiece of the painting of the Italian Renaissance?

The Bamileke people, who form 20 percent of the ethnic groups in Cameroon, are the most important people well known in Cameroon and its surroundings by their practices. Since their long journey from the medieval Egypt in the ninth century of our era up to Cameroon toward the middle of the twelfth century, like the Sawa, the Bassa, the Bakoko, etc., they permanently settled in the region of the highlands of western Cameroon. They live since then in that country, where they suffered an extremely severe genocide from the French army, carried away by the demons of hatred, which was slumbering in the depths of their being, under the command of General de Gaulle—a hatred that continues up to our days.

Their ancestor worship and their cult of divinities, a bipolar religion inherited from Ancient Egypt and its exceptional influence, underwent another atrocity: a brainwashed from the part of the Roman religion after their genocide, but these atrocities could not demolish their belief, and they still believe that God can be reached through these angels (divinities) and that their deceased ancestors can intercede with God for their cause through oracles and mediums. They compose the Semi-Bantu group with the Tikar, an original Bantu ethnic group close to the Bamouns, established in the grasslands of that country. Their neighbors, the Bamouns, established in Cameroon since 1394, founded the Bamoun kingdom from the nineteenth descendant of one of the oldest dynasties of Africa. They belong to the Bantu group of languages within the family of Niger-Congo languages by their tradition to the belief of ancestors worship; the cult of skulls, thoughts inherited from our ancestors, is an important ceremony for the Bamouns, which spread throughout the world, up to the United States of America, having a society practicing the cult of our ancestors, as the cult of the skull and bones.

1 Cor. 15:21–22 said, "For since death came through a man, the resurrection of dead comes also through a man. For as in Adam all die, so in Christ all will be made alive," like a philosophical thought. My philosophical thought leads me to say that God is the law and justice, life and death, and good and evil; for me, without any doubt, no culture can have social norms without philosophical concepts and maintain an inseparable reason from the truth.

Evil is a contingent structure, and good is a surmounted hatred, the chance to express the otherness and the radicalness of the human being to the infinite; without the negative feeling of evil, good will have been trivial to conceive. The thought of my pacifist philosophy allows us to avoid all deviations of insignificance toward the monstrosity of the intolerance, incomparable to the spirit of man to whom a part of the truth escaped, because tolerance is the recognition of the principle of evil with the duty of justice.

The form and the content of racial oppression were set up by capitalism. The close interactions between the social economic functions and the ethnoracial identity of the race and class were the results of the collective suffering of the black communities, caused by the system of oppression, discrimination, and exploitation. The capitalist modes of production have in general practiced this capitalist system based on exploitation of the race in the West. The essentialism of the global society allowed the continuation of the tradition of this Eurocentric cultural hegemony. Optimism ignored the evil of the suffering of black people, a society of freedom and tolerance. The conception of tolerance of these black people is nourished by the anterior thought of man, possessing the virtues of good, love and evil. But at the same time being the transcendent of evil, the lights of good always triumph over the dark forces of evil.

Black radicalism, which is not really one, emerged in the Western capitalist societies. It took place in the cultural degradation, political oppression, and economic exploitation. In addition, it emerged in the New World by the African traditions of resistance. However, the liberation of the black man will be made by the transcendence of space and time. Its cultural heritage that transcended space and time has at the same time, made the movement for civil rights in the United States expressed itself. The African Americans, whose citizenship was not yet permitted, found the freedom of expression, which was denied to them in America. And the concerns of sovereignty and nationalism resulted in the independence of African countries during the sixty decades.

The revolutionary, intellectual consciousness of the nationalism of black people emerged throughout the black continent. In their fight against colonialism, preoccupied by the cultural survival of their people, which was simply distinguished by their freedom of spirit, a spiritual resistance of the African man against the intransigent ideologies of the West was open to the transcendent principles of the mutation of time and space. Justice, freedom, respect for life, and human dignity are universal moral principles of the superior will of the supreme God. These moral principles are located at the highest stage of moral values. They place universal ethics above all other considerations and are establishing the conformism of traditional practices of social conventions, obedience, punishment, the fear of selfishness, the respect of the rights and the individual interests.

Between the Hebrews slavers of the Old Testament and the black intelligentsia, a dialogue must be opened for an inspired mediation, leading to the forgiveness of Christianity and Judaism, aware that the principle of forgiveness is a dimension of the human existence. Luke 23:34 reveals the word of Jesus Christ to us, who said, "Father, forgive them, for they do not know what they're doing." In this case of blacks, they do not know what they did. So forgiveness is possible for humans and allows the person who committed the fault to assume the negationism which reflects on the present and the future, marking the radical historical clashes and misfortunes of the past, which are opposed to the spirit. The commemorative act of memory has a symbolic and educational effect, like an expiatory rite of collective consciousness.

To make a true story be known is a moral and civic education, which alleviates the suffering endured; alleviates the losses incurred and the frustration generated, particularly in the case of blacks that the identity was denied, caused by the amplitude of slavery, but still insufficiently accepted as a cruelty by the West. Even after integrating the black national community in the whole world; they have to undertake a serious conscience examination so that the situation that produced that horrible inhumanity no longer be repeated. The necessity of the knowledge of this history must be the subject of a more precise and reasoned analysis for the memory of the painful history of the past, instead of trivialization or forgetfulness, which cannot substitute the consensus of the unanimity of ethnoracial minorities, which are aiming to continue toward the future, with a view of the constructive actions, and not of the past destructive passions.

The duty of memory allows blacks to not forget their sacrifice. So, say the words that forgive the misfortunes suffered by the immortal black race, and without hatred, your souls will integrate the universal in beauty. The attitude of progressive intellectuals is solely forgiveness and does not exclude the commemorative act of man but is mainly a moral, religious, and rational, obligation, highly moral and highly symbolic, obedient to the divine mercy.

And especially if the spirituality that inspires it is the collective consciousness, it will reach the universality of the reason, the truth, and the values, which are transcendent principles. Religion must inspire a new humanism by the transcendent values to constitute the attitude of principles, not particularly modern values, with Western foreign cultures and civilizations, silent concerning the oppression of black people and ignoring their cultures. The annihilation of their cultures is controversial, and black people are protesting for a new humanism, expressing a rich hope of universal effect with human conditions sharing the experience of the sacred at the heart of the earthly kingdom, manifesting an attitude of tolerance without embodying the idea of the church authority but a new humanism of God. It is in this kind of false pretense that the signification of the truth and natural principles is hidden. Humans live in it—in politics, culture, labor, and economics—which is simply ridiculous and totally devoid of meaning.

A perpetual dilapidation of tradition, culture, and moral values has permanently become a part of everyday life. And man is against this constant disrepair in his life without however losing the sense of truth in this world. This annihilation of cultures was a severe work of missionaries and powerful legislators so miserable of the white human gender of the first ages, very religious in all extreme situations of the nature, who deeply acted intentionally to stain the skin of the black man and still acting deeply on the heart and the skin of all humanity; leaving bad impressions on this austere and rigid institution, which ruined the human race from all views of heaven, of religion, of morality, of his stay on earth, and the subsistence on everything concerning agriculture, civil and domestic economy, education, industry, and work.

The true and only good of the humanity is that the education of the Egyptians, having always been the only one which then had good institutions and also renowned for housing the wisest people of the earth, allowed the establishment of republics and magistrates, who gave birth to the wisest laws, happy fruits of misfortunes of the world, resulting to these deplorable time of disorder of all nature. The Egyptian constitution is the only true evidence of the dark antiquity that still shows us very precious vestiges of the history of that African nation till today. It finally opens the doors of thought to all those who have knowledge to affirm or leave the opportunity for everyone to bubble with the truth given in different theories, leading to that spirit of emulation security of domestic economics, of sociocultural protection policy, and centralized self-education, which animated the sad and unfortunate families escaped from the upheaval world.

This clarification of the history of our ancestors is to give you an idea of the practices and our religious beliefs that were stolen from us to finally use them as weapons on us. The story of the rod of Aaron, which became the supreme sign of the ministry of the family of Levi among the Hebrews, is a primitive story of the ark, the scepter of God out of the sanctuary—a story of priests who were religious ministers, who later on became the real rulers in theocratic governments. The testimony of Hebrews and the ancient pagan revealed its use to us. Among most people, the authority of the sacred law was kept in the ark of a changed religion by deplorable superstition, which confused the laws with God, the legislator. The main legislation of all ceremonial of the pagans auspicious became a secret. The instructive signs were no longer contemplated without fear of dying, and the proper duties of the people were a misery.

To achieve a happy life and good living, man should learn the most hidden splendor in the mysteries of Isis, Samothrace, Cybele, Ceres, Etruscan, etc., which after numerous lessons of great preparations and strong proofs reserved to only few initiates, to whom a dreadful oath made promise a total silence. Theocracy resorted to lie by advocating that these laws kept in the sanctuary were supernatural and wonderful writings of revelations by the divinity of goddesses and gods in a lonely desert, on an inflamed mountain, or in a cave to imagine which way they arrived on earth and for them to appear emanated from God. From this fact, religion wrenched the dignity of reason from man; weakened the honor of his laws so beautiful and so simple, a privilege of the divine gift so sublime that man alone received from his creator on earth, by these horrible lies—the story of Moses, the child saved from the water as the Bible reveals, was a story of a king who lived before Moses. In the book of Mahabharata titled *Adi Parva*, the author told us the story of the demigod Karna. His mother, Kunti, was not yet married but was visited by the sun god. Conceived, she gave birth to a son, who radiated like the sun, the image of his father. Kunti, fearing the loss of her virginity, put the child in a box that she secretly carried to the river. It was Adhirata therefore, who recovered the baby, named him Karna, and raised him like his own son. The story of the child rescued from the water later attributed to Moses—was it the one of Karna? The main mission of Moses was to create a belief in a universal deity. He represented the positive force of general astronomy or animal that could not be represented in human form by the secret knowledge of the Great Pyramid and the sphinx, he himself being Egyptian and a close friend of the pharaoh. The ethical code of Moses, subtle in the use of civilized society, had twelve commandments directly from the formula number 125 of the *Book of the Dead* of Egyptian origin. For the positive contribution to the profit of all humanity, two commandments, very erotic, were kept secret, and ten representing a code.

The misfortunes of the world are at the origin of these laws so suspicious, easily made to lie with more safety; also drawing their sources from the ancient ancestral practices of the great judge so formidable and so terrible; always hidden behind a dark veil in the obscure clouds in a discarded desert, like if the creator could descend to show himself and give laws for the good of humanity without absorbing the universe. These lies are the cause of the docile imbecility of mortals in the opinion of pagan antiquity, and the Jewish belief, assuming that we cannot see God without dying.

The invention of the entire national history of Hebrews is always based on the dark remnants of the ancient natural world events. Each nation saw the emergence of divinations, prophets, soothsayers practicing the art of divination, augurs, and priests who interpreted natural phenomena, considered a manifestation of the gods, to know the future in the Roman religion and the direct revelations of all kind from God. The disguise of the true origin of laws could not completely be erased by these fables, the ancient features of the truth. The hidden Mosaic code by the laws of Hebrews bore a title meaning "the code of the earth saved from the waters" in the Egyptian language.

The errors that came out of these first principles as abuse of these religious institutions established the dogma of the past vicissitudes and all future vicissitudes. This dogma became an instructive fear, a formidable brand filled with religious terror, imposed on all men, like the judgments that God exercised on earth. It perpetually exhibited motifs without borders of recognition to the Supreme Being as if it expected what was to happen and maintained humanity in his instability, with the fear that heaven will render the harmony infernal and the quiet bliss in the world unbearable. I would say that all these religious errors are found united among the Hebrews, who transmitted us the Bible. They dared fix the precise but false moment of the first existence on the chronology of the world, which produced all these strange diversities prevailing between all people. We said that it was natural not to rely on what one does not know either in the nature or in the vast depths of immeasurable times than jumping over the unknown centuries. This lie about its origin has obscured and extinguished the systematic reasoning of supernatural operations of a creator God and the architect of the universe. This state of chaos and confusion is the absurd and the ridiculous birth of the battles between Lucifer against God, Typhon against Osiris, giants against the gods, angels against demons, light against darkness, the sun against the moon, and good against evil. But nevertheless, all the ancient nations of the world tell us about the reign of gods on the earth. Anyway, the effect to consequently want to apply the principles of the reign from above down here below was a fatal error that precipitated the religion and these governments in deep abysses, Phoenicians, Egyptians, Indians, Greeks, Babylonians, and all other nations inhabiting the earth's territories speak of a too familiar time when gods descended to praise men on earth. In the splendors of the ancient state of mankind, the sign of authority, the scepter of the empire, the code of religious civil laws of a united society was deposited in a sacred place; the safest and most respectable representing the siege of the celestial monarch; the sanctuary of a temple confirms the antiquity to us; all recourse of knowledge and the instruction of its duties were held at this place.

Theocracy established an absurd convention of signs to teach the knowledge of its orders and its will to men, since God, being invisible, couldn't command them in a direct way on earth. This imagination suggested that man no longer consulted his reason and even today, where the truth is known to man, he still does not consult his reason; since priests were the religious organs of thought for all nations of the world, everyone became their slaves, their victims, and their dupes without realizing it, believing that their conduct and their actions were a direct revelation from God. I would call such a code of laws the code of institutions of the world drawn from the abyss, made to lie and maintain mankind in fear because of his ignorance of the first natural laws and the first feelings of obedience toward the world in all their traditions. A perfect certainty leads me to affirm that it is after countless sufferings that the law pretended to be given to Moses on the Mount Sinai in the midst of all nature that the primitive church personified the hymns; engendering all old characters who were like Moses, and from which museums were made, and poets sang the sublime origin of the world for the vital aspect of nature.

The Hebrews, still wandering, were always wailing new plagues and new calamities, dwelt for so long in Egypt before entering recently in that puny country that they describe as their promised land in Palestine, today called Israel; knowing themselves to have well suffered endless miseries for forty years in the wilderness. Successively destroyed by chasms, giants, and dragons by thirst and hunger in a wild strange and barren land, renewing their race, so that their former no more live in the new; like ignoring the old state of their human race and the corrupt history of the passage from their old to the new world that they have appropriated themselves; they prefer and pretend to make particular anecdotes of a portion of their turbulent history with a wonderfully hidden origin.

The story of their misery in that land of anguish, almost exterminated by the darkness, pestilence, famine, fire, water, and all apocalyptic plagues, their famous passage through Egypt to the land supposedly promised, immediately preceding their theocratic period, like all old woes of the world preceded theocracies, depositary of laws entrusted to priests, to the officers and ministers of the king, great judges to whom they gave certain powers, and the immanence present in the brightness of time, its movement that was trembling at the hour of nimble, like their current state.

Their theocracy was a gesture by which the first societies presented the fruits of the earth that one held with the charitable hand at each season, since there were no other tributes to pay as an act of gratitude to the Supreme Being, who was made the sovereign king from all universal being, and who needed a real and civil tribute to live. The people knew that he needed a home and that the king was judging with fervor that everyone had to offer him tithes (one-tenth of each one's asset and everyone's own f locks) to his temple, which could contribute to the brilliance and magnificence of the monarch.

Because of the simplicity of the man, who offered himself, his family, and his children as ministers and officers to maintain the one who was holding their freedom, he offered himself without dishonor but recognized himself as a servant. On the other hand, man did not realize that he thus voluntarily became a subject and the slave of priests and his hypocrite ministers, who were devouring all donations for themselves. They did not anymore cease to lay traps on the generous and shared the tenths of the invisible sovereign between them, and the kingdom of heaven made them master of the earth. These priests slaughtered animals, which were gifts offered to the monarch god and exposed before the shrines by shedding blood in his presence, and they roasted some parts and became ruthless butchers.

Their temples were turned into bloody temples, decreasing the priestly portion that familiarized the order as a ridiculous and barbaric order loving blood with a place of carnage in a thousand places in the world for thousands of years, where the human blood, preferred to that of animals, was streaming. There was not a single temple not bloodied or characterized by cruel bloodshed of these primitive times of all people of the world, where one was not presenting the fruits of the earth to the Supreme Being. The Egyptians, the Hebrews, the Greeks, and the Romans, preserved the memory of these primitive days of those dreadful sights of human victims.

If we had not quickly acquired the taste and be familiarized with the blood of animals, imagining that God loved the blood that was offered to him as a sacrifice, to escape the great judgment, we would have continued to offer him the blood of the one who was most precious to us. An inconceivable barbarity and an atrocious way of thinking, which would have never been introduced on earth, would you not say? Here were once again the horrors of the mysteries of religion, particularly of Christianity, valuing the tribute of royalty, the tenths, and the human sacrifice to the pride of the priesthood, which only served to feed, to maintain the great judge, and thus to became his property by divine law. Until today, all religions and all civil governments are still extending new victims to the infinite to increase in abundance the treasures of their ministers and for the purchase of weapons, horses, chariots, shields, and war equipment—things that were in ancient theocracy, the equipages of the invisible monarch, which were dedicated to his gods.

Previously, it was more often a question of the Supreme Being, even as it was so difficult for man to conceive a being so great, so immense yet invisible than he was. The most fatal of all consequences of this story is that theocracy helped to come up with crude carnel comparisons of its representation since the king, regardless of the quality of God, his cup was well filled. Everyone followed his laws, his orders, and his judgments were everywhere. His officers were receiving tributes. His palace, still in its luminous spot, made people talk about him by acts of praise as if one was honoring a religious personality and those of the civil authorities. All acts of religion, civil authority and ceremonial were exercised before the symbolic qualities of a god and a king. Prayers and praises were addressed to the Supreme Being, decorated with all the sublime titles that suited his emblem. In times of misfortune and calamities, nations were coming to bow down before the representations of rough stone or carved stones and brought with them the representative signs of the monarch god, like a cat, a cow, or a goat, for those who believe in the moon and for some who believed in the sun. It was from these awful feelings of idolatry that the fatal door of hatred to the Supreme Being was opened, and men passed from the worship of the Creator to the worship of the creature. It was also through their mistakes that humanity completely ignored his existence and unity.

But by forgetting the past, by the imperceptible progress of ignorance, without wanting it and without knowing it, men gradually found themselves imperceptibly in the gears of a great apparatus of the degenerated sacerdotal worship, which became more avaricious than the idea itself, almost as ignorant as the people, putting two precipices in place, known as slavery and idolatry, and multiplying victims, gifts, and tributes to the monarch god. Every nation has its sensible monarch God and behaves with a religious and intelligent circumspection with respect to his emblem, more by simplicity than by the idea of idolatry. That is why in our courts, the portrait of our sovereign, of his kingship or his excellence, the real sovereign that we do not see, reminds us of his existence at every moment in this or that palace, and before the eyes of all those who seek justice, such was the fate of our ancestors, who did not have the facility to paint divinity, than for us to paint a mortal; such is ours, a commemorative object.

One science was peculiar to the priesthood; it became secretive and mysterious more than it should have been; open and sincere to people, by keeping the true meaning of the symbols and interpretations of all the emblems to themselves, they thought to make religion be respected to nations by all this mysterious darkness and rendered idolatry ambiguous and ambivalent to men, who sincerely sought divinity; but instead of revealing, they extinguished it, leading mankind to the precipitated fall to the point of no longer knowing his God; it was a bizarre and insensible degradation of God, who became figurative and allegorical with a sacred writing, a barbaric theological language, and an inaccessible device to humans instead of an instruction and an explanation as in the beginning.

By multiplying all symbols by themselves, the unity of the cult degenerated, and different nations could not retain the same object and the same symbol as signs of the reigning deity on earth. On the other hand, each nation got used to consider the most holy and the truest divinity, under the sign of the sun, of the moon, of a stone, of a statue or an ox, as its emblem, by seeing in these objects, the true God who was no longer the same symbol of the Supreme Being.

The general religion was extinguished, the unity of nations was broken, all emblems were different, and the earth could no longer imagine that it still had the same God who was everywhere. There only remained a fatal impression and a vague memory of the true old religion of the Supreme Being, who led all people to aspire to the universal monarchy. The priests regarded this universal monarchy like the one who was really supposed to be the Supreme Being, under the form of different names in different languages of ministers, jealous enemies of all the neighboring gods. Thus, under the veil of sacred religion and by the state were the universal sources of all distractions and of all the bloody calamities, which desolated men of all nations of the universe, engendering declared enemies from each other.

The frightful chaos in which primitive religion plunged mankind was also the disfigured result of all disorders of civil administration and theocratic governments, and was also the cause that rendered people slaves by a political edifice built down here as a model of the kingdom of heaven, producing the greatest evils and could only have a fatal success on earth. As the former inhabitants of heaven, the first men in the early days had the instinct to want to be happy and free; but approaching this bliss of fervor and the heroism of the first time, the era of the golden age of their theocracy so sang, the one of the reign of their so-called justice, able to support their government supernaturally established, they soon realized that their transitory religious projection virtues were only passing and could not last here on earth.

These wonderful times existed in all fervor of morals and reason, when man lived in independence and was doing what pleased him. Everyone was free, speaking of the early days of the theocracy, from the beginning of this mystical age, before mankind could be affected with the misfortunes of the world. Terrestrial theocracy was just an object of oppression by disillusioned governments abusing their power and the people and did not resemble the heavenly theocracy with a constant state of bliss, freedom, and justice. Those governments, their ministers, the real despots, and the great judges became symbols of tyranny in all likelihood, but were not the theocracy of the institution of the power of God, however, with essential vice of the theocracy whose priests by the religious abuses, were letting the true origin of their policy be known, and an administration of invisible sultans with all human errors to all humanity.

According to the memory of nations, the abuses and the servitude of men submitted universally, which prevail everywhere on earth, let believe that their visible ministers, worthy of their invisible master, were simply abusing their power and the freedom of men. The supreme and divine power that was first recognized by the good doing of priests made humanity consider them as an organ of divinity, the immutable sovereigns, and the gods. One was accustomed to obey them, to be submitted to their oracles, to not be able to withstand their injustices, to their black projects; we confessed our nothingness, our indignities, not daring to fathom their decrees of an impenetrable providence, and recognized ourselves their slaves by hundred mystical interpretations, of which every day victims are still seeking solutions today. The sacred prejudices of priests, the only sovereigns of the world, covered the earth; they who disposed the honor of the human life were and are still filled with impiety and insolence up to the coat of divinity; the priestly incontinence, the object of a criminal worship, mothers of the miserable victims of their cult, which inhabited the mortals on earth and put at the rank of divinity of the miserable fanatical conquerors, were known as the imposters monsters with unworthy vices of the king's legislators; it is known that they were playing with the human race that they have dishonored and debased on earth.

After a certain time, men left this priesthood and everything concerning religion to priests. Republics were formed by civil magistrates. Men, still religiously affected by the theocracy of a monarch, sought another type of government with more relation of unity, and empires were the preference of all nations, confirmed by the government of one individual than the republican administration, like the republican governments of Europe, the monstrous societies with the ideas of the ancient theocratic principle never extinguished, which we still do not understand.

Here is what the Bible tells us about an example of an imitation that the Hebrews inherited from Africans and later on practiced in Egypt—hiding a monarch god among all people since the dawn of times, in 1 Sm. 8:1–22. When Samuel became old, he appointed his sons as judges over Israel. His firstborn son was named Joel— "the strong God" and the second Abijah — "God the Father"; they judged in Beersheba. But his sons did not walk in his ways; they received bribes and violated justice. All the elders of Israel gathered and came to Samuel at Ramah and said to him, "Behold, thou art old, and thy sons walk not in thy ways: now make us a king to judge us like all other nations." This request displeased Samuel, who prayed to Yahweh, and Yahweh said to him, "Hearken unto the voice of the people in all that they say unto thee: for they have not rejected thee, but they have rejected me, that I should not reign over them.

"As they have done from the day I brought them out of Egypt unto this day, forsaking me, and served other gods, so they're doing to unto thee. Now hearken unto their voice: howbeit warn them solemnly and show them the manner of the king that shall reign over them." So Samuel said to the people, "This will be the right of the king that shall reign over you: He will take your sons, and appoint them on his chariots, and to be his horsemen; and some shall run before his chariots. And he will appoint them captains over thousands and captains over fifties; and others will plow his ground, and to reap his harvest, others to make his instruments of war, and instruments of his chariots. And he will take your daughters to be confectionaries, and to be cooks, and to be bakers. And he will take your fields, and your vineyards, and your olive yards, even the best of them, and give them to his servants. And he will take your menservants, and maidservants, and your goodiest young men, and your asses, and put them to his work. He will take the tenth of your sheep: and ye shall be his servants. And you shall cry out when the day comes because of your king whom you have chosen; and the Lord will not hear you in that day."

The people refused to listen by crying out loud, "We need a king, and we also will be like all the nations; our king will judge us and go on campaign to fight for us." The purpose of this example is to let you notice the theocratic prejudices in the history of Hebrew; the stupid people in a religion that Samuel traces by the greed of a nation wanting a king; their desire for someone to govern them was not foreseeing that by taking a mortal as the representative of the divinity was to give themselves a tyrant, and that his almighty power would defile the sensible feelings of the righteous; and that the public reason could not submit him to the common laws imposed by the society, for acting impurely in a mysterious ark, consequently considered as the emblem of a God—the Supreme Being.

If he were chosen with his fragile portrayal of the monarch God, if one acted against him like one would do with other simple human beings, he will reply without forgiveness because he will consider himself the supreme mystery. But if he were simply chosen as an active and visible sacerdotal emblem, which was to speak as we wanted and which would prevent tyranny, he would represent a symbolic image of a dove, the messenger of peace, sensitive to suffering, and who was to work to alleviate the miseries of life, and he will represent a revealed love in all its divine dignity.

However, this mistake was the mistake of all the people who gave themselves kings, thus substituting a single sovereign magistrate of the priests of bad governance, imagining that they made a great reform. The same chain of false theocracy principles and false reasoning survived and became civil after being sacred and gave birth to despotism. Different people of the world made this transition from theocracy to despotism, differently placing the modified events between the reigns of the gods, who descended to mingle with mortals in times of crises to establish new civilizations and observe mankind obey the laws of the celestial knowledge being preserved for posterity and serve for the good reign of kings, chiefs, and governors in some remote areas and in the world.

Their story, filled with beautiful facts, revealed civil disorders produced by abuses and all evils and false theocratic principles of their time, hidden in the fables to this day. These great changes were not made without tumult and division between priests dethroned by the people. The monarch god was an idol for priests—a strong reason to torment mankind from the first election of kings who were the enemies of the empire for the priesthood since those times up to our days. Always antipathetic to one another, these two supreme dignities never ceased to oppose themselves by alternately giving themselves landmarks and the ideal limits that they have from the undecided people and to dispute the primacy and the empire of the world, always proportioned to the gradual lights of centuries, with the care to note their losses and their mutual successes to reproduce the reason and serenity in it.

These people, being finally resolved, elected a mortal man like them as their monarch god. Their only precaution was to choose the most handsome and the greatest in size than the qualities of the spirit since it was solely the primitive elections under an appearance of the deity than on the real and invisible divinity. This description was attributed to Saul because he exceeded everyone in height, and there was no one like him among all the people; he was the one Yahweh had chosen for all the people, and Saul received the royal anointing from Samuel, according to 1 Sm. 9:1–10.

All people of the world acted like this, according to our ancient authors, the most extraordinary of the ancient world (Strabo, Diodorus of Sicily). According to the Bible, Saul was not sacred. So, the spirit of Yahweh melted upon him, and he prophesied in the ceremonies of coronation of kings. This communication with God transformed him, giving him a new heart, and a proverb was born: Is Saul also among the prophets? I would say yes. Thus, the inauguration to royalty is still up to our days, the subject of an essential ceremony to change the chosen into another man, among all people of the world. It is true that the new kind of government that men embraced in these first elections disclosed less security and precaution than the old theocratic idea and prejudices that existed for choosing a monarch god, representing the mortal, like it was previously a stone ox or goat, with so much simplicity and the same view on the continuation of errors, determining that men were not happy. Despite the discontent over this government with the idea of being governed by revelation, theocracy has not changed from that of the priests and the civil government with the heavenly kingdom that they wanted to represent on earth. Raising a man as God's representative was a burden too heavy for him. This glory of greatness was not originally prescribed for him. For this fact, he succumbed, unable to moderate the feeling of dignity as a mortal instead saw himself being decorated with all titles due to the Supreme Being, not by the reason of the public laws but worshipped as Adonis, Osiris, and other emblems of divinity. The One whom he represented infallibly gave anything to anyone.

The ferocities and the cruelties of that emblem were for man like the judgments of heaven. The dreadful testimony of the rights of the king, who would reign over them and whom Samuel laid against the children of Israel, surpassed in all the imaginary power of the people. They had to religiously and humbly subscribe to his will, his orders, his whims, and his policies, which quickly became the judgments of heaven. The universe belonged to him and mankind with it in that calamity, and those who have always suffered these atrocities with respect humbly kept silent about that stupid idolatry, still believing in the representation of the divinity by a mortal. Such was the government of the monarch man, representing God as a Supreme Being.

This long chain of errors generated false deplorable principles over the entire earth, and it was in these evils that the whole world was educated. I would say that man rushed himself into the abyss by wanting to govern or even still governing by a chimerical revelation, having in view the heavens where any abusive power was above everything, especially in Africa and in some parts of the world, instead of relying on reason. These sublime bitter ideas are up to our days, the inheritance of theocracy.

The idolatry of religion and the despotism of governments are just the same thing that became a monster of all sacred or civil administration, whose brotherhood is so narrow and will forever infect the kingdom of heaven on the earth. If we take a glance in Africa and in other parts of the world, we will notice that the principles of the old theocracy are still the ceremonial and the main uses of the states up to our days, still easily humiliating the majority of the people or the entire world. This theocratic usage is still preserved and practiced by our leaders in Africa, in Asia, in Europe, in Australia, and in America, reminding us of the ancient judges and kings of Ethiopia, of Assyria, of Babylon, of Persia, and Media, a region of Asia Minor that was inhabited by the Medes. Till today, our presidents in Africa are proclaiming themselves to be sons of heaven from the blood of the gods.

They created themselves thrones, where they sit without assembly for an eternity; announcing the happy days of their abundance, of their calamitous serenities predicting the woes of the people every morning according to the season of their moods, or the circumstances of the time with disastrous peace sterility, pierced by the swords of justice in the solemn spiritual law; but believing that with their pestilence burnt convictions of war in themselves, they could shake the world with a movement of their eyebrows. That succession and power are based on all false principles of the ancient theocracies, much older than Christianity, founded on a false truth, which occasioned the misfortune of men and which never could, by their incessantly fatal disorders, applied the true kingdom of heaven to reign down here. It is those false principles, used repeatedly to abuse that are affecting men on earth.

Prejudices are of more than a human soul for them, a risk bore to only see in their actions a foolish pride, and not an authorized conduct received in the plan of its citizens or former fighters for a government of development. Our historians and moralists have not yet seen these follies in everything they supposed to see in them. We are just observing the solemn oath that corresponded to all other usages and to all other errors of nations made on the day of the coronation; they are swearing and promising no fear that their governments would not be inflicted by the sterility of people or by the malignant influences of men.

A promise made as a very peculiar pact, no doubt, to reassure people with no fear, but on which Juste-Lipse only makes vain jokes without determine sources; only comprising traces of woes of the present world. Their beautiful promises are causing all calamities of suffering to the lack of all the people's confidence, like the unworthy words of our African leaders. They're completely ignoring the particular objective, the general purpose of religion and the cult of each government. The hearts of man have only known frightful theocracies of legislators who have governed and still govern societies by terror, which are causing sources of contemptuous rudeness, and which are authentically unveiling a transmission of fable principle fables to us; known very unfaithful like the history of Hebrews with poor collection of false traditions of the ancient times. They misunderstood the world and turned it into a vile place to live; and made numerous slaves with an idea of their God so terrible, an imposture to be compared with the colorful ignorance confirmed in the Bible.

The heart of man, genius of the primitive people and witness of the world's woes, sees atrocities becoming sufferings and miseries of every day in many nations, which up to today only wish for a paternal government of a peaceful nature and friendly to mankind; one that does not and will never need to lead with an iron scepter and the spirit of tyrants. The rigors, the extremes of harshness, the fanaticism, and the cruel atrocities are all abuses that came out of political regimes believed to be theocratic, not the natural vices of man. They use an excessive authority became despotism, where it is impossible to do good but revealing other means of extreme deceptions to manifest their enormous greatness and to dishonor and enslave almost all people of the earth that they do not need to be loved, honored or respected. Since they can only make use of the monstrous power that surpasses their power, they well inflict much evil to humanity. Their actions exciting terror spread fear, abusing the people, since they only show them freedom under the form of a spear or a sword, like the Jehovah of the Hebrews—severe, cruel, ruthless, jealous, vindictive, and decorated with all devices of terror kept hidden and stealing the knowledge of the name of the deity that their God gives himself.

The human race does not seek a storm; it has the fear of everything created for hell and loves the sublime virtues of everything created for heaven. It loves the one who loves men, respects him, honors him, and worships him as a god by the fundamental laws that the people obey without pain and without intrigue, which reasonably favor him and make him unshakable, happy, and distinguished with unprecedented nonviolence of slavery. It is constantly worn out by the unceasing abuses, which the public reason supports by fixed and constant laws; an extreme choice giving to his fellow mortal, the first place like the first of first created men to avoid violence. Our ancestors, who were filled with common sense as moderate humans enjoying the feeling of their civil natural state, did not degrade man; they did not oblige man to slavery. They had a wonderful constitution worthy of all respect; the passions of man were a source of profit for the general well-being.

All these fabulous and deceptive sacred and profane stories known will return to the annals of the empty contempt, which will convince the ignorance and the false silence that the truth precedes. Because creation is just a deluge, the natural, and its deluge is just creation, astrologically, and vice versa, systematically mystic; considered different from one the other; but having a double use of the same fact under two different viewpoints. The unity of societies emerged from the universal dogma that several world religions and different people appropriated themselves. The human being conflict facing the fragility of his existence and in all his creations requires a constant questioning and sees a deep need of transcendence.

The significance of the slavery of the black man had nevertheless, an incalculable scope. It was in my opinion, from the immense moral and spiritual break made between the white society of yesterday and even of today. Their purely racial or mentally sadistic methods failed during the preceding decade. Agricultural science subscribed before this man huge commitments that he could not keep. The hopes that the mechanization of man raised, collapsed one after another, because this same humanity found out that, far from freeing himself from work by the machine, he chained his freedom to the engine, but a great damage was already done. And so far, the white race does not foresee the era of reconciliation, excuse, or even general remuneration for the evil—yes, I do say the evil inserted to the black race throughout the world.

The whole of Africa has lived and is still experiencing phenomena such as the confiscation of countries, as was South Africa, where there is still a very high racial persecution; the exploitation of raw materials and the establishment of a policy of domination, and control of our goods, resulting to a transfer of the African population to the West in search of a new bed. Man escaped from the divine guardianship, believed to be definitively emancipated. He made from the intellectual science, of which reasoning, and deduction are the only tools, his progress. And now, this purely cerebral science turns against him under the form of new plagues and unknown diseases. No one can predict the future in detail, but what is certain is that humanity will no longer find his ancestral root.

He will go from instability to instability until the new equilibrium is found. Thus, the current world is divided between the old humanity that do not want to die and the new humanity that wants to be born. The two conceptions of the society are colliding, and their incessant clash will finally spout out the individual. The cunning and treachery world powers must resort less and less to concealed dealings and underground maneuvers. What is good and what is evil will be spread publicly so that we can quickly distinguish them. Therefore, all international and national misunderstanding will not end suddenly. The sovereign law that sets circumstances and men in motion will require the complete restoration of freedom. Humanity will be somehow put to the rolling mill. What is curved will become straight. What is round will be flat. Any social existence will be reformed to the last molecule. How? When? Where? Nobody knows. No one can deny that the global behavior, especially European and American, of this time is only succeeding in what has already been the history of mankind.

The whole world is sounding with the clamor of threats and the crash of arms. Announcing to us effectively that Armageddon or Apocalypse has begun. The politics of the five continents are upset, and neutrality no longer exists, because the main characteristic of this present period is that nothing of what has been created, adjusted, or imposed is no longer respected. Men are protesting by shouting, "Peace! Peace!" while there is no peace in their lives. Peace can prevail in the whole world only if it first exists in our home. However, we have no peace in us but only fear and hatred.

The present humanity has adopted the motto of modern civilization—which means, the law of the jungle where man eats man and where the reason of the strongest is always the best. No more questions of loving your neighbor as yourself, which was previously the law of love. The tragic truth is that man has forgotten the essential and has built hatred as the edifice out of the humanitarian foundation. In vain, we change the form of government, while governments do not change the bottom of their heart. No authority, whether public or governmental, thinks of realizing the desire of the human; on the contrary, they want the human to realize a certain given authority. However, without understanding that their efforts are tending to compress humanity, give rise to that state of revolt in him, and at the same time raising powerful categorical expansions in him; the greater the material compression of authority is great on him, the greater the spiritual decompression of humanity is considerable in him. Here ends the Christian era and the beginning of oppression took us with full force and is following its course up to our days.

CHAPTER FOUR

SLAVERY

In the previous cycles, the black race (mother of humanity) and the red race successively reigned by powerful civilizations. We see the traces in their gigantic constructions left in Mexico and Egypt, where we could still find understandable traditional monuments of their civilizations.

Civilization itself began on earth more than fifty to sixty thousand years ago with the red race. Let us also note that during the reigning period of the red race in the Austral continent, the entire European continent and part of Asia were still under water. But in this borderless world, the Negro and the white race are forming a marriage, I would say, not as perfect but inseparable. White was the last of races that came out of the glacial caves of the forest ecosystem, where he initially lived in the wild and later on was selling himself into slavery, like merchandise, to the Arabs and as prisoners of the black race to finally get educated in Egypt.

After that education, some whites escaped and returned to the West to apply what they learned from their black masters, only to finally return and overthrow the great African power in Egypt. The inseparable relationship between black and white continued when the white decided to make the blacks prisoners and slaves. The black race has always respected that superiority complex and tolerated the incomprehensibility toward them. The enslavement of black was very rough because of the state of the wild souls of whites and the barbarism that inhabits them than blacks, who had an institutional form of education and well-established civilization. They were and still are inhuman, acting cruelly, brutal, and uncivilized like their white ancestors during the slavery period.

Agenor, whose genealogy was unveiled by Herodotus, Greek historian, of the year 484 before our era, who was also considered as one of the early explorers and first journalist and first prose writer—"the man who wrote in prose" (poet). Also among those who testified about Agenor were Hesiod, the Greek poet of the eighth century, of around 700 BC, who was known for the best story of the origins to the ancient Greeks; the Greek lyric poet Bacchylides of the fifth century BC; Diodorus of Sicily, a Greek historian and chronicler of the first century BC; Aeschylus, known by the dramatic force, the tension, and the anxiety that dwells in his great tragic and satirical Greek drama, toward 525 BC; and Pherecydes, a Greek historian and mythologist of the fifth century BC, who compiled and examined myths; all revealed to us that the name of the European continent was named after the daughter of King Agenor, son of Poseidon and Libya, king of Tyr, the current Lebanon and founder of Thebes in Greece. Neither he nor his wife, were European but both Africans.

So even as I would assume that the superior type of the black race no longer existed in this degenerated race but among the Abyssinians and Nubians, by whom the world was designed, the black race in Africa, particularly in Egypt, which quickly succeeded the red race, was the first true and great power which ruled the world in the light of the living for thousands of years and continued to govern it until today by its dead in the entire history of mankind. The Egypt I am talking about truly existed and had initiates of the first order and sovereign intelligence, creative and instructing.

It is not a historical lie to say and accept that civilization was held for the first time in Africa. And it is well before the white dreamed to set foot on that continent. To get to that civilization, there were confrontations in every country of the continent and between different tribes that gave birth to a very strong and independent clan ruling these countries. This leads me to say that Africa already established a strong state process in some of its countries before the arrival of the Europeans. The arrival of the white man, along with slavery and colonization, came to put an end to a system of political and cultural civilization that already existed since the ancestral reign.

These confrontations were by no means, a cause of human trafficking, in contrary to what is explained by some historians who are lacking honesty about slavery. Africa generally is known as a continent with the kings or queens as members of a royal family prior to their arrival. The proof is that it is the only continent to date that shows us the oldest royal ancestor in the history of mankind. What the scientists call homogenetic conception of humanity is indeed a proven science, asserting that the human being was born in Africa; they concluded by saying that if the phenotype, known as the composition of an organism's observable characteristics, the ontogenetic development of an individual in genetics within the organism, resulting from the dialectic of space and time of the genotype interaction is plural, but the genotype itself remains unique, identical, and universal in all men under Sui generis term; if not, interbreeding between various species of the human race will not be possible. The "dialectic" space and time describes how a thesis and a contradictory antithesis can be reconciled by a higher truth.

Our most civilized, most prosperous, and oldest empires well known to the universe from the sixth century in Africa had constitutions and charters on human rights that were specifying the following points: the right to life, the preservation of nature, the preservation of the physical integrity, respect of the wise, tolerance, the principle of educating children, the involvement of women in politics, the good treatment of servants, the prohibition of slavery, etc. They lost their power with the installation of European ports on the African coast, specifically in Guinea.

I list among others, the empire of Monomotapa, an empire in the 1440s established by Gokomeres, ancestors of the modern Shona people—a people of Southern Africa especially present in Zimbabwe, southern Mozambique, and Zambia. The Bambara kingdom of Segou was founded around 1712 by an association of persons composed of the same age group, of different ethnicities, of traditional African religions, including Muslims, gathering on an equal basis and extending on both banks of the Niger, between Bamako and Timbuktu.

The Fulani Empire of Macina was a theocratic empire founded in the nineteenth century by Sekou Amadou, a Fulani Marabout of the Barry clan, extended on a part of the current Mali to Timbuktu in the north, the Mossi country in the south, Mauritania at the east, and the region of Mopti.

The Congo Empire was an empire founded in the thirteenth century by several Bantu migrations in areas already populated by the Baka pygmies from the seventh to the fifteenth century in territories located in southwestern Africa, specifically in northern Angola, Cabinda, the Republic of Congo, at the western end of the Democratic Republic of Congo, a part of Gabon, and from the Atlantic Ocean at the west of the Kwango River to the east and the Congo River to the south of the river Loje, independently unified under the leadership of one king. It was a very spiritual empire, having supernatural powers and divination, with access to the ancestors. The kings were chosen by ancients among the eligible members of the twelve Congo clans.

The Djolof Empire was an empire founded by Ndiadiane Ndiaye, according to tradition, between the late twelfth century and early thirteenth century. It encompassed the Senegambia space; regions of Kayor, Baol Walo, and Sine, Saloum; a part of Futa Toro, where we would find Fulani of Fouta Toro, established in the region toward the end of the fourteenth century; and part of Bambouk.

Several known empires were also founded by Fulani in the nineteenth century in Africa, among which were the Fulani Empire of Sokoto, north of present-day Nigeria; the Fulani Empire of Macina, in the present-day Mali; and the Toucouleur empire, also in Mali. A theocratic Fulani Empire was more a kingdom than a real empire called *diina* "faith in Islam", the Marabout "Diina" Barry clan of Sekou Amadou, which he founded in the nineteenth century; this theocratic Fulani Empire was known as the Macina Empire.

Within the Cameroonian population, different sociocultural groups characterized by a great linguistic diversity are represented by the mystery that still lingers on the origin of Fulani, led and organized by the equivalent of a village chief, known as a *lamido*; their location is located by many anthropologists in the regions of East Africa, basin of the upper Nile. They're defined as a consistent ethnic group, spread in about fifteen or more countries in West Africa; they're as a visible form of nomadic and seminomadic species living in Benin, Burkina Faso, Cameroon, the Central African Republic, Chad, Gambia, Ghana, Guinea, Guinea-Bissau, Ivory Coast, Mali, Mauritania, a country in northwestern Africa, Nigeria, Niger, Senegal, Sierra Leone, Sudan, and the north of Togo.

Their origin and the one of their identity is composed of an Egyptian Hamitic race of sedentary Africans farmers and practitioners of matriarchy, a government ruled by a woman or women, settled in the southeast of Egypt. Known by Ptolemy and Pliny, their historical context is spread discontinuously from 2500 BC to the era of the Ptolemaic dynasties in 300 BC, where their ethnography appeared in texts and on monuments. A period of an important ethnic mixture occurred from the Lower Egypt with the East and the Mediterranean. The work of their pastors from Egypt, the engravings of symbolic character or mythology, occurred between four thousand and two thousand years; their sovereignty disappeared as a result of the dislocation of the Ancient Egyptian society, which had to migrate quite late. But we would still find that uterine affiliation, which confirmed the black Africans belonging to these people.

Some Fulani are therefore Negroes who were mixed with other races among the black Egyptian population, like the whites coming from abroad. The *Ankh N° 12/13* magazine tells us that the terminology of the pharaonic Egypt power can be found in the titles and names of the Fulani. Stories and tales exist, like the one of Njeddo Dewall, describing the famous country of Heli and Yoyo to us, before their dispersion across the African continent. Linked to Egypt, the origin of the Fulani was not white but black by their culture, their color, and their language, even as hypotheses linking them to the pharaonic Egypt are largely discredited by some modern historians; their abundant literatures for the origin of Foulani are forgetting a very understandable thing, which said that Africa was at first black before any other color came to mix with the mother color.

However, we also find in some a distinction of the mixture of Indo-Europeans and Asians between the Berbers and Indo-European people like Hittites and Hyksos, having penetrated Africa during the Upper Antiquity of Egypt.

The Songhai Empire, product of the interbreeding between the Songhai and the Berbers, was founded in the seventh century in Koukia, the vassal of the empires of Ghana and Mali, and became an empire during the fifteenth century to generate the dynasty of Dia. This empire stretched more or less on Niger, Mali, and a part of the current Nigeria.

The empire of Ghana was one of the known great empires of black Africa from 734 to 1240 by the first Arab-Berbers in search of gold, stretching from the middle Senegal to the region of the current Timbuktu. The West African oral tradition told us that this kingdom was founded toward the fifth century BC by a man named Dinga Cisse of the animist Soninke farmer people from the East to found Ghana in the fourth century, with a belief in the vital force, the soul that animates not only living beings but also natural elements. The Soninkes have an expansion zone located on two-thirds of Mali at the south of Mauritania, with a large part of Senegal, at the northwest of Burkina Faso, a part of the Gambia, and in Guinea and Guinea-Bissau.

The Ashanti Empire was an empire formed by the Akan ethnic group in Ghana from 1620 to the Ghana annexation by the English in 1806.

The kingdom of Oyo was founded in the fifteenth century by Shango, the first king of Oyo in the current Nigeria by the Yoruba, who considered Ile-Ife as their city of origin and was a great rival of Dahomey on the current Benin.

Dahomey was a kingdom of the seventeenth century located in the southeast of the current Benin, which survived until the late nineteenth century.

The Oba of Benin was a former leader of the kingdom of Benin who came from Ife in 1180 and who no longer had a real power since the annexation of the kingdom by the British in 1897.

The kingdom of Kanem-Bornu was founded by the Teda dynasty, originally established in northern Chad around the eighth century.

And the empire of Mali was founded by Sundiata Keita in the thirteenth century and was the birthplace of the Manden Charter; to only name these few kingdoms in our vast Africa.

Forgetting that the African history does not necessarily begin during its discovery, its slavery and colonization by Europe, the entire continent already had original institutions and its sovereign states that the colonizers would ignore in the sixteenth century. It's about these institutional established states in Africa that led Anta Diop to qualify them as not being a compensatory myth, but on the contrary, a truth that we must see in the Bantu pharaohs' dynasties, as an example in the history of which today, we Africans must and willingly accept to make us become worthy by these ancient dynasties of Egyptian civilization with its pyramids, its temples, which were built by blacks and other institutions and sovereign states in that whole African continent.

During that period, Africa had a great conception of integrated urban civilization of cities, state and an organization based on the development of intense economic exchanges divided into four historical and cultural areas:

1. The kingdom of Tekrur, the Mali Empire, the Songhai Empire, and the empire of Ghana constituted the Sudanese area.
2. The coastal kingdoms, agglomerating the Hausa kingdom, the kingdom of Benin, the kingdom of Abomey, and the Ashanti kingdom, constituted the Guinean area.
3. The kingdom of Congo and the kingdom of the Great Lakes constituted the Bantu area.
4. Finally, the kingdom of Ethiopia, Somalia, and a number of kingdoms that were more in contact with the Arab world constituted the eastern area.

Their structures were very complex, constituting officials of customary law, a very well-developed urban architecture, an army, resources and crafts, agriculture, and commercial exchanges, placing them between the eighth and sixteenth century. The archaeologist named Mauny described the city of Kumbi Saleh to us, as the capital of the Ghana Empire in the thirteenth century, before the intrusion of the whites in Africa. He said: the center of town was built around a large square, from which several streets were departing; paving on the ground, epigraphs plates, paintings and inscription on the walls and stairs of stone; all this allowed us to get an idea of what was the civilization that flourished in these places.

Founded between the ninth and tenth century, the cities of Oyo, Ife, Benin, Timbuktu, and Djenn, located on the Bani River on the floodlands, in the southern Mali, became in the sixteenth century very important major trade centers of salt and gold that Europe had ever known. In Bantu language, Zimbabwe—an important great African civilization that unfortunately was exterminated by whites in the sixteenth century by genocide and the slavery industry—and currently a state in Southern Africa, its name meant "large stone house." Apart from the guns, Africa did not have much to envy from the Europeans before their intrusion.

Here is a brief preview of the unfortunate history of our famous Africa, the most beautiful part of the world, which affected historians all over the world and that travelers of insensitive nations and lacking the sense of intellectual and humanitarian knowledge who reached a degradation of mankind thought that, to satisfy their needs, it was necessary that the strongest enslaved the Africa people—the fearful, scared, and weak Negroes but blessed with other virtues by the Creator. They made them slaves but have never been able to subdue them spiritually, morally, or physically. It was in this state of spirit that they believed they were depriving Africans of freedom; for African people, the only reason for Europeans, masters of prejudices who reached this degradation, was to enslave them by their whims.

The analysis of facts marking our societies that I summarized with these letters of fire is uniquely to share our history and the world news with readers because the understanding of the present sometimes requires the ingredients of the past for the preparation of the future. This analysis is also especially for our societies to rise to a higher level of understanding for a moral, physical, and spiritual development. Without some filthy behavior of evil effect, attributed to evil and unsustainable practices of certain black sheep, who go beyond their missions for purely material and radical detriment of human life conditions, come to jeopardize the internal growth of inner necessity and organic progress.

The African society, in his famous history of civilization in the late Middle Ages gave us an impressive fresco, especially during the first cruel racial and colonial contact. Their first contact, the annihilatory progressive measure, was the Negro slave trade. Africa offered hundreds of thousands of full cargoes to the leaders of these expeditions called European conquistadores—adventurous explorers of the fifteenth, sixteenth, and seventeenth centuries who seized vast territories in the world on behalf of the Crown, known more specifically as Spanish or Portuguese, who went to conquer the new countries of America, an episode in the history of the Spanish colonization of the Americas.

The philosopher Christian Delacampagne told us certain truths concerning the entire history of slavery, which I would carefully list here. According to him, the advent of slavery was located in Mesopotamia, the current Iraq; in Persia, the current Iran, since five thousand years; in Indonesia; in China; and in India. During the classical Greco-Roman period, slavery was, for almost a millennium, the pillars of the social organization. We know one of the main old revolts of hundreds of black slaves originating from Africa, historically constituting the rebellion of the black slaves of Zandj against the power of the Abbasids between 869 and 883 in the south of Iraq.

From the fifth century before our era to the third century after, slavery was also important during the peak of the Greco-Roman civilization, which could obtain fresh slaves permanently and in very important quantities by warrior dominating societies. If one combines the synthesis of historical works, the reflection on the ideologies, and the philosophy of that time, we see how the thought of philosophers, especially of Plato or Aristotle, could not influence the justifications of slavery in the Middle Ages and in the modern times, where even the Christian Church never condemned slavery.

The decline and the virtual disappearance of ancient slavery in the north of the West were in no way a philosophical or religious mutation. The victory of Trajan against the Dacians of the current Romania was the last great example of the transformation of the empire and the end of the human predatory wars in the early second century of our era. Each following their sacred text, Islam and Christianity, which forbid the slaves among their community, were directly capturing Ukrainians, Russians, Caucasus, and Slavic people, known formerly as Slavonian Grebe or again were doing business with the Gentiles. On the trade routes of northern Europe, Italy, or Greece, girls and boys illegally kidnapped were marching while chained. Throughout the Middle Ages, the city of Troyes was a place of sale of slaves destined for Italy or the Middle East as in many other cities.

At the late Middle Ages, when slave deposits dried up in northern and Eastern Europe, Portugal was already taking big steps in West Africa. They planted a sinister slave plantation system at Cape Verde, an island that they invaded and occupied during two centuries, and remained the main suppliers of slaves, guaranteed by the papacy on the seventh of June 1494 in a treaty signed in Tordesillas between Spain and Portugal, laying down the line of demarcation and separating the colonial possessions of the two countries by assigning the colonization of Africa, India, and the American continent to Spain.

Portugal and Spain, at that time, were the most powerful states in Europe. But between the two, Portugal quickly became a great power of maritime conquests with their geographical advantageous location. It was a rapid rise for navigation and for those Europeans who dreamed of establishing direct contact with the new world without passing through the Mediterranean, the East, or by passing Africa to the south and across the Indian Ocean to reach India by sea; they went through the islands of the Caribbean Sea and the Pacific, Central America, South America, Hindustan, and Indonesia; a world of states and peaceful people, rattling with diversities, languages, traditions, and culture, was taken violently in possession by the medieval Europe. At that time or later, all discovered lands in the east of that demarcation were to belong to Portugal and at the west to Spain. The world was shared by a treaty in such a way that African slaves exploited in America and the West India Islands were found in the Spanish zone, and slaves that were supplied from Africa were from the Portuguese area for the New World.

During the conquest and the pacification of these territories, the Spaniards founded a vast colonial empire in America and the West Indies in the early sixteenth century, exterminating most of the indigenous population. In Cuba and in Hispaniola, the current Haiti, gold and silver were discovered, and the development of the colonial economy motivated a cheap urgent need for labor in those mines.

Noticing that the native Indians were almost completely exterminated, not being accustomed to intense farming works and not knowing slavery, they began to import African slaves for cheap labor. Spain chose another path; not obtaining the permission to sail from Portugal to the edge of Africa, they accepted the offer of an expedition to the direction of the west toward India, organized by Columbus. The official date of the discovery of America designating the European invasion of the current American continent was placed on October 12 on the island of San Salvador by an expedition of three ships, which left Europe in August 1492, controlled by Columbus.

After this discovery, diplomatic conflicts were extended by the categorical opposition to the Portuguese to cross the Atlantic. And it was the mediation of Pope Alexander IV that delimited the areas of influence between the two countries by special bulls or decrees, definitively ratifying the history of the first division of the world by the Treaty of Tordesillas in Castile, established on June 7, 1494. A version by the king of Portugal on September 5, 1494, and the other ratified in Arevalo by King Ferdinand II of Aragon and Queen Isabella I of Castile on July 2, 1494, fixed a demarcation line in the west of the islands of Cape Verde by 370 leagues. The right for the conquest of Madeira, Porto Santo, the Azores, and the kingdom of Morocco was acquired by the kingdom of Portugal and to the Spanish the Canary Islands. And that was when the slave trade began.

After massacring the American natives, it was the turn of Africa, which suffered the most gigantic deportation of human beings that the history of humanity has known. It is very necessary to note that, when the Europeans arrived in Africa, Africans were practicing a form of servitude, not slavery. Europe, which had a well-known rule of slavery, was the first continent to sell its neighbor for centuries. Despite the rise of the church and the spread of Christian morality, the Frank warriors were still leading battles against the pagan tribes settled on the Elbe and beyond.

After submitting the Saxons of the Germanic language, they attacked the Slavic prisoners, who in large numbers fueled an active trade between Venice and the Arab empire of the southern Mediterranean, passing through the Place de Verdun in Champagne, where they were systematically emasculated.

About a quarter of them did not survive this brutal mutilation. And the other survivors went to Venice by a well-known exit door under the name of a very famous pier at the extremity of the Grand Canal, the Riva degli Schiavoni. In the early days of Islam, the Arab Muslim domination and the reign of Islam in Spain, from 711 to 1492, confirmed to us that this continent was the cradle of slavery. It was also known that, for several centuries, European Christians were selling other Europeans to Jewish merchants specializing in the manufacture of eunuchs. And this process was just a continuation of the slavery supporter institutions of Europe.

Europe first made slavery possible in the Americas with the European expansion in the fifteenth century. Upon the arrival of Christopher Columbus in Hispaniola, the slavery of the American Indians was immediately practiced. In search of a new trade route to Asian markets, Cristoforo Colombo (Christopher Columbus) alighted on the island of Guanahani, a name given to the island by the natives, which he named San Salvador during his first expedition when he landed with the *Santa María*, the *Niña*, and the *Pinta*, three sailing vessels that allowed him to cross the Atlantic Ocean up to the Americas on October 12, 1492. Believing he had reached the Indies, he named the Taino/ Arawak Indians, whom he found for the first time on his path.

Upon their arrival, they anticipated the capture, kidnapping, and enslavement of the Taino/Arawak. These European invasions for the ownership of their lands were a form of war declared legally to non-Europeans, an attack against their culture by an indoctrination program of the European religion of Christianity, and an attack morally sanctioned, which settled on the island of Hispaniola, more precisely in Natividad (today Haiti and the Dominican Republic), as the first Spanish station in the Caribbean for the conquest and for goals well distinct from each other.

It must be said that all those who narrate the history of First Nations often did not have any trace of indigenous blood and placed the wars between nations or internal conflicts in the frame resulting in the practices of slavery between people of the Americas. They failed to say that the ways of the First Nations of performing war, explicitly a practice of warrior people, did not approach in any case the genocidal methods invented particularly in Europe. So their pretext of slavery between these nations was not justifiable since there was no fundamental characteristic with the economic bases for these communities, or racism did not exist as it however was the two reasons which were forming the bases of the slavery practices of the Europeans.

But with strong matrilineal tendencies, the First Nations were forming communal societies without classes, and their political field was in many cases the responsibility of women, not dominated by men. Among natives, elders for their wisdom occupied a place of importance and honor to solve problems in the community. Like among blacks, political decisions were taking after discussions and a consensus between residents according to the elders. The First Nations observed crimes with the principles of natural justice; therefore, there were very few antisocial crimes, and their good ways to solve problems made that there were no jails in their community.

In those days, on the eve of the European colonization of the whole of America, Europeans cruelly confronted the natives of the western hemisphere, a territory densely populated with numerous tribes in the environments of the Arctic and all other regions where the First Nation people inhabited. They were occupying all regions of Americas: from the south of the Arctic to the subarctic region, the Northwest Territories, and the northern regions of Canadian provinces. Today named Alaska, it was inhabited by the Inuit, the Aleutian Chipewyan, the Kaska, the Chilcotin, the Ingalik, the Beothuk, and many other nations. People as the Tlingit, the Haida, the Tsimshian, the Kwakwaka'wakw, the Nuu-chah-nulth, the Nuxalk, the Salish, and the Yurok were found throughout the northwest Pacific coast, the coasts of Alaska, and the British Columbia up to northern California.

The Sahaptin, the Chopunnish, the Shoshone, and the Siksika were known as the occupants of the Pacific Coast Ranges and the Central Plains, today known as the southern British Columbia and the states of Washington, Oregon, Idaho, and Montana. The Lakota (Sioux), the Cheyenne, the Arapaho, the Plains Cree, the Siksika, the Crow, the Kiowa, the Shoshone, and the Mandan were forming the people of the valley who lived in the east, in a vast region going from the south in Texas; at the north in the southern regions of Alberta, Saskatchewan, and Manitoba; and at the east in North and South Dakota, Minnesota, Wisconsin, Missouri, and Arkansas.

The Cayuga, the Kanienkehaka (Mohawk), the Oneida, the Onondaga, and the Seneca (the last five nations, people of the longhouse) and who traditionally lived in what is today New York State, between the Genesee River and Canandaigua Lake, were forming the communities of Haudenosaunee, the Ojibway, the Algonquin, the Micmac, the Wendat (Huron), the Potowatomis, and the Tuscarora as Iroquois Confederacy, stretched further at the east in the Great Lakes region at the Atlantic coast, and in the forested areas extending from Ontario, Quebec, and New York State, up to Carolina.

The Muskogees, the Cherokee, the Natchez, the Tonkawa, and the Attakapas occupied the southern region and part of Virginia up to Florida and the Gulf of Mexico at the west, including Mississippi and Louisiana. The Pueblo, the Hopi, the Zuni, the Hualapai, the Mojave, the Yumas, the Cocopas, the Pima, the Papas, and the Athabaskans were part of the Navajo (Dineh) and the Apaches with locality at the north of Mexico and California at the southwest of the United States in the eastern region.

The Aztecs, the Mayans, the Texcocos, and the Tlacopans (today called Tacuba) in the Yucatan Peninsula were located in Mexico, in Guatemala, and in Belize in the Mesoamerican region. The Arawaks, the Warao, the Yukpas, and the Paganos were living in the coastal regions of Colombia, Venezuela, Costa Rica, Honduras, and several small islands, such as Cuba, Hispaniola, Puerto Rico, etc., including the Caribbean basin. The Incan people constitute the Quechua and Aymara, who lived in the highlands of Andes in Peru and Chile. The Mapuche, the Yanomami, the Gavioes, the Txukahame, the Kreens, and the Akarore are found in the lowland areas, including the Amazon region. The Ayoreo, the Ache, the Matagots, and the Guarani are in the south of the Amazon region, in Argentina, in Paraguay, and in Uruguay. And Qawasgar, the Selk'nam, the Onu, and many others are found in regions more southern.

These people knew themselves altogether as a nation that lived further in the north by hunting musk ox and caribou; in the west, they hunted goat, roe, and bear. In further south, they hunted bison on the prairies and fished marine mammals like (whales, walruses, etc.), and they still live there, but having the vestiges of their culture destroyed. Since 1492, a process of genocide was the cruelty of white men, the best to ensure the approach of a mutually beneficial process, as it was one of the reasons for slave trade; the mortality of Indians was not considered, but allowed labor for the mines and plantations of the Spanish empire. Five hundred years have passed; today, their descendants are crowded in urban ghettos. To have an excuse on their genocide, a parliamentary ambush condemned them, but my god! In which martyrdom life of persecutions must they really believe or have faith in? To live enveloped in duplicities, surrounded with difficulties, to get used to constant dangers, and to agitations of their peril life in their own land.

The population rate of the indigenous, generally recognized at the eve of colonization from 1492 to the present day, is not necessary since until today, despite five hundred years of a genocidal colonization, there are still indigenous people without any rights on their own land and are part of the most exploited section of the population and more disadvantaged than any other territories worldwide.

After the extermination of the Indians in America and their inability to cultivate the lands of their ill-gotten new territories, the European kings and the Vatican took a cruel decision to capture black in Africa to force them to cultivate the land. Being already in Africa, the Portuguese at first were not interested in slavery; they simply wanted to kidnap some black population in Africa and populate Sao Tome, known as a small country in Africa located in the Gulf of Guinea in the archipelago of the South Atlantic, and the Azores, a group of Portuguese islands that are found in the north of the Atlantic Ocean, to exploit the land. It was their fight against Islam that justified the slavery of black people, after the bull or degree of Nicolas V.

That decision was taken without the consent of any African king. When they arrived in Africa, they had to sow discord in a process of independent states already in place in Africa by providing us with weapons of mass destruction, and they divided to better reign. Thus, the small kingdoms, dominated and subordinated, had no choice but to accept with the hope to conquer and grow. The principle was simple: "I give you the guns, and you procure me the slaves after your conquest. If not, you die." From that moment, Africans were caught in a vicious circle with the appetite of voracity that was nourishing their bodies and their cupidity feeding tribal wars, soaked all regions of Africa deeply affected by an explosive blast in a bloodbath. This truth was well known by some historians, who masked it for the simple pleasure of dirtying the black. To not deliver his entire kingdom to deportation, he engaged himself in a ferocious battle against another kingdom that did not have weapons of mass destruction of the European origin to get captives. The loser finally had no choice but to go and meet Europeans to procure himself weapons in exchange, if not provide slaves for deportation. A discord was then established between the kingdoms for their benefit, arming a kingdom that was going to fight against another to deliver captives of the losing side and so on.

Before the unfortunate boat of bad omens crossed the borders of the coast of Africa, Africans were breathing the burning smell of the damp heat on our shores in the open sky. On the other side of the horizon, a plateau of mountains supported by cliffs relatively high constituted the said territory of the proper divination and inhabited by African natives, chiefs, and kings, who were communicating harmoniously with the supreme deity. On the coast where the sun was beating on the trees of life exposed to the open air, monsters were setting their coal boats by a tiny steam, throwing the anchor that was going to disturb the deposit of large oceanic floors and mermaids, ancient deities worshipped and well respected in the African cult, in more than a thousand meters deep, in a strange port that cried woe and to waves murmuring distress.

Without happy stationary of the white ships, the indigenous alerted the unexpected presence of the strange white men with the detonations of tomtoms; and some curious natives' torsos naked, whose black skin always seems to be the most stylish clothing with the sense of hospitality, rushed toward the beach. The costume of indigenous men was a loincloth woven in Africa and attached at the lower bottom of the waist. Those of the women were also handmade, prefabricated fabrics, covering them much more than their men but with naked shoulders and arms and the head with hair braided in noble headdress. And the children, least covered, were coming out of their houses covered with mats of palm leaves, without knowing that they only had some time to live, with domestic animals around those primitive habitations.

Dr. J. B. Danquah—an African writer, the "doyen of Gold Coast politics," a Pan-Africanist, a scholar, a lawyer, and a historian of Ghana—wrote that, in the Akan culture, people have the same haircut and the same pearls and jewelry system, with a background as far back as the jewelry worn on the Eighteenth Dynasty by Queen Nefertiti, the wife of the great pharaoh Akhenaton, and the Fifteenth Dynasty by Queen Nefertari, the wife of Pharaoh Ramses II. That population of West Africa was mainly settled in southern Ghana but also in the south and the east of Ivory Coast. Despite the drums and smoke, a kind of local telegraph that signaled the onset of these terrible aliens with red hair and blue eyes, equipped with firearms that they had never seen, Africans did not inspire any fear whatsoever, but the brutality of their next strangers changed them in such a way that one of the first Portuguese captains by the name of Gonzalo de Cintra, having set foot on the ground of West Africa, was killed on the purlieus of the island of Arguin. They also attacked the ship of Luigi di Cadamosto and Antoniotto Usus di Mare, who had just reached the Gambia for the first time in 1455, with such a fury by poisoned arrows, not by resistance but by a permanent and daily hostility, which proved once again that there was no regular commercial arrangement. From the Gambia River, they stretched the West African coast and discovered the Cape Verde islands, Guinea coast, and notably the Geba River, which emerged in Guinea; they passed through Senegal and reached Guinea-Bissau during their second voyage in 1456.

But the domination of the armed slave traders and sailors on Africans was obvious since, from the fifteenth to seventeenth century, Africa could not in any way oppose the European firearms by the lack of war equipments and the experience as an army of small detachments of isolated tribes of warriors who had only bows and arrows. So they began to construct forts with high walls, endowed with a quantity of heavy artillery, to protect themselves against the local residents of the country and castles that still pierced the skin of ocean waters on the entire littoral coast of African coast, belonging to different countries, whose trade representatives were often in bad relationships against each other.

Sometimes, cannonballs easily passed over the walls and went to strike down an unfortunate village and exterminate that part of the region. These castles once again proved that their intrusion was lucrative compared to the slums of African leaders accused to be their trading partners. They climbed the cliff with their weapons toward a rocky area where lower and thick bushes grew. Just at the distance of forty meters was appearing a distinctive sign of all habitations, where the life of the indigenous was following its course very harmoniously with the nature; but the presence of these foreigners was announcing the turbulence leaning on their arrogant faces to a young girl summarily dressed, crushing wheat in a mortar, harmonizing hands clapping by hitting the pestle that were so well manipulated by an up-and-down movement to pound with a particular elegance worthy of a theatrical show.

They were looking for gold dust, barley, wheat, elephant teeth, etc., in a vegetal land of a sunny and cloudless atmosphere destined for agriculture. With a mountain leading behind a large river shoreline, a firm identity typical of the African landscape saw itself traversed by a torrential conquest that came from afar, without pity and without mercy, to satisfy their interests.

In the fifteenth century, European countries saw the limits of the universe expand by great geographical discoveries. Upon their arrivals at the wide coast of Africa, Europeans saw the shores naturally adorned with a heavenly beauty of our mysterious and fabulously wealthy countries; the Garden of Eden that was the tropical Africa impressively appeared before them.

And on the maps appeared the fantastic islands, formerly inhabited by divines, stuffed with gold, diamond, silver, spices, and many other natural resources, to which it seemed very easy to spawn a road. England, Spain, Holland, France, and Portugal, father of early capitalism, were going to put our Africa in the dizzying methods of chronological order. The Portuguese were the first to hit the road of the ocean toward Africa because of the thirst for gold. They were going to search for gold before on the African coast, in India, and throughout the Far East, driven by the European industry, developed from the fourteenth and fifteenth centuries, since the big country Germany, producer of metal from 1450 to 1550, could no longer deliver.

So, on a newly discovered shore by white, at first, was claiming gold. An expedition landed near Cape Blanco from 1441 to 1442, led by Antao, the Portuguese explorer and slave trader of the fifteenth century sent by Henry the Navigator under the command of Nuno Tristao as the first Europeans to explore the West African coast in an expedition, and captured ten Africans and took them to Portugal. When Goncalves heard the statement of two of them saying that a big ransom would be paid for them in their country, he brought them back in Africa and received various goods, among which were some gold dust and ten slaves, black men and women from different countries, in exchange. The remaining eight captured Africans were sold at a high price in Lisbon.

From that moment on, capturing Africans became a lucrative business for Europe. Expeditions were then multiplied in Africa by Portuguese sailors at the quest for Africans; hoping to obtain big profits since from their first Portuguese expeditions, there was no question of capturing slaves. However, since African expeditions were so expensive, their first yield advantage was the sale of blacks. The Portuguese expansion in Africa for the importation of Africans was sanctioned by the organizers—Henry the Navigator and the Portuguese governors, concerning the adoption of the Christian religion. But their belief did not result in a concrete decision.

Thus, to replace the missing arm in agriculture and housework, the arrogant feudal lords were voluntarily purchasing black slaves at the presence of high dignitaries of the court. A new expedition to Africa was organized by Nuno Tristam two years later. It was then that a special bull of Pope Nicolas V, the 206th pope in the history of the Catholic Church, granted the right not only to conquer lands for King Alfonso V of Portugal but also to reduce the Gentiles into slavery, both in areas already discovered in Africa and those that would be later on discovered, on January 8, 1454, thus opening slave markets that sold black Africans in the Portuguese cities of Lisbon, Lagos, Cadiz, Seville, and other Spanish cities and other parts of Europe.

The first Europeans who reached the bay and the Arguin Island clashed with the indigenous and the resistance of Africans who did not know and did not possess firearms, which the overwhelming superiority of the Portuguese military possessed, but until then experiencing big losses. Near Mauritania, that island of the Atlantic Ocean discovered by the Portuguese in the fifteenth century was the scene of colonial successions. From 1445 to 1633, it was controlled by Portugal; from 1633 to 1655 by the Netherlands; in 1655 by England, which restored it back finally once again to the Netherlands in the same year of 1655 and again controlled it until 1678; and in 1678 by France, who abandoned it on the same year.

The island will remain without colonizers until 1685. However, France came back in the island in 1721 and drove the Brandenburg, one of the federated states compounding Germany trying to settle there from 1685 to 1721 out of the colonial scene and colonized it until 1722. From 1722 to 1724, the Netherlands took it over; but from 1724 to1728, this country that in turns was wrongly and illegally seized again fell into the hands of the French colonizer. France came back and was driven away by the indigenous people, who controlled their territory until the nineteenth century, when finally, France came back to recolonize the region.

The walls of confusion and the towers of the first European port in Africa were built under the sky by the Portuguese on the island of Arguin since 1448—an island in western Sudan and the Sahara, existing for centuries with its salt trade system. But they came and turned off the light of joy and turned on the sound of confusion. That space glowing by the celestial sunshine became something eluding and made them feel the warm thrill of confusion, something not expected to be seen or felt. But like a show, you wanted not to find out what was behind those cold doors of disguised distant claws by beautiful towers.

The sky that looked blue and the sea that looked warm were dragging silent reproaches behind them for their incapacities to fight against that challenge, taking moms, daddies, and children going skating on thin ice of modern life in plantations of different cultures, a million tears staining their eyes. In their deep sleep and out of their minds for a while, a crack in the ice appearing under their feet surprised them, and the fear of the thin ice claws was f lowing in their thoughts. They were shipped across the ocean, just leaving memories to the surviving broken family members left behind with another brick on the wall still standing. But with just that one brick on the wall followed by another, no food and no meat were no longer provided but only thought control; the dark sarcasm and wrongdoings were their daily education.

Without needing anything at all but put on the front line by trusted governments, presidents, and kings, where just bricks on the wall were found, they made all their nightmares come true by putting all their fears right under the wing of the firing line. But like a thought, this song came out on different channels: "Oh! Mother Earth, with this cry breaking my heart, tearing my little body apart, I can see that I am really dying but healthy and clean, and I put all my fears into you, with just one brick in the wall, and will always find out where you're up there in the sky. I am singing this song to not let anyone dirty or anyone dangerous get to me, to frighten me. With the new castle now approaching, lingering pain on the new world unfolding beneath a clear blue sky, I am singing the blues, running for the shelter with just a brick on the wall. Set me free."

Nuno Tristao was sent again by Henry beyond Cape Blanc to reach the Bay of Arguin on the West African coast in 1443; then by taking some fourteen villagers captive and returning to Portugal with them, he noticed the easy slave-raiding grounds in the Arguin banks and the profitable slave trading in Portugal. For that profitable interest, numerous Portuguese adventurers and merchants promptly applied a slave-trading license from Henry. Until today, that lugubrious monument with just bricks on the wall reminds us of the maritime nations that have long coveted that island for its strategic location; not only the Portuguese flag was deployed there in 1443 by the explorer and slave trader Nuno Tristao but also the one of the Dutch, followed by the Brandenburg and French colors. During that period, the island knew a colonial past up to the departure of the last colonizers in 1969.

Spain and Portugal spread that sinister slavery system toward the noble children imported from Africa to India (where till today, there still exists a colony of Negroes in the state of Gujarat), the Americas, and the Caribbean in the sugar cane plantations at the discovery of America and the Caribbean and at the imitation of such a system that they already knew in the Mediterranean. A few centuries later, Holland, France, England, Denmark, and so on ferociously threw themselves into that atrocious triangular trade. Men, children, and African women crammed into the decks of slave trader ships between 1440 and 1870 and were dragged under the heavens in the mud of almost every country around the world for 1,250 years; from the slave trade of the Islamic Arabs of the Christian era around 650 until 1900, there were over eighteen million innocent souls just on the European slave trade for 450 years and twelve to fourteen million of the Muslim slave trade from the seventh to the twentieth century. So, we get a total of thirty to thirty-two million African captives drained out of Africa, without counting the huge loss of life that occurred from the capture up to the auctions on the final drop places.

These miseries, secret messages of our journey, were long decided before our lives to be lived in unsafe hours of nights and daylight; and protected to not be revealed or be exposed to everyone; but only to act so cruel as a fantasy to fill an empty space under the blue sky; by kidnaping us and make us leave our land of refuge covered with forest, plants, and trees with torn heart; only to take us in a new land full of calamities as refugees, where we residence till today, right? Oh my god! I wonder why? But was it just to get a drink of water and walk on its rigorous surface? If you can just let me know as soon as you can, I will understand because miseries and hatred, misfortunes and prejudices are just too great in our world.

And day after day, night after night, in this strange universe, love has turned gray, and we pretend to not see our dying skin, the skin of a man growing older, becoming colder and colder, and nothing much funnier is anymore coming toward his way, but just the sound of a dry funeral drum is slicing his spirit with a cold razor blade, feeling incomplete with just a brick on the wall. However, standing in the aisle of death, a voice is telling us there's no hope at all, with a fading smile and naked hope.

Someone called dead is calling out your name on the other side of a wall so high, saying, "Hey, you out there beyond the wall, will you die? Your time has come. And no matter how hard we try to stay alive out there beyond the other side of the wall, we stand together divided, till we fall and do what we're told to do. And with an open heart, you're to go home where you came from. And without a fight, you will bury the light of your life, leaving just sorrow behind. And none of us will add one cubit to his life by his concern, by wealth acquired in a good or bad way." So, life was not seeing life anymore, because of that fatal fog of slavery that filled life.

Portugal gave great importance to the possessions of West Africa that became a supplier of slaves, spices, and gold in such a way that the trade with that continent became a royal monopoly from 1481. Soon, competition intensified between Portugal, which was running almost total domination of the world located outside of Europe, without sharing with other European countries, like the great maritime power of Spain, which became its most dangerous rival on the shores of the Atlantic. By the order more or less chronological, capitalism hatched primitive accumulation between Portugal, Spain, Holland, France, and England for the advantageous completion of the reconquest in geographical location, etc. At that time, Portugal and Spain were the biggest maritime powers of European States, but Portugal in particular.

In the mid-fifteenth century, they settled on the island of Goree, which became the greatest counter of the slave trade of African coasts in the seventeenth century. The Netherlands was the second country to control Goree Island and then passed under the control of the English; the French came last. With a remarkable strategy, the Portuguese who occupied the current Guinea-Bissau were forced to live there, marry African women, and fathered children, who were to be intermediates for the purchase of slaves in that region of the southern river coast. They also mastered the current Liberia, once known as the coast of seeds or the coast of Malaguettes, known for its masks, and finally Ivory Coast, formerly known as the coast of teeth for its elephant tusks. Before the slavery, Europeans were going there to procure ivory. France took control of that territory of fine sculptures of remarkably particular detail on the seventeenth century.

A rebellion was introduced among Indian workers in the colonies of West Indies by the first African slaves, forcing Nicolas de Ovando—an authoritarian and cruel creature, a soldier, and a Spanish noble who became the Hispaniola governor from 1502 to 1509—to decrease the natives of their new world by burning their leaders and hanging his caciques, Hispanic notable of South-America. This rebellion of the first African slaves in that territory forced him to seek the prohibition of the importation of Africans from Queen Isabella in 1502 or 1503. But he soon changed this idea and ordered the first import of slaves of African origin, having lived in Castile and Portugal or born in Latin America (called Ladino) and speaking Spanish in the Americas.

It was only few years later with the delivery of 250 African slaves in the gold mines of Hispaniola, from 1510, that the European colonies began importing blacks in the New World. The powerful colonies that started to appear, like Holland and England violated the already established monopoly by fortified positions of Spain and Portugal, which were already part of the Spanish empire from 1578 to 1640, and forced the two countries to buy slaves from foreign merchants. The conquests of the colonies in West Africa continued by the Netherlands and England, less than a century later. The colonizers, who were sending Africans to the New World, wished to justify the black slave trade by claiming that their export was to save the extinction of the Indians who escaped the massacre after a few centuries while the struggle to prohibit that traffic was in full swing.

With ambiguous humanitarian purposes, the apostle of the Indians, the Dominican bishop Bartolome de Las Casas, a Spanish Jew converted by force after 1492, a writer and historian who denounced the practices of Spanish settlers and defended the rights of American Indians, proposed twelve black slaves at the disposal of each Spanish colonist; to intensify the importation of African slaves and to replace the Indians in the fields and mines to extract gold in the West Indies. If this intervention had not taken place, such an intensification of the slave trade could have not subsisted. Instead of exercising his influence for good cause, he decided to enter through the back door of history as the one who asked to intensify the routing of slaves from Africa to the king for the development of the black slave trade, even after realizing that this increase did not improve their sad fate and did not result in any Indian freedom, and knowing the injustice involved in the reduction of human in slavery.

And its intensification in that way did not limit or prevent the massacre of slaves, even after a massive evangelism and baptisms. The speech of St. Augustine embodied in the epistle of St. Paul to the Galatians in the New Testament, to the churches of Galatia toward the year 49 of our era was saying that all human beings are in Jesus Christ and that, down here, there is neither Jew nor Greek, neither slave nor free man, and neither man nor woman, and that being far from this faith, or to constitute the opposite belief, would precisely constitute the original sin; by these texts, St. Augustine wanted to say that all men are equal before God, Galatians 3:28. But Catholic authorities, who are describing the thoughts of the God of Augustine as the primitive doctrine of Christianity, demonstrated the contradictory nature of the founding texts of Christianity on the question of slavery and allowed the institution of slavery to its authorities. So, to buy Negroes reduced in slavery was a trade that violated religion belief. But the social organization did not reject this institution; view the circumstances in which Christianity was born in Roman, in a society where slavery was accepted as a fundamental dimension.

Until today, this poor sacrifice in the name of slavery, derived from the European continent and practiced in Africa, will always act in the consciousness of these fathers of the Christian Church as if they were sacrificing themselves.

The Spanish colonizers, who were only seeking to accomplish the satisfaction of their work, bought black slaves captured and well tied up in Africa and sent them to Europe to be baptized, and the Spanish were coming to purchase them in Lisbon, a Portuguese city where the black slave markets were regularly held, to finally take them to India.

This well-known routine was practiced in the early sixteenth century, where thousands of Africans were shuffled from left to right before arriving at a destination not much qualified as a final destination. They were scattered between Jamaica, Hispaniola, Puerto Rico, Cuba, Brazil, etc. All Spanish colonies were receiving four thousand slaves annually from one of the brokers of Charles V in 1517–1518 to whomever he granted the right to sell for eight years; and by the agreements named "Asiento" concluded conditions between the Spanish and Portuguese government, which determined not only the monopoly on the sale of black slaves in the Spanish colonies of the West Indies or Caribbean Basin, a region of the North Atlantic Ocean, includes the island countries and the surrounding waters of three major archipelagoes known as the Greater Antilles, the Lesser Antilles and the Lucayan Archipelago, and America, but also the amount and quality.

A coin of India, the name given to an African slave, should not be sick or have physical defects. He should be thirty to thirty-five years old and at least one meter and eighty feet. Three men aged thirty-five to fifty corresponded to two coins of India. Children of a certain age were treated as a unit and at a young age were not counted at all. These determinations were different from country to country. The conditions in which Africans were found after that long journey were lamentable. Their weight loss made the definition of age impossible. Then, the abuses were very common on the part of Spanish officials, who sometimes fixed the quantity to eleven Africans corresponding to a single unit.

If we based these conditions set by the asiento, it was impossible to approximately establish how many slaves were deported in the Spanish colonies. Also, the quantity of slaves brought through official channels to the Spanish colonies was much lower than the one transported by smuggling from the beginning of the slave trade. It was during the time of the fulfillment of the second half of the sixteenth century, of the absolutism in England, that the Portuguese monopoly in Africa and Spain in the New World crumbled, when the industrial development favored the extension of the English foreign trade, stimulated by the foreign policy of the slaver countries.

The British colonial expansion began when it moved from the export of raw materials to the one of manufactured items. To find markets and raw materials, English-f lagged vessels, differing from the military expeditions, were scouring the coastal waters of West Africa from the mid-sixteenth century. Many times, they did not necessarily want to be engaged in a combat against the Portuguese, seeking to prevent them from anchoring on the coast.

This was the beginning of problems for all of Africa; because, not having immediately understood that these slave traders were using them for their own interests by providing them with weapons, they were encouraging them in wars against their countrymen to create enemies between them and thus to separate them to manage them better. The first journey of John Hawkins in Africa, an English sailor and pirate, was considered the beginning of the British slave trade and was partly financed by the English statesmen. The second and third voyages of the pirate were financially supported by Queen Elizabeth I from 1562 to 1567.

These expeditions were intended to practice the slave trade on slaves which they were going to fetch on the coast of Sierra Leone by the force of arms, by militarily supporting an African leader, by burning villages and reducing the prisoners to slavery, etc. By these cruel means, they got hundreds of slaves which they sold in Hispaniola for a much higher profit to make the expeditions financially profitable. Ennobled by Queen Elizabeth I because of his cruelty to Africans and as the pirate of Portuguese and Spanish vessels, he received the right to be called Sir John Hawkins. Ms. Crete revealed this: "The proliferation of firearms facilitated the forced incorporation of small states into large ones. The territorial expansion by force became the ultimate means to monopolize the economic power of the new order."

Between 1750 and 1807, 283,000 firearms were introduced in the Gulf of Benin, revealed by J. B. Inkori to us; and during the 1730s, according to Richardson, 180,000 guns were introduced per year on the Slave Coast. One of their reasons was to create wars between kingdoms for them not to oppose their request. Another effective and cruel means undertaken by the slave traders to procure slaves was to capture and educate young Africans in Portugal for them to initially master the language, and then give them a racist doctrine, and finally reintroduce them in Africa. These reintroduced young Africans, made racists, could only regain their freedom by each delivering four captive slaves. The Venetian at the service of the crown in 1453 before the Pontifical Bull or degree certified that some slaves, once baptized and spoke the language of their master, were embarked on board of ships and sent to their congeners. They became free men after the delivering of four slaves. Here is another poignant example that proved that, without such cruel methods, the whites could have not reached the deportation of blacks.

Officially, England no longer participated in the black slave trade after John Hawkins for nearly a century, but all those smuggling expeditions were using the same cruel methods used by Hawkins to capture slaves in Africa. The colonial conquests in the New World of England only intensified at the beginning of the seventeenth century on their arrival in Virginia. They were occupying part of the island of St. Kitts and landed in Barbados Island in 1625, which later on became the center of their possessions in the West Indies. In 1631, the construction of their first fort on the Gold Coast marked the beginning of the slave trade on the African west coast.

Their country marching toward revolution could then be settled in Africa, a continent of many opportunities, but a serious political and economic situation came to temporarily stop their colonial expansion, and the Portuguese were obliged to hand over the monopoly to the Dutch, who were expanding the colonial conquests and the slave trade in Africa. When the Dutch came into Africa, despite the opposition of the Portuguese, followed by the end of the bourgeois revolution, they immediately became a great commercial and colonial power in the late sixteenth century. They concluded an agreement with the local chief after they built two forts on the Gold Coast.

In 1611–1612, they built another fort near St. George Del Mina by the name of Nassau. Then the Netherlands continued their monopoly in Africa by purchasing the island of Goree in Senegal in 1617, where they established several small settlements of the European merchants and thus became very great slave traders, barely settled there. They took the fort in St. George Del Mina in 1637, put an end to the Portuguese domination on the Gold Coast, and immediately recovered the one of San Antonio in Axim in 1641. The Dutch quickly acted as intermediaries throughout the period of the slave trade, only constituting small possessions in the New World, as the islands of the West Indies, Curacao, Aruba, etc., where they were selling African slaves to settlers of other countries. The city of New York, well known at that time by the name of New Amsterdam, in the American continent, was founded in 1619 by the Dutch, who were the first to import nineteen African slaves in the current U.S. territory. They were settled in Guyana, Suriname, and Brazil and implanted an economy of plantations in these countries of South America, which were claiming many slaves from settlers. More than fifteen thousand African slaves were sent to Brazil between 1621 and 1624 by the Dutch. The area of Angola and Congo was the only area where most of the Portuguese slave trade took place in that period, outside Ouidah, later founded on the Slave Coast.

After the end of the religious wars, France joined the ranks of the colonial powers of Europe to build itself a colonial empire. It was then that it seized Cayenne, Martinique, Guadeloupe, and a part of St. Kitts Island to build a series of companies and gradually, in the early 1940s, captured slaves in the northwest of Africa, their main area and routed them to their colonies.

The main colonial exploitations in Africa were completed in the mid-seventeenth century, when all these European countries, essential organizers of a colonial system, developed a plantation economy, which could only operate with a massive and cheap workforce in the already owned territories in the American continent and in the West Indies, which they called New World.

In two centuries, exchanges with Africa manifested the founding of many commercial companies of the European countries, which were more interested in the slave trade than the trade in different commodities in general. To obtain capable and cheap workers, they had as advisers the Spaniards, who in their colonies were already using African slaves. The black trade was just a continuation of a system that already existed in Europe. Yes, I would not have enough to repeat that. Its development was characterized by two phases. The flow of slaves from Africa to Portugal and Spain in Europe was the first phase, where European slave traders systematically captured a quantity of men of another race to reduce them as slaves by simple prejudices and a perception of the universe, different from the African reality. The regulation of asiento characterizing the export of slaves directly from Africa first to Europe and then to the New World, marking the beginning of the black slave trade in the Atlantic, was the second phase. The Portuguese were launching raids against Africans to capture a large quantity of slaves by a strong and cruel manner. All those opposed were killed. Many Africans were captured during fights and sold in Europe by Portuguese slave traders. Some natives who could no longer oppose for fear of being killed began to exchange slaves for all sorts of items of no value to Europeans, like cheap fabrics, copper bracelets, necklaces, copper dishes, tin, etc.

And the number increased every year for more than 3,500 slaves only in the coastal areas located between Senegal and Sierra Leone. Some years later, in the late fifteenth century, the slave trade spread wide on the west coast of Africa, on the coast of Senegal, certain regions of the present-day Liberia, on the coast of Sierra Leone, on the Gold Coast, in Benin, and almost throughout the African continent. By passing through Senegal, Ghana, and many other countries, we still find their sites today under the form of large warehouses of goods, like the Goree Island and Citadel of 1874, the Goree Island in 1728, St. Georges Castle at Elmina and St. Jago in the Gold Coast in the late seventeenth century; the European Trading Post at Savi in 1720; Fort Crevecoeur Accra, Gold Coast, in 1679; Fort Nassau (Mowri), Gold Coast, in the seventeenth century; the Christiansburg Castle, Gold Coast, in 1750; Cape Coast castle, Gold Coast, in 1682; the Cormantin (Fort Amsterdam), Gold Coast, in 1704; the Princestown Fort, Gold Coast, in 1688; Fort St. Jacques, Gambia, in 1695; James Island and Fort Gambia in 1727; and Fort Williams, in Ouidah, Benin, in 1727. The existence of another slave port forgotten in the history of slavery just rise in Bimbia, Cameroon. Discovered in 1987, Bimbia, the former state of Isubu ethnic group, was independent until 1884. Well, maybe there are still other strong forts undiscovered nowadays squatting in different dense forests of Africa and so on. These places still emit cries and tears at the coast of the Atlantic Ocean in the open sky by denouncing that harsh and cruel brutality against the mother race of humanity by visitors from various countries.

Each of these forts represented the financial interests of a commercial company in a European country, composed of well-trained soldiers equipped with cannons, rifles, gunpowder, and boats of white slavers heavily armed, waiting captives for mass deportation toward the Americas and the Caribbean, with orders to shoot anyone who threatened their financial firms. After knowing how these forts were protected, one wonders how an outgoing Negro king of the African bush could cross the governors of these forts to go and sell captives to European slaver ships and also wonder why Africa is not enriched with the sale of slaves.

The destruction of the human tissue was caused by the English, Spanish, French, Dutch, Portuguese, etc.; it started the day that the first black slaves departed from the black continent to Portugal in 1441, marking the beginning of the Atlantic slave trade organized by Europe, and in the American continent to the island of Hispaniola, today the Dominican Republic and Haiti, in 1502 after forcing the Indian populations to exploit the gold and silver mines by the Spanish. Europeans were getting slaves mainly by wars or raids and embarked them on the slave ships of certain coasts that were not maintaining slaves. They implanted many centers of trafficking on the coastal countries, having societies grouped into states or very powerful kingdoms, sometimes with or without the European presence. They settled in the Gold Coasts with European fortifications;

in Angola, Mpinda, Luanda, and Benguela, the most important sectors of slave traders; they were in the coast of the Gulf of Benin, invading the cities of Ouidah and Porto Novo; they were found in the coast of Biafra, New Calabar, and Old Calabar; sheltering the Ibo people and other tribes in Nigeria; they were at the entrance of Ouni, the mouthpiece of the slave traders, snooping for the outflow of slaves into the sea, in a place commonly called Lagos, where they left several sea bosoms in a delimited demarcation on which a great series of unpublished events took place; they were in Loango, MaJembo, Cabinda, at the south of the equator; these regions were maintaining many centers of slave trade and other traffic. The walls of these slavery supporter countries are still oozing with the suffering of blacks in chains and letting their blood flow imperceptibly and their sweat in the cellars of slaver hotels carved according to their evil ideas, where their generations live nowadays through the exploitation of slaves.

This outrageous and cruel white race arrived in Africa, where sovereign peace and a concordant harmony with the laws of nature reigned. They organized themselves into troops; one troop that sank in the forests of north and northeast, traditional trade routes in search of native villages; they were capturing the noble Africans that they chained, insulted by beating them and forcing them to walk for days, weeks, and months, up to the embarkations in the slave ships, and this was just to commit that atrocity known of the white men against his fellowman.

The other troops were implanted at the river coasts of Senegambia; from Sierra Leone to the Cape of Palmas; they were implanted at the Gold Coasts (Ghana) in Accra, where a port of embarkation was found; they were implanted in Benin's Bight Coast in the town of (Ouidah), a shipping port and Porto-Novo; in Nigeria, Lagos up to the Biafra New coast and the Old Calabar, way down to the neighboring Cameroon; at the south of the equator, Loango, MaJembo, Cabinda and Mpinda, Luanda and Benguela, as the most important slave traders sectors.

We also cite the eastern coast—namely, Mozambique and Zanzibar, which directly participated in the slave trade toward the nineteenth century through Madagascar, Reunion, Mauritius, northeast Muscat, and the Persian Gulf. This long journey was done in abominable conditions; come rain or shine, these indigenous prisoners—hungry, tired, and thirsty—were forced to continue their journey. Displaying their distressed faces, they were walking barefoot in silence, in the still ghostly shadow of the night that was dying under a pale sky, wet with the legendary tropical rains of the East African coast, which were the hallmark of our ugly days of July and August, dark and foggy to split the heart, up to the destination ports toward the desert or those of the western or eastern coasts.

A huge trade was thus drawn on a specific route, which began in Europe for Africa, where the slavers were going to refuel blacks on all coasts of Africa—Goree, Ghana, Guinea, Gambia, etc.

Europeans were therefore selling their products—wool, brandy, barrels of powder, cotton, iron bars, rum, glass bead, and rifles—or simply with their hypocrisy pretended to present gifts to chiefs of tribes. And up to our days,

Holland remains one of the countries very active in the manufacturing of wax yet aimed specifically for Africans. Africa, therefore, saw the demands of whites multiplying by filling their cargoes with products such as ivory, gum arabic, and ebony wood, which was called black gold of Africa, in exchange with products like bauble, copper, powder, hardware, and weapons.

In exchange for these products, they were receiving chained slaves whom they were loading into the holds of their ships like animals—men, women, and children taken in hostage by raids from the indigenous territories-brutally killing all those who were resisting them. Children under six years old were massacred, and the infirm and elders were killed or abandoned but condemned to die since they could not take care of themselves. They were young, robust, happy, harmonious, and strong with their small families. The white man with blue eyes and red hair landed in their home with his cruel way to destroy the tradition, the pride, the competence, and the united families of the black race of an old civilization of over 5,500 years before Christ. So they attacked families that they were boarding separately—that is, father to Bush, mother to Wilhelmina, child to Piet Botha, aunt to Elizabeth, and uncle to his kingdom come, where his will, will be done on earth, as it is in heaven. It was a real disaster for the initiated African people, who had the habit of orally conveying their knowledge to their first sons who automatically became heads of families or kings when the time comes. But, alas, this was no longer possible because our sages were killed resisting their opponent or transported by force to be sold as objects of no value.

Oh, God, what a horrible fate did you sent us? One of the sages interrogated himself, seeing one of his noble tribes, his children of the former days, out of the ordinary course of nature attacking his brothers of the neighboring village, possessed by the devil. Where are we going to end up? But where do we come from? And what right do they have to make us prisoners? The road was long, very long to determine their fate that no one can convert what they may have experienced as disarray or feel as suffering and anguish; so they started from a very remote village to devastated and terrorized villagers, where they only left the sick and the poor deprived who could not defend themselves against death, and even sometimes, they simply burned the village. These criminal slavers displayed unprecedented barbaric inventiveness with an absolute freedom. They were not threatening; they hurt, they mutilated, and they killed.

After thoroughly have amused themselves by killing some, raping young women in front of their children, burning villages, parents and spouses chained, the embarkation slowly rolled away with women completely naked and walking to the rhythms of lashes; eventually by chasing Kofi, the strongest, the handsome and the robust behind the hill of the village, who wanted not to yield to the authority of the so-called prodigy children. These albinos, children of blacks, rejected in the olden days and thrown into the ocean by the black people because of their chronic heredity and congenital anomaly, due to the lack of a pigment by the name of melanin, a pigment produced by the skin cells to protect the skin from the ultraviolet rays coming from the sun and to give the skin a more or less dark color, which is simply a truth and the pride of the black man born with it. The captured were turning from time to time to cast a brief glance at their village, which was getting far away as they walked away, like to scream for help to that loved cradle unable to help them, and at the same time, unable to wish them whatsoever.

Suddenly, a well-regarded wise of that region cried while singing these words as to say good-bye to his ancestors: "O Almighty Creator of the universe Ptah! You're the one who's in me! And you're the one who is not in him. View his wickedness and fury. The furious in us is opposing our walk-in progress, with a part of our body chained to prevent the execution of any thought, but we just fall on our knees. This nightmare went on in the next village and the village after, before beginning their unknown journey completely out of their villages. And this happens in all key countries, with the will to drain the whole continent or simply to exterminate the black race;" note here that I am using the word "Race" still written in the United States Constitution since 1865, to qualify the white domination that justified the slavery of Africans, distinguished as a lower race for the discrimination purpose. And to distinguish various aristocratic communities from the European people, the word "Race" was used for the first time in Europe in the tenth and eleventh century. Thus, without discrimination, we would have only spoking of the human race in general.

It is the destiny appointed by our proper human symbol of love that despite all our efforts, we end up submitting ourselves, with our heads turned toward our native village, indicating our confusion, abandoning our cherished place of birth, one eye on our beloved country that we are forced to leave by the lashes. Barely, just at the village exit, was the ancestral cemetery, where they turned all their eyes as if to say good-bye once again to their ancestors, who transmitted them the cult of tolerance and love. Further on was the great sanctuary, where those who were performing sacrifices to the Most High God and the most powerful of the universe, the god Ptah, gathered.

The long walk of those noblemen of Africa reduced as slaves began on the small track of the village. It counted hundreds of thousands of men, women, and children. According to experts in this field, the number of Africans involved was impossible to estimate—a tragedy that reached the paroxysm of terror and horror to the point that we still considered the white man as sadistic, cruel, and ferocious, of an extreme wickedness and a savagery not to be imagined, to reduce a human as merchandise essentially to satisfy his economic wish.

For that purpose, they chose to humiliate the child of the Great Architect, simply because he was black, by placing men, women, and children naked for scrutinizing: in front of a multitude of buyers and observers, who were examining, measuring, weighing, and palpating them scrupulously. They had to perform the orders of the white purchaser, who was examining the nigger accordingly, to not say "the slave." They inspect the mouth, eyes, teeth, and ears. They had them bend and spread their legs, jump, and talk. If they had no symptoms of infection, such as scabies, scurvy, ulcer, or intestinal worms, they were admitted to deportation to a new world. If the slave traders discovered a trace of disease or malformation, the price would drop dramatically. After a long discussion on the price, they were finally shipped. Not having any idea of what awaited them on the high seas or even their deportation, they were sorted—men, women, children, and the strongest—chained and crowded into groups.

The mortality rate that I already mentioned above was estimated to be between 13 and 20 percent. Some even estimated it at 40 percent because of the ravages caused by the duration of the nightmare journey. Could that be right? Certainly, the malnutrition, the lack of hygiene in the holds, and epidemics such as dysentery, measles, and smallpox showed the suffering endured by these poor creatures, children of God. The testimony of Olaudah Equiano, born in 1745 in one of the regions of the kingdom of Benin in the current Nigeria, says that when he was deported by Spanish slave traders in 1756, he was first thrown into the steerage of the boat without ventilation and that an ambient heat was added to the overcrowding of passengers, who could hardly turn; there were so many cries of distress to make the heart beat a thousand times, and the dreadful stench caused nausea that prevented one from eating anything. The passengers began to sweat profusely to make the air unbreathable, and it was a sight of horror hardly conceivable for the eyes and nostrils. Among the slaves, a disease spread causing many deaths; aggravated by ulcerations because of chains, afflicting an unbearable pain; they caused pain beyond control to slaves who were screaming; the groans of the dying women who were dropping their children, enduring awful sufferings never seen before in life, was their malediction without explanation; reducing them in slavery, where punishment inflicted serious injuries without any consideration, was a violation of moral, a violation of religion, and all violations of the human rights and the natural laws in the universe.

From Africa, they followed the Atlantic to America. The journey was very long, which made these noble African people sick because they were crowded against each other, hungry, thirsty, chained in the holds of those tangent ships, unventilated, delivered to death in the heat of the tropical equator. Without any medical help, some were dying, and others were decomposing before being brutally thrown into the sea. During the journey, the slaves, exhausted by the transport up to the board of ships, gathered all their forces and fomented a revolt, attacking the crew of the slave traders and at some time even seized the ship; the strongest and most determined waged an active struggle, while the weakest, not having the courage to intervene openly resisted the slave traders with stubborn insistence to regain their freedom. Those revolts made that when Africans slaves, crazy by despair, saw that the slavers were stronger than them, they immediately threw themselves into the sea to put an end to their life.

During the average passage of their journey to the New World, the special conditions of the sailors on the shift duty, during which a part of the crew of a ship was at work for a defined period, they had to ensure that slaves do not jump overboard, as the emerging forms of particular resistance, but devoted mostly to failure.

Abuses, tortures, or cruelties could not stop the captives to rebel, sometimes even twice on the same boat during the trip. Distinguished by a particular violence, both parties were fighting for their lives, knowing that neither the ship's crew nor the slaves could expect help from nowhere.

However, resistance existed; but unfortunately, there are almost no documents to tell us how the different human groups enslaved were behaving. All I could say with serious sympathy about the many revolts is that a deformation of the mentality occasioned the disappearance of the finest qualities, which led to moral degradation and a horrible devaluation of human life. The black slave trade was originally a regrettable division, which caused an incredible isolation from one tribe to another and from one individual to another. Because nobody wanted to be a victim, man had to himself become a slave trader with degraded morality to not be reduced into slavery. It was obvious that to sell others as slaves to Europeans was constantly reminding you that at any time, someone cleverer, stronger, luckier could seize you and sell you. So, everyone was trying to save himself and save his closest relatives without thinking of the others.

In the second half of the seventeenth century, these black men who for over two hundred years were living in the depraving conditions of the disorder of the slave trade, learned to handle firearms that first inspired them a fear of absolute panic; sometimes they succeeded, despite a furious resistance of racist slave traders, to take the strongest and burn the factories. The first time, Europeans almost always succeeded to repel the attackers and to rule by the policy based on the principle of division; and struggling with all the subtleties of cruelty originating from settlers, Africans were so influenced and helpless.

During the period preceding the eighteenth century, the century of the black slave trade, where the entire European policy in West Africa was only conditioned by this trade, the resistance of Africans, if we could call it so, was directed against the slavers. But how could they really resist? Facing a trade that had lasted over two hundred years and that became something usual for Africans? Captives, who were cruelly treated before their relatives to inflict fear as an example, illustrated a general characteristic rule for others. That trade was directed as a permanent source of income that people made as their profession at a time when the most beneficial activity was to kidnap, to steal the weaker, to sell them for immediate concrete benefit: for weapons, wine, or other unnecessary goods; and wars that were intended to make prisoners on the losing side. It was generally impossible to think of escaping because if someone met a runaway slave, all that came into his mind was well-nigh always to sell this fugitive to a European slaver or to an African merchant. That is why there were no resistance or slave revolts in Africa.

Fugitives never managed to return home, for they were again caught on the way and sold to slave traders. Despite all attempts to resistance, at the loading of slaves in ships, because of villages surrounded by very tall wooden palisades capable of protecting against slave hunters raids, the abduction of captives made it impossible to escape; and a cruel punishment to runaway slaves was on the agenda, whether in Africa or in the New World. This cruel irreducible nostalgia forced these noble men to become traitors and supervisors of their unfortunate companions, if not commit suicide or work awaiting death with indifference by the nostalgia of their country. Not having a place to f lee, the trade of African human flesh on that continent, from the time of their capture on the native soil up to the end of their life on the plantations of the West Indies and America, Africans did not cease to fight for their freedom and constantly were protesting against slavery. But in Africa, they could not act against that, for if they seemed to prepare such action or simply speak about it, they were immediately sold to slave traders or killed. These consequences were much deeper and real than we could imagine. Usually doomed to failure, the active resistance was well-nigh always the courage instilled by the despairing spirit of a few individuals. This is why they awaited the arrival in the New World countries to revolt primarily against slavery.

Furthermore, claims that Africans did not protest against slavery because they were accustomed to that state of affairs are absolutely false because they often preferred death than slavery, seeing that there was no hope to break free. It was in spite of the active resistance protests leading to their escape attempts in any favorable opportunity that the slave traders, armed to teeth, were chaining hands, neck, and feet of slaves in guarded caravans and escorted with strict severity. The factories were also well protected with guns pointed at the walls, ready to shoot anyone trying to escape, and a part facing the interior and were aiming the barracks of buildings usually identical and forming one whole to prevent slave revolts. This did not prevent the slaves to try to escape during transportation from the coast up to the ship, to throw themselves on sailors and on the guards, or even to jump into the sea, not caring that they could not swim with chained hands, but they preferred to sink themselves deeper underwater to drown, seeing a boat led by Europeans approaching to remove them from the water. That is why during this operation, the slave traders were monitoring slaves with special security.

The insinuations of the racist sympathizers of slavery, arguing that there were no revolts, did not impress us as there are many hidden documents that could be unearthed showing multiple rebellions before and after the departure from Africa in ships. Africans not only armed with bows and arrows but also with firearms, attacked multiple ships that they burned or raised the anchor so that the boat would drift and disappear without a trace. I could go on listing the examples of resistance, where the slave ships were taken by slaves on board and where the whole European crew was lying dead and the slaves in a state of complete exhaustion, half alive, and on others, there were desiccated corpses of slaves, or only sailors were killed. Some boats conquered by slaves were wrecked on reefs, and by the lack of governance, they were dying of hunger and thirst. The African people who were usually raising a particular disobedience were the Mina, Koromantins, Ewe, and Ashanti, the people of the Kilwa area, Mombasa, the Gold Coast, Sierra Leone, the coast of the Gulf of Benin, and Angola; and those sold from Quelimane and Zanzibar were constantly revolting on ships.

These tribes believed that it was necessary to carefully practice permanent insubordination with boldness, to have the character as strong and impossible to break their proud spirit; so for the uncompromising and unacceptability of their condition of slaves, they practiced obstinacy in the fight, for their desire to be free or just committed suicide; and they were ready to die to let the man who sold them pay; their proud spirits led them to a belief that was the cause of a number of suicides. On board of a caravan or a slave ship carrying slaves, a griot intoned song based on their beliefs. First, they sang to not feel the weight of pain and shame of the yoke that oppressed them. Then they sang in all joy and jubilation with the idea to return one day after death as ghosts to kill those who sold them. The griot intoned, "Oh, you, you sent me on the coast, but when I die, the yoke will fall, and my soul will come back home in my native country to introduce myself to you and kill you." And the entire choir repeated the names of those who sold them as slaves. But because of the tolerance that their ancestors inculcated in them, they never returned to fulfill this wish.

Many examples of resistance remained in the shadows, simply to support a racial theory qualifying them to be accustomed to slavery that deprived them of freedom. Knowing that, even a tame animal could not bear to be deprived of its freedom. Let's think a little! Do you want to? I'm concluding that regardless of the race, all people of the world aspire to live free. Thus, those who survived and arrived in the American continent were repeatedly sold as objects without value at auctions in the Antilles Archipelago, in Brazil, and in the south of the thirteen colonies, forming the East Coast of the United States today, and in Colombia, Mexico, Venezuela, and Peru, countries of the Spanish continental empire; and they no longer thought of returning back home to their ancestors. They stayed in the land to consume products that were manufactured for them in a miserable life. The passion and greed of Africans, as I have already said, initiated whites to manufacture fabrics especially for Africa.

Thus, these African innocent children of God lived every day together with death in the holds of ships—ships that were recognized by the smell of their excrements, vomits, intestinal f lows, children deliveries, corpses of newborns dead on the breast of their mothers, but still holding their children strongly against them, to not even realize that they newborns were dead, to finally be sold with their mothers. However, while naked in their thoughts, they found themselves arrived at a destination where other unpredictable, terrible circumstance was waiting for them with open arms.

Once again, they had to undergo another examination before the sale. Exhausted, tired, sick, and in an unknown land, they saw crowds drawn by them, which were buying them as objects, and forced labor was the result of all that dishonesty. The ruthless and rigid laws governing these slaves in plantations, including unpaid work, undermined their lives.

In that batch of monsters who established that law of the strongest, there were Nazi religious men of extremely racist political parties promoting the extermination of certain human races; they were saints of a rather fuzzy faith, strict followers of Satan, known as not respecting the natural law; the impious, quasi-fanatical outlaws, submitting the black man to occult domination at the psyche level; they were collaborators of the occupying invaders, who behaved at ease by their law; including an army without a shadow of respect, and soldiers without the slightest self-control, no longer keeping the usual order; insane with hatred, whose furious violence exceeded all measures of cruelty in their attitudes of mental delirium unfavorable by excess; they were brandishing an intense carefree horror that went without a punching hand; and never tired of producing terrible howling to my family, the African humanity and my fatherland, Africa. They were constantly whipped at the slightest mistake, with twenty strokes lashes, by a weak white, who could easily be beaten by the one whipped. An escape attempt was assessed as a sentence of death, after slashing his ears for the first attempt and the hock for the second. What a horrible cruelty, what barbarism, an inhuman savagery that I could not describe. Every Sunday, these preachers that some Surinamese Negro slaves or the Netherlands Antilles qualifying as Dutch fetishes were telling slaves that they were all white and black children of Adam; but were they telling the truth, or will you not admit that one couldn't use one's parents in such a horrible way than this? A converted slave exclaimed, "Are we really first cousins? If so, why are dogs, parrots, and monkeys a thousand times less miserable than we are?" Because the master Vanderdendur, the famous Dutch trader gave a canvas underpant twice a year as garment to the sugar workers, and had the habit of cutting off the hand of the slaves whose finger got caught in the grindstone.

Oh, by the name of God! He was cutting their leg when they wanted to flee. So, some slaves found themselves in that horrible state, lacking a left leg and a right hand. My god! In both cases, it was at that price that the Europeans were eating sugar in Europe.

The atrocities committed by the French and all the odious measures implemented by settlers in Haiti were very well known. But let's go to the discovery of Christopher Columbus, where his second son, Fernando Columbus, reported that the indigenous inhabitants of the Caribbean islands were having their hands cut off by his father, punished for not meeting the quota of gold that was to be provided—a bell of gold dust every three months. By this mistake, they were left to death by the loss of blood after cutting their hands. One of the most unspeakable cruelties was the rape and widespread genocide perpetrated by one obscene and inhuman slavery in the American continent on his arrival in the Caribbean islands, today known as Haiti and the Dominican Republic (Hispaniola). He was cutting off the nose and ears of Indians by his draconian law for small offenses. He was setting hunting dogs on the Indians who resisted his tyranny. Bartolome de Las Casas, a Spanish Catholic priest and historian, wrote that he was the eyewitness to this carnage of hunting dogs, sometimes as many as twenty, that ate the Indians by shredding them alive. This same priest also reported that Arawak babies were killed, and the corpses of Indians hunted in the form of sport, were used to feed these dogs. In Haiti and in the Dominican

Republic, a race was completely exterminated by Christopher Columbus and his men. By his orders, his men raped girls as young as nine or ten year's old and aboriginal women.

Miguel Cuneo, a crewman to whom Christopher Columbus gave an Indian teenager on their return to Spain, whipped the teenager mercilessly because she resisted his sexual attempts with all her might, but nevertheless, she was still raped. Las Casas continued by reporting that the men of Christopher Columbus were testing the sharpness of their blades by cutting the children's legs, hacking them and dismembering them and finally roasting them on the spindle. Oh my god! What cruelty? As a precursor of the transatlantic slave trade in 1505, the first exchange of slaves from Africa to the Caribbean was in the charge of Columbus's son, when the Spanish turned to Africa for slaves. This great evil by the name of slavery was the greatest excesses of savage power that could be allocated to man during the period of despotism. By reducing his fellow man by justifications, his supporters despoiled his most beautiful attribute by submitting him to slavery simply because he was African.

The same pretext of violence in black slavery was also used by the French. In America, everything was already concluded; Europeans, who knew that the Indians struck by slaughtering because they lack performance in mining and in their first plantations, therefore did not meet the requirements; the Catholic priest Bartholomew de las Casas directed these vile beings to Africa for a suitable workforce. Thus, by the slaves of other countries, the freedom of Indians was bought. So, since we cannot speak of slavery without speaking about violence, we obviously have to evoke the French colonies.

Therefore, the interest in luxury delivered the entire nation of Africa to the mercy of the natural human being inclinations of violence, to satisfy the desire of their cruelty in the system of slavery. At the sole discretion of the master, judge, and executioner at the same time, he was the only one to order that a slave be "cut," which meant whipped in the French colonies.

For a black in these colonies, the whip of flagellation was only forgotten the day of his death. In the French West Indies, it was the symbol of work; they had several methods for the application of the whip:

1. The slave was tied to four stakes driven into the ground, lying naked, on his stomach.
2. The slave was tied on a scale by hands and feet.
3. The slave was suspended by hands.
4. The suspension of the slave by the four body membranes to apply lashes for punishment.

Cruel as they were, they also invented another way to punish the woman, who did not escape that law. Thus, a hole was dug in the ground to accommodate the big belly of women and supervise their punishment, and regardless of the tearing of the flesh, the application of the whip was to be accomplished. By being whipped, some pregnant women gave birth prematurely or simply lost their babies on that day. The bullwhip was another instrument of torture.

To satisfy their obsessive cruelty, after shredding their flesh, they poured saltwater, ash, lime, chili, pepper, vinegar, etc., on their wounds. For the most horrible conditions, they used mutilations, which I already mentioned above. But the most despicable was the cutting of the genitals of the woman or man. Whenever it pleased them, they were cutting women's breasts, pulling teeth, tying mouths, pulling nails, puncturing eyes, or simply killing them by throwing them into the sugarcane crush machine, in a boiling boiler, or coldblooded in a stove. Hanging was also used; they hanged them by the neck or by the feet on the trunk or smoked them publicly.

Numerous ruthless violence without remorse in their behavior, were taking place with all impunity. And their horrific inventiveness of cruelty did not cease to grow, like coating a human being with sugar and delivering him to the ravenous birds, or leaving him buried up to the neck, with just the head outside, near a nest of red ants or wasps and leaving him to die slowly. But if the death was delayed in coming and taking him, a stone blow on the head alleviated his suffering.

The masters of the French slaves in the French colonies, men and women, loved to burn the black slaves alive. They were even burning them to have a flame for a vigil without any judgment. They brought fire in the anus of slaves stuffed with gunpowder to see him jumping for a while and then blow up like a bomb. To prevent them from eating sugarcane, a collar was placed on their necks and a muzzle on the mouth. This was, therefore, how the whites treated blacks in all their colonies in the New World; were these barbaric acts a simple punishment of blacks in accordance with the natural law, or could we simply qualify them as mere sadists? It would be for you now to justify them. You're just small spirits, unclean and unjust, without any notion of the natural law, non-Christian and inhumane, in need of mercy and pity. So believe me when I say the only being to be at the head of princes, and not just in Europe but also in the entire universe, is just that pure black, whom you formerly threw in the overcrowded steerage of boats with no ventilation, a terrible stench, an ambient heat that made the man sweat to render the air unbreathable with the howls of pain inflicted by chains, whose wearing became unbearable to women, men, and children, muffled by nausea; their cries of despair and the barely conceivable horror of diseases, which spread among them, were killing certain noble African children, but who, always without shaking their faith, experienced all these atrocities, respecting the laws of nature.

God, the divinity of the true tenderness of the unique law, is the close intimate friend of the law in his sovereign authority. His kingdom of glory and joy can only exist here on earth, while there is an intimate relationship of ontological love from him to us and us to him—a very old tradition symbolizing the first African religion, where the monotheism of Moses was born and Christianity of Jesus from Judaism. Without this relationship, religion becomes a theological ideology and a formidable dogmatic theory. Therefore, Christianity should demonstrate love, forgiveness, mercy, and the unique tenderness of God the Father to the beings of the universe—a real sign of the Father, who is mercy. It is basically this moral concept with a political dimension that established the African people, and the power of the Most High Almighty will dominate the universe by imposing in it the law that makes pure; but were these restrictive laws, frustrating and only encouraging contemptuous dehumanization of African people more than the love of justice, laws that governed them, authorizing their indignation and their humiliation without any respect of human rights by the abuses of slavery; were these laws merciful? This question is mainly asked to the representatives of the racial religions—the Catholicism, Judaism, Islam, etc.—the head of these institutions who adopted and practiced laws saying the following:

Art. 2. All slaves that will be in our islands will be baptized and educated in the Catholic religion, Apostolic and Roman.

Art. 11. Defending very specifically, to priests, to make the slaves marriages, if they do not appear with the consent of their masters.

Art. 12. Children who are born of marriages between slaves will be slaves and will belong to the master female slaves and not those of their husbands, if the husband and wife have different masters.

Art. 16. Similarly forbid slaves belonging to different masters to gather in large numbers the day or night, under the pretext of marriage or otherwise, or be in one of their masters, or elsewhere, and even less in the major byways, or places apart, upon which a corporal penalty punishment, which may not be less than the whip and will be marked with the f lower-of-lily; and in the case of frequent recurrences and other aggravating circumstances, can be punished by death.

Art. 22. Masters will be held every week to provide to their slaves aged ten and under two and a half pots of cassava f lour (Paris measure), for their food, or three cassava (cassava cake) weighing each two and a half pounds, at least, or something in this equivalent proportion; with two pounds of corned beef, or three fish books, and children, half of the foodstuffs here above, from the end of their breastfeeding up to the age of ten.

Art. 25. Masters will be required to provide, for each slave, two coats of linen, or four yards of linen annually, at the option of such masters. Art. 27. Crippled slaves by old age, illness, or otherwise the disease is incurable or not, will be fed and maintained by their masters; and if they had abandoned them, said slaves shall be awarded to the hospital, to which masters will be condemned to pay six sols per day for food and maintenance of each slave.

Art. 28. Declare slaves cannot have anything which is not for their masters, and everything that comes to them by industry or by the generosity of others, or otherwise, for any reason whatsoever, be acquired full ownership to their masters; without the children of slaves, their fathers and mothers, their parents or other, can claim nothing by succession.

Art. 33. The slave who will hit his master, his mistress or the husband of his mistress, or their children with contusion or bloodshed shall be put to death.

Art. 35. Robberies, even those of horses, mares, mules, oxen or cows, which have been made by slaves or freedmen, shall be punished with punitive sentences, even death if the case requires.

Art. 38. Fugitive slave who has been on the run for a month, from the day that his master has denounced him in court, will have his ears cut off, and will be marked with the f lower-of-lily on a shoulder; if he recidivism, another month, starting similarly the date of denunciation, he will have his hock cut off, and will be marked with the f lower-of-lily on the other shoulder; and the third time he shall die.

Art. 42. Only the masters can, when they believe that their slaves have deserved it, can enchain them and have them whipped with a stick or ropes. Defend them, giving them torture, or to do them any mutilation of members, under penalty of confiscation of the slaves, and be proceeded against the masters, extraordinarily.

Art. 47. Cannot be seized and sold separately, the husband and wife, and their prepubescent children, if they're under the power of the same master: declare zero seizures and sales that will be made.

Such stipulated the regulatory text of some articles identified in the Black Code meant to organize the slavery society. It notably specified the sacraments that were to punctuate the life of the slave: baptism, marriage, funeral, his rights and his duties, those of his master, and the severe penalties to which the captive exposed himself if he was going to break the rules.

Despite everything, view the current sociocultural and economic developments of these slavery-supporting countries, racist colonizers, and oppressors, most particularly France, which still does not recognize the contribution and the great historical course of Africa, and the United Kingdom, its queen, and its government, which do not want to hear anything about forgiveness or to recognize slavery as a crime against humanity, knowing that many of their fellow citizens have distant ancestors who made a fortune in the slave trade like the case of British prime minister David Cameron. But these countries simply continue to plunder the wealth of Africa at the open sky, so this Black Code is practically implemented toward Africa and countries accommodating the black people in the world today, especially because the extension of this practice in those countries for more than four centuries has largely determined the theoretical system of inequalities, including racial inequality, whose consequences are still valid.

Nowadays, one must still unilaterally explain the law, its attacker, its aggressiveness, its evolution in the religious consciousness, and of those slavery supporters racist countries that imposed it to despise the first people on earth; while they fail themselves to obey it, they disobey the law of nature; love no longer exists between humans, and they undermined the foundations of society and have plunged the world into an absolute mess because they made the law of books, a juridical law. From all eras in the church history, we were told that it has always had a frenetic attachment to the law, not just for the law in general but also specifically the respect for humanity, its environment, its habits, its traditions, and the smallest rites, comprising certain true values poorly exposed or very poorly understood. Isn't it a lie? Knowing the approval, practice, and a strong grip in the history of dehumanization, the worst that could exist?

The relationship between man and God is the one of the subjects to master. It should have appeared as a pedagogical proposal of freedom that leads to a stage of freedom—an initial conception of the law that the slavers forgot and that has nowadays become enslavement, forgetting that it is not the law that counts but the disposition of the heart that expresses fidelity to that law in love and the knowledge of God. It is very important to unmask the false approaches and destroy them to solve problems between different sociocultural environments in the world, instead of questioning oneself with a question of the history of the past sometimes very painful, believing that time will erase the pain. I say no to that because time never erases the pain. If a law must be rigorous, demanding, frustrating, and promoting certain practices, it becomes an unwanted disturbance to humanity and is no longer a universal law but one's small law, which is sufficient to only his small person, who has no joy in life. For that lack of joy in his life, it was absolutely necessary to find a concern to feel fulfilled. So extreme violence was his enjoyment; seeing his fellowmen agonize enormously pleased him and valorized him. It was for these facts that he chose the weak people and submitted them to inhumane conditions. Such was the case of pregnant black women who often underwent painful abortions despite themselves by the fault of their masters who made them work beyond their strength with rigor and often abused them. The slavery society increased by the frequent rapes of masters and was reproduced without the help of male Negroes, who also suffered sexual exploitation from the settlers. Their children were submitted mostly to the rigors of slave labor. And there were certain owners who also sometimes made their biological children work.

To scare the slaves, who easily delivered themselves to death, believing to return to their country of origin by an ancestral belief, the white sadists were cutting off the heads of those who believed that they freed their spirits by death, and suspended them on a pole. Since the effects of the slave trade are still subsisting, they still are the subject of the news up to the present day; alas on this subject, uncultivated slave supports and some historians put forward ideas not always convenient by sometimes confirming very quickly without any evidence that it was the Negro who sold his brother to the slave traders. Let's not forget that this topic is the origin of our current woes; therefore, it concerns us and interests us all. However, many of our black brothers of the New World, by the lack of information or education, believe very quickly, without asking questions, in the propaganda of dangerous Westerners who are accusing Africans of being responsible for their misfortune simply because they do not want to assume their responsibility for the crimes they committed, which is very cowardly from their part; nevertheless, it is very unfortunate for the convinced majority of blacks in the New World who are repeating those crimes unconsciously after being indoctrinated by the education system that whites put in place for these blacks.

Good, my brothers, I have news for you. According to the Black Code, the word *slave* is defined as "personal property." The Jews describe it as a cursed in the Bible: 'Cursed be Canaan! The lowest of slaves will he be to his brothers.' He also said, 'Praise be to the Lord, the God of Shem! May Canaan be the slave of Shem. May God extend Japheth's territory; may Japheth live in the tents of Shem, and may Canaan be the slave of Japheth'" (Gen. 9:25–27). So the Bible translates the first racist text, better known as "the curse of Ham;" slaves were a distraction object or a workhorse, was saying Rome, to qualify slave; for Aristotle, a slave was an animated object; and he was a production tool, believed Ernest Renan. Here you can see that, from the Bible to the Black Code, such definition or the word itself never existed. In addition, Ancient Egypt did not practice slavery, which was very incompatible with its beliefs. So, to conclude, Africa was not practicing slavery in any case. The word or the practice carried on in Africa was "serfdom." The Bible described this aspect in relation to the Jews who were in serfdom in Egypt. Forgetting to think and to ask questions to understand the historical realities of that time, they could not realize that this subject contained more lies than truths, distilled in textbooks and in the media. To better understand, I was obliged to review each of the key information. The first that came to mind and that tortured me was the involvement of the church in slavery. So, was the church right in its mission? To support and justify slavery in the Bible by putting it in practice, since its primary role was to raise awareness and prepare the way for the coming of God's kingdom, which has neither master nor slave? But hidden behind the Bible, their sovereign authorities allowed and made other people to be slaves, to obey with the fear of God to their masters.

It was that same church that owned slaves and much later expelled blacks from their premises instead of protecting them at the time of segregation in the United States. It considered civil rights but practiced intolerable things that Reverend Martin Luther King fought, and for that, it inscribed him on its blacklist. Finally, these same churchmen supported the apartheid regime in South Africa throughout its existence. For a conspiracy of silence from the West, the media generally never covered all these syntheses.

According to many Western historiographers, the reason for the deportation was the evangelization of blacks, but in which way, if I may ask this question? In a belief of hate, were its sovereigns were preaching the opposite of the scripture? This idea is more than absurd if one believes in the story that still designates Ethiopia as the country of the origin of religious practices. But then, where does this idea of evangelizing black's came from? This is a case of simple hypocrisy. A fatal thing here is that the moralist white historians have very limited memory, believing that by letting this period of the history passed in silence, where Europeans were selling their white brothers to Arabs as slaves, that time will be forgotten by them.

But hold on tight, because it is not forgotten. I would like to draw the attention of the historians by saying that the history of Europe is determined by the exercise of this trade in human beings toward its neighbor for a millennium; slave traders were Greeks and Romans, the Indo-European nomads so-called Christians, were unleashed upon the European people of the slavic language that they treated as pagans; established in the major part of Central and Eastern Europe, at the Carolingian time of the Middle Ages, and at the reign of Islam in Spain, from 711 to 1492. The occupation of the Spanish territory was made possible by an African army, led by Tariq ibn Ziyad of Berber Moor origin. They captured Spain under the Visigoths by crossing Gibraltar from northern Africa and invaded the Iberian Peninsula of Andalusia in 711. Most of the knowledge that Europe claimed to be theirs today came through Africa. In particular, those from Arabia, China, and India passed through Africa to Europe. The compass itself was brought from China into Europe by the Moors. A device for measuring the position of the stars and planets, known as an astrolabe, was also introduced in Europe as a new scientific technique. Others such as astronomy, chemistry, geography, mathematics, philosophy, and physics led Europe to progress in science. It is also known that many crops making the pride of Spain today were the work of the Moors, who brought in apricot, cotton, date, fig, ginger, lemon, orange, rice, peach, pomegranate, saffron, silk, and sugarcane. From all these, you could say that the Moors were the center of the culture of the Spanish tradition, if you would note that instruments like guitar, lute, lyre, and several other early instruments came to Europe by them. Because of their long rule, which lasted for almost eight hundred years in Spain, several words were absorbed into the Spanish language from the Arabic language. Note that the Iberian Peninsula includes Spain and Portugal. So, what is today Portugal was also invaded in 711, and Lisbon was captured by the Moors, generally considered to be mostly black of African origin, and occupied the country until 1147. To summarize, in the ancient times, the war of conquest and the crimes associated to the colonial domination that reduced the human being as a slave were already a reality that served for the establishment of trade in human beings at the period of the reign of Islam, which spread to Europe, making the continent a leading provider of white slaves, mostly Slavic men, women, and children, who were feeding that trade between Venice, precisely from the slave Quai, known by the name of the Riva degli Schiavoni, and the Arab-Muslim empire of southern Mediterranean. It was in that corner of the world that the word *sclavus* came to existence, (a name that designated the era of Slavs in Central Europe) at the time when, in the Western languages, the word *slave* or *Slav* replaced the Latin word *servus* to designate the workers deprived of freedom for their embarkation toward the eastern ports. This word was afterward translated into English, and resulted in the word *slave*, which designated white captives according to the Black Code, considered as deprived of freedom. White, therefore, confused us to themselves, who for centuries sold their European brothers to Jew traders for the making of eunuch and, after that, were sold by the Jews in the countries of the Muslim empire.

The Arab slave trade was the one that sent blacks outside Africa for the first time after the seventh century. It was developed in the Mediterranean before the arrival of the Portuguese in Africa. Following the trans-Saharan routes, the Arab slave trade extended to the south of the Sahara, going from Mali and East Africa up to Sudan. The delivery of 325 slaves per year was imposed by the Arab general Abdullah bin Sayd to the Nubian residents of the upper Nile valley in 652. In the eighth century, it reached the Horn of Africa and Morocco; upon their arrival in Africa, a commercial network emerged just in the north around 1200.

The concept that transcends the idea of the sacred leadership of the terms sacred known in English as Kings or Queens was a concept of the members of an aristocracy elite and especially to an hereditary class; but that still governs certain counties in the world. The prophets had supernatural powers and had the ability to predict the future. The coast of Mozambique knew all these ideas because Arab traders settled along the coast of the Khoisan ancestors for several centuries before the Portuguese explorer Vasco da Gama reached the coast in 1498 and politically controlled the country till 1975, when it gained independence.

This Mozambique region appears up to our days, like a commercial center of glass beads and porcelain as far as China and the production of gold and ivory through exchanges and interactions with Muslim traders, who were roaming in the southern Indian Ocean. A vast slave trade was organized in Zanzibar, along the coast of the Indian Ocean, from that time. In sites such as Mapungubwe, archaeologists found many Khoisan objects on the sites of the Bantu settlements, who migrated from the north through the Zambezi River valley between the first and fifth centuries after Jesus Christ. I must precisely add this: in ancient times, the first slaves were always whites, considering the word *slave*. For good understanding, this word is as old in the Western jargon as the oldest texts that we possess, characterizing the sociolect lexicon of a social class. A slave, two thousand years before Christ, was considered as a domestic animal or furniture that belonged totally to his master, who had the right to do anything at all with him—use him sexually, sell him, or kill him was just a play.

A ring was always placed in the nose of the slaves during the Sumer civilization as an ox or a bull. The Greeks and Romans also practiced slavery, either under a form of conviction of a court of justice judgment, or as prisoners of war; they were the barbarian people who spoke neither Greek nor Roman language, whom they regarded with great contempt and at the same time were qualifying them as less civilized people. It was at the second century after Jesus Christ, at the apogee of the Roman Empire, that the slavery system began to decline, making room for serfs, much better than in the Middle Ages, simply linked to the fate of the earth.

At the time of Louis XIV, toward the late Middle Ages, when the countries of North Africa were conquered by the Muslims, slaves of the Slavic countries were still sought. Then suddenly, it was the opposite, and Muslims began to sell their Christian prisoners of North Africa as slaves to whites. It was therefore already at that moment toward the early seventeenth century, where slavery was disappearing in Europe but was reborn in North Africa by settlements between Morocco and Libya, who were already providing two hundred thousand to three hundred thousand Christians slaves in different African ports toward Europe. The Arab Islamic sadists used women first as slaves and second as sexual objects by mutilating the sex organs of male slaves.

It was, on the other hand, during their multiple expeditions of so-called discovery that the Portuguese suddenly found themselves on the west coast of Africa. From that moment on, a jinx under the form of a virus invaded the whole continent. And it has been nothing else since then but only tears and cries of distress up to our days. The Portuguese took the blacks since then to sell them as slaves to finance their journey. Thus, blacks became the main commodity, indeed cheaper than a freed Slav. A new type of slavery was born—the beginning of the black slave trade. Two commodities seriously wanted by whites were coffee and sugar, which caused the misfortune of the two parts of the world—namely America, which was depopulated by genocides, to have land for their plantations, was the same fate for Africa, to procure themselves a nation to cultivate in those plantations. Europe decided therefore to divide Africa between the countries involved in human trafficking in regions or sectors for each European country to own a part. However, there was a small European country that was not yet manifested on the scene of slavery but yet was firmly established throughout Africa and had a high grip on the traffic of blacks. Holland was therefore that country that had the first great center of trade called the Gold Coast, lined with twenty-three forts, among which Holland alone held thirteen, nine for the English and one for the Danes. The second great center of the slave trade, called the Slave Coast, corresponded to countries such as the current coastal areas of Ghana, the current coastal areas of Togo, the Dahomey coastal regions (today called Benin), and a portion of the Nigeria waterfront. That region of the Nigerian slave kingdoms was the most active in the slavery era. The third major center of the slave trade that the French and English were disputing was the most populated part of Africa, in the present Nigeria, between the mouth of the river Osse and Cameroon. Loango and Angola formed the last great center, which took significance toward the middle of the sixteenth century.

Having played a key role in the slave trade, this subject is a taboo topic that men do not like to approach in the Netherlands. But very easily, this small country was mentioned, recognizing its impressive fleet, which operated throughout the world. This fleet was sailed by illustrious Dutch like Piet Heyn, the legal pirate of the Dutch West India Company. He became a vice admiral and was pirating many Portuguese ships for their treasures and also captured Salvador de Bahia, a Portuguese colony in Brazil. He continued his attacks on the Spanish fleets and trapped fifteen of their ships on the Cuban coast, specifically in the Bay of Matanzas, and escaped with a booty worth over eleven million guilders, the treasure of the Spanish New World, on the way to Spain. Willem Barents was another illustrious pioneer explorer of the Dutch expeditions, who navigated in the northern waters; and Michiel de Ruyter was the most famous of all admirals in the history of the Royal Netherlands Navy from generation to generation. It is also known that the creators of the Dutch West India Company were Khazar Jews who immigrated in Holland after being expelled from Portugal and Spain. Their company was the prime slave transporter in the Atlantic.

Today, they only like to associate themselves with the golden age, neglecting the connection between the two. They were wrong, very wrong, to enrich themselves from that trade practiced in distant lands by demoralizing blacks. Let us agree once and for all that colonialism that represented repression and total exploitation could not assimilate itself to the trade based on the exchange to serve the common interest. It turns out that all historical documents relating to the question of African slave raids, the looting of all our goods, and, finally, the slavery of our noble blacks for the new European lands of America, the Caribbean, and the Pacific are once again an unprecedented distortion of facts of the history. As I have already said above, all that is told to us on television, documentaries, news articles, or just historical works on this subject is a form of mendacious cowardice. To say that ships that went from Europe to the coastal trading posts of Africa, with various junk items, were intended for a triangular trade in the equitable form of barter against the captives, for the exploitation of our countries by the Europeans, has no justification. Yes, I assert that these slavers were transporting us to those colonies to work as slaves, but it was against our will and had nothing equitable, if only one refers to the detail of any financial account—whether of a Dutch, English, Portuguese, Spanish, Danish, or French slavers—to note if what the facts relate to us in their time is consistent with what historians tell us today, we realize that they're taking us for fools. For those who do not ask themselves questions, those who do not read, those who really do not want to learn their own history in depth and just believe in hearsay to blame the Africans, here is an example of an account of a certain Theodore Canot, navigator and French slaver between 1806 and 1860, revealing the stock of its cargo to us from Africa for one of his Atlantic crossings.

With this stock, we acknowledged that he made a total of £8,885 for one trip. Now, let's try to imagine how many of these trips were accomplished per month, by the various slaver companies stationed throughout Africa, we would realize very quickly that white men did commit an odious crime not only against humanity but also against our beloved planet Earth, which today summarizes the race to the concerns of the global climate problems. Once again, these same

Western destroyers, who care so much about this problem, have by no means the courage to tell the truth about the devastation of the African fauna and flora. In their multiple documentaries, they're recounting this subject in such a way that when one hears them, he will think that the fault is with Africans. Yet it is the Europeans themselves who devastated our noble and rich mother continent of the universe for centuries. Under silence passed another question—the barter issue, which was certified accurately by historians; and this, was to hide their cruelty, possessing the list of equipment that was very helpful to them and was found in those ships from Europe, such as cannons, gunpowder, rifles, iron bars, flints, soldier's uniforms, stays, etc. Were these war tools destined for barter? No. They were intended for the reinforcement of a cruel force in multiple European castles located in the African coast.

Therefore, was the black slave trade corresponding to the vision worthy of a human being? I would simply say no; the silence that was reigning on this subject in the Netherlands showed that the majority of the Dutch did not know that their country played the main role in the black slave trade.

Oh god! Is it really believable that the people who were not only received by the hospitality and kindness of the blacks to initiate them, bequeathed them secrets of the mysteries, and even gave a part of their land to some of them for them to strive on their native black hosts by misfortune, by making them slaves, is that proper? Cursed by the same people call Jews in a book that they so much consider by the name of the Holy Torah (the law), and who concluded their hatred toward blacks; how should we understand that these Jews and their God, who are preparing the coming of the kingdom of God with some seriousness, honesty, and respect, are they sincere? Where the practice of slavery does not exist but exist in their book called the Bible? Being a people who self-proclaimed themselves chosen people, and without dispute triggered, supported, practiced, and justified the slavery system that led to a great genocide?

The Papal Bull enslaving blacks marked the spirits of our ancestors as the worst day of the black history on Earth; this sanctification of the black race to extinction by the pope of the Catholic Church, designating a call for the holy war against the Negroes, was dated on January 8, 1454. After thirty-eight years, a first decree of Portugal finally decided to expel all the Jewish from that country. On the same year of 1492, after Portugal, they were also ordered to leave Spain. In 1496, forty-two years after that same papal bull against blacks, they were forced to f lee once again from Portugal in large numbers toward the colonies of empires, such as England, the Netherlands, and France, to only name a few; and when the inquisition intensified, they found themselves all over the world. Not having a native country, they enjoyed the hospitality of different countries to reside. They were therefore found where they're still found today as holders of multiple nationalities from all over the world; even though a small territory was given to them, they practiced a kind of extremism never imagined.

Despite this refusal, of having participated in this crime, their history is engraved with the slave trade in the European slavery archives of the world, and well after, leaving Portugal for America. Then they went from America to Africa with the intention of emptying the gold mines in Ghana. And finally, from Africa to the islands known as Santo Domingo today—the Dominican Republic, Martinique, French Guiana, Guadeloupe, the Caribbean, Suriname, and even up to Brazil, etc., where they founded and owned plantations and dedicated themselves by their knowledge to the sugar industry; they were controlling the biggest number of forts and were owners of most of the floats sailing at the coast of Africa, for looting and undertaking a genocidal deportation against African humanity, ever organized for the benefit of their interest. Jews were already precursors at the end of the sixth century. The following testimonies would allow us to conclude that they were the directors of that practice, and the knowledge of all confirmed its support in the Bible. Lady Magnus told us that, in the Middle Ages, the main buyers of slaves were the Jewish. And at the time of Pope St. Gregory the Great, Jews became the largest traders in this kind of traffic from 590 to 604; Julius Brutzkus, Jew and Zionist, revealed that, already in the tenth century, Jews possessed salt mines in Nuremberg. They were arms traders and exploited the treasures of the churches. But their great specialty was slavery.

The *Jewish Encyclopedia* assured us that the first Jews that Poles met were certainly traders, probably slave traders, called at the twelfth century by the name of the *Holekhei Rusya*, or "travelers toward Russia." Israel Abraham confirmed that at the twelfth century, the Spanish Jewish (Marranos) owed their fortune from commercial activities on international markets and the sales of slaves. This effect may be a punishment to them, for not having a specific country forcing them to roam around in the country of others and to have the privilege to speak their languages. Thus, they spoke and still speak Spanish, Russian, German, Dutch, French, Arabic, Persian, Slavic, etc. This skill was the reason for their success in business and the monopoly in international trade. Here is a coincidence that Christopher Columbus revealed to us in his diary: After expelling Jewish out of her empire, Her Highness, the same month of January, ordered him to navigate (sail) toward the said territories of India in any manner whatsoever with six Jews on board his boat; we recalled names like Master Bernal, a scientist; Marco, a surgeon; and Rodrigo Sanchez, an inspector who convinced Columbus to capture five hundred American Indians while in the Americas to sell them in Seville, Spain, as slaves. Among the crew, there was also another interpreter by the name of Luis de Torres; Alfonso de la Calle, a sailor; and Pedro Alonso Nino, a black navigator, probably Moor. We can therefore say that the discovery of America was primarily Jewish business. Among many Jewish historians, the historian George Cohen stated that many wealthy Jews financed the expedition of Columbus. One of those wealthy financers who advanced the sum of seventeen thousand ducats was Luis de Santangelo, a Khazar Jew. In addition, that "Chritobol Colon," known as his real name, being Jew or not, and as proclaimed by many Jewish historians, the fact remains that his expeditions were financed by Jews investors.

The Netherlands, a country that had a monopoly on the slave trade, was a shelter to a strong colony of Jewish and had a well-known Jewish history. The city of Amsterdam is known in the history, to have always had a Jewish mayor since ancient times up to our days. Even as supporters of the religious council forbid us to speak the truth for fear of being accused of anti-Semitism, we will still reveal it. Black history cannot be rewritten. Newspapers, historians, and filmmakers of many documentaries on slavery want to rewrite the history of blacks, accusing them of being the inventors of the slave trade, hammering their truth by saying that the Jew, who is the well-known instigator of slavery, was not involved in the transatlantic slave trade without a doubt; they're cowards, racists, fascists, and cruel beings of a manipulative small spirit. Before crying victim of the World War II, they were and still are the bearers in memories of genocides and crimes against humanity. All Jews and other nations know that the effect of hiding the truth on criminal horrors of their victims is just solidarity, mutual respect, and especially hypocrisy, fear, and shame existing between these nations.

To hide their wickedness, their cruelty, and their superiority complex that they continued to show until today all over the world, even if nobody says anything about their malicious actions, it is by fear to not be accused of anti-Semitism. The book of Prof. Christian Bouyer, an associate in geography and history with a doctorate in European studies, titled *At the Time of the Islands* tells us certain truths about the arrival of the Jews in the American colonies, with reference to religious intolerance. Inacceptable is that, in this crime, another one is added—rape of women and children and slaves who came from all over the continent to be then sold in countless gates of the world, as the terrible expansion of Europeans, of a cold and high extraordinary intensity of physical injuries, characterized by malice, remarkably painful and capable of inspiring terror, completely sealed the black continent and was requiring it to pay its tribute by human, as a plague that lasted for four and a half centuries. Where is justice, therefore? Knowing that the white submitted the Negro in a hellish world, just like an excremental residue that was good to die. So, some whites have quickly passed a negative judgment on the inhabitants of the mother continent of mankind, not even having yet crossed the doors of the African continent. But they quickly took awareness of their intelligence. Other whites, like the Greeks and Romans, who were initiated in Egypt, are more absent in their racial prejudices toward their black initiators. There have been many versions disadvantaging the mother of humanity, qualifying Africans with all kinds of creatures. More specifically of Cynocephali and Acephala, having eyes in the chest; and some as Cynamolgies with long snouts resembling dogs; in addition, saying that some of us had no mouth or tongue, and even nose to breathe, treating us like cannibals by saying that we have frizzy hair, flat noses, and only feed ourselves with human flesh; forgetting that them themselves indeed were cannibals and have also eaten human flesh.

Thomas Jefferson—born on April 13, 1743, in a family plantation in Shadwell in the Albemarle County, Virginia, the third President of the United

States of America from 1801 to 1809, and to whom we attributed the struggle for human rights—died on April 7, 1826, in Monticello; he was saying that whites were superior to blacks, both in body and spirit, even being considered as a distinct race. We should not worry much about his remarks because he was a slaver. Well, say it again but this time louder. What a veritable idiot describing the human being in this way, and why not just say that we are monsters in short? I would say to be precise that these whites, specifically the French who treated the Africans so monstrously, did not know how to obtain the information necessary from Greeks or Romans, the students of black, for them to have a good idea of the black being. In addition, even with the participation of the Koran on the racial equality, which was only practiced during the reign of Muhammad, the Arab Islamic culture of the first conquests of the defeated blacks also contributed to the development of superiority toward Africa.

An African Muslim by the name of Giovanni Leone, captured by a Sicilian during a mission in the East, was the object of a gift to Pope Leo X, who baptized him by the name of Johannes Leo de Medicis after being a slave. It was the memory of this African traveler, written by the request of Pope Leo X, after his several trips in African states, in Arabia, in Constantinople, his stay in Rome, and his multiple remarks that changed the perception that the French and all the rest of whites had on blacks. With these words, I quote his exquisite on the qualifications of whites, saying, "They're crudes, unaltered from their original natural state without reason, without intelligence and without experience. They do not have absolutely any concept of whatever. They also live like beasts, without rules and without laws." The exploration of Africa, centered on geography, information on the life, manners, habits, and customs of Africa, was regarded among his scholarly European peers as the most authoritative treatise until the modern exploration of European geographers interested in African subjects. The book titled *Description of Africa*, of the one known as Joannes Leo, his baptismal name, was published in Italian by Giovanni Battista Ramusio, the Venetian publisher in 1550. The explorer, the said Leo the African, who completed his manuscript on African geography, was born around 1494 in Granada Spain and was originally named al-Hasan ibn Muhammad al-Wazzan. This diplomat and Berber author died according to the sources in 1554 in Tunis, Tunisia, North Africa.

I would therefore determine the slavers who deported blacks from the African continent in four consecutive waves. The first, the Trans-Saharan Trade, is generally referred to as the Arab Trade (or Eastern Trade), known as a trade that was organized by Arab merchants across the Sahara region. It began in the middle ages between several countries of the Mediterranean Sea and Black Africa. From the seventh century on, this commerce flourished and reached its apogee in the thirteenth century to become a thriving trading system toward the fifteenth until the end of the sixteenth century and extended to the third of the nineteenth century.

The second, with the Islamic expansion of the eighth century, which lasted until the nineteenth century, was established on the coast of East Africa, with increased activity toward the end that spread Islam far beyond the Arab area, on a territory comprising some countries in Africa.

The third, the black slave trade, lasted four and a half centuries, and the heaviest damage was the trip across the Atlantic. Organized by Europe in 1441, the Atlantic slave trade was, little by little, abolished in the nineteenth century by all countries of Europe and America, but continued in the world, first legally using slaves and then clandestinely until today. It was practiced by the Europeans to raise the money used for the construction of their beautiful countries through the work, the sweat, and blood of captive slaves.

Finally, the last one is a domestic slavery which continues up to our days and has no estimation on its heaviness in figures. In terms of figures, today accepted with hesitation, the trans-Saharan slave trade of black slaves, who crossed the Saharan region between black Africa and several countries of the Mediterranean Sea, deported 5.3 million individuals. The eastern coast and the Red Sea had 2.9 million individuals. The Atlantic trade deported 11.7 million lives.

Here are some figures that proved how and how much our continent has been deliberately messed up by the Europeans, who did not cease to date to demand from Africa. Approximately 2,400 kilograms of gold were exported from Guinea per year from the period of 1493 to 1580, representing a total of 35 percent of global mining at that time. From 1481 to 1482, another lugubrious fortified building by the name of St. George Del Mina was built on the coast of the present-day Ghana, where significant quantities were exported by the European gold dealers who were adapted to the local conditions to sell not only European goods but also slaves purchased in other parts of the coastline to whites and to African gold merchants, who were trading their gold against commodities and also slaves to transport salt on the coast and take away merchandise as 3,500 animal skins (£1,750); 19 large teeth of ivory of first quality (£1,560); gold (£2,500); 40 slaves (£1600); 600 pounds of small ivory (£350); 15 tons of rice (£600); 36 young oxen (£360); sheep, goats, butter, vegetables (£100); and 900 pounds of beeswax (£ 95) for a total of £8,885. After all this looting for hundreds of years and with the permission from Rome to exterminate blacks, the Catholic and Muslim religions must formally apologize and compensate Africans for authorizing the slave trade and practiced it.

It was therefore Tommaso Parentucelli, born around 1398 in Sarzana and became Pope Nicolas V from March 6, 1447, until his death on March 24, 1455, who authorized the king of Portugal to officially practice the slave trade for the first time. This act emanating from the pope under the reference code PT/TT/BUL/0007/29 was fully reproduced in French under the name of the "Sin of the Pope against Africa." We quote, among others, countries such as Portugal, the United Kingdom, the Netherlands, Belgium, the United States of America, Spain, Germany, France, and many other European countries that founded companies for the enfranchisement and the exportation of Negroes toward the rest of the world.

Although this crime still remains without justice done, it does not mean that it is not severe, even as the international recognition has broken the silence about this crime committed against humanity. A crime that is not only humanitarian but also economic, since it is a crime that has emptied Africa and continued to empty its economic potential until today. This progress of nonmoral and nonpolitical consciousness remains the devastator of the social system, moral conceptions, and the deformation of political systems, displaying the outbreak that caused the slave trade and still caused its outbreak even nowadays by the refusal of those countries that were involved in the slave trade, and at the same time in colonization to present apologies to Africans; but their fear of one or more lawsuits after them recognizing this crime does not exclude this crime.

I would just like to remind those countries that the Jewish Holocaust, which means "to completely burn an animal flesh as sacrifice to God," in their tradition, was practiced on the altar of their temples up to the year 70 in Jerusalem. However, this ritual no longer exists in the Jewish tradition, and the word *holocaust* was only used since the nineteenth century to describe the large-scale massacre of an ethnic and social group.

To characterize the Jew killings after World War II by Nazi Germany, English and French languages began to use this term to describe the victims of that event. For the Jews, it was also a way to exterminate them between 1939 and 1945 and made about six million deaths. But this disaster and crime against humanity was already legally classified, and all claims made by Jews were granted. They were even more than rewarded by dividing a country to create a state for them. According to the Bible, the Jew is a descendant of Abraham, originally from Ur, a tyrannical kingdom that once was located on the other side of Mesopotamia.

Very recently, after the Second World War and more precisely on November 29, 1947, the General Assembly of the UN adopted a resolution on the partition plan of Palestine, which was rejected by the neighboring Arab nations. But without considering their rejection, the Jews literally massacred the Palestinians daily, chasing them from their house and land.

After all these facts well known to the international opinion, the state of Israel, nevertheless, was established on May 14, 1948; and since then, this state is exercising an undeniable law of the jungle and continued to massacre Palestinians in front of the whole world. Is it because they're white?

Furthermore, it is known that Africa, which has been repeatedly brutally attacked by white, torturing its children, forcing them to walk immeasurable distances, chains on the neck and feet, raping its women, massacring some when it seems good to them, and burning villages in their path, dislodged at least twenty million Africans out of the black continent with a deportee mortality rate of 13 percent or two hundred million people; but known as a figure that's still debated by demographers, it is and remains the most deadly practice, resulting in more severe crimes ever orchestrated against humanity; and more specifically, because it is done to blacks, it should not be prosecuted by fear for them to be compensated. What a shame, what human indignity, what cruelty, what an immorality for you who were extolled to be the human rights defenders!

I can shout out loud for their indignity done to others, but does it really worth it? Because here is another one of their shameful doing; I cannot imagine so far that, to satisfy themselves, the white Catholic religion went to all the trouble in the world to paint Jesus with blond hair and blue eyes to change the story that already existed in Egypt for centuries, if not thousands of centuries, simply because they wanted to let humanity believe that they represent God, a pure and good soul. No, make no mistake. I would say that these whites with red hair and blue eyes have a black heart in a white skin, which led them to judge the essence of humanity by the color of his skin. These little spirits, I guess, must not be human beings themselves, who believed themselves superior beings, inflicting injustice to other humans, particularly on blacks.

The Great Architect built the world and placed it at the disposal of man, a chemical creature, with the laws that should be strictly respected. He gave us neither a precise place nor a particular function but simply wanted the human to be able to choose according to their desires and discernment, a way to function in a good way, which could not degenerate into an animal being and harm his neighbor. After all, it is said that the soul will discern and reborn the divine spirit. You're neither heavenly nor earthly, neither mortal nor immortal. You're just human. But after a deep initiation, man must work very hard, as recommended by God, to gain his bread and acquire property or fight to acquire another person's property. Never can we possess a human or force him to do what he does not want to do. In addition, to force a man to work does not mean he is obeying; on the other hand, to force him to obey is an unforgivable crime.

Here is a small parenthesis about the church and its role, a brief comment of Father Fauque to a group of Maroon slaves who tried to escape. He told them, "Remember, my dear children that even though being slaves, you're however Christians as your masters." In fact, slaves were baptized on their arrival in the Caribbean and everywhere where they arrived; a saving mission of the church was there for the pagan. He continued by saying, "You profess since your baptism in the same religion as them, which teaches you that those who do not live in Christianity fall after death into hell." He concluded his preaching with the feeling of compassion and sorrow caused by the suffering and misfortunes of others as if he was feeling sorry for himself by articulating these words: "What a misfortune for you, if after being slaves of men in this world and in time, you become slaves of the demon for eternity after death." What a fool to believe that these noble creatures of God Almighty, removed by force from their country for a forced labor, were not already living in hell and were not already serving the devil on the earth.

And here comes an exclamation to express his frustration: "This misfortune will infallibly happen to you, if you do not keep to your duty, since you're in the habitual state of damnation." This Christian father was preaching the most extreme threat of eternal damnation in hell but did not prevent them priests from committing mortal sins, to not be eternally condemned to hell. What a believer, and what a belief in Christianity! So, if I well understood, this is summarized as such: accept to be slaves of whites in this world to be free in the eternity, provided that the slaves abandon any practice of freedom in this world. Congratulations, Father Fauque. You had to live up to this day to maintain blacks in slavery. This father and many others have forgotten that God was born in Africa by the admission of the ancient Greeks, Egyptians, etc. You and the whole religions of the world knew that the ancient historians nominated Ethiopia as the country of the origin of religious practices. But blacks had to be evangelized; there was the reason for their deportation in America. Was it not what Western historiography said? But in 1844, the statement of the abbot of Castelli, then prefect of Martinique, four years before the abolition of slavery in 1848, was saying that there was never any religious education intended to slaves. These words in capital letters are found in the original text of Mr. Pierre-Paul-the Abbot of Castelli, concerning the slavery in general and the black emancipation. We must dare say that the religious and moral education of slaves, were the basis for their deportation to America. It was therefore required by the royal ordinances and the ministerial prescriptions, so imperiously prescribed, especially by the divine precepts of the Gospel, to evangelize. But "The movement of religious propagation was at or near zero compared to what it should be in the current situation."

To make us prisoners and sell us, it took this cruel great dishonor of religion, a commercial reason and the dishonesty of Europeans to destroy Africa and steal all its wealth, to deport Africans en masse and finally give birth to wars in the mother continent of humanity. And even after so many years of manipulation, of open looting, of unhealthy and destructive hypocrisy, Africans have not yet understood that it is still this dishonesty and this commercial dishonor that are the causes of war and almost continual genocides in Africa. Our desires of wealth and the one of our immoderate, senseless, asshole leaders, particularly without accurate value, is unfortunately destroying our people and giving us the grudge to revolt against them, since ultimately after their death, their wealth is in no way recovered.

When they meet one of our leaders in their sumptuous palaces, it is to excite him, after showing him all the stolen fiches in Africa, supervising him doses of strong destructive liquors, committing him to betray his brother by promising him good life, at the expense of the suffering of the people; to steal the properties of his country and swell the accounts of their banks, they dare give themselves the right to speak of humanitarian law. Knowing what is established for the mistreatment of black people in this world said civilized of our era, they're still qualifying us as human beings born to serve and satisfy the existence of others; considering us as beings that must obey and submit us as oxen to tawny, but must worse again to be human beings without intelligence. I would say without reserve that if blacks were Jews, all Europeans who committed this heinous crime would have already been sent to the criminal court in The Hague.

The slavery of blacks was not only to deprive freedom, or in other words, to perform forced labor but also a well-organized genocide, resulting in the destruction of the black race. For me, the slave trade was a simple and very effective way to deny its human dignity by treating it as slave. This assimilation, which led the whites to believe that they were more precious than the black man, triggered an important displacement of a minimum of twenty million people in the history of mankind.

The Eastern trades remind us of the black slave traders of various origins; they were Berbers, a set of indigenous tribes in North Africa. According to Ibn Khaldun, from 1332 to 1406, Berbers originated from Mazigh, son of Canaan, son of Ham. But the mitochondrial DNA passed on by women to their children, permitting to follow the lineage of a species or of an ethnic group, placed the origin of Berbers at a date more ancient than thirty thousand years before our era, at the prehistoric period, the longest in the Paleolithic, directly from the genetic original of West Eurasians. At a certain time, Berbers were occupying a wide area going from the west of the Nile valley up to the Atlantic Ocean. They founded powerful kingdoms formed with confederated tribes across the Sahara, their favorite territory. Numidia, with names of kings such as Gaia, Syphax, and Massinissa; the ancient Libya; and Libus tribes were the best-known Berber kingdoms. The twenty-second and twenty-third Egyptian dynasties were also Berber kingdoms. Their names, Libyan Moors; Gaetuli, inhabitants of Getulia; Garamantes, a nation dwelling in the Fezzan area of the modern-day Libyan Desert; and Numidia were names known in antiquity. The Berbers have also suffered many conquests and have been victims of the Romans, of Christianization, of the Vandal invasion, and the conversion to Islam by the Arabs. Their oldest expansions across the southern Sahara were the one of the Capsians and most recently the one of the Tuaregs. Their areas are today unevenly distributed and reduced mainly as Berber-speaking areas in Algeria and Morocco and a minority in Egypt, Libya, and Tunisia. Their alphabet, the Tifinagh, still in use by the Tuareg nowadays, was a branch of the family of Afro-Asiatic languages.

The slave traders of various Chinese origins in China invented numerous major tools. They have on their account the compass, the banknote, printing, and the gunpowder, the "fire medicine" in "pinyin spelling," having a controversial date of creation by historians that some placed the invention from 206 BC to AD 220 during the Han dynasty; and some during the Tang dynasty from 618 toward the seventh century to 907. And in the fields of science and arts, China remained the home of numerous innovations, compared to Anatolia, a peninsula located at the western end of Asia, gathering lands strictly and geographically, located at the west of a Coruh-Oronte line, between the Mediterranean, the Sea of Marmara, the Black Sea, and Mesopotamia.

Nowadays, that territory of Asia Minor occupied 97 percent of the territory of Turkey and 3 percent of the territory located in Eastern Thrace. From 1900 to 1200, the civilization of the Hittites was the most important civilizations, developed in Anatolia. Iron was discovered by that Hittite civilization. The hard metal discovered by heating some red stones would replace bronze, tin, and plumb for the making of weapons and tools, unlike the Chinese civilization, that also knew a Neolithic period and the Metal Ages rather later, and sometimes cited as the oldest continuously; it is one of the oldest civilizations in the world that has lasted for nearly five thousand years, practicing Confucianism and Taoism. The sedentary organized societies were practicing agriculture and animal husbandry since the Neolithic period.

Around 5000 BC, rice cultivation appeared. And between 2300 and 2700 BC on the site of the culture of Majiayao, bronze objects were found therein dated in the Bronze Age, around the Xia dynasty, 2100 BC. And the bronze work reached its full development from 1766 to 1122 BC under the Shang dynasty. From the foundation of the empire by the Qin dynasty, China became the home of major civilization, heading the rest of the world generally in technology, arts, and medicine.

As early as the 1990s, Prof. Jin Li, a geneticist and vice president of Fudan University, demonstrated that about one hundred thousand years ago, modern human (*Homo sapiens*) left Africa, and one of his first destinations was Asia, as a place of fairly recent migration. His authoritative theories in the world proved not only that the African man, who entered history one hundred thousand years ago, brought the whole of humanity into the original history of the human race, but also proved that the Chinese indeed came from Africa by the genes highlighted by this same geneticist from Shanghai.

Committed to his work, he undermined the old theories of the eighteenth century, of course unequal, validating the existence of "races," under a "scientific" cover of racist attempts according to which, the modern man would have different origins, by the discovery of the Peking man—the remains of a humanoid of six hundred thousand years old. This discovery, which flattered some nationalists, was proved to be famous to try to validate a "separate" origin of the Chinese, propagated by the German Franz Weidenreich. The first inhabitants of Southeast Asia are probably Homo sapiens, Negritos designating small-size populations. In the Andaman Islands, the Malay Peninsula, and the Philippines, these small-size black-skinned Andamanese with frizzy hair, nicknamed "little blacks" by the first Spanish visitors to the Philippines, lived in these three geographical areas of the Southeast Asia. It is therefore from a single origin, and not from multiple origins, that modern men evolved, and the science of our day continues to confirm, admitting unanimously by disproving the theory of some experts, claiming since some few years that modern men had multiple origins. In the archaeological excavations of the archeologist Kwang Chih Chang, a confirmation of the importance of the black population was recorded, and the existence of an all-black empire in southern China was also reported by columnists. Concerning slavery, the odious human traffic of blacks began in the direction of China, when it was inaugurated in the seventh century by the Arab Muslims, before the first African captive was shipped to the New World. So, the only actors or beneficiaries of black slave trade and slavery are not just Westerners.

And in the imports of Nigger slaves under the Tang dynasty (618-907), Prof. Chang Hsing-Lang, a professor of literature, chemistry, history, and a real author, mentioned the existence of Niggers in China. Speaking of blacks who formerly had a place in the supposedly homogeneous society of China, the black skin of the descendants of the sacred Mangchous dynasty is remarkable; and the black Chinese who once constituted a part of the population before the modern era of China, the roughly 1.3 billion people in China, had sworn to only wash dirty linen in family concerning blacks, and never speak of them, and almost all Chinese are as ignorant of the subject of the Niggers in China. Many testimonies of famous authors like Tcheou Kin-Fei, in his book titled *Ling-wai-Taita*, written in 1178, indicated that thousands of blacks were sold as slaves in China, from Pemba or Madagascar, called K'ounLoun in Chinese. These "slaves resembling the Koui-nou" - demons were mostly owned by wealthy people in Koangtcheaou province (Kouang-Tong). According to the author Chou You, in the P'ing-chuch K'o T'an, these black slaves, considered repulsed by the Chinese because of their appearance, were called Kouinou (demon-like slaves), He-hiao seu (black servants), and treated as Ye-jen—savages. History testifies that the Chinese enslaved thousands of blacks in their homes in total contempt, centuries before a single African was deported by the English, the French, or the Portuguese. China's responsibility in the painful past of the black people was royally an economic ideology than the English, French, or Portuguese, and remains ideologically economic now that it has reconnected with Africa for its raw materials. Yet the African continent was for the Chinese a continent that did not exist and that they despised with indifference barely believable. After slavery, the Chinese royally ignored the Africans, and in the official speeches of the leaders of their empire with the African personalities, they always avoid mentioning the "horrible slavery" crimes. A man named Tchao-Jou-Kou compiled a work titled *Tchou-Fantcheu: Description of the Barbarian Peoples* based on anterior sources in 1226, during the Song period. His book spoke about Alexandria and its light in Egypt, Morocco, Mo Kie La: "Maghreb el agsa," of Wou-sou-Li, meaning Misr, of Libya, and several other African countries like Kan-Mei, probably the Comoros, and Ts'eng-Pa, meaning Zanzibar, as the countries of the east coast. Sicily (Sen-Kia-li-ye) and the southern coast of Spain (Mou Lan-P'i), Arab Mourabit, country of the Almoravids as two European regions, were also cited.

In Java, an inscription dated 860 CE was found, identifying the Zendjs' servants from East Africa sold in China on a list. Other black slaves are mentioned on another Javanese inscription indicating the slaves offered to the imperial court of China by a Javanese king, and more than thirty thousand black slaves were sent to the Ming dynasty by the Javanese. Thus, unlike the "wicked slavers and Western settlers," the Chinese never forget to recall the memory of a peaceful people who left Africa and who never imposed themselves by force, claiming that Zheng He's expeditions were not intended to extend China's sovereignty beyond the seas, unlike the European expeditions of that time. Presumably, their mission was to make East Africa a colony of China, and the effect of sending an army of solid soldiers, plus about twenty-five thousand other men embarked on the Zheng He's Expedition, occupying territories far from the Empire, was far from being a peaceful mission. Yes, it was about making friendships, creating opportunities for trade with foreign countries, deepening geographical knowledge, but the benefits of mutual cooperation were not reciprocal. Well, following the maritime ambitions and conquest in the Western Seas by the last cruise of Tcheng Ho in 1431 of Admiral Zheng He, the Chinese ignored their proven involvement in the tragedies of the black people, but it took a hair breadth for Africa to be Chinese, says Remi Kauffer. In other words, it was under Yong Le, the third Chinese emperor of the Ming dynasty (1368 to 1644), that the genuine Chinese maritime journeys were undertaken by the navigator Zheng He, a Chinese Muslim eunuch, maritime explorer, famous by his journeys in the Middle East and on the coasts of East Africa. But it was at the time of the Han dynasty around 206 before our era that contacts between China and Africa were established. The location of the current Chinese capital was transferred from Nanjing south to Beijing by him in 1409. Huge maritime expeditions were also ordered by Yong Le to explore foreign countries, unlike his predecessors. The map called Da Ming Hun Yi Tu, meaning the map of the great Ming Empire, showing the Nile in Egypt and the Drakensberg mountains in South Africa, and known as the oldest cartographic representation of Africa, dates from 1389. So, for a long journey from the mouth of the Yangtze River, the navigator Zheng He sailed to the South Seas on an expedition of his great armada, called the Fleet of Treasures, with artisans, traders, interpreters, and a whole group of scientists, about thirty thousand men and two hundred sailboats, on July 11, 1405, having the oldest cartographic representation of Africa in hand.

Inscriptions in Chinese characters found in the Cape Province, the Chinese pottery dating from the thirteenth-century in Limpopo province (north of South Africa), and shards of Chinese ceramics, also found in ruins of Great Zimbabwe, proved that Zheng He was the first to cross the Strait of Magellan, followed the eastern coast of Africa, and crossed the Cape of Good Hope and the coasts of Southern Africa on his return. A giraffe, named "Ki-Lin" in Chinese, lions, and zebras were taken to China and were offered during one of his expeditions of 1417. The maritime route of silk, connecting China, the countries of Asia, and Africa, was also actually established by this series of excursions of Zheng He to the West. Today, the Chinese are reminding anyone who wants to hear that the main purpose of their long journey in Africa never sketched the beginning of colonization, while the very other reality was expansionist. Thus, the economic motive for their passage was obvious, consequently affirming that they preceded the Europeans in Africa now that they badly need the black continent. Today united in China-Africa, it is more convenient for them to denounce the "horrible slavery and colonialist crimes of Westerners" and seek kinship ties with the people of the black continent.

It is known that China has historically been one of the oldest civilizations and very advanced society in the world. And finally, their four great inventions formerly also changed the face of world. China was transformed toward the early nineteenth century as the most powerful country in the world and knew a significant period of its history, only to find itself suddenly dominated by the Japanese, Portuguese, Spaniards, and Russians during that century.

These foreign people who hijacked the foundations of their economy surpassed China in terms of technology. At the expense of the Chinese people, their self-sufficiency now rested in favor of foreign occupiers. It suffered a brutal Japanese occupation during World War II, and at the end of that war, it also suffered foreign interventions, the cause of economic and political instability; and thanks to the revolutionary movement of Mao Tse-tung, the country was liberated.

Mao Tse-tung, born on December 26, 1893, in Shaoshan in the province of Hunan, restored the pride and the independence that they once had to the Chinese people by giving back the power to the workers and peasants of the nation, rejecting all foreign influence, forcing the country mostly badly known to become a mysterious country apart from others, and closing itself from 1950 to 1970. Chinese traditions were seriously called into question during the period of this politician, now experiencing difficulty to feed the nation. The country, however, took another very different turn at the arrival to power of Deng Xiaoping after the death of Mao Tse-tung on September 9, 1976, in Beijing.

Gradually, its economy, the Communist base, saw itself transformed into a national market economy; the peasants who were no longer self-sufficient multiplied harvest crops to sell their surplus to merchants in cities. Now foreign investments, which were forbidden, were allowed and accepted by private enterprise to accelerate the development and take advantage of foreign expertise. Through the opening of all their maritime ports, it then went mainly from the isolation to the openness of the country. The central power of the imperial dynasty court during two millennia was the prey of rival factions and the barbarian's intrigues carrying out vast raids in the border regions, from natural disasters to famines, and revolt movements of starving peasants tearing the country that the administration could no longer remedy. Among this quota, there were some warlord chiefs from distant provinces, and sects were born; they could no longer contain the pressure because they do no longer recognize the authority of the emperor.

They divided the empire into rival kingdoms by proclaiming themselves sons of heaven, by showing the Mandate of Heaven lost by the emperor, and by engaging themselves into endless wars. The Mandate of Heaven was considered by a warlord who proved himself cleverer than others, like the founder of the Ming dynasty, who managed to regain control of the entire country to establish a new legitimate dynasty.

The founder of the Qing dynasty, named Emperor Qin Shi Huang from 221 to 207 BC, was the great unifier of China who built the Great Wall of China after the first dynasties of Xia, Shang, and Zhou, only occupying the most central part of the country. China experienced long periods of peace from 206 BC to AD 220 under Han, from 618 to 907 under Tang, and from 960 to 1279 under Song. During those periods, it was ranked first among the most important nations of the world through its innovation, in particular under Song and under Tang dynasties. But it still, of course, experienced periods of civil wars, which troubled their country until the fall of Han in AD 220, which led to the loss of its unity up to the appearance of the three kingdoms in 581 by the Sui dynasty before the advent of Tang.

The five dynasties and the ten kingdoms also had a period of unrest, where the culture of the country at its peak flourished and which separated the Tang from the Song dynasty. The Mongol invasion, which took power from 1234 in northern China, brought a trauma to the Yuan dynasty by the heirs of Genghis Khan, who proclaimed his sovereignty in 1271 on China, despite the fierce resistance of the Song dynasty in the south of the country until 1279. And in 1368, the Han ethnic group finally regained power as a new dynasty. Thus, without regaining its momentum, the Ming dynasty tried to regain its glory of the past without success; this time, it was a new dynasty of Manchu origin, not of Han, who founded the Qing dynasty, the work of Nurhachi; after seizing the throne, he reigned from 1644 to 1912 after the fall of the Ming dynasty, and his lineage led to the last dynasty of the emperor P'u-i, until he was overthrown by the Xinhai Revolution as the last emperor of China on February 12, 1912. And from there, the abdication of the last emperor, P'u-i, generated the Republic of China. In India, the slave trader of various Indian origins, from the Indus Valley civilization was developed as early as 5000 BC. From ancient times, trade routes were present in India, and they housed vast empires in the subcontinent. Buddhism, Hinduism, Jainism, and Sikhism were the four major religions born in the Indian land. During the first millennium, Christianity, Islam, and Zoroastrianism established their domination in their continent; and the British East India Company, with the royal charter of Queen Elizabeth I of England created on December 31, 1600, conferring it the monopoly of trade in the Indian Ocean for fifteen years, gradually annexed them immediately before moving to the nineteenth century under the control of the United Kingdom.

It was the Dutch East India Company (VOC) that drove the first European company founded in the seventeenth century to dominate the f lows of trade with India, also conquering all the possessions of the French East India Company and leading it to ruin. That advantage deeply marked the creation of the future British colonial empire in India. In 1947, after a nonviolent struggle of Mahatma Gandhi, marked by the resistance, it resulted in the independence of the country known as India. In the meantime, an English commercial company became the most powerful of its time and was now controlling the government and the military functions of the vast Indian Territory. With full force in the nineteenth century, the limited company hurt the economy and the politics of the world. Its extraordinary influence from its headquarters in London was extended in all continents and presided among others to the foundation of Hong Kong and Singapore; and to the creation of the British Indies and the Raj by spreading the use of opium in China, and forcing the cultivation of tea in India.

Napoleon, who was directly involved in the political revolt in Boston, the capital of the province of Massachusetts Bay, against the British Parliament by the famous Boston Tea Party, was arrested in 1773 and held captive in St. Helena. The American War of Independence was triggered by that affair. On May 10, 1857, the Indian Rebellion, also called the First Indian War of Independence or the Sepoy Mutiny, began in the town of Meerut by a sepoy mutiny of the army of the British East India Company and led to a popular uprising in the northern and central India to gradually decline up to its disappearance in 1858.

The Indonesian slave traders of various Javanese origins were also supporters of slavery, but there existed other slave trader tribes than the Javanese; the Old Javanese, also called Kawi was characterized as the original Sanskrit vocabulary inscriptions of the Hindu Buddhist period of Java. And besides Java, there existed many linguistic communities, for example, in Suriname in the former Dutch Guiana. Also, at a period, the Javanese ancestors left Java by themselves or by the settlers to other countries such as Australia, Hong Kong, Malaysia, New Caledonia, the Netherlands, Singapore, Taiwan, and East Timor, and they held to preserve their language.

There were also Malaysian populations of the east coast of the Indonesian island of Sumatra, located on the equator and which owes its name from a Muslim kingdom of Samudra in the thirteenth century; the Riau Islands, also Indonesian, on the coastline of the Borneo island, located between Malay Peninsula and Singapore to the north and south of Thailand with provinces such as the city "Yala-Jala," which was part of the Malay Kingdom of Pattani; the Pattani vassal of the kingdom of Ayutthaya of the Pattani sultanate, which ended in 1767; and Narathiwat, a town in the southern region of Thailand, known as a city in the southern region of Thailand, which was also part of the Malay kingdom of Pattani; Songkhla is also a city southern of the Songkhla province of Thailand, having one of the most important port of the eastern Malaysia Peninsular, and made famous on December 7, 1941, by the surprising air attack, launched by the Japanese Imperial Army to start their campaign in Malaysia.

The Javanese country, Indonesia was known as the Dutch East Indies; all these islands speak languages belonging to the linguistic group called "Malay." Two million years ago, that country was populated since the Java man, the fossils of *Homo erectus* were found there; and a supposed species of hominid, the Flores man, was also found on the island of Flores, today no longer existing. *Homo floresiensis*, discovered in the Liang Bua cave in 2003, was small (between 1 and 1.10 meters) and died more than fifty thousand years ago. This new human species that would have coexisted with *Homo sapiens* on the island of Flores for tens of thousands of years disappeared soon after the arrival of *Homo sapiens* that colonized the entire planet in the region.

From seventy thousand to forty thousand years before the present Indonesian archipelago in the Asian continent called Vietnamese: Phu Nam, a name given by the Chinese annals to that ancient kingdom, was a crossing passage of migration. As maritime crossroads of the kingdom of Funan, located in the south of the current Vietnam, Indonesia was part of a port states network between India and China in the first century of our era. Since ancient times, the clove, originally from Indonesia's Northern Maluku archipelago, was first brought in India and then sent to the Middle East by traders from the Indonesian archipelago.

The Clove is mentioned around 200 BC by the time of the Indian Ramayana, as the native spice of the Maluku or Moluccas Islands in Indonesia;" and 206 BC to AD 220, the Chinese Han dynasty was already using cloves. The Indonesian history was fundamentally shaped by trade since the seventh century era. From the eighth century, the Javanese already mastered the technique of rice agriculture at the Central Java, and the ideal conditions allowed the development of prosperous rice crop.

The Buddhist Sailendra dynasty, which reigned over a part of Central Java until the end of the ninth century, and the Hindu Sanjaya of the first kingdom of Mataram, known as the rulers the center of the island of Java, in the "Indonesian classical period," built major monumental temples: an important Buddhist temple of Borobudur; a shrine dedicated to Buddha, built in the eighth and ninth centuries and abandoned around the year 1100; a set of 240 Saivite temples; a shrine dedicated to Shiva, representing Brahma, Ganesh, Shiva, Vishnu, etc., as divinities; and scenes of battles between good and evil inside the temple, built in the ninth century. In the same period, probably in the thirteenth century, important figures of the Hindu Buddhist kingdom and the Hindu of Majapahit and the princes of the north of Sumatra began to convert to Islam up to the fourteenth century by Muslim traders from India, China, and Persia. These important figures of the Buddhist and Hindu kingdom, members of the royal family, wanted to integrate into the commercial network, first in the Indian Muslim kingdoms and then the Chinese and Persian, to make the trade prosper within their archipelago.

The conquest of the kingdom of Mataram began in the late sixteenth century and forced these coastal Muslim port cities to destroy their fleet, and the new the center leader of the island of Java, who proclaimed the heir of Majapahit, banned the maritime trade. A court culture under one of the two states of central Java Island, the Mataram kingdom from the eighth to the eleventh century, which dominated the territory at different times, had models that continued to be represented by the great Indian epics of Mahabharata and of Ramayana. But in Blambangan, an ancient principality of the eastern part of Java, the vassal of Bali escaped the control of Mataram. Thus, in 1770, the Dutch forced their Hindu princes to convert to Islam by fear of subtracting the East Java from the Balinese influence.

The conquest of the coastal regions of the island and the east of the Detroit of Malacca began in the seventeenth century under the reign of the sultanate of Iskandar Muda in Aceh, a kingdom located at the northern tip of Sumatra and West Sumatra. And all the rulers of the reign of Sultan Hasanuddin in the kingdom of Gowa, who reigned from 1653 to 1669 and already converted to Islam in 1605, submitted other important kingdoms—such as the kingdom of Bugis, the Bone kingdom, the Makassar kingdom, the Tallo kingdom, and so on, known as the oldest principalities of South Sulawesi, dating back to the thirteenth century AD—to also convert one after another to Islam. The European conquest began in 1510 by the Portuguese in Goa, India.

In 1511, they conquered the east of Malacca, beyond Indonesia, and allowed Francisco Serrao—the Portuguese explorer of the great discovery periods, who headed west to set foot on the spices islands of the Moluccas—to monopolize the sources of cloves, cubeb, and nutmeg. The lord of Ternate, the sultan Bayan Sirrullah, with whom he formed a binding agreement, became his private advisor. Seeing the expansion of the Muslim kingdom of Demak, Francisco Serrao rushed to sign a treaty, the Luso-Sundanese Treaty of Kalapa, on August 21, 1522, between the Portuguese from Malacca and the Hindu Kingdom of Pajajaran Sundanese to control the production and the trade in spices. And to establish trading posts, they made alliances with the Moluccan princes. The capture of their fort by a prince of Banten, in 1527, would end the Portuguese presence in Java. By a victorious act, the prince of Banten renamed the city as "Jayakarta." Because of disturbances in their colony, they were excluded from Ternate by the natives in 1575. The Dutch adventure in Indonesia began with the entrance of the flotilla of the Dutch explorer Cornelis de Houtman in Sumatra and Banten. It was at that time that this first meeting highlighted the Eurocentric vision of the expeditions and qualified as the sources of discomfort in Indonesia, and the Javanese hardly dared mention that the Dutch East India Company (VOC) received the monopoly of the Dutch parliament by giving it the right of the commercial and colonial activities in Indonesia in 1602. In reverse, taking the Hispanic power on the Asian side of Philip II of Spain, thus the Portuguese Ambon, the North Maluku, and the Banda Islands were expelled by the Dutch from 1605, leaving some cultural influence in language and arts to Malukus, remaining established in the East Timor, where they stayed for nearly four centuries. The west of Java, the city of Jayakarta, was conquered by the Dutch East India Company in 1619, and the city of Batavia (now Jakarta) was founded.

Unlike the Portuguese, the Dutch East India Company delivered a bloody battle to the sultanate of Banten and the sultanate of Mataram, divided them into small kingdoms, and managed to take control of Javanese politics and the spices trade in the archipelago, and settled in the country, which became one of the richest Dutch colonial possessions in the world permanently. After the death of Sultan Agung, in the second half of the seventeenth century, Mataram began its decline and had to cede its territories little by little to the Dutch, who undermined them by the succession of wars financed against the rebel princes and the Mataram kings for the control of the east of the archipelago until the defeat of Gowa in 1664.

The Dutch East India Company, which took advantage, now was controlling all the northern coast of Java in the late eighteenth century, followed by the dissolution of the company by bankruptcy in 1800. After the dissolution of the Dutch East India Company and to reform the colonial administration, the Dutch parliament appointed Herman Willem Daendels, born on October 21, 1762, in Hattem, as governor-general of the Dutch East Indies, appointed by King Louis Bonaparte of the Netherlands, from January 1, 1808, to 1811. Louis Bonaparte, French prince and one of Napoleon's brothers and father of Napoleon III, was born on September 2, 1778 in Ajaccio.

The control of territories, claimed at the south of Singapore, was attributed to the Dutch in 1824, after a London treaty that divided the Malay world in two—the Anglo-Dutch Treaty between the kingdom of the Netherlands and the United Kingdom in London. After the fatal fall of Napoleon Bonaparte on April 3, 1814, Herman Willem Daendels was sent by the Dutch government in Ghana to resume control in those counters occupied by the English under the Dutch Empire.

He died on May 2, 1818, in St. George in the Dutch Gold Coast of Elmina (the current Ghana). Louis Bonaparte, in Dutch Lodewijk Napoleon, king of the Netherlands from 1806 to 1810, died on July 25, 1846, in Livorno (Tuscany) in an old European state, which existed between 1569 and 1801 and then between 1815 and 1859 in the current territory of Italy.

Again, the colonial government found itself taken into the Java War with a part of the Javanese aristocracy. This war, led by Prince Diponegoro between 1825 and 1830, was directed against the occupation of their territories until his arrest. And it was at that moment that they put up a system of forced agriculture in place. Therefore, forced to work in that system oriented toward the production of crops for commercial value to the Dutch government, Indonesian farmers greatly enriched the Netherlands. In 1870, it was abolished for them to appoint the ethics policy, including minor reforms of the education of indigenous people, in 1901.

The slave traders of various Mizrahite origins, descending from the Jewish communities of the Middle East, including the Jewish refugees from Arab countries, the Bukhara Jews, the Caucasus Jews, the Jews of Georgia, the Jews of India, the Jews of Iran, the Jews of Kurdistan, and the Jews of Yemen; the Assembly of the East known as the "Edot HaMizra'h-Bene HaMizrah," designating "Mashriqiyyun" in Arab, and Mizrahi Jews, Mizrahim (Hebrew), are also referred to as "Sons of the East" by opposition to the residents of North Africa (Maghrabiyyun), are originally inhabitants of Iraq, Syria, and other countries of Asia. This term refers collectively to the identification of their country of origin and their immediate ancestors. All these Jews of Iraq, Kurdish Jews, Tunisian Jews, Oriental Jews, etc., going from the Caucasus Mountains via Egypt and Yemen up to the borders of India lost their origin and are roaming for a very long time in other territories in search of a bed. However, long before the arrival of the Sephardim in 1492, there were local Jewish communities in the Middle East. Because of the confusing discrimination in their religious practice, their spiritual leaders take discriminatory positions and put forward statements sometimes very astonishing and very controversial, considering their Sephardic ultra-Orthodox education system; even as there are only about a quarter of the Sephardic Jews of Israel, traditionally attached to the religious practice of Judaism. The example of Rabbi Ovadia Yosef, born on September 24, 1920, in Baghdad, Iraq, gave goose bumps. The former Sephardic chief rabbi of Iraqi descent, first began by qualifying David Ben-Gurion—born in the Russian Empire in Płońsk, nowadays Poland, on October 16, 1886—as a "demon" in 1993; the great renowned spiritual leader continuously considered that the goyim, designating the non-Jew nations, had a place in this world to only serve the people of Israel in October 2010. Referring to the plural of the word *goy*, first quoted in the Bible in Gen. 10:5, it was also used to refer to Israel in Gen. 12:2, when God promised Abraham to make his descendants a "great people of goy gadol." And in Ex. 19:6, Israel became a holy nation of goy kadosh. For the Gentiles, that word means the members of other nations surrounding the land of Israel; he added that they could all die, but may God grant them a long life to serve the Jewish people.

Rabbi Ovadia Yosef did not stop to astonish the world by his statements; he continued by calling for the "annihilation" of Arabs, saying the Lord would return actions against the Arabs themselves, drain their seed, and exterminate them, in his statement made on April 2001. Afterward, he declared that Jews should pray for the destruction of Iran in August 2012 and called for the death of Mahmoud Abbas, the president of the Palestinians.

According to Shas, only the state of Israel should exist and not the establishment of a secular state, and he was opposed to the establishment of a Palestinian state. He watched over the state of the Jewish people in its legislation and said the state should retain its Jewishness in all its decisions, be endowed with a Jewish soul, and respect the Jewish identity. These remarks were denounced by the Anti-Defamation League, modeled from the Masonic organizations to found the Independent Order of B'nai B'rith, an old Jewish organization founded on October 13, 1843, in New York, whose primary purpose was to support the Jews against all forms of anti-Semitism and discrimination. Later on, his words caused several controversies and forced the Palestinian Authority to respond by asking international organizations to consider this rabbi as a war criminal. So even his own community denied him at the end and asked for his resignation. Campaigning still on his decision of supporting slavery and the extermination of other nations, Ovadia Yosef, a Sephardic Israeli and religious rabbinic decision maker, died on October 7, 2013, in Jerusalem, Israel.

These slave qualifications of other non-Jewish nations by the Jewish people caused their expulsion, signed on March 31, 1492, from Spain by the decree of the Catholic kings of Granada at Alhambra; and on December 5, 1496, whether long-established Jewish refugees or newcomers in Spain, were again expelled by

Manuel I from Portugal. The Black Code also expelled them from the French West Indies in 1685 with these words: "All our officers must hunt all Jews, who have established their residence in our said islands; we must make them leave our territories."

Ben-Gurion, meaning "son of the lion" in Hebrew, whom Rabbi Ovadia Yosef was describing as a demon, was a Zionist politician who founded the state of Israel and served as the first minister of Israel from 1948 to 1953 and from 1955 to 1963. He led the implementation of all Jewish people who migrated in Judea, hence the name of the tribe of Judah. Jews were present in Palestine since the Ottoman Empire before 1880; and from the year 1881, the mass of Aliyah farmers of Jewish people arrived in the Palestinian land, mainly from Eastern Europe and Yemen, through the Zionist project before the creation of the state of Israel. Mostly, they were living in Acre, a city in Israel, located north of Haifa Bay, a coastal city of Israel on the banks of the Mediterranean Sea; in Jaffa, one of the oldest ports in the world on the eastern coast of the Mediterranean Sea; in Jerusalem, a city made capital of the state of Israel in 1967 but not recognized by much of the international community, which still considered East Jerusalem as an occupied part. Normally, in 1988, Palestine proclaimed Jerusalem as its capital, even as its authorities did not lay siege there; they were also found in Hebron, a Palestinian city in the West Bank. Since the acquisition of a cave by Abraham, the city was considered by the three great monotheistic religions as a holy city, and it was in that cave that the Tomb of Patriarchs was currently built. They lived in Nablus, a major city in the West Bank, with the Palestinians, its principal inhabitants. They lived in Peki'in; in Safed, a city in northern Israel located in Upper Galilee; and in Shefa-'Amr, an Israeli town populated by Arab, Druze, and half of the Christian religion. They lived in Tiberias, the ancient capital of Galilee and in Gaza until 1779; Gaza was the largest city of the Palestinian Authority. These Jews were all ultraorthodox religious. David Ben-Gurion died on December 1, 1973, in Sde Boker (Israel).

The slave traders of various Radhanite origins of the High Middle Ages were Jewish merchants who were covering routes mostly of North Africa, Central Asia, China, Europe, India, and the Middle East. Primarily in the ninth century, they were trading luxury goods between traders of Christian and Muslim worlds. We got this information regarding the Radhanite traders from the text of Abu'l-Qasim ibn Ubaid Allah Khordadbeh, a bureaucrat and Muslim geographer born in Persia in the northern present Iran and who lived in the ninth century around 820 to 885. His book *The Book of Roads and Kingdoms* described the trade routes and people of the Islamic civilization of that period and narrates regions such as Korea, China, and Japan. Written around 870, it was one of the only sources describing the activity and the existence of the Radhanite Jewish merchants and judging the people of Western Europe as barbaric, where the practice of castration was installed in the ancient times by Greeks and Romans as a source of eunuch male and female slaves and in other parts of the world; it was a traditional punishment and a way to get a job in the imperial service in ancient China at the Sui dynasty up to the end of the Ming dynasty; and a similar system existed in Korea, India, and Vietnam in certain periods. The obligation of this practice was justified by high-ranking officials to retain power since eunuchs could not be tempted to take the power to found a dynasty because they could not procreate.

Also, the Radhanite Jewish merchants were not only selling male slaves, females, and children but also old Chinese brocades, a raised silk fabric of brocaded designs with gold and silver, dating from the beginning of the Christian era; beaver pelts, the largest indigenous aquatic rodent in Eurasia and in the Northern Hemisphere; glue, sable, a small carnivorous mammal of the weasel family, traditionally hunted for its remarkable fur in China, Korea, Finland, Japan, Mongolia, Poland, and Russia; and a sharp white double-edged sword, distinguished from the saber, known from the ancient or middle bronze age, since the Bronze Age, in the first half of the second millennium BC.

The slave traders of various Persian and the Western Persian origins are people sharing a culture and a common history, speaking the Persian language in territories such as Afghanistan (sixteen million speakers), Bahrain minority (Iranian speaking), in Iran (with over seventy-nine million speakers), Uzbekistan (Tajik minority), and Tajikistan (seven million). Apart from Iran, Afghanistan, etc., there are large populations of Persians in Germany, in Canada, in the United States, in the United Arab Emirates, and in Sweden. It should be mentioned that the largest communities of Persians concentrations are in the United States and that they belonged to the Indo-Iranian group of the Indo-European languages, with over one hundred million speakers.

Historically, the origin of the Persian tribe at the southwestern part of Iran, in the present province of Fars, appeared around 550 BC. Iran was the country called Persia until 1935 in the Western world. It was between 2000 and 1500 BC that the Indo-European conquerors of this tribe of the Aryan family arrived in the territory of Greater Iran. But today, in the ethnic sense, Persian is no more precisely distinguished. Therefore, the native language of Armenians, Baluchis, Kurds, and Turkmens is not Persian; and the modern citizens of Iran do not all necessarily have an identity or Persian culture. In the late antiquity, these Oriental trades became mainly Arabs, covering the entire terrestrial surface of the African continent of the historic ancient sub-Saharan kingdoms, counting fifty-four sovereign states nowadays, excluding the Republic of Somaliland, whose constitution of April 30, 2000, is not recognized by the international community and that declared independence in 1991, and the Sahrawi Arab Republic, which the Polisario Front is claiming sovereignty since February 27, 1976.

This territory of Western Sahara is also claimed by Morocco, but the UN does not recognize the sovereignty of Morocco or the Polisario Front because its decolonization is not complete. However, since 1982, the African Union considers the Sahrawi Arab Republic as an African member state in its whole right since 80 percent of the territory of Western Sahara is controlled by Morocco. On the other hand, it was the Arab slave traders which started to designate the inhabitants of the regions of Mozambique going up to the cape of South Africa as an abid, meaning black slave. These groups of Nguni people of Southern Africa—who migrated from Egypt to the Great Lakes as part of the largest group of the Bantu of eastern and Southern Africa; including the Zulu and the Xhosa, "nonconverted to Islam"—were known by the pejorative connotations that the Arab racists addressed in their respect.

The slave traders of the Arab slave trade, the main subset of the Eastern trade, were not exclusively Arab or Muslim; they were Berber, Chinese, Indian, Javanese, Mizrahi Jew, Malay, and Persian. This trade named the Arab slave trade from the Western point of view was associated since the early days of Islam, to the Muslim conquest on the European continent and was described as barbaric by their raids on the shores of the coastal villages surrounding European shores. It stretched from Morocco in Africa and Spain in Europe to India, a country of southern Asia, and China, a country of East Asia, thus encompassing three continents, where they fed the Muslim world at its peak with black slaves, when the northern part of Africa was dominated from the eighth century by the Arabs. It started since the Middle Ages and was more spread out over time in the western region of the present Saudi Arabia, including provinces like Al Bahah, a small province in the southwest near the Red Sea; Jeddah, the second-largest city of Saudi Arabia on the banks of the Red Sea; Medina, the capital of the province of Medina, located in the Hejaz; Mecca, a western Saudi city, the capital of the region of Makkah, eighty kilometers from the Red Sea; and Tabuk in the northwest on the Red Sea border with Jordan, up to the early twentieth century.

Even by the remoteness of East Africa and the hostility of the local population, the Dutch were still able to buy slaves from the Muslim traders of Madagascar, whom the VOC deported to the Cape Colony or to Indonesia.

In the Indian Ocean, slave reservoirs for trade attracted slave traders in Kilwa Kivinje during the Omani occupation. Kilwa Kivinje changed its north-south medieval trade route of navigation, which was completely dominated by the Indian Ocean until the eighteenth century, for a new west-east trade lane orientation between the interior of the African continent and the islands of Zanzibar up to Mozambique; for the good geographical location of the old town of Kilwa Kivinje, we place it at twenty-five kilometers north of Masoko, a capital of the Kilwa district in the Lindi region in Southeast Tanzania; Tanzania is to the south; Kilwa Kivinje and Quelimane are towns originally known as Swahili trade center; Quelimane, founded by the Muslim traders was a port city in Mozambique that evolved as a slave market and was one of the oldest towns in the region, on the eastern coast of the Indian Ocean and the island of Zanzibar toward Madagascar, the Bourbon Islands—"Reunion" and Mauritius in the nineteenth century; and toward Muscat, the capital of Oman, and the Persian Gulf to the northeast, fed the eastern trade by slave caravans.

The sultanate of Oman—bordered by the United Arab Emirates at the north, Saudi Arabia at the west and Yemen at the southwest—is a Middle Eastern country. Oman became the center of true colonial empire in the early nineteenth century and extended the trade from Zanzibar to Baluchistan, a region of Asia shared between Iran to the west, Afghanistan to the north, and the Pakistani province at the east. It must be said that the Arabs who colonized Spain for nearly eight hundred years and at the same time were stopped at Poitiers by Charles Martel, attempting to colonize France in the year 732, did not need the Europeans, especially to use blacks as slaves and to Islamize them in the year 700.

The conquest and the permanent occupation of the Fezzan territory—a deserted region of the modern Libya and Ifriqya, corresponding nowadays to the territories of Tunisia, Algeria, and Libya—were in the Middle Ages the provinces of the Roman Africa at the time of the Muslim Arabs' arrival.

Let us note that Libya was the largest slave distribution center for Muslim slavers. These territories under the name of Ifriqya, which Gen. Oqba Ibn Nafi Al-Fihri, assured the occupation, awarded by the Umayyad Caliph, entrusting him the government in 663, despite numerous resistance opposed to them by the populations of indigenous Christian Berbers, Jewish or pagan of Koceila, Kahena, and Nubia kingdoms, were Christianized since the sixth century; Arabization and Islamization of the Maghreb and throughout the Mediterranean basin were spread rapidly by the Arabs, who conquered North Africa, long occupied by the Berbers.

Gradually, over the development, people of sub-Saharan Africa, who were settled in the areas of the savanna according to geographical criteria, gave birth to the well-organized chiefdoms and to powerful empires of illustrious kings with the democratic vocation for the expansion of state-structured nations. The conversion was done either by constraint to the people who did not want to convert or by peaceful or voluntary conviction. Those who agreed to convert peacefully and voluntarily escaped double taxation and were not taken into slavery. Those who did not want at all to be converted chose to leave the country permanently, besieged by Arab warriors, and went to the South, East, and Central Africa and in nonbesieged and non-Islamized countries for those who wished to remain animists. Moreover, they had no choice but convert to Islam or die by multiple military conquests that the Arabs warriors were leading, justified by the jihad, toward the north and south for its expansion in the eleventh century. Their conquests of Islamization were issues of bloody massacres, expeditions, and manhunts punctuated by wealth looting, accustomed thieves often causing enough damages, and exercised unprecedented cruelty without pity almost throughout the African continent.

In the West African imperial period, marking the three great empires, the empire of Ghana was the first most powerful and the richest political entity at the south of the Sahara, which existed around 300 to 1240 and reached its peak in the tenth century. Designated by its inhabitants as the empire of Ouagadou, it included the regions of Mali and Mauritania and extended to the provinces of Diarra, Mande, Sosso, and Tekrur and comprised the regions of Bambouk, Boure, and Oualata as regions that contained gold and was annexing the neuralgic center under the name of Aoudaghost, which is today found at the southeast of

Mauritania—a shopping center of trade between the north and south, known in the Middle Ages as the great important city of the Berbers, founded in 990.

The empire of the Ghanaian sovereignty was extended up to the Atlantic in the eleventh century, and by the conquest of Wad Draa, the non-Islamized Berbers who lived there saw the destruction of Aoudaghost, which became an important commercial step within the Ghanaian Empire on the trans-Saharan road, and the invasion of Sijilmassa, the former important commercial city in the Middle Ages, dominated in 1055; trade between Egypt and the Ghanaian Empire took a direct route across the desert at a time, but this route was abandoned because of the harsh conditions; instead, caravans passed through the Maghreb to Sijilmassa and then headed south across the Sahara; in 1352–1353, Ibn Battuta, the Moroccan traveler who stayed in Sijilmassa, wrote this: "I reached the city of Sijilmassa, a very beautiful city. It has abundant dates of good quality. The city of al-Basra is like it, in the abundance of dates, but those of Sijilmassa are superior;" these words were qualifying Sijilmassa during his passage there, when he visited the Malian Empire; when comparing the city of Quanzhou in China to Sijilmassa, Ibn Battuta was also describing it by these words: "In this city, as in all cities in China, men have orchards and fields and their houses in the middle, as they're in Siljimassa in our country. This is why their cities are so big."

In the early sixteenth century, Leo Africanus revealed these facts to us concerning the destruction of the city of Sijilmassa, during his journey in Morocco; according to him, the "most imposing and highest walls" were apparently still standing. He described the city as "gallantly built," where water wheels that drew water out of the river Ziz, and many majestic temples and colleges could be found. Leo Africanus says that Sijilmassa was destroyed when its last prince was assassinated by the citizens, and its former residents had moved into outlying villages and castles; and some of its populace spread across the countryside.

This medieval Moroccan city known as Sijilmassa and as a trade entrepot, located at the northern edge of the Sahara Desert, is today known as Rissani in southeastern Morocco. In the trans-Saharan trade, the Sudanese gold played a leading role in the world monetary history, suffering from a frenetic hunger for the yellow metal; therefore, Sijilmassa was a true link between three worlds known as the black Africa—the region of Africa to the south of the Sahara Desert, sub-Saharan; the Maghreb, the region of northern Africa that consists primarily of Morocco, Algeria, Tunisia, Libya, and Mauritania; and, finally, the European continent, before the discovery of America. Sijilmassa comprised the current countries between Senegal and Sudan and a station for large caravans connecting the Sahelian Africa, the land of blacks to the Arab merchants, the Jewish communities of the Middle East, North Africa, or Spain and Portugal; this ancient Maghreb city is today attesting its existence only by ruins. Historically, this town was marked by several successive invasions by Berber dynasties. These merchants were coming to look for slaves, ivory, ostrich feathers, and gold dust. In this important center of Zenata, Berbers, the founders of several Berber states in North Africa and Europe, formed one of the three major Berber groups with Isenhadjen and Imasmouden.

The influence of Islam was not particularly quickly felt in the Ghana Empire, where elite of Islamized politicians, created around a king, remained animist like his population but surrounded by predominantly Muslim traders.

This empire, known by the export of gold and salt, became known in Arabia and Europe in the eighth century; it passed successively under the Almoravid domination from the eleventh century and then under the one of Sosso and, finally, under the Malian Empire.

Toward 1062 to 1071, Youssef Ibn Tachfin, the head of the Almoravid Berber Empire, founded the city of Marrakech. In 1075, they took the city of Fes in central Morocco and in 1080, the city of Tlemcen in the northwest of Algeria. After they were established in the north, the Islamized Berbers of the Almoravid dynasty continued the conquest of the continent and seized Kumbi Saleh, the capital of the Ghana Empire, and converted the king of Ghana to Islam in 1076, with the assistance of the kingdom of Tekrur.

The African dignitaries, who were forming powerful brotherhoods, were converted by force to the syncretisms of the Christianity doctrine and Islam, presenting the typical African initiatics, to safeguard their social positions and their traditional knowledge. The liberator of the Mandinka people against the Sosso invaders of the African king Soumaoro Kante, who reigned in the region of Koulikoro (present Mali) in the thirteenth century, was Sundiata Keita, a Mandinka sovereign of the medieval West Africa, born on August 20, 1190, in Niani in the Siguiri region. King Sundiata Keita of the kingdom of Manding in Guinea, who lived from 1190 to his death in 1255, whose parents hardened life by past experiences in a young age, was mithridatized to guard him against poisons; he was executing hunting with address respect and the shooting of arc with displayed varying degrees of competence.

The revolt of the Mandingos against Soumaoro Kante reached him by an emissary while waiting to avenge the massacre of his family for years with impatience. That day, he decided to put an end to the growing and disturbing popularity of King Soumaoro. Then he gathered an army composed of different small kingdoms and formed an army of ten thousand horsemen and a hundred thousand young warriors well organized to fight against the Sosso. He launched attacks and conquered Fouta Djallon, mainly inhabited by Fulani populations, speaking Pulaar in a mountain range located in Guinea Conakry, West Africa. After this victory, Djegue—sister and wife of Soumaoro Kante, married by force—came to tell him a secret, saying, "Only an arrow bearing a white rooster pin could kill the king of Sosso," her husband. At that revelation, Sundiata, his brother, called to magicians attached to his service to do the necessary and succeeded in 1235 at the Battle of Kirina to defeat the army of Soumaoro Kante. The founder of the Mali Empire formed his empire by uniting all kingdoms to become Mansa, meaning "king of kings," and Niani, his hometown, became the capital.

The Manden Charter, proclaimed by the brotherhood of Manding hunters and considered as one of the first declarations of human rights in the world, was abolishing slavery. But despite his tolerance, he captured Koumbi Saleh, the capital of Ghana around 1240, and then took the title of emperor. Then he sent his lieutenants to conquer a region northeast of Senegambia, corresponding approximately to the Senegal River basins named Bambouk, extending up to the western part of Mali. It was at the end of 1236, the day of his enthronement as Emperor of Mali, that the Manden Charter was solemnly proclaimed. Between the twelfth and the nineteenth centuries, that area was one of the main centers of gold production in the history of Mali, which brought so much wealth to various empires and kingdoms and was part of the empire of Ghana. Bambouk was annexed to the Mali Empire at the death of Sundiata Keita in 1255 by his successor son, Oule Mansa or Mansa Ouali Wullen, named red emperor because of his fair complexion from 1255 to 1270.

Sundiata settled leaders of his armies as provincial governors, implanted a solid political and administrative organization, developed the use of gold trade, and presented new cotton crop to traders; and as leader of his armies, he was known for his wisdom. In his empire, he allowed the peaceful coexistence of animism and Islam.

From the seventh century, the kingdom of Tekrur, living by the gold trade, was partly Islamized and massively in the ninth century. This small state in western Africa, found in the Senegal River Valley, was dislocated by the f light of those who did not want Arabization and Islamization. The kingdom of Kanem, established since the eighth century at the north of the present Chad, was Islamized in the ninth century, and in the twelfth century, it became the kingdom of Kanem-Bornu. At the beginning of the seventh century, the Berber and their Songhai Metis, an ancient people of Western Sudan, originating from several Soninke, Malinke, Fulani, Touareg, and Gourmantche crossbreeds, who settled along the banks of the Niger, also f led the progress of Arabization. These people constitute the major ethnic group in Mali and Niger; living mainly from the cultivation of the soil and handicrafts, were anyway Islamized in the ninth century and founded an empire in the fifteenth century, which extended in the current countries of Guinea, Mali, Niger, and Senegal. The Songhai Empire was a leading trade power in the region, which had a significant influence in the late fifteenth century, and toward the late sixteenth century, was destroyed after the Battle of Tondibi against the Moroccans.

The Islamization of sub-Saharan Africa was not a conquest or even colonization but the propagation of the religion by the traders of the Muslim elite to the populations that remained largely animist. From the eighth century, when an Arab used the word *abid*, he specifically referred to a "black." This word, meaning "slave" in Arabic, became synonymous with black, and it also invoked the racial supremacy of Arabs, and which like among whites, was established by a sordid interpretation attached to the descendants of Ham, the father of Canaan, on a narrative of the curse in the Old Testament but forgetting that they have previously bought and sold the whites. And it continued up to the eastern and Southern Africa to about a thousand years later with the Arab contributions that Muslim called al-Zanj (black) in the medieval times and to a lesser extent, Persians by fiercely attacking and applying an inferior consideration to the blacks as predestined to be slaves because of the color of their skin; the word *Zanjet*, or "slave," designated the inhabitants of the coast of black Africa since antiquity, and *kaffir* or *caffer* were Arab pejorative words associated to the word *nigger* in the United States of America, and "Negro" meaning "black" in Spanish; consequently, the word *nigger* could be used by colonial France, and in several languages, including the English language, designating a Negroid phenotype.

The town of Gede on the Kenyan coast of Swahili culture in the south of Malindi from the thirteenth century was housing an important port of which only ruins remain nowadays. Comoros, a former Federal Islamic Republic of the Comoros Islands, located at the north of the Mozambique Channel in the Indian Ocean, populated by Bantus from the African coast in the sixth century, was Islamized from the ninth century.

In the Indian Ocean, an archipelago named Lamu, located near the Somali border on the "North Coast" of Kenya, sees its days flowing, but filled with sad memories related to the slave trade practiced by the Arabs and the Portuguese merchants. Malindi, a Kenyan town known as a port city for foreign powers, inhabited by Swahili since the fourteenth century, first saw its land be dominated by the Arabs in 1414. However, after a caliph of Malindi established diplomatic relations with China, an embassy of the city of Malindi took the famous giraffe that made a strong impression to the Chinese court in 1414. It is in this city of Malindi that the Chinese admiral Zheng He landed, during his two great expeditions conducted on the African coast, from 1417 to 1419 and from 1431 to 1433, establishing several chines on the spot. And then in 1498, by Vasco de Gama, the Portuguese explorer decided to establish a commercial post there in 1499; finally, he decided and took possession of the city in 1520. Mombasa, a port city in southern Kenya on the Indian Ocean, and the only rival of the city of Malindi, had a foundation that dates back to around AD 900. Historically highly coveted for its strategic position on the sea route to India, this coastal island was very busy for nearly five hundred years because of the shipments of ivory, gold, and spices. And finally, the islands of Zanzibar, in the Indian Ocean, formed by three main islands (Mafia, Pemba, and Unguja), located opposite the Tanzanian coast and several other small islands; this coastal region of East Africa was named Zanzibar by Arab and Persian sailors, who designated that country as *zang*, "black," and *bar*, "land," thus meaning "the land of the blacks" in the Middle Ages; and by extension, this expression meant blacks since the slavery period. All these people of the coast of East Africa shared a number of strictly urban African values and formed a famous Swahili unit living by prosperous African merchandise trades destined for the local and Oriental markets before any Christian and Muslim culture.

The inland area of the Swahili culture escaped the Islamic influences since Muslims limited their activities to the coastal settlements. From the sixth century BC, in a populated region further south, corresponding to the southwest of the present-day Nigeria, a civilization of ancient Yoruba city was developed around the city of Ife from the ninth century and remained a major artistic center most original of black Africa until the fourteenth century.

It is known that Nigeria already took action to populate their wildlife in their geographical environment nine thousand years before Christ, perhaps even earlier, in the southeast of the country in Okigwe, a city located between Port Harcourt, the capital and largest city connecting Enugu with the sea, and located 243 kilometers (151 miles) north of Port Harcourt, and Maiduguri. Okigwe was the second-largest city of Imo State.

In the fourth millennium BC, its farmers were producing ceramic and microlith; and around the first millennium BC, its settled populations lived on agriculture. In the second century BC, they were already working with iron, and the Nok civilization was the first known civilization that emerged in the northeast of the country about one thousand years before Christ on the Jos Plateau. It mysteriously was extinct at the end of the first BC, and in sub-Saharan Africa, it was considered as the oldest producer of terra-cotta.

The Edo kingdom of Benin was one of the few major kingdoms that reached the apogee of its kingdom founded in the thirteenth century before any contact with Europeans and outside the influence of Islam.

Hausa kingdoms were kingdoms of the north occupying these territories since the eleventh century before our era. The Hausa are a people of the Sahel established in northern Cameroon and Nigeria in the north of Benin and Ghana and the south of Niger up to Lake Chad. They're scattered across West Africa in small communities on the road of the Muslim pilgrimage of Hajj, through Chad and Sudan, grouped in seven states: Biram, Daura, Katsina, Zaria, Kano, Rano, and Gobir. Their children, the seven sons of Bayajidda, opposed to the seven sons that their father got from slavery on the Bagwariya River, founded in turn the seven states of Kebbi, Zamfara, Gwari, Yauri, Borgu, Gurma, and Yoruba at the southwest. They're qualified as Banza, meaning "bastards" in English according to legend.

The medieval Ibo kingdom of Nri, from (948 to 1911) was a powerful imperial siege controlling territories at the east of the country by the Igbo of Awka and Onitsha; at the south by Efik, Ibibio, Igala, and the Ijaw; at the north by the Nsukka; and at the west by the Asaba and Anioma. To influence these territories, the kingdom did not use any military conquest but influenced its inhabitants by religious propagation to control trade routes.

The Nupe people established in the west central Nigeria and Yoruba kingdoms, a large ethnic group of Nigeria, were present on the right bank of the river Niger but also in Benin, Togo, Ghana, and Ivory Coast, where they were called Anango. Very early in the history of this ancient kingdom, founded in the fifteenth century by the Yoruba, the Oyo Empire—quite different from other people of black Africa—developed an urban civilization with dozens of flourishing cities of several Yoruba towns, limited at the west by the kingdom of Dahomey, at the north by the Nupe, and at the east by the river Niger.

Its heavy tribute paid to the slave trade was the result of the scattering of the people overseas—for example, in Cuba, Brazil, and the United States. All these territories corresponded to the current Nigeria territories divided into several states from 900 to 1500. During the dehydration by climatic conditions, aiming to remove as much water as possible from the Sahara on the third millennium BC; the prehistoric inhabitants between the forest boundaries and the desert began to widely disperse, and the organized communities in the north of the country covered by savanna began to seek a source of emergence.

It was the birth of the trans-Saharan trade routes; since the earliest times, they connected the western Sudan to the Mediterranean, since the time of Carthage, and the upper Nile. And Islam spread from the ninth century by these same routes in West Africa. The trans-Saharan trade control was assumed by the Songhai Empire. Timbuktu was monitored from January 20, 1468, by Sonni Ali Ber, who began his reign in 1464, made an empire from the kingdom of Gao, and founded the cities of Djenne and Oualata, newly independent from Mali.

To gain the upper hand over his enemy, he used the finest, smallest, and the most faltering virtue to the point of view moral without malice and married the queen mother of the city of Djenne, assailed by a Songhai army; this siege lasted for seven years, seven months, and seven days, according to legend. After taking back Djenne in 1473, he attached it to his empire to consolidate the three major commercial cities in West Africa under a single authority by transforming the country in conquered provinces. He organized his government in an effective bureaucracy different from the previous empires in the region, instituted standards, and appointed governors to govern them.

In November 1492, returning from yet another successful campaign against the Dogons of the Bandiagara cliff and the kingdom of Gourma, he died, and his son, Sonni Baru, succeeded him and reigned for a few months between the death of his father and his overthrow by General Muhammad Toure in 1493.

Sonni Baru was the last king to lead the kingdom under the Songhai Empire, before being overthrown in 1493 by General Toure, who took the name of Askia Muhammad. From 1493, Askia Muhammad founded the dynasty of Askia, native of Tekrur; led the Songhai Empire; changed its name; gave birth to a new dynasty, the empire of Tekrur, which was the first Islamized region of Senegal; and built Gao, the capital of the Songhai Empire. Askia Muhammad gave Djenne a prodigious religious cultural center, and the official religion of the Songhai Empire was based on Islam. Their western Sudan policy made cooperation with Muslim merchants, which became the basis of the income of his regime. Djenne was known as the oldest city, which worked iron from the first days of occupation, inhabited since 250 BC. It was among the oldest cities known by its commercial center and played a role of producer in the iron industry, dating back from the one of the Nok culture, and collector of products such as cereals, ivory, kola nuts, and gold, up to the south; hence the Maghreb and Oriental products from the north. And from AD 850, it became a major urban center of the sub-Saharan Africa.

Askia Muhammad Toure, the emperor of Songhai and founder of the Askia dynasty, built mosques in Gao and made a call to the Muslim scientists. Gradually, as Islam spread, the policy in Nigeria and the trans-Saharan Africa before 1500 had no cultural and economic impact. This trade strengthened the economy considerably, and the biggest party in northern Nigeria was paying a tribute throughout the sixteenth century to the Bornu Empire or the Songhai Empire.

From the arrival of Islam in North Africa and in Spain in the eighth century, many Christian slaves captured by the Arabs in the Mediterranean and on its African coasts were feeding the trans-Saharan trade, especially in the Hejaz region, the Arabian Peninsula, and several Muslim states. Black men, women, and children, captured by wars for enslavement were reduced to animals, and multiple raids were literally burning down people's villages and African states. The captured slaves were transported in different areas of Arab countries and were bought through intermediary characters and enriched the Muslim aristocracy and the Jewish merchants. Some Arab Muslims were using slaves on construction sites or in salt mines as laborers.

For those who mastered the trade, it brought them great profits; and through the slave trade, several cities were enriched and prospered in such a way that the sultan of Oman, who grasped the economic interest of the Arab slave trade, transferred his capital in Zanzibar to better transit thousands of slaves in Arabia to force them to work in plantations. And as the possession of slaves was a sign of belonging to a high social and cultural rank, the fortune that the sultan made by the black slave trade, the sultan being considered a high social rank, that fortune is still reflected on his palace today. We all know that the term *harem* derived from the word *haram* of the Islamic religion, designating what was prohibited by the religion. But the Arab Muslims were using the term *harem* to describe the beauty of a woman or simply the concubines, surrounding the place - the residence of an important person, which justified the need of getting women for sexual purposes.

Ibn Khaldun, born on May 27, 1332, in Tunis and considered as a pioneer of modern sociology, was the person who opened the way to pejorative ideas toward blacks because, in his works, historians and Arab geographers were judging him as a recurring racist. So here was what the Arabs qualified as new ideas of modern sociology in the fourteenth century: because of an inferior degree of humanity, Negroes were the only people to really accept slavery without hope to return, closer to the level of the animal. This Arab historian and philosopher died on March 17, 1406, in Cairo. To wipe out the civilization of blacks forever, Arabs invaded North Africa when Africa was still completely black without any mixture around the year 700 with the support of Europeans.

Their goal to wipe out the civilization of blacks forever did not succeed. It is time for Africa to regain the lead for another five thousand years as it was in Egypt. Abyssinia is an existing proof before King Solomon. My color finally revealed the true story, and it is what it is. Trying at all costs to hide this truth is no longer obvious, and it is today unveiled in broad daylight. That era of Arab, European, and American European domination and cruelty is enough.

The true history of the black African people was hidden by Westerners of the nineteenth century. But we all know that the one who wanted to destroy the black people, first murdered their soul, denying their culture and history, and profaning their beliefs and religions, to kill them intellectually, morally, and physically as white did to the black people; denying the African as a moral and cultural being, and by completely exterminating some of his ethnic groups.

But the gaps in the history of Africa, still largely unknown, are gradually being filled by the prodigious discoveries of archaeologists and historians of the last decades; since our history was transmitted by culture, legends, traditions, jewelry and sculptures representing writing, in the absence of written documents.

For subordination and alienation, the complex and conditioning factors that close the eyes of the evidence were used, leading to violence, more violent than the one that led some species to extinction. From this manipulation, the fight we are waging requires our intellectual sagacity.

Some of the prodigious discoveries in the history of Africa are highlighted when Karl Gottlieb Mauch, five years later, after discovering the first gold mines in the Transvaal, discovered the ruins of the Great Zimbabwe National Monument, and was the first white to contemplate them in 1871. Ignorant that it was the greatest human construction in old African south of the Nile Valley, and not believing that this achievement was made by the ancestors of the black local tribes, he considered them to be the remains of the city of Ophir, known for its wealth.

This city of the origin of gold was given to King Solomon by the Queen of Sheba, according to the Bible. But archaeological research has shown that the construction of this monument was of purely African origin, having no connection with Ophir, contradicting Mauch and his contemporaries. Thus, for their hypotheses on the site of the Great Zimbabwe, archaeologists and modern historians severely criticized the popular ethnocentric paradigm of Mauch and his contemporaries in the nineteenth century.

The German explorer and geologist Karl Gottlieb Mauch was born in Germany on May 7, 1837, in Kernen im Remstal, and died in Germany on April 4, 1875, in Stuttgart. These mysterious ruins, raised in the center of a powerful black kingdom, where the monarchs lived their royal solitude as it suited their royal condition, including their mystery in a fortress, were discovered in the depths of Africa when the world outside Africa was still ignorant of the ancient history of the black people of Africa.

These monarchs embodied the well-being of the people, invested with religious and temporal powers, when the whites who discovered this great stone in the heart of Africa in the first place, were blinded by prejudices; they found fanciful explanations, instead of accepting a possibility of the existence of a truly and exclusively African history, they could not accept the evidence, and spoke only of King Solomon, and the Queen of Sheba, as monarchs of distant rites.

Let's note that racism is a relatively modern evil, since their ancestors who circulated in our kingdoms, were not imbued with any attitude of racial superiority. The whites and the blacks considered themselves an equal digit.

There was no question of qualifying human nature as being at his worst stage, as allusions made later by the Western world toward the black people. In Central Europe, an example of this knowledge of the equality between white and black, which prevailed in the Middle Ages, leads me to quote St. Maurice, including a Venetian illuminated manuscript: "The Passion of Saint-Maurice and his companions (Passio Mauricii and sotiorum ejus in Latin), "is entirely devoted to his legend. The armorial bearings of Cobourg and Saint-Vincent, and on one of the crawling pediments of the Saint-Maurice Cathedral of Vienne (Isere), he is represented as a rider.

In the company of St. Erasmus, one of the fourteen auxiliary saints of the Western tradition, venerated in Central Europe as intercessors, Saint-Maurice appears on an oil on wood of the German painter and hydraulic engineer Matthias Grunewald from (1520-1524) of the Renaissance, contemporary of Albrecht Durer, exhibited at Alte Pinakothek in Munich.

The origin of Saint-Maurice is indicated on a parchment, a banner or a cartouche as of Egyptian origin (Thebae legio, "legion of Thebes", represented dressed as a soldier carrying a shield, a sword, a spear, the palm of martyrdom and the Roman vexillum). From the eleventh century on, he was especially frequently represented in German art, in the guise of a black with woolly hair, camard and lippu," but figured with a western physiognomy in Saint-Maurice and his companions (published between 1475 and 1600, and in several Roman arts depicted as a Roman soldier.

He is also represented as an Egyptian soldier at Magdebourg Cathedral (Dom St. Mauritius), circa 1250. The first German Gothic cathedral on the present site, dedicated to St. Maurice, was founded on September 21, 937 by Otho I, in a Benedictine abbey (Mauritiuskloster). The story of Saint-Maurice, a general at the head of the Theban Legion, is a spectacle both sublime and appalling, lived from a barbarian tyrant Maximian, the Roman emperor who ordered to sacrifice a Roman legion of General Saint-Maurice on September 22, 286, for not wanting to renounce Jesus Christ. Their constancy made them be massacred all en masse in martyrs, devoting their fidelity to the true God.

As a venerated black, who was counted among the five venerated of Central Europe, he is the hero of that story of equality between black and white. The slave trade is therefore the reason for this radical change of attitude among whites, who organized this systematic cruelty for years.

They destroyed kingdoms from the local context since ancient times, like the Kanem-Bornu kingdom of black populations, natives of the northern Chad, originally founded in the eighth century by the Teda dynasty with capital the city of Njimi; the kingdom of Ouaddai, one of the twenty-three regions of Chad, which had Abeche as its capital; or again of Mahdiyah or Mahdist, who attempted unsuccessfully to break British Egyptian rule in Sudan; their political regime, which from 1885 to 1899, ruled Sudan, fed empires market around the Mediterranean, the Middle East, Persia, Rome, the Umayyad Caliphates, the Abbasid dynasty of the Arab Sunni caliphs, who were ruling the Islamic world from 750 to 1258; the Fatimid dynasty of Shiite Ismaili caliphate that between 909 and 969, reigned from Ifriqiya, and an empire encompassing much of North Africa, and a part of the Middle East between 969 and 1171, from Egypt or from the Ottoman Empire; all these empires fed the slave markets with slaves from black Africa.

But we are forgetting the oceanic trafficking in mortality rate, which by no means falls within a triangle of the eastern and the internal slave trades in Africa. The one that was essential transited a major part of the captives of the Atlantic slave trade, connecting Brazil to Africa, and in particular to Angola. We also talked about an archipelago connecting East Africa and the archipelago of Mascarene with the Indian Ocean, formed by three islands of Mauritius, the island of Reunion, the Rodrigues Island and several smaller nearby islands not negligible; and finally, the one connecting Africa to the Caribbean, a subset of the American continent sometimes called the "Mediterranean of the New World," corresponding to the watershed of the Caribbean Sea; and it was in 1920 that the last market of deported African slaves was closed in Morocco.

Even as Europeans never desired to assume and confess their misdeeds, here is what they said about the Amerindians. According to them, some Amerindians were practicing slavery before their arrival in Canada, French Canada and in America in general. Although few people aren't aware, slavery was practiced in French Canada for almost two hundred years, both under the French domination and following the conquest. Obviously, the official history of Canada killed that black episode involving criminal actions and ignoble motives, arousing moral disgust and contempt. And the absence of legal records on the history of slaves in that territory further complicates research. But the discovery of Nigger Rock in Saint-Armand, which is a cemetery of black slaves, brought back the subject into light and requires a little enlightenment.

Documentation of the Historic Centre of St. Armand revealed to us that the number of new slaves from Africa to Canada was increasing from day to day. There were up to forty-four slaves counted from the period of 1700 to 1730 arriving in Quebec. In my opinion, this figure is inaccurate, based on the number of Africans uprooted from Africa and transported by a ship to the New World. It is also said that, in the history of Acadia, slavery seemed to be extremely rare. Yes, but it was difficult to determine the exact number of slaves in those territories because the registration of slaves was made voluntarily by the slavers. This topic, being a difficult problem to admit by slavery supporters of French-Canadian generations and English colonial society, still poses a lot of pain to the passionate hearts of the history of slavery. To expand our knowledge on this issue, let's just say that, more systematically, Canada has intimately hidden the sources and conditions of slavery in its consciousness.

For me, wanting to brave the difficulties of the history of slavery in Canada, without any written documentation of a company engaged in that trade or even a compiled administrative record of slaveholders, is indeed temerity for this enterprise.

Eventually, a very certain and known thing is that whatever darkness settled around the story of slavery in Canada and the province of Quebec, the reasons of slavery remain the same everywhere, where the slave supporters bought slaves as property. But even covered by a thick earth wrongly conquered by these bloody settlers, they still belonged to those who acquired them against their will. And no one can erase that black page of Canadian history and the province of Quebec as being a history that will remain real and will prosecute the life of its generation forever.

Here is the history of the discovery of New France in brief and its illustrious slavery-supporting characters, embarked on the extermination of the indigenous people, known in the history of Quebec and Canada in general.

In 1599, Pierre du Gua, Sieur de Monts—the first colonizer of New France, born around 1560 in the castle of Mons in Royan, the department of Charente-Maritime, the region of Poitou-Charentes in the southwest of France—and his friend Pierre de Chauvin de Tonnetuit – captain of the navy and the French army, and at the same time lieutenant general of New France, born in Dieppe, the department of Seine-Maritime, the region of Haute-Normandie in the northwest of France, before 1575 – he founded the counter of Tadoussac along the St. Lawrence River in 1600. Tadoussac history is known long before the first Europeans' establishment in America. And even though located in the Cote-Nord administrative region in Quebec, Tadoussac history, known as the first permanent French establishment in North America, begins eight years before the founding of Quebec City and the history of Quebec.

Nowadays, the breasts of the two round hills, in the place that the native Innu called "Totouskak," meaning "bosom" located at the west of the village from which the name of Tadoussac derived, is known as a village located in the regional municipality of the county of La Haute-Cote-Nord, the "High Northern Coast" in English, and the administrative region of the North Shore in Quebec. This village of four hundred years is also recognized as the oldest village in Quebec.

Pierre du Gua, one of the founders of this village, was appointed lieutenant general in North America by Henry IV in 1603. And in 1610, he was appointed governor of Pons by the same king, in recognition of his services, and was granted an annual pension of 1,200 crowns. He occupied this post of governor until 1617. In 1628, Pierre du Gua died near Pons, department of Charente-Maritime (Poitou-Charentes), in his castle of Ardennes in Fleac-sur-Seugne at the southwestern France, leaving behind him the town of Tadoussac as a pillar of the colonization history of New France and as the first North American French settlement in the north of Florida. His friend Pierre de Chauvin de Tonnetuit died in February 1603 in a still-existing home, located on Thirty-Five Boulevard Charles V, Honfleur, in a port town of Calvados Department, near the mouth of the Normandy Bridge.

For Quebec, there have been three European figures that turned the first pages of their lifelong history in North America—namely, Jacques Cartier, explorer and navigator who sailed up to the St. Lawrence River on May 10, 1534, during his first trip in the New World; Pierre de Chauvin, Sieur de Tonnetuit (Sir of Tonnetuit) in 1599; and finally, in 1603, Samuel de Champlain.

Jacques Cartier was born in Saint-Malo in 1491 and was the first to reach Newfoundland, a large island of the Atlantic coast of North America and the Gaspesian land, at the east of Quebec in the region of Gaspesia-Magdalen Islands. To claim the region in favor of the king of France; he planted a cross of thirty feet there on a Friday, July 24, 1534.

After getting into contact with the first Amerindian leaders of the Micmac nation on the Chaleur Bay and managing to build trust between sailors and natives, he concluded his trips as successful. Newfoundland was first visited around the year 1000 by the Vikings. Around 1497, the first British colony was established there; and in 1949, it became a Canadian province. On his second trip, he then ascended the course of St. Lawrence, and Jacques Cartier discovered Hochelaga on October 2, 1535. Arrived in this small village on a hill, surrounded by cultivated land and wooden trunks sharpened to a point at the top and buried in the ground, squarely linked against each other, constituting a separation from other spaces, we could see a full cultivated plain of corn. By that beauty, Jacques Cartier named that landscape Mount Royal, Hochelaga. Today, the island and the city that represents a mountain is known under the name of Montreal. The third expedition under the command of Francis I had as aim to establish a colony in search of riches as gold, gems, spices, etc.; for that, men were needed to make them settlers, and criminal prisoners to subdue and exterminate indigenous people were released from their prisons. The expedition of five armed ships therefore embarked livestock and prisoners as future colonists of the New World. After an ominous trip of deadly aim, they finally arrived in August 1541 on the site of Stadacona in an Iroquoian village, known as the present city of Quebec.

The Iroquois formed one of the two largest Amerindian groups, divided in the eastern North America, mostly in the north-northeast and others living further in south. It was these numerous related groups of St. Lawrence Iroquoians that Jacques Cartier met along the St. Lawrence Valley, first in the region of Quebec City in the village of Hochelaga and then in the village of Stadacona. Being in that village, the relationship between Cartier and indigenous people deteriorated, and he decided to go elsewhere to build Fort Charlesbourg-Royal to prepare for colonization and settled at the confluence of the St. Lawrence and the Cap-Rouge River. With the Iroquois of St. Lawrence, Cartier negotiated and accumulated "gold and diamonds" and returned to France to appraise the ore, which did only yield pyrite, a kind of mineral comprising iron disulfide, which may contain traces of Ni, Co, As, Cu, Zn, Ag, Au, Tl, Se, and V, including quartz, mineral species of the group of silicates, subgroup of tectosilicates, composed of silicon dioxide of the formula SiO2 (silica) with traces of elements such as Al, Li, B, Fe, Mg, Ca, Ti, Rb, Na, and OH; therefore very worthless, hence the origins of the expression "fake like diamonds of Canada." After so many exploits, Jacques Cartier died on September 1, 1557. The first French colonial empire consisted of the following territories: Acadia, Canada, Louisiana, the watershed of St. Lawrence River, the Great Lakes, Mississippi, and the Northern Prairie, a large part of the Labrador Peninsula. The rest of New France, which ceased to be attached to Canada in 1718, included more than ten other American states, which are Illinois (somewhat the current American Midwest in United States), a region delimited by the river Mississippi and Ohio Rivers, Ouabache, and Illinois; precisely, these territories located in North America were a viceroy of the French kingdom, which existed from 1534 to 1763, with Quebec as its capital.

On April 13, 1709, in the three urban centers of the French colony in Canada, the Negro slavery and the people named Panis-the first nation slaves became official by an order of the intendant Antoine-Denis Raudot, born in 1679, to revive the economy of New France in agriculture and fisheries, build ships of small caliber for conveying goods, sell these goods in France, and build a new facility on Cape Breton Island, to disrupt the adverse trades in the region. Antoine-Denis Raudot died on July 28, 1737, in Versailles. These ordinances of intendants (E1, S1, P509) of Antoine-Denis Raudot and his father, Jacques Raudot, co-intendant born in 1638, were saying that all blacks formerly purchased would belong in full as properties to slave supporters who bought them as slaves. Jacques Raudot died on February 20, 1728. Another request of Sieur d'Auteuil, requiring an importation of two hundred blacks to the colony of New France, was reiterated by the intendant Michel Begon de la Picardiere in 1720, intendant from 1710 to 1726, ordered with an unjust state of mind to seize the properties and wealth of all people of the colonies, rendering them without resource at the extreme limit of a miser and denying every to the natives to not lack anything. This act was qualified as one of the seven deadly sins defined by Catholicism, described by the church father St. Augustine on the genealogy of sin, yet it was legally supported by the religious communities of slavery officials, and by inhabitants, saying "They were ready to buy blacks, approaching a figure of more than hundred and one slaves from Africa."

Michel Begon VII, born on March 21, 1667, in Blois, established therefore the stinginess as a lack of prodigality of different *onomastismes*, a French word meaning "any word of a proper name" to name misers in Quebec. At that time, this request was transmitted to the East India Company, which had a monopoly of the slave trade, to address the lack of domestics and caring for elderly parents or caring for those who lost autonomy. The hemp cultivation was really favored primarily by the intendant Michel Begon, but we know that, in the early 1670s, Jean Talon, his predecessor, also tried growing hemp. He died on January 18,

1747, in Blois St-Honore, the Picardiere castle. The ordinance of the father and son Raudot, which legalized slavery in 1709, was again published a decade later by the intendant Gilles Hocquart, born in 1694 in Mortagne-au-Perche in Normandy, France. The intendant of New France from 1729 to 1748 died on April 1, 1783 in Paris.

The circumstances of the treaty of the capitulation of Montreal, written in French on September 8, 1760, did not prevent Pierre de Rigaud de Vaudreuil de Cavagnial, the governor-general of New France, to refer to article 47, telling Jeffery Amherst—born on January 29, 1717, in Sevenoaks in England and knighted by King George III—that both sexes of blacks and Panis would remain a possession of the French and Canadians as slaves and that those to whom they belonged would be free to sell or keep their service in the colony.

The major general in the British army and a colonial administrator accepted this proposal by making an exception for those taking prisoners. The first Baron Amherst, holding the highest rank of field marshal in the British army, died on August 3, 1797, in Sevenoaks, England.

These French Canadian border territories comprehended an additional larger number of forced African slave migrants, primarily in Louisiana, in the region engaged in large commercial exchange relations between New France and the French West Indies, where there thousands of black slaves were indeed found. By these revelations, it goes of course without saying that Canada and Quebec change sides accordingly and have the courage to assert the values and pride in their epics, narrating their historical exploits by the swords of massacres with an *onomastisms* spirit, and to commemorate the glory, the honor, and the power of African slaves by a long poem nationwide.

After thirty-one years of existence, the fall of New France was imminent, view its geographical position, which first prevented the gathering of the Thirteen Colonies at the Rupert's Land; the British Empire colonies of North America, which gave birth to the United States of America; as well as the expansion of a territory extending toward the west of Saskatchewan in Quebec, located in the center east, and passing through Nunavut, a federal territory in the north of the present Canada.

This impediment of expansion occasioned many tensions, first on May 28, 1754, with the Battle of Jumonville Glen for the control of the Ohio Valley between the French and English; this one was in the advantage of English.

And then it was followed by the Conquest War or Seven Years' War, which ended by the British victory. With this defeat, Canada and all its dependencies were ceded on September 24, 1760, to the British invasion force in Montreal by Governor Vaudreuil. After three years of negotiations between France and Great Britain, their reconciliation ended the Seven Years' War.

On November 3, 1762, preliminaries were signed at Fontainebleau, where France secretly ceded a major part of Louisiana a year earlier to Spain. And the fall of New France was the final treaty signed in Paris on February 10, 1763. Pierre de Rigaud de Vaudreuil de Cavagnial, as governor of New France, was the only settler born in the colony on November 22, 1698, in Quebec, New France. He was a navy officer before being appointed in 1733 at the post of governor of Trois-Rivières until 1742, and finally, on July 1, 1742, he was appointed governor of Louisiana by the minister of Maurepas navy until 1753. After experiencing numerous lost conflicts, he died on August 4, 1778, in Paris, France.

To designate areas around Stadacona, a St. Lawrence Iroquoian village near present-day Quebec City as well as the river called the Canada River in the sixteenth century, Jacques Cartier borrowed the name Canada, derived from the Iroquois word *kanata,* signifying "earth" or "land" or "village," used by the natives who were living in the present city and the region of Quebec in 1535 to guide the Breton sailor Jacques Cartier toward the village of Stadacona.

This word designated therefore not only that village but also the whole land of Donnacona, generally used by Jacques Cartier. And since then, he was referring to this region by the name of "Canada" from 1545.

At the beginning, it designated a colony of New France, located along the St. Lawrence River and the entire north shore of the Great Lakes, from the fifteenth century to the seventeenth century. Thereafter, the Upper Canada and Lower Canada reunited in a province of Canada used it to designate these two British colonies united in 1841. And when several colonies of British North America were starting the project of uniting to form a country in 1864, the London Conference approved the word *Canada* and federated the three colonies of the British Empire on July 1, 1867, so that, politically, the new monarchy constitutionally federated with the parliamentary system consisting of ten provinces (Alberta, British Columbia, Prince Edward Island, Manitoba, New Brunswick, Nova Scotia, Ontario, Quebec, Saskatchewan, Newfoundland, and Labrador) and three territories (Northwest Territories, Nunavut, and Yukon) bears officially the name Canada as a country. We must finally mention that the village of Stadacona no longer existed when the Samuel de Champlain settled in this village in Quebec City in 1608 because its Iroquois inhabitants were exterminated by even more insidious crimes, and the wealth hunters of France and New France are unpunished to this day. We know that slavery-supporting communities were capturing slaves as in certain societies of Europe antiquity. However, they were first kept as servants; some were handed over to a third person with whom they wanted to cement an alliance and in return received the goods for trade from the counterparty; but a worse serious unpleasant event was still to follow that defective circumstance causing pain, and some were killed after some trouble with the law; very frequently, some slavers were killing slaves to fully satisfy their superiority hunger, their cruel instincts, their thirst for domination, their desire of conquering, or their feeling of revenge. Presumably, the hunting for the history of slavery in French Canada was undertaken through judicial records and parish registers.

As I have already mentioned on the registration of slaves in French Canada, and in general in Canada, and in other parts where slaves were found, the case of the one who was named Matheiu de Costa, of African origin and regarded as the first black slave in the history of slavery in Canada, was not illuminating at all and did not present us any light at the other end of the tunnel, if not that little history of slavery in Canada that Canada presented us concerning his life.

The first black slave, Mathieu da Costa, who left his mark in the history of slavery in French Canada, was a man who learned French, Dutch, and Portuguese from the French, Dutch, and Portuguese explorers—a polyglot who worked as an interpreter for those traders of the European world since their invasion in Africa. Since their first intention was not to capture the blacks and the Portuguese economy was not yet defined by the slave trade but the spices trade, these Europeans traders established a practice to teach their languages to Negroes to assist them as interpreters from the seventeenth century. Enigmatic was his origin, but his name was typical Portuguese, which led me to say that, at that time, Portugal and its navigators who furrowed the African coast as a stopover toward India were still maintaining more or less cordial relations with some African kingdoms. So, it was customary that the Portuguese empire agree to take the son of an African king by diplomatic relations and educate him in Portugal.

One school was even created to specifically educate the children of kings of some African kingdoms in the Portuguese language and culture in Lisbon. We therefore noticed the presence of people of African origin in Portugal by hundreds or even thousands, even when most of them were considered slaves. It was therefore evident that he passed through Portugal before being purchased or voluntarily undertook his interpreter career since he was negotiating his services in return for a sizable sum. His journey will remain a mystery in the history of slavery in New France and Canada. Because before committing himself to Pierre du Gua, he had a contract with the trader Beauquemare, who traveled through the United Provinces of the Netherlands.

In what seemed logical, he started his interpretation services from 1604 up to 1606 for his trips in Acadia and Canada without his purchase agreement with the merchant Beauquemare being fully settled, and that was why he was kidnapped by Hendrick Lonck, captain of the *White Lion* of the United Provinces of the Netherlands, in the Atlantic coast of St. Lawrence in 1607 and took him back to Amsterdam on board the *White Lion*. Being in the company of Dutch, one could say that he learned the language of many aboriginal people of North America because he previously lived in the Dutch colonies of the Americas, like Suriname, formerly Dutch Guyana before independence, located in South America, and the Netherlands Antilles, mainly located in the Caribbean Sea (Bonaire, Curacao, Saba, St. Eustatius, the island of St. Martin and Aruba), especially by this document that certified in February 1607 that he was in the Netherlands. It was after settling the problem of the purchase contract that the French trader Nicolas de Beauquemare retook the interpreter a year later for a sum of £195 in 1608 and brought him back to Acadia in Canada. Since the services of Mathieu da Costa were still interesting to Pierre du Gua, Nicolas de Beauquemare negotiated the purchase of the previous contract with him in 1608, and he gave that previous contract by an intervention of Jean Ralluau, secretary of the head of the mission for the expedition of Monts in 1604, who already moved once to the United Provinces of the Netherlands to buy the contract signed between Beauquemare and Mathieu da Costa to take the interpreter back to La Rochelle, a southwestern city of France.

Like all noble African endowed with a frank spoken and an independent spirit, Mathieu da Costa was not accepting the insolence of the name Negro used against him by the secretary Jean Ralluau and no longer wanted to honor his contract with him; then he let him be imprisoned to force him to honor his commitments. It was therefore when another document of December 1609 attested his imprisonment in Le Havre, France. A century before the time of Champlain, this interpreter practice already existed, whether in Africa or in North America. Also, pidgin being a fusion of European languages and local languages spoken in most African countries and spread along the Atlantic coast, Europeans who were visiting the Americas were frequently using interpreters for their trade with the First Nation people of North America who also spoke pidgin. It was through that asset that Pierre du Gua accepted that previous contract with da Costa, signed on May 26, 1608, in Amsterdam before the notary juror Hercules Falle for a period of three years, and he undertook to sail with him to act as interpreter beside the Mi'kmaq and the Montagnais, living on the north shore of the St. Lawrence River and in Acadia, comprising roughly the north and east of the Canadian province of New Brunswick, the most isolated communities in Prince Edward Island, the Nova Scotia, and the community of Newfoundland and Labrador, increasingly present in that definition, during his travels in Canada.

Although he did not have the condition of a slave, Mathieu da Costa appeared to be the first African to have trodden the Canadian soil 1604, hired by du Gua and accompanied by Samuel de Champlain for his expedition from France to Port Royal, founded in 1605 and the capital of Acadia until 1710. He worked as an interpreter, translating Mi'kmaq into French. However, many Africans who arrived in Canada later were slaves. To believe that slavery only existed in the United States is a widespread idea but erroneous. Canada was perhaps not a slave society like the United States, but it was a society with slaves in large numbers. For Mathieu da Costa, there is only the National Historic Site of Canada at Port-Royal, located in Nova Scotia in Royal Annapolis that honored his coming and the important role that his pluralism played within the Canadian society in Canada; the one that Canada considered to have played a leading role in its history, the one that helped to maintain friendly relations for the advancement of trade and facilitate trade between the French people of New France and aboriginal people in Nova Scotia; the one who is known as a former Portuguese slave of African origin, namely by his importance, animated the evenings of good and bad times in Micmac with poetry and songs, to help build Canada, was Mathieu da Costa. Mathieu da Costa, known for his qualities as a navigator, and his knowledge as an interpreter, sailed and translated with a need of love to help people understand each other, and for them to work together in harmony, died at Port Royal.

The history of New France revealed another arrival to us of what was described as the first slave in its territory, a boy aged about seven years, probably from Guinea or Madagascar, who arrived in New France in 1628 after Quebec was conquered and twenty-four years after the arrival of Mathieu de Costa in New France. So, from 1604 to 1628, there were no slaves in the territory, according to the history of New France, which is very difficult to believe for a nation that was already practicing slavery for centuries. He was the slave of the governor of Newfoundland by the name of Sir David Kirke, the English privateer born around 1597 in Dieppe. Kirke sold the boy to one of the colony clerks named Olivier Le Bailiff; he was the first recorded slave sold in New France. The young slave was again sold to a Quebec resident named Guillaume Couillard de Lespinay, when the French Olivier Le Baillif, at the service of the English, had to leave Quebec. And Guillaume Couillard de Lespinay sold him once again to Fr. Paul Le Jeune. But as the inhabitants of New France wanted to be dissociated from that infamous trafficking, they told themselves that the young slave was a gift to the Jesuit priest. Sir David Kirke died in 1654 near London.

Guillaume Couillard—born on October 11, 1591, in Saint-Servan, a district known today as Saint-Malo (Ille-et-Vilaine) in Brittany, France, knighted by King Louis XIV—was the first French settler of twenty-two years old to immigrate in 1613 in New France. The current premier minister of Quebec, Philippe Couillard de Lespinay, born on June 26, 1957 in Montreal, Quebec, and elected since April 2014, is one of the descendants of many Quebec families of the slavery-supporter ancestor Guillaume Couillard de Lespinay.

After the education of the young slave boy in a school directed by Fr. Paul Le Jeune, the French Jesuit priest and missionary born in July 1591 in Vitry-le-Francois, who arrived in Quebec City on July 5, 1632, died in Paris on August 7, 1664. But earlier before his death, in 1633, the slave boy was baptized in the Catholic faith and received the name of Olivier Le Jeune. Olivier lived in New France until his death on May 10, 1654, at the age of about thirty years.

Kirke is also known to have attacked the town of Quebec that Samuel de Champlain founded on July 3, 1608. And on July 26, 1629, the brothers Thomas Kirke and Lewis Kirke, under the command of David Kirke, sailed up St. Lawrence and took the city of Quebec by the order of the English king Charles I.

New France (Quebec) was giving back to France after the Treaty of Saint-Germain-en-Laye, signed on March 29, 1632, between England and France.

Samuel de Champlain was born between 1567 and 1580 in the former province of Saintonge in Brouage, France. On August 13, 1574, he was baptized in the old province of Aunis at La Rochelle. He remained a local administrator of the city of Quebec until his death on December 25, 1635, at the ancient denomination of Canada as New France in Quebec, nowadays the capital of the Canadian province of Quebec.

Thus, on the island of Cape Breton, three kilometers southwest of a site called "Louisburg" and thirty kilometers southeast of Sydney, in the province of Nova Scotia, we noticed a fortified French town, located in these places because of the contacts of this port with the West Indies. Originally established by two treaties of peace held in the Dutch city of Utrecht on April 11, 1713, Great Britain and the kingdom of France signed the first, and Spain and Great Britain signed the second on July 13 of that year, thus ending the War of the Spanish Succession.

In 1718, the city became the capital of the Royal Island and was captured by a British military force of New England in 1745. Once again, it was a peace treaty of Aachen, gathered in Breda from April 24 to October 18, 1748, in a Dutch city, to end the War of the Austrian Succession. With reference to the conference, a decision was taken for the general restitution of conquests—that is, Louisbourg to the kingdom of France.

Prof. Marcel Trudel—a Canadian historian and researcher on New France and slavery in Canada, born in the northeast of Trois-Rivières in Saint-Narcisse-de-Champlain on May 29, 1917, and died in Longueuil, Monteregie, on January 11, 2011—told us that between the second half of the seventeenth century and 1834, there were 4,185 slaves in Quebec, among whom a quarter was of African origin, who were exploited in urban areas, unlike the slaves of New England exploited in an agricultural context. Yes, but was there any difference since they were all considered as slaves? They were treated not only as their properties but also as machines forced to do hard labor from the time of their capture. They were deprived of their right, the right to move freely or to leave the slavery farms. They could not refuse to work and to seek compensation, and certain slave owners had the legal right to kill them.

Therefore, no slave owner showed the originality or boldness to disqualify this despicable phenomenon, but they continued to own slaves.

In the official history of Canada, this whole episode of the black slave pioneers is not very bright, particularly in Quebec, essentially in modern Nova Scotia. Between 1713 and 1760, the Royal Island in the French colony, from that moment, comprised two islands known as Cape Breton and Prince Edward Island, where black slaves were counted at 90 percent, within the population, and the vast majority was documented. In Montreal, the slaves of African origin were exploited as domestic servants, and those of New France were exploited in urban areas, and some worked in the cultivation of hemp, rice, and tobacco plantations; in the exploitation of skins; and in the production of native plants (indigo) in Quebec for export.

Several members of the Catholic clergy of Mother d'Youville—the first person born in Canada to be canonized, foundress of the Sisters of Charity of Montreal, born Marie-Marguerite Dufrost de Lajemmerais on October 15, 1701—owned slaves, including several religious communities of the Brothers of Charity, an order instituted in 1540 by the founder of the Hospitallers Order of St. John of God, born in Portugal on March 8, 1495, at Montemor-o-Novo. Not even ten years old, his poor parents decided to settle in Spain, more precisely in Oropesa. His order was working for the promotion of justice, for the respect of life, and for the dignity of a person, which put his work, his talent, his time, and his affection to the service of those who were deprived of such properties. It was first established in Spain, Italy, and soon in France and then spread up to Quebec. Joao Cidade, known as his real name, died on March 8, 1550, and in 1690, he was canonized as a Portuguese saint. The Society of Jesus—one of the three most important religious orders of the Catholic Church, founded by Ignatius de Loyola, the first general superior of the order, born in Basque Country on December 24, 1491, in Azpeitia—was approved in 1540 and recognized by Pope Paul III. Ignatius de Loyola, the author of *Spiritual Exercises*, died on July 31, 1556, in Rome.

Another congregation of the Brothers of Charity was of a Belgian priest who spent his life doing good. He was the founder of four different religious congregations and born on August 31, 1760, in Brussels. The priest Pierre Joseph Triest first founded the Sisters of Charity of Jesus and Mary in 1803, followed in 1807 by the Brothers of Charity, and then in 1825 by the Brothers of St. John of God, and finally, in 1835, the Sisters of the Childhood of Jesus.

Because of his relationship with God, he finally understood that the power of the love of God that we give to help others is a love rooted in the divine. To love the poor with all our soul, it is necessary to put four words in the top: the comprehensive cares are the method, service is the way, the joy of resurrection is a prospect, and love is the source. And it's all about love, as divine power to move a special person and conquer his spirit, because its eloquence reached the bottom of hearts. Nothing is stronger than love, thanks to the works of charity in the spirit of faith and our spirit fixed on God; each of us finds himself the true salvation as the source of all things and Divine Providence. Even with these words of the works of the merciful God, all religious representatives possessed and encouraged slavery. The priest Pierre Joseph Triest died on June 24, 1836, in Ghent, Belgium.

The Friars Minor Recollects—Recollect, derived from the word *collected*, in Latin "recollecti"—were members of the Ordo fratrum minorum recollectorum belonging to the religious of strict "observant" tendency of St. Francis; a Catholic religious and founder of the Order of Friars Minor, commonly known as the Franciscan order, resulted from a new policy reform of the order accomplished in Spain in the fifteenth century; it was characterized as the evangelization and respect for creation; the order itself was created in 1209 by Francis of Assisi.

The Sulpicians were from a Catholic society of apostolic life founded in 1641 in Paris by Jean-Jacques Olier de Verneuil; he was the one who established a community of priests and a seminary. It is also good to know that the land of Montreal was granted to Fr. Jean-Jacques Olier by the owner of New France, which was the Company of One Hundred Associates. This handover had as goals to convert the indigenous Indian population into their belief and to provide schools and hospitals for colonists. They trained priests and made Montreal the center of missionary activities in Canada and contributed to the founding of the Canadian city of Montreal.

And the Order of Ursulines was a Catholic religious order founded in November 1535 in Brescia, Lombardy, Italy, by St. Angela Merici, who could not condemn but rather protected slavery. In Quebec, a priest-dean of Saint-Joseph-de-Beauce was saying that black was the evil that sabotaged the established order in this world and was asking God to destroy blacks for there to be social peace. It is surprising to know that these kinds of speeches were coming from a man who was representing God's love in this world.

Slavery in the colonial society of New France was also real. According to reliable sources, a black slave, who was counted as two because she was pregnant and a widow of her husband killed in an attack, was also brought to Quebec in 1745. Another amazing story revealed another possession of a slave named Marie-Josephe Angelique, name given by her last owner. Angelique was born a slave in Madeira, Portugal, in 1715. A certain Nichus Block or Nicolas Bleeker purchased her and brought her to the New World. Before being sold in 1725, she first lived in New England.

She became the property of a certain man named Francois Poulin de Francheville, an important French businessman from Montreal, the province of Quebec in Canada, until his death in 1733, to finally belong to his wife, Teresa de Couagne de Francheville. One of her three children, a boy called Eustace, born on January 11, 1731, died the same year after having lived only one month; and on May 26, 1732, she gave birth to twins, Marie-Francoise and Louis, both deceased also the same year in Montreal after five months. They were children of a black slave of Madagascar by the name of Jacques Caesar. Like their father, they appeared in their baptismal records and were a property of a friend of Francheville by the name of Ignace Gamelin.

Angelique had several times attempted to flee, but afraid to find herself in the Caribbean after being sold and separated from her lover, she tried it no more until the arrival of the salt smuggler Claude Thibault, with whom she wove a passionate relationship. The two led on February 22, 1734, toward the British colonies. But nearly three months later, their f light did not bear fruit, and they were arrested on March 5 and released on April 8, 1734, for her to be handed to her owner and her lover jailed. It was after this escape that a fire, perhaps an action undertaken by neighbors on April 10, 1734, on St. Paul Street, made her jump by shouting for help. "Fire! Fire! Fire!" But that fire, out of control did rage, destroying forty-five or forty-six buildings of the merchant district. She was later captured on April 11, 1734.

After so many interviews, which the first of the six started on April 12 and during which she would deny all statements of the first twelve witnesses, despite her defense to the evidence presented against her, still, the accused denied being the author of that fire. But the judge conducted the conviction and sentenced her to death on June 4. Even the appeal that the prosecutor made at the superior council in Quebec to minimize the sentence and apply another less brutal sentence was rejected. Finally, Angelique was put to questioning, paraded through the city, and tortured in the eyes of everyone until she confessed her crime. Even after helping to save certain properties of the burned houses, she was accused and found guilty of setting the fire that burned much of the city of Montreal, nowadays called Old Montreal.

Public notoriety of the French law, at that time, allowed the community to agree that the suspect was guilty. She was hanged in front of St. Paul Street, and once dead, her body was thrown into the fire to be sure that she was really dead. Finally burned, her ashes were scattered. This kind of treatment, usually known of slavers, of choosing an innocent slave as a scapegoat, without an accredited witness, just for their entertainment showed us the barbaric will manifested by many European people, whether they lost their loved properties or not, not wishing to see the agony of their type of white human species, but wished to see their black scapegoat agonize. Angelique died on June 21, 1734, in Montreal, Quebec. I wondered why France, especially Quebec, denied that slavery was practiced in New France and relied on the words of historians for a national love of shame, who put forward figures that do not collaborate with dates. Some were saying that between 1719 and 1743, there were six thousand slaves from Africa; others pointed out that after 1760, with the arrival of the English regime, the population of black slaves ascended sharply.

Bullshit, I would say; would you not agree? Hello! It is here about the history of the African continent that you're referring to; that you, the slavers of the European continent cruelly organized and orchestrated, and finally distorted by your generations.

Also, between 1730 and 1759, the French were bringing back several black slaves after severe attacks against the English villages as in some societies of European antiquity. Between 1700 and 1759, there were already 323 black slaves in Quebec; that most of the owners were governors, bishops, officers, lords, merchants, etc. I must say that the slave owners of the English regime of British origin owned black slaves in Quebec certainly, but the figures put forward were anyway placing the slave owners as French speaking in majority. Many other black slaves arrived in 1784, with the first loyalist settlers.

The labor that the main companies of New France depended upon was as important for the economy as in other provinces of British North America. But the domination of the royal power, before the signing of the Treaty of Paris on August 28, 1833, finally abolished slavery in Quebec and in all British possessions. But it was only for the official and not unofficial possession. On August 1, 1834, this measure took effect. Despite the official ban, the French planters continued to capture preferably Africans during raids and battles and sent them to the Dominican Republic, in the Caribbean, and even in Canada.

The black community in Nova Scotia is one of the oldest black communities in Canada, concentrated in Halifax; an indigenous population that fled from the United States two centuries ago is still undergoing a form of very subtle racial discrimination; this ancient black community is isolated and forgotten by the Canadian authorities. Thirty thousand African American slaves entered via the secret escape network with the hope of a better life in Canada, but far from the inhuman treatments of whites, they're not so far done with misery up to our present days.

The first black settlers were loyalist slaves confined in the outskirts of white cities and villages. The city is till our present days refusing to recognize their property titles that were promised to anyone who elected a home in the English colonies by the British. Yet the white loyalists received the most fertile land. Their only legacy was Africville, the Nova Scotian black neighborhood in Halifax, which was expropriated, razed, and converted into a park. Today,

Africville is part of the past history that transcends the only black community and still remains a vivid memory of its former residents. It was from 1794 that Nigger Rock, the black slave cemetery at the foot of that big black rock in Saint-Armand that the said cemetery was named after. It is a site up to today not protected, and governments are not involved in the Historical Center of Saint-Armand to prevent undocumented ruins. The Treaty of Paris signed on September 3, 1783, between the representatives of the thirteen American colonies and the British or Great Britain officials, recognizing independence, put an end to the American War of Independence, but Canada was still a British possession. The contribution of black slave pioneers in the history of Canada is almost forgotten. It is forever the only cemetery of dead slaves in servitude known in Quebec; the other provincial court of British Colombia in North America limited slavery through the strictest decisions, obliging property evidences in 1800.

Today in Canada, there are four well-known slave cemeteries, such as Dresden, well known as the home of the former slave Josiah Henson, born into slavery in Charles County, Maryland, on June 15, 1789, and died on May 5, 1883. That illustrious writer, abolitionist, and minister escaped from the United States to Ontario, Canada, in 1830 and founded a colony—a community in southwestern Ontario near Dresden in the county of Kent, the municipality of Chatham-Kent, the terminus of the clandestine railroad at the dawn of the Underground Railroad. A network of routes and secret shelters were used by black slaves in the United States to escape to the Free States and Canada in the nineteenth century, with the help of abolitionists and allies of both blacks and whites sympathetic to the cause.

About 1850 to 100.000 slaves escaped to Mexico or abroad in different routes between 1850 and 1860 by that Underground Railroad created in the nineteenth century, going as far as Priceville, a small village at the southwest of the municipality of Grey Highlands, Grey County, Ontario, Canada, where African Americans set up a small village. Josiah Henson built a church with logs, plus schools in logs for other fugitive slaves, where you could still find a cemetery established by them along Old Durham Road (today known as the Durham Road B) at the east of the village before the development of that city.

The cemetery of Shelburne, a town located in the southwest of Nova Scotia, Canada, and Saint-Armand, a regional municipality in the southern-central of Quebec in Canada, both exists up to our days but are not objects of any official recognition by the Canadian governments. In 1793, it was Ontario in Upper

Canada that first banned the importation of slaves; but as for Quebec, it took time, and we had to wait until August 28, 1833, for slavery to be abolished in New France. So, what do you think about the involvement of Canadians in the slave trade that lasted more than two hundred years in Canada? I think that the misinformation in the history of the slave trade no longer spares doubt of an educated public but that the young Pan-African student and black of other parts of the world receive as teaching is still misinformed by the methods of falsification of the African history in the academia environment.

Faced with this negligence and the repeated falsification of its history by the slavers, their racist children, and the racist bourgeois historians of colonial and neocolonial orientation of our days, the theme still remains very complex for Africanists, not yet having enough materials to proceed to its definitive study, but on the other hand, the lie in its history persists and is accentuated. However, one thing is obvious: the black blood streamed from Niger to Zambezi, from the region of Great Lakes, which became deserted.

At the north of the equator, at the south, at the east, or at the west, a path of corpses, spreading a nagging pain to legs and through the woods, was embracing the air in the open sky, rendering the valley deaf by an inventiveness of barbarous violence, sadistic aggression, torture, assassinations, and mass murder without having to justify themselves.

The scientific council of the quadrennial plan responsible for planning the economy of Nazi Germany, favorable to the extermination of inferior races, used a terrible annihilation ideology with a motivation animated by racism and hatred more sinister than their predecessors, to work for the logic of a continuous system designed for the extermination of so-called inferior beings; during the first decades of the twentieth century, they worked for the extermination of thirty million people in the East, after Adolf Hitler convinced the Germans of the inferiority of the Jews, of Slavs, and other groups; it was a fact that was not revealing any solidarity and a reality without sympathy for the victims. After World War II, the Dutch continued to practice that same ritual of extermination under the pretext of the inferiority of races, also with an animated motivation of racism and hatred of blacks in South Africa, during the first decades of the twentieth century.

The European history of South Africa began in 1488 by Bartolomeu Dias, the Portuguese navigator who reached the Cape of Good Hope, so named because of its storms, and Vasco da Gama, the Portuguese navigator who sailed along the coast of Natal in 1497, followed by the landing of the Dutch in 1652. Because of conflicting relations, the first of the nine Kaffir Wars or border wars began from 1779 to 1878. And the establishment of the Dutch East India Company definitely gave way to the British domination, which became the new colonial power in 1806.

Between 1884 and 1915, all the territory between the Cunene River and the Orange River was placed under the protectorate of the troops of the German colony of Kaiser Wilhelm II, during the Berlin Conference on the partition of

Africa. And they officially named Namibia as the German South West Africa; only the port of Walvis Bay remained in the British hands.

The revocation of the South African mandate in 1968 by the UN, officially renaming Namibia, did not prevent the use of both names until the actual year of the independence of Namibia in 1990.

The Portuguese, who had little competition in the region until the sixteenth century, showed very little interest in colonization. Although being the first to have navigated the rocky shores, constituting a threat to their ships in violent weather conditions, they successfully reached the cape when Bartolomeu Dias discovered the Cape of Good Hope in 1488, only to end up facing indeterminate conflicts during multiple attempts to trade with the local Khoikhoi. They used the coast of the Mozambique bay that they found more attractive as a refueling station of shrimp fishing and to open them a way toward the inward land in search of gold.

In the current natural bay called Table Bay (*Tafelbaai* in Afrikaans), with the flat-topped mountain forming a prominent landmark overlooking the city of Cape Town founded in 1652, at the northern end of the Cape Peninsula of the Atlantic Ocean, extending south of the Cape of Good Hope, came the first Dutch colony in the region. Their ship, the *Nieuwe Haarlem*, was wrecked in March 1647. The abandoned crew established a permanent station named the Sand Fort of the Cape of Good Hope in the bay and stayed there for a year until they were rescued. After being rescued by a fleet of twelve vessels under the command of the task force of Jong, the teammates of this wrecked ship and Jan van Riebeeck, who was part of one of the rescue ships, attempted to convince the Dutch East India Company to return to the cape to open a commercial center. They decided to return with a Dutch expedition of a fleet of five ships, with ninety Calvinist settlers in the Cape Town harbor. This main European trading sailing house, the Dutch East India Company, or (VOC) (*De Vereenigde Oost Indische Compagnie* in Dutch), did not intend to colonize the region. On the other hand, it simply wanted to establish a base camp where passing-through ships could shelter safely and where the hungry sailors could stock up fresh food—such as meat, fruits, and vegetables—and continue the spice route to the East.

On April 6, 1652, Jan van Riebeeck, the small expedition commander of the Dutch East India Company and a Dutch colonial administrator, reached Table Bay and became the founder of Cape Town. Jan van Riebeeck remained in command from 1652 to 1662. The discovery of the first comet in South Africa, with reference number C/1652 Y1, was reported on December 17, 1652, by Jan van Riebeeck. Van Riebeeck was the one who built the first military fort building named Fort de Goede Hoop (the Fort of Good Hope) in Cape Town, which had four corners with four bastions named Drommedaris, Oliphant, Reijger, and Walvisch. It was erected in 1652 and built with wood, mud, and clay for the improvement of natural anchorage at Table Bay. In addition, two other forts (the Redout Kykuit and Redout Duijn Hoop) were also built as squares with clay and wood, having a half bastion at the mouth of the Salt River, leading to

Table Bay, in January–February 1654. The Fort of Good Hope in Cape Town was in use from 1652 until 1674, before being replaced by the star fort, the Castle of Good Hope (or the *Kasteel de Goeie Hoop* in Afrikaans), built between 1666 to 1679 with brick, stone, and cement, with five bastions named after the main titles of William III of Orange-Nassau: Leerdam at the west, with respectively clockwise from it, Buuren, Katzenellenbogen, Nassau, and Orange, on the original coastline of Table Bay, after the departure of Van Riebeeck, in 1662; Cape Town was developed for over two hundred years before the construction of the Suez Canal in 1869.

It should not be confused with the ancient fortress called Fort of Good Hope, or the Cape Town Castle, built with clay and wood by Jan van Riebeeck upon his arrival in Cape Town in 1652 for vessels making long trips between the Netherlands and the Dutch East Indies (today Indonesia). The oldest colonial building in South Africa, built by the commander Zacharias Wagenaer, Jan van Riebeeck's successor, charged by the commissioner Isbrand Goske, is today located near the Cape Town city center because of land reclamation.

The first stone was laid on January 2, 1666. Van Riebeeck recommended the company to authorize the free Dutchmen (Vrijberghe), or simply (burghers) citizens, freed from their obligations to settle freely as farmers and trade along the river Liesbeek; this request was honored by the company by delivering its first authorizations that transformed South Africa into a land of white citizens, with nine former employees of the company in February 1657, while the embryo of colonization amounted to the interior of our ancestors land.

Slaves were imported from Batavia and Madagascar by several expeditions in the same year. In Cape Town, the colony of the East India Company already had 134 employees, 35 free settlers, 15 women, 22 children, and 180 slaves imported from overseas.

Since the new settlement negotiated by necessity with the Khoikhoi was not a friendly relationship, contact with officials of the Dutch company was limited. They were then faced with labor shortage. That is why that small number of Dutch former employees of the company, became farmers and began to provide their harvests crops as fruits, vegetables, wheat, wine, and later, cattle in abundant quantities to remediate the consequences of shortage.

This arrangement of the first small group of bourgeois free farmers proved to be very successful, did not cease to increase in considerable numbers, extending their operations more and more to the north and east in the territory of Khoikhoi. Federated under the authority of the chief Doman in February 1659, the besieged Dutch, following the relational degeneration were forced to retreat to the Fort of Good Hope to finally counterattack the Khoikhoi, who were repressed toward the north or reduced to slaves. The number of these settlers—mostly farmers, artisans, or handlers—increased by eight hundred in 1685. Meanwhile, two hundred Huguenots who represented a component of French identity of a chapter in the history of Protestantism little known in South Africa, joined the eight hundred administered citizens at the trading post and founded Franschhoek, a town in the Western Cape province, about fifty kilometers from the city of Cape Town, in 1688.

These French Protestants left France after the revocation of the Edict of Nantes, signed on April 13, 1598, by Henry IV, which put an end to the religious wars that ravaged the kingdom of France in the sixteenth century, causing the emigration of two hundred thousand Huguenots, an old term given by the enemies to the French Protestants.

In 1685, following the promulgation of the Edict of Nantes, revoked by Louis XIV, granted civil, political, religious rights, and also granted annexes called "patents" to Protestants in certain parts of the kingdom; in addition an annual indemnity was paid by the royal finances, as a request of the winemakers experts and specialists of the olive tree of Gov. Simon van der Stel, considered as the founder of the wine industry in the seventeenth century in South Africa and as a senior Dutch official of the Dutch East India Company; he accepted the request to cultivate land rich in alluvium; the Huguenots of French origin, refugees in the Netherlands, left Holland for the cape on December 31, 1687, and received a portion of land to cultivate for a period of a minimum five years in South Africa. The bourgeois system, established by van Riebeeck and the Dutch company, was mostly of Dutch ancestry belonging to the Calvinist Reformed Church of the Netherlands. Often, its married Dutch settlers imported numerous slaves mainly from Indonesia, Malaysia, and Madagascar. The Metis of cape and the cape Malays were known as descendants of slaves. In that agglomeration of the white race, there were many Germans, joined by the French Calvinists, fleeing religious persecutions in France under King Louis XIV and Scandinavians who invaded South Africa in 1688.

During this series of religious persecutions, nearly two hundred thousand French Huguenot Protestants, inspired by the writings of John Calvin in the 1530s, were expelled from France in the late seventeenth century and ended up in countries like Palatinate region, England, Holland, Switzerland, Northern Europe, North America, and what is the current South Africa.

The small colony of Stellenbosch was founded in homage to the architect of economic development Simon van der Stel, the new commander of the cape in 1679. He was the one who installed the 238 new Huguenot settlers on the land rich in alluvium in the valley of Olifantshoek to develop viticulture there, which very strongly left their footprint on the white South African culture from 1688. In 1691, he was appointed governor of the cape to develop crops. Simon van der Stel granted lands to settlers to plant more than eight thousand trees and transform the entire region. Several years later, his son succeeded him as governor of the cape in 1699. Imbued with his person, the arrogant new governor Willem Adriaan van der Stel sought to monopolize the most advantageous commercial contracts by a greedy feeling of money and his ostentatious love. Thus, scandalized by his behavior, sixty-three persons subject to the administrative authority referred the matter to the higher authorities of the company, causing the first demonstration against the autocratic government of 1706 in Cape Town, to achieve a certain white nationalism. But until then, arguing that he was not Dutch but Afrikaner, he publicly refused to obey the orders of a judge. So, he was expelled from the company and removed from office.

Throughout the eighteenth century, the Dutch colony of European origin in the region prospered enormously, pushing its boundaries further north and east by tripling its population from 1,723 individuals to a total of 1,771 slaves added to it from 1688 to 1708. Deadly clashes, led by the Dutch peasant commandos, decimated many Khoikhoi during the retaliatory operations of that colonial expansion, an expansion into the interior of our ancestors' lands; notably many were killed by smallpox epidemics imported from the West in 1713 and in 1755. So, the cheap labor of certain tribes who were incorporated into the farms of colonial society was recruited to establish themselves near cities, while the majority maintained a monumental gap toward the white men to maintain their independence.

Nearly 3,000 Bushmen established between mountains of Sneeuberg and the Orange River, were captured or killed with superior weapons used in some major wars when they retaliated. Nomadic Khoikhoi were either forced to settle near farms, or to leave the colony of their traditional lands, to settle beyond the colonial border by a new legislation from the Dutch government imposed in 1787. In the eighteenth century, the Bushmen, also victims of the colonial expansion, clashed with the new arrivals. The Khoikhoi who survived had no other choice but to continue the resistance than to work for Europeans in an operating arrangement that did not differ from slavery.

The syndicates and a significant number of white slaves descendants were integrated into the premises as one unit with the white population, creating an additional labor to expand the areas occupied by the Dutch company, followed by the inevitable clashes with the Khoikhoi; the offspring of these union members between the Khoisan, their European supervisors, and the imported slaves formed the basis of the rainbow-colored population of South Africa today.

After the case of the settlers against Adriaan van der Stel, the most important conflicts between the Dutch East India Company and the settlers were just beginning, when it decided to limit the cape function as just a refueling station and completely stop the Dutch immigration in the colony; thus unilaterally imposing its policy of monopolizing the market opportunities of the colony; setting up prices for the local productions, imposing a tax system of the administration of legislative judicial powers, more and more attached to small details and litigious processes to free settlers; its purpose was to discourage any industry development and establish a plan with objectives and means to be implemented for the local economy; but that system of administration of legislative judicial powers did not realize that it could not in any case control the spirit of any individual initiative in South Africa.

Henceforth, the Dutch native farmers of the colony called Boers and the free settlers called Trekboers were going to develop the libertarian spirit with that harassment by crossing borders to settle outside the jurisdiction of its restrictive policy, seeking in this way to escape from their oppressive control.

This bad behavior made that, at the end of the eighteenth century, when the Griquas, born in the seventeenth and the eighteenth centuries, in marriages of mixed sexual relations between European settlers of the Cape and the Khoikhoi living on the west coast between St. Helena Bay and Cederberg Range, equipped themselves with firearms and horses to begin a formidable resistance. The majority of the current population of the Griqua is genetically descended from a mixture of mostly Khoikhoi, Bantu Tswana, and a small contribution of Bushman with European from the time of van Riebeeck. Without doubt, the discontent of these trekboers toward the quests of land and political commitments of the Dutch company, finally united the groups of colored Khoisan; and even white adventurers on their way toward the northeast, before reaching Kimberly—the current capital of the province of Northern Cape; located near the confluence of the river Vaal and Orange River, a historic city of great importance because of its diamonds-mining on the border of the Highveld and the southeastern Kalahari; sieged during the Second Boer War—with the Griqua quickly made a reputation as a formidable military force. They were controlling several political entities in the nineteenth century with their own constitutions governed by a Dutch captain.

Captain Adam Kok, a slave who bought his own freedom, was the first captain and Griqua adviser who led his people at the north inside the Cape Colony because of the discrimination against his people, not yet reached the social or legal status granted to their fathers, yet largely feeling to be the children of Europeans, and speaking the Afrikaans language before their migration; but mainly because colonial laws were only recognizing the forms of Christian marriages, they were not treated with respect; so this time, they headed north, outside Cape Town, near the Orange River just west of the Orange Free State, and on the southern skirts of Transvaal. It was to respond with resistance to the action of the Basters Khoi and San that the colonists easily recruited as paramilitary commandos. Having become experts in combat tactics, they chose to abandon their paternal society and live more the way of their maternal lineages. These groups, Orlan or Griqua, became sadly famous. Before the British intervened at the tip of the African continent toward the late eighteenth century, when the Dutch mercantile power began to fade and seized the colony of the cape in 1795, they found a colony of twenty thousand white settlers there with twenty-five thousand slaves and fifteen thousand Khoisan. The good faith of the newcomers caused them to release one thousand black slaves. They filled the void and briefly stopped the cape from falling into the hands of Napoleonic France, but the cape was waived once again in 1803 to return to the Netherlands. In 1806, the British definitely conquered it and recognized it as their sovereignty in 1815 at the Congress of Vienna. In that period, racial differentiation was already deeply rooted in only one white elite who held power in Cape Town; and in the immediate backcountry, white and black pastors populated the outside of the isolated cape.

Upon their sovereignty, the English immediately tried to solve the troublesome border dispute between the Boers and the Xhosas on the eastern boundary of the colony. Not having initial interest in colonization as the Dutch before them; other than the strategically located port, its use as a trading post was the subject of approximately five thousand immigrants of the British middle class, thereby persuaded by the British authorities to leave England in 1820 and come and settle on the stretches of African soil between the parties in conflict. But almost half of these settlers occupying our ancestral land decided to leave the backcountry after three years to continue the work that they held in Britain in cities like Port Elizabeth and Grahamstown.

The British immediately dominated the political life, mining, finance, trade, and manufacturing; and all operations were under their control. Now two cultures and two bilingual European groups divided the country, thus breaking the relative unity of the white South Africa by an influx of British settlers solidified in the sector and with a model of English speakers, becoming highly urbanized. Although this influx of British settlers did nothing to resolve the border dispute, the space between the British settlers and the Boers further widened. Where before their ideas largely remained unchallenged, the illiterates Boers now relegated themselves largely to their farms.

Thus, conservatism and sense of racial superiority of the British colonists stopped all social radical reforms in 1833 after the abolition of slavery, which the Boers generally regarded as a command of the race given by God. Meanwhile, the British colony increased rapidly in Cape Town at the east, in the current Eastern Cape province, after the discovery of gold and diamonds in Natal, mainly around the current city of Gauteng and in certain parts of Transvaal, leading to a rapid increase of immigration of European fortune researchers in the area, throughout Africa, and in all regions of the globe. And then suddenly, the order of masters and servants that white control perpetuated was exhausted by the British authorities in 1841.

In particular, the military expansion of the Zulu kingdom was described by the Sotho as a period of crushing, a forced migration of dispersion that they call *Difaqane* or *Lifaqane* in the early nineteenth century and that the Zulu called *Mfecane*, a period of generalized chaos and great upheavals qualified as crushing throughout Southern Africa around 1815 and 1840, when Chaka created a Zulu militarist kingdom between the Tugela and Pongola Rivers, led to the creation of modern states such as the present Lesotho and the consolidation of other groups such as the Makololos, the Matabeleland, and the Mfengus. The son of chief Senzangakhona kaJama, Shaka Zulu, of the small Zulu clan became the driving force for change in KwaZulu-Natal, who built large armies. He consolidated the power by proofs in the battle and succeeded gradually by placing armies under the control of his own officers. He began a vast program of expansion in the territories that he conquered. Then he began to enslave or kill anyone who resisted in those territories; death was the conviction of an error in the battle for the warriors of his rigorously disciplined regiment.

I therefore conclude by saying that the upheaval of the political, demographic, and ethnic map across southern East Africa is the *Mfecane*, which began by a fight between Zwide, Dingiswayo, and Matiwane before Shaka came to power, leading to the fleeing of Matiwane and his people.

This was how the ambitious Shaka, a child born out of wedlock, somewhere between 1781 and 1787, began his conquering career. He was a warrior under the influence of the local chief Dingiswayo and Mthethwa for perhaps as long as ten years. He did not have access to a great position according to the legend but was distinguished by his courage. Shaka was best known as the one who united many people of the northern Nguni in the nineteenth century including the preponderance "Mtetwa or Mthethwa Empire," meaning "the one who rules," arose in the eighteenth century at the south of Delagoa Bay and inland in eastern Southern Africa; and the Ndwandwe nation, a Bantu Nguni-speaking people who populated sections of Southern Africa in the Zulu kingdom. Sporadically, the Nguni people entered the present-day South Africa about 2000 years ago from Egypt; their ancient history is part of the oral history, and they still occupy a large part of East and South Africa until today. Between the Pongola and Umzimkulu Rivers, his political sense and vigor marked the beginning of a nation that ruled the greater part of Southern Africa as one of the Zulu's best known leaders in the history of Southern Africa, called genius for his innovations and his reforms; but condemned for the brutality of his reign, separated from the local culture and the previous systems; the methods and influences of the Zulu warrior king threw a glow on the concept of the Zulu state as a unique construction; in particular, the formation of Lesotho, the present states of Lesotho, and Swaziland. Shaka taught the most effective way to become powerful to the Zulus because of his background as a soldier, which promptly gave him control of other tribes by conquest. The development of the Zulu tribe by the mindframe warrior made the construction of these armies easier to Shaka. He moved south to establish his capital at Bulawayo in Qwabe territory, across the Tugela River, and never return to the Zulu traditional center; victim of unclear circumstances of his death, because of a plot orchestrated by his brothers, his aunt Mkabayi with the help of Mbopa, his adviser, one of his trusted men, plotted his death; his death occurred by the dagger of his half-brothers Dingane and Mhlangane in 1828. After assassinating Shaka his half-brother Dingane, a popular leader among the people, seized the power in a very difficult time and became king.

When he took power in 1828, he continued despotism; his lack of leadership and expertise in military strategy that Shaka had, occasioned the detachment of rebel leaders from his reign and the decline of military superiority of the Zulu people in South Africa. Conflicts with the newcomers of voortrekkers were the result of irritation of their dissensions. Even under the domination of Shaka, the fall of the Zulu kingdom was already announced to the European settlers, who took advantage of the situation to enter in the area of the Cape Colony, with multitudes of weapons that they possessed, far superior to the Zulu spears. Because these events were only growing, the independence of the Zulu people began to disappear, jeopardizing relationships that Dingane was trying to establish with the British traders.

The British colony, which proclaimed the rule of equality of races in the Cape Colony, attracted more and more dissatisfaction of Boer slave owners, from which slaves were freed, unhappy with the process of compensation of unfair value of only a quarter, according to the manifest. In search of greater independence, peace, and happiness of their children, several groups of Boers therefore decided from there on to collaborate with the black officials and many Khoikhoi, thus pulling away from the British control in the interior of the South African lands, outside the control of the British administration on the border of the Orange River from the north and the east, which were forming the Cape Colony from 1835, in the middle of the vast stretches of lands seemingly uninhabited. In that Promised Land, the voortrekker settlers (the Dutch Boers) found enough space and independence to graze their cattle and to farm there.

These vast stretches of space were deserted land of disorganized refugees, resulting from the brutality of the *Difaqane*, who scattered them by the lack of firearms and horses. They met little resistance among the people of the plains, except the most powerful Ndebele people centered on Bronkhorstspruit. The advent of civilization to a savage land solidified the conviction of European occupation of Boer by the state of the Zulu weakness. The Basotho nation, which Moshoeshoe I, the first son of Mokhachane, a small Bakoteli chief of the Koena (crocodile) ancestry clan, and who helped his father gain power over some other smaller clans, was born in Menkhoaneng, in the northern part of the present-day Lesotho, founded his own clan and became a chief of the Butha-Buthe mountain at the age of thirty-four, where his followers settled at the north of the city; the mountains that he used from 1821 to 1823, as a fortification and his headquarters, during his war with king Shaka of the Zulus, and the wooded valleys of Zululand.

The series of strong resistance that the Boers met and their incursions triggered a light infantry revolt, commonly known under the name of the skirmishers in the ancient and medieval war, with their light weapons such as bows, slings, and javelins placed on a line to harass the enemy and weaken the treaties governing the increase of white domination for the next fifty years.

It was near the present-day Bloemfontein where they established a republic, specifically in Thaba 'Nchu, a town in the Free State of New Holland, as a homeland for Tswana people, located at sixty kilometers east of Bloemfontein, where they made their first stop. They were separated in groups following disagreements between their leaders, some crossing the highest mountain range in Southern Africa, the Mountains of Dragons (*Drakensbergenen* in Dutch), rising to 3,482 meters (11,424 ft), in Natal, and others continued north.

After crossing the Drakensberg Mountains, with the idea of creating a nation, they elected the Boer representative of that time as leader of the Free Province of New Holland in southeast Africa, who wrote a manifesto seen as a declaration of independence of the voortrekker farmers, in which he was stating his grievances against the British authority, on January 22, 1837, published in the *Grahamstown Journal* on February 2, 1837.

It was less than a month later that Retief, the Boer representative of that period and elected leader, ended up rather quickly at the head of a small group of twenty-six families and left the district of Winterberg to join Thaba Nchu.

The Boer leader Pieter Mauritz Retief—from a family of French origin, born to Jacobus and Debora Retief on November 12, 1780, in the Wagenmakersvallei of the Cape Colony, the present city of Wellington—visited the brother of Shaka, King Dingane kaSenzangakhona, accompanied by his trekboer community of about seventy men.

Pieter Retief settled in the region of Tugela, a historic border of the Zulu people in the Cape Colony, on January 28, 1814. He assumed command of the punitive expeditions in response to raids of the adjacent Xhosa territory and became a spokesman, who wrote the declaration of discontent that manifested the voortrekker farmers at their departure from the colony. Dingane, who lost his livestock, stolen by the Baklava, one of the three main Basotho tribes led by Chief Sekonyela, asked Pieter Retief to go toward them and recover his specific livestock in exchange for a promise of lands as payment, which he kept in his kraal. Dingane honored his treaty with Pieter Retief by giving him all the land between the rivers Tugela and iZimvubu up to the Drakensberg and invited him to drink a traditional Zulu beer by the name of utshwala with all his men on February 6, 1838, to celebrate the recovery of his livestock and the agreements of their treaty; which an original copy preserved for the basic Afrikaner history can still be seen at a museum in the Netherlands. While Retief and all his men were entertained by Zulu dancers, Dingane decided to kill one by one, all the men of Retief by surprise by taking them to Hloma Mabuto, a hill, or perhaps KwaMatiwane, a large steep hill, for some of the cattle that they retained in a site where he executed many other enemies, located at 28°25'37" S 31°16'12" E / 28.42694°S 31.27° E / -28.42694; 31.27.

Leaving Retief alive so that he could watch his men put to death, Dingane exclaimed, "Bulalani abathakathi!" (Kill the wizards!) "Bambani abathakathi!"(Grab the wizards!) The ungodly kings, who were first trained by the Zulu king Shaka, returned to the camp after the massacre. There were a number of five hundred fellow farmers of Retief, their wives, children, and cattle also killed but not without retaliations at the place called "Weenen," a name meaning "cry" in Afrikaans; this place was known as the second-oldest European city in KwaZulu-Natal, established by the Trekkers, after the defeat suffered by the Voortrekkers in the hands of the Zulus, at Bloukrans and Moordspruit, located ten kilometers from Weenen; after they succeeded in stopping the initial attack, many escaped without their animals and firearms.

The Reverend Owen, a missionary who saw everything, and his assistant approached Dingane to give a proper burial to the dead, taking away some personal items in the backpack of Retief, who was also killed at the end, still containing the original treaty of the two men, signed by Dingane on February

6, 1838, with three witnesses each, although dated on February 4, 1838, it disappeared during the Second Boer War. The dutchised Pieter Retief was a founder of the Afrikaner history. However, the battle launched by the Boer army, known as the Battle of Itala to repel the Zulus failed miserably.

The one of December 16, 1838, at Blood River or Ncome River, located in KwaZulu-Natal, led by the commander-general of victory Andries Pretorius, was victorious. Andries Pretorius crossed the Drakensberg into Natal and arrived when the emigrants were leaderless in November 1838 after the death of Pieter Retief. He was born in 1798 as a descendant of one of the first Dutch settlers in South Africa. As leader of Boers, he contributed to the creation of the Republic of Transvaal, as well as the first but ephemeral Natalia Republic, established in 1839 after the Battle of Blood River.

That attack conducted between 470 voortrekkers and about 10,000 to 15,000 Zulu attackers perpetrated with the weapons of mass destruction—namely, three cannons, an elephant gun, and other weapons to their advantage, killed about 3,000 Zulu warriors, including two Zulu princes competing with Prince Mpande for the Zulu throne, and just three Boers suffered minor injuries, including Pretorius himself. Historically, the Zulu mass slaughter of that day, which became a public holiday in South Africa in the 1920s, was also the name given to the Battle of Blood River, known as *iMpi yaseNcome* in Zulu and *Slag van Bloedrivier* in Afrikaans, because of the color of the water in the Ncome River, which turned red with blood, in what is nowadays KwaZulu-Natal in South Africa. The vow made to God by the Boers on December 9, 1838, before the Battle of Blood River to build a church on his name if they were to win, was heard, and they saw their victory as an affirmation of God's approval. Despite their numbers, the region was annexed by the British in 1843 to found a new colony known by the name of Durban, the largest city in South Africa and the third-largest city in the country in the province of KwaZulu-Natal. They established large plantations of sugarcane there but found few Zulu neighbors in those areas willing to work. The voortrekkers saw that their hopes to establish a republic in the Natal subsisted for a short time.

Finally, most of the voortrekkers went toward the north, feeling been squeezed between the British colony on one side and the indigenous people on the other. But facing a nation with a social organization with well-established tradition since the sixteenth century, to wage war in time of national danger, which was applied to a wide confederation governed by Shaka, the British found themselves confronted by a rigid resistance of the Zulus during the first major encounter in the Anglo-Zulu War. The Battle of Isandlwana on January 22, 1879, inflicted a decisive victory that caused one of the most humiliating defeats of the first British invasion to the British Empire. Despite thousands of deaths on the side of the Zulu army, there were more than 1,400 British soldiers killed.

That worst defeat of a technologically inferior force inflicted to the British army led to a much more aggressive reinforcement of the second invasion of Great Britain, which strongly destroyed the king Cetshwayo, to finally establish control over what was then called Zululand and today known as KwaZulu-Natal. From 1872 to 1879, Cetshwayo kaMpande—son of Zulu king Mpande and Queen Ngqumbazi, half nephew of King Shaka Zulu, and grandson of Senzangakhona kaJama—killed his younger brother, Mbuyi, the favorite of Mpande, in the battle in 1856 and became king of the Zulu kingdom, the true leader of the people, during the Anglo-Zulu War of 1879. As the last king of an independent Zulu nation, he died in February 1884. The refusal of the Zulus to adopt the labor position relative to the status of serf pushed the British to turn toward India to solve their labor shortages, importing more than three hundred people, who arrived aboard a steamship in 1860. One hundred fifty thousand Indians followed at the course of the next fifty years, along with many free passengers, to become the largest Indian community in Africa, outnumbering whites in the Natal before the arrival of Mahatma Gandhi in Durban in 1893—a politician par excellence and an ideological leader before the independence of India, born on October 2, 1869, in Porbandar, Gujarat; pioneer of Sanskrit, translated as the "force of the soul," holding to the truth in which the force of the truth is a philosophy; and the practice of nonviolent resistance was designed and developed by him, as a concept that helped India access to independence, and inspired movements for civil rights and freedom across the world; Mahatma, or "great soul," was an honorary title that was first appointed to him by Rabindranath Tagore, a prophet of the West. He was also called *bapu*, or father, and officially honored as the father of the nation in India. October 2, his birthday, is a national holiday in India, commemorated as Gandhi Jayanti and as an International Day of Nonviolence in the whole world. On January 30, 1948, Mahatma Gandhi was assassinated by a Hindu nationalist named Nathuram Godse.

Despite the dotted dispersion of the Boer populations, who persevered in their quest for freedom in the land of South Africa, they were settled without any industry in the Orange Free State, which became independent on February 23, 1854, and in the Transvaal, named after the Vaal River and known as the Republic of Transvaal, also known as an independent region in the northeastern South Africa created on January 17, 1852, and recognized by the Sand River Convention, and successively designating a colony, an independent state, a province, and territories in the same geographical area.

That region of the future Transvaal is inhabited by the ancestors of the Khoikhoi since about ten thousand years ago and was occupied by the Bantu people from Central Africa, from the fourth century onward, and some of them continued their journey in the future Transkei and KwaZulu-Natal, on the Indian Ocean coasts.

The Orange Free State was annexed from 1856 to 1877 and again from 1881 to 1900, after the First Boer War, leaving the region once again under Boer control; the Union of South Africa became the Republic of South Africa in 1961, recognized by Great Britain. The Orange Free State ceased to exist as an independent Boer republic on May 31, 1902, by the Treaty of Vereeniging at the conclusion of the Second Anglo-Boer War; it joined the Union of South

Africa in 1910 as the Orange Free State Province, after a period of direct rule by the British in 1961; both part of the former Boer countries, the South African Republic and the Orange Free State, governed in Southern Africa during the second half of the nineteenth century. Those republics were developed into stable states; one of them, a town near the confluence of the Vaal and Orange Rivers by the name of Kimberley, located at 1,230 meters above sea level in the province of the Northern Cape, the historic Griqualand West region, was abandoned in the nineteenth century to the Métis emigrants from Cape Town; Kimberley is located approximately 110 kilometers east of the confluence of the Vaal and Orange Rivers, where Erasmus Jacobs discovered a small shiny stone on the banks of the Orange River. The first diamond called Eureka of 21.25 carats, weighing 4.25 grams, discovered in South Africa, was found on the banks of the Orange River at 120 kilometers south of Kimberley, more precisely in the small town of Hopetown, located in the desert of Karoo in the Northern Cape province in 1866, by a child—a young boy of fifteen years old by the name of Erasmus Jacobs, who was ignoring the whole nature of the pretty stone, which he used to play as a dice in the farm of De Kalk. A farm of his family rented from Griqua people, a multiracial group from a mixture of European settlers of the cape and the Khoikhoi since the seventeenth and eighteenth century. Hopetown was founded in 1850, when Sir Harry Smith extended the northern border of the Cape Colony to the Orange River.

Daniel Jacobs, the father of young Erasmus, had a neighbor on the lands of Duivenaarsfontein, a farm belonging to the family of van Niekerk. The young Boer farmer Schalk van Niekerk was visiting his neighbor when he noticed that stone that intrigued him and offered to buy it. But the Jacobs family refused and gave it to him as a gift by specifying that there were many others on their farm. That stone was bought by Sir Philip Wodehouse, governor of the Cape Colony, for £500 after being appraised and recognized as being a diamond.

It was cut into a diamond of 10.73 carats, after a universal exposure in Paris in 1867. Schalk van Niekerk sold another diamond named the Star of South Africa, found in the area of De Kalk, for £11,200. After three years, it was also quickly sold for £25,000 in the London markets. The discovery of diamonds followed its course on the slopes of Colesberg Kopje, with another greater diamond of 16.7 g (83.50 carats), this time in the Vooruitzicht farm belonging to the De Beers brothers. It was the cook of the prospector Fleetwood Rawstone of "Red Cap Parti," sent there to dig as a punishment, who made its discovery in 1871. That new discovery practically caused a sparkling hustle, and Kimberley triggered a wave of European and black workers in the region, bringing thousands of prospectors on the banks of the Vaal and Orange Rivers. While the miners of the diamond quest were arriving up to the hill of Colesberg in Kimberley, it disappeared; transforming it into a notorious hole that became the Big Hole, alleged to be the largest mine hole in the world, excavated in the open sky by hand. There were eight hundred claims on the small hill, where two to three thousand men worked frantically in search of diamonds. In less than a month, the leaders of the Griqua (Nicolaas Waterboer), Transvaal, Cape Colony, and Orange Free State claimed all the region of those diamond fields. Since the area was within the natural boundaries created by Orange and Vaal Rivers, the Free Boer State particularly claimed it.

But the mediation overseen by the governor of Natal ruled in favor of Waterboer, the leader of the Griqua, for its territory known under the name of Griqualand West, proclaimed on October 27, 1871, and placed under the British protection. The Boers quickly expressed their anger and transformed it into revolt in the Transvaal, under the British control from 1877, triggering the First Anglo-Boer War in 1880, a first war known as the War of Independence for Afrikaners. The overwhelming victory of the Boers in the Battle of Majuba Hill quickly ended the conflict on February 27, 1881, and Paul Kruger, one of the leaders of the uprising, became the president of Zar Republic, which just recovered its independence. The British pursued their desire to unite the countries of Southern Africa after the aberrant defeat at Majuba, and promoting the highest strategic interests was the best way to reconcile with a white Afrikaner majority in the region. And the Zululand was passed under the British control in 1879, several years later, before the discovery of gold by an Australian prospector in the Witwatersrand, a word meaning "the peak of white water" in Afrikaans, and rather known as a sedimentary range of hills at an altitude of 1700–1800 meters above sea level, running in a west-east direction; locally, Witwatersrand means "Die Rand or the Reef," located in the Gauteng province, at fifty-six-kilometer-long escarpment facing north in South Africa. The greater metropolitan area of Johannesburg, famous for being the source of gold ever mined from the earth, with 40 percent of the gold extracted, accelerated the process of federation and treaties with the Boers. Since then, the great wealth of mines was controlled by Europeans in cities where inhabitants were still ignoring segregation between blacks and whites. The influx of thousands of expatriate migrant workers—almost entirely British, mainly concentrated around the Johannesburg area when the British government wanted to extend its colonial power in South Africa—changed the situation. The initial exploitation of gold fields of the Witwatersrand in the Transvaal favored the influx of workers, both blacks and whites, particularly worrying the Boers pressed on the corner.

The European states, which were already more than present in North Africa and sub-Saharan Africa, categorically settled there this time with a grip in Africa after the abolition of slavery in the nineteenth century. These colonial countries nevertheless shared Africa despite the resistance of African people. And under the European administration, human exploitation of African continued but in another form, without counting the exploitation of many natural resources, until the twentieth century. The link between colonization and slavery also deserved to be clarified. Colonization was a system of political, economic, cultural, and religious domination, followed by demographic expansion. It started with the Portuguese conquests, which established protectorates in Africa, India, the Spanish Brazil of Central America, English, and French meridional, and the

North Netherlands America from the sixteenth to the eighteenth century; their administration, an ideology, and a doctrine practiced by certain states on other states were both a compulsory practice for more or less close narrow relations of dependence accepted as an expansionist process under the influence of foreign occupation; and both consisted of establishing colonies in other territories and subduing their inhabitants to the racial political domination of imperialism, as an implementation of prejudices to the detriment of the citizen, and grant rights, legal status to the colonizers, for the benefit of their vital space; their strategic position was for the exploitation of the country's raw material, and its workforce was announcing the development of civilization that never materialized. Those colonizers were managing the abducted people from their notable group to establish them far from their homeland without however letting their original ties to melt in a different civilization. When a group was banned by an internal political and juridical conflict, it preferred to f lee its homeland.

Following the global process of decolonization without decolonization, the colonizers were forced to assume neocolonialism of a much sharper theatrical representation, offering the capacity and quality to destroy as a new form of policy led by certain developed countries aimed to establish their dominance over the independent states formerly colonized. It was a new ideology for decolonization to establish international law, which obliged cooperation between the economic and political organizations of colonized countries for the economic and political profit of the new powers, like the English, the Germans, French, Dutch, etc.

The colonial domination under the ideology of civilization, developed moral justification in the West by a colonial administration always unjust and oppressive, centralist and directly authoritarian, which was juxtaposing local notables by relying on some ethnic groups subjected to forced labor and the collection of forced taxes that the indigenous had to pay to finance their projects. Everything was freely bequeathed to the colonizers, who always confiscated anything that interested them for the benefit of their reign. They humiliated leaders who refused their collaboration by beating them with lashes in the public square or even just simply killing them all. Justice did not exist for the colonized.

Religion also played a very important role in that colonial expansion because there was always a priest present in the first expedition. As example, we know David Livingstone in Central Africa, Mungo Park in West Africa, David Jones and Thomas Bevan in Madagascar, etc.; the army of the colonial administration occupying countries was always present throughout states, to protect American British, Norwegians protestant missionaries, etc., participating in a private action of spreading the word of Christ.

Christianity, Judaism, and Islam participated in the establishment of the ideologies of racism to justify colonialism. Humanism was not a concept in the spirits of Muslim and the European colonizers since these religions disregarded the culture and human rights of those colonized countries but at the same time claimed the generous feelings of Mohamed and the Christic dimension for themselves. The effects of knowing that 80 percent of the African continent was free toward the 1880s made several European powers launch themselves into a fierce confrontation to consolidate a position, except the few coastal areas, such as the Belgian Congo, a part of North Africa, and South Africa, which were already under colonial domination. Congo, for example, was the victim of King Leopold II, who, to enjoy its prodigious wealth, reduced the entire population to slaves, after personally seizing the immense territories crossed by the Congo River, at the beginning of colonization from 1880 to 1908; making them suffer, undergo tortures, mutilations, and killing some in cold blood, to the point of exterminating at least ten million of these Congolese by forced labor. The formation of colonial empires from 1881 to 1898 continued until 1914 and led to the expansions marked by a sort of Europeanization of the world. The great colonial powers took possession of vast territories.

Southeast Asia and the Pacific were already dominated by Great Britain, which now tended to expand toward Egypt, South Africa, and East Africa. After the conquest of Algeria, the submission of Tunisia to its protectorate, and the seizure of the countries of the western coast of Africa, from the Gulf of Guinea and Madagascar to Indochina, France reconstructed its colonial empire. Germany was already very active in Oceania (New Guinea, Samoa, Marshall Islands) and Africa (Togo, Cameroon, East Africa; Congo) to the Belgium of the sovereign Leopold II, and Italy, groping from left to right; sometimes in Somalia, Eritrea, and finally in Libya, without success, because the Italian East Africa occupation was established after the Second Italo-Abyssinian War from October 3, 1935, to May 5, 1936, that defeated the Ethiopian Empire, resulted in the annexation of territories by Fascist Italy as Italian colonies in the Horn of Africa.

The declaration of war on Britain and France, by Italian military forces in Libya, on June 10, 1940, was a threat to Egypt and a danger to the British and French territories in the Horn of Africa; these territories were occupied by a force led by the British during the East African Campaign of the Second World War in 1941; their colonial unity in East Africa, known as Somaliland, Eritrea, and the newly annexed Ethiopia Empire became the British administration after the Second World War; while Ethiopia regained its full independence, Somaliland, reconstituted as the Trust Territory of Somaliland, in 1949, was administered by Italy from 1950 until its independence in 1960; putting an end to the invasion act of social imperialism, and the downfall of the Fascist regime in East Africa. An international conference of Brussels and Berlin, at the initiative of King Leopold II of Belgium, was organized by Chancellor Bismarck. More than fourteen colonial nations were gathered at the Berlin Conference in 1884 for the division of territories to be decolonized and had as aims to define the rules of colonization, resulting in an agreement with a general act on February 26, 1885. For them, the partition of Africa was legitimate. Here is an excerpt of that February 1885 act by the European leaders after the Berlin Conference.

The Heads of States gathered, wanting to settle in a spirit of mutual understanding, the most favorable conditions to the development of trade and civilization in certain parts of Africa, wanting in the other hand to prevent misunderstandings and disputes that may arise in the future for the new taken of possession on the coast of Africa, and concerned at the same time by the means of increasing the moral well-being and material of indigenous people, they resolved:

1. The trade of all nations shall enjoy a full freedom in all the territories constituting the Basin of Congo and Its tributaries.
5. All power which is exercising or will exercise the sovereign rights in the above territories will not be able to concede, neither monopoly, nor privilege of any kind in commercial matters there.
6. All the Powers exercising sovereign rights or influence in the say territories engaged themselves to ensure the preservation of indigenous populations, and to the improvement of their moral and material conditions of existence, to contribute to the abolition of slavery, and especially the black slave trade. They shall protect and favor all institutions and religious enterprises, scientific or charitable created institutions and organized for the above ends, or which aim to educate the natives and make them understand and appreciate the benefits of civilization.
34. The power that takes possession of a territory on the coast of the African continent will notify the other signatory powers. Signed by Germany; Austria; Belgium; Denmark; Spain; the United States; France; the United Kingdom; Italy; the Netherlands; Portugal; Russia; Sweden, and the Ottoman Empire. Burundi, the Democratic Republic of Congo, and Rwanda fell under Belgian colonization. Around 1870 to 1880; the British Empire, which could not simply be limited to Cape Town, took root in Africa by passing through Sudan. The control of Egypt up to South Africa was to secure the route to India from Cape Town.

The total conquest of South Africa by the United Kingdom began in 1899 with the invasion of the Boer states, such as Transvaal, a region in the northeast of South Africa, and the Orange Free State, an old Boer republic of the nineteenth century; then their possessions extended to Botswana, Rhodesia, etc. The Seven Years' War, known as a global conflict involving every European great power to span the five continents of the world at that time, divided Europe into two coalitions; on one side, it was led by "the Kingdom of Great Britain, Prussia, Portugal, Hanover, and other small German states;" and on the other side, "the Kingdom of France, the Holy Roman Empire, the Russian Empire, Bourbon Spain, and Sweden." The conflict fought between 1756 and 1763, affected Europe, the Americas, West Africa, India, and the Philippines. Meanwhile, the French supporting India tried to crush a British attempt to conquer Bengal. It was finally the treaties from the Seven Years' War that allowed the British Empire to constitute itself as great colonial empire in the world.

It seized the French colonies in Canada and in India, representing 458 million inhabitants; the majority located in India, in which 22 percent occupied 33 million km2 of land. Let us add that, for England, colonization was of economic nature. In 1884, after the Berlin Conference, the Western powers shared Africa between them, and all the territory between the Cunene River and Orange River was placed under the one who proclaimed the German protectorate. The explorer Gustav Nachtigal, at Luderitz, was named as a special envoy in Central and West Africa to negotiate land annexations by the chancellor Otto von Bismarck. And it was thanks to his interventions that Togo and Cameroon became German colonies. It was from that moment that the strategy of colonization began, which first took place in 1891 to 1897 by the German colonies in East Africa and then from 1904 until the beginning of the First World War in West Africa. In the German colonies of West Africa, the conquered people, after participating in the uprisings, agreed to sign collaboration agreements. In that case, the protection pact was signed between the commissioner of the Reich, Heinrich Goring, and the father of Samuel Maharero. That pact stipulated the essential points that ensured the nonabuse of nature, the protection of nature, how to exploit nature, and most importantly the respect for the human in all its forms.

The successor of Gustav Nachtigal, Heinrich Goring, newly appointed German governor of South West Africa from 1885 to 1890, instead of respecting the clauses signed in the agreement with the head of the Herero, began playing a brutal political expediency of the third thief by ordering displacements without consideration, executions and confiscations without standards between 1884 and 1890. The forced use of the Herero by the German farmers because of expansionism to build the railway was protested shortly before his return to Germany in 1889.

He was replaced by Commander Curt von Francois. The father of Samuel Maharero was an important Herero leader Kamaharero, before his death. The Herero, the Ovambo Bantu, and the Kavango crossed the Cunene River toward 1550 to colonize the South West Africa. The Herero are of the Bantu language group. They live in Angola, Botswana, and Namibia, the northwest area of Botswana with agricultural activities and their cattle breeding, large attic with a potential to establish agro-food industries, including people that his father conquered; two of these people were precisely well known by the names of Nama and Oorlam: the first people, the Nama of the chiefdom of Hendrik Witbooi, born near the Fish River in what is today Namibia, was also chief of the tribe like his grandfather David Witbooi, who was the tribal chief of a native clan of the Cape Colony; their language family is the Nama language of the Khoe-Kwadi, and many of them speak Afrikaans. Moses Witbooi, father of Hendrik Witbooi, who was the second tribal chief of the Nama tribe, a subtribe of the Khoikhoi as his uncle Jonker Afrikaner, sovereign of the territories between Orange River and the mouth of Swakop River, was killed by Paul Visser to take his place as tribal leader on February 22, 1887. He was avenged by his son by killing Paul Visser and replaced him on July 12, 1888, with the connections of other Nama tribes who rallied to his command; he then became the new leader of the Witbooi clan of the Nama people from 1825 to 1905.

The Namaqua people of the traditional Nama language, allied with the Herero against the German power, was one of the main branches considered by some as the true Khoikhoi descendants in Southern Africa. Most of them nowadays speak Afrikaans, mainly in Namibia, South Africa, and Botswana. They were known as pastoralists with a tradition of pastoral life as herders of goats and sheep and harvesting honey thousands of years ago. The people whom the first settlers were calling the Hottentots were living in southern Namibia on the Orange River in the north of South Africa, where in the 1920s prospectors discovered diamond, followed by the appropriations of traditional lands—a system put in place from the early colonial era. The last shepherds were settled in villages under an apartheid regime in a region built as the cities of Alexander Bay and Port Nolloth.

The second people, the Oorlam, the Metis of the Dutch settlers in the nineteenth century, f led from the discriminatory laws and the expansionism of European settlers of the Cape Colony to emigrate and took control in the center of the current Namibia, an area located between the Orange River and Swakop River. They imposed themselves on the enslaved Nama, Herero, and Damara and drove away the German missionaries in the region. With their good knowledge of firearms, they imposed their hegemony throughout the center and the south of the current Namibia from 1820 up to the 1870s.

It was Hugo Hahn and Heinrich Kleinschmidt, who settled in Winterhoek in 1842, who forced to conclude an unequal peace between the Oorlam and the Herero. Finally, the Herero coalition of the chief Maharero and the Nama, armed by the Swedish merchants, ended in the signing of the peace agreements with Jan Jonker Afrikaner, consecrating the new supremacy of the Herero in 1870. They settled in the South West Africa and led the battle by using horses under the reign of Jaager and then of Jonker Afrikaner, son of the captain Jaager Afrikaner, from 1760 to 1823. They were defeated on December 12, 1880, by the warriors of Wilhelm Maharero at Otjikango and at Osona.

These two important people were under the leadership of Kamaharero, father of Samuel Maharero. When his father died in 1890, he, who already had a good relationship with the German government, had also very well educated his son on these same principles. His son, educated in a school of the Lutheran mission, had just replaced him. He was a well-educated and well-respected chief in the region of Okahandja, located in the center of the Otjozondjupa region of Namibia, founded by the Herero and the Nama toward the 1800s.

Around twenty-seven years after its foundation, Heinrich Schmelen, a German pastor, became the first European to go there in 1827. Seventeen years later, Okahandja received two other missionaries assigned permanently in 1844 and founded the Herero church there in 1870. Finally, fifty years after the Christian dogma, Okahandja was invaded with the help of the missionaries of the German army, who established a military base there, to officially receive the status of a village in 1894. But not considering that the West must impose its values on traditional cultural institutions and oppress all other traditional civilizations already inked in the indigenous community, he refused the protection and the German sovereignty, which led him directly in an intense conflict in 1893, in the third year of his reign, against the German colonial troops of Curt von Francois and later against Theodor Leutwein up to 1896.

The claims of the native lands confiscated from the Heroes began in 1885, when an Ovambo murdered William Worthington Jordaan, a Metis explorer from the Cape colony. William Worthington Jordaan, left South Africa where he was born in Wynberg, to explore the territories of the current countries known as, Angola, Botswana and Namibia, to finally go to South West Africa, where the King Kambonde Kampingana, King of the Ovambo of the Ndongas, ceded a territorial concession to him, in Grootfontein and Otavi, in 1884.

Grootfontein, meaning "the large fountain territory," was a town in Namibia, located in the northeast of the country in the region of Otjozondjupa on the road leading from Windhoek to the Caprivi Strip. And Otavi was a small town in north-central Namibia, located in a district of the province of Otjozondjupa.

That concession gave a certain power to William Worthington Jordaan to bring forty-five Boer families from Angola to settle near Grootfontein and proclaim the Republic of Upingtonia. It was then that the rival ethnic groups of Ndonga claimed that territory, which led to hostilities, causing the death of William Worthington Jordaan in Omandonga, to put an end to the small Boer republic, on June 30, 1886. Finally, the territory was acquired by the German South West Africa Company after the departure of the Boer settlers in Angola and in Transvaal.

Appointments continued, followed by successions, and this was how Curt von Francois was sent to South West Africa, the British enclave at Walvis Bay, to raise the fortifications, in charge of his brother Hugo, and pacify the region by Otto von Bismarck on June 24, 1889. Heinrich Goring, the German high commissioner, was already placed under British protection because of the multiple denunciations of non-respect of the protection treaty by Maharero and conquered Tsaobis and Heusis.

On October 18, 1890, he landed on the site of Winterhoek, with a battalion of twenty-one German soldiers. Very quickly, he built a headquarters there—the strong Alte Feste for the colonial forces of the Reich. He settled his quarters at Otjimbingwe in the South West Africa. On December 7, 1891, Curt von Francois was already appointed as imperial commissioner at the departure of Heinrich Goring and then moved the colonial administration of Otjimbingwe in Windhoek.

In the colonial historiography, it was by error that he was named the founder of Windhoek because Windhoek, then called Winterhoek was already an ideal city founded by Jonker Afrikaner in 1840 at the center of the country near the water sources, located between the Nama and Herero territories.

And it was next to the former Berg hotel, the current South African high commission, that he built his first house before the laying of the first stone of the fort on October 18, 1890 by the German colonizers, today known as "Alte Feste," for the German colonizers, to say they were the founders of the same city and named it Windhuk. Note that in that city of three hundred to four hundred blacks, mainly Nama, there were more than eighty-five white residents, including five women, and already five hundred soldiers of the German colonial troops were counted there from 1891 to 1894. The first German war was launched in that territory by him, attacking the headquarters of the Nama chief Hendrik Witbooi in Hornkranz.

Because Hendrik Witbooi, who became the main enemy of von Francois, refused three times in a row to be submitted under the German protection in 1893. For this fact, seventy women and children were killed in Hornkranz. Chief Hendrik Witbooi, who escaped the attacks of von Francois, counterattacked and freed the horses of the colonial German troops on the outskirts of Windhoek; the attacks therefore became a common thing, since von Francois attacked Hornkranz again, this time by eliminating the Rehoboth Basters of Captain Hans Diergaardt so that the Germans could occupy the site.

Forcing the colonial troops to abandon Hornkranz, Chief Hendrik Witbooi counterattacked once more, first in Naos and then directly in Windhoek. Throughout 1893, there were just attacks of the colonial troops and counterattack, sabotage, and retaliation of Hendrik Witbooi resistance. But in December of that same year, the Witbooi Nama were for the first time severely beaten by the fourth attack of von Francois in Hornkranz. That victory did not bear him fruit and could not calm the pressures that were already mounting against him in Germany, blaming him of only been able to deal with weapons and not conquering by that way either. So, after establishing a military station at Warmbad in southern South West Africa, von Francois yielded his title as imperial commissioner to Theodor Leutwein on March 15, 1894.

On January 1, 1894, Theodor Gotthilf Leutwein (1849 to 1921) arrived in the German protectorate and then engaged with the Nama tribes of Chief Hendrik Witbooi. He met the chief of the Herero, Samuel Maharero, in February 1894 in Okahandja. Repressions started when he gave order to execute the chief of Khauas Nama, Andreas Lambert, who was still refusing to sign the protection treaty of the German Reich on March 19, after he participated in the attack of Khauas Nama in Aais and Naosanabis (Leonardville) on February 24.

That signature was finally granted to him by his successor, Eduard Lambert, but if he was not afraid of also being executed, he would have not signed it. Then in the Naukluft Mountains, Leutwein, this time attacked the Nama of Hendrik Witbooi now that he was officially in command of the colonial army of the protectorate, on August 22 after the final departure of von Francois from the German colony in August 1894. It was then after that attack, with a loss of 27 percent of the German workforce, that Witbooi proposed a conditional agreement, accepted by Leutwein and signed the treaty of protection, which would be respected for ten years.

That treaty of protection guaranteed their autonomy by giving them the right to possess firearms but still managed by the seductive diplomacy to convince many Herero chiefs, including Tyiseseta Manasse of Omaruru, as well as all Herero and Damara, to submit themselves on November 26; then after the neutralization of the hostile clans in December 1894, he set boundaries for the protection of southern Herero land with Samuel Maharero on August 27, 1895. By his political divisions, he organized a punitive expedition in alliance with Hendrik Witbooi, this time to fight against the Khauas clans, the Fransman Nama, and the Bondelswarts in January 1895, thus establishing a garrison at Gobabis, a city in the Omaheke Region in the east of Namibia and a military post in Olifantskloof to control trade with the Bechuanaland, a neighboring protectorate established on March 31, 1885, by the United Kingdom in Southern Africa, which gave birth on September 30, 1966, to the current Botswana. To accommodate multiple losers in a one-way battle, concentration camps were built for the convicts of Khauas Nama and several victims of the revolts or rivalries of disadvantaged clans to forced labor authorities by the Germans, who simply were executing tribal leaders after a false judgment in their court martial by a repressive jurisdiction under the order of Leutwein in 1896. On April 18, 1898, he was officially appointed governor, with the slogan "To colonize peacefully without bloodshed in the territory."

From 1894 to 1904, Theodor Gotthilf Leutwein was the governor of South West Africa. To better reign, he spent ten years of his command in South West Africa to create divisions in the indigenous policy by a combination of diplomacy, such as seduction, deceit, and military coercion, to establish an administrative and economic infrastructure of the German protectorate and decentralized all administration offices divided between Windhoek, Otjimbingwe, and Keetmanshoop. The seduction policy was committed to intervene in a dispute between the natives of Samuel Maharero and Michael Tyiseseta of Omaruru in November 1899. He favored Samuel Maharero, the one who needed to fight against the Ovaherero clans and who made the advancement of the interests of the German authorities impossible.

By ceding him a part of his land in exchange for European goods, Samuel Maharero, the chief of the Herero people in South West Africa of the current Namibia, from 1856 to 1923, restored the protection treaty denounced some time earlier by his father. By respecting the German colonial authorities, he then undertook a consolidated collaboration policy by maintaining good relations to exchange European goods with colonial troops led by Gov. Theodor Leutwein for a part of his land. But during a heated argument in Warmbad, the Bondelswarts of Jan Abraham Christian, the chief of Bondelswarts, protested because of a judiciary procedure, which gave reason to Jan Abraham Christian, against the use of violence by Walter Jobst, the German official of that district, on October 25, 1903. After putting their heads at price for two thousand marks for the head of the new Bondelswart chief and five hundred marks for each Bondelswart involved in the killing of Warmbad, the troops of Hendrik Witbooi gave their support to the German authorities. But unfortunately, there was no peace in that side of the world. Since some time after, the uprising of the Herero ended the uprising of the Bondelswarts, which stopped in January 1904 at Kalkfontein.

The German administration of coercive diplomacy did not inspire peace at all in South West Africa. Divisions in the indigenous politics, favoritism, unjust confiscation, and perpetual injustice to the indigenous were producing uprisings and frequent rebellion. The chief of the Herero, Samuel Maharero, dissatisfied with that situation of non-respect and the enfranchisement of the Damara serfs, found himself once again forced to an uprising after unsuccessfully attempted to rally the chiefs of the neighboring tribes to his cause, and disavowed by the German government after an attempt to negotiate with its officials. But the missive extermination of this people was already hovering in the German commandment, which divided its colonial troops under the command of Colonel Leutwein, in four sections to deal with rebellion troops of Samuel Maharero on February 11, 1904.

The evidence of this policy retained the attention of Leutwein, who did not stop warning the German government against that policy. However, the destruction of that entire people was just a total fantasy for the partisans who wanted the total annihilation of the rebel tribes, because the colonial troops were recording losses toward the rebellion troops. It must be said that Colonel Leutwein was not in favor of that idea, by asking to stop the dismantling of indigenous structures, trying to find a peace agreement by the end of May 1904.

Meanwhile, Kaiser Wilhelm II had another plan in mind. His real chastisement was the total annihilation of an entire people. In that regard, he did not hesitate a moment to send Gen. Lothar von Trotha to take command of the colonial troops. In June 1904, he put an immediate end to negotiations undertaken by the Colonel Leutwein, who printed a proclamation in Otjihererro, the Herero language, saying, "You know well that when you uprise against your protector, the German emperor, nothing else awaited you than a fight to death. Until then, I cannot stop the war; however, you can stop it by coming toward me to hand over your weapons to me, and receive the due punishment."

In December 1904, Major Leutwein, repudiated by the emperor William II and the majority of German settlers, left South West Africa and ceded his position to General von Trotha as governor of South West Africa. Born on July 3, 1848, and died on March 31, 1920, Dietrich Lothar von Trotha was sent as commander of the colonial forces in a former German protectorate of East Africa, known by the name of Tanganyika, in 1894 and then in South West Africa when the war of the Herero against the German troops, with little victories by the German side, raged for five months, thanks to his reputation of repressor, who exercised a brutal and ruthless repression on the movements of the African rebels who were against the German colonial forces.

In a word, he was a real German, bloodthirsty without forgiveness. But sure of himself and treating the Herero to be just savages by underestimating the intelligence of their combativeness, which continued to increase the loss of life among the German troops, he opted for a new military tactic and encircled the Herero on three sides, just leaving them the Kalahari Desert as the only escape door. Thousands of Herero died of thirst by trying to find refuge in the depths of the Omaheke Desert because he poisoned all water points. Dietrich Lothar von Trotha was also the one who signed the extermination order regardless of age or sex after setting up guard posts at the regular intervals, with orders to shoot every Herero man, woman, and child, armed or not, within the Germany borders without warning.

On June 11, 1904, in Walvis Bay, von Trotha led a military battalion for the war against the Herero in South West Africa. The last great battle, the one of Waterberg in Namibia, took place on August 11, 1904. The German army massacred the Herero in 1904 in South West Africa, consequently for all those tensions. And as highlighted by a German report of that time, that terrible conflict completed the explicit extermination of the entire Herero nation, which the German army began from their first settlement in that territory.

That organized killing was considered as the first genocide of the twentieth century; the first crime properly named genocide, planned by a state for inscribing a rebellion against the German colonizers; from a submission refractory of populations by military expeditionary force of terror of their colony, under the command of Lothar von Trotha to an explicit extermination of the entire Herero nation. The extermination took place without any coordinated reaction against that policy, which at the same time generally, was directed against other people—namely, in Tanganyika—making about one hundred thousand deaths in two years from 1905 and against the Nama in Namibia from 1908. Tanganyika was a colony that extended on the current territories of Burundi, Rwanda, and the mainland portion of Tanzania. Fragmented by the First World War, after its creation in the 1880s, it gave rise to the colony of Belgian Empire, Ruanda-Urundi, and the British Empire, Tanganyika.

Thus, the British and the Germans drove out the original people from their lands during the war between the Germans and the English for Tanganyika, the area where the Kalanga-Rozwi local languages were spoken. The Herero warriors of Chief Samuel Maharero, estimated to be eighty thousand people before the start of the war, only remained fifteen thousand individuals after the war in 1911 in that country.

These revelations reached us through detailed accounts of operations documentation written by von Trotha and his subordinates, available in the archives. The most common difference between two values ranged this number between ten thousand, twenty-five thousand, or forty thousand Namaquas killed; but according to Serge Bile, there were about sixty thousand deaths. This massacre shows us all constitutive elements and a political will on racial or ethnical criteria, deliberately chosen with the consent of the emperor Wilhelm II, to eliminate the Herero, and free lands for the German settlers and prevent racial mixtures, causing a massive number of civilian casualties by a colossal military power, different from the other opposing party.

In 1890, a law prohibiting the voting rights or the citizenship of all expatriate migrant workers who were not residents for at least fourteen years was adopted by the government of the Transvaal, under the presidency of Stephanus Johannes Paulus Kruger. Better known as Paul Kruger, he was a German immigrant and descendant of South African, born on October 10, 1825; he was also having an international renowned of resistant Boer, against the British during the Second Boer War of 1899 to 1902, but who already saw the power passed to the British. Eventually, these rights that limited corruption, high tax and inefficient administration in the Boer Republics were factors of the Second Boer War in the region. Thus, a considerable dissatisfaction of the public administration resulted in a raid, the Jameson Raid.

Consequently, before the war, a group led by Capt. Leander Starr Jameson, a British colonial statesman, from the family of Jameson of Edinburgh in Scotland, born on February 9, 1853; also known under the name of Dr. Jim, was the first to trigger an uprising in 1895 in the Witwatersrand with the initiative to establish a British administration. Jameson wanted to foment unrest among expatriate migrant workers and use the outbreak of the revolt as an excuse to invade and annex the territory. Therefore, a private army was gathered from Transvaal to overthrow the Boer government by violence, and they managed to push the Boers' superior forces nearly twenty miles of Johannesburg before these same Boer forces forced his private army to surrender. Capt. Leander Starr Jameson arrived in South Africa after he achieved a professional career in London. He settled in Kimberley and opened a medical practice. Very quickly among his patients, he gained a great reputation with President Kruger and Chief Lobengula, chief of Matabele, a Zulu branch separated from King Shaka by the name of Mzilikazi. The medical success of Jameson earned him the joy expressed by Chief Lobengula by awarding him the rare status of induna during the opening ceremonies related to that honor, although being white.

He immediately had more contact with Cecil John Rhodes, a British mining magnate, politician, philanthropist, and businessman. Jameson became prime minister of the Cape Colony from 1904 to 1908 and had a successful political life following the invasion by receiving numerous honors at the end of his life. Cecil John Rhodes also arrived in South Africa, specifically in Natal, removed from the grammar school for health reasons by his family, which thought that the warm climate would improve the state of his asthma; the teenager had Herbert Rhodes, already in South Africa, as his older brother that he should also assist in the exploitation of a cotton farm located in the Umkomazi Valley, which finally failed to operate. So Herbert and Rhodes left the Natal to go to the Kimberley diamond fields in October 1871, where Rhodes was able to found the diamond company of De Beers by purchasing all small-scale mining of diamonds in the Kimberley region, and over the next seventeen years, he became a businessman and the tycoon of the mining industry, financed by N M Rothschild & Sons. He implemented the provisions of the Rhodes scholarship, financed by his estate. Rhodes entered in the public life in 1877 with the prior incorporation of Griqualand West in the ministry framework of Sir John Charles Molteno, prime minister of the Cape Colony. Rhodes became a member of the parliament in Cape Town and chose the district of Barkly West, a rural district located on the northern bank of the Vaal River at the west of Kimberley, where the predominant Boer voters remained faithful to him, even after his support for the Jameson Raid against the Transvaal, which ended in fiasco. The main objective of the assembly was to help decide on the inability to control the territory of Basutoland, a British colony founded in 1884 after the Cape Colony. As prime minister of the Cape Colony and CEO of the Cecil Rhodes Company, born in 1853 in Bishop's Stortford, Hertfordshire, England, wishing to put South Africa under British rule, he encouraged expatriate migrant workers to openly resist the domination of the Boer Republics for their protection and their rights.

Through that policy, as a strong advocate of colonialism, imperialism and the founder of the state of Rhodesia, Rhodesia was named after him. Rhodesia, which is no longer generally used nowadays, formed two territories, which are today Zambia and Zimbabwe.

The intransigence of Stephanus Johannes Paulus Kruger and the British insistence peaked and busted the Second Boer War (Netherlanders) in 1899. Transvaal and all its subjects became a British colony after its defeat in 1902. His government excluded all foreign franchises, rejecting any British request.

That Second Anglo-Boer War of October 11, 1899, to May 31, 1902, was the bloodiest conflict between 1815 and 1914, which lasted longer than the first; the British preparation exceeded the one of Majuba. That Second Boer War gradually became less popular, especially after the horrible revelations on conditions in the concentration camps killing tens of thousands of children, men, and women by malnutrition, negligence, and diseases. The signing of the Treaty of Vereeniging, the peace treaty ending the Second Anglo-Boer War, was held on May 31, 1902. The promise of autonomy by the British Empire, the recognition of the British sovereignty by the Boers under its provisions, and the reconstruction of areas under their control led to the creation of the Union of South Africa; the mining industry, particularly of the Witwatersrand, after the war years produced almost a third of the annual world gold production in 1907.

A law called the South Africa Act of 1909 was adopted to encourage the union of four British colonies—namely, the Cape of Good Hope, the Natal, the Orange River, and the Transvaal, and the admission of Rhodesia as a fifth province in closer union. A referendum held in 1922 by settlers of Rhodesia rejected the third draft of the union, but it continued on its way under the direct rule of Great Britain after its division into two countries. Such laws also united the Upper Canada to the west, created by the Constitutional Act of 1791, which separated the former Lower Canada, province of Quebec, to the east to form the United Canadas; and the union of Australian colonies, united by the Australia

Constitution Act in 1900. The Union of South Africa was internationally respected, setting the equal states up with the other three major British possessions and allies—Canada, Australia, and New Zealand. But the concentrated attention of the British on the reconstruction of the country was disputed and weakened peace through harsh taxes and wages cuts imposed by the authorities. On all sides, the system completely marginalized blacks, Metis, and Boers, finding themselves in a shameful position of being poor peasants throughout the country. In particular, their anger made them irrelevant when the Great Britain administrator-imposed English as the official language in workplaces and in all schools. To compromise any resistance, large mining and foreign companies were encouraged by the government to bring thousands of Chinese for immigration. In 1906, the Zulu revolt against the onerous tax legislation and the British rule in Natal were led by Bambatha kaMancinza, chief of the amaZondi clan of the Zulu, who was living in the Mpanza Valley, a district near Greytown, KwaZulu-Natal. That revolt claimed between three thousand and four thousand Zulu lives and some fighters on the side of the Natal government. There were more than seven thousand jailed and four thousand f logged.

The franchise of blacks and Metis remained as before the union in the republics of the new Union of South Africa, and Afrikaans only became the official language in 1925. The first major piece of the legislation of segregation by the name of Natives Land Act of 1913 was a historically significant part of the apartheid system and regulated by legal reasons, the acquisition of lands from indigenous people in South Africa, a system of land tenure that denied the right to own land to the majority of people in South Africa and that caused significant socioeconomic repercussion.

Before the 1990s, apartheid was strictly regulated under this act, which regulated the ownership of black land. Finally, this segregation law was replaced by the current policy of land restitution. More importantly, although lamentable, many other projects of laws were legislated, giving full political control to white people. Here are some of those projects of laws adopted for racial segregation.

In 1853, the Cape Constitution allowed a voting right to all males living in the colony in a permanent manner. But to be eligible for this right, you had to own a property of £25 value. This necessary condition was never respected until 1887 under the form of an electoral secret, noticing that Africans could be decisive if they exercised this right to vote by the law existing in the cape. Rhodes said clearly in a parliamentary speech in June 1887 that the native was to be treated as a child to deprive him of all concession. He decisively admitted the adoption of a system of despotism toward the barbarity of Africans in South Africa, just like the one instituted in India.

To completely disadvantage the right to be elected to the legislative council, the property was to have the value of £1,000, and £25 for the house of assembly. Finally, the property qualification amount of £25, giving the right to vote to Africans, was increased to £75 by a voting act of 1892, inscribing a disadvantage to poor whites, their Metis children, and all Africans.

And the Indigenous Representation Act removed African voters of the Cape from the communal ballots, registered since 1854. In 1905, the general regulation on that project of law removed the voting right from blacks by limiting them to fixed areas, and the famous pass system was introduced. So, Africans had no vote in the Orange Free State and in the Transvaal, and almost all Africans were effectively excluded from the granting of votes.

The Cape parliamentary registration law of 1887 excluded the tribal forms of ownership concession, comprising all families grouping in the cape, and denied the civil rights of citizenship to Africans in the Eastern Cape, particularly the right to vote. The Legislative Assembly on the Natal project of law (1894) was depriving the voting right to Indians and to elect representatives at the assembly of the state of Natal. The withdrawal of this project of law was obtained by Mahatma Karamchand Gandhi, who made ten thousand people sign a petition by raising their awareness to unite and fight against racial discrimination perpetrated by the British and the Boers, dominating the black populations and immigrant communities without sharing, by the Native Locations Act of 1904, which established the segregation of urban Africans.

Without violence, Gandhi convinced three thousand delegates not to submit to the new segregationist law in 1906. That Black Ordinance of 1906, also known under the name of the Asiatic Law Amendment Act, was ordering Asians to register on the lists to closely monitor their activities. An extension of laws put in place, specifically for each Asian male, was an identification system with the thumbprint on an affidavit. If upon request the foreign immigrants failed to produce this affidavit, expulsion without right of appeal was considered. Severely, it closed the cape door to Asians over the age of more than sixteen years old and limited their entry in other parts of South Africa. Whatever the cost, Gandhi succeeded in resisting those three thousand delegates. Following that resistance, the British government repealed that law the same year after the action of a delegation of a lobby led by Gandhi, which resulted in the reconstitution of that decree in 1908. Gen. Jan Smuts, as colonial minister, was forced and finally signed an agreement on the repeal of much of the racial laws with Gandhi on June 30, 1914, after constantly opposing the segregationist laws for eight years. And forever, he left South Africa and returned to India on July 18, 1914.

Residential segregation according to the color of skin was a creation of a racial group in that apartheid system known as the Natives (Urban Areas) Act of 1923, which prohibiting non-whites from living in the most developed areas, and also to provide cheap labor in multiple white mining sites and in the agricultural sector in South Africa; the one of 1926 prevented blacks to practice skillful professions, subjected to painful and complete control of the South African political system; it established an unpleasant domination of white on all other racial groups by the law in 1910. A racial legislation, followed by a series of laws adopted to resolve the indigenous question on the concession, promoted two parallel systems of law, amended in 1932, which was not allowing any African to move freely in South Africa.

Any sale of lands was forbidden to Indians by the laws of apartheid. The native administration crowned the British as the supreme leaders of all African affairs in South Africa.

During the First World War, since the British territory was part of the Union of South Africa, it automatically joined the Great Britain as an ally and part of the major military operations against the German Empire. Louis Botha, born on September 27, 1862, in Greytown, currently in KwaZulu-Natal, who headed the government, was a Boer hero of the Second Boer War. He was also a representative of his countrymen in the peace negotiations and a signatory of the Treaty of Vereeniging, signed on May 31, 1902. That treaty ended the Second Anglo-Boer War between the alliance of the South African Republic and the Orange Free State against the British Empire. Considered too conciliatory with the Great Britain, his own party rebelled against him.

He became prime minister of Transvaal on March 4, 1907, and the first prime minister of the Union of South Africa in 1910 after obtaining the domination of state. Louis Botha and the defense minister joined the Allied side of Great Britain in the First World War, which was mainly held in Europe from 1914 to 1918, as a member of the dominion without hesitation.

In a certain number of areas, the Union Defense Force of the Union of South Africa sent its army to take control of the former German colony of South West Africa. The *Deutsch-Südwestafrika* from 1884 until 1915, which was supported by South Africa under the wing of the British Empire, is nowadays known as Namibia. And Gen. Jan Smuts was sent to the region of German East Africa (*Deutsch-Ostafrika*), a colony in East Africa in the 1880s, to try to capture the elusive German general von Lettow-Vorbeck in the colony, which today includes countries like Burundi, Rwanda, and Tanzania. After the defeat of the imperial Germany in the First World War, the territory was divided between Great Britain and Belgium until its conversion to a mandate of the League of Nations. It had 30,000 men on the western front, 43,000 in West Africa, 83,000 blacks, 2,500 Metis and Asians, and more than 146,000 whites. South Africa lost about 18,600 during the First World War. The Union of South Africa, so closely linked to Great Britain, found itself in a military and political impasse on the eve of World War II. Before World War II, the Statute of Westminster 1931 from the United Kingdom Parliament was created for autonomous legislative dominions of the British Empire and the United Kingdom (22 and 23 Geo. V c. 4, December 11, 1931); and to be in the same footing under the Statute of Westminster 1931, its head of state was the king of England. But constitutionally, South Africa was obliged to support Great Britain against Nazi Germany on the night of August 31, 1939, when the forces of Hitler attacked Poland, concerning the agreements between the UK and Poland, as a Second Republic of Mutual Assistance, signed in London on August 25, 1939, stipulated that, in case of a military invasion by a European power, the treaty required that the UK and its possessions must help Poland.

That Polish-British pact of mutual defense forced Great Britain to declare war on Nazi Germany, understood as a European power in the agreement and which disregarded the Munich Agreement. Without the presence of Czechoslovakia, which was not invited to the conference held in Munich between the great powers of Europe to discuss the future of the Sudetenland against territorial claims by Adolf Hitler on areas inhabited mainly by the German parent tree along the Czech border; the Czechs and Slovaks sometimes called this agreement the Munich Diktat. It also represented a military alliance with France, which despite all was not honored. That agreement dated September 29 was signed in the early hours of September 30, 1938 by France, Great Britain, Nazi Germany, and Italy.

The Parliament of South Africa held a brief debate in the corridors of power, opposing furiously those seeking to support the British side in that war. J. B. M. Hertzog, a Boer general during the Second Anglo-Boer War, was determined to encourage the development and protect the Afrikaners from the British influence throughout his life. Born on April 3, 1866, in Wellington, Cape Colony, he became prime minister of the Union of South Africa from 1924 to 1939. He approved the Statute of Westminster in 1931. Despite all, his National Party and the South African Party merged to form the United Party in 1934. That party refused to accept the decision of the neutral position of Hertzog in the Second World War in favor of the former general, former prime minister Jan Smuts, on September 4, 1939, and against the Ossewabrandwag (OB) movement of South African pro-Nazis, called the Ox-wagon Sentinel in English. Jan Smuts took severe measures to capture the members of that anti-British organization, founded in Bloemfontein on February 4, 1939 by Afrikaners who were opposed to the participation of South Africa in the Second World War and who were committing sabotage by blowing up railway lines, cutting power lines, telephone and telegraph lines. Those acts, far from being accepted by most Afrikaners, made the future prime minister B. J. Vorster to be imprisoned among leaders, interned for the duration of the Second World War.

The Hitler fascism of the Second World War was not only limited in Europe. The Eurocentrism of some historians, who always claimed that Africa did not interest Hitler, forgot that there were secret archives relating to the history of the Second World War. For Hitler, one of the main goals of that war included modeling a fascist Africa from north to south and from east to west after recovering the former German colonies lost in 1918 to transform Africa as an immense colony of a unified Europe and put it at the service of a Greater German Reich, in case Hitler won the Second World War. Hitler was thinking to undertake the implementation of racial Nazi theories in Africans.

The outlook of the maximum economic exploitation of our country and the militarization of the African continent were to serve as the basis of aggression against the United States of America. In addition, he was planning a strictly strategies program with certain racist politicians in South Africa, who after that war managed to establish apartheid, once in power. He therefore did not intend to abandon Africa to the English and the French since their supreme ambition of the African policy of Germany before the war already stretched from the cape to Cairo and from Lagos to Dar es Salaam and across different countries in Africa.

In 1935, during the invasion of Abyssinia, the present Ethiopia, the army and the South African Air Force contributed to the defeat of the Italian Army of the fascist Benito Mussolini. These same forces participated in another armored operation at the side of the British forces from May 5 to November 6, 1942, for the liberation of the eastern Madagascar from the control of Vichy France, who were allies of the Nazis, known as the Battle of Madagascar. That operation was mainly initiated by the British, who feared that the Japanese forces would employ Madagascar as a base to cripple the trade and English communication in the Indian Ocean.

To its prestige and to the national honor, South Africa fought tirelessly for the Western Allies in other well-known battles, at a time when the struggle of the third world against colonialism had not taken a stage in the international community. Let's also note that it was prime minister Smuts who signed the peace treaty of Paris and represented his country in San Francisco, USA, during the drafting of the UN Charter. After the Second World War, South Africa entered an intolerable policy phase of discrimination based on race and accepted throughout the world. It was at that moment that the 1948 elections were held, and only the whites and Metis could vote. The differentiation of that system on race eventually began the isolation of South Africa, with a mainly poor, marginalized, and disgruntled community, led by the National Party after the war, leading to the defeat of Smuts. Since the establishment of the Union of South Africa in 1910, the history of South Africa held important general elections up to the one in 1948. It was therefore in 1948 that the postapartheid National Party withdrew the right to vote from the Metis of Cape Town and from the mixed-race people until 1994, giving the right to vote to only white voters. Nevertheless, constituting over 75 percent of the population, the act of the new union refused voting rights to blacks in the Transvaal, in the areas of the Orange Free State, and the Cape Town. Shortly thereafter, instead of freedom, they adopted the oppressive legislation. As a blatant betrayal, whites, representing 20 percent of the population, rendered work illegal for blacks.

Reserving skilled jobs for whites, they only limited blacks to military service. It was at that moment that the black nontribal opposition began to form political groups, bringing together representatives of various African tribes into a unified national organization to represent the interests of blacks and ensure that they had an effective voice in the new union. Above all, the South African Native National Congress (SAANC) was founded on January 8, 1912, in Bloemfontein. At that time, we could recognize as personages a certain poet and author called Solomon Plaatje, born in 1876 in Doornfontein in the Orange Free State. He was the son of a descendant of Modiboa, a dethroned king of the sixteenth and seventeenth centuries, belonging to the Barolong tribe, a subgroup of the Tswana; he died in 1932. A certain Thomas Mtobi Mapikela was an entrepreneur and politician born in 1869 in Cape Town and died in 1945.

A certain John Langalibalele Dube—philosopher, poet, educator, editor, novelist and politician, born in the British colony of Natal in 1871—was the first president of the South African Native National Congress from 1912 to 1917; he was from a royal lineage of the Zulu tribe of the Qadi; he was the son of James Ngcobo Dube, one of the first African ordained pastors of the American-Zulu mission, and the grandson of the first Zulu woman who was converted to Christianity during the evangelization of Zululand in the 1840s, by American missionaries. He died in 1946. And the one born on February 21, 1858, in Somerset East by the name of Walter Benson Rubusana, an ordained evangelist pastor of the London Missionary Society in 1884; he was a politician and the first black man to serve on the provincial council of the cape from 1910 to 1914. He died in 1936.

These illustrious politicians were all founding members of the SAANC. This organization, which campaigned to increase the rights of blacks in the South African population, became the African National Congress (ANC) in 1923. Governing the left-wing political parties nationally, the African National Congress, banned by the administration of Charles Robberts Swart on 8 April 1960, was again legalized on February 2, 1990, whereas, in June 1991, apartheid was abolished. After apartheid, this party in power since 1994, allowed Nelson Mandela, born on July 18, 1918, in Mvezo, South Africa, to be elected as the first black president of the Republic of South Africa during the first multiracial elections in the history of the country from 1994 to 1999.

The regent Jongintaba Dalindyebo to the Thembu throne, informally adopted Mandela at the age of nine from the death of his father, Gadla Henry Mphakanyiswa, the village chief of Mvezo, dethroned from his function by the colonial authorities but nevertheless remained a member of the king's private council and played a vital role for the rise of the new regent. Known as the first member of his family to go to a Methodist mission school located beside the palace of the regent, he found himself subjected to a common custom practiced in Africa at that time; probably because of the English, German, French, Spanish, or Dutch influence, the colonists of their education, requiring that the teacher gives English name to each student on the first day of school; and also because those settlers could not easily pronounce African names; so, as a colonial legacy, Mss. Mdingane, his teacher at that time, named him Nelson; it was an English name that he had never heard of, and he had no idea why it was particularly given to him. After obtaining his junior certificate in two years instead of the usual three years at the Clarkebury Boarding Institute, he entered in a Methodist school in Healdtown in Fort Beaufort, where most of the Thembu royal family studied, in 1937. His traditional initiation teaching according to the Thembu custom took place at the age of sixteen, giving him both African and European education. Mandela Rolihlahla, now called Nelson, continued his studies in law to obtain his degree in the only university in Fort Hare that accepted blacks at that time. Mandela Rolihlahla was his birth name; and because each name in the African culture has a special meaning and story, the name Rolihlahla of the late Mandela "vulgarly means troublemaker" but correctly means pulling the branch of a tree," and his "tribal clan name was Madiba," fitting a truly great man and meaning "father" in the Xhosa language.

It was in that university that he met his friend and colleague Oliver Tambo, discussing with comrades about differing views on South African whites and Jan Smuts, who served as prime minister of the Union of South Africa from 1919 until 1924 and from 1939 until 1948; including the impending conflict between the United Kingdom and the Nazi Germany, and concerning the support or the neutrality of South Africa; it was then that Nelson Mandela decided to principally support the British politic; and by applauding the deputy prime minister Jan Smuts, who came for the graduation ceremony at Fort Hare; and it is also at that time that Nelson Mandela discovered the existence of the ANC.

Already, he was soon involved in the claims of the rights of students at the Fort Hare University. Despite the boycott of the elections organized to obtain the improvement of food and increase the representative powers of the student council, in which he was participating, Nelson Mandela was designated unwillingly to one of the six seats of the student representative council. He was discharged from the university after resigning twice, the first time with his five companions; then he submitted his resignation alone after being reelected with the same five comrades. But the principal of the Fort Hare University was reserving him the option to return if he agreed to still accept to serve on the student representative council.

That possibility was not honored by Mandela, who was explaining that he was ready to revolt against the social system of his own people and their traditional customs but not against whites. In addition, his decision proved that his ideas were more advanced on the social plan than political. It was at that moment that the king Jongintaba, his tutor, came to announce an arranged marriage for Mandela and for his son, heir to the throne, shortly after leaving Fort Hare; dissatisfied with that arrangement, the two young men chose to flee to Johannesburg. Very soon, he began to work on his arrival in the economic capital of Transvaal, first as a mine guard, and he suddenly saw this job canceled by his employer, who afterward realized that Mandela was the adopted son of the regent on the run. Afterward, through his relationship with his friend and mentor Walter Sisulu, he obtained a job in a law firm and finished his degree by correspondence at the University of South Africa, to finally continue his law studies at the important and prestigious University of the Witwatersrand. That English-speaking university was located in Johannesburg in the Gauteng province, a historic region of Witwatersrand.

During the apartheid era, its peculiarity was that it welcomed black students in limited numbers and was also known as the first university to end the policy of racial segregation in its institution, where many futures antiapartheid activists were presented. Mandela joined the young and radical Youth League of the ANC to fight against the political domination of the white minority; to encourage the mass actions with his comrades Anton Lembede, Walter Sisulu, and Oliver Tambo, against the racial segregation laws, or the ongoing discrimination uniformity in the four South African provinces that the country already knew since the foundation of the South Africa Union in 1910 and outlawing strikes of black workers in South Africa. It was at that moment that the ANC Youth League showed itself determined by dismissing Alfred Xuma and imposed James Moroka, physician and politician, born on March 16, 1891, in Thaba'Nchu at the Orange Free State, as president from 1949 to 1952 to prepare a wide defiance campaign.

In December 1951, the African National Congress presented "the defiance campaign" at a conference held in Bloemfontein, against unjust and discriminatory laws, which advocated civil disobedience. The term was coined by the American Henry David Thoreau—teacher, philosopher, poet, and amateur naturalist, born on July 12, 1817, in Concord, Massachusetts, where he died on May 6, 1862. The term civil disobedience, practiced long before his personal opposition testimony abhorred on the slavery of blacks toward the slavery supporter authorities of that period, was popularized in his essay "Resistance to Civil Government," published in 1849. He put forward the idea of "nonviolent" resistance to a single government considered unfair. ANC decided to implement that concept into the national action against racial segregation, a practice of refusing to be submitted to unjust laws, to regulation, and to the power judged unfair by those who challenge it, culminating with a demonstration at the date of the first installation of whites in South Africa and the three-hundredth anniversary of the founding of Cape Town, on April 6, 1952, after electing Nelson Mandela as president of the ANC in the Transvaal and as national vice president.

According to the noncooperation, the conference made a long public statement on a historic decision as follows: "All persons, regardless of the national group they belong to and whatever the color of their skin, belonging to South Africa, have the right to live a full and free life. This right to live a free life included the full democratic right with their word to say in government affairs, is the inalienable right of all Africans in South Africa, including the entire continent. A right that must be realize immediately, if South Africa wants to be saved from the social chaos, from the tyranny and evils, resulting from the existing denial, from frankness of the immoral norms pre-established in the vast mass of population, on the basis of race and skin color."

The law amendment on public security (Public Safety Act of 1953) of the government of prime minister Daniel Francois Malan, between June 6, 1948, and November 30, 1954, authorizing him to govern by decrees suspending civil liberties, proclaimed a state of emergency. To achieve demands of the movement on the community demands of Alfred Xuma party, which introduced the requirement of universal nonracial suffrage (one man, one vote) for the first time, constituting a struggle against racial discrimination leading to political power, was initiated in 1945.

The Congress of the People, which adopted the Freedom Charter that gave the fundamental bases of the antiapartheid movement, took place in 1955. Nelson Mandela and his friend Oliver Tambo, born on October 27, 1917, in Mbizana at Pondoland (Eastern Cape), were running the law firm Mandela & Tambo as the first two black lawyers in Johannesburg who were legally advising numerous blacks who could not afford the lawyers' fees for free or at low cost during that period. After the legalization of the party by Frederick de Klerk, Oliver Tambo—who chaired the ANC in exile for thirty years—returned to South Africa in 1991. He died of a heart attack on April 24, 1993.

The struggle that the national organizations of non-European people still lead in Africa is not directed against any races or national group. It is against unjust laws that cause perpetual submission and unimaginable misery of large sections of the population. It is for the creation of clean conditions and to restore human dignity, equality, and freedom in every country of South Africa and the entire African continent. About 8,500 of the 10,000 people who protested against the unjust laws of apartheid were jailed, including Nelson Mandela. He led the struggle against the policy of apartheid, segregation laws, and the mandatory bearing of a pass for blacks as a politician before becoming president of the Republic of South Africa from 1994 to 1999 by the ANC, which he joined in 1944.

In 1961, he founded the military wing of the ANC, Umkhonto we Sizwe ("the spear of the nation" in English), which he directed in collaboration with the Communist Party of South Africa to conduct a campaign of sabotage against government installations and against the apartheid military regime, after founding that the nonviolent struggle against the apartheid laws, which he led, gave no tangible results. He was therefore one of the historical leaders who fought against the political domination of the white minority and racial segregation. The Sharpeville massacre, in a black township of the city of Vereeniging in the Transvaal, perpetrated by the repression of the South African police on March 21, 1960, was the result of his foundation. On March 28, 1960, anger triggered a general strike. Spreading radio news bulletins put the event in one of the evening newspapers, and the news went up to the cape. The insurrection of the people was enormous, despite warnings of the government, which later on declared a state of emergency and triggered the process to prohibit the ANC and the Pan-African Congress (PAC).

March 21 was declared the International Day for the Elimination of Racial Discrimination by the UN, in memory of the Sharpeville massacre and to honor the victims. That massacred crowd was essentially composed of women, children, the elderly, workers, and employees in a good mood, dancing and laughing. But suddenly, the police took the good humor of those people for aggression and provocation against them. It was at that time that a shot rang out from one of the loaded weapons of the police line, facing the protesters at the entrance of the police station. And for a minute or more, a burst of gunfire followed, killing 69 people and wounding 178 from gunshot to the head, chest, and back; this was very impressive for the world to once again live the white brutality, occurred just because an officer in function tripped, causing an impulse of curiosity in the glowing crowd; but for the misinterpretation of the good humor of those people by the police, they showed their racial intention by fatal deliberate shootings, followed by an absolute silence, and a deafening cry was announcing the result of their fatal cruelty pleasure of causing pain and suffering. The brutality of whites in South Africa, generally in the African continent and subtly in the United States of America, would continue to fascinate the free world. But the West, keeper of different maritime routes of Africa, specifically the one of the cape, and depending on the minerals and metals—like diamonds, gold, uranium, manganese, chromium, and antimony—of the African continent, supported one of the leading global producers by a sadistic ideology, which was called apartheid.

In collaboration with the Central Intelligence Agency (CIA), Nelson Mandela, considered a terrorist and Communist in the context of apartheid ideology, was arrested on August 5, 1962, after seventeen months of hiding, by the South African government. He was first sentenced on October 25 to five years in prison under very harsh conditions. Then in a trial that began on October 9, 1963, he was found guilty in the Rivonia Trial, chaired by an Afrikaner judge in the court of Transvaal by the name of Quartus de Wet, before the Pretoria high court. Quartus de Wet, born in 1899 and died in 1980, was appointed by the government of Jan Smuts during the period of the United Party. On April 20, 1964, Nelson Mandela exposed why he did resort to violence as a tactic, revealing that the peaceful methods used by the ANC to resist apartheid for all those years up to the Sharpeville massacre did not stop the apartheid system. In front of the Supreme Court, he demonstrated that their only choice was to resist against the banning of the ANC and the declaration of the state of emergency by the government, which showed the failure of the National Party policies. For them to do otherwise would have been the same with a capitulation without condition. He concluded by stating, "All my life I have dedicated myself to the struggle for the African people. I have fought against white domination, and I have fought against black domination. I have cherished the ideal of a free and democratic society in which all persons would have lived together in harmony and with equal opportunities. It is an ideal which I hope to live and accomplish, but if necessary, it is an ideal for which I am prepared to die for."

That statement was fully reproduced in the great liberal English-language daily newspaper named the *Rand Daily Mail* of Johannesburg. On June 11, 1964, Nelson Mandela was put to question with his companions, and it was Quartus de Wet who judged him guilty of sedition and pronounced the sentence of life imprisonment of Nelson Mandela and his companions on June 12, 1964.

Through the international pressure, they escaped the death penalty, which they were liable by the influenced verdict that recognized them guilty of four charges. Jailed in the prison of Robben Island at the coast of Cape Town, Nelson Mandela spent eighteen years of his twenty-seven years in prison there. Then along with the main leaders of ANC, Mandela was transferred in March 1982 in a suburb of Cape Town at the prison of Pollsmoor. Living very rudimentary conditions in the prison and separated according to their skin color, black prisoners were receiving smaller rations. Political prisoners of which Nelson Mandela was part were separated from criminals. They had fewer privileges and common right. Mandela was only allowed one visit and one letter every six months. Often, it was a letter made unreadable by the prison censorship and delayed for a long time because he was of the lowest class D of prisoners not only political but also black. He was sleeping in a tiny cell, which has become a tourist attraction nowadays, and was bathing with cold seawater. If the Robben Island prison was to break the will of Mandela, it could not, but it only seemed to strengthen him because he was not accepting any treatment of favor. By refusing to call the guards and senior of the prison (boss; in Dutch, *Baas*) as required, he was continuing to fight for racial equality, his dignity, and the one of other prisoners despite the very harsh regime. On a nonviolent manner, he continued to resist the system. The man who long resisted the apartheid system and white settlers' domination was also an intellectual, and in what became the Mandela University, he was reciting and teaching the undefeated poem "Invictus" by William Ernest

Henley and was also speaking of politics as well as William Shakespeare.

The separated development of races or the policy of segregation (apartheid), established by the National Party, put to power in 1948 until its abolition in 1952, was forbidding blacks to live in the same cities as whites, and the Natives Act was also forbidding them to use the same infrastructure as them, unless they were working there for limited wages. In their own country, Nazism principles thus became the basis of a racist dictatorship, depriving them of the right to own property or just limited them to certain areas, excluded them from political rights. This was maintained officially in the eyes of all Western regimes with their tacit consent up to the end of the Cold War.

The Union of South Africa was created after the war of the Boers from 1899 to 1902, against the Boers who were seeking to resist British rule. Defeated, the Boers and the British colonists decided to join forces to create the Union of South Africa in 1910. To reinforce apartheid, the Union of South Africa left the commonwealth on May 31, 1961, by numerous critics of other members, and became the Republic of South Africa, and the country ceased to be a British dominion. It was the First World War that ended the German protectorate over South West Africa. To administer South West Africa, the League of Nations gave a type C mandate to the Union of South Africa on December 17, 1920. The South West African lands belonged to 41 percent of whites, and 43 percent of the territory consisted of reserves, under the supervision of tribal chiefs of Damaraland (country of Damara), located in west of Namibia, between 1980 and 1989; the Damara ethnic of Bantustan autonomous, speaking the Nama language; the Kaokoland (country of Kaoko) or Kaokoveld (Kaoko forest), located in the northwest of Namibia; the Himba ethnicity, a Bantu tribe of Namibia; the autonomous Bantustan, speaking Himba, mainly living in the Kaokoveld

(Kaoko forest), related to the Herero of the Bantu language group speaking Herero; the Kavangoland (country of Kavangos), located in the northeastern Namibia, between 1973 and 1989; the Kavango ethnicity, a group of Bantustan ethnic autonomous of the northern Namibia, living near the border with Angola, speaking the Rukwangal language; the Hereroland (country of Herero), located in the eastern Namibia, between 1970 and 1989; the Herero ethnic, Bantustan autonomous; the Namaland (country of Nama), located in the southern Namibia, between 1980 and 1989; the Nama ethnic, Bantustan autonomous, speaking the Nama language; the Ovamboland (country of Ovambo), located in the northern Namibia, between 1973 and 1989; the Ovambo ethnic group, Bantustan autonomous, speaking the Oshiwambo language; and the Rehoboth Bastards of the Rehobothers State, at South West Africa (present Namibia) occupied the rest of the territory in 1925.

The *Basters*: a word that contains the origin and the history of those who proudly claimed it to distinguish themselves from black Africans to whom they absolutely do not want to be assimilated to; but having a pejorative sense designating a people of Rehoboth or Rehobothers descendants of matrimonial relationships between African women and Dutch as baster settlers of the seventeenth century; living mainly in Namibia and in South Africa as a whole, left the Cape Colony in 1868. The Basters arrived in the Free Republic of Rehoboth, former Bantustan, Namibia, a city located on highlands at ninety kilometers from the center of Namibia, at the south of Windhoek, capital of Namibia; and they founded the Free Republic of Rehoboth in 1872 but originally a Nama territory. The first vote on universal suffrage took place in the 1994 general election, allowing each racial group to vote to mark the end of apartheid. All three referenda were held during the era of white minority government of the National Party in control during that period. The first referendum of 1960, at the request of prime minister Hendrik Verwoerd, was intended to renounce the status of commonwealth kingdom and become a republic since the Afrikaner National Party entered in power in 1948, considered the kingdom of the commonwealth as a relic of the British imperialism. Thus realizing the dream of an independent Afrikaner republic, the prime minister Hendrik Verwoerd, the "great architect of apartheid" born on September 8, 1901, in Amsterdam, north of the Netherlands, prohibited the African National Congress (ANC) and the Pan-African Congress in 1960.

He was assassinated on September 6, 1966. The second referendum of 1983 was an implementation of the tricameral parliament, a legislative body composed of three chambers, from 1984 to 1994. That regime adopted it to simplify the discussion of the elaboration of laws and therefore undemocratic. The tricameral parliament of the National Party (NP) was giving a limited political voice to the colored groups and Indian groups, totally excluding the group of the black majority population. That proposal was a continued response to a request of P. W. Botha, president of the council at that time, for the implementation of shared power between the Indian communities, whites, and colored groups—a presented series of proposals for the reform of the political constitution in 1982.

The implementation of that council president's proposal in 1983, which Botha continued to favor, introduced a new institutional framework to liberalize the institutional apartheid regime.

That reform aroused the discontent of a group of deputies of the right wing of the National Party (NP), headed by a cabinet minister, Dr. Andries Treurnicht, leader of the National Party in the province of Transvaal. To maintain the original form of apartheid, Dr. Andries Treurnicht broke away from the National Party to form the Conservative Party (CP) and fought for a return to apartheid. The third referendum was held on March 17, 1992. A white vote, resulting in 68 percent, favored the dismantling of apartheid through negotiations. This one was a proposal of reforms negotiated two years earlier, started by the state of President F. W. de Klerk that whites had supported, to put an end to apartheid. As the leader of the National Party, Frederik Willem de Klerk, born on March 18, 1936, in Johannesburg, Transvaal, the dominion of the Union of South Africa, was the last president of the apartheid state consolidated in 1948 in South Africa. Later on, his National Party became the New National Party. He is known to have supported the transformation of South Africa into a multiracial democracy and for engineering the end to racial segregation of apartheid. F. W. de Klerk announced the legalization of the African National Congress and the Pan-African Congress, as well as the release of Nelson Mandela, historic leader of ANC, on February 2, 1990, after meeting the first president of independent Zambia, Pres. Kenneth Kaunda, born on April 28, 1924, in Lubwa, Chinsali, in northern Rhodesia, the present Zambia, on August 28, 1989.

However, we know that Thabo Mbeki was ordered to leave South Africa on the instruction of ANC after the arrest and the imprisonment of his father, of Mandela, and Sisulu to lead a clandestine life. To complete his studies, he arrived in England at the age of nineteen and continued his studies in economics and African studies in an antiapartheid political training at the University of Sussex, located near the village of Falmer (East Sussex) four miles from Brighton. In the same university, from 1967 to 1985, a professor by the name of Harold Kroto carried out research leading to a Nobel Prize for Chemistry in 1996 after discovering the famous molecule used in nanotechnology called fullerene. Once Thabo Mbeki completed his studies, followed by the receipt of his diploma in 1966, he became a high officer of the armed wing of the ANC, the Umkhonto we Sizwe, still living a clandestine life. As a former foreign student in England, Thabo Mbeki received an honorary degree at the University of Sussex. In exile in Lusaka and Zambia, where the party had its headquarters, he was appointed assistant secretary of the revolutionary council of the ANC in 1971. From 1973 to 1974 in Botswana and from 1976 to 1978 in Nigeria and Swaziland, he represented ANC to foreign governments and negotiated for the opening of ANC office in Botswana. Specifically, he was appointed minister of foreign affairs of ANC and head of external relations department in 1989. And it was he who led the delegation of ANC, which secretly met the representatives of the South African government to continue talks leading to the legalization of the

ANC, started in 1985, and for the release of political prisoners. Zambia then housing several camps of ANC and its staff, Pres. F. W. de Klerk secretly met the representatives of ANC there. After Nelson Mandela's release from prison, Thabo Mbeki returned to South Africa, specifically in 1990, after spending twenty-eight years in exile.

Unconvinced by the ideology of Marxism spread by the South African Communist Party, the African nationalism was embodied in him, and he decided to initiate himself to the doctrine that Gandhi started in South Africa.

So he advocated a nonviolent resistance, a method that influenced not only Nelson Mandela and several generations of antiapartheid activists but also several generations of activists in different parts of the world, seeing in it a method to fight against oppression and colonialism. I quote the nonviolent activist Martin Luther King, an African-American Baptist pastor born on January 15, 1929, in poverty in Atlanta, Georgia, a state southern United States, and the leader of the black civil rights movement, for peace, and against poverty in the United States; an African American decades-long struggle to end racial segregation, discrimination, the state of depriving a right, especially the right to vote, and depriving the natural rights of black community, generally legalized between 1945 and 1970. Martin Luther King was known for his famous historic speech "I Have a Dream," generally considered as one of the greatest highlights of the twentieth century, pronounced to a number of participants varying according to police from two hundred thousand to over three hundred thousand, on the steps of the Lincoln Memorial in Washington on August 28, 1963. There were about 80 percent of African Americans and 20 percent of whites, including other ethnic groups, protesting in a political march on Washington for jobs and freedom. He inspired, he educated, and he guided not just the people who were there to listen to him speak as he did, but also people throughout America, as well as the future generations around the world. In his struggle against racial discrimination, the thirty-fifth President of the United States, John F. Kennedy—born on May 29, 1917, in Brooklyn, who took office on January 20, 1961, at the age of forty-three and was assassinated on November 22, 1963, in Dallas—expressed his absolute support for him. The Montgomery bus boycott was organized and led by him to defend the right to vote and employment of minorities.

The desegregation aimed at ending racial segregation in the United States was also because of him. It was under the presidency of Lyndon B. Johnson—born on August 27, 1908, in Stonewall, Texas, the thirty-sixth President of the United States elected in 1965 and who succeeded John F. Kennedy, assassinated during his term—that an act of Congress on voting rights (the Voting Rights Act) was signed on August 6, 1965. The Voting Rights Act abolished other bureaucratic restrictions that prevented blacks the right to vote in some southern states, subjecting them to pass a quite demanding formal literacy test, which most poor African Americans failed, including poll taxes that most did not have the means to pay before voting; although theoretically the vote of the Thirteenth, Fourteenth, and Fifteenth Amendments, proposed on February 26, 1869, and ratified on February 3, 1870, in the United States Constitution was disposing the voting rights to African-Americans; the extension of that act for another twenty-five years was signed on July 27, 2006, by the forty-third President of the United States, George W. Bush, born on July 6, 1946, in New Haven, Connecticut. He was in office from January 20, 2001, to January 20, 2009. Lyndon B. Johnson also signed the Civil Rights Act, originally designed to protect the rights of Africans-American, outlawing discrimination based on race, color, religion, sex, or national origin.

He created Medicare, Medicaid and launched a war program against poverty. Most of these rights were promoted by his nonviolent struggle against racial segregation and for peace. In 1964, Martin Luther King received the Nobel Peace Prize as the youngest laureate. He was assassinated on April 4, 1968, in Memphis, Tennessee, by James Earl Ray, born on March 10, 1928.

Sentenced to ninety-nine years in prison, he died on April 23, 1998, from hepatitis C. His participation in a conspiracy and his guilt in the assassination of Martin Luther King are still debated. In 1977, Jimmy Carter awarded him the Presidential Medal of Freedom as a posthumous title; in 1978, the United Nations Prize in the Field of Human Rights; and in 2004, the Congressional Gold Medal. And a holiday to commemorate the memory of one of America's and the world's greatest orators was assigned to his name since 1986 in the United States.

Clearly, he illustrated his desire to see the future with blacks and whites coexisting in harmony and living as equals by that most famous passage of his speech "I Have a Dream," a message of hope well beyond the United States borders and nowadays celebrated around the world, saying, I say to you today, my friends, even though we face the difficulties of today and tomorrow, I still have a dream. It is a dream deeply rooted in the American dream.

I have a dream that one day this nation will rise up and live out the true meaning of its creed. We hold these truths to be self-evident, that all men are created equal.

I have a dream that one day on the red hills of Georgia, the sons of former slaves and the sons of former slave owners will be able to sit down together at the table of brotherhood.

I have a dream that one day even the state of Mississippi, a state sweltering with the heat of injustice, sweltering with the heat of oppression, will be transformed into an oasis of freedom and justice.

I have a dream that my four little children will one day live in a nation where they will not be judged by the color of their skin but by the content of their character.

I have a dream today! I have a dream that one day, down in Alabama, with its vicious racists, with its governor having his lips dripping with the words of "interposition" and "nullification," one day right there in Alabama little black boys and black girls will be able to join hands with little white boys and white girls as sisters and brothers.

I have a dream today! I have a dream that one day every valley shall be exalted and every hill and mountain shall be made low, the rough places will be made plain, and the crooked places will be made straight; and the glory of the Lord shall be revealed and all flesh shall see it together.

The historical event that partly materialized elements of this speech was the election of the first black American Barack Obama, born on August 4, 1961, in Honolulu, Hawaii, as the forty-fourth President of the United States, who took office on January 20, 2009.

On February 11, 1990, Nelson Mandela was released by the government of Pres. Frederik de Klerk, with whom he supported the negotiation of reconciliation, thereby avoiding a civil war between the supporters of apartheid, those of the ANC, and those of the Inkatha Freedom Party, a conservative political party of Zulu founded by a former member of the Youth League of the African National Congress, Prince Mangosuthu Buthelezi, head of the territorial authority of KwaZulu in the Natal province in 1975. The Inkatha, which advocated a territorial separatism, became a staunch opponent of the African National Congress in the 1980s after being deployed in three other provinces.

That party was born from the National Cultural Liberation Movement; the Inkatha cultural organization was founded by King Solomon kaDinuzulu in 1920 to deal with British imperialism and the Afrikaner domination and fight against the extinction of Zulu culture. The Inkatha fought racial discrimination, alongside ANC in its beginnings, and then banned by the apartheid regime. But since the whites were accustomed to sow discord among people, Inkatha could not resist the proposal of the white governments. It was then that Mangosuthu Buthelezi, born on August 27, 1928, in Mahlabathini, Zululand, Natal province, was appointed prime minister of the autonomous Bantustan of KwaZulu, from 1976 to 1994, causing personal rivalries between black leaders. Since then, he was accused of being a collaborator of the apartheid regime with an indigenous military force, which was receiving weapons from a deadly squadron by the name of Vlakplaas, name of a farm twenty kilometers from Pretoria. The headquarters of the C10 unit (later C1), created in the early 1980s, commanded by Col. Eugene de Kock, was linked to the security services of the South African police engaged in the repression of the inhabitants of the ghettos in revolt. It was a phenomenal catastrophe for the most radical nearer to black consciousness. The Inkatha became a fierce potential rival backed by the government, and Buthelezi broke his connections with the ANC in 1980. Vlakplaas was used as a place of torture, assassinations, and executions of opposition members against apartheid. While a civil war was raging at the Natal between the Zulu of ANC and those of Inkatha, with over ten thousand deaths, the Inkatha was enjoying more or less the direct support of white paramilitary groups, and security forces were guaranteeing them certain impunity. In 1990, Buthelezi tried to appear as the key figure during the final negotiations with ANC at the release of Nelson Mandela.

Claiming the establishment of an independent Zulu state in South Africa, officially, he wanted to save his more practical privileges. He was then invited to participate in the elections of April 27, 1994, by ANC and the government. Buthelezi accepted and won by fraud in the new KwaZulu-Natal province.

To ensure civil peace, ANC renounced to report fraud; thus, under the aegis of Nelson Mandela, he allowed him to participate in his party in the national unity government. He became minister of internal affairs of South Africa from May 1994 to 2004 under the Nelson Mandela and Thabo Mbeki regime. Thabo Mbeki, born on June 18, 1942, a politician, was with Frederik de Klerk, one of the two vice presidents of Nelson Mandela from 1994 to 1996. He became the only vice president from 1996 to 1999, following the resignation of Frederik de Klerk. He was elected president of the South African Republic for the African National Congress, succeeding Nelson Mandela, and Jacob Zuma was chosen as his vice president.

Thabo Mbeki dismissed Zuma during his second term in 2005 for a corruption case of €3.7 billion related to an arms deal. The abandonment of the lawsuit in April 2009 by the party in power caused a serious split within ANC. For their peaceful actions favoring the end of the apartheid regime and for the elaboration of the democratic foundations of a new South Africa, Nelson Mandela and Frederik de Klerk jointly received the Nobel Peace Prize in 1993. Nelson Mandela retired from active politics after one term while condemning the excesses of the African National Congress (ANC), which he was publicly supporting.

Considered fully as the instigator of multiracial democracy and father of the South African nation, called the "rainbow nation," he was listened worldwide about human rights and continued to fight against community retreat caused by serious problems of economic inequality in the social mix up to his death on December 5, 2013, at Houghton Estate, Johannesburg, South Africa. Since then, the South African political life is dominated by ANC in the various general elections of 1994, 1999, 2004, and 2009, with 60 to 70 percent of the vote. The Chief Albert Luthuli House of twenty-two floors, which bore the name of Shell House, located in Johannesburg, is the headquarters of the ANC, and Jacob Zuma was the current president of the Republic of South Africa.

The apartheid, which settled in South Africa, was granted a mandate in South West Africa after the First World War. In that German territory, today Namibia, Germany reigned as a dangerous, sadistic member of violent criminal groups, mobsters in a word, seeking to affirm its unity since 1871 as a great world power. However, that colonial protectorate of apartheid definitively ended in 1990. That colonial protectorate of colonization dismembered Africa without taking into account the realities of the people but simply used the regrouping of different countries in subregions in a practical concern that was not a historical truth. Because of the expansion of colonial empires, the African continent only numbered two sovereign states: Abyssinia (former name of the Ethiopia Massif) and Liberia in 1914; in 1922, Egypt; and in 1931, the South African Union were added to the two first sovereign states.

After the Second World War, the independence of African countries did not cease to increase—four in 1945, twenty-seven in 1960, for a total of fifty-three in 1993—generally among which North Africa, black Africa (also known as the sub-Saharan Africa), and Southern Africa were distinguished. And all its borders were from colonization; they dismembered Africa by initiating hatred, separating some ethnic groups by ethnic layers, sprinkled with germs of wars and promoting wars in noncleaved ethnicities; then wars exploded, resulting in the separation of a once united community, in small communities without agreement; depriving some funding of projects initiated by those same communities of those colonized countries not only proved us the failure of their system but also expressly made specifically to create poverty, by sinking them into the wrong management, which is today preventing the development of the industry—a fatality in Africa.

The strong African empires of Ahmadou, of Rabah in Chad, of Almamy Samory in Sudan, of Mali, of Niger, and the real African resistances quickly crashed, facing the conquest, with violent resistances in the interior of countries, truly devastating indigenous populations. Blacks were enrolled by force in the battalions of the conquest to form black troops to oppress their fellow indigenous in forced labors and lead the unjust systematic looting of the populations. Thus, the resistance that was opposing weapons and the colonial penetration into the interior of countries was significantly reduced.

Commercial products such as cocoa, coffee, cotton, rubber, palm oil, etc., have always been their monoculture farming exploitation and are still essential for their infrastructure that they have put in place; favoring the depletion of the soil, leading to the collapse of food production and the disappearance of rural self-sufficiency, thanks to forced labor for products directed entirely toward exportation.

Their intention was to speculate but not at all to develop. It was from that point that the living standards of the African population stagnated, and life was regressing since then despite an exploitation of agricultural products and raw materials and the productive investments of investors, who were using Africa as a reservoir for metropolitan manufactured goods since the time of slavery up to the present day. Their administrations relied in fact on local notables to fight against the former local leaders of the overexploited rural mass, a strategy that appeared with colonization. That mass was and is still especially opposed to the brutality, to the authority without limit, to uncontrolled looting, and to the destruction of nature—for example, killing animals for the pleasure of killing. On behalf of a civilization of superiority, racism, used as a mode of government, was destroying cultural heritage and still does because they were juggling humanity, particularly Africans, not only in Africa but also beyond Africa, by their will. Colonization, I would say in general, was therefore not a civilization mission but a strong international export competition, a vast movement of capital for the aim of capitalism, a fierce competition between imperialist powers. The colonial conquest made substantial profits, which rapidly benefited the capitalists, supported mostly by the indigenous people. For these quick benefits, the administration costs of those European colonial capitalists left Africa in the financial abyss.

These effects of intensive clearing of African territory to make place for agriculture, ranches, and the intensive mining exploitation eventually caused increased deforestation and damaged territories. The indigenous people of those regions, in particular those who lived by subsistence farming, were victims of the dismantling and destruction of land resources, replaced by agricultural export products. Consequently, they had no choice but to enter into an unhealthy relationship of forced dependency with the landowners and manufacturers, leading thereby to a barbarous social class war, particularly when the Industrial Revolution (fed by the expropriation of the materials from the Americas and African) gained momentum. The African ethnic groups and ancient kingdoms were victims of boundaries set by multiple bilateral treaties from the principle of territorial compensation between artificial compromises of Europeans. This is how the image of our rich and populous black Africa became wrongly dangled by these intruders. Prejudices against African people pushed them to migrate away from their colony by vexations and countless losses. The intentions of that departure beyond the borders, in the spirit of the native tribes, never had the evidence to break the sacred bond that united them to the land where they were born. In addition, the dishonesty, the unjustifiable hatred of the white authorities, manifested under the guise of religion led to huge losses of life inflicted by forced submission, infested all African countries; Africans since then, not foreseeing future for themselves and for their children in our countries so rich but troubled, saw them only resulting in total ruins throughout our continent.

The principles of freedom waved everywhere in the universe did not really succeed to reprimand crimes and prejudices or care to maintain specific rules to preserve respect for humanity. The interference of our colonizers did not let us govern ourselves in our rich land that saw our birth but pushed us to enter the wild and dangerous territories by humiliation and the loss of all our dignity by believing and obeying humbly to the omniscient, just, and merciful being.

Up to our days, the intellectual superiority of the human being has not convinced the limited white species, who are continuing to believe in the inferiority of races, are inflicting them the most frightful abuses. How is it that, in the history of mankind, your intellectual superiority, which you so undoubtedly presumed to have, only led and still leads you to carry out barbaric acts of uncivilized savage beings against other weak beings by military power or by killing one black today, and maybe ten tomorrow like in the United States? Be aware that Negroes are proud to be Negroes.

Oh, yes, believe me a thousand times. They have never, to my knowledge, asked the white men to be elevated to the level of the white men and certainly never asked for help or to be protected by white men, who have no concept of intellectual or moral relationships. So, know that if sociologically our species is susceptible to mingle with yours, it is because of our common nature.

Europeans were assimilated to the lions because only the lion killed to satisfy his hunger. And for a European, massacring the black was a glory, a right, a cruel quality, and a trickery, which led him to believe in his intellectual superiority to overcome his complex beside the weak. A winner is only praiseworthy if the opponent has competitive skills, not chasing the weak natives in their territory with firearms that he did not have; capture him, enchain him, treat him more than anything disgusting with strong indignation by boasting to be superior; and simultaneously forbid him to defend himself by qualifying him to be bloodthirsty; but approving his own act worthy by mass killing of his fellow, the white race was characterized from its earliest emergence as uncivilized; by its cruel law and its barbarism toward itself and by the invasion of other nations for wealth. Till today, we still find traces of this cruelty at the coasts of the African shoreline, complaining to the nature, by old forts formerly armed with cannons, guns, and bodyguards who raised the bridge day and night in an environment that had never known such cruelties.

These kingdoms, beyond the lagoons at several days of walk from the coast, where our kings lived deep in their palaces in a pleasant atmosphere, were subjugated by foreigners, by tormentors surrounded by their bloodthirsty dignitaries, leaning on a power of a strong contingent of their army wearing a kind of uniform and speaking a kind of awful language. Their number was not estimable. They surrounded the king's army, which was without a doubt, the strongest core of the kingdom, with approximately two to four thousand soldiers armed with light archers with ivory bangle, where rested the arrow to aim, and sometimes old popguns, and the cohort of elephant hunters, not more trained than their European opponents.

Alas, their black god could not operate miracle before such horrible infernal machine of savagery, which on the littoral coast chastised the Cameroonian tribes; horrified the Congo, amputated Nigeria of its population, fiercely emptying the coast of gold, damaging the Dahomey kingdom, and from Senegal to where you would like to limit them, etc., invaded the coasts of Africa with on board ships, English, Dutch, French German, Portuguese, and Spanish, equipped with fire guns, cannons, multiple ammunition and were affirming their requirements with a rare insolence inhumanity, on the poor, helpless children of Africa.

The great provinces of our Africa were now controlled by the Western powers, who continued their criminal works in the depth to consolidate my Africa. There was only one way to reach this goal. They could only use the combined action of force and seduction. But the insubordination of populations unfortunately made this very difficult. Their policy was to destroy and ruin to better build. So, did they build? No. Their interests were only to prepare the ground for their future undertakings, destined to compel submission of the people, who would later on be their main agents and collaborators to well carry out those undertakings. Their seduction policy attracted the most important part of the inhabitants of our countries, having a great power of knowledge; their goal was to extract this knowledge and determine the political organization to give it, and the means to be used for its submission and to use it against us.

Their first efforts were to study the races that occupy a region and successfully develop a sufficiently accurate ethnographic map of the territory for any territorial command by opposing people, tribes, families, any agglomeration of individuals, and by opposing the manners and customs to be respected with racism; unravelling one another to obtain rivalries and hatreds by relying on some to better defeat the others; these practices were their cruel strategies for them to establish a political action of common interests used for their profits.

It also consisted in neutralizing the usable local elements primarily for profit above all and destroying unusable local elements by dragging the African people into deception; momentarily, they had a soft face for the working mass of the population to not feel their cruelty, but quickly understood that they were manipulated for the interest to generate them wealth; this is what our African brainless leaders do not understand till today that, that system was deliberately set up in Africa, like elsewhere. First there was slavery, barbarism, and crimes to break the African moral, followed by colonization, the role of a soldier, who took the trade to open markets; then the administrator went to study the submissive populations and satisfy their social needs; on the other hand, he created opportunities for European trade, by developing the natural wealth of the African soil for the extension of colonization.

These conditions imposed on us, qualified as the economic development of a colony, are completely contradictory to the life of the native, which generally has very few needs. The new mode of existence that whites made us adopt leads us to live in a neighboring state of misery by creating in our countries, essential needs that we absolutely do not need, and to get to those resources that we no longer have, we must find them somewhere else to improve our lives. The consequence of this need for the well-being is naturally the importation of items that we lack for the benefit of trade and for the European economic development. Today, the industrial footprint in the African continent—whether banana, rubber, palm, the installation of fecund cultural models that we do not know the processes, the establishment of national industries of subsidized factories presented as a way to create free markets but very gradually imposed laws thereafter, or again, providing labor assistance to European settlers, etc.—are just methods allowing the Europeans to remain the master. Always obedient to the noblest ideal of formidable forces, natives have braved the greatest dangers and endured all sufferings.

Their value, their sense of nobility helped them to enfranchise that odious domination up to the disappearance of that shameful scourge of slavery from the face of the world. But the battle is not yet over. The scandal of evil abuses in the supposed called properties of European countries continued—they who brought their views on countries overseas, with the moral and material interests to radiate beyond their narrow borders, for opportunities of all its manufacturing workers of a trading nation like theirs.

At the beginning of that labor creation, powers applauded the place taken by another state to grow their capital there, thanks to the support of those with capital and the labor in mind. Channels of rapid communication and economics were quickly opened, thanks to the vast fluvial network, which allowed its direct penetration up to the center of our African continent. These were the conditions that determined the creation of the African workforce for the benefit of those who have never benefited from that national interest exploited with great pomp to date. The realization of this daring African work continues to this day, in the same thought of interest, guided and supported so far by our African leaders.

Since 1884, some European countries like Belgium appropriated Congo under private ownership. In that country, chiefs were arrested and held prisoner because the natives who were subjected to the payment of a tax by a determined number of kilograms of rubber or copal, peanuts, or food was late or in default of payment. In addition, women and children were often held hostage by the state. Harvesters who had not completely supplied their imposition were whipped by belts or long strips of leather. Some natives had to pay very high fines, imposed on villages by civil servants or military officials. Moreover, natives were called to do certain work and were paying tax at the same time.

The history of the black race in America from 1619 to 1880 and from 1800 to 1880 is a work published in 1882 to 1883 in two volumes by George Washington Williams, born on October 16, 1849, in Bedford Springs, Pennsylvania, USA. George Washington Williams participated in combat on the side of the Union Army during the American Civil War at the age of fourteen years old. He studied theology at Cambridge, Massachusetts, after the war. Then he worked as a Baptist pastor in Boston and Cincinnati in Ohio. He became a black jurist and the first African American to be elected in the legal system of Ohio. In his book, one of the first on the history of African Americans, he summarized the history of Africa and reported on the black governments of Sierra Leone and Liberia. Then activist for the cause of the persecuted African Americans by the splinter group of the Ku Klux Klan, he struggled to obtain their civil rights to put an end to racial segregation, especially in the southern states.

He presented us blacks as slaves, blacks as soldiers, and blacks as citizens. As a politician with a preliminary consideration on the unity of the human family, he tried to obtain the repeal of a law banning interracial marriages by raising fury. As speaker, he hosted several conferences on the black cause. In 1889, despite the objections of King Leopold II, he traveled to Central Africa, was especially brought to meet Leopold II for an interview, and saw the living conditions of the Congolese.

Because of his Metis origins, he was nicknamed Mundele Ndombe, meaning "the white black," by the Congolese Lingala, a Bantu language used by over eight million people in the northern parts of Congo (formerly Zaire), today the Democratic Republic of Congo. When he discovered the Belgian colonial work on the field, he criticized King Leopold II, describing the actions of colonization as crimes against humanity. George Washington Williams severely condemned the oppression and colonial brutality that the Congolese people suffered in his famous open letter of ten pages to Leopold II in 1890, a letter that was widely distributed, raising vivid outcries in America and Europe against the Belgian political class and more particularly against Leopold II.

He also mentioned the role played by Henry Morton Stanley, a British journalist and explorer born in Wales on January 28, 1841, in Denbigh, who was sent to Congo by the king, who met him on June 10, 1878, and made a five-year agreement with him. To make ensure that this agreement was in formal order, Leopold II took care of funding, and Stanley acquired Congo by tricking and mistreating Africans.

Because upon his arrival in Congo, he collected purchased contracts of lands around the river by making tribal leaders sign documents in an unknown language, in which a contract clause indicated not only that the workforce of the inhabitants of Congo would become the possession of Leopold II but also that the Congolese soil, with a reputable subsoil so rich, which contained minerals such as copper, cobalt, silver, uranium, lead, zinc, cadmium, diamond, gold, tin, tungsten, manganese, and coltan, would become his private property. He thereby made Leopold II guilty of the exactions committed in Congo.

Before his death in 1891 in Blackpool, England, George Washington Williams appealed to the international community to create an international commission to investigate the above charges perpetrated on behalf of humanity.

An Open Letter to His Serene Majesty Leopold II; King of the Belgians and Sovereign of the Independent State of Congo by Colonel, the Honorable Geo. W. Williams, of the United States of America, 1890.

Good and Great Friend,

I have the honor to submit for your Majesty's consideration some reflections respecting the Independent State of the Congo, based upon a careful study. Every charge which I am about to bring against your Majesty's personal Government in the Congo has been carefully investigated; a list of competent and veracious witnesses, documents, letters, official records and data has been faithfully prepared.

About the submission of villages: thanks to few boxes of gin, whole villages were abandoned by a signature away to your Majesty. Lands purchased by such means are territories to which Your Majesty cannot claim legally.

About military bases established on the river: These piratical, buccaneering posts compel the natives to furnish them with fish, goats, fowls, and vegetables at the mouths of their muskets; and whenever the natives refuse to feed these vampires, they report to the main station and white officers come with an expeditionary force and burn away the homes of the natives.

About the manner in which justice is rendered: the government of your majesty is excessively cruel to its prisoners, condemning them to be chained like slaves for the slightest offences, to the chain gang, not seen in any other Government in the civilized or uncivilized world...Often, these oxchains, the neck collars, were gnawing the neck of the prisoners and caused wounds infested by flies, aggravating the festering wound...The courts of the Government of your Majesty are abortive, unjust, partial and delinquent.

About the slavery: The Government of your Majesty is engaged in trade and commerce, competing with the organized trade companies of Belgium, England, France, Portugal and Holland...

The Government of your Majesty is engaged in the slave trade of wholesale and retail. It buys sells and steals slaves.

The Government of your Majesty gives three pounds per head for slaves physically fit for military service...The workforce in the government stations of your Majesty on the upper river is composed of slaves of all ages and both sexes; and the black soldiers, laborers of your Majesty's, many of whom are slaves, exercise the power of life and death on these natives, the greatest curse the country suffers now.

Geo. W. WILLIAMS
Stanley falls, in Central Africa,

18th of July 1890.

The insolence and shame of intellectuals toward the crimes committed by their ancestors led them to always insult the intellectuality of the African people. But whatever you do, these crimes will remain in your memory like a cancer and will only free you when you would have accepted them. So do not believe that saying that the African populations were drawn from the primitive savagery gave you the right to steal our resources, to kill them, and to rape African women. Tell us, did we ask you to come and remove us from our primitive savagery? No and a thousand times no. You came on your own initiative, in the territory of someone with your savagery, to take what did not belong to you. By these facts, none of the African countries that have been besieged by whites never could evolve, even after fifty years of the so-called independence of those states. Belgium should be pursued by the international court for all the crimes committed in Congo.

That royal family still lives to this day with the blood money that Leopold II stole, and his government was fully involved in that fraud. That abuse of Negroes by whites was always explained by a need to create a legal framework in which political chaos would be ordered. Come on, you have only created chaos and let chaos happen wherever you passed.

The boundaries that you traced have messed up Africa; the economic tools that you started did not work. So, tell us, how long must it take for it to work since, according to you, the foundation of an empire would not be a day work? Leopold II was saying that we couldn't accomplish a great work without the part of evil. For him to seize the property of someone else was a great work. He continued by giving this example during the construction of a cathedral, where many inevitably unfortunate incidents occurred by saying, there will be injustice, accidents, fights, and sometimes violent brawls. We've heard insults and profanity, but ultimately, the monument was completed for the glory of God and the salvation of souls; it was the same in Congo. Bravo! Only fine words were from your speeches but nothing good. But what do you build as a monument in Congo, or elsewhere in Africa? Nothing at all. After so many protests from both sides, he was obliged to correct his mistakes, his serious abuses, the injustice toward the indigenous and the serious imperfections reported in the administration of his judicial system and his colony. That correction was a way for me to recognize his exactions.

The examples of injustice abuses of power, and orchestrated killings by the regime of colonization, which treated us as primitive savages, proved to be more savage than the word savage. I must say that you really have to be a thousand times inhuman to know that the treatments prescribed by those settlers were frankly administered frequently by white humans to black humans in Africa and all over the world. The young people who freshly landed in Africa were racists of first class and were arriving in Africa without any education. They were people who had never worked or occupied a lesser responsibility—a nobody you may say, without experience, and without moderation. Immediately, they found themselves invested in positions of power and became true pain inflictors, establishing a system of good pleasure within their range of action; and that good pleasure was to inflict maximum pain on Africans. It must be said that this behavior was intolerable to those you called savages but tolerated by the administration of the colonial regime. In general, these governments, which came from afar to arrange chaos according to them in Africa, had no control over how their administrators applied regulations.

The station chiefs, soldiers, agents of various concessionary companies, each one was a wren, and that is why they left Africa in a chaotic state, pretending that they came for a civilizing mission, while they themselves were not civilized. I do not believe that giving 50, 100, 150, or 200 blows of Chicot to workers explained any sort of civilization. But believe me; that measure was a corporal punishment and the favorite penalty used, not only against the workers but also on all natives, noble or not. And very often, the one who inflicted that pain by whipping was not even realizing that the native was dead, but continued to tear his skin without any remorse; and if he did not die there, he would let him die without care, with his bleeding skin completely torn. All this was happening after a disturbing period on the moral plane, requiring a personal questioning concerning a period where this same white at first, voluntarily captured and chained the ancestors of these same African people to deport them overseas as slaves.

Imprisonment was also one of their cruelties, an absolutely murderous retribution. The coercion—a detention system of women and children—was especially recommended as a very effective system, practiced for persuading them to do something by using threats or strength. All prisoners were chained and treated like real prisoners, with orders to shoot fugitives. An escape attempt was inevitably punished by death. The women prisoners were subjected to the hardest work one could ever imagine and were continuously raped by the department chiefs, guards, soldiers, and agents of various operating companies.

It is in all likelihood deplorable to know with which easiness they were using firearms, because blacks were killed as worthless objects.

A medieval principle known by the name of "glebe," literally meaning field, a piece of cultivated land or land of an estate, used to provide income for the settler's benefice; meaning here that the natives, the serfs: the agricultural laborers, bound under the feudal system to work on their lord's estate, were attached to a village that they had to cultivate to provide benefit as a mandatory rule imposed upon them; in addition, they could not go to another village without a pass issued by the chiefs of various companies or factories, which had each about twenty or more armed soldier-workers, not having the right to inflict corporal punishment on workers, but administered it anyway with a frequency more than great; meaning that women living in other villages had no husband and were not also allowed to leave their village to marry natives in other villages. Don't be surprised, but it was a system that was tacitly accepted.

Blacks were working like slaves in rubber-producing regions for faster and maximum harvest of that product. Violating that rule was lethal. The sole purpose was for commercial purpose and not the welfare of the country or the natives. Military expeditions were ordered against villages not satisfactory from the standpoint of harvesting rubber.

The state officials—such as district commissioners, station chiefs, and senior military officers—even received high premiums from concessionary companies, generally for agreeing to be the instruments of inflicting inhuman corporal punishment to the natives. The absolutely incontestable freedom of the agents' actions was generally of unquestioned legal impunity; they were considered as omnipotent and having no limits on their ability to inflict punishments of any kind. Natives were imprisoned by the chiefs of post for not bringing more food than required. These excessive impositions were a ridiculous situation for the natives, who had to be submitted to the heads, who were exceeding their rights, knowing that they would be whipped for expressing their grievances to the magistrate. The administration' tolerance for these abuses favored repression and made difficult the role of judicial authorities to enforce punitive justice against bad officials in the military expeditions commanded by those same officers, and companies were accomplishing less control in their operations.

The sanitary conditions in which the natives lived were absolutely devastating and favored epidemics as sleeping sickness, which greatly ravaged the natives, from the carelessness of colonial states. The cause of the slave trade and the enslavement of blacks murdered, forced to commit suicide after being tortured and raped, must be heard, but their history—the slavery of Negroes in the Bible by the Jews, who launched all these negationists gossips, embarrasses, bothers, alienates, terrifies, and importunes revisionists to the point that could lead to reality; if we do not carefully deny it, it will always seem real in everyday life; knowing that this history of the Jewish concerning Negroes never existed. Your cruel Jewish nature made the history of the dead blacks, who received you with open arms disappear. It also made the traces of their generous hearts disappears, which you once begged to give you hospitality, and their footsteps and honorable works were destroyed.

Oh, Africa! On your wild land of Africa, everything has been erased, and those same people you protected for a long time have soon forgotten thy divine goodness. Before our eyes, pursue your present history, and your past is inscribed on the nefarious efforts of your colonials. But beautifully, you will be accomplished without fault and with such enormous invocative philosophies.

Oh, Africa! As the breath with strength and vigor suggests it, your dead ancestors are not dead; they're pursuing your present history in the shadow that thickens and the shadow that enlightens.

No, your dead are not dead; they're acquiring your memory in truth and vigilance on your part. No, they're not dead but buried because of their spirit of free examination, which animated with wisdom and nobility. Yet they're continuing your history with full attention, and the one of a rewritten era between the beginnings of capitalism, founded for that same slavery system, and held for the destruction of humanity, once their slavery system reached mature. Your history of thousand sheets is their history of economic and political development, under the pressure of each era's events.

Pursue your present history in a historical part of the world, where you were born with nobility and where you engendered mankind. It is the right of all governments of Africa to request a correction on that passage of the Bible, bearing that injury toward the black humanity, and it is even their duty to associate themselves to various economic and social actors, who loudly clamor for our wealth, to remedy this disastrous situation confronting our continent since the beginning of time; and start investments in the economic and social infrastructures of our countries, for a vigorous, sustainable, and more equitable development; but apparently, nothing concrete worthwhile will be done for future generations without boldness nor generosity; otherwise, the continent will continue to decline and darkens the future of the entire African population. Definitely, the moral secular authority of our generation will be evaluated in terms of our positions and subjected to comparison, to the permanent struggle for freedom and for the dignity that our ancestors and their predecessors waged, and that our fathers and ourselves, have not ceased to extol to the world, and could not be abandoned.

Before the Slavery Abolition Act, entered with vigor on August 1, 1834, in all regions of the British Empire, slavery remained legal. After the American War of Independence, the Sierra Leone Company was created through the work of ardent abolitionists, such as Granville Sharp, one of the first Englishmen involved in the correction of social injustices who campaigned for the abolition of the slave trade. The English hero of abolition, born on November 10, 1735, in Durham, England, fought and obtained a positive right recognizing the freedom of a fugitive slave on the British soil who escaped from his master by the legal judgments of Lord Mansfield, the lord chief justice of Great Britain. For his theoretical effort and judicial action, before his death on July 6, 1813, in Fulham, the abolitionist Granville Sharp started legal proceedings for the trial of the African American slave James Somerset, judged by Lord Mansfield, born on March 2, 1705, which ended with his liberation in 1772; it was decreed that slavery was illegal in England well before its abolition in 1833.

This first Earl of Mansfield, politician and British judge, died on March 20, 1793. The British scholar Granville Sharp was one of the founding fathers of Sierra Leone, called the Province of Freedom; he elaborated the plan and founded the precursor of the Sierra Leone Company, named St. George's Bay Company. With the help of a freed slave of current Nigeria by the name of Olaudah Equiano, born around 1745 in Biafra, precisely at Isseke, Granville Sharp tried in 1783 to advance the abolitionist cause. The story of this child of African origin became abolitionist is remarkable; let us take a look at his journey.

The ten-year-old Olaudah Equiano was kidnapped and transferred to Barbados. He became a slave sold several times. From Barbados, he became the property of a British naval officer to serve him as a sailor and began to serve his master. Meanwhile, he was renamed; and as a mockery accompanied by contempt, he was named after Gustav Vasa, the one who was first the regent of Sweden from 1521 to 1523 and then from 1523 to his death, king of Sweden.

His owner took him to Virginia and to England and served during the Seven Years' War. After the Seven Years' War, an English trader bought him, but his former owner, needing to free him, bought him back on July 11, 1766, for £40, and he became a free man. In 1767, he worked in London as a barber.

In 1773, Constantine John Phipps, a British naturalist, embarked him again for an expedition in the Arctic regions, New England, and Nicaragua. This was how Olaudah Equiano, the British Calvinist writer who mainly lived in the British colonies of America, became an influential figure in the abolition of slavery in the United Kingdom. Thus, in 1783, he accompanied Granville Sharp in Freetown, Sierra Leone, founded in 1787, for the installation of the first formerly freed black slaves in Africa. As one of the very few direct testimonials of the slave trade, he published his autobiography, at the request of abolitionists under this title: *The Interesting Narrative of the Life of Olaudah Equiano, or Gustavus Vassa, the African* in 1789; his testimony about his separation from his family, his fear of childhood, and his conditions of slave life largely contributed and used by the British abolitionist movement.

For this struggle, Lord Mansfield addressed the British courts by saying that the case of slaves was exactly similar to the one of horses, that this was so shocking. Olaudah Equiano died on March 31, 1797, in Cambridgeshire, United Kingdom.

On the list of these spokesmen for African slaves, added the name of Ottobah Cugoano. This young man of African origin was born in 1757 in what is today Ghana. At age thirteen, he was kidnapped and transported to Granada against his will and became a slave. Then he was transferred to England to be baptized in 1773 under the name of John Stuart, and it was in England that he was released. After his liberation, Quobna Ottobah Cugoano obtained a post the date of his baptism from the first painter of the Prince of Wales as a servant.

His privilege in the court of the first painter of the Prince of Wales allowed him to see the injustice suffered by his brothers still slaves in England. And his experience in plantations in Grenada, an island, a country in the southeastern Caribbean Sea, and the appalling living conditions of the slaves which horrified him, led him to write to express his thoughts toward the slavery. In 1787, he published his ref lections on the slavery of Negroes and became a staunch spokesman of the African slaves. Quobna Ottobah died around 1801 in England.

Henry Thornton was an English reformer and activist for the abolition of the slave trade, born on March 10, 1760; he was one of the most active English supporters of the abolitionist cause and one of the creators of the Sierra Leone Company, who played a major role in its creation. He was a politician aiming to end the slave trade from Africa with his close friends and collaborators William Wilberforce and Zachary Macaulay. He died on January 16, 1815.

William Wilberforce, a lover of life, who was putting humanity at the forefront of his priorities, was born in Yorkshire on August 24, 1759 in Kingston-upon-Hull. As a politician and reformer, with Thomas Clarkson, Granville Sharp, Hannah More, and Charles Middleton, he quickly became the most influential man in Britain for the abolitionist cause in 1787.

Those two sons of Africa and other freed black slaves wrote open letters that provoked debate in the societies that newspapers and enthusiastic, influential people took to support the campaign against the slave trade. Respectively, in 1787 and 1789, they also wrote influential books on the slavery and the slave trade.

William Wilberforce campaigned and defended causes for the abolition of slavery. He fought the slave trade led through the means of exchanges between Europe, Africa, and the Americas during the sixteenth century in Britain. The British involved in the trade were transporting manufactured goods from home to exchange them in Africa and buy slaves to ensure the distribution of black slaves in the colony's plantations of the New World. This transfer of slaves in the New World was in exchange for coffee, cocoa, cotton, tobacco, and gold for the benefit of the transporter to the European ports in 1783.

Since the ships of Great Britain dominated this trade, which represented about 80 percent of their foreign income, it supplied other colonies of Europe- namely, the Spanish colonies, the Dutch and the French colonies, etc., with slaves. This trade was active upstream; first, they had to find excuses to justify this traffic and then raise capitals, the necessary ships, men, and finally, the goods, while the processing of commodities was done downstream. The routing of chained African captives enslaved in the Americas was not only in places where captives were transiting but also in the residence of the ideology which led the system of the slave trade, with Rio de Janeiro as the first slave port in the world. To provide those colonies by ships, Great Britain was transporting up to forty thousand slaves annually to the other side of the Atlantic. Knowing that Africans deported from Africa to the New World were dying en masse during the voyage and their frightful living conditions in plantations, prompted the abolitionist William Wilberforce to focus on activities of the causes for the abolition. Convinced, he campaigned for the creation of a colony for freed slaves in Sierra Leone up to his death on July 29, 1833, three days after the passing of the Slavery Abolition Act 1833, abolishing slavery in most of the British Empire, and was buried in Westminster Abbey.

During the crossing with the deported, there were about 1.4 million death Africans. Zachary Macaulay was a colonial governor born in Inveraray, Scotland, on May 2, 1768. After serving in the army of the East India Company, he later became an abolitionist activist. With some of his spearhead friends and emblematic figures of the Protestant humanitarian movement, the Briton was invited to visit the colony of Sierra Leone in 1790. In 1792, Sierra Leone became the first British colony in West Africa, and Zachary Macaulay became governor there in 1794. That colony of Sierra Leone, founded by the Sierra Leone Company, was set up by his new companions Granville Sharp and Henry Thornton. Throughout England in the nineteenth century, it was a chartered organization with about forty thousand members, intended to receive black loyalists and to send freed black slaves away from the former American slave colonies, who chose the British side during the American War of Independence.

After transiting through Nova Scotia, some of them mingled with the poor black community and moved to London, and the plan conceived at the same time in Britain allowed the installation of the majority of this community in countries such as Liberia and Sierra Leone, considered to be the original territory of these freed slaves in Africa. And in 1796, the reconquered Negro Maroons of Jamaica deported in Nova Scotia, completed the settlement of Freetown.

Those black Americo-Liberian slaves, freed by the American Colonization Society established in 1816 by Robert Finley of New Jersey, supported the migration of free African Americans to the continent of Africa. This Society for the Colonization of Free Color People of America helped to found the colony of Liberia in 1821–1822 on the coast of West Africa as the birthplace of free or manumitted American black back in Africa. These blacks, once in Africa, decided to establish a slavery lifestyle as masters, which installed tensions between the indigenous Liberian population and them. The Americo-Liberian elite retained power for a century, after the independence of Liberia from its first president, Joseph Jenkins Roberts, in 1847, with a threshold of imposition against the right to vote and the eligibility of indigenous citizens.

On behalf of the United States multinationals, the Germans and the Swedish etc., in the rubber industry, they imposed forced labor conditions to the indigenous, which they were placing as second-class citizens, until the League of Nations (LN) condemned forced labor in 1931. The voting rights for indigenous Liberians was granted by Pres. William Tubman in May 1945, after a scandal forcing the government to resign in 1936, and it was on that date that forced labor was prohibited by the new government.

The obtaining of the abolition of slavery in 1807 did not lessen his fight, so he concentrated his activity in the British Empire for the total abolition of slavery until the Slavery Abolition Act 1833. Macaulay died on May 13, 1838, in London. At the Westminster Abbey, where he was buried, a memorial was erected in his honor. And a medallion symbolizing the fight against slavery was engraved under his bust, representing a kneeling slave with this inscription: "Am I not a man and a brother?"

The moralist Hannah More was a woman dealing with social works and patronage. Born in 1745 in Fishponds near Bristol, the talented British poetess, woman of letters, and spiritual woman published several works. To only name a few of her works, I would begin with the first original publication in 1766 called *The Search after Happiness,* written in 1762, which sold more than ten thousand copies in the mid-1780s. From the five dramas she wrote, the last one not intended for performance called the *Sacred Dramas* was published originally in 1787, written in 1782; in 1786, the poems "The Bas Bleu" and "Florio" were published; in 1788, she wrote *Thoughts on the Importance of the Manners of the Great to General Society* (based on ref lections on the influence, the manners of people quality on the rest of society); and a poem about the Slave Trade titled "Slavery," also in 1788. In 1791, she wrote *An Estimate of the Religion of the Fashionable World.* And without a stop, Hannah More wrote numerous books and moral manuals; one of them published in 1799 was *Strictures on the Modern System of Female Education.* She continued writing about subjects based on the Bible, on Christian morals, on freedom, on politics, etc., until her last book called the *Spirit of Prayer* in 1825, originally published in 1833. After meeting the leading figures of the abolitionist movement here above, she became an abolitionist. And on September 7, 1833, Hannah More died old, retaining all her faculties till two years before her death. John Clarkson was a conscientious solidary, fair and reasonable colony administrator younger brother of Thomas Clarkson. He was born on April 4, 1764, in Wisbech, England. Universally respected by the settlers, he was designated as one of the central figures of the abolition of slavery in Britain and the British Empire in the late eighteenth century. He contributed to the founding of Freetown, today the capital of Sierra Leone, as an agent of the

Sierra Leone Company for the resettlement of some former American slaves on the west coast of Africa, mainly moved to Nova Scotia.

Lieutenant Clarkson did not only found Freetown but also was the first governor of the colony, one of the most popular in Sierra Leone and respected for his work with the settlers in Nova Scotia, Canada, and Sierra Leone. He struggled to represent black communities of Nova Scotia with great respect and to ensure the installation of volunteers in the region of the mouth of Sierra Leone River. He died in Woodbridge, Suffolk, East Anglia, England, on April 2, 1828.

Thomas Clarkson was the one who helped found the Committee for the Abolition of the Slave Trade and campaigned against the slave trade in the British Empire. He was born on March 28, 1760, in Wisbech, Cambridgeshire, England. His support helped put an end to the British slave trade and in other countries of the British Empire by the adoption of the law on slave trade in 1807. The abolitionist died on September 26, 1846, in Playford, Suffolk, England.

The Republic of Sierra Leone, today known as a state of West Africa, was formerly known under the name of Granville City; this state is located between Guinea at the northwest and Liberia and bordered at the southwest by the Atlantic Ocean. Sierra Leone was created in 1787 by the Committee for the Relief of the Black Poor in London to arrange the transport of supposedly poor blacks from London to Sierra Leone by the early English settlers. These poor black loyalists had to leave the United States after the War of Independence, and several escaped from enslavement in the United States for Nova Scotia, another Canadian province of British settlement in North America. And some from the West Indies decided voluntarily to return to Africa, where a colony was established in Sierra Leone, Freetown, in 1792 after being destroyed in 1789 and rebuilt in 1791.

Granville Town, named after its benefactor, was established as the first city of the Province of Freedom. Granville Sharp died on July 6, 1813. After the independence of the United States, two emancipated slaves led the free blacks and slaves of the French colony of Saint-Domingue to rebel. That chain of insurrections constituted the first antislavery revolution of the American continent known under the name of the Haitian Revolution, which began in 1791. Francois Dominique Toussaint Louverture, a descendant of black slaves of African-Caribbean origin and French politician of the Caribbean, was one of the leaders of the Haitian Revolution from 1791 to his arrest in 1802; and Jean-Jacques Dessalines, an African-Caribbean who was first a slave in the house of Henry Duclos in Santo Domingo, also headed the Haitian Revolution.

Jean-Jacques Dessalines was the lieutenant of Toussaint Louverture, who had after so many troubles led the island on January 1, 1804, to the proclamation of independence of Haiti. He became the first emperor of Haiti under the name of Jacques I in 1804, to his murder on October 17, 1806, in Pont-Rouge. Haiti then became the second independent state proclaimed a republic in the American continent. In the history of the Haitian Revolution, Jean-Jacques Dessalines and Francois Dominique Toussaint Louverture are cited as two great figures of the anticolonial movements, abolitionism, and the emancipation of blacks. That point of Organ with a lot of tree trunks of freedom was many times overthrown, but it grew back by the light of abolitionist philosophers of conscience, because its many roots were very deep.

The meager profitability of the slave trade after the industrial revolt was the real reason that pushed companies of that trade to the abolition of slavery. In fact, despite its importance, the maintenance costs of forts necessary for the trade on the African coasts, the death of sailors and slaves in ship holds, and shipwrecks no longer justified its continuity to subsidize trips to Africa. The first country to officially abolish slavery in Europe was the smallest of the Scandinavian countries, Denmark, in 1792, then associated to the kingdom of Norway.

Sweden also prevailed in 1824, associated with the kingdom of Norway, at the signing of the Treaty for the Suppression of the Slave Trade with England. In Northern Europe, the kingdom of Denmark, inhabited since thousands of years, was controlling England, territories in Germany, Norway, the Baltic, and Sweden. It is from 958 that the King of Denmark Harald I, also called "Harald blue tooth," who lived until 986, realized the unity of Denmark at a time he long held a leading role in Northern Europe. After the fall of Napoleon I, with whom Frederick VI allied during the Napoleonic wars in 1814, the Scandinavian Union of Denmark, Sweden, and Norway, created in 1397 in Kalmar, under the authority of Queen Margaret I of Denmark, nicknamed "the Northern Semiramis," was amputated from a part of his territory by the treaty of Kiel. Denmark, which invaded Sweden, was once driven out of Sweden before the reign of Frederick VI, during a rebellion led in 1520 by Erik Johansson Vasa, father of Gustav Eriksson Vasa, murdered in 1520.

That rebellion day, called "Stockholm Blood Bath," allowed Gustave I Vasa, to be elected regent of the Kingdom of Sweden, from August 23, 1521, to 1523, and regained his independence as king of Sweden on June 6, 1523, thus breaking the union of Kalmar, until his death on September 29, 1560. Notably, the union with Norway was dissolved in 1814, after the defeat of Napoleon I. And Frederick VI was forced to cede the territory of Norway to Sweden.

That treaty ended hostilities between the parties during the Napoleonic Wars, where King Frederick VI of Denmark, and Norway allied with Napoleon I, first opposing the United Kingdom, the Kingdom of Sweden, and second between the Kingdom of Denmark and Norway, concluded, on January 14, 1814, in Kiel.

For that tragic page of history that was the Arab and European slave trade, the rise of claims for repairs after a fierce struggle revived public interest, under the leadership of Ms. Christiane Taubira-Delanon, former deputy of Guyana, from 1993 to 2012, and former Minister of Justice, appointed Minister of Justice of the French Republic in "the governments of Jean-Marc Ayrault one and two," and then in "the governments of Manuel Valls one and two" since May 16, 2012; she resigned from that post on January 27, 2016, after six years in the office of the French Minister of Justice. The law of May 21, 2001, which she was responsible, finally made the slave trade and slavery practiced from the fifteenth century by Europeans, recognized by the French Republic as a "crime against humanity." It remains the recognition of the one of the Arabs, a main subset of the eastern slave trade, practiced from the eighth century to the present day, by the Arab slave traders on some populations in Africa.

The importance of the fight to obtain reparations is not yet really grasped by the black world. Historical analyses of the slave trade remain under the influence of a dogmatic and hypocritical Eurocentrism, immobilizing the reason of this tragic history. They put in place huge mediatic means to spread colossal false truths, saying that, at the arrival of Europeans in Africa, Africans were all living wildly and claiming that they were buying captives from African kings; tragic again concerning their pejorative conception is that it was necessary to evangelize and civilize Negroes still cannibals, etc.; nevertheless, blaming Negroes is the most common idea and the major excuse to cover their guilt.

Generally, in school textbooks, no mention of this history is made; and their consequences of a truncated history are ignored, dealing with the slavery distorted ideas of the slave trade, of colonial domination filled with white ferocity, a significant deficiency of whites to non-whites to non-Aryans; like Nazism, transposing non-whites to non-Aryans, and the racial hierarchy illustrating the moral debacle of Europe. The slave trade, the conquest of America, and finally the occupation of Africa are the ferocities hitherto reserved for others and between different continents.

These unforgivable crimes committed between the differences of races and the mentality of superiority of the whites are unjustifiable for the enslavement imposed on blacks, the total extermination of certain races, their annihilation, and their destruction by Europeans, are poignant testimonies in the heart of the quickly freed world from the traditions of slavery, and the prejudices of their master slavers; these testimonies are briskly expressed like a cry of a sick who needs attention—is this cry heard? But in the meantime, the relationships of Europeans to other people are inevitable, even as the principal reason of their relation is officially declared to be superior to other races.

The sadistic and fertile spirit of the European man is able to produce aberrations. They involved themselves into it by all ages with much ardor; as soon as they settled in; cries of family fathers, of women and children of all ages, were heard, and little boys and girls, abandoned in the hands of haywire perverts—perverts but perfectly respectable men who will sodomize them every night and then kidnap them for exportation; they supported these sufferings, despite the pain that ignited their butts, as an anesthesia effect, which gave them the strength to continue.

The height of disgust was achieved with the introduction of new sexual practices such as the coprophagia, ondinism, and the scatology of the malicious mature adults inflicting pain on immature organs, which have not finished being formed, were screwed to death, as the wildest delirium inflicted on girls who had the fecal bolus down, but paid a very dear tribute to the unpleasant human beings, who imposed such barbaric things by a completely outdated practice, like an unjustifiable unbearable aberration, to bathe with the seminal fluid and urine of these girls; and it is also a sexual disgust if man must copulate with male animals or be sodomized by animals of different species in all senses. These practices were certainly not from our culture; the geographic ethnic and cultural unity of the Nilotic countries or the Nile regions, where various relations existed between Ethiopia, Egypt, and Libya; the founding influence of Ethiopia, Nubia-Sudan on Egypt, and the Sahel-Maghreb world. Their solidities in the field of archaeological information, the philological rigor, total mastery of the international way of working in Egyptology, to the knowledge of the ancient Black Africa, are evidences of an immense intellectual and scientific contribution.

Silence and shame still weigh on the Europeans for what forms a black page in the history of our countries. But slavery still raises multiple questions, from the slavery mechanism up to its abolition; its axes of thought must be taught, and how to approach the understanding of slavery must be easily transmitted by educational means; these neglected facts are raising awareness in my spirit and in the spirit of ignorant.

A historical perspective exists between the beginnings of capitalisms—in this case, concerning the English capitalism and the black slave trade, and the entire colonial trade in the seventeenth and eighteenth centuries, the black slave trade played a role in the constitution of capitalism. The slavers and the colonizers of Africa must strive to establish the real facts on the African slave trade and the colonization of Africa before moralizing. Before turning toward Africa, the Europeans had already sold their fellow man.

Therefore, I would like to honor all victims of all trades with abominable character. Western or not, they should not be minimized. I do not see why some are outraged, quantitatively correlating important figures. We know that between 650 and 1920, the Muslim eastern trades, with the creation of a vast Muslim slavery empire, made about seventeen million victims of black Africans. On the other hand, the transatlantic European slave trade, between 1450 and 1869, made more than eleven million slaves of blacks from Africa to the Americas and the Atlantic islands. Let us understand that these figures are just estimations of all deported blacks from Africa. I do not also think that the difference in figures between the transatlantic trade and those that I rather prefer to call Eastern than Muslim, which lasted thirteen centuries, justifies them. Patrick Manning, the American historian, believes that the inter-African trade is equivalent to 50 percent of twenty-eight million. Martin Klein, the famous specialist in the history of precolonial Africa, explained that there were more than seven million slaves of trades quoted here above only in French West Africa around 1900, which led me to conclude without exaggeration that there were over a period of thirteen centuries, perhaps more than fourteen million slaves in the African continent.

The Muslim slavers, like most societies in the seventh century of our era, were importing slaves from Asia, Central Europe, and sub-Saharan Africa, and at the same time deported them to these territories; since Muslims could not be reduced to slavery, and its Koran expressed no race or color prejudice.

The Atlantic slave trade took off around 1650, at the sugar revolution, after a long period, from the discovery of the coasts of the Gulf of Guinea by the Portuguese in the fifteenth century. The Europeans, who were in search of gold, discovered human as a commodity, a lucrative trade. The exchange therefore did not constitute anything between Europe and Africa. Europeans were then going to purchase slaves, which cost them nothing, but also gold, ivory, etc., for two centuries until the mid-seventeenth century.

It will seem less daring for me to say that the guilt of all Europeans is pushing their complex to seek for invalid reasons to try to explain the inexplicable. What should then be the impact of African slavery to finally satisfy the historians? Descendants of the slavers with their multiple declarations, very Eurocentric, not accepting that the demographic revolution was prior to the Western industrial revolution, but what then if it has not caused a demographic decline? According to you, how many Africans had to be deported from the continent to justify a decline? Numerous testimonies confirmed that Africa was stable before the arrival of whites; after their arrival, the continent experienced a total instability in growth. Deporting seventy-six thousand Africans a year may be minimized nowadays but not at the time of that trade because slavers were only seeking strong men, men in good health, and intelligent men who could work, therefore leaving an Africa booming in full without strong hands, without intelligent men, without protection but with a weakened morale.

The former slave trader elites in West Africa who came to power in the twentieth century were collaborators of the armed slavers to oversee their interests and for the oppression of the society as a whole, only encountered some resistances. Societies which were previously better organized and tremendously strengthened were separated by wars to the detriment of other small societies. If slavery was not all that profitable, as the work of economic historians claim it, all Europe would have not ventured in it. A percentage of 4 to 6 percent for France and 10 percent for England were published. But to my knowledge, not only those two countries were in that slave trade. The most curious thing in all this case is that these same historians who were determining who were African collaborators of slavery and who made such or such gain haven't tell us how much these collaborators earned throughout the slave trade, since these same historians were confirming with certainty that there was a question of trade between Europe and black Africa, an equitable trade in short. So, if that was the case, where did the funds generated from these exchanges in terms of percentage or in terms of investment go?

The European countries made huge profits during the four centuries of the slave trade, which were then invested in industry and so on. If the Western Industrial Revolution could not be explained by the slave trade, why not simply deny the existence of slavery?

The Atlantic slave trade was the cause of the sugar revolution and big plantations in the Americas, essentially in Brazil, the Caribbean, and the Old South in the United States toward 1650 up to its abolition in 1807. For years, a large labor force was desired, and only the black man was to meet that demand, because the slave system was profitable for the planters and their plantations. Until the nineteenth century, all states were more than listening to them.

The slavers quickly turned toward Africa, toward a workforce that already knew the profession, after a papal bull forbidding the reduction of Native Americans to slavery. The legitimization of the slave trade was the origin of racism; I think everyone would agree on that. The Eastern slave trade played a very important role in the economy of the Muslim world; we know it by the development of sugarcane in Morocco in the sixteenth century, in the large plantations of Zanzibar in the nineteenth century, and in the large exploitations of lower Iraq. But the volume of slaves involved during the thirteen centuries, a total of seventeen million for the Muslim slave trade, is much lower compared to the four centuries of European slavery, resulting in eleven million slaves. Really, can this figure of 17 million of the Muslim slave trade be accepted, considering the thirteen centuries of its duration?

However, if this figure of the Muslim slave trade is considered, we immediately imagine that if it was Europe that made thirteen centuries of the slave trade, Africa would have been completely empty. Another reason so understandable is that the Eastern slave trade usually generated a good part of its slaves by wars, and since there existed a trade considered as an exchange, we do not consider them as slave trades like those of Europeans who raided, chained by force, and killed anyone who were opposing their orders. Some blacks of the Caribbean and America in general believe in multiple antagonist stories, in the writings of historians, criticizing Africans for trading Black ancestors in the past. The memories that aroused a story must be true to be part of a histoire. The objective considering these memories and render them history belongs to the state through the law, since the slave trade was generally a global affair of state.

After the abolition by abolitionists, essentially white Protestants philanthropist in 1807, England no longer needed slaves in the Industrial Revolution. But despite the blockade and the resistance of slaves themselves, the slave system continued, especially because it was still useful and very profitable toward the late eighteenth century to its complete end around 1920. The slave trade by the Europeans was a crime against humanity, although policies do not want to agree on it. In fact, it is a much higher crime compared to an inferior genocide like the Holocaust.

The reality is as it is, and nobody can change it. The words are also as they're, but it is the consciousness of the statements that is the reason of being. Africa, as we have said many times, has never known slavery before the arrival of foreigners. All this is to say that the ancestors of the ancestors were completely free men. Thereby, to say that the ancestors of the ancestors were either freemen or slaves or slave traders is untrue. We cannot also minimize the intellectuality of those artists, those of African intellectuals who call themselves descendants of slaves, to create an immediate memorial ceremony between the past and the present.

So, since there is no Richter scale of sufferings, pay tribute therefore to those who deserve it and recognize the fathers of African-born slaves. Solemnly glorify them for the prominent role they played in the history of mankind and revive the scorned memory of slavery and the slave trade. Particularly, publicly recall the crimes committed by the French, the English, the Dutch, the Portuguese, the Spanish, etc., during the slave trade, which carefully wiped out civilization and that the Westerners want to carefully erase and strictly speak of colonization; especially not hiding behind revisionist research to publicly insult the memory of the descendants of slaves.

The highest institutions of all republics and kingdoms of the world must explicitly confirm the recognition of all genocides without the exception of the slave trade by refusing revisionism.

Let all the descendants of slaves and all those who are against the denial of the colonial genocides immediately take measures and prosecute all those who advocate insulting doctrines, aiming to teach or spreading the denial of the inadmissible colonial genocides to tarnish the memory and the honor of millions of men, women, and children from Africa deported by force.

Let all united in honor and dignity make it clear that we are a force. Know that the African man will not one day be a father or a genius of humanity; he is already the father and a genius of humanity, an indivisible genetically distinct nature, a fraternal order of the world, like that kind of genius that humanity loves so much, transmitted from one generation to the next, as a reminder that he already existed in this world and that from good to the raining weather, millions of humanities succeeded the right of his kinship.

It was on February 4, 1794, that the proposal for the slavery abolition of Deputy Danton was acclaimed for the first time, abolishing slavery in all the territories of the French Republic. Bonaparte restored slavery by the law of May 20, 1802, thus revoking the principles of the law of February 4, 1794. And the general regulations of April 25, 1803, led Victor Hughes to restore slavery in French Guiana. It was final in the French colonies only in 1848. It took until September 25, 1926, for the international community, under the auspices of the League of Nations, to sign an agreement abolishing slavery; and entered into effective on March 9, 1927, after the relentless struggle of the English against slavery practices in other colonies in the nineteenth century.

The dictator Napoleon Bonaparte restored the crimes against humanity by restoring slavery and the slave trade in the French colonies on May 20, 1802. Upon the reestablishment, gassing and drowning were used to destroy the people of Haiti and Guadeloupe, resisting the restoration of slavery and the slave trade from the autumn of 1802. Napoleon, the first racist dictator in history, banned Negroes and colored people to enter the French territory on July 2, 1802. He prohibited mixed marriages in France on January 3, 1803.

From all these facts, the dictator Napoleon Bonaparte, emperor of the French, morally fell under the blow of a French Parliament law declaring slavery and the slave trade, as crimes against humanity. It was a law adopted in May 2001 to respect the memory of slaves and their descendants. This law must triumph over the truth of the hypocrisy of that period. All forms of discrimination and exclusion, all crimes against humanity from the days of slavery and colonization should be sentenced before the eyes of everyone with the utmost firmness. A way to no longer be worried about our appearance or our origins; in addition to no longer judge us by the color to better qualify us; adding that we are black men and talk about our African identity with honor and dignity; accepting that there is something different, special, and that something different should be special than our skin color.

Let States adapt themselves to situations and to people who are worthy in this world of the twenty-first century. Let there be a very respectful expression, a consideration of the purity of blood, and a belief in the race to no longer suffer the gaze of others; to no longer insult the dignity of the spirit or soul, already offended by the painful injustice made to its ancestor; deported in the abominable conditions in the holds of armed ships; by whip blows, by the rapping humiliations of their women, tortures by mutilations, and finally death. After the death followed the oblivion of a decimated continent, and a trampled civilization, of which he would never have the freedom to get rid of.

What is certain is that by establishing the Black Code of King Louis XIV in 1685, the French slaveholders and slavers of other countries were abusing African deportees in various colonies, who were legally treated as chattels; no one knows it, but contrary to what we believed concerning the declaration of the Human Rights of 1789, it only concerned whites, and it was necessary that men of color wait three years for them to be recognized as free men; and under the pressure of a revolt that could not be contained, slavery was abolished after five years.

But before getting to the human rights, the glory was to the terror, massacres, looting, rapes, and tortures perpetrated against African civilians, leaving ineffaceable sequels in the spirits and souls of our ancestors. The gas chambers for these slaves were the holds of ships, in which men, women, and children died by suffocation to sulfur, demonstrating thereby the secret existence of a plan of extermination. It is only natural to recognize slavery as such. Multiple examples can be scanned to justify the slave trade, in its courses, as a crime against humanity. But these examples are they really without foundation? To only be content with words without taking action? And is it that these slave trades did not occur? For the reason of its statements to have a conscience, if not, why does France recognize the transatlantic slave trade as a crime against humanity?

Article 1, promulgated on May 21, 2001, affirms that the French Republic recognized that the transatlantic slave trade and trade in the Indian Ocean, on one hand, and slavery, on the other, perpetrated from the fifteenth century in the Americas, the Caribbean, the Indian Ocean, and Europe against the African people, Amerindians, Malagasy, and Indians, constituted a crime against humanity. Since France has already officially recognized the transatlantic slave trade, the abolition of slavery, and the memories of the victims of this crime against humanity, this crime must be solemnly for the first time, accepted by all states of the world.

All states which practiced the slave trade must implement a law recognizing the slave trades and the practice of some forms of slavery as a crime against humanity. Whether for the Eastern Muslim Arabs slave trade from the seventh century, the transatlantic slave trade, or the trafficking held for the practice of slavery, still active today in Mauritania, Niger, Sudan, and in the states of the Persian Gulf, all should advocate the recognition of that law, and grant an increased concern as a mission, and a consequent place to the slave trade and slavery, for a day of commemoration worthy of that name throughout the whole world. This new commemorative celebration of masses, which will bear the name "Splendor of Slavery," should not be a bath confusion of opinions, since such legislation will not perhaps completely abolish slavery in the world, where a considerable part of this practice is still continuing nowadays. On the other hand, no longer close our eyes on the humiliating slavery traffic dishonoring humanity.

This is to take a big step toward raising awareness against racism, racial discrimination and once and for all, abandon that primitive mentality to finally live in the civilized world of intellectuals without prejudice.

This mercantile spirit of many European slavery-supporters and colonization generations, installed very serious repercussions on the survival conditions in Africa, and yet it possessed a total balance of stable African societies in full blooming harmony, between the mental activity and a constant pondering calm of the esprit, view expansion, powers and well balanced in every burst of harmonious civilization with a system of well-formed bodies, whose composition of states does not vary; but from 1441 to about 1865, that trade resulted in an extraordinary demographic puncture in Africa. That trade stagnated its spiritual growth, its mystical growth, its demographic growth, and its political, economic, cultural, social, and population growth, throughout the period of the slave trade.

The consequences of that trade demonstrated the systematic way, the mercantile spirit, the market mechanisms, and the powered system fed with the need of gain and greed, known as the economic and social values of the Western works. Fundamentally conflicting, that mercantile system of economic values and the dislocation of traditional society created a tragic dualism, which inhabits contemporary Africa. This disastrous situation of mankind, inhumane to his born-free fellow, still follows Africa in the sappy road that it has traveled from its known existence to date.

Generally, these Romanesque European generations and supporters of slavery have nothing scientifically proven concerning the slavery era or the colonial period, if not that razor all too full of our riches, the destruction of our already established powers, and the opportunity to take advantage of our unorganized creativity in a peaceful African world.

They may refuse to admit and may hide the marks of our real history that occupy a prominent place in the blazon of our African countries, carefully deposited in its different parts of the universe to men, but pretending to ignore the collections of its presence in our spirit is simply cruel; despite all, hide the great scientific and technological discoveries of numerous disturbing facts, revealed by our prophets to govern by controlling, guiding us in a life without a future, and manipulating the world toward a new ferocious stage by certain particularly financial lobbyists, pretending to develop the planet; and increasing in prevision, the animated adjectives of curious characters known by material desire of those distant times to build themselves a better life. Nevertheless, they're still unable to clearly translate the spurs received from the highest spirit, but which they pretend to ignore and forget, yet showing a serene face, often discreet, while in the meantime sparing knowledge expressed in metaphors or mysterious symbols of our ancestors, appearing in the religious art of our present civilization, and letting us live in this same world full of pitfalls for us who must accomplish a certain mission in a world completely different from the one that heavenly beings descended from heaven, have already visited since the dawn of time to inculcate us love, knowledge, respect, and moral responsibility.

They can graciously ignore problems erected by their evil force of darkness, specifically illegal and of undesirable quality, but which has always recruited mankind; create diseases and implant them with known references on earth; at the same time, categorically refuse to protect and respect nature, which is maintaining itself at a distance here among us, to observe us in occasion by hiding the true purpose of its existence and its intentions toward humanity; in addition, make black men believe that they were born by chance, originally to maintain the security of their great secret societies alive and direct us toward the hazard for purely economic interests, as a consequence of a stolen know-how and their eager desire completely inexplicable but existing in their universe, and not comprehensible. Despite everything, it was with this mercantile spirit and their greedy desire that they took the decision to govern us but forgetting that no one will be able to prevent man constantly aided by his inspiration from governing himself.

An evidence repeatedly demonstrated by the secret vision of some prophets, for the knowledge is a source where everyone can come to drink and transcend in majority to a new stage on the endless ladder of the liberation of our lives and achieve the hermetical expensive transmutation, which appears today as a miracle, if one really wants it. Can we really deny that, that endless source of the liberation of our lives is also the reason why the European slavers, leaders, kings, and chiefs of governments transformed free men into slaves in African countries but were nevertheless not able to subjugate them? It is therefore unreasonable, incomprehensible, intolerable, and not a philosophical way of thinking to even presume that our heads of state even think of governing us as still savage men, submitted to one man, a tyrant who is governing by the police nations of violence, using a cruel force of oppression, launching a formidable and sanguinary attack against humanity.

This kind of government, belonging to a dangerous belief, spontaneously born from the rebellious blood of mortals, cannot in all likelihood take place in our country after so much shame of the bad management and the contempt of its supporters of slavery, who have forced thousands of their fellows, enchained them voluntarily, and forced them to be their slaves.

Reasonably, I'm not only looking for the origin of those numerous universal spirits, who created harmful beliefs and everything that it contains as contempt by a proven hatred, by actions and pejorative words of people knowing good and the impermissible evil, but also of that cruel degeneration of the white race, to a height increasingly high on a scale of evolution toward the animal man, as a human created by an act of creation committed illegally without authorization in a special chosen isolated place, and breathed the breath of life into his nostrils; nevertheless pure but at the same time evil, the same so-called civilized race at its passage on earth, where it extended its limits and engaged itself in abominable enterprises.

They established governments, born from conqueror ambitions with the cruel pride of their unique sense of inhospitality to strangers, as a false conjecture justified since the history of mankind. Thus, my justification is to put forward an idea, a combination of events, a truth that we cannot refuse to subscribe to, for an evolution, a development so requested for the well-being and for the pride of our citizens.

History is showing us that all Europe was very jealous of the freedom enjoyed by the freemen of the universe, particularly the African freedom. A reasoning that seems extreme to me, but true, since their influence at the expense of an infinite of moral, political and economic cause, was attributing itself only two spells known as servitude and the slavery of men; men neglected and regarded as a worthless machine, and using the effects of a secret cause of mass destruction, genocide, and prejudices even stronger than all influences of heaven and earth; but despite all, no inhabitant of the earth is able to fully extinguish the natural feeling of freedom in man.

These motives spread prejudices and bitter influences like a virulent infection throughout the vast region of Africa, in the same sky, the same climate, the same law, the same rights, and subjecting the same spells to humanity. These wandering and savage nations, which retained and still retain the freedom of mankind in America, Asia, Australia, and Africa, have only generated a mixture of large and small nations of slaves without self-esteem, close to those vagabonds still wandering in adventure in a foreign soil to oppress them and prevent any sort of development.

I would therefore like to say that this hideous system of slavery and servitude that very quickly and very well destroyed the natural moral was a mistake and a series of errors put in place to make mankind suffer by a degraded mankind and a thinking creature. It is necessary to stop philosophical chimeras to explain these errors because it is not in the philosophical system that man must look for the source but on facts, details, and customs of that creepy, horrible, and shameful practice. That recognition, after a big mea culpa and a considerable material or spiritual compensation, will be necessary for a reconciliation to first of all, bring the victims of slavery closer and finally cut that great human error chain, this time to willingly reconcile but not by force but by accepting these errors as a sad consequence of the debased mankind. A human race so handsome, so dignified, a magnificent universe model of a Supreme Being, having fatal original projects with a plan filled with horror and misery that precipitated it, and will still precipitate it again and again in undesirable events of bad grade; in addition with a too great false conception of heaven and earth; and it then led this same human race to write a page of a senseless cult in the history, degraded by a principle that was only covering it with glory; consequently, it is a real discovery of truth concerning these evil spirit of men, established here on earth. However, in their distraction, truth and freedom have always been in the bottom of their hearts during those deplorable days when white human species degenerated after exterminating, destroyed, and disturbed the order of universal nature by the miserable bestial insensitive feeling, and a passing contentment of joy; always ready to watch and memorize the suffering of the opponent like a good dream in a state of silence; believing to forget all in the following centuries, under the penalty of inner sufferings. These extreme disturbances of the order of nature have precipitated our universe in calamities, and the world has lost the light to make room to darkness. Thousand plagues succeeded since these deplorable scenes of calamity.

The Humanity, collectively considered as the human race in the world nowadays, has become the desolating hatred for the benefit of his own humanity, not having neighbors to appeal to for urgent assistance; thus, without any source of strength, his comfortless is drowning him in his own bad doing, and all nature is irritated. Thunder growls and hidden torrents in the bowels of the universe are falling on earth, burying all living. Salvation is no more, but the sun and the planets are still seeking to restore calm, harmony, peace, freedom, and the dignity of men and the ruins of the earth. This appalling disaster creates overwhelming difficulties, which are destroying the cosmic cycle for centuries—a chimera of an indelible history forever engraved in the spirits of Africans and other victims, with an unknown history to almost everyone. Slavers neglected to educate people and keep the history of slavery to date by studying its civil institutions, its causes, its effects, its progress, its customs, its laws, and the vulgar inconstant and insensitive Christian religion, which supported and still supports the establishment of that thought to perpetuate the fragile misfortune of the human race throughout the world for good.

Christianity, Islam, and other religions keep a profound silence after being the true legislators and organizers of slavery. The Bible, the Christian book of the holiest worship of the world, insists until today on that famous invented fable and truncated history of slavery on earth and in heaven, according to its believers. If I was to question myself about that strange and sordid history of the Old Testament, which tells us that Noah cursed Ham, from his three children and his descendants, for the simple fact that he made fun of him because he was drunk and undressed, I conclude that this manipulation of information by its protagonists and this belief, which led the Europeans who exterminated the people of America, to decide to make blacks slaves; this belief is neither religious nor moral or spiritual and goes against all the laws of nature and all the rights of the human nature.

To give themselves good conscience, those poor Jewish protagonists are to my knowledge, the only ones who are the subject of a qualification of the inferior beings of the brachycephalic race; they're inert, poor, and racist of the slave trades, who invented this infantile nonsense mythological story of Noah's curse. Unfortunately for the leaders of a supposedly universal religion, the work of researchers has resulted in the restitution of the Nigger essence of a great brilliant civilization of Ancient Egypt.

The Europeans who believed that only slavery would allow Negroes to be cleansed from the curse of the patriarch Noah by Christianizing them made a great mistake; despite their humiliating description, qualifying Niggers as people having a brain inadequately structured, as people with a flat nose, graded as barbaric savages, attested as ugly people, confirmed as dirty lazy thieves and rapists; in short certifying them as subhuman, only having emotions denoting worse performance than most humans, and having animal instincts. They were also questioning themselves to know how the Supreme Being named God, the wise creator of the mother being of humanity, managed to put a soul, a good soul in a black body from its feet to the head. They were asking themselves this despicable and stupid question, forgetting that black is the mother not only of humanity and civilization but also of the highest philosophy with a very great consequence that initiated our entire universe.

I would conclude that with such absurdity, they're the ones who had no concept of religion and would never reach the knowledge of the true religion that they once stole from him.

I wonder how these religions of the world can still be proud religiously after having so miserably treated human beings, claiming to show them the sources of their origin by evangelizing them. The misfortunes, the bad impressions, and all political and religious errors that these religions have made to men on earth have become the torches of dark spaces and imposture to the existence of humanity. The means by which we could manage to forgive these wonderful enigmas of all multitudes errors with ease, to lead mankind in the solution that would offer new scenes in the world, is to penetrate the feelings and the impressions of the victims, illuminate the truth in darkness, examine the how of the principles of those same feelings, and get away from all the sacred chimeras of ignorance, is to put ourselves for a moment in the place of those victims, by crossing the boundaries of their affected feelings, as if to go and search those sacred chimeras of ignorance and the principles of suffering beyond in the gloomy spaces; the cult applied by all those extreme governments, and also the slavers who were compounded of Dutch, English, French, Portuguese, Spanish, etc., produced a mixture in the air smelling like something bad; intensifying the negative aspects that prohibited themselves from prosecuting a felony, in exchange for money or other consideration.

There is a fume here to extinguish, since the perpetrators knew that they cannot be tried again for the same offence. Let me try to make wrong things right by not considering acquittal, since this effect is not compounding an offence but worsening it by aggravating it and exacerbating it. So let's talk a dialect compounded of Dutch, English, French, Portuguese, Spanish, etc., because there is still time to penetrate the feelings of those victims, examine the principles of their sufferings, and illuminate the truth in darkness.

After this being done, you will notice the difference between the victims and those slaver governments; and with a new surprise, the world will reveal itself to our eyes and thereby a more natural truth than what is in existence. In that examination of conscience, I will never imagine that the white human race of that time is different from the white human race of today because they still increase the extreme difficulties of mankind and discard themselves actually more from the reason. In addition, the white man today still identifies himself with those same striking prejudices, despite scholarly knowledge that we have acquired since the savage mankind.

In this regard, I think that the circumstances that give rise to these ideas, formerly the world's woes are transporting us through thousands of centuries of the primitive world. That is why these exciting woes of the world are extinguishing the harmonious strength of the sunlight and bring back the old calamities, which again return to besiege mankind nowadays. It is no longer necessary to ask metaphysical questions or to philosophize much to guess what we think of the sacred dogmas of the end of the world; my question is, what will man do if the earth was to raise against itself at the last great judgment of the rashness of men that the Great Spirit retraces for the future life with strength and that profoundly affects the heart of all men today? What will man do if the waters of the seas were to flood the whole earth, bringing out the sulfur and the bitumen by torrent from the deep bosom of the entire earth, in the days of God's vengeance? And what will become the sacred dogmas if a thousand and one volcanoes were to be opened everywhere in the world, by exalting all nature with all its strength and changing its emotional harmony into chaos?

Oh! That the day of justice has come; if the sun ceased to give us its light and lets us sink into the dark spaces of the broken continents under our feet, we will say that the great judge of the universe has descended to reward the just and punish the calamities of plagues and the desolation of all kinds. Our aggressors and oppressive nephews who affected our ancestors will also be affected in these same fatal circumstances, when the universe will decide to no longer give us its primitive harmony. Our ancestors saw the polytheists of a polytheism that was never the fruit of a rational and meditated system, walk toward a narrow and fatal road of Africa, never followed or pioneered previously. They arrived at their source without embracing the ancestral humanitarian assumptions of those who preceded them. The ancient thinking creatures of the human race, naturally human in the universe of respect for human rights, at the origin of the history of humanity in which he is an essential part, obliging us to seek happiness and love that always cherished the bottom heart of the ancestral human race; and with ardor the children of the children of their children have sought happiness and love throughout their life; and our grandfathers and their children have sought happiness and love too; but our fathers, we and our children are still seeking the same happiness and love until our days.

Is it so difficult to seek the truth and freedom in a higher sphere, to bring societies and those religious or secular institutions to conceive the felicity so high and sublime, so comforting and powerful? I strongly remind you that a conjecture of different circumstances of this perambulation will increase horror, death, and the feeling of sadness that already inspired us the choices established in their principles, more unfortunate than we can imagine, and more criminal than we can believe, arising from these multiple unexpected sources, are presenting a distressing sadness of terror to men and to humanity.

Telling you the shameful and barbaric terrible stories that our noble Africans lived is necessarily horrible; they were horribly dislodged for countries overseas, for a simple reason purely economic; yes, telling you the shameful and barbaric terrible stories with the sad and tragic scenes that still produced the revolt of the spirit is horrible; but our young Africans till today still undertake crucial adventures to get to the West and undergo the same dreadful, shameful, and barbaric experiences of our noble African ancestors, looking for a new bed. Sometimes even accepting to live certain horrible conditions that lead to mass death, at the shores of the ocean crowning our borders with the West, simply because they're fleeing from their beautiful countries, their beautiful destroyed continent, Africa of statesmen without moral will, Africa that no longer has any honor, any insured fortune, and without property to offer them, to encourage them, to secure them or again, to give them hope that one day, they could be able to lead a better life in their beloved African continent; but only living in the fear of the whims of a ferocious dictatorship of moron leaders, who are undermining their lives; known as the only asset they have as gracious gift from God, and which, according to them, should be without existence. All this because of the long journey that Africa has been forced into, since its advent by a foreign body equipped with slavery, colonization, the plundering of its riches, and finally the corruption inflicted on its kingdom and its leaders. Know that I am not in any way, trying to set up a community against the other by my comments.

Nevertheless, without me being wrong, my many interventions are asserting the bad faith of Arabs, Europeans, and Jews against the Negroes. In addition, if we analyze historical documents and check the consistency of the facts, we will see that the damage has been done and continues to persist.

I will be very humble and admit beforehand that, even if I cannot guarantee the good faith of universality concerning everything said in this book, I am certain that all my theories are more related to the truth than the officially distributed theories. Here is one example of what we are taught in schools as fair knowledge: the theory of evolution of species of Darwin; the prehistory as described in the schoolbooks is increasingly contradicted by facts and puts the researchers in question. Just because you believe it to be true because it seems true to you does not mean that it is true; is it because a thesis seems wrong that it is? Check and make your own inquiries and tell yourselves that it is not because what seems true is not false and that nothing is preventing what you think is false to be true. Whoever wants to know the truth must seek the knowledge portal that provides the means to discover the truth. So, all those who will read this book will be overwhelmed by some of my comments and will not be stopped in considering me as a haywire or an eccentric for having such thoughts. Nevertheless, in the end, open the doors of thought to all those who have knowledge to assert and give the opportunity to everyone to see the truth—the truth in different exposed thesis that I gathered from my different ideas and teaching. I think and believe that my readers are already sufficiently aware of certain truths, so I do not have to remind them.

But if not, learn to think in the light of what others tell you but without taking their word for it. Study and do not swallow without thinking. Let this be a valid rule for all. My goal is not to impose the truth on you but to open that door of reflection in the thought after you read mine. Invite a close friend or acquaintance so that together, we end up discovering and contemplating the truth. The truth, a source of happiness, gives rest to those who are responsible for a significant burden of peace, of pain, of sin and to those whose struggle is overwhelming. Whoever tramples the heart and soul of his brother does not love God. Whoever seeks to obscure his mind by the fear of hell does not love God. The one who seeks to hinder his neighbor or to hate him does not love God. The universal spirit always appears in all truth and not only in a single truth. The one who does not rejoice in this truth has not yet understood the ultimate goal, which crowns man with a radiant halo. A meaningless word of natural law sends some and others at the stake. The true love of sweetness and purity surrounds all, you and me. It embraces all humanity and is not limited, so why such divisions between us, which raise walls that separate us? Why not understand love in the true sense of the word and fill every heart with it? Know it well that humans have only one balm for pain, and only one thing matters.

The only thing that the world has always needed to know is love, a mutual sympathy, the only path that leads to heaven, to an absolute satisfaction that crucifies the betrayal, which is received as a small child, the kingdom of God. Mark 10:15 says, "Whosoever shall not receive the kingdom of God as a little child, shall not enter therein." A new philosophy that everyone welcomes in a different way is thenceforth offered to the world. The importance given to this teaching in the Christian religion is recognized.

Obviously, from all kind of new philosophical essay, certain endeavor to put into practice these principles in their daily lives and concord them with their personal ideas. Here, your first merit is the justification of your own ideas because, for you, philosophy in itself is of secondary importance. If my ideas meet your expectations, you will adopt them with a partisan spirit, and you shall be bound to them with enthusiasm. But disappointed, you will reject them, disgusted probably, as if they personally insult you. Do not contain yourself within a skeptical attitude as soon as you discover something that you have not yet read or heard somewhere or that you do not yet conceive in your proper thought. Nevertheless, the truth that you reject without examination is hidden in your closed spirit. However, your mental attitude is the height of your suffering and your intolerance.

Do not turn your back from the light. Do not let your preconceived ideas prevent the truth. In addition, let the truth penetrate its rays in you. Impregnate yourself with the inevitable feeling of the superiority of your knowledge. Eminently, be receptive. However, do not accept everything in that beautiful attitude of trust, in which there is no shadow of a doubt.

Human being is born to live in the lethargy of boredom and anxiety in this materialistic and spiritual world, beautiful and crazy at the same time, where everything is true, with nothing being exact. Very precious is that day when you're touched with love, with glory, and with beauty, the only words that govern a lifetime from a distance of reflection, to the analysis capacity and the maturity of the spirit, necessary to powerfully guide all our steps, throughout our lives in happiness, success, and prosperity.

This spiritual and physical sensation is the motherland of a terrible conflict ripping the spirit, agonizing men, isolating and rejecting us African people. By the symbolism of a pernicious ideology of racial oppression and racism, explaining the intensity of the suffering that we all carry in our hearts. The African humanity will again host those foreign outlaws of yesterday in its bosom and will take possession of its victory, conquered with dignity, peace, freedom, and justice.

We will face the challenge against racism and against sexism, the challenge to build and work for democracy. Continue to stand beside those off-laws of yesterday and play the infinitely traditional democratic and cultural role against the bloodthirsty forces, offensive forces, and other discrimination as enslavement, which takes us to sexism, which has reached the end of its justice.

Fight against deprivation engaged to refuse freedom to see the light; fight against poverty, suffering, and the refusal of freedom, the most inalienable right to the human dignity, the reason of what pleases them to the indignity of considering it as being the outcast of this world and to not see a lasting peace, political empowerment, and human security, whatever its rank is.

Let us note that the battle that our perfect ancestors led, always dedicated to our fathers, devoted to their sons, and that we, their descendants are leading against this earth, directed by the black sheep who go beyond all rules of nature, is always won by this earth. That born from the infinitely small to the immensely large in this immensity, which is earth, will eventually die one day. Finally, swallowed up by earth, we disappear, and the earth continues to live its disappointing life of time. The destiny of man, the one of the earth and of those who direct it make our sons undergo the same atrocious spells of horrors and suffering that our ancestors and fathers have already endured for centuries. Furthermore, it is only our imagination of love that's for us always better than the reality of the atrocities experienced. The work that this infinitely small to the infinitely large imposed upon me envelops me, locks me up, withdraws me from the present, and makes me a prisoner of myself; and for this work to be a scholarly work, it is necessary that the beauty of my verses mingle with concordance and become an inspired melody on the written pages, since my geniuses are just the result of a painful long labor, because the sparkling erudite action is a result of a patient long work.

The time has come! Will we be able to fill the ditches that are separating us? The least is found in the soul—heart of society, the rainbow of peace within itself, hero and heroine, priest of life, trapped in so many issues of human unity, currently serving its amnesty sentence in all categories. The freedom to be born today by the cosmic will glorify in itself all our hopes. The drama of the human disaster has lasted too long already. A proud society of humanity must rise with the acts of nobility of the human soul to strengthen the faith of humanity in justice, true justice of the supreme—the symbol of intelligence, the human consciousness, and the irreversible freedom—so that our lives bloom with faith and a deep sense of happiness and exaltation. Without hesitation of joy and enthusiasm, when the grown herb of our continent becomes green again, the f lowers of harmonization and the f lowers of initiation will open the petals of knowledge.

Africans must build a society in which all can walk without fear. Make a decision, African people; the unit of success is implanted in your nation. Make a decision now toward the consciousness of freedom with a humble faith as proud nation; from the birth of a nation to the birth of unity, as peace existing for all; soul, spirit, and body at last liberated; Africa! Oh, Africa, do not suffer anymore. Thy reign is the experience, the reward of freedom, peace, and justice that exists for all; you're blessed by God, the blazing sun that never sets and which manifests itself in human achievement. Rise up as God, the sun that never sets, and do not ever set anymore.

Memory is nothing if it is not at the same time an awareness. It becomes very important at that moment because it is an educational value reconstructing the past and improving understanding for future generations. Our ancestors suffered moral, spiritual, and physical harm, whose consequences we still suffer; we still struggle to ask for repair to the governments of countries involved in slavery, the looting of our properties, the Atlantic trade, and finally for those school textbooks to include the history of slavery and honor the memory of slavery victims.

The absence of European, American, Canadian, English, French and other heads of states on this subject proves us their will is to want to forget or even to put an end to the officialization of the history of slavery. All these societies remain indifferent, if not reluctant to change their minds. So why are those operators who led the slavery, barbarism, colonialism, and Nazi extermination policy in Africa taking their time? This question still remains without answer.

The undeniable prosperity of these countries today owes much to Africans and to the ancestors of slaves, victims of a crime that still makes a mutilated continent mourns and a people living with psychological trauma until today. From 1672 to 1837, only France carried out nearly five hundred maritime expeditions to deport some 130,000 slaves from Africa toward the French Antilles. And for this black dehumanization to be legal, it took a codified lawmaking by the French Black Code of 1685 for countries like the Netherlands, Portugal, England, Germany, Spain, etc., to remain in force until the second abolition of slavery in the French colonies in 1848.

It's about admitting that there was a deliberate desire as direct manner of the Europeans to promote the political development and the ideological blossoming of a black dehumanizing enterprise as the Nazi barbarism to destroy the African economy. This approach is useful and contributes in putting an end to all forms of discrimination, starting with that discrimination of choosing which crime to convict depending on the identity of the victims, the one that advocates racial inferiority of non-whites and the superiority of the white race, which were written in the law consecrated by Christianity and reinforced in practice. It is necessary that Europe and America accept that the destruction of people, whether natives of America or Aborigines of Australia; the establishment of colonial domination and racial inequality; and the dehumanizing system of blacks was never before recorded in the history of mankind, and assumed responsibility of that crime.

A true genocide and crimes against humanity, whether on the European slave trade or the slavery across the Atlantic, are all thereby multifarious harm done to humanity, and especially to Africa without repair, after 170 years of French slave abolition, on April 27, 1848, and 70 years of the Universal Declaration of Human Rights, adopted in Paris by the fifty-eight member states that then constituted the General Assembly of the United Nations, on December 10, 1948. After much harm inflicted on the black African man, it is more than great time to try to unearth the psychological defects of our subconscious and take on the challenges and lancinating pains for the real liberation in the twenty-first century and the state of rights of our people, to snatch our countries from dictatorship and neocolonialism for democracy and dignity to achieve the unity of the African people, and to build the United States of Africa from Algeria to Cape Town and from Senegal to Somalia and create the great World Council of Black People (WCBP) for economic and social development and a lasting culture viable in Africa. The purpose of this book is to permit a reflection on African history concerning slavery, colonization, its economic policy, and especially its future; far from being a fence, but just to remind those countries involved that a story should not be confused or be forgotten, but recognized as history in the history of the world.

It is this recognition that allows the whole entity to recognize itself in the history for what it has given, suffered, lived, and what it has to receive. Africa and its noble children, therefore, must first know who they're and where they come from and then ask themselves where they're going and how they will get there.

Despite the influence of the eternal gravediggers of its history, it is, however, very important today to inform and educate our African children of tomorrow on the true history of our ancestors so that they draw pride from it and be capable of over amplifying their pride as a source of viable and reliable development. This logic dictates that those who have the skills must continue the work initiated by several African historians. This great task of educators and African intellectuals of the twenty-first century is the reconstruction of the African past. A colossal challenge, isn't it? However, their duty is to exhume or supply old or newly hatched hatreds. I even encourage that associations be created, having as one of their objectives to facilitate access to writings on all subjects of the black people.

Learning is a process that changes the future behavior, and memory is our ability to remind us of all learning of the past experiences since it allows the storage of learned information. Our so-called African leaders do not know, or do not want to properly use different types of memory that are at work in humans, particularly the one used not only to store all significant events that mark our existence but also the long-term memory memorizing an information, the sense of existence in itself, with an unlimited capacity far infallible during days, months, years, or even a lifetime; the one that is qualified to remind us of all the things that can be described verbally and of which one is conscious of remembering is the declarative memory, also referred to as explicit memory.

The know-how memory, a nondeclarative memory, an unconscious memory of skills and how to do things is a special type of memory that only expresses itself with words. The memories of our African statesmen are not basically associative since they do not link new information to the knowledge already acquired and firmly anchored in their memories for a relatively permanent modification of behavior that marks a gain of knowledge, understanding, or skills, like riding a bike or playing the guitar, thanks to memorized remembrances. A more effective link is that it should have a meaning for us because a fruit of that learning can pay at the end of the line, rather than a simple evocation of fixed traces. Their prefrontal cortex, known as the great planificator, the cerebral center responsible for this planification activity and coordination of our activities; a part of the brain that is precisely the most developed in humans is the region where the thought is elaborated, the kingdom of reason and consciousness, which intermediately coordinates a series of actions and activities to organize our lives accordingly, etc., is damaged, and is obviously not functional in the heads of our despicable leaders, resulting precisely in the problems of planification of their African states, while their memory is intact. But still under the influence of neocolonialism drugs and the desire of power, they're failing to go and see the content of their memories and thoughts to manage the activities of the traditional African policy of African states; known as a solidaristic policy nature, qualified as assistance between generations; the traditional policy nature of collectivist, unifying people and the continuity of cultures; a cantonalistic policy nature, as partisan of the decentralization of power to the cantons; the communitarian politics, connecting individual and the community; the culture of a traditional nature, as a complementarity between genres; the tradition of a religious nature, as tolerance between civilizations and natural observation of the tradition; the educational policy nature, as professionalism, respect for morals, more operational to realize, and achieve a sustainable development; "the art of managing the city," as a branch of traditional religion; and the practice and participation in social and community well-being. The prefrontal area is therefore essential not only for managing multitasking actions but also to realize complex operations, such as decisions or judgment; (should I do this or that?) or the realization of contingent activities (what to do if . . .?) These are factors that have never been a source of constructive intelligence among African leaders.

The plagues and social syndromes that African states are suffering by this lack of factors listed above make that frequent constitutional amendments are made to stay in power, guaranteeing poverty, and promoting misery through the perpetual indebtedness of our countries; the succession syndrome or subsidiary transmission of presidential power to cover themselves and protect the party after the departure of the paternal candidate; the instrumentalization of corruption by favoritism and the erection of the privileged class; the embezzlement of public funds for the enrichment of offspring and the safeguard of regimes for indefinite periods; and the electoral frauds discredited in many countries that orchestrate recurring coup attempts and state coups. I say that the fiftieth anniversary of the independence of African countries has opened old wounds and has thrown a harsh light on the long reign of invisible African heads of states, who do not respect the customs of traditional African politics, conceiving that every citizen, every farmer, and every villager must imperatively participate in the management of the city, of the country, and the village.

We all know perfectly well that, when we were subjected to a subordination that tended to a condemnation of always been enslaved, Africa exclaimed itself with these words: "Freedom, freedom, freedom," followed by the slogan, "Peace, peace, peace," and well after, "Independence, independence, independence."

Isn't it a challenge, but also a very useful thing that allows us to be masters of our own destiny? To cease to hear that we are subjects, to eliminate that notion of master and subject, to do better than when the master was present or to do as much as him at our home and elsewhere, and to show that we did not deserve to be subjects? However, it turns out that after the so-called masters, nothing is developing in Africa, been at the political level or in infrastructure, yet we definitely have a converging point, a common denominator, which is that Africa, rich in the true sense of the word, which must be developed by its leaders and take care of its children.

"But, no," say our leaders. Yes, young Africans, we non-nationalist leaders from across Africa, we initially refused you freedom and peace; we refused you freedom and officially not to aspire to freedom of expression. On the other hand, to deprive you sons, daughters, mothers, fathers, aunts and uncles, of good medical cares; we deprived you of a good education; we refused you a good job and all forms of good easy life, and we will put you against the current aspirations of your people. The anger of the African people, the abused victims for over half a century by the violation of human rights and social injustice of governments, still founding nonhumanist regimes and bad governance in general with neocolonialist ideology, making us victims of aggression as presented above, has literally and clandestinely transformed the despairing African people without conscience toward the West. This leads me to say out loud that it is necessary that intellectual honesty must get our arrogant Africa out of today's archaism and introduce it into modernity. But being still the product of autocracy backed with badly assumed nationalism, which have governed consciences and mentalities of men and women of our country for several decades, it is important that African leaders of today or those who aspire to become leaders understand that the period of leadership by force is over. Even if it is based on noble intentions, the consent of a public voice is today essential on the road to the construction of the collective welfare. Let us cultivate the garden of our thoughts and our emotions to get the best out of it.

Silently, let us look at our reflections in the mirror for a beginning of wisdom, which is the true royal path toward the development that we have invented from the bottom of our hearts for ourselves and by ourselves and which will lead us toward the better future we all want for all.

To achieve this paradigm change, it is necessary to change the autocratic habits based on a badly assumed nationalism; question methods that combine violence, intimidation, humiliation, impatience, impolitic, recklessness and perkiness, which primarily constitute the failure of our policies and development; fight against corruption; the iniquity in contracts binding multinationals to Africa; and know that when we want to manage men and lead them to operate a profound change of values and build a better future, the content and the form must be very important. If the roads that Africa tacked without knowing, without noticing, and without wanting to achieve its liberation, its total independence, peace, and freedom are diverted and long, it is because the slavers, monster despots of immoral colonization, who set up the system of independence, produced it and chained it like a legacy in Africa.

That is why the inheritance of that shameful and unjust cruel barbaric constitution is making that simple presidents in Africa are absolutely important; for me not to say they're like God or everything supreme that does and have everything it desire and the African people are nothing and have nothing. Their actions are testifying us men without foundation; men who are abusing their authorities without will; they're tyrants without any knowledge of honor, having no respect for humanity or even its reason of being; they're insensitive men to their own existence with ferocious whims of imbecility, which are producing tragic scenes ever seen in our sad African regions.

Our sad people in all nations of Africa have tried almost everything to do right by going to fetch ideas sometimes in the moral sources for a good state of mind, addressed exhortations of good management, subjected recommendations for changes, for the importance of the judgment of values valid in life, which must establish the standards operating in a society.

Sometimes, in our conclusions on moral precepts, we organize demonstrations with the aim to attract the attention of our governments by human actions, to express our demands and as a practical general rule intended to regulate behavior or thought of a government; but the moral fear and physical response of these governments lead them to commit acts resulting to the death of many civilians; because they're opposing the demands of their citizens; and more often again in their imagination, they're lacking the necessary knowledge to solve problems.

With all these events, the insensitivity of our statesmen, and the dictatorial policy of the colonial system, it is like living around the ages of wildlife, where forced and fearful men were submitted to the stronger by force. Our leaders have not learned. They remain submissive and feel better in their wild state and fail to achieve a revolution at the cost of freedom, the only property of the human race. But how can they despoil it, since that freedom is still the unique property that Africa and humanity in general possessed? Men, women, and children are suffering, squatting in misery without any hope of returning to prosperity. We who are living outside the continent also share the same pain because we maintain good relationships with our families back in our various countries in Africa. The impoverishment of these countries affects all Africans wherever they're in the world and spares nobody directly or indirectly.

The voices in all edges of the world are rising and are intoning the same melodious song of disarray to recognize the failure of their political systems, the failure of a generation, the suffering of a people by the existence of two, three, or even four regimes in fifty-seven years after independence, which are part of the causes of widespread corruption, hence the beginning of the decline of mores, which reveals that generations still rising have been sacrificed and forgotten. We simply find nonrespect, and very few existing security standards in it, the urbanizations standards almost nonexistent—no infrastructure, no proper health care, a poorly organized system of education, an inflation that kills, no work for graduates and for our parents. Roads are ramshackle, there are no traffic code and no road signs, and the law enforcement agents are all requesting bribes without proper uniform in all offices. Motorcycles, as urban transportation mode, are completely polluting our environment, where the highest record of accidental deaths on poor roads, etc., is recorded. And the pollution caused by motorcycles generates all sorts of unimaginable diseases, essentially resulting in tears, leading toward the road of tombs. All this demonstrates the most visible signs of a total mess of countries, which do not care about the fate of their futures.

Since the sovereignty of Africa, no progress has been accomplished, but good significant efforts of the unusual architecture of all African presidents are put in place to roll back prospects of putting their skills at the service of development in the course of these last years after independence. They're unable and have no intuition to elaborate a work plan leading to the modernization of Africa; to preserve the achievements and recommendations of our pioneers, their loyal ideals ensuring the patriotic fidelity; to recognize the merit of their struggle for independence since independence; and continue to operate our countries smoothly in a spirit of tolerance and in accordance with the general interest. But by breaking up with traditional construction, they're prescribing tasks to accomplish in the prelude of inequality, which are affecting all aspects of life; food, health, education, living conditions, etc., or the fight against poverty, are basic necessities essential to life, but affecting over 40 percent of our population; and the refusal to elaborate challenges from inequality to equality at the international order are issues that we still face in Africa; and the intolerable in our society places the human dignity at the forefront of their valuable codes of conduct without values.

In my spirit, things are clear; and according to my thought, we could only overcome poverty at the cost of a stronger commitment, which will be inscribed in duration if our heads of state of the new generation of the coming decades could give a place to the dream of an immediate intergenerational alternation. What is therefore a distressing truth is that there is no prospect for a new generation to succeed, the only way to guarantee our stability and to ensure our economic progress and social life. The political, economic, or sociocultural situation of Africa in general denotes all the evil that still undermines Africa. The treacherous Europeans, many of whom carry the same official identities of corruption, have not yet completed to sell out everything in Africa. It should be noted that facts are almost the result of the organized crime of corrupt European traffickers, without any concern for the dignity and security of Africans in the African territory.

The Europeans in corrupt accomplices, filled with contempt, greed, and disorder, still dictate the law to African heads of state, allowing the presumed prevaricators to embezzle funds, extraversion of capitals, and the export of these astronomical sums of money, sometimes three to four times greater than the budget of our own countries in foreign banks, or to own real estate and other properties in those foreign countries, which ultimately serve the economic development of those countries, leaving the entire population in suffering and paralyzing an Africa still on its knees.

We have repeatedly in vain reported these facts to attract the world's attention on this because you can read their expenses through their investments and realizations that they made for the development of their own progress. We must not forget that these barons of our regimes are supported by European regimes for years, helping them put a system of kingdom in place, explained a Ponte of a regime under anonymity in Africa. This situation is seeking an urgent and violent intervention of the UN to put an end to this sacrilege. The current governance of the UN for the development of Africa will not contradict any of my remarks because of having been adequately informed of the issue, and having repeatedly intervening to ascertain the truth, the involvement of African heads of state in these troubling acts remain unpunished. It is urgent to put an end to these extreme probate actions of gangsterism at the open sky, and perpetrated by all those band of rogue heads of state, who are scornfully mocking the fight against poverty, corruption, the social inequality of the entire population within the continent and their nonpatriotic intellectuality that contributes to tarnish the image of Africa; and to ruin the trust of African citizens, who are observing the death of the soul in their governments, they're trampling on the authority of the whole UN institution concerning this problem.

The incapacity to follow the path of a problem from point A to reach point B of the solution is one of the facts that Africans are reproached for, particularly to their leaders. The effect of knowing that we are cruelly lacking action has never been an insult but a reality that we must acknowledge. And it is only through questioning that we can come to accept it and start projecting ourselves forward effectively. Because the thought is only awakened in the intensity of the crisis, and it is in deep meditation that the necessity of questioning arises; this thought in its epistemological horizons was philosophized by the priests of the school of Amarna, Heliopolis, Memphis, Thebes, and the ancient school of the city of Sais, where the grave of Osiris was located in Egypt, "Kemite," the universal cradle of philosophy. The prestige of their doctrines and their main works attracted the whole world, and it is in these schools that the first Greek thinkers received their morning lessons to effectively project themselves forward, but today they find themselves beyond the precept of millennium amnesia.

A beginning of communication with all spirit is necessary to exchange, to inform oneself, and finally to be mobilized in the black continent, as a means to be freed; according to my opinion, this mobilization should be the vector of the revolution of all African people, not at all in good march toward the evolution at the speed of the present century, but unfortunately still imprisoned between the barbed wire of the neocolonial regimes of the West, this vector of revolution is necessary for a march toward evolution; a creed put in place for the states of censorship in the heart of Africa's administrations, where freedom, chastened by severe measures, constantly oppressing men is killing and imprisoning without being trialed; journalists are muzzled, intellectuals called to orders to be maintained in power at all costs; the bullying of minds depriving freedom in societies, where death is today considered as a banal thing and life not representing anything anymore have become common in life.

Whatever that may cost, a great educated world and patriotic elites must urgently take charge of billions of Africans in the black continent and profoundly educate them so that its population can achieve intellectual honesty in the coming years toward the evolution and the development of economic, cultural, and sociopolitical reality of our countries. I am well aware that a great number of compatriots are making their opinion on the conduct of public affairs in our countries, but with respect to the views of each other, I will say we cannot always be on the same wavelength, knowing many disparities, both on the political, ethnic, linguistic, cultural, and intellectual issues. My idea is to create a convergence of ideas for the awareness of all statesman and intellectual to the culmination of a real success that we can retain as essential for all Africans, wherever they're or whichever tribe they belong to. Freethinkers should particularly have the commitments of an intelligent thought, permanently communicating nationalist ideas, and try to fill a good part of the existing free spaces in the stupidly authoritarian regimes, always under pressure of the Western power, with widespread corruption and a difficult economy. We need those rare patriots who can work for a lifetime for Africa.

This tireless struggle for democracy; the freedom of men, women, and children and justice arouses objectivity in the process against the infantilization of an indescribable timorous apparatchik justice at a time when the rulers of the continent want to transform the symbols of a vibrant and bold civil society of since the heroic times. Despite the persecutions of the ruling regimes of heads of state with a keen interest in keen longevity reigns of esotericism, with mystical-exoteric practices at the heart of African regimes, they do not govern or reign but float and fly at a distance for the needs of their colonial homologous. The mooring lines of the colonial era still placed across the torn continent, reflect a climate of extreme tension in the entire African territory.

The freedom of Germany, the Netherlands, England, Portugal, Spain, France, etc., is at the end of the cannon. And the pack is just growing since the sharing of Africa in Germany in 1884. Dear Africans and dear readers, let's open our eyes to see the face of our executioner; what we have suffered to obtain, peace, freedom, and independence are just empty words in Africa. Make an effort and find out that African dictators are protected and loved by those colonial leaders. So, let us not be easy preys because, even if a wolf changes the pattern of its movement, it will always remain a wolf. The officialization of the dismemberment of Africa occurred at the meeting of the ancient slave trader powers in Berlin from 1884 to 1885. After slavery, everything was set up by the same ancient slave trader powers to continue their domination on our people. This allowed Germany to take control of Cameroon, Togo, and South West Africa, later called Namibia and today corresponding to East Africa and present territories of Rwanda, Burundi, and Tanzania, where a dehumanizing and enslavement system coldly set up was providing unbearable conditions.

Africa has therefore also known Nazi undertaken in the German colonies by the German colonizer, who committed an intolerable genocide in Namibia.

The Belgian king was content to cut the hand of those who were fleeing from forced labor or just kill half of the Congolese population for his dissatisfaction. Finally, we also know that the genocide committed overseas exterminating the Native Americans in North America was repeated in Australia with the extermination of the Tasmanian Aborigines by the British colonizers at the outset of the nineteenth century; and as it was the tradition of the colonial powers to invent a legal system of "bestialization" of blacks in the concentrationary universe of America, which was done in all legality, because from blacks, a cry was heard up to the celestial vault, announcing the great niggerchronoholocaust cataclysm. This cry of distress, expressing a desperate and dehumanized soul, intended to be heard by those who wanted not to hear it, was explaining that this dehumanizing enterprise marked by barbarism still continues without interruption, even after these same victorious powers of barbarism, ironically decreed that there was no rationality behind its fearsome and incomprehensible atrocities of Nazism.

I hereby draw your attention to the condescending testimony of some so-called intellectuals of the most prestigious scientific societies of the nineteenth century who believed in the extermination of races. Some of those are the Royal Geographical Society, the Anthropological Society of London, and the Geological Society of Paris. A very amazing thing is that the Anthropological Society of London organized a round table on the extinction of inferior races on January 19, 1864. The worrying issue, which was discussed on that famous round table, was the right of superior races to colonize the territorial spaces considered vital for their interests. Sometime later, a report of the discussion proceedings of that round table was published in the journal vol. 165 of 1864 of the said association. Surprisingly, the results of the report revealed an interrogation on an inevitable extinction of inferior races for all colonization or if there would be a possibility for them to coexist with the superior race without being eliminated. Bullshit! Can you believe it? By the way! Of what are you really superior?

Albert Sarraut, then interior minister at Constantine in Algeria and the French politician and servant of the Radical Party, declared on April 23, 1927 during a speech, the ideal of a radical-socialist, which he pronounced in front of students of a colonial school, saying, "It would be childish to oppose European colonization undertakings with an alleged right of occupation of our continent for its wealth;" according to him, "this wealth, which would have perpetuated into the hands of unables, could have resulted to the possession of wealth in vain, without exploitation." He was also opposing the political theory that advocates the possession of all property by the public and advocated the abolition of social classes by strongly condemning that same pooling of means of production derived from Karl Marx, called "communism" to the favor of French "imperialism." I would simply say, God bless you wherever you are.

Georges Vacher de Lapouge, a French sociologist full of racial hatred, openly supported him by saying there was nothing more natural than the enslavement of inferior races by pleading for a single superior race, leveled by selection. According to him, only the dolichocephalic white Aryan race is the bearer of greatness, unlike the brachycephalic inert and poor race, of which the Jew is the worst figure. So, we could not rejoice by knowing that the abolition of slavery was only for economic reasons and not for striking moral reasons.

Because of the cost of recruitment and maintenance reasons, slavery was no more profitable during the revolution of modern industry. I especially want to pay tribute to black people without forgetting other nations who experienced the same suffering by emitting a cry of distress to the awareness concerning the magnitude of the consequences of slavery, a practice that denies rights to be recognized as human beings but as certain arbitrarily defined categories, a well-recognized and rare practice, today recognized as a serious crime against humanity in the strictest sense of the term; and because America, Europe, and the Middle East do not want to undertake the genuine repentance to demonstrate a sincere regret or remorse, and the remembrance work for the faith that could save their relationship, this denial of rights to be recognized as human beings still ethically and sustainably sully their social relations, affected by the absence of all values toward the black man; these reasons make that slavery has of course not disappeared from the living conscience. That suffering, including the shame of the enslaved, the destroyed individuals and the humiliation of an entire continent left in the heart of each human being, to live in the open and festering wound.

The South American historians agreed and revealed a truth to us, but as always, it is disputed by Europeans. According to them, on the eve of 1550, there were approximately one hundred million inhabitants in the American continent, and there only remained ten million after the conquest as a result of a genocidal extermination of ninety million human beings. Oh, Lord! What cruelty; while Europeans, to lessen the figure, are considering that there were only eighty million Amerindian inhabitants in the whole American continent, resulting to a sudden subtraction of twenty million civilized Amerindian inhabitants, and that there were only ten million remaining after their genocide escapade. Anyway, whatever the figure may be, we acknowledge in relative terms that there has been a massive humanity destruction of 90 percent.

This posterior unjustified and not judged criminal act, has conditioned the sociocultural, the ideological, and the political evolution of white supremacy in respect of other non-European people, and ultimately, it has only been for the interest of Europe. This disturbing impunity favoring those slavers, led them to have fun by burning the natives alive in pyres or throwing the indigenous and infants snatched from their mother as food to hungry dogs.

Remember that the racialization of slavery in the concentration camp of America and Africa, as a totalitarian idea of the white race with their famous superiority belief toward the Negroes, and qualifying them as inferior beings, has nowadays become an unavoidable truth imposed by the Western culture.

That dangerous legacy, harmful to the whole society, was adopted by the European colonizers and combined with nocuous classified effects, which stimulated the emergence of a culture favoring the extermination of groups considered inferior.

Hope is allowed when nothing works. And suddenly, the premonitory sign deciphers an end of the first political generations committed to the obligations of neocolonialism but also those committed to nationalism by their unconditional loyalty, which nobody can really significantly define better than themselves.

My premonition is the law of the age, and known as an irreversible era of changes revealing facts with enthusiasm, is calling for the responsibility of the young people, who should define their project and the political commitment of the society of tomorrow in our countries; to accordingly form states in accordance for the people unity, and the establishment of good institutions; consequently with the logic of the architect of life, they must be as great servants of our nations; therefore symbolizing the continuity of political regimes of renewal in Africa. This illustrious new succeeding generation will put an end to the political system of the former barons' regimes of looters and killers of ancient days, which aroused fear and terror after gaining access to the highest office in our countries determined to constitute the policy of their illustrious colonial predecessors.

The afterlife has definitely taken over the lions of various African governments, having contributed to the establishment of both mystical, and Republican institutions; and a severe repression of an autocratic regime of heaven here on earth, governing men as if earth does not exist, and lacking a total indefectible democracy, causing upheavals in the disastrous national political sphere against freethinkers; these upheavals are arose by the opposition on the intellectual future of the African populations, whose governments did not hesitate to qualify as enemies of our independent nations; demonstrating a desire to track down their opponents with the fallible democratic political system up to the sumptuous hiding places of their palaces.

In conditions never elucidated, the amnesia of these first Africans, who reached the summits of knowledge, reveals to us that it becomes normal that they're not using their intellectual lucidity to detect social injustices as a shocking wave; this way of doing saddens, and it justifies a feeling that influenced the conscience of young aspirants into politics in the African continent; they found themselves not having any apparatus of sociological example deemed gentle and without a simple praise of love or solidarity, but called to be undisputed master of many disciplines of both mystical and Republican Institutions, which, however, practically remained without respect in our countries. It is that mode of management without satisfaction of human needs that the man who meditates, who reviews with all his strength, and devotes all his existence fights, fifty-seven years after independence in some African countries.

An irreducible, unending poverty explains a dehumanizing system of colonialism of long ago that Africans still experience in their conscience; hence, some all-powerful civilize leaders who are squandering the assets of our countries, do not aim at any productivity or the economic well-being of all people in a world where nothing been certain, dominate the unexpected by the parody of absurdity, contrary to the reason at any time possible.

The perpetual struggle imposed by the need for shelter, as the rudimentary facility for health, the facility intended to help the populations to feed themselves, to clothe and to be educated or intended to protect them from dangers and bad elements, and to determine the cause against political pressure, etc., remain projects that are still defying the common sense of African man; drawing his attention on the question to know of what future his present was bearer.

Here I am summarizing my thought with all my bliss and agree to submit myself willingly to certain obligations to justify the impious, the impetuosities of African politicians who are depriving generations of vivifying sources, without which life has no meaning or no germination is possible. This loud deafening cry of protest has plunged Africa in misfortune, in which the silent extinction of civilizing voices is characterized as a great contempt of all ages. In this, a disturbing sense of acceptation of the acts practiced by tyranny as an arbitrary sublime spell of life for African society sacrificed at a genital stage. But how do we transform that knowledge of our patriotic intellectuals into a permanent presence to hasten the advent of love, peace, and freedom and to develop democracy and progress, banished by the very undemocratic powers of the continent?

In the African tradition, the hope of becoming a worthy successor and an heir to the father's intelligence is permitted; it is permitted to know the intellectual and spiritual skills to perform domestic tasks of our nations; to evaluate vocations of different missions on the moral, spiritual, and intellectual plan; to seduce people through freedom of thought and expression, to give a significant place that the theme of democratic life occupies in the knowledge of civilization, concerning the historicity of the African world with its constraints, its disciplinary requirements, and put the pedagogical qualities endowed with great skills into practice on African culture; a cultural identity in all likelihood known as the black Africa culture, tied to the authenticity of mysticism, the mysteries of traditional art, its techniques, the meaning of symbols, but also and above all, to affirm African realities.

The African continent must come out of its present great drowsiness and make Africans walk in the center of gravity to draw itself an important place in the international world, to forget the lost age of narcissism, to rediscover the resources of its regeneration, to create something eminently new, to reconstruct itself as a force to advantageously negotiate with its people and subsequently with the world, to cease maintaining quarrels, and to simply erect a new will that gives a mark to the African people turned to losers in the eyes of the world. Strengthen material foundations, local potentates, and social classes in flesh, in bone, and in spirit by the renewal of postcolonial powers bequeathed by the mediocre colonization of the former colonial power, which decolonized our countries without self-decolonization, and whose the smallness minds of our leaders are still dependent toward their colonial masters, and do not do much better to develop Africa. However, a transfer of power took place without radical decolonization, leading to a new beginning. The colonial system and the neocolonial regime exerted state terrorism on African populations for decades through the constant practice of torture, the historically known oppression in its worst forms, the forced exploitation without compensation of its workforce, the sacking of its natural resources, massacres and genocides guided by colonial principles against the first nationalists, and the bloody crackdown against all opposition. It turns out that in this summarized sentence, defined by the culture of violence and conflicts, which founded the Western society, are practices completely rejected by African traditions and cultures. Let us remember that the black nationalism of the past was asserting to never renounce the natural right, rightful to independence.

The Black Nationalism also confirmed that our people preferred to live in poverty with freedom than to be rich in slavery, and that we can only exist richly free in the memory of our people to better exist in the cradle of authenticity and the originality of the African. It is therefore clear that the deprivation of good mores regarding democracy arouses a radical change for the establishment of traditional African democracy, which does not resemble the ancient Greek random democracy drawing in any African society; for Africans, the existed consensus among the Meru, or the inter-African mode of decision making, was the only complete form of any democratic expression, rather than the universal suffrage dominating the world today.

The direct democracy known as the citizen expression by consensus is an essential element in any system truly called democratic system, having an image acceptable by many people of the world, as a government thirsty for the well-being of the whole population in a nation; consequently, the African people demand the change of the current neocolonial system, which is governing them since the early twentieth century; it is pinpointed by poverty, despair, and the state of unrestrained degradation of their living conditions by its officials, who are stifling initiatives of any economic expansion by a dominant reign, and whose external relations are those of dependency toward the neocolonial networks and the international assistance; this dependency on our neocolonial masters leads us to think of a new autonomous way of thinking for the introduction of democratic politics, leading to the general well-being of our citizens. Injuries of its multiple illnesses are evils of hatred and grudge inhabiting hearts and gnawing the society and are asking to be healed for the inevitable return of the internal and social peace. Let us get out of the shackles of the colonialism misery, and struggle for our liberation from the violence, insecurity, and injustice currently in power, and let us solemnly commit ourselves to operate a fundamental change toward a democratic state.

The following four areas are precisely needed to reach a consensus:

1. Make a generational change in the leadership of African states from the meritocratic aristocracy of the administrative elite of the colonial era, mostly in control of the current centralized and individualistic power of the colonial and neocolonial practices; this change must be made by young people.
2. Establish a democratic state instead of the current neocolonial French state.
3. Replace the management of public affairs by a social ethic.

4. Create a new economic vision with new strategies of the twenty-first century.

Because democracy does not exist in self-proclaimed democratic countries that, at the same time, are said to be exporters of democracy in Africa; they cannot offer us democracy, which all presidents of the United States of America and their allies wanted to export in Iraq by the bombing of the Iraqis, launched on March 19, 2003.

Every human being endowed with the slightest intellectual capacity of judgment and appreciation does not prevent himself to ask question about that kind of Western democracy, whose legitimacy is only based on one fact: the bombing of a sovereign country to establish democracy.

This beautiful country of western Asia occupying the most part of Mesopotamia, the cradle of ancient civilizations of Sumer, Akkad, Babylon, and Assyria, was practically calm compared to how it is today; it is a part of the world with an exceptional prehistoric history. Among others, Sumer, a historic region located in southern Iraq, the first settlement of Eridu, ancient city of Lower Mesopotamia in the "Obeid period," known as a proto historical stage of the Mesopotamia development, which goes from about 5000 to 3750, and from about 3700 to 2900 BC, the period of Uruk which succeeded that of Obeid approximately in the sixth millennium BC; the Uruk period is development phase of the Uruk culture and started in Mesopotamia in the fourth millennium BC.

The third millennium BC, during the dynastic periods called early dynastic or pre-Sargonic period of the city-states of Lower Mesopotamia, up to the beginning of the second millennium BC, at the rise of Babylon, the first truly urban civilization marking the end of the Middle East prehistory. From a single reference in Gen. 10:10, Akkad is presented as Accad; Akkad is an ancient city of ancient Lower Mesopotamia, the capital of the Akkad Empire founded by Sargon the Great of the "Old Akkadian" dynasty, was known as the first ruler of the Semitic-speaking Akkadian Empire. From the twenty-fourth to the twenty-third centuries BC, Sargon the Great was also known for his conquests of the Sumerian city-states. The "Sargonic" dynasty, ruled for about a century, and after his death in the late third millennium BC, the Gutian dynasty conquest took the power over Sumer in Mesopotamia; the single mention of the name Sargon is in Is. 20:1, referring us Sargon II in the Hebrew Bible. From the eighteenth to sixth centuries BC, Babylon was a key kingdom in ancient Mesopotamia; and known as an ancient capital of Babylonia, it was known for its luxury, its fortifications, and particularly for its Hanging Gardens of the early second millennium BC, and it is located on the Euphrates, nowadays Iraq; and finally Assyria, also an ancient region of northern Mesopotamia; Assyria was a kingdom and a major empire of the ancient Middle East and the Levant; that name Assyria is derived from the city of Assur, and from its tutelary deity, known as the god Ashur. This region experienced a powerful kingdom, formed in the second millennium BC, and later became an empire, which controlled all or part of the territories extending on several countries, such as current Iraq, Syria, Lebanon, Turkey, and Iran. For the reason of that democracy, Iraqis are living with atrocities day by day, which they did not experience before the American invasion. The same reasons motivated France and all those who declared war on Libya.

Before our eyes, African children are hurt by the looting of Africa, causing the suffering of its citizens and killing the entire continent in silence by a nebula history of *Françafrique*, a pejorative word used in French pronunciation to designate the neocolonial relationship of France with its former African colonies without any powerful country of the world intervening; to talk about it or taking action against it. *Françafrique*, a parodying unsuitable term in form as in substance, which is akin to attaching two words indicating France: a western country, and Africa: a very faraway continent, connecting France to the entire continent of Africa only by a very damaging history, known as an occult aspect of French politics in Africa.

This expression was invented by the former president Felix Houphouet-Boigny of Ivory Coast to define the relationship with France in 1955. Mr. Francois-Xavier Verschave, an economist by profession and passionate about Franco-African relations, who described the concept, transformed its form to became what we call *Françafrique* today.

According to him, the logic of this aspiration was to prohibit initiative out of the circle of initiates, organized in the networks and lobbies, as a nebula of economic, political, and military actors in France and in Africa, and polarized on the grabbing of two rents in foreign countries; first, on raw materials, and, second, the famous public development aid that became an inescapable debt for our countries. However, that self-degrading system, naturally hostile to democracy, is recycled by the neocolonialism to the criminalization of France as the only country exercising this crime in an entire continent of Africa.

Francois-Xavier Verschave let us know the issue of *Françafrique* through his two main works titled *La Françafrique*, published by Stock in 1998, and *Noir Silence* (Arenas, 2000), which became references for the Survival association, of which he was a founding member and president from 1995 to 2005 to fight social injustice that strikes as a mental illness and return to the root of a concrete economic activity through a small woodworking company of Arti wood that still operates today; it was founded in the 1970s, on one hand, to motivate a half of workers composed of able-bodied, and on the other hand, half of workers with mental disabilities, to help them regain dignity through work before writing *Françafrique*, denouncing the control of the French National Grand Lodge action of Freemasonry on *Françafrique* in particular.

In 2001, he also published other works known as "The Black File of the African Policy of France No. 16," called "L'Envers de la dette," "The Underside of the Debt"; in 2002, he wrote the number 17, "The Criminal Operations in Africa," called "Les pillards de la foret," "The Plunderers of Forest"; in 2004, "De la Francafrique a la Mafiafrique," "From Francafrique to Mafiafrique";"The Franco-African Neocolonialism," called "Au mepris des peuples," "In Contempt of the People," also published in 2004; and so on. The lawsuit filed against three African heads of state, friends of France—namely, the deceased Omar Bongo, Idriss Deby, and Denis Sassou-Nguesso, linked to his last famous book called *Le silence noir* (*The Black Silence*), which narrated the black trial earned them a lawsuit, he and Laurent Beccaria, the former director of the publishing house that published that same book, for insulting foreign heads of state. To comply with the European Convention on Human Rights, the court declared them not guilty, given the absence of criminal intent in the legal context of the case. It is well known that France has a great history with a certain number of countries in Africa.

These ties woven with Africa through the means of *Françafrique* received no political review and no criticism from any so-called democratic country, not daring to tackle up the questions posed by these ties weighing so much on the privileged relationships between France and developing countries; inscribed in the history as the longest scandal of the politics of the French Republic, the so-called homeland of human rights without any dignity, containing the pre-square of all compromises of madness of *Françafrique*, marking the calendar of crimes known as a striking spirit of France overseas. In theory, democracy is only an appearance in France. We do not find a repressive system or compulsory labor camps there certainly, but that great country draws up the history of intellectual disorientation, giving harmful effects on the African economy as a whole. This is why *Françafrique* was founded as the main axis to undermine the economic and political development of African countries.

On the eve of the decolonization of the Fifth Republic of General de Gaulle—the unique grand master of the Order of Liberation, president of the provisional government of the French Republic from 1944 to 1946, last president of the council from 1958 to 1959, and instigator of the foundation of the Fifth Republic, of which he was the first president from 1959 to 1969—was designed as a partnership between France, a sovereign state, and African states having internal autonomy, not forgetting that the economic integration between France and its colonial empire has reached its most complete form in the'50s. It was therefore under the authority of de Gaulle that the networks of *Françafrique* were set up, exporting 30 percent of exports in the framework of the empire in 1960. He pretended to accept the will of French colonies in the south of the Sahara and faced a new international situation, affirming their desire to gain independence. The relations between France and its colonies remained a neocolonial geopolitical strategy, combined with military regime and completely looting the economy under the Western control for its oil, its raw materials, and its countless treasures. The effect of arming the resistance in those regions justified the grip of Europe toward Africa. They import mediocre goods at low prices and sell them at the highest price possible to Africans, against an exportation remuneration of primary goods as low as possible for producers. The reason of being part of their colony until proven otherwise is to bring to the metropolis the macroeconomic plan to always have control over its colonial empire.

From 1958, a reactionary right-wing, conservative, rear-guarded system, elaborated by the Mafia networks and occult channels was set up with parallel forces of political, economic, and military cooperation agreements, which swaddled the former colonies and placed them entirely under guardianship. The ingenious idea of creating the franc (CFA) is actually a wonderful instrument to convert a number of African wealth in Switzerland. The development assistance, the economic, military, and the political cooperation agreements, the franc (CFA), and the diplomacy are several components of *Françafrique*.

The relationship between France and African states was transformed after independence into a kind of infectious and incestuous relationship—a relationship formed by African presidents and multinationals with the aim of maintaining corrupt leaders in power for the systematic looting of our fabulous wealth. Making the French economy competitive is the aim and the fundamental principle of *Françafrique*. The fight against scarcity for economic needs ensures the survival of France by providing it with all the natural resources that its economy needs. To impose docility on African presidents, *Françafrique* is organizing coups to allow French companies to improperly exploit our natural resources. And to obtain or retain contracts and concessions, multinationals were instrumentalizing and are still instrumentalizing regional or local conflicts. Through this diplomacy, France thereby helped some French companies through all dirty tricks to exploit the natural resources of the Francophone countries in Africa, which became a protected area where impunity was guaranteed to the powerful to share the juicy African cake between themselves, a kind of criminal relations in a globalization transformed into a military plan by *Françafrique*, since the dawn of time, to eliminate nationalist partisans. In Cameroon, Ruben Um Nyobe—born on April 10, 1913 in Eog Makon, the Nyong-et-Kelle department, leader and precursor of independence in Francophone Africa, one of the emblematic figures of the struggle for the independence of Cameroon, as Felix-Roland Moumie and Ernest Ouandie, with whom he shared the same tragic end—was assassinated by the French army on September 13, 1958, in the Bassa County.

The majority of the French population does not know until today that their army was engaged in a hidden war at the origins of *Françafrique*, which caused tens of thousands of deaths—a real butchery inscribed in the lineage of the worst colonial conflicts, including those of Algeria, Indochina, etc., from 1955 to 1962. It was seven years of total genocide, radical, and unmerciful event, to eradicate a rebel movement that was demanding the independence of an African territory from 1948 by the name of Union of the People of Cameroon (UPC) in Cameroon by targeted execution of the leaders of the rebellion, torture erected as a weapon of mass terror, and by psychological action on a large scale, causing at least 20,000 to 120,000 deaths.

In the former Zaire, the current Democratic Republic of Congo, Patrice Lumumba was born on July 2, 1925, at Onalua in the Belgian Congo, who was the first prime minister of the Democratic Republic of the Congo from June to September 1960 and one of the main figures of the independence of Congo, with Joseph Kasavubu. He was murdered on January 17, 1961, in Katanga by the colonial power of the Belgian Congo. Sylvanus Olympio was a politician and the first president of the Republic of Togo, born in Kpando on September 6, 1902, and murdered on January 13, 1963, by the hands of Gnassingbe Eyadema during the coup.

In the Central African Republic, Barthelemy Boganda, born on April 4, 1910, in Ubangi-Shari, was a politician and deputy mayor of Bangui and considered as the founding father and president of the government, who gave its flag, its motto, its anthem, and the RCA denomination to the Central African Republic. He who led a struggle against the exploitation and abuses of the French colonial empire and a struggle for the emancipation of the black man, rendering his personality unavoidable during the process of decolonization, died on March 29, 1959.

In Congo-Brazzaville, Marien Ngouabi, born on December 31, 1938, at Ombele, first followed a military career as a sergeant officer and was part of the second battalion of the skirmishers of Cameroon from 1958 to 1960. He participated in the colonial war that the French delivered to the Cameroonian people and became at the age of thirty, the third president of the Republic of Congo, from December 31, 1968, to his death, murdered on March 18, 1977.

In Ivory Coast, Ernest Boka was a doctor in law. He was a politician and chief of staff of the governor-general of Ivory Coast in 1957. He held the position of minister of education in 1958 and minister of public service in 1959 and was named president of the Supreme Court of the Ivory Coast in 1960. Boka died in 1964.

In South Africa, Steve Biko, founder of the Black Consciousness Movement, born on December 18, 1946, in King William's Town in the Cape Province, who was a black activist and a key figure of the antiapartheid fight in South Africa, died on September 12, 1977, tortured in prison by the police.

In Burkina Faso, Thomas Sankara, born on December 21, 1949, in Yako, was a Pan-Africanist politician, anti-imperialist, and Third Worldist. He changed the name of Upper Volta, given by the colonization, to Burkina Faso, a name taken from the African tradition, meaning "the land of honest men" after the revolution that he headed on August 4, 1983, until the coup by Blaise Compaore, who led his assassination on October 15, 1987, in Ouagadougou.

On this long list of French crimes overseas, we also remember the military intervention of France, against three thousand Congolese rebels of the Congolese National Liberation Front (FNLC) in the 1970s that threatened to expel Joseph-Desire Mobutu of Zaire from his regime by their two attempted invasions of Katanga Province (renamed Shaba) in Zaire in 1977 and 1978. In support of the dictator, who abandoned his first names to be called Mobutu Sese Seko Kuku Ngbendu Wa Za Banga, when he was leading a campaign of "Africanization" in 1972, the FLNC became a member of the political life of Zaire, nowadays Democratic Republic of Congo from 1991.

In Niger, Hamani Diori was one of the charismatic figures of the country's independence, the first president of the republic, and one of the architects of the Agency for Cultural and Technical Cooperation (ACCT), today International Organization of La Francophonie (IOF). President Diori, born on June 6, 1916, at Soudoure, wanting to sell uranium elsewhere than in France, contributed to hasten the military to bring down his regime on April 15, 1974 by a coup, in which the tragedy cost him the life of his wife, Aichatou Diori, the dearest person in his life. He was imprisoned for six years in Zinder and then kept under house arrest from 1980 to 1987 in Niamey. He left his country to Morocco, where he died in Rabat on April 23, 1989.

France is more active than the past to destabilize our states. Since it does not disarm, there are only operations, such as those in West Africa, where the political crisis seems to be permanently installed, more specifically in Congo-Brazzaville, where the president of the republic, Pascal Lissouba, a scientist born on November 15, 1931, in Tsinguidi, who had the misfortune of wanting to increase royalties on the oil prices to 33 percent instead of 17 percent of Sassou Nguesso, was ousted from power by the *Françafrique* on October 15, 1997.

In August 2003, the overthrowing of Mr. Charles Taylor by the rebellion in Liberia for the reconquest of Liberia from the western Ivory Coast caused a destabilization that is following its course until today; in West Africa, the year 2003 was announcing the policy backwash in Senegal; in September 2003, Guinea-Bissau was trembling by a coup, and Sao Tome and Principe in July 2003; a coup attempt took place in Burkina Faso in October 2003; and in Mauritania, an attempted coup also took place that same year 2003.

These destabilizing effects of coups, which normally present the contrary as true, are highlighting their typical absurdity and manifesting an expression of tragic humorous effect of very different natures in our continent; their meanings, which have basic definitions, evoking the violent and illegal seizures of power, are many phenomena that still structure African geopolitics. Therefore, the effect of incoherent and drastic structural adjustment policies, reducing to nothing our already fragile young independent states, is just a complete legacy of the staggering domination of our sovereignty by presidents, multinationals, and powerful banks; a big and very heavy colonial legacy of the former European colonizing owners constituting dangers, mainly for the exploitation of our natural resources by uncivilized privatizations, disguised social plans of disadvantageous trade measures, the shameless exploitation of our workforce, frauds and the low prices of raw materials, the war of Katanga in the current Democratic Republic of Congo, which took place in 1978, by the French and Belgian military forces; followed by the funds investors with a poorly controlled democratic injunction, etc.; but we Africans being the only ones responsible for those ills, which are overwhelming our continent, are certainly rushing it into a certain death by relying on foreign strangulation, which marks out the development paths of our African countries.

Regional or local conflicts instrumentalized by those multinationals lead to wars, such as the one named Barracuda, instrumentalized by France, began on September 20, 1979, to overthrow the Emperor Bokassa I of the Central African Republic; the French military operation known by the name of Tacaud, which took place between February 1978 and May 1980 in Chad; the war of Katanga, in the current Democratic Republic of Congo, which took place in 1978, by the French and Belgian military forces; the Operation Sparrowhawk (*L'opération Epervier* in French), code name for the French military power in Chad; the Operation Turquoise, a military operation organized by France and led by French general Jean-Claude Lafourcade, at the end of the genocide in Rwanda; the participation of French Armed Forces under French command since 2002 in Ivory Coast was distinguished under the name of Operation Unicorn; and in Comoros in 1995, the Operation Azalea.

Since oil is at the top of the headlines, the geopolitical strategy, seeing the army resistance in the Persian Gulf and the depletion of oil wells in those regions, reminds us that the Gulf of Guinea should be fully under Western control; the populations in those countries that have oil in their land see themselves being subjected to the power of those multinational oil companies.

We then forget more often that it is for its oil, its raw materials, and its innumerable treasures that Europe is nowadays turning more than ever toward Africa, justifying that all countries of the Gulf of Guinea will experience the same fate of destabilization in a more or less near future. And France is doing everything to keep a few despots in power, devoted with body and soul to its homeland to the detriment of our motherland, Africa.

And I will add that *Françafrique* has clearly demonstrated the impostures, the shenanigans and a thousand intrigues by the support of that tiny club of rich states, which is the United Nations, where no African country has a seat in its security council as permanent member. Unfortunately for Africans, the African Union cannot be free, especially since it is financed by the European Union. Nevertheless, the improvisation of the economic plan of those multinational oil companies, from which Elf draws about 70 percent of its production and from which the new Total Fina Elf still draws 40 percent of its production, has become the first French private company and the fourth largest oil company in the world since its fusion in March 2000, with 50 billion francs profit and a turnover of 761 billion, the half of the budget of France.

The oil group Total posted the biggest adjusted net profit ever recorded by a French company of 12.585 billion euros in 2006, which increased by 12 percent to 153.802 billion euros. The group's profit growth followed the rise in oil prices in the recent years; in 2003, 7 billion, and in 2004, going over 9 billion. And in 2005, Total's profit reached an unprecedented record of 12.003 billion.

These oil companies are involved in the political and economic life of the countries concerned for decades by the sponsorship of regimes responsible for massive violations of human rights, the establishment of France on food, the encouragement of corruption circuits, and the total destruction of the environment; in North Africa, particularly Libya with the company called Fina; in the sub-Saharan Africa, Angola, Congo Brazzaville, Gabon, Cameroon, Chad, with the company called Elf; and Total is mainly active in Asia and Burma. The United Nations ranks the effect of this monstrous industry as the instigator of poverty in the two main African oil-producing countries—namely, Nigeria and Angola, among the poorest nations, impoverished by three decades of oil exploitation. All African countries are on the bottom of the table of the World Health Organization (WHO) global ranking; Angola is at 187 out of 191, Chad at 178, the Democratic Republic of Congo at 188, Nigeria at 187, and Sierra Leone at 191. Since the extraction of the first oil in those countries rich in raw materials, $653 billion have been received by Anglo-American, French, and Malaysian companies, and only $62 million remained for Chad. Eighty percent of the population of Nigeria, the second-largest oil producing country in Africa, still lives till today with less than a dollar a day while having 2.5 billion barrels of oil in reserves; the idea of conceiving that a fertile continent like ours with such rich subsoil be humiliated and raped gives goosebumps and sends cold shivers through the body out of shame; African people have the right to enjoy the riches of their continent and to live in dignity and peace in their countries. Mother Earth watches silently at the mafia politico-business of the foreign multinationals with the complicity of our satraps in power, bleeding our continent in white and leading our future to shreds.

The new African youth will soon have its word to say for the defense of its interests and the importance that some French multinationals are taking, exercising their control not only over many public services in our countries like the company of electricity, telecommunications, building, and public works, but also on the production tools, without the local population benefiting from the fruits of the dividends growth. It is well known that the black gold is drawn without shame from our countries regarded as the milk cow to the Westerners who are leading our countries in ruins, putting our beloved Africa at risk by multinational companies and by some wealthy African shareholders.

The oil manna, in my opinion is irrigated particularly to France and to the Western countries; but which profit can we truly attribute to our African oil-producing countries? If not to the so-called developed countries that are playing the benefactors, where virtually all dividends are registered by leaving Africa asleep in poverty? The addictive products that are pushing France to plunder our subsoil with the help of our presidents, and whose weight in the trade balance is very heavy, are oil, copper, manganese, silicon, platinum, chromium, molybdenum, titanium sponge, and cobalt. One of the main economic players in *Françafrique* maintaining close relations with African dictatorships, benefiting from all the political and financial ties with our great government support and the militaro-business tendency is Vincent Bollore, and is registers as Bollore-Rivaud, a French bank by the name of Rivaud; it became Rivaud Group, and it is Vincent Bollore who is in control of this group; he controls maritime transportation, Thomson (electronics), the paper industry, Dassault (aviation),

Bouygues (building), Bouygues Telecommunications and Communication, advertising, Suez-Lyonnaise-Dumez (water), Castel (beer), ultrathin plastic film, the automobile construction, and media. The French group Bollore is the owner of the dredging company for the clearing of the bottom of ports, rivers, or "another water zones" of the Coast of Africa (SDCA); Bollore Africa provides logistical services in Algeria, Angola, South Africa, Benin, Botswana, Burkina Faso, Burundi, Cameroon, Djibouti, Ethiopia, Gabon, Gambia, Guinea, Ivory Coast (Sitarail), Kenya, Liberia, Mali, Madagascar, Malawi, Mauritania, Mozambique, Namibia, Niger, Nigeria, Rwanda, Senegal, Sierra Leone, the Central African Republic, Chad, Togo, Tunisia, Zambia, Zimbabwe, up to the Reunion Island.

Regarding the activities of the French entrepreneur, the actions of his companies do not benefit the manpower population because their employees are not well remunerated at their fair value. Thereby, it's more than shameful to know that our Africa, which wants to liberalize everything, cannot establish a minimum-wage scale in the society, knowing that those most industrialized countries are imposing minimum wages on workers because they're subsidizing all their productions, which means that Africa is a land blessed for the welfare of France and that tiny club of rich multinational states. Evaluating these multiple problems, we must conclude that Africa must regain its control, especially in terms of labor. A society is organized by rejecting everything that is faulty and laying down rules to redress what is considered necessary for the common life and not the intellectually dishonest individualism of any multinational company. Unfortunately, France uses this weakness to conduct its inhuman business in Africa, but what can we truly do to definitively liberate Africa from this neocolonial yoke?

African countries must take the example of this fact determining a desire of domination relative to France in a decisive manner, a fact that shook France after collaborating with Hitler in 1940; and because it lost the war against the Germans, America wanted to colonize France by printing the French franc made in America in banknotes and put them in circulation in France. This action, undertaken by the thirty-second President of the United States from 1933 to 1945 was because Pres. Franklin Delano Roosevelt and the principal allies of France wanted not to recognize the new provisional government of France that General de Gaulle just created in Algeria. Speaking specifically of President Franklin Delano Roosevelt's action, General Charles de Gaulle made this remark about the United States: "The United States has no friends, it only has interests."

According to President Roosevelt, there was no question that De Gaulle, a soldier, and not democratically elected soldier, governs France. Franklin Delano Roosevelt's hatred for "the dictator apprentice" Charles de Gaulle, wanted to spare the dictatorship to France after Petain, and establish a universal democracy from 1941 to 1942, imposed by Washington and governed by the Allied Military Government of Occupied Territories (Amgot). This American military government of the Occupied Territories (Amgot) Allied Military Government of Occupied Territories of Washington wanted to impose a protectorate status on France, abolishing all its sovereignty, including its right to mint money. This protectorate was governed by a model provided by the Darlan-Clark agreements of November 22, 1942; and on December 24, 1942, Darlan-Clark was murdered in Algiers, North Africa, by a young student named Fernand Bonnier de La Chapelle. His assassination was sponsored by a Companion of Liberation named Henri d'Astier de La Vigerie; a member of the Order of the Liberation, founded by General de Gaulle as leader of the Free French, on November 16, 1940.

Finding himself on the "loser's camp," the camp of the defeated, Charles de Gaulle appealed to the French nation to liberate the occupation of France with the main allies from July 6 to the liberation of France on May 8, 1945. This appeal for the destruction of the Germans by General De Gaulle was well obeyed by the French, who carried out terrible actions during eleven months to liberate France and reaffirm its sovereignty and currency, thus rejoining the camp of the winners to avoid American colonizing France. This history of the colonization of France by America is a hidden story not known by the majority of people in the world, especially in Africa. It is just like the formation of an imperial economic protected zone adopted by the creation of a common currency area in Africa, at the outbreak of World War II, imposed by France as the franc (CFA), a currency for its former colonies, officially born in 1946; this currency was founded based on the complementarity of colonial exchange and the metropolitan productions of our natural resources.

After the Second World War with the creation of franc (CFA) in Africa for French colonies, connecting them with colonies which were nationalized and systematized; its primary characteristics were the introduction of exchange regulations and the centralization of foreign exchange reserves for the benefit of the metropolis, valid for all residents of the empire. This structure of colonial state management of the franc (CFA) zone has better survived the decolonization because French companies are operating in this area without significant risk; in its operation, where workers are still experiencing some forms of servitude, its mechanisms ensure the supremacy of France, who keeps the control of the economic system of its former colonies and the free transfer of capital in the area. By all and in all understanding, the economic strength of our countries depends on its ability to exercise protectionism, through which domestic products are valued.

Our countries must again be re-educated in real schools, but not where corruption is currently taught. This re-education must teach them that it is the same French slave traders—traitors of modern times fundamentally supporters of slavery—who perpetrated genocide in various African countries, and that they're the true enemies of the African nation, to generate significant regression of this eternal dependence toward the West in an environment inclined to fraud and asphyxiated by corruption, nepotism, and tribalism, which undermine the existence of the African citizen and allow everyone an equal opportunity. African leaders should know that the inventors of Bosch and Siemens are self-taught. It is the great importance granted to them that awarded them the titles of engineers after their inventions; they were not doctors or engineers before their inventions. It is obvious that we can still improve everything for our young people to be ready, thanks to changing times.

Our leaders, born under the colonial era, swearing by honor and loyalty to the settlers by hypnosis, will never cease to consider them as their master. By reducing their own countrymen as slaves at the expense of individual interests in the land of our forefathers, they're explaining the inertia facing the monopolization of our countries, both politically and economically. We must quickly recover the courage of our fathers of independence today to fight the French political system of intellectual masturbation in Africa, under the voice of the question of independence, which is requestioned in the same way but in a more complex context, the one to have a predominant capacity over the fate of our continent; to reclaim freedom tools for ourselves without hindrance or restriction for the becoming of our lives and to awaken nationalism in the spirit of our citizens. This French political system aims to serve itself from the lack of patriotism, has made that our local vassals are doing this work better than those worst French racists.

Neocolonization has educated Africans to accept mediocrity. To break off with the palpable expression of neocolonialism, nationals should be more involved in the management of companies in their countries, and the crucial sectors such as port, water, electricity, railway, and aviation must remain in the hands of the state. The real change will happen justly by political will and respect for the jurisdiction over generations because the current generation has its hands and feet tied with shady deals; it crucially lacks men filled with political vision, encouraging enamored progress and freedom; and in that atmosphere, the actions of multinational are one day too much at the straight line with the colonization, leading to another day and night, passing judicial sentence, and leaving crucial proceedings behind through towns and villages; and we could see one more day pass slowly without sovereignty. The culmination of colonization is materialized through the support at the highest level of the state. A model of neocolonial growth of those same men, who are hitherto accommodating the confusion of objectives, is conceived to preserve an area of influence in Africa for France.

The cooperation policy is today at a crossroads from inadequate to the maladjustment of structures, lenifying speeches, falsifications, lies, propaganda, and waste of resources that have characterized this policy for fifty-seven years for its favor. France, which is not the messiah of Africa, has the interest to re-establish its relations with our great continent; avoid the proliferation of extremist attitudes, breeding ground for international terrorism, and throw away its colonial glasses. We will fight *Françafrique* with all our strength to eradicate that dictatorship, which advocates misery in the management of already poor countries by opting for conservatism and stagnation. The normal functioning of political and diplomatic institutions must prevail on unofficial circuits that have done so much harm in the past. It is necessary that France, once and for all, turn the page of complacency, secrets, and ambiguities, especially with the Africans, and get rid of the networks of other times and of unofficial emissaries who have no other mandates than the ones they're inventing for themselves.

Thomas Sankara, the assassinated former Burkina Faso president, said this: "There is a crisis today because the popular masses assembled as one body are refusing that wealth should be concentrated in the hands of a few individuals. There is a crisis because few individuals are depositing colossal sums of money in banks abroad, which would have been more than enough to develop Africa. There is therefore a fight, and the exacerbation of that fight is leading financial authorities to be worried about it. Today we are asked to be accomplices in the search for equilibrium; equilibrium in favor of the financial power holders; equilibrium at the expense of the popular masses. No! We cannot be accomplices;" he uttered these words before his peers, exhausted enough intellectually, at the tribune of the Organization of African Unity (OAU), nowadays African Union (AU), on July 27, 1987.

And it was the exacerbation of that fight of financial powers that triggered the Ivorian and Libyan crisis. In that period, Nicolas Sarkozy, of Hungarian origin, was the president of France. Let us enter his universe; Hungary was for centuries inhabited by the Celts, Romans, Huns, Slavs, Gepids, and Avars. The Slovak territory, named after the Slavs, extending over the territories of the present Czech Republic, of eastern Germany, of Slovakia, and Hungary in the northwest, was a Slavic kingdom from 833 up to the beginning of the tenth century. Historically, the Hungarian language derived from Indo-Iranian, Turkish, German, Latin, and Slavic languages. When its independence came to an end in the early sixteenth century by the conquest of the Ottoman Empire, the western and northern parts of Hungary, which were not conquered, became the kingdom of Hungary, consisting partly of the Slovak territory; and from the year 1001 to 1946, it became a political regime of the Hungarian state, where Nagy-Bocsay Sarkozy Pal Istvan Ernő came from, who Frenchified his name to Paul Etienne Ernest Sarkozy de Nagy-Bocsa. He is the father of Nicolas Sarkozy and Andree Mallah, and his mother was from a Greek Sephardic Jewish family in Spain. The Mallah family took refuge in Salonika after the expulsion of Jews in 1492 from Spain. It was on February 8, 1950, in the seventeenth arrondissement of Paris, that the couple got married after their establishment in France, and they got separated in 1959. The father of Nicolas Sarkozy remarried a second time and then went through another divorce.

After that second divorce, he got remarried a third time to Christine de Ganay; and after the third divorce, his ex-wife Christine de Ganay remarried in 1977 with Frank G. Wisner II, son of Frank Wisner, who was from 1951 to 1959 the deputy director for plans of the CIA. Before the Office of Strategic Services (OSS) was dissolved in October 1945 and became the descendant of the CIA, he was promoted in their office in southern Europe as director of operations and planning. In the 1950s, alongside Allen Dulles (who was the first civil director of the CIA from February 26, 1953, to November 29, 1961) and Richard Helms (from 1966 to 1973 director of the Central Intelligence Agency), Frank Wisner was one of the main founders of the clandestine action doctrine of the CIA, founded in 1947 by the National Security Act and signed on July 26, 1947, by the President of the United States Harry S. Truman under an act of Congress (Pub. L. No. 235, Eightieth United States Congress, 61 Stat. 496, United States Code ch. 15). Under George H. W. Bush, who took office on January 20, 1989, as the forty-first President of the United States, Frank George Wisner II held the position of undersecretary of state for arms control and for international security from 1992 to 1993, in his administration of 1989 to 1992, and then beaten by Bill Clinton, whose real name is William Jefferson Clinton, born William Jefferson Blythe III. He was first the acting secretary of state of the United States in 1993 and then the undersecretary of defense for policy from 1993 to 1994 in the administration of the forty-second President of the United States from 1993 to 2001. This politician was remarried to Christine de Ganay, when Olivier Sarkozy was seven and Sarkozy then twenty-two years old in 1977; she was divorced from Sarkozy Pal Nagy-Bocsa, father of the former president Nicolas Sarkozy, but had Olivier Sarkozy with her. Frank G. Wisner, who raised Olivier Sarkozy the half-brother of the former French president Nicolas Sarkozy, favored the get-together of the half brothers and sister during weekends and during the summer months at their childhood, if he was outside France or the United States.

He who had the post of ambassador in Zambia, Egypt, the Philippines, and India was the best occult counselor of Nicolas Sarkozy in the corridors of power and remained in the shadows of the depths that no one ever saw. He was a man of networks in American and international politics, having a French passport, one of those who do not put themselves at the forefront of international political scenes and who contributed to the meteoric rise of the former French head of state Nicolas Sarkozy by taking advantage of the remarriage of his stepmother, Christine de Ganay, to Frank George Wisner.

He who inherited a heavy burden from the political career of his father, cofounder of the CIA, would also pursue his ambitions in the world of espionage but would not work exactly in the footsteps of his father. After long operating in the hushed world of diplomacy and information, Frank George Wisner was involved in the anomalies of economic espionage. So it would not be surprising to know that the several anomalies in which he was involved put him on the list of those persons considered as eminent terrorists in the United States, whose common point can be found at the junction of intelligence and finance crisis, at the eve of the famous crime initiated on September 11, 2001; that crime is evoked as the deed of American citizens.

The origins of former president Nicolas Sarkozy of the French Republic and his governance caused a rupture with the principles that founded the French nation, hustling all markers on the right and the left, creating a complete confusion not only in France but in some parts of the world as well. That agent of the United States and Israel hides his ties to the French to be elected leader of the Gaullist Party up to becoming the president of the French Republic, probably by the favor obtained from Frank George Wisner, the Western superpower, and the support of other politicians and the agents of the CIA listed here below. From the beginning of its history, CIA has always dislodged the leaders of several countries by coup. It was the case of the military coup in France aimed to destabilize the government of Pres. Rene Coty, which was jointly organized by the directorate of plans of the CIA, headed by Frank Wisner Sr. and NATO in 1958, to protect North Africa against Soviet influence by a possible victory of the FLN in Algeria, worrying the United States. A pressure of the French generals forced the French civil power to vote General de Gaulle to full power without the need to use force.

But it was the successor of Wisner, by the name of Allen Welsh Dulles, who supervised the coup, during the two mandates of Dwight David Eisenhower, the thirty-fourth President of the United States, from January 20, 1953, to January 20, 1961.

After that event, the CIA and NATO, as those who led Charles de Gaulle in power, felt betrayed. Unable to manipulate him, they attempted to support territories overseas in the bosom of the French Union by giving them broad autonomy. The fierce repression campaigns led against the independentists of colonized people, no longer believing in the promises of the metropolis, did not save the French Empire, which was facing the requirements of their independence; and independence was granted to each colony. So, a volte-face was settled; then they began all kinds of methods such as assassination attempts to eliminate independentist leaders and heads of states overseas not meeting their demands. At that moment, there was a certain character named Achille Peretti. His rise started as a lawyer in 1935 at the branch of the administration of the law dealing with the prosecution of crimes in Ajaccio and in 1937, as a police commissioner. He was transferred to Nice in the services of Colonel Paillole and continued his action in the Second Bureau of Intelligence in April 1941. He made contact with the Free French Forces in January 1942 and managed to reach England by air through a phratry network under the name of Paul Vatier on June 13, 1943. After performing a special internship, he created a new network of information under the pseudonym of Ajax and directed it in the southern zone at his return to France on July 22, 1943, and he was also the cofounder of SAC.

With the government of Algeria, Achille Peretti was appointed deputy director of the national security in 1944 after being the honorary chairman of the committee of the former network leaders of the French fighting forces and promoted as the prefect of the third-class senior executive in August 1944; and from 1947 to 1983, he was mayor of Neuilly-sur-Seine. In the economic life, he held various responsibilities as president of the mining company of the East Oubangui, the French Company of Upper and Lower Congo, and director of the Societe des forges et chantiers de la Mediterranee in 1947. From 1952 to 1958, he was a councilor of the French Union, and in 1958, the Seine deputy of UNR. On June 25, 1969, he was elected president of the National Assembly; and in 1977, he served on the Constitutional Council until his death on April 14, 1983, in Neuilly-sur-Seine. The former bodyguard also ensured the protection of General Charles de Gaulle during his days in Paris in August 1944.

Charles Pasqua was the second character to play a great role in the formation of Civic Action Service, qualified as a terrorist organization in which he became vice president and created with Alexandre Sanguinetti on January 4, 1960, at the service of General de Gaulle. It was originally created to form faithful guards and often qualified as a parallel police force in 1958, dedicated to the unconditional service of the general after his return to business. That Civic Action Service was led by Pierre Debizet, who was the first president, but it was Jacques Foccart, the confidant of Charles de Gaulle, who was certainly the real boss.

Etienne Leandri, a friend and the close intermediary to Charles Pasqua, had a secret financial role and intervened on many large international contracts. Etienne Leandri was representing the interests of Dumez, Elf, General Waters, GMF, Lyonnais, and Thomson-CSF. At that time, criminals like Joseph Brahim Attia (called "Jo Attia"), a Parisian gangster of the 1940s to 1960 and member of Gang des Tractions Avant, and Christian David (called "the Beautiful Serge"), a small robber involved in the war in Algeria, to only mention a few, had a SAC card. David Christian even became a trafficker and pimp, mixed with the networks of the French Connection. Both were involved in the controversial operations attributed to the French special services during the Gaullist era, the case of Col. Antoine Argoud, and the kidnapping of Ben Barka.

Thus, from 1944 to 1946, the head of the provisional government settled in the French Republic; from 1958 to 1959, he was the president of the French Council of Ministers. And from January 8, 1959, to April 28, 1969, he became the eighteenth president of the French Republic, the first to occupy the supreme judicature under the Fifth Republic. As its instigator, the Fifth Republic was founded in 1958. By affirming his membership in the Atlantic camp, Gen. Charles de Gaulle designed a policy of national independence with panache to challenge the Anglo-Saxon leadership with much opposition, such as, in 1961, the deployment of UN peacekeepers in Congo, and in 1961 and 1967, the entry of the United Kingdom into the European common market. In 1964, during a speech in Mexico City, Latin American states were encouraged to get rid of the U.S. imperialism.

In 1966, NATO was expelled from France and withdrew from the integrated command of the Atlantic Alliance. In 1966, during a speech in Phnom Penh, the Vietnam War was denounced. In 1967, during a speech in Montreal, Quebec, independence was supported. And in 1967, during the Six- Day War, the Israeli expansionism beyond its borders in Palestine and other neighboring countries was strongly condemned. After implanting a décor consolidating the power of France since the beginning of time, the French wrongly elected a man named Nicolas Sarkozy, whom they believed was free yet tossed in a recomposed family; closed to his stepmother Christine de Ganay, who was at a certain time the secretary of Achille Peretti, then mayor of Neuilly; to his half-brother Olivier Sarkozy, CEO and codirector of the international financial services of the Carlyle Group, appointed on March 3, 2008, and to his half-sister Caroline Sarkozy, specialized in interior design; he grew up in a school of vices, practicing habits considered to be selling evil and illegal ideas, qualified as degrading, immoral habits of wickedness, depraved conduct, corruption, desperadoes, pirates, and certain other forms of criminalities and violent behavior. Nicolas Sarkozy ended up marrying Marie-Dominique Culioli, the niece of Achille Peretti, in 1982, and his witness was none other than Charles Pasqua, who literally let Sarkozy steal the town hall of Neuilly-sur-Seine the following year.

Charles Pasqua was a senator of Hauts-de-Seine in 1968, chairman of the General Council of Hauts-de-Seine from 1986 to 1988, and minister of the interior affairs in 2004. He became senator of Hauts-de-Seine once again but got involved in several political and financial affairs and was held liable. Achille Peretti was also linked to the famous French Connection and seriously held liable for his involvement in that secret criminal organization, which was controlling much of the drug trade between Europe and America in 1972. From his involvement in the organization named the Unione Corse, Achille Peretti escaped a suicide and gave up the presidency of the National Assembly. In that case, the name of Jean Venturi, the trade commissioner of Charles Pasqua in Ricard, a liquor company was mentioned; his Pasqua network extending up to Africa made him the trusted man of French-speaking African heads of states, who initially retained a strong hand over Moroccan marijuana, retained games and races in Francophone Africa, and took control of casinos.

This Corsican bandit married the Quebecois Jeanne Joly in 1947, daughter of Maurice Joly, a Canadian bootlegger. This smuggler made his fortune during the prohibition period of beer, rum, wine, and liquors. In January 1952, as a representative, Charles Pasqua was hired by Paul Ricard, the creator of Ricard pastis, a French public limited company founded in 1932 in Marseille. In 1955, he became inspector of sales; in 1960, the regional director; in 1962, the general manager of sales; and in 1963, the director of export. He then became the number-two man of Ricard group after climbing all those steps. During his leadership in Ricard, he marketed a prohibited alcohol, absinthe; then by selling anisette, he became respectable.

Charles Pasqua evokes the name of several Mafia families, including the names of two Italian New Yorker Genovese families, the Morello family, ancestor of the future Genovese family, who was involved in the early 1910s in the extortion and the smuggling of alcohol, and the one of Lucky Luciano, a Corsican mobster who was controlling the U.S. ports; his influence in the high sphere made the investigations of the secret services of the United States very difficult, since their investigation on Ricard's Company producing prohibited alcohol failed, and it continued to serve as a cover for all kinds of illegal trafficking by Jean Venturi, the Mafia boss arrested a few years earlier in Canada, and who was recruiting him big arms for his school of vice and crime, to let the absinthe pass as anisette, introduced in the United States and Canada between the years 1917 and 1935.

The Ricard alcohol company that Charles Pasqua left in 1967 is the second-largest group today in manufacturing and the distribution of beer, rum, wine, and liquors by the name of Pernod Ricard. From Peretti, Pasqua, Leandri, and

Venturi to Frank Wisner Jr. of the central administration of the State Department of the United States of America and many others, Sarkozy has always had familial, friendly, or professional ties with politicians, who traditionally are or were involved in the organized crime in the Unione Corse, his mentors that he defended the interests as a lawyer.

Thanks to his stepmother, America was open to him; and with the help of the CIA during the time of Frank Wisner Jr. as undersecretary of defense of President Clinton in 1993, and then as vice president of AIG, American International Group; he was also the vice president of the Business Council for International Understanding; the director of formerly Enron Oil & Gas Company, known today as EOG Resources, and many other titles of responsibility in different companies, including institutions founded by him, he gradually began to plan for the end of the Gaullist current and the advent of Nicolas Sarkozy. He in 1984 betrayed his wife Marie-Dominique Culioli by maintaining a secret affair with Cecilia Ciganer-Albeniz, whom he met during the celebration of her marriage as mayor of Neuilly with Jacques Martin, the most famous French television and radio host from 1984 to 1989; and he married her in 1996, after the divorce of his first marriage with Marie-Dominique Culioli (married in 1982 and divorced in 1996). With Cecilia, Nicolas Sarkozy led a brief relationship with Claude Chirac, daughter of Jacques Chirac, who started to advise her father about his permanency policy, being mayor of Paris in 1989, and continued to advise him about "communication opinion" at the time he became president of the republic.

She married the political scientist Philippe Habert in 1992, and it was Nicolas Sarkozy who was his best man. But because of that relationship of the deceived husband, he died on April 5, 1993, by suicide after absorbing drugs; while Claude Chirac was seeking forever to deny those rumors of adultery, the relationship between Chirac and Nicolas Sarkozy took a brutal rupture, and without any amelioration with this phrase of Bernadette Chirac: "He has pierced our privacy," referring to Nicolas Sarkozy. He divorced Cecilia Ciganer-Albeniz in 2007, and on February 2, 2008, he married Carla Bruni-Tedeschi.

The history of the Gaullist leadership first collided with the right by the right; and finally on the left by a mechanism of betrayals, elaborated between 2002 and 2007, for Sarkozy to win the election by eliminating all his competitors; when Jacques Chirac was betrayed by Charles Pasqua and Nicolas Sarkozy, or when the famous tape fell into the hands of judge Eric Halphen; a videotape containing a long narrative recorded in form of a confession of Jean-Claude Mery, three years before his death, for the occult financing of the political party called "Rassemblement pour la Republique," RPR.

In 2004, Nicolas Sarkozy became the interior minister as president of the "Union for a Popular Movement," UMP. Nicolas Sarkozy was slandered in the Clearstream affair, declaring that Dominique de Villepin was aiming to oust him from the presidential candidacy, and with a firm voice, he initiated a complaint implying a conspiracy. In the 2007 presidential elections, he won the election against the Socialist candidate Segolene Royal and became president of the republic. Claude Gueant, the former right hand of Charles Pasqua, became his secretary general at the Elysee Palace. At the request of Wisner Jr., to resolve the issue of Kosovo's independence, he appointed Bernard Kouchner at the ministry of foreign affairs, as a lift back to Wisner Jr., who had, during the election campaign of Nicolas Sarkozy, chosen David Wisner's son as an English-speaking manager. History remembers, without doubt, that the mandate of the former president of the French Republic Nicolas Sarkozy was marked by a break in style than those of his predecessors.

During the mandate of the former president Nicolas Sarkozy, a case of murder sponsored by him to assassinate Hugo Chavez was stifled. France did everything possible to keep secret that operation, concluded by a total fiasco. On that subject, the substantial compensation granted by France forced the Venezuelan authorities to silence. But Philippe Lalliot, the spokesman of the Quai d'Orsay, confirmed these facts, released on December 29, 2012, in the Twitter account of the Member of the Venezuelan Parliament known as a political deputy from 2001 to 2011 before being appointed minister of correctional services from July 26, 2011, to June 16, 2017.

Maria Iris Varela Rangel blew the wind of the fiasco of France that no human ear heard concerning her country; she was ringing the bell for the fall of France by announcing the expulsion of one of its nationals, known under the name of Frederic Laurent Bouquet, under article 39, paragraph 4 of the Foreigners and Migration Act, for endangering the national security of Venezuela. By Order No. 096-12 of the first judge Yulismar Jaime, he was extracted from his cell after serving his sentence of four years for illegal possession of weapons.

She thereby disclosed a secret that hitherto was refrained from communicating, the one to silence the enemy. On June 18, 2009, Frederic Laurent Bouquet, an agent of French military intelligence secret services (DGSE), arrested in Caracas with three Dominican citizens, admitted during his trial to be in possession of 7 military uniforms, 14 assault rifles (1 noiseless, 5 fitted with telescopic aimer, and 5 with laser aimer), 5 shotguns of the 12 caliber, 4 guns of various calibers, 3 machine guns, 19,721 cartridges of different calibers, 2 bulletproof vests, 500 grams of C4 explosives, 9 bottles of cannon powder, special cables, 11 electronic detonators, 8 grenades, 1 combat knife, 3 walkie-talkies and a radio base, 1 gas mask, and 11 radio equipment. This arsenal was seized by the forensic police of Hugo Chavez in an apartment purchased by Frederic Laurent Bouquet in Caracas. He said he was trained in Israel to assassinate Pres. Hugo Chavez, constitutionally elected by his people. Like his stepfather and mentor Frank Wisner Jr., Nicolas Sarkozy continued to destabilize countries through attempts that went on in silence.

Under the Fifth Republic of the former president Sarkozy, the secret war led by his government was an act that violated article 35 of the French Constitution without precedent; but by the lack of an obligation of relevant treaties, that violation constituting a crime punishable by the high court (article 68) was not applied, which made him enjoy absolute freedom without trial for his crimes.

Before his death, when Hugo Chavez introduced the idea of socialism in the twenty-first century, the United States sought, by all means, to discredit that idea by the failed coup attempts throughout his presidency. But his thoughtful social policy allowed the realization of many things that made Venezuelans happier than most people in America. After the death of Hugo Chavez, that trend intensified to destabilize his successor. For that fact, the arsenal of destabilization was mobilized by Washington, which was playing a major role against Venezuela.

The country of Nicolas Maduro was infiltrated by the United States intelligence agencies. First, the psychological war propaganda was established. Then to carry out terrorist attacks, the Colombian paramilitaries infiltrated the country; and by the use of social networks on the Internet, there was economic and financial sabotage. That destabilization arsenal of the United States to change governments was applied in Iraq, Iran, Ukraine, Libya, Venezuela, Syria, etc., to prove that, in different regions of the world, Washington was still capable of directing as a superpower and discouraging leaders who were present in those countries but escaping it.

So, by synchronizing efforts, the United States governments destabilized those countries to forge other alliances. However, the Operation Jericho, which wanted to terminate the administration of Pres. Nicolas Maduro, put in place on February 6, 2015, and planned by the National Security Council (NSC) for the overthrowing of the democratic institutions of Venezuela, failed once more on February 12, 2015. That attempted coup was planned to change Venezuela's political regime, which motivated them to kill Pres. Nicolas Maduro, to be replaced with the former deputy Maria Corina Machado. It was a question of bombing the presidential palace and killing Pres. Nicolas Maduro to prevent the redistribution of the wealth of his country and continue his way into independence. Venezuela was, since the adoption of the 1999 constitution, one of the most endangered states by the doctrine of the National Security Strategy of Washington. That phase of the Obama administration, which organized that putsch by disguising a plane of the Academi (formerly Blackwater) as an aircraft of the Venezuelan Army, presaged the worst.

The United States allies, who were to subcontract certain parts of the coup during the stroke, were Germany (responsible for the protection of NATO nationals), Canada (responsible for monitoring the civil international airport of Caracas), Israel (responsible for the assassinations of Chavistas), the United Kingdom (responsible for the propaganda coup), and those who were to recognize the putschists as political networks who were already ready; on the list were Senator Marco Rubio in Washington, the former president of the Spanish government Jose Maria Aznar, the former Colombian presidents Alvaro Uribe and Andres Pastrana, the former Chilean president Sebastian Pinera, and the former Mexican presidents Felipe Calderon and Vicente Fox. Not long ago, agents disguised as gangs, paid four times the salary of the average income, to infiltrate the crowd, attacked the police during demonstrations concerning essential commodities that the White House encouraged by asking large

Venezuelan companies to store goods of first necessity rather than distributing them, and causing queues at the shops to justify their coup since it was known that in the Venezuelan history, the Venezuelan nation never attacked trader shops when it came to problems of supply but politely queued in front of shops. That plot aimed to assassinate President Maduro was marked by the vigilance of the Venezuelan military intelligence, and the personalities suspected to have plotted it were arrested.

Nicolas Sarkozy claimed to have overthrown the former president Laurent Gbagbo by the Constitutional Council and the barbarity of the French army to invest Alassane Ouattara to control huge natural resources that abound Ivory Coast. The use of military violence to install Alassane Ouattara as the head of Ivory Coast was never the choice of Ivorians.

The declared winner after the presidential election of November 2010 by the unique judge of elections in Ivory Coast and under the supervision of the international community requested the recount because he was sure to have won, but he was overthrown by a coup, simply because he was not meeting the requirements of France. Nicolas Sarkozy admitted to being the initiator of the tragedy that killed thousands of Ivorian children, women, and men by recognizing its improvisation in Mali and the Central African Republic, where a military intervention was not necessary, those two countries being just a cash cow for France. The truth about his confession reached us through Nathalie Schuck and Frederic Gerschel, two French journalists to whom Nicolas Sarkozy made secret confidences during his two and a half years of political retirement. They unveiled his coup confessions motivated by economic reasons. He chose not to respect the choice of the Ivorian people expressed at the ballot box, against a personal matter toward President Gbagbo, by brandishing arguments clearly contradicting the truths of the electoral disputes at the beginning of his offensive.

France should be ashamed of its leaders with such unworthy revelations, accompanied by unhealthy behaviors and mobster acts. Once again, with those mobster acts, the will of the process of democracy by a choice expressed at the polls to peacefully choose a president was categorically endangered by Sarkozy. The role of the imperialist international community still raises many interrogations to date in African affairs; its problematic insertion issues in the international relations at the emergence of the independence of the continent, and to the modern life are its references made on the predation and extraversion; that initial handicap could not be eradicated by colonization or by the wave of decolonization of the '60s.

The reconstruction of the foundations of the architecture of its civilization, the knowledge of its origin, and the unprecedented liberation heritage are buried under the rubbles of the African intellectual generations, dominated by the European ideology, from slavery to the World War II until the fall of the racist regimes of Southern Africa and the end of the Cold War.

Africa is still far from overcoming centuries of contradictory domination and the racist ideology condemning black people as an inferior race but bearing the universal history. This structural handicap of negotiating its relation to the world to its advantage prevents its outbreak from expanding, and its cry on this subject could be heard beyond infinite kilometers, to begin the new century for an appearance of glory. That relation must be a definition of something called global-worthy community, with moral and human attributes that do not exclude and do not justify verbal, physical, or moral abuse against those excluded, having no rights, and exercising no policy of force whatsoever, to conquer another sovereign country without any condition or reason to redefine in law which is common to all contours of human by powerful international campaigns of that community; but having the right of self-determination, to govern itself without driving another nation to conquer, to occupy, to define itself as colonizer, and to exploit inferior countries in technological powers.

The dazzled gaze of the yardstick of time has seen several centuries of all kinds of reasons pass since the dawn of time, concerning the right that other countries should have for the colonization of civilized nations; the colonialist, son of the enslaver, justified that domination by denying all intelligible historical existence, by falsification, and by a montage of history without the writings of the black people—a group of humanity deprived of historical foundations of antiquity since the advent of the Western domination.

Foreign interventions in African internal affairs are at the heart of Africa since time immemorial of occupation, of slavery, followed by colonization up to the decolonization and the implementation of neocolonialism. Those former colonial powers still use an imperialist policy toward our countries to make a profit, generally by methods of occult influences of their big companies.

The foreign policy of France in Africa by the term *Françafrique* is a maneuver of the French state put in place to protect and support the vast majority of African dictator presidents of the former French colonies. That policy of France in Africa maintains them in power for decades for the interest of France. It is qualified as a set of pejorative networks of influence devoted to vast scandals. The most famous are: the vast scandal and long political financial affair, which erupted in 1994 as the "Elf affair"; an exploitation French oil company of refining and distribution of petroleum named Elf-Aquitaine, concerning the case of "Sniffer Aircraft" in 1979 to the early 1980s, later revealed to be a scam; since the Second World War, Elf scandal was "the biggest fraud inquiry in Europe;" at that time, the richest men of Britain, France, German, Iraq, etc., received illegal commissions linked to the Clearstream scandal. Its involvement after its transformation into a private bank favored political executives to have mistresses, jewelries, fine arts, villas, and apartments. In the former East Germany, more than 2,500 vacated gas station allotments were taken over by Elf Aquitaine without paying the rightful owners; and the money for the Oil-for-Food program transited through the escrow account of BNP Paribas in 2001. The scandals of Elf-Aquitaine are multiple in the world of business, resulting from a political will of General de Gaulle; in fact, his idea, destined to ensure the "grandeur" of France, was to maintain French access to the strategic oil resource in Africa despite the decolonization according to Francois-Xavier Verschave, until 2003 when it merged with TotalFina to form TotalFinaElf and changed its name to Total.

The military interventions in the crisis countries like Ivory Coast, Libya, Mali, Central Africa, etc., and the institutional architecture and international finance concerning the origins and consequences of the Third World debt are other vast political famous scandals in which France and international monetary system are involved.

The elaboration of radical alternatives, aiming universal satisfaction of rich countries, and financial methods to manage and maintain the odious debt are methods of foreign policy of France and international policies; this foreign policy requires the development of freedoms, leading to a radical transformation to guarantee the fundamental human rights, which still challenge political representatives at the international level to respect the tradition of the proud south, glowing with the ardor of the sun.

In the Congolese drama, the United Nations played a big role in the early '60s for the traumatic assassination of the nationalist Patrice Lumumba by the CIA, stationed for the first time in the Belgian Congo in 1961, when Allen Welsh Dulles was the CIA director. By misinterpreting the will of Pres. Dwight Eisenhower, Allen Dulles ordered the operation of his assassination to prevent that Congo bascule in the Communist camp of the Soviet Union to put a dictator in place—a kind of flexible person easy to manipulate; this method was used in time elsewhere in the world; to put the one who come to their mind in power at the episode of the so-called decolonization by preserving the stranglehold of that international organization, on the systematic looting of resources like Congo's riches and in other countries of Africa, during the period of the Cold War, historically marking spirits of our noble Africans. When the nationalist leader Patrice Lumumba, perceived as a major threat for the western interests was eliminated, the entire country was opened at the disposal of the United States and Belgium, including the United Nations secretariat.

He who wanted to have full control over Congo's resources to achieve genuine independence and freedom to utilize these resources to improve material prosperity and the living conditions of Congolese in a country torn down under four separate governments divided in four cities of the country, known as the "then Leopoldville central government, in a city known today as Kinshasa; the then Stanleyville, rival central government by Lumumba's followers in a city known today as Kisangani; and then in the mineral-rich provinces of Katanga and South Kasai, the secessionist regimes;" but he who was fighting to unite his country is no more.

His assassination, a stumbling block to the independence for a Pan-African solidarity, a block of national unity ideals as well as a good economic hope, led international efforts in August 1961 to unite the Lumumbist regime in Kisangani in September 1962; the secession of South Kasai, and in January 1963, the Katanga secession to end separated governments in the country, and restore the authority of the pro-western regime in Kinshasa and over the entire country. As a culmination point of two assassins interrelated by the American and the Belgian governments, Americans used the Belgian execution squad, and the Congolese as accomplices, to carry out the deed of this heinous crime. At the outbreak of the Cold War and the eve of independence, it was inevitable known that the United States and its western allies would not let Africans have effective control over their strategic raw materials or let them fall into the hands of their enemies.

The claims of the Congo Basin territories by King Leopold II of Belgium in April 1884 were recognized by the United States, which as the first country in the world had already recognized the Congo Basin as the property of King Leopold II, seven months before the Berlin Congress. Then at the sharing of Africa, the United States, together with other world powers, forced Belgium to take over the Congo as a regular colony, for the United States to require a strategic interest of the enormous natural wealth of the country during the colonial period, resulting in millions of fatalities. Well, it was the period of interest and of course, a time when all hell was completely unleashed in Africa as it still is nowadays. Till today, the predation in favor of the international actors continues by endless wars of plunders in that country. On the other side, in another past war, humanitarian organizations took action against a part of the citizens in the secession war of Biafra, seeking to restrict the right of an independent state and the sovereignty of that country. It took a great moral coalition of an extensive global network of solidarity to force Western governments to apply sanctions ending the racist apartheid regime in South Africa; and the principle of non-intervention by the United Nation of not becoming involved in the war in Rwanda, a country in East Africa; resulting from a trend implemented by the European colonial authorities favoring the Tutsi since 1895, continued anti-Hutu policies in the nineteenth century.

In 1959, Belgian support for the Hutu revolt caused a sudden reversal of the situation, finally in 1962, establishing an independent state dominated by the Hutu, killing those who fought and by burning Tutsi houses. That war, the "final solution" to exterminate all Tutsi, led to a resurgence of violence against Tutsi, conducted during a supposed support brought to the Hutus by France for the Tutsi genocide; practiced and qualified as a collective psychosis protein catalyst that speed up chemical reactions in cells, prepared by mutual hatred of the west, triggered from April 6 to July 4, 1994.

Thus, pursuing various unequal treaties, which are serving the same form of objectives, they give a right of sovereignty and the absolute control of our African subsoil resources to the imperialist Western powers. Directly, that historic task prevents our continent to become its own strength in the economic system. It is important to emphasize the term *democratization*, proposed for the counter-models with the intentions of a great equal openness, and a connotation of positive judgments, values that appear more neutral and more objective, seeming to be broken by the majority of the people. Democratization is a transition, from authoritarian regimes to a more democratic political regime, from a state of dictatorship to a state of royalty that gives a favorable image to criticized phenomena. It also refers to substantive political changes, moving toward a democratic regime, toward the direction of freedom, according to the history and cleavages that mark a society.

Democratization in the economic sense of the term—that is to say the particular process of social change or access to something, who's very high cost restricted access; rising incomes and facilitating a significant drop in prices, which restricted access to a great group of populations. Democratization of education, health care system, leisure, sport, etc., and create a new age of creativity in institutional development to radically transform the democratization of societies under the guise of the globalization, and the right of the advent of a culture as a model of a new power, and put an end to internal wars and external interventions, fundamentally historical questions for the Western countries to have the right of interference in Africa.

Sometimes, the imperialist international community amused itself to stitch a diplomatic ideological strategy, truly conceived with all characteristics of the imperialist global-liberal world, seeming to lead to the foundation of the true values of international civility, marking to evoke a consensual state of consent agreed, and founded by the legitimate authority for the international order. A legitimate ideological perspective on the existence of a moral consensus, to the evolution of the global international life, which should be institutionalized as a convenient concept of peace for the international community, should be legitimized. This diplomatic ideological strategy had to be a respective strict significant and unequivocal meaningful right, first of all, to identify the matrix of problems in that concept, its concrete configuration, and render them effectively easy, evoking a consensual state of a consent agreement agreed by the collectivity to define the social, political, and cultural dimensions of the entire planetary order and for the international community; to synthetically determine a strategic cultural and structural environment of symbolic activities, largely corresponding to an international and transnational framework of sociability without considering constraints formed in the spheres of international relations, as an ordered pragmatism and regulator of the consensual processes of a sociability of coexistence to render reason analytically and justified by socio-political analysis. Methodologically, a critical sociopolitical analysis of the intellectual instruments that clearly reveal the semantic elements so much targeted is attentive to the conditions of enunciating uninteresting montages of the international imperialist community.

To those montages, the diplomatico-strategic lexicon of the international imperialist community makes use of the organizational and institutional functions of complexity in the final vacuity of its presentation and its representation in different acts, according to the logics of the situation. It supports those post-bipolarized montages to characterize it with the relevant use of diplomatic strategies, which are operating as forces to ensure the coherence of utterances, and particularly important to control the core of senses of its implementations. As sphere, its diplomatico-ethical values, oriented toward the resolution of crises with a validity of legitimacy are questionable. View the immediate observation of its implementations, multiple conflicts are not enunciated with the same intentionality corresponding to the same ethical-political formulations in the moral and democratic targeting to be developed toward a situation of globalized international crises in Africa.

The United Nations system, the Bretton Woods institutions of Washington consensus with Western original values and norms of inspiration, intervenes selectively, expressing the cultural rhythm of globalization on the moral management of African international crises; forgetting that they had to rationalize an image based on humanistic values and a morality of an idealistic solidary humanity, inspired by the justice of Maat, the cosmic order, and as truth in the universal community; a natural right for the human rights, as an ethic of the institutionalism of liberal rationalism; decisive in the international order, to the reason of universal reign, open to the global liberal light of orientations to the idealistic pluralism of interculturalism, of functionalist type as an order of values, principles, norms, and consensual rules for the foundation of the constitution of this world. In view of the postelection crisis aggravation, Laurent Gbagbo denounced a betrayal of the resolution of the major challenges in Africa for the benefit of the major powers of the United Nations by using the African Union, dedicated to marginalization to legitimize their actions and authorize their selfish interventions during the tragic events in Ivory Coast. It is not surprising to know that the Ivorian people, Laurent Gbagbo, and his wife, the former first lady Simone Gbagbo, continued to suffer to this day as abused and humiliated victims, by the interests of a system of international relations that high and loudly advocates the universal human rights.

Not long ago in Ivory Coast, it was under the control of this same international community of the UN that the electoral dispute that caused the outbreak of the Ivorian crisis began on the basis of the support for Mr. Alassane Ouattara, received mostly from international institutions. How can we trust Mr. Alassane Ouattara, the president recognized by the international community, who served institutions like the IMF or the World Bank? The majority of African public opinion sided with Mr. Gbagbo, who embodied the endless struggle of Africans against the Western imperialism without reservation. Today, the authority of the United Nations is severely compromised as a neutral force in the resolution of internal conflicts, like the one in Ivory Coast.

Consequently, it is no longer questioned to accept this organization in the hands of great powers of the world as a single instrument of peace, and its development can no longer convince Africa and the rest of the world. How many flagrant violations of perverse and harmful powers should still suffer Africa and the rest of the developing countries before realizing a democratic system of global governance? According to the Ivorian Constitution, Alassane Ouattara was ineligible to run for presidential election in Ivory Coast. At the initiative of Alassane Ouattara with the support of France, a coup attempt to overthrow Laurent Gbagbo by an army of rebels was followed by a civil war that divided the country between north and south. After years of tensions established at the era of former president Henri Konan Bedie related to ethnic policies of "ivoirite" (translated in English as Ivoirity), an Ivorian political concept, defining the national preference characters of Ivory Coast dating back from 1995, caused a split between the mainly Christian Ivorians, concentrated in the south of the country, and foreigners from neighboring countries of Muslim denomination, living in the north of Ivory Coast.

General Robert Guei, former head of the junta, defeated by Laurent Gbagbo in the October 2000 presidential election and chased from power by the street because he was trying to keep it, was killed on the day of the outbreak of the rebellion against Laurent Gbagbo on September 19, 2002. Both presidents were successors of Konan Bedie, who in turn perpetuated the same policy to exclude election campaigns of a political opponent of Burkinabe origin by the name of Alassane Ouattara. On September 19, 2002, when former president Laurent Gbagbo, democratically elected in 2000, was outside the country, soldiers and rebels of the Patriotic Movement of Ivory Coast launched their attacks and tried to control the cities of Abidjan, Bouake, and Korhogo, dividing the country in two.

The rebels who obtained several positions—including those of prime minister, minister of justice, and minister of economy and finance—in exchange for their disarmament pledged by the peace agreements never respected them; in that institution, even the presidency of the electoral commission and the absolute majority of seats taking part in it respected nothing. On November 28, 2010, Alassane Ouattara refused to accept the election results, announcing Laurent Gbagbo as the winner; but with the interference of the French army and the United Nations, they generated an electoral dispute by their support for Ouattara. The one elected, Laurent Gbagbo, was sworn in by the Constitutional Council as president.

On April 11, 2011, the French forces under UN mandate captured the one elected and recognized by the highest jurisdiction charged to proclaim the final results, and handed him over to the hands of Ouattara, his opponent who did not win the elections.

The existence and the relevance of the perspectives of the Western imperialist international community send back impure influences, which are shaping the social spheres to morally and culturally register an African crisis in the agenda of global diplomacy. It used its ideological influence in the diplomatic and moral treatment of the Ivorian postelectoral crisis of November 2010, whose unanimous acceptance and unilateral support to Alassane Ouattara contributed to make a point of significant attention from that crisis in the international news.

That support was not part of a consensus to uphold the sincerity, the integrity, and the democratic will of the vote in Ivory Coast. And the wrongdoings of the Ivorian postelectoral crisis could not be attributed mainly or exclusively to Laurent Gbagbo. Thus, in an unknown location in the north of the country, he was held prisoner, despite the requirement for his and his relatives' immediate release by many organizations and by thousands of people in Africa and around the world. The legitimacy of Alassane Ouattara, elected under questionable circumstances, and the systematic physical eliminations of a community of Ivorian elites, presented many questions in a country where it was not clear who an Ivorian was and who was not at all. But in a country governed by the hands of newcomers to power, those of some leaders of the Ivorian Popular Front (IPF) after separating the country, despite the tone raised against the UN by many African intellectuals and dignitaries of the world, France and the UN continued their catastrophic hostilities in that country, making Laurent Gbagbo the elected president prisoner, responsible for that conflict and against human rights violations. The former president Gbagbo, arrested since, is still held in The Hague, the Netherlands, suspected by the International Criminal Court (ICC) to be the indirect co-perpetrator of crimes against humanity during the crisis of 2010 to 2011 in Ivory Coast. And since April 2011, the former first lady Simone Gbagbo was incarcerated in the Ivorian northwest, precisely in Odienne, a city of Mali and Guinea, located in the north of Ivory Coast. She was tried and convicted on October 3, 2015, to twenty years in prison by a marathon trial of the Abidjan Assize Court. The eldest son of former president Laurent Gbagbo, Michel Gbagbo, was sentenced to five years' deprivation of rights and five years in prison; but thanks to a suspense appeal, he remained at liberty.

Simone Gbagbo, the former first lady, who was already convicted for "violating state security to 20 years imprisonment in March 2015," was still prosecuted by the Ivorian justice for "war crime and crime against humanity" by the prosecutor who asked for life imprisonment, and was finally acquitted on Tuesday, March 28, 2017. Apparently, as it was the interests of the West, everyone had forgotten that Ivory Coast had a constitution, which said that it was necessary to take an oath before the Constitutional Council before being considered as president; and without that formality, no legitimacy was given to any president, therefore not to Ouattara, nondeclared elected by the highest jurisdiction of the Constitutional Council, which was responsible for proclaiming presidential final results and which already had declared Gbagbo as the winner to lead the country. What Laurent Gbagbo had already done, take an oath before the Constitutional Council and established as president of Ivory Coast, gave no legitimacy to Ouattara without that essential formality. But the Western world, blinded by interests, ignored the Constitutional Council of Ivory Coast and accepted that the president, considered as having taken the oath before the Constitutional Council and whose judicial act of swearing was in the archives of the Constitutional Council, be put under house arrest by an unknown person of that court, taking decisions and making speeches to force generals to obey and be faithful to him as a sovereign.

That performance before the generals was an affirmation of President Gbagbo's dismissal and confirming the allegiance of a sudden legal status that conferred legal legitimacy to Ouattara. Not having come to power legally, he used weapons, opponent arrests, and elimination by torture or simply killed those who were at the head of the state. That painful reality of the support attitude of France and the international community to Alassane Ouattara will always be seen as a coup for Ivorians and the rest of the world and as a usurper who took the reign of the country, established at the head of their state by weapons with the help perpetrated by France as foreign country, and the UN as the international community. Legally, as a mode of operation, there can only be one president at a time in Ivory Coast. He is the one whose oath is in the archives of the Constitutional Council; and not the brutal seizure of power that predicts somber days, and that the famous international community no longer distinguishes its ass from its elbow and otherwise wants us to believe in their nonsense by considering us as bladders for lanterns.

Ten years after independence, Laurent Gbagbo became very active in the Ivorian politics. But it was well known that upon the taking of power in Ivory Coast, Houphouet-Boigny ruled as a dictator, consolidating his power without any opposition. During that period in Ivory Coast, progressive African graduates returned from France, and Ivorian Communist sympathizers impregnated with Marxist-Leninist ideology were expressing a certain antipathy toward change. To reduce opponents to criminal conspirators against the state, the creation of a six-thousand-men militia, at the service of the Democratic Party of Ivory Coast on August 26, led to a climate of terror in Ivory Coast after its independence on August 7, 1960, during the drafting of a new constitution. But on July 27, 1960, before independence, Houphouet-Boigny had already created the National Armed Forces of Ivory Coast, whose defense was entrusted to the French Armed Forces. The Democratic Party of Ivory Coast, of which Felix Houphouet-Boigny was the founding president, as the only party in the country, was subscribed to the arrest of many poor citizens, opponents of the PDCI, or the destabilization of progressive African leaders like Ahmed Ben Bella, Gamal Abdel Nasser, and Kwame Nkrumah or again the partisans of multipartism as well as the Freemasons, when French interests were threatened.

The active syndicalist Laurent Gbagbo made his first entry into politics in the 1970s. He was imprisoned with his wife, Simone Ehivet Gbagbo, by Houphouet from March 1971 to January 1973 in Seguela and in Bouake because his teaching as a member of the National Syndicate of Research and Higher Education was considered subversive. In 1980, he became the director of the Institute of History, Art, and Archeology of Africa (IHAAA) at the University of Abidjan, where he worked as a researcher after his release from prison. On February 9, 1982, during the student demonstrations, he was revealed as one of the main instigators. Those events caused the closure of colleges and universities in the country. During that year, the future Front Populaire Ivoirien (FPI) was born clandestinely, ideologically close to the French Socialist Party, with the idea of promoting a multiparty system.

That Ivorian left political party, which since constituted the main opposition party in the country, created by Laurent Gbagbo and his wife, under the form of a clandestine movement of Marxist-Leninist obedience, was officially recognized in 1990.

In 1988, its incorporation into a political party marked the establishment of a multiparty and militated against colonialism as a Socialist Democratic political party, aiming to fight against the dictatorship of the Democratic Party of Ivory Coast, then a single party. He went into exile in France in 1985 and promoted his opposition to the government program of Felix Houphouet-Boigny. On September 13, 1988, Laurent Gbagbo finally returned to Ivory Coast by the French pressures, believing he had obtained Houphouet-Boigny pardon by this statement: "The tree does not get angry at the bird." Stirring his opposition much more cumbersome in Abidjan, he stood in the presidential election of October 28, 1990, as secretary general of FPI; that he became during the constituent congress of November 19 and 20, 1988.

That presidential election, marking the first candidacy against the one of Pres. Felix Houphouet-Boigny made him win 18.3 percent of votes and consecrated him the status of the opposition leader. Being one of the first under the banner of multipartism, he was elected in the constituency of his hometown, Ouaragahio, and obtained 9 seats out of 175 in the legislative elections of November 25, 1990. In the meantime, important student demonstrations took place from 1990 to 1992. But first, on March 2, 1990, protesters demonstrating in the streets of Abidjan were emitting these slogans: "Houphouet corrupt, Houphouet thief," against his thirty years of reign as president; they were slogans never heard before. So, these strong social agitations that created a real climate of insecurity reached their height in May 1991 and in February 1992. On May 31, the president was forced to launch a democratization of the regime, authorizing a political and syndicate pluralism. But he was reelected for a seventh term in office with 81.68 percent of votes; Laurent Gbagbo called for clear differentiation between nationals and foreign migrants and denounced a manipulation of the Nationality Code.

In that perspective, those foreigners practically had the same civil, political, and social rights as Ivorians; and their votes were automatically offered to Houphouet-Boigny, their protector. Questioning the properties acquired for decades by those Burkinabe foreigners, Laurent Gbagbo even laid a legal recognition claim of the rights of nationals on Ivorian soil. In the southwest forest of the country, these Burkinabe farmers were already occupying the Ivorian land. Unfortunately, Houphouet-Boigny, who had already declared to prefer injustice to disorder, authorized the occupation of the campus of the university in the city of Yopougon, in the district of Abidjan, by his paramilitary commandos sent on the night of May 17 to 18, 1991, to commit numerous abuses. On February 13, 1992, the Student Federation of Ivory Coast organized another demonstration in Abidjan, resulting to the first one leading to an army raid on student residences of Abidjan's Yopougon University. Three hundred people were arrested in the raid of the 18th, including the president of the Ivorian Human Rights League, Rene-Degni Segui, and Laurent Gbagbo.

It was following the rejection of the inquiry reports of brutality by the army of Pres. Felix Houphouet-Boigny, resulting in May 1991 to the raid of protesters, the student residence of Yopougon University in Abidjan, and of the two raids since February 1992 of demonstrators demonstrating against him. The office of the prime minister, unoccupied from 1960 to 1990, was eventually occupied by an economist by profession, having notably worked at the IMF.

Houphouet-Boigny appointed Alassane Ouattara as prime minister of Ivory Coast on November 7, 1990, to December 9, 1993. On February 18, 1992, Laurent Gbagbo was arrested, and sentenced to two years in prison on March 6, 1992, after Alassane Ouattara made the head of state sign an anti-breakers law on the eve. Finally, in August of the same year, he was released on July 24, 1992, pardoned by Houphouet-Boigny. He eventually participated in several conflicts of presidential elections, particularly in 1995. Because of the reform of the electoral code, he called for a boycott of the presidential election scheduled for October 22. Henri Konan Bedie was then, from 1980 to 1993, the president of the National Assembly, ensuring the interim after the death of Felix Houphouet-Boigny until 1995, and elected president of the Republic of Ivory Coast with 96.44 percent of votes from 1993 to 1999. Laurent Gbagbo was reelected in his constituency, during the partial legislative elections, and won five of the eight seats on December 30, 1996.

In the presidential election of October 22, 2000, the opponent Alassane Ouattara was eliminated by his opponent Henri Konan Bedie on the Ivorian presidential election of 1995, according to his established concept of Ivoirite, which only allowed a person of a father and mother of Ivorian origin to run for the Ivorian presidential election; but denying the concept of Ivoirite, he presented himself as a candidate once more. Gbagbo officially presented his candidate on that Ivorian presidential election, designated during the third FPI party congress, held from July 9 to 11, against General Robert Guei, who overthrew President Bedie on December 24, 1999; and several candidates, including that of Alassane Ouattara, were eliminated by the Supreme Court because of falsification and forgery on filiations and doubtful nationality. The winner of that presidential election against Guei was Laurent Gbagbo, declared president on October 26, 2000, after contestations from General Robert Guei, who finally, on November 13, recognized his legitimacy; Laurent Gbagbo won from then a majority of ninety-one seats against seventy of the PDCI and sixteen independent on the legislative elections of December 10. Longtime opposing Houphouet-Boigny, he was elected president of the Republic of Ivory Coast, from October 26, 2000, to December 4, 2010; and according to his supporters, until April 11, 2011, when he was arrested in Abidjan by French forces, he was given to Alassane Ouattara. He was extradited and jailed by the International Criminal Court in The Hague in the Netherlands since November 30, 2011. It is known that since the creation of the International Criminal Court, ICC, on July 17, 1998, in Rome, Italy, having the statute with 124 member states, it is reasonable to believe that this court is only targeting Africans, because the list of Africans judged before this judicial division is very long. While trials continue in this court, impartialities, proofs of "mounting evidences," and indictments, are critics of certain milieu and countries against this International Criminal Court. However, it seems that the Rome Statute, created for a more just word in accordance to seek the justice we all yearn for, and do all within its power, independently, impartially, and objectively, unfortunately has forgotten its aim of dedication and integrity, but finds itself facing scandal upon scandal.

In the case of Laurent Gbagbo, the former president of Ivory Coast, deliberate impartiality and ruthless accusations by this International Criminal Court were already criticized by numerous countries in the world. Certain allegations since the start of his trial were revealing "mounting of evidences." These revelations were suggesting that the arrest of the former president Laurent Gbagbo by the French men of Alassane Ouattara was planned from the outset, because the prosecutor at the time of the former president Laurent Gbagbo arrest, called Luis Moreno-Ocampo, sent an e-mail on the day of his arrest to the French officials of the Ministry of Foreign Affairs, asking them to maintain him in prison. This accusation against the International Criminal Court was very serious; while Ivorian officials or any African country did not ask to refer the case to the ICC; and to this accusation with a lot of deviations, the Ivorian statesman named Pascal Affi N'guessan, who became minister of industry and tourism under the military leader named Robert Guei from December 24, 1999, to October 26, 2000, and then from 2000 to 2003 as prime minister of Ivory Coast under the former president Laurent Gbagbo, asked the International Criminal Court "to relinquish the case of Laurent Gbagbo," and that if "it continues to prosecute him the Court will become an accomplice of the political plot against the former president Laurent Gbagbo."

The Libyan scandal is the second revelation against the International Criminal Court, ICC, connecting the former prosecutor Luis Moreno-Ocampo to Libyan officials of Muammar Gaddafi, during the crisis that led to his fall caused by Nicolas Sarkozy. Nicolas Sarkozy is a man to fear, because after receiving funding for his presidential campaign financed by Colonel Gaddafi in 2007, he contested it and still formally contests it; but the picture that this story forms, once assembled, is very frightening and leaves us with a rude voice and gives nausea toward the French Republic. Even if in the judicial file, the former French president is not yet prosecuted, the elements of the Libyan financing were published, but since he had already concocted the war with the international force against Libya, the word of Gaddafi did no longer worth a dime. Consequently, Kadhafi assured on television, *"I was the one who helped Sarkozy to take power"*; *"I gave him money before he became president,"* after the announcement of the official Libyan Jamahiriya News Agency, JANA, on March 10, 2011. Four months later, the colonel insisted in front of a *Figaro* reporter, *"We have given him the necessary funding so that he can win the election at home."* One of his sons then stated, *"First, Sarkozy must return the money he accepted from Libya to finance his electoral campaign,"* in front of Euronews cameras.

Certainly, but the contestation of Nicolas Sarkozy concerning this Libyan financing prompted two journalists of *Mediapart* by the names of Fabrice Arfi and Karl Laske to investigate these allegations, and their result is very damning; today, toward the end of 2017, after a close synthesis of six years of investigation, they published a carefully documented and wellargued report on the financing of the Sarkozy campaign by Colonel Gaddafi.

This investigation was based on forty thousand documents, including personal e-mails of Mr. Luis Moreno Ocampo and obtained the support of the European Investigative Collaborations and eleven press organs participating and treated by them. Although there is nothing to indicate that the system of the International Criminal Court, ICC, is compromising, allegations against its former prosecutor are in the light of recent media reports. At the time that Mr. Ocampo was the ICC prosecutor, the financial reporting system for senior management—namely, the president, the prosecutor, the deputy prosecutor, the clerk chief of the court, and the entire Secretary-General Office—was not put in place; and it is only since 2015 that an obligation to submit an annual financial statement that the court put this financial disclosure system in place, so prior to the establishment of this system, the financial arrangements of the prosecutor of the International Criminal Court were not known to the court. But what do we say about teeth in the mouth? To my knowledge, "It's a tooth that spoils all the other teeth in the mouth;" and "the tongue is often bitten by the teeth yet must always be together and remain good friends." As such, I would say that the entire system of the International Criminal Court, ICC, is rotten, since Laurent Gbagbo is still maintained without reason by the ICC, after the revelation of the e-mail of Luis Moreno-Ocampo, exhibited by *Mediapart*, asking to keep him in prison, after his arrest by Alassane Ouattara.

In addition, on these recent media allegations concerning the former prosecutor, his office, and some current staff members of the International Criminal Court, ICC, these allegations totally affected Ms. Fatou Bensouda, who worked as a legal counsel and prosecutor, and formally appointed senior legal counsel and head of the Legal Advisory Unit, who was elected deputy prosecutor (prosecution) on August 8, 2004, with an overwhelming majority of votes by the Assembly of States Parties to the International Criminal Court.

The rise of Ms. Fatou Bensouda in her international career continued its apogee when she was sworn in as deputy prosecutor (prosecution) on November 1, 2004. As a prosecutor, she took the initiative to report two members of her personnel to the Independent Oversight Mechanism, IOM, involving those allegations in her legal framework. In accordance with IOM's standards and procedures, the case will conduct a full investigation in an objective and impartial manner in full respect of the procedure and the fair treatment concerning the staff will be taken into consideration, because she took these allegations very seriously and considered them with concern. Having served at the International Criminal Court in The Hague since 2004, she was chosen on December 12, 2011, as attorney general, after she first served as deputy attorney general of Luis

Moreno Ocampo, she succeeded him; and on June 15, 2012, she was officially sworn in, after being selected from 52 candidates by the 120 member states of the tribunal.

During that election period in Ivory Coast, a UN official considered himself above a constitutional institution. The African Union recognized that victory without contrary conclusions of its proper observers sent to the field. Could we get the respect we deserved just by satisfying our former masters? If the opinion of one of our leaders, who represents one billion Africans, could immediately change the lapel of his jacket after a trip from Paris, Jacob Zuma, the president of South Africa, who had initially declared that Ouattara had not won the election, could not maintain his decision or his respect for expression, but simply accepted to be a serf; that means that it's really deplorable for Africa. Contrary to his own convictions, he made a rotation of 180 degrees and changed his statement.

In 2000, those who voted for Gbagbo, after being seduced by the nationalist speech, were hoping that he would put the ideology of Ivoirity policy in application upon his arrival to power; but, alas, this was not the case. Following that lack of position, he lost the votes that he had won in the north of Ivory Coast in 2000 and also lost the bet of national reconciliation, the Marcoussis Agreement, on behalf of Mr. Alassane Ouattara, who won two departments in the extreme south of Ivory Coast. Henceforth, after ten years in power, Ivory Coast was divided in two, but what were we to do now that Mr. Alassane Ouattara held a power that he was not to have, according to the pro-Gbagbo communautarist drifters marking a great need to solve politically unavoidable problems of that population since 2003? Mr. Laurent Gbagbo claimed the sovereignty of nationalism that was not compatible with internationalism; and social democracy did not prevent its relations to endorse old imperialist costume to the international level. But wanting to correct that situation by electoral manipulations did not validate the perspective of such election; considering the clear presumption of a fanatical communitarianism of the Ivorian people, who was summoned to choose one party against the other by the modalities of its possible postcolonial history resolution, and its consequences for Africa; as an uncontrolled choice of passions that provokes an outburst, leading to the violence of supporters in both parties engaged in a democracy process using bazookas. Alongside Mr. Alassane Ouattara, France and the international community were determined to find a solution to that increasingly deadly civil conflict with infantry weapons by favoring Ouattara.

Whatever the 1961 secret agreements of independence were stipulating, it must be admitted that France and its Licorne force, installed in Ivory Coast since 2002 and which was not costing less than two hundred million euros per year (131 billion CFA francs) to France then, were only for the interests of France and not to resolve the Ivorian conflict; in that country that the Licorne force was considered as a force of occupation by a certain fringe of the Ivorian and African opinion, since it clashed with Laurent Gbagbo armed forces in November 2004, neutralizing the Ivorian aviation military force. That war action and humiliation inflicted on the Ivorian people by France reminded us the old colonial methods, which precipitated the already difficult relations between the former president Gbagbo and France into an abyss. The order to bomb the entire Ivorian air force was given by the former president Jacques Chirac personally.

That war action precipitated an unprecedented crisis in Ivory Coast. The march organized by the leaders of the Young Patriots on the airport, the camp of the Forty-Third Marine Infantry Battalion opposing Ivorian militaries, and 2,000 young Ivorian civilians rampaging killed 64 and injured 1,300 young Ivorians by soldiers who opened fire from their tanks, positioned near the residence of the former president Gbagbo. The killings of demonstrators in November 2004 by the French Licorne military were muted in the past and until our days; those crimes remained unpunished without any investigation.

It was a French soldier who testified those events in Paris match. This was another chapter in the long colonial history that really produces its objective. It just took Ivory Coast, as its shopping window in Africa; their evil force, mobilized against the Ivorians, caused chaos, and a disorderly fight was plainly contemplated. Jacques Chirac warned the Ivorian president Gbagbo after being informed of the offensive that the troops of Gbagbo were preparing against the rebels. He declared that such action would constitute a breach of the Marcoussis Agreement. After that interference and breach of sovereignty by Jacques Chirac, the fighting continued between the French Legionnaires and the soldiers of the Ivorian army, perpetrating massacres by Sarkozy's support to Ouattara, attempting to impose his rule to Ivorians even by his recognized defeat by the board of the highest Ivorian constitutional jurisdiction.

Know that that imperialism, with the conquest policy and cynical desperate barkings, which do not lack the doctrine of romantic seduction to a certain point of view, is a voluntarily opportunist pragmatism that must be examined very closely for the future of Africa. Furthermore, at the economic level, its forms of monopolistic capitalism of domination established by its nations over our countries are put forward nowadays by its numerous Marxist leaders. So from the protectionist nature, they're opposing the rise of our ties with nationalism of a sociological nature by extending their exploitation in the colonial world, controlled by banks of great capital and the financing of wars, allowing the emergence of racial conceptions, exploited by the Nazis, to the average trend profit rate.

Their idea, at the genesis of totalitarianism is based on the policies of control of our resources, the exploitation of our earthly wealth, and their system of domination is collaborating with our modern states for the control of our economy; their direct support involving unhealthy policy is leading to the indirect territorial capture for the destabilization and the establishment of inequilateral trade treaties between our countries; Its policy adoption can only lead to an unqualified commitment, a heartbreaking-causing fire on all sides, to disadvantage the destiny of Africa. Following the principle example of states sovereignty, the Ivorian case raises the problem of credibility principles of the international right, to the conscience of the same so-called international community, known as the major principal actors of the said right.

I would say immediately therefore that the UN forces (UNOCI) stationed in Ivory Coast and the indefinite extension of the Operation of the French Unicorn peacekeeping force in support of the United Nations, admitted without consensual agreement in that country, were executing their mandate from resolution 1962 of the UN Security Council, which eventually guaranteed them full freedom of movement in an independent and sovereign country. The UNOCI's mission and the French Licorne force posed and still pose a respect problem from the said United Nations right for the reality of the sovereignty of that country, if it was really determined as real. Today, January 21, 2015, twelve years later, France formally decided to put an end to Operation Unicorn, which began in September 2002 by France and officially changed its mandate by this name: the French Forces in Ivory Coast (FFIC), thus continuing the role of soldiers in that country since the days of the armed rebellion in the north. The French Forces in Ivory Coast are today created as prepositioned forces and will constitute an advanced base on the African continent for military and logistical operations. The anti-imperialists, the sovereignists, and the nationalists no longer stop nowadays to question themselves about their mission. This so-called interposition mission, which constitutes ramparts against the sovereignty of that country and the exercise of democracy of African people, was set up by France regardless of the sovereignty of this country.

Let's talk a bit about human rights toward the United States before continuing. Have we forgotten the atomic bomb crimes of very large magnitudes committed against innocent civilians by dropping the first on August 6 in Hiroshima and the second in Nagasaki on August 9 on the United States initiative in 1945 as the first nuclear tests in the world? Organized by the Allied powers of the United States to determine the fate of enemy nations, after the rejection of the ultimatum of the Potsdam Conference by Japanese leaders and not mentioning any nuclear weapons? Those allied powers represented by Harry Truman of the United States, by Joseph Stalin of the USSR, by Winston Churchill and his deputy prime minister Clement Attlee in the coalition government in the period of war from 1940 to 1945, led by Winston Churchill, who eventually was elected prime minister of the United Kingdom from 1945 to 1951, who all signed the Potsdam Agreement promulgated on July 26, 1945—were they prosecuted? Has the United States not continued to extend its violation of human rights in Iraq and finally in Afghanistan? Let's end this summary by mentioning that on a power equivalent of about 20,000 tons, that atomic bomb of mass destruction caused considerable damages, estimated to have 60,000 to 80,000 people killed on a population of 250,000, according to the most recent estimate.

What is most disturbing about this story is that the U.S. government let pass the immediate effects of this bomb in silence, and the consequences of long-term radiations without common measure, are still ravaging its survivors more and more in slow agony than the time of the explosion in Hiroshima.

Thus, the so-called international community, which advocates the establishment of disarmament or the demilitarization, is undertaking the destruction of the freedom of expression by referring to the Nazism laws for the dismantling of the democratization of our countries.

We know that Prescott Bush, the grandfather of George W. Bush, was one of the executive directors of the Union Banking Corporation (UBC). Before and during World War II, Prescott Bush and his father-in-law, George Herbert Walker, joined forces with Fritz Thyssen, the German businessman, to finance Adolf Hitler. Fritz Thyssen compensated the victims of the war after admitting his involvement in the rise of Nazism. U.S. government records and the Dutch intelligence services confirmed the profits drawn from the dead by their direct collaboration with Adolf Hitler.

Among that group of companies that helped arm, educate, and pay the Nazis of Hitler were Standard Oil, the Chase Bank of Rockefeller, and major American car manufacturers. Because the interests of Prescott Bush were much higher and sinister at his time, valued at $1.5 million profited from the Holocaust, by using Jews designated as an inferior race by the Nazis ideology and other deportees as slaves, his memory, assimilated to the "evil" genius (devil, demon) inherited by the grandfather of the former president George W. Bush, kept secret for more than seventy-two years, and considered as one of the worst acts of genocide in the history of humanity, is committed by well-educated, modern, civilized men, and not by "bullies."

Prescott Sheldon Bush Sr. who in 1918 exhumed the skull of the apache chief named Geronimo, to give it to the secret organization called Skull and Bones, and considered the patriarch of the Bush family, was the son of Samuel Prescott Bush, who was the father of the former president George H. W. Bush, who also gave birth to the former president George W. Bush; and by the marriage of Prescott Bush to the daughter of George Herbert Walker, named Dorothy Walker, both families encouraged and assisted the Nazis before and during the war.

The former president, vice president, and director of the CIA, father of George W. Bush, also a former U.S. president, reached the top of the political ladder of the United States. Their aid to Adolf Hitler in World War II constituted a significant share of the financial foundation of the Bush family as it was during the war in Iraq. The media did not inquire directly about the crimes of the two former presidents Bush of the United States naturally to not admit betrayal against their country. It all started by the despicable railway tycoon by the name of W. Averell Harriman, an American businessman, Democratic political man, diplomat, and former governor of the state of New York. The then founder of the W. A. Harriman & Co. bank in 1922 had as employees the grandfather of the former U.S. president George W. Bush and George Herbert Walker, also employed in the Union Banking Corporation, founded in 1924.

The U.S. government closed the Union Banking Corporation in 1943, accused of being a Nazi organization, after the entry of the United States into World War II by an act giving the president the power to oversee or restrict any and all trade between the United States and its enemies in times of war; this act is known under the name Trading with the Enemy Act, a United States federal law to restrict trade with countries hostile to the United States, making the Union Banking Corporation a criminal offense trading with the enemy. The shipping United American Lines Company, which he founded in 1921, was sold to HAPAG in 1926. W. Averell Harriman took the initiative to found a subsidiary bank in Europe and went to Berlin to meet Fritz Thyssen and members of his family in 1922. Fritz Thyssen founded the Union Banking Corporation, with the help of the investment bank W. A. Harriman & Co., and the one who became the president of that bank was George Herbert Walker.

His official shareholders were W. A. Harriman, with 3,991 shares; Cornelius Lievense, 4 shares; Harold D. Pennington, 1 share; Rae Morris, 1 share; H. J. Kouwenhoven, 1 share; Johan Groeninger, 1 share; and Prescott Bush, 1 share, in a bank officially a solely American investment, where a handful of former Yale classmates of Prescott Bush belonging to the Skull and Bones were investors.

The Thyssen family had three extremely important banks: in the Netherlands, the Bank voor Handel en Scheepvaart; in the United States in New York City, the Union Banking Corporation, which was created to transfer funds between Manhattan and the Dutch banks of Thyssen, assisted by the Dutch royal family, which cooperated to hide their accounts in a number of their banks; (Prince Bernhard, who was a native of German, was himself making his operations in that agency); and in Berlin, the August Thyssen Bank. From 1923, Fritz Thyssen publicly supported the new National Socialist German Workers' Party (NSDAP), often simply referred to as the Nazi Party, commonly classified on the far right. Founded in 1920 and attached to the fascist political family, Adolf Hitler took office on January 30, 1933, appointed by Marshal Paul von Hindenburg, president of the Reich, as the chancellor of Germany of the Nazi political ideology. Fritz Thyssen was funding the party through the Bank voor Handel, a family business based in Scheepvaart in Rotterdam. Allen Dulles, the lawyer of the bank, who later became the CIA director, first worked in New York for Sullivan & Cromwell, an international law firm with offices located in Europe, Asia, and Australia. Kurt Baron von Schroeder, a German general who served during World War I, was a member of the Nazi Party; both Kurt von Schroder, the banker-financier of the Nazi regime, and Johann Groening worked with the Democrat W. Averell Harriman, the one who became the vice president of W. A. Harriman Company. E. Roland Harriman, his little brother, was also an American financier; W. Prescott Bush (father of George Bush Sr. and grandfather of George W. Bush) were both directors of a steel mill of Thyssen, a factory producing steel in large quantities; all these directors were equally represented by the sworn enemy of the Americans named Allen Dulles, who was a lawyer of the Sullivan and Cromwell lawyer firm to hide their business deals increasingly elaborated with the Nazis and the fraudulent assets of "sixty of his closest friends"; these businessmen, who collaborated with the Nazis, really only wanted "absolute power" but were really never interested in the American ideals of "freedom" and "democracy." Allen Dulles was also the lawyer for the Thyssens' Rotterdam bank and represented other German firms, including I. G. Farben.

Prescott Bush was appointed by George Herbert Walker as supervisor of the new Thyssen/Flick United Steel Works. As the three owners of the biggest Polish industry, Bush, Harriman, and Walker held a third of the Upper Silesian Coal and Steel Company of Flick. The new holding company was named the Consolidated Silesian Steel Corp., which owned a third of the Upper Silesian Coal and Steel Company, and Frederick Flick held the remaining two-thirds.

The Consolidated Silesian Coal and Steel Corp. of Flick was directed by John Foster Dulles. Just like the United Steel Works, the last one also depended on forced labor, performed at Auschwitz during the war. The establishment of "storm troopers" of the NSDAP, a paramilitary organization of the Nazi Party from the SS, founded by Adolf Hitler, resulting in the rising popularity of Nazism in Germany, was helped by Thyssen's Bank voor Handel, and millions of dollars transited through the Bush-Harriman Union Banking Corporation (UBC). The Bush family has always been particularly involved in shady dealings, and its fortune mainly resulted from the Hitler project, undertaken only to exterminate Jews during World War II.

It is also known that it is an information manipulation of his administration on armament programs of Saddam Hussein, wrongly accusing him of possessing weapons of mass destruction to justify the invasion of Iraq during the presidency of their son named George W. Bush at the supreme judicature of the United States who provided the specific strategic justification for the war in Iraq, held to procure himself the wealth of that country by heavily investing in the Carlyle Group in which he and his family made several billions from the war also known as the Second Gulf War.

Prescott Bush was supervising all investments as the director of UBC; his responsibility was to know people who were performing transactions in his bank and their destinations. In that Nazi war machine, Rockefeller also invested huge sums, and it was UBC that laundered dirty money paid by the Nazis, coming from the Rockefeller family investment in Germany.

John D. Rockefeller, who was aiming to become a great businessman, started to make money by raising turkeys with a loan of a few dollars from comrades with interest. From those small businesses—namely, an assistant bookkeeper at the age of sixteen as an office clerk selling and shipping grain, coal, and other commodities for commission—he also sold candy and did some jobs for neighbors; combining his attraction for the railways, the organization of banks and factories to acquire a monopoly in the industry; in addition, he was devoted specifically to art, music, literature, and concerned with social and political values. He joined forces in 1862, with two partners who created oil refining company; experienced many adventures in job as accountant and investor in oil extraction; and created an oil refining company. John D. Rockefeller traveled to Pennsylvania after hearing about a former employee of the railway, by the name of Colonel Drake, who was hired to find oil and examine the wells more closely. Immediately, convinced of the possibilities offered by a handful of businessmen in that new field, he decided to invest. It was then that he set up his first refinery with the chemist Samuel Andrews, his new partner, in Cleveland to produce naphtha and kerosene in 1863. John D. Rockefeller followed thereby the footsteps of his father, William Avery Rockefeller, of English and German origin, who was selling "miracle drugs" without the title of Doctor of Medicine, but as a traveling merchant officer of health.

Under that title, he sold bottles made of oil mixed with laxative and pretended to be a specialist of certain remedies against cancer. John D. Rockefeller rapidly expanded his business by keeping costs and wages the lowest possible and constantly reinvesting his profits, and with Henry Flagler, another partner, he founded the firm Rockefeller, Andrews & Flagler in 1867, and Cleveland became one of the five main refining centers, along with New York, Pittsburgh, and the northwestern region of Pennsylvania, from which most of the oil came from, in the USA. But it was in Poland, at the southeast of Galicia near Krosno in Bobrka, that the first oil well, which became the true birth of the oil industry in the world, was drilled in 1854 by Ignacy Łukasiewicz. At the end of the War of Secession, a civil war occurred between 1861 and 1865, his company that produced naphtha and kerosene, including the profits of two refineries, made his company the largest oil enterprise in the world.

S.O, the initials of Standard Oil, an oil refining and distribution company created by John D. Rockefeller and his associates in January 1870, formulated the one that became Esso, the Eastern States Standard Oil, before 1911 and finally replaced by ExxonMobil brand, an oil and gas company. Esso then became a brand associated with the oil company ExxonMobil after buying the Humble Oil Company. A law aimed to counter the actions of the Standard Oil Company, which at the beginning was a "Trust" was recognized at that time as a large legal enterprise managing the assets in the best interests of the trustor, possessing strong dominant positions in an industrial area and not in the form of a limited liability company. The Standard Oil of John D. Rockefeller, which had already taken the form of a company, was dismantled, and ironically, the Sherman Antitrust Act, countering Standard Oil, for it to take the form of a company, did no longer apply to trusts.

The US government's Sherman Anti-Trust Act was intended to limit corporate anti-competitive behavior. The expression of antitrust was applied to the trusts of various companies controlled by Standard Oil, by closing thirty-one of the fifty-three refineries of Standard Oil and concentrating the production in three giant refineries. It was the application of the Sherman Antitrust Act in 1911 that led to the fragmentation because of the monopoly of John D. Rockefeller's company in thirty-four firms, which became companies of which the best known are the following: Chevron, Esso (SO for Standard Oil), Exxon, and Mobil. The Sherman Antitrust Act bore the name of Senator John Sherman of Ohio as the first attempt of the U.S. government to rise against the emerging power of some companies to limit anticompetitive behavior. The birth of the modern competition law, constituting the U.S. law against the monopoly of companies, was signed on July 2, 1890. It was launched in automobile, aviation, and real estate projects after handling the monopoly in the oil sector. The name Esso remained the one used everywhere in the world, with US$ 416 billion on March 31, 2014; ExxonMobil Corporation held the second-largest stockbroker capitalization in the world.

After the Second World War, Chase Manhattan, the Rockefellers'bank, became the owner of Thyssen group with 31 percent. Nowadays, that group is one of the richest companies on the planet, which began businesses with the Nazi funds worth $50 billion, and then on the same lineage, the Bush family, all members of the Skull & Bones fraternity since Yale. Formally, the original name of this secret society today known as the Skull and Bones secret society in the United States was called the Brotherhood of Death. Despite the denial of conspiracy theories on the construction of the CIA by members of this group, it is known that the first known members of CIA who were old students of Yale University belonged to a secret society and a number of other members who reached great fame and fortune while being members of one of the oldest student secret societies.

This secret society, open to only a few elite members, practiced rituals inspired by the Masonic rituals that usually gathered its members in a building called the "Tomb"; the Order of Skull and Bones was founded in 1832. As members of the Skull and Bones fraternity, the Bush family also had business relationships with the family of bin Laden, both belonging to the Carlyle Group, which over the past thirty years has benefited from the blood money on the backs of innocent people. Now, let's get back to the subject of Rockefeller. After his death, being the richest man in the United States, and one of the most powerful in the world in 1937, his son and successor John D. Rockefeller Jr. (1874 to 1960) succeeded him accordingly. His son took over the family business as the head of an empire dating for nearly two centuries; David Rockefeller was among the former presidents of Chase Manhattan Bank from 1946, up to his retirement in 1981.

The investment bank merged in January 2001 with J. P. Morgan & Co. to form the financial holding bank JP Morgan Chase. He continued as the nonexecutive chairman of the Rockefeller Center Properties Trust and RCP Holdings and chairman of the Council on Foreign Relations with Prince Bernhard of Lippe-Biesterfeld, a German prince who became prince of the Netherlands during his marriage on January 7, 1937, with Princess Juliana van Orange-Nassau of the Royal House of Orange-Nassau; Juliana was the only child of Queen Wilhelmina; and Henry of Mecklenburg-Schwerin, also a German Duke, became the prince consort of the Netherlands as her husband; Juliana, as a princess of the crown, who succeeded her mother, became the queen of the Netherlands from September 6, 1948, to April 30, 1980.

Prince Bernhard had four children among whom included Beatrix, the former queen of the Netherlands; as the father of the former queen Beatrix and the grandfather of the current king Willem-Alexander, he cofounded the Bilderberg Group with David Rockefeller, who was partly a supporter of the orchestration doctrine of economic globalization, inaugurated in May 1954 in Oosterbeek, bringing together the world financially, leading to both the manipulation and camouflage of shady enterprises, and the contacts with "wrong" regime and dictator governments, which are nothing new for us, throughout the famous history of the royal Dutch family.

Prince Bernhard of the Netherlands was also involved in scandals of contributions of $1.2 million he received from the officials of U.S. aerospace company Lockheed to "facilitate the signing of a contract for fighter aircraft," as a series of bribes from the late 1950s to the 1970s. The aircraft manufacturer called Lockheed Corporation scandals, which encompassed bribery in the process of negotiating the sale of aircraft, caused considerable political controversy in West Germany, Italy, the Netherlands, Japan, and the United States, exploded precisely in 1976.

In the Netherlands, the Dutch continue to consider the prewar past of Prince Bernhard, father of Queen Beatrix and grandfather of the current king of the Netherlands, as a delicate subject like Belgium, their close neighbor; yet in July 1936, the proclamation of Belgian neutrality and the controversial behavior of King Leopold III concerning the Second World War faced with the German threat, provoked long polemics and a national crisis. But despite his opposition to the war, "new overwhelming documents" of anti- Semitism, demonstrating that the king did not like Jews very much, make "headlines," and the same war was a subject of serious debates in books of great scientific significance. Historians on this subject preferred to speak of a certain passivity of the king, like the majority of the European institutions at that time. These three European countries, including England, Belgium, and the Netherlands, had monarchs with the Nazi spirit. In England, the husband of Queen Elizabeth II, named Philip Mountbatten, Duke of Edinburgh, the only boy, fifth child of Prince Andrew of Greece and Princess Alice of Battenberg, belonged indeed to the Nazi party NSDAP before the war.

Before his engagement to the future queen Juliana of the Netherlands, Prince Bernhard, at the age of twenty-two, was a member of Hitler's party and returned his party card after his engagement on September 9, 1936. In the Netherlands, Prince Bernhard managed to hide the truth since the end of the Second World War. This revelation came in addition to the splash of bribes paid by Lockheed and the authentication of Prince Bernhard's membership to the Nazi Party NSDAP came from two Dutch historians who discovered a document in the United States. So we can see that whether King Leopold III, the fourth Belgian king who massacred, of Congolese with that Nazi spirit to exterminate them during colonization, or the husband of Queen Elizabeth II of England, whose families were significantly involved in slavery and colonization, or Prince Bernhard of the

Netherlands, also known as a country that made its wealth not only by slavery and colonization of some countries in the world, but literally confiscated South Africa, and under the eyes of the whole world, practiced a horrible system of segregation than the Nazism of which they all belonged without this German citizen called Bernhard zur Lippe-Biesterfeld raising a finger.

In England, it is now clear that the refusal of Queen Elizabeth II to ask for forgiveness for the crimes against humanity perpetrated by her citizens during slavery at the order of her kingdom is a refusal motivated by this Nazi ideology. "An aberration to know that in the lineage of Windsor—the British monarchy enthusiastically financed and supported Hitler and the Nazis." In fact, the entire Windsor Political Chamber did everything to build the Nazi war machine long before and after the abdication of King Edward VIII from the throne because of his support for the Nazis in 1938; the geopolitical war between Germany and Russia was planned by the British, and the merry Windsors maintained their direct Nazi ties and supported the Nazi genocide wholeheartedly. At the same time, Philip and his three brothers-in-law, who until today remained a subversive force in Germany, were Anglophiles and pro-Nazis and were part of a group of German aristocrats.

Prince Philip was trained in the Hitler Youth curriculum, and all his German brothers-in-law with whom he shared and lived together became high-ranking figures in the Nazi Party. So, we can usefully start to truly understand the House of Windsor today. The school founded by Max von Baden, near Lake Constantine in German, is where young Philip studied; he was sent there through the influence of his sister Theodora, who also studied in Germany. Max von Baden, known as Maximilian Alexander Friedrich Wilhelm Margrave of Baden, was a German prince and politician who briefly served as chancellor of the German Empire during World War I in October and November 1918; he was a chancellor of Germany and minister president of Prussia.

His son, Prince Berthold of Baden, married the daughter of Prince Andrew of Greece and Denmark and his wife, Princess Alice of Battenberg; she was known as Princess Theodora of Greece and Denmark from 1906 to 1969 and as the sister of Philip; they celebrated their wedding in Baden-Baden, on August 17, 1931, which made Prince Berthold the brother-in-law of Prince Philip. Margarita, Philip's older sister, married a great-grandson of England's Queen Victoria named Gottfried von Hohenlohe-Langenburg—a prince of the Kingdom of Wurttemberg—within the German Empire before 1918. Cecilia also married a great-grandson of Queen Victoria named Georg Donatus, grand duke of Hesse-by-Rhine, and Sophie, the last of the youngest of the four sisters of Philip, married Prince Christoph of Hesse. These marriages took place from 1931 to 1932. The German aristocratic ties were definitely strengthened by the marriages of Prince Philip's sister to Prince Berthold, including his other sisters.

The German educator, whose philosophies are considered internationally influential named Kurt Hahn, also known as Kurt Matthias Robert Martin Hahn, was commander of the Order of the British Empire. He is the one who, in 1963, founded the International School of Ibadan, Nigeria, and several new boarding schools all over the world; he worked as the personal secretary of Max von Baden and as the first headmaster of his Schule Schloss Salem. Hahn first served as head of intelligence service of the Ministry of Foreign Affairs of Berlin, trained by the Oxford University, and then in the Versailles Treaty negotiations, he served as a special adviser to Prince Max; furthermore, employing a combination of monasticism and the Nazis' "strength-through joy" system, a school wing of Schloss Salem was set up by Hahn. As a Jew, Hahn soon found himself in trouble with the SS, after he first supported the Nazis, and became the centrist elements of the Nazi Party. Hahn became the termed "universal fascist," like the born-in-Germany Jewish refugee who f led the Nazis regime with his family in 1938 called Heinz Alfred Henry Kissinger and his antifascist friends; Michael Ledeen, the left wing and antifascist activist, placing the human freedom at the heart of his action; the antifascist count Coudenhove-Kalergi; the sense of Vladimir Jabotinsky, who was a leader of the Zionist movement of the right wing and who founded the Jewish Legion during the First World War; the antifascist Strasser brothers, who opposed Adolf Hitler's anti-Semitism but first occupied a leading position in the Nazi Party during its formative period; and other fascists who had no dealings with the hard-core of Nazis.

Hahn established a new school in Scotland called Gordonstoun after he escaped from the concentration camps by his powerful connections before Philip's arrival in the school he founded in Germany, and then became the Nazis science school "curriculum for race" and controlled by Hitler's Youth and the Nazi Party. His school in Scotland will play a major role for the education of all male children of Queen Elizabeth II. Upon appeals to the "centrist Nazis," London appointed him as an adviser to their Foreign Office, urging policies against the SS.

The son of King Ludwig of Bavaria became King Otto I, a Bavarian prince who became the first modern king of Greece in 1832 after a British-run coup, under the Convention of London; and in 1862, he was dispatched after thirty years of reign, and London selected Prince William as the successor; he was the son of the designated heir and nephew to the Danish king, the Crown Prince Christian. Prince William of the Danes married the granddaughter of Czar Nicholas I in 1866, after being installed on the throne as King George I of Greece in 1862. As the grandson of Queen Victoria, Prince Philip is related to seven czars, including most of the current and former crowned heads of Europe.

Prince Philip was in the line of succession to the Greek throne before being forced into exile with his family, but before his marriage to Princess Elizabeth, who later became Queen Elizabeth II; he renounced his rights to the Greek and Danish throne as well as his Greek titles on February 28, 1947. The king of the United Kingdom, the last emperor of India, and the first head of the Commonwealth—and the dominions of the British Commonwealth from December 11, 1936 to August 15, 1947, until his death on February 6, 1952, was King George VI. King George VI, who was born on December 14, 1895, awarded Prince Philip the title of the duke of Edinburgh on his wedding day in 1957. Prince Philip became duke of Edinburgh styled Prince, and on June 1, 1973, the Greek monarchy was abolished by the then-ruling military regime.

In 1933, Prince Christoph joined the Nazi Party, embraced by the Nazis, and became the chief of the Forschungsamt (directorate of scientific research) in 1935. The Nazi Party saw this husband of Sophie, Philip's sister, as a channel faction in the Great Britain of King Edward VIII, who was a good friend of Adolf Hitler. Prince Christoph and Sophie's eldest child was named Karl Adolf after Hitler, and his education was later on promoted by Prince Philip.

A daughter of the king of Italy married Philip of Hesse, the brother of Prince Christoph, and became the official liaison between the Nazi and Fascist regimes. Prince Christoph was under Hermann Goring, the SS and the Standartenfuhrer (colonel), who directed the special intelligence operation; Col. Hermann Goring, one of the most powerful figures in the Nazi Party (NSDAP), ruled Germany from 1933 to 1945, under Heinrich Himmler's personal staff, one of the highest dignitaries of the Third Reich. Heinrich Himmler, the Reichsfuhrer of the Schutzstaffel (Protection Squadron SS), was a leading member of Adolf Hitler Nazi Party (NSDAP) in Germany; he was known to be one of the most powerful people directly responsible for the Holocaust in Nazi Germany. He died by cyanide pill poisoning in the headquarters of the Second British Army in Luneburg after his arrest; and at the Nuremberg trials, Goring was convicted of war crimes and crimes against humanity after the war.

Prince Philip attended the Gordonstoun Academy in Scotland, four years after leaving the Schloss Salem. During their trip to London for Georg's brother's wedding, one of Goring's Junker aircraft, transporting Georg Donatus, the inheritor grand duke of Hesse-by-Rhine, his wife Cecilia, the sister of Philip, heavily pregnant with her fourth child at the time, their two young sons, Georg's mother Grand Duchess Eleonore, the children's nurse, a family friend, a pilot, and two crewmen, crashed when the pilot was attempting to land despite the poor weather conditions because Cecilia was to give birth, killing all those on board, on November 16, 1937.

Prince Philip, who developed secretive ties with King Edward VIII, learned about the crash the same day, and the funeral became a gathering point for Nazi leaders and their partisans; he continued his secretive ties in 1938 after the dispatch of King Edward VIII, according to the British magazine called *Private Eye*. Philip's parents were working for the SS; in fact, Lord Louis Mountbatten (originally Battenberg, Philip's uncle, a branch of the House of Hesse) was one of the central figures in the Nazi-British back channel and sponsor in the 1930s, backed by King Edward VIII. Between the British royal family and their pro-Hitler cousins in Germany, secret channels of communication were maintained through much of the World War II by Lord Mountbatten and through Prince Philip's aunt, the crown princess of pro-Nazi Sweden Louise Mountbatten, the elder sister of Lord Mountbatten. These channels of communication included messages from Prince Philip's secret ally and those of the former Duke of

Windsor Edward VIII; but Buckingham Palace tried to depict this collaboration with the enemy as mere family correspondence during wartime. The duke of Windsor, in close collaboration with the Nazis in Spain and Portugal, planning to foment a revolution in Great Britain, was reported by the *Washington Times*, on November 12, 1995, based on the Portuguese Secret Service files discovery, first published in the *London Observer*. Walter Schellenberg, head of the gestapo counterintelligence, was the contact point in that plot, according to the Portuguese surveillance revelation. This plot was revealed by the Portuguese surveillance after the Spanish ambassador to Portugal, Nicolas Franco, met with Schellenberg.

This first published Portuguese Secret Service files in the *London Observer* led the Churchill government to a slow fall, forcing him to destitute King George VI, his brother; and with the American divorcee Queen Wallis Simpson, he allowed him to regain the throne, but at her side, he abdicated the throne. In June 1945, King George VI dispatched Anthony Blunt, the former MI-5 officer, to gather whatever correspondence was hidden in the Kronberg Castle of Sophie and Prince Christoph; but Anthony Blunt was summoned by Queen Elizabeth II, insisting that no interrogation should be revealed about his secret trip to the castle. The House of Windsor's close collaboration with the Nazis was desperate to keep those Kronberg Castle documents classified, starting with an exchange between King George VI and President Eisenhower, but long beyond the normal length of time, they fell into the hands of the U.S. Army, which quickly found that those documents of Kronberg Castle were not just the exchange of Christmas greetings of Lord Dickie Mountbatten, Princess Louise, and Philip's brother-in-law, Prince Christoph of Hesse, but an official link between the Nazi and Fascist regimes.

His Royal Highness Prince Bernhard of the Netherlands cofounded the World Wildlife Fund for Nature with Prince Philip, the Duke of Edinburgh; it was formerly named the World Wildlife Fund, as an international nongovernmental organization founded in October 1961; its official name is still used in Canada and the United States. Prince Bernhard, who recruited Prince Philip for the eco-fascist cause, had a well-laid Nazi root much earlier, and both had very strong roots in the Nazi movement. In 1971, Prince Philip replaced Prince Bernhard, forced to resign from his most important public functions because of the Lockheed scandal.

Joop den Uyl, prime minister of the Netherlands from May 11, 1973, until December 19, 1977, during the monarch of Queen Juliana, finally privileged Prince Bernhard from criminal investigation and ruled out prosecutions, which could have caused him serious consequences of jail and damaged his reputation as the "head of state" and as the consort of Queen Juliana. Joop den Uyl then saved him from jail by the request of Queen Juliana, saying that if her husband was prosecuted, she would abdicate the throne in August 1976, when the Lockheed scandal erupted. During his last year of study at the University of Berlin in 1934, Prince Bernhard became interested in the Nazis. He first worked openly in the

SS motorized infantry regiment after a member of the Nazi intelligence services recruited him.

To build concentration camps and convert coal into synthetic gasoline and rubber, Prince Bernhard was sent to work for the IG Farben firm in Paris, in a German chemical and pharmaceutical industry conglomerate, both known as the largest company in Europe and the largest chemical and pharmaceutical company distributing antibiotic and medicine overall in the world. It is this firm that developed the Nazi system of the slave labor camps in Germany and throughout occupied Europe by the Germans during World War II, introduced by Hjalmar Schacht, aiming to improve the German economy.

Among the 190,000 people IG Farben employed, there were eighty thousand forced laborers. This company, founded in 1925 as the world's leading chemical company, under the presidency of Carl Bosch until his death in 1945, was producing the Zyklon B gas used in the Nazi concentration camps to exterminate those whom they considered "racially inferior" by their Nazi racial ideology, not only aiming Jews but also extending its racial ideology to exterminate homosexuals, blacks, Poles and other Slavs, the Tziganes, also called "Gypsies," and Jehovah's Witnesses.

This chemical conglomerate, representing a scandal in the eyes of the world, only counts six million Jews in Europe, forgetting that there were many blacks dead in these Nazi concentration camps. These "Niggers," the first target of Nazi discrimination, were Burundians, Cameroonians, Namibians, Rwandans, Tanzanians and Togolese of the German colonies in Africa, who lived in Germany, including black Americans f led from the U.S. segregation, and the Antillians of the West Indies Islands—brought there by European colonizers, and having a significant cultural history of African descendants throughout the region. Among these Africans, many Cameroonians already brought to Germany were once again transferred from Germany to the United States in considerable numbers to work in all fields of the economic development possessed by the Germans in America before the Second World War, but without ruling out the f low of Cameroonians taken to the United States during slavery and after slavery, during the German colonization in Cameroon.

In the concentration camps, these blacks considered as subhuman, between the monkey and the Jew, suffered Nazi horrors; specifically practiced by the laws of racial discrimination promulgated toward blacks from 1933 to 1945 in Nazi Germany and in territories occupied by that same Nazism, derived from a single and same text of the Nuremberg Laws. However, medical experiments such as sterilization, brutal incarceration, isolation, and killings, manifested toward blacks, we will never know the exact numbers decimated in those death camps. The Nazis considered these Niggers brought by the Jews in the region of western Germany, also called "Rhineland," and that Hitler accused Jews of wanting to intentionally destroy the white race, were portrayed by German racist propaganda as black carriers of venereal diseases and threatening the purity of the German race. John William, the first voice to have sung the cause of blacks, both religious and secular, born Ernest Armand Huss in Ivory Coast, from an Alsatian father named Ernest Charles Huss, was kidnapped at eighteen months of age from his mother of Ivorian origin, whose name was Henriette Amoussan, and entrusted to a distant relative in a small village in Seine-et-Marne at the age of eight. At the age of seventeen, after studying at a French boarding school in 1939, he became an apprentice toolmaker at the Renault plant in Boulogne-Billancourt; then from June 1943 to August 1943, in Charente-Maritime; afterward, he was engaged in a Sagem factory that manufactured radars for German planes at Montlucon.

He took part in a sabotage of the Nazi equipment workshop and exploded it the following night in March 1944. Ernest Armand Huss, who was covering a young worker in laying explosives, was arrested and had a tragic existence; he was tortured by the gestapo and was deported to the Neuengamme concentration camp in March 1944, where he worked in an arms factory until the collapse of Nazi Germany during the Second World War. John William, the only black survivor of the Shoah, and an illustrious singer with his baritone voice, born in Grand-Bassam on October 9, 1922, died on January 8, 2011, at the age of eighty-eight years old in Antibes, a region of the Provence-Alpes-Cote d'Azu, located in the Alpes-Maritimes department in the southeast of France. He believed that between twenty-four thousand to thirty thousand blacks died in the Nazi death camps and that their sacrifice is a neglected and forgotten part of the history of Nazi Germany, which puts only six million Jews ahead as the story of the Second World War. The Nuremberg war crimes trials after the collapse of the Nazi regime revealed that the Nazis helped German companies like Audi, known as Auto Union during the Nazi period, BMW, the electric giant Bosc, Daimler, which owns Mercedes, Deutsche Bank, a Nazi ammunition factory near the Dachau concentration camp, and VW, just to name a few, to become very wealthy during the Second World War.

IG Farben Cartel, literally meaning in German language, *Interessen-Gemeinschaft Farbenindustrie*, "community of interests," or *AktienGesellschaft*, AG abbreviation, known as a German word for a corporation limited by share ownership, was known as a public limited "international capitalist Jewish company." As a large government contractor after the Nazi takeover Germany, IG Farben became embroiled in the Nazi regime's policies. Several large American trusts such as Standard Oil, the U.S. Steel company created in 1901 by J.P. Morgan, the International Paper and Alcoa, as large businesses with significant market power were its collaborators. Originally, it is an American lawyer named Samuel Calvin Tate Dodd who was working for John D. Rockefeller, who helped him and created the business trust arrangement in January 1882 to consolidate his control over the many acquisitions of Standard Oil, already the largest corporation in the world, and enabled Rockefeller's control of many oil companies; and as one of the earliest largest holdings companies, he organized Standard Oil.

The Rockefeller's model of American Standard Oil Company, exercising an absolute control over the Council of Businesses, the government, the people of the United States, and foreign relations, was largely adopted to establish IG Farben Cartel model, seeking monopoly during its heyday, which, thanks to it, developed several very important industrial processes put in place for the Nazi system of slave labor, introduced by Hjalmar Schacht. In 1930, Hjalmar Schacht developed the right wing of fascist political ideas, and then Hitler appointed him as minister of economics in August 1934. He started immediately to disagree with what he called "unlawful activities" against Jews, like other Nazis extremely hostile to Germany's Jewish population, and agreed to raise funds for the Nazi Party by his good contacts with the Germany industrialists; furthermore, he persuaded Albert Voegler, an engineer who worked with the United Steel company; Gustav Krupp, an ardent supporter of Adolf Hitler; and Alfried Krupp, whose family company, formally known as Friedrich Krupp AG Hoesch-Krupp, supplied weapons and other materials as cannons and shells from Ruhr, intended for the Nazi regime and the Wehrmacht during World War II; he also persuaded people like Fritz Thyssen, a German businessman; Emile Kirdorf, the son of a textile manufacturer; Carl Bechstein, the founder of C. Bechstein Pianofortefabrik; and Hugo Bruckmann, a German publisher, to provide money for the party. Hjalmar Schacht was arrested in 1944, accused of being involved in the July plot against Hitler.

At the end of the war, he was released from Dachau Concentration Camp still alive. At the Nuremberg War Crimes Trial, accused of crimes against humanity, he was found not guilty but rearrested by the German government and sentenced to eight years' imprisonment for other offences, but on September 2, 1948, he was freed. Hjalmar Schacht, who provided funds in 1926 to found IG Farben, died in Munich on June 4, 1970.

IG Farben cartel, the German chemical conglomerate and one of the most powerful corporations in the world, which was at its peak in the 1930s, supported the Nazi party financially and morally; and their support of the Nazis placed their story into the historical record of the world, including the industrialist leaders of the Krupp Arms Companies; both Companies were later charged with war crimes at the Nuremberg Tribunals after World War II.

IG Farben cartel soon had a network controlling some five hundred firms, and other industrialists like Henry Ford, interested in their success, set up a branch of Ford Motor Company in Germany and began a close association with Adolf Hitler, supplying him with much-needed funds and political influence. In 1922, the funding of Hitler and his SS came in part from affiliated or subsidiaries U.S. firms, including Henry Ford. In 1933, the IG Farben and General Electric payments were followed by the subsidiary payments to Heinrich Himmler up to 1944, and by the Standard Oil of New Jersey and ITT.

The American law firm Sullivan and Cromwell, where John Foster Dulles worked, appointed him as the U.S. legal counsel for IG Farben cartel. In 1936, the new organization investment firm called Schroder-Rockefeller Company, set up by Avery Rockefeller, and also had John Foster Dulles as attorney. From 1927 to 1934, John Foster Dulles was the director of GAF and International Nickel, which was part of the IG Farben firms' network. The Rockefeller's Schroder-Rockefeller Company was combining its bank interests with the personal bank of Hitler, and the Rockefeller family was related to John Foster Dulles through the Avery connection.

Prince Bernhard of the Netherlands joined the board of directors of IG subsidiary, Farben Bilder; it is from the IG subsidiary Farben Bilder that he took the name of Bilderberg to form the group's supersecret policy after the war and organize the Circle of Friends of Farben executive personalities and provide sufficient funds for Heinrich Himmler, the man initially known as Keppler, the chairman of IG. The Keppler's Circle of Friends had eight executives of IG Farben or its subsidiaries among the forty members of the Circle of Friends. In 1933, like other officials of IG Farben, enthusiastic to support the Hitler regime, it first received 400,000 reichsmarks; a total of 4.5 million reichsmarks were given to the Nazi Party as contributions, and their contributions were paid to all other beneficiaries during that period, equaling all contributions that reached the sum of 40 million reichsmarks by 1945. The reichsmark was a currency used from 1924 to June 20, 1948, in West Germany, replaced with the deutsche mark, then in East Germany until June 23, 1948, replaced by the East German mark.

This money, considered to be a tragic history that allowed the Nazi Party to finance a disaster, including using slave labor at a specially constructed factory in Auschwitz called Monowitz, was not a funny matter concerning what the IG Farben financing to the Nazis did to the world.

The IG Farben cartel, with firms under its control, contributing directly to the pioneered Hjalmar Schacht, the Nazi minister of the economy and president of the Reichsbank of Hitler, is indeed known as a firm where Prince Bernhard worked; and other industrialists and bankers who funded Hitler had their contributions processed through an account of Hjalmar Schacht at the private Delbruck Schickler Bank, administered by Hitler's deputy, Rudolf Hess. A testimony at the Nuremberg trials revealed that Prince Bernhard conducted espionage on behalf of the SS as part of a special SS intelligence unit with code number "NW-7" in the IG Farben industries, according to April 5, 1976, issued *Newsweek*. When Prince Bernhard, a right-wing playboy SS man, who begged money for Hitler, married Juliana, he left the SS and signed his letter of resignation to Adolf Hitler, "Heil Hitler!" Despite his deep Nazi roots and all these endless corruption scandals, he received titles and honors, first from the Netherlands, from all European countries, and from countries all over the world. The tradition of the whole House of Orange continued with the marriage of a former member of Hitlerjugend, Hitler Youth; this marriage was held between a German diplomat named Claus von Amsberg by a formal union to Princess Beatrix on March 10, 1966, by a civil and religious ceremony, and she reigned from April 30, 1980 to April 30, 2013.

Following the tradition of marrying the German Nazi's members, the current Dutch king, the Greatly Honorable Willem Alexander, who succeeded Queen Beatrix, is married to Maxima Zorreguieta Cerruti, the daughter of the minister of the Argentina fascist junta, on February 2, 2002, at the Nieuwe Kerk in Amsterdam. During the last civil-military dictatorship of Argentina from 1976 to 1983, Jorge Horacio Zorreguieta Stefanini, the father of Maxima Zorreguieta Cerruti, was the secretary of state for agriculture, in the regime of Gen. Jorge Rafael Videla. A big party was given on the occasion of the royal wedding, which took place in Amsterdam, the Netherlands.

Moreover, considering the Netherlands as the country that siege in the International Criminal Court, none of these adherents to Hitler's party have ever been charged, either for their atrocities of the Second World War after its end or those inflicted on blacks in South Africa by the Dutch of a Nazi past for decades. We can more or less see that the attitude of King Leopold III of Belgium, Prince Bernhard of the Netherlands, and the husband of Queen Elizabeth II of England, Prince Philip, the duke of Edinburgh, simply created societies for the conferences of the Nazi elites and companies with their collaborators in the United States to handle the hefty sums acquired before, during, and after the Second World War.

Dozens of Nazi leaders suspected of war crimes and twenty-four directors of the chemical conglomerate of IG Farben were prosecuted by the Allies of a military court in the Nuremberg Courthouse and were sentenced to sentences ranging from six months and varying from two years and ten months, from three, six to seven years' imprisonment, and some were sentenced to prison terms ranging from nine, ten, to twelve years' imprisonment in 1948.

In 1945 and 1946, according to the prosecutor chief named Telford Taylor, assistant to Robert Houghwout Jackson, chief prosecutor for the United States at the Nuremberg Trials in the birthplace of the Nazi party, he declared that without the organization of IG Farben, World War II would not have been possible, before indicting the twenty-four directors and other industrialists charged with slavery, genocide, and other crimes against humanity.

The IG Farben cartel was thus closing one of the darkest episodes in the German history after the collapse of the Nazi regime, guilty of the deaths of six million Jews and as many as thirty thousand blacks in Europe, and the Allies decided to dismantle that company with a direct link to Nazism. The denazification policy of the group's activities became a powerful cartel of the German chemical and pharmaceutical companies such as Agfa, founded in 1867 as a dye factory in Germany, and by share, Agfa was for more than ten years under the control of IG Farben for the manufacture of aniline; BASF, meaning Badische Anilin-&-Soda-Fabrik, originally created in 1865 with headquarters in Ludwigshafen on the Rhine in Germany; Hoechst, a German chemical and pharmaceutical group founded in 1863, today Aventis; Bayer AG, the manufacturer of aspirin, a German chemical and pharmaceutical company founded in 1863 in Barmen; and Dynamit Nobel, more exactly named Dynamit Nobel AG, founded by the Swedish chemist and industrialist Alfred Nobel in Hamburg on June 21, 1865; all these companies were dissolved by decree in August 1950 and divided into twelve companies, to be finally placed in judicial liquidation in 1952; but as huge actors in the pharmaceutical and chemical industry, many of these unscrupulous criminals later played a key role in the recovery of several IG Farben companies; they're initially owners of these same companies, and the main successors are AGFA, BASF, Bayer, and Sanofi, as four largest original constituent companies remaining the largest chemical and pharmaceutical companies of the world. Following several mergers in West Germany, they operate as informal cartel and play a major role in the "economic miracle"—*Wirtschaftswunder* in German language—describing their rapid reconstruction of West German and Austria economies development, based on social market economy after World War II. Many of these former Nazi Germans, who would later be at the center the development of the trade association throughout Europe and the United States, became pan-Europeans in the current European Union. Of the twelve heir companies of IG Farben, we can note the close link of these few companies and personalities quoted below with the Nazism; AGFA, since 1936, invented color film and was for more than ten years under the control of IG Farben Company, and we all know that all its leaders were supporters of Nazism.

Bayer became Bayer AG, a German chemical and pharmaceutical company, which later also became part of IG Farben in the 1920s, producing the Zyklon-B gas used by the Nazis in the gas chambers of the extermination camps.

BASF, the largest German company producing chemical products in the world, founded IG Farben with Hoechst, Bayer, and three other companies, under the direction of Carl Bosch; IG Farben, the multinational family enterprise, achieved its notoriety by producing deadly Zyklon B used in the Nazi extermination camps.

BMW/owners of VARTA batteries, is a German-based company that first produced aircraft engines until 1945 and currently producing automobiles and motorcycles, including Altana AG chemicals divisions of the Varta Group; it was founded by Gunther Quandt, a German industrialist; it is known that in Germany, the current eight hundred richest Germans are among his descendants; Quandt joined the Nazi Party in 1933 after Hitler's election; today, the industrial empire is overtaken by its Nazi past.

Hugo Boss, who used the forced labor of deportees in concentration camps, had 324 workers in 1944: mostly French and Polish. He joined the NSDAP party (former Nazi party) in 1931 and made uniforms for the Nazi army from 1933 to 1945. The company that still belongs to the Holy family passed into the hands of his son-in-law, Eugen Holy, after his death in 1948.

Liliane Bettencourt, daughter of a clever chemist named Eugene Schueller and the wife of Andre Bettencourt, were both fascist leaders during the Second World War. As heiress, she pockets 45 million euros a month to become the richest in the world.

Christophe de Margerie, grandson of the champagne magnate Taittinger, pro-Hitlerite named "Jeunesses Patriotes" in the 1930s, and sponsor of the fascist gangs.

Renault, collaborator of the Nazi occupier; out of eleven articles, this car manufacturer was convicted for its Nazi collaboration in 1945.

Ford and his anti-Semitism, was more violent against the Jews in Germany; the fantasies of Ford that portrayed Jews as a "seed" that must be "cleaned up" were applied by Adolf Hitler and his government and took that same orientation and words. In the war years, Ford built Fordwerke, a factory in Germany and Poissy in France, which built a very large number of military vehicles for the Nazi army. Opel, a German subsidiary of General Motors, was building Nazi aircraft, and both were supplying 70 percent of the German car market. Henri Ford preferred to hide his American anti-Semitism and his Nazi past to embody such a model of industrial success.

The companies of JP Morgan bank first took off in the nineteenth century by the practice of loan to slaves. John Pierpont Morgan, the true founder of the company, as a former friend of Nazi Germany, maintained discreet support with Nazi Germany during the 1930s; he was also a virulent anti-Semite who loudly said the discomfort he felt in the presence of his Jewish confreres, including his business friends who refused to deal with Jewish companies known as First Boston or George F. Baker, precursor to Citigroup, Kidder, and Peabody & Co. The financial operations of the Catholic Church worldwide were taken over by the Rothschild in 1823. By 1885, "the World Order," fixed upon the Rothschild monetary power, reached a point of world control; and becoming the Bank of England's bullion brokers, the Rothschild Bank set up agencies in California and Australia in 1840.

The Royal Institute of International Affairs and its London political group, re-established the colonial government in the United States since 1900, essentially as political decision-makers; and it was through the Council on Foreign Relations, the subsidiary of the Royal Institute of International Affairs, that the colonial and the government or the occupation, primarily functioning through the Foundation of Rockefeller, controlled the educational establishments, the media, religions, the state legislatures, and governmental functions.

The Rothschild Bank, beyond banking services, still controls the financial system, the United States Federal Reserve, and still belongs to the Rothschilds, a German-Jewish family of multiple nationalities. Both entities were created by the Rothschilds' empire and funded Hitler, confiscated Jews properties, supplied machines to produce punch cards to manage their identification to the Nazis, organized the expulsion of Jews and the extermination of over forty-two million people during the Second World War. These agents of the World Order are still operating freely in Europe and the United States as "terrorists"; but they prudently avoid any mention of this fact, well aware by both Departments of Justice.

IG Farben was controlled by the Rothschilds and went on using Jews and other disaffected people as slave labor in the concentration camps in 1939. A giant step was taken by the Rothschilds when the second "League of Nations" was later on approved as the "United Nations;" that giant step led the Rothschilds toward their goal of world domination.

The Rockefeller's business interests to develop the world economy revolution at the height of the century led the Dutch Royal Petroleum company to find itself in a fierce competition for the lucrative control of the European market with the Standard Oil Company of Rockefeller. David Rockefeller was the president of the American private Rockefeller University, specializing in medical and scientific research, founded by the oil magnate John D. Rockefeller in 1901, and president emeritus of the Museum of Modern Art, inaugurated in 1929 in New York.

The Foreign Relations Council of the United States Senate Committee on Foreign Affairs also had David Rockefeller as president. That organization having as aim to analyze the foreign policy of the United States and the global political situation, founded in 1921, has housed personalities as Allen Dulles, an important figure of the OSS, the Office of Strategic Services, an American intelligence agency during the Second World War; he finally became the third director of the CIA, known to be the longest-serving director to date, during the early Cold War; he was also a professional lawyer dedicated to promoting the interests of the Nazi Reich and a banker with treacherous behavior; followed by Wesley Clair Mitchell as one of the professors of economics and as a researcher, who founded the New School for Social Research; there were also over twelve foreign ministers such as John Foster Dulles, Dean Rusk, Henry Kissinger, Madeleine Albright, Colin Powell, etc.; several politicians like Gerald Ford and professional lawyers and bankers were protected by this organization.

Listed among the one hundred richest people on the planet, David Rockefeller's family still held shares in the multinational ExxonMobil. David Rockefeller was succeeded by his son David Rockefeller Jr., who had the idea to create the Trilateral Commission, initially launched in June 1972, and was soon joined by Zbigniew Brzezinski and Henry Kissinger, and officially established on July 1, 1973 in Tokyo, at the initiative of the main leaders of the Bilderberg Group and the Council on Foreign Relations. Being a member of numerous boards of administration of the family institutions known under the name of the cousins of the prominent Rockefeller family, he was considered as the first plan of the member of the fourth Rockefeller generation, founder of the Standard Oil Company.

Since the founding of the Rockefeller Foundation in 1913 by John D. Rockefeller, he was the sixth family member to serve on its board of directors since his appointment in October 2006. So rather than democracy and freedom, through those large banks, United States led secret operations around the entire world with the help of CIA to serve the financial interests of large American groups. To continue that strong enterprise, its monopoly on the transport of exotic products, African oil, and other natural products, the doctrine of the United States since the nineteenth to twenty-first century is characterized as a foreign policy overthrowing democratically elected governments, under the guise of protecting American interests and those of Europe, which is involved in the same financial links to influence African governments as guardians of the American continent of Europeans. Whether in Central America, Latin America, South America, Africa, or elsewhere in the world, their foreign policy is purely inspired by economic intentions. It recognized the government of the Republic of Ivory Coast of President Ouattara since May 6, 2011, appearing as the president of a segregation ideology; a paradox rendering the possibility to feel love difficult; presiding over an ideological policy of a single side in a defined area; to cause a heavy pain in the conscience of people, and finally, developing a territorial apartheid, questioning the way in which the original thoughts should be considered, capable of identifying maladaptive thoughts to the point of view of others.

The same international community recognized the insurgent government in Libya by taking the low position and by pretending not to know the problems that would result, especially to get their hands on natural resources and pass them reconstruction contracts under the guise of being humanitarian or under the cover of the new role of gendarme by the name of security. Unfortunately, that American intervention only darkens the future of Europe by current events in Iran with the Hezbollah, playing a decisive role in the Islamic Cultural Revolution against secularists and modernists; followed by events in the Middle East and the Maghreb. The Maghreb, sometimes reduced to Iraq, Syria, Lebanon, Jordan, and the region of Palestine or the Arab world, is not subjected to the Arab-Berber influences, whose uncertainties concerning oil make some French and the Western world fearful.

Openly, their will and the international decision have deliberately biased analysis, manifesting a geopolitical bias rather than being interested in the virtuous democracy. The imperialist Western powers had already chosen Alassane Ouattara as the legitimate presidential interlocutor, valid for their benefit; actioning their diplomatic networks of mediatic intelligences and the lobbying of the global imperialist liberalism for the electoral recriminations against Laurent Gbagbo.

From that moment on, the indisputable democratic virtue of Alassane Ouattara was seen as an innocent victim against an electoral hold-up by Laurent Gbagbo; orchestrated in such a way as to create substantial distortions of vote after canceling seven votes of the northern departments for wrong reasons and declared himself the winner by the Constitutional Council. The international dignity of Alassane Ouattara was thus constructed, passing the electoral turpitudes in silence, consecrating the diplomatic indignity of Laurent Gbagbo, and accusing him of all electoral perversions. Technologically, the Western media devices prepared the mighty steamroller, making use of their influence within the United Nations and supported by the European Union against the regime of Laurent Gbagbo, undoubtedly launched by all weight.

That African crisis led the Economic Community of West African States (ECOWAS) and the African Union in a political diplomacy. It concentrated all political and diplomatic attention of other African countries and the world to that country. Yet the same determination was not demonstrated during the vote in the Central African Republic by the liberal global powers of the Western imperialism to defend democratic sincerity and the integrity of the electoral process in that country—a country that experienced a civil war that led the UN to structure an integral peace created for the purposes of the cause.

The electoral process in that country of Central Africa was openly neglected. And deliberately, the same postelectoral actors of the imperialist international community in Ivory Coast did not bother to enforce the respect of moral and democratic election in sub-Saharan Africa in general. Despite reservations about the conduct of the Central African Republic electoral process, the policy of Gen. Francois Bozize Yangouvonda was militarily supported by France. Francois Bozize was born in Gabon at Mouila on October 14, 1946. This Central African politician and Masonic member of the Great French National Lodge (GFNL), founded in 1913 as the only French obedience, based on the precepts of regularity proclaimed by the United Grand Lodge of England in 1929, brought a real confusion in that country of the core region of the African continent. He came to power on March 15, 2003, by a coup during a presidential visit of Ange-Felix Patasse in Niger, politely let down by France. The presidential reelection of Francois Bozize in the first round of the 2011 elections was decisive with 64.37 percent of the vote against 21.41 percent of the former Central African president Ange-Felix Patasse and 6.8 percent for Martin Ziguele, his former prime minister. The nonmoral, democratic, and electoral sense of that election triggered many protests leading to appeals alleging fraud, filed by several candidates before the constitutional court.

After some time, Ange-Felix Patasse, born in Paoua, a city located in the prefecture of Ouham-Pende, on January 25, 1937, and who led Central Africa from 1993 to 2003, died at the age of seventy-four on April 5, 2011, at the Douala General Hospital in Cameroon. Francois Bozize Yangouvonda was also overthrown on March 24, 2013, because of oil. He dared to sign an agreement with China National Petroleum for the exploitation of Gordil oil at the Chadian border. Since then, the Central African crisis cast a chronic instability in that country up to today.

Since the death of Ange-Felix Patasse, Central African Republic is in a deplorable situation. Currently, with the country completely divided, one wonders whether one day it will even see a better future in its near future.

The juridical limits and the ethic of the diplomatic policy of that imperialist international organism and the European Union, which particularly presented themselves as watchdogs of democracy in Ivory Coast, did not show the same interests in that country.

Their honesty to analyze the postelection controversies according to the requirements concerning the integrity, sincerity, and respect for the democratic freedom of the Central African presidential vote, was partial. Were they seeking for the truth? Not having paid attention to the complaints of the Central African opposition? Such questions remain unanswered. The same international community on the other hand, had a discriminatory attitude but supercilious concerning the electoral process in Ivory Coast.

The announcement of a return to peace in Ivory Coast, despite all, did not benefit the same political and mediatic interest in a sovereign zone of politicomilitary crisis and the electoral conjuncture. Its sociopolitical configurations are not understandable on a simple moral and ethical basis, but only by the consistency of variable content of power configurations, not established on the basis of ethical, moral and rewarding considerations.

The global Western and liberal international community, with predominant imperial powers of geo-economics and geo-strategy interest, is engaging powerful global multinational companies, like the international financial and economic institutions, linked to the Bretton Woods system in dealing with African crises, for the operational structure of the decision-making networks that are concretizing and organizing the same international community.

We all know that, at the end of the Second World War, the elaboration and discussion of international institutions started in the middle of World War II, more precisely from 1941 when sovereignty was still more a matter of degree than an absolute condition. In May 1942, Harry Dexter White, a senior economist working in the U.S. Treasury department during the Second World War, and a senior official at the Bretton Woods conference in 1944 after the war, presented an established ordered economic plan for the funding of stabilization of the United Nations and associates of the United Nations Bank for the Reconstruction and the Development, to the former president Franklin Roosevelt; he was a major architect of the International Monetary Fund and World Bank, at the Bretton Woods. The main objective was to put a world monetary organization in place, promoting the reconstruction and the economic development of countries affected by war. Several proposals were abandoned between 1941 and July 22, 1944—a period when the Bretton Woods conference ended, after three weeks of debates, among 730 delegates representing all 44 allied nations, including one Soviet observer present at the debates. There were two main protagonists in that conference who established the postwar economic order.

The one on the American side was Harry Dexter White, an American economist and assistant to the secretary of the United States Treasury, born in October 1892 and died of a heart attack on August 16, 1948. That child of a Lithuanian Jewish immigrant played an important role in the creation of IMF and the World Bank. And the other named John Maynard Keynes, an internationally renowned British economist, headed the British delegation, born on June 5, 1883, in Cambridge, England, United Kingdom. He won over the objections of John Maynard Keynes, dominated and imposed his vision at the 1944 Bretton Woods conference.

John Keynes was the founder of modern macroeconomics and recognized as one of the most influential economic theorists of the twentieth century. He participated in the discussion and negotiations that led to the agreements of the Bretton Woods's system. The economic agreements, having outlined the main features of the international financial system, were signed on July 22, 1944, in

Bretton Woods, a town in eastern New Hampshire in the United States. He died on April 21, 1946, in Firle, Sussex, United Kingdom.

The Keynes plan was drafted in 1941 and was preparing a global monetary system based on a nonnational reserve unit. He proposed the creation of an international compensation union and a supranational currency, the bancor. But against the plan that restored the gold-exchange standard of Harry Dexter White, he lost. Thus, to ensure his leadership on the world after World War II, the White's proposal, with a nominal attachment to gold, organized the world monetary system around the American dollar. Finally, two bodies were created: the financial institution that indicated that the economic impact on the entire African region was worsening, since the contestation of the election results on November 28, 2010, in Ivory Coast, on the West African Economic and Monetary Union (WAEMU), mainly of the former territories of French West Africa, is an organization of eight predominantly French-speaking states, encompassing Benin, Burkina Faso, Ivory Coast, Mali, Niger, Senegal, Togo, and Guinea-Bissau, a Portuguese former colony, which shares a customs union established in 1994; and its currency union is using the franc (CFA), pegged to the euro; these eight WAEMU countries are also members of ECOWAS, within a group also including the six member countries of the West African Monetary Zone (WAMZ), encompassing the Gambia, Ghana, Guinea, Nigeria, Sierra Leone, Liberia, and Cabo Verde. This financial institution, as the first created body, known as the International Monetary Fund, IMF, estimated that the WAEMU countries will continue to face difficulties, given the convergence criteria.

The World Bank (WB), formed by the International Bank for the Reconstruction and the Development, was created on December 27, 1945. This account allowed the cofinancing of expertise in short or medium term for the benefit of the bank's customer countries. All sectors are concerned, bringing together two international institutions: IBRD, International Bank for Reconstruction and Development, and to advise states in difficulty by providing financial support for poverty alleviation with IDA, the International Development Association, founded in 1960 as part of the World Bank, complementing the IBRD.

The International Monetary Fund, created in 1944, allowed the cofinancing of activities with the Training Institute of the International Monetary Fund, essentially intended for African countries. At the absence of agreement, the third body in charge of international trade, which was to be created, could only be created in 1995, with the creation of the World Trade Organization (WTO). That fund was created to help finance technical assistance activities of the WTO.

These financial institutions are the armed wings of neoliberal globalization, which plunged the third world in the spiral of debt from the late '60s. These same countries of the third world were subjected to the absolute requirements of structural adjustment programs, imposed by them, the strongest so far, mainly to transfer their economic assets in the portfolio of foreign multinationals. I could spot behaviors of avaricious power and greedy inspirations of influences acting for motives much more prosaic constantly. Those behaviors are primarily masking chains of power, structuring the orientation of real negative and passive intentions beyond the good principles of the state of law or human rights. Mainly, these foreign multinationals forms the core of the geo-strategy systemic demarcation, leading to the geo-economics and to the economic strategies for the action units, attached to the North-Atlantic and the Euro- Western Politics preponderance power centers; they're envisioning African crises for a recolonial perspective and a semicolonial paternalism.

These topics of hard proofs are imposing misery upon me because I'm an African in heart, soul, and spirit—son of the cradle of humanity. And nobody will therefore tax the son of the cradle of humanity, because the unthinkable cause has no form. And above our conceptions is the cause without cause but driven by the values of the formation of all states of the world.

My thought on the state of law is to promote African humanity by the enormous potential that specifically abound its African continent and generally for all the inhabitants of the entire universe. Because the cult of divinity, revealed in the living shrine is the only legitimate cult in the psychic state (terrestrial), and in the physical state, man is the supreme evaluator. He is the work of the one who possessed attributes, the work of the psycho-intellectual man, divine and human from his emanation and his formations. Since there is only one law, the law of charity, which is with justice, violation of this law creates a total imbalance to the excess. Passionate with the perpetual evolution toward the perfection for the development of that magnificent African continent and confronted with the idea of its bad governance, against its excessive exploitation, and the one of the entire universe by multinationals for many years, the suffering imposed upon me is too strong.

The eternal and natural way to reach earth's immortality is its formation; unfortunately, the globalization of the law, to let the state of law advance, remains a strong lesson to learn, however very far from the justice of natural laws that lead to eternal immortality. Every child of the cosmos has a right to be guided and led in the development of his individual faculties and to live as he can and as he wishes. He has the right to take his own place in the cosmos and fulfill his special role as a human being, but justice with its earthly laws remains a rampart upon which come to break a vague desire of various abuses by the manipulations of all kinds, inflicted to humanity by the holders of executive power on the only sacred life on earth, known as undivine manifestation without royalty of an aristocracy without intelligence; therefore, lacking the divine nature, I assert that there is still a real deficit in the ethical dimension of the judiciary power. With a justice system of orders, corrupt and laxist, it is absolutely necessary to redo everything to give a real place to justice as a power that can play a leading role in the development and preservation of democracy. Currently, the idea of its mutualization is deviance toward its community (citizens of the world).

Nevertheless, its recurrence demonstrates that its conducts are escaping social norms, therefore threatening the system in its globality by behaviors not complying with the sociology concepts. Because its civil and citizen representativeness remains embryonic to the four classifications of the terrestrial formations, which are animal, mineral, psycho-intellectual, and human divine—an order that has no division.

Numerous trips that I made in other continents of the world made me a citizen of the world. So, it is these accumulated experiences, for the sake of respect and truth, which gave me the right to demand a reward from the multinationals for the citizens of the world; because in my opinion, defeated by poverty, they remain "spectators" of the mundane game with legitimacy.

My humanistic approach, an ideology based on the exercise of my spirit, from an analysis point of view, is simply a fact of nature. Thus, my form of authority takes me to the distinct ref lection of the philosopher in a conceptual framework of the most varied subjects to defend values generally of a human nature. Consequently, I engage myself intellectually in the practical affairs to indicate the responsibilities of the people in the public sphere, men, of sense, created from the preestablished technical laws. Therefore, my idea, put into situation as a concept of social birth concerning this award from the multinationals is an extremely positive vision of a human being with a tendency of innate humanist principle, wanting the realization of his vision resting on the unique postulate of every human being.

Thus it is here about self-determination of these multinationals, presidents of the world, judges, lawyers, magistrates, all religious leaders, traditional and spiritual leaders, humanists, and finally all those who do not want to see the world in poverty and misery anymore, must realize their potential in a positive way.

Within my thought, a thought, thought to be thought with the "Third Force" known in Psychology, and mobilize the forces of psychological growth as psychotherapy, and give that place to the human being on earth, confirming that every human being is unique. This existentially humanist approach requires a humanist will and a political will to develop toward the norms of democracy, which are expressed in full autonomy and full independence, without harming the intuition.

Get rid of all conditioning that limits freedom, and follow your own conscious experience to evolve positively, under any circumstances, choose a behavior dictated by profitability, ease or the principle of pleasure, and the fruits of despair known as violence and predation. Thus, my humanism, our humanism will join my humanist sociology, our humanist sociology, because basically, the human being is good and has the ability to make good choices. So to calm the pressure of the human beings who have experienced difficulties and ensure equity, I request and require that the operation of the judicial machinery of the world seize the temples of the courthouses in Africa, Australia, Asia, Europe, and America-the United-states, to baptize a tradition of the world's fertile soil preserved by humanity in trust and respect, and implement a reward program for the exploitation of natural resources by multinationals who are exploiting them.

Don't let the existential tradition longer grants limitations to the human beings as anti-determinism in their intention, to their choice, and the responsibility of important values granted to freedom, for an orientation toward the awareness, which defines the specific qualities of the human nature.

By a conception of courtesy and moral elegance, of solidarity toward the other members of the human species, grant this reward as a reward worthy of that name to all citizens of the world, to benefit from the benefits made from the natural resources of the world, by this name: "Proud to be Citizens of the World," to stop the cycles of poverty around the world; therefore a right of 10 percent restitution of all the benefits of natural resources of the world, since their exploitation by multinational companies.

My great design, the spontaneous creativity of man, gives you free rein on a feeling of civility, of attachment characterized by the taste of politeness and science. We trust you and respect you; since, in conditions of trust and respect, the human being tends to evolve in a positive way. My challenge is launched to all lawyers of the world, and now the ball is in your camp, to execute the law according to the spirit of the universal law, and for the magistrates to administer it by using various systems of governments according to the natural laws of the universe, and to exercise their profession in righteousness, to give reason to all terrestrial humanity. I assure you that, with a strong worldwide union, we can with effort, win this good cause for humanity; "yes, we can," with the inspired will because the cosmos has offered everything that is found as wealth on earth to mankind, and for the cosmos, no one owns its properties; so humanity also has every right to benefit from it; for humanity to enjoy, because death claims its life after only a few short days spent on earth; "yes, we can," referring to the words of the former U.S. president Barack Obama, and rightly only the dead have the right to decide over humanity.

Here, the bitter observation, a fact that promptly retains optimal attention is made grandiosely in its views of the past and the future; the deeper it will be in foundation, the closer it will be to the effective realities of the cosmos; and the more precise and extensive it will be, the more it will require psychointellectual power to be considered, accepted, and executed.

Let the magistrates all over the world resume their role, to get out of their prerogatives, and adopt a code of penal procedure, and maintain its necessity and its scrupulous fidelity, with respect and stronger filial love, opening on relative advances certainly perfectible and take this humanity program that I call "Proud to be honored Citizens of the World," with attention, with lucidity, and with intelligence; otherwise, it will be perverted and eventually die.

Nothing will justify your apathy on this subject, or the renouncement by fear of this right, apparently obvious; especially in the art of instructing exclusively against the multinationals for the well-being of humanity as a fact, for the process of an agreement to understand the difference between good and evil, and award this material good, for the advancement of humanity in the field of love, lasting peace, progress, and prosperity, and thus demonstrate to the face of the whole world that the executive is the sole master of the game in the treatment of files said to be sensitive. Because the laws that animate the immensity of the universe, of time and space, are governing the forces of the entities that inhabit it; and these entities are requiring a conscious awakening of consciousness for these laws to be correctly grasped, to guarantee their representativeness before justice, and instruct this cause in the annals of the law to illustrate the influence of the law, the individual right to profit from our natural resources, and for mankind to reach the higher level of wisdom; the fine the smooth f lower received as fact, information, skill, or acquired knowledge, through a quality experience, known as good judgment, courageous practice, and theoretical understanding of the law is the wisdom of the Most High, before which, one is constantly in presence. The one who receives it complies himself to its usage, to the purpose for which man was created; I know that the satisfaction of some personal needs remains the only true motivation on the material, metascientific sources; the metascientific sources consisting to expose what man can learn about that mysterious wisdom from the Most High. That is why beyond all that precedes knowledge, wisdom, essential for a particular purpose is required for this program; therefore, the collective verdict of all leaders of the world would put an end to the insidious and devious proximity of the multinationals who are plumbing the good functioning of humanity, and its impoverishment in the world manifesting itself up to man and beyond him.

Consequently, a fierce battle against these practices should be conducted, whether in physical or spiritual domains, to sanction such abuses; otherwise, the free consent of multinationals must be registered; relying on the knowledge of the past, describing what they have learned as process of abuses, accumulations, violences, sprains inflicted on common morality that history is hiding behind "legality"—power that manages to pervert the law for its own benefit on a global scale, and that humanity is claiming today, must be subjected to the many vocations of memorative consciousness in the framework of the normal operation of this program.

Their statements must be properly recorded as minutes and must be considered the best of wisdom that has been revealed for millennia, resulting in a real manna that will be inscribed on the budget of each state of the world for an equitable sharing to every citizen of the world; because even as it has taken so long to believe that the citizens of the world could benefit from natural resources under the hidden appearances, they were discovered and exploited and are still exploited thoroughly to sumptuously enrich only few individuals among the mass of the population of the universe.

It is said that where men and women are requiring public power for a long time, the public authority must be renewed under the guise of great movements, vociferous by a slow work and patient—the one of human evolution—and ensure the proper execution of the legal procedures between them, whatever the balance of power is. Challenging illegal acts and claiming the rights from the branches of the highest psycho-intellectual mysticism, which are hiding under the seal of secrecy is essential to wake up the executive and legislative powers of each government of the universe and address the intellectual elite of the multinationals so that the democratic state lives a mystical adhesion, and successfully produce the intended result.

Know God as an accomplishment and prosper in an equitable judicial system, effective and accessible to all. Let the great launched philosophical momentum spread throughout the world. Let the freedom of the citizens of the world assert their rights, to require a legal execution and ritual practices of understanding. To create an environment for human rights as it should be, institutionally and culturally perform a genuine work of propitious quality for the hatching of individual freedom, because the relational principles require democracy and the duty toward the democratic ideal to earn the nation. To no longer abuse by perverted effects of the saddest kind of multinationals with reckless actions and their beliefs in superstitious opulence, because of the ignorance of most of them, which, since a very long time, is animating and will continue to animate their spirits; that branch of all things that does not favor is unveiled, and leads to a much lower level of development. The permanent neutrality and the impartiality of humanity are for the democratic state to prosper and for the egalitarian to prevail in the sacerdotal practice that condemned and confiscated the conception of justice from blacks, and from all citizens of the world by favoring the multinationals to plunder the natural resources of our countries and break down the trust of other races trust in the society of the world.

The control of natural forces must not be hidden, pretending to obtain a good account from it, but be revealed only to guarantee that the cause of the citizens of the world, with that feeling shared by a system of laws, which regulates the rights and duties in society be heard; let it be heard by judges at the service of the law and not from the authority that appointed them and remunerates them to not apply the rule of the remunerated judges, which is not the law, given the serious dangers that this science involves. In the most important field of life in societies, the state must provide the capacity of a state of law and justice, to legal persons recognized as having legal rights that did not agree at all with the multinationals' rules, plunderers of natural resources, and for the citizens of the world broken trust, to implement the rule of laws according the power of justice; not as signs of decline, but the legal rights of the nation for the citizens of the world, if they aspire to penetrate into the arcane of the high and pure science of justice.

The time has come for all magistrates and all legal actors of the law to inscribe themselves on the pediment of humanity; to denounce the pressures and the instructions that we called high hierarchy by addressing the different systems of laws under the strict legal point of view that does not accommodate arbitrariness, but that establishes their responsibilities before our preserved history and the true science of justice.

Today, my choice is a call to the conscience that was lost in the fearsome psychic life never heard before. Now, the whole world has the eyes fixed on you—magistrates who have the obligation to accept and accomplish this official order for the citizens of the world, in the history of the world. Now, it is time to act in honor like those who preceded you in honor for the history of the African continent leading to the history of the world. It is a challenge to you magistrates of the whole world to put the executive power in execution to assume your responsibilities and to lift the citizens of the world from the traps of the low maneuvers of poverty.

With the globalization of the judgment authorities, it is time that the magistrates and all parties operate their credibility at trial, in front of those who have worn out the trust in the society of the world. Ensure that a cosmic sociology, a divine unity, will be addressed and manifested by the collective humanity.

History will record it in justice, in freedom, and in peace. Considering the dominant lines of prosperity networks in the United States, the European Union, and Canada, located in those areas of crisis in African states, and at the planetary scale, they're known as the belts of enrichment of the Western development. In those African states, the diplomatic management of crisis takes place around the utilities of strategic companies, which are necessary for the beneficial operations of those multinationals and for the advancement of their community at the international level embodied in the preponderance.

Their applicable presence and pertinently engaged by their timely spirits in the crisis of the Democratic Republic of Congo (DRC) is systematically for their interests, launched without agreements by the powerful Western global liberal lobbies, which are not acting for the virtues of democracy and for a peace process to get this country out of crisis, but just drowning it in a deep abyss engulfed in the f lames of hell; I referred them to the virtuous pagans who never had the opportunity to recognize the love of Christ in their lives, but who nevertheless lead virtuous lives.

These actors of the autocratic legacy and of disastrous murderous power have literally taken control of our immense wealth in tutorship, for the Western economic reorientation, through the politico-military process by structuring the political institution and political-economic management of our countries, located in the Ugandans subregion, Rwanda and the Democratic Republic of Congo. To better reposition their industrial interests, commercially, economically, and financially, these industrialists take advantage of mines and mineral rents by political and economic considerations, to requisition certain countries by exploiting the Southern Africa, generally including Angola, Botswana, Lesotho, Malawi, Mozambique, Namibia, South Africa, Swaziland, Zambia, and Zimbabwe, by immoderate desires, and the international reasoning that supposed to resolve African crises do not valorize the democratic legitimacy requirements of good governance. Where the effectiveness of civil peace, however, is presented as strategic reasons for the solidarity of Western lobbies but is revealed by the ability to strangle certain governments, to get rid of crisis and electoral controversies in African.

Thus, it supports the efforts of certain governments with effort to preserve its domination in our territories. Toward the Ivorian presidential elections in the late 2010, it was very intransigent with Laurent Gbagbo; yet shameless, it is committing scandalous, reprehensible acts, manifesting an obvious cynicism and implementing a political system of shameful, hypocritical, untruthful, and monopolistic tradition in our countries.

So solicitous, the French authorities showed their so-called attachment to democracy in Abidjan; Barack Obama and Hillary Clinton were also resolved to support the pro-democratic mobilization in a winded-broken way for the revolution, even being so demanding in terms of democracy. In the same opportunist registry, that pro-democratic mobilization was placed in the diplomatic and strategic category, which gave place to the dire straits characterized by a selective perception of changing political crises and fluctuating usages in Africa. At the discretion of the strategic and systemic interests of the West, using liberalism and the multifaceted capitalist system as a tool to maintain its status of global hegemony of increasingly aggressive nature for export; the mobilization of variable geometry to legitimize their moral involvement in the strong selective management of African crises was put on the agenda. In November 2010, in Ivory Coast, the systemic interests were played for the conquest, the exercise and the preservation of political power. The young African democracy was in extreme danger at that election time. The respect for democratic rules was more exceptional than normality.

Why do we fail to organize free and transparent elections in Africa, at the South of Sahara, to bring about changes and stabilize the political system on the respect of democratic rules that have become the factor of social organizations? In the field of economic, political, and cultural interest, and consolidate the social and economic development of African states, and not the destruction, the destabilization by the political fight of violence in the shadow of various conflicts and intercommunal rancor? That denial of democratic rules gives free rein to ethnic conflicts, prey of violence and insecurity, arising from a bad supervision of the electoral process by the international community in the democratic socle of states in our continent, still very fragile, and where many contestations of results called into question are a congenital crisis in Africa, knowing that voting is a moment of sovereignty expression. It is known that to avoid dramatic situations of a delicate sensitive legitimation of political power in a democracy, the framing of democratic rules is necessary. That legitimacy in a democracy, where people have the possibility to freely express their choice by voting, is lacking to good numerous African leaders and undermines our sovereignty. Failure to not respect its choice in terms of the process by electoral tampering to gain access in power without the transparency to all citizens prevents the people from benefiting from the same facilities subjected to the same conditions.

The international community that monitors the process of African presidential elections differs depending on the context by the vulgarization principle of the electoral code to certain international organizations, such as the UN, the EU, and the AU; the commonwealth and the OIF, as intergovernmental organizations that provide financial, material, and technical support, are attached by legitimacy to those elected, conducted by the government authorities. That is why, depending on the context, it countersigns the minutes after the results of elections, consigns their observations as a whole, elaborates a report and makes a formal judgment on the validity and credibility of the electoral process.

Their compilation determines the absence of a genuine independent electoral code because of the legislative power and the judicial power, as well as the national commissions; their ambition is the preservation of political power in a good number of African states. The involvement of the international community is simply a relatively symbolic value. In case of noticed irregularities in the electoral process or any fact leading to the denunciations of massive frauds and other major irregularities, despite reports produced by the international observers, the electoral authorities in the country assigned to this task have the right to cancel the election. Unfortunately, the electoral authorities in almost all elections in Africa are lacking audacity to monitor electoral operations, ratifying all results with their own results. The international community does not defend the fundamental and constitutional law and does not wish to encourage the principles of democracy. Its effectiveness, the real reason for its strong mobilization—often erroneous and one-sided—is to ensure the desired maneuverability of future politicians, defenders of great powers with interests on the African continent. Consequently, those future presidents are devoid of substance in the general interest of their nation and those of their populations. Its sympathy toward a given governing body in office produces reports that prevent various future constitutional developments, and its reason to negotiate solutions to get out of crises, is alas, a source of discord. A certain degree of political immaturity and the absence of a real democratic political will are giving credit to the recommendations of the observations, and the idea of transforming the electoral process of the majority of African states into kingdoms is leading the conscience of our sovereignty in a very difficult position today; and the diktat of the international community is not very well adapted to the international scene.

Its recognition of a state as a state is contrary to the principle of sovereign equality of states. Without its agreement, the new state cannot integrate the international community. That theory gives it a supreme, unlimited, and unconditioned power to privilege a preferred state and a position of an organized political power in a country exercising sovereign skills. Consubstantially to the existence of the state, which needs organs to represent it and express its will as a moral-legal person, holder of the power, which makes the government function through its same organs, and which is exercising jurisdiction within the government, its maintenance of order and security inside and outside that same government, its organs remain largely politicized, but must "proceed" eternally before all "eternal ages" like a family father, so that its spirits "proceed" as well eternally as a family father.

Oh, Africa! Your discretionary policy, which is effectively imposing an offensive practice by its inadmissible evidence, is objectified and unappreciated because of the selfish interests of other sovereign entities. That violation of your principle of sovereign equality by other foreign nations is lacking the object of appreciations toward legitimate juridical plans, by surrounding it with objectives of nonlegal marks of the legitimate process of depoliticization, and the neutralization of interests; it rejects the thought of the consecration of international law of sovereign states, and rather guarantees the legitimate contradictory divergences, sometimes with the state of intolerable interference by the simple fact of the recognition of government; its juridical acceptance is not dissociated from the one of consubstantial policies of nowadays, to replace the notion of intervention with intention, to promote negative political positions within other borders, without taking into account the representatives of the human rights as a whole in the international society, to prohibit a sovereign state from doing what it is entitled to do; intervening by force in a sovereign state, which validly authorizes the said international requirements under its jurisdiction, governing the general practice objectified as law.

Government recognition by the international community, for the specific case of Ivory Coast, is an unhealthy juridical interference constituting an infringement of the said state by the certification of the United Nations, if a valid juridical title exists. However, the recognition of government lacks juridical foundation mainly because of a lack of prior electoral consent; only a sovereign state is authorized to take action in self-defense by individual military force in accordance with the principles and purposes of the United Nations. For many, the United Nations Security Council must abandon the vote of confidence of Article 24 of the Charter 18, in the field of peacekeeping and international security of states as a whole; mentioning to intervene militarily in the affairs of a state and justify the intervention by one of the legal cases provided by the Charter 14–15 of cooperation, or military assistance of actions carried out for the goals and principles of the United Nations of Charter 15 and the Charter 16.

For an improvement in different areas of knowledge concerning the vote of confidence, these articles and charters in the area of peacekeeping and international security in foreign countries must be abandoned by the most impressive literary work, indicating the end of military interventions in the affairs of a state to work in favor of peace, worthy of that name, thus following the last wishes of Alfred Nobel for the considerable progress in the field of social knowledge, culture, peace diplomacy, and other disciplines.

After rendering the greatest services to humanity, over the past years, the Swedish Academy of the Nobel Peace Prize, instituted by the will of the Swedish Alfred Nobel, and which will choose the laureates for two of the Nobel prizes later on, to reward the outstanding achievements of international significance of men and women. He established the price, leaving much of his wealth in writing, at his last will, requiring that the works of the last exercised year on international level be awarded to achievements in chemistry, literature, medicine, physiology, and physics, to developers and peace workers, in all corners of the globe since 1901, but not to be awarded to those who do not deserve it. Alfred Nobel was born on October 21, 1833, in Stockholm, Sweden, and died on December 10, 1896, in San Remo, Italy. Even possessing an armament company named Bofors, converted from a steel company to an armaments' company, and then to a chemical company, he was the chemist industrial manufacturing the Swedish armaments and inventor of dynamite; he advocated peace by honoring men and women who work for peace.

Thereby, the well-inspired sages of the Swedish Academy wisely awarded the Nobel Peace Prize to one of the so gentle, so inoffensive, but the spearhead of the destabilization operation of Libya by anticipation. I cannot still believe that former president Obama authorized and handed over that operation to the unspeakable, intolerable claws of the disgusting coalition of the Western imperialism, to destroy the war machine power of the Libyan people, killing their leader and ravaging that poor country, victim of hatred, without nonetheless attempting any kind of peaceful negotiation.

President Obama did not realize that there are countries like Palestine and its people who are not living in paradise during his two mandates at the White House, but cajoled by the brutality of the supposedly wise, pious Israeli leaders and by the sickening coalition of Western imperialism. In addition, forgetting that the West constantly relies on the element of separation since antiquity, to destabilize the traditional development of any form in our countries to better reign, as was the case in Libya; constantly relying on the known element of tyranny, such as the great usurper of the throne of Judea, named Herod I, king of the Jews from 37 BC to 4 BC, born in Ascalon in 73 BC, placed on the throne of Jerusalem by the Romans, exercised tyranny with support and in favor of the Roman Empire, after the overthrow of Antigonus Hasmonean's legitimate dynasty, following a three-year war between 37 and 34 BC.

To foment an Arab uprising, the English used Lawrence of Arabia and King Faisal I of Iraq by supporting him against the Ottoman Empire as the answer to the Eastern Question, leading to the arbitrary dismemberment of the Ottoman Empire, supervised by the League of Nations. It was a fake bait allowing the great Western powers to disguise the principle of self-determination of people and legitimize unprecedented crimes against humanity under the international law and intended to deceive by the name of the so-called international law in the history of mankind. Obviously, that dangerous disease, which is prevailing from that patronizing musketeer condescending concept of small intellectual spirits, manifestly loss of the imperialist international Western coalition, deeply hampers the Pan-Africanism and goes against the will of the leaders and intellectual African Pan-Africanists.

It is here about the perverse effects that do not concede with any good faith, but of mentally deficient, sometimes miserably disguised to my knowledge in a model that does not seem to suit humanity, and that only fight to safeguard some personal interests. I wonder why the international community was not called to get rid of that plague that seemed to be former President Sarkozy, and arm the French citizens accustomed to regular manifestations, during his mandate as French president. Why did the former president Obama—a charming intellectual gentleman, a model, usually of humble posture—dared to naively accept their grievances, without the slightest trace of expressiveness, the prospect of mental retardation? Consent to the honor of beggars, known as men who are perpetually behind the masks of charitable organization, unfortunately qualified by all as an intellectual pandemic, to carry out a largescale missile cruises in Libya, letting his own image be mystified? It is to be feared that he was already trapped in the mirror of horror and had already lost his spirit; he whom each of us considered as the one who would really question that imperial structure, which is haunting Africa from its ancestors for decades, will he let believe and establish the intellectuality of that continent to the great world? No.

Africans cheered your speech delivered in Accra on Saturday, July 11, 2009, with joy; that speech was seen as a founding act for Africa, and in my opinion, a truth—a message for Africa to take its responsibility in hand and transform its destiny, especially through good governance and through democratic practices, and place Africa on an essential position in the world. To transform the political vision of our African leaders, who are always content to reach out and receive aid for the development of their proper countries, only to prosper their personal wealth. That speech was clearly articulated with an intense emotional reaction caused by a joyful emotion as an African, rationally, according to what must become Africans in the world of tomorrow, by reminding us that your grandfather was a cook for the British in Kenya and that your father grew up raising goats in a tiny village before going to the United States.

The first African American president, Barack Hussein Obama, did not only confirm his African identity but also wanted to show the importance of the work there is to do to achieve this transformation for Africans. As the first African American president, you qualified Ghana as a country that has always been devoted to Pan-Africanism by citing Kwame Nkrumah as the spearhead of its implementation through various leaders; that Ghana has made an explicit and voluntary choice toward its modern version of political renewal to show to the world that a political change was quite possible in Africa; and that what would favor the self-esteem of Africans was the review of a rich history that Africa possesses, to forge itself an identity in the world. But since your speech, Africa is still experiencing the humiliation of the unequal feudal treaties of the West and its international community, blinded by the hatred of wealth that it possesses, and that it has lived throughout its history for several millennia. Still, Africa is suffering from similar barbarities like those experienced at the time of Greece and ancient Rome. That prospect is more and more frightening for the leaders of all African intellectuals, who are unable to effectively solve their own problems.

It must be said that Africa does not deserve this kind of Western humanitarian complacency without any romantic vocation, to work for its happiness without any complex. Africa must overcome the superiority complex of the West, which is killing the African life; and this must be done neither by the love for the capitalist world, nor by hatred of the West, but simply by pragmatism. African leaders and intellectuals, faced with these tragedies, must do their part of things.

Their role is to objectively and carefully analyze all problems opposing the imperial capitalist world in Africa without complacency and make a great leap forward, toward a cultural revolution to henceforth get rid of that metal collar used to tie them as prisoners to that demagogic neocolonial Western policy, with the intention to demolish all the bases of the erection of a viable state in Africa. You pointed out to the Westerners that it was their colonial and neocolonial map that fostered the birth of current conflicts and problems in Africa, placing the hope of generations born of Pan-Africanism in a cynicism and despair that undermine the present generations.

How do you think, dear Mr. Obama that Africans could be able to build an identity for themselves other than the one the West has given them since time immemorial, or has always willing to give them? If you still allow the West to maintain the power to essentially strike down one of the African leaders, who believed and worked for that Pan-Africanism? When will we get out of that unproductive hatred of the West? From that hysterical romanticism of doubtful quality, carried by some of our intellectuals, and in which our leaders are sinking, known to be very damaging to Africa, and known as the only real passion it reserved for humanity by a vice developed in complacency from the slavers' mentality, preventing them to rebuild the foundations of our own internal and external power? These questions are asked to you with so many question marks, and not only deserve answers but also concrete actions, leading to the restoration of the African identity. Because Africans thought that your speech describing Africa as a partner and friend of America will fundamentally change things, related to the messages of pity and insult toward African countries that we commonly hear from *Françafrique* and the commonwealth, of which African countries still remain in the status of victim, whose effects are extending to the populations living in Africa. Was it an irony from you, to make fun of your own continent?

You said: Africa does not need powerful men, but that it needs strong institutions. I thought those words meant the liberation of Africa from the control of other nations. You also declared in your speech in Africa that: freedom was our inheritance and that it was our responsibility to build on the foundation of that freedom, knowing yourself that the West has not yet liberated Africa. That proclamation marked a historic day between the United States and Africa, but that historic day—evidence of a powerful, symbolic change in the global politics of the world—ended when you, the son of a Kenyan goat herder and leader of the free world, authorized the control of other nations on the African soil. I would therefore conclude that it was you, son of the South, who should have killed the paternalism of the old Western colonialism and neocolonialism model for Africans to merit that freedom, the legacy of Africa, but on the contrary, you authorized it; because you, Mr. Barack Obama, as the former President of the United States, yielded to the pressures of Nicolas Sarkozy, for the multinational military intervention, officially placed under the auspices of the United Nations (UN), and it was only in 2016 that you recognized that military operation in Libya as "the worst mistake of your presidency" and will then judge Libyan "chaos" as a part of Washington's responsibility. But what do you think will change after you recognize that military operation in Libya as your worst mistake? Can you imagine what an abuse of power your decision caused to Libya and generally to Africa?

The support of the United States for the democracy of the African continent and for its socioeconomic development that you promised ended in zero value without any action, and was the same arrogance of Western leaders, since the emergence of the so-called independent nations of Africa. Independence is not given but is taken as the inheritance of our freedom. On the other hand, it is explained with great bitterness in the voice of political figures, charmed by its intelligence and its diplomatic depth of vast culture, naturally open to the Western, through an intensification of extraversion behaviors, on the basis of accentuating inequality procedures; the grabbing of annuities and a deadly labyrinth debt, linked to death by space, time, and distanced, whose primary stake is the war, having a different meaning at the level of moral responsibility of the one who is engaging it, to the one who is the main target.

The law in Africa is a law of interference, a right of perversion, conquest, and occupation of the rich countries for the alternation of power, justifying the subjugation of inferior races, declared incapable of governing themselves at the time of slavery, of colonization, and even nowadays, the neocolonialism in the sovereignty of these countries. They do everything to promote all things absolutely contrary to the interests of Africa, encouraging or instrumentalizing ethnic wars and consecrating the absence of symmetry at the heart of international relations, where it is possible to quickly grasp the universality of black man, earlier caught in his beautiful cultivated, inhabited, and hospitable region, leaned against the wall of our land and our cosmogonic forests, where our ancestors taught us the secrets of life and how to fertilize the land, practices that we kept very dearly, helping us to participate in its fertile manifestation, beautifully in blossoming today, for an absolutely promising harvest in the near future. Essentially, based on the refusal to see our laborious dynamic freedom, taken in hostage by the selfish interests of another race, signatory of the dark pages of our history, and a past that still damages our lives and the well-being of a heavily mortgaged people, who have paid a heavy tribute not only by physical and moral violence, but also by political, economic, social, and distinctly cultural; while focusing on a dangerous character of an image preciously described as evil. Well, behold that the other has colonized us in the cradle of the culture of false *entricity*. But is that forever? I say no and conclude that things must change right now to righting the capsized dinghy.

It is time to return to base and correct errors committed by our ancestors, which allowed our knowledge to be colonized by the others; it is now up to us to colonize the expertise and technicality of the other, to achieve a civilizational project; an opportunity to gather the basics of ref lections of our most distant ancestors, like the first modern humans in the history of humanity, and define ourselves as Africans, the first being to build our own civilizational project at a time, revealing exceptional memories at the sight of all.

In search of that recognition, to identify the gratitude of this subject as a true right, I invite you to join your efforts so that together, we accomplish this quest, to enjoy the ravishing thoughts of our ancestors who built this exceptional earth, and who are still seeking to consolidate each day of the year; and by all peaceful means, demand further vocation for peace in the world, as a manifestation of supreme beatitude. I am stunned by the seemingly unanimous position of the moral, social, and traditional authority, generating more and more serious and urgent questions concerning the real motives of that authority, exacting urgent answers on the true motivations of that authority. Our ancestors taught us altruistic values in the universal sense, but we accepted the animal behavior of the West, a priori characterized by disinteresting acts and the countersense of their culture and their dominant society. They also bequeathed us the values of sharing and solidarity that helped to found the earth and the culture of a story worthy to humanity.

From a very early point of view, we understand the mixture of races and cultures, which occurred in the universality of the humanity; and from the inside as well as the outside, we perceive a sharing of traditions at all times; it is that sharing, known as the information element of that civilization in general that enriches, and not autarky: "self-sufficiency or the economic independence," but known as wealth, fruit of the cosmic labor of our cosmos, whose daily life has made life painful for humanity by the absence of love. Our relations with sharing are also as old as our own history. Some of our animal neighbors are resolutely testifying that fact, because in this world, sharing is the rich history that we must engage in our future, not the withdrawal into oneself or in fear. Our multiple sciences, having a definite objective, have been experienced and tested, and proved that our knowledge is the knowledge of the intellectual experience of our ancestors. To reinstate an economic post and the cultural tradition that was taken from us and give a positive image to the African continent, we must recognize the ancient foundation of that knowledge; especially, knowing that its mathematic basics are unique foundations to Africans. The eyewitness testimony of Herodotus, certifying that the Ancient Egyptians had black skin and frizzy hair is not debatable; this declaration was confirmed by Aristotle, specifying also that the Egyptian natives of Ancient Egypt were black-skinned people and asserting that Egypt was the cradle of mathematics.

Integration is a very good thing and is essential to Africans living outside the continent, but it does not mean losing the African dimension. It all began in Africa; let us not forget that and let us not also forget the heritage of our historic beauty on the history of humanity, transmitted to the Greeks.

Let us realize our nonrealization and irresponsibility toward history, because without history, we have no culture, and without culture, we have no economy. So let us take note of our history and stop looking for modernity in others; let us recognize that we are Africans with the potential to realize our potential and meet the challenges of the century, because the man with frizzy hair is an extraordinary opportunity for humanity, a dynamic force toward the development and for the cosmos expansion.

His nature is the carrier of human genius. He is the only being of all beings in the universe that captures the sun's rays through his hair. His scientific genius is knowledge in itself, with a great divine civilization project. African must realize that the civilizational project of the other was subjected to him by force and that it is negative for him.

You know very well that in the reign of our continent, neocolonialism succeeded the colonial powers of traditional colonialism that we thought were dead, but in any case, still firmly involved in the future of Africans. To drown the dreams of internal development and the hopes of Africa, it took the intervention of the World Bank and the International Monetary Fund (IMF). Private investors, general managers and CEO's of multinational companies quickly replaced monarchs and European leaders. The abuses committed against Africans by the neocolonial societies, belonging to the West and the global financial institutions, are many since centuries.

These European companies, specialists in mining are feeding decades of civil war in our countries, particularly today, in the Democratic Republic of Congo, for the acquisition of minerals such as coltan, a black or red-brown ore containing two minerals associated with: the columbite (Fe Mn) (Nb, Ta) $2O6$ and tantalite (Fe, Mn) (Ta, Nb) $2O6$, used to power cell phones, iPods, and laptops. Even the two atomic bombs dropped on Hiroshima and Nagasaki were built from the uranium originating from the Shinkolobwe mine; the symbol of its chemical element is U, and the atomic number 92 of the family of actinides, used for the construction of atomic bombs made of uranium, and which became the main raw material used by the nuclear industry. Its nuclear reactors, fueled by uranium for the production of plutonium, are still exploited. These mines of the radioactive heavy metal of alpha emitter—a radioactive isotope that emits alpha particles—types of decay in a state of decomposition, such as alpha caries; to support it, its process must have an atomic nucleus of minimal size, unlike other types of alpha particles emitted by all radioactive nuclei, known as alpha-disintegrating particles of heavy-weight atoms (106 atomic atoms), such as uranium, thorium, actinium, and radium (with the exception of beryllium-8); the lightest nuclides of tellurium (element 52) are nuclides with massive numbers between 106 and 110, emitting thorium particles and transuranic elements.

All these electromagnetic and nuclear forces are the fundamental effects that produce significant long-range forces that can be seen directly in everyday life, and the strong and weak effects that produce forces at minuscule subatomic distances are governed by nuclear interactions that ruined the health of the Congolese population that produced uranium for United States, allowing the construction of the two largest bombs ever constructed.

This very heavy metal, used as an abundant source of concentrated energy for sixty years, was discovered in the mineral known as pitchblende by a German chemist called Martin Klaproth in 1789. Generating 0.1 watts/ton as disintegration, it is enough to warm the terrestrial core. Its effect, causing convection and continental drift is provided by the main source of heat inside the earth, from its slow radioactive decay, apparently formed about 6.6 billion years ago in supernovas. This ore, deriving from various locations in the Shinkolobwe quarries, believed to be officially closed since 2004, continues to be exploited illegally to smuggle it minerals; and one of which emitting a radiation value fifty times higher than the value authorized by environmental authorities, raises fears in the scientific sectors of the world and the international community, concerning the traffic of uranium and other minerals. The blockade of the former president of the Democratic Republic of Congo, named Laurent Desire Kabila, extending to the assets of the state of Congo, was to be applied by all African states to protect themselves from the monopoly of the World Bank and the IMF, aiming to establish rights for a traditional logic of the Western strategy that has lost an immediate cohesion.

The numerous inconsistencies of media political speeches of dissimulations revealed in fragments have experienced a strong interesting contradictory evolution. We have been constantly told about democracy, concerning several leaders accused of rage, who have transformed the legislative power of our countries into Shereefian dynasties, but the strategy of the imperialist discretion that veils our eyes is a powerful engine in our countries, maintaining our leaders in power sometimes for more than forty years, cannot be explained, but confirmed by its legality allegation containing some secrets that time will discover at a time.

The maintenance of the endless immoral strangulation, drowns Africa in the grief of a solid mass, from a democratic point of view; revealing old strategies of ancient behavior, which have proved their destructive efficiency in every circumstance, restored to the taste of the day up to date; like that NATO intervention launched in Libya, causing the Libyan blood to stream afloat and continuing to do so, after the proclamation of their victory over the death of its leader Mouammar Gaddhafi; and the Arab world could not stop that infesting interference at that time, and will not be able to stop that Libyan bloodbath in the near future, where a total destabilization has been established to the satisfaction of the international community. Obviously, a civil war well known for oil production took place in Libya. Why and how did it explode? Only the international community knows it. Now, it is Libyans who are paying and would continue to pay the consequences for the fault of others. In Iraq, more than a million innocent Arab lives were sacrificed by Bush's invasion under false pretexts. The consequences of that Bush and NATO war, where children are born with malformations, are not at all mentioned because of the shame, but they have enriched themselves and left the country that was so prosperous, in a poor condition.

That cynicism of NATO and the United States continued in Afghanistan and Pakistan, killing innocent civilians every day. Is it not time for the world to say no to the death of innocent civilians? Never was there question of a systematic repression against civilian populations in Libya by their leader. The Libyan conflict has always been tribal and remained tribal, but in this case that killed Gaddhafi, forged by the Westerners, the first victims were migrant workers, brutally forced to leave Libya. That departure was intentionally misinterpreted by the international community to make people around the world believe that hundreds of thousands of people just wanted to escape a massacre and spoke of crimes against humanity. In political terms certainly, there have been deaths between loyalists and insurgents but not in the exaggerated proportions.

On that day, the international community decided to demolish Libya at the sight of all, by the disproportionate aerial bombardments of the international coalition, related to the objective of the UN resolution for purely economic reasons. The disproportionate entry into action of these imperialist air forces on Saturday, March 19, 2011, in relation to the objective set by the Security Council in its resolution 1973, deeply aggravated the crisis, resulting to a country without peace until to today.

That action did not allow, in any way, the preservation of a full sovereignty or the preservation of the territorial integrity and the preservation of unity and did not solve the crisis peacefully and permanently for the respect of Libyans. On the other hand, they acted intentionally to destabilize that country that had no problem and whose leader, with Pan-Africanist ideas, had distinctive projects for the development of Africa, and his ambitions were not pleasing the West, particularly France.

Those bombings against the regime of the former Libyan leader Muammar Gaddhafi, born on June 19, 1942, in Qasr Abu Hadi, still arouse a lot of comments, and critiques have taken place since that Saturday. Very early the next day, on Sunday, March 20, 2011, critics of the Arab League were heard. Its former chief, Amr Moussa, the secretary general of the Arab League from 2001 to 2011 and an Egyptian politician, explained that they were misinformed, and that the resolution was misinterpreted, differently to the goal that was just to impose a no-fly zone. To sow chaos and misinformation, the governments of the Western imperialist empire published all sorts of figures and versions through its media to draw the biggest benefit from the unfortunate events caused in Libya.

Currently, the genius of hatred has escaped from the bottle, and no one is anymore able to know who controls or what is really happening in that country; the continuation of the brutal and bloody repression against the Libyan civil population is repugnant, declared Nicolas Sarkozy, the former French ally of the

NATO. In Kuwait, David Cameron, the former British prime minister, admitted in a speech that an error was committed by the Western countries by supporting nondemocratic governments in the Arab world. Franco Frattini, a former Italian foreign minister, spoke of tragic figures of thousands of deaths in a bloodbath in Tripoli. The bloodshed is absolutely unacceptable and must stop, said Hillary Clinton. The use of violence in that country is absolutely unacceptable, stated by Ban Ki-moon, the eighth secretary-general of the United Nations, succeeding Kofi Annan; he served two terms from January 1, 2007, to December 31, 2016. But of which bloodbath were they talking about? And today, what are those same politicians saying concerning Libya? Ban Ki-moon was opening the door to consider the systematic control of the wealth of that country by pronouncing these words: "The Security Council will act in accordance with the decisions of the international community. . . We are considering a series of alternatives." Thus, the main NATO leaders were jubilant, and Ban Ki-moon was only waiting for the final word of Obama, who was letting us know that Hillary Clinton, his secretary of state at the time, would leave for Europe to meet the NATO allies to decide with them what measures was to be taken. With these words, the American former president Barack Obama wanted to guarantee his investiture by the Democratic Party by competing against John McCain, the Republican senator of right-wing, Joseph Lieberman, the pro-Israel senator from Connecticut, and leaders of the tea party. The ground was thus prepared by Westerners for a military intervention in Libya.

There was nothing surprising than to know that that action would guarantee almost two million barrels of light oil per day to Europe. For this imperial empire, if it did not occasion those events ending the leadership or the life of Gaddhafi, it would have continued to import that light oil. And Obama was rather involved anyway. He gave bullets to his right-wing opponents for his own execution. For this first black American president, the false step of Nicolas Sarkozy, the incarnated evil, managed to make him follow suit in infamous insinuations by following him obediently like a sheep in the reality of classic imperialist aims. And the first victim of that war is the truth of disastrous consequences. The obvious barrier that was difficult to cross, would not certainly delay falling. As the first step in the remodeling of Africa, Libya, inhabited by the theory of conspiracy invented from scratch by France, was put into perspective after Sudan and Ivory Coast. We know that France was already infallibly asking the end of Colonel Gaddhafi's reign and that that approach and the intention of Sarkozy, was suffering from a certain selfishness or even an egocentrism to end the power in Tripoli; but that undertaking was hampered by the iron hand of Rome, which had just signed trade agreements by transferring large funds to Libya.

Aligning himself with the adage that says that "The end justifies the means," Sarkozy used means, methods, and direct operations to achieve his goals and his objectives focused on jealousy and envy, testifying a certain motivation prompting to harm others, socially and/or physically, most often insidiously or openly. I would conclude by saying that his past insidious venom was mixed with the present to insiduously poison the life of the Libyan leader.

What we did not know was that the attack against Libya and the Benghazi revolt were prepared by the French secret services since November 2010. That hypothesis probably had many causes. But as long as we could not read their secret maps, we would never know the truth. So the truth, the first victim of that war against Libya, was that France did not accept the serious problems that the French companies were facing, against those created by the guarantor of Libya to large Italian companies, strongly supported by their government, for an energy to run its big business in Italy.

Historically, the French state has approaches, behaviors and relationships that neglect others, but much more serious with the African states than the Italian state, which shows a certain temperament of will or even a certain conscious ambition to accomplish a choice under the form of socially acceptable personal desires; and productively in the professional senses, particularly economic and relational, Italy largely invested in Libya to allow the center-right to survive electorally. Thus, agreeing to make conditions very favorable to the Libyan government, it wins the supply of Libyan oil, and since then, this annoyed the Elysian activism. In that respect, the vengeance of France was unclear. Has it decided to swindle their Italian colleagues? If that is the case, so much better, but what is interesting us is for us to understand.

For the first time, Italy will have to pay a very high price, permitting itself to support the attacks against Libya than the luxurious support against Iraq and Afghanistan. The journalist and former deputy director of the Italian daily *Libero*, Franco Bechis, the media bodyguard of Berlusconi, revealed to us that many isolated and individual voices of the left against that interimperialist conflict were heard. But the real opposition, due to very materialistic causes, came from the center right base, and those who were in control were from the Northern League NdT and the daily *Libero*, clearly pro-Berlusconi, are those who were to pay the price for the Italian entrepreneurs. Franco Bechis also told us about the contradictions and the pettiness of the comical national opponents, by often presenting us interesting material—we who considered those representatives of both factions with the same contempt; but even if the sources of Bechis are not verified to the satisfaction of some people, the West always uses the help of rebellion of an international variety for regime change in Africa and everywhere in the world; that was the case in Libya, where it was highly improbable that the rebels would ever overthrow Qaddafi, but they engineered his overthrow, the overthrow of another unpopular regime, just to get an easy supply of oil. He presented an interesting documentation for a future research on the real causes of that war, based on documents of the French secret services. It must be said that even when nobody yet knew that Benghazi was boiling, Maghreb Confidential already knew it. And it is this same (Maghreb Confidential No. 957, a paid version) which in their confidential letter propagated the smashing news from the French diplomatic circles concerning Libya. He described the story of the chief of protocol of Muammar Gaddhafi, named Nuri Mesmari.

Arrested on November 29, 2011, after fleeing to France to escape the accusations against him; Nuri Mesmari was put under the Libyan interpellation concerning his extradition to Tripoli; Mesmari was claimed by an international arrest warrant signed on November 28, 2011, for embezzling public funds, and released on the order of the Court of Appeal of Versailles, which judged his detention unlawful in relation with the provisions of the European Convention on Human Rights. Thus, one after another, he began to reveal all secrets of the military defense of Col. Muammar Gaddhafi.

Describing the map of disagreement, he outlined details of the forces on the ground, denouncing the diplomatic and financial alliances of the regime. He decided to work with the General Directorate for External Security (DGSE) for the preparation of a curious mixed expedition of French entrepreneurs and soldiers disguised as businessmen who met Abdullah Gehani, an aeronautical colonel who allegedly prepared the Libyan revolt in Benghazi.

Consequently, France had all the keys in hands to try to overthrow the colonel toward mid-January 2011, when a leak of secret information from Gaddhafi regime authorizing the arrest of Col. Abdallah Gehani, the secret referent of the French since November 18, 2010, reached the French Secret Service DGSE; and the one who was to arrest him was a loyal friend of Colonel Gaddhafi, Gen. Oudh Saati, the Secret Service chief of Cyrenaica, who on January 22, 2011, arrested him and imprisoned him in Tripoli with the accusation of creating a social network in Cyrenaica, formerly a Roman province of North Africa, located between the provinces of Egypt and Numidia, a part of Libya today. It was a social network that praised the protest of the Arab world in Tunisia, leading to the departure of Ben Ali. However, Gaddhafi didn't know that it was too late, since the revolt of Benghazi was already prepared with the help of the French by Gehani.

Because on February 17, 2011, the revolt against the colonel's militia entered Libya, particularly in Benghazi, after Tunisia and Egypt; without even knowing why, we were already at war. The documents of the French Secret Service DGSE testified the visit of Mesmari, which lasted only a few hours in Tunis. Surely, he was seeking to obtain the alliance of the Tunisian opposition and the one of Nicolas Sarkozy of France to prepare the final blow against Gaddhafi. These revelations were qualified as a rivalry in the bosom of European capitalism, especially encouraged by the Italian Secret Services.

The overthrow conspiracy was revealed by a French nonprofit association, founded in 1994 in the European Parliament and dissolved in 2007; it aimed to promote freedom of expression and secularism, considered threatened by a legislative disposition introduced in the New French Penal Code, working toward the emancipation of individuals against dogmas and empires. It was presented following a crisis, like a nonaligned press network in the early 2000s. Established in Lebanon, the association changed its statutes, abandoned its French form, and continued its development in the Arab world and in Eastern Europe. From 2005, it was formally designated as the International Voltaire Network; it was this network that specified that Paris quickly associated London to its project to overthrow Colonel Gaddhafi, victim of the blind repression in reality for the classical imperialist aims. That declaration gave reason to the German former vice-chancellor and minister of foreign affairs, Guido Westerwelle, sustaining his strong reservations about the military operation of the international coalition; according to him at risk, and preoccupying Vladimir Putin, the then Russian prime minister, who was qualifying that ongoing military operation as a call to the Crusades, testifying a strong tendency of dissatisfaction by saying that the United States always used force against weak third world countries. Let us note that these two Western countries were among the five countries that were abstained from voting on the resolution on Thursday, March 17, 2011. It is unacceptable to use the mandate of the Security Council, solely providing measures to protect the civilian population, to carry out objectives of hatred that clearly go beyond its provisions.

An imperialism violating the need for "consent", and which legitimates itself within the communitarianism belief against the anti-imperialism of the exterior, opposed to colonial empires, to colonialism, and the territorial expansion of a country beyond its established boundaries, still gives birth to divided entities in a sovereign country affirming the fundamental unity of African origin, known as the African nationalism ideology. Because of its internal fragility, the misdeeds of colonialism and imperialism, made it pay the highest price through the bombardments authorized by the United Nations, an organization that has failed on its vocation and which on the other side, has legalized and legitimized terrorism of its allies, which has become increasingly unbearable and intolerable in a mission condemned by South Africa, Brazil, China, India, the countries of the Middle East, and Venezuela. This African nationalism of since the heroic times of Lucy and the fossil skull of the primate (Toumai, "hope of life"), dated about seven million years before the present, discovered in 2001 in the Djourab desert in Chad, that African nationalism, up to the current events, still exists. Does the history of Africa, a continent facing the challenges of globalization really exist for the international imperialism? And what is Africa, therefore? After more than fifty years of independence and the creation of the Organization of African Unity, whose ideology was first ignored by some presidents, and which after their so called conscientization was transformed into an African Union, is still searching for its original unpublished archives on the five continents? Yesterday, its children were forced into slavery born from the constraints of yesterday in the diaspora, and today, the children of that Africa of the noble lands, are leaving that continent that wants to remain standing and are migrating voluntarily, edifying thorny problems, preoccupying the international imperialism in the current globalization, and insurmountable problems for Africa.

That international imperialism has only one purpose—to defend interests that are not African but prosaically their own interests. Africa must try to subtract those voracious appetites of colonial imperialism that exist on all sides, first in each of the internal forces of our countries and then between the forces of the international markets established since the late nineteenth century.

The Western imperialist powers deliberately prepared that intervention to simply use the situation as their usual traditional method of exploiting rich regions. That new intervention in Libya was the result of the Arab desert areas, where the irregularity is the rule, due to the rise of cereal prices, the widespread poverty of the people, with very low incomes from privileged sectors, linked to the vast oil resources of those countries in crisis, imposed by the U.S. policy of plunders and their NATO allies in the Middle East. In the framework of the colonial order that existed at the end of the Second World War, the victorious powers that founded the UN imposed the rules governing trade and the global economy. Not respecting any of the basic obligations before its creation, that Arab world of culture and predominantly Moslem religion, felt more humiliated by the establishment of fire and blood of a system that only encrypted the treasures of aristocratic minority in trillions of dollars.

The Western aggression against Gaddhafi put the detractor coalition of that operation named "Dawn of Odyssey" before its irresponsibility. The African Union stood out immediately by the name of its sovereignty, its independence, its unity, its territorial integrity, and its legislative rights, by reminding its historical opposition for the use of foreign international military actions in its continent; its committee was always in favor of a peaceful action, specific to an African solution that must be in accordance with our commitment for the respect of unity and territorial integrity; thus, also strongly denouncing their maneuver as regrettable, they regret that their rejection of that foreign military intervention on the African continent was not heard.

The Bolivarian Alliance for the Americas (ALBA) testified its concern by the Bolivian president Evo Morales, concerning the interests of the coalition to appropriate themselves oil from Libya through a resolution leading to the violations of human rights. For a continent that was in the same configuration as Asia thirty years ago, the moment is crucial, for the children of Africa. It is time that the interest of investors and their benefit in the unprecedented growth of the continent's natural resources truly profit African diversity, which first knew how to keep its generalizations. The path that leads to progress inspires us, nourishes our thinking, enriches our cultures, and is also a key asset for our development. The exclusively negative image that you made of our continent is systematically false. Africa is full of potential resources. We can no longer accept instability and conflicts that continue to plague our people with poverty, hunger, and disease without a good health and education system.

We Africans clearly know that there are so many unavoidable challenges to improve living conditions on the continent. But despite significant progress in the development, our problems cannot be solved by externally imposed solutions. Our development policy must now focus more on the indigenous people, both on the national and local levels, to overcome those challenges, not by the international community, no matter how well intentioned those solutions are. So, let's integrate all African communities in the elaboration and management of development programs for the creation of more effective and suitable civilizational projects—a culture followed by the diversity of our continent for its own development for millennia. Those ambitions are meeting African needs, which are sharing our continent.

All African states knew that the real reason for the war—that murdered civilians, women, and Libyan children and destabilized that country—was for France and its allies, a punishment for Gaddhafi, for making them lose US$500 million of taxes per year that Europe obliged African countries to pay on telephone conversations, even for communicating within the same African country, for the transition of voices on European satellites such as Intelsat; for Gaddhafi, the vase was full, concerning that system that generated interest in billions of U.S. dollars debt to the infinity, and to maintain the occult expropriation system in Africa; while an African communications satellite would have only cost US$400 million; but for the first time in the history of Africa, the company RASCOM was created by forty-five African countries in 1992 and just cost US$400 million, payable once.

The Regional African Satellite Communication Organization (RASCOM) is a Pan-African intergovernmental organization, with headquarters in Abidjan, responsible for defining the telecommunication services at low costs, based on the space technology in conjunction with telecommunication operators in its member countries. Before its creation, the price of the telephone from the West to Africa and vice versa was the most expensive in the world. US$300 million were put on the table in 2006 by the Libyan guide Gaddhafi. Those millions of U.S. dollars were destined for the sustainable development of telecommunications in Africa, after several consultations that resulted in the awareness of the leading role of telecommunications in the process of economic development, constituting a motivating factor for any investor.

Telecommunications could also drastically improve the quality of life through various development projects and raise the effectiveness level of productivity of all other sectors. In addition, US$50 million from the African Development Bank and US$27 million from the West African Development Bank were added to that amount to enable the first communication satellite to emerge in Africa, since December 26, 2007. Its mission is the universal coverage of the continent in multiple applications, such as radio broadcasting, television, telephony, telemedicine, and distance education. The first real revolution of modern Africa was therefore offered by Gaddhafi. Thanks to the WiMAX bridge system, a low-cost connection became available even in the rural areas across the continent. Meanwhile, Algeria, Angola, South Africa, and Nigeria got the opportunity to launch new satellites thanks to the technology transmitted to them by China and Russia.

In July 2010, a second African satellite was launched. And notably in 2020, a very first 100 percent African satellite would be expected to compete with the best in the world at a cost ten times lower; it would be built on African soil, precisely in Algeria. Would it be born, now that the first true revolutionary of the modern time of Africa is no more? There remains the question. The rage of France against Gaddhafi was also characterized by the initiative of his contribution for the financing and the total stability of the African federation. In the Libyan Central Bank, US$30 billion seized by Mr. Obama were scheduled for three flagship projects, with offices in various African countries—namely:

I) - On headquarters of the African Investment Bank in Sirte, Libya
II) - One head-office in Cameroon, precisely in Yaoundé, where an African Monetary Fund was to be created as soon as 2011 with a capital of US$42 billion to replace the International Monetary Fund, created initially to rebuild Europe, and secondly to ensure a smooth financial development in the world but which, for all its activities, has managed to put our entire African continent on its knees from its creation, with US$25 billion of capital only, and whose role was to guarantee the economic stability of the international monetary system (IMS) and to reduce poverty in the world has completely failed. And one office of an African Central Bank in Nigeria in Abuja, which was to signify the end of the domination of France on the CFA after fifty years on certain African countries and to issue the first African currency.

Those same Western countries that have forced African countries to move from public monopoly to privatization were unanimously rejected on December 16 and 17, 2010, in Yaoundé; by a greed qualified as a bad joke in lieu of a request asking if they could be part of our new African financial institution in sight; but the unanimity of the African countries was without ambiguity, specifying that that institution of the African Monetary Fund (AMF) was only for African countries. So will the financial independence and economic security of Africa see that day be born, to put an end to the multitude of currencies and forge a single African currency to promote trade integration between African states, significantly weakened by numerous currencies in circulation on the continent? I very much hope that the Twenty-Third Assembly of Heads of State and Government of the African Union, held in Malabo, Equatorial Guinea, on June 20 to 27, 2014, would continue the work of Gaddhafi in good and due form.

Those same countries of the Western coalition who were bombing Libya, all have bankruptcy problem in common and are afraid of that African institutions, which at its establishment, would prevent them from continuing to play the role of debt collectors; debt problems caused by their ancestors to keep the developing Africa countries under their financial control. It turns out that financially, the debt of France in the form of loans taken by the state, calculated according to the European Maastricht criteria, was amounted to €1,995.3 billion in the first quarter of 2014, approximately 94.5 percent of GDP. According to the National

Statistical Institute, in the second quarter of 2014, their debt officially exceeded €2,023.7 billion. The one of Italy was €2,120 billion, or 135.6 percent of GDP. The British government had already reached €1,795 billion, or 91.1 percent of GDP; and €2,139 billion for Germany, or 77.3 percent of GDP.

However, that level still remains very much higher than the criterion ceiling of the Stability and Growth Pact of 60 percent of GDP set by the EU treaties. These debts are to further increase in percentage of GDP far higher than the wealth produced by the economy of each government of these countries each year. Since, in the United States only, it already exceeded the threshold of US$36,000 billion, up to a specific date, reaching therefore a historical record for a population of 318,407,968 people at the time: or about US$114 million per inhabitant of the country. Their debt level reached will then be reactivated on March 16, 2015, and seeing billions adding to that debt each year, the ceiling of their debt looks less and less stable every day.

That failure in the absence of economic action of Western countries is the reason of different problems that prompted Berlusconi, Sarkozy, and the international community to slaughter the Libyan leader. But until now, after years in their assize court of vulgar thieves and the justice of deception, the undertaken efforts are not sufficient for them to emerge from their economic abysses, which only amount in billions of euros and only rise on the same accentuated rhythm as the time of Sarkozy; and not a single European country, or the United States, Japan, China, and other industrialized countries that do not have a problem with their debts in GDP. That increasing importance of their debts placed the sovereign states of Africa in the snap-hooks of those United States countries fraudsters and looters of the African continent wealth with their insolvable debts, which is holding the financial world execution in hostage.

The World Bank, which analyzes the economic outlook of Africa, reported according to the forecasts that the economic growth of Africa increased in 2014 by 4.6 percent and predicted a growth in 2015–16 of 5.2 percent of GDP, with a GDP per inhabitant of 2.1 percent in 2014 and 2.6 percent in 2015. This 4.6 percent of GDP of the region in 2014 is expected to grow at an annual rate of 5.3 percent in 2017 compared to 5.2 percent in 2015–16.

This rise in GDP, which generates more endogenous growth, is significantly higher than the average for developing countries by (3.9 percent), according to the economic forecasts of the United Nations, the African Development Bank, and the Organization for Economic Cooperation and Development (OECD). The prospects of that economic growth in Africa remain very favorable, with a population of 1.14 billion, but to maintain that growth, different African countries will have to face the many challenges for the total economic awakening of Africa, despite the unfortunate international economic condition. The mortgage of our young and poor African countries by public debts called load or burden by economists, frequently under the spotlight of problematic prospects numbering in billions of dollars that the World Bank and the International Monetary Fund (IMF) are not willing to deal with, is not a recent problem.

That debt accumulation is from savings and borrowing from various sources to the developing countries of sub-Saharan Africa, on which we limit the remarks. These elements are determining a representation of the development of African nations through time, and the only solution to deal with that debt issue to improve the living standards of its booming population is its cancellations, since we all know that the acceleration of the development of rich countries is largely due to the loan growth of young and poor countries of Africa for almost a century. Lenders devoted to very rigid acceptance preferential ratings provide loan terms and set the estimated interest rates at risky to borrowers. With these very high loan interest rates, loans are accrued in interest rates, which engaged our states in these loans paid for year after year. For that consequence of accumulation, states engaged become unable to repay their loans to national or international public institutions; even after their payment efforts, inscribed on the very long repayment terms to facilitate repayment of loans they cannot pay, but they agree to grant loans, and sometimes, the grant time could reach a period of forty years or more. That increasing acceleration of debt does not always make it possible to reach deadlines facing commitments rarely favorable to the borrower for repayment. After years of imagined deadlines to enable them to honor their commitments, these economist moneylenders are initiating a set of action procedures to penalize the borrower's defaults by recovering the loan balance on his assets. That debt then becomes a hindrance under the form of bad influence for the development of African states and absorbs a growing share of the government revenue, financially justifiable from the account of lenders. That transfer of our wealth to the major Western banks and international financial institutions prohibits all real and sustainable development of our countries to grow financially but allows these developed states to play a role of dominator with a powerful destabilizing mechanism on our countries forever subordinated by public debts and plunged our countries into an infernal spiral of a breathless context, ruining our natural resources with an increased rhythm of impoverishment of hundreds of millions of people by their world economic system of inequalities across the world.

These northern states and international financial institutions are using the debt to impose the same economic and financial logic to maintain African regions that however possess enormous wealth in poverty. That strategy of rich countries to subordinate and dominate poor countries to their dominant ideology is the consequence of their geopolitical or geostrategic choice.

These Western banks, which were looking for opportunities everywhere in the poor world, were overflowing with Eurodollars from the Marshall Plan to help rebuild Europe after the Second World War. On the other hand, they simply pushed the southern countries, particularly those of Africa especially in search for funds to finance their development, to borrow from them. Each of these northern state banks and international financial institutions had an interest for our countries to go into debt after gaining their independence in the "60s and 70s." We therefore will see that these debts, a derisory sum in the global finance, issued by the international financial institutions to the developing countries are the cause of suffering resulting to thirty thousand children dying every day across the world, which could be avoided if only they had access to adequate care, according to the United Nations Development Program (UNDP), which advocated change by helping developing countries by giving them knowledge, experiences, and resources and by working in collaboration with many other programs that their populations need to improve their lives. What's very surprising in this entire story is that the public debt of all African countries makes a total of less than US$700 billion. It totalizes US$2.8 trillion for all developing countries with about five billion individuals, comprising 85 percent of the world population, and US$60,000 billion in debt globally; that great difference in higher public debts in the West is so detrimental to Western countries and their economies; to me, it is obvious that the greed of all those countries that were bombarding Libya were aiming one thing—to get oxygen with the hope to continue plundering our resources to cure their economic apnea. For that fact, they need motives that they fabricate in their great UN offices and in the European community in Brussels. It is well said that to better manage, it is necessary to divide; since not very long ago, one of those great ideas, according to some, suddenly emerged.

In a conference organized to separate North Africa from the rest of black Africa, the European Union failed to destabilize and destroy the African Union by the creation of another union with some African countries. That union is called the Union for the Mediterranean (UFM), an initiative of Nicolas Sarkozy, former President of the French Republic.

That famous international intergovernmental organization, with regional vocation, was officially founded on July 13, 2008, and was to link Europe in partnership with the countries bordering the Mediterranean. All the then twenty-seven countries of the European Union were invited to this conference.

Let's specify that the European Union today has twenty-eight member states. A total of forty-three heads of state and government attended. Except the African Union was not among the guests and was not even informed of what so far, simply associating a few North African countries—namely, Algeria, Egypt, Morocco, Mauritania, and Tunisia; Sarkozy wanted therefore to favor a union than the other, which would have greatly harmed the credibility of the ruling African Union. That project rightly thought for the UFM was a very dangerous project in itself. Indeed, it would have not avoided the foreign policy outbreak, whether European or Mediterranean. We must, however, understand that the foreign policy of the EU has already been unveiled to the general public, and their empire policy is only sinking into a decline—a decline that took off during the famous Berlin Conference for the partition of Africa in 1884. So, it tries to sow mess here and there on essential topics of discord, subtly thought to work subversively in agreement on all, as the case of Libya and Ivory Coast. But to whom does it benefit? France, of course; the killed president Gaddhafi, assassinated by France very quickly understood that well-prepared and well-studied mixing of disorders that was looming on the horizon and that, insidiously willingly or by force. Thus, the assassinated president Gaddhafi, the main driving force of the African federation of that time and of all times, officially declined the invitation of the French president and categorically refused to go to France. With his strong belief in the progress of the African Union, the hand of that master was leading the African Union toward the United States of Africa.

Constituting a cultural, political, and economic project, which absolutely encompasses everything, this African Union, is proving to be very dangerous for the West. At the opening of the Arab summit in Tripoli, Muammar Gaddhafi was lucidly engaged in a veritable diatribe against the UFM. The former Libyan leader monopolized the speech by proclaiming, "We are members of the Arab League and also of the African Union, and we will in no way take the risk of dispersing our ranks." The UFM could jeopardize the mutual consent of the African Union and the Arab League by competing with the already existing organizations. To prevent that, he said, "If Europe wants to cooperate with us, let it do it with the Arab League, or the African Union. We do not accept that Europe deals with only one group of countries, meaning with solely those bordering the southern shore of the Mediterranean, as proposed by the Union for the Mediterranean project." Let our European partners understand that well, warned the former Libyan leader by adding, "We are neither famished nor dogs for them to throw us bones." He denounced the project of cooperation between the countries of both shores of the Mediterranean in front of the Algerian, Mauritanian, Tunisian, and Syrian presidents and the Moroccan prime minister.

The initiative of the division of Africa by our dear friend Sarkozy was strongly rejected by the deceased colonel Gaddhafi and at the same time by Europe. Traditionally, he was qualifying those economic projects promised to the countries of the southern Mediterranean as bait and a sort of humiliation for those countries. To enable the Arab countries to take a common position, Colonel Gaddhafi took the initiative to organize a mini summit in Tripoli, which unfortunately did not produce results on consultations with the leaders who were present, before the official proclamation of the UFM on July 13 in Paris. Colonel Gaddhafi was right because there was a divergence from that first meeting among countries of the southern shore; and the participation of Israel in the UFM, particular sparked clarifications, given the fragile relations between Israel and Arab countries. I wonder why our prominent leaders who say they're competent did not use their intelligence; and for that reason could not immediately distinguish that particularly sensitive subject and officially give their opinion on things well parceled out by France to keep Africa in slavery. You're very unbelievable and very remarkable, since your endless conversations concerning your policies of deception do not change. And the agreements that have been reached between you leaders are useless. Especially if it concerns the prodigals of France, they do not necessarily reflect the reality. For France, Algeria and Libya represent little on the chessboard of the world. Since it is on its decline, its last roar is to tear down the whole of Africa, to shift its era in the global issues to meet tomorrow's planetary challenges.

I wish that our African presidents have the goodwill to attentively lend a listening ear and learn from the gigantic intelligent work done by Colonel Gaddhafi in the sense of history. With his arrogant neighbor Abdelaziz Bouteflika, where oil is at the highest level, Algeria has enormous energy resources; and in 2013, it was prognosticated to have a monetary reserve of $224.1 billion by the IMF, which was forecasting a growth in 2014 of 4.3 percent, and in 2015, 4.1 percent.

But Bouteflika was not realizing that there would not always be a forest behind the tree, not having the policy of constructive ideas, but the style of the old perpetual colonialism of France and the imperialist international community, practicing hatred toward the rich African countries by demonstrating their origins, will declare him the next war after Libya, to the point that he narrowly escaped because he had also suspended the question of his presence at the summit, which should launch the Union for the Mediterranean.

Following a meeting between Nicolas Sarkozy and his Algerian counterpart, President Bouteflika finally indicated that he would be present in Paris. The policy of scheme of the imperialist international community is more and more interested in misinformation campaigns full of evil. Sometimes it announces an extremely important central role that played an African country around the negotiating table, if only that suits them; sometimes it dismembers a country in pieces by bombs because it dared take a position or expressed its interest to truly implement development projects and safeguard its resources.

Africa can only advance if our relations are warm and renewed with the intellectuals of our entire continent. With everything that is happening before our eyes, I believe it is time to expel that style of old colonialism, exercising less and less respect for human rights. The hunt of money makes us all lose respect in the eyes of the universe and does not stop humbling us. We need a bit of pragmatism because we know that power is money. This style of old colonialism is making fun of us. We cannot trust it because it has not yet turned the black pages of its history of pleasing the master, that it delicately lets us know it.

Many concealed traps are always strained for us by the children politician leaders of that old style of colonialism. A good efficient head of state must be clear-sighted, thoughtful, and proud. Gaddhafi met all these criteria and reincarnated Pan-Africanism. He was saying aloud what several African head of states could not dare say and what they were to reincarnate. The worst is that his thoughts and actions were what many heads of state were thinking and saying in a low voice all along. It is a cruel irony but just. I remind you that this is a true lesson in diplomacy, knowing that the sacred Nicolas Sarkozy was indeed in a good school of racist from the eighteenth to the nineteenth century. And he reserved us a lot of slavery service, with the same racist terms of inequality between the African people and the rest of the world, particularly the white, who still considers himself the most advanced and civilized than the rest. The investment of Gaddhafi in several African countries really proves that that man had always loved the black continent. The incarnation of his dignity is the very symbol of a certain idea of Africans for Africa. For fourteen years, the European

Union, the United States, the IMF, and the World Bank uselessly stripped our countries.

A simple symbolic gesture of a small US$300 million of Gaddhafi was able to put an end to the agony of unnecessary begging the alleged Western benefactors practicing servile exploitation of master. That kind of symbol worthy of Africa is what the black continent must embody. His gesture, which we all acclaimed, changed the lives of an entire continent for his Pan-African convictions, his fight against imperialism, and his desire to liberate Africa, captivated without embarrassment, with physical and mental hindrance, preventing our countries to break freed from their chains and become emancipated since time immemorial. He, this time, suffered an international terrorist aggression, which caused his death in Sirte, Libya, on October 20, 2011.

But whatever the West and its imperialist international community do, he will always remain in the hearts of almost all Africans as a generous and humanist man. The theory of the moral feelings of the imperialist international community is described on the origin of its individualistic capacity, a disinterested character of certain judgments of human nature, which is only asserts through selfishness and interest. It must be said that each of us possesses an inner self within oneself; an inner-self testimony, a judgment capable of rising beyond its own passions and interests to constitute oneself in life, and capable of condemning one's approbation or the moral disapproval of oneself, since we do not ignore the judgment of our own actions; which means to my knowledge, a superego, one of the three elements of the psychic structure with the id and the ego; as one of the three instances of personality; it exercises censorship against the instinctive impulses condemned by society; our inner self is a moral conception of good and evil and a judicial capacity able to reward or punish all the psychic character of our psyche. Here, the synthesis of my ideas represents the disappointment of time in the sense of empathy that man faces. It is revealed by events in time without requiring putting ourselves in the place of the other. Distinct from any global system of coherent comprehension in the field of knowledge, it contains rules of efficiency and inefficiency of man who dies in time without taking time to consider his neighbor. My thought is based on the principle of a wise man as the head of the family who agrees with time to demonstrate the same wise principle of time in the management of an empire of knowledge by the laws of nature that govern time.

With an ability to first know and understand oneself before knowing or understanding others, that ability requires us to put ourselves in the place of others, in the place of a humble being who in its actions, must take into account the empathy of others in empathy—a sympathy in the sense of empathy, which occupies a central place in the field of common knowledge, of the one allowing the control of passions and which founded the rules of the system of peace, freedom, and justice.

In the international community, the United Nations is an organization guarding the general interest, governing fair rules, and not of the regal interest attached to royalty. A president's right of grace is to protect his citizens against injustices and violences from another state by justice. Logically, the foundations of the international laws were instituted by the natural law. That is why the American Society of International Law (ASIL), an educational organization founded in 1906, with headquarters in Washington, was mandated by the United States Congress to study the international law in 1950.

It is for the United Nations to implement the maintenance and relations of these international laws. The United Nations cannot give itself the right to function as a police, especially involving economic intervention, to guarantee the productivity of wealth to any state. The United Nations comparative measure described that crisis as a nation wishing to end the reign of its tyrant; so was the situation in Libya described; the first African country according to the criterion of human development index by the French media and very little mediatic light resulted in an underexposure, to distinguish the impact of its policies and standards of living in that country, was generally too dark and had no details in the shadows.

The statement of Mr. Alain Juppe, the former foreign minister of France, before the vote on the desire for democracy in the Arab nations was saying, "It was good news for all of us, inviting the Security Council to support that evolution with confidence to help each nation to build its future," referring to Gaddafi's actions as "criminal folly;" his statement was disgusting, because of the other major Western powers, France has uncommonly distinguished itself as historically maintaining a closer relationship with the Arab states. He was masking the dark intentions of the former president Sarkozy and France, already installed in the Arab world, praising King Mohammed VI of Morocco, like one of those revolutionary militants. Not saying anything about the bloody repression taking place in Bahrain and in Yemen, the former French foreign minister was contributing to strengthen the disastrous image of France. I would like to remind him that he was several times the minister of budget, foreign affairs, ecology, and defense, and the prime minister from 1995 to 1997.

During that time, he did nothing for democracy in African countries than that systematic plundering of our resources, ardently fought since then by the Libyan leader Gaddhafi. And it was the declaration of his ineligibility in politics that forced him to quit his parliamentary duties in 2004 with a ten-year sentence, reduced on appeal to one year of ineligibility, before he became the minister of foreign and European affairs to replace the resigning Michele Alliot-Marie, also named the French FBI, in intelligence matters, and who chaired the merger of the Central Directorate of General Information (CDGI); informing the government on any movement affecting the state within the Central Directorate of Internal Intelligence (CDII); an intelligence service of the Interior Ministry of French, within the Directorate General of the National Police, and the Directorate for Territorial Surveillance (DTS) in charge of counter-espionage in France, founded on July 1, 2008. As appointed minister of interior on May 18, 2007, she faced contestation created by her reforms, attracting the reservations of the Commission nationale de l'informatique et des libertes (CNIL)-the National information science and Liberties Commission.

For Nicolas Sarkozy, those interventions were a disavowal for observers toward the very poor management of a ministry he himself led for four years. Michele Allot-Marie was the one who defended the imposition of very restrictive criteria for the implementation of universal competence in France before the Law Commission of the National Assembly in spring 2010. It was therefore intentionally that the French Coalition for the International Criminal Court (FCICC) launched a campaign for the adoption of a bill, making possible the prosecution and the trial in France of those presumed accused perpetrators of international crimes (war crimes, crimes against humanity, and genocide) and leading the French Coalition for the International Criminal Court FCICC to remain on the sidelines of the globalization and the fight against impunity of dictators and torturers. That bill was voted in accordance. She took office as the minister of state and minister of justice and freedoms, appointed on June 24, 2009. She finally was appointed minister of state and minister of foreign and European affairs on November 14, 2010.

Three days before the fall of Zine el-Abidine Ben Ali, she proposed a violent universe of the French power in the midst of the Tunisian revolution, claiming that the Tunisian police should use the know-how methods of the French security forces to solve that type of safety situations during demonstrations and discord, and to support the Ben Ali regime. Indeed, that proposal was directed to both countries, Algeria and Tunisia, as part of the cooperation of France. Criticized by French journalists, those of the whole world, and by the parliamentarians' left-wing, she asserted that her comments were out of context. The "regrets" of Frederic Mitterrand, the minister of culture of that period, presented in a letter published on January 23, 2011, were in relation to the support already given to the power of Zine El-Abidine Ben Ali and his opinion qualifying that country to not be an "unambiguous dictatorship" followed in the same week.

Sometime later, Francois Fillon, the French prime minister of that period, admitted that as the minister of foreign affairs, she authorized the delivery of tear gas to the Tunisian police. On January 12, she herself made that authorization final. But the delay of the French customs awaiting a confirmation before delivery did that, it was finally canceled on January 18, 2011, by the minister, four days after Ben Ali f led. The revelations of the newspaper called *Le Canard Enchainé* asserted that she spent her holidays of late 2010 in Tunisia, while the demonstrations was going on for several weeks.

Finally, it was the series of details on those holidays, unveiled by the weekly newspaper in its successive editions that nourished controversy. We know that two trips were made by Patrick Ollier, the companion of Michele Alliot-Marie, and her parents, in the private jet of a certain man in business with the relatives of Ben Ali, by the name of Aziz Miled, and that a real estate acquisition was concluded by the parents of Michele Alliot-Marie and that businessman. A *Mediapart* newspaper, designating a company having started and practicing in a sector of unique activity on the Web as "pure player type," revealed that during her holidays, she had a brief telephone conversation with the former president Ben Ali. She asserted however that, repeating lies does not make them truth, denouncing an outrageous campaign waged against her. But in her successive replies, the opposition and a part of the press detected contradictions revealing her proximity to the former Tunisian regime and demanded her resignation, which she refused many times, including those of the president and prime minister. Finally, she handed over her resignation letter to the president on February 27, 2011. Her leaving the government became inevitable, because her voice as chief of diplomacy became inaudible, declared the former prime minister Francois Fillon.

It was a government reshuffle for the reorganization of the Ministry of Foreign Affairs that Nicolas Sarkozy appointed Alain Juppe in that ministry on February 27, 2011, without mentioning the name of his predecessor, Michele Alliot-Marie. I would say that it was the same story for Alain Juppe, who was indicted for breach of trust, concealment, abuse of social property, of corporate assets, and illegal taking of interest in 1998. Considered a key element of an occult financing system, financed by the City Hall of Paris from 1983 to 1995, his personal secretary at the *Rassemblement pour la République* [RPR], who joined the Chiraquian party in 1977, was taken in charge by the Ségur group between 1989 and 1990, and was paid around €21,300 by the real estate company eager to quickly receive public contracts, and finally, was also paid by the city of Paris in exchange for good favors. That occult banker of the black box of the RPR was Mrs. Louise-Yvonne Casetta. She was also the former assistant to the executive director. She acknowledged having served as link between the treasurers and executive directors, financers, and corporate directors. But she quickly added that it was on the orders of politicians.

Jacques Chirac, who was the direct supervisor of Juppe, enjoyed immunity as president of the republic throughout that period of illegal activity; because he had knowledge of the rigged market deals and the occult role of "companies' donations," which the former treasurer Louise-Yvonne Casetta of the black box of RPR was playing, when he was the president of the RPR. She also worked with Alain Juppe when he was appointed to the directorate general of the RPR.

She was accused by a witness, the former commercial director of Mazotti Construction Company, on October 18, 2001. The president of the republic came to her aid on November 13, 2001, followed by a conviction on appeal of six months in prison with suspended sentence on December 19, 2001. At the trial of Ile-de-France contracts on May 17, 2005, she denounced the cowardice of the RPR leaders by complaining that she was abandoned by the leaders of the Chiraquian party in the court of Paris.

In her role as an executor, she denied any involvement in that huge corruption case, with groan in her voice, accompanied by a crisis of tears on her face, saying that she never contacted a company, never was awarded a contract, and was never informed of the high school markets by denouncing the politicians above her, to whom she rendered account. Those politicians— treasurers, national and general secretaries—who were giving orders were Jacques Boyon, Jacques Oudin, and Robert Galley, known as the three former treasurers of the RPR. Jacques Toubon, a former secretary general of the RPR from 1984 to 1988, whom Alain Juppe succeeded from 1988 to November 1994, was not judged in that trial. Apart from the three former treasurers heard as witnesses, Jacques Toubon was never prosecuted. For the fictitious jobs of the RPR, the conviction of Ms. Louise-Yvonne Casetta was confirmed on September 22, 2005, by the court of cassation. The closure of that case, declaring the last appeal filed by the former intendant of the RPR was inadmissible and her ten months in prison with suspended sentence, indirectly benefiting Alain Juppe, the former prime minister, who in that same case was sentenced to fourteen months in prison with suspended sentence and one year of ineligibility for taking illegal interest in December 2004 by the Appeal Court of Versailles. In the case of rigged markets of public high schools in Ile-de-France, she was sentenced to pay a fine of €10,000 and twenty months in prison with suspended sentence on October 26, 2005, followed by an aggravated sentence on appeal for the emissaries of Lycees de l'Ile-de-France in February 2007.

She was prosecuted for complicity and concealment, corruption and twice sentenced to prison with suspended sentences in the RPR trials as officially the secretary from 1984 to 1987 and as an intendant from 1988 to 1996. After being retrial on appeal, the occult treasurer of the RPR received a two-year suspended sentence and a €10,000 fine on February 27, 2007. That occult system of officially financing political parties, established by the longstanding leaders of RPR, continuing to circumvent the law from 1988, was put in evidence by the opening of an investigation led by the Judge Patrick Desmure in 1996.

That same year, a first law was adopted under a government led by Jacques Chirac. But under the Balladur government in 1995, the most recent promulgated law, which could not change things with a magic wand, was the one that predicted Alain Juppe's ineligibility as a member of the party. In a report handed over to the judge on March 25, 1999, investigators of the judicial police concluded that, in their discoveries, the seized documents made them to presume the knowledge of a mechanism of malpractices committed for the benefit of the RPR. That criminal system, organized with the approval of its governing bodies, incriminated its president Jacques Chirac and its secretary general. On June 30, 1999, the Court of Cassation validated most of the investigation of Judge Desmure, and the delay strategy chosen by Alain Juppe ended in failure.

Since August 21, 1998, as I already mentioned above, Alain Juppe, a close associate of Jacques Chirac from 1976 and his deputy in charge of finance at the mayor's office of Paris from 1983 to 1995, was indicted in the investigation on the financing of the RPR. The judicial calendar that would hamper his political ambitions caught him after delaying the proceedings, risking him a court appearance. Living a battery of indictments since 1998, he was finally pursued in

June 2002, presiding (l'Union pour un mouvement populaire UPM) from 2002 to 2004, and at the same time, presiding the (Rassemblement pour la Republique RPR) from 1994 to 1997. He would be the main defendant in the course of the next few years of a trial in the criminal court of Nanterre (Hauts-de-Seine) on the financing of the RPR.

But before that, he was continually involved in the establishment of that practice for years, where he held senior positions within the Gaullist Party; and through which, at a time from 1988 to 1995, dozens of RPR executives were fictitiously employed by the city of Paris. Alain Juppe was facing charges of aggravated breach of trust in the framework of fictitious jobs in the Paris City Hall, misappropriation of public funds, complicity and concealment, abuse of trust, taking of illegal interest, and abuse of corporate assets. Already, on November 17, 2002, he was the leader of (l'Union pour un mouvement populaire UMP). Exercising his power, he will commit a lot of blunders that he would recognize. He admitted having made a mistake, by loudly protesting against the support of the transport minister of the UPM Gilles de Robien, brought to Christian Blanc, and by judging unacceptable the candidate of the UDF to the partial legislative of the department of Yvelines on December 10, 2002. Also, in 2002, with the second political party listed to the right of the political spectrum that Jacques Chirac founded on November 17, 2002, Alain Juppe entered into a rivalry with Nicolas Sarkozy three weeks after its official birth. The UPM, l'Union pour un mouvement populaire, whose initials were inherited from l'Union pour la majorite presidentielle of the early 2000s, with the aim of gathering the Gaullist, centrist, liberal, and conservative French tendencies, supported the governments appointed by former Pres. Jacques Chirac from 2002 to 2007, after accomplishing its purpose of supporting his presidential candidacy, in fusion with the Rassemblement pour la Republique (RPR), created by Jacques Chirac on December 5, 1976. From May 17, 1995, to May 16, 2007, Jacques Chirac was the twenty-second president of the French Republic. After the investiture of Nicolas Sarkozy from 2007 to 2012, the former president of the republic left the presidential palace on May 16, 2007. He was put in withdrawal because of the state of his health on December 9, 2010, after serving on the Constitutional Council as the former president of the Republic and ex officio member. His legal troubles in connection with the case of fictitious jobs in the municipality of Paris, after investigation, estimated his guilt and sentenced him to two years in prison with suspended sentence in 2011.

Well, now let's get back to the rivalry between Alain Juppe and Nicolas Sarkozy. Facing that rivalry of the former interior minister Nicolas Sarkozy, appointed from 2002, openly criticizing the president of the UPM without naming him, he was openly denouncing his sectarianism repeatedly.

Consequently to that closure of Alain Juppe, Nicolas Sarkozy could not contain his anger and did not prevent himself from showing his annoyance in front of the elected UPM politicians of Paris, gathered in Enghien-les-Bains (Val d'Oise), saying that it is only the weak that deprive themselves of the skills of others by closing themselves and that the division resulting from sectarianism will not satisfy any ambition. He continued by adding that he did not appreciate that on November 17, 2002, the day of the founding congress of the UPM, none of the tenors of the UPM were invited, including himself, to speak at the podium, consequently to the closure of Alain Juppe, justifying himself for not wanting to create chapels within the UPM. Few days earlier, Alain Juppe angered the minister of interior with his total refusal to appoint Brice Hortefeux, his closest collaborator, in the team of deputy secretaries-general of the UPM. Also, before the press, the former minister of interior indicated that upon his arrival in the convention hall, the new president of the UPM, by pushing the sound system, was trying to mess up his sound; but the new president of the UPM, not letting anything appear then, even claimed that he appreciated the efficiency of Nicolas Sarkozy in the matter of security on several occasions.

Those mistakes prompted by the words of Alain Juppe against one of his ministers and Gilles de Robien of the Union for French Democracy (UFD), minister for transport, caused many reactions. To calm down the spirits in the quarrel aroused by the words of Alain Juppe, Jean-Pierre Raffarin had to rise to the crenel, and as a call to order, the former head of government in Enghien-les-Bains exclaimed that, the unions that are made by special interest are not durable and that basically, the union is built and deserved. But it took the intervention of several members of the UPM, even in the entourage of the former president of the republic, to assert that there was no problem between the two tenors of the majority and in the entire government, even if the confrontation between the two men was inevitable. For the entire government to be on the same wavelength, he reminded everyone that the UPM, which was just especially seeing the day under the leadership of Alain Juppe, had allowed a second term to the tenant of the presidential palace. Therefore, it was important for everyone to focus on the essential missions entrusted by the French, six months ago to be honored with respect and rigor and not give importance to confrontations than what already exists. Similarly, man was trying to relieve the pressure of a catastrophic assessment, caused by the scheduled crushing of its partners in the new UMP, but Alain Juppe doubly lost by his excessive stiffness and was punished once again at the first test by the fiasco of his authoritarian behavior, clumsy and even more disturbing for the majority of the UMP and UFD.

The annoyance hindering the political ambitions of Alain Juppe by legal affairs continued its judicial calendar for the illegal taking of interests. The president of the UMP, who was to be judged, wanted the prosecution on May 7, 2003, in a trial that could take place in November 2003, preconizing the abandonment of a part of the charges; pursued since 1998 in this case for the existence of an occult care system of permanent salaries set up by the then president of the UMP Gaullist party, it was unveiled at the end of the investigation on the financing of the former RPR. The referral to the criminal court of Alain Juppe was required by Bernard Pages, the public prosecutor of Nanterre (Hauts-de-Seine), on Monday, May 5. In that case, the Gaullist Party officials received occult salaries from companies and from the city of Paris between 1988 and 1995, when Alain Juppe was responsible for finance as the deputy of Jacques Chirac at the Paris City Council and secretary-general of the RPR.

On the offenses of illegal acquisition of interest, committed to the prejudice of the municipality of Paris, the appearance of the former prime minister offered conditions. The prosecutor advocated abandoning prosecutions for breach of trust, concealment and abuse of corporate assets, considering the lack of evidence establishing the knowledge of the fraudulent scheme set up for the benefit of the former RPR and the former prime minister. On that recommendation, obtaining a dismissal on that part of the file might be possible if Alain Philibeaux, the investigating judge, follows those requisitions.

On the other hand, if the investigation established evidence, the prosecutor would order the prosecution of Alain Juppe. For offenses committed, the referral order leading to the appearance of several former Gaullist leaders to the justice will be signed in the coming days to allow the trial to be held in November. Alain Juppe became the interim president of the RPR during the presidential election of Jacques Chirac on November 4, 1994, then mayor of Paris. The new president Jacques Chirac elected to the supreme office on May 17, 1995, definitely left his post of president of the RPR to Alain Juppe and appointed him prime minister of his government on the same day of his inauguration at the Elysee Palace, the official residence of the French president in Paris since 1870. After having long relied on the stagnation of the procedure, Alain Juppe changed his tactics in 2002, following the reelection of Jacques Chirac, again invested in the Elysee Palace on May 16, 2002. He had at that time, wished the acceleration of the process for reasons related to his political agenda, hoping at best that a trial will offer him the opportunity to appeal a conviction in 2004, when his term as head of the UPM since 2002 will end, and hoping to be done with his legal troubles by then to present himself in 2007 as a presidential candidate.

So far, Yves Bot, appointed in October 2002 at the head of the prosecutor's office of Paris, and Patrick Desmure, the examining magistrate, promoted prosecutor of Chartres (Eure-et-Loir), considered that the requisitions of the prosecutor of Nanterre, dismissing some accusations brought against him, are against the position adopted during the investigation by their predecessors; these accusations declared that Alain Juppe was well aware of an uncovered system in his capacity as general secretary of RPR.

He challenged the reality of such a system during his interrogation in November 1999 before the investigating judge Desmure by saying, "I was not unaware of these practices, because I was not invested in the daily management of the movement," "asserting that he was unaware of the existence of fictitious jobs and that his task was essentially political in the RPR.

In addition, Jacques Boyon and Robert Galley, treasurers of the RPR, and twenty-five people, prosecuted for concealment and complicity in abuse of property and breach of trust, the prosecutor advocated the referral before the court. For breach of trust and concealment, Patrick Stefanini, closed to Alain

Juppe, the lawsuits was dropped; but for unlawful taking of interest, suspected of having benefited from a fictitious job at the general inspection of the city of Paris in the 1990s, the proceedings would be postponed. At the time of facts, when Jacques Chirac was the mayor of Paris and president of the RPR, the file on the financing of the former RPR, the leader of the Gaullist party was also aware of the system of the provision of personnel at the opening of the investigation in 1996, and that situation led to his direct questioning; and on those facts likely to be imputed, Judge Desmure declared himself incompetent to investigate the case of Jacques Chirac on April 15, 1999, in view of his presidential immunity. At the time of that finding, a file expressly targeting the president was opened by Judge Philibeaux on December 12, 2002, stating that he should be indicted when he leaves the Elysee Palace. Thus, the referral order was signed by Judge Alain Philibeaux, the successor of Judge Patrick Desmure, sending Alain Juppe, former prime minister, Jacques Boyon and Robert Galley, two former RPR treasurers before the court, in the case of the alleged fictitious jobs of RPR and for illegal taking of interest, along with twenty-six other persons, mostly entrepreneurs. Addressing that last judicial taking of position rather favorable, the mayor of Bordeaux was risking a fine of €75,000, a sentence of five years' imprisonment, and a penalty of ineligibility. Apart from the criticism of Judge Philibeaux to the RPR former leader, the judge declared that in what constituted an illegal taking of interest, Alain Juppe was aware of the availability of employees of the city as the former director of finance of the city of Paris. Nevertheless, he estimated that the prosecutor's office of Nanterre could not allow imputing the disposal of RPR president for the employees of private companies by the seven years of instruction and decided to abandon half of the proceedings against Alain Juppe in a trial in the autumn. So instead of explaining himself for thirty people paid by third parties, he will only explain himself for a dozen of agents who worked in the RPR, letting the majority of his bodyguards escape pursuit. On Friday, January 30, 2004, after a conditional eighteen-month suspended prison sentence for illegal taking of interest, Alain Juppe, the president of the UPM, appealed, resulting in an automatic suspension of his eligibility for the conviction of the criminal court of Nanterre. And the inscription of his conviction on the criminal record was clearly excluded by Katherine Pierce, the presiding judge, having as effect to automatically dismiss the ten years of his ineligibility. By making himself guilty of illegal taking of interest in the case of fictitious jobs of the RPR, the court in its judgment wrote in a severe tone ensuring particularly that Alain Juppe deceived the confidence of the sovereign French people, contrary to the general will expressed by the law and unbearable to the social body.

Invested in a public elective mandate, the nature of the acts he committed was unanimous to judges. But he announced that he would appeal the decision of that conviction through Francis Szpiner, his lawyer, who was to intervene formally within ten days. By attacking the justice, the lawyer described the conviction as wanting to put itself above politics and eliminate his client from the political life, which was censurable and unfair in a case whose elements were questionable. He was accused of having covered the remuneration of seven people who were actually working for his party but paid by the city, in that case of a French politician of fifty-eight years old.

He was interrogated as the one who incited the regularization of that occult system of financing, a situation that everyone knew in the world of French politicians. At his trial, he denied everything and reiterated that he was only made aware of those practices on October 7, 2003, and that he was at no time informed of fictitious jobs before 1993. He said, with an emotionless face that when he became aware of that situation, he immediately ordered its end. After the investigation, the judge estimated his culpability and said that criminal offenses were likely to be imputed.

So Jacques Chirac was still dreaming of whitewashing his friend by the court of appeal by the end of that year or early coming year, but with the severity that the judges' showed at the first trial, that former Giscardian was still raising doubts among the Chiracquians. And by a relationship of trust established between them, the Elysee still needed him for the presidency of the UPM, and not being able to say no, he decided to obey to render that last service to his chief Jacques Chirac. Convinced by the head of state, his favorite son remained officially in command to prepare the succession, because he was not seeing how to replace him and do without that centerpiece key device in the middle of the electoral campaign.

He said, as long as the court of appeal has not decided, I will not throw out the sponge. At that verdict of Nanterre, many UPM parliamentarians had tears in their eyes with this statement: "I fell as if the sky fell on my head." For long minutes, they applauded him and believed that with dignity, the mayor of Bordeaux had just said farewell.

Announcing that in his case, justice was heavier compared to so many others but that he relied on the wisdom of the court of appeal as a private citizen, because the law must be applied to everyone and does not seek to pity anyone, he said; even being cruelly condemned for violating the will of the sovereign French people by the judges of Nanterre and suffering from not being loved by that moral lesson.

But in the case of the trial of fictitious jobs of the RPR, which sentenced Alain Juppe on January 30, 2004, to eighteen months of suspended sentence for illegal taking of interest and to the automatic penalty of ten years of ineligibility by the judges of Nanterre, the former finance assistant of the city of Paris proposed to repay €1.2 million to the mayor of Paris. On that topic, the spokesman of the mayor expressed himself by these words: "It is not appropriate to change the situation between the judgment of first instance and the appeal." He asked for that refund to the city hall in exchange for the withdrawing his civil suit, his which was refused by Dominique Perben, "the Minister of Justice keeper of the Seals," asserting that there is no study that could allow Alain Juppe to be exempted from punishment, therefore, to be ineligible for such refund to the chancellery. This being said, he would be retried from October 13 to 29 before the Versailles Court of Appeal, including six other people on appeal for their sentences. But clenching on his positions, the former prime minister repeated in the court of appeal that he played no role in the provision of agents of the city of Paris, in all tones almost detached. He said, "But on me, I am ready to take all the sins of Israel, and not the criminal responsibility; punish me because I was the nigger of Jacques Chirac from 1976 to 1986, and perhaps even beyond," in an almost joking tone by insinuating that, since he wrote dozens of speeches for Jacques Chirac without keeping any trace, his work could pass for a fictitious job. In any case, it was not for that, that the charges of the former head of the UPM will drop.

On December 1, 2004, Alain Juppe was convicted of illegal taking of interest in the Versailles Court of Appeal to fourteen-month suspended prison sentence and an additional penalty of one year of ineligibility and forced to resign from his mandate as mayor of Bordeaux and president of his UPM but may come back to run for the 2007 presidential election. However, it was inferior to the one pronounced on January 30—namely, eighteen-month suspended sentence and ten years of ineligibility—by the Correctional Court of Nanterre.

The accusers specified by testifying that a traffic of influence was established for the secret commissions requiring 2 percent of the received contracts to officially help the political parties through occult financing.

Bribes in exchange for obtaining the markets from the mayor of Paris were received in cash, by the treasury of the black box as a golden rule at the time, called commercial expenses or "Perfume the dog." They added that the president knew that intention of scam and "donations" of companies within the state. In that operation of the system of 2 percent of the contract amounts that companies were to retrocede to parties, the sharing was 1.2 percent for the RPR and its Republican Party ally PR, and 0.8 percent for the Socialist Party-PS. In the 1990s, that corruption pact was linking the main political parties to big companies and entrepreneurs who had to pay a commission to political parties represented in the regional council to win public construction or renovation contracts.

In that case of fictitious jobs of the Paris City Hall within the Rassemblement Pour la Republique (RPR), ancestor of the UPM, today the main parliamentary opposition party, he was first deprived of the presidency of the UPM and his duties as the mayor of Bordeaux, deputy and president of the urban community. Alain Juppe suffered a shame and humiliation engraved on his skin as a politician, undermining the entire French political class. The court particularly considered that, in the quest of human means, appearing necessary to him for the action of RPR, he deliberately chose certain efficiency by resorting to illegal arrangements.

Did Alain Juppe, appointed by that plague that seemed to be Mr. Sarkozy, already had the ability to properly manage international affairs without deliberately making use of illegal arrangements? He who pleaded for an intervention by the international community in Libya, voted on March 17, 2011, by the United Nations Security Council, for the urgent protection of civilians against the alleged violence committed by the troops of Muammar Gaddhafi?

The accreditation of that decision of Nicolas Sarkozy and his foreign minister remains to be reviewed, knowing that his foreign minister has already deceived the confidence of the sovereign people in France.

In the case of Gaddhafi, Alain Juppe, the former French defense minister, began with misleading statements saying that he wanted to see the last moments of the Libyan head of state Muammar Gaddhafi. He called for sanctions by a hardening voice of all kinds and did not exclude a closure of the airspace or even stop the purchase of oil, all this against the Libyan regime; this was because Muammar Gaddhafi refused to do business with France.

To deceive the international community, he forged a sordid story against the Libyan leader, saying that he was shooting on his people with heavy weapons and by evoking the UN's responsibility to protect any population in danger and by taking a very clear position for the fall of Gaddhafi. It is terrible to know what jealousy can make the jealous people do; naturally, it was unacceptable to procure the property of the other. In that case, there was another case hidden behind those allegations; the Libyan oil was the cause. The France of Nicolas Sarkozy and his foreign minister Alain Juppe concocted a reorganization program and decided on a strategy against the regime of Muammar Gaddhafi, and already sequences were making teeth grind; since in the Belgian capital, the European Council devoted a meeting concerning Libya. But Alain Juppe, as former French foreign minister already in the Belgian capital with his European counterparts, was not present at the meeting held at the Elysee Palace. For him, one thing was clear: he was wishing with open heart that Gaddhafi, the Libyan head of state, live his last moments; the one who had trouble working with Nicolas Sarkozy found himself rallied by the Elysee Palace strategy of scheme concerning the crisis in Libya. They legitimized the Libyan National Transitional Council (NTC) after a meeting held at the Elysee Palace, against the interests of the one whom they called dictator Gaddhafi, while validating the principle of targeted air strikes as a diplomatic sequence played in solo by the Elysee. The game was played in that part of Africa, because they were everywhere in Africa as ants. Another protagonist entered in that unhealthy game—the Algerian Jew Bernard-Henri Levy, the controversial looter of the precious African woods operating in Cameroon, Ivory Coast, and Gabon, with the family import company by the named of Becob, who earned its billions by slave labor of Africans. This gentleman hid very troublesome affairs of his family company, until Forests Monitor, a leading British NGO specialized in the fight against deforestation put its nose in his business in June 2000.

Mandated to investigate the impact of deforestation activities in Africa, the Inter Youth Association Committee for the Environment was going to conduct investigations against European forestry companies on the local environment and its impact on the population. In Gabon, the study was focused on three representative operating sites, but it was the Mboumi site—where the Societe de la Haute Mondah (SHM) operated—that interested them.

The group of the Levy family exploited the concession of 170,000 hectares of land from 1983 to 1997 via Interwood, subsidiary of Becob, and mainly with some two hundred Gabonese employees. Workers of that forestry exploitation were observed by that NGO for several weeks, discussing the conditions of their work with them. That study encompassing all of Central Africa produced a damning report, describing the sanitary conditions in that project as deplorable. Bernard-Henri Levy—the African Jew, who called himself a champion of human rights and selfproclaimed friend of black Africa—was on the contrary, a man enjoying the deprivation of civil rights, and his crimes committed by his capitalist state were severely unveiled by an extremely critical report under the weight of his faults. Contrary to what was known of him, he was a two-headed snake.

His reaction was to overthrow those who accused him by denouncing anti-Semitism. That kind of ridiculous pedant no longer works today, my dear. Bernard Henri-Levy stole all precious African timber by causing deforestation in those countries, leaving their inhabitants without wood and enriching himself by billions before selling Becob, estimated for €120 million at that time, to the Pinault group.

Under the aegis of newspapers led by his faithful friends, he published articles of disinformation with the connivance of Sarkozy and his government members. He would have by all means, convinced Wade to invite Gaddhafi to quit power and go and help his friends in the NTC in Libya. Not neglecting his interests, he converged with his departure, interested in the Libyan oil than the fate of Gaddhafi's compatriots. Belonging to a nation condemned by the law of disinheritance, he was at the source of the diplomatic turn of the international community and was at the heart of the recognition of the National Transitional Council by Nicolas Sarkozy. His trip to Libya had one goal—to meet the opponents of Gaddhafi regime—and it was after that trip that he found himself a few days later face-to-face with the former French president at the Elysee Palace, with the company of the Libyan National Transitional Council representatives, a meeting suggested to Nicolas Sarkozy by him. Like so many Jews and Zionists, he committed himself to the heart of the Libyan spring for the total destruction of Libya to take the maximum advantage of the wealth of that African country. Under the technical shadows of a coup in Libya, he certified to have played a role for the definition of the French diplomatic strategy, and all the government ministers concerned were on the same wavelength as the presidency to that rule of the game.

His recent peregrinations to the city of Benghazi in that remote country were released to the Elysee Palace, following which the 1973 resolution presented by France and the United Kingdom was adopted with ten votes in favor and five abstentions of (Germany, Brazil, China, the Russian Federation, and India), which banned all f lights in the airspace of the Libyan Arab Jamahiriya. The resolution also stated that, "The resolution further strengthens the arms embargo imposed by resolution 1970 (2011), which considered that the widespread and systematic attacks against the civilian population could constitute crimes against humanity." Here, France, the United Kingdom, and concerned member states of the UN Security Council were not seeing the widespread and systematic attacks committed against Palestinian civilians by Israel instead of those that did not exist in Libya, but what an injustice. The Security Council reminded the Libyan authorities to not have complied with resolution 1970 (2011) and expressed deep concern for the deterioration of the situation, the escalation of violence, and the heavy civilian casualties. But at that same time, the Israelis were in the process of massacring Palestinians with weapons of mass destruction and by air bombings without a resolution passed to prohibit all f lights from Israel to protect the Palestinian airspace and population, wounded since the creation of that country by the UN, and declare its systematically generalized crimes as crimes against humanity.

Since Israel does not respect the international law, including the human rights and the territorial law. That disrespect of Israel does not call the attention or the responsibility of the UN Security Council. It's here concerning the defective verbs, the true grotesque spirit of violence, mainly of degeneracy to political corruption, emanating immoral authoritarian injunctions to individuals, as obligations to human lives that the history of the international community has legitimized, established, and naturally producing suffering for an ignored people. We remember that a similar resolution was already adopted—the resolution 748, adopted on March 31, 1992, by the same UN Security Council, establishing military and air embargo against Libya, accused to have organized the bombing of Lockerbie, a village in Scotland, during which a Boeing 747-100 of the U.S. airline Pan Am exploded on December 21, 1988. Of the total fatalities of 270 people on board, 243 passengers and 16 crew members died, including 11 villagers on the ground areas of Lockerbie, Scotland.

That f light 103 was securing the connection between Frankfurt to Detroit via London and New York, and the attack of UTA f light, the DC-10, linking Brazzaville (capital of Congo) to Paris via N'Djamena in Chad and Niger, exploded above the Tenere Desert in Niger on September 19, 1989, killing 170 passengers and crew members. That attack occurred a year later than the one of Lockerbie as reprisals of the Libyan state against both Western powers. But the funny thing is that the resolution 748 also prohibited all f lights in the airspace of the Libyan Arab Jamahiriya but was not strengthened by the bombing of war amenities. It was Mandela, who decided on October 23, 1997, after five long years, to go and undo that injustice against Libya, barely released from his twenty-seven years in the apartheid prison. Before his intervention, no plane could land in Libya because of that embargo. But because of his gratitude to President Gaddhafi, Mandela made a calvary journey to arrive in Libya.

To get there, there were two options. One was to take a flight to Tunisia. Upon arrival in Djerba, an island of 514 km2 (about 25 km by 20 km and 150 km of coastline) located in the Gulf of Gabes, he had to continue by car for five hours to Ben Gardane, a city south of Tunisia, and then cross the border to take the road through the desert for three hours up to Tripoli. The other option was to go through Malta and spend a whole night crossing on poorly maintained boats to the Libyan coast. That Mandela's visit to Gaddhafi was unbearable for Westerners, those who supported their racist brothers on racial segregation, affecting populations according to racial or ethnic criteria in the specific geographical areas, only protecting their interests in South Africa.

Even the former U.S. president Bill Clinton deemed that visit unwelcome. But the then-strong man Nelson Mandela, who was still considered as a dangerous terrorist, including all members of the ANC, replied, "No state can arrogate itself the role of the policeman of the world, and no state can dictate to others what they must do. Those who yesterday were the friends of our enemies, today have the nerve to forbid me not to visit my brother Gaddafi, they advise us to be ungrateful and forget our friends of yesterday."

It was on July 2, 2008 that the U.S. Congress passed a law to definitively wipe the name of Nelson Mandela and his ANC compatriots from the blacklist to honor his ninety years of life on earth, but not because they judged such a list as stupid and unjust. I must say that even when Nelson Mandela was the president of South Africa, he was still on that list. Although Gaddafi maintained that he had never given the order to bomb Lockerbie, he accepted the responsibility for the attack and compensated families by paying the victims in 2003. In 2004, the resolution was lifted, allowing Libya to trade freely again. After the suspension of the embargo in 1999, Libya strengthened its cooperation with European countries, marking its return to the international community. That return ended with the visit of Nicolas Sarkozy, the former president of the French Republic, on July 25 to 26, 2007, in Libya. Before him, a first visit took place since the independence of Libya, when a French head of state Jacques Chirac went officially from November 24 to 25, 2004 in Libya; both visits and the one of Colonel Gaddhafi in Paris, from December 10 to 15, 2007, were confirming the normalization of the renewed relationship foundations. For France, that normalization was translated in particular through a creation of a delegation of the International Police Technical Cooperation Service in Tripoli in September 2005—as his cooperation on internal security matters and the fight against terrorism.

Historically, France has always been indispensable to Mr. Africa; the indispensable France, which orchestrates the support of some and the destabilization of others without emotion. It has indeed the upper hand on the diplomacy and the secret service activities since the independence of our countries in Africa. The implementation of that strategy in Africa was the work of two well-known French personalities in the French political milieu. One was called Jacques Foccart, technical advisor and the confidant of General de Gaulle and Georges Pompidou; he was from 1960 to 1974 the secretary-general of the Elysee for African and Malagasy Affairs. He met Houphouet-Boigny in Abidjan in 1953.

Since then, he became a central figure in the creation of *Françafrique*. And the other was Pierre Guillaumat, the first president of Elf-ERAP. He was first appointed minister of Armed Forces by Charles de Gaulle from June 1958, and in the government of Michel Debre, he continued as minister of Armed Forces to 1960; and from February 1960 to April 1962, he was minister delegate to the prime minister. It is known that the technics of the French atom bomb were realized when he was the responsible for research as the general administrator at the Central commission of nuclear energy and public service from 1951 to 1958; from November 22, 1960, to February 20, 1961, he was the interim minister of education.

In all African countries of the former French colonial empire, Guillaumat was considered as the instigator of conspiracies and coups. That was how he restored Emile Derlin Zinsou as the president of the Republic of Dahomey, the present Benin from 1968 to 1969; supported Mobutu in Congo-Kinshasa; and supported Sekou Toure's opponents in Guinea. In the secessionist war of Biafra in Nigeria, he was a major player for the supply of arms and the interposed mercenaries from 1967. He was the one who established the oil El Dorado of Gabon and as a cornerstone of the African policy of France. He actively helped shape the administration of Pres. Leon M'ba, the first president of Gabon from 1961 to 1967. Reinstalled to power after a military coup, he was asked to appoint the promising Omar Bongo as vice president, and in that case, most faithful to the allies of France, who enjoyed a particular friendly treatment in Africa.

The engineer, politician and French businessman met Jacques Foccart at the Third Army, after his entry into clandestinity at the (BCRA): Bureau Central de Renseignements et d'Action during World War II, which took place from September 1, 1939, to September 2, 1945. The engineer Guillaumat was working in the French secret services, an office created by General de Gaulle in July 1940 for intelligence and clandestine actions of Free France. It merged with the General Directorate of Special Services (DGSS) in 1943. Jacques Foccart was at that time, integrated in the General Directorate of Studies and Research (DGSR), at the state intelligence services. That office was known as the future Foreign Documentation and Counterespionage Service (SEDSCE) when the engineer met him; that French intelligence service, created on December 28, 1945, was replaced by the Directorate General for External Security (DGES) on April 2, 1982. All these two men with a French political base of Gaullism linked to two criminal enigmas, dealt with African issues and were the most influential French authorities that decided the fate of Africa by using conspiracies against African states, implicitly assuming the role of policeman in Africa. That history of the role of policeman in Africa, played by France, still continues till today. This time, it was Libya's turn to pay the price as a victim because of its oil; and on the other side of sub-Saharan Africa, Ivory Coast. As long as we do not completely get rid of that old neocolonial system and no longer accept that the African Union be financed by the European Union, there will be no effective independence, because if the African Union continues to function by the conditions of the European Union, we will always be at the starting point.

In the same vein, the European Union has encouraged and financed regional groupings in Africa. It was obvious that the Economic Community of West African States (ECOWAS), created on May 28, 1975, with fifteen member states known as Benin, Burkina Faso, Cape Verde, Gambia, Ghana, Guinea, Guinea Bissau, Ivory Coast, Liberia, Mali, Niger, Nigeria, Senegal, Sierra Leone, and Togo, will suffer the same fate as the African Union because of the European funding. Among the fifteen countries, Guinea and Niger were excluded from the decision-making bodies of the current regional institution.

To these, added Mauritania, which decided to leave ECOWAS in 2000; it had therefore sixteen member countries in total before 2000. Twelve West African states are currently classified as having the status of least developed countries and four (Cape Verde, Ivory Coast, Ghana, and Nigeria) non-leastdeveloped countries out of the sixteen states. Their decision to leave ECOWAS is today qualified as an error, no matter the reason given by Mauritania. So, it reconsiders the decision and requests reinstatement within that subregional organization to get closer to their brothers and southern neighbors from January 1, 2015, if the reintegration process is granted with the objective of being a full member. But the slavery and racism still practiced in Mauritania against the Haratines by the name of Islam in our black continent bear all qualities of a feudal cultural, ethical, political demographic imbalance system, carefully perpetuating the obligation of services and the Marxist-Leninist obedience still justified by fears. After being a taboo for a long time, this question of slavery, because of its racial implications, raises considerable debates and controversies for democracy, development and stability, both of course on the national and international political scene.

We must recognize that the civilizing message, despite its attempted liberation alleged by the colonization had done nothing to improve the fate of slaves in Mauritania. They're not eager to grant them the status of respect so coveted by that homogenous black color community that rhythm each action throughout the life of our countries. But Mauritanians do not understand that that country must be shared as the colonist and the previous regimes did and improve the status and living conditions of the first damned of the earth.

Thus, with everyone's indifference, the Haratines are murdered, exploited, humiliated, and marginalized and have become victims of contempt; they, who hoped that their return to the south will be glorious, are forced to depend on their masters who quickly found out that, without the integration of their agricultural vocation, the Mauritanian colony will not be vital. So, the Haratines, also called black moors and natives of the northwestern oasis of Africa, are subjected to terrible pain, whose aim is death by the rulers (consisting of feudal Arab-Berber oligarchy).

Nevertheless, being a member of the Arab Maghreb Union (UMA) inspired in 1956, with the independence of Morocco and Tunisia, the idea of a Maghreb economic union was launched to strengthen the independence of the member states, to guarantee cooperation "with similar regional institutions," and to safeguard their assets; in 1988, thirty years late, five Maghreb states—namely, Algeria, Libya, Mauritania, Morocco, and Tunisia—met in a summit for the first time and joined the Union to create the Constitutive Act for the same aim. The Arab Maghreb Union (UMA) was then created on February 17, 1989, which, in fact, never existed as the economic zone of its member countries. Since 1994, having little influence on the policies of its member states, the council of the five signatory heads of states constituting the union with the headquarters of the general secretariat located in Rabat, Morocco, after its transfer to Tunisia and Algeria, there was never again a new meeting held beyond its official constitution due to the traditional problems of rivalry within the AMU.

The diplomatic tensions between the leaders of its member states, continuously refusing to attend AMU meetings held in Algiers, justified the decision to transfer the AMU presidency in Libya. But because of the lack of all required conditions to relinquish the presidency as stipulated in the Constitutive Act, which states that the presidency should in fact rotate on an annual basis, made that the transfer could not take place, forcing Muammar Gaddafi to put the Union "in freeze," following the announcement of the decision to transfer the presidency of the union to the Libyan leader. Mauritania, which for fifteen years remained outside ECOWAS, as a founding member, decided to correct its decision of quitting it, describing it as one of the most active and dynamic organizations and for the future of the African continent as a major asset that will contribute to accelerate the economic and social development of its countries.

Will ECOWAS honor the request for the reinstatement of Mauritania within the organization in which members are speaking English, French, and Portuguese and benefit from its advantages, even knowing its position in the practice of slavery? As early as 2016, the Economic Community of West African States, which instead of the travel certificate that was in vigor and the restrictive residence card for integration, will both be replaced by a biometric identity card. The aim is to avoid annoying holders of a biometric identity card to ask for a resident card in each country in the ECOWAS area. This confirmation was made on December 11, 2014, in Abuja by the council of ministers of the intergovernmental organization and the integration of West African.

In 2014, its population was estimated at just over 334.6 million, with a projection of 350 million in 2020 and 500 million in 2030. It is hosting in total, nearly a third of the sub-Saharan population, which was 960.1 million in 2014. Knowing that 60 percent of its population lives with less than US$1 per day, ECOWAS has a gross domestic product (GDP) of around US$600 billion; its mission is to promote cooperation and integration for the creation of an economic and monetary union to favor the economic growth and development of West Africa. From year to year, strong growth has been registered, with a rate of 6.5 percent in 2012 against 6.2 percent the previous year, to finally settle at 6.6 percent in 2013 against 6.5 percent in 2012; and in 2014, the expected growth rate was 6.3 percent. The GDP growth was projected to hit 7.1 percent in 2015 against 6.3 percent in 2014. Nigeria alone represents a growth rate of 78 percent of the ECOWAS countries in GDP.

Within ECOWAS and the African Union, this country of West Africa has become a leading diplomatic actor and is contributing to promote the economic partnership of states that compound them in Africa. And in addition to its 183.5 million inhabitants, Nigeria has one sixth of the population of its continent; its GDP is US$2,688 per capita on average, according to the IMF in 2014.

That main structure of ECOWAS, intended to coordinate the actions of its countries, must concretize its ambitions to promote the cooperation and the integration of a union, especially by the establishment of a common external tariff, the harmonization of economic and financial policies, and the creation of a single currency. Abuja, its headquarters, is housing the three main institutions: the commission, the parliament, and the court of justice.

The specialized institutions are spread across the member state countries. The ECOWAS embassy in Brussels, which gets most of its funding from the EU, is a major obstacle against the African federation. When Lincoln was fighting in the Secession War in the United States, that's what he was fighting for, knowing that if a group of countries was to gather around a regional political organization, it would weaken the central organ. The year 2015 symbolically represented the forty years of ECOWAS; May 28 was scheduled as the day that highlights very important festive events to better promote the organization, and to make its objectives and its achievements known to the youths of all its fifteen member states.

Europe therefore wanted to weaken the central organ by also creating the (COMESA), the Common Market for Eastern and Southern Africa. It replaced the former preferential trade area, which existed since December 21, 1981. Its member countries are Burundi, Comoros, Democratic Republic of Congo, Djibouti, Egypt, Eritrea (member since 1994), Ethiopia, Kenya, Libya (member since 2005), Madagascar, Malawi, Mauritius, Rwanda, Seychelles (member since 2001), Sudan and South Sudan (member since 2011), Swaziland, Uganda, Zambia, and Zimbabwe. It also included Angola, among the countries that left the organization in 2007, Lesotho in 1997, Mozambique in 1997, Namibia in 2004 and Tanzania in 2000. These five former members are no longer part of the international organization with a regional vocation of East Africa, whose objective is to create a customs union between its twenty member countries.

The COMESA area covers a total population of 340 million and a total GDP of US$170 billion. (The average GDP per capita is US$690.) Its business transactions volume reaches US$60 billion annually between its member countries and the rest of the world. It also houses four Arab member countries, which are Comoros, Djibouti, Egypt, and Sudan. Its treaty was signed in November 1993 and ratified in December 1994. The Central African Customs and Economic Union (CACEU) was replaced by the Economic and Monetary Community of Central Africa (EMCCA). Its treaty was signed on March 16, 1994, in Chad in N'Djamena and entered into force in June 1999. Its headquarters are in Bangui (Central African Republic). The Southern African Development Community (SADC) took over on August 17, 1992, from the South African Development Coordination Conference (SADCC), founded on April 1, 1980. That organization, which aimed to promote the economic development of Southern Africa and the Greater Maghreb, has never functioned. Let's thank Gaddhafi one more time—he who had very well understood what other Africans did not understand. That assassinated symbol, activist of Africanism, was one of the few Africans who fought for the liberation, the sovereignty, and the unity of Africa. In my opinion, his assassination was ordered by the UN Security Council, issuing his death warrant by a resolution. Nowadays, the said Security Council, as the organ of the United Nations, does not reflect the universal conscience but is permanently recognized by its numerous resolutions to crush the majority of its members by force, having of course the principle of sovereignty. The revision of its mandate, functioning, and representativeness, excluding any subordination on the organic plane, does not constitute a superstate or the International Court of Justice. Its consequence is the logic of the principle of sovereign equality of states, included in article 2 and paragraph 1 of the United Nations foundation.

This knowledge is for us to recognize that no major organ could be invested with any powers; therefore, we do not have such a global organization, having an ideal of values and principles followed by all; concerning the well-being of the global community and having objective reality around its consecration with the natural, social, and the typical supernatural phenomenon, which cares about human beings in time; born of solidarity interests, good values of the state sovereignty that guarantees the protection of individual rights as a true international community organization—a simple society organ—a unified community of the human race of all mankind, founded on the principles of freedom, love, and peace, of which the individual would be worthy of, with the realization of an ultimate sovereignty, not opposing the interstate community but reuniting the states. The one we know today limits the exercise of the state sovereignty and good principles commonly wanted by its member states.

It is in that conception of denied sovereignty to its member states that they're calling for an indisputable initial legal requirement, for a conception that could guarantee the protection of individual rights, the fundamental freedom of its member states, the respect of the human rights, and the foundation of progressive affirmation at the international level, promoting the principle of democratic legitimacy and constituting a state of mind of goodwill as a progressive practice, consecrating a theory considered legitimately democratic for new governments and producing real effects determined by the democratic legitimacy of the former governments.

In a system of government, the democratic conception must gradually be developed to consolidate and reaffirm democracy in a strict sense of the legitimacy of the state in a nation. The dictate of the most powerful international states has not allowed the principles of freedom, democracy, and respect for human rights in Africa be developed legitimately on the formal level but has preserved a character of law increasingly restrictive to intervene in African states. The whole Africa and all its citizens reject that unconstitutional subordination to the international community power, governing the current member states as a serious threat for the stability, peace, security, and the development of Africa. In fact, the mobilization of this imperialist international power serves the interests of their well-understood powerful states, of course, of values opposing certain ideals and the universal legal norms necessary for the constitutional normality of democracy. That consequence of the selfish interests of the imperialist international community, at the detriment of reason, makes us doubt the existence of a true international community.

Their detention of a coercion power depends on the military, economic, and political power for a radical solution, because of the incestuosity of their interests by a strategic action of force to collectively procure them wealth and to favor the erection of a hegemonic policy, having a controlling selfish behavior, accompanied by the theory of fear and the guilt of not having assisted people in danger. It opposes the liberal model but favors the multiplicity of approaches of ethnic divisions, constantly used for inadmissible ideologically discriminatory purposes, imposing the principles of justice by wars, and opened to a unilateralist imperialist policy interpreted as sovereignty. That coercion without state of mind determines the confiscation of power from African states, and it is fatal to an ideal of liberal values.

This control between the controller, the Western, and the controlled, being Africa, was a pun on words of one of the Western leaders considered as an ignorant uttering an emotional blackmail of African history for their assuring self-esteem, described Africa as a continent subjected to a process of their little thought and opinion; excited and inspired by the thought of fear but not expressing the true expression of "Africa" by its ornamental plant, which has flourished velvety and delicate f lowers in the history of humanity; while a close relationship was established between them, he came and obscured it and confused the situation.

The emotional blackmail climate was used by Nicolas Sarkozy to describe Africa, already subjected to a form of dependency, to make it feel a desperate sense of hopelessness, rather than being the conscious plan that it represents in reality. With his main speeches written by Henri Guaino, his special adviser during his five-year term, they stirred the knife in the plague of the black history with racist quotations throughout his presidential mandate.

That son of a Hungarian immigrant Nicolas Sarkozy de Nagy-Bosca, born in the seventeenth arrondissement of Paris on January 28, 1955, on a trip to West Africa in July 2007, also believed that the African man has not entered enough in the history and that Africa was living too much in the present with the nostalgia of the lost paradise of its childhood, categorically ignoring Africa in the history of the world. In October 2007, he stated in another speech in Constantine (Algeria) that "the colonial system could not be lived otherwise than as an enterprise of enslavement and exploitation." Why not start your own enslavement and exploitation enterprise? But let me tell you Mr. Nicolas Sarkozy de Nagy-Bosca that, "your colonial system of enslavement and exploitation was unjust to humanity as well as to the nature."

During his first official visit to Libya to sell weapons and surveillance equipment in October 2005 to the Libyan leader, Nicolas Sarkozy was still the interior minister. He announced his intention to run for the presidential election, requesting financial support from Colonel Gaddhafi in Tripoli a year later in November 2006. But the former French president has always denied having benefited from Libyan funds, until the document published by *Mediapart* on April 28, 2012, and the mysterious white notes from the secret services found by chance in the office of a Parisian business lawyer concerning the Libyan funding for Sarkozy's presidential campaign in 2007, be authenticated by a panel of handwriting experts appointed by judges in charge of the investigate. That unjustifiable indifference and nonrecognition of the former president of the French Republic Nicolas Sarkozy, by fear to face the truth, was of judicial importance for the death of Muammar Gaddhafi.

The corruption of a French political clan was brandishing clearly contradictory arguments of truths about the receipt of money from that foreign country but displaying it as a dictatorial regime. The Gaddhafi regime decided to release the funds of €50 million, according to an official Libyan document. His shameful secrets of the hidden financing of his presidential campaign played a role in the French military intervention in Libya in 2011.

Another president of a corrupt French political clan in control of the apparatus of African states was saying, "They have served us as labor for the toughest tasks, then we colonized them; we used them as cannon fodder, we looted their raw materials, and we are continuing looting them. Now we are taking their gray matter;" and finally, he added that "the African dictators must be supported, otherwise they would not organize elections."

Thus, Jacques Chirac, a French statesman born in the fifth arrondissement of Paris on November 29, 1932, and the twenty-second president of the French Republic from May 17, 1995, to May 16, 2007, exclaimed about Africans in one of his confidences to a French investigation journalist, Pierre Pean, born on March 5, 1938, in Sable-sur-Sarthe. That French investigation journalist played another active role in the diamond case involving the former president Valery Giscard d'Estaing concerning diamond plates (two stars of small fine stones), with an estimated value of four thousand and seven thousand francs at that time, and African ebony fruits. Valery Giscard d'Estaing received several gifts from the Central African president, the former emperor Jean-Bedel Bokassa or Bokassa I, in the 1970s in lieu of friendship—namely, diamonds of around thirty carats and a decorative panel of ivory—shortly after his election to the presidency of the French Republic. He again offered him elephant tusks and three squares of brilliant compositions during an official trip in Bangui in March 1975. Despite the contrary speech of Giscard d'Estaing, a French statesman born in Koblenz in Germany on February 2, 1926, the twentieth president of the French Republic, from May 27, 1974, to May 21, 1981, had indeed received these diamonds;

affirmed by numerous testimonies—namely from Albert de Schonen, the former ambassador of France in the Central African Republic, and the national diamond administrator, the former British honorary consul in Bangui in 1973, who says that Henry Kissinger notably received a similar diamond plate, and that the value of the diamonds offered by Bokassa to his distinguished guests never exceeded US$10,000.

Edouard Balladur—also a former French politician, born on February 5, 1929, in Izmir in Turkey, who held many key positions in the French government before being appointed prime minister on April 29, 1993, to 1995—denigrated Africa during a TV show in 1994, saying, "We have a moral duty toward these people. We are the ones who brought them civilization." Again, here was a stupid quote from a man who was said to be intellectual. So, Mr. Balladur, was it in Turkey that you learned that, or was it simply discrimination? Or again, did all other European leaders know that Bulgarians, Hungarians, and all Central Europe of the Slavic language were hunted down, captured, and condemned by other white Christians to be sold to the Arabs as worthless objects in the years 1200 to 1300? The political crisis in the Republic of Ivory Coast, Libya, and many other African countries is a question of several unhealthy historical memories on the evolution of African political powers, born from the presence of the omnipresence of the multifaceted imperialist international community. The considerable self-weakening of African political powers stems from the powers of different European colonial systems, which have mutually delivered themselves the two great wars by dragging nations of the world into them and killing most of their populations.

Their subsequent evolution, downgraded to the rank of the new superpower countries, is a planned resurrection conditioned by the bipolarization of the political ideology of the postwar world. Faced with that new American planetary superpower, the said protector of the Eastern bloc, materialized by the constitution of a Soviet continental territory, dominated by the United States and Europe divided, sought to reposition itself, but forced to decolonize Africa, by the United Nations. Thus, the thesis of the French exception, of a zone of territorial cultural influence of franc CFA in the French-speaking world in Africa will be defended with some success by the African nationalist forces on an African continent consisting of states more artificial than real. The reorientation, subordinated to the agreement of the European allies and NATO, was set up to invest more in African affairs and pretended to support the work of the African Union; their great powers have put multiple initiatives in place, in transit zones, of harborages and secret activities.

In that cradle of humanity, the entire Middle East submitted the Horn of Africa vigorously to Islam. The geostrategic oil exports of the Middle East, a region between the eastern shore of the Mediterranean Sea and the line drawn by the border between Iran, on one hand, Pakistan, Afghanistan on the other hand, and the Middle East, a region of Asia and Africa, including the southeastern countries of the Levantine Basin the (Mediterranean Sea), played an important role in the strategic history of France; these regions are not absent in the development history of France because of their petroleum resources.

In accordance with the logic of State accountability, France is seeking to Europeanize the Reinforce African Peacekeeping Capacities (RECAMP) program since 1994, by equipping it with technological means, reconfiguring its military device, training it gradually for the proper supervision, to increase the control of its territory and ensure the so-called security of the continent, as preconditions for the economic growth, under the auspices of the United Nations.

That program is governed by the multilateral principles of the Economic Community of West African States ECOWAS; a West African intergovernmental organization created on May 28, 1975, and the Economic Community of Central African States (ECCAS), created by a treaty signed on October 20, 1983, in Libreville, the political and administrative capital of Gabon; it entered into force on December 18, 1984, in the Gabon Estuary, a state located west of Central Africa across the equator. Like the vast majority of French colonies in sub-Saharan Africa, it accounts about fifty ethnic groups. The majority includes the Fangs, the Gisir, the Kota, the Myene, the Nzebis, the Obambas, the Punu, the Teke, and the Vungu. Other ethnic groups, counting only a few hundred individuals, tend to melt gradually into the mass and culturally lose their language and their particularities. The prefix *Ba* is often known as the plural mark in the Bantu languages, considered in plural or singular, as a more Frenchified form but differently spelled from the same word. It gained independence on August 17, 1960. It was populated by successive waves of Pygmies and the massive immigrations of Bantus, up to the nineteenth century, as a former French colony, neighboring Cameroon.

SADC, the Southern African Development Community is more broadly to the service of the continent's stability and the bilateral cooperation, the development aid and is a complement to the New Partnership for Africa's Development (NEPAD). That policy of military deployment of the European Union's operational forces, within the framework of the Common Foreign Security and Defense Policy (CFSP), is engaged by the Artemis Operation of the European Union Force (EUFOR) for several years in the Democratic Republic of Congo, Chad, and Central Africa since 2007, officially in 2008. For the edification of a regional system of collective security, the Security Council voted to deploy a joint force of the UN and the African Union, adopted in 2005 by the EU Strategy for Africa, and to support the African Union by the resolution of July 31, 2007.

Those ambitions of diplomatic and economic rivalries of the European Union and the investment of the United States in Africa are psychologically disastrous and simultaneously considered as a phenomenon of social disorder on the African continent. But history will stammer once again by a new confrontation of strategic geopolitical data of new global superpower, known as the emergence of China and its financial allies, including Russia, are seeking to conquer the African continent. As the potential founding members of the

Asian Infrastructure Investment Bank, here are few names that have joined China: Australia, Bangladesh, Brazil, Brunei, Cambodia, Denmark, Egypt, Finland, France, Germany, Iceland, India, Indonesia, Iran, Israel, Italy, Jordan, Kazakhstan, Kuwait, Laos, Malaysia, Maldives, Mongolia, Myanmar, Nepal, Netherlands, New Zealand, Norway, Oman, Pakistan, Qatar, Russia, Saudi Arabia, Singapore, South Africa, Spain, Sri Lanka, Sweden, Tajikistan, Thailand, Turkey, United Kingdom, Uzbekistan, and Vietnam. The first objective of the Chinese government in Africa, the continent known as privileged to Europeans, is the economic cooperation and trade development between the two continents.

China is one of the most important donors of funds countries in the African continent; the amounts granted as development aid amount to two billion per year. Corruption and the violation of human rights do not stop them to invest in our country, and the non-interference in the internal affairs of African countries is their basic policy. Principally, 70 percent of the oil and 5 percent of the mineral resources are African exportation to China. From China, the imported products are electronic devices, shoes, telecommunication equipment, textiles, cars, etc. A new record of US$114.8 billion, which is €87.7 billion, was published by the Chinese authorities for the first eleven months of 2010. Reaching a 43.5 percent increased trade between Africa and China, after more than US$106 billion in 2008. They jumped from $127 billion to $166 billion between 2010 and 2011 and reached $198.49 billion in 2012, an increase of 19.3 percent compared to the previous year.

In 2013, the bilateral trade amounted to $210 billion; and China plans to double that amount of its trade with Africa, to $400 billion by 2020. The growth forecasts for the global economy, revised again by the International Monetary Fund (IMF), decreased by 3.6 percent in 2014 and favored the total volume of Sino-African trade, which not only represents challenges but can also be explained by opportunities to support their respective growth and highlight their enormous potential for economic and commercial exchanges.

The Sino-African trade, referring to the historical relations is more active in political, economic, military, social, and cultural ties between China and the African continent. Thus, heading the United States and France, China has become the main trading partner of Africa, with investments started in the 1980s for a growth rate estimated at 33.5 percent in 2009. In terms of commercial exchanges, $1.44 billion was invested that year—namely, $17 billion of bilateral trade with Angola, $16 billion in South Africa, $6.39 billion in Sudan, and $6.37 billion in Nigeria. Unlike Westerners, China's help is not subjected to any political conditions; Angola is providing 30 percent of oil supplies at this moment, and about 55 percent of Sudan's production is exported to China, where a deadly game for the control of huge Africa's resources is played—a vessel in which all nations are embarked for the rudder of the world, defined by the new Chinese superpower. Yes, China, which wants to make Africa the showcase of its economic and military power outside Asia, also wants to change the situation of an old idea that the West still defends in Africa. It is willingly accommodating mass misery and poverty, and through its henchmen, controls everything. Yes, approximately sixty-six years ago, the United States and Europe decided to make Africa one of the pillars. But the steamroller of the Chinese superpower is crushing them terribly, proceeding exactly like them in Africa.

That new situation is the visible consequence of the international geopolitics caused by the Ivorian political crisis since it is on that presidential domination that the pure and simple cancellation of African states' sovereignty was played—an illustration of a new division of an African territory, still on the menu of the great imperialist powers of this world and relatively under the domination of international organizations controlled by the United States; they also control the management of its files. Generally, its domination is at stake, through the analysis of their diplomatic notes disclosed in the WikiLeaks site, demonstrating that they were very happy about France erasure, leaving them a free field on the entire African continent. It is well-known that the colonial imperialist powers are inevitably making use of violence to cause the chronic political instability that is prevailing in the postcolonial society by a multitude of small civil wars, causing the death of more people than anywhere else on earth in the last two decades.

The estimation of the International Rescue Committee numbered people's death following the conflict in the Democratic Republic of Congo to 3.3 million, more than the eight hundred thousand deaths in Rwanda during the genocide in 1994, well after the colonies formed by Great Britain, France, Portugal, and Germany. Today, the Democratic Republic of Congo, formerly known as the Belgian Congo, only emerged in 1908, yet discovered by the Portuguese sailor Diogo Cao, when the Europeans recognized that African region from 1482 to 1483; but until November 15, 1908, that country was under the possession of King Leopold II of Belgium for twenty-three years (1885 to 1908). A year before the death of the king, on December 17, 1909, the Belgian Federal Parliament regained guardianship over the territory, henceforth known as Belgian Congo.

That independent state of Congo was designated at the time of the Berlin Conference from 1884 to 1885. Considered as the property of King Leopold II of Belgium, the international humanitarian pressure led Belgium to assume its colonization by its serious and numerous abuses from the time of its formation. Generally, in 2014, Africa represented 16.14 percent of the world population, with more than 1.2 billion inhabitants. The Nigerian population would double by the year 2050—to a population of 440 million inhabitants in total, given the highest birth rate already experienced in that country; we are counting nearly one in ten babies born on that land. That African population recorded in 2014 would double and reach about 4.2 billion people by 2100 on the continent.

So, the African population would be 40 percent of the world population. Our Africa, which comprised forty-eight countries including Madagascar, and fifty-four including all archipelagos with an area of 30,221,532 km2, is including the islands, covering 6 percent of the terrestrial surface and 20.3 percent of the emerged lands. From the perspective of cultural, philosophical, and political values, the 192 states that constitute the UN are all different from one another and are also very variable in their decision-making process, concerning the borders of African states, largely derived from the colonization, bringing together different countries in subregions that they use more for practical reasons than the historical truth, by taking little account of the realities of the populations.

Black Africa, known also as sub-Saharan Africa, and Southern Africa, only had two sovereign states because of the expansion of colonial empires in 1914— Namely— a country in East Africa, long known under the name of Abyssinia, whose Hebeshe Semitic root means "mixture," between the Sabean and the indigenous cultures; or also called "Ethiopia," the second most populous African country located in the Horn of Africa, consisting mainly of highlands, rising from the Danakil Depression at 120 meters, up to the snowy peaks of Mount Ras Dashan at 4543 meters.

Since ancient times, Ethiopia has always been a sovereign state in Africa. In its history, it is known that on March 1, 1896, it inflicted a defeat on the attempt of colonization, known as the first decisive victory of an African country against the colonialists, and managed to repel the Italians at the Battle of Adwa. After a phase of prosperity, which started with the formation of the D'mt kingdom, appeared around 800 BC and lasted until the seventh century BC, the D'mt kingdom was entirely an indigenous civilization without the Sabaean influence since the ancient Semitic language, the Ge'ez language of the northern Ethiopia and Eritrea did not come from the Sabaean language.

Various other less influential entities followed the fall of the D'mt kingdom in the fifth century BC, without the continuity being clear, until the emergence of the kingdom of Aksum, the capable unifying power of the region in the first century BC, at the transition in the mid-twelfth and the late thirteenth century, to a Christian Orthodox family of Lasta, the province of the former Zagwe kingdom. It has been almost three thousand years that the independent states located on the parts of the present territory of Ethiopia were identified.

The constitution of the Solomonic kingdom, which was initiated toward 1270, would continue in various forms up to the empire of Ethiopia, designating the set of policies established by the Zagwe toward 990. That region shelters 11 medieval stone churches. Yekuno Amlak was the one who claimed patrilineal descent from King Solomon of Israel and the Queen of Sheba, to create the ancient ruling Imperial House of the Ethiopian Empire, after overthrowing the Zagwe dynasty. From 1270 up to the Zemene Mesafint (Age of Princes), the name of the dynasty derived from the Agaw Kushitic language of northern Ethiopia, when the Solomonic dynasty was governing the Ethiopian Empire.

Under Lebna Dengel, it ended in the early sixteenth century, and the outbreak of wars began in 1527, with the population growth and the economic troubles, first between Muslim forces led by Ahmad ibn Ibrahim al-Ghazi, supported by the Ottomans and the Ethiopian Christian Empire. The Ethiopian Empire was on the verge of collapsing in 1535 after a series of victories won by Ahmad's troops. At that time, Lebna Dengel appealed to the Portuguese; and from 1541, the course of the conflict would change by the Battle of Wayna Daga, where Ahmad was killed on February 21, 1543, inflicting a defeat on its army. After the Islamic sultanates, the fragility and weakness of the empire allowed the population movements that would last three decades from 1550 to 1580, to finally impose Catholicism to Susenyos the sovereign, at the second half of the sixteenth century. What is interesting in this whole story is that a company of Jesus was followed by protests, transforming the country into a real civil war and forcing Susenyos to abandon the sovereign power in favor of his son Fasilides on June 14, 1632.

Many other sovereigns followed, marking the periods during which the doctrinal divisions of the church took place, leading to the collapse of the breakthrough of Islam and the fight against Oromo offensives up to the coronation of Haile Selassie I, on November 2, 1930. From that date to September 12, 1974, the Empire of Ethiopia ended on September 12, 1974, after overthrowing the něgūša naga Haile Selassie I, due to a coup d'etat by the revolution of the Provisional Military Government of Socialist Ethiopia and the abolition of the monarchy by the military junta on March 12, 1975. And the Marxism-Leninism proclaimed the new official ideology of the state.

The People's Democratic Republic of Ethiopia succeeded the Provisional Military Government of Socialist Ethiopia at the official dissolution of that government, and the entry into force of a new constitution on September 10, 1987, instituting the name of the People's Democratic Republic of Ethiopia in the country. Those political movements of a Marxist-Leninist ideology moved to a social-democratic approach with the seizure of power by the "Regionalists Nationalists" on May 21, 1991, to restore the ethnic federalism before gaining access to the current government of the Federal Democratic Republic of Ethiopia. The parenthesis of attempting to westernize the African blood in that African country by the Spanish, Portuguese, and Italians took nearly a century of European presence in the Ethiopian Nation.

The Aksum's elite had already established a tradition of sharply hewn and carefully etched stones called stelae to adorn their graveyards or obelisks for their cities in memory of an important event. Their occupation of Ethiopia by Mussolini's armies in 1937 destroyed one of the Aksum's obelisks and taken to be erected in front of the building that housed the Ministry of Africa up to 1945, near the Circus Maximus in Rome, Italy. Finally, the restitution of that dismembered monolith only took place in 2005 by a commitment undertaken by Italy in 1947; its three pieces found their location in Aksum in August 2008.

Ethiopia is also the site of Lucy's discovery, considered as the cradle of humanity. With Kenya and Chad, Ethiopia is one of the countries where the oldest hominids of *Homo erectus* were discovered dating back three or four million years and the oldest specimens of *Homo sapiens* between 1.7 million and two hundred thousand years before our era since 2003. The fertile land of Ethiopia, where numerous discoveries took place is also where the coffee grows in the wild state, probably originating from that country.

Religion in Ethiopia is divided in three streams. The Ethiopian Orthodox Church comprises 43.5 percent of the Ethiopian population; it is part of the churches of the three councils and is one of the oldest and largest churches in the world within the Eastern Christianity, which are grouping the churches of Armenian, Syriac, and the Coptic liturgical tradition. The Ethiopian Orthodox Church is the only precolonial Orthodox Church in sub-Saharan Africa since 1959. It was part of the Coptic Orthodox Church. Those churches only recognize the liturgical tradition of the First Council of Nicaea of 325, the First Council of Constantinople in 381, and the Council of Ephesus in 431, among the ecumenical councils; following the Council of Chalcedon in 451, they were separated from the Christianity of the Byzantine Empire. As the members of the Ethiopian Orthodox Tewahedo Church, the Protestant Ethiopian Church of the Lutheran tradition has 18.6 percent of the population, and the Ethiopian Catholic Church claims 0.7 percent of the population.

Finally, about 33.9 percent of the Ethiopian population would practice Islam, and it was between 325 and 328 that Christianity was introduced in Ethiopia and then Monophysite, when the father of peace, St. Frumentius of Tyre, converted King Ezana of Aksum, making Ethiopia, after Armenia, the second-oldest Christian state in the world. At that time, the symbolism of the sun and the moon was replaced by the cross, and they were the first to affix that cross on all the kingdom coins at the late third century. And from a refusal of the formulations of the Council of Chalcedon in 451, adhering to the unique nature of Christ, the "nine saints," a group of monks introduced monasticism as a state and way of life of people who have pronounced religious vows. Its adherents were part of a separated order from the world and living under a common rule.

The word *monasticism* came from the ancient Greek *monos*, meaning specifically "bachelor" or "solitary." Twenty-five centuries ago, the first institution possessing its own form of monasticism was Theravada Buddhism, and the heart of its practice to this day is meditation. It was in Egypt that monasticism appeared in Christianity toward 329 under Pachomius the Great, the founder of Christian cenobitism, according to tradition. The Catholic Church celebrated this holy event on May 9 and the Orthodox Church on May 15. Around the temple of Serapis, Ancient Egypt experienced a reclusive tradition (*katochoi*), which significantly differed from the Christian vision of monasticism. Established in the Hellenistic period by Ptolemy I, Serapis—the syncretic deity of the first pharaoh of the Ptolemy dynasty, gathering traits of Hades, the bull god Apis and Osiris, which was first Osorapis before becoming Serapis—had to be accepted by the Egyptian world.

The name of the "Ptolemaic dynasty" came from the son of Lagos, who reigned over Egypt from 323 to 30 before our era, counted as the thirty-second Egyptian pharaonic dynasty, from the Macedonian general Ptolemy. It was the continuation of the Macedonian king Alexander the Great, one of the most famous figures of antiquity, who was proclaimed pharaoh of Egypt in 331. He was officially crowned in the temple of Ptah in Memphis, and the oracle of Luxor declared him "son of Re." His meeting with the oracle of Amun/Zeus in the Oasis of Siwa confirmed him as a descendant of the god Amun.

The Ptolemaic period of the Egyptian pharaonic dynasty from 304 to 30 is a Lagid period that preceded the birth of Christ, known as a period of weakening and definitive decline that determined the Roman colony in Egypt. The artificial birth of the god Serapis in Alexandria was summarizing the fundamental objective points, recalling the vital renewal of Osiris and Apis to the Egyptians and to the Greeks, the appearance of the god Zeus who illustrated the link to the Greek religion, by the reunion in the same religious orientation. In the third century of our era, Serapis became one of the most beloved deities of the Egyptian pantheon. And Monophysitism, a Christological doctrine that appeared around 480 in the Byzantine Empire in reaction to Nestorianism, was a doctrine claiming Christianity and affirming that the Son Jesus Christ has only one nature-human and that he is divine. In its variant miaphysite, a doctrine also Christological developed by Dioscorus, the patriarch of Alexandria in the fifth and sixth centuries, of Severus of Antioch, a leading theologian and a saint of the Syriac Orthodox and the Coptic Church, Patriarch from 512 to 518, and by Cyril of Alexandria, father and doctor of the Catholic Church, saint for the Catholics and the Orthodox, who promoted the formula of the doctrine, strove to eradicate paganism, Judaism, and all what he regarded as heresies, designated their church professing the doctrine or a person belonging to that church as "Monophysite."

Following the report of the Jacobite bishop, the Syriac-speaking writer, historian, doctor, and Arab philosopher of the Christian religion known by the name of Bar Hebraeus, the Antioch theologian patriarch, was exposing the cream of his wisdom concerning the Monophysite doctrine, saying that there was only one nature in Christ, the divine and not human, which was without corruption, without confusion, and without mixture, just as the nature of man is of two natures, soul and body. That nature, divine and human, remains what it is; and the one of the body is also composed of two natures, the form and matter, without the soul being changed into the body and the form into the matter.

There was therefore no question in terms of Monophysitism when it comes to miaphysism. In the sense of Eutyches, a personality of ancient Christianity fiercely opposed to Nestorianism, was also affirming that two personalities, one divine and the other human, coexisted in Jesus Christ; closed to Chrysaphios, a Greek eunuch typically attested as being a castrated man, depicted as a sinister figure at the Protobyzantine time and in all the ancient accounts, his doctrine was also teaching that there was only one nature in Jesus Christ, the divine nature, refusing to consider two distinct natures of the Christ. That refusal, describing on the contrary the unity of Christ as the fusion of two natures in one, absorbed the human nature of Christ like a drop of water absorbed by the sea. Thus, the Council of Chalcedon, the fourth ecumenical council, held in St. Euphemia Church of the Asian side of Istanbul from October 8 to November 1, 451, condemned the doctrine of Eutyches on the basis of the letter of Pope Leo I, entitled Tome to Flavian, reflecting the significant influence of Orthodox

Christianity throughout the Ethiopian history. But among the Coptic populations of Egypt and Byzantine of Syria, Monophysitism continued to be developed in its provinces throughout the sixth century up to the Persian invasions and in the early seventh century, followed by the Arabs. Today, Ethiopia, a country constitutionally secular, is a nation where many beliefs coexist. There are, among others, animists and the Falashas as religious minorities, Catholics, Monophysite Orthodox, and Protestants. And finally, Muslims represent one-third of its inhabitants.

Coming from a Christian background belonging to the Elcesaite sect, Mani or Manes, the Persian Mesopotamian prophet born in 216 who was preaching the Manichaeism of the Nordic god Mani, the personification of the moon, was the founder of a religion in the third century, which today disappeared. In the footsteps of the community of the apostle Thomas, one of the twelve apostles of Jesus, he began to preach toward 240 and considered himself as an imitator of Jesus's life. He was influenced by the Greco-Buddhism during his trip in the Indo-Greek kingdom and joined the court of the Sassanid king Shapur I, faithful to Zoroastrianism, on his return in 242 and presented him Manichaeism as his doctrine—a syncretism of Christianity, Buddhism, and Zoroastrianism.

Today qualified as a thought or an action without nuances, good and evil are clearly defined and separated. According to Manichaeism, human nature is twofold; it possesses a spirit (the immortal part, belonging to the kingdom of light, kingdom of the divine life) and a body (the mortal part, belonging to the kingdom of darkness, kingdom of the matter, the realm of the dead), where what is space/time is expressed.

Coexisting without ever interfering, a catastrophic event gave birth to man from that conflict of the kingdom of light and the kingdom of darkness. And it is death that could transform the natural man from the secret of obscurity (the kingdom of darkness) toward the secure reality of truth (the kingdom of light, the kingdom of the divine life). As the sunlight draws the seed upward, so do the light attracts the spirit of men from the dark neighborhood of ignorance to the state of existence and dignify the plane of existence, the one of the creator of heaven and earth, in a process of supreme elevation of the spirit liberation. He cited the civilization of the Ethiopian kingdom of Aksum as the first great empire to convert to Christianity, among the four most important powers in the world in the third century. The northern city of Aksum, in the province of Tigray, was the center of the Aksumite Empire from the fourth century BC to reach its apogee in the first century of our era. It was also one of the religious centers of the Ethiopian Orthodox Church, founded by the Bible's unknown son of Kush named St. Frumence of Aksum. According to tradition, the most important church in Ethiopia, the Church of St. Mary of Zion, built in the course of the fourth century during the reign of the first emperor Ezana in the year 320, is housing the Ark of the Covenant.

It was King Menelik I, considered one of the oldest and most famous Metis in the history, who established the Solomonid dynasty and became the first king of the first Solomonid dynasty of Ethiopia. That kingdom was promised by Solomon to Makeda, the mother of Menelik I, the day of her departure after her visit by telling her, "Take this ring on which the Lion of Judah is engraved, to not forget me; and if I ever have a son as offspring from thy womb, let him come to me, to be the representative of the sign of this Lion."

The Ark of the Covenant was entrusted by Solomon to King Menelik I, his heir, upon his departure from Jerusalem, after his education at the age of twenty-two and after being impregnated with the wisdom of his father, to hide it away from Jerusalem in the kingdom of Saba. He placed it on an island of Lake Tana, not stolen as claimed by some legends. He brought the ark, containing the tablets of the law, from there to Ethiopia in the fourth century. He also ordained the great elite of Israelites, exacting that the eldest sons of each family of the twelve tribes and some twelve thousand Jews belonging to the twelve tribes should accompany him. He was obliged to send Menelik I, back to his mother because the pressure of the high priests accusing him of giving him too much affection worried Solomon. On the order of Solomon himself, those Levites, the close guards of Solomon, left with Menelik I, as his faithful initiates, for the handling of the ark. From that moment on, the "Falasha," an important community living in Ethiopia, today qualified in Israel as Ethiopian Jews from the house of Israel (*Beta Israel* as Ethiopian Jewish) fled into exile, and obeying the laws of Israel as the Ethiopian descendants of the Jewish religion, settled in the kingdom from the first Solomonid dynasty of Ethiopia. In accordance with the original text of the Bible, their priests were practicing animal sacrifices and still do it nowadays. For centuries, led by a priest council, they were living particularly in the provinces of Gondor and Tigray in northern Ethiopia. The Ethiopian Empire conquered them after benefiting small independent states until the seventeenth century. They became a marginalized minority, and accused of having the "evil eye," they were forbidden to own lands by an origin wrongly defined. These Ethiopian Israelis were descendants of one of the "ten lost tribes" of the tribe of Dan, deported in 722 BC by the Assyrians.

They had an important monastic tradition of Christians, and their place of worship was called masjid, where they were reading the Bible based on the version of the five books of the Pentateuch. Their version of the Bible includes the book of Tobit, the book of Judith, the Sirach, the book of Enoch, and the book of Jubilees. They were sacrificing the Passover lamb there. This biblical custom of the Falasha in the Ge'ez liturgical language specific to the Greek Septuagint, different from the one that Ethiopian Christians were using, was abandoned by other Jewish communities. The current Hebrew version of the canonized Septuagint was not useful to them until the twentieth century, since they did not speak the Hebrew language. In ancient geography, the name of the kingdom of Aksum designated Africa from the fourth century. Aksum, which was developed during the first and fourth centuries of our era, was a construction of the development built by natives. Initially, the control of northern Ethiopia, Eritrea, northeast Sudan, southeastern Egypt, Djibouti, and the Yemeni area of

Tihama in South Arabia was taken when Aksum was quite powerful in the third century, with a total of 1.25 million square kilometers of territory.

The prophet Mani mentioned that kingdom—with Persia, the Roman Empire, and China—as one of the four greatest powers of his time when Aksum struck its own currency and put it in circulation around the middle of the Aksumite period toward 270, under the reign of King Endubis, and constituted a monetary system based on metal (gold, silver, and copper). That currency was the only one in circulation in sub-Saharan Africa; it spread from the third century up to the first half of the seventh century, and it was in Tanzania at the tenth century that the sultanate of Kilwa, the most important of the Swahili culture, issued its own currency. Its decline began at the beginning of the sixth century, after a second golden age, and at the beginning of the seventh century, that kingdom ceased its production of Aksumite coins, finally dissolved by the Jewish pagan Yodit Gudit, the legendary queen who devastated Aksum, destroying monuments and burning churches and religious literature in the ninth or tenth century, during its invasion. She began a violent campaign of misdeeds to exterminate members of the ruling dynasty by killing the emperor and ransacking Debre Damo, a monastery founded in the sixth century by Za-Mikael Aragewi, the group leader and one of the nine saints from the Byzantine Empire in the kingdom of Aksum, to spread Christianity. That Ethiopian Orthodox monastery is established at the flat top of a mountain about ninety kilometers north of Ethiopia in the province of Tigray. In the historical accounts, the tradition mentioned the acts of that non-Christian who reigned during a dark period for forty years until the ascension of the Zagwe dynasty, an Orthodox Christian family in Lasta, who reigned in the eleventh or twelfth century after a Jewish monarchy. At that time, on August 10, 1270, Yekuno Amlak, king or negus, killed the last Zagwe king and ascended to the throne of Ethiopia until his death on June 19, 1285. I must underline that we should not confuse negus, a title of Ethiopian nobility, with něgūša nagašt, equivalent to the title of emperor and meaning "king of kings" already negus since 1928.

Haile Selassie I, accessed the supreme title of něgūša nagašt at his coronation in 1930. That country where the Ark of the Covenant is resting and the home of the Queen Sheba, who reigned on the kingdom of Sheba, reached its peak in the first century. It was one of the few among the fifty-four states that retained its sovereignty over the dismemberment of Africa in the nineteenth century.

Historically, the kingdom of Saba, located in Yemen, the southern Arabia, the northern Ethiopia, or the present-day Eritrea, dated from 716 BC. Usually mentioned by the Bible and the Koran, that kingdom had an existence posterior to the Solomon's reign.

The city of Marib, capital of the kingdom of Sheba, was built around 1500 BC, even before Rome was built. The biblical kingdom of Sheba was considered as the richest of the earth at that time, and its people were in contact with the entire Mediterranean world. The Bible highlights the biblical period of the reign of the Queen of Sheba by her visit to King Solomon in Jerusalem toward the late tenth century BC.

The Queen of Sheba was described by others as a spiritual or a magician temptress, but King Solomon saw a sublime woman in her—a personage of profound wisdom, of high intelligence, and a breathtaking beauty as the virgin creatures of paradise, the reward of the blessed celestial characters. She was assigned different names; she was called "Makeda" in the Ethiopian tradition, "Sheba" in Hebrew, "Balqama" in Yemen, and "Balkis" in the Islamic tradition, through the words of the prophet Muhammad in the sura 27 of the Koran.

Luke 11:31 called her the "queen of the south" in the New Testament. The Hebrew Bible recounts her meeting with King Solomon in 1 Kings 10:1–13 and his many rich gifts (gold, precious stones, and perfumes) from Ophir. According to the Bible, King Solomon was receiving a cargo loaded with gold, ivory, peacocks, precious stones, sandalwood, silver, and monkeys from Ophir every three years. Notably, the region of Ophir was known for its wealth as mentioned in the Bible. Saba, impressed by the splendor of the palace and the yard of Solomon, was devoted; the story of the Hebrew Bible tells how Solomon proved his great wisdom to her after attended to the services rendered to God in the temple of Jerusalem. She returned to her country breathless, praising God who had chosen her to reign over her people and for the Wisdom of Solomon. She was invited by Solomon because she was not faithful to God, and her people worshipped the sun, according to sura 27, verses 23–44, of the Koran, to finally be converted to "the faith of the unique God."

In the gospel according to Luke, to Jews refusing to believe in him, Jesus of Nazareth compared her to those who would not deign to approach him at that very place where the queen of Sheba traveled to meet Solomon; saying that he still deserves greater efforts from that generation, and that the Queen of Sheba will condemn it because Christ is more important than Solomon. In two Masonic rituals, the Queen of Sheba is briefly mentioned:

> (i) - In the rites of English origin, the Emulation Rite, introduced and defended by Irish regiments, was exported to North America as a masonry ritual of pure tradition, related to the name of York rite, by the sense of a mythical origin, as the oldest Masonic customs and traditions. Subsequently, it took its secondary denomination from the American rite in the early eighteenth century. In its context of the resolutely theist appearance, the York Rite is fundamentally from the Old Testament and relies on the Bible; its belief or doctrine, which affirms the existence of at least one divinity, is the religious theism, since it is through the intermediaries of religion that the relation of man with God is established: God is an action in the universe and a personal existence; theism clearly affirms the divine interference in human affairs and opposes atheism, contrary to the deist view that affirms the existence of God and his influence in the creation of the

universe, without relying on sacred texts or depending on a revealed religion; its "natural religion" is lived by individual experience and does not rest on a written tradition; according to philosophical theism, God directly governs the universe.

Certain characteristics of God can be understood by the intellectual faculties of man. God, "the Supreme Architect," neither alters nor interferes with human affairs, nor suspends the natural laws that govern the universe, and rejects all supernatural events as prophecies and miracles. All that the theistic religion sees as divine revelation in the structured holy books is at the origin of religions, and its divinities have an influence in the universe; but we can also cite several forms of theism that are not necessarily religious, among which deism - irreligious theism, particularly the pantheism, monotheism, and polytheism are included; the theistic doctrine is claiming that it is inconceivable that nothing is at the origin of everything, that all that is created by God—as an original universal and intelligent source—is not the work of man, and that in the universe, God has an action and personal existence. Unlike the deist vision, religious theism is claiming that the only way for man to unite with God is through religion, that revelations are at the origin of religion and in sacred texts like Koran, Bible, Torah, and Veda, and that for the salvation of man, respect for religious rites is essential; the deist sees these affirmations as simple interpretations made by man and concludes that no religious source can be authoritative. The emulation ritual or rite of union is practiced particularly in the ritual called "installation of the venerable." It was in the presence of the Queen of Sheba that Solomon made this gesture, which became one of the signs of recognition in the Masonic rituals. A Masonic Lodge is a civil fraternity that brings together a small group of members of Freemasonry at the local level; its members are characterized by a "distinctive title called degree; so the American York rite is divided into many degrees grouped into four categories:

1. "Blue Lodges"
   Apprentice
   Companion

Master of the Blue Lodges
These are degrees of the Blue Lodges.

2. "Royal Arch"
   Brand master
   Virtual pass master
   Very excellent master
   Mason of the Royal Arch

The royal arch, which takes its symbol on the Ark of the Covenant, is contained in the Temple of Solomon.

   3. "Council—Cryptic Masons"
      Royal Master
      Chosen Master
      Super excellent master

The Council's ritual completes the chapter's degrees under the mythological reference to the Temple Crypts of Solomon. These rituals of the council are much more modern.

   4. "Commanderies—Knights Templar"
      Knight of the Red Cross
      Knight of Malta
      Knight of the Temple

The Commanderies, which moved from the Temple of Solomon to the Knights Templar, have a more Christian dimension than the chapters or the council.

   (i) - Equally, in the American jurisdictions, the Most Excellent Master degree, which can be received after a past master's degree, by those who have proved themselves worthy, by their virtue, skills, and fidelity, they're then inducted into the Oriental Chair of King Solomon. This degree is originated in the York Rite system and by far the most spectacular degree in all Freemasonry. A candidate receiving this degree represents King Solomon and acknowledged holding a scepter in his hand, wearing a crown, and dressed in a crimson robe.

It is the Para-Masonic American Order, known as the order of the Eastern Star that inspired the degree of Queen of the South. This Masonic philanthropic organization of ladies and gentlemen patriotic members is mainly based on the Bible and has approximately ten thousand chapters similar to the Masonic lodges with the current of esoteric thought, attached to the Judeo-Christian mysticism, in particular asking its members to belief in God. Christianity, Islam, Hinduism, and Judaism are theistic religions; on the other hand, Buddhism, Confucianism, and Taoism, not being based on one or more deities, are philosophies not explicitly theistic. So before the preaching of Jesus of Nazareth around the year 30, from Judaism to Abraham, the "true" religion before the Hegira—the departure of Muhammad and his followers from the point of view of the first congregational religious immigration in "exile" from Mecca toward the oasis of Yathrib, later renamed Medinat *an-Nabī* by him in 622, literally meaning the "*city of the prophet,*" it was soon dropped and named "Medina," meaning "the city"—Christianity existed already in Genesis, under different forms successively abstaining; but claims to have been founded by Mohammed in 622, in another form as a kind of temporal "ecumenism."

However, the "true" local variant religion, such as the polytheistic religion that never knew these religions closest to monotheism, was the henotheism and the animist religion of the Great Spirit, up to the valid form of monotheism. Thus, after the appearance of Islam, and since its chronology for all the people encountered, Islam abrogated those previous versions of henotheism.

The temple of the moon god, a sacred site called Mahram Bilqis in northern Yemen, was used between 1200 and 550 by pilgrims. Dating back from three thousand years, it could be the evidence of the existence of Queen of Sheba, located near the ancient city of Marib, the capital of the kingdom of Sheba, according to the Bible and the Muslim tradition. The palace of the Queen of Sheba was discovered in Ethiopia, according to the University of Hamburg, below the palace of a Christian king. It reported that the building, oriented toward the star Sirius, was the first version of the palace. According to the Bible, the Queen of Sheba and her son Menelik I became its worshippers.

Jerusalem—which holds a central place in the Jewish, Christian, and Muslim religions—is a city of the Middle East. In the twentieth and fourteenth century before our era, that city, "Jerusalem," is mentioned in the Egyptian texts of hatred, violence, and what is worthy of maledictions for the first time at the time when Egypt reduced "*Ka-na-na*," Canaan, as its vassal state for some two centuries under the name of Rushalimu and Urusalim, which did not spring out clearly from the Egyptian hieroglyphs. As it was customary to give the name of a local god to a city, the city of Jerusalem was named Urushalimu, reflecting the cult of the god Shalem, a god of creation, of completeness, and the setting sun, known as the Canaanite god.

That Canaanite god was known as a god of Canaan, adopted during the major historical periods up to when the city was baptized Jerusalem, the problematic capital of Israel. We must remember that for 3,500 years, Canaan—the black territory, a land then called Palestine—has always been a mix of populations but also the object of struggles for influence and has repeatedly changed powerful hands. Those powerful influences were the Hebrews, Philistines, Egyptians, Persians, Romans, Arab Muslims, the Christian crusaders, Ottomans, British, the Palestinians, and Israelis.

From 1942, Ethiopia became one of the fifty-one founding member states of the UN and a signatory of the United Nations Declaration. Ethiopia was the oldest independent state in Africa, almost three thousand years, and was the first to have its own coins, deeply involved in trade between India and the Mediterranean and the leading supplier of African products to the Roman Empire. The port of Adulis an Ethiopia city on the west coast of the Red Sea, at the bottom of the bay of Adulis or Ansley, became the port of Aksum under the Romans, today Zoulla, exporting ivory collected by the slaughtering of our elephants on the Kushite territory, instead of passing through Meroe, the capital of Kush. Away from the Nile corridor, a caravan bound for Egypt was created. The kingdom of Aksum continued to extend its control over the basin of the Red Sea during the second and third centuries.

Its history began around the eighth century BC with the formation of the ancient kingdom of D'mt or Da'amot before the Sabaean migration of the fourth and fifth centuries BC. That ancient kingdom appeared around 800 BC and extended on the current region of Eritrea, in the northern Ethiopia, and lasted until the seventh century BC. It spoke the Semitic languages called Habesha, known as a Kushitic family language and as a family of languages spoken in East Africa; constituting a branch of Chamito-Semitic languages, also called Afro-Asian languages, as a family of languages spoken in the Middle East and North Africa; and Nilo-Saharan languages, such as a family of languages spoken in sub-Saharan Africa in the regions of Upper Nile and Upper-Chari including Nubia. In addition, the Ge'ez, the ancient Semitic language of Eritrea and Ethiopia, is today known not to be derived from the language of Saba, and there are signs of the presence of Semitic languages in Ethiopia and Eritrea at least 2000 BC. Yetbarak, the last sovereign of Ethiopia's Zagwe dynasty, who died in 1268, overthrown by Yekuno Amlak in 1270, marked the restoration of the Solomonid dynasty that ruled almost continuously until 1974.

Ethiopia, Eritrea, Somalia, and the coast of Sudan are also possible locations of the country named the land of Punt, which means "the country of God," or *Ta Netjeru* in Egyptian ("land of gods"), who's first mentioned by the Egyptians, dates back to the twenty-fifth century BC. On the Egyptian monuments, the representations of the Somali people as children of Punt country show striking resemblances to the Egyptians to demonstrate their ancestral historical family ties. These countries are considered as the original place of God and gods.

Liberia, founded in 1822 by the American Colonization Society, is an American Society denounced from 1829 by William Lloyd Garrison, the abolitionist, and in 1832 in his book entitled Thoughts on African Colonization, followed in 1833, by the main organization known as the American Anti-Slavery Society. Those denunciations, which were against the objective of the United States and Robert Finley, to reduce the number of black people in their country, once again organized their deportation back to Africa and installed the freed black slaves there. Liberia, which was controlled from the founding of the American Colonization Society in 1817, became an independent republic on July 26, 1847, as the first African nation to have achieved independence.

Subsequently, Egypt saw the prosperity of one of the most brilliant civilizations in the history of the Nile valley and of mankind for nearly three millennia; shortly after, the appearance of the wedge-shaped (cuneiform) signs from the earliest known writing system, this form of wedges was developed in lower Mesopotamia around 3400 and 3200 BC; but the human species came out of the prehistory with the invention of an original writing in the form of ideogram symbols, hieroglyphs, based on pictograms, "images that look like what they signify," to reach its peak in the eighteenth century BC and known by a monumental work of the world heritage.

It was in the first century that the Christian community was formed, converted by St. Mark, nicknamed Marcus, and also called John in the Acts of the Apostles. He was the author of the gospel according to Mark, one of the three synoptic gospels of the New Testament, and a bishop of Alexandria. Despite a long Ottoman rule and then British, the kingdom of Egypt became independent in 1922, after numerous invasions and various occupations, mainly by Persians, Greeks, Romans, and Byzantines.

Finally, the South African Union, discovered by Bartolomeu Dias, who discovered various bays on the coast of the present-day South Africa, including Algoa Bay, eight hundred kilometers east of the Cape of Good Hope, the Cape of Agulhas, at the southernmost point of the continent, and the Cape of Good Hope in January 1488, looking for another way to India.

The Dutch and English also stopped at the southern tip of the continent, along the trade route, when they started to challenge the Portuguese. This made that the cape became a regular stop. One of the parents of the navigator Bartolomeu Dias, named Dinis Dias, was the first navigator arrived in the country of blacks up to Cap Blanc in 1442. He was the first navigator to go beyond Mauritania, traditionally called the Moors country, along the Northern coast of Africa, to capture slaves, sell them, and finance his expeditions. He discovered Cape Verde, the most westerly point of the African continent, the Cape Verde Peninsula, in the present Senegal, not the Cape Verde Islands discovered in 1456, and the Goree Island in 1444. From that period to the present day, the natural rights of Africans and other people worldwide were confiscated.

We need a permanent democratic process to reaffirm the natural rights of humans. But all countries of the world are usurping the word *democracy* because they're just able to scream louder than others. Unambiguously, good morals are from Africans, regarding the true meaning of the term *traditional democracy* from a primitive idea with African origins. The Africans relied mainly on the myths that put assemblies in performance, where men or deities intervene.

In the region of Meru, the eastern province of Kenya in East Africa had a true democracy. Since it had only one and unique geopolitical district for many years, they easily gathered their people; and since each citizen easily knew all the others, voting was an act of democratic foundation in a tribe, in a village, or in a great nation. The structure of the generational systems of Meru in Kenya, was based on the ranks of fathers, a tribal based, which was regrouping people by definition in small entities in a new type of policies devoid of central power but with clean features to societies and to the state. The exercise of a judicial and legislative function, the control of violence, and territorial sovereignty legitimacy were the attributes ingredients of the fathers who were gathered in assembly. The democratic feeling was present around the life that revolved around the same common points, bringing a kind of self-regulation and self censorship as a positive result; an organization of the state with the ideal of tending to help and not of appropriating wealth or power; without forgetting what voting a member from members meant. I vote for the one I know and that I speak to concerning the democratic debate that precedes every election, expressing myself on the future of my nation by knowing all its members. It was in the process of initiation that this new model of democracy draws its origin and legitimacy.

That mode of government of citizenship was turned upside down during the colonial conquest. That system was aggregated into simple age groups, which provided comparative insights on political institutions specific to certain cities. It was not speaking of justice, of tribunal to find solutions to multiple quarrels of various interests that their society naturally generated.

It is up to Africa to export its expertise in the redistribution of direct democracy with citizen expression by consensus, the legality in ranks, in fortunes distribution, and not the opposite. Those who want pompously to export the so-called democracy are only claiming the necessity of luxury, of wealth that has become their virtue, the objective to reach happiness at all costs, and not caring or wanting to share fortunes with the people.

The most unbalanced and most unequal country in the world is the United States of America, which is exercising a subtle dictatorship of elites with a sufficiently repressive dictatorial system like other Western countries; preventing any attempt of rebellion, and where 5 percent of the population owns 60 percent of the national wealth. The rich and the poor are both corrupt, whether through possession or through envy, where luxury, seducing each other for vanity, deprives the state of all its citizens and sells them to a defective constitution mark and where forty-three million civil servants and military actually control the country. Thus, Nations are accepting the system that oppresses them stoically everywhere in the world without reacting.

Democratization in Africa and in the black world was implemented without problem, and it remained consistent because the black question was not arising. It led a lucid and courageous politics of the ethnic groups but exposed to the anti-contextualism, without face or gaze and wandering like Narcissus. In the situation of ethnic groups, rather than judging according to absolute moral standards, it took into account the particular context of acts, when evaluating them ethically; thus within each context it evaluated them with the law of love, not with the universal law that had to be followed; but the type of love that showed the concern about others, caring for them as much as one cares for himself with a totally unconditional love, conceived as having no strings attached to it and seeking nothing in return with some important respect, having a reason and possibly even "being true" or "being right," and only having relative meaning understood in a specified context increasingly popular among ethnic groups.

That situation was often closely associated with ethics situational, or with moral relativism point of view, preoccupied by differences in moral judgments between different people and cultures, disagreeing about what is moral; whereas in such disagreements, nobody is objectively right or wrong; and because nobody is right or wrong, democracy had to tolerate the behavior of others even when disagreeing about their morality; that was the debate on democracy for thousands of years in Africa. In various fields of democracy, like the authoritarian democracy, the direct democracy, the dominant-party system, the electoral democracy, the illiberal democracy, the liberal democracy, the parliamentary democracy, the presidential democracy, the representative democracy, and the totalitarian democracy, to only name a few, including art, philosophy, religion, and science, Ancient Greece and India adopted them to the present day. Consequently, to the profoundly divergent interests that we have after five hundred years of the dominator and the dominated relationship with the West; how can we not define good from the wicked, from the same criteria since then proven as racist theory of Europeans? Does Africa still have its place in such a democratic organization? No, because none of these Western countries have the power to assign us any democracy.

The fifty-four African countries should leave the United Nations; to return in it one day is to put their reform on the agenda, for the entire African federation to have at least one permanent member in the Security Council, with the same right of veto, because its hierarchy and its configuration are at the service of the strongest. That conception of the world is solely based, since then, on the crushing of the weakest. We need to have thoughtful acts of union to become a force, to reach true freedom, respectability, and dignity for Africa, as a price to pay that will restore that respectability, not to guarantee the comfort of other nations but toward our respect. It's time; we must assume the consequences. An agreement to thwart any action allowing to bomb this or that country has always been signed silently; this scenario already seen before is simply repeated today without reprisals from anyone. It is what happened at the end of the Second World War. To not be fooled or manipulated anymore, learning his history is important. The history of men, as we know it today, has the duty and the responsibility to transmit a democratic future for generations to come; convey a consciousness of African humanity beyond humanity, which is not written in the ideological obscurantism; revise the multidimensionality of African history with scientific objectivity, particularly on the cumulative negative impacts of the historical facts on the cultural, economic, demographic, political, psychological developments, and social factors in the explanations of contemporary realities; and correct the falsification of the historiography of the African slaver raids and the slavery, the nature of the patriarchal contact of Europe/Africa at the imperial era, the influence of the historical cradles from the nomadic societies, and the importance of the African resistance, which led to the abolition. All whams of the Eurocentric speeches of the last five hundred years through the history of slavery should be criticized.

The African civilization of direct democracy among the Meru generally operated through a conference, gathering everyone involved near or far, to resolve a situation of disagreement that required solution. The representatives of multiple functions, with the primary role of resolving problems without bias and without legal challenge of appropriate ranks to settle disputes, gathered delegates, of course with the existing rivalries, but which remained within the acceptable limits. As one of the most vivid historical examples of the proper functioning of the direct democracy in Africa, initiation was the institutional rite that regulated the democratic succession to power in the Meru nation before the German colonial invasion in 1908. In fact, all citizens of that democratic society of over ninety thousand souls were governing the country of Meru.

This process is the healing general solution offered since by the traditions of African communities to establish the necessary reconciliation of a fraternity, located on the possible reparations, and to settle the political affairs in a direct and total democracy, which brought welfare to the people as they wish; particularly, giving the historical possibility to freely establish the new constitution of their new states, which will allow to establish the kind of democratic institutions that the people will decide to put in place. Stipulating clearly that, whenever the people's trust rate falls below a figure decided by the people (for example, 50 percent), the legal representative leader must immediately resign from his functions because of insufficient people's confidence and must be replaced by the people according to the procedure defined by the law. The people thereby become the sovereign, the trust, an important unequivocal principle that had to justify the legitimacy to exert any state or popular power for any individual or group of individuals, with the power and authority to dissolve all political institutions of our countries became democratic, exercising a direct democracy, through its free decisions of laws that are automatically applied by the popular legitimacy. To fraud the inviolable popular expression without the law that imposed a particular form of its expression was the most serious crimes of high treason against the people who freely decided its form of popular expression, in the scale of the penal crimes code of the country, as a basic unit of the popular expression of the legislative power. A National Assembly designated the members of the Supreme Court who were responsible for judicial power. A panel composed of magistrates was publishing the candidates at the functions of judges at the Supreme Court, which were to ensure the functioning of courts in accordance with laws applicable throughout the national territory, adopted by the National Assembly to maintain the ethic, morality, and virtue in the field of public defense, of all management of men and public properties, susceptible to undermine the well-being of the public, in accordance with the guidelines given by the people.

This is to let the colonial and neocolonial administrative units disappear in the political, economic, social, cultural, and environmental affairs of Africa—a wish so much desired by the public as a constitutional requirement. Thus, in any decision-making of a group, the consensualism, which already existed very long ago in the African historical society, will become a universal rule in the contemporary society and a new African democratic custom in the democratic state based on tradition of the African people's wisdom who must decide on the consensus matter for an effective management of the African community in Africa.

Europe, as a former slaver and colonizer still feeds the psychic structures with racism and institutions with a formidable racial logic, having been a primitive form of racial domination not until today dismantled at home, but still possessed by a spirit of demon, a desire for apartheid, hatred of foreigners, and folded in its traditions that we all know. That process of decolonization without democratization is making that Africans are turning around in circle, still having a long way to go to positively achieve the decolonization of their world.

Africa must achieve that decolonization by centralizing its energies and forces scattered by the European cruelty, to reconstruct the internal disorders and stop the waste of its natural resources by the structures of the unequal exploitation on a global scale, whose consequences are disastrous. Evidently, we need a particular context of thoughts, of real critics and self-struggle to open the paths of the future, if we want to accomplish this work.

Slavery and colonization formed the legacy of the political class of African elites who are governing with the behavior of servants subordinated to masters, the foreign occupiers of a tradition of savagery toward our country. These elites are demonstrating a savage manner and are leading their countries in a beastly way, encouraged at all times by that same tradition of foreign savagery, historically generalized across the world. Their recognized model of existence continues to undermine the spirit and life of Africans through the cruel fog and smoke of a burning fire with violence in Africa. Despite that calamity and a catastrophic management of those money avids in power in our continent, a new cycle of massive Chinese unprecedented immigration with a tendency to newly colonize us comes and join a heavy evolution of a civilization already reaching a population of more than one billion inhabitants; a real contrast, establishing the truth of a fact, the desire of thousands of worthy African sons and daughters seeking to leave their continent to live elsewhere than at home. I would say without hesitation that a structural mental realignment of our institutions should regulate the smooth circulation of new Diasporas in Africa—a continent generally known for its hospitality—opened to newcomers.

Affected by millions, they're going out in desperation; fleeing our governments led by heads of state like greedy masked chiefdoms with disastrous politics, for a recomposition of their uncertain life beyond the borders of their African continent. Africa needs intellectual creativity, economic growth, a sociocultural physical process properly African; a sense of development and mental evolution at work, without which, the inherited borders of colonization will never fall. These key factors are forming the rules concerning reforms that so many Africans want at the continental level to allow their return in the continent.

Officially, I also wished that an idea be realized—to give the right of belonging to the people of African descent all over the world, who want to belong to the continent or make a final return to Africa. A black leader of the twentieth century, considered a prophet by the followers of the Rastafarian movement, by the name of Marcus Mosiah Garvey, born in Jamaica on August 17, 1887, in St. Ann's Bay, had already proclaimed that wish of Pan-Africanism by declaring during one of his speeches that he did not believe that the descendants of black slaves could live free and respected outside Africa.

Obstinate about the union of blacks around the world and their return to Africa, he requested the right of repatriation in Africa and undertook steps to unify blacks internationally. A black king will one day be crowned in Africa and will lead the black people of the whole world to the deliverance. He will be the God of all ages and the eternal God—God the Son and God the Holy Spirit, to whom we niggers will believe and whom we will worship, God of Ethiopia, meaning Africa in the Anglo-Saxon Bible of (King James). Often referring to Ethiopia, Garvey generally designated Africa, following the Rastafarian doctrine that was attributed to him, following the prophecy created by him. Jamaica, substantially formed by the slave trade, is the birthplace of the Rastafarian Abrahamic religion during the 1930s.

Haile Selassie I, the righteous leader of the earth for most Rastas, who believed in his spirituality based on his divinity, was the direct descendant of the said dynasty of King Solomon and David by Queen Makeda of Saba. According to the Jamaica tradition, the Ethiopian emperor was regarded as the messiah of the Rastafarian prophecy and the central figure in the Rastafarian ideology. The history of his ancient dynasty was traced in the sacred book *Glory of the Kings* or *Kebra Nagast*, indicating his birth on July 23, 1892, in a city called Ejersa Goro in eastern Ethiopia, located outside the city of Harar, the region of the Ethiopian Empire; Ras Tafari Makonnen, his real name meaning — Tafari, the "one who is respected or feared," and the name of his father, Makonnen, meaning the "great, noble," was the last emperor in Africa.

At his accession to the throne of Ethiopia, proclaimed on April 3, 1930, after the sudden death of the Empress Zewditu, the one who never adhere to the Rastafarian movement changed his name to Haile Selassie I. It is from his pre-regnal title name "Ras Tafari Makonnen" that the word "Ras derived from, meaning "head," the equivalent of chief, a duke or prince, is the basis name of the Jamaican "Rastafarian" religion. Thus, his first earthly name Ras Tafari means Chief Dread or Head Dread.

Nowadays, the name "Jah" as a deity is most commonly associated with Rastafarians in the English-language context, as the name of God or Haile Selassie, who some Rastafarians regard as the incarnation of God, also believe that "Jah" is inherent within each human, and that "God is man and man is God;" rather than simply believing in him, by seeking the narrow distance separating humanity from divinity, forgetting that knowing "Jah," is embracing mysticism.

As head of one of the first officially Christian nation since 1,500 years in the history and historically known as Abyssinia, Tafari Makonnen was crowned with the sacred crown of *nĕgusä nagašt* on November 2, 1930, in Ethiopia and became the emperor (*atse*) and his name meaning "elect of God" in Ge'ez (*Seyoume Igziabeher*) means "power of the Trinity," as the last King who bore the title of negus. The Power of Trinity, "King of Kings, Lord of Lords," or the

Conquering Lion of the Tribe of Judah, as the title of Moa Anbessa Ze Imnegede Yehuda, always preceded the name of the emperor. Up to Yohannes IV, king of Zion (*Negusse Tsion*), his reference to Christ marked the imperial submission to the superiority of Jesus. Dead on August 27, 1975, in Addis Ababa, Haile Selassie I was the last emperor of Ethiopia from 1930 to 1936 and from 1941 to 1974. He was the only African leader to have honored the request of Garvey by opening the doors of his country and accepting the return of blacks in Ethiopia. In Shashamane, thanks to this opening of the Ethiopian borders by Haile Selassie I, we still find a Jamaican community, mainly Rastas and black Jews coming from America, who settled in that country from 1955, thus regaining their "Mother Earth" from which they were brutally snatched by white slavers.

Despite his enthusiasm and love for Africa, Garvey died in London on June 10, 1940, of a heart attack, without ever reaching Africa. Kwame Nkrumah would retake the idea of the black Moses, the precursor of Pan-Africanism, by organizing the first conference of the independent African states by the Sixth and Seventh Pan-African Conferences in Kumasi in 1953 and Accra in 1958 with the father of Pan-Africanism of the twentieth century, the Caribbean George Padmore. He advocated the formation of a supranational identity of the United States of Africa. According to him, this goal would allow the continent to become one of the greatest powers of the world by establishing a common policy with his African homologues in 1958. As an example, to support his idea, he granted a loan of £10 million to Ahmed Sekou Toure, the man who led Guinea to independence in 1958, born on January 9, 1922, in Faranah, Guinea, in an environment of Sarakolle traders, and the president of Guinea from January 15, 1959, up to his death on March 26, 1984. Sekou Toure was a descendant of Almamy Samory Toure, a Mandinka emperor who led a fierce battle with his army against colonialism. Kwame Nkrumah became the first to make that gesture of good comprehension by forming a union for the concrete realization of Pan-Africanism with Guinea on May 1, 1959.

On December 24, 1960, Mali adhered to that union initiative. Born on September 21, 1909, at Nkroful in Ghana, he became the prime minister from 1957 to 1960 after his studies in England and the United States of America. And from 1960 to 1966, as president, after forcing the United Kingdom to the proclamation of independence on March 6, 1957, finally, Kwame Nkrumah proposed the creation of an African central government in March 1963. It is an idea that unfortunately hasn't been retained since then as a real African Union but remained embryonic and purely symbolic until today in the Ethiopian capital of Addis Ababa, its current headquarters. That great independentist politician and Ghanaian Pan-Africanist died in Bucharest, Romania, on April 27, 1972.

This would have been a vast horizon for the future if African leaders of today attempted to flourish such a good idea for the generation of a promising future, seized by the challenges of globalization of the present tumult. The new African intellectuals and civilized societies must embrace the process of that idea and reactivate the dormant political dimensions, with a voice capable to make a great cultural movement emerge, resulting into a traditional African aesthetic policy of esoteric philosophies, and a centralized sociocultural economy, which comes from our faraway ancestral thoughts; in this world where the return of the political walls of racism and fear is building the reason of the prejudices that we thought were abandoned on the psychic limit, with a greater and most ferocious partition aiming to reduce the logic of Africa that absolutely wants to build up an autonomous force. All African countries are struck by that well-advanced shift rooted in the postcolonial authoritarian culture, developed from the slave trade, practiced by the leaders of each of their societies, since the independence in Africa. So, our governments still operate on the basis of the political belief of the succession to the throne of our states from father to son or the everlasting reign, like in the good old days of colonization.

The abilities of organizing themselves in our continent remain manifestly the structures of the Western institution structures with the legitimate forms of corruption, widespread looting, waste without purpose, and a machine of prefabricated consumers to spend unreservedly, conditioning the daily and political life of the people since the independence of Africa. The modernity of the globalization implied in our lives consists of deploying powers to venal lamentations. The particular senility inflicted on African citizens by the whites and by the old age does not necessarily help the production of generations that can study the multiple ways of sociocultural logics and their everyday practices for solidarity in communities, how to communicate the distress and claims of a life leading to the expressive joy, as a principal and symbolic resource, which constitute the effective actions of the institution of democracy, and achieve the organizational goals of the transcendental tactical intellectual reappropriations for the benefit of Africa.

Establish its constitution by building the democratic foundations of its republics and legitimize its state by building a modern and stable state of law, for humanitarian actions, a legitimate power under sacred values, vibrating with love, freedom, and peace; to represent institutions with patriotic objectives, including a policy and a viable organ that can defend the interests of multidimensional resources that constitute the wealth, leading to the development of our countries.

The obscurantism organized by politicians is using diplomatic weapons against all adversity to achieve the objectives of an instructive reason leading to progress and maintain the people in the pauperization offered by the contemporary modernity, which protects the neocolonial manipulations, and the unilateral agreements imposed by the colonial pact determined by the influential leaders on the political plans throughout the world. The strategic and operational decisions of our partnership relations preserved an autosomal structure of decentralized action and logistics as the driving forces within our countries, to cut the civil society from an alternative society project, fighting to achieve the actions of a unifying framework beyond ethnic groupings, to achieve an influential political, economic, and financial capacity; having the appropriate patriotic competent commitment and aiming to defend the legitimate interests of our countries, in a policy of inertia dictatorship and by the reign of forces demoted with strong force.

The struggle must be perpetuated until the true liberation of Africa in a memorable manner. This is how the traditional collaboration will accompany the logic of communities and enthrone a proud dynasty as a witness and victim of the incessant repression of the violation of human rights of any kind, corruption, persecution, and reprisals by the postcolonial power. The fight against tribalism, a political instrument of division mounted by the colonizers from scratch, still prospers strongly in our countries but still advocates neutrality to symbolize unity and reconciliation.

At the twilight of independence, the total lack of will and the greed of the material desire of the politicians who took power in our countries made that they're still ignoring the grievances and claims of their community until today, with an immense arrogance and the illegitimacy of permanently unfailing abuses of life, preventing freedom to people by the violations of human rights, the right of democratic expression, but freely testifying their abuses against human beings in general by their respective ruthless governments in Africa.

The experiences already lived and which are still lived today in Africa do not form any peaceful structural alternation to the authoritarian postcolonial culture, which refuses a rooting of freely chosen institutions, which can lead to a development leading to a radical democratization of African political life.

The geniuses of different African traditions of solidarity must rise beyond imagination and organized traditional institutions as a symbol of unconditional rapprochement between people through social and cultural forces to support democracy, which is one of their common denominator, and root it in Africa to ensure the bridge between the forms of democratic politics of the society and the state on one side and the credible legitimacy of social and cultural logics on the other. Such a project is far from being accomplished intellectually under the current conditions where the consciousness of the African political class is not revived, but still significantly requiring certain proportion of ethnicity, preventing the definition of the outline idioms of our communities, which could inspire the policies necessary for a new vision of the community that transcends the kinships lineage or tribes; particularly in these difficult moments of suffering and political turbulence, where senility is striking thousands of men publicly, generally lucid only a few hours a day, at all levels of life.

It is imperative to know and to submit oneself to the cup of death, which requires killing everything that lives and breathes. But they do not want to die because they want to quench their thirst for power. It is unfortunately not possible to avoid that feeling that has no alternative than death. Today, the need for an urgent revolution is weighing forever in our societies, likely to lead the actions of all that could help to unblock the impasse. This situation is constantly giving very painful headaches and causes insomnia to weight loss, the energy not revitalizing the body, weakening the immune system and leading to multiple diseases.

This is a risk of a social implosion toward that lack of democracy; a situation particularly occurring currently in a very complementary way in a spirit supporting the need for a common Pan-Africanist denominator in Africa. However, instead of inspiring for the principle of conduct, of the three duties necessary for humanity which are the following:

1. Love – a very intense feeling to love, of having a devotion as dedication, has become like a drop of water that hurts the passionate eye; a passionate love of oneself to the loved one, making a difference in an entire ocean no longer exists in the reasoning of humanity.
2. Estimate – to recognize the value of humanity, to determine a visceral impulse, to consider making more appeal to reason, to have the same opinion, and believe to be loved.
3. Respect – the fear of the judgment of men, a civility allowing someone to treat his neighbor with great respect. Respect the reason to make men wise and happy; as far as they're here on earth, they must be the basis of all reasonable reasoning education, to one day change the face of the world toward the happy centuries, and not always so easily making us see the horrible principles of the Europeans with their ancient Christian principles.

Our leaders are exterminators, destructive conquerors, and worshippers of python worship, a monster snake that lives in them. They're singing the victory of darkness to us, the sanguinary victorious rites of the character of the public calamities, constituting false commitment and non-instructive commemorative principles.

They eat the victims of their people and drink the blood of our children for excellence with the greatest exquisite delight in their altars of nonpatriotism. Is it understandable to have such an idea that does them honor, to alter the human blood of their people by carnage, requiring the approval of their governments? What an honor or happiness these poor African leaders have, who believe that the blood of a whole population is not enough to satisfy their greatest exaggerated fanaticism by the greater barbarism. Those errors have become a custom in a number of the political yards of Africa, without respect, without truth, and without consequences for these leaders. The expectation of the people is just announcing the pleasure of their future life and the perpetual consolidation of fear and terror in various unhappy aspects. But considering them as the inexorable ruthless exterminating dictators, these snakes can be judged by allegorical names.

They have excessively perverted, crushed the character of men, forced a large number into slavery, repelling the gentle and peaceful people of these too unhappy nations in different continents; muzzled a hundred times the dupes who became the victims of the monsters worshipers; horrible governments of cruelty with the result of unreasonable legislation, and which correlatively have degraded the true character of the human race.

To date, the governments of America have already proven that injustice and cruel tyranny do not make free men happy, but the sumptuous and tedious governments of despots in Africa are still carrying very high that flambeau and sheltering their people in a foster asylum, with their extreme policies supported by the governments of the world, advocating the exercise of human rights.

These leaders are spending their time abusing their people by false principles of their governments bearing bad imprints with boundless power. By the wisdom and the humanism of nations, the exercise and the administration of politics by the constitution in Africa were to make the happiness and safety of the people.

Indeed, these foreign states with magistrates and respectable scholars who are tolerating and supporting forever these African despots were to teach lessons of remonstrances, tell them boldly or compelling them not to abuse their power, but to moderate it, by establishing instead of destroying passions, and rendering people inferior to the unhealthy conditions of the earth, which do not allow their prosperity and glory in our glorious continent; African governments would not let us see what was the great and sublime speculation of the first politicians, who sought not only to be independent but also to render men happy by shaping their governments on the African tradition to show us a justified example and the flattering appearance under the same views considered by our ancestors.

It is important to point out that African people have never been freed but have for long struggled for their honor and dignity. As far away it may seem, martyrdom imposed on our heroes of the struggle for our independence is part of that perpetual struggle for the advent of new and prosperous African people. Until today, the continuation of the popular uprisings for that fight represents for us a decisive battle of that long and difficult road toward our freedom. Let the patriotism of all those who gave their lives for Africa enlighten us, their death to inspire us so that their sacrifice may not be in vain.

It is necessary to strengthen a democracy guided by a patriotic leadership of wisdom, courageous, and full of compassion oriented toward the advent of our freedom, offering real opportunities to all regardless of political affinity, religion, ethnicity, and gender. Only an urgent action of the international level can stop and prevent the explosion of criminal impetus of hollow persuasive speeches of corruption, of poverty caused by the embezzlement of public funds, and the insecurity that currently governs the cradle of our ancestors, developed as a time bomb since our independence. Let us rise as a unit against the tyranny at the head of the cradle of our ancestors. It's now or never; our martyrs are watching over us, protecting us, and Africa will win because these leaders will pass, but Africa and its sovereign people will remain.

To preserve peace in the world, a powerful international organization was created after World War II. A United Nations Charter was the founding treaty of the international organization called the United Nations, signed on June 26, 1945, at San Francisco War Memorial and Performing Arts Center in San Francisco, United States. On October 24, 1945, it entered into force after being ratified by the five permanent members of the Security Council, with the objectives of maintaining international security, for the realization of the world peace, and the social progress of human rights, to facilitate the economic development and the cooperation in the international law. Unlike the League of Nations (LN), an intergovernmental organization created on January 10, 1920, in France, following the Paris Peace Conference, resulting to a peace treaty signed on June 28, 1919, after the First World War; as the first international organization, it determined the sanctions taken against Germany, which was deprived of its colonies, but failed to prevent the Second World War from 1939 to 1945.

Yet under the same law of the United Nations, the sovereignty of our African countries is an illusion, knowing that, in many African countries as in other continents, forces are stationed here and there to consistently and courageously maintain dictators hated by their people in power. The ambiguous nature of the United Nations cannot fail to ask itself a question; question that generally arises in terms of sovereignist, nationalist, and anti-imperialist, who are seeing this international organization called the United Nations not lift a finger to prevent genocide, massacres, collective rapes, and other crimes against humanity. We know as well that the American imperialism that enters a country already torn apart to officially accomplish a mission makes of that situation the bitter experience considered as a force of occupation, pretty much everywhere during the twentieth century in the world—namely, in the Philippines, Japan, Germany, Indonesia, Lebanon, Central and Latin America, and today in Afghanistan, Iraq, as well as in Libya—and supported the Ivory Coast crisis. That self-determination to prolong their missions indefinitely on the land of others, especially in our valleys of tears and happy souls, is for the use of force in a sense, for a deep intellectual satisfaction; but also in the context of their sexual enjoyment is awaiting the eternal decision of its supreme condemnation, and it can only become an unfriendly decision, and considered as a sworn enemy force, for their legitimized presence particularly pretentious.

This Africanist and anti-imperialist feeling, generated by the French forces with different names of animals, against the exercise of democracy and sovereignty of African people, represents a violent anti-European feeling in particular and the anti-Western feeling in general. The most active part of all the victims of the colonial and neocolonial dictatorships is naturally recruited among the mass of scholars and intellectuals of different protagonists for the authoritarian regimes of our countries. These literate protagonists and intellectuals of our countries perpetuate aggravating clumsiness with regard to the African policy for France, to the point of provoking the greatest anger of Africans intelligentsia. This type of aggravating imperialist clumsiness, qualifying Africa as not having made history, was pronounced at a bad time by Jacques Chirac, Nicolas Sarkozy de Nagy-Bosca, and Edouard Balladur, to only name a few; and at the same time a lack of intelligence that could hardly be described as idiotic; but exercising a continuity of an obstinate policy to vassalize Africa, they're wishing it the worse criminal intentions, of which the imperialist will of these French antagonists is considered as amply proven.

From the European Union (EU) and the countries of the world belonging to the United Nations led by the United States, there is no difference between interests; the weight of the American leadership in this supposedly international institution that took care to clean up the ancestry vices of the sad fate of the defunct League of Nations that was formed by the official political base of the United States president Woodrow Wilson, and that the United States will never integrate, still advocates the secret diplomacy submitted by this American president; but that leadership remains powerless when it comes to Africa, given the positioning of the actors of the European states in the field, the demotion of Russia to the rank of European power since the disintegration of the Soviet Union, the goodwill of the United States and its affirmation in the management of international conflicts, depends solely on the systematic alignment of these European Union States and the member countries of the United Nations.

It is well-known that the tactical perspectives of the Western imperialism—even though still in the Cold War pattern, in connection with capitalism, colonialism, socialism, decolonization, and self-determination—hated and still hate nationalist and the Africanist resistances who occasionally turned their backs on all revolutionary inclination for a political vision resolutely reformist in Africa. But being rather anchored in the liberal world is an intention of good conduct and a recommended progressive force in the eyes of third world. Thus, from November 1, 1814, the Congress of Vienna began the reconstruction of Europe, deeply destabilized by the Napoleonic and revolutionary wars. And June 9, 1815, marked the date of the signing of the final act to redefine the contours of Europe after the fall of Napoleon, to establish a new order to rule the new balance and perpetuate the return of peace in Europe, but taking into account the territorial upheavals related to the French Revolution. After the Russo-Turkish War of 1877 to 1878, a conflict between the Ottoman Empire and Russia, Romania, Serbia, and Montenegro, the international conference of June 13—held in Berlin, ended with the Treaty of Berlin on July 13, 1878, laying the foundations of a new order of things, allowing to share and reshare Europe, the Middle East, and the Eastern Question—was well ordered. But already, the fate of Asia and the Americas was resolved.

When all the rest of the world was shared, reshared and taken, Africa, the mother continent of humanity, which aroused low interest, was found behind the collimator. The Berlin Conference in 1884 allowed the European powers to avoid tearing themselves for the sharing, as it was the case elsewhere in Europe and the Middle East between England, France, Prussia, Russia, and Austria-Hungary, without forgetting the Ottomans. From then, the Middle East escaped all external control, even if it constituted a space of uncertainty at the moment.

Between Great Britain and France up to North America and South America, and between Portugal and Spain up to Latin America and Central America, the multiple naval companies engaged in the slavery initiated the Atlantic slave trade through the deportation of African captives to the Iberian Peninsula for several decades in 1441—namely, from 1422, the Portuguese navigator prince called

Don Henri, named "Infante Dom Henrique in Portuguese," financed the first maritime exploration of the Atlantic coasts. And to circumvent the Ottoman stranglehold on the trade routes with the East and restrain the worldwide expansion of Islam to the detriment of Christianity, in a nation long known by the Westerners as a powerful Christian nation, the legendary Prester John wanted an ally against the Muslims, and Ethiopia became the center of research for his Christian kingdom, which some historians referred to as the monarch of Prester John. However, since the rise of Islam, the Western contact with Ethiopia was sporadic, and they did not understand that there was no honorary indigenous title in the list of royal names of Zara Yaqob, and that the admonitions Ethiopian thoughts never called their emperor Prester John; insisted the Westerners claimed that Ethiopia was at the origin of the Prester John legend for many years; already, since 1442, the religious considerations were added to the political and commercial considerations, allowing the first sale of black captives raided from the Atlantic coast in the Portuguese city of Lagos in 1444.

That wave followed the slaves conveyed to the Caribbean and South America in the following century, resulting to the decisions of Popes Eugene IV and Nicolas V, who endorsed the conquests of King Alfonso V of Portugal in 1452. Thus, Henry the Navigator was the one who gradually established the relations between the sub-Saharan Africa and the Western world after the fall of Constantinople, which deprived European traders of the trans-Mediterranean traders in 1453. And in 1455 and 1456, two other expeditions were organized by the Venetian Alvise Cadamosto. The company of the adventurers of Africa was founded by King Charles II during the English Restoration in 1660. King Charles Stuart II, falsely represented as a white man, was a black man, since his name Stuart, meaning "black" in Old English or "swarthy," comes from the Old Norse root *Svart,* meaning "black." He was therefore known as the "black boy" of a Stuart lineage in England by his subjects found throughout the British island but in clear contradiction to the famous description of the happy king commemorated in the famous name of the Black Boy Inn. Equally, the current queen of the United Kingdom, Elizabeth II, carries the African blood in her veins, because Charlotte of Mecklenburg-Strelitz was the mother of Edward-Auguste I, duke of Kent and Strathearn, the father of the deceased Queen Victoria, therefore the great-great-grandmother of Queen Elizabeth II. Thus, the African blood has been flowing into the Western kingship of several European countries since the sixteenth century. Queen Charlotte of Mecklenburg-Strelitz was born on May 19, 1744, from a princess named Elizabeth Albertine of Saxony-Hildburghausen (1713–1761) and from the Duke Charles I of Mecklenburg-Strelitz (1708–1752).

She is the first queen of England of African descent. A Portuguese woman named Margarita de Castro y Sousa, a black branch of the Portuguese royal chamber, was her direct descendant. Charlotte of Mecklenburg-Strelitz had Negroid features of a beautiful and elegant African woman very well pronounced. George III of the United Kingdom (1738–1820) was her husband, and their liaison, led to their marriage on September 8, 1761; they had fifteen children, nine sons and six daughters. Her descendants were mighty queen and kings in Europe, including George IV, William IV, Edward-Auguste, and Queen Charlotte Augusta Matilda. The official residence of the present British sovereigns, known as the Buckingham Palace, was purchased by George IV and Charlotte of Mecklenburg-Strelitz in 1762 and served as a second home for the couple and family. The queen of England, Charlotte of Mecklenburg- Strelitz of African descendants, died on November 17, 1818, at Kew Palace, Richmond, United Kingdom.

The Duke of York James Stuart succeeded his brother Charles II; he created the new Royal Company of Africa in 1672; that company, which built dozens of forts in Africa, received the monopoly of importing slaves to the new world; a palpable example of their monopoly in African is the one of William Brew, a slave ship captain who erected the "Brew Castle" on the coast of Ghana as a vast, richly furnished, well-fortified home that homed numerous soldiers and slave traders; that native of a family of Earl of Clare, slaver and brewer, married the daughter of an African chief to easily procure slaves in the Ghanaian tribes and on the African coast. But how could he live with an African by capturing, mistreating and killing her brothers, sisters and children? I will love someone to tell me how.

The Danish historian Per Hernaes initially estimated that from 1451 to 1870, the Danish ships deported 10,000,870 slaves, but today, he changed the number to 85,000 slaves deported between 1660 and 1806, in 250 crossings from Europe to West Africa and from West Africa to Europe for the new world. But it is known that to complete the annexation and the settlements of the Swedish Gold Coast, the Christiansborg Fort and the Carlsborg Fort were seized by the Danish on April 20, 1663. And the Danish West India-Guinea Company administered these settlements from 1674 to 1755.

Furthermore, the Christiansborg Fort was occupied by the Portuguese from December 1680 to August 29, 1682 and was occupied by the Danish crown colony in 1750, to be occupied by the British from 1782 to 1785. Finally, to incorporate the forts of the Kingdom of Denmark into the British Gold Coast, the United Kingdom, bought all the Denmark's Danish Gold Coast Territorial Settlement, on March 30, 1850. These Fort, known as the Fredensborg Fort founded in 1734, the Prinsensten Fort founded in 1784, the Kongensten Fort founded in 1784, the Augustaborg Fort founded in1787, were all in the possession of Denmark in 1850, before been sold to the United Kingdom. Several forts and trading posts like the Carlsborg Fort founded in 1658, the Frederiksborg Fort founded in 1659 and the Cong Heights founded in 1659, were temporarily held by the Danes, apart from these main forts mentioned here above. In the 1660s, with the Gold Coast colony establishment in that period, their navy, the "mercantile marine" was classified as the fourth largest slavery Company involved in the slave trade from the mid-seventeenth century until the early nineteenth century in Europe.

"The Danish exports accounted for about 5 percent of enslaved Africans from the Gold Coast, throughout the eighteenth century, and a total of up to 10 percent by the 1780s. The Danish slave trade embarked about 100,000 Africans who were captured directly from Africa."

Admiral Jean-Baptiste du Casse began his service in the merchant navy with the East India Company, and much later in the Company of Senegal created by Louis XIV in June 1679, where he became a director in 1677, and in 1678, he took possession of Goree; and before being appointed governor of Santo Domingo from 1691 to 1703, he passed into the Royal Navy and obtained the royal privilege of selling slaves to the West Indies, where he acquired a large plantation; in that slave trade, he was the first French actor to take part in that heinous crime of selling slaves in Africa. The Guinea Company was created by Louis XIV in 1684; Antoine Crozat took its administration in 1701; between Nantes and the island of Santo Domingo, it became one of the most important companies of slave trade and the triangular trade; Antoine Crozat imported slaves into French Louisiana, which he acquired as the first owner in 1712, and collided against the Amerindians; Louisiana, the first fortune of France, was a place where most "color people" who fled from Santo Domingo lived at the end of the reign of Louis XIV.

The Angolan Company was founded on September 7, 1748, in Nantes, France, by the Walsh family, and it was practicing the black slave trade along the Angolan coast. In 1664, the French East India Company was founded by Jean-Baptiste Colbert; it was to navigate in almost all the Indies and Eastern Seas from the Cape of Good Hope, and forming a real power in the Indian Ocean with a monopoly of distant trade for fifty years. This French colonial enterprise was to compete with the British East India Company and the Dutch East India Company and to give France a tool for international trade with Asia.

Three slave ships were held by the French East India Company, financed by the king's banker, the Marquis de Laborde, who acquired the monopoly for the provision of piasters in the French colonial enterprise in 1751; "piastre" was originally known as a currency of the republic of Venice in the sixteenth century. In Santo Domingo, he owned 1,400 hectares on three plantations, and in 1794, he was guillotined; but after only a century of existence, the war of attrition with the Dutch and the frontal clash in India with the English, forced its end in 1769. The piracy of the 1800s in the Caribbean, supplying the French planters in Cuba and Louisiana, was led by Jean Boze and Jean Lafitte in 1803.

Other naval companies, or those of the imperial armies in Asia, engaged in the naval battles with the loss of innumerable ships, many men and goods, were sent to the bottom of the Atlantic Ocean and the Indian Ocean. Among all these slave trader naval companies, it is the Royal Navy of the United Kingdom that was a winner, thanks to its power for the reasons of economic equilibrium. Consequently, thanks to the black slavery, six countries—namely, England, the United States, Spain, France, the Netherlands, and Portugal—became very rich. Certain continents like Asia and Latin America territories in the Americas were already awakened in the early twenty-first century to form large local powers and did no longer permit foreign power to come and dictate their laws; but what is Africa waiting for? Nevertheless, for the elites of the current African intelligentsia, all are accepting this international unanimity since the dawn of the Berlin Conference in 1884, which shared Africa more or less without conflict; it appears once again as one of the rare regions of the world where the external forces of the imperial mode can always come to exploit.

The "Eastern Slave Trade," from the seventh century to 1920, was the triggering element of the intra-African slave trade and was intensified by the "slave trade" from 1441 until its abolition in the field of human rights.

The intra-African slave trade remained one of the most controversial trades in Africa that African leaders are not debating the structure to prohibit its practices, and that the Western donor countries, seeking to improve their economic management, continue to exert pressure to influence the shape that should be given to the African continent. While the mechanism of evaluation of the exercise of democratic power and the settlement of the conflicts of these western countries in our continent only lead to more tribal wars, the intra-African slave trade increases its existence and often serves as a humanistic pretext for the benefit of the former colonial empires.

The intra-African slave trade, which became dominant in the nineteenth century, is the least documented and the most obscure; it is in all three trades the one that has strongly increased by about a third of the African captives before 1850; today, their number has increased for the reasons of exploitation in those countries where the West claimed to establish democratic power, but rather created conflicts and tribal wars, as the case of Libya currently.

I do not therefore understand the silence of the African intelligentsia on the situation that Africa is currently experiencing, knowing that it is considered as an experimental ground of new forms of enslavement. This exceptional phenomenon is always brushed aside at the gaze of the fragmented international geopolitics, and the former president Barack Obama, a son belonging to the African ancestral land, promoted to the American high magistrature, did not say anything.

The society transformation programs must be implemented. We must invoke the immortals of our ancient beautiful world, from all considerations beyond some intelligent African people, and break the chain of that sociopolitical, economic, and cultural imprisonment for liberation and lead Africa to its destiny, because the understanding of the sacred is not already so bad but cannot be confused with the fraternity that seduces most of our Africanist intellectuals.

African presidents have all greatly far surpassed the pride of temporal presidents, regardless of their independent state and their status character; they're pretending to be kings in the federated and united republics. Their immortality in power and their credulity are affecting the greater majority of the people. Their treacheries serve neither the evolution nor the development of Africa; to deftly replace a very rare and difficult aspect hidden behind a veil like a block of marble for their eternal theocratic invisibility of evil in power, many lies, many statements contrary to the truth, betray nature, and their sovereigns considered as representatives of God, who last longer in power than any other leaders in the world, still end up dying like any other human being on earth. Africans countries must wake up in this century to form a great power because their insensitivity is still allowing the foreign powers to come and dictate their laws in our countries. This insensitivity is at the origin of several centuries of our history pages darkened by slavery, colonization, and neocolonialism, begun after the indoctrination of the black man, claiming an uninterrupted and infallible succession, continuing in the progressive light of future centuries. Our African presidents are continuing to govern us in that ignorance of past centuries, in the light of time without future progress.

Frightening examples have shown us all our destroyed centuries and the infinite evils derived from the extremely disproportionate cruelty of their ancient slavery institutions, and for their success, they implemented harmful principles in our spirits than reasonable principles in Africa. These principles were to be the only torch to illuminate the beautiful features of the history of our planet; but the nature decided otherwise and unveiled the black man in the eyes of those slavers as being the history of humanity, to counterbalance the cry of all nations, their lived experience during all those periods, and rise up against the system with which they ruled the world or pretending to govern it currently or govern men.

I profoundly hear that voice of God to man, between heaven and earth, between the state of the righteous up there, and the state of societies down here, saying that our leaders must again and again learn all the shocks that shook our empires and change several times our unsatisfactory course of life, solely for the sublime monsters' secret vices, like Nero and Sardanapalus and their ancestors. The boundless abuses of power were played to ruin the human nature of Africa and plunged Africa and its people in the awful false principles that have produced all religious and political disasters, to put in place the chimeras and fabulous annals of the history, to which our governments owed their birth. Africa is however, the only continent in the world, despite all these problems, that has preserved more traces of primitive institutions concerning the history of humanity; as a great intelligent species that produces proofs of the development of its rare and human race in general without equivalent example for its good habits and customs, singularly placed at the first rank, and always revealing the secrets received from our ancestors to all mankind.

That development, more reasoned than mechanical gestures but wrongly inherited by Westerners, puts a great deal of obstacles for the progress of the human spirit, particularly in the West, indicating everything that does not advance in their morale, therefore, as a result, has actually belittled the African man but never lost his moral values known as courtesy, honesty, hospitality, humility, Integrity, loyalty, respect, and sharing. Everything will change the day these unfortunate nations of Africa will be perfected by the progress of their reason, when those who are today evil will disappear everywhere, all these changes will be implemented for good in the world.

The causes of these changes must be noble, also known as being at the origin of the human race, at present just a monster from its birth, the source of degrading plagues, dishonoring forever, and assuming extreme principles that are not made for earth; that human race of white men has produced degraded governments, wicked for one to another, and boundless servitude has taken the place of the prestigious freedom, becoming a shame for its instigators. And from that woe of the world, we are plunged in horrors and despair in the reign of hell. Instead of a reign of public reason, we watched a multitude of nascent false principles from that gangrene implementation, which corrupts, perverts and amputates the hearts of humans, who have constantly been deceived; and continuing to be deceived without cease, they cannot be on earth without degrading. It is therefore good to know that the kind of government that the West implemented and supported in Africa was contrary to the common sense and healthy reason. After reaching the awareness of all the circumstances of progress and the reign of terror, the same Western people decided to put an end to intolerance and unlocked the chains of the intolerable yoke of the African people, to engage themselves in another manner, to another inhumanist aspect of the human race in Africa, without doubt that these nations have consequently chosen among several nations of the earth. Consequently, no one is ignoring that it is from religion that monarchy, despotism, and well after, republicanism was born. It is these same governments that established and are still establishing new contempt, the character of new legislations, suitable to their nature, and all curiously necessary for the reign of false principles of their new governments. In this multitude of monarchical nations or republicans, all despots did not see human inequality in slavery. Distinctly, the world history teaches us that the establishment of the republican governments throughout Europe was a means of rendering honor more glorious and the freedom to human nature after overthrowing the kingdoms of the ancient kings of Greece, France, and Italy, to only name a few, because they were tired of their tyranny.

These republican governments, which overthrew these tyrannical ancient kingdoms, caused the extinction principle of their kingdoms, which were governing by one will, one Supreme Being, and were producing bad abusive consequences in each of their society. But the truth is that Europeans, who always say that they're the most sensitive men on earth, bequeathed all these old prejudices of the new kind of governments they previously gave themselves to new republics in Africa, and they're causing the greatest devastation to African nations. In that disgusting commotion, old speculations awakened old prejudices extinct in Europe; they inflicted them in the new arrangements caught in projects of freedom and independence as a new contempt, therefore, are the source of all disorders of political constitutions in Africa. Nevertheless, the reality of these horrors could not be annihilated without recognizing their power, since that spirit and the necessity of those ancient prejudices are still held in the attachments of the European people.

They preserved the ominous shadow to satisfy all their prejudices of hatred. They're still inspired to bring them back and boldly support governments of all discord, offering perpetual fermentations of republics and the state of one man in Africa. They're so illusory to hope for their success, knowing that they're practicing false aristocratic principles; never could these governments succeed in establishing freedom, equality, and happiness of every citizen on a fixed and quiet basis in our countries.

To maintain violence, it was necessary to discard equality, that essence of freedom; and resorting to forced means never imagined to share our lands, and constantly dividing our countries in weakened numbers, by legislative votes, their legislation, to the abolition of thousand moral values and increase the psychic problems of African humanity, long tormented by dreadful storms of slavery, colonization, and neocolonialism, for all extreme benefits, in a land they qualified as wild. And that was the end of peace by a multitude of laws on luxury and frugality. Governments of the world must remember that these horrific past abuses have rendered the conquering spirit against the well-being of a whole society in certain countries of the world and more particularly in Africa; these unbalanced governments, built like empires, having no exact dimensions and not being easy to measure, since they're from the inconstant characters of man, are not able to make the happiness of the spirit here on earth with their perpetual divisions between ethnic groups, their constitutions devoured by their leaders, sitting on the gold mines for the uncontrolled looting of the Western countries, for their own enrichment, and for the benefit of their family members.

They shed so much blood to reign without the unanimity of the people within the limits of our territories, where the power of a president is sacred and accepting the dithyrambs; but with differing opinions on the quality of their very unpopular governance. They're known as dictators for their implacable cruelty toward whoever opposed them, was considered as opposing God with violence. These leaders of our countries are marking our lives with sufferings that shorten our lives for a short period on earth by the reign of God, but not having the salvation and wisdom of God. The omerta that reigns over the state of health of our African heads of state is a state secret ballot, yet some of them are unable to govern their respective countries; they do not tirelessly pursue the noble mission entrusted to them, therefore do not fully exercise their constitutional prerogatives but cling to power until their death. To not be seduced by these astonishing features, we must be conscious because the causes of their vices with respect to man are greater than slavery and are causing serious damage. However, their virtues still seem to speak in their favor, as principles rose above all still acting excessively, capable of constantly supporting a state that isn't that of man. Thus, these virtues, the main cruel sources of their prodigies allowing us to discover the unexplored corners of their cruelty so disproportionate, not being part of the ordinary course of nature, but found in the causes of all republics of Africa, are only for a time. It is high time that man gives himself a moment of silence for a while to rise above himself and regain the supernatural state to examine his faults and inequalities that must be avoided, to remodel himself and become the man in whom the sublime virtue dwells, the source of equality made for the human being to be what he is. That human nature is itself able to banish the inconceivable inequality and take a very wise humanitarian motive necessary for equality.

The dangers of these abuses must teach us to think how to found a government by the laws of reason on which reign a society unanimously wise and happy. These laws must describe precisely what is allowed and what is forbidden to a government and what will be its duration after a vote in our countries. These rules formulated by the nature of man with the true motives that direct them wherever human beings live on earth, must govern the conduct and social relations of man in society, to the honor of his reason. They must also be able to make man enjoy all possible happiness, all possible freedom, and all possible advantages that can be enjoyed on earth, like abliss, a sublime truth more solid and more constant, and as a masterpiece of the human reason. Society was established on the basis of the character of natural things here on earth, for a safer existence of love, and not on false principles, rays of the sublime virtues of a republic, which believed to be based on true principles; but practicing the inappropriate rules and the abuses on the public reason and on the progress of the citizens. Mainly these republics are lacking criteria that lead toward the perfection of human life. Yet it is this progress and perfection of human life, which were to be the effortless victorious nature of the new lights of politics in Africa and in the world.

All the fastidious observers of good faith in the African political scene have agreed and affirmed that drastic measures must be taken to eradicate the situation of the current notorious corruption, which from the top of the state affects all social categories, and which gangrenes our countries, to prevent a normal social life in our African continent; since the powers at the exercise are concealing a virus of corruption that became generalized, it seizes anyone, attacks those who undergo it and against whom do not exercise its power. Its economic political system offers no credible alternative to ensure effective control for the benefit of Africa but holds men who are governing by an iron fist, placed at strategic locations, carefully selected as managers of our countries and as a heritage to ensure their prosperity. Certainly, reforms seem to be engaged under the pressure of donors, the bilateral and multilateral partners to reduce the effects of highly symptomatic corruption, to a less monstrous level in our countries, requiring them to create governmental structures respecting the ratification of the United Nations Convention against Corruption.

The scale of posturing has not led to a reduction of abuses by the officials of our regimes under the so-called campaigns against that scourge that plagued the economy and flushing down the development of African countries over the years. Through the grotesque stagings, donors who are often content to complain verbally to African government structures are fighting against corruption, rooted in the society of the political system of the current African states. This grotesque staging means fighting against a political system that needs corruption as a central operating element to perpetuate itself in power.

The security system of the regime in our countries was shaken before a political system based on the accumulation of wealth by leaders putting all productive processes in place to be maintained in power. This is probably why it is almost impossible to draft a law against that scourge. It has affected justice, law enforcement, and a whole body of the weevilled governance, became a mafia system, where the speculation of dirty money reigns, motivating the development of all sorts of crimes and the spoliation of individual rights. Generally, all social life concerns this scourge; the respect for human rights, inspiring all decisions and actions in our democracy, is not applied to the benefit of the services due, yet the human rights is an integral part of the universal constitutional law. In a word, what breathing, nutrition, and reproduction are to physiological life is what the fight against corruption and human rights are for the politics and social life. The humiliations inflicted on the people by the officials of different rotten clans I power are revelation of a colonial system, a prelude to an implosion in Africa for more than fifty years.

Respect for economic, social, culture and environmental rights in Africa presents a contrast between the existing legal texts of several treaties and signed agreements, and their applications by the political authorities in place are unfortunately not respected. The hazardous management of public institutions is trampling the human rights. The embezzlement of public funds without respect to moralization, but they respect the hierarchical bases of corruption, and the top of this political jungle is characterized as particularly anchored in the structures of the technocratic political system of the state for several years, resulting in the extreme impoverishment of poor households and the loss of their civil, economic, social, and cultural rights. The reign of our African heads of state and its followers, qualified as a handful of privileged, is assimilated to a cold dictatorship, animated by the flagrant and permanent violation of their constitutions, which has never been the expression of the general will of the people, thus totally unable to implement certain provisions of the actual constitutional laws that could have ensured transparency and some democratic progress. Unfortunately, they're haunted by the sole concern of entrusting power to new political elite, a new leadership filled with patriotism, courage, wisdom, and a lot of compassion for our countries. But this handing over of power to new political elite is a concern perceived as a declaration of war to new political elite by our current African heads of state, whose main objective is only to reflect on the means of not ensuring alternation at the top of the state.

This effect of restoring sovereignty to the people is an essential means for them to put their know-how together to find appropriate strategies, to fight against the holding hostage of our nations by these bloodthirsty and intolerant regimes that only work for the interests of the Western countries. Their will is also an explicit way of providing a new impetus for economic, social, and infrastructural changes. The task of the new team is titanic by the poor governance of the current policy, having the lack of infrastructure, like education, electricity, health, water and sanitary insufficiency, in view of many vicissitudes that overlap in the administrative management of the poor public services of our countries, where the French influence still plays a very important role. The intermediary for the matter of promotion, protection and the sensitization of human rights, an African and international mechanism summarized in three words: to defend, educate, and inform, conceived in the African continent since 1999—namely, in Benin, Burkina Faso, Cameroon, Congo, Ivory Coast, Central African Republic, Gabon, Mali, Mauritania, Madagascar, Niger, Senegal, Togo and Chad, to just name a few—is a Pan-African nongovernmental organization for the improvement and effectiveness of the African human rights system. This African Commission on Human and Peoples' Rights, a judicial Pan-African institution based in Banjul, The Gambia, does practically nothing against the violation of the law establishing the human rights conditions of the charter prescribed by that said law, article 13 stipulating that all citizens have the right to participate in the management of their country's affairs.

The liberal thinkers of the nineteenth century elaborated and put this policy in place to better theorize the end of the story. So, a repartition of power gives advantage to some and endangers others, gives the power of decision to some and disadvantages others, and gives a prestigious position to some who give and to others, the humiliating position of those begging. Africa needs very strong bold social policies and venerable cultural institutions that can replace the disappearance of a spy, a dictator, a traitor, or a tyrant in a country by a patriotic group of politicians to preside on the current destinies of African countries going through a period where history transcending different periods, has always been the liberation against tyrants and regarded as a guarantee for the security of a community deprived of all freedom to found fair laws and clear regulations.

The confiscation of the democratic process by this political system hampers the progress of our African countries by the embezzlement of public funds. The impunity of prevarication, transgressing the laws and the duty of a moral obligation, leads to the drying up of natural and financial resources affected by those corrupt governments. The permanent use of torture explicitly made by the police and gendarmes is treating citizens demonstrating their discontent as if they were wrong to put their freedom of expression in practice for the alternation of the governance, voluntarily eternalized in power and violating the peoples' rights; by blocking the promotion of African values, and exercising an obscure aspect of human rights is not at all for the democratic process. Beyond a morbid arithmetic of compatriots, the loss of a *tyrannical politician* always inspires the people to live in a renovated political environment regardless of his ethnic and political convictions, religious beliefs, or the color of his skin. The institutions of African politics must be rebuilt, putting into practice a definitive cohesion of the rule of law, and not the current damaging supreme power of humiliation of our citizens, engendering feelings of revenge in our African countries.

In recent years, the rhythm of certain African political personalities of the postindependence years is pointing out the end of the reign of a generation of men who made African political history by their disappearance. These men, symbolizing the cold dictatorship of brutality, are not an isolated case, and it's not difficult to believe that by the mere mention of their names in the slightest retrenchment provoked terror within the population. The introduction of multipartyism, whose positions taken in view of democracy, is one of the major controversial issues up to the present day. Since the postindependence years, some of these African political personalities have unfortunately built themselves an image of baobab in Africa, and in certain countries, we can only count two or three president changes for a period of fifty-seven years, like in Cameroon with only two presidents since its independence. The Nationalists' policy, which is led by leaders of the nationalist populations, is not welcomed by the authorities of the current neocolonial administration, who are strongly criticized by the people; in spite of any claim of regime change by taking a stand against men who remained in the political seraglio of the postindependence generation, they remain attached to power. The aim here is to restore respect for human rights, economic rights, social rights, cultural rights, and environmental rights of the current period, and their consequences for the years to come. Let them learn without necessarily being astonished that all the harmonious spheres of everyday or public life in our countries are based on the respect for one's neighbor by African politics.

The extinction of the voice of protest of the people, summoning to determine in what continuity or rupture our societies must be inscribed, has plunged us into a deafening silence, resulting in the foundation of a weak civilization. All this exists in a context of a long history of ever dangerous oppression imposed on everyday life and drawn up for injustice and tyranny. Some of these African governments with powers usurped for fifty-seven years are already known without democracy, freedom, or peace, and they're afflicting misfortunes and bad image to the conscience of the African continent, where the life of human beings has always been treated with contempt. Instead of elevating the human sublime dignity embodying that ethic that life is never a fight for justice, the African man is continuing to fight not only injustice but also cruelty and violent acts. The necessary urgency to follow for the progress of the African culture is refused to him, and no compromise is tolerated.

They're approving the imbecile dogmas at the foundation of tyranny disturbing our people who must imperatively pursue their hideous memory, indignant at the feeling of anger and revolt like thousands of other personalities, dead for the struggle of that independence that only transformed Africa in cruel campaigns, revealing the radical uncertainty of security. A complete lack of development that colonialism spread in its moral project since the agitated immobility of slavery; it is rather important to reopen the dark pages of the history, to reinvent the absence of the past advent, to look far ahead and remember, to recreate the future as the desired life expectancy, and the ascending progression of knowledge; to remobilize the vigorous energies of the maternal conversion that will serve as a teacher of primary education in our political institutions, to transform the amnesia that thrives in the tyranny for our decolonization. It is time to address the question of knowing once and for all who the white man is and throw away the cursed fate of all their heroes. To prepare the only partition of the social sciences and its consecration according to the norms of a general set of respective humanitarian rules necessary for the administration of our countries. This unique partition of the respective humanitarian rules will give rise to the new special organizing commission designated for the proclamation of the functions for Africa. It is these functions of a very great exceptional capacity and a prototype of the intellectual intelligence—including a multitude of facts and the concepts of men behind these facts that henceforth, will be engaged in the reading and the writing of the respective humanitarian rules and will take over the economic, cultural, and political challenge in our continent.

On the eve of independence, the European had and still has the hand very well established in the African politics as the man who will remain closer to the realities of a system that he entrusted to Africa when he began the writing of independence. An independence that must question its historical period in relation to the end of colonialism, known as a real mission of destruction and massive looting of the natural resources of the black nations. Unjust tribulations are requiring to be justly and prosperously explained. The daily refusal of justice to African residents is a perpetual celebration of injustice, which produces individuals capable of unprecedented cruelty, and should draw our attention on the reasons for its hatred. From birth, the existence of a generation, bearer of a deadly virus in their DNA, is a diabolical dialectic without any compromise. Educated African elites developed a chronic complex of the colonized, especially by the cruel dissatisfaction; often reflecting a feeling of betrayal toward certain laurels of knowledge and scientific knowledge, they become even more dangerous for themselves and their society. Their feeling of insecurity and inferiority leads them to a need of repetitive demonstrations for the reaffirmation of their existence on the international scene, to constantly distinguish themselves from their former status of the colonized and the oppressed. Especially voluntarily greedy, ignorant, and dishonest, not being afraid to display an animal instinct of the power of despotic obscurantism, barbaric in broad daylight, and faithful apostles of a school of dictatorship, built of crime for the African humanity; they strew many corpses in the cemeteries of the continent by permanently planting multi-ethnic and multicultural negation in all values of African societies.

Nationalism does not exclude the right of self-determination of people, the fullness of competence, the concept of diplomatic practice of national interests, the national independence, and the national sovereignty. The nationalism crowned with the abuse of rights sometimes clumsy, contradictory to the spirit of justice and collective security, cannot be of a political positivity. For a true nationalism, it is first of all a question of an aspiration to dignity, the autonomy of management by popular movements at the international recognition, easily presented as an evidence in the political and social life, tending to legitimize the existence of a nation-state for every nation fighting against the usurpation of the basic rights of the people by the mentally incapable individuals, aspiring for the territorial extension in Africa.

A fundamental theoretical reality of the law for the economic reconstruction and development focused on the effective defense of national interests, for the liberation and the intellectual emulation of a diplomatic political philosophy, and the systematic peace of the internal independent systems of our countries must be unquestionably considered.

The unity of societies emerged from the universal dogma that several religions and different people of the world have appropriated themselves. For many mystics, idolatry is an old frenzy rejuvenated by Christianity after the ancient revolutions in the world. At that time, people truly believed in the reign of God and the reign of the righteous, which they once thought to have ruled on earth. This was a contempt for the dishonored, hated and disgraced nations with ardor. These two mythologies: paganism and Judaism can correspond to the different things that happened in the idealistic philosophy, to the things that happened in spirituality to formulate their religious history. So, they have a real common source as an abuse of the history of nature. That is why all heroes and heroines of the Judaic theocracy are just a glow of the Greek mythology inherited from Egypt. Their religions have therefore, interpreted this close resemblance of a multitude of characters and facts that are found among the pagans and the Hebrews; but generally, they ignore the provenance of their original sources.

Representing the home of God, the monarch, in the middle of the society was one of the first abuses of the theocratic reign. It is from there that man had the idea of the master's representation, and it is from there that all idolatries came out, ancient or modern. There still reigns nowadays, a continual spirit of that belief in the African governments, as the smallness spirits never imagined and not to doubt; inherited from the origin of abuses drawn from the history of ancient figures and endowed with symbolic attributes of nature.

In my opinion, this resemblance is the primary conduct of our leaders, especially through the obvious relationships of the West, which forcibly excites our leaders to hold a hand so badly served for the material. Those who are part of these mysterious governments are ensuring themselves sweet hopes up to their death and for eternity to all their families. They have established despotism in Africa to regulate the life of men in perpetual poverty and disorders as a pendulum but forgetting that we only need to adjust our conduct here on earth and to know the means of subsistence to live in peace with moderation between us to die with the hope of a better future. If there had never been despotism in these great truths easily preserved as mysteries in our governments, if priests of religion did not transform themselves as masters of the universe, and if all religions of the world were subjected at all times to the natural laws, history would have been worthless to good morals; but since slavers are accused for this frightening description of reason, their crimes, because of the horrors of their mystical lawmakers, are almost irreparable. Teaching man to conduct himself by revelation is an abominable system that annihilates the human reason, debases humanity, and produces the greatest evils in societies on earth.

Democracy responds to a form of government of the assembly and all people. It is a political system that has existed for thousands of years in Africa. It is known that our ancestors chose the consensus policy that was to lead them consensually, a concept of a political organization as the expression of African people for direct democracy. Africa must know that the West has no real democracy. History tells us that Greece, the center of the political life in the European antiquity, was nothing more than an aristocracy, a government of just a few in a political class, the senate. From the aristocracy, Europe followed the hideous road to the theocracy to finally achieve the republican concept—a concept that was bequeathed to Africa on the eve of independence. And up to today, precolonial Africa has not yet understood that this political thought is a very dangerous foreign policy system for the African continent.

I will say therefore that it is time for Africa to establish true democracy—a democracy with consensus expression of citizens, a democracy that must guide our proposals of the state in a political system of thought exchange, since the borders of acceptability are endued with the meaning of the history and culture, a conception of social norms of every nation or human community, are for the true well-being in any African society. This foreign concept of historical religious confrontation created a lot of cultural differences that caused a transplantation of terrorism and palavers between nations to the point that the harvesting of a miracle for the general well-being is no more a principle to hope for in the spirit of the political system of precolonial Africa of the current world. This political system that brought back the model of aristocratic government in almost all contemporary republics, copied from France, is a story totally different from the African political concept; it is a concept of a monarchy, governed by an aristocratic class that, unfortunately, is at the origin of multidimensional failures in all known domains, therefore very damaging to pursue the goal of the general well-being in our African countries.

Among the 192 states that form the United Nations in today's world, there are 167 republics; 131 are unitary republics, including 13 federal republics, 7 democratic republics, 6 people's republics, 4 Islamic republics, 3 Arab republics, 2 Socialist republics, and 1 constitutional republic. In the diversity of each of these republics guided by domination, it is very difficult to find a sense of the common well-being of the populations. However, some of these African leaders, easily qualified as ignorant, are from the Schools of Administration and Magistracy of a concept purely founded by the Western republican societies, defined by the seeds of violence and conflict, completely rejected by the traditional African populations, is known to them as a concept opposing the culture of the continent and the historical reality of Africa.

Popular discontentment against the dictatorship of that foreign concept, the cornerstone of all existing tyranny, has become impossible to contain and makes every effort to organize effectively rather difficult to canalize the general lines characterized unquestionably laconic, to fulfill the specific duty of a decisive history of liberation of every patriot, caught in the spiral of obligatory reverence from the African and Mediterranean antiquity up to the present day. This dissonance between word and action reveals all incoherencies of an imperfect governance model caught in the brotherhood of power, relating to the interests of senior officials of the system of our African states. The general instability and insecurity of our institutions displeases Africa, boiling with discontentment of presidential monarchs who are trying to impose the wacky, hypocritical, and misleading apologetic omerta to an entire community.

In other words, beyond promoting the efficiency and the effectiveness of the state services, to mitigate the inconsistencies and observed antagonism, it actually seems real for me to say that the meritocracy of our states is a purely republican objective without democracy, far from pursuing the goals allowing the survival and a good life of a community against the forces of nature, but having a hidden face of power rather for selfish interests to the conquest of power, during the exercise and for the conservation of power to achieve their objectives and political power. Mainly, the fierce confiscation of the state system by these puppets at the services of those informal organizations of France and the Westerners in general, does no longer escape the humiliation device of the common sense set up by the monstrous militancy of solidarity between criminals and irresponsibles of the first occult lodge of our republics, at the heart of the governing system in the ultimate optic to undertake the historical problematic actions against the forces of nature. Much more, it is in that fierce confiscation of the state system that henceforth reigns all the revelations that sow discord between the states, where an injustice in which the origin of the crazy bulimia lies is the instigator of difficulties without conscience, consisting of determining the necessary and permanent intentions to terrorize the populations. A perfect mastery of strategic and geostrategic issues to be feared and not invested in the field of knowledge has been well established. These strategic and geostrategic issues need to be carefully eradicated for the training required to improve intellectual comfort.

Government actors are guilty of corruption, of economic criminal operations, and yes, they're guilty of embezzling several millions of dollars by the support of Western collaborators, forced by the deceptive protocol without nobility or definitions at the height of task. In addition, knowing that the state is the robber of freedom, evoking a malevolent indignity in particular to the mind, it is criticized by compatriots and traditional leaders, indeed with a historical decline in the practice that lacks modesty; deciphering the sociopolitical evolution in secret ideologies whose key is not known, generated by the enchantment idea; and not able to really make the true sociopolitical thought work to obtain a positive answer, but delivered to the foolish manipulations with force.

This seemingly difficult synthesis, which is inflicting a strategic dissociation to the real sociopolitical thought by the point of view of the republican ethics, is against the fundamentalist ready to serve the authentic renewal. The mortgage of the human rights limitation to my understanding is interpreted as an insult to the formation and the professionalism of our governments. This fact confirms the lack of accredited expertise, security, relevance in state services, and a conviction to do things for success. Government institutions are controlling and managing the state affairs without adequate intellectual experience, and its high officials are pretending to be great leaders of our states.

Manipulation, corruption, injustice, imposture, and poverty have become the claws of our countries. The rise of oppression reveals all inconsistencies of these governments toward all African citizens. All this unfortunately is reinforcing my testimony to qualify our states as the generalized institutional debacles having no sociopolitical, socioeconomic, and sociocultural context, and as powerless administrations that do not bode better future for Africans.

Their moral depravity has reached unprecedented proportions in our countries. The evils that undermine African societies are well known, but the African states aren't doing anything to put an end to the multiple mechanisms known as the widespread banditry, favoring the misappropriation of public funds, the widespread corruption leading to road insecurity, and the pervasive ambient poverty, facilitating the HIV/AIDS pandemic and spreading other serious diseases in our countries. Prostitution and homosexuality have become cultural mechanisms; the exploitation of children by labor and for sexual purpose have let them at the mercy of pedophiles, thus preventing them from enjoying their childhood freedom; and the illiteracy, the gigantic networks of gangsterism in all fields, and the installations of migratory movements with the complicity of the state summit, etc., are also added to the mechanisms that are upsetting our societies in Africa.

These practices that frustrate and hurt are factors aggravating the situation and leaving incurable sequelae to which are added incalculable cruel consequences, exposing them to unwanted pregnancies, hemorrhages, the maternal death occurring before, during or shortly after childbirth, followed by sleep disorders, malnutrition, and chronic pain on their mental and psychical. In these circumstances and without any exaggeration, how do we conceive such a destabilization, which presents significant risk and very serious danger in our countries, abandoned in the hands of a network of mafia gangster's groups at the international level, who cares about nothing, regrets nothing but simply concerned about their durability on the throne of power? Actually, it is a perspective, I would once again say, which distances us every day from the opportunity to prepare the political change between the governors and the governed that can lead our countries to the rupture of numerous dissatisfactions of pauperization, and the inequality that foments a real lobby within the administration, placed forever above the law in the entire population in Africa.

The enrichment of these high state authorities is authorized by our acephalic presidents of great potential instability, who are making constitutional low hand for the embezzlement of public funds through the brotherhood that controls all the state-owned companies. Moreover, the honesty of professionalism is escaping the configuration of their logic, constituting the implosive dysfunction of a state's potential. The many heads of state that are generating victims of our political system in Africa are known to be sponsored by Western states. As usual, our history has just once again lived a remarkable insult. This time, what is amazing is that it suffers the insult in collaboration with our alienated leaders at the gaze of all the former colonizers during the celebration of the independence of the French Republic on July 14, 2010, fifty years after the African independence. That commemoration, marking the taking of Bastille on July 14, 1789, was a surrender that made a seism in France as elsewhere in Europe, symbolizing the end of despotism of the old political regime, a period in the history of France from the late Renaissance up to the beginning of the French Revolution marking the end of the kingdom of France and the advent of the French First Republic of the sixteenth to eighteenth century.

After the slavery and three-quarters of a century of colonization, the monarchy of France then embarked on the establishment of the subguardianship of colonies as a mission to plunder Africa for the account of France. Throughout the world, the sprain of the adventures suffered by the history of France, which embedded its contradictory roots in the bowels of Africa, was not always complimentary in the face of these ransacked countries, whose entire formation holds a funny pride.

For me, to celebrate that launch of the placing of our countries under the guardianship by the Armed Forces of those countries which hold a sublime pride to carry the national colors like those of France has enough to make history laugh. Because to endeavor to pay tribute to sharpshooters—African black soldiers, known liberators of France who fought two wars of 1914 and 1939, and several others that killed Africans in attacks whose logic escapes them—is not propitious to history.

It is known that they were always sent alone in missions when all hope of return was excluded, where they fought at that time as lions to conquer Madagascar from 1895 to 1905; the one of the said fighters of North Africa, the northern end of Africa called Maghreb, which was forming the French North Africa (AFN), before the independence during the colonial period by the Army of African, from June 14, 1830 to 1902, is today made up of three states, known as Algeria, Morocco, and Tunisia. The war in Morocco cost the lives of thousands of African victims from 1911 to 1937, for the pacification of Africa; they also participated in conflicts in Indochina, in the Levant (Syria, Lebanon), and even during the Suez battle, after the two world wars; these sharpshooters—black African soldiers—could not, in any case, claim a rank beyond sergeant. The Army of Africa, from June 14, 1830, was dissolved in 1962. These facts are part of the construction of the very ancient French history of two wars by ambiguities sometimes very embarrassing. It was in September 1944, after the Second World War, when German officers vigorously opposed to mention black troops among the men who defeated them, when De Gaulle signed the decree of laundering the French army that the supreme insult was definitely established toward the sharpshooters—black African soldiers. Until today, a vast field dotted with white stakes without a single name is the only witness of that carnage done by German tanks in the cemetery at the entrance of the city. For propaganda, the sharpshooters were replaced by schoolboy soldiers in a hurry to occupy positions conquered by those blacks, who were despite then, well and truly French citizens, acting under the account and the authority of France, just for the photo. Pretending to honor their memory with a nice farce of very bad taste is a useless scorn of Europe, which owes them the vast foundations of the elite unity of its present army of which France is so proud today. It is therefore time for France, the French army, and especially the naval commandos to honor those black sharpshooters for the loyalty in their history. The representatives of the French republic must organize a parade of truth and put it on the agenda for the alliance formed in particular between Africa and France for the French benefit, but also especially by the French of heart and conviction, and governors of the new times that so cruelly lack clarity.

Fair enough, I would say once more that these refounding presidents of the African republics, derived from their founding masters in the Western republics, were summoned to witness a repetition of the solemn oath of France on its empire eternally rooted in African politics by the parade of sharpshooters—black African soldiers—on July 14, 2010, on the Champs Elysees. True politics respects authority by the vision of the first magistrate and gives advices on the necessity to protect and promote human rights, which are fundamental to all nations.

A nation cannot be created without the fundamental freedoms and the rights of a society. Respect for the human rights is the tantalizing cohesion of freedom, of the national and social unity, which creates the conditions of justice and citizen equality before the law and develops a sense of belonging to a nation in the general population. African countries are confronted with a bitter fatalism of immobility of regrettable degradation and blockage phenomena originating from the economic and political backwardness without hope of boosting a new dynamic of adapted business on the black continent, before the one of the most barbaric dictatorships that this earth has ever known, to vampirize the last energies that still remain to its people in African countries; like the Roman dictatorship and the one of its local accomplices, the Jewish church, known as the Pharisees, scribes, and elders, who, by Herod, the Jewish king, decapitated John the Baptist and asked for the crucifixion of Jesus Christ. Tyrants will be neutralized one of these days for the neocolonialist dictators to disappear permanently from all political power in Africa.

Africa is the threshold of the history of universality, fully developed in natural history and the reason of the spirit. But if the Nigger is superior to the apes, as Voltaire cited, oysters are superior to the whites, who are more qualified to animals of the human species, to have captured Africans, transported them from their different warm climate to countries sometimes colder in climate, sold them like goods and subordinated them to slavery to serve the white men and treated them as beasts. The intelligence evaluation of the white man, considered superior to the intelligence of Africans as he himself is saying it, has put between him and other human species in different degrees of understanding, which contradict the nature of the understanding principle of creation. For me, the superiority, or should I say the inferiority of his intelligence has besotted him and led him to direct different judgments with regard to the Nigger, the father of humanity. This species of a prodigious man with round eyes, flat nose, thick lips, differently figured ears, and frizzy hair like wool on his compressed skull—in short, a cannibal deprived of progress, invention, desire to know, of no pity or any feeling but having an emotion—is capable of great attention. As said in a stupid quote by Senghor, "Emotion is Negro as reason is Greek." Here I'm designating the polytheism as *Hellene*, a generic term used since the sixth century for those who are not Christian, thus the polytheistic *pagan* religion after the establishment of Christianity by Theodosius I, the last emperor to reign over the unified Roman Empire. The Greeks designated themselves as "Greeks" and "Romans" at the late Antiquity (around the third and seventh century CE), and then after 212 CE, all Greeks were Roman citizens. His thinking ability is the philosophy, art, and science of his actions of illustrious spirit combining the advantages of his influential nature, naturally deposited in the nature of his civilized nations. The white man stole them during his famous conquest before the colonization and personified them to finally paint him as a man without the slightest sign of intelligence.

The abuses of the white man even led him to deny his mulatto-born children, from a white father and a black mother or from a black father and a white mother, which he qualified as a bastard race. Yes, the Nigger is from Africa like elephants and monkeys; he is a different species of men that thou hast scattered as slaves around the world, as yourself, always wandering in the land of others for purely economic reasons. My positive philosophy leads me to say that no individual is distinguishable from the nature of the black man; whether in the field of action by the magnitude of appreciable superiority, or by the personality above the common ladder or the body and spirit, at the level of attaining the strength of the Nigger spirit, his sense of beauty and the sublime that rise above understanding and his intelligence, are all above the nature of man.

The white race is the most degraded of human races, whose forms of brutality made of barbarism rise above animality. On the other hand, the Nigger is the mother idea of God; he is wisdom and a good soul. His selfrefolding, absolutely valid, is a state of an existing reality in itself and for itself, which generated religion for the recognition on the universal scale; and his consciousness that attained the contemplation of a solid objectivity; he is the law to which must adhere the will of man and reach the intuition of his own essence, the essence of God, for example; obviously, you who assume that the Nigger is not a human being are not Christians.

Oh, white child of nature par excellence, despite your manifestation of the lack of reason and gratitude for the humanist, you distinguish yourself by serenity. But terror, the art of cruelty, animated by the fear of your childhood, is omnipresent in your life, without the slightest mark of patience in your disappointment and your attitude toward the colonized people. Agitated, you're hatred—indeed a wild demon, a figure of barbarism, blamed by those you have tired with work, with ingratitude for years by the spells of slavery, followed by wild colonization. But the African people, your captives, opposing the benefice of others through slavery, only need protection and the light that establishes peace and imposes peace. But when you will meet humanism, you will then meet humanity, the ancestor of blacks.

Oh, white, thy strong race carries a heavy burden summoned from far by the crimes toward thy neighbor and rather putting your son in exile. Your dark captive half-child, freshly badly conquered on the shores of Africa like beasts and scattered by the stick blows, has served your fugacious heavy diabolical harness and intellectual character of a savage, by the lack of intelligence and the structural assimilation with a wild heart moving constantly. The civilized child of the race of man, having a place in the scientific geology of the terrestrial globe, has been treated and still is treated as an inferior animal by the fantasy of baliverne imbecile rogues, peddlers of the European man repeating the words of such a low demagoguery. And for how long are you going to treat him as an inferior animal under the government of a unique God to all? But know that God is great enough to create and direct the universe in equality with a feeling of a distinct race with body and spirit, due to time, to the observation of beauty and the sublime recognition of universality and an existing reality in itself and for itself.

His raison d'etre is the threshold of the history of the universe, originating in this part of Africa. His intelligence is of another understanding; his principled nature, his degree of tolerance, and the characters of his notions in the nations of the earth, influence a higher cosmic intelligence genetically elevated, capable of a great philosophical attention different from other human species. The intellectual and moral reform of the whites has nothing but sketching intelligence, knowing that the conquest and the colonization of a country of a weak race with heavy weapons and as a well-armed race is a political abuse of the first order. Their science does not believe in the issues of judicious unions.

Oh, white, for the abuses of the Niggers and generally to other human species, you yourself became naturally very inferior to other races that appeared in all texts and literary theories of each race of man, native of the world. Know that all that can be qualified as a democratic government was held for the first time in Africa. The imbecile remarks, coming from illustrious intellectuals such as Bellon de Saint Quentin, a theologian, wrote a dissertation on the trafficking and the trade of Negroes that he published in 1764; he justified the possession of Negro slaves at the time of the Enlightenment by saying, "The possession and service are not contrary to the natural law, nor to the written divine law, nor even to the Gospel law;" Rousselot de Surgy treated the Negroes by these words: "Among the Niggers, no spirit, no aptitude."

To prove the natural inferiority of blacks, an awful campaign of opinion was published in 1803 by Louis-Narcisse Baudry Deslozieres, justifying the physical criteria, the beauty of the faces, etc.; he was defining the hierarchy between the blacks and whites as the racial sign of the white race by the enslavement of the black race.

Deslozieres justified the Nigger inferiority in "The Distractions of Negrophilism," giving rise to the worst racist expressions in the history of humanity; Alfred Michiels qualified Niggers as the bloodiest of all human races with no pity or feeling and that it was the most stupid and perverse race without any invention, no progress without the desire to know, and that their color was the sign of depravity. He was even afraid that the black blood would attack France and distort the complexion of its population to the heart of its nation through crossbreeding. He also declared that, "The color of Negroes in Africa is the color of darkness;" Victor Hugo wrote, "Africa has no history;" from 1880 to 1881 and 1883 to 1885, Jules Ferry was twice the prime minister of France during the Third Republic. Before the French Chamber of Deputies, on March 28, 1884, he justified his colonial policy and the economic expansion system connected to three sets of ideas: the most far-reaching ideas of civilization ideas, the economic ideas, the political and patriotic sort of ideas of the superior race that vastly extended the French colonial empire. His promoting education in France was to let the French Chamber of Deputies know their duty concerning Niggers by uttering these words: "The duty to civilize the inferior races." On July 20, 1885, during a parliamentary debate, Jules Ferry continued his justification of slavery, the slave trade, and the superiority over inferior races by openly declaring the duty to civilize the inferior races, summarizing his reasons against socialist opposed to French imperialism after annexing Tunisia, parts of Indochina in Southeast Asia, and exploring parts of Africa; Jules Ferry, the Freemason of La Clemente Amitie lodge of the Grand Orient of France, who will belong much later to the Alsace-Lorraine lodge, was hereby confirming the intangible differences between the black race and the white race by the duty to civilize the inferior races.

In 1853–1855, the famous work of the French writer named Joseph Arthur, Comte de Gobineau, was published under this title: "Essay on the Inequality of the Human Races;" the theologian J. Teilhard de Chardin, Keer-Lez-Maastricht, tells us about the work of missionaries in the far-off lands of African people, evangelized by the Missionaries of the Society of African Missions of France. His oeuvre recounts us of the deep misery and the state of our people so degraded on the African continent by the old Europe, irresistibly pushed toward the desire to so contemptuously colonize and civilize. They were saying to themselves that God had sent them to extend the reign of their Christ and to begin the conquest of our people, whom they considered so barbarous for the good and only true civilization.

The dreadful pages of these so-called envoys of God and apostles of Christ, whose missionary work was the gospel presented as the only true civilization, will last for more than four hundred years; the manuscript titled "The Upper Guinea and its Dutch Missions," written by J. Teilhard de Chardin, wanted to put these so-called missionaries of the old Europe without fruits, so degraded and so disdainful to the attention of the world. The vast majority of the imperfections of their success, maintained intentionally, left the state of their works as a perversion in the history of humanity. Charles Richet (1850–1935), Nobel Prize awardee in medicine and physiology, considered "blacks to be inferior to monkeys." This racist, who was an influential member of the Grand Orient of France, advocated the science of eugenics and the elimination of the inferior races.

Here are some excerpts of his treated subjects in his book titled Human Selection, which reflects his eugenic, negrophobic, and racist views. I quote: "It is about thirty thousand years ago that there are blacks in Africa, and during these thirty thousand years they have not been able to achieve anything that raises them above the apes." "Niggers continued even in the midst of the whites, to live a vegetative existence, producing nothing but carbonic acid and urea." "Turtles, squirrels and monkeys are well above the Niggers in the hierarchy of intelligences," "excerpt from" The stupid man." "When it comes to the yellow race, and even more so to the black race, to preserve and above all, to increase our mental power, we will not have to practice individual selection as with our white brothers, but the specific selection, resolutely rejecting any mixture with the inferior races." "After the elimination of the inferior races, the first step in the path of selection is the elimination of the abnormal," extract from "The Human Selection." Bertrand Russell (1872–1970), a mathematician, said, "The Negroes, on the other hand, represent the greatest failure of democracy in the United States, and until some justice is accorded to them it cannot be maintained that democracy exists here in America." He continued by saying, "The police will always suspect a Negro first if possible, and the courts will condemn him more readily." Bertrand Russell was explaining that the use of the word *Negro* was not meant to be offensive. In 1942, his speech was delivered at a time when the word *black* was considered more offensive; and both as exonym and endonym, Negro was accepted as a normal superseded colored and as the politest word for African Americans. By then, Martin Luther King Jr. was even identified as "Negro" during the later African American Civil Rights Movement; but some black American leaders disapproved the word *Negro* during the 1950s. Malcolm X, Martin Luther King Jr., and other well-known black leaders of the Civil Rights Movement associated the word *Negro* with the long history of slavery, followed by segregation, accentuated by discrimination that treated them as second-class citizens, or worse. These black Americans started using the term *Afro-American*, and after the one born as Malcolm Little, who adopted the pseudonym of Malcolm X, and finally left the Nation of Islam in 1964, preferred the word *black* to the word *Negro*, after the famous Martin Luther King Jr.'s speech titled "I Have a Dream" in 1963.

Albert Schweitzer, Nobel Peace Prize awardee, was an Alsatian musician, a medical doctor, a philosopher, and a Protestant pastor and a theologian, who died in Lambarene Gabon, on September 4, 1965. His exposing quotations of racism and racist remarks are found in his books titled, "*On the Edge of the Primeval Forest,*" published in 1922; "*More from the Primeval Forest,*" published in 1931; and "*Out of My Life and Thought,*" published in 1922. In page 88, he said, "The Negro is a child, and with children nothing can be done without the use of authority." "We must, therefore, organize the circumstances of daily life so that my natural authority finds its expression." With regard to the Negros, I therefore invented this formula: "I am your brother, it is true, but your elder brother." Ernest Renan (1823–1892) reaffirmed the same story illustration in "The intellectual and moral reform in 1871," with dimensional perspectives; Guy de Maupassant was qualifying Africans by these words: "Girls in Africa are maleficent and rotten; a greasy and blackish exudation that stains the linen spread an unpleasant smell;" Pope Leo XIII was affirming that "God created the earth for the whites, Amen," by sanitizing the grouping of the black nations as slaves.

Pius XII categorically refused the black guards at the Vatican during his pontificate between 1939 and 1958; these bishops and popes of the Catholic religion, who wanted the black man to remain a slave, were accomplices in this racial hatred and wanted not even that the black men should be freed. Friedrich Hegel, the German philosopher who taught philosophy in the form of a system presented as a "phenomenology of the spirit and as an "encyclopaedia of philosophical sciences," united all knowledge according to a dialectical logic. His work had a decisive influence on the whole of contemporary philosophy as one of the most representative of German idealism. Georg Wilhelm Friedrich Hegel, who was born on August 27, 1770, in Stuttgart, and died in November 14, 1831, in Berlin, thundered as follows: "Africa is the country where men are children, a land far from the light of its own historical consciousness and bathed by the dark colors of the night; At this point let's forget Africa and do not talk about it anymore, because Africa does not belong to the history of the world." He said this in 1831 without even setting foot in Africa and totally ignoring its people. An English explorer named Richard Burton, the first European to climb the summit of Mount Cameroon, the culminate point of West Africa, and a Sufi master of an initiation path called tassawuf or tariqa for the spiritual elevation, representing an esoteric and mystical tendency of Islam, was a passionate experimenter of the most human perversions. Apart from the well-known negationist remarks of Friedrich Hegel, Richard Francis Burton said, "The study of the blacks is to study the human spirit at its most rudimentary stage; beings which resemble more a degeneracy of civilized man than savages liable to become so, if not by their incapacity to progress. Their naturalness being peculiar to education or culture seems to belong to one of these infantile species, unable to access the condition of men, like an interrupted Mayon of the great chain of nature." This British polymath erudite writer, ethnologist, linguist, poet, and translator, who studied African languages and customs, and who knew Africa well, and who was describing the African as an interrupted Mayan of the great chain of nature, was born on March 19, 1821, in Torquay, and died on October 20, 1890, in Trieste. It must be said that there were several whites who thought like these two characters mentioned above, since the explorer Samuel Baker, in his memoirs, wrote this: "The human nature, at its most rude stage as I have been able to observe it among the African savages, is precisely at the level of the brute and cannot be compared to the noble characters of the dog; we find no gratitude on them, no pity, no love, neither self-gift; nothing but greed, ingratitude, selfishness, and cruelty."

These insults and prejudices of the Europeans of the eighteenth and nineteenth centuries are unforgivable, hiding what their ancestors knew well as those who were educated and initiated by many sumptuous African kingdoms, which were developed and well governed than others in medieval Europe.

All these illustrious so-called intellectuals were expressing a perverse reasoning against the Negroes. These racist criteria and expressions put the idea of a common history of humanity into questioning and excluded the Africans who were destined to be enslaved by the history of civilization. For these imbecile remarks, can I also qualify you? Well, according to me, yes, you're monsters and the people affected with a serious defect, usually hereditary, but at the same time uncivilized people that civilization had not yet reached; and without your timely and brutal interventions for your appropriation of that Africa that was walking in a civilization worthy of that name, Africa would have been a great power in the world today; that Africa with its ancient tribes of primitive people, which taught different conceptions and an infallible intuition in the world to the European humanity that only had elementary values, who became a lion as a king in the African jungle.

If man must speak louder and truer, the principle of your light is a legacy of an eternal light inherited from Africa. Its veracity, its inner dignity, and its moral personality are a sublime divine consciousness among Niggers. Your cruelty, with so many lies of your impure generations and your evil spirits to establish yourself as a master, certainly helped you to monopolize the noble applications of the highest intellectual levels of the Nigger. The number of genes of intelligence among blacks that you qualify as intellectual inferiority, an IQ of less than 100, is an influence of academic sciences, compared to the American Nigger inventions that you hide for a long time but known throughout the world without knowing the inventors.

In the American society, more precisely in the United States, where blacks occupied and still occupy an inferior position after the slave trade, that intellectual inferiority has not been forgotten, given the required claims to put an end to the discrimination in the constitutional legislation in the whole country. We can here again see an inhumane manner of whites, who even after the abolition of slavery continued to make blacks suffer by subjecting them to an immense feeling of insecurity and inferiority. Yet they're indeed bourgeois from Nantes, Rochelle, Bordeaux, Marseille, Netherlands, London, Bristol in England, Copenhagen, Lisbon Portugal, Spain and other counties across Europe, to a continent that is not really theirs.

They were unjust and still are disloyal to judge the black population in the United States, denying them access to a better education to finally get a better job or better housing, a stable life. A certain number of seats were exclusively reserved for blacks after World War II in schools, in universities, and in the public sector. Despite these draconian measures, their intellectual efforts enabled them to surpass the middle class and developed themselves up to a superior class with a well-distinguished professional personality, which I quote here below:

Asa Philip Randolph (1889–1979)

Philip Randolph, who opened the labor movement for blacks, was indeed a writer endowed with the endowment deeds. He contributed to the founding of the union and published an opinion and review magazine called the *Messenger*. This radical monthly magazine was qualified as "the most able and the most dangerous of all the Negro publications" by the U.S. Department of Justice.

His writings also dealt with the subjects of the Brotherhood of Sleeping Car Porters, which he founded with Chandler Owen, whom he met at the Columbia University and helped by the Socialist Party of America in 1917; he organized and led the Brotherhood of Sleeping Car Porters in 1925.

This African American labor union was the first effort to form a serious labor institution as a labor movement for employees of the Pullman Railroads Company. Pullman was not only manufacturing streetcars, buses and trolleys for the use in cities, but also started developing train sleeping cars and operated them on most of the railroads in the United States.

Employees of the Pullman Company were coupling the cars to trains and in charge of cleaning, making beds in the sleeping car passenger trains, etc.; as a major employer of African-Americans, his employees requested assistance from Mr. Randolph as the first predominantly African-American labor union supporting labor rights against unfair labor practices in relation to black people. His employees believed that if they were to form a syndicate, they could obtain better working conditions. However, the leaders of the railway companies were not interested and did not listen to the requests of this group.

Mr. Philip Randolph worked for twelve years for that syndicate, and the Brotherhood of Sleeping Car Porters was recognized by the railroad. Finally, in 1937, an agreement was signed. In a few years, the salaries of porters were doubled. Mr. Randolph was therefore the first spokesman for all black workers.

When the Second World War began in 1939, more and more workers were requested by factories manufacturing war materials in the United States. During that period, the only jobs reserved for blacks were sweepers, attendants for the maintenance of those factories, residence attendants, etc., and were not called to perform other jobs. So, Mr. Randolph once again committed himself to do something about that subject and concerning poor conditions of black workers.

In 1941, to show that blacks were not satisfied with job inequality, he organized a march in Washington; regarded by the government of the United States as one of the main speakers against discrimination, his action was acknowledged by Pres. Franklin D. Roosevelt, after cancelling that march; and decided to order all factories to engage the black population in all jobs they could handle. Several thousand black workers got better jobs as a result of that action. For his work in the syndical movement, he was awarded the NAACP Spingarn Medal, in 1942.

Up to then, in the army and the navy, the discrimination and segregation of blacks from white soldiers and sailors in their government institutions, in 1948, forced Mr. Randolph to call on President Truman, letting him understand this time on his trip in Washington D.C. that blacks were tired of fighting for democracy in other countries when they have no freedom in their own country. After his appeal that convinced Pres. Harry S. Truman on the issues of discrimination and segregation, components required in the army were integrated by President Truman, a few days later.

To show the need to establish new civil rights laws, he asked the people of the United States to ones again travel to Washington, for a very important event in the fight for fraternity. In that march in Washington, more than two hundred thousand people participated in 1963.

Up to our present days, the labor and civil rights movements are still resonating, while the union movement was just beginning to organize itself at its birth in 1889. For a better life and good working conditions for everyone, the tools of speaking and writing were used as a writer to fight discrimination, segregation, for good working conditions for everyone, for the civil rights and for a better life for blacks in the United States.

Charles Richard Drew (1904–1950)

This American surgeon and researcher, born in the ghetto of Washington D.C., on June 3, 1904, dedicated himself for the storage of human blood while it was not necessary for transfusion to save someone's life. Blood preservation techniques, which he perfected and the organization of the first blood bank, which he planned were the main contributions of Dr. Charles Drew to science and medicine.

He researched on the nature of human blood and created what has today become known as the blood banks for the conservation of blood. These places are where blood is kept in a special form (plasma) until required by injured or sick patients.

Mr. Drew established a program of blood bank in Great Britain at the course of the Second World War in 1940, asked by the British. Thanks to his conservation techniques, thousands of lives were saved for their country by British doctors and Allied forces transfusing blood.

The American Red Cross appointed him as the first director of their blood bank after the war. Then, the armed forces of the United States of America were supplied by his conserved plasmas.

As one of the most famous African American physicians of his time, he was recognized as an excellent surgeon, teacher and civil servant. He was the one who protested against the segregationist measures, not having scientific basis, related to the donation of blood. In 1944, he received a Spingarn Medal. Following a car accident, he died on April 1, 1950, in North Carolina, specifically in Burlington.

Granville Tailer Woods (1856–1910)

Mr. Granville T. Woods was granted patents of more than fifty electrical inventions. As an American of African descent, originally from Columbus, Ohio, he was the first to be a mechanical and electrical engineer, already at that period. Many of his ingenious inventions were concentrated on street electrical systems and electrical systems in general. They're included in the devices of General Electric Company, founded by Thomas Edison and JP Morgan in 1878; and which in 1892 merged with Thomson-Houston Electric Company.

His inventions were also included in the devices of Westinghouse Electric and Telephone, founded by George Westinghouse on January 8, 1886. He invented the Telegraph Multiplex on October 11, 1887 and sold it to the Bell Telephone Company. More than a dozen designed devices were invented by him who was born on April 23, 1856, to improve electricity in railroad cars and better control the f low; and for the "Conductor" who was also called "Engineer" of a train to know how his train was necessary to travelers, Mr. Granville T. Woods invented a system as his most notable invention, reducing accidents and collisions between trains.

Among his other main inventions were an artificial incubator, invented in 1890; an electric circuit interrupter, invented on January 1, 1889; a steam boiler and an automatic oven; compressed air brakes used to slow down or stop trains, invented in 1905; an electronic brake, invented in 1887; a parabolic antenna, invented on June 7, 1887; and a reliable rheostat, invented on October 13, 1896.

He also invented the tunnel for electric trains on July 17, 1888; the telegraph of the railways on August 28, 1888; telegraphony, combining telephone and telegraph, in 1885, whose rights he sold to the Bell Telephone Company; an interrupter on January 1, 1889; an amusement apparatus on December 19, 1899; devices for the transmission of messages via electricity on April 7, 1885; and the third rail for the subway after the War of Secession on January 29, 1901.

Garrett A. Morgan (1875–1963)

Mr. Garrett Augustus Morgan was an award-winning inventor. His very first invention was a strap clasp for sewing machines, invented in 1901. He then invented the first hair fixer. At that time, it was known as the refining cream, invented in 1909 in his clothing shop in Cleveland.

In the early 1900s, firefighters in many American cities widely used his safety helmet, developed on October 13, 1914. That prototype would later become a gas mask. When he and his brother used the mask to save more than two dozen men who were trapped under Lake Erie in Cleveland, Ohio, during an explosion in a tunnel under construction, his invention became popular.

For his heroic rescue, the city of Cleveland awarded him a gold medal. At the Second International Exposition of Safety and Sanitation in New York later on, he was awarded another gold medal for his gas mask. Best known for his invention, the automatic stop sign, invented on November 20, 1923, today called "Traffic light or stop light" is controlling the flow of vehicles through intersections of roads around the world.

Theodore Kenneth Lawless (1892–1971)

Through his studies that he started at Straight College which offered an elementary education up to college level before merging with the University of New Orleans and became the University that is today known as the University of Dillard, his practice and the development of drugs, Dr. Theodore K. Lawless became a millionaire as a renowned skin specialist (dermatologist).

His contribution to a disease that destroyed the muscles of the body known as leprosy, and to a much better understanding of the venereal disease called syphilis, was indeed a real relief to poor people. He created one of the most important and most known dermatological clinics, by setting up offices in the heart of the city of Chicago's black community. Black and white, children, men and women crowded his waiting room from morning till evening, for many years.

To share his knowledge with other doctors, he worked with the staff of the Chicago Provident Hospital, and always found time to teach at the Northwestern University. Dr. Theodore K. Lawless received many distinctions to honor his work.

Among others, honorary doctorates in science from the American city of Talladega in Alabama, a state in the southern United States, and Howard University, Washington, were awarded to him; he also received one (LL.D.) from Bethune-Cookman College, located in Daytona Beach, Florida, one (LL.D.) from the University of Illinois and one (LL.D.) from Virginia State University located in the north of the Appomattox River, in Petersburg, United States.

Historically, this black university in Washington D.C., known as Howard University, was non-sectarian since its creation; it was open to people of both sexes and all races, and that's why it was nicknamed "Black Harvard." It trained students in pharmacy, law, social work, medicine, dentistry, divinity, etc., and was classified as a research university with a great deal of activity in the field of research in sciences; after obtaining an A.B. in 1914, from Talladega College in Alabama, he continued his doctorate in medicine at the University of Kansas and received his MD in 1919 and a MS in 1920 from the University of Illinois.

This Northwestern University Medical School in Chicago offers a fulltime doctor of medicine degree program and grants competitive research in science; the University of Illinois, which comprises 17 colleges offering more than 150 programs of study, is also a public research university known as the second-largest library after Howard and different from the one of the states of Virginia but also historically a black university of subsidization, located in the north of the Appomattox River in Ettrick and from the one of Bethune-Cookman College, a private university historically black in Daytona Beach, Florida, United States. As an instructor at the Northwestern University Medical School, he taught dermatology and syphilology to students. In 1929, this professor of dermatology and syphilology, who directed the Marina City Bank and the Supreme Life Insurance Company, won the Harmon Award in Science for his outstanding work in medicine.

He received the Spingarn Medal (NAACP) Award, for his contribution as educator and philanthropist, and for his distinguished achievement as a physician in 1954; for his acts of charity and medical service in 1966, a Distinguished Service Award from Phi Beta Kappa, the oldest honor society for the liberal arts and sciences, was awarded to him; the City of Hope Golden Torch Award, and the Distinguished Service Citation from the University of Kansas in 1967.

Benjamin Banneker (1731–1806)

This astronomer, essayist, inspector, mathematician, slavery abolitionist and inventor named Benjamin Banneker, built a wooden homemade clock, which was probably the first entirely built in America; it kept an exact time until his death at the age of seventy-five years in 1806. From 1792 to 1806, the man who published a widely used almanac, using his mathematical skills to establish it annually was an autodidact and was born free in Ellicott, Maryland.

To render his calendar as accurate as possible, numerous nights were spent studying stars. As an expert, in 1791, he was called upon to assist Andrew and Joseph Ellicott, as well as Pierre Charles, to trace the new streets and build buildings in Washington, the capital of the United States. That same year, he decided to take the defense of African American by writing to Thomas Jefferson, the author of the Declaration of Independence.

At that time, the black race was still considered as an inferior race, unable to understand the meaning of citizenship. Jefferson approved the words of Mr. Banneker but did not help him in his struggle for the abolition of slavery. He wrote about the misdeeds of slavery as an essayist and became one of the most famous African-Americans in the history of the United States, at the beginning of those years because of his work.

Louis Tompkins Wright (1891–1952)

Being a physician and surgeon, Dr. Louis T. Wright invented an operative method on fractures of the knee joint, a fracture apparatus of the vertebral column, and the vaccination against smallpox, which earned him a prize of merit. He received the Purple Heart after a gas attack during the First World War, when he was stationed in France.

He supervised the first testing of a miracle drug called Aureomycin on men. Aureomycin (trade name for chlortetracycline) is a tetracycline antibiotic drug for the treatment of venereal diseases, and he initiated the cancer research and also advanced a new theory on the treatment of skull fractures (cervical fractures).

During the First World War, he was appointed lieutenant in the Medical Reserve Corps offices in 1917, after his graduation in 1915 with honors from Harvard Medical School and became lieutenant colonel in the U.S. Army.

In a municipal hospital in New York City (Harlem Hospital), he became the first black to be appointed as doctor in 1919 and contributed to raise professional standards and lower the mortality rate. Dr. Tompkins Wright published extensive research with great influence in a number of fields throughout his career, including antibiotic treatment, cancer, chemotherapy, the treatment of head injuries and the treatment of bone fractures. To his honor just before his death at the age of 61 in 1952, the new Harlem Hospital library that bears his name was renamed at its inauguration in his name.

Lewis Howard Latimer (1848–1928)

The one who was believed to have invented the electric bulb of Mr. Thomas A. Edison, the inventor, became an electrical engineer-inventor, on June 17, 1882, after he invented the fine carbon filament, used in lightbulbs for a long lasting effect than the original electrified paper filament of Mr. Thomas A. Edison.

As an improvement to Edison's inventions, the incandescent lamp was finally put in the lightbulb. Mr. Thomas A. Edison, the inventor of the electric bulb, and Mr. Alexander Graham Bell, the inventor of the phone were his employers. It is with enthusiasm that the ideas of this son of a fugitive slave were received by these two inventors and businessmen for his development of electrical appliances and telephone.

Together with Joseph V. Nichols, Mr. Howard Latimer invented the electric lamp on September 13, 1881. On January 12, 1886, he inscribed a cooling and disinfecting apparatus on his name. He represented one of the pioneers of Edison, one of his first twenty-eight employees and was the only black man dedicated to maintaining alive the ideals of the Edison General Electric Company.

Also classified as an author, draftsman, expert in patent and musician, Mr. Latimer supervised the installation of public electric lights through New York, Philadelphia, Montreal, and London.

Daniel Hale Williams (1858–1931)

The Provident Hospital in Chicago, the first nonsegregated hospital in the United States, existing till today was the foundation of Dr. Williams. Well before the open-heart type of surgery could be performed in the world or elaborated in the United States, he performed the first open-heart surgery on July 9, 1893, and was the first African American to be accredited for it.

By sewing the heart of the named James Cornish, stabbed in the chest, Dr. Williams saved the life of this victim without blood transfusion or interventions of modern surgery. During that period, black doctors were denied positions, and African American citizens still could not be admitted to hospitals because of daily discrimination.

Appointed chief surgeon of the freedmen hospital in Washington D.C., where he moved in 1894, he devoted himself to provide care to former African-American slaves by improving surgical procedures through diligent work on the revitalization of life by a cardiac surgery performed on July 10, 1893, and which fell into deep oblivion for four years; and would only be reported in 1897 and acknowledged as a successful pericardium surgery to repair a wound and to decrease a much higher mortality rate at that time in that city of the United States of America.

His growing specialization in institutions allowed the public to know more about surgery. He was pledged to fight and provide opportunities for black doctors and nursing students by adding a multiracial team to launch an ambulance service and cofounded a professional organization for black doctors, named the National Medical Association, which did allowed service to African-Americans as an alternative in 1895.

Working in an operating room of very small fortune with an operating team of six people who were helping him wasn't without complications, but by exposing the beating heart without modern miracle drugs, X-ray aid, or blood transfusion, he was opening a patient's chest, a fraction of centimeter from the heart, and sewed the dagger's wound with competence.

To remove some fluids from the thoracic cage, Dr. Williams operated again on August 2. The patient was discharged from the hospital, on August 30, and twenty years later, he was known to be alive and healthy. This surgeon, born in Hollidaysburg, Pennsylvania, on January 18, 1858, continued his career as a pioneer in medicine up to his death on August 4, 1931, at Idlewild, Michigan, United States.

As a member of the Chicago Surgical Society, the American College of Surgeons elected him as its only African American founding member in 1913, and the Howard and Wilberforce Universities awarded him honorary degrees.

William Augustus Hinton (1883–1959)

In 1927, when syphilis was on the rise in the United States, Dr. William Augustus Hinton was best known for the Davies-Hinton test; as a specialist in the study and development of drugs to fight against diseases, he used the test to detect venereal diseases like syphilis.

This disease is transmitted by the source of *Treponema pallidum* bacterium through unprotected sexual act. It is contracted by anal, oral, vaginal intercourse, and blood transfusion. And the child is contaminated during the second and third trimesters of pregnancy by the mother's transplacental route. If she presents a primary or secondary form of syphilis, it can result by the death of the newborn and in other cases, lead newborns to congenitally acquired malformations occurring after birth, if it is latent.

Its incubation period is from three weeks to one month, but some manifestations may occur several years after contamination. This contagious sexually transmitted infection is manifested by an initial chancre and by the visceral organs or central nervous system.

His humanity spared countless long pains with lower and more accurate treatment costs than his predecessors. These treatment costs were putting the poor patients in the black communities at risk, particularly affected by this fearsome scourge, sometimes leading to blindness, madness, heart disease, and paralysis for those harshly affected.

In the world of diagnosis and treatment of syphilis, Dr. William Augustus Hinton became one of the most important authorities by the book he wrote on his studies in 1936.

Dr. William Augustus Hinton was appointed instructor in preventive medicine and hygiene at the famous university, the Harvard Medical School, three years only after obtaining his doctorate in 1912. Dr. William chose to serve humanity by working in the field of public health, refusing to make a fortune in private practice, but it was said he could.

Jean-Baptiste-Point Du Sable (1745–1814)

An unusual man, born in Saint-Marc, Haiti between 1745 and 1750, made a long journey for more than two hundred years ago, from Haiti to the Great Lakes in the United States. It was a long journey that this Metis made, known as a son of a former slave mother of African origin and a French sailor. He was born a free man in Haiti, the former French colony of Santo Domingo. When this young man judged that he was in danger to be sold as a slave, he decided to go to Louisiana. To escape up to the Mississippi River, Mr. Jean-Baptiste-Point Du Sable built himself a small boat and first moved to St. Louis, where he learned the Indian language, living and hunting with them.

Now that he could speak the Indian language made a great difference in his life, having already learned French and English, he could help them sell their furs. Thus, in the fur trade, he became the confident man before deciding to make his way up to the rich region called *Chekagou* by the Indians in Mississippi in 1772.

The word *chekagou*, deformed by the French and derived from the Indian word *sikaakwa*, Chicago in English, could mean "skunk" or "wild onion," named because at that location, these two products were found in large quantity! "*Sikaakwa* or *Chekagou*," could also mean "great" or "powerful." At that location, because of its two watercourses, as well as Lake Michigan, one of the five Great Lakes in North America, was a good position for a commercial site; he quickly realized it by opening a prosperous trading post, a good place to stop, being able to speak to all who met him in French, English, and Indian.

Chicago is on the southwest shore of Lake Michigan, the largest city in the Midwest region, the third largest city in the United States, which formed the main economic and cultural center located in the northeast of the state of Illinois. Mr. Du Sable being the first to settle there was therefore the founder of Chicago.

To sell his furs, he made several trips toward French Canada, to which he was very closely connected. He was later on identified as a French-Canadian origin by the Michigan historian named Milo Milton Quaife, putting forward a theory that he was a French immigrant from Canada.

Traders and men all over the world decided to raise families there; close to his post, they built houses and stores. Pioneers came west, trappers, hunters, missionaries, and explorers, all had confidence in him as a pioneer, because he was honest and treated everybody fairly. The waters of Lake Michigan were where they fished, to grow the colony in that city of Chicago as it is known today. Deceased on August 28, 1818, this great pioneer is resting in peace in St. Charles, Missouri, United States.

Frederick Douglass (1817–1895)

The daughter of his master taught the young Frederick how to read and write, although it was against the law of Maryland to teach and educate slaves in 1820, but in a house where he was a slave, he learned to read. Mr. Frederick Bailey wanted to be free, but knew he could not be, knowing that some slaves in that period bought their own freedom; therefore, he so much wanted to be free, the more he acquired knowledge.

In 1838, with a lot of planning and little luck, he escaped to New York and therefore left Col. Edward Lloyd, his owner, one of the richest men in the state, who possessed according to his estimations, nearly a thousand slaves. Although finally a free man in a free land, he had to be very careful not to be captured because he was still a slave; and because Mr. Frederick Douglass wanted freedom not just for himself but for all slaves, he started therefore to call himself Douglass by dropping the slavery name of Bailey; but still a slave, the story of his life that he began to tell deeply moved People in 1841.

Traveling throughout the North shortly afterward, uttering speeches against slavery, been hired to speak to groups who wanted to hear his story by the Massachusetts Antislavery Society, and writing the story of his life in 1845, his friends, who persuaded him to f lee to Europe for his security were fearing that he might be recognized and be returned to slavery at that moment.

For the continuation of the struggle against slavery, he was touring to raise funds to be used for his cause being in Europe, which his friends also did meanwhile, to buy his freedom in the United States. Mr. Frederick Douglass returned to the United States, after the proclamation of his freedom, where he set up his own newspaper, which he called the *North Star*, in which he wrote things never been written before in the United States, against death penalty, the lack of attention paid to the education of poor people, the Chinese newcomers to the United States, and the bad treatment of Indians.

To recruit black soldiers into the Union Army, Mr. Frederick Douglass had to speak to President Abraham Lincoln, asked to do that by his community for a change in the law before the war. More than two hundred thousand black men followed the example of the two sons of Mr. Douglass, who were among the first to join the Union Army. He became active in politics, now appointed marshal of Washington D.C. after the War of Secession; he was speaking on many issues, issues like women' right, the voting right, the national system education right, and many other subjects. He continued to do that even after being appointed minister of the United States in Haiti in 1889.

On February 28, 1895, Mr. Frederick Augustus Washington Douglass died in Washington D.C. This politician, who was (despite himself) a candidate for the vice presidency of the United States for the National Equal Rights Party in 1872, designated as the running mate of the nominated candidate for presidency called Victoria Woodhull, Frederick Douglass was known not only as one of the most famous American abolitionists of the nineteenth century but also, especially for his speeches against slavery—the speeches that helped to convince the white supporters of slavery. In addition, he refused the designation of the National Equal Rights Party, because he was a radical Republican activist and went to support the presidential campaign in New York State, for Pr. Ulysses Grant. This slave son nicknamed "The sage of Anacostia" or "The lion of Anacostia" was during the candidate for the presidential election of Victoria Woodhull, the first black to be a candidate for the vice presidency of the United States.

Norbert Rillieux (1806–1894)

In the United States of America, there was already a quarter of a million free blacks in the South only in 1860; therefore, all Blacks who lived in America were not slaves before the Civil War. Norbert's father, Vincent Rillieux, mechanical engineer, expert and machine builder, and his mother, Constance Vivant, a free black woman in New Orleans, Louisiana, were wealthy parents; therefore, he was born with a golden spoon in his mouth on March 17, 1806. Norbert, being an excellent student who wanted to study engineering, was sent to Paris, France, by his rich and prosperous parents, like many other wealthy parents who sent their sons to study in Europe at that time.

He became a teacher in a French engineering school at the age of twenty-four. Throughout Europe, the book he wrote on steam engines became very famous; finally interested in how sugar was refined or made pure, while eliminating the impurities or dirt from sugar, forced him to commit himself to innovate that industry, and change the method that took several hours, too much fuel and a lot of work at that time. That method, consisting of boiling sugar cane juice, then allowed it to get cool for the white sugar crystals to be formed was very slow.

For the development of the sugar industry, a pan to remove water from sugar was invented by this African American Creole, after many studies on December 10, 1846. It was an effective and an important method known as a system of multi-effect evaporation, with the publication number US4879A. His pan to remove water from sugar, which improved sugar production, was installed in the manufactures of sugar cleaner in America and France. This system of evaporation pan was used to produce a better and cleaner type of sugar faster, and considerably made the price of sugar cheaper.

This quotation: "The invention of Mr. Rillieux was the largest in the history of America in chemical engineering," was written at that period of his invention by the American government. His invention, a system used not only in the production of sugar, but also in the production of glue, condensed milk, gelatin and for the recovery of liquid waste in factories and distilleries, as well as in the production of soap, is still in use until today.

His decision to return to France was therefore because of the racial prejudices; and the pain he felt in the United States, made him became very unhappy, including the violation of their rights, their well-being and interests; him himself been often insulted and badly treated in his hometown Louisiana, and the bad treatment of free blacks in the South.

His decision was motivated by the rejection to patent one of his inventions by the authorities for race relations in the United States. In the late 1850s, Mr. Norbert Rillieux was also wrongfully believed to not be a citizen in the United States but a slave like all blacks before the Civil War in American, caused by the seceded eleven states of the South from the United States. It occurred between 1861 and 1865 and was led by Jefferson Davis on the Confederate States of America side and Abraham Lincoln on the United States side. In France, where he lived until his death at the age of eighty-nine, he worked as a researcher and professor.

An inscription on the bronze monument in the Louisiana State Museum reads as follows: "To honor Norbert Rillieux, born at New Orleans, Louisiana, March 17, 1806, and died at Paris, France, October 8, 1894. Inventor of Multiple Evaporation and its Application to the Sugar Industry."

Note that even today, the condensed milk production, distilleries, the gelatin and glue productions, the sugar and sweet industries, owe a debt to the genius of this great African American inventor.

Hiram Rhodes Revels (1822–1901)

At the time that some blacks were born free and some had bought their freedom before the Civil War, years were very difficult for blacks in the South of the United States. Moreover, blacks were prohibited from learning to read or write, slave or free man. To thwart that decision, Mr. Hiram Revels therefore moved to northern Ohio as soon as he was old enough to go to school because he wanted to learn.

He, who was born in North Carolina in 1822, became a reverend in the African Methodist Church, after he graduated from the Knox College in Illinois, and was preaching at the border states of Kentucky and Missouri. He, who organized the first black regiment of the state, was preaching in Maryland when the Civil War began; believing that black citizens should participate in the war like whites, he taught free slaves after the war.

Mr. Hiram Revels eventually settled in Mississippi, since his work as an educator became notorious, made him one of the most popular reverends in the state, traveling to the southern state to organize churches and schools. I must say that his work as an educator and preaching the gospel were not at all appreciated by the United-States government because "he later recalled the great opposition he sometimes encountered" with these words: "I was imprisoned in Missouri in 1854 for preaching the gospel to Negroes, though I was never subjected to violence." As the first black to sit in the United States Senate, elected in the senate of Mississippi in 1869, he made history for being appointed to the United States Senate in Washington D.C. in 1870.

Mr. Jefferson Davis, who became president of the confederation after his resignation from his Senate seat, was replaced by Mr. Hiram in 1861, to represent the state of Mississippi for two years. After the Civil War, a new black leadership group emerged, called the reconstructionists; this group wanted to help rebuild the South, and Mr. Hiram was part of those advanced men, black or white reconstructionists. Today, this African American is remembered as an educator and a builder.

This half-breed man, born in Fayetteville, North Carolina, on September 27, 1827, from a white mother of Scottish origin, and a free nigger father, fought against racial inequality, segregation, and discrimination practiced in Washington D.C. and at the West Point. He tried to reason with his white colleagues who were in favor of a ruthless "radical" treatment to assume the civil rights of the former slaves and other niggers without infringing the civil rights of whites.

After so many years of struggle, of evangelization to whites and black slaves, of helping as a military chaplain in the army of the union, and of supporting a speedy restoration of the rights of states, accepting fidelity to the union, the first black parliamentarian who favored racial equality in the history of the United-States died in Aberdeen, Mississippi, on January 16, 1901.

Carter Godwin Woodson (1875–1950)

In 1875, Mr. Carter Godwin Woodson was born in a poor family in Virginia with little luck or money to send him to school. At the age of seventeen, he had to work as a miner to support himself, until he was twenty-two, when he finished high school. In 1912, he received a PhD from Harvard University, after college education.

In Washington D.C., he taught the history of the United States as a high school teacher but in the history of the United-States, he realized sooner that he was not teaching the history of African-Americans, missing in the history of their country. He felt that if the history of blacks was taught to all, relations between races could be improved. A group called the "Association for the Study of African-American Life and History" was founded by this wise teacher in 1915.

The journal of black history, published four times a year in America, is still published by this group. The loss history of his people, the history of blacks in the history of the United States was for the first time an issue of research, which he began and wrote sixteen books over the years of this research on the history of blacks and their contribution to the history of the United-States.

In the United-States celebrations, such as special Brotherhood Week and Education Week were celebrated, but not Negroes' history week, but why not a Negroes' history week? He questioned himself. The answer, which was another idea conceived by Dr. Carter Woodson in 1926, finally became a reality, for him to become the Negro History Week founder that became the Black History Month in 1976.

Commemorating the anniversary of the great spokesman against slavery, Frederick Douglass the abolitionist, publisher, speaker, and US official, including Abraham Lincoln, who preserved the Union after the American Civil War and who abolished slavery, the Negro History Week was celebrated; became the Black History Month, it is celebrated every year in February nowadays as the foundation of Dr. Carter Woodson.

To teach the black history, programs were organized throughout the country, such as listen to discussions, attending lectures and reading books, during that special period.

The one, who died in 1950, was awarded many honors such as the NAACP Spingarn Medal, for collecting and publishing documents on the history of blacks, in the course of his life. He is remembered by his books, his accomplishments, and especially the encouragement of the population. We will never forget his classics of the African-American emancipation literature titled *A Century of Negro Migration*, published in 1918; *Free Negro Owners of Slaves in the United States in 1830*, published in 1924; and *The Miseducation of the Negro*, written in 1933.

The provocative works of the distinguished scientist were relating these facts to us concerning blacks from the South toward the North and West, from the colonial era up to the early twentieth century were stipulating that: "If you can control a man's thinking, you don't have to worry about his actions.

If you can determine what a man thinks you do not have to worry about what he will do. "If you can make a man believe that he is inferior, you don't have to compel him to seek an inferior status, he will do so without being told and if you can make a man believe that he is justly an outcast, you don't have to order him to the back door, he will go to the back door on his own and if there is no back door, the very nature of the man will demand that you build one."

This African-American historian, author, teacher, founder of the "Association for the Study of African- American Life and History," journalist, father of the history of blacks, and the initiator of the Black History Month died on April 3, 1950, in Washington D.C.

Vance Hunter Marchbanks Jr. (1905–1988)

As an African American colonel, surgeon, and scientist in the air force of his country, Dr. Marchbanks received a bachelor's degree from the University of Arizona and a PhD in medicine from Howard University. And at the Freedmen's Hospital in Washington D.C., he completed his internship and residency in internal medicine.

He was one of the two black doctors to have completed aerospace medicine of the United-States Air Force School Academy. He discovered a method to measure fatigue in pilots who were involved in aircraft accidents, after designing a gas mask testing device.

In various types of aircraft, he did extensive research for their noise control. To determine the effects of space f light on man, he was appointed chief medical officer of the project before the first American space launch of Project Mercury, tasked to collect medical information on astronauts before, during, and after the f light.

For the launch of Apollo on the moon, he helped design the spatial combination suits and monitoring systems, as head of environmental health services of the United Aircraft Corporation in the 1960s. Both in the aeronautical history and the black history, he became famous as one of the first in his field for his achievements.

This first black in the air force and one of the first black f light surgeons in the army was the one who made many dreams possible to blacks and to all other astronauts. They resolutely decided to continue their historic aeronautical journeys that he started until the end. This African American colonel, the first black doctor in the air force, and a space pioneer, born in Fort Washakie, Wyoming, on January 12, 1905, died on October 21, 1988, in Hartford, Connecticut.

Otis Boykin (1920–1982)

Being a scientist in electronics, inventor, and African American engineer, Mr. Otis Boykin designed a regulator for cardiac stimulator or pacemaker controller, a control unit used in artificial pacemakers; this device essentially used electrical pulses to maintain a regular cardiac rhythm. Many other devices were invented by this wise inventor, including a variable resistance apparatus used in many guided missiles, thick resistance films, used in IBM computers, an antitheft box, and finally, a chemical air filter.

On June 16, 1959, the obtained patent for his wire precision resistor, today used in many computers, radio, and televisions was developed very earlier, when he started as an assistant in the laboratory testing airplane of automatic controls, improved their functioning. Other notable inventions in electronically controlled devices were subscribed on the list of his inventions.

In Paris and throughout Europe, products from his devices were manufactured with success. For the common market, one of his products was approved for the use in military equipment. This creative inventor was living at a time when African Americans lived a life of segregation, but he managed at that period to triumph despite the obstacles of the time when electronics was just beginning to be known in the world. During that period, he reached the top level of technology to help the world reach the technology we know today.

In his lifetime, Mr. Otis Boykin only had twenty-six patents in his name from more than twenty-eight appliances he invented. Born on August 29, 1920, in Dallas, Texas, this inventor of pacemaker died ironically from heart failure himself on March 13, 1982, in Chicago, Illinois.

Rufus Stokes (1922–1986)

On November 5, 1940, Mr. Rufus Stokes was engaged in the American Army at Fort Benning, Georgia, at the age of eighteen, just before receiving his high school diploma from an Alabama public school. He then received training as a car mechanic in an army technical school. Records of the American army indicated that he was released in 1945 and began working.

After having worked as a car mechanic and as a worker in metal pipes and metal sheet, he continued his job search and worked specifically in the sanatorium section of tuberculosis at the Veterans Administration Hospital in Chicago by searching for his vocation. He then worked at Brule Inc., an incinerator manufacturing company in Chicago, after leaving the hospital.

At that moment, he became quickly familiar with the combustion process and thought he had found his vocation; seeing that he was never accredited by his competence or for his work, which strongly contributed to the design of new incinerators, he left that employer and pursued his own interests. To demonstrate his unrestricted versatility in design, configuration and skill, his applications remained excellent and efficient, whether industrial or residential.

A patent on an air purification device that reduced gas and ashes to a nondangerous and invisible level from the smoke was obtained by Mr. Rufus Stokes in 1968. That device, which not only improved the health of people with breathing problem, who should thank him in the future, also improved other things exposed to the air as animals, plants, cars, and the appearance and durability of buildings.

To show that his invention could be used in many ways, a mobile model of small and large dimension was built in 1973, after successfully constructed and tested several models of that same machine. This African American, born on September 3, 1922, in the city of Phoenix, and died on June 22, 1986, in Claremont, California, left us an unforgettable legacy.

Gordon Parks (1912–2006)

Mr. Gordon Parks was that kind of person talented in numerous fields but for his talent in photography, he was classified especially famous. Mr. Gordon Parks, who was born on a farm in Kansas in 1912, and went to school in Minnesota, dropped out of high school discouraged by racial segregation to play piano and held various other jobs until 25-year-old, when he started his career as photographer in Chicago in 1937; he was a writer and a composer of classical music, and his work with the camera was encouraged by artists of the South Side Community Art Center Chicago, Illinois, where he moved, and became a fashion and personalities photographer.

Many jobs were offered to him soon after, as a result of his success as a good photographer to have his own show in the center. For his photography, he won the first Rosenwald fellowship, and for the Farm Security Administration, a photo report was made as an objective assessment of the living and working conditions of rural Americans for its photographic section.

Most often in life, it is through the medium of photography that history was told, and nowadays, it is much so. That was why some important reportage of Mr. Parks—telling life stories were highly regarded —including segregation in the South, the life and crime in the United-States, one photo-reporter on Harlem leaders, and the poor Brazilian boy sad life—were and are still very emotional. Concerning the poor living conditions of a black family in Harlem, he made a very moving photo-reporter for *Life magazine* in 1968, which employed him as a photographer and photo-reporter in 1949.

Mr. Gordon Parks, who believed that photography was an important way to tell about life and learn from humanity, gave the same attention to the photography of high fashion, as he did with the crude and pesky subjects; this made him be considered as one of the best photographers in the United-States, to be granted numerous awards, and named the magazine photographer of the year in 1961.

At a concert in Philadelphia in 1955, three of his piano pieces that he always found time to compose as musical works, despite such an exciting career were performed by this orchestra. His several written books including one on photography were a success. Him himself produced and directed his transformed novel titled *The Learning Tree* published in 1963 into a film. Three years later, *A Choice of Weapons*, was published as his autobiography.

Before he left us on March 7, 2006, he gave us dignity, the beauty of life; he showed us harmony, the beauty of love and the horror of life, and was doing it with absolute skill. He's resting in peace in the Kansas Evergreen Cemetery in Fort Scott, Bourbon County; death at the age of ninety-three.

Edward Brooke (1919–2015)

The mother of the young Edward Brooke, born in Washington D.C. in 1919, gave him some advice: "People are as they're, and we accept them as such." He followed this advice as he grew up, and he thought people would accept him for his potentials, he, accepting people as they were.

Mr. Edward Brooke continued his studies at Howard University, after his education at Paul Laurence Dunbar High School. In 1941, he graduated from Howard University, and was called into the army, soon after the war broke out, where he worked behind the enemy lines in Italy as a lieutenant and received the Bronze Star Medal for his bravery.

Interested in how the government worked, and then wanted to be part of the government, made him to continue his law studies at the Boston University School of Law after the war. To attack dishonesty in the organizations of the city, Mr. Brooke was appointed by Mr. John Volpe, the governor of Massachusetts, as chairman of the Boston Finance Committee in 1961. Mr. Brooke worked very hard to achieve his goals, and was crowned with success for his work, leading him to run as a candidate for the position of attorney general of Massachusetts, which he ultimately won in 1962, in the largest law firm elected in that state.

Mr. Brooke was the first black to be elected attorney general, and in 1964, was reelected to the same position, although governors or president had already appointed senior posts to blacks. By a direct vote of the people, whom he trusted, he decided to apply for a more important post as a Senator of the United- States, and his trying paid and finally became the first black to be elected to the Senate of the United States. Devoted to the service of his state and his country since his election, Senator Brooke became an important and respected member of the Congress.

In 1972, the reelection of Senator Brooke was a very good thing for the Republican Party; and because he has proven that what really mattered was how to do his job well, the inhabitants of Massachusetts were equally proud of Mr. Edward Brooke.

Mr. Brooke was decorated in 2004 by Pres. George W. Bush and received a Presidential Medal of Freedom, which could only be granted by the president of the United-States for his contribution to security, peace in the world and the national interests of the United-States, public or private. This first African-American to be elected by a popular vote to serve as senator for two terms and to be at the front line in the battle for civil rights and economic equity died on January 3, 2015, at Coral Gables, Florida.

Carl Burton Stokes (1927–1996)

The city of Cleveland being at the same time, the largest city in Ohio, one of the main commercial centers of the Midwest, is also the eighth-largest city in the United-States, facing many problems major cities in America and around the world are facing. Very high taxes, air and water pollution, crimes, and of course, its slums, are known problems of that city.

In that city, at a very bad time, a black man named Carl Stokes became mayor on November 7, 1967, with Mr. Richard Gordon Hatcher, elected mayor in the state of more than one hundred thousand people known as the state of Indiana, they became the first two black mayors of larger cities elected the same day; so both of the largest cities in America had black men as mayors, the sons of slaves.

But in the city of Cleveland, with Mayor Carl Stokes, while expectation was an assumption, hope on him was the wish of the country for something to happen; because there were no schools and transportation infrastructure or enough money for their construction. Although the history of Mr. Carl Stokes' politics often overshadowed some achievements of his compatriots and other African-American mayors, the history of American politics would tell us that Mr. Robert Clayton Henry was the first African-American mayor of an American city of any size, specifically in Springfield, Ohio, from 1966 to 1968.

To remove his city from problems that haunted it so much and prevented it from progressing, Mayor Stokes had a plan. Being aware of the difficulties emanating from one of the most difficult jobs in politics, to face the management of a city in the United-States, how was he prepared for this task? Well, of course, his advent was a real success. "My son, learn to be somebody," his mother said, who raised him from his birth on June 21, 1957, in Cleveland, and his father who died when he was a baby, was the advice giving to him since his childhood. But not listening at first at the age of seventeen, he left high school and joined the army.

However, in 1957, Mr. Stokes began practicing law after completed his college and law school, attended after being released from the army. And, after being attracted to politics, to fight for civil rights and the well-being of laws, he served in the state legislature of Ohio for three terms. He ran for mayor and lost in 1965, and was retained in office, two years later when he presented himself again.

In considerable numbers, black citizens of Cleveland went to the polls because he became a source of pride, elected for his ability to represent the entire community. By putting in place program after program and a gigantic effort to rebuild and renew the city, Mr. Stokes organized Cleveland; and because he has always gotten federal money for his projects, he built new housing, created new jobs by helping small businesses worked to overcome pollution.

Mr. Stokes, who died on April 3, 1996, at the age of sixty-eight, his programs were crowned with success until proven otherwise. And he also made the participation of black voters and the presence of politicians a real force, to make him the symbol of a new chapter in American politics. The ballot power importance was shown by his election and record in office.

Dean Dixon (1915–1976)

He who had the decisive hand of his mother on him, as a little boy with his short young legs, was climbing up to the balcony of the New York's Carnegie Hall; in that Carnegie Hall where the mother of the named Dean Dixon took him to see the performance of symphonic orchestras when she could afford it, in many concerts because she loved symphonic music. He who was born from the West Indies parents on January 10, 1915, in Harlem, New York, as soon as he could read, could learn to read music, and at the age of six, took violin lessons.

Mr. Dean started to play violin in his high school orchestra, and in 1931, he founded his own orchestra at the age of sixteen at the YMCA of Harlem after graduating. Numerous famous people came to listen to the Dean Dixon Symphony Orchestra, with seventy-two years as the oldest member of the group, and twelve as the youngest, and open to blacks and whites.

Among them famous people was the president of the National Broadcasting Company, who invited him to be the conductor of the NBC Symphony Orchestra and then in 1941, the guest conductor of the New York Philharmonic; with the Philadelphia Orchestra and the Boston Symphony Orchestra, he also worked as guest conductor.

To all music lovers, his fame spread, allowing him to obtain the title of the exceptional conductor of the year, and received the year 1948 prize of $1,000. But as conductor, no American orchestra gave him a permanent position because of his African origins, in spite of his talent. He was therefore forced to migrate in Europe, where he received an immediate invitation to serve as a musical director in 1949 from an orchestra in Paris, and then served for eight years as head of a symphony orchestra in Sweden.

To spend his first six hours of the day planning and doing paperwork, he wakes up every day at six o'clock in the morning, and spend his last six hours as conductor; the life of a conductor, being demanding and difficult, led him to lose nearly five pounds in a real concert. In 1944, he created the American Youth Orchestra, for his dedication to help young people composed of young musicians of all races.

To young people who did not otherwise have the opportunity to listen to good music, he gave the opportunity to listen to good music by organizing concerts. To familiarize with the European public, numerous works were also presented in Europe, like William Grant Still and Gordon Parks compositions, as black music composers.

Because he took good music and goodwill wherever he went, many were already calling him the American ambassador of music, before being the head of the German Radio Symphony Orchestra. He directed almost all the great symphonies in the world. Mr. Dean Dixon returned to the United States with triumph in 1970, where he was once again invited to conduct at Central Park, New York, before seventy-five thousand auditors.

Having obtained the bourgeoisie honor, Mayor Lindsay awarded him the Golden Key of New York. His contribution earned him the Award of Merit of the American Society of Composers, Authors, and Publishers for having opened the doors of his heart to other talented musicians. The world lost a great artist and a distinguished man at his death on November 3, 1976, in Zurich.

Ralph Bunche (1904–1971)

Only few black children were lucky to go to high school in Los Angeles, in the early 1900s; but the grandmother of Mr. Ralph Bunche knew how important to have a good education was for life, which other children did not have, however mostly supporting their families by working. According to her, whatever our race, we could control our future with a good education, so stay in school, Mr. Ralph Bunche' grandmother insisted.

The young Ralph, born on August 7, 1904, in Detroit, Michigan, from an African American family with Irish roots, had good grades at the high school, following the advice of his grandmother. To study at the University of California, where he graduated with honors, he received a scholarship. Harvard University graduated him to receive a doctorate in philosophy in 1934. After completing his master's degree, he became a professor in 1928, at Harvard University in Washington D.C. He became famous because of his skills and knowledge in world affairs, and in that field, he gave courses.

To help the United States improve its relations with Africa, Dr. Bunche left teaching at the course of the Second World War, and the State Department employed him as the highest-ranking black person. In the United Nations, where he held several important positions, he contributed to the writing of the United Nations Charter, after the war. With Eleanor Roosevelt, he also participated in the elaboration of the Universal Declaration of Human Rights.

A peace agreement between the new nation of Israel and the Arab nations in the Middle East was organized by his help in 1940. In the peacekeeping establishment, Dr. Bunche became successful all over the world for his help for the independence of Israel and bringing peace to the Middle East.

This first black who received the Nobel Peace Prize in 1950, also contributed in 1956 to the peace in the Suez region; in 1960, the Congo, in 1964, the island of Cyprus, Kashmir, and Yemen. In 1963, he was awarded the highest distinction awarded to a civilian by the United-States government, the Presidential Medal of Freedom, awarded by Pres. John F. Kennedy. In Selma and in Montgomery, Alabama, he attended freedom marches, although been ill in 1965.

He who died on December 9, 1971, at the age of sixty-seven, served for twenty-two years, up to his death as a board member of the NAACP, the National Association for the Advancement of Colored People, as an American organization of civil rights defense.

Robert Clifton Weaver (1907–1997)

In the United States, the entire population of about 80 percent was already living in large cities in the year 2000, sheltering numerous problems such as the lack of employment, the rise of criminality, and the slums' growth, created by a massive movement of the population, made Pres. Lyndon B. Johnson to quickly realize that he had these problems as serious problems in his country.

For that, in 1966, the new Department with the initials generally known as HUD-Housing and Urban Development was created by him. After the president organized his cabinet by the advice of several heads of major ministerial departments, Mr. Robert C. Weaver, as the first black member of a president's cabinet, was also the one called to rebuild cities and stop the spread of slums, as the first secretary of HUD to do the job.

Mr. Weaver obtained a PhD in economics from Harvard University, after graduating from high school. The secretary of interior, Mr. Harold Ickes, welcomes him as an aide, when he returned to Washington in 1933. The non-white messengers' lunchroom in the building where Mr. Weaver worked was where all blacks supposed to eat; but without anyone asking him to leave, he entered in the white cafeteria with his friends for breakfast as a black man.

Related to discrimination in housing, employment, and education, he held several jobs, working with Mr. Ralph Bunche and Mr. Roy Wilkins, during his first days in Washington; they contributed together to the integration in ministries. Mr. Weaver taught in several colleges and worked for the UN later on; on the city problems, he wrote four books. He, believing that cities should be rebuilt and render more pleasant to live in, led him to attempt to persuade middle-income families to continue living in cities, as a secretary of HUD.

Given the great demand and the need for his services, he accepted the new job, as president of the Bernard Baruch College of the City University of New York in 1968. Today, for the more than 125 million people living in cities, he did much to make life better, and as an active member of thirteen boards of directors of large corporations, people owe him a lot for his hard work. Mr. Weaver, who was born in Washington D.C. in 1907, died in the State of New York, United States on July 17, 1997.

Elijah McCoy (1843–1929)

On May 2, 1844, Elijah McCoy was born free in Canada, precisely in Colchester, Ontario. His parents were former fugitive slaves of a plantation in Louisville, Kentucky, who escaped from the United States in 1837 by the clandestine railroad to Canada.

It must be said that, while in Canada, his father, George McCoy, briefly joined the Canadian Army, which awarded him 160 acres of farmland in the township of Colchester as a reward for his services rendered to the Canadian Army during the rebel war.

His parents, Canadian citizens, returned to the United States at Ypsilanti in 1847, when he was about five years old. He became an American citizen and lived the rest of his life in the United States. His father, George, was a train conductor from Ypsilanti to Michigan.

For the slaves fleeing from Kentucky up to Canada, that line was a very important stop for the escapees. While his cigar business was prospering, he helped several African Americans to escape from Kentucky. He was hiding them under cigar boxes he had to deliver in Detroit. He and Emilia Mildred Goins McCoy, his wife and Elijah McCoy's mom, were black.

Mr. Elijah McCoy was sent to Edinburgh, Scotland, in an engineering school at the age of fifteen, after completing the local secondary school in 1859. This African Canadian turned African American returned immediately to the United States, where he expected to work as a mechanical engineer. But despite his qualifications, his expertise was not considered because of his race and the color of his skin. He was therefore unable to find work as an engineer.

At that time, little interest was accorded to African Americans for professional positions, considering them less than nothing even with their professional training because of racial barriers. He then decided to work for the Michigan Central Railroad as a firefighter and oiler as it was impossible to find work as a black engineer.

After exerting more highly skilled work in that machine shop in Ypsilanti, Michigan, he developed and invented a lubrication device to improve and render railway operations more efficient. Mr. Elijah McCoy succeeded in solving the problems of engine lubrication and overheating, which periodically stopped the trains. His engine lubrication, using steam pressure, pumped oil where it was necessary in such a way that the train no longer had to stop to be lubricated.

This prototype, patented on July 12, 1872, as his first invention, proved to be valuable to the industry. It allowed the lubrication of blades, pumps, brakes, cylinders of an engine, etc., all while moving, reducing thereby some noisy friction to silence. This genuine and self-regulating system was used on steamships, locomotives, engines, and factories.

But up to then, not having yet lived all emotionally loaded subjects required as a victim of ostracism, he was rejected at the door of seminaries or councils when the color of his skin was discovered; and surely far from having seen everything, he had not yet said his last word concerning the enormity of his ingenuity and the quality of his inventions, which, at the level of his distinctions, would bear his name.

He used his first creation to develop another sophisticated self-lubrication containing a stopcock. For the same concept, he deposited more than fifty patents and other grass sprinkler mechanisms and ironing board. Although his name was unknown to most people, this father of lubrication, born with ingenious qualities, died on October 10, 1929, in Detroit, Michigan.

Fred McKinley Jones (1893–1961)

The "Model A" for the refrigeration system of the vehicle, which was later named Thermo King, the first unit of transport refrigeration, was patented by Frederick Jones and Joseph Numero on July 12, 1940. Mr. Fred Jones was certainly one of the most important black inventors who formulated many inventions throughout his life. Born from a white father of Irish origin and from a black mother on May 17, 1893, at Covington, Kentucky, he was raised by his father, a railway worker, after the death of his mother when he was young.

For Mr. Frederick Jones to have a better chance for an education, his father took him to Cincinnati, Ohio, and exhorted Fr. Edward A. Ryan of the Catholic Church of the St. Mary Parish, who exposed him in that educational environment in the parish priest's house from the age of eight. He showed great interest in mechanical functioning at a very early age. Whether it was a toy, a watch, or a kitchen appliance, Mr. Frederick Jones was disassembling everything.

In the house of the priest, where he only did small tasks like rubbing floors, shoveling snow, and mowing the grass around the church to be lodged and fed, he also learned to cook until he was twelve years old. That interest in mechanical work prompted him to take an interest in car mechanics. He eventually left the priest's house and began working in the R. C. Crothers Garage as a sweeper and garage cleaner.

In that garage mainly designed to repair cars and also used as a racing car construction studio, Fred became the owner's foreman after three years. He developed incredible knowledge about automobiles and their workings by watching with enthusiasm the mechanics working on cars and by spending a lot of his time collecting information with a voracious taste for learning.

That is how he started his diversities based on the great number of his inventions by starting with the construction of his cars after a few years. He also became one of the most famous car racers in the Great Lakes region by driving cars so speedily that he himself constructed, after a brief work aboard in a steamboat and in a hotel. One of his particularly well-conceived cars not only defeated other automobiles but also triumphed over an airplane, under the number 15, in a race. For the new radio station of his city, he built a transmitter and invented a device that combined sound with moving pictures after learning electronics by himself.

His portable unit designed for cooling trucks carrying perishable goods, the refrigeration for the preservation of blood, medicine, and food, brought a great improvement to the long-haul carriers to refrigerate the interior of semitrailers.

Mr. Frederick Jones was inducted in the National Inventors Hall of Fame in 1977 and prizewinner of the National Medal of Technology in 1991 for his innovations, precisely forty for the refrigeration equipments and others for portable X-ray machines, sound equipment, and gasoline engines. Sixty-one patents were received in the course of his life. This African American was the first to be elected to the American Society of Refrigeration Engineers in 1944. It was in Minneapolis that Mr. Frederick Jones died on February 21, 1961.

George Washington Carver (1864–1943)

The botanist and inventor named Man of the Year by the Federation of Architects, Chemists, Engineers, and Technicians in 1940, and by the United States Department of Agriculture in various councils and committees, was also honored by the University of Rochester and Simpson College; this illustrious figure named George Washington Carver evenly received honorary doctorates in science.

From the beginning of his inventions, he became one of the most famous scientists and the most respected in the history of the United States, who allowed farmers across the South and Midwest to become profitable and prosperous by his methods and important discoveries despite the early difficulties.

For most of his childhood, this sickly child—born a slave on January 1, 1864, in Missouri at Diamond Grove by two slave parents—remained fragile and could not work in the fields but had a great interest in plants. At that time where it was common to steal slaves and resell them, he and his mother Mary were kidnapped from their family one night by a gang of thieves. These Confederate thieves were stealing and reselling blacks, freed or slaves for their own profit. Thus, found safe and sound by the neighbors a few days later without his mother already resold, he was the object of an exchange by a race horse so that he could be returned to his owners.

Eager to learn more about plants, his master, a German immigrant named Moses Carver, sent him to Neosho, Missouri, for an education whose maturity and development occurs before the usual age; and at the Minneapolis High School in Kansas, where he graduated. The one who was formerly named the Doctor of Plants by the neighbors of his owner was because he had acquired knowledge of plants. Not only wanting to be satisfied with a high school diploma, he then sent a request to the Highland University in Kansas, where his acceptance and scholarship were offered to him, but immediately withdrawn by the president of the university because he was a nigger. After discovering the painted f lowers in the kitchen of one of his farmer neighbors whom he had helped, he decided to become as much an artist as a botanist.

In Indianola, Iowa, the Simpson College accepted him in 1887. His artistic talent earned him great respect for the school newspaper to publish his poems and enrolled him in the spectacular World's Columbian Exposition for his art. This exposition, which commemorated the four hundred years of Christopher Columbus's arrival in the New World, and which exhibited two of his paintings, took place from May 1 to October 30, 1893 in Chicago, Illinois. In addition, it inscribed an incredible and unforgettable story in its archive concerning a criminal case that fascinated and horrified the public. It is a story of a killer considered in the United States as the first officially recognized serial killer.

This serial killer, named H. H. Holmes, was murdering some of his hotel guests to seize their possessions and make their bodies disappear during that exposition attracting twenty-seven million visitors. Fortunately, Mr. Carver was not one of his victims, and he had not lost interest in agriculture but put more effort into sciences, which eventually won him a transfer from the Simpson College to the Iowa Agricultural College and became the first African American in that establishment in 1891.

After receiving his master's degree in agriculture in 1896, the faculty of the school, today the Iowa State University, offered him a post as the first black to be awarded that honor for his distinction. Two mushrooms discovered by him were named on his honor in 1897. Convened by Booker T. Washington of Tuskegee Normal and Industrial Institute to teach, the most crucial moment of his life arose at that stage when he was appointed as the director of agriculture.

Quickly, he taught his methods of improving the soil to his close friends and farmers, which they were to exploit easily, for the abundant harvests; and encouraged poor farmers to grow groundnuts, sweet potatoes and soybeans as a substitute for the repeated cultivation of cotton; not only to help replenish the soil by plants containing proteins to improve the cultivation and the harvest of cotton, but also for their source of food and to improve their quality of life.

His methods drove the farmers in heaven by overflowing warehouses. George Washington Carver invented soap from groundnut, toilet powder from groundnut, flour from sweet potato, ink from sweet potato, tapioca from sweet potato, starch from sweet potato, and the synthetic rubber from sweet potato, to only name his few inventions.

The Royal Society for the Encouragement of Arts Manufactures, and Commerce of Great Britain elected him as a member of its institution and was one of the few Americans to receive this honor at that time in 1916. The Spingarn Medal of the National Association for the Advancement of Colored People was awarded to him in 1923. And for his distinguished research in agricultural chemistry, this "Black Leonardo," who was dubbed by Time magazine received the Theodore Roosevelt Medal in 1939.

Six months after his death, occurred on January 5, 1943, a national monument dedicated to his discoveries was constructed and inaugurated to his honor by President Frank Delano Roosevelt on July 14, 1943, with this inscription on the grave: "He could have added fortune to fame, but caring for neither, he found happiness and honor in being helpful to the world." It is in that park, including the first bust of Carver as national monument near Diamond Grove, Missouri, where he spent his childhood that this monument, devoted to an African-American in the United States, was recognized as the first to honor someone other than a president.

By this national monument, President Frank Delano Roosevelt wanted to support the fight against segregation that this "Black Leonardo" led throughout his life and recognized his contribution and scientific expertise in the field of plant pathology to the American nation and to the world.

Jan Ernst Matzeliger (1852–1889)

It was at the age of nineteen that this man born in Suriname in Paramaribo began to work. At that age, Mr. Jan Ernst Matzeliger was a seaman in a merchant vessel. This brave young man was born on September 15, 1852, from a Netherlander father and a black Surinamese mother in Dutch Guiana, today the Republic of Suriname in South America.

In the seventeenth century, this region, colonized by the Republic of the United Netherlands, took the name of Dutch Guiana. The country Suriname, with Paramaribo as the capital, has a border with French Guiana to the east, Guyana to the west, and Brazil to the south and is located on the coastline of the Atlantic Ocean, in the northeast of the continent, in the heart of the Guiana plateau.

This son of a Dutch engineer was already showing a certain interest in mechanics in his country of origin. At the beginning, when he moved to the United States, he settled in the state of Pennsylvania in Philadelphia in 1873. Speaking very little English, he only got small jobs, although he was mechanically good with his hands to earn his living. He was pitied by some black residents active in a local church with which he became friends. Decided to remain in the United States, he moved once more and settled in Lynn in the state of Massachusetts in 1877.

At Lynn, a shoemaker gave him a job at a certain moment when he could not find work at Lynn and was still unable to speak rudimentary English. It was at that time that Mr. Jan Ernst Matzeliger became interested in the fabrication of shoes. After passing some considerably difficult time, he began working in a shoemaking workshop as an apprentice and operated the McKay machine to stitch the sole and to assemble the different parts of a shoe; after he worked as a sailor, which allowed him to explore other parts of the world during the two years he worked aboard that merchant vessel of the East Indies.

Mr. Jan Ernst Matzeliger became interested in the fabrication of shoes at the time when the small town of Lynn, Massachusetts, held the monopoly on the manufacture of shoes, producing more than half of shoes in the United States.

At that time, the upper part of a shoe was attached to the sole by hand sewing. Unfortunately, there were no machines for this operation.

It was at that moment that his efforts to invent a machine to assemble shoes began. Then to learn English, he took evening classes, after long days of work, to study books of physics and mechanics, allowing him to invent a number of inventions. Incapable of patenting his inventions for the lack of financial means, he watched others patent his creation helplessly and receive rewards for his inventions, but he continued to develop a few crude working models of his invention with whatever materials he could find and needed better materials to improve his device because he felt he was on the right path.

For that, he decided to make a deal not bearing to sell his device. So two investors by the names of Charles H. Delnow and Melville S. Nichols took notice of his work and offered him a financial backing of two-thirds interest, and they retained a 66 percent interest for his device, to financially allow him to finish the machine he was developing.

Though he had enough money, he already thought of a more important invention and did not despair over his fate. That important invention was the shoe laster machine. After finishing the second and third model of the machine, he filed a patent for his second invention and received it on March 20, 1883, after five years of work. Quickly, in Lynn, his invention supplanted other hand lasting methods of boots and shoes machine in two years; and he received several other patents for the model of improved shoe manufacturing machines.

The inventor, who revolutionized the footwear industry and proved wrong those who were saying that no man could build a machine to replace their work unless he builds a machine that has fingers like them, died three weeks before his thirty-seventh birthday on August 24, 1889, in Lynn, Massachusetts.

In his honor, precisely on September 15, 1991, a 29-cent postal stamp was issued by the United-States, but it was until recently that he was mentioned in the history books of his country because of the color of his skin. Thus, Mr. Jan Ernst Matzeliger was never able to profit from the benefits of his invention because of his early death from tuberculosis.

C. J. Walker (1867–1919)

The first African-American woman who managed to be rich by her own efforts, showcasing her ambitious business potential by inventing her products, elaborated unique marketing strategies to become a homemade millionaire; and as widow at the age of twenty, she was living daily with the hair loss problems that she and her black sisters were experiencing.

The problem of hair loss was a real problem and waited for solutions. So, after working for Annie Malone as a sales agent in 1905 and cooking in an embarkation house, the one who worked as a laundress decided to settle for solutions and find a treatment for hair loss problem.

The opportunity for her to become an African American businesswoman occurred when a pharmacist wholesaler in Denver by the name of Edmund L. Scholtz proposed to analyze the formulas of Annie Malone for Mrs. C. J. Walker. She followed the advice of that pharmacist, who suggested that she put aside her sales activity and put more time in making money for herself.

Thus, on the basis of the formulas of Malone, she dedicated herself to the modification for her own hair care products. She developed a system after so much research for the treatment of that capillary anomaly and created a line of cosmetics and care products, including a shampoo and an ointment to help grow the hair faster and stronger.

Under the name Roberts and Pope, she was selling her products door to door in the compact black community in Denver directly to black women. Her method of applying the iron comb to the hair with intense brushing was transforming the brittle and dull hair into luxurious soft hair.

The image of the medium-length hair that boosted hair growth and conditioned hair scalp after a treatment of only two years appeared in July 1906 as the first advertisement for her hair care products. It was designed to promote her products through the setting up of her own marvelous production, but that caused her the detachment from the Malone, Roberts and Pope Company.

Her most effective strategy, the multilevel marketing, significantly increased her customer base between February and April 1910. Her talent of self-promotion allowed her to create a booming business, the C. J. Walker Manufacturing Co., a manufacturer of African American cosmetics in the United States, incorporated in Indianapolis, Indiana. In the twentieth century, that company was better known for its cosmetic products and African American hair care products.

Born Sarah Breedlove on December 23, 1867, in Delta, Louisiana, her two parents were former slaves. This civil rights activist, philanthropist, and entrepreneur, who was financing women's scholarships at the Tuskegee Institute, was also donating significant funding to the National Association for the Advancement of Colored People, to the (Black YMCA, or Young Men's Christian Association) gathering more than 15,000 local youth associations, and to dozens of other charitable organizations. She bequeathed nearly $100,000 for orphanages, institutions, and individuals.

In 1917, two years before her death, she was saying that she was not yet a millionaire but that she hoped to be at a certain time. She died in her Villa Lewaro in Irvington-on-Hudson, New York, on May 25, 1919, and the Walker Company was closed in July 1981. She was considered in America as the richest African American woman at her death.

In 1993, the National Women's Hall of Fame honored her by perpetuating her memory as a woman who excelled in the field of humanities affairs, at the origin of inventions and in politics and sciences. And as part of the Black Heritage series, a commemorative stamp was issued to her honor by the United States Postal Service in 1998, followed by many other honors.

Percy Lavon Julian (1899–1975)

The synthesis of the physostigmine and the extraction of stigmasterol from *Physostigma venenosum* of the natural product, which occurs naturally in the Calabar bean, is a highly toxic alkaloid; the seed of a leguminous plant, is known to be a native plant of West Africa; its toxic-to-humans, a substance that stimulates the parasympathetic nervous system was for the first time, synthesized and known as the realization of this researcher chemist and pioneer of herbal medicines in the industrial chemical synthesis at large-scale in 1935.

He also invented the fireproof foam used for the suppression of fire, the synthesis of progesterone, and the synthesis of cortisone on August 10, 1954. The chemist, Percy Julian was very interested in herbal medicines; in particular, the Calabar bean, whose active ingredient is physostigmine. This toxic seed of a tropical plant containing physostigmine was once used for tribal events. *E-ser-e*, its indigenous name, meaning "bean of the Ordalia," was administered to people accused of witchcraft or other crimes by the court ruling of the ancient inhabitants of Calabar in Nigeria; known precisely as the people of Efik, closely related to the Ibibio, were among the four main ethnic groups targeted during the slavery period; including the Igbo, and the Yoruba, they were deported in unimaginable numbers as slaves in Barbados.

In some duels, each of the opponents was to eat half of the seed, preventing any uncontrolled physiological action, and in a reversibly manner; the acetylcholinesterase, an enzyme naturally existing in humans, increased its local concentration of acetylcholine in a functional contact zone, between one or two neurons, and another cell (muscle cells); its synaptic cleft allows the stimulation of nicotinic receptors.

During a deep relaxation, in the paradoxical phase of sleep, the decrease or disappearance of tonus and most often muscular contractility, the physostigmine of this generic molecule deriving from an African leguminous plant was used. And in case of atony of the digestive tract, the myasthenia of glaucoma as an antidote for acute intoxication, and as a decurarizer in anesthesiology, it was used in therapeutic use.

In 1931, his prominence on organic chemistry qualified him for a doctoral degree in Vienna, Austria, after receiving a scholarship from the General Education Council in 1929. From the beginning of his studies, because of racial concerns, Mr. Percy Julian was always discouraged from seeking admission to a graduate school, given the racial potential of coworkers and future employers.

After two years in Fisk University as a chemistry professor in a black college in Nashville, Tennessee, he was unable to obtain a position as an assistant teacher at major universities because of the refusal of white students objecting to learn under a black professor.

In Vienna, the interesting properties and the capacities of soybeans made him develop a fascination in its composition with an associate in Vienna, Dr. Josef Pikl, with whom he worked on the synthesis of physostigmine.

For his achievement, Dr. Percy Lavon Julian, born on April 11, 1899, was internationally hailed as the one who developed a drug that was used for the treatment of glaucoma, and also used to treat Alzheimer's disease. He did not disappoint those who were asking him to develop compounds that could be used for the production of paints and other products from soy.

This pioneer, both known in the world of chemistry and as a defender of the critical situation of black scientists, died on April 19, 1975.

Andre Pinto Reboucas (1838–1898)

Andre Reboucas was born in Brazil on January 13, 1838, in Rio de Janeiro. Became engineer after studying in Europe, Andre Reboucas designed an immersive device known as torpedo, which could be projected underwater, causing an explosion to a ship, during the time ships became more and more integrated in the war.

Being trained in the military school of Rio de Janeiro, the former lieutenant in the Paraguayan War of 1864 and former teacher at the Polytechnic School of Rio de Janeiro used his wealth to help the abolition movement to put an end to slavery in Brazil; he still had to concede of being supervised at the age of twenty-two; but deeply offended by seeing slaves carrying water through the streets of Rio de Janeiro, he modernized the city's sanitation network and founded the "Brazilian Antislavery Society" to live and see the day of the slavery abolition.

Thus, disgusted with the Brazilian conditions, he moved to the coast of Africa, in Funchal, the capital of Madeira, in the autonomous region of Madeira, comprising the islands of the archipelago located at the offshore of Morocco in the Atlantic Ocean, where he died on April 9, 1898.

The death of this dominant African-Brazilian figure was striking. It was at the foot of a cliff in Funchal near the hotel where he lived that his body was found. This slavery abolitionist, who was living the stories of blatant racism against him, undoubtedly found himself faced with a frenzy of racial hostility.

So, the image of freedom requires our interrogation; because the example of these black men represents the image of equality that we are demanding and the goal that we are still pursuing up to this day for freedom. What have we learned about seeking equality as a path toward freedom? Excuse me gentlemen, nothing.

These black men, well-trained professionals, members of the social elite who were able to achieve their full talents, considered middle class and proud as they were, are still considered to be subhumans that have brought nothing to human civilization; but on the other hand, who have been victims of racial hostility. Nevertheless, centuries after slavery, this old interrogation from whites, asking themselves— "Why are blacks so angry?"—continues to hang in the air; have they gotten the answer? Hell, surely not.

But for blacks, who are suffering this injustice so far, forgetting the racial issues that they know so well is an impossible task for the white community to understand, however, who is continuing its racial hostility toward niggers; thus lacking them the least intellectuality, they will never be ready to understand the point of view of niggers, who are vacillating between uncontrollable hatred and skepticism.

That feeling of frustration often expressed by the black man was conceived by all the psychological activities, doctrines, disciplines or European values, not having good faith. In response to the opposition, related to anger, annoyance, bitterness, disappointment and the resistance to the fulfillment of an individual's will or goal, it arises and is likely to increase when a will or goal is denied or blocked. It is real and it matters in all giving perspectives. Because with acuity, it makes us live, the overwhelmingly incredible trauma inflicted on black in Africa but very severely on blacks, uprooted from Africa, dispossessed of their identity, their family, their languages, their religious beliefs and deported to enslavement; a stolen identity all short.

William F. Burr (1825–1861)

William F. Burr, born on March 29, 1825, and died on October 22, 1861, was the one who filed a patent for a railroad switching system, a railroad device used to change lanes to a train, on October 31, 1899. Shifting a train is usually assigning it a direction.

F. J. Wood

The harvesting of potatoes was a slow and difficult process before the invention of the potato shovel, invented by F. J. Wood on April 23, 1895. For farmers, this tool, with a patent filed by the inventor, became a very important tool.

Albert C. Richardson

On February 17, 1891, Mr. Albert C. Richardson patented the butter churn, a device for an easy way to make butter that forever changed the food industry. In 1882, a hame fastener was patented by the same inventor. Before the invention of the coffin lowering device of Mr. Albert C. Richardson, the burial of the dead was done in shallow graves because of the difficulties of the gravediggers, who also proceeded to the lowering of the coffin; or if the hole was deeper, the lowering of a coffin required many people; but since they were using an archaic technique, the coffin was most often damaged because gravediggers, who required a certain physical and mental strength, for a good progress of the before, during and after funerals, were dropping the coffin, because of the lack of good secure method offering a balanced descent for the lowering of the casket.

The coffin-lowering device was therefore also invented and patented by him on November 13, 1894. That invention consisted of a series of pulleys and ropes or rags. It allowed the lowering of the coffin with assured uniformity in a deep hole, thus making the task easier for cemeteries guards. This very important process is used up to the present day in all cemeteries and is considered as the most durable device among his inventions, to definitely solve the problem of lowering coffins in the tomb.

In February 1899, he invented an insect destroyer; and in December 1899, he brought an improvement in the design of the bottle. This prolific inventor, who displayed his talent, designed and created simple, durable and inexpensive useful devices, used in various fields, used his skills for the improvement of human life on Earth.

John Standard

We attributed the invention of the refrigerator to John Standard because he was the one who filed the patents on July 14, 1891, allowing the industrial development of the refrigerator in the United States, forty years later than the previous inventions.

But it is known that in 1748, William Cullen at the University of Glasgow discovered and demonstrated the first known artificial refrigeration that he did not particularly use for any practical purpose. And the first refrigeration machine was designed by Oliver Evans, known as an American inventor in 1805.

In 1834, Jacob Perkins built the first practical refrigerating machine that used ether in a steam compression cycle. And to cool the air for his yellow fever patients, John Gorrie, an American physician started experimenting with making artificial ice in 1844, and then he built a refrigerator to make, ice based on Oliver Evans' design on Mai 6, 1851, after giving up his medical practice in 1845.

This secretary of the Masonic Lodge and one of the founding members of the Episcopal Church of the Trinity used this ice in a suspended basin on the ceiling of the hospital rooms to maintain a cool temperature in the rooms of the hospital. As an early pioneer of the artificial manufacture of ice, of refrigeration and the father of air conditioning, a humanist, inventor and physician, he obtained the patent N° 8080 for his invention as the first patented in United-Stated; and till today his principle is still most often used in refrigeration system.

The water and sulfuric acid refrigerator was invented in 1850 by the French engineer and inventor Edmond Carre. He imagined a sulfuric acid reservoir to heat the carafes of water successfully. These methods would be perfected in 1857 by Ferdinand Carre, who revealed his major invention, the absorption refrigerator using water and sulfuric acid.

The French Ferdinand Carre, known for his work in electricity, was the one who invented the electric regulator, an important machine that bore his name, or again, the absorption refrigerator using older principles of his brother, including two pressure levels and two fluids (water as an absorbent and ammonia as a refrigerant), in 1959. His method of cooling is still more widely used.

In 1851, the Scottish James Harrison, a pioneer in refrigeration techniques, tried to use the same principle of ether gas evaporation of the first mechanical machine for making ice; after noticing that the fluid used to clean the moving metal characters of his press called sulfuric ether left the type of metal cold to the touch after evaporation. This publisher, journalist, and politician used this principle of evaporation and cooling for the design of his own refrigerator.

He registered the patent of the first mechanical ice machine, the commercial version, in 1854 for his ice-making machine system by compressing ether vapor, which was producing up to three thousand kilograms of ice per day in 1855; and both of his processes, "747 of 1856," and his apparatus "2362 of 1857," were patented in London.

After proving that meat remained perfectly edible when preserved frozen for several months, the engineer James Harrison won a gold medal at the Melbourne Exhibition in 1873.

And in 1876, the German Carl von Linde invented a refrigerator based on the cryogenic gas liquefaction, which became the basis technology of modern refrigeration. As a member of scientific associations, Linde successfully liquefied air in 1895; but other inventors attributed themselves this paternity because this technology took a long time to be developed.

My desire on this quote of black inventors is to insist on their so great achievements, to recall their role of the past often obscured by the history against the progress of humanity. At the course of the last millennia, and for those who do not know it, the rich history of ancient civilizations of Africa did not begin with Europeans, or when the first Europeans arrived on the African continent.

They simply wanted to systematically erase black history by excluding Africa from the history of the world, to rationalize the nigger slavery. Stop this ignorance right now; because the cosmic never created two creations as the white man claims, while the only human creation created on earth, and scientifically proven is the black man.

Today, this history of the world cannot really be written without referring to the Negro people for it not to result in a scientifically erroneous consideration or sociologically dangerous conclusions. Stop this ignorance right now, albino son of the black man, and start considering the one you are calling Nigger as your true parent; it's a pure and simple truth from which you cannot escape and should not be ashamed of, but simply be pride of, for the restoration of one Human Race worthy of that name.

Thus, I seek to remind readers that forgetting to explain the decisive role played by Africa in the history, the present condition of humanity cannot be explained correctly. It is under the influence of the past that the awakening of the present is diversified and enriched by facts of all that has been closely lived by the spirit, the faith, the senses of the scholar between space and time, of elements that inscribe Black pioneers into the chronology of the world, bringing all the enriched sources into the annals of the history of mankind.

Universally, the chronology, beliefs, cultures and civilizations, started to bloom from the times of the chronology derived from the furrows of our distant lands, to vigorously irrigate the periods of the world history.

It is therefore a fact to know that the elevator was invented by Alexander Miles on October 11, 1867; this African-American inventor, born on May 18, 1838, was awarded the U.S. Patent 371, 207 for an automatic doors opening and closing elevator. He died on May 7, 1918.

The photographic print and negative wash machine that neutralized the chemicals in each bathing process was invented by Clatonia Joaquin Dorticus on June 7, 1893. Over the next one hundred years, he filed five more patents for the photographic film and print washers. On July 12, 1894, he filed a patent for an improved machine for embossing photographs, designed for mounting and/or embossing a photographic print.

In the 1950s, this invention was referenced by two other patents from the year 1950, and the spring of 1895, both patents, although filed about a year apart, were published only days apart. A device for applying coloring liquids to the sides of the soles or the heels of the shoes was patented on March 19, 1895; the embossing machine for photographs, on April 16, 1895; the photographic print washer, on April 23, 1895; and the hose leak stop, on July 18, 1899.

This African-Cuban descent, born in Cuba in 1863, often noted on the list of African-American inventors as a citizen of the United States, residing in Newton, Sussex county and the State of New Jersey, died in 1903 at only thirty-nine years of age.

The wagon-mounted fire escape ladder was invented by Joseph R. Winters on May 7, 1878; he also received an improvement patent for his ladder on April 8, 1879, and for a fire escape ladder that could be affixed on buildings on May 16, 1882. However, his metal frame and parallel steps replaced the wooden ladder twenty-nine years after the initially introduced ladder in 1849 by George Huttman and George Kornelio. As an African-American inventor, he was born on August 29, 1816, in Leesburg, Virginia, to an African-American brickmaker and a Shawnee Indian mother, known as a "female Indian doctor." This abolitionist, who was active in the Underground Railroad, died on November 26, 1916.

The portable weighing scale was invented by John W. Hunter on November 3, 1896; it is used to determine the weight, the mass of an object or an individual. This African American also received a patent for a hair dressing device on January 19, 1909.

The steam cooktop was invented by Carter William on October 26, 1897. The overshoe was invented by Alvin L. Rickman on February 8, 1898; its light oversize was designed to cover the sole, heel and the space between the sole and the upper shoe only, leaving the shoe upper part free and uncovered; it can be made of rubber, rubber and fabric combined, or of any suitable waterproof material.

The automatic clothes dryer was invented by George T. Sampson on June 7, 1892; his clothes dryer was a frame that suspended clothes above a stove so that laundry dries more quickly; but in 1881, he first invented the sled propeller. This African American inventor was born on July 24, 1861, in Palmyra, New York, and before he died in 1902, his Alzheimer disease made him forget all memorized information.

The street mailbox with a hinge at the door was invented by Philip B. Downing on October 27, 1891; this African American inventor, born on September 3, 1871, also patented an electric switch for railroads. At an appropriate time, this device allowed railroad workers to supply or shut off the trains' energy a year earlier, on June 27, 1890. Innovators later on created electric switches such as light switches used in homes based on his design.

Apart from being an inventor, Philip Downing was elected in 1948 and was reelected in 1952 as a member of the Wisconsin State Senate and was also a representative of the Republican Party. He died on January 17, 1961.

The composting machine was invented by William Barry; he also invented the stacking device, the mail-canceling machine, the postmarking and the canceling machine, and the postal machine or "obliteration;" all his inventions were patented on June 22, 1897. In the United States, the stamp cancelling machine and mail distributing machine are still widely used as two of his most important inventions.

The typewriter was invented by Lee S. Burridge and Newman R. Mashman on April 7, 1885. Lee S. Burridge was the son of a renowned dentist by the name of Levi Spear and Emma Francs (Ogden) Burridge. This genius and inventive manufacturer was born on September 22, 1861, in Paris, France, but in 1878, he moved to New York City and quickly directed his attention to the manufacture of mechanical toys where he invented moving toys, helicopter, switching device for railway lines, and a bicycle. On May 4, 1915, he died in New York City at the age of fifty-four.

Newman R. Marshman was the son of a real estate agent, Benjamin Marshman, and Rachel Newman Marshman. Born on April 7, 1847 in New York City, this music professor and a successful typewriter manufacturer and designer passed away on November 2, 1930; he died in the Bronx County, New York, at the age of eighty-three.

Joseph H. Dickinson invented the "Reed Organ" as an instrument that produces sounds by free reeds (vibrating through a slot with close tolerance) with no pipes, on February 5, 1899; he invented two volume-controlling means for mechanical musical instruments, one on March 23, 1909, and the other on June 29, 1909; this device was a mechanism or a ring, which allow the control of the intensity and the frequency of the wave.

"The mechanical piano or player piano," is a self-playing piano, containing a pneumatic or electromechanical mechanism that operates the piano action via programmed music recorded on perforated paper" he invented on June 11, 1912; the rewind device for phonographs, is a backup and restore system to broadcast the peripherals of the band, followed his inventions on June 23, 1916; he brought significant improvement to phonographs by inventing the motor drive for phonographs on March 20, 1917; his automatic musical instrument, invented on April 11, 1918, is a machine that plays music automatically and designed to sound like an orchestra or band for entertainment; in addition, his recording machine, the "phonograph," "was a device for the mechanical recording and reproduction of sound" that he invented on January 8, 1918; the sound box for sound-reproducing machines that he invented on December 16, 1919, was an automatic musical instrument that produces sounds by the use of a set of pins placed on a revolving cylinder; after his first piano-player invented on June 11, 1912, he invented the improved model on June 8, 1920; his automatic musical instrument was also improved on April 20, 1921; followed by the improvement of the automatic piano on December 22, 1922; then the multiple-record-magazine, the phonograph, was also improved by him on March 20, 1923; and the music roll magazine was a mechanism for the player piano, known as the sheet music that made the piano more reliable and able to play music in forward or reverse mode invented on October 15, 1928.

Joseph Hunter Dickinson was born on June 22, 1855, in Chatham, Ontario, Canada; he was elected in 1897 and reelected in 1899 to the Michigan House of Representatives as a Republican candidate, and the information on the place of his death can't be found in his bibliography. This African American, with a trained and active intellect, who invented several improvements to different musical instruments to hold a significant position in the American society and in the world, was a man of genius for our race.

The car brakes, invented by John Y. Smith, on May 25, 1815, their conduct was put under vacuum, instead of putting it under pressure; thus, unambiguously, they constituted a clear new improvement and useful safety accessories for the vacuum brakes of railway oars, using a reverse process.

The determination of melanin dosage that gives color to the skin, known as the dark brown to black pigment found in the hair, skin, and iris of the eye in people and animals, was first tested by Cheikh Anta Diop; he was the one who invented the method of determining the level of melanin in the skin of human beings, responsible for the tanning of the skin exposed to sunlight. It is also known that the Egyptian people have a melanin concentration that corresponds only to the black race; this is attested by the tests performed on their mummies.

The first lawn mower with rotating blades on traction wheels was invented by John Albert Burr on May 9, 1899; as an African-American inventor, born in 1848 in Maryland, the state of the North-East of the United States, this child of two slave parents, held other inventions, besides the patent of the lawn mower, but this one was the most famous of his inventions.

John Albert Burr was not really included in his country's history as an intelligent human being, since racial profiling and segregation of Niggers still continued at that period. But its more than 30 patents were also good for lawn care and in the field of agriculture; and his mechanical engineering skills greatly helped the evolution of agricultural equipment. And the way he improved the shape of the blades has had an impact on the life of humanity by positively influencing the scientific community; and today, his blade in lawnmowers fields and farms is still used; so acknowledge this inventor who made this task a little easier for you, the next time you mow the lawn. Burr lived a long life, enjoyed the fruits of his success, until his death by influenza in 1926 at age seventy-eight.

The sterilization of food was invented by Lloyd A. Hal on February 8, 1938; he studied pharmaceutical chemistry at Northwestern University after graduating from the East Side High School in Aurora and received a BS; and at the University of Chicago, a master's degree. This African American chemist was born on June 21, 1894, in Elgin, Illinois.

Lloyd Augustus Hall patented fifty-nine devices for food preservation techniques based on Sodium chloride in the United States toward the end of his career, and other countries also patented his inventions in considerable numbers. After his contribution to the science of food preservation, he received honorary degrees from the Virginia State University, the Howard University, and the Tuskegee Institute, and several other honors were awarded to him during his lifetime. He was inducted into the National Inventors Hall of Fame for his work in 2004 and picked the Northwestern University among four colleges he had the opportunity to choose. He sat on the American Food for Peace Council from 1962 to 1964, and he consulted for the Food and Agriculture Organization of the United Nations after his retirement from Griffith in 1959. Lloyd A. Hal died on January 2, 1971, in Pasadena, California.

The organic pheromone synthesis and the oligosaccharide synthesis were invented by Bertram Oliver Fraser-Reid. In 1956, he moved to Canada after attending the Clarendon College in Jamaican. He established a research group known as Fraser-Reid's Rowdies, at the faculty of the University of Waterloo in Waterloo, Ontario; his work at that stage was the synthesis of chiral natural products.

He moved to the University of Maryland, College Park, in 1980. Then in 1982, he went to the Duke University in Durham, North Carolina; at Duke University, where he finally became the James B. Duke Professor of Chemistry in 1985, he continued his research using carbohydrates as the starting materials and on the role of oligosaccharides in the immune response.

This widely recognized chemist, born on February 23, 1934, in Coleyville, Jamaica, explored the role of oligosaccharides in the immune responses to particularly know what role these molecules play in human diseases like malaria and AIDS. Fraser-Reid is often cited in the Canadian civil law for his prevailed lawsuit that went all the way to the Supreme Court of Canada against a building contractor who did not follow the municipal building codes in the 1970s. He is still an accomplished musician apart from his interests in science.

The Merck, Sharp & Dohme Award from the Chemical Institute of Canada awarded him an award in 1977; the Claude S. Hudson Award in carbohydrate chemistry from the American Chemical Society also honored him with an award in 1989; in 1990, the West Germany's Alexander von Humboldt Foundation recognized him as the Senior Distinguished United States Scientist; in 1991, he received the Percy Julian Award from the National Organization of Black Chemists and Chemical Engineers, and was elected Fellow of the American Academy of Arts and Sciences; he was given the Haworth Memorial Medal and Lectureship by the Royal Society of Chemistry.

He was named North Carolina Chemist of the Year by the American Institute of Chemistry in 1995; and for the Promotion of Science, he was elected Fellow of the Japanese Society.

The polytherapy therapy (chemotherapy) against cancer was invented by Jane Cooke Wright; she was recognized for her contributions to chemotherapy as a pioneer cancer researcher and surgeon using the methotrexate drug to treat breast and skin cancer. This highest-ranked African American woman physician was accredited for developing the technique of using human tissue culture. Jane Cooke Wright was born on November 30, 1919, in Manhattan, New York, and worked in Ghana in 1957 and in Kenya in 1961, treating cancer patients.

The Women's Medical College of Pennsylvania awarded her the honorary title of Doctor of Medicine and received numerous awards. Jane Cooke Wright died on February 19, 2013.

Samuel L. Kountz invented the kidney transplantation and the kidney preservation. He was born on August 20, 1930 and became the first African American admitted to the Arkansas School of Medicine, where he graduated in 1958. This international African American leader in transplant surgery, who made the kidney transplants to be fairly a routine today, won numerous awards.

In 1974, he was elected president of the Society of University Surgeons and shared his expertise with the world. During a trip in South Africa in 1977, Samuel L. Kountz contracted an unknown disease that caused serious brain damage until his death on December 23, 1981, after a long illness at the age of fifty-one years old.

The ultraviolet camera/spectrograph invented by George R. Carruthers was transported for the first mission of *Apollo 16* lunar observatory. It is found today at the shadow of the lunar module of Orion, on the mountainous Descartes region of the moon, since astronauts of *Apollo 16* placed it in April 1972 on the moon.

When the general audience of the developer asked him to explain the highlights of his instrument's findings, Dr. Carruthers said, "The most immediately visible and spectacular results were really for the Earth observations, because this was the first time that the Earth had been photographed from a distance in ultraviolet light, so that you can see the full extent of the hydrogen atmosphere, the polar auroras and what we call the tropical airglow belt."

The National Medal of Technology and Innovation, the highest national honor in technology achievement, was awarded to him in 2012. This African American physician and space scientific, who was born on October 1, 1939, in Cincinnati, Ohio, invented devices as the "image converter," patented in1969.

One of his inventions captured an ultraviolet image of Halley's Comet in 1986, and he also invented a camera that was used in the Space Shuttle Mission in 1991. For his achievements in the field of space science, he was honored at the Office of Naval Research as a Distinguished Lecturer on February 12, 2009; he received the 2012 National Medal of Technology and Innovation from the former president Barack Obama at the White House on February 1, 2013, and several other awards, such as the NASA Medal for Scientific Excellence, for his inventions which helped the NASA in 1972. And for his work in science and engineering, he was inducted into the National Inventor's Hall of Fame in 2003.

The (airport beacons, of cranes and high buildings) as signalization light was invented by Lewis W. Chubb on March 30, 1937; a few months later, precisely on July 20, 1937, he invented Vehicle Lighting System. This inventor, electrical engineer, radio broadcasting pioneer, who was the research director of the Westinghouse Electric Corporation laboratory, registered 150 patents on his name; and in 1947, the John Fritz Medal was awarded to him. Or the fire extinguisher, invented by Thomas J. Martain, on March 26, 1872; his fire extinguisher, used to spray burning fires, could wisely be attached to a reservoir of stored water as a quite notable device patented by him. To only quote these few examples of African American inventors, all these inventions were the works of black geniuses.

These achievements were a great work of the greatest accuracy and supreme perfection, the great significant black exquisite with great value. Note that is by looking into the occult past to see where we come from that we can fully live the present and build the future, especially in our present position as blacks.

Knowing that the basis of the world civilization is practically the work of blacks pushes us to ask these questions: what mistakes did we make, and how did we get there? Instead of deceiving oneself and thinking that one can fully live the present and build the future without going through it, we should know that it is only after answering these questions that we can elaborate new strategies to build a future. I therefore claim the right of recognition for them, even if their exploits remain unrewarded.

Our identity is today broken to the point that we no longer know where we are going because we have almost no landmarks anymore. But a place has been given to us by Westerners for their interests. Should we be satisfied with that place? What will you say? I would say no. Spending our time wanting to do things as they do, contributed gradually to the disappearance of our traditional African cultures. To ignore it is an illness and an alienating error to expressly not accept Africans as the basis of the world history; but the truth is that we are already part of the history of the world; in fact we are the history of the world, and the father of all mankind.

Let's learn from the present and act accordingly for the future. And I believe that, without the inventions of my ancestors, traveling in space would have not been possible today. So, these symbols will remain the true symbols of peace. The choice is given freely. All present elements seem to make us believe that we are the last of the humanity on earth. Analyzing the past, its ingenuity and the memories of our ancestors will allow blacks who still doubt the skills that we possess to know that we are capable to accomplish great achievements as our ancestors did, who accomplished the work of civilization in this world; and that in their past, there were challenges, methods of conjuncture that are incomparable to the stakes of the present days, with an imperfect future furnish with different real ditches, which were draining their blood at the edges of their heart.

The context of the past belongs to the past, the present belongs to the moment we all well love, and as an opportunity that can overtake us, is what this present is; and the future, which remains a mystery to us, is the unknown that it will reveal to us—will it be such as the Great Architect wants? Nobody can guess it. All these moments have a dimensional value: the memory, the reality, and the principle of love, are unavoidable realities in everyone's life. And thanks to our aspirations and our failures, we will succeed, because the past is more a generator of models than the present.

Without these inventions of the first earthly black beings of the distant past, the experimental result of the current technological terrestrial progress would have not been possible. The Space Shuttle is one of their results; and the prototypes of autonomous stations in an immense air bubble have already been manufactured by our scientists. These space crafts, would they be equipped without the knowledge of blacks? Where would we be without these black inventions, which they started implementing from the archaic times to modernity? In the weightlessness, where there is no presence of inventions, or in the comfort, aboard our spacecraft without a knowledge acquired by a long practice and without a real mission? Know then that the order of this new world was first established by blacks since time immemorial.

Black surgeons have achieved open-heart surgery with scholarly intellectuality; it must be said that we could not have imagined this kind of operation possible without their undeniable contribution, or be able to achieve all kinds of operations impossible to achieve before on earth without the inventions of these blacks full of competence.

Black-skinned men realized all these inventions for themselves as they invented fire for humanity, simply by building them as they built the pyramids, the Sphinx of the Giza plateau, known as the world's largest monolithic monumental sculpture in Lower Egypt, and we all know that every person in this world has his own geniuses as a natural ability and great creative faculty.

Therefore, the monopoly of beauty, full of admiration and the intelligence of a secret complicity, is not the possession of any race. And even as blacks will still have many geniuses ignored by white men, telescopes invented by black man are scrutinizing the sky and filming all the spatial regions without stopping, observing the spheres activities and the terrestrial influences by retransmitting the images of their entire trip to the world. These numerous programs are connected in this world permanently, with the hope to better know it and to discover the signs of life there.

Some Nobel Prizes have also been awarded to some of them—like the Nobel Prize in Literature, awarded to Derek Walcott, and the Nobel Prize in Economics awarded to William Arthur Lewis. The best mathematician in the world, David Blackwell, won the John von Neumann Theory Prize and was the first African American to be a member of the National Academy of Sciences and received several other awards. Born on April 24, 1919 in Centralia, Illinois, this renowned mathematician died in Berkeley, California, on July 8, 2010.

In the invention of the atomic bomb, the design and construction of a special distillation system, was mainly under the responsibility of Albert Lloyd Quaterman; this special distillation system was built for the purification of large quantities of hydrogen fluoride and for the separation of the U-235 uranium isotope he accumulated for the construction of atomic bombs and the one released above Hiroshima. He also worked in the Manhattan Project that produced the first nuclear weapons led by the United States and support by Canada and the United Kingdom. Including Edwin R. Russel, an Africa-American chemist who worked on atomic bomb, at the University of Chicago's Metallurgical Laboratory, on the Manhattan Project and on the isolating and the extracting of plutonium-239 from uranium, placed top-secret research at the Chicago Met Lab. Benjamin F. Scott was an African American chemist who worked on the Manhattan Project in World War II.

This notable African American scientist also worked on one of the most important scientific projects of the twentieth century at the University of Chicago's Metallurgical Laboratory, which ended World War II after the development of the atomic bomb. Ernest Wilkins, an African American qualified as "Negro Genius" in the media as a nuclear scientist, mathematician and mechanical engineer in the United States. Harold Delaney was one of the only few African American scientists who also worked at the University of Chicago on the Manhattan Project. Jasper Jeffries, an African American scientist, as a physicist at the Met Lab at the University of Chicago, worked on the Manhattan Project. Moddie Taylor, was a chemist who worked on the Manhattan Project; and for his research focused on analyzing the chemical properties of rare earth metals and his contribution to the Manhattan Project, he was awarded a Certificate of Merit from Robert Patterson, the Secretary of War in 1946. Ralph Gardner was one of more than a dozen African-American scientists who were involved in the research on the atomic project, classified as a plutonium research that resulted in the development of the atomic bomb in the United States, etc.

All these black scientists who were involved in the development of the atomic bomb and other devices in various fields were the "founding fathers, mothers and inventors" in the scientific field. The contribution of the black world to science and modern technology deserves to be emphasized with respect, because we can say that the ancient African cultures of several thousands of years ago, have invented agriculture, astronomy, writing, fire control, mathematics, medicine, philosophy, and early tools of all kinds, etc.

It is the genius of these black inventors and innovators, comprehensive pioneers in the field of invention that they must be recognized; meanwhile, they're often unrecognized because of the color of their skin; but they cannot be unrecognized because they contributed to the development of science and in other inventions in the world, and their merit must be perennial.

My duty is therefore to raise awareness and inform the public about the real unjust issues of our world, which are obscuring the real ambitions of our elite in all areas; whether prophetic, religious, scientific, or at the level of democracy, and the massive inequalities that characterize our world; such as freedom, the freedom of expression, the social injustice, the socioeconomic injustice, the sociopolitical injustice, the global peace, or today, the forms of slavery put in place by the said democracy of the governments of the world, under the cover of the world prosperity, are the much deeper tragic issues that humiliate our people, transforming the social organization of our world, and destroying our cultures. My words are expressing the evils we still live every day; so I am fighting against the inequalities of the human beings plunged in the distress and the solitude without hope or opportunities, and which dissolve the social bond, for a right reaffirmation of Freedom and Truth; and I'm asking God to show the way to humanity; because whoever is afraid of making a mistake will never make up his mind to rectify the error situation destined to be rectified.

Let humanity realize that there is what is right beyond what seems to be honest; therefore be just and honest, imperialism; you who control the people and the resources of our world; economically and politically to the social causes of violence by wars, so that the Spirit of God may enter into your heart and cleanse you from all that is not according to the divine law. Open your heart oh humanity! To the causes that create blindness, vulnerability, the feelings of humiliation and the desire of revenge against that violence, which prevents us from evolving without prejudices, and without overwhelming hatred limiting our freedoms. Align your thoughts and agree to do what needs to be done without violence, because God dwells within everyone.

Thus, I'm expressing what my soul is asking me to do, no matter their allegiance in madness; but sometimes, my words are not enough to express the evil that I feel; because beyond words hides the truth and my obligation to fidelity and obedience to my nation. Not denouncing these injustices that turn adults into murderers is not informing the population and it is condoning these injustices and accepting those dominant elites as evil in what we call the New Order of the World today.

May the heart of humanity be flooded with the Love of God, to redistribute the benefits of cooperation; to respect each one for what he is, and above all, to fight for a more just world, for a "restoration of freedom and peace for all in the divine energy." I wish.

ABOUT THE AUTHOR

These irrevocable writings of providence, proclaiming the spiritual unity in equality, used poetry, meaning the universal father God: I am the rhythm of laws and the sacred magic sense of art, the nature mysteries and the most sublime moral conception for you to prelude.

Its work is an inspiration conceived to reveal the eternal truth that vibrates the mysterious lyres of souls, singing the birth of love, invoking joy and satisfaction and the conception of hatred in our hearts, recalling yesterday's every memory of our past life; to strive to the surface that gives birth to many forms of our expression.

And like a star among multiple, its mysterious song will awaken a divine soul. Will its action lead to the advent that is assigned to it? Its advent constitutes an exceptional exemption to save. It is genuinely at the end proud of its accomplishment to honor.

ACKNOWLEDGMENTS AND GRATITUDE

First of all, I would like to express my love to God for the blessing and to have opened the well of truth in me to realize this book from its preliminary planning stage until its publication. From you and through you, I believe that my work is not in vain, and I show you my greatest gratitude. I am truly indebted to the many people who have helped and encouraged me throughout the various stages of writing this book.

My special thanks go first to my mother and father, who gave me the word and who were my first spiritual guides. I dedicate my greatest gratitude to my great spiritual masters who guided me in spiritual doctrine—a moral code allowing enlightenment and dedicated to the truth. It is to you that I entrust . . . with my best wishes of deep peace, sincerely and fraternally.

My deepest appreciation to my wife, Chantal Nyangon Dipanda, for being a loving wife; you were so helpful in sharing brilliant ideas in the best of humors and encouraging me to the completion of this book. I am grateful and recognize your love and delightfulness in giving me cool attention when I was working and for empowering my inner heart and body up to the finishing of this project.

Without your presence well valiant and luminous, this book could not have seen the day; thank you very much. And finally, to all my friends around the 808 world, I direct my utmost gratitude; because in this world where everything is just passing by, if anything of me were to survive among my brothers and friends, I would like my testimony to be this book; I vow it to you and to the Winged Soul-God, the one who led me to the bottom of its realization as a conquered and shared faith, to spread its sacred fire; because He did not cease to follow me and hold my hand for this work.

For its guidance on the way to our settlement, after freeing us from the terrestrial chains, both in life and during periods of isolation, I felt His faithful ray exhorting me from the bosom of the heavenly light to communicate His thought watching on us, to you, favoring our resources by His boundless compassion, His immeasurable help, and His qualities of pure authenticity, up to the end of our predestined hatching.

R.M. Dipanda

www.ingramcontent.com/pod-product-compliance
Lightning Source LLC
Chambersburg PA
CBHW021436070526
44577CB00002B/189